Training and Development Handbook

Training and Development Handbook

A Guide to Human Resource Development

Sponsored by the American Society for Training and Development

Edited by
ROBERT L. CRAIG

Second Edition

McGRAW-HILL BOOK COMPANY
New York   St. Louis   San Francisco   Auckland   Bogotá
Düsseldorf   Johannesburg   London   Madrid   Mexico
Montreal   New Delhi   Panama   Paris   São Paulo
Singapore   Sydney   Tokyo   Toronto

Library of Congress Cataloging in Publication Data

Craig, Robert L
  Training and development handbook.

  Includes bibliographies and index.
  1. Employees, Training of. I. American Society for
Training and Development. II. Title.
HF5549.5.T7C7   1976   658.31'24   76-15295
ISBN 0-07-013350-6

    890   KPKP   854321

The editors for this book were Harold B. Crawford and Patricia A. Allen,
the designer was Naomi Auerbach, and the production supervisor
was Frank Bellantoni. It was set in Baskerville
by University Graphics, Inc.

Printed and bound by The Kingsport Press.

American Society for Training and Development
TRAINING AND DEVELOPMENT HANDBOOK, Second Edition

PUBLICATIONS COMMITTEE

The members of this Committee assisted in the planning of this Handbook and in the manuscript review process.

ROBERT D. JOHNSON, *Chairperson*
Consolidated Edison Company of New York

ARTHUR S. KING
American Arbitration Association

JAMES H. McCORMICK
Industrial Training Specialist

JOYCE M. PARKER
State Compensation Fund of Arizona

SHIRLEY SCHMITZ
Port-A-Bookstore

HOWARD R. SHELTON
Sandia Laboratories

CHARLES H. VERVALIN
Gulf Publishing Company

Contents

Section 3   APPLICATIONS IN TRAINING

Section 4   MEDIA AND METHODS

Section 5   TRAINING AND DEVELOPMENT RESOURCES

Index follows Chapter 47.

Foreword

Human resource development is growing steadily in size, outreach, and impact. Increasingly, the HRD professional is recognized as a prime contributor to organizational effectiveness and individual satisfaction and productivity in the world of work. No longer confined by earlier narrow definitions of "training," the profession has evolved to encompass a multitude of disciplines and approaches, all focused on the central goal of developing human potential in every aspect of lifelong learning.

This second edition of the *Training and Development Handbook* reflects the current body of knowledge of our emerging field. Because there exists no single traditional academic base for the comprehensive set of skills and information required by the profession, works such as this become an increasingly valuable resource for all practioners at all levels of experience.

The first edition served a broad need—and served it well. And now the second edition, greatly expanded and updated, seeks to meet the contemporary need of a profession far more dynamic, complex, and challenging than it was just ten short years ago.

It is an important sourcebook—and the American Society for Training and Development is proud to have assisted in its creation.

KEVIN O'SULLIVAN
Executive Director
American Society for Training and Development

Preface

Much has happened in training and development in the nearly ten years since the first edition of this Handbook was published. We are seeing an almost explosive growth of the field as this edition goes to press. Education and training in the world of work has become a major part of the real education system. Employers are increasingly recognizing the pragmatic need for the continual development of the knowledge and skills of the work force as essential to organizational success and individual employee achievement. Job competences constantly interface with technological advances, economic change, employee advancement, and a host of other demands. As a result, organization management, in both the public and private sectors, has come to have greater and greater expectations from the training and development function. Human resource development is now considered essential in most organizations.

Concurrent with this growing demand, the body of knowledge in HRD has grown enormously, too, and that's why this new edition of the Handbook is so needed. The advances have been so great that this second edition is virtually a new work. Only two chapters bear close resemblance to their counterparts in the first edition—Cloyd Steinmetz's "History of Training" and Don Kirkpatrick's classic "Evaluation of Training" required only modest updating. The rest of the book is new.

The new material includes the major recent applications of the behavioral sciences in management practices and in the development of human resources; an emphasis on systematic and quantitative methods for determining training needs and assessing training outcomes; an overall updating in instructional methods and media; and coverage of newer concepts in human resource development such as organization development, work design and group behavior. We've also extended coverage in the applications to broad employee populations such as minorities, secretarial and clerical, sales, and international.

The result of all this new material is a considerably larger handbook—47 chapters developed especially for this purpose by 59 authorities. (The first edition had 32 chapters by 36 contributors.)

Assembling all this required the diligent help of a lot of people and I want to express my thanks. First to the 59 contributors—their expertise and their willingness to share it made the whole project possible.

I want to give my special thanks to the members of the ASTD Publications Committee who were so essential in the original planning of the Handbook and in the extensive manuscript review process. The committee members were: Chairperson, *Robert D. Johnson,* Consolidated Edison Company of New York; *Arthur S. King,* Director of Education and Training, American Arbitration Association; *James H. McCormick,* Industrial Training Specialist; *Joyce M. Parker,* State Compensation Fund of Arizona; *Shirley Schmitz,* Port-A-Bookstore; *Howard R. Shelton,* Sandia Laboratories; and *Charles H. Vervalin,* Gulf Publishing.

I also want to thank Agnes, my wife, and Bob, my son, for their forbearance and help during the many months of putting this Handbook together.

Human resource development in the workplace faces a demanding, and exciting, future which will require the highest levels of professional competence. This Handbook is intended as a contribution to that need.

I hope the Handbook serves that purpose well.

ROBERT L. CRAIG
Editor

The Training and Development Function

Chapter 1

The History of Training

CLOYD S. STEINMETZ

Cloyd S. Steinmetz *was, since 1968, a consultant on personnel development for companies from coast to coast and a speaker at management and sales meetings. For many years he was Director of Sales Training, Reynolds Metals Co., and director for both production and sales training for Owens-Corning Fiberglas Corp. He was one of the early members of the American Society of Training Directors and had participated in many of its conferences and clinics. He was an innovator in the use of voice recording as a supervisory development tool. Mr. Steinmetz was a former president of both the American Society for Training and Development and the National Society of Sales Training Executives. He died in November 1975.*

As man invented tools, weapons, clothing, shelter, and language, the need for training became an essential ingredient in the march of civilization. Whether our ancestors stumbled upon or invented these facets of civilization is of relatively little significance. What is more important is that man had the ability to pass on to others the knowledge and skill gained in mastering circumstances. This was done by deliberate example, by signs, and by words. Through these devices the development process called *training* was administered; and when the message was received by another successfully, we say that learning took place and knowledge or skill was transferred.

It is generally thought that man began amassing knowledge at the beginning of the Stone Age. For reasonably logical reasons, especially since it marked the advent of the industrial revolution, the date 1750 has been selected by many thoughtful people as signaling the close of the first period of man's knowledge accumulation and the beginning of a new phase.

Technical and mechanical inquisitiveness took a tremendous spurt after 1750, resulting in the doubling of human knowledge in only 150 years—to about 1900. In the next fifty years, by 1950, it doubled again! The single decade of the '50s witnessed the firing of the technological rocket, and again our sum of knowledge doubled. But now a new problem has arisen. The "fallout" of information no longer valid or pertinent has grown to threatening proportions. The seriousness of the situation is further accentuated by the fact that another doubling of total human knowledge is estimated to have occurred in the five-year period ending in 1964. The rapidity of change has become a dramatic challenge to training—a challenge of both addition and subtraction.

TRAINING'S BEGINNINGS

As archaeological excavations continue to unearth clay or brick tablets on which is inscribed information about the life of people living six thousand or more years ago, the place of training and learning in the skyrocketing development of knowledge and civilizations has become dramatically evident.

The Sumerian Palace at Kish, in Mesopotamia, built in 3500 B.C., exemplifies the ancient use of brick, and the Bible tells us that the Tower of Babel was also built of brick. The astounding architectural and masonry accomplishments embodied in the pyramids and ancient temples, such as Solomon's First Temple, are memorials to the stonemasons, the brickmasons, the carpenters, the artists, and the scientists of ancient times.

Apprenticeship

It must be remembered that in early civilizations, literacy reached neither the craftsman nor the peasantry. The skills and knowledge of the crafts could be transmitted only by direct instruction. Thus was developed an apprenticeship system whereby an experienced person passed along knowledge and skill to the novice, who, after a period of apprenticeship, became a journeyman or a yeoman. Provisions for governing apprenticeship were instituted as early as 2100 B.C., when such rules and procedures were included in the Code of Hammurabi.

The apprenticeship system was not restricted to artisanship alone. It was also the vehicle for instruction in medicine, law, and education. As recently as the 1920s, it was possible in the United States for a young person to "read law in the office of a local attorney." This was a form of apprenticeship and guidance which, after an extended period of study, was followed by the apprentice's taking a governmentally supervised examination. A passing grade on this examination qualified the apprentice to practice law.

The ancient temples taught religion and frequently art. The armies took the responsibility for teaching soldiers. The private schools taught statesmen, and the industrial class developed an intricate apprenticeship system which, in turn, developed into a business social system.

One outgrowth of the Crusades was the establishment of universities as a form of protest against monastic education. Although some church domination lingered, the higher levels of education began to supervise their own activities.

Guilds

Another development was the formation of guilds, which were associations of people whose interests or pursuits were the same or similar. The basic purpose was mutual protection, assistance, and advantage. In essence, guilds created private franchise and at the same time established quality standards of products through quality standards of workmanship.

The workers composing the membership of a guild were of three kinds: the master workers, who owned the raw materials and the tools and directed the work; the apprentices, who usually lived with a master and who received practically no pay, except maintenance and training; and the journeymen, who had passed through the stage of apprenticeship but were not yet qualified as masters. Journeymen worked under a master and received fixed wages for their labor. Of course, both apprentices and journeymen hoped that they would ultimately become masters.

As markets expanded, more machinery and tools were required, and this meant that becoming a master craftsman required a greater capital investment. These conditions reduced the opportunities of journeymen to become master craftsmen.

The necessity of the journeymen to have their own organization resulted in the development of yeomanry guilds. This need was accentuated when the master craftsmen sought to make their guilds even more exclusive by raising their standards of skill, thereby making it increasingly more difficult for a journeyman to qualify as a master.

During the peak of the guild system, between the twelfth and the fifteenth centuries, the privileges of the members were protected by strict regulation of hours, tools, prices, and wages. The system required that all have the same privileges and pursue the same methods. Thus it was that conditions forced the skilled workers, the journeymen, to band together for their own protection and advancement. These yeomanry guilds became the forerunners of the modern-day labor unions. In the craft unions of today, we still find restrictions as to numbers of apprentices, regulation of the quantity and quality of work, and the establishment of a basic system of financial reward.

Craft Training

The nineteenth century ushered in an era of social legislation and, with it, sizable changes in the concept of the workers' organization. Through all these changes, however, one constantly developing emphasis has been upon quality training of workers, and this has culminated in the staunch support of the unions for any legislation that provides a wide range of vocational education.

In the United States, early seeds of vocational education were planted in the form of craft training in such areas as gardening and carpentry. As early as 1745, the Moravian brothers established such training as Bethlehem, Pennsylvania, and in 1787 the Methodists instituted similar training at Cokesbury College in Abington, Maryland.

Industrial Era Emerges

The change from an agrarian to an industrial economy in the United States is evidenced by the rapid increase in the number of patents issued by the United States Patent Office. An average of 77 per year were issued between 1790 and 1811, and an average of 192 per year between 1812 and 1817. Then there was a startling spurt to a figure of 540 in the year 1830. Just 30 years later, in 1860, the average was 4,819.

This outpouring of industrial ideas has obviously been reflected in the manufacturing volume of our country. By today's standards the figures are small, but in terms of speed of growth they are very significant. For example, the approximate manufacturing volume in 1850 was $1 billion. In 1880 it was $5 billion. By 1909 it had reached $20 billion, and by 1914, it was $24 billion. In other words, it increased by $4 billion in the 30 years between 1850 and 1880. It increased again by $4 billion in the five years between 1909 and 1914. This kind of geometric progression has been the rule rather than the exception ever since.

The history of the growth of the training which accompanied this industrial expansion is fascinating. As early as 1809, the Masonic Grand Lodge of New York, under the leadership of DeWitt Clinton, established vocational training facilities. In 1828 the Ohio Mechanics Institute was started in Cincinnati, Ohio. Manual training began in the United States in about 1825. Most of the early manual training institutes that sprang up after 1825, however, were more disciplinary than vocational. The so-called state industrial schools were really places of incarceration for "bad boys." Nevertheless, the basic concept was correct, namely, to give idle hands training in such a manner that in accompaniment with a trained mind, they would be able to make a contribution to society rather than constitute a liability to it.

By 1886, private manual training schools were established in Cincinnati, Cleveland, Toledo, and Chicago, and public institutions of a similar sort were established in Philadelphia, Baltimore, and Omaha. An educational factor then unique, but now exceedingly common, was instituted at Cooper Union in New York in 1854, when evening classes of a vocational nature were established.

One of the great steps forward in the effort to free workers from the limitations of their immediate craft requirements was the passing of the Land Grant Act in 1862. When Abraham Lincoln signed this act, he initiated a means of higher education for the average man's children, which previously could be enjoyed only by the wealthy.

Factory Schools

With the growth of industry there came a new form of training—the factory schools. One of the first was established at Hoe and Company in New York City in 1872. This manufacturer of printing presses had such a volume of business that it was necessary to establish a factory school to train machinists. The old-style apprentice system was inadequate. Similar factory schools were established at Westinghouse in 1888, at General Electric Company and Baldwin Locomotive Works in 1901, and at International Harvester Company in 1907. Rapidly this became a common practice. Such companies as Western Electric, Goodyear, Ford, and National Cash Register were in the forefront of this educational activity.

Another key influence in the development of training was the YMCA. In 1892 the Brooklyn YMCA offered a course in freehand drawing, and the Springfield, Ohio, YMCA offered trade training in patternmaking, toolmaking, and cabinetry. The West Side New York YMCA, in 1905, offered 63 courses, 36 percent of which were commercial and 26 percent industrial and scientific.

An innovation in education took place during the first decade of the present century when Dean Schneider, of the University of Cincinnati, College of Engineering, introduced cooperative education. The student would go to school for a time and work in a factory for an equal period of time, returning to school for additional training and then going back to the industry for additional practical experience.

Association Beginnings

By the early 1900s vocational education was sufficiently extensive that there was a greater and greater need for mutual assistance in this field. The natural outgrowth was the realization that in unity of action there is strength. In 1906, 250 key educators interested in industrial education met at Cooper Union in New York City and formed the National Society for the Promotion of Industrial Education. In 1914 the Vocational Association of the Midwest was originated with similar goals. The development of these two associations was quite rapid. It was also paralleled by the organization in 1913 of the National Vocational Guidance Association at Grand Rapids, Michigan. Thus we sense the special interests that were developing more and more as a vocational educational consciousness became dominant.

In 1918 the National Society for the Promotion of Industrial Education changed its name to the National Society for Vocational Education. One of the major reasons for this change was the fact that in 1917, President Woodrow Wilson signed the Smith-Hughes Act, which provided for public moneys to assist vocational training efforts. It was now felt that the promotion of industrial education had been fairly well accomplished and that the title of the National Society for Vocational Education would better describe efforts at furthering the development of conditions from within rather than securing outside support.

In 1925 the Vocational Association of the Midwest and the National Society for Vocational Education merged into the American Vocational Association. While this association is composed of men and women in industry, education, and politics, it has been very much dominated by a preponderance of members from the field of public education. Before the Smith-Hughes Act, the membership was composed of a sizable number of people from both industry and education. Their points of view differed decidedly, although their basic goal was a common one. Industry members felt that the academicians were trying to dominate the situation, and the educators felt that "big business" was trying to run the show. As the educators' influence grew and the industrial participation waned, a new element entered into the picture. It could be called the "element of politics," but we must certainly define this factor so as not to give a wrong implication.

FEDERAL GOVERNMENT

Why should the politician be a part of vocational education? A good answer is provided by a story told by P. E. Browne, a retired director of vocational training for the state of North Carolina, concerning an effort that was being made to get legislation that would provide additional support for vocational education in the state. During the hearings for the bill a man stood up and asked for permission to speak. He said:

> I am George Patton from a country community in the mountains of Macon County, where I would still be if your state director of vocational education had not found me. You see this empty sleeve? I lost my right arm in a corn shredder when I was very young. It had always been my ambition to work my way through the State University and become a lawyer, and with the help of vocational education funds and my aunt, who is a school teacher, I succeeded. Today I plead for the same chance for every North Carolina boy and girl. What I have done, they can do.
> This sounds like a lot of money to many of us, but it can be found. Can we deny any child the right to serve humanity in his chosen field? Can we refuse to let any handicapped person develop his brain as well as his body? I shall devote my time to this project. Will you join me?

What this young legislator did not tell us was that he did so well at the university that he was taken into the best law firm in his hometown and later became mayor. He served in the state legislature, was appointed assistant attorney general, was made a superior court judge, and then became attorney general of the state of North Carolina. There was and still is a rightful place for the politician who has a sincere interest in providing vocational education for the people.

United States Federal Legislation

The outcome of this interest is indeed a march of progress. The Smith-Hughes Act of 1917 provided a permanent appropriation of approximately $7 million annually for vocational education in agricultural trades, home economics, industry, and teacher training. This act was sponsored by Senator Hoke Smith and Congressman Dudley M. Hughes of Georgia. In 1929 the George-Reed Act was passed and sponsored by Walter F. George of Georgia and Daniel A. Reed of New York. It authorized an appropriation of $1 million annually to expand vocational education in agriculture and home economics.

In 1934 the George-Ellzey Act was passed; it replaced the George-Reed Act and expanded still further vocational educational privileges. Again Senator George was senior sponsor, and Congressman Lawrence R. Ellzey of Mississippi was cosponsor. In 1936 the George-Deen Act was passed with Senator George and Congressman Braswell Deen, both of Georgia, as sponsors. It authorized, on a continuing basis, an annual appropriation of approximately $14 million for vocational education in agriculture, home economics, trades and industry, and, for the first time, distributive occupations. In 1937 the National Apprenticeship Act authorized the Secretary of Labor to formulate labor standards for the welfare of apprentices and to cooperate with the Office of Education in providing related instruction for apprentices.

In 1946 the George-Barden Act was passed with Senator George of Georgia and Congressman Graham A. Barden of North Carolina as cosponsors. It was an amendment to the George-Deen Act and superseded it. It increased the appropriations to $39 million annually and authorized the use of funds for guidance and research in vocational education. In 1958 Title 8 of the National Defense Act provided for the training of highly skilled technicians. In 1961 the Area Redevelopment Act sought to correct the economic imbalance of the economy by means of an educational approach. In 1962 the Manpower Development and Training Act provided funds for training the unemployed, the underemployed, and those displaced by technological change (see also Chapter 25, "Vocational and Technical Education").

INDUSTRIAL TRAINING ASSOCIATIONS

It will be helpful to go back and reexamine the history of vocational education between 1912 and 1920. It is interesting to note that in 1914, a young man by the name of Alvin E. Dodd was named assistant secretary of the National Society for the Promotion of Industrial Education. It is quite evident that Dodd's philosophy closely resembled the philosophy of many of those in industry who were operating the training schools of their organizations. These were the people who could not agree with the "educators" and felt that their problems were different and needed a different approach.

In 1913 a meeting was held at New York University, at which time the National Association of Corporation Schools was organized. Attending this meeting were two men whose names were to become extremely well known in training circles: Channing R. Dooley, of Standard Oil Company of New Jersey, and J. Walter Dietz, of the Western Electric Company.

The National Association of Corporation Schools started with 60 members representing 34 corporations. It held its first convention in 1914 in Dayton, Ohio, and printed proceedings of that meeting were 438 pages long. The following year, the proceedings were 548 pages long. Both issues were beautifully printed and bound in hard covers. Four annual conventions were held.

It is quite natural that as business educators began to examine the training needs of their organizations, their understanding of the process continued to develop and to expand into many categories. By 1918 the National Association of Corporation Schools' major interest had become "personnel." In 1920 it changed its name to the National Association of Corporation Training, and shortly afterward it merged with the Industrial Relations Association of America to become the National Personnel Association. Less than three years later, in 1923, the name was again changed to the American Management Association. The guiding spirit and executive director of this association was Alvin Dodd, who continued to occupy that position for many years.

Thus we see that modern personnel management may be said to be based on an alert training consciousness. The functionalization of training into its parts and the development of techniques for each of these parts constitute today's modern concept of human resource development.

WORLD WAR I PERIOD

A tremendous training impetus was unleashed shortly after the passage of the Smith-Hughes Act of 1917, but had no relationship whatsoever to it. On September 12, 1917, the Emergency Fleet Corporation of the United States Shipping

Board set up an educational and training section. Charles R. Allen, affectionately known as "Skipper Allen," was chosen as head, and Michael J. Kane was his assistant. At almost the same time, the War Department Committee for Educational and Special Training appointed Chan Dooley its director and Walter Dietz its secretary. It was their job to develop material for colleges so that almost 100 trades that were desperately needed in the Army would be developed with Army recruits. These four men became well acquainted with one another, and, as we shall see, this acquaintanceship bore fruit about 20 years later.

Training has always grown best where emergency is the dominant thought. This was the case when business began to expand and the need for more and better-trained labor became evident. Industrial training programs were called for. The need for better industrial instruction in industry had been apparent to many managers, educators, and consultants for years. As early as 1910, Allen, while still a vocational instructor under the Massachusetts State Board of Education, was pleading for improvement in instruction, pretty largely to deaf ears.

With the outbreak of World War I, emergency became the key word. There was a vital need for a "bridge of ships" to Europe so that the United States could do its part to "make the world safe for democracy." The Emergency Fleet Corporation of the United States Shipping Board set up an education and training section. It was found that 61 shipyards with 50,000 workers had an urgent need for 10 times as many workers, but none were available. The only answer was to train them. Charles Allen, as head of the program, had an opportunity to demonstrate the practicality of his philosophy. He ordered that all the training be done at the shipyards and that the instructors be the supervisors of these organizations.

Four-Step Method

Adopting the Herbartian steps of "show, tell, do, and check," Skipper Allen and Mike Kane launched a four-step method of job instruction training which helped to solve this World War I training problem. This was the fertile ground in which the seeds were planted 20 years later, just preceding and during World War II, for the War Manpower Commission's Training within Industry activities.

So effective were Allen's four steps that in the early 1920s they were, for the first time, printed in card form at Dunwoody Institute, where Allen was a staff member and Dr. Charles Prosser was head of the institute.

Many lessons were learned during World War I. At the time of the United States census in 1920, it was said, "The public is again reminded through this census of the lessons which the war should have taught regarding the tremendous loss in the inability of the public schools to reach out to all alike, and give them the educational and training equipment necessary for a life career."

THE 1920s

About this time, industry was being served by a unique and valuable training service, the Federal Board of Vocational Education. The industrial education staff of this organization was headed during the early '20s by Frank Cushman. One of their main objectives was to develop a sound program of part-time instruction of youth who had definitely left school and had entered into wage-earning employment. Many of their early bulletins were directed to this responsibility. For example, Bulletin 85 was entitled *Program for Training Part-Time School Teachers*, and Bulletin 114 was called *Training for Leadership in Trade and Industrial Education*. Much current-day training material would have more acceptability if it contained as much well-developed material as these bulletins.

The prosperity of the '20s tended to discourage the application of training to industrial situations, or at least it gave a minimum of encouragement. In the meantime, another type of training, that provided by the correspondence school, was serving the American wage earner. Van Liew Morris said in 1921, "Probably more men in American industry have gained the technical phases of their trades from correspondence schools than by any other means."

THE DEPRESSION YEARS

The economy that gorged itself at the prosperity feast of the late 1920s was cataclysmically plunged into the greatest depression in American history. Now the phrase "We don't need training," mouthed by shortsighted management, was changed from a complacent comment to a plaintive cry of managerial bewilderment. The Depression years of the '30s wrecked many internal training programs. It was obvious to management that their needs for workers could readily be met from the ranks of the unemployed.

On the other hand, a great influence to the furtherance of training was stimulated by this same set of depression-laden circumstances. Unemployed people had time on their hands and nothing in those hands. Even if they were fortunate enough to have money enough to feed themselves and their families, they still had the problem of what to do with their time. This problem became acute. A major effort to meet it was instigated by local, state, and federal governments. Perhaps the most widespread program was that involving the appropriation of federal funds for training in the handicrafts.

This training was usually scheduled in the late afternoons and evenings and was conducted in public school facilities. Hundreds of thousands of men and women occupied their spare time by learning leatherwork, weaving, painting, chair caning, jewelry making, etc. These people came to discover that they could pleasantly and profitably occupy their hands and minds. They could make useful things. Many times these articles were sold to help relieve the economic insecurity of the early '30s. People became training-conscious and, likewise, became conscious of their learning potential for maintaining and promoting their personal welfare. To resort to new vocational efforts when the need arose became a part of their philosophy.

Strangely, a corollary of this objective of training is finding growing validity in a new and expanding socioeconomic fact of national life. The combination of earlier retirement, improved health, and increased longevity has renewed and extended the need for new training efforts in the growing sector of retired people in our population. Improved morale and health and even economic betterment are some of the benefits thus afforded.

WORLD WAR II

It was quite logical, then, that as the World War II crisis approached and as the United States moved into the "defense era," these same men and women were ready to accept the call for service in the defense industry to replace young men drafted into the Armed Forces. They took to welding training, machinist training, and specialized job training of many kinds without fear or undue urging.

But who would do this training? By now the supply of vocational school instructors was fairly well exhausted. At last, business and industry came face to face with the reality that they had too long ignored. Suddenly the training function of the supervisor became paramount. In fact, management found that without training skill, supervisors were unable to produce adequately for the defense or the war effort. With it, new production records were being established by the aged, the handicapped, and industrially inexperienced women.

Someone had to bring leadership and coordination to this supervisory and job training. The training director became a necessity, and soon this was a common title in the management hierarchy. The process of selection was often crude, arbitrary, and fortuitous, further demonstrating the imperative need for the training director's services.

Now came the tremendous training impetus accomplished by the establishment of the War Production Board and, within that organization, the Training within Industry group. Here we find as leaders the people who had faced the war production manpower problems of World War I. They capitalized upon that experience by refining the techniques that had proved so effective in the prior conflict. Five men stand out in this vital change of direction in training: Chan Dooley, of Standard Oil of New Jersey; Walter Dietz, of Western Electric; Mike Kane, of AT&T; Glenn Gardiner, of Forstmann Woolen Mills; and Bill Conover, of U.S. Steel. They were frequently referred to as "the five horsemen."

The J Programs

Starting with the reformulation of an on-the-job training approach, the Job Instructor Training program was developed—quickly shortened to JIT. It was a program oriented especially to the first- and second-line supervisors whose skill in explaining their job know-how was essential to the mushrooming defense industry. Institutes were held all over the country with anywhere from 15 to 30 persons in attendance. Initially the participants were given a three-day training program in how to train supervisors to use the JIT formula. Later the institute grew to a 45-hour program.

JIT was all-inclusive. It not only taught how to instruct but also put emphasis upon the related problem of human relations between supervisor and worker and the equally important matter of determining the best job methods. It was quite natural, then, that a Job Relations Training program (JRT) was developed. This was quickly followed by a Job Methods Training program (JMT). With so many workers unfamiliar with the industrial environment, a safety emphasis was needed. Hence a Job Safety Training program (JST) was a natural development. A Program Development Training course (PDT) was developed for executives unfamiliar with training techniques. Each program was a specialized facet of the fundamentals inherent in the JIT card, which by this time had become famous. These 10-hour training programs for supervisors and training officers were given to almost two million war production and essential service management men. What an indoctrination in the needs for, and the rich rewards of, the training function! (See also Chapter 32, "Job Instruction.")

Management Training Emerges

Meanwhile, another very important influence was adding its emphasis to the growing realization of training's contribution to meeting the complexities of production and distribution. In order to meet the need for upgrading workers in college-level-type subjects, the Engineering, Science, and Management War Training program (ESMWT) was instituted. ESMWT programs were conducted under the sponsorship and guidance of universities and colleges, with competent academicians steering their progress. College-level courses in almost every aspect of management and technology were offered.

Not only did the ESMWT provide a service to war production companies, but it also gave higher educational authorities a most encouraging "peek under the tent" at the expanded opportunities for colleges and universities (and enterprising professors). They discovered new needs for their services which had enticing income benefits.

The ESMWT programs were made available both on and off campus. In many communities they became the forerunners of junior or community colleges. They were also the strong roots from which were developed centers for continuing education and management training centers as vital facets of higher learning. They also influenced the blossoming of the American Management Association into an institution offering a kaleidoscopic array of business training programs, extending from the first-line supervisor into the highest echelons of management—chairmen of boards of directors, presidents, directors of finance, etc.

Emergence of the Training Director

The combination of extensive training of supervisors and the ESMWT programs made obvious the necessity for two elements besides students and curriculum. Instructors were needed, and within companies the programs had to be scheduled, implemented, and supervised. The obvious source of both services was the industrial training director.

It was natural that in various localities and in various industries—for example, the petroleum industry—people who had the responsibility for directing the training efforts in their company or industry should want to get together and exchange ideas about training services and their related problems. It even went further than that. The foremen who were bearing the brunt of so much of this training effort also appreciated the value of exchanging ideas. A great ground swell of interest in foremanship resulted. The National Association of Foremen (NAF), with headquarters in Dayton, Ohio, accepted the responsibility for supplying this need. Hundreds of foremen's clubs were formed throughout the country. These in turn affiliated with the NAF. The prime function of the NAF was education. Its national conferences were dominated by orientation programs in how to become a good trainer, counselor, or manager and also in how to become a good club officer. Their annual conferences drew many thousands of delegates. More recently the association's name was changed to the National Management Association in order to establish more firmly the line foreman in the management hierarchy.

A parallel outgrowth of the Depression period was a greater consciousness by business that economic recovery would occur only as people's confidence was reestablished in terms of their buying mood. They needed to be persuaded that the habits of restraint in buying the products of industry, cultivated during the Depression, were hindering the recovery. Accomplishing this attitudinal change required salesmanship of high ethical and persuasive order. This was the responsibility of the sales training directors whose companies were actively seeking new outlets for their products. This group of sales executives founded the first national training directors society. In 1940 in Cleveland, Ohio, the National Society of Sales Training Executives (NSSTE) was organized.

AMERICAN SOCIETY OF TRAINING DIRECTORS

National conventions of the NAF and the NSSTE did not adequately supply the demand for training skills and knowledge by business, industry, and government. Therefore, in 1944 the NAF sponsored the First National Conference of Educational Directors in Industry. It was held in Columbus, Ohio, and was highly successful. Two more such conferences were held in 1946 and 1947 in Pittsburgh and Cleveland. Each conference had strong support from local training director societies in major cities such as St. Louis, Indianapolis, Cleveland, Pittsburgh, Detroit, and New York.

When the American Society of Training Directors (ASTD) was formed in 1945, many of the local societies became its chapters. This condition created a duplication of effort, and after trying to hold a conference under joint sponsorship, the NAF decided to concentrate on foremanship and management education, leaving the training director activities in the hands of ASTD specialists.

The American Society of Training Directors was born late in World War II. In fact, it was born at the very time when many people predicted that training would go into a tailspin. Now that the war was nearly over, surely this function of training and the training director would be abandoned. The fact that it has grown each year to far exceed anyone's previous estimate shows the lack of foresight that dominated the thinking of many personnel seers at the close of the war years and shortly thereafter. With all these influences at work and with many local training directors' associations scattered throughout the country, a catalyst was needed to bring these influences into a common cause.

The petroleum industry had, since 1939, been holding meetings of the training directors of its various companies. At a meeting in New Orleans on April 2, 1942, a group of these training specialists gathered to swap training ideas and experiences. Thomas Keaty, of Esso Standard, Baton Rouge, is credited with having pointed out the need for a national society of training directors cutting across all industries. The others agreed. By means of correspondence by petroleum companies in seven states, training directors were invited to become a part of an organization called the American Society of Training Directors. The interest which ensued was so encouraging that by 1945, the American Society of Training Directors held its first annual convention in Chicago at the Morrison Hotel. Fifty-six men responded to that conference call from among the 200 members who had signed up during the previous three years. Officers were elected, and definite organization plans took form. Thomas Keaty was elected president, and Andrew Triche became secretary-treasurer.

The second annual conference was scheduled to be held in Pittsburgh in 1946, but because of a hotel elevator operator strike the meeting was, at the last moment, transferred to New Castle, Pennsylvania. Despite the disruption in plans there was a decided growth in attendance, and this trend continued in the years that followed as conferences were held in various parts of the country, usually alternating between the Midwestern and Eastern cities.

The society's headquarters for the first nine years was in the business office of the member holding the position of secretary-treasurer. This was changed in 1954, when a permanent headquarters was established in Madison, Wisconsin. With a rapid growth in membership, chapters, and staff, several local moves were made, and ultimately the society moved into a headquarters building of its own.

The original interest in, and emphasis on, the training of manufacturing and marketing personnel has continued to expand greatly. Since the '50s training has also come to encompass workers in government, utilities, and financial institutions, for example—in fact, it is now an essential in every area of employment. Similarly, as the realization grew that training and development was the transmission of knowledge and skills as such and also their successful transmittal *to people* and *by people,* suddenly a whole new group of educators found these various fields interesting, challenging, and financially rewarding. The interest of academic educators was now aroused. Their opportunities to serve in terms of behavioral understanding and modern management practices brought a strong surge of educational professionalism into the membership of the ASTD. With 11,000 members in 100 chapters covering nearly every segment of the United States, the exchange and contact opportunities offered by the society are staggering in terms of quantity, of quality, and variety. Only the imagination of the individual—whether training administrator, novitiate, or educational doctorate—limits the extent of the benefits that society membership makes available. Specialized divisions greatly enhance in-depth studies of sales training, organizational development, community development, instructional media and other special interests.

Many services have been developed to help fulfill the basic objectives of that organization. Unquestionably, one of the great services is the publication of the *Training and Development Journal.* (Originally it was called the *Journal of Industrial*

Training and was later changed to the *Journal of the ASTD;* in 1963 it became *Training Directors Journal,* and in 1966 it was given its present title.)

This society also conducts high-caliber institutes, one and two weeks in length, seeking to give professional emphasis to the development of the capabilities needed for the effective direction of training activities. The quality of all these efforts has been applauded by business, government, and social agencies. Dwight Eisenhower was the first President to recognize formally the services of this organization. The broadening scope of its responsibilities forced a change in the society's name to make it more inclusive. Fortunately it retains the letters for which it had become famous. With this change of name it became the American Society for Training and Development.

THE PAST IS PROLOGUE TO THE FUTURE

Whether the past is truly prologue to the future is entirely dependent upon the attitude of the individual. One thing is certain: Dynamic development forces are needed now and will be needed even more in the future. They will be forthcoming to serve the needs of minorities, including older persons and the handicapped, and to provide for equal opportunity and nondiscriminatory treatment. Such social growth factors are among our greatest assets and are needed in the release of human greatness.

Chapter 2

Organization and Management of Training

RICHARD B. JOHNSON

Richard B. Johnson *is an international training and development consultant. In 1970 he retired as Director, Organization Development and Training, Consolidated Natural Gas Company. Prior to joining Consolidated Natural Gas, Mr. Johnson was Training Coordinator for The Port of New York Authority; Chief of Training, U.S. Department of the Interior; Director of Training and Retraining, War Relocation Authority; and Instructor, School of Education, New York University. He is past president of ASTD; Fellow, American Management Association; and a member of honors and professional societies. He holds B.S. and M.A. degrees from New York University.*

ROLE OF TRAINING

An organization, whether public or private, exists and grows because it provides the community with goods or services the community sees as worthwhile. To do this efficiently, the organization must function at an optimum level of productivity. This level is a direct result of the collective effort of all employees. Yet not every employee works at the level established by the standard of performance for the job he or she holds. Similarly, groups of employees may not consistently produce up to standards.

When there is a difference or gap between actual performance and what is needed (the standard), productivity suffers. Training can reduce if not eliminate this gap. It does so by changing the behavior of individuals—by giving them whatever additional specific items of knowledge, skill, or attitude they need to perform up to that standard.

Changing behavior, then, is the function of training. The terminal objective is to help achieve the goals of the organization through optimum use of manpower. Some ways of doing this are explained in other chapters of this handbook. Here we are concerned with ways to organize and manage the training function.

What Problems Can Training Solve? Training can solve a variety of manpower problems which militate against optimum productivity. Included are operating problems having a manpower component. These problems can emerge within any group: exempt, nonexempt, line, staff, unskilled, skilled, paraprofessional, professional, and lower, middle, and upper management. These problems will differ in nature, and yet all have a common denominator: The solution requires individuals to add to their apperceptive backgrounds specific, identifiable items of additional knowledge, skill, or understanding. Organization-wide, these problems include needs to:

- Increase productivity
- Improve the quality of work and raise morale
- Develop new skills, knowledge, understanding, and attitudes
- Use correctly new tools, machines, processes, methods, or modifications thereof
- Reduce waste, accidents, turnover, lateness, absenteeism, and other overhead costs
- Implement new or changed policies or regulations
- Fight obsolescence in skills, technologies, methods, products, markets, capital management, etc.
- Bring incumbents to that level of performance which meets (100 percent of the time) the standard of performance for the job
- Develop replacements, prepare people for advancement, improve manpower deployment, and ensure continuity of leadership
- Ensure the survival and growth of the enterprise

Where Can Training Become a Functional Part of the Organization?   Training can become a functional part of the organization anywhere. All that is needed is evidence that an operating problem exists which can be solved in whole or in part through structured and controlled training activities. The following are examples of such problems: (1) Newly employed persons need to become acquainted with the organization's goals, policies, structure, products or services, etc. This information can be disseminated economically and uniformly via group sessions. The training department is the unit best equipped to give such instruction. (2) A new policy is to be implemented. Supervisors and others whose work will be influenced by the policy are brought together. The people who structured the policy explain the need, answer questions, and get feedback. (3) A new procedure, a new record form, or a new machine (or a modification of present usage) is being introduced. Everyone concerned is brought together for explanations, demonstrations, question periods, reactions, and practice. Instruction is given by the person(s) responsible for the proper use of the procedure, form, or machine. (4) The quality of written reports, letters, or other documents needs to be improved. All persons concerned are scheduled into one or more training sessions in which they review or develop standards, study or compose samples of desired material, practice, etc. If the organization is not itself capable of supplying needed instruction, resources outside the organization can be used. A number of these are described elsewhere in this handbook.

How Can Training Become a Functional Part of the Organization?   Training can become a functional part of the organization by helping to improve productivity. The performance of an employee is the responsibility of his or her immediate supervisor. This performance reflects in part the supervisor's interest in training and ability as a trainer. Understandably, results vary. They also are unpredictable. Instruction usually is informal, sometimes on an "if, when, and as needed" basis. It is limited largely to immediate on-the-job application. Finally, it often is done on a one-to-one basis; i.e., the supervisor works with a single subordinate.

As the organization grows, so do the kind and number of operating problems. So also does the number of people needing guidance and help. A felt need emerges for something beyond informal training. Line managers and others see a planned approach as a better way of solving some of these problems. Evidence accumulates that group training would pay off. The time has come for a formal, structured, controlled program of manpower development. The time is ripe for the addition of a training function to the organization structure.

At this point the executive traditionally expected to take the initiative is the one in charge of "people." In the past, this person was often the industrial relations officer or the personnel officer. There is now an increasing trend to assign the broad people function to a top management level with a human resource development kind of title. Regardless of title, the person in charge of people factors is approached, accepts the assignment and now we have training as a functional part of the organization.

The person in charge moves to get answers to some basic questions.

- When is qualified manpower needed—immediately or during the next several years?
- What kinds of operating problems involving manpower exist for which training can provide solutions in whole or in part?
- What kinds of training are already going on? *Note:* It is possible that some managers have been quietly carrying on excellent training within their own units. They may have some ideas which should be made available to others.
- When is training needed—immediately, next year, or within the next five years?
- Will top management support a viable program?
- Who can be tapped as a training manager?

GROWTH OF THE TRAINING FUNCTION

Embracing the "promotion-from-within" policy, our human resource officer looks around for someone to invite to become the training manager. He or she should know the organization, be respected by fellow workers, like people, want to get into training, have a college degree, and who ideally has had previous training experience. If such a person can be found and accepts the offer, he or she is transferred to training and is given every support. We now have a training manager

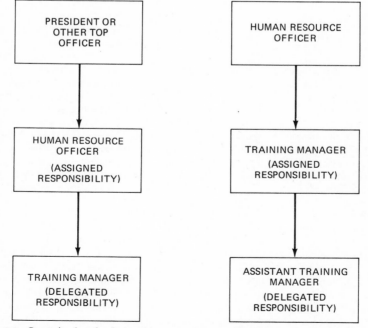

Fig. 2-1 Organizational relationships.   **Fig. 2-2** Human resource department relationships.

(TM). If no one can be found within the organization, outside recruitment is pursued. Here the criteria can be designed to attract true training and development professionals. Of the two methods, the latter often is the safest. The organization gets someone who can handle a challenging job right from the start (see Fig. 2-1).

Let us assume that a woman has been chosen as TM and that she does a good job. Calls for her services increase. Soon her workload as consultant, program designer, presenter, etc., becomes too heavy. She is given a full-time assistant (see Fig. 2-2).

Time passes. The organization continues to grow, and so does the training function. More help is needed. Additional manpower is assigned. Our first instructor is promoted to assistant TM. One of the new instructors works into skills training, and the other into supervisory development (see Fig. 2-3).

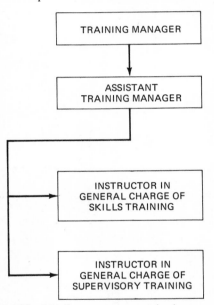

Fig. 2-3 Four-person organization.

Organization by Specialty

Some organizations in both the public and private sectors have had large training departments for years. Many professionals and support personnel share a wide variety of assignments. The division of labor among these practitioners reflects the kinds of training and educational needs which have emerged as the organization has expanded. Some corporations, government departments, and other large entities have organized on a functional basis. Specialists handle the training needs of homogeneous groups of employees: clerical workers, production workers, salespeople, engineers, foremen and supervisors, managers, executives, and others. For control purposes some large organizations have structured a central training and education (T&E) group at headquarters, with counterparts in subsidiaries (see Fig. 2-4).

In these large organizations, T&E support personnel also are assigned by specialty. Some handle program design, and others handle the development of training materials. Some are concerned with tests and records, with audiovisual and computer-assisted instruction installations, with the supervision of instruction, with research, or with off-site courses including education refund programs, etc. (see Fig. 2-5).

Expanding Role of the Training Manager

As the training function expands and activities proliferate, the role of the TM becomes less that of a program creator and presenter and increasingly that of a line manager. Now our TM must direct and control a diverse activity. He or she must use effectively all the management techniques. The TM has to do long-range planning geared to manpower projections; implement and audit policies; structure the training operation for maximum productivity; establish and maintain standards; select, train, and motivate staff; evaluate performance and administer rewards; develop and implement career patterns for staff; employ operations analysis and cost-reduction techniques; budget skillfully (both performance and fiscal); be aware of current and emerging manpower needs and problems; serve

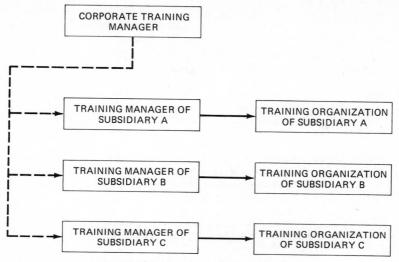

Fig. 2-4 Structure of a multiunit system.

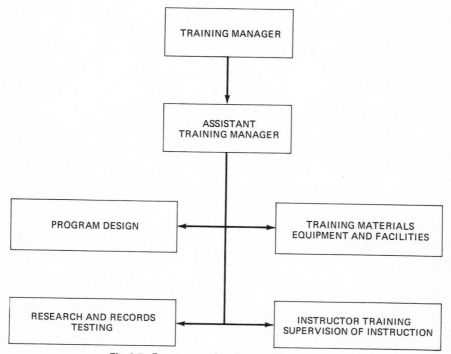

Fig. 2-5 Support services in a multiunit system.

management as an in-house consultant; work creatively and cooperatively with a large number of people throughout the organization; keep up with education and training technology; and be active in the professional association. The selection and development of the training staff are discussed in the next chapter of this handbook.

POLICIES

The organization and management of the training function stem from its implementing policy. This is the basic statement giving the function its license and character. It defines its scope and responsibility. It has its root in the basic policy of the overall organization. It shows clearly just how training is expected to contribute to the achievement of the goals of the organization. The writing of this basic policy is one of the first steps to be taken when setting up a training function. In general terms this basic training policy should identify:

- The reasons for establishing the function.
- The title of the person under whose general jurisdiction the function will be carried out.
- The title of the person to whom specific responsibility has been delegated. *Note:* This usually is the training manager.
- The broad areas of activity with which the function will be concerned.
- Other basic aspects which answer the question: How will training contribute to the goals of the organization?

For an example of a basic policy, see Fig. 2-6.

As training activities expand, specialized policies may be needed. Each will have its root in the parent statement. They become additions to the training and development policy manual. They identify what is to be done, how, by whom, and in what manner. Each will be revised from time to time as conditions and experience make this desirable, for all policies are but aids to administration. No policy should be regarded as a law of nature. However, if each is carefully constructed as a general guide, its life should be quite stable. Each, of course, will have been approved by top management for harmony with the overall goals of the organization (see Fig. 2-7).

Organizational Attitudes

Organizational attitudes directly affect the training function. These attitudes are subjective feelings people have about an activity. They are held by everyone. At a given moment each employee, regardless of level or specialty, likes or does not like training, depending upon his or her personal experience and perceptions. Where there has been no personal involvement in training, feelings can mirror those of the boss, other authority figures, or peers, for example. Friends who have been through a training program return to report on what took place, how things went, the quality of instruction, the personalities of the leaders, the degree of class participation, the adequacy of facilities, and the relevance of the whole thing to personal needs. Listeners are influenced accordingly. Successful indeed is the program which the returning trainee describes as "good stuff—I can use it."

The decision to support a training function is made by top management. The decision to conduct specific programs generally is made by middle management (heads of divisions, departments, sections, etc.). Personal attitudes toward the training of these leaders contribute to the organizational attitude. In a real sense these middle managers determine how far training will get—the amount of money, personnel, facilities, and other support that will be allocated. Therefore, where training is based on a valid need, where it is performance-oriented, and

Guide Number: 313

Supersedes: 313 dated June 28, 1968

SUBJECT: Management Development and Planning

APPROVED: By Management - March 12, 1975

Date: April 16, 1975

Page: 1 of 1

Objective

To assure continuity of management leadership necessary to meet the everchanging needs of the System:

1. Through identification of each manager's individual needs for increased skills and knowledge.

2. Through the provision of means to assist each manager to attain his goals of self-development for improvement in current job performance in preparation for greater responsibility.

3. Through providing a System mechanism for the exchange of information as to subsidiary company personnel needs and as to the availability of highly qualified employees.

Policy

1. Each System Company will:

   a. Maintain a continuing formal inventory of its present and future needs for management leadership and available replacements.

   b. To the extent possible, maintain a management personnel work force sufficient to allow the use of such techniques as rotation, participation in extended study and training assignments, etc.

   c. Provide means appropriate for various levels of management to establish objectives and measure performance. This will normally be accomplished through manager to manager consultation held periodically for this purpose and should at all times be separate and apart from appraisal for salary administration.

   d. Assist each manager in his self-development effort by providing the opportunities, both within and outside of the Company, for such improvement.

2. Such individual company programs will be coordinated on a System basis in an effort to achieve a goal where each incumbent in a management position is the best qualified individual available in the System.

Procedure

1. Each System company will establish procedures and forms and assign responsibility for the maintenance of such Management Development Programs.

2. Quarterly meetings will be held by the heads of the Employee Relations function in the Consolidated Processing Service Company, Consolidated Reserve Corporation. The Bar Operation Company, and The Airport Maintenance Company. They will meet as representatives of the four Management Manpower Planning Committees. At these meetings (and when necessary between meetings) information will be interchanged to be communicated to the respective company committees concerning the following situations. (This interchange will be restricted to positions and their incumbents for all key personnel as defined by each Company Committee. Positions reporting to the President would be excluded from this interchange.)

   a. Positions for which adequate replacement cannot at the time be identified.

   b. Cases of a highly qualified individual with potential for at least two levels beyond his current assignment, for whom at the time no reasonably foreseeable advancement possibilities can be identified.

   c. Positions for which a Committee in one Company is considering as a future replacement an individual from another Company.

3. Before hiring from the outside for a position as qualified under 2 above, each Company will contact the other companies in the System as to whether or not qualified candidates are available.

Fig. 2-6 Sample of a basic policy.

THE ABC CORPORATION

EMPLOYEE RELATIONS POLICY AND PROCEDURE

Date: August 17, 1974

SUBJECT: Education Refund Plan

Approved by R. B. Johness, Vice President - Employee Relations
Supersedes Policy and Procedure issued September 1, 1971

I.   Policy

Policy Guide 308 states the objective of this plan is -

"By means of the Education Refund Plan, it is the intent
to assist employees to attain optimum performance on
their present assignment and to prepare for additional
responsibilities."

II.   Administration

The administration of the Education Refund Plan is the responsibility
of the Training Manager.

III. Reimbursement

1. An eligible employee will be reimbursed in full for expenses
    of tuition; required fees, books and materials.

2. Employees receiving allowances from other sources such as
    G.I. Bill, scholarship, grant-in-aid, etc., may participate
    to the extent that approved costs exceed allowances from
    other sources.

3. Internal Revenue Service rulings consider such reimbursements
    as income. Therefore, arrangements will be made for the
    necessary tax withholding from any such reimbursements.

IV.   Eligibility

To be eligible for reimbursement, an employee must:

1. Have regular active employee status at time of application for
    and completion of the courses. Employees on leave of absence
    status are ineligible, except those on educational leave of
    absence. Note: an employee will not be reimbursed if he or

Fig. 2-7 Sample of a specialized policy.

-2-

she leaves the employ of the Company before completing the course, or in cases of course completion, before a reimbursement check can be processed.

2. Have sufficient background, and show sufficient initiative and promise in his work to warrant his undertaking of the training at Company expense.

3. Select courses which bear a relationship to the employee's present job or possible future assignment. All courses required for an approved degree are reimbursable. However, courses which are job related shall be given priority over other listed courses and electives.

4. Select courses which will not interfere with his normally scheduled work. The number of courses authorized will be determined with this in view.

5. Select courses offered (a) at any accredited secondary school, college or university, (b) at any business school, technical institute. trade school, association, professional society, or similar organization sponsoring after-hours educational or vocational courses approved under the Plan, (c) at any correspondence school certified by the National Home Study Council. In cases where there is a significant difference in tuition costs for courses leading to comparable educational objectives, the employee may be requested to select the course with the lower cost.

6. The applicant must obtain approval of the immediate supervisor and the Training Manager prior to enrollment in any course.

7. Within three months of completion, submit receipts for monies paid, certification of passing grades and duplicate copy of application form. Employees authorized to take refresher courses for a professional license (such as professional engineering license) will be reimbursed for such courses upon evidence of completion even though the professional license or other certificate is not received.

V. Application Procedure

1. Application for authorization of outside study courses is to be made in duplicate on Educational Refund Application Form.

2. The applicant sends to his supervisor the application, in duplicate, together with a copy of the current school catalog describing these courses.

3. The supervisor evaluates the application in accordance with the requirements of section IV above. He forwards both copies of the application (containing his reasons for approval or disapproval) and the catalog to the Training Manager through

Fig. 2-7 (Cont.) Sample of a specialized policy.

-3-

his Department Head. He may attach records or other information which might help in judging the application.

4. The application must be filed with the Training Manager at
least two weeks before the course begins. If, for valid
reasons, the application cannot be so submitted, the employee
may be requested to attach a memorandum addressed to the
Training Manager, explaining the delay.

5. The Training Manager approves or disapproves the application,
signing same.

6. If the application is approved, the Training Manager notifies
the employee's supervisor by returning the duplicate to him.
In turn, the supervisor returns the duplicate to the employee.
The employee then may enroll.

7. If the application is not approved, the Training Manager
notifies the supervisor by returning the duplicate and the
catalog together with a written explanation. In turn, the
supervisor returns the duplicate and the catalog, together
with the written explanation to the employee.

VI.   Refund Procedure

Refunds are made only on receipt of evidence of payment and certification of passing grades or successful completion where appropriate. Request for refund should be made within three months
after the completion of the course.

1. The employee forwards to the Training Manager his duplicate
copy of the application to which he has attached:

a. receipts for fees or other monies paid,
b. certification of passing grades, or successful completion
where appropriate.

2. After being checked by the Training Manager the duplicate copy
and/or request for payment will be forwarded to the Payroll
Department for reimbursement.

Fig. 2-7 (Cont.)   Sample of a specialized policy.

where management has a voice in determining what will be done, how it will be
done, and how results will be evaluated, the organizational attitude will be supportive. Of course, some managers and trainers always see training as "good" on the
basis that any program is good for the employees and therefore good for the
organization. As a result of such attitudes, time, talent, and money are sometimes
invested in programs not related directly to valid needs. "Training for training's
sake" is to be avoided.

WHEN IS TRAINING JUSTIFIED?

Training is expensive. It ties up manpower, time, money, facilities, equipment,
and supplies. It can disrupt production. When, then, is training justified?

- When there is no better way to solve the operating problem involved
- When other interventions have been considered and found less effective
- When the training is performance-oriented
- When changes in the behavior of the trainees can be measured

- When the new behaviors will be used on the job
- When the job environment will permit the use of the new behaviors
- When the training has been delimited and only what actually is needed at a given moment is provided
- When the trainees can profit from the instruction
- When the trainees are in a state of readiness and each sees a personal advantage in completing the program
- When the trainees can, and do, transfer their new behaviors to the job
- When the program has been carefully structured, objectives are valid and clear, instructors are capable, and equipment and facilities are adequate

Who Determines When Training Is Needed?

The need for training is determined by the head of the line or staff organizational unit in which there exists an operating problem which can be solved in whole or in part through training. Each manager is responsible for the productivity of his or her organizational unit. Training, then, is the responsibility of management. Management determines when training is needed and what kind of training there should be. The training professional determines how it shall be done, under what conditions, at what costs, and by whom. Management can be held accountable for the content validity of a program, and the training professional for the educational validity.

This does not mean that training managers sit in their offices waiting for business. Rather, they are consultants to management. They help management to see training needs. They then personally (in small organizations) or through their staff (in large organizations) help management to meet these needs.

In doing this, however, training managers resist the temptation to meet automatically *all* requests for their services. They question management and otherwise evaluate each request until they are satisfied that a valid training need exists. They do their best to determine that no other intervention will work, such as a better job (by management) of planning, organizing, assigning work, controlling, or changing a process or procedure. Some managers are quite willing to pass the buck to training. At this point, then, the training manager can be seen as a roadblock to training—and properly so.

The training professional works closely with line and staff, establishing relationships everywhere. When our TM sees a need emerging, this need is discussed with the manager concerned. Preventive training can be as profit-producing as corrective training.

Must Training Be "Sold"?

The answer to this question is "Never!" Where a valid need exists, where a program has been carefully designed to meet this need, where the program has brought about the desired changes in behavior on the part of the learners, and where the new behaviors are being used back on the job there is no need to sell training as a "good thing." It sells itself.

SCOPE OF THE TRAINING FUNCTION

As stated above, the function of training is to ensure that each employee makes a required contribution to the achievement of the goals of the organization. The required contribution is represented by the standard of performance for his or her job. Employees on all levels work in homogeneous groups (mechanics, typists, lawyers, engineers, salespeople, accountants, etc.). Some are paid by the hour; others are on salary. Each is employed because his or her contribution is needed. Each is unique and changeable.

The organization itself is in constant flux. It is growing or dying. It is expanding or shrinking in its particular marketplace. It changes pace and direction under the impact of an ever-changing environment.

New products, new processes, new materials, and new services; new uses for old products, processes, materials, and services; the expansion of technology; the activities of competitors; the responses of those served; the influences of regulations and other controls—all these and other factors combine to help or hinder an organization's ability to survive and grow.

One key to this survival and growth is the efficiency of the work force. Therefore, a major effort in successful organizations is directed at optimum use of manpower. This in turn calls for constant attention to the growth needs of each employee, even in organizations with large numbers of volunteer workers, such as hospital auxiliaries. To meet these needs efficiently, many organizations augment on-the-job supervision with formal off-the-job training.

This training takes many forms, depending upon the needs of particular groups of employees. Thus we have vocational and technical training, secretarial and clerical courses, sales training, courses for scientists and engineers, supervisory and management development, and other work groups. Resources outside the organization also are used, including trade and technical schools; correspondence courses; colleges, universities, and other educational institutions; consultants; special programs; and training packages. Each is described elsewhere in this handbook.

How to Get Started

The organization has decided to add a training function to its structure. It has given the training manager overall responsibility. How does the TM get started? He or she makes a study of the organization's needs for training and then prepares a recommendation for the boss.

In making the study, the training manager interviews key executives and others to get answers to such questions as:

- In what ways is present employee performance inadequate?
- What new skills or knowledge is needed by what kinds of workers?
- What planned changes in the operation of the enterprise will require workers to possess new abilities and insights?
- What plans, if any, does the organization have for expansion of the work force? If it has such plans, what kinds of workers will be needed to permit the expansion?
- Can present employees be trained or retrained for upcoming jobs, or will new employees with the needed skills have to be recruited?
- What needs exist for replacements of all kinds?
- What kinds of training are already going on?
- What do individual managers feel should be done to increase manpower productivity?
- In what order should these things be done?

Making this study is not a quick or easy exercise. Every key person must be interviewed; no one must be left out. Also, the comments of these people provide clues about their attitudes toward training. From their responses you can estimate the extent to which they are "for" the function. Finally, your meetings give you an opportunity to establish relationships. These can be helpful as time goes by. As a group, key officials are dedicated and capable. Their help can enrich the value of your survey. *Caution:* Some officials will talk to you in confidence. Respect this. Protect them.

Your approach to each official is easy. Each is expecting you. The survey and its purpose have been announced. A schedule of visits shows with whom you will meet and when and where you will meet them. This schedule is not tight. Enough time (two hours?) is allowed between visits to accommodate an occasional spillover. You also have time to polish your notes from the last meeting, for you should take notes—right in front of those with whom you are meeting. They will see this as efficient and will know they are to be quoted accurately. They will give better thought to their inputs. *Suggestion:* List your questions on your pad ahead of time, thus ensuring coverage of each.

Each interview can be opened with a single question put to the host: "In your opinion, Miss X, what are desirable next steps in training and development?" The answers to other questions will emerge as the interview progresses.

It is possible that a survey will be made before a training manager is employed. The results can give clues concerning the kind of training manager needed. This aids recruitment. When the TM comes aboard, he or she starts with the recommendations of the study. The survey committee represents all units of the organization in which significant training needs exist.

In preparing your recommendation for your boss, consolidate your notes into a summary which will

- Identify apparent needs
- Propose ways to meet these needs
- Suggest a timetable for implementing stages
- Include other items you feel appropriate

ORGANIZING THE TRAINING FUNCTION

In a one-person training unit the work is apt to be organized on a priority basis— at any given moment the hottest job gets the attention. When the load gets too heavy, temporary help can be recruited from outside the training division. Persons from other units can be detailed temporarily into "training." Instructional duties can be shared with others either inside the organization or outside. Clerical help can be tapped elsewhere in personnel.

When the training unit has grown to include several people, formal organization is needed. The unit usually is structured on the following basis:

- The work is divided functionally. Clerical training is handled separately, and so are production training, sales training, management training, etc.
- All activities are covered. Each is the whole responsibility of a named person; i.e., each is assigned to only one person.
- All persons know to whom they report.
- All persons know who reports to them.
- All persons know the boundaries of their assignments.
- Each position has a written job description.
- Each position has a written standard of performance.
- The structure of the unit is shown on a published organization chart.
- The workload is balanced.
- Responsibilities are delegated so that decisions can be made as close to the point of action as possible.
- All persons have the authority they need.
- The organization is as simple as possible; levels of authority are kept to a minimum.
- The organization has the approval of the person to whom the training manager reports.
- The organization pattern is free of nonessentials, overlapping assignments, conflicts in lines of authority, and foggy areas of responsibility.
- Each position has an identified backstop.

- An organization manual is available to everyone. This manual covers:
  - All policies
  - The organization chart
  - All job descriptions
  - All standards of performance
  - Grade and salary-range charts
  - Career patterns
  - Other pertinent items

MANAGEMENT OF THE TRAINING FUNCTION

After the training function is organized, it must be managed. Managing here is the same as managing anywhere: each of the management functions must be handled skillfully.

Research

Research is the basis for planning. It answers important questions such as: What is going on? How will it affect our organization? How will it affect training? What should we do about it now, in the near future, and next year? Additional questions concern events outside the organization: What are the trends in the industry, the profession, the marketplace, the technology, and the regulatory agencies? What is new in the training business—what methods, procedures, materials, equipment, concepts, interventions, successes, failures, programs, publications, and media should we know about? Should these things influence what we are trying to do? If so, in what ways?

Planning

Planning is the key to optimum use of training manpower and resources. It is based on the results of research and also on constant reference to the goals established as a result of the organization survey of training and development needs. Planning answers such questions as:

- What should be done?
- In what sequence?
- When?
- How?
- By whom?
- For whom?
- In what ways?
- At what cost?
- What specific results can be expected?
- What constraints will operate?
- What problems must be resolved?

An *annual* plan pictures what the training function will attempt to accomplish during the ensuing 12 months. A *long-term* plan will identify targets over a period of several years. Interim and *short-term* plans treat specific projects, individual courses or programs, expansion of facilities, additions to equipment, etc.

Plans must be developed carefully. All persons concerned should contribute inputs. Final agreements must have the approval of the person with final responsibility for the function, usually the TM's boss. Plans also should be flexible and amenable to adjustment as conditions inevitably change.

Scheduling

Scheduling is based on the plan. It identifies the sequence in which events will take place and pinpoints when an event will occur, who will be in charge, where it will take place, for whom it will be held, and how long it will last. Scheduling ties down people, places, facilities. All concerned must participate in the setting up of a schedule and must agree with its final format. Schedules, of course, are not fixed in cement. Unexpected events can crop up suddenly and throw off even the best schedule, at which point the schedule is restructured.

Operating

Operating is based on the schedule. It involves all the things training personnel do with and for others to achieve the objectives of a given program, action, or event. Operating, for instance, embraces the preparation for, conduct of, and follow-up steps pursued in presenting a training seminar, workshop, course, lecture series, tour, hands-on clinic, or any other structured activity. Operating integrates people, facilities, equipment, and other components into a coordinated effort. Operating also includes the day-to-day management of the training function, the maintenance of a climate which motivates, the identification and on-the-spot solution of problems, the integration of diverse personnel and other resources, and the recording and analysis of experience for guidance purposes. Operating success can be measured by responses to such simple questions as: How are things going? How are we doing? Are we on the beam? Are we within budget? Are we on target re our schedule (short-term, long-term)? Operating puts planning and scheduling to the test. It also reveals the abilities of personnel to carry out assigned roles. It reveals strengths and pinpoints needs for improved performance.

Controlling

Controlling keeps things on the beam. It fosters constant surveillance of operations against targets and assures compliance with goals. Familiar control devices include records and reports, inventories, surveys, questionnaires, analysis of performance, kinetic responses of trainees, subjective data including people's opinions (the grapevine), observation, and measurement of such things as compliance with budget allocations, maintenance of schedules, and depletion of supplies. Control procedures give warning of deviations from plans and goals. Causes can be identified and examined, and corrective action can be taken. Broad controls are provided by policy statements, and other controls by supporting statements identifying specific objectives for particular activities.

Evaluating

Evaluating is the payoff step. It determines whether the training function is doing what it was set up to do—whether it is worth the cost. The basic question is a simple one: Did the seminar, workshop, class, course, program, or whatever accomplish what it was supposed to accomplish? The same question can be applied to the training function itself: Is the training division doing a good job? Is it accomplishing the things it was created to accomplish? The answer is easy to get. Just take the stated goal of an activity and turn it around. It now becomes the criterion for measuring effectiveness. For instance, in Fig. 2-6 policy item 1-a reads: "Each System company *will* maintain a continuing formal inventory of its present and future needs for management leadership and available replacements." This is the goal. To get an evaluative criterion (a gauge for measuring effectiveness), change the first five words of this policy statement to read: "*Does* each System company maintain . . . ? At the moment of evaluation, the System companies do or do not—or they do to some extent. If they do not, or do only to some extent, the next question also is simple: Why not? The answer, of course, may reveal very good reasons why the criterion has not been met. Maybe the evaluation has been made short of the deadline for creation of the inventory. Maybe the inventory is waiting behind other programs for processing into the computer. Maybe other perfectly valid reasons obtain. The point is that evaluation must be done in the light of circumstances. Yet it must be done, for the reasons also may reveal inefficiency, procrastination, poor planning, etc. One of the easiest training activities to evaluate is an individual course: Did behavior change as planned? Is the new behavior being used back on the job?

Evaluation also provides clues useful in controlling the pace and direction of the training function. Ask yourself and others questions such as:

- What policies should be revised, and in what way?
- What new policies should be promulgated?
- What activities should be phased out, and what new ones should be instituted?
- Should training personnel be redeployed?
- What additional services should be implemented?
- In what ways should we increase the productivity of the training division?

Other sources of evaluation include:

- Performance of trainees on tests, in demonstrations, and in other situations in which behavior can be observed
- Opinions of trainees (expressed either in written form or orally)
- Opinions of supervisors concerning improvement (or lack of improvement) in the performance of subordinates following training
- Recommendations of training personnel during staff meetings or at other times
- Observations of the person to whom the training function reports
- Comments of other management personnel interested in the particular activity under discussion
- Other situations from which clues can be distilled

Revision

Revision keeps training and development viable, relevant, up-to-date, and on target. It restructures organization to optimize productivity, and it eliminates dips in the management performance curve. A training department is dynamic. It changes pace and direction constantly. The need for revision of structure and activity is ever present. Clues to needed revision come from experience with program controls and from the results of evaluation. *Caution:* Revision must be approached with care, assuming that research, planning, organization, and operation have been done as carefully as possible. Do not revise anything until there is clear evidence that such revision will indeed improve something. Change for the sake of change is to be avoided.

Reportability

As mentioned earlier in this chapter, the training function generally reports officially to the top human resource development officer. TMs can report to other persons, depending upon the particular organization. For instance, TMs are known to report to vice presidents, presidents, plant managers, division managers, sales managers, employee relations managers, and others.

Unofficially, the TM "reports" to at least two other persons:

- The head of any line or staff unit of the organization with whom the TM or staff is working at any given moment (i.e., anyone who is planning to or actually is running a training activity in the unit)
- Any member of top management who has an interest in training or who wants to be kept up-to-date concerning training activities

Accountability

Accountability is a synonym for responsibility. The TM is accountable for all that he or she does within the bounds of the basic policy implementing the training function. This includes accountability for the results of all actions taken in the name of training, including program development, operation, and evaluation; the management of budget; the deployment of staff; the maintenance of relationships everywhere in the organization; etc. The TM rightfully can be, and is, held accountable for all that happens. Realizing this, experienced TMS never hesitate to seek guidance from their bosses or others who can help them arrive at decisions and take actions which will properly further the goals that all have in view.

Relationships

Relationships are critical to the success of the TM and his or her staff. To do the job properly, the TM must be able to move throughout the organization with complete freedom, thus developing relationships with many people. The way in which others perceive the TM as a person helps or hinders this individual's efforts. If the TM is seen as ethical, capable, and likable, the way will be smooth. The TM's style will elicit confidence and therefore cooperation. Occasionally, a training problem will have an element of tension. Here the TM's dignity, reserved judgment, and face-saving questions addressed to others will bolster that feeling of "comfortableness" between the TM and others which is the touchstone in relationships.

BIBLIOGRAPHY

An Introductory Course in Teaching and Training Methods for Management Development, International Labour Office, Geneva, 1972, especially chaps. 19, 21.

Training Methods for Skills Acquisition, American Society for Training and Development (cosponsored by the Agency for International Development, U.S. Department of State), Madison, Wis., 1972, especially chaps. 5, 7–9.

Chapter 3

Selection and Development of the Training Staff

PAUL H. CHADDOCK

Paul H. Chaddock *is Director of Personnel Development and Management Manpower Planning, J. L. Hudson Co., Detroit, Mich. He was formerly Director, Organization/Manpower Development, Addressograph Multigraph Corporation, Cleveland, Ohio. His career at Addressograph Multigraph began in marketing. Mr. Chaddock has given many presentations on training-staff development to ASTD and business and academic groups and has published widely. A member of the Association for Educational Communications and Technology, the National Society of Sales Training Executives, and ASTD, he holds a B.S. degree in business administration from West Virginia Wesleyan College.*

OVERVIEW AND DEFINITIONS

The objectives of this chapter are to provide an overview of the kinds of personnel required to staff a training department, where to find them, how to select and develop them, their career-path options, and ways of evaluating their performance. To accomplish these objectives, it is important to define the various roles a trainer may assume and how these roles may be employed to accomplish the many tasks that a total training department should address.

Training departments must be designed, staffed, and resourced so that they can assist in achieving the goals of the organization. Although this chapter will attempt to be broad enough in scope to apply to all types of organizations, it will be specific when discussing techniques and tools used to select and develop a staff.

Definitions of Roles of the Training Staff

Too often the label of "trainer" is synonymous with "one who trains"; translated, that may mean "instruct" or "teach." Although conducting training programs is usually an important function, it is only one of the many roles an effective trainer should assume. If a training department is performing its mission of contributing to the achievement of organizational goals, it will be staffed by people trained to detect, analyze, and solve the performance problems of those who make up the organization. The various roles that are needed may all be assumed by one person or given to individuals who specialize. In any event, the total staff should be prepared to handle the following specialized roles.

Learning Specialist Gordon L. Lippitt and Leonard Nadler, in an article appearing in *Training and Development Journal,* identified three roles of a training director. When delegated to his or her staff, these can be seen as separate training roles. The first role is that of learning specialist. Lippitt and Nadler define a learning specialist as one who is "skilled in the ability to use learning theory and methods to meet training needs."[1] This definition implies that there is much more to being a trainer than instructing. It means that the trainer must be able to identify needs solvable by training, to design appropriate training, and to present it in such a way that the process of learning is maximized. For the purpose of staffing a department, this role can be divided into the roles of designer and presenter.

The designer is responsible for defining training needs, analyzing them in terms of training requirements and objectives, designing program content to achieve those objectives, developing evaluation and validation procedures, and field-testing the program to ensure that trainees have the necessary skills.

The presenter is responsible for ensuring that the environment in which the designed training is given and the manner in which it is presented assist the trainees in their learning. This involves establishing the climate for learning, presenting material clearly, responding to trainee concerns, and providing ways for trainees to evaluate their own progress toward achieving the training objectives. The presenter must be able to use all types of training devices and aids. He or she must be able to conduct training in the mode most closely approximating the work setting. An understanding of the dynamics of communication and motivation and a knowledge of the principles of learning are important.

Although the roles of the designer and the presenter have been discussed separately, there is a close relationship between the two; in fact, they are often performed by the same individual. The net result is that the role of the learning specialist consists in the design and presentation of training.

Administrator   In referring to this role, Lippitt and Nadler state that the administrator "will need to recruit, select, and develop his staff team; plan programs; set up the process of coordination and communication; carry out financial planning of the training effort and all of the other administrative steps of leading a staff function in the organization."[2]

The administrator is the manager of the training function. He or she is responsible for seeing that the training staff is organized, resourced, and skilled to provide training activities responsive to the organization's needs. The person assuming this role must be knowledgeable about the total organization—its goals, unique characteristics, politics, sources of real power, and competition.

The administrator must strive to gain organizational credibility. He or she must recognize the obligation of helping line management solve its training needs, but must also keep in mind that line management is usually not knowledgeable enough concerning the appropriate role of training to always suggest its best use. Therefore, the administrator must gain enough respect in the organization to operate proactively as well as react to requests. The administrator gains respect by managing the training staff's activities in a cost-effective manner and by directing its resources toward solving real organizational problems.

Consultant   The third role to be found in a training staff is that of internal consultant. The internal consultant has been described as a "consultant on problem solving, change and organizational development."[3] This role is both the most difficult to staff for and the one with the highest payoff for the organization. It is also the one most difficult to define and compartmentalize because the activities performed in this role are varied and depend on many factors, including the skill of the consultant; the consultant's relationship with the organization and its management, familiarity with the pending problem, and personal style of behavior; where in the organizational hierarchy the training function is located; and the ability of the consultant to recognize problems in the organization.

Lippitt and Nadler list the following tasks of the internal consultant:

1. Helps management examine organizational problems.
2. Helps management examine the contribution of training to these problems.
3. Helps examine the long-range and short-range objectives of the training.
4. Explores with management alternatives to training–problem solving approaches.
5. Develops, with management, the training plans.
6. Explores appropriate resources to implement plan.
7. Provides consultation for management on evaluation and review of program.
8. Explores with management the follow-up steps necessary to reinforce problem solution.[4]

As this list illustrates, the consultant must have many skills and perform many tasks, and the role is influenced by the manner in which he or she performs it—in other words, the "what" of the job is varied, as well as the "how."

Again referring to Lippitt and Nadler, Fig. 3-1 shows various approaches the training director can take, from directive to non-directive (consulting).

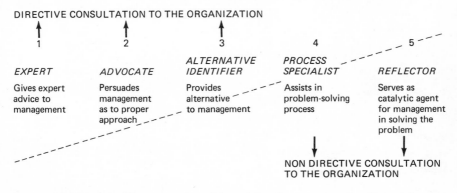

Fig. 3-1 Multiple consulting approaches of the training director. *(Reproduced by special permission from Training and Development Journal, August 1967. Copyright 1967 by the American Society for Training and Development, Inc.)*

One final point to be made here is that the specifics of the consultant role need to be tailored to the organization.

Interdependency of Roles

One might get the impression that the three roles are fairly discrete and independent. It is true that on a given day or in connection with a particular project a consultant's activities could be quite far removed from those of a learning specialist. However, the total training function should be collectively providing advice and service aimed at correcting the human performance deficiencies of the organization.

Deficiencies in human performance exist for a myriad of reasons. The training staff will therefore be engaged in many different activities, depending on the deficiency they are trying to correct. Because these activities can be traced to one of the three trainer roles discussed above, there is both separation of task, skill, and knowledge and commonality of purpose. This commonality of purpose results in an interdependency of roles because the ultimate goal of the training function cannot be reached unless all roles are performed. Common knowledge and skill support the roles.

The implication of this role relationship for recruiting, selection, and development is that it is desirable for candidates for all roles to have certain characteristics, knowledge, and skills. It is important for total departmental success that trainers who are assigned these roles understand their interdependency.

Objectives of Training-Function Organization

We have already discussed the organization and management of a training function in Chapter 2. However, it is important to say a word here about the objectives of a training department and their relationship to staffing and development.

The department's objectives need to reflect the organization's current stage of development. If the organization is in a growth period, there will probably need to be heavy emphasis on the training of new people in various skills required to realize this growth. The fact that the organization has entered new markets or adopted new technology may have created a significant need to retain longer-term employees in new skills. This situation might make the learning specialist's role the predominant one in the training department.

In another organization the emphasis might be on changes caused by new management or by a move from strong central control to a decentralized structure with autonomous functions or profit centers. The training department might be the resource looked to for assistance in making these changes or resolving conflicts caused by them. In this situation the most important role for the department to provide would be that of consultant.

The point is that the training department needs to look first to the priorities of the organization before establishing its own mission statement and supporting objectives. This should be done on a periodic basis to ensure relevance in staff and other departmental resources.

SOURCES OF MANPOWER

The problem of staffing for any position always involves the decision concerning whether it is better to choose someone who has all the skills required (an external candidate) or someone who has some of the necessary skills and knowledge and appears to have the ability to learn the rest (an internal candidate). The issue of choosing between in-house and outside manpower for a training staff deserves some discussion.

In-House versus Outside Manpower Sources

Successful performance of any of the roles in a training department requires (1) the skills demanded by the specific role and (2) a knowledge of the organization. The latter includes a knowledge of how things are done, the informal organization, and the culture that makes up the organization.

Acquiring the necessary skills and knowledge costs money. A direct expenditure may be involved, such as the cost of attending a seminar or course, or there may be an indirect expenditure which is more difficult to measure but which is nevertheless significant. Expenditures that fall into the second category include the costs of operating at less than top performance, taking longer than necessary to perform a task, and making bad decisions.

Often overlooked is the cost of orienting a person recruited from outside the organization. One company has reported that orientation costs 190 percent of the first year's salary for a new employee regardless of level.[5] That cost is incurred even if the person recruited has all the job skills and knowledge required for that position.

A candidate selected from within the organization will probably have fewer job skills but more organization knowledge. A danger associated with selecting internal candidates is that the organization may not invest the money necessary to provide them with the opportunity to learn job skills.

Current "master performers" are one of the most frequently used sources of candidates for the learning-specialist role (both designer and presenter). People are chosen to be trainers in a given skill area because they have demonstrated their competence. There is no denying that knowing how to perform a task well is a great advantage when training others to perform it, but there is a big difference between being good at a task and designing instruction or teaching others. If an organization is to realize the total benefits of a skilled training department, it must recognize that unique skills are required, and it must provide the opportunity for employees to acquire them.

Frequently the impact of the trainer is underestimated. Ineffective or inefficiently designed training can be very costly, particularly when many trainees are going through a given program. The consultant who provides bad advice to resolve organizational conflict can cause irreparable damage. Decisions to choose someone from inside the organization versus a proved professional from the outside should take into consideration the criteria of (1) economy, (2) the availability of resources to orient skills, and (3) the total training department's priorities at that point in time.

Qualifying the Opening

A critical step that must be taken prior to generating candidates for a position is that of qualifying the opening. This requires gathering two kinds of information: objective data about the candidate and the position and subjective data about the opening. Subjective information about the opening includes factors such as the following:

- The dynamics in the department. Staff members feeling strong team loyalty, versus a strong individual professional loyalty.
- The personality and management style of the department manager. Does he or she exercise tight control rather than relying heavily on individual subordinate motivation and competence?
- The biases that the organization or the department manager might have about the person who is to fill the role. Does the manager feel that candidates must possess certain physical characteristics, height, youth, etc.?
- The conceptual biases held by the current training staff. Do they feel that the training design has to be based primarily on the thinking of B. F. Skinner or on that of Carl Rogers, for example?
- The sociability of the group. Do the existing staff members like to create occasions for social gatherings, or do they tend to avoid outside social contact?

Being able to respond to such issues is an important determinant of the success of any department member.

Finding Inside Talent

Recommendations by supervisors are valuable in the search for internal candidates. Frequently supervisors will say of subordinates:

- "He really likes to help people."
- "She has good communications skills; she can really get an idea across."
- "I can always rely on her to help new people in the department get started."
- "He is a real people developer."

Such comments may indicate the presence of real skill, or they may reflect simply the subordinate's desire to perform a training role in the organization. The desire to assist in developing others is important for a trainer. When a supervisor observes this attribute in a subordinate frequently enough to make a recommendation, it will probably be worth investigating.

The observations of the current training staff are also valuable in uncovering inside talent. Being alert to the performance of trainees attending a program can be productive; frequently a trainee who wants to become a part of the training department will express this desire during such a session. The training staff can also uncover candidates while working throughout the organization, for example, when conducting a training-needs analysis or implementing a new program.

The training staff should further investigate the inside candidate's potential by creating an opportunity for him or her to be part of a training effort; for example, the training staff could ask the candidate to assist in evaluating a new program or to contribute design ideas. People in other functional areas such as employee relations, personnel, compensation, placement, or manpower planning may be good candidates.

Many of the "people" systems installed in the organization may uncover candidates. For example, a performance appraisal system may provide an opportunity to record subordinates' personal development and career goals, including specific transfers or assignments for growth. The performance appraisal might indicate that a move into the training function would be desirable. Similar information can come from succession or manpower planning systems, skills inventories, or career-path planning.

Some organizations have adopted the philosophy that a career path should move in and out of staff positions. This is often the case where the career path is aimed at making generalists out of people who started as specialists. The rationale for having key generalist line-management candidates go through training, personnel, or employee relations assignments is that such experiences better prepare them for top management. These career-path systems can be a good source for candidates.

Some general comments about using these internal sources are in order:

- The move into training may be just a stepping-stone. This may cause candidates to have a somewhat negative attitude toward developing good trainer skills because they feel the assignment is temporary.
- Moving internal candidates into training may create turnover in the training function at a more rapid pace than is desirable.
- Candidates selected from some of the internal sources discussed may have aspirations but not skills. The amount of time and money required to develop their skills may be prohibitive.
- Supervisors may recommend an employee because they are dissatisfied with the employee's performance. Supervisors' recommendations must be carefully qualified by the training manager.

A few of the ways in which the training manager can qualify internal candidates are by testing them, interviewing them, using them for temporary training task forces, having them assist in training-needs analysis, and using them as subject matter experts in the design of a new training program or as part of an evaluation team for a new training package.

Outside Sources

Outside sources used to obtain candidates include newspaper ads, employment agencies, professional organization placement services, and trade publications. Three steps should be followed when using any of these sources: specification of position and candidate requirements, candidate generation, and candidate selection.

In specifying the requirements of a position it is important to include exact responsibilities, accountabilities (products of the position), salary range, reporting relations, and the timing for filling the opening. Candidate specifications should include skills, experience, desired specialty areas, education, and personal attributes required by the job. A sample position requisition form is shown in Fig. 3-2.

Before reviewing the various methods of generating candidates, it is important to consider some factors which would impact the decision: how fast the opening needs to be filled, how much time the training manager has to screen résumés or interview candidates, the past experience constraints, and the ease or difficulty of obtaining approval for extensive relocation expense. The choice of a candidate source should be made in light of these issues.

The second step is to generate candidates. Using the position and candidate specifications, many sources can be tapped. If a newspaper ad is the means chosen, the first decision concerns the geographic area in which the search will be confined. Once the area is isolated, this will dictate which newspaper to use. Ads which appear on Tuesday, Wednesday, and Thursday for positions open have historically produced more candidates. It is advisable to use an advertising agency to assist in layout and placement of the ad, and in some instances it does not cost anything to get this professional help. Having responses returned to a blind box number may prove successful. This is especially important if the existing training staff is not aware of the recruiting effort.

Very often employment agencies have people qualified to recruit in speciality areas, such as training. There are employment agencies whose entire thrust is training, personnel, or industrial relations. One measure of the professionalism of any agency is its insistence on getting a position specification sheet from you. A good agency will also spend a considerable amount of time interviewing you to get an idea of the responsibilities, reporting relationships, and types of projects involved in the position. Any constraints should be made clear to the agency. Such things as limiting the recruiting to a given geographic area, salary range, or specialized previous experience will narrow the agency's search activity. The result should be a faster generation of qualified candidates. One major advantage of using agencies is that they will prescreen candidates, thus reducing the training managers' interviewing and selection time.

There are many professional organizations to which candidates might belong, such as the American Society for Training and Development, the National Society of Sales Training Executives, the National Society for Performance and Instruction, the National Audio-Visual Association, the Association for Educational Communications and Technology, the American Psychological Association, and the Organization Development Network. Many of these organizations maintain national offices with a continuing placement or referral service. Position and candidate specifications can be sent to the association, which will then forward résumés of appropriate candidates. Often this is a free service.

All such organizations hold annual or semiannual conferences and conventions, and it is common to find a placement booth at such meetings. Either the booth will be staffed by representatives of the organization who attempt to get openings and candidates together, or there will be a book of positions wanted and a book of positions open. Contact with candidates can normally be made during the meeting. These organizations also have local chapter or regional meetings at which similar services are provided. Their publications or newsletters can be used to advertise for candidates; this is normally a very inexpensive service and will yield good candidates.

Many commercial magazines in the training and development field have classified advertising sections. Such magazines include the *Training and Development Journal, Training, Personnel Journal, AV Communications,* and *AV Instruction.*

One frequently overlooked source is the personal contacts trainers have with

ADDRESSOGRAPH MULTIGRAPH

REQUISITION FOR PERSONNEL

NUMBER ______ UNIT ______ DATE ______

☐ Addition	☐ Replacement	☐ Permanent	☐ Temporary

Position:	Code:	Department:

Description of Duties:

Qualifications:	Education: ☐ High School ☐ College		
	Degree(s)	Field	

Work Experience Desired:

Approximate Salary:	Date Required:

ORIGINATOR ______ DEPARTMENT MANAGER ______

APPROVALS ______ MANPOWER PLACEMENT MANAGER ______

Fig. 3-2 Requisition for personnel. *(Addressograph Multigraph Corporation company form.)*

others in the field. Phone calls to people outside the organization may quickly produce highly qualified candidates known personally to the referrer. This source may uncover people who are currently unhappy or feel stymied in their jobs, but not to the point of active job hunting. In such cases, discreet inquiry can be made. It is also useful to ask the consultants or training firms you deal with about possible candidates.

In making the decision about which vehicle to use, there are two main considerations: cost and timing. Using an employment agency may be the fastest method but also the most expensive. The decision about which way to recruit will depend on the relationship of these two factors to the criticalness of filling the opening.

CANDIDATES										
DATE	NAME	SEX	SOURCE	C	N	SA	AI	O	ACTION	

ADVERTISING

PLACEMENT:

NAME   SALARY

CLASSIFICATION   CODE

STARTING DATE

Fig. 3-2 (Cont.)   Requisition for personnel.

SELECTION

Before discussing specific tools and methods, it is important to identify the relationship of the selection process to the accomplishments of the training department's goals. Malcolm Warren, in his book *Training for Results*, states:

> Once missions have been established and the organizational training unit designed, staffing it can be undertaken. Both the missions established and the organizational design contribute to setting the selection criteria for searching, screening, and selecting this staff. The organization's ability to successfully compete in the manpower market and

to attract individuals with the competence to meet the selection criteria will determine whether it will meet its design requirements. In other words, the organization may be forced to modify both mission and unit design to meet its ability to pay for or locate individuals who meet the selection criteria. Without a search of the market and its own organization, however, it is unrealistic to modify the training unit. An attempt to obtain staffing to meet organizational needs rather than modify organization requirements for available manpower is, from a systems point of view, a more realistic approach. True, modification may be necessary, but any modifications should be made grudgingly as a last resort rather than lower the potential contribution of the training function to the organization at the outset.[6]

Criteria for Selection

Before making a selection decision, it is important to identify the things to be learned about a candidate and how they will be measured. The following areas encompass what the process should reveal about the candidate.

Organizational Knowledge   This includes a knowledge or awareness of the culture of the organization and its history; the level of sophistication training has reached; the informal and formal organizational patterns; the organization's purpose, mission, and objectives; and the impact of external forces on the organization.

Professional Knowledge   Here it is important to determine the candidate's depth of understanding, pattern of experience, and levels of accomplishment. Does the person approach the training function with an innovative view or just mimic the "in" jargon of the day? Is the person affiliated with professional organizations in the field, especially in leadership roles?

Personal Qualifications   Is the candidate able to travel? Healthy? Does he or she project enthusiasm and sincerity?

Education and Training   Has the candidate been prepared through formal education and had appropriate management experience for the situation? Is the candidate's level of scholastic achievement acceptable? Has he or she had any postcollege training?

Skills and Abilities   Are the candidate's past responsibilities and accomplishments indicative of the abilities the position requires?

Personal Goals and Motivation   Are the candidate's aspirations for employment in the direction of the opening? Are his or her reasons for making a move acceptable?

If the candidate lacks qualifications in any of these areas, it is important to recognize that there will be an additional investment for training and development.

Tools for Selection

The following tools are listed in the order in which they are used. They serve as a means of obtaining information about the candidate that will be helpful in making a selection decision.

Résumés   The written résumé may well be the first contact with the candidate. A well-written résumé will be informative to the point of arousing interest, but will not be complete enough to eliminate the need for a personal interview. A good résumé will contain the objectives for employment, previous responsibilities, the accomplishments within those responsibilities, personal data, outside affiliations, and educational background.

Telephone Interviews   After selecting a résumé that describes a candidate you wish to pursue, a telephone interview should be the next step. The purposes of this call are to qualify the interest of the candidate, learn more information than the résumé provided, and (if warranted) arrange for a personal interview.

Personal Interviews   The expense of bringing the candidate to the organization should be incurred only if the first two levels of inquiry make it appear that the candidate is really attractive. Since coming to the organization for an interview usually requires some investment on the part of candidates, it is unfair to ask them to come if you are not sincerely interested in them. During this contact it will be possible to select out those candidates who for some reason have not been able to verify their experience or seem to have voids in their backgrounds that are unacceptable. You should conduct in-depth questioning concerning experience, desires, and personal qualifications. At the conclusion of this stage you will have eliminated many candidates, and your choice should be narrowed substantially.

References   It is advisable to ask candidates to supply references with whom you can get in touch. Questioning of these people should be aimed at uncovering new information, verifying information the candidate has provided, gathering opinions about performance, and confirming personal data about the candidate. Such things as outside interests, known organizational affiliations, and outstanding accomplishments would fall in this area. After you have described the position, one useful question might be: Would you hire the individual? This may give some real insight into the candidate's match with the position's requirements.

Samples of Work   Reviewing samples of work can be very useful. Asking the candidate to explain the process of design, the steps in analysis, or the results after implementation can produce valuable information about how he or she approaches the job. One extremely profitable question can be: How did you measure the results of this program in terms of payoff for the organization?

Sample Problems from the Work Setting   Describing a real problem you face within the organization and asking the candidate for ideas about how to approach it can be very productive. You can also choose problems you have already attacked. In this case it can be useful to compare the candidate's on-the-spot thinking ability with the solution your staff has designed and implemented.

Evaluation by Staff Members   Having existing staff members interview a very promising candidate can produce many mutual benefits. It will allow the candidate to assess potential associates and get some insight into the dynamics within the department. Existing members of the staff will be able to assess the candidate and share in the decision-making process about selection. This evaluation can even produce additional information about the candidate.

The information that the above steps provide about the candidate should enable you to make a fairly confident selection decision. Although there is no question that selecting the right department member requires a substantial amount of the training manager's time, professionalism and team compatibility are important enough in the training function to justify this effort.

TRAINING AND DEVELOPING THE STAFF

Because of the need to improve skills, expand individuals' capabilities into other roles, and keep abreast of the developments within the training field, training and developing the staff is a continuous process. Numerous resources provide help in these areas. Selecting one from the array available is simplified if the objective of development is decided on first.

There are many commercial and academic sponsors of training activities to which the trainer can turn for assistance. Also, within the job setting the trainer will find many opportunities to develop his or her capabilities.

Outside Sources

Workshops, seminars, institutes, and programs are run on virtually every facet of the training function. They may be sponsored by universities, professional associations, individual specialists, or consultants.

The selection and evaluation of these programs deserve some discussion. In reviewing the promotional material for a program, one important piece of information to look for is the stated objectives that participants are expected to achieve. If objectives are not printed in the advertising material it may be a sign that the program is more of an orientation toward a given subject than one in which specific skills will be learned. After selecting what appears to be the program with the most relevant content, the next step is to try to determine the quality of that program. The sponsoring organization is usually more than willing to produce a list of organizations that have sent people to the program. Asking those organizations for their opinion may result in a valuable evaluation of the program. Once this has been done, the decision may well be reduced to one concerning economics, logistics, and the timing of releasing the person from the training department.

Another outside development opportunity is membership in professional organizations, which provide contact with others in the field and also offer various services and programs. These personal relationships can frequently produce more individual learning and growth than the programs.

Many consultants within the training field specialize in one or two areas. Spending a day with a consultant to learn about a particular specialty area may be an appropriate use of a trainer's time. Preparation for the day with the consultant is critical. A list of learning objectives should be developed. It may be profitable to send the list to the consultant prior to the day of the meeting so that he or she will be prepared with resources.

Writing for a trade journal or magazine presents a very definite learning opportunity. Preparing a manuscript requires researching a subject in great depth—and perhaps doing some thinking about a system design or developing criteria for measuring the effectiveness of a training program. Such a venture may result in more relevant and profitable learning than attendance at several outside seminars.

Inside Sources

Many organizations design and present workshops and seminars for the trainer. The decision to attend should be measured against the same criteria as the decision to attend an outside workshop. The advantage of using inside sources may be that the jargon and examples used are particularly relevant to the organization. Frequently participants will be part of a peer group of other trainers, and this mutual sharing and discovery of ideas will be useful.

The trainer may develop a personal learning plan or map. This kind of tool would contain the specific objectives the trainer would like to achieve. The training manager or other people within the organization would serve as resources to the trainer in deciding the most appropriate way to reach those learning goals. The learning plan should also include the criteria of measurement for successful achievement of objectives. This kind of self-directed activity may produce much more commitment on the part of the trainer than an activity prescribed by the organization. It has the further advantage of allowing the trainer to progress through the plan at an individualized pace, taking into consideration the pressures and the commitments of the job as well as his or her individual abilities to absorb and apply new knowledge.

Work assignments involving the trainer with people who have other training roles can be used to expand his or her skills and knowledge. Asking a presenter to participate with another member of the staff on training design may help the participant gain insight and skill in this new area. Asking a designer to be part of a brainstorming session in which a consultant is trying to analyze data learned from a recent interview can help the designer gain some appreciation of the role of the trainer as consultant.

The training function should be managed in an objective way. This means that each member of the training staff has negotiated performance objectives to be achieved within a given time period. Upon review and apprasial of performance, the trainer and the superior should also be mutually committed to personal development needs. Development will then have become another performance objective that both the trainer and the organization are committed to achieve. Regardless of the method chosen to expand the skills of the trainer, it is important to decide ahead of time how training effectiveness is going to be measured. This should mean that the trainer and the manager have decided on very specific performances on the job that will be changed as a result of the learning experience. In other words, the manager will be able to do things that he or she could not do before the learning experience or to do things better than before. This will ensure that the learning experience is relevant to actual performance requirements on the job.

Dr. Dugan Laird has summarized the development of the training specialist in an unpublished paper (see Fig. 3-3).

Career Paths: The Need

People need to achieve and to feel that they are advancing. Advancement may occur in a variety of ways, including being promoted upward into the hierarchy of management, taking on greater responsibility within a functional specialty, and developing into a generalist. Advancement can occur as a result of increased competence, i.e., when the person grows from a practitioner into an innovator.

Organizations have installed systems to help foster this process of advancement, partly because of their need to have human resources ready to assume new roles as the organization grows. Subsystems frequently are designed to fill specific parts of the total need for human resource planning. Examples of these subsystems are management succession planning, career counseling, career-path planning, and assessment programs. One irony is that frequently the training and development department or the personnel who design these systems install them in all the functions of the organization except their own. Another unfortunate fact is that people in the training department often see themselves as staying in the same role indefinitely. With no internal feeling or external system forcing change, trainers can become stale and "ivory-towerish." In order to counteract the negatives in this situation as well as capitalize on the positives for the person and the organization, some system for planning the growth and the advancement of people within the training function should be adopted.

Career Paths: How to Develop

When solving any problem, the first step is always to gather data. Applying that principle to career pathing, the first step would be to assess (1) the organization's needs now and in the future, (2) the role the department should play in responding to those needs, and (3) the growth goals and aspirations of the people currently in the training department.

In looking at the future needs of the organization, it is important to determine what changes are likely to occur. New organization structures, new areas of endeavor, and a change in the work-force size or technology will impact the things the training function will be required to do. Once this picture of organizational evolution is painted, the role of training, the types of skills the training department will require, and the organization of the function can be determined. The result should be a manpower plan for training. Included would be requirements for staff size, supervision levels, timing for filling openings, and skills—in effect, the action steps needed to cover the time period of the manpower plan.

Succession Planning

In order to implement orderly planning for the future, it is necessary to have information about (1) function and staffing needs for the future and (2) the current and potential performance of the staff. To obtain data about the staff's strength and potential, two sources can be assessed: (1) the supervisor and clients of the trainer and (2) the trainer.

Collecting information from superiors can be accomplished by means of a form such as that shown in Fig. 3-4. The purpose of collecting this information is to

WILL HE/SHE. . . ?   THEN HIS/HER TRAINING SHOULD INCLUDE;

	MINIMUM REQUIREMENTS:	WORTHWHILE ENRICHMENTS:
CONDUCT TRAINING?	Behavioral objectives Learning theory Reinforcement theory Listening skills Questioning skills Discussion leading Lecture and demonstration Job instruction training	Case methods In-basket Sensitivity training Use of media Open classroom Incident process Action maze Role playing

When training people who design and conduct training, stress applications rather than knowledge. At least 50 percent of training time should go to workshops and clinics.

DESIGN TRAINING?	Behavioral objectives Learning theory Reinforcement theory Questioning techniques Feedback systems Logical outlining Use of media Discussion leading Case methods Job instruction training	Conference design Programmed instruction Open classroom Incident process In-basket Critical incident Writing skills Role playing
ADMINISTER TRAINING?	Planning skills Organizing skills Listening skills Writing skills Questioning skills Speaking skills Discussion leading	Sensitivity training Organization development PLUS All skills listed for conductors and designers
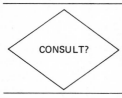CONSULT?	Listening skills Questioning skills Reinforcement theory Sensitivity training Problem-solving skills Performance analysis	Organization development Speaking skills Writing skills PLUS All skills listed for the other three roles
NONE OF THESE?	Do not train people in skills which they cannot use for their organization. Such "educational overkill" is detrimental to the training function, to the specific training programs, and - above all - to the person who acquires behaviors he/she will never use.	

Fig. 3-3 Developing the training specialist. (*Source: Unpublished manuscript by Dr. Dugan Laird, Atlanta, Georgia.*)

SUCCESSION PLANNING WORKSHEET

1. NAME OF EMPLOYEE _____

2. PRESENT POSITION _____

3. LAST POSITION _____ Within AM (yes or no) _____
   If no, what company _____

4. OVERALL JOB PERFORMANCE RATING

	6 mon ago	Today		6 mon ago	Today
Distinguished	☐	☐	Fair	☐	☐
Superior	☐	☐	Marginal	☐	☐
Competent	☐	☐	Not enough time to determine	☐	☐

5. RATING OF EMPLOYEE'S PERFORMANCE ON CURRENT OBJECTIVES/PROJECTS

   ☐ Exceeds standards of objectives   ☐ Meets standards of objectives

   ☐ Good – but not all objectives achieved   ☐ Unacceptable achievement of objectives

6. ANTICIPATED NEXT STEP JOB(S) OR OTHER AM JOBS FOR WHICH HE/SHE SHOULD BE CONSIDERED
   (Be as specific as possible, i.e., job title, division, etc.)

	Ready now	6-12 mon	1-2 yr	3-5 yr	Over 5 yr

7. DEVELOPMENT NEEDS

   _____
   _____
   _____
   _____
   _____

8. DEVELOPMENT PLANS

   _____
   _____
   _____
   _____
   _____

Fig. 3-4 Succession-planning worksheet. *(Addressograph Multigraph Corporation company form.)*

compare performance and potential ratings of individual trainers within the total training function. Asking line managers who have had dealings with staff members to record similar information will add to the basis of judgment. Recording these data in a manpower data box would be the next step. Arranging these boxes in an organization-chart format (see Fig. 3-5) will give a picture of both present strengths and weaknesses and future departmental needs. It also will identify

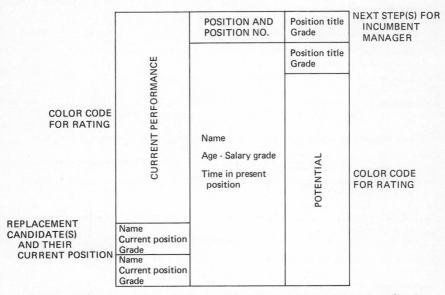

Fig. 3-5   Manpower data box. *(Addressograph Multigraph Corporation company form.)*

actions necessary to capitalize on potential, people who need development, people who are blocking others, and those who will need to be replaced.

The other input to this process is the opinion of the individual staff members. Through interviews or questionnaires, trainers can be asked to evaluate their own performance and future aspirations. There will probably be an amazing similarity between their own ratings and the ratings of others. If anything, people tend to underrate themselves.

The result of this total effort is (1) information necessary to build a plan for the training function in total and (2) individual development plans for staff members.

EVALUATING TRAINING-STAFF PERFORMANCE

It is necessary to make a distinction between evaluating the performance of an individual trainer and evaluating the total performance of the staff. The reputation of the department will be established in part by the contributions of individual members, but the means of evaluation employed will be different.

Evaluating the Individual

There are several ways to measure a trainer's performance and contributions. These are based on various factors: the trainer's performance, economic impact on the organization, and internal and external reputation.

Position descriptions should contain accountabilities as well as standards of effective performance. The total of all accountabilities should be the umbrella under which specific responsibilities of the role fall. When responsibilities are grouped under a common accountability and standards are identified for satisfactory performance, the measurement of performance becomes simplified. Thus measurement of performance against accountabilities becomes the first means of evaluation.

Ideally, the training function should be managed under some version of Management by Objectives. If it is, all staff members and superiors set objectives against which performance is measured. Objectives should include the standards of acceptable accomplishment. By reviewing performance throughout the time frame of the objectives and appraising performance at the end, a very objective evaluation of the trainer's contribution can be made.

A third basis of measurement is the economic impact the trainer makes on the organization. Is the value of the training solutions designed and implemented greater than the cost? This evaluation is possible only if the trainer is making decisions about expending time and other resources on the basis of economic payoff for the organization. One would hope that this will be true the majority of the time.

The impact of the trainer's activities on solving human performance problems also provides a means of evaluation. Here again change brought about through the trainer's interventions would be the measurement of his or her contribution. Even though a change may not be measurable in economic terms, there should be few trainer activities performed that cannot be measured in terms of some quantifiable change they have brought about: new skills learned, a problem solved, a new system set up and running efficiently, fewer grievances, less scrap, or fewer errors on orders entering the system, for example.

A fifth basis of measurement is the reputation the trainer has earned within the organization. Elements of this reputation include comments by line managers about the trainer or the results of training. The frequency and volume of requests for the trainer's services are a measure of worth, particularly if requests for solutions to different problems come repeatedly from the same part of the organization.

Last, external reputation is a measure of trainer performance. Has the trainer been asked to hold office, chair committees, or appear on programs for professional organizations? Is he or she asked to speak, conduct seminars, or write articles? Do people volunteer comments about the individual's innovations or worth? Admittedly, these are more a measure of the trainer's visibility and marketability than of performance on the job, but there is usually a definite, positive correlation.

Evaluating the Total Staff

There are four distinct elements that can be measured when evaluating the performance of a department. The first is the accomplishment of departmental objectives. Were they achieved? Within the budget? Using appropriate response time? If specific projects and objectives have been planned, departmental performance in relation to them is a very objective means of evaluation. The source of such information could be the upper management that training reports to, the line organization it serves, or both. This evaluation is activity-based only.

A second basis of evaluation is the economic accomplishment of the department. In much the same manner as was suggested for individual trainer measurement, the value of training is compared with the cost. If the department approaches projects with an eye to payoff, it determines the worth of a project before embarking on it. Ideally, the payoff will be measurable in economic terms; if it is not, certainly some measurable change in the organization should be apparent. Keeping a record of the results of each project, program, or activity and making comparisons with the department's total training budget will yield the department's evaluation. Training should not cost an organization anything. The results of its activities should be worth more than the cost of staffing and running it.

How effectively the department uses its resources is a third basis of evaluation. One method of measuring this is to have a system for establishing priorities of departmental activities. First, criteria for accepting projects would be identified. Each criterion would be given a value. A minimum value for a project would be determined as acceptable for the department's use of its resources. Reviewing the work of the department against these criteria and values would result in the evaluation. For example, a department could establish the criteria as (1) economic payoff of a project, (2) the probability of its success, (3) staff time required to complete it, (4) its cost, and (5) its relevance to the accountabilities of the department. Assigning values (numbers) to the criteria enables the administrator to weigh each one for a given request or project, multiply by the value, and thus determine priority. Analyzing departmental performance at the end of the year against this system would result in a very objective look at contribution.

Fourth, the department's reputation and the budget-request trend can be evaluated. Does top management think the department is performing a valuable role? Is the training department asked for opinions about solutions to specific problems? Is it brought in at the discussion stage, or is it told what solution it should implement? Are the training department's staffing requests approved? Is the requested budget approved? Are facilities and location adequate? These are all indicators of the organization's evaluation of the worth of the department's performance.

CONCLUSIONS ABOUT SELECTION AND DEVELOPMENT

Throughout this chapter we have been looking at the various aspects of the problem of providing a training staff equipped to meet an organization's training and development needs. The intent has been to offer some practical "how-to" advice as well as to present some conceptual, broader-based ideas. At this point it would be well to identify some of the organizational factors against which previously stated guidelines for selection, staffing, development, and measurement of the staff should be matched.

Taking the view that the purpose of a training staff is to assist the organization in solving performance-deficiency problems, what problems and factors should be considered? Those which would influence how large the training staff should be? Those influencing where it should report? Whether training should be centralized or not?

- Complexity of skills required. Are the skills the organization requires of its people complex and changing? Are they used widely throughout the work force? Are they unique to your organization?
- Availability of skills. Is there a ready labor market with the required skills? Are schools providing graduates capable of performing on the job? Can schools be convinced to train for these skills? Is the trained labor market available in all locations where the organization recruits or hires?
- Size of the organization. Is it getting larger, and at what pace? What is the five- or ten-year plan for growth, expansion, and diversification?
- Economics of the organization. Is the profit margin small? Does the organization operate each department on a budget? Does the organization have short-range operating plans? Is there a cost-cutting climate? Is there more payoff for finding ways to cut operating expenses than increasing revenue?

- Turnover. Is there a high rate? Does the work force have a substantial number of retirements planned for the next five years? What is the rate of turnover by group, such as new hires, sales organization, and engineering?
- Impact of external forces. Is the organization regulated strongly by government legislation? What is the influence of ecology? Do special-interest groups have a strong influence?
- Analysis of these factors will provide a framework for the role of training, its need for staff, and its priorities.

REFERENCES

1. Lippitt, Gordon L., and Leonard Nadler: "Emerging Roles of the Training Director," *Training and Development Journal,* August 1967, Vol. 21, No. 8.
2. Ibid.
3. Ibid.
4. Ibid.
5. Warren, Malcom: Unpublished research. Toledo.
6. Warren, Malcom: *Training for Results,* Addison-Wesley Publishing Company, Inc., Reading, Mass., 1969, "Staffing the Training Organization."

Chapter 4

Budgeting and Controlling Training Costs

JOHN S. JENNESS

John S. Jenness *has been Director of Manpower Planning and Development at Consolidated Edison Company of New York since 1970. He had formerly been Manager of Training and Development for Levitt and Sons, Inc., and Vice President and General Manager of Levitt Job Opportunities, Inc., a subsidiary operating construction skills training programs under contracts from the U.S. Department of Labor. Before joining Levitt, he held personnel and training positions at Uniroyal, Continental Can Company, and Ambac Industries. A past president of ASTD, he is also an Adjunct Assistant Professor of Business Administration at Adelphi University and Lecturer on Training and Development in the School of Continuing Education at New York University. Currently a member of the National Advisory Committee of IAESTE (International Association for Exchange of Students for Technical Experience), ASEE (American Society for Engineering Education), and the Alumni Council of Dartmouth College, he is a frequent lecturer on manpower development and personnel management topics.*

For training to become fully accepted as an integral part of an organization's operating plan, it must first be recognized as a function which makes a positive contribution to the success of the organization, within the cost limitations imposed on it. To achieve this goal, cost effectiveness must become a vital part of the design and development of the training plan, and, in turn, sound budgeting and control of costs must become a vital responsibility of the training director and staff.

TRAINING TO PRODUCE SAVINGS OR PROFITS

Every training program is an instance where money spent *now* is an investment so that improved efficiency or increased profits will be realized later. The training staff has a basic responsibility to make this statement come true. Training for the sake of training or for the purpose of achieving hazy, ill-defined goals can cast the entire training function into disrepute and lead to continuation of the philosophy under which training, like advertising, is an early casualty of an economic downturn.

As a matter of practice, each training plan should contain financial objectives as well as conventional learning objectives. And, like the learning objectives, the financial objectives should be based on the need analysis that preceded the development of the plan. Such objectives presuppose two things: that costs of training can be identified and controlled and that operating costs, both before and after training, can be calculated and compared so that savings can be identified.

True Costs

In planning for savings from training, it is essential that training directors include *all* appropriate costs in the financial plan to avoid deceiving themselves or misleading top management about the quantitative benefits which can be achieved by the program. Providing incomplete or misleading figures—and then having to admit the error—will cause the next sales pitch to be looked at with an even more jaundiced eye than usual. Too often, training plans are developed without accurate identification of all the costs involved, and this can lead to incorrect decisions or inaccurately stated results. To prevent this, the training director should be careful to ensure that all costs have been considered in the program planning and in the analysis of the alternative methods of presentation.

Identification of training costs would hardly seem to be a problem. Yet, too often, costs truly attributable to training are combined with other operating costs and are in effect hidden. This is particularly true when training is done on the job, such as when the immediate supervisor, with primary responsibility for training newly assigned personnel, is credited with an allowance for reduced productivity in recognition of training costs involved. As a result, the organization may not realize the true magnitude of its training costs until analysis of the reasons for low productivity or high operating costs pinpoints the training element built in.

For example, if the standard production for a trained employee is 30 units per hour, a new employee may produce only 15 units initially. If new employees are assigned directly to foremen without being given prior training, the expected production of each work unit is reduced by 15 units per hour per new employee for the first day (or week). This is, in effect, a credit or allowance to cover the low productivity of the learner. The reduction decreases each day (or weekly) according to a plan which is usually based on historical data but which has no impact on the foreman's skill in teaching and motivating the new worker.

Savings from Training

Savings, whether directly or indirectly attributable to training, may also be hard to calculate. In skills programs, where "before" and "after" costs can be collected and analyzed, they are probably easiest to identify. Often, not only increased output but also improved quality can be figured.

Savings which result from operating improvements traceable to supervisory participation in a training program should not be forgotten. For example, when, as part of the training process, participants are assigned special projects to be accomplished on their jobs before the next phase of training, savings from these projects should be counted.

Many indirect savings from training cannot be realistically quantified, and yet they should not be overlooked in developing the "plus" side of the financial plan. Absenteeism, tardiness and turnover, equipment breakage, tool loss, and the like can often be traced back to operating problems and the operating climate within the organization. Effective training, and management's interest in helping individuals achieve their maximum potential, can play an important part in improving the climate and reducing such costs. Often these savings may be estimated from data on the cost of hiring a new employee, reduced overtime to replace absentees, etc.

Comparative Costs

The training financial plan may also include comparison of the cost per trainee day for one program with that for a previous one or a comparison of the costs under two alternative methods or approaches. In certain instances it may be practical to compare the costs of an entire project with the training done two ways: For example, by all OJT with the foreman responsible, or by vestibule training, off the production line, with the training staff responsible for providing the foreman with at least partially-trained workers.

The training financial plan has a single message to get across to top management: The training department is concerned with making a financial contribution to the enterprise in terms of profits or savings, and every effort will be made to calculate (realistically) the financial benefits from each training program planned for the coming year.

PROGRAM COST CONSIDERATIONS

Once a training need has been established, several questions come to mind: What kind of a program is required to achieve the training objectives? How much will it cost? What are the potential cost reductions, savings, or other benefits that can be expected to result from this program?

Savings may be a key element of the program, or it may be only incidental. Knowledge of the degree of its importance is vital for the training director. Particularly in safety training, the cost of the program itself is immaterial (within certain limits, of course); the primary consideration is that the trainee, at the end of the program, will be able to perform a certain task or function in a specified, safe manner. For example, the duration—and cost—of a program in artificial respiration are usually in direct relationship to the foreseen need for its use. Only a casual knowledge of the process is required by most individuals as part of a neighborhood Red Cross or PTA activity. On the other hand, firemen, lifeguards, and utility linemen, who often find themselves in situations in which they must administer artificial respiration, require an intense, thorough, and often-repeated program.

Cost Factors

When the financial factor is vital—as is usually the case—careful cost control and financial planning become imperative. Determination of potential savings from the program, on a per-worker basis, is the starting point. Then, as the training program is developed to meet the identified training needs, certain cost factors should be considered which affect both the design and the per-trainee cost of the program:

1. What is the total population to be trained?
2. How many can be released from their jobs at any one time?
3. How long can each be released each time—for one hour, one day, one week?
4. What is the *optimum* trainee-instructor ratio, and what is the absolute maximum number of trainees that an instructor can handle and still achieve the training objectives?
5. How will the added benefits, impact, and reinforcement from an off-premises, sleep-in program compare with the added costs?
6. How will benefits derived from the use of closed-circuit television, special simulators or simulations, and the like compare with the added costs?

Cost Effectiveness

It is generally preferable to develop and cost out a program designed to produce optimum results and then analyze the various cost-effectiveness alternatives. For planning purposes, the development costs should be allocated over the original target population or the first 12 months of the program, whichever occurs sooner. Even though the program *may* go into a second or third year without major revision, prediction of such a long life without major redesign expenses is not realistic.

Cost-effectiveness alternatives come in a wide variety, as noted in the above list. For example, if the topic is common in industry and the population is small or intermittent, will using an outside program be more practical than developing an in-house one? Will it be less expensive to adapt an outside, prepackaged program to meet the need than to develop one from scratch? Should a consultant be hired to teach the program, or should another trainer be added to the staff? How great a reduction in potential learning will there be if one more trainee is added to each group or each instructor load? If two more are added? Three?

Schedule Effect

The training schedule itself also affects the program costs. The number of days or hours of room or space rental is one factor; another, less obvious factor is the added staff time spent checking (or making) room setups and preparing topic summaries and reviews at the end and start of each session. Thus more new material can be covered in one eight-hour, all-day session than in two four-hour sessions, four two-hour sessions, or eight one-hour sessions. But, on the other hand, what of the benefits accruing from the shorter sessions—improved attention span, better digestion of material, and opportunity to practice on the job between sessions? The program content or the operating requirements—or both—may dictate the schedule regardless of the cost factors involved, but the costs certainly should not be ignored.

BUDGET DEVELOPMENT AND PLANNING

The requirement for presentation of its operating and capital budgets provides the training department with an annual opportunity to present to top management a comprehensive package to justify its continued existence. The package should contain both operational (training) objectives and financial ones and, in effect, should say:

1. These are the training programs which the department plans to conduct next year to meet specific needs which have been identified by the organization's objectives or its operating elements.
2. Here is the cost of each of these programs (broken down into as fine detail as necessary).
3. Here are the estimated savings, or increased profits, which will accrue from this training, calculated from increased productivity; improved quality of work; reduced expenditures for tools, equipment, and materials; and improved supervisory performance.

The budget is normally divided into two parts: operating and capital. The *operating budget* includes wage and salary costs for the professional training staff and its clerical support, expenditures for supplies, operating expenses, and other direct and indirect costs.

The *capital budget* generally includes major items of training equipment such as audiovisual projectors, closed-circuit television cameras, monitors and playback units, simulators, and chalkboards.

Climate and Strategy   In the preparation, and defense, of the training department operating budget, some things may be more important than actual dollars. A certain budget climate exists in the top levels of every organization; the training director must understand it and must gear the budget strategy to it. Merely adding excess dollars to an amount really needed, for the purpose of allowing higher levels to whittle off enough to give them a sense of accomplishment, is not necessarily effective and may only damage the training director's credibility. An understanding of top management's attitude toward each type of training, and toward the budgetary process in general, is of prime importance.

If the budget has a control function and cannot be exceeded under any circumstances, the training director must think accordingly. If it is used as a tool for both planning and measurement of performance, the director has more latitude. Under this concept, justification is possible for exceeding the original budget, if circumstances later in the year so dictate.

Similarly, knowledge of the significant budget items may be of prime importance. For instance, what is scrutinized most carefully by top management in the budget review? Total salary costs, total departmental costs, total costs in comparison with costs in prior years, total number of staff—which is most important? The degree of emphasis given by top management to each of these points out where the training director's justification should be concentrated.

Budgeting Influences   In addition to knowing the attitude of top management toward each kind of training, the director should also be aware of other factors which could influence the budget. Knowledge of long-range plans involving an employment expansion or contraction and requiring retraining or development of a new capability is vital. An equipment changeover, such as from a manual system of customer accounting or inventory control to a computer-based one with video display terminals, can create a massive retraining requirement for a definite period of time. (In such a situation, the training department *must* be involved in the planning and scheduling of the entire changeover if it is desirable to hold training costs to a minimum.) Customer complaints which force remedial action within the organization can also lead to training requirements and should be reflected in the training budget.

One primary item of budget strategy is the Boy Scout motto—"Be prepared!" To sell the budget effectively and protect it from indiscriminate cutting by upper-management personnel who do not understand the savings potential of effective training programs, the training director needs to justify each program and each cost item thoroughly.

As part of this strategy, programs should be listed in descending order of priority so that the executive to whom the training director reports is fully aware of the impact of budget reductions and of reduced staff manning.

Backup Data   Details need to be identified for each program in terms of learning objectives, population to be trained in the year, program length, class size, space requirements and costs, AV equipment and other supplies and materials required, and development and administrative costs involved. These backup data should be structured so that a variety of alternatives can be presented during the course of negotiations. As a cost reduction, for example, a program can be eliminated completely, it can be presented less frequently and to a smaller number of participants, or it can be reduced in length or content (with learning objectives reduced to compensate), depending on the amount of reduction required. (Some forms used recently at Consolidated Edison are shown in Figs. 4-1 to 4-3.)

TRAINING AND DEVELOPMENT Program Activities 1975 (Proposed)			ORIGINAL TOTAL $202,000 REDUCTION 57,000 REVISED TOTAL $145,000	
Activities	No. Sessions	No. Participants	Man-Days Training	Operating Cost (Tuition & Expense), $
Management Training & Development				
College Graduate Orientation	3	80	800	6,000
Engineering Lectures	2	60	600	1,000
Management Orientation	4	120	180	300
Supervisory (1st & 2nd Level)				
Central Operations	20	400	2,000	20,000
Division Operations	20	400	2,000	20,000
Other	5	100	500	5,000
Management/Leadership				
Central Operations	5	75	225	10,000
Division Operations	10	150	450	20,000
Other	5	75	225	10,000
Management Follow-up				
Seminars	4	80	160	1,000

Fig. 4-1 Section of proposed training activities and budget showing both original and reduced data.

Budget Justification   In the course of the budgetary negotiations, as the financial executives struggle to bring together total expenditures and total requirements, the training director will generally have to fight vigorously since training objectives are normally given lower priority than operating objectives by operating executives. However, advance discussions sometimes can set the stage to advantage.

A system of clearing accounts, charging the costs of a training program back to the using organization, could be installed. This device reduces the final training department budget and transfers costs of training directly back to the using agencies. (Effective operation of such a system is predicated on controls so that the users cannot divert the funds in these accounts to support other production objectives.)

As another alternative, one or more profit centers could be set up within the department, particularly if any training services can be made available for sale to outside organizations. Under such a plan expenditures are offset by cash income, resulting in either a net income or a lower net expense figure for comparison against the budget. In costing out a program for outside sale, the basic financial objectives need to be considered—the decision to recover only direct costs, to recover all costs (direct, indirect, and allocated), or to recover costs plus fee or profit can result in dramatic differences in the fee charged outside participants.

Human Resource Accounting

Another approach to overcoming budget problems is through the use of human resource accounting. Espoused by the R. G. Barry Company and by Dr. Rensis

1975 OPERATING BUDGET JUSTIFICATION   Department (Gas Operations)

Manpower Planning & Development

Function*	Work Unit	Est. 1973 Units of Work (per Month)	Average Units per Union Employee (per Month)	Number of Union Employees Required (to 12/31/73)	Average Units per Mgmt. Employee (per Month)	Number of Mgmt. Employees Required (to 12/31/73)	Total Annual Salaries for Function	Reason, Remarks, and Impact of Elimination
General Utility Man	Trng. Manday	60	–	–	60	1	16.0	8 classes 5 days 20/class 160/yr
Mechanic B	"	450	–	–	150	3	53.0	15 classes 17 days 20/class 300/yr
Mechanic A	"	200	–	–	100	2	34.0	8 classes 17 days 20/class 160/yr
Foreman	"	80	–	–	80	1	16.0	9 classes 15 days 8/class 72/yr
Inspector	"	60	–	–	60			12 classes 5 days 10/class 120/yr
Welding	"	200	–	–	100	2	35.0	6 classes 40 days 10/class 60/yr
Automotive	"	200	–	–	100	2	37.0	10 classes 10 days 10/class 100/yr
Administrative & Clerical		–	–	1	–	1	29.0	Typing & Section Administration
		1,100		1		12	220.0	
Additions since 8/1/72								
Contractor Training		200	–	–	100	2	35.0	Train outside contractor personnel per requirements of Public Service Commission. Follow-up on posttraining field performance to analyze results, determine need for curricula revision, etc.
Gas Mechanic	"	40	–	–	40	1	16.0	
		240		1		15	271.0	

*Programs support company's 1973 Goal A26: "Develop a real capability for training . . . (c) gas training school—for gas mechanics and their apprentices and (d) mobile equipment maintenance school for auto and equipment mechanics."

Fig. 4-2 Budget justification sheet showing detail of staffing and programs in technical skills training activity.

1975 BUDGET JUSTIFICATION TRAINING & DEVELOPMENT

SECTION CUSTOMER SERVICE (CS) ACCOUNT NOS. 7051, 7055

Course or Function	Duration (Days)	No. Trainees per Class	No. Classes per Yr.	Trainee Days (TD)	No. of Instructors Mgt.	Wk.	Manpower, $	Terminals, $	Suppl. & Exp., $	Total, $	Cost/ TD, $
		8-12	162	19,690	20	1	386,000	100,000	152,000	638,000	
Administration					2	1					
New CS System	5	8-12	20	1,000	2		22,100	4,400	1,810	23,910	28.25
CS System-Remedial	5-20	10	10	1,500	1		27,200	13,200	5,075	45,475	30.00
New CS Representative	62	10	17	10,540	8		198,615	56,000	24,330	278,945	26.50
Advanced Accounting & Credit	25	10	10	2,500	1		40,250	12,000	6,125	58,375	27.25
Customer Field Rep.-Collection	2-3	8	20	350	1		14,675	—	3,250	17,925	29.00
Customer Relations	1½	10	40	400	1						

Fig. 4-3 Sample justification sheet showing cost analysis by course and type of expense.

Likert, of the Institute for Social Research at the University of Michigan, it provides a technique for categorizing training and development costs as capital items. This concept is based on the premise that an organization's employee group should be considered one of its primary assets, on the same basis as its physical plant and equipment. It contends that training and development costs should really be considered similar to those for technological repair and overhaul, aimed at keeping the organization's human equipment in the most effective operating state. Thus, it provides a justification for amortizing these costs over several years, rather than including them in a single year's expenses.

As a concept, much can be said for it, particularly if top management recognizes the analogy between human and physical resources. However, most organizations have not yet been willing to build it into their budgetary and accounting processes. Even if they did, it is doubtful what benefits would accrue to the training director who has an ongoing, comprehensive program. Deferring some costs over the life of the training benefit onto a depreciation-type basis only smooths out marked increases in the costs. The process tends to render less visible marked changes in training requirements which would otherwise be reflected in the department's budget. (As a personal preference, I feel the training function should be visible and responsible, rather than invisible and forgotten.)

Capital Budgets

Particularly with the expanded use of equipment such as closed-circuit television for training, the training director must be more aware of capital budgets. If the organization permits free transfer of funds between operating (expense) and capital budgets, the distinction is of little concern, other than advising accounting to tag each new capital item purchased. However, if the capital budget receives different treatment—and particularly when capital funds are limited—the training director may need considerable initiative to obtain the desired hardware.

As a starter, discussion may be required with accounting to determine how their basic definition of a capital item applies to training and development hardware and software. Accountants generally classify as "capital items" things which cost over a certain amount (usually $100 to $250), have a useful life of five years or more, and can be readily tagged and accounted for. With a little persuasion they can be convinced that training software items (films, TV tapes, workbooks, etc.) are noncapital items, regardless of initial cost, because of their relatively short life and lack of residual value. More persuasion may be required before accounting will classify most AV hardware similarly, regardless of cost, since design changes and technological improvements in overhead projectors, sound-slide units, and the like occur rapidly, making current equipment obsolete before it wears out. For example, certain early sound-slide units had a fixed timing requirement for each slide that late ones did not have. Thus purchasing a new unit may be more desirable than restricting the programming to the limitations of the earlier equipment.

Purchase versus Rental Illustrative of typical capital budget problems is an unexpected request to schedule a program that utilizes a sophisticated tape-slide machine for immediate extensive, additional presentations in another part of the organization. Meeting the request will require a second machine, which must be either purchased (a $400 capital expense) or rented (a bigger expense if the rental will be for an extended period). There are two ways in which the purchase could legitimately be included as an operating cost if no capital funds are available:

1. Convince accounting that, despite its total cost, the short life of the unit, due to the rapid technological obsolescence in that field, makes it a noncapital item.

2. Negotiate a rental agreement which is in reality a deferred payment contract. Such an agreement is often available upon request from vendors. In it, the purchase price is divided into several parts, each less than the capital limit, and is paid off monthly, with the organization taking title with the last payment. As long as the total cost is not substantially above the original price of the unit, this may afford a practical solution to a limited capital budget.

Construction and Facilities   Similar questions can arise during the construction of new training facilities. From a tactical point of view, it is generally more advantageous to ensure that all ancillary items are identified and ordered as part of the total package. This includes the necessary tables, chairs, chalkboards, screens, storage shelving, audiovisual equipment, simulators, and miscellaneous items that can make life so much easier for a training staff.

For equipment used in vestibule skills training programs, one basic criterion applies both to budgeting and to sound learning: *All* equipment must be the same as, or technically ahead of, the equipment used in the operating units. From a funding viewpoint this may permit purchase of the equipment against the capital budget of the operating unit, with the provision that the equipment will be transferred to that organization as soon as its use in the vestibule training center is completed. From the training viewpoint it ensures that when trainees are assigned to the field, they will not be baffled by more modern equipment than they had become accustomed to in the vestibule school.

COST IDENTIFICATION

A primary step in effective budgeting and control is to identify the kinds of costs which result from operation of the training department for a given period of time. These costs can generally be classified into two groups: (1) *direct costs* of operating a particular program and (2) *indirect,* or *overhead, costs* of the program (some of which are often overlooked); the latter include costs of operating the entire department.

Totaling these costs for the year is the next step in the budget process. Dividing the total by the number and kind of programs and by the number of participants in each provides a target of cost control against which to measure performance from one year to the next or from one program to the next.

Direct Costs

Direct costs are generally obvious. Wages and/or salaries and fringe benefits of the participants and instructors; supplies and materials for the particular programs; services (including consultants' fees for development and/or presentation of the program); the cost of the facilities (even for presentation in-house); and incidental costs for travel, meals, lodging, etc.—all fall within this category and are easily identified. The organization's accounting and budgetary system may create variances in actual charging and payments, but, for the purpose of the training financial plan, they must all be included.

Indirect, or Overhead, Costs

Indirect training costs are more difficult to calculate and are more often overlooked in costing a program. Program development and support costs are the primary items—the costs of all those activities which made the program possible and of those which operate behind the scenes to keep it running effectively.

Development Costs   If it appears that the program will run in more than one calendar year, development costs can be calculated and then allocated by individual participant or group across the total population to be trained. Items such as: outside consultants' fees and expenses; hours spent by staff professionals, clerical workers, and line managers; research costs for film rentals, simulations, audiovisual aids, etc.; and the cost of "train-the-trainer" sessions.

Support Costs Support costs should not be overlooked, although they tend to be lumped into the general operating costs of the department. To arrive at a true picture of the cost of each program, costs should be identified and charged as they are accrued. Personnel involved in such activities as mailing of program announcements, maintenance of attendance records, AV setup and operation, message service, and analysis of evaluation should be charged into this category.

General Operating Costs General operating costs should be allocated across all the department's programs. Their extent can generally be predicted and budgeted from year to year. Any general and administrative organizational overhead allocation should be included, as well as charges for space, telephones, and janitorial services. Staff development (books and periodicals, membership dues in professional societies, attendance at seminars, conferences and professional society meetings, etc.) is vital for the stimulation and growth of the professional staff, and its cost must not be forgotten or ignored. Salary and fringe-benefit costs for the training director, for any other supervisors whose time cannot be allocated to specific programs, and for clerical personnel should also be included.

COST CONTROL AND COST REDUCTION

Each month the training director and any subordinates responsible for subunit budgets should receive a summary of actual costs against the budget for the previous month and the year to date. This summary should be based on a chart of accounts that provides enough detail for an easy analysis of performance and identification of problem areas. Continuing cost comparison—against the original financial plan for each program, against costs for the last similar program, or against the targeted cost per trainee day—is necessary to ensure that actual performance against standard measures up.

As a means of staff development, the training director should delegate responsibility for cost control as widely as practical. Each professional should be held responsible for cost performance as well as instructional performance on assigned programs. Similarly, all professionals should be involved as much as possible in developing program costs that can be consolidated into the departmental budget.

On the other hand, the training director should take steps to retain control of training accounts. If operating personnel are able to charge labor hours against a training code without approval of the training staff, this account can be used as a place to dump miscellaneous charges (which would otherwise reduce the operating unit's productivity) rather than measure true training costs.

The director should also initiate a program that will result in cost improvements outside the training department. A skills training unit can pioneer or pilot many operational cost reductions through such initiative. Since line supervision may be too busy getting production out to pay enough attention to this responsibility, the instructional staff can more easily place greater emphasis on it, to the benefit of the entire organization. At Con Edison, all electrical construction and gas operations schools (for splicers, overhead linemen, network mechanics, and gas mechanics) pilot new methods and operating techniques. Most of these are initially developed by electrical or gas engineering, but on several occasions the impetus has come from the school staff, who were aggressively seeking a "better way" as part of their operating procedures.

Because the training function is eligible for professional discounts, discussions with purchasing and accounting may be appropriate to realize the benefits from such discounts.

SUMMARY

A training director's interest in budgets and cost control generally can be traced back to two questions:

1. How thoroughly does the boss insist on justification of budget and plans for training for the coming year?
2. How close control of operating and capital costs for training does the boss expect during the year, and how will this affect the training director's performance evaluation?

Really, though, as a matter of professional pride, the effective training director should be interested in, and concerned with, providing truly cost-effective training—the maximum possible learning experience for the minimum practical cost. To accomplish this requires a thorough understanding of the costs involved in each individual program, a well-documented analysis of the savings that should result from each, and a careful comparison of planned program costs against those for alternative methods and media. It also means continuing comparisons of actual costs against budget, against last year's programs and costs, and against the organization's cost and human resource goals established for the year.

BIBLIOGRAPHY

Brummet, R. Lee: "Accounting for Human Resources," *The New York Certified Public Accountant,* pp. 12–15, July 1970.

Brummet, R. Lee, Eric G. Flamholtz, and William C. Pyle: "Human Resource Accounting: A Tool to Increase Managerial Effectiveness," *Management Accounting,* pp. 62–66, August 1969.

Friedland, Marianne: "Putting a Value on Human Resources," *International Management,* pp. 42–44, October 1970.

Jauch, Roger, and Michael Skigen: "Human Resource Accounting," *Management Accounting,* May 1974.

Jauch, Roger, and Michael Skigen: "Is Human Resource Accounting Really Practical?" (digest), *Management Review,* pp. 40–42, September 1974.

Likert, Rensis: "Improving the Accuracy of P/L Reports by Estimating the Change in Dollar Value of the Human Organization," *Michigan Business Review,* March 1973.

Likert, Rensis: "Human Resources Accounting: Building and Assessing Productive Organizations," *Personnel,* May–June 1973.

Likert, Rensis, and William C. Pyle: "Human Resource Accounting: A Human Organization Measurement Approach," *Financial Analysts Journal,* pp. 1–10, January–February 1971.

Pyle, William C.: "Monitoring Human Resources—'On Line,'" *Michigan Business Review,* pp. 19–32, July 1970.

Chapter 5

Training Records and Information Systems

NANCY D. MARSH

Nancy D. Marsh *is the Director of Development for the Government Employees Insurance Company in Washington, D.C. She is responsible for the design, coordination, instruction, and evaluation of middle-management and executive development programs as well as all other nontechnical training programs. She has spent a number of years exploring learning systems for upper-management cost systems and evaluation techniques and has conducted programs for such organizations as Bell & Howell, the U.S. Department of Labor, and ASTD.*

Training directors are professionals—experts in sophisticated methods of educational design and in the relationship between organizational objectives and developmental needs. Yet they are constantly beseiged by questions, often requiring simple, one-word answers. They have neither the time nor the space for overstuffed computer print-outs.

Meanwhile, the computer has come of age. American business is strongly influenced by sophisticated management information systems made possible by computer science. But real communication (the *right* information going to the right people) is more difficult now than ever before in history.

The information which the training director provides is critical to the success of his or her operation. Corporate policies and legal requirements necessitate complete, accurate records—available at a moment's notice. Providing that information, however, is one of the least productive aspects of the training director's job, and it can be one of the biggest time-eaters. Phone calls, memos, and requests often occupy as much as 20 percent of the training director's daily activities.

The effective training unit reduces those information contacts and, at the same time, makes sure that the right information is available when it is needed. This chapter tells how to gain valuable time by building a training information system. A two-step process is involved:

1. Carefully assessing information requirements
2. Designing a system that will track training needs, communicate programs and schedules, handle registrations, and communicate results

ASSESSING INFORMATION REQUIREMENTS

Analysis of Information Needs

Regardless of the size of the organization, at least five kinds of people ask questions about training and development activities. They include the following.

1. *Line Managers or Supervisors*
   - Who completed various programs?
   - How well did they do?
   - What future programs are available?
   - What should the next step be?
   - When are future programs scheduled?
   - What areas of performance have improved?
   - How much did it cost?

2. *Trainees or Participants*
   - How well did I do?
   - How do I compare with others in the class?
   - Does my boss know the results?
   - What is the next step?
   - What other programs are available?
   - When are they scheduled?

3. *The Training Unit*
   - How well did the program go?
   - What results were actually obtained?
   - How much did the program cost?
   - What programs are needed in the future?
   - How many people will attend?

4. *The Personnel Department*
   - What courses has an employee completed?
   - How well did he or she do?
   - What should the next step be?

5. *Top Management*
   - What programs are being run?
   - How effective are they?
   - How much do they cost?
   - How well do people do?
   - How many people attend them?
   - What results are expected, and what results are achieved?
   - Are the programs cost-effective?
   - What skills will we need in the future?
   - Who has those skills?

This information is easily translated into information "bits" upon which a system can be built (as shown in Fig. 5-1).

Information contacts per day (ICPDs) are cut drastically when the training director can anticipate information that will be needed and can design a systematic way of providing it.

Since the amount and kind of information needed can vary significantly with the size of the organization, the following factors must be considered.

Small Organizations   Organizations with fewer than 1,000 employees often assign the training function to the personnel department or to an administrative assistant. Such a function becomes one more duty in a long list of other things to do. And frequently the responsibility for providing information is split among a number of people; hence information is rarely systematic.

Most "training" occurs on the job or is provided in technical programs—training in operating a cash register or (in a manufacturing organization) in soldering and

	Line Mgrs.	Train-ees	Top Mgmt.	Trng. Dir.	Pers.
TRAINING NEEDS					
1. Analysis of Individual Needs	X	X		X	
2. Analysis of Organizational Needs			X	X	
3. Analysis of Future Individual Needs	X	X		X	
4. Analysis of Future Organizational Needs			X	X	
RESOURCES AND SCHEDULES					
5. Internal Programs Available	X	X	X	X	
6. Internal Programs Being Developed	X		X	X	
7. Published Materials Available	X	X		X	
8. Public Seminars/Conferences	X	X		X	
9. Dates/Times/Eligibility/Locations	X	X		X	
REGISTRATIONS/CONFIRMATIONS					
10. Number of Registrations Received			X	X	
11. Number of Times Program Required			X	X	
12. Notification of Dates to Attend	X	X			
RESULTS					
13. Individual Results	X	X		X	X
14. Compiled Individual Results				X	
15. Reactions to Programs				X	
16. Objectives Achieved			X	X	
17. Cost of Program			X	X	
18. Cost/Benefit Ratio			X	X	

Fig. 5-1 Training information needed by various members of the organization. Time spent on calls is cut when the training director can anticipate information that will be needed and can provide it in a systematic way.

assembling, for example. Personnel may periodically run special courses and provide published materials, but usually this is done on a special-request basis. Managers get information on programs the easy way—by phone. The information system is informal, time-consuming, and often not very comprehensive. Local and long-distance calls, memos, visits, and questions occupy already busy hours.

Medium-sized Organizations   By the time a company has 1,000 employees, a training specialist has usually been appointed, and as the size of the organization grows, the size of the training unit grows also—often on a 1-to-1,000 basis. The people in the training unit now are responsible only for training and can focus on analyzing needs and defining objectives. The unit develops or purchases course materials, enrolls employees in programs, and usually provides instruction in the programs and makes periodic evaluations.

The organization is now big enough so that people do not know one another anymore. Promotional activity is often based on file reviews or career planning; course information becomes an important part of promotional decisions. All too often, though, course information is still sketchy. The same information problems exist as in the small organization, but they are now multiplied. Depending on how active the training unit is and on the degree to which the organization is decentralized, it can become virtually impossible to track all necessary information by hand.

Large Organizations   The organization of 10,000 or more employees is usually computerized and generally widely decentralized. Employees constantly transfer from one area to another. Central and regional training schools often exist. Educational assistance, tuition assistance, and continuing education unit programs* supplement regular internal training programs. The information problem is further complicated in many organizations by the existence of corporate, regional, and branch training units.

In such an organization, effective use of human resources depends on complete, current files of employee skills and on a record of the total management capabilities of the organization. Often, however, the cost of developing these data is exceptionally high.

With a careful analysis of the organization's needs and resources (time, money, personnel, and computer access), the training director here too can build an information system which provides the necessary data without a multitude of administrative activities. The system need not be expensive; it needs merely to be thought out carefully in terms of the organization's specific needs.

Tools for Providing Information

Hundreds of tools and formats exist for communicating training information. Most organizations will gladly share the forms they have developed for tracking information or their report formats. Generally the tools cover four major areas:

1. *Employee Information.*   The best single source of information about the employee is the personnel file. It will give information about educational background and work experience. As time goes by, it should also provide information about additional education or training programs the employee has completed since inception into the organization. The personnel file is extremely useful for obtaining performance information, salary information, and information on promotional potential.

Either a single file jacket, with information clipped in, or a preprinted file jacket can be used (see Fig. 5-2). The file shown in the figure was preprinted specifically for training information.

2. *Registration Information.*   Regardless of the size of the organization, a simple registration form can save the training director more time than any other single item. A well-designed form has multiple uses: It becomes a permanent record of registrations, a way of evaluating programs, a method of telling conference leaders who is involved, a way of being sure that employees know they are registered, a way of confirming registrations, and an automatic feedback of completion information.

In a small organization, the form (see Fig. 5-3) can simply be photocopied; as the organization grows, it can be preprinted in three or more parts.

---

*The Continuing Education Unit (CEU) was designed as a uniform unit of measurement to facilitate the accumulation and exchange of standardized information about individual participation in noncredit continuing education.

3. *Announcements and Schedules.*   Program announcements and schedules take various forms. One-time program announcements, slick brochures, bulletin-board notices, memos, and even phone calls all make the work force aware of the program. Semiannual or monthly schedules provide the additional advantage of allowing managers to plan ahead. Once the schedule is worked out, the communications or publications unit in the organization will often be happy to publish it in employee publications.

EMPLOYMENT APPLICATION
PLEASE COMPLETE

NAME

POSITION DESIRED

DATE

GOVERNMENT
EMPLOYEES
COMPANIES

GOVERNMENT EMPLOYEES COMPANIES
WORLD-WIDE SERVICE

Fig. 5-2 Personnel file jacket and forms.

HELLO, AND WELCOME!

WE APPRECIATE YOUR INTEREST IN OUR COMPANY AND WILL BE HAPPY TO EXPLORE WITH YOU THE POSSIBILITIES OF YOUR JOINING OUR STAFF. EMPLOYMENT DECISIONS ARE MADE SOLELY ON THE QUALIFICATIONS OF THE INDIVIDUAL APPLICANT, AND ARE NOT AFFECTED BY RACE, COLOR, CREED, AGE, SEX, NATIONAL ORIGIN, OR MARITAL STATUS. THANK YOU, AND BEST WISHES!

PLEASE COMPLETE ANSWERS TO ALL QUESTIONS THAT APPLY TO YOU

PLEASE PRINT

LEGAL NAME ► (Last)   (First)   (Middle)   (Maiden— For reference check purposes only)   SOCIAL SECURITY NUMBER

PRESENT ADDRESS ► (No.)   (Street)   (Apt. #)   (City, State, ZIP Code)   (How long at this address)   HOME TELEPHONE

PRIOR ADDRESS ► (No.)   (Street)   (Apt. #)   (City, State, ZIP Code)   (How long at this address)   BUSINESS TELEPHONE

PRIOR ADDRESS ► (No.)   (Street)   (Apt. #)   (City, State, ZIP Code)   (How long at this address)   PRESENT HEIGHT   PRESENT WEIGHT

POSITION DESIRED ►   SALARY DESIRED   ARE YOU WILLING TO RELOCATE? ☐ YES ☐ NO   DATE AVAILABLE

HAVE YOU EVER BEEN EMPLOYED BY THIS COMPANY? ☐ YES ☐ NO   HAVE YOU EVER APPLIED TO THIS COMPANY BEFORE? ☐ YES ☐ NO   IF SO, WHEN?   AGE   DATE OF BIRTH

The Age Discrimination Act of 1967 prohibits discrimination on the basis of age with respect to individuals who are at least 40 but less than 65 years of age.

EDUCATION AND TRAINING

	DATES ATTENDED (YEAR AND MONTH) FROM TO	NAME AND LOCATION (CITY AND STATE)	MAJOR COURSE	DID YOU GRADUATE?	DATE AND DEGREE RECEIVED
HIGH OR PREP SCHOOL					
COLLEGE OR UNIVERSITY					
OTHER, I.E. BUSINESS, SECRETARIAL, TECHNICAL, LAW, ETC.					

ARE YOU STUDYING NOW? ☐ YES ☐ NO   WHAT SCHOOL?   CLASS HOURS   WHAT SUBJECT?

LIST YOUR CHIEF HIGH SCHOOL SUBJECTS   SEMESTER HOURS

LIST YOUR CHIEF COLLEGE SUBJECTS

SPECIFICALLY, HAVE YOU HAD COURSES IN THE FOLLOWING; CHECK: LIST OTHER SKILLS

☐ TYPING____WPM   ☐ COMMERCIAL MATH   ☐ ACCOUNTING
☐ SHORTHAND____WPM   ☐ TRANSCRIBING MACHINES   ☐ PBX OPERATION
☐ KEY PUNCH   ☐ COMPUTER OPERATIONS PROGRAMMING
☐ BOOKKEEPING   ☐ OTHER (SPECIFY)____

IN WHAT ACTIVITIES DID YOU PARTICIPATE IN HIGH SCHOOL OR COLLEGE? (OPTIONAL)

Fig. 5-2 (Cont.)   Personnel file jacket and forms.

EMPLOYMENT RECORD

PLEASE ACCOUNT FOR ALL PAST EMPLOYMENT

APPLICANT, PLEASE DO NOT
WRITE IN THIS MARGIN

PRESENT OR LAST POSITION	FROM (DATE) TO (DATE)	POSITION		BEGINNING SALARY	LAST SALARY

COMPANY NAME | NO. AND STREET / CITY / STATE

TYPE OF BUSINESS | BRIEFLY DESCRIBE YOUR DUTIES

NAME OF LAST SUPERVISOR | REASON FOR LEAVING | DID YOU RESIGN?

PREVIOUS POSITION	FROM (DATE) TO (DATE)	POSITION		BEGINNING SALARY	LAST SALARY

COMPANY NAME | NO. AND STREET / CITY / STATE

TYPE OF BUSINESS | BRIEFLY DESCRIBE YOUR DUTIES

NAME OF LAST SUPERVISOR | REASON FOR LEAVING | DID YOU RESIGN?

PREVIOUS POSITION	FROM (DATE) TO (DATE)	POSITION	LAST SALARY

COMPANY NAME | NO. AND STREET / CITY / STATE

TYPE OF BUSINESS | BRIEFLY DESCRIBE YOUR DUTIES

NAME OF LAST SUPERVISOR | REASON FOR LEAVING | DID YOU RESIGN?

PREVIOUS POSITION	FROM (DATE) TO (DATE)	POSITION	LAST SALARY

COMPANY NAME | NO. AND STREET / CITY / STATE

TYPE OF BUSINESS | BRIEFLY DESCRIBE YOUR DUTIES

NAME OF LAST SUPERVISOR | REASON FOR LEAVING | DID YOU RESIGN?

OTHER PREVIOUS POSITIONS OR ACTIVITIES

AFTER LISTING YOUR OTHER PREVIOUS POSITIONS YOU MAY, IF YOU WISH, INCLUDE IN THIS SPACE ANY PERTINENT CIVIC, WELFARE, OR ORGANIZATIONAL ACTIVITY WHICH YOU HAVE PERFORMED, EITHER WITH OR WITHOUT COMPENSATION. SHOW ACTUAL TIME SPENT IN SUCH ACTIVITY.

DATE | NAME AND ADDRESS OF COMPANY OR ACTIVITY | TITLE OF JOB
FROM   TO

UNITED STATES MILITARY SERVICE

BRANCH | DATE ENTERED

DATE DISCHARGED OR PLACED ON INACTIVE DUTY | TYPE OF DISCHARGE   HONORABLE ☐ YES   ☐ NO | OTHER

PRESENT OR LAST RANK | MILITARY OCCUPATION

PLEASE TURN PAGE

Fig. 5-2 (Cont.) Personnel file jacket and forms.

OTHER PERSONAL INFORMATION

IT IS HELPFUL THAT WE KNOW YOU AS WELL AS POSSIBLE IN ORDER TO EMPLOY YOU AND TO ASSIGN YOU TO THE JOB MOST APPROPRIATE FOR YOU. WE THEREFORE REQUEST THE FOLLOWING INFORMATION:

| THIS COMPANY REQUIRES A PHYSICAL EXAM BY OUR DOCTOR. WILL YOU AGREE TO AN EXAM? ☐ YES ☐ NO | HAVE YOU EVER BEEN CONVICTED OF A CRIMINAL OFFENSE OTHER THAN A MINOR TRAFFIC VIOLATION? ☐ YES ☐ NO |

DATE OF LAST PHYSICAL EXAM | EXAMINING DOCTOR'S NAME | ARE THERE ANY OUTSTANDING TAX LIENS OR LEGAL JUDGMENTS AGAINST YOU? ☐ YES ☐ NO

RESULTS OF EXAM | ARE YOU ☐ RIGHT HANDED ☐ LEFT HANDED | ARE YOU A UNITED STATES CITIZEN? ☐ YES ☐ NO | IF YOU ARE NOT A U.S. CITIZEN, DO YOU HAVE A LEGAL RIGHT TO REMAIN IN THE U.S.? ☐ YES ☐ NO | ALIEN REGISTRATION NUMBER

IN AN EMERGENCY WHOM SHALL WE CONTACT IN THIS AREA? | PHONE NUMBER DURING DAY

ADDRESS

HOW DID YOU HEAR ABOUT THIS JOB? | LIST ANY FRIENDS OR ACQUAINTANCES WHO WORK HERE

APPLICANT'S COMMENTS AND ADDITIONAL INFORMATION

Public Law 91-508 requires that we advise you that a routine investigation may be made whereby information is obtained through personal interviews with your neighbors, friends or others with whom you are acquainted. This inquiry includes information as to your character, general reputation, personal characteristics and mode of living. You have the right to make a written request within a reasonable period of time to receive additional, detailed information about the nature and scope of this investigation.

In submitting this application I understand that withholding information or making a false statement will disqualify me for employment or cause my subsequent dismissal. I further understand that permanent employment is contingent upon my meeting Company standards for a medical examination and background check. I authorize the Company to make a thorough background investigation, including the personal information mentioned above and all statements on this application.

► SIGN YOUR NAME _____   DATE _____
(MUST agree with signature on your Social Security Card)

APPLICANT, PLEASE DO NOT WRITE BELOW THIS LINE

DATE | INTERVIEWER | COMMENTS BY PERSONNEL DEPARTMENT

COMMENTS BY INTERVIEWING DEPARTMENT

IF ACCEPTED, TO BE COMPLETED BY INTERVIEWING DEPARTMENT — PLEASE PRINT

CHECK APPROPRIATE COLUMNS

PART-TIME	FULL-TIME	TEMPORARY			REHIRE	Night or Other Shift (Days & Hours)
(Give hours)		Summer	Medical	Other		

D-8#_____

REPORTING DATE | REG/DEPT/DIV | SEC. CODE | JOB TITLE

GRADE	JOB CODE	SALARY		TELEPHONE (7 digits and non-restricted extension if applicable)	LOCATION (Bldg — ie., Oper, Barlow, etc.)
		Yearly	Weekly		

COMMITMENTS

APPROVED BY

D-35 (9-74)

Fig. 5-2 (Cont.)   Personnel file jacket and forms.

DATE _____

COURSE INFORMATION SHEET

To the file of: _T. B. SANFORD_____

This employee has attended the following education programs:

Clerical and Written Communications

Title of Course _____ Dates _____ Completed _____

Title of Course _____ Dates _____ Completed _____

Title of Course _____ Dates _____ Completed _____

Title of Course _____ Dates _____ Completed _____

Title of Course _____ Dates _____ Completed _____

Title of Course _____ Dates _____ Completed _____

Management and Supervisory Programs

Title of Course _IIA - MGT 41_____ Dates __10/73____ Completed _EXCELLENT_

Title of Course _BASIC MGMT_____ Dates _AUG/72___ Completed _SATIS____

Title of Course _____ Dates _____ Completed _____

Title of Course _____ Dates _____ Completed _____

Title of Course _____ Dates _____ Completed _____

Title of Course _____ Dates _____ Completed _____

Outside Programs - Programs Offered by Other Departments

Title of Course _____ Dates _____ Completed _____

Title of Course _____ Dates _____ Completed _____

Title of Course _____ Dates _____ Completed _____

Title of Course _____ Dates _____ Completed _____

Title Of Course _____ Dates _____ Completed _____

IIA PROGRAMS

___ Ins. 21 _____	✓ Mgt. 41 _____	___ Adj. 31 _____
___ Ins. 22 _____	___ Mgt. 42 _____	___ Adj. 32 _____
___ Ins. 23 _____	___ Mgt. 43 _____	___ Adj. 35 _____
	___ Mgt. 44 _____	___ Adj. 36 _____
___ CPCU I _____	___ CPCU IV _____	
___ CPCU II _____	___ CPCU V _____	
___ CPCU III _____		

CODES FOR IIA PROGRAMS: (E)= Excellent--passed exam; (G)=Good--passed exam; (P)=Passed exam
(C)= Completed course to GEICO Standards; (I)=Incomplete--did not take
ER-3 (NS)   exam; (D)=Dropped

Fig. 5-2 (Cont.) Personnel file jacket and forms.

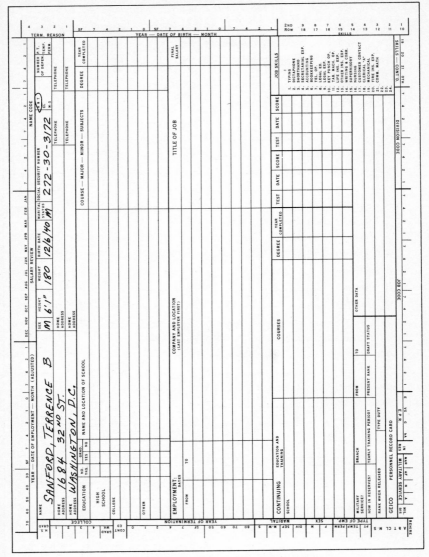

Fig. 5-2 (Cont.) Personnel file jacket and forms.

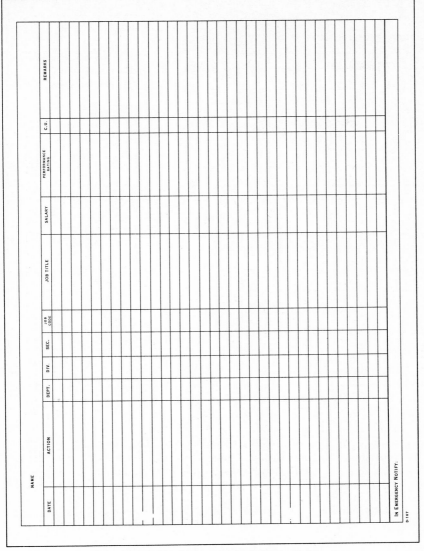

Fig. 5-2 (Cont.)   Personnel file jacket and forms.

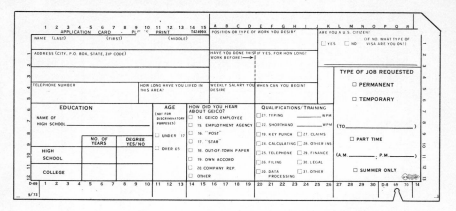

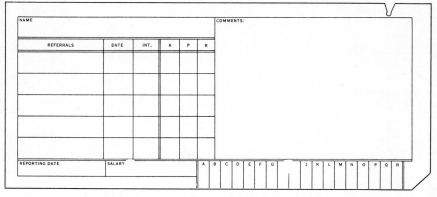

Fig. 5-2 (Concluded)   Personnel file jacket and forms.

Some companies now also publish handbooks (see Fig. 5-4) listing all available training programs, self-instructional programs, and audiovisual aids. Various formats are used, but most handbooks include information about (1) program objectives, (2) program content, (3) participant requirements, (4) registration, (5) whom to contact for more information.

4. *Information Summaries.*   Reporting results is time-consuming but critical to the development process. The training director is involved in research, problem analysis, surveys, program evaluations, and often personnel evaluations. Summaries of this information can be provided in three ways:

- Manual reports. All information is tabulated and typed or written in a report format.
- Semiautomatic reports. A card-sort or similar system is used which allows for some automation in the tabulating process. Often this is an inexpensive, easy way to tabulate hundreds of responses (see Fig. 5-5).
- Computer runs. An already existing program is used or a new computer program is introduced to compile some specific information. If the company has a computerized payroll system (as many do), a great deal of information about employees is already available to the training director who requests it. Additional information may often be programmed for special studies, but

often computer time and programming time become significant barriers. Computer studies and reports require a great deal of advance planning and the assistance of the data processing department.

Lots of tools exist—almost as many as the training director can create to do the job. The key to the *effective* training information system is to find a way to apply the tools systematically and to use only those which pay their way.

DESIGNING THE SYSTEM

Regardless of the size and degree of sophistication of the organization, the effective information system includes four key elements:

1. Methods of determining and classifying needs

2. Communication of resources
   a. Existing and planning programs
   b. Schedules—semiannual, monthly, or one-time program announcements.

GOVERNMENT EMPLOYEES COMPANIES
COURSE REGISTRATION FORM

DO NOT FILL IN
Completed _____

TRAINING & DEVELOPMENT PROGRAMS

Title of Program and/or Course   (Please type)

Course Dates (mo./days/year)

Name (Last)   First   Middle Initial)   Extension   Location

Department or Field Office   Division   Section

Job Title   Grade   Your Supervisor   Extension

D—120 (10/72)

This registration form should be completed and routed through your Department Head for approval. Registration forms must be received by Training & Development before the registration deadline listed on the announcement.
IMPORTANT: If this is an outside study program (IIA, CPCU, Law for Claimsmen, etc.) please complete the back of this card.
CONFIRMATION INFORMATION

EMPLOYEE'S SIGNATURE _____
DEPARTMENT
HEAD'S SIGNATURE _____

Approved as registered [   ]   Confirmed, but rescheduled for [   ]

Comments _____

Front

OUTSIDE STUDY PROGRAMS

If you are in a field office, fill in this section.

OFFICE

I meet the following qualifications:

COLLEGE/UNIVERSITY ATTENDING

_____ High School Graduate or the equivalent.

CITY   STATE

_____ Employed by the Companies for at least three months.

_____ Any additional or special criteria required for the program by a local college or university.

Beginning Date: Tuition Cost:

I understand that:

a. Whenever possible the Company will provide all facilities and instructors for the program - either in the Operations Building or at an approved site.
b. If I register through the Training & Development Division I am eligible to be reimbursed as outlined in the course bulletin.
c. I must pay the examination fee when due, but will be reimbursed when I take the examination regardless of the results.

ADDRESS: _____ CITY: _____ STATE: _____ ZIP: _____

DATE: _____   SIGNATURE: _____

Back

Fig. 5-3   Course registration form.

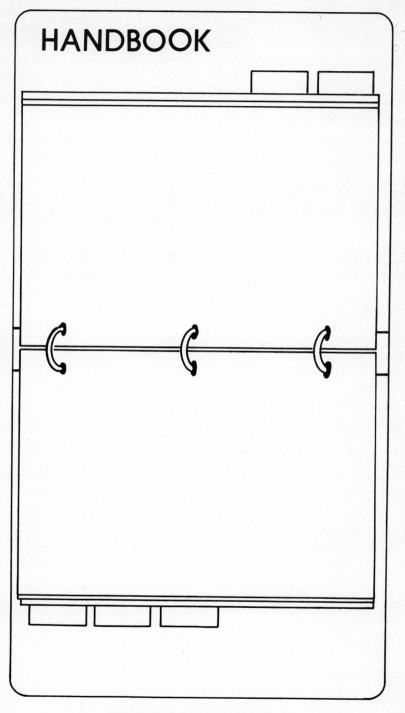

Fig. 5-4 Training program handbook

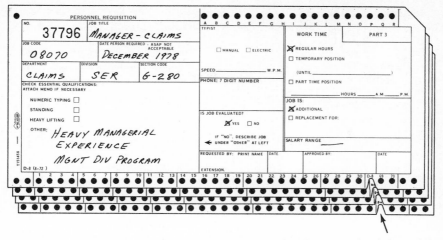

Fig. 5-5 Punch-card system. Card holes are coded and punched for appropriate information. A quick sort can be done by stacking the cards and sticking a needle through the code wanted. All punched cards will fall out.

3. Registration and confirmation procedures
4. Methods of determining and communicating program results

Each of these four elements plays an important part in cutting down the information contacts per day. The effective training information system anticipates these needs in the organization and handles them on a systematic basis (see Fig. 5-6).

Summarizing Training Needs

Hundreds of different kinds of training are going on in organizations. Each supervisor teaches employees how to do their jobs; people learn to manage, run meetings, operate computers, use tools, develop budgets, plan systems, and control operations. They learn through classes, self-instructional programs, textbooks, trial and error, outside programs, and other aids that supervisors provide for them. Literally thousands of training needs exist in any organization; often hundreds of good programs exist too. Frequently, though, few people know about the programs. One of the biggest problems the training administrator faces is that of developing a simplified method of collecting and communicating this information.

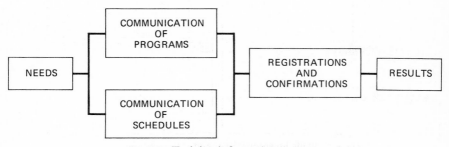

Fig. 5-6 Training information system.

Personnel Records   Personnel records can be an excellent input for training needs, but to be effective they must be monitored carefully and summarized regularly.

Large organizations such as the Hartford Insurance Company use computerized personnel systems which are constantly updated by line managers. A single turnaround form serves many purposes. The manager simply indicates each change on the form and submits it to the personnel department. The form (Fig. 5-7) becomes the input to the computer; it, in turn, is updated and then returned to

PERSONAL				RECORD DATE

NAME:
SOC. SEC.:
DATE OF BIRTH: CATEGORY:
                         SEX: MARITAL: **career profile**
INCEPTION DATE:
MILITARY OBLIG. COMPLETE DATE:

EDUCATIONAL ATTAINMENT   JOB/WORK LOCATION
                 LEVEL   SUBJECT   SCHOOL   YEAR   CO.   DPT:
HIGHEST LEVEL   DIV: SEC:
ADDITIONAL DEG 1   JOB CODE: JOB DATE:
ADDITIONAL DEG 2   JOB TITLE:

EDUCATION IN PROGRESS   TRAINING
DEGREE SOUGHT   CREDITS REQUIRED: COURSE   STATUS/GRADE   CLASS   DATE
MAJOR SUBJECT   CREDITS OBTAINED: COMPLETED
MINOR SUBJECT   YEAR CREDITS LAST OBTAINED:
SCHOOL

PRIOR WORK EXPERIENCE
COMPANY/MILITARY BRANCH   FROM   TO   TITLE/DUTIES

                                                           UPDATE INSTRUCTIONS
                                                           To add one year experience enter 'U' in action column.
               Work Experience, Management Experience, Work Specialties and Preferences,   To delete a term enter 'D' in action column.
WORK EXPERIENCE   Relocation Preferences, Languages, Licenses   To add a new term use reverse side of form.

DATEGORY	DESCRIPTION	YRS EXP COMM	LST YR	COMMENT	CODE

SIGNIFICANT ACHIEVEMENTS   YOUR CAREER PLAN
      DATE   DESCRIPTION   JOB TITLE   FUNCTIONAL DEVELOPMENT NEEDS
                                                       Skill   Description
                                                       Code

OUTSIDE ACTIVITIES

Fig. 5-7 Skills inventory form and career profile form.

the manager until the next change. Many reports (including companywide skill inventories) are generated by this same system.

Smaller companies use a combination of computer and manual systems based on the cost-benefit ratio derived from their system. The organization with few employees can usually screen personnel records on a semiannual or annual basis; organizations with hundreds of employees must rely on a semiautomated system.

Training-Needs Survey   Surveys do not work unless they include a clear definition of the kind of information needed and are easy to complete and tabulate.

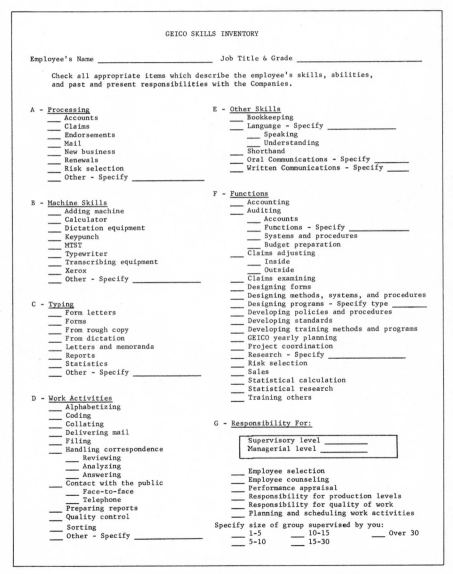

Fig. 5-7 (Cont.)   Skills inventory form and career profile form.

PRIORITIES FOR MANAGEMENT TRAINING

	Room for Improvement Score	X	Frequency of Mention Score	=	Priority Index
Organizing, Planning, and Taking Action	14.19 (1)*	X	40.0 (1)	=	596.00
Feeling Pressure for Performance Improvement	13.8 (2)	X	18.6 (2)	=	256.68
Feeling Committed to Goal Achievement	13.2 (4)	X	14.2 (4)	=	187.44
Understanding GEICO's Goals and Policies	9.3 (8)	X	17.7 (3)	=	164.61
Feeling of Warmth, Support, Responsibility to the Work Groups	10.6 (6)	X	10.0 (5)	=	106.00
Receiving Feedback and Reward on Performance	13.6 (3)	X	7.0 (7)	=	95.20
Setting Mutually Agreeable Goals	11.9 (5)	X	7.1 (6)	=	84.46
Being Encouraged, Helped, and Developed by Manager	10.5 (7)	X	3.1 (8)	=	32.55

*Numbers in parentheses refer to rankings.

Fig. 5-8 Management training-needs summary.

Broad, general surveys provide only general information, while specific questions elicit a clear set of needs and objectives. Surveys may be conducted (1) by questionnaire, (2) through personal interviews, or (3) through a combination of the two. The survey of management training needs shown in Fig. 5-8 was conducted by questionnaire and confirmed by a proportionate number of interviews. The summary sheet was designed to provide the training director with the critically needed course content at a glance. It was also used to communicate the basis of the program to participants and eventually became the foundation of a pretesting program.

Surveys may be tabulated manually, through card-sort systems, or, if the employee base is large enough, through a computer system.

Performance Problems Performance reviews, warnings, and exit interviews often reveal performance problems for specific individuals or, when tabulated, for whole areas or sections. To be effective, the performance review or warning should include a section on development and/or improvement needs and should be audited on a regular basis. In a large organization, this is an extremely time-consuming process unless the training director can develop a simplifed system. The system should include:

- Improvement areas listed (specifically) on performance appraisal forms and coded for easy tabulation (see Fig. 5-9)
- Quarterly summaries completed from codes

Quarterly or semiannual summaries by region or department provide an excellent means of verifying information gathered from other sources.

Exit interviews also provide a check on performance problems, but by the time the exit comes through, it is too late! Like performance reviews, however, exit interviews can be tabulated on a quarterly basis to provide an overview. Figure 5-10 shows a quarterly summary of exit interviews. The personnel department in this organization simply added one new segment to an already existing report. No additional tabulation was required, and yet the training department then had a ready reference of performance problems. *Remember:* The training director can accomplish more by adding to already existing tools (tabulated by others) than by inventing new ones.

The Training Committee   A training committee, if carefully chosen and representative of the major sections of the organization, can provide the organization with an ongoing analysis of:

1. Organizational training responsibilities
2. Organizational training needs

____ March   19___
____ September   19___

PERFORMANCE APPRAISAL
Goal Setting Supplement

NAME_____ JOB TITLE _____ CODE _____

REGION/DEPT. _____ DIVISION_____SECTION CODE _____

Instructions to the Supervisor

Discuss overall responsibilities and specific goals for the next rating period with this employee. When you have reached agreement, record goals and "measurement of success" below. Keep one copy for your records, give one copy to the employee.

SECTION II — MUTUAL GOAL SETTING

Responsibilities/Objectives	Applicable Goal Scale OR Other Measurement of Success	Completion Date

SECTION III — MANPOWER PLANNING AND DEVELOPMENT

A. Areas of Improvement (Goals)	Completion Date
TYPING	10/74
TELEPHONE HANDLING	10/74
KNOWLEDGE OF MATERIAL DAMAGE PROC.	1/75

Supervisor's Signature _____   Employee's Signature _____

D-146

Fig. 5-9   Performance appraisal forms.

PERFORMANCE APPRAISAL

_____ March 19_____
_____ September 19_____

Name		Region/Dept.		Division		Sec.	Employee No.

Date Employed	Date Assigned Present Job		Job Title			Code	Grade

Last Rating

SECTION I — APPRAISAL OF PAST PERFORMANCE

A. **Responsibilities/Objectives** — list responsibilities/goals set at last performance appraisal. Use additional sheets or attach last Goal Setting Supplement if appropriate.

RESPONSIBILITIES/OBJECTIVES   RESULTS

1.   1.

2.   2.

3.   3.

4.   4.

5.   5.

Percent of job covered by these objectives

B. **Summary Statement of Overall Job Performance**

C. **Overall Performance Appraisal** — Consider the total job responsibilities, actual results achieved and the summary statements in arriving at your rating.

	Less Than 100% Trained			**100% Trained**	
Average Training Time _____	_____	(5) Far Exceeds Requirements	_____	(5) Far Exceeds Requirements
Time in Job _____	_____	(4) Exceeds Requirements	_____	(4) Exceeds Requirements
Percent Trained _____	_____	(3) Meets Requirements	_____	(3) Meets Requirements
	_____	(2) Meets Requirements in Some Areas	_____	(2) Meets Requirements in Some Areas
	_____	(1) Does Not Meet Requirements	_____	(1) Does Not Meet Requirements

_____ Eligible for Promotion   _____ Not Eligible for Promotion At This Time

D-91 (Rev. 11/74)   (OVER)

Fig. 5-9 (Cont.)   Performance appraisal forms.

SECTION II – MUTUAL GOAL SETTING

Complete the Supplemental Goal Setting Form (see attached). Goals and responsibilities should be realistic, specific, and measureable.

SECTION III – MANPOWER PLANNING & DEVELOPMENT

A. **Areas of Improvement** – List specific areas in which the employee needs to improve his skills and set goals for the next rating period.
(See supplemental form).

B. **Additional Training and/or Other Development Activities to Help the Employee Improve.**

	TECHNICAL	SUPERVISORY/MANAGERIAL	PERSONAL SKILLS
1.			
2.			
3.			

C. **List Two Possible Future Career Opportunities for This Employee.**

1.

2.

SECTION IV – EMPLOYEE'S COMMENTS – to be filled in by the employee.

Rated By _____ Date _____ Approved By _____

Reviewed By _____ Date _____ Date _____

Fig. 5-9 (Concluded)   Performance appraisal forms

EXIT INTERVIEW

The confidential information requested of you goes directly to Personnel. Insert and seal in the envelope provided and give to the Personnel interviewer. In field offices you may send in Company mail or mail it through Post Office. Postage is provided.

NAME

☐ PART TIME   ☐ TEMPORARY

☐ PERMANENT

DEPARTMENT   DIVISION   SECTION

☐ GEICO   ☐ GELICO   ☐ GECO   ☐ CRICO   ☐ GEFCO

YOUR SUPERVISOR'S NAME

GRADE AND TITLE

INCEPTION DATE   TERMINATION DATE

PLEASE USE A BLACK PEN AND WRITE OR PRINT CLEARLY.

WHAT MADE YOU DECIDE TO LEAVE YOUR JOB?   *Explain*

WOULD YOU CHECK THE BLOCK THAT MOST PERTAINS TO YOU? *(This check is for statistical purposes.)*

Reason for termination

☐ Pregnancy	☐ Family Resp.	☐ Transportation	☐ Other
☐ Marriage	☐ Relocation	☐ Dissatisfied	
☐ Another Job	☐ School	☐ Did Not Return From Leave	☐ Allowed To Resign
☐ Military Service	☐ Health	☐ Abandonment of Job	☐ Released

DID YOU LIKE YOUR JOB?

☐ YES
    Why?
☐ NO

HOW DO YOU EVALUATE THE TRAINING RECEIVED?

☐ VERY GOOD

☐ AVERAGE   *Explain*

☐ POOR

DID YOU HAVE ENOUGH OPPORTUNITY TO DEVELOP YOUR CAPABILITIES IN YOUR PRESENT JOB?

☐ YES
    If not, Explain
☐ NO

WHAT DO YOU THINK OF THE AMOUNT OF WORK EXPECTED OF YOU?

☐ NOT ENOUGH

☐ AVERAGE   *Explain*

☐ TOO MUCH

DO YOU THINK YOUR SALARY WAS FAIR?

☐ YES
    Explain
☐ NO

D-62 (11-72)   *(OVER)*

Fig. 5-10 Exit-interview form and summary form.

DID YOU SEE OPPORTUNITY FOR ADVANCEMENT?

☐ YES

Explain

☐ NO

WHAT DID YOU THINK OF YOUR PRESENT SUPERVISOR?

Very Good   Average   Poor   *Explain*
☐   ☐   ☐

DO YOU THINK YOU WERE FAIRLY RATED ON YOUR PERFORMANCE REVIEWS?

PERFORMANCE   ☐ YES ☐ NO
                                      Explain
SALARY ACTION   ☐ YES ☐ NO

HOW WAS THE MORALE IN YOUR AREA? *(How did most people feel about their jobs, their supervisor, the Company, etc.?)*

☐ VERY GOOD
☐ AVERAGE   *Explain*
☐ POOR

WERE WORKING CONDITIONS SATISFACTORY?

☐ YES
                  If 'no', Explain
☐ NO

WHAT DO YOU THINK ABOUT THE COMPANY'S BENEFIT PROGRAMS AND LEAVE PLANS? *(Temporary & Part-Time Employees please omit)*

☐ VERY GOOD
☐ AVERAGE   *Explain*
☐ POOR

SUMMARY: Please give any other suggestions you have for changes or improvements

Fig. 5-10 (Cont.)   Exit-interview form and summary form.

EXIT INTERVIEW SUMMARY

Department _____

Division   _____

Total Terms _____ (%) _____ (%) _____ (%) _____ (%)

Total Exits _____   _____   _____   _____

	1st Quarter	2nd Quarter	3rd Quarter	4th Quarter	Annual
Did you like your job?	Yes No	Yes No	Yes No	Yes No	Yes No
How do you evaluate the training received?	VG G F P	VG G F P	VG G F P	VG G F P	VG G F P
Did you have enough opportunity to use and develop your capabilities?	Yes No	Yes No	Yes No	Yes No	Yes No
Did you feel your job was important?	Yes No	Yes No	Yes No	Yes No	Yes No
What do you think of the amount of work expected of you?	NE A TM	NE A TM	NE A TM	NE A TM	NE A TM
What did you think of your supervisor?	VG G F P	VG G F P	VG G F P	VG G F P	VG G F P
Do you think you were fairly evaluated on your EPR's?	Yes No	Yes No	Yes No	Yes No	Yes No
How was the morale in your area?	VG G F P	VG G F P	VG G F P	VG G F P	VG G F P
Were working conditions satisfactory?	Yes No	Yes No	Yes No	Yes No	Yes No

Comments:

Fig. 5-10 (Concluded)   Exit-interview form and summary form.

3. Existing programs
4. Planned programs or programs already being developed

The committee can become a clearinghouse for information about existing programs and a means of publicizing new ones. Skillful direction is needed, however, if the committee is to be successful.

At the beginning, such a committee should meet monthly to establish an effective communication vehicle and define priorities. The committee's first major project which impacts significantly on the information system is to develop a statement of "responsibility" for training. Although managers think that the training unit *trains*, literally every supervisor and manager and a number of staff units are involved in the training effort. The training committee should define that responsibility precisely and publish it in such a way that others in the organization accept their roles. (Figure 5-11 outlines responsibilities for one organization.)

With a clear definition of responsibility, the training director can draw on many more people to provide information. His or her job then becomes one of compiling what line people have already submitted. A by-product of this approach is that the information is readily accepted by the line.

A second project the committee may become involved in is determining organization-wide training needs and translating them into program objectives. This can be tracked through careful discussion, committee notes covering major projects, and review dates which prevent projects from being "lost."

The third project is a definition of, and report on, programs that are currently being developed in various areas of the organization. The novice will be surprised to find out how many people in the organization are developing training materials. Distribution of this information prevents duplication of effort from one area to another, especially in large companies where many staff units are engaged in overlapping responsibilities. Critical to the success of this project is the committee membership and their understanding of their responsibilities and committment.

	Corporate Trng. Unit	Line Mgr.	Regional* Trng. Coord.	
Analysis of Need		PRIMARY Responsibility		
Definition of Objectives	PRIMARY Responsibility	Approval		
Design	PRIMARY Responsibility			
"Do" the Training	Assists as needed	PRIMARY Responsibility	Maintains courses, equipment. Instructs	
Evaluate Revise	PRIMARY Responsibility	Feedback	Assists and collects data	

*May not exist in all regions.

Fig. 5-11 Training responsibilities.

The final information project for the committee is the definition of existing programs and the careful description of them. Course descriptions which include clear-cut objectives make it easy for the manager to determine whether the course covers the needed behaviors; more importantly, however, they make it possible for the training needs and resources to be classified in an orderly manner. (A publication like the handbook shown in Fig. 5-4, for example, is frequently a product of committee effort.)

Converting to Objectives

For many years program descriptions gave general information about programs, conference leaders, and daily schedules of what would be taught. The descriptions did not provide, however, a clear understanding of what the participants would actually get out of the program. Managers send subordinates to programs to learn; however, subordinates often do not know what they should learn or how they should use their new knowledge in their work. A great deal of training goes on, but often only a small portion is actually used back on the job.

The introduction of behavioral objectives into the educational process[1] has made it possible now to state precisely what a participant will be able to do at the end of the program. If the course does not take the participant far enough in learning the required skill, the manager knows ahead of time and can schedule additional activities. If the course is too general, the manager can schedule another program instead.

Use of objectives has short-cut research and training time significantly. Courses are aimed at specific results; research into existing programs can be categorized. Over a period of time, the training director can develop an inventory of major training objectives for the organization and a listing of various programs and other available resources. Today's trainer has many more resources to draw on, and it is now possible to cut through the thousands of existing programs to find appropriate ones.

To convert training needs (or subject matter) to objectives, the trainer simply turns the information around and states the content in terms of what the participant will be able to do after completing the program, as illustrated in the table below.

Training needs (from Fig. 5-9)	*Objectives*
■ Typing	■ Type 55 wpm on company forms
■ Telephone skills	■ Take correct messages; handle complaints; transfer Centrex calls
■ Material damage	■ Estimate damage (within 10% of guideline) to an American-made car

It is easy to see that not all typing or telephone training programs would teach the specific skills listed in the second column. Similarly, a general insurance course would not cover the skills needed in the material-damage area.

Classifying Objectives   Complete classifications of learning objectives run into thousands of pages.[2] Obviously the training director cannot handle that volume of information, nor would it make sense to try. It is possible, though, to set up a 3×5 card file for each of the major training objectives in a particular subject area. As resources are identified and programs are obtained, they can be listed along with other information. Both objectives and resources can be included in the program handbook. Remember too that the training committee and others involved in the training effort can help significantly in developing this information. The volume of information and the extent of the classification should not exceed what is needed by the organization *at this time.* As the organization grows, the system and the sophistication of classification grow too.

Communicating and Scheduling Programs

Most of the calls that the training director receives during the day are requests for particular programs or for information about program schedules.

What Programs to Offer Getting started is the hardest part. Ask yourself: Where do the priorities lie? Which contain the biggest "payoff" over the next six months for the organization? The training director who is starting out in the small or medium-sized organization should:

1. Carefully analyze his or her own responsibilities
2. Determine the major training needs
3. Calculate the payoff for each

Needs	How Critical	Time	Savings	Reaction	Comments

Fig. 5-12 Training-needs matrix.

This analysis can be informal, determining which programs are most immediate and which will best set the pattern for the future. Once the training director has a "winner," he or she can go on to set priorities based on both short- and long-range needs, considering far less measurable and often far more critical payoffs. The key question is: Which program should be first? Which will be the winner?

Three simple steps help define the winner: a careful review of compiled training needs, a historical forecast to check receptivity, and a decision as to whether this course should be a one-time, low-key program or a regular course offering.

1. *Review of Training Needs.* Regardless of which methods were used to summarize training needs and objectives, a matrix like that shown in Fig. 5-12 can now be constructed to identify priorities. A summary of this sort should help immensely in determining where the payoff lies.

2. *Historical Forecast.* If the programs have been run in the past and records of registration and attendance have been kept, the training director can accurately forecast the programs that will be needed during the coming year and the ones that will be successful. Registration and attendance records clearly show the interest in the program during previous years, the number of people turned away because of overregistration, changes which should be made in candidate requirements, and requests for additional programs.

3. *The Decision Maze.* Regular course offerings versus one-time program offerings. All managers in an organization have their own ideas concerning what training programs should be offered, and about 20 percent of the managers or supervisors in an organization will request specific programs sometime during the year. Which requests should be accepted?

The training director has two alternatives: develop programs on a request basis (often a "crash" basis) or rely on interviews, surveys, and past registrations to determine priority areas and fill those requests. Development dollars and time should be plowed into programs which have a wide impact on the organization. Managers are willing to wait if they know their requests have been considered and are being worked on. Outside seminars or published materials can be used for those managers who need other programs immediately. One-time programs,

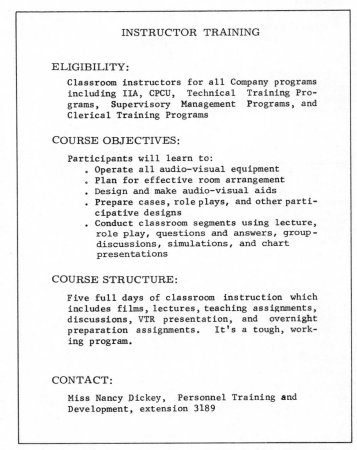

INSTRUCTOR TRAINING

ELIGIBILITY:

> Classroom instructors for all Company programs including IIA, CPCU, Technical Training Programs, Supervisory Management Programs, and Clerical Training Programs

COURSE OBJECTIVES:

> Participants will learn to:
> - Operate all audio-visual equipment
> - Plan for effective room arrangement
> - Design and make audio-visual aids
> - Prepare cases, role plays, and other participative designs
> - Conduct classroom segments using lecture, role play, questions and answers, group-discussions, simulations, and chart presentations

COURSE STRUCTURE:

> Five full days of classroom instruction which includes films, lectures, teaching assignments, discussions, VTR presentation, and overnight preparation assignments. It's a tough, working program.

CONTACT:

> Miss Nancy Dickey, Personnel Training and Development, extension 3189

Fig. 5-13 Program description. *(GEICO Development Opportunities.)*

designed for a limited group of people, should not claim a major share of resources.

After several years of systematic development, most of the crash-request areas will have been included on the regular schedule anyway.

Making Managers Aware

Regardless of the size of the organization, the training director must find some way—as a result of either planning or happenstance—to alert line managers to the programs and resources which are available to them. All too often the director assumes that the only "available" programs are those which have been developed by the training unit. A few minutes of careful analysis, however, will quickly show that many, many other programs exist within the organization and could be available if only people knew about them. Thousands are also available on the open market.

A systematic approach to making managers aware includes:

1. *Program information*
   - Programs existing within the company
   - Other learning resources
   - Programs available soon

2. *Schedule of programs to be conducted*
   - Annual or semiannual programs
   - Monthly programs
   - Special one-time programs

Program Information   The behavioral sciences made a great contribution to the training profession, in terms of design and communication, when they introduced the concept of learning objectives (see the section on converting to objectives). Objectives communicate clearly the desired outcomes of programs—without the necessity of constantly updating the information because of format or content changes. Some companies use a format like the one shown in Fig. 5-13 to publicize programs within the organization. The key to an effective listing, however, is to list not only those programs which have been developed internally but also those which are commercially available. The training director can also use his or her resources to "publicize" programs produced by other departments in the organization—much to the credit of those who have developed them.

Other Learning Resources   The distinction between training programs as such and other learning resources is becoming more and more difficult to make. Are training programs always classroom-based? Self-instructional? Combined? How should they be listed? The same method of describing a classroom program can be applied to other learning resources. If the resource is a complete entity, it should be listed separately. If it is simply an aid for another program (such as a film or textbook), it should be listed on a single page, by use. For example, a page of management development program aids might look like Fig. 5-14. Programs should be cross-referenced in all applicable categories.

Programs Being Developed   Sixty percent of the calls involve "current" programs. The rest are about programs managers would like to see. And, of course, everyone in the organization has his or her own idea of what programs should be provided. It is impossible to meet all requests. Informing managers of what is being developed can eliminate many of these request calls.

The program development report should be sent to key people only. It should answer new program questions, coordinate the efforts of all those in the organization who are developing programs, and clearly communicate the present status. The development report takes about a half hour to prepare and is issued quarterly. It includes seven categories (as shown in Fig. 5-15).

Announcing Program Schedules

Many callers ask for program dates, times, and locations. Each time there is a call, someone must look up the information or ask to have the coordinator return the call. In organizations with more than 500 people, some regular communication will save considerable time. Most commonly used are (1) semiannual or annual training schedule, (2) the monthly training announcement, and (3) the one-time program brochure or announcement.

"Great idea, but we can't possibly plan that far ahead." Maybe. But maybe it is possible to plan six months ahead. Even if plans change along the way, the semiannual or annual training schedule is one of the best methods of communicating the programs that will be available. And, with it, managers can plan their "development" programs around work schedules. Calls are cut significantly. Keep it simple—-one page if possible, including only the program name and scheduled

```
The Appraisal Interview. . . . . . . . . Filmstrip
Capitalizing on Group Dynamics . . . . . Filmstrip
Disciplinary Interview . . . . . . . . . Filmstrip
Why Appraise . . . . . . . . . . . . . . Filmstrip
What to Appraise . . . . . . . . . . . . Filmstrip
EFFECTIVE COMMUNICATIONS SKILLS SERIES:. Filmstrip
  . General Principles of Communications  (Series)
  . Effective Group Communications
  . The Supervisor as a Communicator
  . Improving Personal Communications
DEVELOPING MANAGEMENT SKILLS . . . . . . Filmstrip
  . Developing Effective Management        (Series)
  . Organize for Results
  . Decision Making
  . Perception
  . Leading People
THE HUMAN SIDE OF MANAGEMENT . . . . . . Filmstrip
  . What's Behind Behavior                 (Series)
  . Working More Effectively with People
  . Management for Results
  . Coaching
SOUNDS OF SUPERVISION. . . . . . . . . Audio Cassette
  . Controlling Absenteeism                (Series)
  . Preventing Employee Theft
  . How to Give Orders
  . Your Role in Safety
  . Managing Your Time
  . Controlling Alcohol, Drugs, Gambling
EXECUTIVE SEMINAR IN SOUND . . . . . . Audio Cassette
  . Make the Most of Your Time             (Series)
  . How to Get Your Ideas Across
How to Communicate Your Ideas. . . . . Audio Record
```

Fig. 5-14   Training-aids list. *(GEICO Development Opportunities.)*

week (see Fig. 5-16). Managers can look in the handbook for additional information. The report provides a direction for a specified period of time and allows for advance scheduling of space and audiovisual equipment.

Even the best schedules have a way of getting lost or left in the bottom drawer. A monthly training announcement—with specific information—serves as a regular reminder. Such an announcement includes:

- Program name
- Dates, times, and location
- Instructor or coordinator
- Brief description of the program
- Registration deadline (important)

The registration deadline is the best method of controlling registrations. Once the organization gets used to the idea that there is a single time when registrations will be accepted, calls and late registrations drop to a minimum.

New or one-time program announcements call attention to a new program or a special program. The easiest way to make such announcements is by means of

TRAINING ACTIVITIES REPORT - MAY, 1973

Program	Description	Coordinator	Proposal	Approval	Development	Piloted	Completed	Comments
CLAIMS PROGRAMS								
Injury Claim Evaluation	Seminar for experienced Grade 19 Examiners	B. Woolner	X	X				Program dropped—to be replaced
Total Theft Package	For Managers and Supvs. use on the job	B. Woolner	X	X	X	X	X	Completed
Suit Handling	Seminar for experienced Grade 19 Examiners	B. Woolner	X	X	6/2/73			
No-Fault	Michigan Plans & New York Plans	B. Woolner (same)	7/1/73 10/1/73					
Intro. To Fire and Allied Lines	Program developed by Property Loss Research Bureau specifically for GEICO	John Erickson	X	X	X	X	X	Completed
Civil Trial	Simulated trial for Claims Training to show how recorded statements, pictures, etc., are use in actual trial	T. Baxter Walt Smith	X	X	6/30/73			

Fig. 5-15 Program development report.

Training & Development CONFERENCE SCHEDULE SPRING 1973	COURSES	JANUARY 1 8 15 22 29	FEBRUARY 5 12 19 26	MARCH 5 12 19 26	APRIL 2 9 16 23 30	MAY 7 14 21 28	JUNE 4 11 18 25
	TYPING TRAINING	Every Day For Four Weeks	Every Day For Four Weeks		Every Day For Four Weeks	Every Day For Four Weeks	Every Day - Four Weeks
	REFRESHER TYPING			Every Day For Three Weeks			Every Day For Three Weeks
	TELEPHONE TRAINING			W W W			W W W
	MINI MESSAGES		M,T,W,Th			M,T,W,Th	M,T,W,Th
	DICTATION TRAINING	Th,F Th,F		Th,F	Th,F	Th,F	Th,F
	LETTER WRITING	For Und. Dept. - Every Tues. / For Claims Dept. - Every Wed.		For Und. Dept. - Every Tues. / For Claim Dept. - Every Wed.		For Und. Dept. - Every Tues. / For Claim Dept. - Every Wed.	
	REPORT & MEMO WRITING		T,Th T,Th T,Th T,Th		T,Th T,Th T,Th T,Th		
	CRITIQUING MADE EASY		W		W T	T	
	D-22 WORKSHOP		F		F		F
	SECRETARIAL TRAINING			Every Day For 2 Wks		Every Day For 2 Wks	
	ENGLISH FOR SECRETARIES					T,Th T,Th T,Th T,Th	T,Th T,Th T,Th T,Th
	PROCEDURE WRITING	T,Th M,Th F					
	INSTRUCTOR TRAINING	DATES TO BE ANNOUNCED					
	SUPERVISORY INTERN		W,Th	T Th	T W	Th	W
	BASIC SUPERVISION		M,T,W,Th	M,T,W,F	M,T,W,Th T,W,Th		
	BASIC MANAGEMENT	M,W,Th,F T,W,Th			T,W,Th M,W,Th		
	COMPUTER CONCEPTS		T,Th T,Th T,Th T,Th				
	EXCEPTIONAL MANAGER		M,T,W	M,T,W M,T,W	M,T,W M,T,W	M,T,W	M,T,W M,T,W M,T,W
	IIA - 21	STARTS JANUARY 24, 1973 - Will Meet Every Wednesday for Fourteen Weeks					
	IIA - 22	STARTS JANUARY 22, 1973 - Will Meet Every Monday for Fourteen Weeks					
	IIA - 42	STARTS JANUARY 23, 1973 - Will Meet Every Tuesday For Fourteen Weeks					
	IIA - 44	STARTS JANUARY 25, 1973 - Will Meet Every Thursday for Fourteen Weeks					
	LAW FOR THE CLAIMSMAN	REGISTRATION Once a Month Every Month - Consult The Monthly Class Announcement for Course Registration Deadline					
	ENGLISH AS A 2nd LANGUAGE	DATES TO BE ANNOUNCED					
	SPANISH FOR SUPERVISORS	DATES TO BE ANNOUNCED					
	FIELD OFFICE CONFERENCES	DATES TO BE ANNOUNCED					

Fig. 5-16 Program schedule.

preprinted letterheads (see Fig. 5-17), which can be prepared inexpensively and used in many ways. The letterhead flashes your program to all who are interested. Information can be written exactly as the handbook will eventually be written. The announcement can be posted on bulletin boards, attached to monthly training schedules or newsletters, and eventually added to handbooks.

It does not have to be expensive ($20 per thousand), but it should be attractive and eye-catching.

REGISTRATIONS AND CONFIRMATIONS

How much does the training director need to know about program participants? New training directors typically spend the first year or so taking registrations by memo or phone—all they do is list the participants' names. Someone in the training unit then looks up all the rest of the information: job title, grade, salary, supervisor, extension, etc. Then, about an hour before the first session, one or two participants call to say that they did not know they were scheduled for this program.

After about a year of this nonsense, a registration procedure is instituted. Why not start that way? A simplfied registration procedure might use preprinted or Xeroxed cards. The registration cards then become a ready reference and can be arranged alphabetically, chronologically, or by program. They can be used (as in Fig. 5-3) to confirm registrations, make sure that employees know they are registered, alert managers and instructors, and keep track of people attending.

Simplifying Registrations

Few programs require more information than is already included on the registra-tion form. Regular programs can be handled easily. Training directors, however, are often tempted to announce special programs on a "special" basis and ask for registrations by memo or phone. Why? If the registration procedure exists and works, why not include the special programs in the same procedure? Managers react better because they already know the procedure, and all master records are automatically set up.

Tuition reimbursement or other programs requiring billing and reimbursements may require additional information about employees and their reasons for requesting the program. In this case, the training director can set up a separate registration form or, preferably, a "supplementary" sheet. The supplementary sheet usually works better because the master registration card is completed and available for tabulation at a later date.

Announcing
A New
Training Program

PUT IT IN WRITING

This program is designed to improve clarity, speed, and image in your written communications. It will help you write more clearly - so clearly your reader cannot possibly misunderstand you. You will learn to write faster - perhaps twice as fast - without wasting time fumbling over false starts and rewrites. And you will develop techniques to present your ideas in a way that pleases the reader and presents a pleasant, thoughtful image of you and our companies. In addition, this workshop should make you a better reader, speaker, and listener by enabling you to recognize and overcome weaknesses in your writing.

We're going to achieve these goals with no sacrifice in the intelligence or detail of what you write!

This course is divided into two parts. The first half stresses clarity (How); the second, organization (What). Each of the six sessions provides 1/2 hour of audio-visual input followed by 1 1/2 to 2 hours of discussion and workshop. You will be given two outside assignments in addition to workbook exercises.

STRUCTURE: The workshop meets for 2 1/2 hours twice each week for three weeks.

        Session 1: Clarity - Your First Objective
        Session 2: Changing Some Old Attitudes
        Session 3: Measuring Your Clarity
        Session 4: Practical Tips on Organizing
        Session 5: How to Outsmart the Deadline
        Session 6: The Finishing Touches of the Pros

ELIGIBILITY: All those who spend at least 20 percent of their time writing memos,
        letters, or reports are eligible to participate. A pretest will be
        given to exempt those whose written skills are well developed.

TO REGISTER: Submit a D-120 Course Registration Form, signed by your department
        head, to the Employee Relations Department, Development Division (3T).

FOR MORE INFORMATION CONTACT MARY BISHOP ON EXTENSION 2350.

► Please keep this sheet in your files

Fig. 5-17 Special program announcement.

Confirmations

A multiple-copy registration form makes the confirmation process exceptionally easy. Participants know they are signed up for the course because they have already signed the registration form. The training unit simply has to check the approved box on the form; fill in the date, time, and location; and return the form to the participant.

The second copy of the form can then be filed by program and—on a specified date—given to the instructor along with all other registrations for that program. The instructor then has a ready record of participants and a great deal of information about them.

In some organizations, it is not necessary to confirm registrations to managers. If it is, however, the training director might send the participant confirmations *through* the manager.

How did the program go? Evaluation of training and program participants is one of the most difficult tasks the training director faces.

PARTICIPANT RESULTS

Participants need immediate feedback, and the training director needs information about the combined group of participants and how well they did. Grading is one way of summarizing results, but it is effective in adult education only when it is possible to quantify desired results. Many organizational training programs are aimed at behavioral or attitudinal changes, which cannot be measured quantitatively. One way to handle grading is to use letter or number grades only for those programs in which testing is an integral part of the program and relates specifically to the course objectives. A three-point system of "satisfactory" or "complete" for successful completion, "unsatisfactory" for unsuccessful completion, and "incomplete" for attendance or drop-out problems can then be used for all other programs. Unfortunately, this does not provide enough information for the participant, but it does make it possible to summarize results. The instructor can conduct follow-up discussions with the participant if additional information is necessary.

Completion information should automatically be communicated to the participant and to the manager. This can easily be done by routing the completed instructor copy of the registration form back to the participant and the manager.

PROGRAM RESULTS

Evaluating training programs is extremely difficult and expensive. Spend money and time on evaluation only when you will get the information you need. In general, look for information in the following areas:

1. *Participant results*
   - Reactions to programs
   - Actual learning that took place
   - Changes in on-the-job behavior

2. *Changes in organizational structure, work flow, or other management systems*

3. *Costs of the program*

4. *Problems or obstacles preventing changes*

At the end of the program year, a single program evaluation sheet can be written for each major training program conducted. The individual sheets can then be combined in cost-outcome order. This type of summary is extremely useful for future planning and allocation of resources.

A word of caution about communication. Communicate only information that is actually needed to those who need it. Summary sheets are primarily for the training director to use in evaluating his or her unit's activities and in planning future activities. Information from these sheets can be communicated to top management, but this should be done selectively and for a specific purpose. A clear communication of participant and program results can cause major changes in the organization. And that is what training is all about.

EVALUATING YOUR INFORMATION SYSTEM

To test your information system, take a few minutes to fill out the checklist below. In the first column, check those items needed in your organization. In the second column, check those already provided. *(Be honest!)* Total your scores, and you will have an immediate assessment of the job ahead.

If your column 2 score is more than your column 1 score (although this will probably not be the case), you need to cut back. If your column 2 score is less than your column 1 score, subtract it, and you will see how far you have to go.

Type of information	*Definitely needed*	*Provided now*
1. Communicated to managers		
■ Participant completions	_____	_____
■ Grades	_____	_____
■ Future programs	_____	_____
■ Future program dates	_____	_____
■ Performance improvements	_____	_____
■ Cost of program	_____	_____
2. Communicated to participants		
■ Grades	_____	_____
■ Standing in class	_____	_____
■ Future programs	_____	_____
■ Future program dates	_____	_____
3. Available for training director		
■ Summary of training needs	_____	_____
■ Reactions to programs	_____	_____
■ Actual program results	_____	_____
■ Cost of program	_____	_____
■ Future programs needed	_____	_____
■ Number that will attend	_____	_____
4. Sent to personnel for files		
■ Courses employee completes	_____	_____
■ Grades	_____	_____
5. Available for top management		
■ Programs being run (summary)	_____	_____
■ Cost of programs	_____	_____
■ Program results	_____	_____
■ Participants' grades	_____	_____
■ Number of attendees	_____	_____
■ Future programs needed	_____	_____
■ Future schedules	_____	_____

Total possible: 25
Your score—column 1 _____
Your score—column 2 _____
Total score _____

REFERENCES

1. Mager, Robert F.: *Preparing Instructional Objectives*, Fearon Publishers, Inc., Palo Alto, Calif, 1962.
2. Bloom, B. S., M. D. Engelhard, E. H. Furst, W. H. Hill, and D. R. Krathwohl (eds.): *Taxonomy of Educational Objectives*, David McKay Company, Inc., New York, 1956.

Chapter 6

Legal and Legislative Aspects of Training

JOHN WALSH

J. ARTHUR WAITES

John Walsh *is the Administrator of Management Development with the Lockheed-California Company, Burbank, California. He has been active in managerial and technical training for over 20 years at Lockheed and at Montgomery Ward and Spiegel, Inc., Chicago. A past president of ASTD, he has also been a part-time Professor of Business Administration, California State University at Northridge. He received his B.A. from the University of Illinois and his M.A. from the University of Southern California.*

J. Arthur Waites *earned his M.A. and Ph.D. in psychology from the University of Manchester, England. After serving for three years as academic adviser to the Governor of British Guiana, he became Area Chief of Psychology in the New England states for the Veterans Administration. For eight years, Dr. Waites served as Director of the graduate program in hospital administration, U.C.L.A. He has been a consultant in management development and organization over a period of years to industrial companies and hospitals here and abroad.*

The total body of legislative matter which bears upon the field of industrial relations, and therefore to some extent upon training, is wide. Many of the legal aspects are oblique, however, and concentrate more upon compensation, labor relations, or industrial safety than they do upon training.

However, the coverage here is limited only to the legal matters which the training manager may be called upon to understand because of his or her position as an administrator of training activities. Legislation or directives with some qualities of legal direction are discussed in the areas of (1) wages and hours, (2) apprenticeship, (3) the Manpower Development and Training Act, (4) reproducing copyrighted material, (5) civil rights, and (6) the Occupational Safety and Health Act. Finally, there are matters of company policy and agreements which may bind the representatives of a company or agency, particularly the training manager.

WAGES AND HOURS

Hours of pay and pay practices are regulated under the Fair Labor Standards Act, often referred to as the "wage-and-hour law," and under the Walsh-Healey Act. An understanding and appreciation of the Fair Labor Standards Act is of critical importance to the training manager in the establishment of a training program. To those employees who are employed under federal government contracts, the Walsh-Healey Act is also significant, although the same principles are applicable to both acts. The primary substantive distinction between the two enactments is that the Fair Labor Standards Act requires the payment of the overtime rate after 40 hours of work in a workweek, while the Walsh-Healey Act requires the overtime payment after eight hours of work in the workday.

The major area of concern in the field of training is whether time spent by employees in training activities must be considered as compensable work time within the meaning of this legislation. This problem is particularly important with respect to training programs which are conducted at the end of the workday because if the hours are to be considered as hours worked, in all probability they will have to be compensated at the overtime rate. It is apparent that the training manager must be acutely conscious of the provisions of this legislation since the cost to the employer of such a training program could become prohibitive, and if appropriate payment is not made, the employer could be subjected to serious and time-consuming litigation.

While the provisions of the legislation relating specifically to training programs are of primary concern, it is also important for the training manager to recognize that other provisions of the legislation may also relate to the question of whether time spent in training programs may be compensable. As an example, the acts provide exemption for the so-called white-collar employee. The regulations defining these exemptions are extremely complex but nevertheless must be reviewed in order to determine whether basic coverage exists.

Neither the Fair Labor Standards Act nor the Walsh-Healey Act specifically deals with the question of training programs. The responsibility for defining the application of the legislation in this area has been delegated to the Administrator of the Wage and Hour and Public Contracts Divisions of the Department of Labor. The Administrator has issued specific regulations on this subject under which time spent on training programs will be regarded as compensable time unless all the following conditions are satisfied:

1. The training program must be conducted outside the employee's assigned working hours.

2. Attendance at the training program must be voluntary on the part of the employee. In this respect, if employees' continuation on their present jobs is conditioned on their attending the training course, it is not voluntary. However, if only future advancement is dependent on attendance, and it is in fact optional, it will be considered voluntary. It is suggested that prior to the commencement of the training program, employees be specifically advised as to whether attendance is optional or mandatory. It should not be left to employees to make their own determinations concerning whether attendance is a condition of continued employment.

3. The training program must not be directly related to the employee's job. Of all the criteria, this is the most elusive of precise definition. As a general rule, however, if the course is designed to make the employee perform his or her present job more efficiently, it will be considered job-related, but if it is designed to prepare the employee for a better job, it will not be considered job-related. While a training course falling in the latter category would in all probability have some

indirect effect on the performance of the present job, it would not be considered job-related within the meaning of the regulation. It should also be noted that if employees, on their own time and as the result of their own initiative, take a course which is job-related, time spent attending the course will not be considered as compensable time.

4. The employee may not perform any production work during the course of the instruction. If products or data are produced during training, they should not be used by the employer for any purpose if the exclusion is to be maintained.

Under the specific wage portions of these legislative pieces, there can be subminimal rates paid under certain conditions for learners, beginners, probationary workers, or apprentices. Apply to the Administrator of the Wage and Hour Division of the Department of Labor if your company seeks less than prevailing minimal rates for learning workers. Generally, in the case of doubt about the application of federal wage-and-hour legislation to a specific training program, a ruling may be obtained from the Department of Labor.

APPRENTICESHIP

The American apprenticeship system is based on voluntary cooperation between management and labor, between industry and government, and between the company and the school system. It is a businesslike system of training in which the young worker entering industry is given thorough instruction and experience, both on and off the job, in the practical and theoretical aspects of the work in a skilled trade.

State apprenticeship agencies are established in a number of states, where they are usually a division within the state department of labor. A number of the state apprenticeship agencies have staffs to assist management and labor as they develop and operate apprenticeship programs; this work is carried on as an integral part of the national apprenticeship program.

An effective apprenticeship program, as recommended by the Federal Committee on Apprenticeship,[1] should contain certain prescribed provisions:

1. The starting age of an apprentice to be not less than 16.
2. A schedule of work processes to give practical training and experience on the job to each apprentice.
3. Organized instruction to provide apprentices with knowledge in technical subjects related to their trade. (A minimum of 144 school hours per year of such instruction is normally considered necessary.)
4. A progressively increasing wage schedule.
5. Proper supervision of on-the-job training, with adequate facilities to train apprentices.
6. Periodic evaluation of apprentices' progress, in both their job performance and related instruction, and maintenance of appropriate records to show their scheduled progress.
7. Evidence of employee-employer cooperation.
8. Recognition of the individual apprentice's program.

The Veterans' Readjustment Assistance Act of 1952 provides monthly training allowances to eligible veterans employed as apprentices in establishments certified as qualified and equipped to provide such training. In addition, the Disabled Veterans Vocational Rehabilitation Act of 1950 provides monthly subsistence allowances and other means of rehabilitation to eligible veterans employed as apprentices who have service-connected disabilities incurred since the start of the

Korean conflict. If you have any such cases, check with the appropriate Veterans Administration office.

As a final general qualification, occupations recognized by the Federal Committee on Apprenticeship are those which customarily have been learned in a practical way through two or more years' training and work experience on the job and which are clearly identified and commonly recognized throughout industry. Occupations that have not used apprenticeship are selling, retailing, and similar occupations in the distributive field; managerial occupations; clerical occupations; professional and semiprofessional occupations; and agricultural occupations.

MANPOWER DEVELOPMENT AND TRAINING ACT

The Manpower Development and Training Act was signed into law in March 1962. The U.S. Department of Labor's Office of Manpower, Automation and Training is the responsible federal office, assisted by a National Advisory Committee representing labor, management, agriculture, education, training, and the public in general. The Secretary of Health, Education, and Welfare also shares a responsibility with the Secretary of Labor in providing training under this law, which has become a bench mark in domestic economic legislation.

The purposes of the Manpower Development and Training Act are to recognize several pertinent factors:

1. That differing job skills are required as a result of technological developments, foreign competition, relocation of industry, shifts in market demands, and other changes in the structure of the economy
2. That the differing skills required as a result of these technological and other changes could result in widespread unemployment, as well as unfilled jobs
3. That improved planning and expanded efforts will be required to assure that men, women, and young people will be trained and available to meet shifting employment needs
4. That many persons currently unemployed or underemployed must be retrained in new skills
5. That the work force will continue to grow at an uncommonly rapid rate, especially with regard to young people

The provisions of the Manpower Development and Training Act include:

1. Programs of research in the field of manpower requirements, development, and utilization
2. Information and communications programs to develop an improved understanding by the public of the nation's manpower requirements, development. and utilization, including an annual Manpower Report of the President of the United States
3. Training and skill development programs in public and private institutions and on-the-job training programs, particularly for youth, including allowances for subsistence and travel
4. Supplemental basic education programs for those persons who otherwise could not qualify for, or benefit from, occupational training
5. Programs of research to develop new techniques for training those with especially difficult employment problems

REPRODUCING COPYRIGHTED MATERIAL

The training manager may frequently want to copy materials directly from other sources, especially those known to be copyrighted. Always obtain permission and give credit for the use of such materials.

The reverse of the title page of any standard publication bears the usual copyright imprint, which states in whose name the copyright is held, whether it be publisher, author, or organization. A brief, definitive letter to the publisher stating what you wish to reproduce, in what form, and for what purpose usually brings the required permission.

In summary on this point, general information about limitations imposed by the copyright law indicates that its source is the United States Constitution (Art. 1, sec. 8), empowering Congress "to promote the progress of science and useful arts by securing for limited times to the authors . . . the exclusive right to their writings." Copyright protection and limitations are contained in the Copyright Act, Title 17, of the U.S. Code, and extend to books, pamphlets, periodicals, lectures, monologues, maps, drawings, photographs, commercial prints, labels, motion pictures, and plastic works of a scientific or technical character. The copyright term endures for 28 years from the date of publication and may be renewed for another 28-year period.

Technically, if any literary work susceptible to copyright protection is published without the word "copyright," the abbreviation "copr.," or the symbol ©, it will fall into public domain and is not protected by the copyright law. However, it is good business practice to request permission to reproduce in any case.

In a 1973 copyright decision, the U.S. Court of Claims ruled that making single photocopies of journal articles by the National Library of Medicine and the National Institutes of Health staff library does not violate copyright laws. The judgment was in response to a petition filed in 1968 by Williams & Wilkins against the federal government. The petition alleged that the National Library of Medicine and the National Institutes of Health library had infringed upon the journal publishers' copyright by providing on interlibrary loan single copies of journal articles to libraries for the use of health professionals.

The Court said that medical research would suffer since "the supply of reprints and back numbers is wholly inadequate" and since it is "wholly unrealistic to expect scientific personnel to subscribe regularly to large numbers of journals which would only occasionally contain articles of interest to them."[2]

The Court's majority opinion raised points for Congress to consider in its deliberations on copyright legislation: the extent to which photocopying should be allowed; whether copiers should be licensed; how much they should pay publishers; and the special status, if any, of scientific and educational needs. A dissenting opinion predicted that the decision could "encourage unrestricted piracy" of all authors' works. A copy of this Williams & Wilkins copyright decision may be obtained from the U.S. Court of Claims, Washington, D.C.

CIVIL RIGHTS

On July 2, 1965, Title VII of the Civil Rights Act of 1964 became legally effective. It is known as the Equal Employment Opportunity Act and has affected to some degree almost every job applicant, employee, and employer in the country.

Basically, Title VII prohibits discrimination on the basis of race, color, religion, sex, or national origin. No training manager can afford not to be fully acquainted with the update of this act as described in Public Law 92-261 approved March 24, 1972.

This part of the chapter will summarize the major elements of the act in the hope that training managers will become aware of the scope of the act as it may affect them in their relationships with management and employees alike. As in most legal issues, direct reference should be made to the appropriate congressional documents.

Equal Employment Opportunity Commission

The Equal Employment Opportunity Commission, established under Title VII, is composed of five members, not more than three of whom can be members of the same political party. The members are appointed by the President, with the advice and consent of the Senate, for a term of five years. The President also designates one member to serve as chairperson of the Commission and another to serve as vice chairperson. The President also appoints a general counsel—with the advice and consent of the Senate—to a term of four years. The general counsel has the responsibility for the conduct of litigation as provided in the act. The Commission makes a report to the President at the close of each fiscal year.

The Commission is concerned primarily with discrimination practices from four major sources to which Title VII applies: (1) employers of 15 or more persons; (2) labor unions which have 15 or more members, which refer persons for employment, or which represent employees of employers covered by the act; (3) employment agencies doing business with employers of more than 15 persons; and (4) joint labor-management apprenticeship programs of employers and unions covered by the act. (It is to be noted that prior to March 1973, the numbers referred to above were 25, not the present 15.)

Exemptions to the above may apply under certain circumstances to the "employment of aliens outside any state, a religious corporation, association, educational institution, or society with respect to the employment of individuals of a particular religion to perform work connected with the carrying on by such corporation, association, educational institution, or society of its activities."

The Commission is largely an investigatory body examining charges of employment discrimination. Usually, its members like the solution to the problems to come from conciliation, but they can, and do, advise the Justice Department and the Attorney General in more recalcitrant cases; action may then be taken in a U.S. district court.

Discrimination

The Equal Employment Opportunity Act of 1972 added *applicants for employment* and *applicants for membership to a labor organization* to those protected from discrimination on the basis of race, color, religion, sex, or national origin.

It is an unlawful employment practice for an employer to "fail or refuse to hire or to discharge any individual or otherwise discriminate against any individual" with respect to these factors. Nor can an employer "limit, segregate, or classify his employees or applicants for employment in any way which would deprive or tend to deprive any individual of employment opportunities or otherwise affect his status as an employee."

Basically the same conditions apply to employment agencies, labor unions, and programs such as those listed above.

However, there are certain situations where this practice may be exempt. It is well for the training manager to read the details of these exemptions in the Equal Employment Opportunity Act of 1972; the major exemptions are briefly listed here.

It may not be an "unlawful employment practice" where any of the major categories listed "is a bona fide occupational qualification reasonably necessary to the normal operation of that particular business or enterprise." Nor is it unlawful to require, for example, that in a school, college or university, a faculty member be of a particular religion "if the curriculum of such a school, college, university, or other educational institution of learning is directed toward the propagation of a particular religion."

Other exemptions include members of the Communist party of the United States, situations in which national security may be involved, and employees who are measured strictly by a "bona fide seniority or merit system, or a system which measures earnings by quantity or quality of production or to employees who work in different locations." There are also special exemptions regarding businesses near or on Indian reservations and, finally, situations in which "an imbalance may exist with respect to the total number of persons or percentage of persons of any race, color, religion, sex, or national origin."

Guidelines on Discrimination The Equal Employment Opportunity Commission has published guidelines on discrimination which may be obtained from the Office of the General Counsel, 1800 G Street N.W., Washington, D.C. 20506. Training managers should have their own copies on hand. The following discussion, however, will give some idea of the scope of these guidelines.

Sex. The intent of the Commission is seen in the statement that it "believes that the bona fide occupational exception as to sex should be interpreted narrowly. Labels—'Men's jobs' and 'Women's jobs'—tend to deny employment opportunities unnecessarily to one sex or the other."

The Commission does, however, consider sex to be a bona fide classification in the case of an actor or actress, for example. The legislation has much to say about sex-oriented state employment legislation, and training managers would do well to be thoroughly acquainted with the laws of employment in their own state.

The Commission also gives special consideration to the problems inherent in separate lines of progression and seniority systems "where this would adversely affect any employee unless sex is a bona fide occupational qualification for that job." One has to be careful not to distinguish between "light" and "heavy" jobs on the basis of sex; the Commission may regard this as a disguised form of discrimination. Discrimination against married women in any way is unlawful under the act.

Job-opportunities advertising in a help-wanted column is unlawful if it "indicates a preference, limitation, specification, or discrimination based on sex." Columns headed "Male" or "Female" are thus considered unlawful under the act.

This is extended to the referral practices of employment agencies. In fact, the employment agency "will share responsibility with the employer placing the job order" if it knowingly fills an order that does discriminate on a sex basis.

Both equal pay and equal fringe benefits are areas of concern for the Commission in the sense that it is an unlawful practice for an employer to discriminate between men and women with regard to these factors. The employment policies relating to pregnancy and childbirth are spelled out in the act.

National Origin. Part 1606 of the act deals with guidelines on discrimination on the basis of national origin. The Commission uses strong language to support this section of the law; "it intends to apply the full force of the law to eliminate such discrimination." The concern appears to match the Commission's awareness of the widespread practices of discrimination on the basis of national origin.

The *Federal Register,* vol. 35, January 13, 1970, gives some usual examples of this form of discrimination: the use of tests in the English language when the person did not use English as a mother tongue and where the use of English is not mandatory to the performance of the job; denial of equal opportunity to persons married to those of certain national origins; denial of benefits to those who support organizations seeking to promote the interests of national groups; and denial to those whose spouse's name reflects a certain national origin or to those who as a class of persons fall outside national norms for height and weight.

It is well to remember that these rules apply equally to a lawfully immigrated alien who is residing in this country, except in certain cases where national security is involved.

Religion.   The Commission's concern with discrimination on the basis of religion centers largely around the problems of employees who, because of their religion, regularly do not work on certain days, Friday evenings and Saturdays, for example.

However, the act stipulates that this applies only "where such accommodations can be made without undue hardship on the conduct of the employer's business." It is up to the employer, though, to prove that an undue burden or hardship renders the required accommodations to the religious needs of the employee "unreasonable."

The Commission promises to review each case on an individual basis in order to seek an equitable application of the guidelines concerning religion and the observance of religious holidays.

Employee Selection Procedures

The training manager would be well-advised to obtain the Commission's *Guidelines on Employee Selection Procedures,* which constitutes one of the most comprehensive sections of the act and which is quite likely to affect many persons in business settings where the use of tests is common.

The Commission recognizes that "properly validated and standardized employee selection procedures can significantly contribute to the implementation of nondiscriminatory personnel policies." However, the Commission also guards against any form of unprofessionalism and lack of fairness in the use of such tools. It has expressed concern for the "marked increase in doubtful testing practices" as the basis for making personnel decisions; it questions the use of tests for employment decisions "without evidence that they are valid predictors of employee job performance." It is, in fact, quite concerned about test validity.

The Commission defines as a test "any paper-and-pencil or performance measure used as a basis for any employment decision." This definition includes tests of ability, general intelligence, learning ability, aptitudes, dexterity and coordination, knowledge and proficiency, interests and attitudes, personality, and temperament. It includes "all formalized, scored, quantified or standardized techniques of assessing job suitability" (see also chapter 16, "The Assessment Center Method").

The *Federal Register,* vol. 35, August 1, 1970, spells out in great detail the Commission's regulations regarding the use and the validity of the tests used for the purposes of the act. It makes clear that copies of the tests used shall be available for inspection.

As evidence of the tests' validity the Commission spells out certain checkpoints: Have a sufficient number of minority individuals been obtained to "achieve findings of statistical and practical significance"? Are the tests designed to reflect the persons who have been at a job long enough to warrant consideration for promotion? In multiunit organizations care must be taken to see "that no significant differences exist between units, jobs, and applicant populations."

Generally, the standards used for checking the tests are those described in *Standards for Educational and Psychological Tests and Manuals,* published by the American Psychological Association.

The *Federal Register* describes numerous areas of concern with testing as used in industry, such as how to present validity evidence, the use of other validity studies, the assumption of validity, the continued use of tests, tests' relationship to employment agencies and employment services, and retesting.

In conclusion, the guidelines on this section read: "Specifically, the use of tests which have been validated pursuant to these guidelines does not relieve employers, unions, or employment agencies of their obligations to take positive action in affording employment and training to members of classes protected by Title VII."

It is clear, then, that the civil rights issues are both firm and complex. The training manager may well become both the guardian and the clarifier of these concerns.

THE OCCUPATIONAL SAFETY AND HEALTH ACT

The Williams-Steiger Occupational Safety and Health Act of 1970, known familiarly as OSHA, actually took effect on April 18, 1971. The declared congressional purpose of the act is "to assure so far as possible every working man and woman in the nation safe and healthful working conditions and to preserve our human resources."[3]

Because safety is virtually an automatic part of every training plan and because it has now been legislated with strong penalties for violations, the training manager has the twin responsibility of being familiar with OSHA and of assuring that supervisors and employees are aware of its requirements and penalties.

The provisions of the law apply to every employer engaged in a business affecting commerce. The law applies to all 50 states, the District of Columbia, Puerto Rico, the Virgin Islands, American Samoa, Guam, the Trust Territory of the Pacific Islands, Wake Island, the Outer Continental Shelf Lands, Johnston Island, and the Canal Zone.

Duties of Employers and Employees

Each *employer* under the act has the general duty of furnishing each of his or her employees employment, and places of employment, free from recognized hazards causing, or likely to cause, death or serious physical harm. The employer also has the specific duty of complying with safety and health standards promulgated under the act.

Each *employee* has the duty to comply with these safety and health standards and with all rules, regulations, and orders issued pursuant to the act which are applicable to his or her own actions and conduct.

Looking at the provisions of the act from both points of view, violations produce complaints; complaints cause investigations, which may possibly incur a citation and penalty; and thus managers and supervisors must act to avoid the violations.

Administration

Administration and enforcement of the act are vested primarily in the Secretary of Labor and in an agency newly formed when the act took effect, the Occupational Safety and Health Review Commission. The Commission is a quasi-judicial board of three members appointed by the President. Research and related functions are vested in the Secretary of Health, Education, and Welfare, whose functions are carried out, for the most part, by the National Institute for Occupational Safety and Health, established within HEW. Regional officers for OSHA were established in Boston, New York City, Philadelphia, Atlanta, Chicago, Dallas, Kansas City, Denver, San Francisco, and Seattle.

Enforcement

Labor Department safety inspectors may enter any establishment covered by the act to inspect the premises and equipment and to question the employer or employees. Should an investigation reveal a health or safety violation, the employer is issued a written citation describing the nature of the violation. The citation also prescribes a reasonable time for elimination or abatement of the hazard. Also within a reasonable time after the citation, the Labor Department notifies the employer of the penalty, if any, which is proposed to be assessed.

Willful or repeated violation of the act's requirements by employers may incur monetary penalties up to $10,000 for each violation. A citation for a serious violation requires a penalty of up to $1,000 for each violation. A serious violation is one involving a substantial probability that death or serious physical harm could result. An employer who does not correct a cited violation may be penalized $1,000 for each day the violation persists beyond the elimination or abatement date.

A willful violation by an employer resulting in the death of an employee is punishable by a fine up to $10,000 or imprisonment up to six months. A second conviction may double the criminal penalties.

Hence the training manager has more to consider in safety training than the humanitarian requirements; industrial safety has now been legislated, and there are stiff penalties for employers and their managers and supervisors.

OSHA Training Programs

The act provides for programs to be conducted by the Department of Labor, in concert with the Department of Health, Education, and Welfare, for education and training of employers and employees so that they may recognize, avoid, and prevent unsafe and unhealthful working conditions.

Training personnel are referred for information to the regional offices of OSHA or to the Office of Information Services, Occupational Safety and Health Administration, U.S. Department of Labor, Washington, D.C. Where the state government has taken over OSHA, refer to the state's division of industrial safety or to its department of industrial relations.

COMPANY POLICY AND UNION AGREEMENTS

It is to be understood that there may be legal or tacitly legal requirements placed upon the training manager through interpretation of company policies or through a contractual agreement with a bargaining agent, licensee, or customer. These matters are local and vary among industries, agencies, and companies. Training managers are well-advised to be aware of the precedents which prevail and to seek the guidance of their company's legal counsel.

Policy or agreements may include statements on matters such as the following.

Financial Incentives to Learning Should the company's education program have a policy reading "to provide educational counseling, work-study programs, evening educational courses, and partial tuition reimbursement as inducements to employees to further their education," it seems evident that the training manager lays out some clear guidelines. A work-study program makes it possible for an employee to work part time while attending college to obtain a basic or advanced degree. Matters of implementation are selection and counseling of proper candidates; setting a proportionately reduced workweek and pay; and the expense of tuition, books, and other required fees. A tuition reimbursement program makes it possible for an employee to work full time while adding to his or her education or pursuing a degree program through evening or extension courses. Matters of implementation again include counseling, the percent of tuition reimbursement (usually between 50 and 100 percent), maximum allowable reimbursement for courses completed in any one calendar year, and the minimum amount of tuition for which reimbursement may be requested.

Training Requirements for Licenses, Subcontractors, or Customers as Called out by Contract or Policy Customer or licensing contracts and agreements often call for instruction of the customer's or licensee's personnel. These agreements usually specify the number and kinds of people to be trained, the hours of instruction, housing and travel arrangements, the type of equipment to be used, and the exact instruction and technical printed information to be furnished. In cases of foreign personnel, responsibility for interpreters and the language of instruction is fixed. Company policy often affirms by practice that field representatives carry an understood obligation to train even when that obligation is not stated contractually.

Admittance to Classified or Restricted Areas and Control of Classified Material Used in Training   Customarily, well-defined rules exist for the handling of company- or government-restricted matters. For the training manager this often poses the twin responsibility of educating employees about security and of strictly observing the restrictions when employees enter the training environment. This concern obviously has special importance for companies engaged in government contract work.

Transportation to and from Training Sites   The company-union agreement often contains a section calling for certain insurance or pay provisions if trainees travel between working and training sites. In the absence of a contractual agreement, provisions like these are often covered in procedure or policy statements.

LEGISLATION AND THE TRAINING MANAGER

Rapid organizational, professional, and technological changes have become commonplace for the industries, companies, and agencies whose training activities are represented by a training manager, whatever his or her title. The cultural environment embracing the total activities of industry and government is also in constant change.

A striking example is the federal government's recognition of a training need and its attempt to meet this need through the program known as MDTA (Manpower Development and Training Act). Yet another is the Equal Employment Opportunity Act (EEOC), directed toward a cultural impact in the industrial world. A third acronym (OSHA) identifies the human-centered Occupational Safety and Health Act.

The training function may be affected swiftly by more state, national, and international legislation; training managers are the logical persons to help fashion legislation within their field and to help assure the appropriate implementation when it is fashioned.

REFERENCES

1. *Apprentice Training: An Investment in Manpower,* U.S. Department of Labor, Bureau of Apprenticeship, 1956.
2. *National Library of Medicine News,* vol. 28, no. 12, U.S. Department of Health, Education, and Welfare, December 1973.
3. *A Handy Reference Guide, The Williams-Steiger Occupational Safety and Health Act of 1970,* Government Printing Office, Washington, stock no. 2915-0001. (Some additional points in this section are also taken from the reference guide.)

Chapter **7**

Training Facilities and Equipment

JEROME MENELL

Jerome Menell is President, Chief Consultant, and Design Engineer at Menell Associates, Inc., in New York. He has developed visual communication concepts and space planning for training centers and management centers and has designed data-handling and internal communications systems for major corporate and government clients. He has also designed and engineered the implementation of these concepts. Over the past 25 years, he has designed and planned audiovisual communications systems and facilities for clients in business, industry, education, and government, as well as for exhibits and museums. He has been awarded United States patents covering operational innovations he has developed. A member of the National Academy of Television Arts and Sciences, the National Audio-Visual Association, and the Society of Motion Picture and Television Engineers, Mr. Menell has lectured at the American Management Association and the Audio-Visual Institute at Indiana University.

The success of any activity is affected by the quality of all its component parts. From the inception of an instructional program's development until the attainment of its ultimate goal of adding to an individual's knowledge and understanding, each element affects the degree of its success.

This chapter is addressed to an important aspect of this learning process—the physical facilities and their environment.

Planning facilities in such a way as to take into consideration the preparation procedures and the requirements of the attendees and the presenters plays an indirect and a direct role in the achievement of instructional programs.

The effect of well-planned facilities is indirect in that comfortable and efficient work areas, conveniently located in relation to support activities and the classroom, diminish distractions normally present in preparation environments. A positive ancillary effect of well-planned work and instruction areas is the increased utilization that occurs. Time and again, a program content has been given new life because the instructional team was inspired by an improved environment facility. The team makes the extra effort buoyed by their more favorable surroundings and the lessening of their operational limitations.

Well-planned facilities have a direct effect on the attitudes of the people to whom a program is presented. The culmination of all the planning, and all the creative and technical efforts of the training group occurs when the information is actually communicated, received, understood, and retained. For optimum results, the students should have a sense of well-being and be in a receptive frame of mind at this time. Their environment and the technical aspects of the information transmitted play an important part in supporting these attitudes. Any aspect of the environment or the presentation that is distracting or in some way adversely affects the students' concentration will lessen the program's chances for success.

Definitions   Some commonly used terms relating to new or renovated space are explained below.

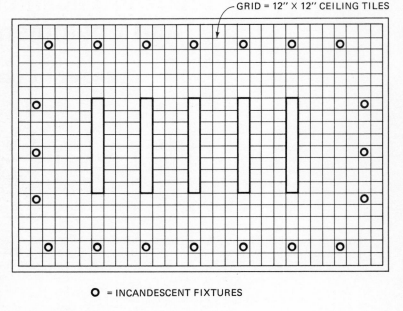

O = INCANDESCENT FIXTURES

▭ = FLUORESCENT FIXTURES

Fig 7-1   Reflected ceiling plan.

Reflected Ceiling Plan.   The drawing in Fig. 7-1 shows the ceiling and room light configuration as it would appear if you were above the ceiling looking through it to the floor below. Such drawings sometimes illustrate the furniture layout so that the lighting can be seen in perspective.

Plan View.   A plan view is similar to a reflected ceiling plan except that the ceiling is not shown (see Fig. 7-2). The figure shows what you would see if you were looking at the room from above without ceilings to block your view. Door swings, room dimensions, furniture, and other related items best shown from this perspective are usually included in a plan view.

Elevation.   This is a view indicated, on the plan-view drawing, of a vertical surface such as an internal or external wall; it usually shows doors and other apertures such as windows. This drawing shows the room as it would appear if you were standing in front of the wall but well back from it (see Fig. 7-3).

Horizontal Section.   This is a part plan on a drawing showing specific details. It is a section of a wall, door, or cabinet, for example, that has been cut through horizontally; you are viewing up or down from the cut, depending on the direction of the arrows showing the cut on the elevation drawings (see Fig. 7-3).

Vertical Section.   This is similar to a horizontal section except that the cut is vertical and you are looking to the right or left according to the arrows on the elevation or plan view (see Fig. 7-3).

Ceilings.   Plaster and plasterboard ceilings need no explanation; however, some readers may not be familiar with acoustic tile ceilings using concealed or visible splines.

The spline itself shown in Fig. 7-4 is generally a length of T-shaped metal that fits into a slot in the tile so that is is not visible; the tile can also rest on the spline, in which case the spline is visible.

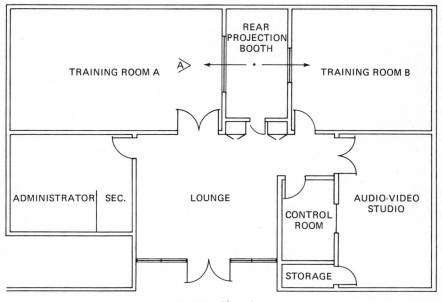

Fig. 7-2   Plan view.

Sheetrock or Dry Wall.   These are usually plasterboard, rather than composition or prefabricated, wall sections.

Plasterboard consists of two pieces of flat paperboard bonded to a plaster cone; it is normally applied to metal or wood studs.

Duplex Convenience Outlet.   This is a standard electric receptacle for two plugs.

HVAC.   This is the abbreviation for heating, ventilating, and air conditioning.

DETERMINING SPACE REQUIREMENTS

When planning new facilities or renovating existing ones, preliminary information should be gathered to help formulate the operational parameters.

List current and future programs by type of audience, group size, length of program, and media to be used. Charts to use in correlating this information as it is collected are shown in Figs. 7-5 and 7-6.

Once this information begins to be developed, additional questions must be answered, and long-term decisions made, in order to fill in the information required for the chart. As these data are correlated, a workable program evolves. It is a matter of developing all aspects to their fullest and evaluating them in

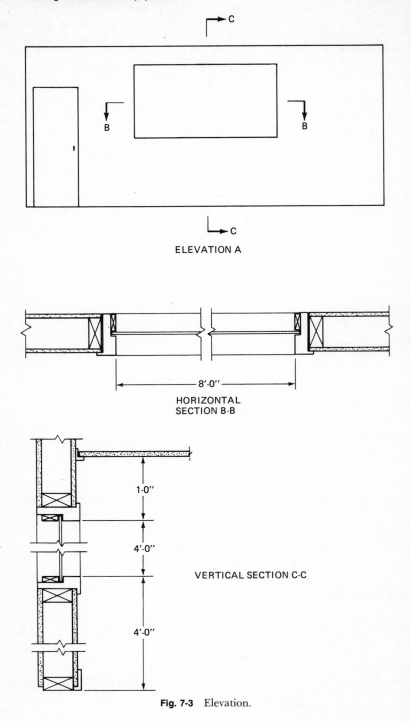

ELEVATION A

HORIZONTAL
SECTION B-B

8'-0"

1-0"

4'-0"

4'-0"

VERTICAL SECTION C-C

Fig. 7-3 Elevation.

relation to the resources which can be expected to be made available or which would be needed to implement the program.

This method will also enable you to detect any factors that might delay the completion of a program or, for that matter, any conflicts in the use of resources, facilities, and support requirements.

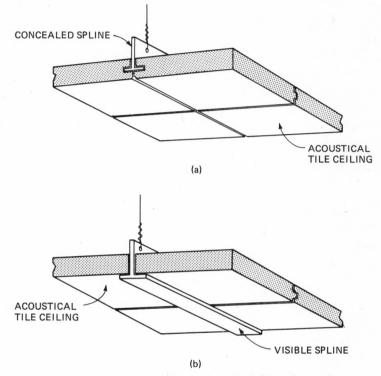

CONCEALED SPLINE

ACOUSTICAL TILE CEILING

(a)

ACOUSTICAL TILE CEILING

VISIBLE SPLINE

(b)

Fig. 7-4   *(a)* Concealed spline section; *(b)* visible spline section.

A detailed listing of existing classrooms and support facilities, available instructors and support personnel, and current output capabilities should be made. The quality of printed material, media, and other related output should be tabulated and used as a guide to determine increases in personnel, space, and equipment required to support the instructional programs.

The chart will illustrate the location and type of space needed as well as media and staff requirements. Recognizing the limitations is helpful in planning programs for the highest utilization. Adjustments in class size, frequency, and location may be necessary to schedule the desired programs. Collecting and reviewing all the relevant factors actually pinpoints decisions and commitments that must be made to achieve the desired manpower development goals. Projected manpower requirements at all levels become one of the growth factors to be dealt with in making long-term plans. Widening coverage of existing programs and projected widening of new programs after they have proved themselves complete the information development phase.

DATA	PROGRAMS (C–Current, F–Future)						
	Mgmt. #1 (C)	Mgmt. #2 (C)	Sales #1 (C)	#590 Term (C)	Sales #2 (F)	Sales #3 (F)	Supvr. #1 (F)
LOCATION							
Training Center							
Branch							
Hotel							
INSTRUCTION							
Resident Staff							
Travel Staff							
Part-time Staff							
Visiting							
SEATING FORMAT							
Classroom							
Theater							
Conference							
"V" or "U" Shape							
Carrels							
"Break Out"							
Random							
MEDIA							
Filmstrip							
Slides							
Movies							
Audio Tape							
Video Tape							
Role Playing							
CLASS SIZE							
LENGTH (DAYS)							
# GIVEN YEARLY							
ESTIMATED COST							

Fig. 7-5   Program characteristics.

INTERRELATION AND INTERDEPENDENCE OF SPACE

Training facilities should be as self-sustaining as possible. Quite often, however, the media used are planned by the instructional group but produced by an in-house graphic arts department or by outside sources. This is a satisfactory arrangement if some control can be exercised over the quality and availability of special techniques and over adherence to production schedules.

If the working arrangement is satisfactory, it is suggested that the training group's staff include people experienced in graphic arts and instructional writing. They are indispensable for preparing the material for the graphic arts department or outside producer as well as for reviewing the completed work for quality (color, resolution, contrast, sound, etc.) and acceptability.

With a graphic artist on staff, some equipment should be made available for the preparation of overhead transparencies if your program requires their use. A copying machine that copies on paper or transparent material is ideal for this purpose and will meet the department's copying needs.

In addition to the graphic arts, space allocations should be given to the following.

Preparation and Rehearsal Room for Instructors.   This space can be part of a projection booth (depending on the projection-system concept) or other space adjacent to the graphic arts space.

Library and Reference Materials.   This space would be used by instructors and students alike. It would also be a good area in which to have study booths or carrels for individualized programs and review of course material previously studied.

Laboratories and Shops.   Certain courses will require a "hands-on" activity, and space should be allotted for this purpose.

Conference Space.   This can be part of the instructors' preparation space; it would be used for conferences with other instructors, students, and media specialists.

Projection Booths.   Depending on the selected projection method, this space should accommodate other activities without disrupting its primary purpose. Factors affecting ancillary uses will be covered later in the section on the projection-system concept.

Training Rooms.   Depending on their size, these rooms can be divided into smaller rooms and used for smaller classes, break-out sessions, and role playing, as well as basic instruction. Their proximity to other rooms and services is important to multiple use and flexibility.

	John Doe	Jane Smith	Mary Doe	Frank Smith	Future	Future
Photographer	x					x
Chartist			x			
Graphic Artist		x				
Writer				x		
Producer					x	
Director	x			x		
Camera-Film	x					x
Camera-Video	x					x
Darkroom	x					x
Slides	x					
Movies	x					
Audio Tape					x	
Video Tape					x	
Headliner		x	x			
Varityper		x				
Transparencies	x					
Copy Camera	x		x			

Fig. 7-6 Resource requirements.

Peripheral Considerations

1. Coffee service can be accommodated in a central location during a pre-scribed period, or each room can contain a hidden counter that is set up from the

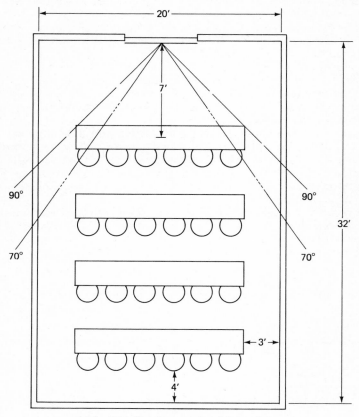

Fig. 7-7   Classroom style—24 people.

corridor while the class is in session. When the class is ready, doors are opened to expose the refreshments. The counter is cleared in a reverse sequence.

2. Lavatories. It is important that these be large enough and convenient to the training center.

3. If smoking is permitted, cigarettes should be available nearby, and ample ashtrays provided.

DETERMINING ROOM SIZE

Seating capacity and configuration are major factors in determining room size. Generally speaking, a 20 × 32 foot room will seat about 49 people theater style, 24 people classroom style, 18 people at a U-shaped table, and 15 people at a conference table (see Figs. 7-7 to 7-10). Round tables are highly recommended for break-out, and a large doughnut-shaped table with a section facing the communication wall removed is extremely effective for programs involving interaction within the group (see Figs. 7-11 and 7-12).

To carry this further, the image size for the furthest viewer at 26 feet is 4.3 feet on a front-projection matte white screen and 3.5 feet on an average rear-projection screen. Seating capacity is also affected by the 90-degree viewing angle[1] of the

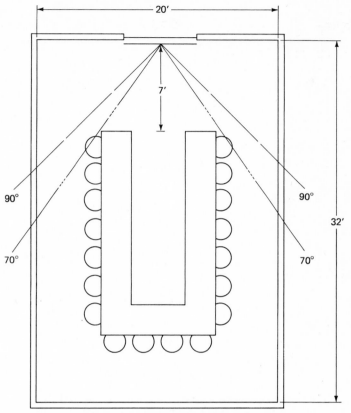

Fig. 7-8   U-shaped table—18 people.

matte white screen and the 70-degree angle[2] of the average rear-projection screen. (The angle of view must be determined for each image in multi-image systems.)

Many factors must be taken into consideration when determining the ideal room configuration and projection mode. Techniques are available which can provide acceptable combinations even though they do not meet the minimum rule-of-thumb standards. Space limitations preclude coverage of these special situations here.

At this point, however, we shall discuss how some basic training-room determinations can be made using suggested guidelines and formulas. This information is based on the assumption that good-quality projectors, lenses, screens, and mirrors will be used; that ambient-light conditions are properly controlled; and that adequate projector-light output in relation to picture size and ambient light is selected.

The foregoing qualifications are intended to reinforce the understanding that the following information is to be used only as a guide to develop a preliminary plan. The standards presented are minimum acceptable standards and are based on alphameric character sizes discussed later in this chapter.

Theater Style

Training-room space requirements are based on class size as determined by previous experience and future projections. For theater style, the seating area is

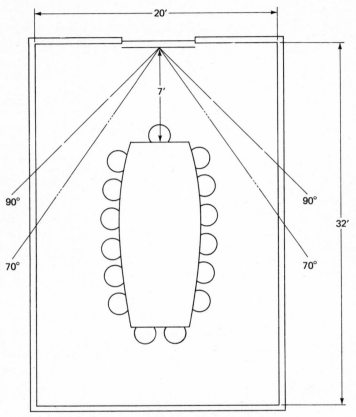

Fig. 7-9   Conference table—15 people.

determined by allowing 6 square feet per person,[3] 2 feet wide by 3 feet deep. This is a comfortable arrangement and allows for a cross aisle in very deep rooms. Adding space for 3-foot aisles, a 4-foot back aisle, and the distance to the front wall (which is calculated by multiplying the number of rows by 1 foot or adding 1 foot for every 3 feet of depth in the seating area) determines the overall room size.

Using a theater-style arrangement for a class of 49 students (or a classroom plan for 24 students, as shown in Fig. 7-7), we start by blocking out the audience area as shown in Fig. 7-10.

Using the 2-foot width by 3-foot depth for each person and a desired ratio of 2:3 for the room configuration, we come up with a 14 × 21 foot seating area. The seating arrangement would be seven rows of seven seats in each row.

We then add the 3-foot aisle on each side and the 4-foot aisle at the rear. In order to calculate the front space, we multiply the number of rows by 1 foot, for a total of 7 feet (7 × 1.0 = 7 feet).

In order to check the seating-area space, we multiply the number of students by 6 square feet (49 × 6 = 294 square feet) and prove that our calculations are correct by multiplying the dimensions of the seating area, or 14 × 21 feet = 294 square feet.

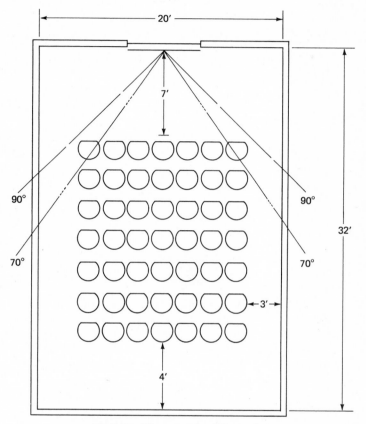

Fig. 7-10   Theater style—49 people.

Image Size

Image-size requirements are derived by dividing the distance to the last viewer by the factor 7.5[4] for rear projection and 6[5] for front projection*; 28 (21 + 7) divided by 7.5 equals a 3.7-foot-wide image for rear projection, and 28 divided by 6 equals a 4.6-foot-wide image for front projection.*

If a screen exists, the farthest viewing distance would be 7.5 times the image width for rear projection and 6 times the image width for front projection. The distance to the closest viewer should be no less than twice the image width for rear projection and 1½ times the image width for front projection.

The reason for the difference in image-size requirements is that visual acuity is enhanced when projected images are viewed in a lighted room. Tests have proved that the lighted area adjacent to the screen provides a point of reference for the

*See the following section, Artwork Standards.

eyes and makes it possible to read characters up to 20 percent smaller than can be read in darkened rooms.[6] The special Eastman Kodak Ektalite front-projection screen is an exception, because of its unusual reflection qualities, and it too can be

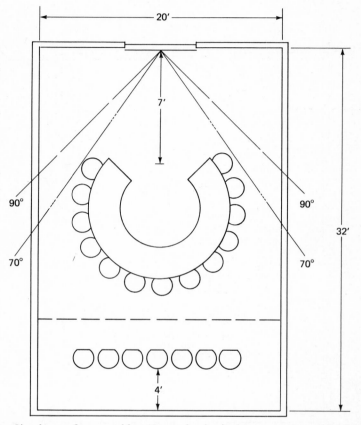

Fig. 7-11   Circular conference table—13 people plus 7 observers or use of 24-foot room.

used in a lighted room. The Ektalite screen's use is limited to small rooms, however, since it is available only as a 40 × 40 inch screen.

A few additional points are worth noting:

1. The bottom of the screen should be at least 4 feet above the floor. Exceptions can be made in the case of stepped-floor rooms and conference or U-shaped seating arrangements.

2. An entrance door should be positioned near the back of the room if possible. This permits late arrivals and visitors to enter without causing too much distraction.

3. The last 4 feet can be used to increase capacity if the traffic flow permits it.

ARTWORK STANDARDS

Projected alphameric character sizes are really what is referred to when satisfactory image sizes and viewing distances are discussed. When we say that the minimum viewing distance for front projection is six times the image size (6 × 4 =

24 feet), we are assuming that graphic arts standards are being adhered to. Unfortunately, this is not always the case.

In order for the character to be legible at 24 feet on a 4-foot front-projection

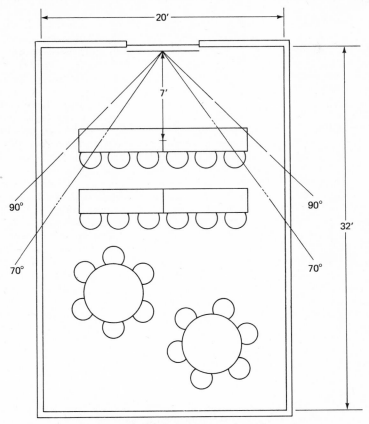

Fig. 7-12 Modified classroom style—12 people.

screen, it must be projected to ¹³⁄₁₆ inches and ¹¹⁄₁₆ inches for a 3.2-foot rear-projection screen.* Actually these character sizes would be legible at 24 feet on any size screen; however, in the interest of standardization, it is recommended that a basic format be used so that no matter who makes your visuals or where they are shown, they will be visible at the expected distances if the projection system used roughly follows the general standard. The format that is recommended here is quite conservative, and a comfortable margin is built in. The example described above utilizes a minimum ⁵⁄₃₂-inch original character†, we recommend the use of a ³⁄₁₆-inch minimum character‡ which would produce a 1-inch character in a 4-foot front-projection image and a ¹³⁄₁₆-inch character in a 3.2-foot rear-projection image. In addition to the safety factor, it reduces the amount of information that can be accommodated.

*Based on 20-35 visual acuity.
†Based on 20-35 visual acuity.
‡Based on 20-40 visual acuity.

The viewing distances are based on black characters on a white or lightly tinted background with comfortable spacing between characters. Reversals require wide spacing, lines of heavy weight, and high contrast ratios. Extremely high contrasts such as white on black or midnight blue require wider spacing or a light-colored tint to reduce the white flare.

The recommended standard is the use of a 6 × 9 inch copy area for 35mm slides (2:3 format) and a 6.75 × 9 inch copy area for overhead transparencies and other 3:4 format visuals on a 12 × 12 inch art board for rectangular format and a 9 × 9 inch copy area for square format. The minimum character size should be $\frac{3}{16}$ inch and have at least a medium line weight. Except for intermixing of slides and special slide formats, the information above is all that is needed. The projection systems used should be set up with lensing to fill the screen from the appropriate media. Of course, any mathematical progression in artwork up or down is permissible, though extra care should be exercised with line weight and opacity. For example, a $\frac{3}{8}$-inch character in a 12 × 18 inch copy area for 2:3-format slides and a 13.5 × 18 inch copy area for 3:4-format visuals (or an 18 × 18 inch copy area for square format) on a 24 × 24 inch art board would be satisfactory.

Slides.   The standard slide format is 22.9 × 34.2mm or 0.9 × 1.34 inches and has an aspect ratio of 2:3. Unless there is a special application, most audiovisual systems are designed to fill the screen with the largest dimension.

In order to accommodate square images within the same system and maintain the same parameters, slides of 38mm square (1.5 inches square) should *not* be used since they will project a 10 percent larger image than the standard 34.2mm (1.34-inch) slide. These slides are usually called *superslides.* There are times when it is advantageous to use them, but when they are intermixed with standard slides, either the latter look disproportionately smaller, or the superslides bleed off the screen.

The solution to this problem is to have these square slides shot in the same way as superslides but masked down to the standard 1.34-inch format. Die-cut slide masks are available for this size, and the cost of producing them should be the same as that of producing superslides.

In this way horizontal, vertical, and square images can be utilized in the same projection system with large size compatibility.

Special Note.   In addition to following standards for good visibility, it is necessary to assure proper slide density for highest light transmission as well as high contrast ratios in the visuals to enhance overall image quality.

SEATING ARRANGEMENTS

Classroom Style   The most popular style for instructional facilities is the classroom style, which usually consists of 5- or 7-foot-long by 2-foot-wide tables with two or three people at each table (see Fig. 7-7). The tables are usually foldable so that they can be stored when another seating arrangement is desired.

Stepped platforms can add to the visibility of the communication activity and can help the instructor to make eye contact, which increases the audience's level of attention.

The tables are especially useful when books and looseleaf binders are used in a course and when individuals are working at their own levels using programmed texts, with an instructor in attendance for support.

Theater Style   This arrangement provides the largest seating capacity and is best used for opening sessions, special or guest-lecturer situations, and general orientations (see Fig. 7-10).

This arrangement can be set up on a level or stepped floor. For certain requirements, folding writing tablets add to utilization.

U-Shaped Style   This style of seating (see Fig. 7-8), along with the conference style (see Fig. 7-9), oval style, elliptical style, etc., is most effective with programs designed for group interaction. When people are seated facing one another, they are more likely to form a cohesive group and to work together comfortably. Seated in this manner, the participants are less dependent on the instructor as a sounding board or as a go-between in class discussions as is usually the case when classroom- or theater-style seating is used, since these styles encourage interaction predominantly with the instructor.

The tables used for the classroom style can easily be set up in the U-shaped or conference-table arrangement.

Random Seating   This arrangment is normally used for executive presentations, marketing presentations, and high-level orientations. Generally, upholstered swivel armchairs are provided, with enough space between them so that each participants can rotate 360 degrees without colliding with objects or another person's knees.

The 360-degree swivel is required when the participants are expected to face one another for discussion periods and when they might be asked to direct their attention to any point in the room as part of the program.

This seating is usually semipermanent, and should be used when no rearrangement is anticipated.

ENVIRONMENTAL ASPECTS

As mentioned earlier in this chapter, it is important that the recipients, as well as the presenter, feel comfortable in their surroundings.

The level of decor is determined by several factors in addition to cost. Budgetary considerations, of course, will determine expenditures for materials and accessories, but the overall feeling of the room should not be adversely affected.

Although expensive and luxurious fabrics, carpets, and wall coverings are certainly not required, buying low-quality materials is a false economy when maintenance and a high incidence of replacement or repair over a period of five to ten years will cost two or three times the amount originally saved—not to mention the time lost while the carpet or wallpaper is changed or while the heating or ventilating system is upgraded.

Suggestions   A simple but nicely appointed look should be the goal. (By "simple," we mean clean lines—not exposed pipes or concrete blocks.) A little subtle architectural detailing can go a long way toward enhancing the room's appearance.

Warm, soft colors and textured wall coverings are recommended.

Interior space is best for environmental and lighting control. Windows are potential sources of distraction and should be avoided for training rooms.

If possible, one opposing wall should have a soft or at least a heavily textured surface to absorb and diffuse sound waves. Acoustic tile or a heavily textured ceiling will also absorb and diffuse sound waves.

Heating, ventilating, and air conditioning (HVAC) are as important to comfort and attentiveness as any of the other factors discussed in this chapter. Many a program has been adversely affected by improper smoke removal, underheating or overheating, too little or too much air conditioning, etc. Most of these problems can be quickly corrected if localized control of the room or at least the training area is possible. Ideally, the training rooms should have separate HVAC systems with local control. In addition to the obvious advantages of this arrangement, it makes it possible to utilize the facilities evenings and weekends without having to depend on a major HVAC building system.

A rear entrance location is suggested to accommodate late arrivals and visitors with a minimum of disruption. Of course, a front entrance may be more conve-nient for participants and the instructor, but where possible a rear entrance should be provided as well.

Other important items that are sometimes overlooked are local and state requirements concerning safety lighting, flame-retardant fabrics, wood paneling and doors, and number of exits.

Seating   Seating should swivel and tilt, except in the case of theater style and other arrangements where space does not comfortably permit it. Being able to swivel into and away from a table or to move with an instructor who is utilizing the front and side walls for display surfaces during the presentation enhances the students' sense of well-being and improves their attentiveness.

Tilting is not as important as swiveling, but a limited tilt in some formats can provide welcome relief after periods of concentration.

The seating should be upholstered with materials that "breathe." Any natural or synthetic material which permits air movement through pores, through the weave, or by other means dissipates body heat that would otherwise make the participant uncomfortable. Sitting in nonporous seating for long periods usually produces a damp, tacky feeling that is uncomfortable and distracting.

Lighting   Remember that incandescent lights are warmer in tone and create a more interesting ceiling than fluorescent lights. Incandescent lights also produce more heat and can sometimes require more air conditioning. A combination of both types usually meets the aesthetic and mechanical requirements best.

For work sessions where participants will be reading and writing, the lighting pattern should provide at least 70 footcandles at table height. This can be reduced to 50 footcandles for note taking with a 100- to 150-footcandle level to accentuate static visuals or writing surfaces that the presenter may be using.

When projectuals are used, the lights immediately in front of a rear-projection screen should be switched off to reduce the amount of direct light falling on the screen. For front projection, the room lights must be turned down (if dimmer-controlled) or switched out so that ambient light reaching the screen is no more than 0.3 percent of the screen brightness. The front-projection screen in this room light condition would appear very dark to the eye.

In existing rooms, lighting adjustments are generally limited to new switching arrangements. For rear projection, it is suggested that the first row or two of fluorescents be switched out as well as half the tubes in the remaining lights—fluorescent lights are usually more directional, and fewer need to be switched off.

With front projection, it is necessary to darken the room somewhat more than with rear projection because any ambient light reaching the screen is reflected with the projected image, reducing its contrast and visibility. In most instances fluores-cent lights must all be switched out in small rooms and also medium-sized rooms unless a special directional louver is used. This commercially available mirrored louver directs most of the fluorescent light straight down and is ideal for rooms in which projection of visuals is to take place. In large rooms, the rear lights can usually remain on. When directional downlights are used, it is likely that more of the room can remain in a higher light level.

When light dimming exists, incandescent lights will provide a lower and more even illumination than fluorescent lights, without affecting the projected image. This is due partially to the relatively high threshold of the lowest light-level limit that can be sustained by fluorescents without experiencing flickering.

The light level and ambient-light condition should be worked out and preset so that the desired lighting is easily attained when needed. New construction and renovation permit full consideration of the desired lighting and switching require-ments. The suggestions in the previous paragraphs will be helpful in formulating these plans.

Display and Writing Surfaces   Requirements of programs determine the extent and type of surfaces needed. Commonly used products are listed below.

1. *Chalkboards.*   These are available in several colors and materials. Slate is still the best surface, and porcelain on steel is the next best (it is also magnetic); the composition of porcelain on steel is lighter, but it is generally more difficult to clean.

Black or dark brown chalkboards are recommended, but any dark color is satisfactory. A good grade of white or pastel-colored chalk should be used.

White chalkboards are acceptable as projection surfaces, but the blue chalk that is usually used with them leaves a dust that is extremely difficult to contend with.

2. *Felt-Tip Pen Boards.*   These have several good features and are available in embossed white vinyl laminated to steel and in glossy white porcelain on steel. Both take water-soluble and semipermanent colors, and both are magnetic; however, the vinyl makes a good front-projection screen, while the porcelain does not. The porcelain, however, permits use of chemical "dry" markers, which are removable with a chalk eraser or dry cloth.

3. *Nylon Hook and Loop Material.*   Also known as Velcro, when this is installed properly, it holds light as well as relatively heavy objects, comes in many colors, enhances the room's appearance, and improves acoustic control.

PROJECTION FACILITIES

Projection methods for meeting and training rooms fall into two categories and several configurations.

1. Front Projection   Here an image is transmitted by light beams originating in a projection device to a flat, opaque surface (usually a white or silver screen) which reflects a visible image.

Front projection then produces a reflected image which is viewed on the same side of the screen as the projection equipment.

2. Rear Projection   Here an image is projected from the same source as in front projection to a flat, translucent surface (usually a specially formulated medium-gray screen for normal use), forming a visible image on the back surface—from the viewer's standpoint—as it passes through the screen and is viewed on the opposite side.

Rear projection then produces a transmitted image which is viewed on the opposite side of the screen from the projection equipment.

Methods of projection are discussed below.

Direct Projection.   Once the image has left the objective (or prime) lens, a projector (or projectors) projects it directly onto the screen surface.

Indirect Projection A.   This is similar to direct projection except that once the image has left the objective lens, it is reflected by one or more mirrors or prisms attached to, or in close proximity to, the objective lens before it reaches the screen.

Indirect Projection B.   This is like indirect projection A except that the image is reflected from a mirror (or mirrors) at least one-third of the distance to the screen.

PHYSICAL CRITERIA FOR PROJECTION SYSTEMS

General

1. The screen-image area should be square to accommodate vertical, horizontal, or square images using the standard aperture for the selected format. Exceptions should be made only if all media to be used are completely controllable or have a special limited application. See the detailed explanation in the section on slides.

2. The vertical and horizontal center of the projector lens must be aligned with the center of the projection screen for undistorted images. This is a more critical concern for rear projection than front projection because of the closer proximity. However, 2 degrees off center vertically or horizontally is acceptable.

The centering alignment holds true if for some reason the screen or equipment is angled off perpendicular with the floor. When this occurs, the projectors and screen must be positioned on the same center line (see Fig. 7-13).

3. The bottom of the screen-image area should be at least 4 feet above the floor in most instances.

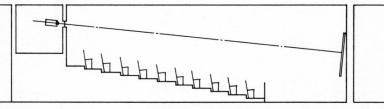

FRONT PROJECTION

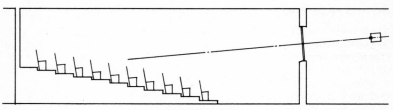

REAR PROJECTION

Fig. 7-13   Projector and screen positioning.

Front Projection

To solve the problem of the distracting noise and physical intrusion that accompany the use of exposed projectors, it is recommended that the machines be enclosed within the training room or, space permitting, within a separate projection booth.

A cabinet to contain a standard motion picture projector and one or two 35mm slide projectors can be as shallow as 20 inches, including sound-absorption material, using an indirect projection A format for the motion picture projector. Using a simple two-mirror arrangement, the motion picture projector can be positioned parallel with the screen, requiring very little depth (see Fig. 7-14): The front-projection cabinet can, of course, be affixed to the wall or mounted on casters for mobility. In either case, wiring for audio reproduction and slide-projector control should be installed so that when the equipment is to be used, it is simply plugged into existing wiring, making it unnecessary to run wires around the room, which is time-consuming, unsafe, and amateurish.

Overhead Projector

Although the overhead projector is most effectively used by the presenter in the front of the room, this usually creates some problems for the viewer; there may be image distortion, obstruction of the view by the machine or the presenter, or both.

Image distortion is relatively easy to correct. The axis of the screen and projector head must simply be put in the same plane.

The projection method most often used is unfortunately the one that produces the most obstruction. The screen hangs straight down from the ceiling wall, and the projector is positioned on the conference table or on a stand in front of the screen so that the head of the projector is approximately on a level with the center of the screen. This eliminates image distortion (keystone) but also blocks a portion of the image for just about everyone in the room. Several approaches can be used to solve these problems:

1. Place the projector on a low stand so that its head is just about table height; angle the projector up toward the screen, and the screen down toward the projector (by pushing the bottom of the screen toward the wall or pulling the top of the screen away from the wall) and have the presenter sit next to the projector. This all but eliminates the major problems.

2. Angle the projector and screen alignment across the front of the room. Unfortunately, this also diminishes eye contact.

3. Use a conference-table arrangement with projector and screen alignment parallel with the table; this may also diminish eye contact, however.

4. Use a special overhead projector with long throw optics. Sometimes this enables the projector to be positioned at the back of the room or in a projection booth attended by an operator. This arrangement precludes some of the advantages of the overhead projector, and a review of the need for this medium would be advisable.

The typical front-projection booth should be at least 5 to 6 feet deep to contain standard incandescent 16mm motion picture and other projection equipment. The booth's minimum depth is based on a 16mm projector because this is the longest standard machine and requires 30 to 40 inches front to back with 2,000-foot reels, depending on manufacturer and model.

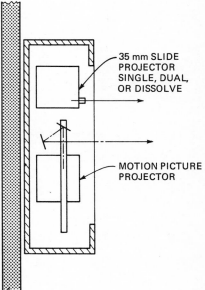

Fig. 7-14   Minimal depth front projection cabinet.

35 mm SLIDE PROJECTOR SINGLE, DUAL, OR DISSOLVE

MOTION PICTURE PROJECTOR

Larger equipment or equipment made larger by the addition of high-light-output adaptations may require more booth depth.

As a general rule, the projection port should contain optically clear glass and permit the projected light beam to pass well above the audience's heads. Two trade names for glass to be used in projection ports are Water White and Crown Quality.

Rear Projection

As in front projection, the equipment should be enclosed. For plans that do not or could not allot space for a separate booth, the equipment can be designed into a cabinet within the room parameters. These arrangements can be specially engineered or selected from among a number of prefabricated designs. Almost all these units use a mirror or mirrors to redirect the projected light beam in a minimum depth while maintaining a satisfactory projection distance.

Unlike front-projection systems, rear-projection systems vary in depth with image-size requirement and design concept. Generally, they are engineered to be as shallow as possible to consume the least number of square feet and for ease of handling. The typical rear-projection booth depth is generally about twice the image size. Therefore, a 10-foot-deep projection booth should be allocated for a 5-foot image system in the preliminary plan.

This suggestion is based on the accepted minimum standard of projecting a distance at least twice the image size, which is a ratio of 2:1 projection distance to image size.[7] The 2:1 ratio can be achieved in less booth depth, but the people in charge of the early planning stages are generally not familiar with the engineering concept unless an audiovisual system consultant has been brought in.

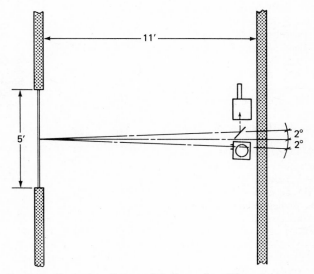

Fig. 7-15   Projection distance 2:1. Reversing slides necessary.

We shall now discuss the projection methods one at a time as they relate to rear-projection booth sizes in obtaining a 5-foot image.

Direct Rear Projection   This method, which is *not* recommended, would require about 11 feet of booth depth (see Fig. 7-15).

This method is not recommended because all slides would have to be inserted in projector magazines in a reverse manner, which is time-consuming and confusing. Using a mirror permits the slides to be loaded as they normally would be for front projection, making any standard loaded magazine compatible for front or rear projection.

If two projectors are to be used, either they must be shifted back and forth to be on center, or each one must be slightly off center. If more projectors are to be used, they generally must be shifted. This, of course, can be accomplished manually or automatically.

Indirect Rear Projection A   This method is similar to direct rear projection except that each machine uses a mirror, and the booth would be a minimum of 10 feet instead of 11 feet (see Fig. 7-16).

The centering requirements are the same.

Indirect Rear Projection B   Because the projector can be a greater distance from the mirror which redirects the light beam, the 10-foot booth would permit a longer projection distance providing a 3.5:1 ratio (see Fig. 7-17). The image

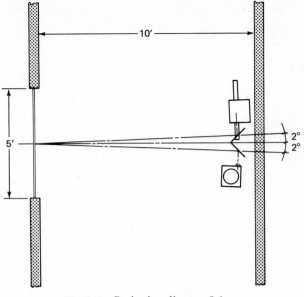

Fig. 7-16   Projection distance 2:1.

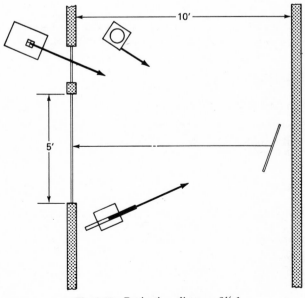

Fig. 7-17   Projection distance $3\frac{1}{2}$:1.

projected in this format would be more resolute and would have less apparent falloff and a much wider angle of view.

Of course, the minimum ratio of 2:1 could also be used for comparison purposes. As shown in Fig. 7-18, the booth-depth requirement is a minimal 6 feet.

Additional advantages of this method are that when the mirror is rotated, all the projectors remain in true vertical and horizontal alignment; the large mirror also permits an overhead projector to be used in the training room next to the instructor, while the image it projects reflects from the mirror to the back of the rear-projection screen. This places the projector and instructor out of the viewers' sight lines to the screen.

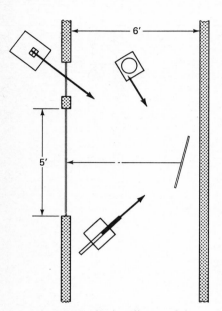

Another method of utilizing less space for a rear-projection system is to periscope the projected light path as shown in Fig. 7-19. This method provides additional projection distance and simplifies operation of the system, especially when the screen is unusually high, requiring an angled screen and platforms for the operator. An ancillary advantage is that the operator is less likely to block a projected image from one projector while loading another.

Special Notes. Any light falling on the back of the rear screen will transmit through the screen with the image, reducing its contrast and clarity. To eliminate this problem, the booth should be painted flat black or dark brown, and if possible the light path should be en-

Fig. 7-18   Projection distance 2:1.

closed. An ancillary advantage of the enclosure is that the booth can be used for other, related activities without affecting the projected image.

PROJECTION-METHOD POINTS FOR ELEVATION

Front Projection (Matte White Screen)

The viewing-distance factor is 6 when using the character sizes discussed earlier in this chapter (e.g., if the image size is 5 feet, the alphamerics would be clear at a distance of 30 feet to a viewer with 20-40 vision).

Advantages

1. There is a very good angle of view and virtually no apparent falloff to the sides.

2. This method is recommended for checking lab quality of all projectuals.

3. This is a good method to use in large auditoriums where orientations and dramatic presentations are taking place and where note taking is not important.

Disadvantages

1. High ceilings are required to utilize a square screen to accommodate vertical as well as horizontal images.

2. A distraction is created when the presenter or the viewers interrupt the light beam.

3. Any ambient light adversely affects the image quality. The room must be relatively dark to achieve the desired picture contrast.

4. This method precludes the most effective use of the overhead projector.

Rear Projection (Rigid or Flexible Material)

The viewing-distance factor is 7.5 when using the character sizes discussed earlier in this chapter (e.g., if the image size is 5 feet, the viewing distance would be 37.5 feet).

Advantages

1. A 20 percent smaller image can be used than is required by front projection. This method also permits minimum standards to be met in low-ceilinged rooms.

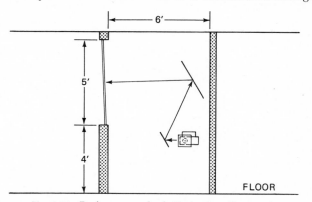

Fig. 7-19 Periscope method. Projection distance 2:1.

2. This method can be used under higher ambient-light conditions, permitting note taking.

3. There is no distracting light beam; thus the presenter can more comfortably point at details.

4. Because the room is brighter, the presenter easily maintains eye contact.

5. An overhead projector can be used without the machine and the presenter blocking the image from the viewers.

Disadvantages

1. The inherent grain and directional quality of the rear screen eliminate it as a viewing medium to determine the lab quality of projectuals.

2. The projection system must be designed to overcome apparent illumination falloff at the sides and to improve the angle of view.

3. This method requires a mirrored image for proper use.

4. More space is required than for front projection.

5. The cost is usually higher.

The basic visualizing concept for an audiovisual facility is not affected by a manual or automated system. The important thing to keep in mind is that in a complex arrangement, automation is much more efficient and in the long run more economical. It is more economical because technicians do not have to be in attendance once the equipment is loaded.

Multimedia

A multimedia system is one which can project visuals from more than one type of source. If a projection system can project images from 35mm slides and motion picture film, it is a multimedia system.

Multi-Image

A multi-image consists of more than one nonoverlapping image on a projection screen. Since multi-image presentations require much more preparation, coordination, and rehearsal than single-image presentations, their use is limited to outside specially produced industrial shows, fairs, and museums. In training facilities, having two slide images or one slide image and one overhead image is generally the extent of multi-image usage.

Sophistication versus Complication

This distinction refers to projection systems, not the visual presentation, though there appears to be some confusion in this area as well. An effective sophisticated presentation can be single-image or multi-image. Concept, preparation, technique, and cohesive result are what make it sophisticated. Too often a presentation with a lot of theatrical effects and flashing images which submerge the message is accepted as sophisticated when it is just an elaborate complication.

In a sense we have a similar situation in system design. When system requirements get beyond a slide projector or two and a motion picture projector in a single-image system, the operational aspects become very complicated. This is where an audiovisual system design engineer can make an important contribution. The designer's optical and physical plan can simplify the operation of the most complex requirement by positioning the equipment so that it is easily accessible and by eliminating the necessity for readjustments by means of preset alignment positions. Operating the adequately designed system is then simply a matter of loading the equipment and operating it from the booth or remote-control position. Where elaborate multimedia, multi-image presentations are made several times a year, the services of a programmer should be considered part of the equipment package.

Television

Television in the instructional environment is generally a vehicle for role playing and reproduction of commercial and in-house productions. Live closed-circuit transmission is used to a lesser degree because real-time situations are difficult to schedule and have limited application.

Where instruction is concerned, video single reproduction is excellent for small groups and individuals through monitors, but it has rather limited use for medium-sized or large groups. Classroom situations normally use monitors which permit a high room light level, though this method directs the attention of the participants away from the instructor.

Insofar as video projectors are concerned, their light output is inadequate for semilighted rooms, except for one or two very expensive units.

For darkroom viewing, there are a few reasonably priced black-and-white video projectors and one color projector (which requires a special screen) that do an acceptable job for role playing and specially prepared visuals.

The above-mentioned projectors, except the small color unit, can be used with some rear- and most front-projection systems.

The limitation in rear-projection systems is space. The projectors usually require a 2:1 ratio of projection distance to image size, with a minimum image size of about 6 feet. This means that a 12-foot projection distance is required, and since most video projectors have very low light-level output, a mirror should be avoided if possible.

Visuals for television require special attention. Subject matter, illustrations, and alphameric characters must be larger than the normal size required for slides. This can be accomplished by using a ¼-inch original character size in a 4.5 × 6 inch copy area photographed on a 6 × 9 inch field to approximate transmission loss at the edges and corners of a standard television receiver.

Support Functions

In addition to the graphic arts support activity discussed at the beginning of this chapter, a technical support activity is also required. Some relatively small operations require only one person, who may also have other assignments. However, one individual or a group should be designated.

The support group should be familiar with the concept and operation of each system and machine as well as its maintenance requirements. Unless your facility is very far away from an outside service organization, all that should be necessary from a maintenance standpoint is a knowledge of how to change bulbs and fuses. Beyond this, the audiovisual contractor should service any electromechanical devices, control circuitry, and optical alignment.

The technical support group should also be responsible for setting up a stock of projection lamps, tapes, cassettes, and any expendable items and for determining the reorder level and quality.

It is suggested that some standby equipment be considered in highly active, multisystem facilities.

Regional Facilities

At the beginning of this chapter we discussed facilities from the standpoint of permanent in-house space utilization. However, it is quite possible that all or some programs will be more efficient and economically feasible if presented in the field. There are several options in terms of field instruction.

Depending on the size of the organization, its dispersion, and its instructional requirements, the main alternatives are the following.

1. *Permanent Regional In-House or External Facilities.* These can be served by:
   a. Traveling instructional teams with specific programs
   b. A permanent instructional staff at each location with traveling specialists
   c. Managers or supervisors
2. *Transient Facilities.* Although these facilities can be served by the same alternatives as those listed above, much more coordination is necessary to assure smoothly running facility functions and operational stability. Many varied accommodations are available at hotels, motels, conference centers, universities, colleges, resorts, and convention centers. It is imperative that the physical facilities be examined as well as the audiovisual equipment, if this is to be supplied locally. Check the adequacy of:
   a. Audio facilities
   b. Power availability and capacity
   c. Light control
   d. Ambient-light conditions
   e. Screen—type and size
   f. Privacy
   g. Ambient noise
   h. Adjacent functions
   i. Related requirements:
      (1) Lavatories
      (2) Coffee service
      (3) Lunch facilities
      (4) Anteroom or space for congregating
   Advantages and Disadvantages of Permanent Facilities
   1. There is full control.
   2. There is more efficient use of time and facility investment.

3. Students come to the facility (transient facilities are less costly in this respect only).

4. There is good cost control.

Advantages and Disadvantages of Transient Facilities

1. They provide flexibility (especially since they can accommodate traveling programs), and they are ideal for one-time programs.

2. Instructors go to students, which is less costly.

3. They may place limitations on display techniques.

4. They are not under full control; there is limited privacy.

5. Costs are higher and there are more limitations than with permanent facilities.

Purchase Equipment For

1. Permanent facilities—in-house or external

2. Traveling program with permanent staff

3. Program formats that will continually be repeated

Rent Equipment For

1. Short-term or test programs

2. Externally produced programs that require special equipment

REFERENCES

1. Eastman Kodak Company, Motion Picture and Education Markets Division: *Legibility: Artwork to Screen,* Pamphlet S-24; *Projection Calculator and Seating Guide,* publication S-16, Rochester, N.Y.
2. Dreyer, J.: *Operational Characteristics of Rear Projection,* Society of Motion Picture and Television Engineers, Scarsdale, N.Y., 1959, pp. 521–524.
3. Eastman Kodak Company: op. cit.
4. Crouch, C. L.: "The Relationship between Illumination and Vision," *Illuminating Engineer,* pp. 747–784, November 1945.
5. Eastman Kodak Company: op. cit.
6. Crouch: op. cit.
7. Dreyer: op. cit.

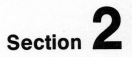

Program Development

Chapter **8**

The Behavioral Sciences in Training and Development

HAROLD M. F. RUSH

Harold M. F. Rush *is Personnel Development Advisor for Exxon-Esso Europe, Inc. in London, England and has been associated with Exxon Corporation at its headquarters in New York, responsible for manpower development and training. His background includes research, teaching, consulting, and line management of human resources. His industry experience includes plant-level and corporate positions with Thiokol Chemical Corporation as training specialist, corporate employment manager, corporate personnel administrator, assistant to the corporate secretary, and special assistant to the chairman and chief executive. He served "on loan" to the White House during the Kennedy and Johnson administrations, managing a joint industry-government program to employ and train minorities. For nine years Mr. Rush was a member of the professional staff of The Conference Board as senior specialist in organization development and behavioral sciences. He has published widely and is the author of five books and scores of articles appearing in business and professional journals. He is a visiting lecturer at the major universities and business schools in North America and a member of the International Quality of Working Life Project.*

Manager: a leader who enables people to work most effectively together by performing primarily the work of planning, organizing, leading, and controlling.[1]

Of the four basic managerial functions, none is more crucial to the success of the organization than leading, for it is in performing this function that the manager's ability to manage is put to the acid test. It is in leading, more than in any other function, that the manager must deal directly with the human resources of the organization, and as any experienced manager knows, this is often a complex and difficult job, requiring knowledge and skill beyond that which the average person naturally possesses. People are variable; their behaviors are sometimes predictable, and sometimes not; people both think and feel; what worked well for management in the past often seems less effective when dealing with a more mobile, better-educated, more aggressive, and more affluent work force.

For these reasons, the managerial profession has looked outside the traditional business disciplines for insights and guidance in formulating strategies to manage the "people" part of the enterprise. Increasingly, the assistance is sought from a loosely bound collection of academic disciplines referred to as the *behavioral sciences*, which may include sociology, anthropology, socioeconomics, the various subspecialities within psychology (clinical, social, experimental, etc.), and a host of other disciplines concerned with human behavior in social settings—in this case, the world of work and the work environment.[2]

An understanding of the contributions of the behavioral sciences and the implications of their theories and research findings is essential to the contemporary manager, who is, more than ever before, concerned about employee motivation and an accompanying increase in productivity. To sharpen his or her ability to manage people effectively and thereby help the organization to realize its objectives, it is incumbent upon the manager to know something about the inner workings of people and the resultant behaviors they exhibit in relation to the work they perform and the relationships that develop on the job between superiors, subordinates, and peers. One of the prime movers of the current generation of behavioral scientists, Douglas McGregor, pointed out that a substantial body of knowledge, based on research and scientific observation, now exists to enable the manager to manage people on a logical, professional basis, and not according to outdated myths and old wives' tales about what truly motivates people. In fact, he made an impassioned plea for enterprises to "exploit" the behavioral sciences and tap their contributions toward making management a science, as well as an art.[3]

While the coming together of management and the behavioral sciences has been a gradual process that continues to evolve even today, the heightened interest on both sides of the fence can be traced back only about three decades. However, there are some significant series of events which can be identified as precursors of the contemporary behavioral science–business interface. Principal among them are the so-called Hawthorne studies, the emergence of group dynamics research, and the group theory of organization.

THE HAWTHORNE STUDIES

Beginning in 1927 and continuing for five years, the Hawthorne studies were conducted at Western Electric's Hawthorne plant near Chicago. A group of social scientists from Harvard was brought into the plant to study "the relation between conditions of work and the incidence of fatigue and monotony among employees." To do so, they set out to assess the influence of physical and environmental influences such as temperature, light, and humidity at the workplace and the relationship of rest periods to subsequent efficiency on the job. They selected experimental groups of employees, manipulated work conditions, and recorded the results. While they were able, in some instances, to determine cause-and-effect relationships between work conditions and efficiency, they also found that, almost regardless of what changes they made in the work environment, efficiency increased among their experimental groups of workers. This gave rise to what is called the *Hawthorne effect;* that is, the theory that employees perform more efficiently simply because they are given special attention.

More significant than the findings based on the original premise that physical conditions at the workplace affect efficiency were the unexpected findings that were gleaned from the Hawthorne studies. Because the researchers were, in effect, set back each time they tried to relate the various physical conditions to worker efficiency, the project, which was designed to last only one year, extended to five years. The reason: There were influences affecting efficiency and productivity much more strongly than working conditions—namely, group social structures, group norms, and group pressures. The researchers found, for example, that employees were more productive when working in groups than when working in isolation and that wage incentives alone did not determine product output, even on a piecework basis. Workers would sacrifice greater output for group acceptance.[4] Modern managers will find this no surprise, since they know and understand what happens to "rate-busters," but in the late 1920s—when most of industry was influenced heavily by "efficiency experts," time and motion studies, and incentive plans that were based on purely economic considerations—the social-group influences and interpersonal factors that were operating came as a surprise both to management and to the social scientists.

As a result, the research evolved to measure the human and social factors at play, and the investigation began to be concentrated on attitudes and motives of workers as individuals and on the social organization of work groups. With these findings documented, further research on the special roles of supervision and its relationship to the work groups began to be incorporated into the Hawthorne research, which served as the impetus for other groundbreaking behavioral research.

GROUP DYNAMICS RESEARCH

Although the principles of gestalt psychology had been applied to other areas of behavioral research, it was not until Kurt Lewin, the German-born American psychologist, and his colleagues began their experiments on interacting, face-to-face groups that the gestalt was adapted to social units or groups. The *gestalt* principle, most simply stated, is, that the whole is greater than the sum of its parts. With this orientation as an underlying theoretical framework, Lewin and his colleagues made studies of groups as phenomena that were quite different from studies of individuals who compose groups. The research findings suggest that groups do, indeed, take on a distinct personality that supersedes the aggregate personality of its members, and for the first time in the history of social psychology, such terms as "group feeling," "group atmosphere," and "group goals" had an established scientific basis.

Moreover, it was found that the behavior of individuals acting in group situations is determined partially by the group's interaction and behavior, while influencing the norms and behavior of the group. In other words, there is a dynamic interaction, a give-and-take which occurs whenever groups function, that gives rise to what is referred to as *group dynamics*. Lewin and his associates studied group dynamics in the context of the "field" or "life space" in which the behaviors take place, and they posited that behavior can be understood only in the context of this field, thereby creating an analogy, however tenuous, to field theory in the physical sciences. Field theory in social psychology has been variously expressed in mathematical formulas, but the equation $B = f(PE)$, or behavior as a function of personality plus environment, underscores the situational nature of group dynamics and field theory. The personality of individuals may have many determinants, including heredity, early maturational experiences, beliefs, needs, etc., but any given behavior is a function of that personality *plus* the environment or field in which the individual interacts with others—therefore, behavior is changing and dynamic.[5]

GROUP THEORY OF ORGANIZATION

Group dynamics research, which later produced the learning techniques of laboratory training (discussed later), clearly reinforced and gave explanation to the social-group phenomena that the Hawthorne research uncovered in factory work groups. It also formed the basis for large-scale research by Likert, Pelz, et al. on the roles of leadership and work groups, commonly referred to as the *group theory of organization*.

Prior to the Hawthorne studies, supervisors generally dealt with employees as individuals, using a corresponding managerial style designed to supervise on a one-to-one basis. With the research which demonstrated that organizations are actually composed of distinct and identifiable social groups, both formal and informal, and the complementary research on group dynamics and group behaviors, behavioral scientists—mainly from the University of Michigan—undertook extensive action research to identify where these groups exist in organizations, the patterns of group interaction in work situations, and the factors that encourage or impede group cohesion and effectiveness, the relationship of particular groups to other groups, and the individual's role in the several groups and subgroups to which he or she belongs.

Consistently it was demonstrated that the key to successful leadership lies in managers' recognition that they are not managing a collection of individuals—that they must couch their managerial strategies in terms of their relationships to the various groups to which they belong and particularly to the groups they supervise. This may involve an understanding of the function of informal groups in the organization, whose influence may be greater than is indicated by the work grouping that appears on the formal and official organization charts.[6]

Since an organization is more than a large collection of individuals, it is actually a series of overlapping groups—groups with the characteristics of individuals (norms, beliefs, values, feelings, inputs, outputs, etc.) but reinforced and modified by group interaction in any given situation. Crucial to the effective manager's role in relationship to these groups is the matter of *perception*—the way the manager perceives his or her roles with the groups and the way the groups perceive the manager.

BEHAVIORAL THEORIES AND THEORISTS INFLUENCING CONTEMPORARY MANAGEMENT

With the backdrop of the foregoing breakthrough research findings, the behavioral sciences have produced a wealth of subsequent research and theory that have special relevance to the management of modern organizations. Some of these were produced quite independently from business organizations and were adapted by business enterprises because the problems they address are common in business organizations; others were carried out as developmental or action research in and for business organizations. It is impossible in this space to discuss in detail even the most significant findings, let alone others that may have made contributions to the growing body of behavioral research. However, some of the theories and research which seem to have most influenced the managerial process can be treated briefly in overview here. Since most are identified with the initiating researchers, they are categorized and discussed under the names of their principal promulgators or champions.[7]

Kurt Lewin

As mentioned above, the group dynamics research which was headed by Kurt Lewin has had a weighty impact on subsequent behavioral science applications in contemporary organizations. The most widely applied facet of this research is one that has special interest to executives concerned with training and development: *laboratory training.*[8]

Laboratory training is the generic name for a variety of educational experiences designed (1) to increase individuals' sensitivity to their own motives and behavior, (2) to increase their sensitivity to the behavior of others, (3) to give them an understanding of how others perceive their behavior and are affected by it, and (4) to determine what factors facilitate or impede group effectiveness. The most common method of laboratory training used by business organizations, especially since the early 1960s, has been *sensitivity training* labs, the heart of which is the *T group* ("T" for training).[9]

While there are many variations on the basic T group, the traditional or "classic" one involves about 12 participants, usually strangers to one another, who meet for two weeks in an isolated spot without agenda and without hierarchical status to interact in face-to-face groups. Although designed to be an educational experience, the sessions are intended to encourage emotional or visceral learning, as contrasted with intellectual or "head-level" learning, which characterizes more traditional education. Further, there is no appointed leader or teacher, though an experienced "trainer" may act in the role of process observer and interpret the behavioral interactions of participants. The group's behavior is both the content and the process of the learning experience—totally experiential in nature. Participants learn to give and receive feedback on a completely candid and instantaneous basis, and the behaviors of individuals and the larger group are reacted to in terms of the "here and now," thereby underscoring Lewin's emphasis on understanding behavior in the "field" in which it occurs.[10]

Laboratory training is still widely used as a developmental technique, though in recent years organizations have tended to replace laboratory training or to supplement it with exercises designed to bridge the gap between the "pure" lab experience and on-the-job problems and situations. These exercises, however, owe much of their methodology to laboratory training. Among these are the Managerial Grid (discussed later in connection with Blake and Mouton), team building, intergroup building, and other methods associated with organization development.[11]

Rensis Likert

The name of Rensis Likert looms large in social psychology. Likert is widely known as the developer of one of the most popular opinion and attitude measurement scales, which has been in use for more than four decades. His more recent contributions, however, are directed more toward organizational behavior and the managerial process. A proponent of the group theory of organization, Likert has been actively involved in some of the most significant action research to be conducted in the world of work. His name is most often associated with the linking-pin concept and its companion, the interaction-influence principle; the four systems of organization; and human resource accounting.

The *linking-pin concept* concerns the manager's role in relation to the groups he or she supervises and the group's perception of their manager. The manager serves as a vital link between subordinates and his or her peers and superiors. Thus the manager is the channel of communication between organizational levels; the interpreter of objectives, policies, directives, etc., for subordinates; and the representative and advocate of the members of the work group for his or her peers and superiors. There is nothing new here, so far, since this is a primary function of *any* manager. The difference—and a crucial one—is that the linking pin is a *member* of at least two groups, and thus his or her behavior reflects the values, norms, and objectives of both groups. Usually the manager is the subordinate in one group (e.g., top management) and the superior in the other (e.g., middle management). Further, in order to be an effective linking pin, the manager must be perceived by both groups as a real member of the group, with corresponding identification with each group's activities, problems, accomplishments, etc.[12]

Interaction-Influence Principle   Even if the behaviors and perceptions of both groups are favorable in relation to the so-called linking pin, the *interaction-influence principle* must also be operative for the manager to be effective in an organization composed of overlapping and interfacing groups. Research on leadership styles and managerial effectiveness supports the necessity of a positive operation of the interaciton-influence principle, with two essential variables at work.

First, the amount of influence a manager (linking pin) exerts upward in an organization directly determines the amount of influence he or she exerts downward. Stated simply, the more a manager is respected and listened to and can influence peers and superiors, the more effective he or she will be in managing subordinates. Managers who carry little "weight" with higher levels of the organizational hierarchy are apt to have little influence on the work groups that report to them.

Second, the more that managers allow themselves to be influenced by their

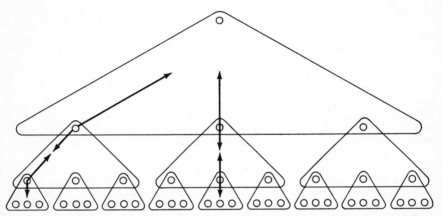

Fig. 8-1   The linking-pin function. *(Source: Rensis Likert, New Patterns of Management, McGraw-Hill Book Company, New York, 1961. Used with permission of McGraw-Hill Book Company.)*

subordinates, the more influence they, in turn, exert on subordinates. For example, in making decisions that will affect subordinates, the manager is more apt to get commitment and involvement from the work group in carrying out the decision if the work group has had some voice in determining the course of the decision. (See Fig. 8-1 for a graphic presentation of the linking pin and the directions of interaction and influence.)

The Four Systems   The interaction-influence principle clearly has strong implications for the development of a managerial style that is participative and involves the work group. And this is the style that Likert champions in his exposition of the *four systems of organization,* which is a comparative analysis of organizational and performance characteristics of four distinct types of organization. The systems are arranged on a continuum as follows:

System 1: Exploitive-authoritative
System 2: Benevolent-authoritative
System 3: Consultative
System 4: Participative-group

Several organizational variables are analyzed in terms of their existence in organizations typified by the respective systems and their corresponding organizational climates and management styles, including such variables as leadership processes used, character of motivational forces, communication processes, decision-making processes, control processes, and so forth. The four-system construct can be used to identify and describe organizations that are characteristic of the various points on the continuum, as well as to provide a model for normative organizational change.[13]

Throughout his work, Likert advocates a management that is based on the application of scientific research to human behavior in the social setting of the workplace. He sees the climate and managerial style inherent in his System 4 as the ones best founded on behavioral research and most conducive to effective achievement of organizational objectives, since System 4 relies most heavily on work-group participation and fuller utilization of human resources. Likert carries his emphasis on treating the "people" side of the organization as a resource to a logical extreme by developing a model for a method of accounting for the human resources.

Human Resource Accounting Likert proposed formulas for assigning monetary values, often very specific ones, to the recruitment, hiring, training, and utilization of human beings, much as an organization would account for acquisition and usage of capital equipment. In human resource accounting, the human resources are accounted for in terms of gain or loss, appreciation or depreciation, and asset or liability, much as the material resources of the organization are accounted for, and they appear on the balance sheets as such.[14] While it remains to be seen whether human resource accounting is a viable or practicable technology for most organizations, a few firms have undertaken the practice on an experimental basis.

Douglas McGregor

Although Douglas McGregor made contributions to the body of behavioral research and had an active career as professor of management, management consultant, writer, and college president, his name is most often associated with his formulation of philosophical views of mankind, which he called *Theory X* and *Theory Y*.[15]

Theory X, basically a negativistic set of beliefs, includes the following assumptions (paraphrased):

1. People have an inherent dislike for work and will avoid it whenever possible.
2. Because they dislike work, people must be coerced, controlled, directed, or threatened with punishment in order to get them to exert sufficient effort toward organizational objectives.
3. People prefer to be directed, want to avoid responsibility, have little ambition, and seek mainly security.

Theory Y, in contrast, is an optimistic view of human nature:

1. Physical and mental work are as natural as play and rest.
2. People will exercise self-direction and self-control in achieving objectives if they are committed to the objectives.
3. Commitment to objectives is a function of the rewards associated with their achievement.
4. Under proper conditions, people learn not only to accept but also to seek responsibility.
5. Creativity, ingenuity, and imagination are *widely* distributed among the population; most people are capable of directing these abilities toward solving organizational problems.
6. Under conditions in most existing organizations, the average person's intellectual potentialities are being utilized only partially.

McGregor called these sets of assumptions *managerial cosmologies,* and he recognized that they represent only two of many possible "cosmologies"—a term related to *weltanschauung,* which is used in psychology and philosophy to denote a comprehensive conception of the world. They are therefore fundamental orientations or perceptions about the basic nature of human beings, particularly in relation to work and organizational life. While managerial styles and strategies logically are based on these theories, McGregor insisted that he was not proposing a "cookbook" for managing. He adds, however, that Theory X most nearly sums up the view traditional management has taken toward the work force, while Theory Y represents an enlightened view of how most people are constituted, based on a considerable storehouse of research on human behavior.

"Consensus" Management?   Any management style starts with one's beliefs about the nature of people, and in most cases the sets of beliefs or assumptions held by managers become self-fulfilling prophecies when it comes to actual managing. If one's beliefs about people are consonant with those of Theory X, there is only one way to manage: by exerting external control on subordinates. On the other hand, if one views people in a way characteristic of the Theory Y assumptions, there is the possibility of allowing people to exercise self-control. This is what McGregor stated in his compilation of Theory Y, not a "soft" or "consensus" management, though critics often have leveled this charge.

There are qualifiers in Theory Y, and they are important to an understanding of what McGregor intended. For example, he specifies that people will exercise self-control and self-direction *if* they are committed to the objectives; people will accept and seek responsibility *under proper conditions*. McGregor realized that not all people are psychologically mature and that work is, in fact, a burden to some people, and he also realized that some people are passive and dependent and need to have external control. He adds, however, that people are not like this by nature; instead, their experiences in organizations have made them this way. While McGregor's own style and purpose reflected a Theory Y view of human nature and a management style consistent with Theory Y, he realized that if the manager cannot create the conditions that will lead people to use their creativity or if he cannot gain commitment and involvement, authority and imposed control must be exercised. The key to understanding the differences between the two theories is rigidity versus flexibility. Theory X allows for no flexibility in managerial style, while Theory Y suggests a wide range of styles, depending upon the work force and the situation.

McGregor argued that managing requires a special kind of skill and expertise because the manager's success is dependent upon effective utilization of the talents, minds, abilities, and efforts of other people. He therefore advocated a professional management founded upon scientifically obtained knowledge of human motivations and behaviors.[16]

Abraham H. Maslow

Maslow, a leader of the humanistic psychology movement, was concerned primarily with the fullest development of human potential; thus his burning interest was the study of superior people. He did not set out to develop a model of employee job motivation, though his theory of human personality has become probably the most influential conceptual basis for employee motivation to be found in modern industry. It is based on Maslow's theorizing and research into how the personality develops and grows and on the cardinal relationship of growth to motivation.

Starting with the assumption that human beings are wanting animals and are forever striving for goals of various kinds, Maslow posited that people want because they *need* these goals. Furthermore, while the finite expression of these needs may vary from individual to individual and from culture to culture, there are certain fundamental stages of need and growth common to all human beings—or at least the potential is present in everyone. Whether a person reaches the upper plateaus of these potential stages of growth depends upon the degree to which lower-level needs are adequately fulfilled. In fact, Maslow categorized these needs into a conceptual hierarchy, called, logically enough, the *hierarchy of needs.*[17] The five levels of the hierarchy, here represented in their ascending pattern of emergence, are

- self-actualization needs
- esteem needs
- love and belongingness needs
- safety needs
- physiological needs

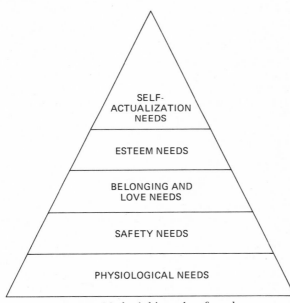

Fig. 8-2 Maslow's hierarchy of needs.

Physiological Needs.   These are the needs for food, warmth, sleep, sex, and other primarily bodily satisfactions.

Safety Needs.   These include the need to be free from actual danger, as well as the need for psychological assurance of security.

Love and Belongingness Needs.   These are the basic needs for other people, social acceptance, and group membership, as well as the need to give and to receive love and affection.

Esteem Needs.   These include the need to have the respect and esteem of others, as well as the need for self-esteem.

Self-Actualization Needs.   These are the needs to realize one's potential fully, to become what one is capable of becoming, and to actualize the real "self," which is more than the basic organism.

The hierarchy implies that needs occur in the order in which they are presented, with physiological needs appearing first, then safety needs, etc. (see Fig. 8-2). This theory of personality and maturation states that until one level of need is fairly well satisfied, the next higher need does not even emerge. Moreover, once a particular set of needs is fulfilled, it no longer motivates. One is not driven to find safety if one is already safe, although if safety is taken away or threatened, it once again becomes the person's driving force or motivation, just as a fish is not motivated to seek water unless it is taken out of water. Stated simply, people are not motivated to achieve goals that they have already reached.

While Maslow posits these five sets of needs as inherently possible for all people, there are impediments of various kinds that can cause a person to reach a certain level of the hierarchy and cease to grow further. Even in relatively mature people, the lower-level needs remain and must be constantly maintained in order for motivation to be directed at the upper-level social and egotistic levels. In fact, the necessity of keeping the lower, more basic and primitive needs satisfied is a key factor in the Maslow model of personality and motivation. Because the lower-level needs are more immediate and urgent, if they are not constantly satisfied, they again come into play as the source and direction of a person's motivation. For example, a person who has climbed up the emotional ladder of the hierarchy of needs to the level of "esteem" will fall back to satisfy the safety needs if his or her safety is threatened.

While Maslow posits a serial nature of needs, it is important to keep in mind that an individual's motivation is not static, fixed, or "set in concrete." Whatever need is operative at a given time becomes the focus of an individual's striving to achieve satisfaction. Despite the tendency to fall back to a lower level if a lower-level need is insufficiently met, this lasts only until the need is satisfied. Then the individual's motivation is once again directed at the appropriate higher-level need. Maslow states explicitly that a person can be identified as being primarily at a given level— the level of prime motivation—at any given point in life. Emotionally healthy and mature persons are found striving to satisfy upper-level needs.

Self-Actualization Is Rare   However, while everyone may have a self-actualizing potential, Maslow's study of superior people indicates that few reach the level at which self-actualization is their prime motivation. Truly self-actualizing people are rare specimens. They are realistically oriented and are accepting of themselves, other people, and the natural world for what they are; they are greatly spontaneous; they are problem-centered, rather than self-centered; they have an air of detachment and a need for privacy; they are autonomous and independent; they have a fresh, rather than stereotyped, appreciation of people and things; they have had profound mystical or spiritual experiences, though not necessarily religious ones; they identify with all human beings rather than a subgroup; they have intimate relationships with a few specially loved people, and these relationships tend to be profound rather than superficial; they possess democratic values and attitudes; they do not confuse means with ends; they have a philosophical, rather than hostile, sense of humor; they have a great fund of creativeness and resist conforming to the culture; and they transcend the environment, rather than merely coping with it.[18]

The Maslow studies and the hierarchy of needs contain a wealth of personality theory and insights into human motivation, but the hierarchy alone has minimal relevance for average managers, except to broaden their understanding of human nature, unless it is related to the environment in general and the facts of organizational life in particular. This may be done by looking at the hierarchy in terms of the motivations of employees who compose the work forces in Western industry today.

Translation of Factors   Physiological needs—for food, shelter, clothing, etc.— require a job and a salary as a means to satisfy them. Safety needs are fulfilled through physical safety on the job, job security, and many fringe benefits. Belongingness needs may be satisfied by off-the-job relationships, by membership in work groups in modern industrial society, to a certain extent by work-connected social activities, and by unions and professional societies.

The pungent part of this analogy is what may *not* be satisfied: the need for esteem and the need for self-actualization. The key to real motivation lies in providing people the opportunity to satisfy their upper-level needs, rather than the lower-level ones, which most employees have already satisfied. It is important to remember that "a satisfied need no longer motivates."

Frederick Herzberg

Many managers, though intrigued and fascinated by Maslow's theory of personality and motivation, find it difficult to translate into concrete on-the-job application. However, the research and subsequent job redesign prescriptions of Frederick Herzberg and his colleagues are seen by large numbers of managers as a practical and workable means of increasing employee motivation. Yet the work of Herzberg can be understood only in terms of its extrapolation from Maslow's work, although on some fine points the connection is tenuous or represents an interpretation somewhat different from that of Maslow.

Herzberg's research, which has captured the imagination and loyalty of a host of followers (and has infuriated and alienated many others), began not as an inquiry into job redesign as such, but as an investigation of job factors and their relation to employee mental health. Herzberg and his colleagues were attempting to identify which kinds of on-the-job sequences contribute to job satisfaction and which ones cause dissatisfaction.

The research design is a simple one. Employees (originally accountants and engineers) were asked in semistructured interviews to recall specific events in the course of their work which made them feel particularly satisfied in their jobs; they were then asked to recall specific events that caused them to feel dissatisfied in their jobs. The interviews netted a large number of different kinds of events or circumstances, which Herzberg and his associates synthesized into several categories that describe in substance the multiple responses.

They found that rarely were the same sorts of events listed as sources of both satisfaction and dissatisfaction. In fact, allowing for some overlap, the things that caused satisfaction had a distinctly different character from that of the things reported as causing dissatisfaction.

Two-Factor Theory   Herzberg hypothesized, then, that the opposite of dissatisfaction is not satisfaction, but simply no dissatisfaction, and that the absence of satisfaction is not dissatisfaction, but no satisfaction. His postulating these sets of factors as different in character, separate, and discrete caused the theory to be called the *Herzberg two-factor theory of job satisfaction*. A listing of the basic factors—which he called *satisfiers* and *dissatisfiers*—may illustrate the substantive differences in their character, though not necessarily in order of importance within each set of factors.

Satisfiers
Achievement
Recognition
Responsibility
Work itself
Growth
Advancement

Dissatisfiers
Working conditions
Policies and administrative practices
Supervision
Interpersonal relations
Salary (all forms of financial compensation)
Status
Job security
Personal life

Further analysis of the responses suggests that the satisfiers are all integral to the performance of the job, and therefore are referred to as job-*content* factors, while the dissatisfiers have to do with the environment surrounding the job itself, and thus are referred to as job-*context* factors. Herzberg called the satisfiers *motivators,* and the dissatisfiers *hygiene factors,* since they serve merely to support the climate for the job-content or motivating factors; therefore, the theory is often called the *motivation-hygiene* theory of job satisfaction.[19] He referred to the dissatisfiers as *replenishment needs* (they always go back to zero), since they must always be provided for, but their importance is realized only when they are inadequate or absent. The motivators are called *growth needs,* since they are the work elements that provide real motivation in this theory of job satisfaction. Generally speaking, the dissatisfiers, or hygiene factors, represent the lower-level needs on Maslow's hierarchy, and the satisfiers, or motivators, are *roughly* analogous to the upper levels of the hierarchy—esteem and self-actualization.

Job Enrichment versus Job Enlargement   Building on this model, Herzberg and his colleagues coined the term "job enrichment" to describe the process of redesigning work in order to build in or emphasize the motivators. They prefer the term "job enrichment" over the older term "job enlargement" because, in their view, enriching the job is quite a different thing from increasing the number of tasks. In fact, they refer to job enlargement as *horizontal job loading,* meaning that the job is redesigned to include additional tasks or operations of about the same difficulty as the core job. They insist that little, if any, real motivation will result from this kind of job redesign, since none of the motivators are accounted for, and that adding additional boring jobs to what is already a boring job may even decrease motivation. In contrast, job enrichment, or *vertical job loading,* involves building into the job the motivators by delegating some of the planning and controlling aspects, as well as the "doing" of the job.[20]

As already noted, there is considerable controversy over the motivation-hygiene theory of job satisfaction. There are many research studies which were designed to test the theory on various occupational groups, and the results are mixed. In general, those studies which follow rather closely the original Herzberg research design tend to support his findings, while those which attempt to validate the theory with more complex research designs tend to develop different, and often opposing, results.

There has been widespread criticism of the theory from within the professional ranks of psychology as well as from practitioners in business and industry. Critics charge that the research design is simplistic and that people tend to tell an interviewer what they think the interviewer wants to hear. Perhaps a more telling criticism is based on people's innate ego-defensiveness, which may make them attribute satisfaction or success to themselves and dissatisfaction or failure to the environment or to other people. Nevertheless, Herzberg and others using his basic research design have replicated the original research on at least 16 different work populations, in addition to the accountants and engineers who composed the first sample, with similar results.[21] And cross-cultural studies, including ones made in the Soviet Union, Finland, and Israel, produce data similar to those gleaned from American work groups.

Robert R. Blake and Jane S. Mouton

Blake and Mouton are known among business people and organization development professionals principally for their development of a unique approach to management and organization development called the *Managerial Grid.*®*

In the late 1950s, when laboratory training came into usage in business organizations, the Grid was developed to meet the need for a means to bridge the gap between pure laboratory training and the real problems and behaviors in the

*Registered trademark of Scientific Methods, Inc.

"back-home" culture of the organization. It also served as a vehicle for experiential learning—of the sort that laboratory training provided—without outside trainers, thereby facilitating wide-scale exposure to the basic laboratory experience on an in-house basis by using trainers from the sponsoring company.[22]

The Managerial Grid's underlying thesis is that two fundamental concerns most often determine managerial styles: people and production. Too often these concerns are polarized in the manager's mind and resultant managerial style. Blake and Mouton hypothesized that the dichotomy of people and production concerns is both unnecessary and dysfunctional. In contrast, the two concerns are actually complementary and mutually reinforcing, since a manager achieves results by and through the efforts of others and since managing human resources effectively to meet organizational objectives is the manager's primary obligation. However, most managers adopt a managerial style that reflects an unbalanced concern for either production or people, with consequent neglect of the other. The Managerial Grid is a systematic program of management and organization development that is designed to increase both the human and the economic or material concerns.[23]

The Grid is actually a graphic representation of the prevalent managerial styles, with concern for people on the nine-point vertical axis and concern for production on the nine-point horizontal axis (see Fig. 8-3). While theoretically there are 81 positions on the Grid, five points, representing five distinct managerial styles, are those used for analysis of the manager's relative concerns and his or her typical mode of managing. Ideally, the 9,9 position is the optimization of both the people and production concerns.

The Six Phases   The Grid is used by managers as an aid in assessing their own managerial styles, as well as in assessing the styles of their fellow participants in a laboratory training session called *phase 1*. While many of the pedagogical techniques in this basic laboratory are akin to those in more traditional laboratory training, the focus is on analysis of managerial behaviors in relation to the job, as contrasted with behavioral patterns in general.

Phase 1, the first of six overlapping and complementary phases, .is called *management development,* since it is designed to increase the *individual* participant's awareness of his or her own managerial behavior and since it does not provide for the larger organization's development.

Phase 2, a logical extension of the basic lab, is called *work-team development* or, commonly, *team building;* in this phase managers begin to apply what they have learned in phase 1 to their back-home work situations with their colleagues. Individual and team standards of excellence are set, and personal and team barriers to their achievement are analyzed in group or team sessions.

Phase 3 is the first phase called *organization development* because it has impact upon the larger organization. It uses techniques similar to those of phase 2, but it is concerned with work units and teams at their interface, whether line and staff or different functional groups (e.g., manufacturing and sales). This phase is referred to as *intergroup development,* and its principal aim is identification and resolution of barriers to intergroup cooperation.

Phase 4, *organizational goal setting,* involves top management in setting long-range organizational improvement goals and the development of strategies to reach them. The phase 4 plans deal with every aspect of the organization's operation, and the plans often detail specific objectives, e.g., 10 percent increase in profit or 10 percent reduction in employee turnover.

Phase 5 is *implementation* of the phase 4 plans, and—depending upon the nature of the various developmental goals, their time span, etc.—phase 5 may extend over several years. In this phase, task forces made up of members of the organization from different functional levels and multiple hierarchical levels are charged with the responsibility for monitoring and implementing the respective plans.

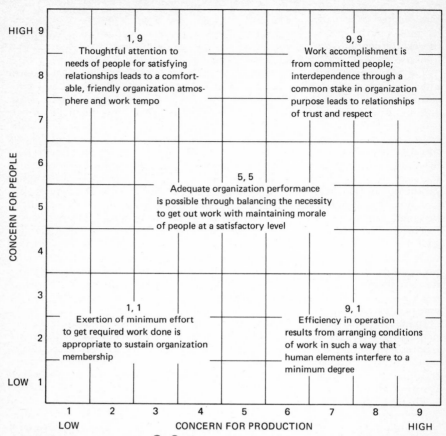

Fig. 8-3   The Managerial Grid.® (© *R. R. Blake and J. S. Morton and Gulf Publishing Company, Houston.*)

Phase 6, the *stabilization* phase, is primarily a measurement and evaluation phase to examine the organization's success in reaching its organizational goals. It involves critique and analysis of failures and shortcomings, as well as remedial action. It further involves recycling of the OD process at any or all of the preceding phases, whenever indicated.[24]

Grid organization development, while set up in six conceptual and implementation phases, is clearly a *systematic* method of organizational improvement that involves both the human and material aspects of the organization's operation. Just as in the phase 1 lab, in which production and people concerns are seen as complementary, the larger Grid program of OD is established to account for both concerns in its long-range effort to revitalize and renew organizations.

Not only is Grid OD designed to be followed in a set of logical sequences, but it also provides for a kind of "operation bootstrap" approach to organizational improvement. Even from phase 1, which often uses line managers as trainers, the OD process calls for participation and leadership from members of the organization, rather than reliance on outside trainers and resources. The people affected by the process are those most intimately involved in its implementation; therefore, the Grid is one form of *organic* organization development. Throughout the six phases, managers concerned with Grid OD use printed guidelines and forms to aid them in their efforts and to ensure that all relevant factors are considered and taken into account. These forms and guidelines are referred to as *instruments,* and the Grid is called *instrumented organization development.*[25]

While the Managerial Grid is intended as a basic format for any organization, the underlying concepts and techniques have been modified into several "spin-offs," with exercises and case materials adapted to the needs of various specialties, notably sales.[26]

Chris Argyris

A recurring theme in research and writing is the effects of organizational life upon the human personality. Because people are social animals, they construct organizations, formal and informal, to meet their need for social contact and to accomplish objectives that individuals cannot accomplish. Since the industrial revolution, there has been an ever-increasing tendency to institutionalize and formalize the aspects of organizations that capitalize on the economy of scale in order to increase output of goods and services.

One outcome, according to Argyris, is the alienation of the persons who make up the organization—a result of the fact that the view of "economic man" underlies and determines the operation of organizations. Ironically, the social and egoistic needs of the people in the organization are largely ignored, when taking them into account could result in the tapping of vast resources of creativity and in the obtaining of employee commitment to organizational objectives. Argyris states that modern organizations are often the source and *cause* of human alienation, apathy, and antagonism because such things as formalized structures, rigid channels of communication, prescriptive job designs, and pyramidal or hierarchical levels of authority are imposed on people in most organizations. People possess psychological energy which could be channeled toward making organizations more effective if these organizations allowed room for individuals to realize their needs. Instead, the psychological energy is often directed at fighting the system, or it is dissipated by individuals' frustrating attempts to realize their own needs within the context of organizational life.

Individual or Organizational Needs?   Argyris sees a fundamental dichotomy between individual and organizational needs, and because individuals by nature tend to place their own needs before those of the organization, neither their needs nor those of the organization are optimally fulfilled. Argyris argues that this will always be the case if individuals perceive that the organization's needs are given precedence over their own, and he contends that this is the case almost universally in contemporary organizations. He proposes as a solution a radical revamping of organizational practices to allow individuals the opportunity for self-realization in order for their psychological energy to be directed more toward organizational objectives.[27]

Argyris's complex prescription for improved organizational health includes an "open" organization, in which there are challenging goals for its members, work that permits some self-actualization, a highly developed sense of trust and supportiveness, interpersonal competence, a democratizing of decision making, and a decentralization of influence and authority, plus an awareness throughout the organization of the interdependence of its parts. He stresses, too, the dynamic nature of organizations, as opposed to a static view. Furthermore, for increased individual and organizational effectiveness, the dynamic nature of both must always be maintained by keeping the organization flexible enough to change, grow, modify, and adapt its internal structure, roles, processes, practices, and objectives to cope with pervasive change in its members and the environment in which it exists.

David C. McClelland

"Achievement" and "motivation" are ubiquitous concepts in the literature of the behavioral sciences that address themselves to the world of work. While some theories posit a connection between the two concepts, e.g., Herzberg's categorization of achievement as a motivating factor, there is a group of behavioral scientists whose central subject is the motivation to achieve. The best known of these researchers and theorists is David C. McClelland, noted for his studies of the degree of *need for achievement* in persons with varying personalities and social histories.[28]

McClelland and his colleagues have over the years studied individuals to determine how strong their need for achievement is. The research is based not so much on empirical observation of the subjects as on their response to several projective tests commonly used by psychologists in assessment of personality traits and in clinical diagnosis, notable H. A. Murray's Thematic Apperception Test (TAT). From among the 20 cards composing the TAT, which are untitled pictures, McClelland selected those with implicit "achievement imagery." The subject taking the TAT is given each card in succession and is asked to study each card and to imagine who the people in the picture are, what their relationships are, what the scene depicts, what led up to this scene, and what will happen afterward. Essentially the subject projects himself or herself into the picture and becomes one of the "actors" in the scene. The interviewer is alert to the various themes that emerge from the subject's narrative. An important theme, of course, is the need to achieve, a weighty personality and behavior variable.

Relevance of Need Achievement   In McClelland's model, persons are characterized as having either high or low need for achievement (nAch), which may be determined by the overall culture in which he or she was raised, familial relationships and experiences, interpersonal relationships, life experiences, etc. The nature of the nAch, as interpreted by McClelland and others who study achievement motivation, is a strong determinant in occupational choice and in the way people respond to the challenges or tasks that arise out of the job. For example, entrepreneurs predictably test out with high nAch, and among nonentrepreneurial types salespeople tend to demonstrate a high degree of need achievement.

People with high nAch typically are found to:

1. Prefer situations in which they can take personal responsibility for finding solutions to problems
2. Tend to set moderate and realistic achievement goals and to take "calculated" risks
3. Want concrete feedback on how well they are doing

There is a tendency for these people to make decisions themselves, not only to have better control over the outcome but to gain personal satisfaction from achieving. They usually are not given to sharing responsibility or to gambling on chance.

In setting moderate—or what they perceive as realistic—goals, people with high nAch are again selecting situations in which their need for achievement can be satisfied. If the goal is too easy to reach, they gain little sense of achievement; if it is too difficult, they are likely to fail and thus derive no sense of achievement.

The desire for concrete feedback on how they are doing is merely another example of such persons' need to do and achieve. Without the feedback, they do not know whether they are successful.

People with high nAch more frequently resume interrupted tasks after interpolated failure than after interpolated success. Once their need for achievement is satisfied—in this case, returning to a task repeatedly until they have completed or mastered it—they tend to go on to other challenges. On the other hand, people with low nAch tend to resume or to repeat tasks after success rather than after failure.

Cultural Determinants of nAch   The achievement motive, as already noted, can be determined by a complex interaction of experiences. The research indicates that the degree of emphasis placed upon achievement per se may vary from culture to culture; e.g., some American Indians test out with higher nAch than others, and the test results underscore the relative emphasis that the respective tribal nations place on achievement. But within a given culture or subculture there are discernible differences between individuals in terms of need for achievement, e.g., how much or how little the parents stressed achievement, what opportunities the individual encounters for psychological success, and how he or she copes with these opportunities. Regardless of the degree of nAch, two significant findings stand out in the diagnostic research on the achievement motive and the empirical research that correlates with the clinical assessments: (1) Rather than being an innate characteristic, the need for achievement is *learned* through a series of reinforcing learning experiences, and (2) it can be taught under the right circumstances.[29]

These two points are the most pungent parts of the achievement-motive research and theory. By first determining the degree of nAch in the individual and then ascertaining the maturational and other learning experiences that were responsible for it, new influences, experiences, and emotional climates can be created to raise the need for achievement. Whereas persons with high nAch require freedom to take risks, pursue challenging goals, and receive their gratification from successful completion of tasks, people with low nAch tend to be more concerned with acceptance by their peers, superiors, and subordinates; with affiliation; and with material rewards for relatively unchallenging tasks. People with high nAch more often seek the *intrinsic* rewards, represented by higher-level needs (à la Maslow), while people with low nAch tend to be motivated by the *extrinsic* rewards that are represented by lower-level needs.

B. F. Skinner

Sporadically throughout the history of psychology as a recognized discipline, the behaviorist school of thought has enjoyed a vogue, only to fall into disfavor with the majority of psychologists after a period of popularity. Virtually every introductory course in psychology includes a review of the early psychological experiments of Pavlov, the Russian physiologist, and his work with dogs. Other names associated with the behaviorist approach, Watson and Thorndike notably, are probably familiar to the layperson too.

Behaviorist psychology, also know as *stimulus-response* (or *stimulus-organism-response*) psychology, is actually a branch of experimental psychology (as contrasted with other branches, such as social and clinical) which is concerned with the kinds of stimuli that will produce a given response or responses and under what conditions. Members of this school tend to be interested in behavior per se and are not very concerned with the more abstract aspects of psychological theory— unconscious motivation, genetic predisposition, etc. Rather, they study the effects of the various stimuli and their ability to induce or modify certain behaviors by accompanying the stimuli with some kind of reward. Once a desired behavior or behavioral pattern is achieved through response to stimuli and rewards, the organism (or subject of the experiment) tends to maintain the behavior, even after the reward is taken away. All that is required, once the behavior is "locked in," is the stimulus associated with the reward, which produces a *conditioned response.*

For example, in the famous Pavlov research, there is the oft-cited experiment in which a bell was sounded simultaneously with the presentation of meat to the dog in his laboratory. After the dog had come to associate the repeated stimulus (bell) with the repeated reward (meat), Pavlov discovered that he could cease providing the meat, and the dog's response (salivation) would still occur each time the bell sounded.

Roots in Stimulus-Response Psychology   The work of B. F. Skinner follows generically the stimulus-response approach, though with some considerable modifications. Like his fellow behaviorists, he is concerned only with overt behavior that can be observed, predicted, and changed. He does not deny the existence of unconscious processes and motives or of genetic and cultural determinants of personality or behavior. He simply does not attempt to study them or take them into account in his highly scientifically controlled research. He states that modification of such things as genetically produced motivations is an extremely difficult and long-term task—because they are fundamentally resistant to change—while modification of overt behavior is relatively much more simple. He feels, therefore, that the minds, energies, and talents of psychologists ought to be directed toward changing behaviors, rather than delving into complex or metaphysical origins of behavior. Moreover, even when it can be shown that some aspect of behavior is due to season of birth, gross body type, or genetic constitution, the fact is of limited use. It may help in predicting behavior, but it is of little value in an experimental analysis or in practical control because such a condition cannot be manipulated.

Focus on Modifying Behavior   Skinner's chief interest is thus the manipulation and control of behavior. He proceeds on the assumption that all behavior is orderly and lawful and that the greater the understanding of cause and effect, the greater the potential for behavioral change, or, to use his term, *behavioral modification.* So far his position is not unlike that of other stimulus-response psychologists. The principal difference, however, is Skinner's emphasis on the *operant,* which he defines as "a response that operates on the environment and changes it." Operants are factors not necessarily directly associated with an applied stimulus—for example, a direct response to a stimulus, after the response has been sufficiently conditioned, such as the reflex of dropping a hot coal. Operants, while also logical and stimulated by something in the environment, cannot always be traced to an observable stimulus—for example, crossing from one side of the street to the other.[30]

The crux of Skinner's method of behavioral modification is *reinforcement.* Whenever a desired behavior occurs, whether in direct response to an applied stimulus or to an operant, it is rewarded, in order to increase the probability of its recurrence. This is positive reinforcement. Conversely, whenever an undesired behavior occurs, it is punished, in order to decrease the probability of recurrence. Frequent reinforcement of the operants will cause the behavior to become conditioned; therefore, the theory is often referred to as *operant conditioning* or *operant reinforcement.* The behavior becomes "locked in" if the reward (or punishment) follows the behavior immediately, because the subject more readily associates the reinforcing factor with the behavior. While this is an important factor in operant reinforcement, an almost equally important consideration is the schedule of reinforcement. Once the subject has associated the reward with the behavior, rewards are withheld and given irregularly. For instance, rather than administer the reward after each demonstration of behavior (which could lessen the subject's association of the operant and its reinforcement), one gives intermittent rewards, which are apt to increase the rate of response: the subject keeps performing the behavior until he or she is rewarded. Variable or intermittent rewards further tend to make the learned response more resistant to extinction.

While most of Skinner's research has been in laboratories using animals, mainly rats and pigeons, he and his disciples show no trepidation in extrapolating and generalizing the applicability of their findings to human behavior. In fact, the Skinnerian model has been adopted in a wide range of applications, including missile control, aspects of space technology, educational technology, treatment of the mentally ill, behavioral assay of psychoactive drugs, and the development of experimental cultures and societies.

Programmed Learning   The training and development professional is likely to be familiar with at least one educational technology that can be traced to Skinner, not only for its rationale and methodology, but also for its actual development as well. One of the first examples of "programmed learning" was developed by Skinner and his associate, J. G. Holland.[31] The Skinnerian principles are readily discernible in programmed learning systems, in which the learner gets immediate feedback on the solution to a problem or the answer to a question. The learner is usually told when an answer is correct (desired response) and instructed to continue (reward), but if the answer is incorrect or insufficient, the instruction is to try again or revert to previous material (punishment). Moreover, until the desired response is given, the learner may not proceed, and no further material will be supplied.

Recently there has been an upsurge of interest in operant reinforcement and behavior modification in business organizations, quite apart from interest in programmed learning. Increasingly, companies are applying Skinnerian techniques to improve on-the-job performance in a systematic way. Employees get instantaneous feedback on, and evaluation of, their performance of daily tasks. If a job is done well, the employee is rewarded for it, possibly by direct recognition from a superior, or possibly by the posting of his or her accomplishments for peers to see. The "reward" may also take the form of giving the employee a preferred work assignment.[32] And in some instances companies are trying to effect that often-heralded ideal of tying financial rewards and promotion to *actual* performance and, further, of associating performance with reward in employees' minds.[33]

Since the focus and aim of operant reinforcement are manipulation and control of behavior, many critics reject the approach as unethical and demeaning of human beings because of the "Big Brother" implications if behavior modification is carried to its logical extreme. Skinner acknowledges this possibility, but he argues that operant reinforcement *ought* to be used to improve broad social conditions and to resolve societal problems.[34]

Eric Berne and Thomas A. Harris

The names of Berne and Harris are not as familiar to most people as the theory of interpersonal relations most often associated with them: *Transactional Analysis.*

In a relatively short time, Transactional Analysis (TA) has captured the imagination and attention of professionals and lay people to an extent enjoyed by few other developments in psychology and psychiatry. This has been due mainly to the publication of Berne's *Games People Play*[35] and, later, Harris's *I'm O.K. —You're O.K.: A Practical Guide to Transactional Analysis,*[36] both of which were "sleepers" in the publishing business. Both had been in print for some time and largely ignored; then suddenly they became runaway best-sellers.

Originally a method to improve face-to-face communication and a framework for analyzing emotional and behavioral states of persons in group therapy, TA rapidly gained adherents outside the realm of psychotherapy.

Transactional Analysis is a system of defining and analyzing what goes on when people communicate and interact. A transaction is defined as any unit of social interaction between two or more persons. The theory holds that the nature of the transaction is determined by the *ego states* at that particular time of the persons interacting. In the TA model there are three ego states: *Parent, Adult, and Child* (the terms are capitalized to differentiate them from actual parent, adult, and child). These ego states are present in everyone and coexist throughout a person's lifetime. Depending upon the individual's degree of maturity, the circumstances under which transactions take place, the type of communication and interaction desired (either consciously or unconsciously), and the relationship of the persons interacting, one of the ego states will be in control at that time and will determine the character of the transaction.

The term "transaction" connotes transfer from one to another, and the transactions are analyzed in terms of a *stimulus* from one person and a *response* from another (see Fig. 8-4).

The *Parent* represents the behaviors that children learn from their actual parents and other authority figures. Their perceptions, feelings, and reactions to these figures are "programmed" into personality and become a permanent part of makeup. The Parent ego state is one of superiority, authority, and command, whether it be nurturing or punitive.

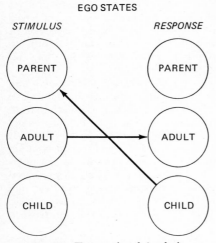

EGO STATES

STIMULUS   *RESPONSE*

Fig. 8-4 Transactional Analysis.

The *Child* reflects early childhood experiences—dependent, immature, inadequate, exploratory, playful; sometimes pliant and passive, sometimes irresponsible and rebellious. Like the Parent ego state, this one is also "programmed" into the personality of the physically mature adult.

The *Adult* ego state is objective, thinking, emotionally mature, and reality-based. In TA theory, it is the only state that is capable of "computerizing" data from previous experiences and the here and now to determine a "sane" and rational approach to transactions, whether acting as stimulus or as response. Only the Adult thinks logically, while the Parent and Child feel and react.

Kinds of Transactions   While an Adult stimulus from one person ideally elicits an Adult response from another person in most transactions involving mature persons, more important than achieving Adult-Adult in all situations and circumstances is achieving a complementary stimulus and response, called a *parallel transaction*. For example, if the stimulus is Parent addressing Child and the response is Child to Parent, there is a parallel transaction, as much as in Adult-Adult, Child-Child, or Parent-Parent. On the other hand, if the transaction is not complementary, it is called a *crossed transaction*. For example, if an Adult stimulus (aiming for an Adult response) gets a Child response, a crossed transaction has occurred.

The significant point is that complementary, or parallel, transactions are conducive to continued communication, so that communication can go on indefinitely; if the transaction is crossed, communication is short-circuited.

TA analyzes individual transactions as they occur, but the TA model is also utilized to interpret interpersonal problems of a continuing nature. Sometimes a person adopts a particular role when dealing with a certain person or with people in general. If the role is not appropriate to the circumstances and the people involved, there is a pattern of crossed transactions that may create long-range interpersonal difficulties (e.g., when someone who is working with peers, in what is supposedly a team situation with its members on an equal footing, assumes a lecturing and criticizing Parent stance toward the others).

Transactional Analysis is designed to open communication between people and to facilitate supportive, cooperative, and productive relationships—authentic, honest interpersonal transactions. TA theory posits that whenever people, for whatever reason, want to avoid authentic relationships, they resort to *games*. A *game*, in TA parlance, is a set of transactions which, on the surface, appear plausible but which really represent ulterior motives or gimmicks for the person playing the game. Games inhibit mutually productive relationships for those involved, but they satisfy some hidden need of the players and contain a "payoff" for them. Games are played in temporary encounters, but they also become part of people's basic behavioral patterns. In either case, players resort to games to avoid real interactions on an adult and authentic level: they are avoiding intimacy.[37]

As previously stated, TA is used to help people develop meaningful and game-free relationships. While Adult-Adult is sought in most instances, people may revert to the Parent or Child ego state in any one of a variety of situations. This may be quite natural if the person is aware of doing it and if it elicits a parallel response. Yet it may be carried to such an extreme that a person's whole personality can be characterized as composed of games, and the resultant *life position*, or world view, is affected. In TA, there are four basic life positions, each representing ego states ranging from "out of touch" to emotionally mature.[38] They are

1. I'm not OK—You're OK (Child).
2. I'm OK—You're not OK (Parent).
3. I'm not OK—You're not OK (pathological).
4. I'm OK—You're OK (Adult).

TA has received a lot of criticism for being too simplistic a model, with all the earmarks of a fad and a panacea, while the issues it addresses are complex and often deep-seated in personality. However, many people report that it has helped to provide them with valuable insights into emotional problems in a short time, as contrasted with some other types of psychotherapy, which may involve long periods, even years.

The nontherapeutic uses of TA have included, since 1969, several adaptations for training and development in business organizations. In fact, it has recently become extremely popular as a development tool in a variety of business situations.[39] Training and development specialists, as well as other managers, frequently report that members of their organizations have found TA an easily understandable and a practical and useful tool for improving their on-the-job relationships; yet the investment of time, effort, and expense required to provide TA training can be minimal.[40]

SUMMARY

Any review of the behavioral science research and writings reveals that there are many aspects to the complex subject of human behavior. There are differing points of view concerning the facets of personality that are the most relevant to human motivation, a point that usually comes through strongly, even in a cursory overview of a few of the leading theories, such as the one presented here. However, it becomes equally clear, despite the variety of approaches, that all are concerned with gaining greater understanding of the causes and forms of human behavior, especially in the context of organizations.

In some instances the contributions of the behavioral sciences offer specific guidelines or "how-to" action steps for improving the motivational climate. In other instances the contributions are in the forms of insights into the inner workings of personality and behavior, which are translations of research findings but which remain in the realm of theory. Even these theoretical or "philosophical" contributions can be useful, insofar as they provide a conceptual framework for understanding people and the behaviors they exhibit.

This is no small consideration for the manager, who, by definition, accomplishes objectives through and with the efforts of other people. In fact, the manager's skill is greatly dependent upon his or her ability to look beyond the overt behaviors of people into the sources and causes of those behaviors. Most managers who are successful in their jobs exhibit an understanding of the human as well as the material side of enterprise. To do this one need not be an "armchair psychologist" or an "office sociologist," although in managing today's work force the inputs of the behavioral sciences are in many ways as relevant as the physical or material concerns facing the manager.

Despite the tremendous advances of modern technology, successful management of the enterprise is greatly dependent upon effective utilization of the most important asset of any organization—the human resources.

While the process of motivation is always complex and often elusive, it is incumbent upon the manager, *at the very least,* to work toward removing the demotivating factors in the organization's culture and in his or her own interpersonal style in dealing with peers, superiors, and subordinates. This is not an easy task, regardless of the degree of sensitivity and insight the manager possesses, but at the heart of the matter is a recognition that motivation is inextricably linked with individual growth and development.

Development of subordinates is properly a line responsibility. But the training and development professional has a special role to fulfill in the process, which consists in keeping abreast of the developments within the field of human behavior and in serving as a valuable resource for the manager who is trying to create a climate in which motivation flourishes.

REFERENCES

1. Allen, Louis A.: *Professional Management: New Concepts and Proven Practices,* McGraw-Hill Book Company (UK) Limited, London, 1973.
2. Rush, Harold M. F.: "What Is Behavioral Science?" *The Conference Board Record,* January 1965.
3. McGregor, Douglas: *Leadership and Motivation* (edited by W. G. Bennis, E. H. Schein, and C. McGregor), The M.I.T. Press, Cambridge, Mass., 1966.
4. Roethlisberger, F., and W. J. Dickson: *Management and the Worker,* Harvard University Press, Cambridge, Mass., 1939.

    Roethlisberger, F., and W. J. Dickson: *Counseling in an Organization: A Sequel to the Hawthorne Research,* Harvard University Graduate School of Business, Boston, 1966.
5. Lewin, Kurt: *Resolving Social Conflicts: Selected Papers on Group Dynamics* (edited by Gertrude W. Lewin), Harper & Row, Publishers, Incorporated, New York, 1948.

    Cartwright, Dorian, and Alvin Zander (eds.): *Group Dynamics: Research and Theory, 2d ed.,* Harper & Row, Publishers, Incorporated, New York, 1960.
6. For a discussion of what constitutes a true group, see Rush, Harold M. F.: "Work Units, Teams . . . or Groups," *The Conference Board Record,* January 1967.
7. Rush, Harold M. F.: *Behavioral Science: Concepts and Management Application,* National Industrial Conference Board, Inc., New York, 1969.
    (This book deals in greater depth with the nature and contributions of the various behavioral sciences, the work and writings of most of the theorists discussed in this handbook, and three approaches to behaviorally oriented training. It includes 10 case studies of business applications of behavioral science technology.)
8. Schein, Edgar H., and Warren G. Bennis: *Personal and Organizational Change through Group Methods,* John Wiley & Sons, Inc., New York, 1965.

9. For a discussion of typical sequences of events in T groups for business people, see Rush, Harold M. F.: *Behavioral Science: Concepts and Management Application,* chap. 3.
10. Marrow, Alfred J.: *Behind the Executive Mask,* American Management Association, New York, 1964.

    (Marrow discusses the rationale for laboratory training for managers and gives an excellent narrative account of behavioral interaction in a "classic" T group.)
11. For a discussion of organization development, see chap. 20 of this handbook. See also:

    Kuriloff, Arthur H.: *Organizational Development for Survival,* American Management Association, New York, 1972.

    Rush, Harold M. F.: *Organization Development: A Reconnaissance,* The Conference Board, New York, 1973.
12. Likert, Rensis: *New Patterns of Management,* McGraw-Hill Book Company, New York, 1961.
13. Likert, Rensis: *The Human Organization: Its Management and Value,* McGraw-Hill Book Company, New York, 1967.
14. Ibid.
15. McGregor, Douglas: *The Human Side of Enterprise,* McGraw-Hill Book Company, New York, 1960.

    (Although McGregor wrote many articles for business and professional journals, *The Human Side of Enterprise* is his only book-length work published before his death. Its influence on the behavioral science movement within the business community is inestimable.)
16. McGregor, Douglas: *The Professional Manager* (edited by Caroline McGregor and Warren G. Bennis), McGraw-Hill Book Company, New York, 1967.
17. Maslow, Abraham H.: *Motivation and Personality,* 2d ed., Harper & Row Publishers, Incorporated, New York, 1970.
18. Maslow, Abraham H.: *Toward Psychology of Being,* 2d ed., Van Nostrand Reinhold Incorporated, New York, 1968.

    Maslow, Abraham H.: *Eupsychian Management: A Journal,* Dorsey Press, Inc., Division of Richard D. Irwin, Inc., Homewood, Ill., 1965.
19. Herzberg, Frederick: *Work and the Nature of Man,* The World Publishing Company, Cleveland, 1966.
20. Rush, Harold M. F.: *Job Design for Motivation: Experiments in Job Enlargement and Job Enrichment,* The Conference Board, New York, 1971.
21. Ford, Robert N.: *Motivation through the Work Itself,* American Management Association, New York, 1969.

    Myers, M. Scott: *Every Employee a Manager: More Meaningful Work through Job Enrichment,* McGraw-Hill Book Company, New York, 1970.

    Work in America, report of a special task force to the Secretary of Health, Education, and Welfare, The M.I.T. Press, Cambridge, Mass., 1973.
22. Blake, Mouton, Barnes, and Greiner: "Breakthrough in Organization Development," *Harvard Business Review,* November–December 1964.

    Rush, Harold M.F: *Organization Development: A Reconnaissance.*
    (The article by Blake et al. reports the development of the Managerial Grid and initial validation research with Humble Oil Company (now Exxon Company, U.S.A.), using a pseudonym for the company. The book by Rush includes a capsule discussion of this development research in a case study which also deals with Humble's experience with several approaches to organizational improvement.)
23. Blake, Robert R., and Jane S. Mouton: *The Managerial Grid,* Gulf Publishing Company, Houston, 1964.
24. Blake, Robert R., and Jane S. Mouton: *Corporate Excellence Diagnosis,* Scientific Methods, Inc., Austin, 1968.
25. For a comparison of instrumented OD with other forms, see Rush: *Organization Development: A Reconnaissance.* This work also compares practices in "OD" and "non-OD" companies.
26. Blake, Robert R., and Jane S. Mouton: *The Grid for Sales Excellence: Benchmarks for Effective Salesmanship,* McGraw-Hill Book Company, New York, 1969.

27. Argyris, Chris: *Integrating the Individual and the Organization,* John Wiley & Sons, Inc., New York, 1964

     Argyris, Chris: *Interpersonal Competence and Organizational Effectiveness,* Dorsey Press, Inc., Division of Richard D. Irwin, Inc., Homewood, Ill., 1962.
28. McClelland, David C., et al.: *The Achievement Motive,* Appleton-Century-Crofts, New York, 1953.
29. McClelland, David C., and David J. Winter: *Motivating Economic Achievement,* The Free Press, New York, 1969.
30. Skinner, B. F.: *Science and Human Behavior,* The Macmillan Company, New York, 1953.
31. Holland, J. G., and B. F. Skinner: *The Analysis of Behavior: A Program for Self-Instruction,* McGraw-Hill Book Company, New York, 1961.
32. Laird, Dugan: "Why Everything Is All Loused Up, Really (and What to Do about It)," *Training in Business and Industry,* March 1971.
     (Laird's article reports on widespread *conscious* application of behavior-modification techniques within Emery Air Freight, a company that pioneered adaptation of Skinnerian principles to day-to-day operations.)
33. "Where Skinner's Theories Work," *Business Week,* Dec. 2, 1972.
34. Skinner, B. F.: *Beyond Freedom and Dignity,* Alfred A. Knopf, Inc., New York, 1972.
     (This best-seller is a defense of Skinner's position on the use of operant reinforcement as a means of control over people to accomplish broad social goals of societies and cultures. It is also an excellent exposition of operant reinforcement theory and method, couched in lay terms.)
35. Berne, Eric: *Games People Play,* Grove Press, Inc., New York, 1964.
36. Harris, Thomas A.: *I'm OK, You're OK: A Practical Guide to Transactional Analysis,* Harper & Row, Publishers, Incorporated, New York, 1967.
37. Berne: op. cit.
38. Harris: op. cit.
39. Rush, Harold M. F., and Phyllis S. McGrath: "Transactional Analysis Moves into Corporate Training," *The Conference Board Record,* July, 1973.
40. Meininger, Jut: *Success through Transactional Analysis,* Grosset & Dunlap, Inc., New York, 1973.

Chapter 9

Determining Training Needs

JAMES H. MORRISON

James H. Morrison *is a Kansas- and Canadian-registered management psychologist who specializes in the design and conduct of executive develop- ment programs. As a lecturer, author, and group leader, he is recognized for his contributions to the advancement of professional skills in the develop- ment and training field. Now residing in his home city of Overland Park, Kansas, he is a Director of Lawrence-Leiter and Co. of Kansas City, Missouri. First selected for inclusion in* American Men of Science *in 1962, he teaches management sciences in five continents.*

The concept of training and development needs emerged originally from a basically simple, oft-asked question in management circles: Do we or do we not have a need for training? Unfortunately, this relatively good question is too often short-circuited into the statement: "We certainly have a training need here!" And therein lies the beginning of a vast wasteland of unnecessary and expensive training programs which have given rise to the odious label of "training programs for training programs' sake."

Educational, training, and developmental programs should be a response to a *need,* not merely a reaction to a problem. When a problem has been identified, the next step is to develop alternative solutions. Sometimes the most feasible answers are better materials, methods, and machines, or more money, rather than a training program.

Definitions

A *training need* may be described as existing any time an actual condition differs from a desired condition in the human, or "people," aspect of organization performance or, more specifically, when a change in present human knowledges, skills, or attitudes can bring about the desired performance.*

This definition would largely rule out, as constituting a training need, the problem of obsolete plant equipment that is unable to manufacture products to tolerance or at economical production rates. If, however, procuring machinery of the latest type to get quality production faster was adopted as a solution, this would

---

*The author includes "attitudes" as a determiner of behavior (and performance) which can be shaped by new experiences often provided by activities included in training programs. See Bloom et al.[1] for a complete identification and classification of training and education objectives in the "affective" domain.

in turn require operator training programs to update the skills of operators using the obsolete equipment so that they could master the new machinery. If a compensation program for store managers is not providing incentives that "motivate" good managers to increase sales results, the answer may be (among many possibilities) an updated incentive program rather than a training program in "how to improve sales results." If the new incentive program is adopted, this might initiate the need for a brief training program in "understanding the new sales incentive program for store managers."

A *developmental need,* as differentiated from a training need by many training professionals, deals with the total growth and effectiveness of the individual, particularly as the person expands realized abilities toward the potential that he or she seems capable of achieving. To others, developmental activities are pointed toward future, usually higher-order, responsibilities than those held by the individual at present.

Organizational or corporate goals often provide clues to future performance requirements and possible training needs. Expansions, new products, new markets, modernization, new system installations, adoption of new managerial techniques or organization structure, revised financial requirements, and new legislation all create a demand for training programs to produce changed behavior.

Broad Approaches

In general, there are three ways to get at training needs:

1. Assuming a performance problem has been identified with a particular group, survey that group for whom training may be needed, their supervisors, the receivers of the product or services provided by that group, and their subordinates, if any. Here the focus is on the group responses which, when analyzed properly, can lead to the preparation of training for individuals, usually in groups.
2. Conduct organizational audits that review production financial, personnel, and other operational data from records and reports to uncover problem areas susceptible to correction through training and/or development. A full functional audit of an area may need to be conducted to get a thorough analysis of the situation. Here the focus is on "results" of activities, and you work backward to the causes to identify training needs.
3. Assess an individual's achievement levels, knowledges, potentials, behaviors, skills, and performance; prepare a needs analysis; and plan development and training specifically for that individual. Similar techniques may be used with groups of individuals, but the focus is on the individual, and the outcome should include individual development plans.

We shall consider each of these approaches, beginning with the survey technique.

SURVEY TECHNIQUES

Survey techniques range from one-page "yes" or "no" response sheets to highly sophisticated methods requiring a multidisciplinary approach—from the "felt-needs" response of the participants to the carefully constructed questionnaires which scientifically cross-check the responses two or more times.

Educational-Needs Survey

The educational-needs survey has, in the 1970s, attained a new level of accuracy and usefulness. The major steps in making the survey are:

1. *Review.*   Review the past and current training programs and the reactions to them. Review the educational and training policies and how they have been

implemented (in-house programs, tuition refund, association-sponsored programs, university short courses, on-the-job training, etc.).

2. *Determine the scope and utilization of the survey.* Who and what will be covered by the survey, and why? Do you want a 100 percent survey, or will a sampling be sufficient? Will you take action on the findings? What are you trying to accomplish by using the survey instead of other needs-determination techniques?

3. *Conduct personal interviews.* Key people on several levels should be interviewed. If the survey is assessing supervisory training needs, interview not only the supervisors who will receive the training but also their supervisors and their subordinates. In the case of a salesperson training-needs survey, interview representative customers and sales managers as well as selected salespeople.

4. *Construct the questionnaire.* The questionnaire should get at the needs of the group for whom the training is intended. If persons other than the group for whom training needs are being determined are to be surveyed, a questionnaire specifically worded for such people should be designed. Test the questionnaire on a sample group in order to "debug" it before printing.

5. *Administer the questionnaire.* It is often best to give the questionnaire on company time so that a 100 percent return (or thereabouts) can be obtained.

6. *Analyze results.* The computer can be used to advantage when there are large amounts of data or when the analysis and correlation of results are complex.

7. *Develop training objectives and design programs.* This step is covered extensively in other chapters of this handbook.

The Employee Attitude Survey

The attitude survey has long been used as a method of uncovering training needs. Employee attitude surveys frequently are conducted to obtain reactions to supervisory and managerial personnel for use in designing management training programs.

Presurvey investigations are necessary. There must be some idea of the "openness" allowed in the company. (How receptive and nonpunitive is the company atmosphere in terms of individual ideas, feelings, and attitudes?) Usually an organization brings in a third party with an objective view to conduct an employee attitude survey. The respondents in an attitude survey should feel free to express their true attitudes. Care must be taken in forming the questionnaire to avoid questions that lead to preconceived answers.

Currently, questions about worker and managerial satisfactions with employment are often grouped within a structure of leading motivational theories. When the motivational frame of reference is à la Herzberg, for example, questions relating to job satisfactions and dissatisfactions are designed to explore the "hygiene" and "motivator" job factors and then are sprinkled throughout the attitude questionnaire. Using computer approaches, the clusters of questions about each factor can be analyzed and cross-checked to determine with fair accuracy the extent of the satisfactions or dissatisfactions. The steps for devising this survey should be similar to those for designing the educational training-needs survey. It is best to correlate answers with normative, or demographic, information. This information should be asked for in such a way that employees can maintain their anonymity if there is any question or fear of reprisal. Once the responses have been analyzed, the training department should recommend any training that might be appropriate.

The Consumer, or Customer, Survey

Sometimes needs exist which are not apparent to those involved in the production of the goods or services, but which might cause friction among the receivers of the service or the product. Such problems are revealed by means of a consumer, or customer, survey. The design of customer surveys follows the pattern of other surveys:

1. A review of the past and the current situation leads to a determination of the objectives of the survey.
2. Will you question only those who have already been or who are presently customers, or will you question people who are not now customers to try to find out why not and how they could be persuaded to become customers?

The format should be simple, since customer responses are apt to be difficult to obtain because the benefits to be derived are not obvious. The same techniques of correlating answers should be followed as those used in the educational-needs survey. The value of the survey lies in the interpretation of the answers received and in the follow-up actions. Data should be obtained on what changes are indicated, how strongly they are indicated, and whether making the changes is feasible.

Responses may indicate areas of training needs (the case of the permanent employee who is not able to furnish information about stock items) or possibly the need for closer supervision (the case of the employee who handles sales indifferently or who alienates customers). Analysis of the results obtained from a customer survey can uncover areas of training needs that have not been noticed within the organization.

The Delphi Technique

The Delphi technique is a method of systematically soliciting, collecting, evaluating, and tabulating expert opinions, usually in long-range forecasting. It is conducted anonymously in order to reduce distorting factors common in committee decisions, such as the unwillingness to contradict publicly expressed opinions, the bandwagon effect of majority opinions, or the impact of a highly articulate or powerful advocate of a particular stance.

The Delphi technique works typically as follows:

1. An opinion is asked on a particular question or problem. The statistical results are then gathered, indicating the distribution of responses, the median response, and the interquartile range (the interval containing the middle 50 percent of the responses).
2. The results of this tabulation are again distributed to respondents, who are asked to reconsider their answers and revise them if they want to. Respondents whose answers are outside the interquartile range are asked to state briefly why they feel their answers were much lower or much higher than the majority of opinions. This produces a responsibility toward "extreme" answers. It also allows an opportunity to justify and defend an answer.
3. The statistical results of the second survey are gathered (and typically there is a move toward the median). The reasons for the extreme answers are also summarized and presented.
4. These results are redistributed a third time, and respondents are asked to revise their opinions once more if they choose. The median of the final responses gathered is taken to represent the group consensus.

Based on a combination of experience, judgment, and a sort of intuitive perception, the Delphi technique has been described as a "quantitative intuition." In terms of assessing training needs, it would probably be most useful for forecasting future training needs in relation to long-range company plans or objectives.

Problem Survey

The problem inventory is usually administered to a group of people for whom training is to be provided. It is therefore a "problem-centered" approach that leads to practical, specifically targeted program planning.

In applying the technique, for example, at a meeting of district sales managers for whom training needs are being assessed, a supply of 3 × 5 cards is distributed to each sales manager. The group is instructed to write down problems they are now facing in their districts—one problem to a card. The best way to develop problem statements is to begin them with the words "How to. . . ."

The group is asked to avoid large, catchall, umbrella-type statements, such as "how to increase sales in my district next year." Far better are more specific problems, such as "how to identify new prospects for product X." The managers are requested to write down as many problems as they can think of for which they would like some practical ideas for solutions. The cards are then picked up, and a small committee, including a training staff member, sorts through the problems, clustering them into groups and arranging them into a logical sequence. "Commonality" can be quickly determined by the number of cards identifying a particular problem, although a problem mentioned only once may turn out to be a most insightful guide for preparing objectives and program subject matter outlines. The latter can be ensured by providing the committee members with a list of the "once-mentioned" problems prior to a committee meeting. Ask the committee members to consider each problem statement as to its originality, creative insight, and possible value for inclusion in the training. At the next meeting, discuss each of the problems on the list, as a group, before discarding any.

ORGANIZATIONAL AUDITS

Audits may be conducted of organizational units and may deal with activities, inputs, outputs, costs, or efficiency and effectiveness studies. Operating records and reports are examined and verified. Systems and procedures are analyzed. Deficiencies exposed and improvement potentials assessed often provide a basis for planning education and training activities. The needs determinations discussed in this section emerge from "results."

Efficiency and Production Records

A wide variety of operating figures may be audited to determine trends and variations from period to period, from department to department, or from division to division. In some instances comparative figures are available, enabling an organization to compare its performance with that of the industry as a whole. Some of the common ratios or indexes are:

1. Return on investment (or return on invested assets)
2. Actual hours (or dollars) compared with standard
3. Piecework earnings or points
4. Overhead cost ratios (burden)
5. Labor costs and variances
6. Quality records
7. Reject and scrap rates or costs
8. Output per worker-hour
9. Ratio of salary costs to sales (or units produced)
10. Units of sales per salesperson

Personnel Records

Several commonly available personnel statistics may be referred to in the process of determining training needs. The following list is suggested primarily because of the frequency of availability.

1. *Personnel Turnover.*   Turnover is commonly expressed in terms of the monthly separation rate or the annual separation rate.

$$\text{Monthly separation rate (\%)} = \frac{\text{total separations for month}}{\text{average number on payroll for month}} \times 100$$

The average number on the payroll for the month is determined by adding the number on the payroll at the beginning of the month to the number at the end of the month and dividing by 2. This monthly figure is convertible to an annual figure by the following formula:

$$\text{AR} = \text{MSR} \times \frac{365}{\text{actual}}$$

2. *Absence Rate.*   The absence rate includes both justifiable and unexcused absences, but it is an index that serves to highlight trends and provide a comparison with other companies in the same industry.

$$\text{AR} = \frac{\text{worker-days lost per month}}{\text{worker-days worked plus worker-days lost per month}}$$

3. *Accident Statistics.*   The American National Standards Institute provides the following formulas:

$$\text{Frequency rate} = \frac{\text{number of lost-time injuries} \times 1,000,000}{\text{number of worker-hours of exposure}}$$

$$\text{Severity rate} = \frac{\text{number of time charges in days of lost time} \times 1,000}{\text{number of worker-hours of exposure}}$$

4. *Grievances.*   There are no official formulas for indexing grievances. The in-house versions deal with such variables as number, rate (number within a given interval), and qualitative evaluation of type of complaint. Types of grievances may be classified according to (*a*) physical origin that can be verified by observation ("the machine won't work"); (*b*) physical origin, but depending on employees' subjective reactions ("the work is too hard" or "the work is too messy"); and (*c*) subjective origin expressing employees' hopes and fears ("they don't recognize ability around here"). The number of grievances not settled by supervisors at their own levels is another criterion used.

Functional Audits

Functional audits can be conducted to review the effectiveness of almost any functional unit of the organization: marketing audit, EDP audit, and many others, including an audit of how the management development function is being administered.

Using the management development audit as an example, the usual approach is to develop a checklist of questions to answer in order to determine the extent and quality of the management development efforts in the organization. Typically, two major aspects of the function are assessed, and 15 to 30 questions are developed in order to explore each aspect:

1. What has been accomplished in organizational long-range planning, including assumptions, objectives, potentials, and probable trends, which will serve as a basis for planning for managerial development
2. What has been accomplished in the past (both activities and results) in the development of managers

When the answers to the questions have been obtained, a report is prepared which serves as an evaluation of the current status of management development activities.

Skills Inventory A skills inventory not only permits an organization to make fullest use of the skills and abilities of the entire work force but also can guide the training director to an awareness of in-house deficiencies which can be corrected by training. A skills inventory, at first glance, may be regarded as a compilation of technical skills and knowledges most useful in technologically oriented industries, but it is equally useful in cataloging managerial experience and abilities. When the aspirations of the individuals are recorded, as well as their achieved skills, this can serve as an assurance to each individual that career goals are being considered as well as education and experience.

Manpower Planning Data

The manpower planning function in an organization typically collects and analyzes data of immediate usefulness to training and development managers. Two types of data are of major importance:

1. *Management Replacement Organization Charts.* These are usually prepared annually to give a quick, overall indication of the need for trained individuals to replace the current managerial team. They consist of organization charts of the management levels, with the "backups," if designated, being identified as to when they will be ready for the responsibilities toward which they are being pointed (see Fig. 9-1).

2. *Annual Personnel Inventory.* The annual personnel inventory seeks to record present performance, future potential, promotions or transfers in the near future, and what kind of developmental activities should be provided each individual. It is most often developed by a committee which has access to the performance records of each individual and consists of management people who are familiar with the individual's work as well as his or her supervisor. It is confined largely to management positions, but key positions, such as in engineering or sales, may be included.

A form which permits summarization of the information is important for giving a quick, overall visualization of the situation (see Fig. 9-2). The *kind* of management development activities deemed essential by the committee is coded (Fig. 9-2, column 21) to alert the individual's supervisor to the planning activities required during the coming year (see Fig. 9-3).

INDIVIDUAL NEEDS DETERMINATIONS

A third major concept in determining training needs is the "individual" approach, although this may range from a personal interview to observation of a person in a group situation. The end result of the use of any of these methods is primarily the design of a developmental plan or an activity for a specific person. Even though the training recommendations for an individual may include structured group learning activities, the emphasis is still on obtaining information from, or about, the individual in order to develop a tailored plan for that person.

The Interview

The personal interview has long been the basis of tailoring a developmental program to the needs of the individual. It is customary to develop a structured interview covering questions about:

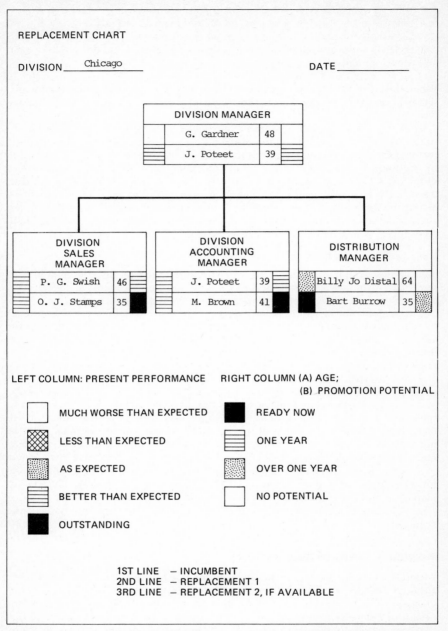

Fig. 9-1 Replacement chart (With the common availability of black-and-white reproduction equipment, the most popular method of coding is shading and hatching.)

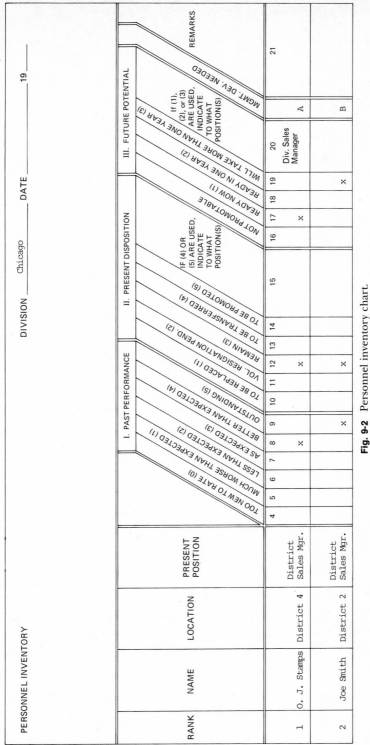

Fig. 9-2 Personnel inventory chart.

1. Problems encountered on the job
2. Improvements that could be made in the department
3. The most liked and least liked aspects of the job
4. Accomplishments on the job
5. Relations with associates, subordinates, and supervisors
6. Outside interests
7. Personal goals and career goals
8. Felt needs for acquiring additional skills or knowledge

It is extremely important that confidentiality of the interview be assured. Accordingly, an outside psychologist with the privilege of confidentiality is sometimes

---

C. Needs training and development in day-to-day aspects of the job. Can be handled by his supervisor through individual training and coaching. (Local programs and courses to improve technical skills may be recommended under a tuition refund plan.)

B. Needs C, plus special courses, seminars, executive development programs, etc. These may be outside-the-company programs, or they can be presented internally. (Courses usually of one week duration or less.)

A. Needs C and B, plus programs for planned growth in various functions in the Company. Planned rotation, special assignments, etc., should be specifically planned for "A" class people. Also, top level executive development programs at universities, usually of three weeks duration, or longer, may be included in the program.

Fig. 9-3 Classification of A, B, and C management development activities.

employed. Information requested to be kept off the record by the interviewee should be so treated, but a written report and training recommendations should be prepared by the interviewer.

When the employee's immediate supervisor conducts such an interview, it is usually held in conjunction with the periodic work review and planning discussions.

As with educational-needs surveys, it is wise to interview people from at least three levels. In addition to the person for whom the training plan is being prepared, interview his or her supervisor and subordinates. In the case of programming for salespeople or public contact people, interviews should be conducted with customers or the receivers of services.

The Training-Needs Questionnaire

A favorite "quick and dirty" method is to develop a list of skills required to do the job effectively and then to ask employees to check those in which they believe they need training. The person completing the questionnaire is identified by name so that the information can become part of an individual developmental plan (see Fig. 9-4).

In more sophisticated applications for managers, the checklist is a much more detailed listing of tasks a manager is normally expected to perform (see also the references to task analysis in Chapter 12, "Instructional Systems"). Instead of simple "Yes," "?," "No" responses, each manager is asked to give two items of information about each task:[2]

1. The relative importance of the task as the manager's own training need on a four-point scale ranging from "not important" to "very important"
2. The relative performance *frequency* of each task on a four-point scale ranging from "never" to "often"

The obtained data are treated statistically to provide training priority levels based on estimated training *importance* and *frequency* of utilization of a given task.

TRAINING NEEDS CHECKLIST

Instructions: Please read the list over thoroughly before answering. Check "Yes" if you believe you need training in that skill, either for use in your current job or for getting ready for promotion to a better position. Circle the "question mark" for uncertain. Check "No" if you feel no need for training in that area.

1. How to supervise minority workers. . . . . Yes   ?   No

2. How to train subordinates efficiently . . . . Yes   ?   No

3. How to handle discipline problems. . . . . Yes   ?   No

4. How to conform to OSHA safety requirements in my department . . . . Yes   ?   No

5. How to develop better objectives with my subordinates. . . . . Yes   ?   No

6. How to improve my personal productivity . . . . Yes   ?   No

7. How to implement participative management concepts . . . . Yes   ?   No

Fig. 9-4 Training-needs checklist.

Needs-Analysis Rating Method

A needs analysis is best accomplished jointly by the person for whom the analysis is being made and one other person—usually his or her supervisor, but sometimes a personnel counselor. Basic to good needs-analysis rating is the preparation of an analytic checklist based on a sound concept of the functions and responsibilities of the position.

For example, in the case of managerial positions, it is possible to list the significant skills in each of the major management functions, which are then rated as to the individual's mastery of them. Those which are considered "developmental needs" are identified, and a plan is devised whereby the person can acquire satisfactory competence in them (see Fig. 9-5).

Achievement Testing

Separate from the problem of personality, trait, aptitude, and attitudinal testing, with the attendant difficulties in establishing predictive, construct, and content validities, is the relatively straightforward testing of achievement. A comprehensive achievement test can provide for proper placement in the sequence of courses leading to a qualifications status required by the trade, the profession, the law, or the educational institution. The process of "testing out" permits elimination of senseless repetition of training for skills already acquired and, at the same time, reveals the magnitude of the training job yet to be accomplished.

TRAINING NEEDS ANALYSIS

EXPLANATION:

S = Outstanding Strength

M = Meets Requirements or
Not Applicable to Job

D = Development Need

SUPERVISOR: Discusses strengths with subordinate during postappraisal interview.

INCUMBENT: Discusses needs and goals with Supervisor during postappraisal interview.

	Management activity	S	M	D
PLANNING	Promoting improvements			
	Developing original ideas			
	Applying new ideas			
	Gathering information			
	Analyzing information			
	Planning objectives			
ORGAN-IZING	Organizing ability			
	Selecting people			
	Utilizing people			
	Delegation			
DIRECTING AND COORDINATING	Coaching			
	Training and developing people			
	Oral expression			
	Conducting meeting			
	Written expression			
	Keeping supervisor informed			
	Keeping subordinates informed			
	Achieving results through others			
	Personal acceptance by others			
	Setting standards for others			
CONTROLLING	Maintaining control of operations			
	Willingness to follow-up			
	Measuring results of operation			
	Control of costs			
	Control of quality			
	Expanding income			
	Improving net earnings			
OTHER				

Signed: _____ Date: _____
Incumbent

Fig. 9-5 Schoeller training-needs-analysis form. *(Adapted from a form created by V. Donald Schoeller appearing originally in a private paper entitled "The Management Process.")*

Achievement tests can deal with knowledge or skill levels, or with both at the same time. The proficiency test, in which a sample of the actual task to be accomplished on the job is to be performed, is one of the most powerful demonstrations of skill mastery, or lack of it, available today. Such a test must incorporate the following elements:

1. A description of the product or service or result to be accomplished during the test
2. A standard, or measure, with limits and tolerances (how much, how well, or the measurable effect), of what is to be accomplished during the test
3. Under what conditions the test is to be taken (the "givens," tools, time, distractions)—in general, the assumptions about the test environment

Proficiency tests are not confined to basic manual skills and information, but can be applied to higher-order cognitive skills or analysis, synthesis, evaluation, and complex decision making.

Performance Appraisal Data

Since the earliest days of merit rating, the review of performance evaluation data has been essential to planning performance improvement activities. Members of the personnel training staff may review all performance rating sheets and tabulate weaknesses, or poor ratings. In the case of first-line supervision, a frequent appearance of comments such as "poor skill in training subordinates," "does not communicate well," or even "poor initiative" would be the basis for developing appropriate supervisory courses in such subjects as how to train, communications, or leadership.

As Management by Objectives programs became increasingly popular, performance evaluation tended to deal more with *results* than with traits or functions, and it became more difficult to plan subject matter courses which would correct performance that was "below expectations" (see Chapter 13, "Management by Objectives"). The search for ways to deal more effectively with the analysis of behavior leading to specific results led to one significant approach, which in turn was incorporated into new styles of performance evaluation devices: the *critical incident method.*

Critical incidents are specific behaviors that have been found to make the differences between success and failure in carrying out a job. Furthermore, there are effective and ineffective critical incidents. An ineffective critical incident leads to significantly worse-than-average performance (waste, scrap, time lost, omissions, errors, etc.); an effective critical incident leads to significantly better-than-average performance (production, services, customer satisfaction, etc.).

Critical incidents are collected from incumbents in the job as well as their supervisors and other personnel involved in the activity. After establishing that an incident is truly *critical,* the behavior descriptions are grouped into major performance areas and into subgroups within major performance areas. These are next incorporated into a performance evaluation record with provisions for checking both effective and ineffective critical incidents as they are observed by the supervisor. The record is maintained during predetermined performance periods as the behavior is evidenced to provide a factual basis for performance review.[3] An example of a subgroup of one major performance area for a department manager is shown in Fig. 9-6. Each time an incident is observed, the manager records the date and the item identification letter and makes a brief note about the participants and the outcomes (see also Chapter 35, "The Case Method").

How can this information be applied to training needs? First, the supervisor of the person being rated has a basis for individual coaching and on-the-job training. Second, the personnel training staff can review the history of the progress of each individual by reviewing the sequence of the past performance evaluation reports. Third, when a sufficient number of employees in a given job category exhibit ineffective critical incident behaviors or when a less than reasonable amount of effective critical incident behaviors are being recorded for them, the personnel training staff can organize courses designed to produce more effective behavior patterns in that job category.

Major Performance Area: I. Managing the Work of Subordinate Supervisors

Subgroup: A. Setting Objectives

1. Critical Incidents

Effective	Innefective
a. Asked experienced supervisor to prepare objectives in advance of objective setting discussion. b. Provided information about corporate and division goals to subordinate prior to interview. c. Developed yardsticks for measuring results of a targeted objective.	a. Permits use of words like "improve" or "upgrade" in objectives. b. Provided too short a time to adequately discuss objectives experienced. c. Told subordinate the objectives he was to accomplish.

Date	Item	What Happened	Date	Item	What Happened

Fig. 9-6   Critical incident performance evaluation record.

Observation and Measurement of Behavior

Instrumented devices that provide a measure of individual behavior—ranging from tests of attitudes or knowledges to self-reports—are increasingly a basis for revealing training needs to the individuals most concerned with the learning process—those who need to change themselves. The vehicles may be opinionnaires, tests, simulations, competitive games, or any devices which permit measurement of individual and/or team results.

Tests and Questionnaires   Standardized tests have the advantage of specific scoring systems which lead to a measure of the degree of mastery of the subject matter content. Sometimes the standardized scoring system based on so-called right answers is no longer applicable because of the passage of time or because the conditions in an organization differ from those contemplated by the author of the test. Therefore, whenever possible, it is best to develop your own "right-answer" key to the test by applying statistical processes to answers given by the relatively more successful individuals in a given job category. This has been done in the case of tests such as *How Supervise?* [4] as well as nonstandardized tests such as those found in the *The Human Side of Management.* [5]

The procedure for determining training needs and helping each individual confront the reality of his or her own deficiencies is as follows:

1. Give the test or questionnaire prior to any discussion of the subject. The key factor is to get *written* commitment to an answer.
2. Ask the individuals to discuss in small groups their answers to each question and their reasons for answering as they did. Tell them to listen to the others in the group as they discuss their own answers and the reasoning behind them.
3. Have the individuals score their questionnaires according to the right-answer key developed by successful managers in your organization.
4. Plot the scattergram of scores for the entire group so that individuals can see where their scores lie in relation to the range of scores of the other members of the group.

This process makes evident to each individual his or her relative mastery of the concepts covered by the test questions in a private but highly impactful way (see also Chapter 10, "The Role of Testing in Training and Development").

Team versus Individual Interactions   A slightly different version consists of having each person respond in writing to specific items; this might include ranking the importance of, or priorities involved in, managerial decisions. Small groups, or teams, are asked to discuss the questions and arrive at a group consensus on each item. Scores are computed and team effectiveness is evaluated by completing information for each team as shown in Fig. 9-7. In Fig. 9-7, while team 3 is the highest-scoring team (the "winner"), it is decidedly the poorest in production efficiency.[6] While there are implications for teamwork training, participants are also aware of their own individual scores and of their approximate standing relative to the scoring of the others.

Simulations and Games   Teams are formed to "play" a competitive game with measurable outcomes. At the conclusion of the play, each group is asked to examine its behaviors during the game. Frequently, observers are appointed who report on individual behaviors and group processes during a feedback period. Additionally, each member may be asked to comment on the contributions of his or her teammates, sometimes using a rating sheet on which are recorded in measurable units specific items of behavior. Thus the members of the team provide feedback to every other person on the team, which can provide a basis for forward planning of individual developmental activities. This is best assured if the personnel training staff administers the games and organizes and

#1	#2	#3	#4	#5	#6
Team Number	Average of Individual Scores on the Team (Perfect score = 100)	Team Consensus Score	Gain-Loss Team vs. Average (Col. 3 less Col. 2)	Possible Improvement (Perfect Score less Col. 2)	Production Efficiency of Team (Col. 4 ÷ Col. 3 X 100)
#1	62	70	+8	38	+11.43
#2	75	68	−7	25	−10.29
#3	85	75	−10	20	−13.33

Fig 9-7   Scoring team results.

records the feedback data for later use in individual developmental planning conferences.

MISCELLANEOUS METHODS

A list of devices for determining training needs would be incomplete without some mention of the following, sometimes extremely important methods.

Personal Observations   Get out where the action is! Walk the mill, ride the territory, and talk with workers, supervisors, customers, and field personnel. Look for small but important indicators of housekeeping standards, hazards, time-wasting practices, and overtones of conflict versus cooperation. A heightened awareness of what is going on in the human side of the business is essential.

Training Advisory Committee   If an advisory committee is appointed, ask for representative and typical members of various segments of the organization as well as outstanding leaders. Avoid "has-beens" and semiretired personnel who can easily be spared from their regular duties. Plan the agenda carefully and distribute it in advance to committee members. Be sure to record decisions and recommendations and distribute them to top management as well as to members of the committee.

Requests from the "Brass"   Top-management requests for training can be a curse or a blessing. If the request results from a personal feeling, even whim, of a top executive without the existence of a clear-cut need, it can divert your energies from more important training activities. If the request involves a bona fide, high-priority need, the top executive can give you the support you want for the training effort. Ask questions of the "brass," such as What do we want these people to be able to do? What results are we really trying to accomplish? Is training the best solution, or are improved equipment, materials, or methods more likely to give us the desired results in the operation?

The important point is: Don't ignore requests from top executives, for they can be the strongest supporters of high-priority training; also, don't overreact to every suggestion. It may be only a casual thought, and you don't want to launch a major training program on the basis of every remark dropped, even if it is made by the president of the firm.

TRAINING OBJECTIVES

Once specific training needs have been identified, training objectives should be formulated. A definition of a training need is not, per se, a statement of a training objective. The need must be restated as a training objective or as a series of training objectives.

Many kinds of objectives have been loosely labeled "training objectives" in the past, with little thought given to the relative complexities of attaining them. The major classifications of objectives which have been considered training objectives are:

1. *Operational Objectives.*   These are measured in terms of organizational outputs, such as increased sales, reduced costs, and improved productivity.

2. *Performance Objectives.*   These have to do with an individual's performance, such as achieving higher departmental efficiency, staying within budget limitations, and attaining performance objectives of various kinds.

3. *Instructional Objectives.*   These can usually be measured at the end of the training program by some sort of (one would hope) objective "test." Robert Mager has provided a classic explanation of instructional objective writing.[7]

4. *Reaction Objectives.*   These are usually subjective in nature and are obtained by asking the participants to report their feelings and reactions to the training

program. There is considerable merit in obtaining feedback from participants for use in improving the program content and instructional methods. In many cases, however, these may be considered "training director" objectives when reaction ratings (sometimes referred to as "happiness" ratings) are termed "evaluations" and are used to justify training expenditures or to sell training to top management.

5. *Personal Growth Objectives.* These may cover some, all, or none of the preceding objectives and may or may not be related to measurable results. These objectives have to do with feelings of self-confidence, self-competence, enhanced self-image, and other aspects of self-realization.

The major point is: In the 1970s personal growth objectives have emerged as more important than professional trainers had previously considered them. Increasingly, the key to assuming the maximum effectiveness of the program is to have program developers identify individual growth objectives and build them into the training design. The participant easily identifies the advantage to the organization in most training activities. The additional element of providing an opportunity for the attainment of personal growth objectives will help participants answer the pervasive, human question of "what's in it for me—as an individual, as a human being, as a person." If participants can find honest, satisfying answers to this question within the framework of training programming, the basic problem of creating positive motivation toward organizational training may be largely solved in the last quarter of the twentieth century.

REFERENCES

1. Bloom, B. S., D. R. Krathwohl, and B. B. Masia: *Taxonomy of Educational Objectives,* handbook II, *Affective Domain,* David McKay Company, Inc., New York, 1964.
2. Stewart, William J.: "Determining First-Line Supervisory Training Needs," *Training and Development Journal,* pp. 12–20, April 1974.
3. Mayeske, George W., Francis L. Harmon, and Albert S. Glickman: "What Can Critical Incidents Tell Management?" *Training and Development Journal,* pp. 20–34, April 1966.
4. File, Q. W., and H. H. Remmer: *How Supervise?* The Psychological Corporation, New York, 1948.
5. Morrison, James H.: *The Human Side of Management,* Addison-Wesley Publishing Company, Inc., Reading, Mass., 1971.
6. Blake, Robert R., and Jane Srygley Mouton: "What Is Instrumented Learning?" *Training and Development Journal,* pp. 12–20, January 1972.
7. Mager, Robert F.: *Preparing Instructional Objectives,* Fearon Publishers, Inc., Belmont, Calif., 1962.

BIBLIOGRAPHY

Byham, W. C.: "The Assessment Center as an Aid in Management Development," *Training and Development Journal,* December 1971.
Finkle, Robert B., and William S. Jobes: *Assessing Corporate Talent: A Key to Managerial Manpower Planning,* Interscience Publishers, a division of John Wiley & Sons, Inc., New York, 1970.
Kirkpatrick, Donald: *Practical Guide for Supervisory Training and Development,* Addison-Wesley Publishing Company, Inc., Reading, Mass., 1971.
Mager, Robert F., and Peter Pipe: *Analyzing Performance Problems,* Fearon Publishers, Inc., Belmont, Calif., 1970.
Odiorne, George S.: *Training by Objectives,* The Macmillan Company, New York, 1970.

Chapter **10**

The Role of Testing
in Training and Development

ALBERT P. MASLOW

Albert P. Maslow *is Director of the Center for Occupational and Profes-
sional Assessment, Educational Testing Service, in Princeton, New Jersey.
He has had extensive experience in personnel management and research,
especially in the public service as Chief of the Personnel Research and
Development Center of the U.S. Civil Service Commission. Dr. Maslow, a
University of Maryland Ph.D., consults with a number of personnel management staffs; he has contributed to professional journals and to a book,*
Recruitment and Selection in the Public Service. *His academic experience includes part-time appointments at the University of Maryland and
George Washington University, and he has participated in numerous
seminars and special programs such as workshops in 1972 and 1973 on
improving and validating personnel selection, conducted by the International Personnel Management Association, and in the ETS programs for
continuing education. A fellow of the American Psychological Association,
he has been on the Executive Council of the International Personnel
Management Association. His professional honors include the Cushman
Award of the IPMA Eastern Region (1965) and the Distinguished Service
Award of the American Psychological Association's Division of Psychologists in Public Service (1959).*

In managing a training and development program, the training director must
answer many questions: Which of the employees are to be trained? Where do
these employees now stand in relation to the desired outcomes of training? How
can it be determined whether the trainees are progressing? How can it be
recognized when, and how fully, the trainees have met the training objectives? Is
the training, in fact, useful to the employee's career and to the company's business
purposes? Do the skills or knowledge attained at the end of training stand up well
over time, or are they merely transitory gains?

In answering these and many other questions, the training director must apply
measurement tools and concepts. These may be informal judgments of employees
and their records or partly structured interviews. They may include a more
systematic "test," that is, an assessment procedure in which prescribed problems or
questions are presented to the employee in a standard way and are designed so as
to stimulate responses which can be evaluated objectively. In general, all these
procedures are expected to yield cues or information based on past or present

behavior of the employee from which dependable predictions can be made as to how he or she will probably behave in some future situation.

The growth of testing and its widespread impact on our society—and the many uses (and abuses) of personnel tests—are well known to training specialists. In recent years, however, the national efforts toward equal employment opportunity, based on Title VII of the Civil Rights Act of 1964 as amended by the Equal Employment Opportunity Act of 1972, have focused greater attention on the role of testing.

Tests and related assessment methods in business and industry have over the years been especially prominent in the hiring process; as a result, the most direct and immediate impact of the law and federal regulations has been on selection procedures. Yet the guidelines on employee selection procedures issued and enforced by the Equal Employment Opportunity Commission, the Office of Federal Contract Compliance, and the Bureau of Apprenticeship, Department of Labor, apply to "tests" which are designed not just to measure eligibility for hire but also to use in decisions concerning transfer, promotion, membership, training, referral, or retention. The term "test" as defined in these guidelines is almost unlimited. It encompasses not only the typical paper-and-pencil multiple-choice objective test but also any measure of intellectual abilities; of mechanical, clerical, and other aptitudes; of dexterity and coordination; of knowledge and proficiency; of interests; and of attitudes, personality, or temperament. The term also includes specific personal history requirements, scored interviews, rating scales, application forms, etc., and all other formal scored procedures of assessing job suitability. Beyond these more or less structured procedures, the guidelines also extend to unscored procedures such as casual interviews or judgments based on informal appraisal of application forms.

The specific guideline that directly affects the use of testing procedures in connection with training and career development is the provision that the use of any "test" which adversely affects an employee who is in one of the classes protected by Title VII—that is, classes defined according to race, color, religion, sex, or national origin—constitutes illegal discrimination unless performance on the test can be shown to be an effective and relevant basis for the personnel decision that is made.

Stated simply, what the laws and current regulations mean for training specialists is that any employer who is in an industry affecting commerce and who regularly employs at least 15 persons may not discriminate against any individual because of race, color, religion, sex, or national origin in relation to apprenticeship or training, and retraining, including on-the-job training programs. In practice, this means that employees or applicants may allege that they have been denied access to training opportunities on the basis of such group membership; the burden then shifts to the employer to demonstrate that the methods used in selecting and rejecting persons for training and career development opportunities are in fact fair and not biased against members of such protected groups.

It should be quite obvious, therefore, that employers and their training specialists should at the very least be fully familiar with the current regulations of the Equal Employment Opportunity Commission and other regulatory agencies concerned with carrying out the provisions of the Civil Rights Act of 1964 as amended and that they must become much more sophisticated in the development, selection, and use of assessment procedures in connection with training and career development.

Tests have had a widespread acceptance by our society as one basis for decisions affecting access to school and work, as well as to other activities such as driving an automobile. The use of tests has grown with technical advances in their construction, administration, and scoring.

In recent years, however, public concern over the invasion of personal privacy has extended to the impact of testing and access to test records. This issue, coupled with the demand for fair employment practices, is resulting in a widespread reexamination of the nature and use of tests.

TESTS RELEVANT TO TRAINING AND DEVELOPMENT

There are many ways to classify the measures that may be useful and available to the training director. In considering using or preparing tests, the training director will find it helpful to examine their characteristics by asking the following questions.

What Employee Characteristics Is the Test Designed to Assess?

General Intellectual Abilities.   Measures of the various facets of "intelligence" typically emphasize cognitive abilities, such as verbal comprehension, reasoning, and spatial orientation. These abilities are among those which contribute to successful learning and performance in many jobs. However, a given test may not measure other abilities important for a job, such as perceptual ability. The extent to which a general ability test might be useful will therefore vary with the content of the test and the requirements of the job.

People differ from one another in the degrees to which they possess these abilities, and each person has, to some degree, a higher level in some abilities than in others. A test which provides separate scores for these abilities will be of greater use than one which yields simply a total score or "IQ." It permits weighting and combining the several parts in different ways to fit the differences in job requirements.

Aptitudes.   In contrast to *abilities,* which are the skills a person has already mastered, an *aptitude* may be best thought of as the capacity to attain, from learning or training opportunities, new kinds or levels of knowledge, skills, abilities, or personal characteristics. Aptitude tests measure a relatively well-defined area, such as mechanical aptitude, clerical aptitude, arithmetic aptitude, spatial orientation, and perceptual speed. Again, as with general ability tests, learning to perform a job will call on a complex combination of these aptitudes.

It should be recognized that this distinction between abilities and aptitudes is somewhat arbitrary. The same kind of test material may be considered a measure of achieved or developed ability or a measure of aptitude for further development, depending on the purpose of the test and the use of its results.

Achievement.   Achievement tests are intended to measure what the employee knows, understands, or can do in relation to quite specific areas of job knowledge or skill. Such a test can present an entire task, such as actually operating a lathe, or translating a foreign-language manuscript; it can *sample* from the domain of knowledge, such as selected concepts in biology; or it can be an "in-basket" which presents a typical array of administrative problems for consideration and action by the candidate.

Psychomotor and Sensorimotor Abilities.   Important in industry and elsewhere are tests of the employee's ability to do work involving predominantly muscular activities or predominantly sensory activities. Visual, auditory, and tactile acuity are examples of common sensorimotor requirements. Dexterity (both gross and fine), eye-hand coordination, and strength and agility are important psychomotor abilities.

Some of these abilities are assessed as part of entrance medical screening. However, other well-developed tests can have considerable value for selection, training, and placement. These may be of special value in the training of handicapped or disabled employees.

Interests and Motivation.   Efforts to use measures of interest and of motivation toward work and training have not been very effective except, perhaps, in a counseling setting. Difficulties arise from the "fakability" of these measures. Also, such measures often require the employee to express preferences as to jobs or other situations concerning which he or she has little firsthand knowledge or experience. Certain variants of the usual questionnaire attempt to disguise the material so that employees are not clearly aware of the interpretations that may be made of their responses. These are objectionable to employees and difficult to defend. The general scoring procedures of current tests seem to require very substantial research in order to adapt to the needs and purposes of the company.

In summary, the evaluation of interests as related to training needs and opportunities is more likely to rest on expressed statements of employees and on review of their records than on formal test procedures.

Personality and Temperament.   Attempts to assess personality characteristics and temperaments by structured paper-and-pencil tests, such as self-administered inventories, or by less structured means, such as projective situations (inkblots, ambiguous scenes, etc.), have serious drawbacks for use in business and industry. Whatever value they have as clinical diagnostic instruments does not seem to carry over to personnel selection. In addition to their problems with subjectivity and fakability and their intrusion on individual privacy, there is essentially little research evidence to support their use in training and development programs.

Interpersonal Skills, Leadership Qualities, etc.   Information as to these characteristics is often based on work history and on reports from previous or present supervisors. Some methods, such as situational tests or leaderless group discussions, provide for observation of employees' skills in working with others and in handling and solving typical problems of the kind they would confront on the job. These methods are a major component of the range of appraisal procedures used in assessment centers.

Personal History Data.   The evaluation of personal history is a widely used process. It can take the form of a review of an application blank and other information in the personnel file—work experience, previous education, credentials, relevant memberships and activities, military records, special awards and other personnel actions, etc. The personal history data may be supplemented by forms calling for highly detailed and specific information (perhaps self-rating) about particular competencies related to the specific job or training situation. It is possible to work out a systematic plan for evaluating such records qualitatively. In addition, when there is evidence linking certain specific kinds of experience, or biographical items, to success in training or on the job, it may be justifiable to develop a scheme for "scoring" and "weighting" these items as a basis for personnel decisions.

To biographical data from the candidate may be added information from personal references, previous employers, academic records, and other sources. These may simply supplement or verify material submitted by the candidate; they may also be "scored" as part of the total evaluation. In some cases, candidates may also submit examples of their work, such as a drawing, a model, an article, or a book.

Current Performance and Potential.   Evaluations of the performance of employees on their present jobs and estimates of their potential are widely used in assessing trainability and likelihood of success in higher-level or other kinds of work. Typically supervisors at first and second levels, and occasionally coworkers, may be asked to appraise the employee on a variety of aspects of job behavior and effectiveness. Rating scales, checklists, and many other forms are used, and extensive work has been directed at trying to improve such essentially subjective appraisals. In general, ratings can be useful if the purposes are clearly defined, if the rater is asked to describe behavior rather than to evaluate it, if adequate guidelines are available, if the raters are trained, and if they share an understanding of the standards and goals of the process.

How Are the Assessment Procedures to Be Administered?

Paper-and-Pencil Tests. This is the familiar format used for most general abilities and achievement tests, as well as many others. Its popularity is based on the ease of administration to small or large numbers of people. This form supports objectivity and economy in scoring, reporting, and research evaluation. Paper-and-pencil tests can range from highly structured measures, such as multiple-choice or checklist forms, to quite unstructured ones, such as essay forms. In another dimension, they can present material that requires verbal or language responses, or they can present problems in pictorial or graphic form which require little language facility. Ratings, reference forms, and biographical data forms are also paper-and-pencil procedures.

Test problems may be presented orally by examiners or by audiovisual means. The employee's response may be made orally to the examiner or to recording equipment, it may be written, or it may be made by manipulation of equipment. Oral presentation is useful when this represents the job situation closely, as in shorthand dictation or following oral directions.

Performance Tests. Typically, these tests assess an employee as he or she uses tools, equipment, data, and other facilities in a realistic work setting. Driving a car, operating a band saw, playing a tune, and typing a letter are examples. This category may also include observation of the employee's performance in a group setting.

Simulation Modes. These are similar to performance tests. Here a situation is designed to replicate as closely as feasible important features of the "real" work site. Using driver-training equipment, building scale models, or demonstrating nursing skills on other than actual patients represent simulated work.

Interactive Methods. These are another class of test situations. Here the candidate does not simply respond to a series of separate problems; rather, the test technique provides some continuing feedback that influences how the candidate responds to the next phase of the test. "Patient management" case problems in medical tests are an example. In some instances, as in an employment interview, the employee interacts with the interviewer(s). Other interview settings—where a group of management trainees, for example, deal with a common problem—provide group interaction. Computer-based devices may also be used as an interactive assessment method.

How Will Information from Use of the Assessment Measures Be Recorded and Interpreted?

A basic characteristic of any of the measures listed above is the kind of information that it yields and the form in which that information is recorded for use in later decisions. The data may range from scores on written tests, to check marks on biographical forms, to prose statements or essays by and about the candidate, to interview notes. They may be based on evaluation by one person or on the consensus of several. For any such data to meet the test of relevance and fairness, they must first of all be reliable. This means that the methods used to gather data about an employee should yield accurate and consistent information.

Standardized structured measures in short-answer or checklist form, with set procedures for administration and with predetermined scoring keys or evaluation schema, have become a widely accepted and preferred method to help ensure the reliability of tests and other assessment measures.

In addition to discussing the dependability of the measure, it is useful here to distinguish several different ways to interpret tests. One is called the *norm-referenced* form. In this plan, the strength of the employee's score or performance is judged in relation to the range of scores made by some defined reference group. Thus the person's score may be among the top 10 percent of the scores of all new hires, it may be at the average for all journeymen, etc. The relative standing of the score will vary with the group against which it is judged. Frequently, however, a norm-referenced measure will not indicate clearly just what knowledges and skills the employee has; it will show only that the employee has to the measured degree the knowledge and skills assumed to be present in the reference group.

In a second model, known as the *criterion-referenced* form, the employee's test behavior can be related to (or predict) some standard, such as production records or supervisory evaluation of performance.

A third form, often called *content-referenced,* is one in which the test samples directly from a domain of behavior, e.g., a reading knowledge of Latin or skill in conference leadership. This kind of measure is most useful in determining whether the employee has mastered a desirable level of competence in the subject matter or skills area being tested. The construction of such instruments involves the detailed specification of what the employee is expected to know or be able to do in order for decisions to be made about his or her training, placement, or promotion.

The following section discusses the several uses of assessment measures in training and development in terms of objective-test concepts. Other kinds of measures are also employed and are useful to the degree to which they provide dependable (reliable) and relevant (valid) data for the decisions to be made.

ASSESSMENT MEASURES IN TRAINING AND DEVELOPMENT

The training director will recognize many steps at which dependable measures will be helpful, if not critical, to the design, conduct, and evaluation of an effective program. These steps involve both decisions about individuals and decisions about the program. Both of these are preceded by, and based on, the company's clear definition of the desired effects or outcomes of its investment in the training effort. This requires a detailed analysis of the instructional objectives of the program, stated in terms of the knowledges, skills, and abilities that are the goals of the program. These objectives need not be so detailed as to be trivial, but they should be specified clearly enough to provide some way of judging whether these desired outcomes have, in fact, been realized.

For Evaluation of the Individual

Diagnosing Training Needs and Present Status.   Decisions about employees require a clear picture of where they now stand with respect to the desired outcome of training. For this purpose, written tests of their knowledge, work samples of performance, and similar measures related directly to the training objectives are important. These will be helpful not only for making decisions about the individual employee but also in reviewing the differences in employees' readiness for training and in their training needs. Such data will help in the decision as to whether a single program and instructional plan can be reasonably effective or whether there must be tailor-made plans that will take into account the different needs and present status of the employees concerned. This kind of information is also useful in advising individual employees about the steps they should be taking in order to facilitate their entry into a structured training program.

Placement in Formal Training Programs.   This decision involves information about both the needs and present status of the employee and the instructional alternatives that are available in the training program. It also implies a review of the probable interaction between the employee's characteristics and the nature of the different instructional alternatives so that the choice for the employee can be made in terms of that alternative plan of training from which he or she is most likely to benefit. For example, the diagnostic stage may suggest that for certain employees, training that involves close monitoring, tutorial assistance, and much practice is particularly desirable; similarly, the training program might recognize that other employees can work with much less direct instruction, with greater independence and self-pacing, etc. Judgments on such issues will be facilitated not only by information as to the competences of the employee but also by biographical data and review of the kinds of education or training programs in which the employee has learned best.

Prescribing Individual Remedial Work.   When remedial work is considered important for particular employees, the tests and measures are useful in determining how effective the remedial work is and at what point the employee may be considered to have reached the desired level of mastery to justify being placed in the regular training program. Here it is useful to distinguish between remedial work designed to compensate for general educational deficiencies (such as a deficiency in basic reading skills, which can be diagnosed by standardized educationally related achievement tests) and remedial work which is much more specific to the work situation and has to do with job-related knowledges, skills, and abilities. It is particularly important that these different purposes of remediation be recognized and that attention be paid to general educational deficiencies if they will in fact influence the likelihood of an employee's success in specific job-related programs.

Monitoring Progress and Self-Appraisal.   During the course of training, the use of objective measures, sample skill exercises, and other measures of progress serves a dual purpose. One purpose is to provide to the program director information as to the effectiveness of the program. The second is to provide information to employees that will assist them in making a self-appraisal of their progress and will operate as a motivator for further progress. Systematic measures here can also assist the instructional staff in pacing the rate at which the employee is learning most effectively. It can also pinpoint specific problems, such as inadequate mastery of certain units of information or certain skills, which are basic to the attainment of higher-level abilities.

Recognizing Achievement.   A major requirement of any formal training program is an indication as to the gains in that program and the level of competence resulting from the employee's participation in it. Thus end-of-course objective measures are a major tool for recognizing the achievement of the employee, particularly in programs which are aimed at developing the competence required for formal certification or licensing.

Retention of skills.   It is becoming more widely recognized that in many occupations and professions, it is important for employees as well as others to know whether they are retaining their skills and maintaining their knowledge so that they can continue to work effectively in their chosen field. This is particularly critical in cases where, as a result of many factors, skills as well as knowledge may become obsolete over time. Objective instruments are a method of choice in the periodic assessment of the current competence of employees and the identification of those areas in which they need retraining or continued education and training programs to maintain a satisfactory level of competence.

For Program Evaluation

Evaluating Instructional Alternatives.   In the development of training programs, a training director will consider and may experiment with alternative ways of presenting and monitoring the instructional program. The director will then be faced with the need for evaluating their comparative effectiveness. Assuming that the desired outcomes are the same, systematic measures are necessary to determine what gains in knowledges and skills and other abilities employees have made in the alternative programs.

Making a Skills Census for Manpower Planning.   Just as it is necessary to diagnose the training needs of employees for particular programs, it is also important in the overall planning of the training program and of the allocation of resources for development to have knowledge of the competences and deficiencies of the present work force. A skills census then becomes a highly useful way of mapping the characteristics of present manpower for planning purposes. Here, survey instruments of achievement and skill in the areas relative to the company's work will help identify the competences of the present work force. They will also identify whether certain employees have strengths that would suggest reassignment or better utilization of their skills. They will identify those areas where, in consideration of the possibility of shortages in the labor market, training efforts by the company will have to be undertaken.

Evaluating Training and Development Program Objectives.   In addition to examining the outcome of specific training programs, from a manpower and management standpoint it is also desirable to evaluate the extent to which the training and career development program as a whole has attained the company's objectives. For this purpose, systematic surveys of the skills of the employees in broad categories may be introduced and maintained over time to provide a continuous picture of the overall success of the program in meeting the company's manpower needs. Such an analysis must of course take into account factors other than measured success in training, e.g., fluctuations of available skills in the labor market, turnover figures, and data as to the relative rate of development of employees in various occupational groups in the company.

Assisting in Accountability.   In some situations the accountability of training directors for the company resources which they use may be based in part on measurable outcomes of the training program. The most relevant index, the performance of employees on the job, will in many situations be difficult to obtain. Dependable observations or records and information from the use of objective tests of knowledges and skills, for example, may be a useful second-order indication of the gains to the company related to its training investment.

CHARACTERISTICS OF USABLE PERSONNEL MEASURES

Any personnel appraisal methods should have those characteristics which will permit the training director to decide on its relevance for the purpose and on its technical usefulness. This applies alike to measures available from recognized test publishers, to methods tailor-made by consultants, and to those developed in-house.

Definition of Purpose   Any measure should be explicitly described as to the rationale underlying its preparation and the purposes for which it can properly be used. The fact that a form may carry a name, such as "mechanical ability" or "leadership aptitude," is no assurance that it is, in fact, a defensible measure on the basis of which judgments about employees can be made. There must be a statement, supported by reasonable information based on theory and research, to support use of the measure for its intended purposes; this information should make clear the necessary qualifications of users, and it should be written so that the users will be able to choose, give, evaluate, and interpret the test properly, for their own or for others' decision making.

Performance is multidimensional; in learning or working activities, the employee accomplishes the tasks by applying a complex and interacting array of underlying factors—abilities, skills, knowledges, and other characteristics. Similarly, all assessment measures are complex to some degree. The description of the measure should make clear whether it is designed to yield a total score or rating that is usable for prediction of defined characteristics or whether there are "part scores," as in a test battery, each of which has a somewhat different meaning.

If personnel measures are to meet the standards of relevance and fairness, a higher degree of professional competence will be required in their development. "Tests" or other measures put together casually by employers with little or no special training carry a high risk. Furthermore, it is difficult for a company to argue that its measures are "professionally developed" unless those who prepared them can establish their competence. However this competence is attained, the measures used should meet this standard.

Reliability of Measurement   Basic to any usable measure is evidence of its "reliability," that is, its consistency in measuring the employee's ability. The employee's performance in any test situation may be broadly viewed as comprised of his or her basic status, or "true score," and errors in measurement. A multitude of sources contribute to this inaccuracy. At a given time, many conditions—such as the individual's interest, state of mental and emotional health, and degree of preparation for the test situation—will affect performance somewhat. Also, there will be variance due to technical inadequacies in the measuring instruments themselves. But most important will be the inaccuracy resulting from the personal involvement of other people in the process of testing, interviewing, reviewing biographical personnel files, etc. Each of these people will have somewhat different perceptions of the situation, somewhat different standards, and different competences. Thus the scores or ratings of the employee will almost surely differ from one situation to the next, from one appraiser to the next, and from one form of the test to the next. Standard procedures for estimating reliability exist and should be applied. If measures are not adequately reliable, it is almost impossible for them to be satisfactorily valid and to bear the weight of decision making. Clearly, it is unfair to employees to make critical judgments on the basis of unstable information.

Validity

Issues in Determining the Validity of Measures.   The term "validity" is widely used and misused. Validation can best be looked at as a process through which the company can determine the relevance of its personal measures to the decisions that are based on them. Since personnel measures generally are constructed for the purpose of assigning scores or ratings to employees or making judgments about them that represent some larger area or domain of performance, one validity issue is the degree to which a measure is a good index of a particular domain. Since the measures are normally used as a predictor of later performance in training or on the job, a second validity issue is the degree to which the measures provide a sound basis for making such predictions about the employee.

It is somewhat artificial to talk about the validity of a single measure, such as a test score or interview rating, as if it were in fact separable from the entire system of selection. Furthermore, it is of little practical value to spend time and money to determine the validity of measures if, in fact, the personnel decisions do not rest on those measures. For example, test scores might be used in arraying employees in a rank order of predicted success in training. However, if other information or policies are used for selecting the employees who will be given the training or for choosing different treatments, the outcome is the same as if the test had not been used at all, and the question of its validity becomes irrelevant.

Validation Models.   Professional consensus recognizes three broad models of the validation process. In one approach, the predictive utility of personnel measures is evaluated by comparing the employee's performance on the measure with some index of his or her ability on a criterion of success in training or effectiveness on the job. Most desirably, to establish the predictive validity of instruments, the scores on such measures should not be used in actual selection for training or employment. Rather, the measures should be administered experimentally and then related to the criterion data, after which decisions can be made as to the value of the predictors if they were to be made part of the selection process. In cases where it is not possible to experiment with measures on applicants, they may be tried out with current employees. While such a "concurrent" study is often easier to accomplish, a number of serious drawbacks should be understood. First of all, employees normally have been selected by one or more measures probably similar to, or correlated with, the trial tests. Thus the restriction among employees in the range of the abilities that are of interest, as compared with the wider range found among applicants, will raise some serious questions as to the interpretation of the results. Second, if the employees in the study have been on the job for some period of time, their abilities have been modified through their job experience, and they no longer fairly represent the competences of applicants or new employees. The approach described in this paragraph is called *criterion-related validity*.

In adopting the criterion-related strategy, the company should be sure that in using current employees as its model, it is satisfied with their performance and will be satisfied with selecting from the labor market new employees who are similar to those already on the job. A final precaution is to guard against contamination through which the predictive measures themselves have a direct influence or weight in the criterion measures. If they do, a false overestimate of the value of the predictors will surely result. For example, personnel data collected at the time of appointment or selection for training are often made known directly or indirectly to supervisors, trainers, and others. If these people are later called upon to evaluate the trainee so that their evaluations can be related to test scores, for example, their prior knowledge of the person's test scores and their attitudes toward the meaning of those scores will affect in some way their expectations and their appraisal of his or her performance.

A second general model of validation is known as *content validity*. This model is often used in developing measures of knowledges, skills, and other behaviors where the testing situation can reproduce and sample from the domain of knowledges or skills that are of concern. Achievement tests, performance tests, and similar measures would fall under this broad definition. The value of measures based on a content-validity model is in proportion to the degree to which the domain of instructional objectives or of job performance is specific and to the extent to which the test adequately samples from the various areas within the broad domain. However, since even content-valid tests are used to make statements about the future behavior of employees, it is desirable that the accuracy of these predictions be verified where possible through follow-up studies.

A third validation model, called *construct validity*, is based on a theoretical principle or concept used as an underlying basis for the description of human behavior. Examples of constructs are reading comprehension, supervisory ability, and management judgment. Many specific behaviors might be considered expressions of the operation of a general construct. It is a very substantial research task to establish the soundness of such theoretical ideas and to define a variety of measurable behaviors which are commonly, and perhaps uniquely, explainable by the construct. The way in which an individual responds on accepted measures of a construct permits making generalizations or predictions about how he or she might behave in a variety of different situations where the same construct is considered to be operating. Thus, for example, knowledge of how well the individual does on a construct-valid test of mechanical ability would be helpful in estimating how well this person might respond to training in mechanical work or might carry out other tasks that rest in part on mechanical ability. Since the establishment of a construct is normally based on the research evidence in psychological literature, training directors should be particularly cautious about undertaking short-term studies with the intention of defining constructs or about attempting to justify their use of measures simply because the names of those measures seem to describe employee characteristics that are thought to be important for training or job performance. They should also be alert to the fact that whereas determination of the construct in certain tests has had substantial research, there is very little guidance at present as to how one goes about developing the constructs in training or job performance that can then be matched to known constructs in tests. Attention is now being given to this issue, and some procedures for demonstrating the constructs in training or performance may become available in the next few years.

Interpretation of Data   For measures to be useful, there must be a way in which the scores or ratings can be interpreted. Tests which are "standardized" are typically accompanied by norms or similar information which provides a basis for the training director to judge the relative standing of the employee's test performance. This requires that various norming populations be defined, and their performance on the measures arrayed. Typically this calls, for example, for percentile tables showing what proportions of the norming populations made particular scores on the test. Norms may also be in the form of "standard scores" which relate a raw test score to the variability of the scores for the population. It is particularly important that the characteristics of the norming groups be specified in terms of sex, age, educational level, experience, and other relevant characteristics. In using norm tables, the training director should ask whether the norming group is at all comparable to the applicant or employee group with whom he or she is working and therefore whether the use of the norm tables is justified. Where there are sufficient local factors that make normative information (based, for example, on nationwide samples) not very useful, the company can over a period of time collect and organize the test performance of its own applicants and employees to develop local norms. These give a picture of the range and level of tested abilities of a known employee group and provide a very useful template against which to judge the relative strength of groups of applicants in the local labor market or of groups of employees in particular units of the company or against which to make individual judgments. At the very least, however, companies should maintain descriptive information and records of the results of personnel assessments; these should include computation of the average scores, of the distribution of the scores around the average, and of the reliability of the scores. Where any substantial volume of hiring or training occurs, the data should be tabulated and evaluated separately for subgroups identified by race, sex, age, educational level, and other relevant characteristics; this makes it possible to observe the relative performance of different subgroups and be alert to any adverse effects of, or unfairness in, the tests.

In addition to normative comparisons, the question as to how test scores might best be used to make predictions of success in training or on the job can be examined through a display of test and criterion data in the form of "expectancy tables." Such tables, usually in two-way form, are often expressed in terms of the probability that an individual who makes a certain score on the predictor will fall at a particular level or range on the subsequent training or performance criterion. These tables permit judgments as to the degree to which companies are willing to risk hiring or training employees who have very low likelihood of success. However, since the labor market, as well as training and job conditions, change over time, such tables need regular updating and reevaluation so that they continue to support the decision process.

Administrative Factors   A major consideration in the selection and use of personnel tests and measures is their ease of administration, including the time and cost required to give, score, and interpret them and to maintain records of their use. Good administration calls not only for good facilities but also for standard instructions so that all people subjected to these procedures are treated in a uniform manner. The security of the test material must of course be controlled. If material is lost or unnecessarily exposed or made public, its use is compromised, and the confidence of applicants or employees in the objectivity and fairness of the personnel procedures is undermined; as a result, the company may have to go to very great expense to develop new materials to replace those which have been compromised. Applicants and employees are also entitled, of course, to some feedback as to their performance and the resulting decisions. The way in which this information is provided should be carefully worked out and consistently applied. Finally, the records must be maintained in a usable form, and the policies governing access to them must be made explicit in order to protect their confidentiality. While records of an employee's performance in the personnel assessment process and training may have long-range historical and research value, training directors and personnel staff must be mindful that their measurement significance is degradable and that judgments about an employee today should be based on today's evaluation rather than on records of his or her abilities and competences made four or five years ago or even further in the past.

RESOURCES

The demands on personnel staffs for "professional" standards in the assessment of applicants and employees are increasing steadily. The sophistication in preparing, selecting, and using personnel measures referred to early in this chapter implies that the training director and staff need to have a working knowledge of concepts of assessment of human abilities and of the general literature on personnel measurement. They should understand the methods of elementary descriptive and analytic statistics, both for application in their own work and for the evaluation of data presented by others. If they prepare tests, rating procedures, and other methods for company use, they should be able to apply sound practices in developing, pretesting, norming, and validating these instruments. And if special competence is required to give and evaluate certain measures, they should have the needed training. A training director who does not have the special skills called for is responsible for seeing that the staff does have the required formal training and experience.

For professional consultative or training assistance the training director can consult with the faculties in appropriate departments (such as psychology, education, or business administration) in nearby universities. The director can locate specialists in the directory of the American Psychological Association or write to the APA Washington headquarters for referrals. Many colleagues in the ASTD will have relevant experience and competence.

The following selected references, in addition to journal literature and relevant ASTD publications, will be helpful for training in the effective preparation, selection, and use of tests and measures.

BIBLIOGRAPHY

Anastasi, Anne: *Psychological Testing,* 3d ed., The Macmillan Company, New York, 1968.
Anderson, S. B., S. Ball, R. T. Murphy, and E. J. Rosenthal: *Anatomy of Evaluation: Important Concepts and Techniques in Evaluating Education/Training Programs,* Educational Testing Service, Princeton, N.J., August 1973.

Buros, O. K. (ed.): *The Seventh Mental Measurements Yearbook,* Gryphon Press, Highland Park, N.J., 1972.

Guion, Robert M.: *Personnel Testing,* McGraw-Hill Book Company, New York, 1965.

Standards for Educational and Psychological Tests, American Psychological Association, Inc., Washington, 1974.

Thorndike, Robert L. (ed.): *Educational Measurement,* 2d ed., American Council on Education, Washington, 1971.

U.S. Equal Employment Opportunity Commission: "Guidelines on Employee Selection Procedures," *Federal Register,* vol. 35, no. 149, Aug. 1, 1970.

Chapter 11

Manpower and Career Planning

JOHN E. McMAHON

JOSEPH C. YEAGER

John E. McMahon *is Manager of Human Resources Development at SmithKline Corporation in Philadelphia, where he directs manpower training and development. He joined SmithKline in 1972 after 20 years with Union Carbide, where he designed and conducted manpower planning and career planning programs for a major division. He graduated with a B.S. in chemistry from St. Vincent College and added an M.S. in chemistry from Canisius. He also attended advanced courses in personnel administration (NICB) and organization development (NTL—National Training Laboratories). For the past few years he has conducted workshops in career planning and human resources development at the University of Michigan (Division of Management Education) and the University of Cincinnati and at Educational Testing Service in Princeton, New Jersey. He has also conducted life/career planning workshops for many other universities and business organizations. He is a member of the Philadelphia and National Organizational Development Network and the Philadelphia chapter of ASTD.*

Joseph C. Yeager *is a consultant on the corporate staff of Pfizer, Inc., New York, and is the Vice President of Research and Development for Personal Dynamics, Minneapolis, Minnesota. Dr. Yeager has been Director of Staff Development and Internal Consulting at Educational Testing Service in Princeton, New Jersey. At ETS he held previous positions as Director of Personnel and Director of Professional Personnel. He was previously Director of Personnel at Allegheny Airlines, where he was responsible for management development, recruiting, wage and salary, general personnel administration, and training programs for ground personnel and flight crews. He has also developed and implemented programs on organizational change and executive career planning and has consulted with numerous commercial organizations and schools. During the last few years, he has authored many papers on management, personnel, and psychology. He earned his B.A. in psychology from Thiel College, Greenville, Pennslyvania. He later received a master's degree in counseling psychology and a Ph.D. in organizational and consulting psychology from the University of Pittsburgh. He is a member of ASTD, the American Psychological Association, Eastern College Placement Officers, the Employment Management Association, and the AERA Systems Group, and he is currently serving on the Bureau of National Affairs Personnel Policies Forum.*

Manpower planning has been defined as having the right number and the right kinds of people, at the right places, and at the right time, doing things which result in maximum long-term benefits for both the organization and the individuals. This definition has as much relevance today as it did when it was proposed by Vetter, the dean of manpower planning, in 1967.[1]

Vetter's foresight in delineating the manpower planning concept is yet to be matched in practice by many organizations. A central issue in this delay is the clarification of an emerging "psychological" contract or interdependent relationship between the organization and the individual.

Especially prominent are the demands of individuals for a more meaningful role in the corporate environment in which most spend their working lives and for a sense of reasonable control over their destiny. Demands upon organizations for responsiveness to individuals have generated an important new facet of manpower planning, i.e., career planning as a means of integrating the relationship between the individual and the organization.

This relationship is emerging as the focus of manpower planning and career planning. Although the issues involved are well known, implementation of manpower planning lags behind the knowledge in the field. In a recent survey of manpower planning activities, the Bureau of National Affairs received a disappointingly small response to its questionnaire.[2] Rather than indicating lack of interest, the results of a follow-up questionnaire revealed that in many companies little is being done in the manpower planning area. Yet it was also learned that interest is increasing and that more firms will have manpower planning programs in the future. This is supported by the experience of the authors, who have observed an increasing rate of interest in the manpower and career planning workshops offered at the University of Michigan's Division of Management Education.

The Basic Unit

The basic unit of manpower and career planning (MP and CP) is the individual. And two different viewpoints are involved: the organization's perspective and the individual's perspective. The relationship between the organization and the individual, while reciprocal and interdependent, is also quite distinct. MP is often viewed as the macroscopic system that provides guidance for the optimum use of the organization's human resources. The MP system must, however, incorporate programs and subsystems which maximize the growth of the individuals who collectively make up its human resources, and it must determine ways in which these two will interact. CP is used to identify those programs which deal with the issue of individual growth and productivity within the organizational environment. CP deals with the determinants which will facilitate the individual's ability to perform given tasks as needed and to smooth the interface between the individual and the system.

The Nitty-Gritty Process

Manpower planning (the corporate focus) and career planning (the individual focus) derive from a universal sequence of events which, for the sake of the illustration and mnemonic value, we call the *nitty-gritty process*. Manpower planning as a macro system derives from business objectives and tends to be a demographic process handling large numbers of individuals. Career planning involves programs and actions which capitalize on the idiosyncratic needs, abilities, aspirations, goals, etc., of the individual—in a competitive social and business system.

The nitty-gritty process as it applies to the individual (Fig. 11-1) simply illustrates the idea that each individual is recruited, is given some introduction to the job, is observed for performance characteristics, is compared with criteria (either present- or future-oriented), is advised of options, and finally makes a career choice that is based on personal preference, the wishes of management, or both. The process recycles and is continuous. This is a universal process. The corporate organization needs to cope with great numbers of individuals. MP and CP systems have emerged as vital corporate activities. Unsystematic methods in large or growing organizations produce numerous administrative problems.

Three Components   During the nitty-gritty process, three significant factors are operating which determine the outcome for any given individual: the ultimate decisions which must be made about the individual, the source of those decisions, and the methods used in arriving at those decisions.

First, the decisions which must be made about the individual are commonsense choices, i.e., to promote, transfer, terminate, make a salary change, freeze in a current position, demote, or retire. These decisions are facilitated by CP programs which will enhance their accuracy, objectivity, and validity from both the individual (I) and the organizational (O) point of view.

Second, the source of the decisions that are made about the individual will vary according to the mechanisms which operate within an organization. The employee's supervisor will have considerable influence, but in many situations a supervisor one or two levels removed from the employee will make or heavily influence the decision. There are CP systems in which either the employee and/or a committee submits information for the decision-making process. The decision makers are influenced by current business conditions, organizational objectives, and the prevailing legal climate.

Fig. 11-1   The nitty-gritty process.

Third, the methods used in arriving at the decisions vary considerably; the range includes traditional performance rating forms, MBO, skills inventories, assessment centers, and interpersonal skills training.

The administrative problems arising from the nitty-gritty process create the need for both MP and CP systems. These lead to delivery systems, or programs, for the sake of economy and efficiency in handling large numbers of people in organizations. The way decisions, decision makers, and methods relate to the individual are depicted in Fig. 11-2.

The Point of Reference   The nitty-gritty model is the anchoring point for MP and CP programs because the individual *is* the irreducible and productive keystone of the organization's human resources. From the CP perspective, programs are designed to elicit comprehensive and relevant information on the individual's career. Simultaneously, the organization will generate a symbiotic relationship with the individual. From the MP perspective, individuals and their characteristics, when combined with all others in the system, create the need for macro-level systems to provide demographic data relevant to organizational objectives.

The final form of the MP and CP programs must make sense to the user organization, and it is here that an organization's philosophy, climate, traditions, etc., come into play in the selection of strategies and methods which will contribute to its economic objectives. For the sake of discussion, MP has been treated as strategic and demographic (or macro) in nature, and CP has been treated as tactical and person-oriented (or micro). This distinction has heuristic value, but in the operation of many organizations it is difficult to separate one type of program from another.

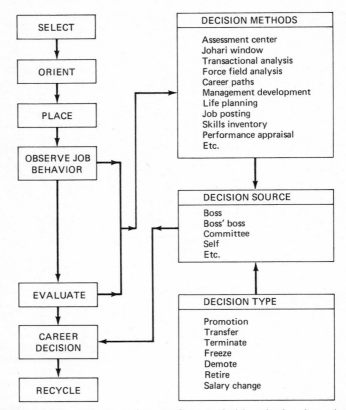

Fig. 11-2 The sources, methods, and types of career decisions in the nitty-gritty process.

The I-O Psychological Contract

The issue of the individual's relationship to the organization (I-O) demands a special note. During the interaction between the individual and the organization, conflicts of interest inevitably arise; the organization often demands commitment to the organization, and the sacrifice of personal desires, and it has the power to enforce its wishes. In contrast, the individual searches for maximum gain in terms which are personally meaningful. This push and pull generates conflict. It is the prevention or resolution of these vested interests in harmonious ways which is a major function of MP and CP. Luft,[3] a behavioral scientist, illuminates the individual's point of view with the concept of *habeas emotum*. In paraphrase, the concept summarizes the individual's sense of fair play and emotional logic in the I-O relationship; there is a focus especially on the fact that organizations usually win any conflicts. The point of the I-O idea is to repeat the axiom that people in organizations want to be treated as ends as well as means.

The Place of Feelings   Because operation of the nitty-gritty model contains the primary elements of the I-O relationship, the basic decisions facilitated by MP and CP systems will often generate a great deal of emotion. Habeas emotum expresses this emotional experience; it is analogous to the legal concept of habeas corpus which outlaws all forms of illegal custody. Thus, in parallel logic it represents the sense of justice and fair play in the exercise of one's psychological freedom not to have one's emotional space arbitrarily violated by organizational actions. But institutions are changing rapidly, and a sense of emotional justice and fairness often is lost in the press of events. The design of MP and CP strategies and tactics must take this notion into account if real success is to be achieved. Institutionalizing a sense of fairness consists simply in showing overtly that the organization does care about its employees. Without this, an impoverished emotional environment is assured. Plans which generate a sense of emotional injustice are sure to be full of problems and very costly.

Mature Processes   There is a search for psychological order which recognizes the fundamental fact of human beings and their feelings. The index of a group or organization's maturity is its concern for human emotion. Yet it is difficult to find institutionalized forms of concern for human emotion in the typical large organization. In terms of one's performance on the job, there is a deep longing for fair acknowledgment and recognition of one's contribution. This sense of justice or fair play is often insufficiently served. While some behavioral scientists would factually point out the demotivating effect of the absence of habeas emotum, Luft sees its absence as a major pathological symptom for the organization.

All the above is finally related to MP and CP systems as they in turn relate to the gathering of data about individuals and the forming of judgments and decisions which intrude on the life space of the individuals within the organization.

In the press of events, interactions generate information about the individual, and the processes of collecting and measuring impressions are of prime importance. Forming judgments calls for a difficult combination of involvement and objective observation. The quality of consensus varies with the caliber of the members in the group, but even more crucially with the nature of the processes involved. The resolution of this interaction of the individual as both end and means leads to the fundamental questions of the kinds of programs or processes to be implemented. Every organization has MP and CP, even if they are only the effect of organizational practices. But planned approaches are naturally superior to the artifacts of neglect if the desire is to optimize human resources for both the individual and the organization.

DIAGNOSIS OF MP NEEDS

In order to optimize human resources through MP, it is first helpful to define the nature of the human resource system, evaluate how it is doing, and learn how the key people involved feel about it. One method of doing this is illustrated in Fig. 11-3, which illustrates a device that can be used to analyze the perceived status of the human resource system and to develop ideas about what might be done to improve it.

This particular questionnaire has been used as a diagnostic aid serving a number of useful functions for the innovative manpower planner. Its use as the basis of a patterned interview with senior managers reveals what is perceived as the level of functioning of the current system. It is a multifaceted way of surveying the situation. The particular questions may, of course, be varied considerably. To initiate change, it is necessary to have some sense of a felt need, and by guiding a discussion through a list of subjects such as this, one develops a very concrete idea of the nature of the felt need.

As J. C. Yeager[4] has pointed out in his model for change, there are numerous

WHAT IS THE HUMAN RESOURCE SYSTEM DOING?

Human Resource Functions	Our system does not do this:		Our system does this now at this level of effectiveness:			
	and it shouldn't	but it should	needs great deal of improvement	needs some improvement	generally adequate	no real weakness
1. Generating interest among potential young managers in the organization.						
2. Actually hiring the best prospects interviewed for the available jobs.						
3. Effectively utilizing the newly hired and making them productive.						
4. Providing meaningful job assignments.						
5. Providing sound promotional and career opportunities.						
6. Identifying meaningful career patterns for managers.						
7. Successfully filling key middle and higher management positions.						
8. Keeping the management compensation system up to date and effective.						
9. Adequately evaluating the performance of managers.						
10. Adequately evaluating the potential of managers for higher responsibilities.						
11. Maintaining a sound and flexible organization structure.						
12. Controlling attrition at all levels.						
13. Reducing attrition among capable younger managers.						
14. Anticipating future managerial manpower requirements.						
15. Maintaining an adequate information system on manpower.						
16. Developing managers for higher level responsibilities.						
17. Motivating managers to accept greater responsibilities and assume initiative.						
18. Preventing experienced managers from growing obsolete.						
19. Motivating experienced managers to effectively develop subordinates.						
20. Providing needed cross-training for managers with high potential.						
21. Developing personnel policies.						
22. Implementing personnel policies						
23. Selecting the right person for the right job						
24. Complying with EEO requirements (minorities and women).						
25. Explaining personnel policies to employees.						
26. Building morale through company programs.						
27. Training new staff in line positions.						
28. Conducting personnel research (attitude surveys, turnover, etc.).						
29. Rewarding individuals on the basis of performance.						
30. Improving individual productivity.						
31. Providing adequate fringe benefits.						
32. Conducting an effective health and safety program.						
33. Facilitating cooperation across and within divisions.						
34. Producing a growth-oriented climate.						

Fig. 11-3 Patterned interview questionnaire.

prerequisites for change in any given social system. Primary among them are the existence or elicitation of a felt need and the support of influential individuals to attempt any systematic, consciously designed change in a system.

The Change Agent's Role

There is also the question of the change agent's role. Will the change agent be active or passive, proactive or reactive? That is, in producing an MP system from information gathered in the questionnaire, what issues on the list do you want to handle? Does the change agent have the desire, the power, and the initiative to begin change? Should one start at the policy or the program level? The questionnaire will have at least two results: (1) The current perception of the state of the organization's human resources will become apparent, and (2) from the choices in the column labeled "should not do," boundaries will be clearly labeled. This produces a clear statement of whose opinions must be changed in order to implement a program. It also is useful to ask who the powerful persons are in the organization. The collected answers produce a network (or sociogram) of expectations and a definition of the power system. The clusters of powerful people are then identified for special persuasive efforts in order to gain support for the MP or CP system. Sorting them into special-interest groups such as top, operating, and personnel managers can give comparative data and guidelines for analysis and follow-up.

Manpower Planning and the Data Base

To restate the definition, manpower planning is that process by which management prepares to have the needed types and numbers of people in the right places at the right times to fulfill both corporate and individual objectives.

Manpower planning is becoming more synonymous with the idea of a total human resource system, especially in determining how an organization should move from its current manpower position to its desired position. And it relies very heavily on an accurate data base describing the human resources needed to function. Manpower planning, synonymous with a human resource system, is essential to the health and growth of organizations.

Roles and Devices   Important roles of the function are to assess the organization's existing manpower resources, evaluate the current organization, and project future manpower requirements and combine them with financial and technological planning as well. These roles require at least two specific devices:

- A manpower inventory. An objective assessment of existing resources based on data derived from the methods of the nitty-gritty process.
- A manpower forecast. The collection and analysis of future manpower requirements based on the effects of internal and external influencing factors for the organization and for individual operating centers.

These devices are most efficiently managed by a centrally controlled data handling system which will answer questions with reports as quickly as they are asked.

Manpower planning is one of the key units of business planning, like sales projections, strategic planning, facilities planning, and finance planning. To be effective, it must be integrated with these other business elements.

It should result in a specific definition of future needs, and it should also provide a vehicle to set goals for women and minorities in management in terms of specific departments and specific levels of responsibility on a periodic basis. It should provide data which will permit better prediction and control over those influences which will determine the availability of the right person in the right place at the right time.

Thus the development of manpower planning forecasts is dependent upon the creation of an administrative and informational data-base matrix consisting of descriptive characteristics of both the employees and the organization.

Data-Base Content   Items in the data base which can integrate programmatic subsystems from the nitty-gritty process can be limited or far-reaching, according to the particular needs. For the employee, the items may range from the general, such as age, sex, education, assessment center data, and performance appraisals, to extremely detailed skills inventory data involved in technologically intensive companies. For the organization, the terms might include job classifications, cost center number, reporting relationships, and other, similar data concerning each employee.

But regardless of the scope of the data base, it is useless unless the information is stored in such a way that questions can be answered with a reasonably efficient retrieval mechanism which will allow the data to be assembled as they are needed and to be anchored to the individual.

The mechanisms for handling the data-base elements vary considerably and range from manually manipulated card decks, to mechanically operated card methods, to electronic data processing systems; these have been described by Morrison.[5]

The ability to capture the elements in summary, tabular, graphic, or other formats allows a wide variety of potential reports, i.e., questions which can be answered or forecasts and trends which can be identified as the data are tracked over given periods of time. In many advanced applications with computers, this kind of a system can be maintained and used with minimal effort. But in smaller applications with employees numbering in the hundreds or a few thousand, manual methods of MP can be very effective. Much of the information that might possibly be generated about an employee has only indirect use in MP at the strategic level. Thus a dozen or two items which can be easily manipulated may well serve to meet the needs of the smaller organization. These methods have been described by Casey et al.[6]

Data Uses   Also from the CP perspective, it is imperative that the data which are generated by the many methods available through the nitty-gritty process be entered into the data base as major contributing variables to the overall manpower plan.

The information which is generated by a data handling system must then be put to use. At the demographic level a series of important reports can be retrieved from the system and used as the basis of discussions and planning among those who are responsible for planning. Figure 11-4 shows how reports such as these can be assembled for use as the agenda for a series of planning meetings to interpret the meaning of the data and plan for their use. The secret of MP data is to keep them visible, according to Phillip Morgan,[7] of Information Science, Inc. They are samples of what the MP products might be, but they are valuable only if they are used and answer pertinent questions as they are asked. The EDP system may produce information, but unless it becomes integral with the organization's planning, generating it will become an academic exercise. Thus building it into a workshop or committee structure where it will be processed assures some degree of assimilation, interpretation, and action by important decision makers in the organization.

On Implementation and Change

Once MP data are discussed, a basic decision must be considered, i.e., the scale of influence at which the change agent wishes to operate. There are two basic ways of approaching organizational change. One is to attempt to change the structure within which one operates. The other is to change the behavior of the people in the system. In both approaches the object is an actual, measurable change in the

```
REPORT A ....... PAGE NO.   1     REPORTING RELATIONSHIPS — ECHELON CODING
```

DEPT #	ECHELON CODE	POSITION TITLE — — — — — —	EMPLOYEE NAME
010	B	SENIOR V.P.	SMITH
010	C	VICE PRESIDENT, FINANCE	GRUBER
010	D	TREASURER	MCWIT
010	D	CONTROLLER	

WHAT DOES THE ORGANIZATION ACTUALLY LOOK LIKE?

```
REPORT F .........    PAGE NO.   1    PROJECTED RETIREMENTS FOR THE NEXT THREE YEARS
```

EMPLOYEE — — — LAST NAME — — —	LOCATION — — — — — — — — NAME — — — — — — — — — —	JOB — — — — — — — — — — TITLE — — — — — — — —	BIRTH MO-DA-YR	YEARS OF SERVICE	ANNUAL EQUIV
CHEEVERS	CORPORATE FINANCE	CONSOLIDATION ACCOUNTANT	12-04-08	22	12,500
MILLER	CORPORATE TREAS. OFFICE	SENIOR ACCOUNTANT	08-16-08	10	11,700
BILLMEYER	DIVISIONAL HEADQUARTERS	STAFF CONSULTANT	06-04-08	30	18,000
SMITH	HOUSTON SALES OFFICE	STENOGRAPHER	03-29-08	5	7,500
BURROWMEISTERN	INTERNATIONAL SALES	CORRESPONDENT	09-17-08	16	15,200

WHO IS RETIRING IN THE NEXT 3 YEARS?

```
REPORT B ........ PAGE NO.   1    POSITION PROMOTION REGISTER
```

TITLE	INCUMBENT	PROMOTION NOMINEE 1	PROMOTION NOMINEE 2	PROMOTION NOMINEE 3
V P, ADMINISTRATION	BROWN	IRWIN	BRENNON	DALY
V P, DATA PROCESSING	KINGSTON	DONNELLY	REYNOLDS	CARSON
V P, MARKETING	JONES	JACKSON	CROSS	WATKINS
V P, OPERATIONS	MOORE	MARKS	GRAY	THOMAS
V P, FINANCE	EDWARDS	DAVIS	HOWARD	NASH

ARE KEY POSITIONS BACKED UP?

```
REPORT C ........ PAGE NO.   1    EXECUTIVE TIME IN POSITION
```

DAPT	NAME	TITLE	POS YR	DEPT YRS
010	ABACROMBIE	VICE PRESIDENT	5	5
010	CHRISTIANSEN	CONTROLLER	8	15
010	ZAMBINE	SENIOR VICE PRESIDENT	4	10

ARE EXECUTIVES BEING KEPT TOO LONG IN ONE POSITION?

```
REPORT D ....... PAGE 1    MANPOWER PLANNING TALENT LIST
```

DEPARTMENT	TITLE	NAME	EXPERIENCE SPECIALTY	NUMBER OF YEARS	YEAR LAST USED
001	DIRECTOR, ADMIN SERVICES	CHAMPION	BENEFITS ADMIN	2	71
001	ASSISTANT VICE PRESIDENT	HOLLISTER	BENEFITS ADMIN	4	72
001	ASSISTANT VICE PRESIDENT	NORRIS	BENEFITS ADMIN	8	69

CAN WE STAFF A NEW DEPARTMENT WITH IN-HOUSE TALENT?

Fig. 11-4 Manpower planning reports.

ways in which work of one sort or another is accomplished. As a general rule of thumb it is useful to note that MP tends to focus on causing change at the structural or program level and that CP tends to focus on causing change by direct interventions into the behavioral patterns of individuals. Relatively speaking, it is more efficient to change the structure of an organization, for this in turn will cause much individual behavior change. Of course, one could attempt to persuade or train individuals, but resistance to change is in the natural order of things since habits tend to persist. It is more efficient to change the situation in which the individual is functioning so that it calls for a more desirable pattern of response. Some behavioral scientists think of situational change as constituting behavioral engineering, as Yeager[8] has pointed out in his analysis of management development.

Policy vs. Persuasion   In other words, a well-designed policy or program will generally net more behavior change per unit or effort than specific attempts to train or persuade individuals to behave differently. Perhaps an obvious case on the current scene is the implementation of equal employment opportunity laws. Few would challenge the notion that in the wake of these laws, a great deal of individual behavior has been changed which had been previously considered unchangeable. The major point to be made in this vein, however, is simply that one may implement career planning programs with many of the methods which are described later in this discussion. Without supportive organizational structure, climate, and policy at the macroscopic manpower planning level, the chances of cost-effective success are less probable.

The concern now shifts to the issue of career planning.

OBJECTIVES OF CAREER PLANNING

The origin of the need for career planning is at least two-dimensional. Organizations are under pressure to maximize the utilization of their human resources to ensure profitability, yet they are under counterpressure from changing social values to meet the demands of individuals for satisfying employment experiences. Increasingly, individuals are restive about how organizations impose upon what is considered "personal space."

Kellogg[9] has identified at least four challenges in the career planning function: culturally deprived minorities, women, demands of young people, and the shift in age distribution. Kellogg concludes that new concepts are needed to give both the individual and the organization greater flexibility. And we need ingenious devices to facilitate careers so that talents can be applied and developed at the rate demanded by our challenging times. She also makes the concomitant observation that these systems remain underdeveloped. Corporate CP can fill the void with measurable and positive impact.

The issure then is how to generate processes which will optimize the interdependent individual-organizational (I-O) relationship.

Ends and Means

Career planning often means job rotation, succession planning, performance appraisals, etc. Organizations often use results from these processes to decide how to utilize the individual as a means for achieving organizational objectives. Resulting decisions are usually one-sided in favor of the organization's needs.

Individuals have been used as means for attaining the organization's ends, a result of the fact that at decision points where individual and organizational needs conflict to any significant degree, organizational pressure can overwhelm the individual. Effective career planning programs can mediate this traditional conflict to the advantage of both I and O.

Human resource management, through innovative career planning, is rapidly becoming a more formalized institutional activity, although not always successfully. With some CP attempts there has been a corresponding sense developing in individuals that the organization tends to do things *to* rather than *for* them as McMahon and Yeager[10] have observed in their University of Michigan seminar series. From the suspicion which is generated by this conflict, organizations may recognize that career planning is a weak link in their manpower programs. Individuals resist even benevolent attempts by the organization to solicit information from them. Effective CP could counteract this problem. Thus with a CP process to meet both sets of needs, the employee can emerge from the position of being merely a means and be an end as well.

Organizational Resistance

Since adults in our culture have a strong tendency to define themselves in terms of the work they do, facilitating a CP process would seem to be of self-evident value and a means of maximizing the individual's contribution to the organization. Yet some organizations resist career planning efforts in attempts to manipulate the decisions of individuals under their control. Usually this is rationalized as an attempt to preserve organizational stability or to limit decisions by individuals which are inconvenient to the organization. But a contrasting attitude was recently observed during a career planning program conducted by McMahon[11] at the Career Dynamics Center of the University of Cincinnati. As a result of a life planning exercise in that program, a staff member resigned to pursue a career in industry. Dr. Phil Marvin, director of the center, responded with the enlightened comment that "I would rather have people here because they plan to be here than because of accident or apathy."

Individuals should be primarily responsible for their own career planning. Even in apparently hopeless organizational settings the individual always has the option to leave. But it is certainly a desirable goal for CP programs to facilitate the individual's achievement of personal objectives. Where there is choice, there may be more commitment from the individual, and a more productive relationship may result.

One other item is important to mention. Career planning is not always synonymous with upward mobility, for only a few make significant upward strides. Rather, CP is more comparable to the notion of growth and development, which is for everybody.

Thus the objective of CP is simply the mutual I-O establishment of a course of action which seems reasonable in terms of what is known about the individual and the environment of the organization. There are criteria which are important in developing CP programs. Five important ones are discussed below.

Five Career Planning Criteria

There are five features or criteria which are important to the success of any CP effort. They are dialogue, guidance, the individual's involvement in the process, feedback to the individual, and the mechanisms by which the process operates.

Dialogue represents the relationship between the individual and the organization. It might be between the individual and his or her immediate manager, the manager's manager, other interested parties, or a third party who can facilitate and help increase the objectivity and validity of the decisions. Through dialogue, openness and trust can be generated to the advantage of both the individual and the organization. Dialogue may be implemented in a number of ways, but the essential point is that without it, there is no career planning.

Guidance from management is, in essence, the provision of information about the career milieu in which the individual must function. An individual can plan intelligently with knowledge about options, opportunities, and goals available. The information can be provided by means of seminars, or third-party counseling, or it can be given informally if no systematic program is developed.

To ensure a high degree of *involvement,* means must be established to allow individuals to input their career objectives, timetables, values, and other personally meaningful issues. Provision must be made to use this information once it is solicited in order to optimize the relationship between what the individual wants and what is possible. It may be necessary to structure a sequence of events in order to obtain clear statements from individuals of what they, in fact, want. This is not easy since experience shows that individuals' desires are often poorly defined and are sometimes in conflict with the organization's goals. Special career planning workshops can be developed that will help identify and resolve this problem; these are described later in the chapter.

Feedback to the individual is important in that it provides the basis for calibrating his or her behavior or for initiating appropriate changes in terms of what is learned. It may take the form of one-to-one discussions with superiors, or often it emerges from developmental experiences which point out areas requiring change.

The *mechanisms* of CP (the processes and the techniques) must interface with one another as subsystems. The potentially useful devices are rather numerous. Because they are the means by which the above four items are brought into being, considerable discussion will be devoted to several of them in the following sections.

The Thrust of Career Planning Program Content

For the individual, career planning programs should serve some specific functions. Kellogg[12] indicates that to manage a career to best advantage, the individual will view the comments and assessments of others as information to be combined with personal awareness of strengths and weaknesses. Weighing all the available information then makes an effective career decision possible. The supervisor, the individual's performance history, career planning programs, and job possibilities all will generate facets of this information matrix. Other variables typically include an inventory of goals and values, an assessment of skills and (potential) hidden abilities, the individual's standing in the eyes of significant decision makers, and so on. All this information is most usefully synthesized into a source document as the basic career plan and is entered in the EDP data base in coded format.

It is critically important to the organization that the information gathered contribute measurably to having the right person at the right place at the right time. Beyond any altruistic motives which might be operating, there is the legal imperative to make valid corporate decisions from the equal employment opportunity perspective.

Matching versus Uniqueness   A great deal of effort has been expended in the past to match individuals to jobs by comparing their characteristics with composite profiles of successful people. But this pigeonholing method has not been valuable in assessing uniqueness. In contrast to traditional job matching, Ginzberg[13] has identified two important facets of career planning which should be provided. First, he feels it should be a joint probing and evaluating of the individual's strengths, weaknesses, and potential. In the second stage of the process, the individual learns more about the career milieu in which goals can be realized.

In other words, career planning can be visualized as a means for providing two types of information: (1) affective and cognitive information about the person and (2) information about his or her career context. But to add a third facet to represent the corporation, this information should be translated into a form which can add to the manpower planning system's data base. That is, the information must be collected in a systematic way so that it can be manipulated for comparison with the demographic problem of knowing how many of what kind of human resources are available.

The *small-group model* as a facilitating method for generating this kind of information has been used widely and successfully by both business and academic institutions. It has a number of advantages. For instance, individuals participate at a personally comfortable rate and exchange useful information. Interaction between participants produces a controlled forum for the testing of individual thoughts and positions, and it can produce useful additions to the MP data base.

One component of the authors' programs has consisted of sets of instructions and projects to stimulate guided group interaction on shared concerns and to ground the interaction on a base of data which relates directly to participants' needs and to the environmental conditions affecting career planning. A great deal of experience has also been gathered by other organizations and experts on the usefulness and cost effectiveness of the small-group model in CP to generate action-oriented information.

A unique combination of corporate career information and personal experience delivered through small-group techniques is seen as an advantageous feature of economical CP programs. Group techniques are often selected for their relative efficiency, supplemented by one-to-one sessions as needed. One program objective should be to produce comparative indices by means of which individuals could evaluate themselves in relationship to items such as peer achievement, salary, technical obsolescence, interpersonal and managerial effectiveness, life-style, and especially, personal goals and values. From these base-line data, individuals can assess objective and subjective career progress, in terms that are personally meaningful and from which short-, medium-, and long-range career plans may be plotted in a source document. The resulting plan must be worked out in dialogue with the cognizant individuals who represent the corporate point of view in order to harmonize the needs of the parties involved, and appropriate data should be entered in the MP data base.

The authors have developed and implemented CP programs containing group interaction modules. Hundreds of employees at Educational Testing Service, SmithKline Corporation, and the state of Pennsylvania's Department of Public Welfare have participated in CP workshops with a program format similar to that described below in the section on life/career planning. The response to this method has been extremely positive. R. Stull and R. Mitchell,[14] of Pennsylvania's Department of Public Welfare Training Unit, have based a CP program on the life/career planning process for application to over 40,000 employees. This pioneering effort has demonstrated the cost effectiveness of the small-group model on a very large scale. As in this case, when such a method is designed to mesh with other existing methods in the organization, a very effective program can result.

The Career Development Window

Underlying many emerging CP systems is an assumption that the more the individual and the organization know about each other, the better. This issue, concerning how much reciprocal knowledge there is about the individual within the context of a career, can be represented by the Johari window. This device was named after its creators, Joseph Luft and Harry Ingham—hence the name "Johari." The assumption made about career planning is that the more open and honest the relationship between I and O, the better.

The career development version of the Johari window provides a way of conceptualizing the individual's relationships and the criteria for evaluating the effectiveness of his or her role in the building of these relationships in the career planning setting (see Fig. 11-5).

The upper left-hand square of the window represents the area that the individual knows and the area that the supervisor or manager knows. This is the common-knowledge or OPEN (PUBLIC) area in their relationship.

The area in the lower left-hand block indicates the things which the individual knows but which the supervisor does not know. This is referred to as the HIDDEN (DEFENSIVE) area. These are things the individual does not tell his or her supervisor.

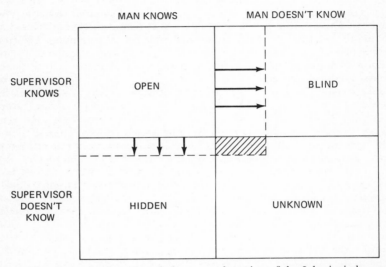

Fig. 11-5 The career development window—an adaptation of the Johari window concept of exposure and feedback process in personal growth in the employee-supervisor interview.

The upper right-hand block shows the area of knowledge that the supervisor has but does not tell the individual; and since the person does not know about the things in this area, it is referred to as the BLIND area. Without feedback from the career planning process, this can be a debilitating and sometimes dishonest area.

The bottom block on the right indicates an area about which neither the individual nor the supervisor knows. This is called the UNKNOWN area. In this area one may find undiscovered potential and creativity or other untapped capabilities or resources.

In line with the objective of the career planning process—to foster a clearer understanding, a sharper definition of purpose, and commitment between an individual and his or her supervisor (or with a third party in many cases) through a frank, participative discussion of climate, needs, strengths, feelings, aspirations, performance, and compensation—the Johari process might be applied in the following way.

If the person tells the supervisor some of the things that the supervisor does not know, the HIDDEN area is reduced, and this may stimulate some response or feedback from the supervisor in the area about which the person does not know, thereby reducing the BLIND area. In both cases it increases the "arena" or OPEN area between them and may expose more of the UNKNOWN or potential areas.

This concept and the emphasis on future planning can be helpful in meeting the objectives of career planning.

I-O and the Third-Party Role

Of critical importance in the CP process is the interview facet of the I-O dialogue, which often takes place between the individual and the immediate superior, at least. It is normally assumed that an effective dialogue can be managed between the two. In practice, a great deal of suspicion and anxiety are often involved in this part of the CP process. It might be asked whether it is desirable or even possible to have a candid dialogue between the individual and the supervisor. The critical variable in an individual's career is often the immediate superior. Many successful managers list a supportive supervisor as the crucial ingredient of career success. With such a great deal at stake in this relationship, caution on the part of the individual is likely to inhibit the flow of intensely candid information in a great many exchanges. This is a least one reason for the emerging felt need for some sort of facilitating third party in the CP process and for other mechanisms to mediate these conflicting needs. For instance, the authors have found in work with Stull and Mitchell, at the Pennsylvania Department of Public Welfare, that the third-party career counselor provides an integrating mechanism by taking the information emerging from the dialogue between the employee and the supervisor, as generated by the CP methods, to a career review committee. Then feedback is provided to both the supervisor and the employee. This feedback is then used to develop a career plan for the employee. This serves as useful mediating process to alleviate conflicts of interest in the CP program between the individual and the supervisor. At Educational Testing Service, the recruiters in the personnel department also specialize in third-party services to individuals and the organization.

   The Supervisor's Role   Another approach is to produce life/career planning workshops for employees which give them the basis for initiating career changes without necessarily involving their supervisor. Still another method is the external third-party career planning mechanism described by the authors in an article in the *Journal of College Placement*[15] outlining the use of the University Career Planning Office as a means of helping to mediate the I-O conflict of interest.

   The CP process should generate data in a form in which at least a great deal of these data are compatible with a central storage and retrieval system so that they can be used in the MP process too. One advantage of a computer system which is capable of comparing individuals against vacancies is that individuals are not wholly dependent upon their supervisors to pursue opportunities or growth experiences for them. Job posting is another avenue for accomplishing this, as is third-party career counseling. This responsibility can hardly be handled very well by a supervisor who has other pressing duties. In short, the CP process must take note of the fact that not all managers are apt as career facilitators, that supervisors are prone to human frailties, and that some provision must be made to prevent these realities from intruding on the purposes of the process. Naturally, this is an important concern, the subject of much lip service and worry from those designing CP programs. If the safeguards are inadequate, it is sure to emerge, for according to Murphy's law, "nature always finds the hidden flaw." But in today's environment it is more likely to be found by an agressive, ambitious individual who just may turn out to be a minority-group or woman employee with a great deal of familiarity with the law. Thus, leaving the initiative of the process of advancing an employee in the hands of a supervisor almost guarantees some degree of inequitable treatment. In contrast, some system of CP that is more or less self-initiated or automatically maintained is to be preferred.

   Skills finders, third-party help, job posting, and specialized workshops are several devices that can help minimize dependence on the supervisor, with all those intrinsic hazards of a threatening or inadequate I-O interaction.

TECHNIQUES AND METHODS OF CAREER PLANNING

A component of the nitty-gritty process model (Fig. 11-2) labeled *decision methods* lists a number of specific means which have been used in CP efforts. There are many other devices available in addition to those listed in the figure, but space limitations prevent detailed consideration of them. Full descriptions are available in the literature in the field. For instance, assessment centers and Transactional Analysis are discussed elsewhere in this handbook, and they are very useful components in CP program designs of many organizations. Three other methods will be described briefly: the life/career planning process, career paths, and job posting. Assessment centers are noted also.

Life/Career Planning

The life/career planning process is instrumental for career planning activities in a growing number of organizations. It is a reasonably simple method to use and can be administered independently of any other program or system. Its costs are negligible, requiring only blank paper and a pencil for each participant for recording thoughts and reactions to stimulating career questions. An ordinary conference room can be used as long as chairs can be arranged in small circular groups of three or four people. There are many variations of this process, but common to most is the idea that the individual is primarily responsible for his or her own career and that the result of the process is to have a written career plan in the individual's hands at the completion of the workshop. This plan can be used to fit together the purposes of the individual and the organization.

Many people make the assumption that their future (life or career) is determined largely by their past or is controlled largely by people other than themselves.

Career planning, dealing with a base of "here and now," has often slipped back into the past. It might be more effective if the process could slip more into the future. The following sequence of exercises is a way of bringing the future of one's choice into being. Any of the exercises, or the entire sequence, could be done by individuals, pairs, or groups. The latter method permits more sharing of one's plans with others and may generate more self-growth goals than could be achieved through self-insight alone.

The following exercises should help participants to confront various issues in their own lives and work and to begin making choices that will lead to greater fulfillment of their potential. Once these issues are met, the choice of future actions, plans, and projects becomes easier:

1. Draw a line which represents your life. This line may take any form or any direction to represent your life from the beginning to the end. Now mark an X on the line to indicate where you are right now. In your small group, show, explain, or discuss your life line.
2. Now that you have indicated where you are, answer, in as many ways as you can, the question: Who am I? For instance, goals, roles, values, responsibilities, traits, and needs may define who you are. After you have prepared this list either on one sheet of paper or on several cards, rearrange them in the order of importance to you. Did the sequence of the answers change from the order in which you wrote them? Did the sequence of the answers change from the order of importance to you? Share these also with other members of the group.
3. Look at the above and determine:
   a. Which are temporary and which are permanent?
   b. Which are things you wish to take with you into the future?

    c. Which are things that you would like to leave behind?

    d. Are there other things that you would like to add or modify?

4. Select a partner from a small group and ask each other the following questions:

    a. When do you feel fully "alive"? In other words, what things really turn you on? (These could be events, activities, achievements, etc. If certain things do turn you on and excite you, perhaps you should arrange your future so that these things happen more often.)

    b. What do you really do well? For example, what outstanding skills do you have, or in what kind of relationships do you function best?

    c. Given your circumstances and your desires, what do you need? What do you need to learn? (This is a pivotal question—sometimes there may be no correlation between *a* and *b* above, and you may find some things that you do not need or do not need to learn.)

    d. What dreams could you be turning into plans? (This is a question not casually answered, and it may reflect some things that you have often wanted to do, some ideas, some wishes, etc.)

    e. What should you stop doing now? What should you start doing now?

    f. What resources do you have that are underdeveloped, misused, or not used at all?

    g. Set up tentative life planning policies for yourself. (These could be fairly general or fairly concrete.)

The person asking the questions should act as a "consultant" to develop the data from the "client" and should write down only what the client says. When all the questions have been answered, the consultant should read it back. Then the client and consultant switch roles.

5. Write your biography—from now on. As an alternative, write your eulogy or your retirement-dinner speech. What will you have accomplished? What values are foremost in your thinking?

6. Describe the ideal job for you.

7. What resources do you have? How can you use them?

8. What sequences of steps can you initiate to begin your career plan?

There are numerous variations and extensions of this process; Lippitt[16] illustrates another version, as does Bolles.[17] Experience has shown the authors that a one-day workshop is very flexible and revealing. In between questions and group interaction on sharing responses, information is given to participants about the organizational career environment. When the first half of the workshop deals with life values and the second section focuses on career issues, there is a helpful integration of the goals the individual wants to actualize through the medium of the career. This process has been used by the authors at numerous organizations with very positive results.

Transactional Analysis

Among the newer devices to come to the attention of the career planning specialist is the methodology of Transactional Analysis (TA). The brainchild of Eric Berne,[18] it is a systematic way of analyzing interpersonal and intrapersonal dynamics. In the CP context it applies primarily to the process of analyzing those behaviors which unnecessarily limit growth and development. The logic of TA is an outgrowth of psychoanalytic psychology. The language used to describe the psychology of intrapersonal and interpersonal relations is understandable and meaningful to a large audience. It provides a common vocabulary for individuals to use in working through the relationships which affect their careers. Workshops based on TA can be very fruitful in pinpointing areas which are amenable to corrective action.

In *I'm OK, You're OK,* Harris[19] gives us a fresh frame of reference, in the lay person's language, to help us understand ourselves and our interaction with others.

McMahon[20] applies Transactional Analysis to the individual manager relationship established in the career planning process, for it can be intriguing and liberating indeed for individual and manager to recognize these facets of themselves and use the data of TA in effective career planning.

Career Paths

A common device very often confused with career planning is the method known as *career paths* or *career ladders.* In essence, career paths imply a structured series of predetermined on-the-job experiences which result in movement up a hierarchy.

Career paths can be a two-edged sword. While they do provide some closure for a career plan, they do not easily provide for the dynamics of either the organization or the individual in a changing environment. A major argument against "pathing" is that it assumes that an individual is being prepared for a job whose date of availability and content are known. It also assumes that the "when" and the "what" of the job are not likely to change prior to the individual's arrival. But there are intervening variables such as reorganizations and maturation of the individual which occur, and the requirement to avoid preparing for tomorrow's job according to today's I and O needs emerges.

Where structured experience is a technical necessity, there may be a place for career paths. But in many situations where organizational environments have become volatile, it makes little sense to structure careers much more than two to five years into the future. Structuring careers only a short distance into the future also avoids the embarrassing problem of having to explain to an individual why a career path must be abandoned after the individual has been sold on the long-range idea. New organizational structures such as the matrix concept (nonhierarchical work environments) and project management may eventually provide many optional ways of arranging developmental experiences which allow more flexibility in dealing with opportunities as they arise in a dynamic organization. They also point out the need for continuously assessing the individual's cognitive and personal growth in order to optimize opportunities for I and O as they occur.

Job Posting

Job posting is the intraorganizational equivalent of publicly announcing position vacancies in the classified section of a newspaper. Candidates apply according to their aspirations and career plans. As Yeager and Yeager have shown,[21] individuals, motivated to apply for vacancies on their own, produce a vastly superior organizational climate for I-O optimization than can be attained through any other single method of CP. Systems combining job posting with other devices such as life/career planning, assessment centers, organizational development, and manager development are experiencing efficient and effective results. There is a great deal of management resistance to the openness of announcing vacancies and their relative positions in the hierarchy, usually stated in terms meaning that individuals cannot be trusted to behave conveniently and rationally if they are given options. But in terms of the Johari window, mentioned earlier, openness and honesty are assumed to be ends in themselves. Organizations which cannot fathom this concept are the same organizations from which an individual would be well-advised to plan an intelligent departure. Openness and honesty are the foundation of the habeas emotum, and job posting can be a keystone in the development of such an environment.

Assessment Centers

The purpose of the assessment center is to create miniature situations, or simulations, of job functions and processes under controlled conditions where individuals may be systematically observed by judges and where their readiness to advance in the organization may be evaluated.

This is a distinct advance over the traditional paper-and-pencil personality tests, which attempted to answer the question: What is the person like? The assessment approach focuses more on the question: What can the person do? What a person *does* is a much better predictor of performance than what that person is *like*.

Byham[22] has developed a series of exercises which elicit observable problem-solving skills from individuals being assessed. Such exercises can be administered in a wide variety of combinations as needed by any organization. The process of assessment is usually carried out by a designated unit of the organization or a consultant; during the course of the assessment, the dimensions common to success in management are displayed by the assessees as they work through the assessment tasks. On the basis of the results of the process, placement decisions can be made. (See also Chapter 16, The Assessment Center Method.)

SUMMARY

Manpower planning as a function in its broadest sense is very much like a comprehensive list of personnel functions, old and new, ranging from wage and salary and recruiting to OD and behavioral science. It is the operational concept of human resource management in action.

Often, reading the list of functions carried out by a manpower planning or human resource planning function is very much like reading the table of contents in a comprehensive textbook on personnel. Policy, procedure, practices, legislation—all these things are subsumed under the concept of MP and range from the traditional to the exotic. Often, the MP function will be circumscribed to personnel planning, but human resources are one-third of a corporation's resources (money and physical facilities being the others). Human resources are perhaps the most important because of the human element involved. These are the resources which "wear out" with disuse or improper use. MP is synonymous with the scope of the personnel or human resource function and is not merely a narrow planning role within a corporate personnel operation. It is the total human resource concept or system.

Career planning, on the other hand, can often be translated into programs and procedures which are designed to give the individual leverage in carving out a personal career within the corporate environment in dialogue with the organization. If, at the decision point in the nitty-gritty process, the corporation wins in any conflicts which arise, the results are often turnover, depressed morale, difficulty in recruiting high-caliber individuals, or, especially, suboptimization of available resources.

It is hoped that CP will open a facilitating dialogue between the individual and the organization in order to optimize their mutual needs as they are set in the context of manpower planning.

Some desirable features or criteria of CP programs are the ideas that individuals should be able to articulate and specify their desires (consistent with the jobs available), that the corporation will endeavor to match those needs as much as possible and not be capricious or arbitrary, and that the corporation will follow through on commitments and expectations which are raised. It is not desirable to determine that individuals want to transfer to Kalamazoo, only to send them to Kokomo. A great number of techniques are available which contribute to the decisions reached in the nitty-gritty process, some of which have been mentioned.

The data which are elicited from the individual in CP programs tend to age rapidly because people are dynamic, changing entities. The half-life of CP data seems, as a rule of thumb, to be reached within 18 to 24 months in many cases. Family circumstances change, career aspirations are modified, interests shift, new goals emerge, etc.

Of course, at appropiate points in the CP dialogue, individuals have the obligation to achieve whatever developmental goals are required to prepare them for the career objectives which have been delineated.

From a programmatic point of view, it is preferable to have CP programs which are easily administered and maintained. If CP can transcend being viewed as "just another personnel program" overlaid upon the busy line manager, the chances of success are increased.

REFERENCES

1. Vetter, Eric W.: *Manpower Planning for High Talent Personnel,* University of Michigan, Graduate School of Business Administration, Ann Arbor, 1967.
2. *Manpower Programs: Bulletin to Management,* Bureau of National Affairs, no. 1192, part 2, Dec. 14, 1972.
3. Luft, Joseph: *Group Processes,* 2d ed., National Press Books, Palo Alto, Calif., 1970.
4. Yeager, Joseph: "A Model for Inducing Change in Social Systems: A Preliminary Report," paper for the American Educational Research Association, annual convention, Chicago, 1972.
5. Morrison, Edward J.: *Developing Computer-based Employee Information Systems,* American Management Association, Research Study 99, New York, 1969.
6. Casey, J., R. Perry, and D. Berry: *Punched Cards,* 2d ed., Reinhold Publishing Corporation, New York, 1958.
7. Morgan, Phillip: Personal communication, 1974.
8. Yeager, Joseph C.: "Management Development: An Act of Faith," *Training and Development Journal,* May 1971.
9. Kellogg, Marion S.: *Career Management,* American Management Association, New York, 1972.
10. McMahon, John, and Joseph Yeager: *Corporate Career Planning Workshop,* University of Michigan, Division of Management Education, Ann Arbor, 1973–1974.
11. McMahon, John: *Life-Career Planning Seminar,* University of Cincinnati, November 1973.
12. Kellogg: *op. cit.*
13. Ginzberg, Eli: *Career Guidance: Who Needs It, Who Provides It, Who Can Improve It,* McGraw-Hill Book Company, New York, 1971.
14. Stull, Robert, Robert Mitchell, John McMahon, and Joseph Yeager: Career Planning Workshop Series, Commonwealth of Pennsylvania, Department of Public Welfare, Harrisburg, 1973.
15. Yeager, Joseph C., and John McMahon: "Adult Career Planning: A Needed Solution," *Journal of College Placement,* Spring, 1974.
16. Lippitt, Gordon: "Developing Life Plans," *Training and Development Journal,* May 1970.
17. Bolles, Richard N.: *What Color Is Your Parachute?* Ten Speed Press, Berkeley, Calif., 1972.
18. Berne, Eric: *Transactional Analysis in Psychotherapy,* Grove Press, Inc., New York, 1961.
19. Harris, Thomas: *I'm OK, You're OK,* Harper & Row, Publishers, Incorporated, New York, 1969.
20. McMahon, John, and Joseph Yeager: *Womanpower Resources Workshop,* University of Michigan, Division of Management Education, Ann Arbor, 1973–1974.
21. Yeager, Joseph, and David Yeager: "Optimizing Human Resources with Transfer and Promotion Policies," *Career Planning Workshop,* University of Michigan, Division of Management Education, Ann Arbor, 1973–1974.
22. Byham, William: *Catalogue of Assessment Exercises,* Development Dimensions, Inc., Pittsburgh, 1973.

Chapter **12**

Instructional Systems

JOHN P. CICERO

John P. Cicero *is President, Management and Educational Consulting, Leesburg, Virginia. Until recently, he was Manager of Instructor Training, Xerox International Center for Training and Management Development where he directed the design, implementation, and evaluation of instructor training programs for sales, service, and management development as well as administrative, manufacturing, and corporate headquarters and personnel and other training operations. At Xerox he was also Manager of Performance Analysis and Manager of Service Education Development. Currently Adjunct Associate Professor at George Washington University, College of Government and Business, he also taught at Rochester Institute of Technology, College of Business Administration, and Syracuse University, College of Business. Dr. Cicero was Instructor in Business Administration and Research Associate dealing with NASA/APOLLO program management, and Instructor in Business Communications for the Central City Business Institute. His articles include "Behavioral Objectives for Technical Training Systems"* (Training and Development Journal, *1973*), *"The Project Manager: Anomalies and Ambiguities"*(Academy of Management Journal, *September 1970*), *and "A Concept of Project Authority: A Multidimensional View"* (IEEE Transactions on Engineering Management, *May 1970*). *He holds a Ph.D. from Syracuse University (1971) in instructional technology (his dissertation was entitled "A Program Management Approach to Instructional Technology"), an M.B.A. from Syracuse University (1969) in organization and management, and an A.B. from the University of Rochester (1966) in English and history. He attended Syracuse University Law School for one year (1967).*

SYSTEMS PERFORMANCE

To utilize a systems concept effectively, designers must assume the management science stance. In other words, they must *overview* those elements which may have an impact on outcomes and/or performances. The key is to tie the system to some performance.

A performance approach considers a multitude of factors that interrelate to affect the outcomes of *specific people in specific positions.* If, then, you are talking about an *instructional* performance system, you want to focus the system on the position and consider what combination of elements is going to affect performance within that position. For example, consider Fig. 12-1.

While the six factors outlined below are not intended to be all-inclusive, given their somewhat generic applicability, a brief discussion of each is appropriate.

Instructional Systems   The total instructional system involves the design, carry-out, and evaluation functions on a per-program basis. Pivotal considerations are a *learner-based orientation* and *job-relevant content evaluation*.

Perhaps the most common error is that of an instructor orientation. If the question of what to teach underlies the basic design philosophy, a performance system will never be the ultimate outcome. The approach must ask: What do we want the trainee to learn and to be able to do? *What trainee behaviors are we looking*

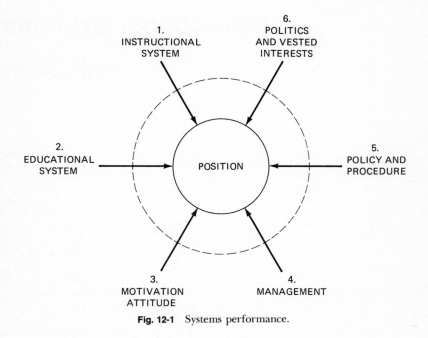

Fig. 12-1   Systems performance.

for? The focus begins and ends with the trainee. This concept will be dealt with in more detail later.

Job-relevant content is another area in which mistakes often occur. What can happen is that program development, even if learner-oriented, may take place in a vacuum. It is possible to develop educationally sound training programs that are not relevant to anything specific. Work the process from the position and the desired performance backward. If training is developed with a view toward *the learner in his or her position performing some task,* much ineffectiveness can be minimized.

Educational Systems   Seldom does training consist of a single program. More often there is a multitude of programs, cross-training considerations, refresher training, continuing education, and any number of other learning forums confronting trainees at different points in their development. This larger learning environment must be evaluated in terms of sequence and continuity. This total system impacts performance in a more comprehensive way than any single program can. Questions might be:

- Have conflicts or contradictions in information moving from one program to another been avoided?
- Has duplication in the total training process been avoided?
- Have "gaps" in the total training process been avoided?

- Have unnecessary or unexplained methodological shifts from one program to another been avoided?
- Is there reinforcement of previous learning from one program to another?
- Is there some centralized "control" of the total training package?
- Is there consistent feedback to the trainee throughout the training process?
- Is timing such that new skills can be practiced and reinforced both in training and on the job?

A "no" response to any of these questions may have a significant negative impact on performance. The instructional systems individually affect performance, and they also collectively are interdependent and affect one another and *together* affect performance. This interdependence works throughout the factors of the performance model.

Motivation and Attitude   While the total realm of motivational concepts may be relevant, consider, for the moment, potential negative fallout. Negative motivators can, in effect, cancel any gain derived through effective instructional and educational systems. Enough research evidence exists to support the contention that attitudes and/or feelings toward the learning environment are as important as any content considerations. This area will also be discussed in more detail in a later section.

Management   The ability to monitor a performance system effectively represents a critical input. Any instructional (educational) system is only as effective as the management support and understanding behind it. For example, a system without appropriate logistics, financing, and evaluation from a cost-effective and trade-off perspective cannot achieve a meaningful performance output. Even more basic is communication of simple procedural techniques. For example, how can a manager evaluate an instructional system if he or she is unaware of how it operates? A classic misinterpretation occurs when the manager looks at traditional classroom evaluation techniques while judging a self-paced criterion-referenced program.

Policy and Procedure   The formal structure and operation of the organization need to be consistent with training objectives and motivational considerations. Policy that precludes desired performance outcomes will have an obvious negative impact. Too often policy may have the effect of rewarding nonperformance and punishing performance. For example, a task may take an hour to complete effectively, and yet a policy may exist constraining completion time to 45 minutes. The effective performer will be "punished," and the ineffective performer "rewarded," over the long run.

Politics and Vested Interests   Often embarking on a systems approach generates a change-paced environment. The rapidity and frequency of the change sometimes make a clear distinction between the old and the new at best difficult, but more often this distinction becomes impossible to make because of the absence of any true comparative base. This may lend an air of ambiguity to the total systems process. Where flexibility and maneuverability are the key to successful completion, resistance may predominate. The resistance is generally subtle, even to the extent of being unconscious. The reason for this is that from a logic base, there is little with which to openly attack a systems approach. Furthermore, open attack can be confronted directly and dealt with directly.

The more subdued resistance falls prey to politics and vested interests. The status quo is the hue and cry. Change for the sake of change is the formally defined enemy. The factors that operate include habit, the natural inclination to do things the way one has always done them, the risk involved in changing a previously successful strategy, the reaction to ego models as examples for our own action, basic insecurity about changing any mode of operation, and group norms and pressures. The issue for practical purposes is not the kind or frequency of resistant traits, but who and/or what groups have them. The system cannot be implemented without management support or implementer support. A nonresistant management cannot command away this type of resistance; nonresistant implementers cannot survive a resistant management. The impact, then, of politics and vested interests in a resistant mode infiltrates the whole systems performance model.

THE GENERIC INSTRUCTIONAL SYSTEM

A Model   An instructional system contains three basic elements:

1. A definition or statement of the behaviors that the trainee must be capable of demonstrating at the completion of training
2. A definition or statement of the relationship between the behaviors achieved in training and actual on-the-job performance
3. A recognition and simulation of the on-the-job conditions under which the trainee must demonstrate the behaviors

The above elements can be broken down into several steps which take the program design from initial establishment of a course goal through the development of an ongoing feedback and revision cycle. Figure 12-2 represents a generic model showing the flow of this development process.

Goal Analysis   To formulate the overall direction of the system effectively, it must first be broken down into logically identifiable subsystems. For example, a program for auto mechanics might look at any number of subsystems such as the fuel system, the electrical system, and the steering system. It is important to identify the relationships between these subsystems and the logical sequence in which they might be taught. However, the most critical input at this stage is the development of a task listing which describes, for each subsystem, the *behaviors* the mechanic is expected to *perform.* This listing will help clarify the relationships and interdependencies between system components and the sequence of presenting information. At this stage information may be collected from product experts or from engineering, training, or any other group associated with the desired outcomes. Once this procedure has been followed, a course goal can be formally written.

The reasoning behind this process is to focus the system immediately on learner behavior and/or performance outcomes. Without yet going into a lot of detail, the system takes on a direction and specificity not possible as a result of simply speculating about what its outcomes should or should not be.

Target Population and Assumptions   To purposely move a trainee from one level of skill or knowledge to another, it is necessary to know the trainee's level prior to entering the system. What skills and knowledges does the trainee already possess, and where is his or her level in comparison with the expected performances the training program is designed to achieve? This must be measured at the point of entrance into the program. However, be certain that you look at the skills and knowledges specific to the instructional system you are dealing with. Too often a measure of *potential ability,* rather than specific program-relevant skills, is taken. For example, you cannot determine entry level in the auto mechanics program by testing generic mechanical skills—you must test those skills which are specific to what you are going to teach. The potential ability to use a screwdriver, for example, is not the same as the acquired skill of being able to use a screwdriver to adjust the air intake on a carburetion system.

In many cases, the entering behaviors of the target population are assumed rather than measured. While measurement is the acceptable approach, there are at least three basic reasons why it becomes feasible for the program developer to make assumptions:

1. To take precise measurements would either cost too much or take too much time with respect to the payoff.
2. Certain types of measurements are difficult to get or are valid for only a specific point in time, e.g., measurements of attitude, mood, or motivation.
3. The behavior is obvious, and no benefit would be gained by precise measurement.

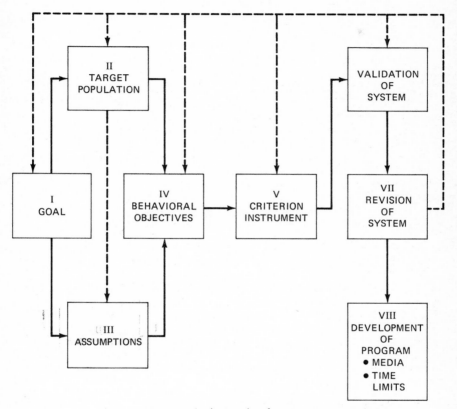

Fig. 12-2 An instructional system.

Whether to measure a behavior exactly or to make an assumption is always a trade-off situation balancing measurement results against cost, time, and possible impacts on learner and/or program performance and effectiveness. An incorrect measurement obviously adversely affects the program. Keep in mind, however, that an incorrect assumption will also negative impact the system—the fact that it was merely an assumption, and perhaps a subjective one, does not lessen its importance.

Behavioral Objectives   The behavioral objective fine-tunes the learner behaviors necessary for the trainee to complete the program successfully. In effect, the objective is the core of the system. Each objective must contain three criteria:

- what you want the trainee to do;
- under what conditions; and
- a measurement.

In developing objectives, the two most frequent errors are (1) focusing on what the *instructor* should do and (2) making objectives too complex by combining several behaviors into a single objective.

While there is general consensus on the above comments, the process of developing a system with objectives poses a central issue: Where should development start, and what can be traded off when time, cost, and manpower constraints prevent the "perfect" theory from reaching its ultimate realization (See Fig. 12-3)?

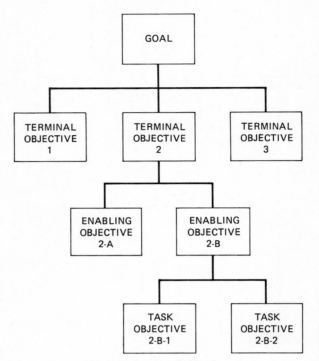

Fig. 12-3 System of objectives.

The system of objectives themselves may be compared with an organization chart. The goal is the president. It gives overall direction. Working for it directly are terminal objectives; for them, enabling objectives; and for them, task objectives. The issue is: Should initial system design move from the goal down or from the task objective up? It is the opinion of this writer that to achieve and maintain system continuity, the system should be built from the terminal behavior down to the task behavior. This is especially critical in an industrial environment where time, cost, or manpower constraints may curtail total design efficiency. For example, if a task objective is used as the starting point, it is not meaningful until *all* related task and enabling behaviors have been identified to *collectively* determine where the system is going. On the other hand, a series of terminal objectives clearly identifies the end points in the system and gives a continuous flow. The trade-off is leaving the detail up to the expertise of the instructor; at least, however, the instructor knows exactly where he or she is going and also knows exactly what trainee behaviors are expected.

Criterion Instruments   For all practical purposes, once a behavioral objective is developed, an internally consistent testing program is immediately available. The objective states a behavior, the conditions, and the measurement. The test item need ask only for the performance, under the conditions stated, and to the level of proficiency demanded. For example, how would you test for the following objective? "The trainee will be able to write a behaviorally stated objective without the use of any resource materials. The objective must include a behavioral term, conditions, and a measurement."

To make the test, you would ask the trainee to write the behaviorally stated objective and evaluate it in terms of whether the three criteria were present. The method of evaluation is not norm-referenced, but criterion-referenced. In other words, each trainee is rated against a performance, *not* against his or her peers. In this mode the traditional grading structure breaks down. It does not become a question of percentages or of A's versus F's; instead, trainees meet the objective (the performance), or they do not.

Validation and Revision   It was suggested earlier that it is possible to develop a system that is relevant only to itself—one that is educationally sound, but not related to on-the-job performance. In this context, the validation of the system must take place with a view toward actual on-the-job performances.

Look at the trainee's job and explore the following kinds of questions with respect to the training program:

- Is the emphasis in training the same as that in actual field performance, or are you training heavily on the exceptions and perhaps not at all on day-to-day routine operations?
- Are you overtraining skills that can be affected only by continuous practice and undertraining skills that can be mastered with limited in-training practice?
- Are you setting objectives in training that are unrealistic in terms of actual job conditions? How closely do the conditions in an objective simulate the work environment?
- Are you training for performances today that will not occur on the job for many months?
- Is there a skill-level difference or a shorter learning curve between formally trained personnel and untrained personnel?
- Is your training program addressing only trainable activities, or are you focusing on problems not resolvable through training, such as inconsistent policy or inefficient management?

By answering questions like these, you can validate the system or, if necessary, revise it to meet the performance criteria it is designed to achieve.

MANAGING THE AFFECTIVE DOMAIN

While most training programs strive for specific task achievement and often within compressed time parameters, research in human learning has shown that emotions, attitudes, and feelings are important to effective learning. The implication is that to the extent that training programs fail to generate positive affect (emotions, attitudes, and feelings), they fail to generate effective learning.

Six areas are briefly considered: (1) negative affect and job dependency; (2) communication skills, knowledge, and attitude toward the subject matter; (3) reinforcement and contingency management in the classroom; (4) the target population; (5) interactive instruction; and (6) the use of media for stimulus intensification.

Negative Affect and Job Dependency   While the thrust is to look at positive affect, the effect of job dependency on training cannot be ignored. All too often, trainees are motivated primarily by the belief that their jobs and/or opportunities for advancement depend upon successful completion of the training. Learning itself may run a distant second. In terms of long-range vested competence, a positive attitude toward learning must be maximized, and the threat to job security minimized.

If trainees are forced to succeed to minimize their risk, that is not the same success gained through concept, principle, and problem-solving learning. "Playing the game" and learning produce substantially different long-term results. It is, then, management's responsibility to provide a true learning environment. This responsibility includes (1) generating a positive attitude toward training, stressing individual growth and development (and deemphasizing job dependency); (2) developing an educationally as well as technically competent training force; (3) keeping abreast of new technology in education; and (4) giving appropriate financial and facilities support to technical training areas.

Communication   Beyond   management   support,   communication   skills, knowledge and attitude toward the subject matter itself play important roles in generating positive affect. However, each of these factors must be viewed from a dual perspective—from the point of view of the trainer-instructor *and* from the point of view of the trainee-learner.

Communication skills are relevant whether we are considering a traditional classroom environment, a programmed instruction module, or any other medium. Examples using language are obvious—either the instruction matches the learner's language skills, or no effective learning can take place. The classic discrepancy occurs when the instructor talks "above" the students. Another common error is assigning written programs at a level above the learner's reading skills. A less obvious problem occurs with the use of visual images. While a visual can, indeed, communicate a multitude of concepts, the clarity of that communication is dependent upon the learner's visual perception.

The question is: How often are these factors considered in the design of a technical training program? Recently, in my own organization a programmed instruction module used to teach basic circuits and symbols to new-hire technical representatives was evaluated to be approximately four grade levels higher than the average reading skill of the user. However, the same module matched the skill level of the designer almost perfectly. There are two choices: (1) Bring the learner's reading level up, or (2) bring the reading level of the module down. Even more important, however, is increasing the designer's awareness of the problem.

The example may seem almost too simple. However, communication skills are often assumed and seldom measured. The measure is relatively simple and can, perhaps, be even subjective. If a discrepancy is allowed to exist, the motivation level of the learner must go down as a result of pure lack of attention and/or an inability to attach any meaning or understanding to the technical training program.

Teacher versus Learner Orientation.   Knowledge also affects the learner's motivation. However, a discrepancy between the learner's knowledge and the instructor's knowledge is not a liability, but in fact is a necessity. The assumption is that the instruction will increase learner knowledge. This increase is a factor of learning, not teaching per se. In other words, the instruction itself is merely a vehicle to enhance learning and therefore should be learner-oriented and not teacher-oriented, as already expressed.

This is a rather subtle point and can be expressed through the following example. In a recent training program a student was unable to recognize the conceptual distinction between teaching and learning. The argument was that there is a one-to-one correlation between what the teacher teaches and what the learner learns. This may be true in the case of simple memorization tasks, but not in the case of more complicated problem-solving tasks. In the example of the student, for instance, the subject matter (or what the instructor was teaching) was the distinction between learning and teaching. If indeed they are related one-to-one, the problem should never have occurred.

The point is that when developing a training program, you should focus the instruction on learner behaviors rather than instructor behaviors. This would apply particularly to the instructor's guide itself. Such guides tend to focus on timetables and instructor activities to the exclusion of any learner activities. It is only through learner behavior that one can measure the effectiveness of the program.

The final area in communications is attitude toward the subject matter itself. Here the instructor plays an important role; positive attitudes on the part of the instructor will generally have a positive effect on the student, and negative attitudes will generally have a negative effect. However, keep in mind the distinction between a negative attitude and constructive criticism. There is almost always a place for the latter. Take a simple example— a problem area in a machine in terms of reliability and/or maintainability. The instructor can imply that the designers must have been asleep on the job, or the learner can be honestly cautioned about certain problem areas and told that one of the challenging aspects of the work will be to keep these in check. In either case the "self-fulfilling prophecy" will take over. The learner will develop a negative attitude or accept the challenge.

Reinforcement Perhaps the most powerful tool available in training is positive reinforcement of desired performances. Trainees must be constantly made aware of their progress. Reinforcement, to be most effective, must occur in three modes: (1) performance/contingency management in the classroom, (2) content and skill practice and critiquing during training, and (3) performance evaluation on the job.

In the classroom the instructor needs to give learners feedback consistent in terms of their progress in meeting the objectives of the performance system. The single most important consideration is the immediacy of the feedback in relation to the performance. Beyond simple one-time acknowledgment of a performance, important skills need to be reinforced throughout the training cycle. Seldom will one-time feedback assure skill acquisition over an extended period. If proper attention is paid to a system sequence, the program becomes self-reinforcing through a behavior-building and/or behavior-shaping approach. Finally, an on-the-job evaluation of skill usage is the single most important step in tying training performance to on-the-job performance.

The Target Population Apart from any skill considerations, the performance system is also dependent upon an awareness of the environmental conditions from which the trainees are emerging. To deal effectively with attitudes in the classroom, to get trainees to make a critical judgment about the content, and finally to get trainees to develop a philosophy about the conceptual input they are exposed to, some understanding of their background and work environment is essential.

When "perfect" content is presented to a group in an unacceptable manner, much of its potential impact is lost. Ask yourself questions such as the following:

- Are there cultural distinctions between the various groups of trainees?
- Do the trainees have reason to believe the training is a waste of time for them?
- Were the trainees properly prepared to come into a formalized training session?
- Will the trainees' past work experiences pose particularly difficult problems in teaching them "our" system?

- Are there on-the-job pressures that make the trainees reluctant to take time out for further training?
- Are the trainees particularly sensitive about who or where they are?
- During training, are the trainees provided a proper living environment?

Again, any of these factors may have an impact on the performance system.

Interactive Instruction and Media   The final points to be made involve simply maintaining attention. From a communications viewpoint, learning cannot take place in any meaningful sense unless the attention of the learner is maintained. The more interactive the instruction through the use of questioning techniques, role playing, simulations, labs, and the like, the better the chance of maximizing attention. The media used should be directly associated with the learning objective and also, by virtue of their very characteristics, should enhance the process of maintaining attention. This is especially relevant in industrial training where programs run over a 40-hour week.

SUMMARY AND CONCLUSIONS

The primary focus of a system, then, is the learner, the trainee. The system needs to specifically designate, measure, and reinforce performance. The performance itself needs to consider the on-the-job skills and knowledges. And finally, while the system provides content consistency and relevance, the attitudes surrounding that system—on the part of the trainer, the trainees, and management—are paramount to achieving the desired outcomes. In the final analysis, the instructional system is a learner-oriented, position-relevant, performance-oriented training tool that considers content and attitude and is designed for constant evaluation and update.

BIBLIOGRAPHY

Butler, F. Coit: *Instructional Systems Development for Vocational and Technical Training,* Educational Technology Publications, Englewood Cliffs, N.J., 1972.

Mager, Robert F.: *Preparing Instructional Objectives,* Fearon Publishers, Inc., Belmont, Calif., 1962.

Mager, Robert F., and Peter Pipe: *Analyzing Performance Problems,* Fearon Publishers, Inc., Palo Alto, Calif., 1970.

Tracey, William R.: *Evaluating Training and Development Systems,* American Management Association, New York, 1968.

Tracey, W. R.: *Managing Training and Development Systems,* AMACOM (Division of American Management Associations), New York, 1974.

Chapter 13

Management by Objectives

GEORGE S. ODIORNE

George S. Odiorne *is Dean of the School of Business and Professor of Management at the University of Massachusetts in Amherst. Prior to joining the staff at the University of Massachusetts, Dr. Odiorne was Dean of the College of Business and Professor of Management at the University of Utah for five years; before that, he was Director of the Bureau of Industrial Relations at the University of Michigan, a position he held for 10 years. He has taught management and economics at Rutgers and New York Universities. His experience includes positions with General Mills, Inc.; American Management Association; and American Can Company. He has also been a consultant to many major American corporations. His education includes a bachelor's degree from Rutgers and an M.B.A. and a Ph.D. from New York University. Dr. Odiorne serves on several boards of directors of corporations and civic institutions. He is a member of several learned societies and is also the author of 10 books and 100 articles. His most current books include* Management and the Activity Trap *(1974),* Personnel Administration *(1972),* Green Power: The Corporation and the Urban Crisis *(1969),* Management Decisions by Objectives *(1969), and* Management by Objectives: A System of Managerial Leadership *(1965).*

The relationship between ends and means is no new question. Machiavelli advised his Prince on this matter. Philosophers have noted it as a moral question. In more modern times Max Weber described the bureaucracy as a form of organization which often produced "bureaucrats," persons who were stuck on methods rather than results. Robert Merton, in 1940, wrote on the "Disfunctions of the Bureaucracy," pointing out that one such ill effect of the bureaucratic form is that people lose sight of their goals. He called this *goals displacement*. By this he meant that people become so enmeshed in procedures that they lose sight of the reasons for the procedures, and the true goals (results) are displaced by false goals (activity). All of these sociological observations are a conceptual background for the idea of Management by Objectives. The MBO idea is a conceptually simple one: People who pay unremitting attention to purpose are more likely to attain their objectives than people who lose sight of them because they are diverted from them.

   The Cure for This Diversion?   At the beginning of every period, each manager and each subordinate sit down and jointly work out agreements concerning the subordinate's objectives, with specific criteria for performance in each area of subordinate responsibility. Thus the subordinate is clear in advance as to what is expected and as to what would constitute good performance and bad performance. This, it is proposed, will improve subordinates' performance and facilitate their motivation and growth. If during the period they can assess their own performance and at the end of the period show how well or how poorly they have done, the growth is further accelerated. This is, of course, not an addition to their work, but a way of doing it.

MANAGEMENT BY OBJECTIVES: THE CURRENT STATE OF THE ART

During the sixties Management by Objectives (MBO) was *discovered* widely and changed from a narrowly applied kind of criteria development for performance review into a general management system.

Business Origins

The organizers of large corporations in the last half of the nineteenth century learned some painful lessons about management: (1.) It was a giant feat to organize a large organization, and (2.) it was *something else* to manage it profitably for survival.[1]

What they learned, and what many modern conglomerators have not yet learned, is that although no individual can direct all the activities of a large organization, a person who can control *results* can indeed manage even the largest.

Peter Drucker, whose original studies were in General Motors Corporation, noted this distinction,[2] spelled the idea out clearly in his lectures at New York University in the forties, and published it as a chapter in his *Practice of Management* in 1954.[3]

The application to a narrow usage, that of establishing results-oriented appraisal systems where stated goals replace personality traits as appraisal criteria, occurred in a number of large corporations. It was applied in General Mills, Inc., in 1955,[4] an application noted by McGregor in a well-known article appearing in *Harvard Business Review* in 1960.[5] Likert also noted it as a means of implementing participative management at about the same time.[6]

Yet in such a narrow context it sometimes failed to stick. Sometimes it was seen as another personnel department gimmick.[7] In other cases, a change of management caused it to exit with the old guard. It was this single use which constituted its greatest weakness.

Schleh, a consultant who made the commercial mistake of being ahead of his time, has treated it as a general system of management.[8] Odiorne,[9] following five years of monthly seminars for executives at Michigan, published *Management by Objectives: A System of Managerial Leadership* in 1965, which was widely read in executive circles. This book ties the MBO idea to the systems approach. It went through 14 printings, including foreign ones, between October 1965 and June 1970. Numerous other books and articles have followed.

The Systems Approach   Of the numerous kinds of "systems" which could fall within a general systems theory[10] the cybernetic, or feedback, system is usually identified as the most typical. Among its applications is that to the economics of the organization. Three elements make up such a system (see Fig. 13-1).

Inputs are the resources committed to an idea to make it a tangible, going concern. They include capital (fixed, working, cash, receivables, inventories) labor, and materials.

Activities are the behaviors of people—designing, making, selling, keeping books, engineering, bargaining, and the like—which *add value* (presumably) to the inputs.

Outputs are the goods and services—hardware and software—which *come out* of the system. These outputs are more valuable than all the inputs which were used up to make them, and a *value added* can be computed.

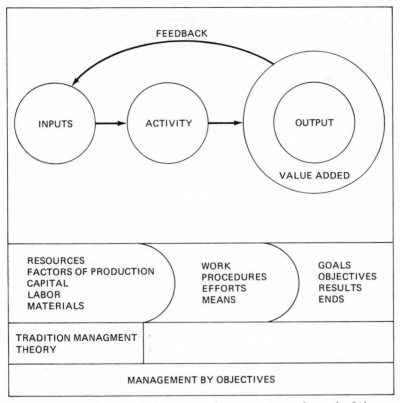

Fig. 13-1 Schematic of a cybernetic system—the most commonly used of the systems approaches.

This value added is the profit, the need being filled, the *purpose* for which *the input is being committed and the activity is being carried out.* Two ways of disposing of this surplus value are customary: (1) They are *fed back* into the system, and (2) they are distributed to the beneficiaries of the system as dividends, learning, satisfactions, benefits, needs met, and the like.

While this short course in the economics of an organization as a system is instructive as a map, it is also a diagram of the traps that await managers and other people who are *part* of the system.

The easy trap to fall into is that of becoming emotionally overattached to one element of what must be a three-element system:

1. Some become *input*-obsessed and spend their time preventing expenditure. (Think of the person who will disapprove your expense account.)
2. Others become *output* fanatics and heartily resist considering whether the inputs and resources are adequate, or the activities possible. (Think of the desk pounder and "I demand results, not alibis" type.)

3. Far more prevalent, however, are the activity-obsessed people. They are competent, professional, and often dedicated, but they have lost sight of inputs used up or even of *results* sought.

Thus, in system terms, *Management by Objectives is a system which begins by defining outputs and applies these output statements as criteria to judge the quality of activity (behavior) and to govern the release and effectiveness of the inputs.*[11]

In more ordinary language, MBO is a system under which the manager and subordinate sit down at the beginning of each period and talk until agreement on job goals has been reached. During the period, the subordinate is given wide latitude in choice of method. At the end of the period the actual results are jointly reviewed against agreed-upon goals, and an assessment of the degree of success is made. The process is begun again.

MBO OBJECTIVES

As a result of this procedure, several normal benefits of value to the *organization* and the *individual* should be more likely:

1. *A natural tendency toward goal displacement will be alleviated.* There is some research which tends to show that in human organizations, a normal and perhaps natural (at least an explainable) tendency exists for people to *start out* toward momentarily clear goals, but shortly to become so enmeshed with *activity* that the goal is lost.[12]

In its most aggravated form the "activity" management becomes a matter of deep-rooted procedures (as with salary administration, job descriptions, etc.) and attempts to revert back to basic purposes meet with strong resistance. ("Do it my way.")

MBO from the top-management perspective is a direct attempt to build into management systems an unremitting attention to purpose.

2. *MBO should clarify role conflict and ambiguity between individual managers and subordinates.* There is evidence that, left to their own devices, the average manager and subordinate manager are not apt to be in agreement about the subordinate manager's responsibilities in terms of outputs for any given period of time ahead.[13] Such a lack of agreement makes it impossible for subordinates to "succeed," with corresponding ill effects to them in terms of pay, bonus, promotion, and recorded performance reports. Even further ill effects ensue when coaching to "improve" them probes matters such as personality, attitude, motives, background, or similar proposed explanation of "failure."

MBO attacks directly the gap between expectations and performance and directly defines "success" in specific output terms.

3. *MBO should be causally associated with the overall success of the organization.* Drucker has noted that in leading corporations—General Motors, Ford, IBM, GE—where size has required divisionalized forms of organization, "Management *is* Management by Objectives."[14] My own prolonged observations in leading firms have convinced me that more people are aware of their goals in the more successful firms (the ones that achieve charted goals) than in less successful organizations. Sears managers know their goals better than failing small merchants.

Participative management is not as uniformly present but is perhaps more possible under MBO than under intuitive or autocratic centralized management. This style is discretionary, but in many kinds of organization (where the people have been taught to expect it) it is mandatory to avoidance of disruption.

Clarity of objectives between all links of individual managers is more likely to produce cumulative clarity of objectives.

Thus, MBO should improve overall organizational performance and increase the level of participation.

4. *When individuals are clear about their own job objectives, their performance is better than when they are not clear about these objectives.*   It is to be expected that individual performance will improve when goals are clarified, without seeking to achieve directly other side effects, even though they might well be predicted also.[15] The questions of motivation, attitude, enthusiasm, and the alleviation of barriers to such activating forces I must leave to others.

5. *MBO should bring about such individual improvement and growth.*   The assumption here is an important one. MBO should be both *functional* (get the job done) and *developmental* (help the individual grow). This congruence is vital to the survival of our economic system and the social and political system so intimately associated with it. If individual growth and corporate success were necessarily antithetical, the system could be self-destructing.

In adopting MBO as a system, we recognize that organizations create products and produce people who are workers as well.

MBO thus appeals to higher-ranking, profit-oriented chief executives and to humanist personnel and developmental staff persons.

EMERGENT APPLICATIONS OF MBO

Among the chronic areas of concern in administration to which MBO is being applied are the following:

1. *Management Strategy.*   The system of five-year (or multiyear) plans, adjusted annually, takes on immediacy if there is added to it, as an integral part of such planning, the achievement of one-year commitments and quarterly reviews through MBO.[16] Both the multiyear plan and MBO are parts of a single aggressive and humanist strategy of administration.

2. *PPBS in Government.*   In the federal establishment since 1965 (Executive Order No. 66-3) the use of Planning, Programming, Budgeting System in management has been mandatory. This system calls for an adoption of multiyear planning with one-year commitment and quarterly reviews for all agencies and departments of government. For most administrators and professionals, this implies that MBO will be the system used.

3. *Budgeting and Accounting.*   Changes in accounting systems ("responsibility accounting") and extension of accounting to previously untouched areas ("human resource accounting") have been closely allied to MBO.[17]

4. *Changes in Personnel Administration Practices and Procedures to Reflect MBO, in addition to Performance Appraisal and Selection by Objectives.*   A system in which desired job outputs become the basic criteria for selection has been described and is being experimentally applied.[18]

5. *Salary Administration.*   The restructuring of job descriptions along the lines of responsibilities and outputs has already become viable in the accountability system widely used by the late Ned Hay and his associates, and it provides a most logical rationale for the "job cluster" phenomena described by Jay Otis.[19]

6. *Training by Objectives.*   Much of the new hard technology of training is rooted in definition of training goals in behavioral terms.[20] In education, Mager has proposed a reconstruction of teaching in his approach to *defining educational objectives.*[21]

The insights which come from application of an output-oriented system of management have not yet been fully explored, described, or tested. Its possibilities are great.

PROBLEMS AHEAD IN MBO

The major areas for productive study and development seem to be concentrated most heavily in those positions identified with the management of intangible outputs. These are normally identified as "staff" positions but would include all the professional and service occupations, including research, education, and social service occupations. The fervent attachment of staff people to activities, per se, seems to be the major barrier to their using MBO. If they were convinced of the merits of so doing (or the motives of those who propose it), they would have ample capability to define their own objectives with great skill and clarity.

The most successful approach to defining staff outputs to date has been made by Juran.[22] He has proposed that staff outputs be classified in the categories of (1) advice, (2) service, (3) controls, and (4) research, which lend themselves to specifying goals.

Juran's approach requires that the staff department view itself as a producer and seller of *softwares* which are made and sold to internal captive customers. Such a perspective removes much of the ambiguity attendant upon activity management, looping constantly between inputs ("We need more budget") and activity ("Let's fool around with this idea") and back again.

Obviously, it is easier to define output goals in production and sales and other measures used long before MBO was described. In staff positions we miss the natural discipline of things to be counted. Therefore, it is much more necessary that we work consciously at defining softwares as goals and that we construct an ordering of values which describes the conditions which could exist for all possible levels of output.

The Problem Of Ordering Criteria   While some insist that every objective must be stated in quantitative terms, experience reveals that not every area of a business lends itself to such specificity. Staff work, research, and service professions often involve goals which can only be *described*. If measurements are forced upon such goals, they become meaningless, if not diversionary from real purposes.

Yet an objective needs criteria to describe all the possible outcomes. At least it needs to describe the conditions which exist if the goal is fully achieved or not achieved at all.

THE MECHANICS OF IMPLEMENTATION

Admitting that such a systematic way of thinking about management is perfectly sound, how do you get it into an ongoing organization? I suggest the following four steps as constituting the best system for implementation.

1. *Diagnosis.*   The first step is to describe your own management system. Do people know what is expected of them? Do they get collaboration or obstacle creation from their superiors? Is the organization output-centered, or is it activity- and input-centered? Are good people left alone to work in their own way once they are clear about their job purposes? Are rewards related to performance? Have outputs slipped with relationship to inputs over the past few years? If the answer to any significant number of these questions is "yes," then you may be ready for the introduction of MBO for the benefit of the organization and its people.

2. *Educational Program.*   Starting with a top-management familiarization program, the development of an implementation plan requires that extensive training in the "why" and "how" of MBO be professionally executed. Sending top people away and obtaining detailed training for the MBO administrators and trainers is also sound strategy.

The use of top managers as trainers is to be encouraged. When they are trained twice—once as learners and again as teachers—their commitment grows, and their store of information is increased.

3. *Operational.*   From the training environment, the setting of goals and their use in management must be moved back to the job. This often requires counseling, advice, and help in application. A qualified person to serve as MBO administrator is really an extension of the classroom training, converting the training into one-by-one tutorial training. This means that an in-house residential expert should be trained and on board, usually in the training or management development department.

4. *Follow-up and Evaluation.*   When all the goals are set, continual training and research into the effects must follow. Attitude and opinion samplings, special guest lectures, newsletters, and reading assignments may be used to keep the practice of MBO alive. It is certainly not a one-time course, but a way of managing. Rather than being an addition to anybody's job, it is a way of doing it.

REFERENCES

1. Dale, Ernest: *The Great Organizers: Theory and Practice of Organization,* McGraw-Hill Book Company, New York, 1960.
2. Drucker, Peter: *The Concept of the Corporation,* New American Library, Inc., New York, 1964.
3. Drucker, Peter: *The Practice of Management,* Harper & Brothers, New York, 1954.
4. Balch, D. E.: *AMA Business Report,* American Management Association, New York, 1959.
5. McGregor, Douglas: *The Human Side of Enterprise,* McGraw-Hill Book Company, New York, 1960.
6. Likert, Rensis: *New Patterns of Management,* McGraw-Hill Book Company, New York, 1961.
7. *Managing by Objectives,* National Industrial Conference Board, Inc., New York, 1966.
8. Schleh, E. C.: *Management by Results: The Dynamics of Profitable Management,* McGraw-Hill Book Company, New York, 1969.
9. Odiorne, George S.: *Management by Objectives: A System of Managerial Leadership,* Pitman Publishing Corporation, New York, 1965.
10. Boulding, K.: "Toward a General Systems Theory," *Journal of Management Science.*
11. Odiorne: op. cit.
12. Merton, R.: "The Disfunctions of a Bureaucracy," *Social Forces,* 1940.
13. Maier, N. R. F., L. R. Hoffman, J. J. Hooven, and W. H. Read: *Superior Subordinate Communication in Management,* American Management Association, Research Study 52, New York, 1961.
14. Drucker: *op. cit.*
15. Filley, Alan and Robert J. House: *The Process of Management,* Scott, Foresman and Company, Glenview, Ill., 1960.
16. Schleh: *op. cit.*
17. Bullock, James: "Responsibility Accounting: A Results-oriented Appraisal System," *Management of Personnel Quarterly,* 1966.
18. Odiorne, G. J.: *Personnel Administration by Objectives,* Richard D. Irwin, Inc., Homewood, Ill., 1971.
19. Otis, Jay: *The Job Cluster Method,* California Institute of Technology, Pasadena, 1960.
20. Odiorne, G. S.: *Training by Objectives: An Economic Approach to Management Training,* The Macmillan Company, New York, 1970.
21. Mager, R. F.: *Preparing Instructional Objectives,* Fearon Publishers, Inc., Palo Alto, Calif., 1962.
22. Juran, J. M.: *Managerial Breakthrough: A New Concept of the Manager's Job,* McGraw-Hill Book Company, New York, 1964.

Chapter **14**

The Performance Audit

GEARY A. RUMMLER

Geary A. Rummler *is Managing Director of Praxis Corporation in Morristown, New Jersey. Prior to forming Praxis in 1969, he was founder and Director of the University of Michigan's Center for Programmed Learning for Business, with responsibility for planning, design, and implementation of workshops and seminars in a wide range of industrial management areas. He was formerly Assistant Director of the Institute for Behavior Research and Programmed Instruction, Inc. At Praxis Corporation, Dr. Rummler has directed projects to analyze and improve the performance of machine operators, first-line supervisors, managers, and entire organizations. Dr. Rummler is coauthor of* Programmed Learning: A Practicum *(Ann Arbor Publishers, Inc., 1965) and* Labor Relations for Supervisors *(Addison-Wesley, 1968) and is editor of* Managing the Instructional Programming Effort *(Bureau of Industrial Relations, University of Michigan, 1967). He has published articles on training and behavioral technology in such periodicals as* Training Directors Journal, Michigan Business Review, Personnel, Educational Technology, *and* Human Resource Management, *and he has contributed to* Handbook for Modern Personnel Administration *(McGraw-Hill, 1972). He served as president of the National Society for Programmed Instruction in 1968. As a member of ASTD he served on the Educational Services Task Force and the Professionalization Task Force. He is a member of the Training Research Forum.*

Because of the increasing demand for better utilization of the work force, the training function is becoming the most important service function in many organizations today. However, it frequently is underutilized itself, and its limited resources are often squandered. This situation is due largely to the difficulty of identifying *significant* training problems and of evaluating the impact of training. The result of this difficulty is an organizational attitude toward training that is often described as "lack of management support."

The cause of this difficulty is most certainly not a lack of desire for effectiveness on the part of trainers, or (hard to believe as it may seem at times) a conspiracy on the part of management to frustrate trainers by purposely stating problems

NOTE: The technology and procedures described herein have been developed to a large degree by Dr. Thomas F. Gilbert, Technical Director, Praxis Corporation. The various applications described were carried out by the author and other staff of Praxis Corporation.

vaguely and providing little money for their solution. The culprit would seem to be the lack of a technology for problem identification, solution design, and evaluation. (*Some* blame might be put on trainers for not having vigorously pursued the development of such a technology and on management for not having demanded it.) The performance audit is an approximation to such a technology of performance problem analysis. It is one of the analysis approaches to come out of the relatively new field of performance analysis.[1] It is a framework for viewing human performance problems and a set of procedures for systematically determining the worth of correcting the problem, finding the causes of the problem, and designing solutions to the problem. An evaluation system for determining the impact of the solution on the problem is inherent in the procedures.

The benefits of making the performance-audit procedures part of the training procedures include the following:

1. The *organization* will have its real problems solved.
2. The *training function* will be able to direct its energy to solving training problems, rather than continuously trying (at management's suggestion) to solve nontraining problems with training solutions. It will also be able to evaluate its impact on, and contribution to, the organization.
3. The *trainee* will receive relevant and efficient training.

In addition, there are significant implications for an altered and increased role of the training function in improving the performance of organizations.

Before beginning to describe the performance audit, we acknowledge that organizations generally have low tolerance for "analysis" of activities which they feel smack of "research." It is also true that there are legitimate limitations on the time and money that can be put into analysis. Therefore, after presenting a comprehensive look at the performance audit, we shall discuss some intelligent compromises or "short forms" of the system for use in the less-than-ideal circumstances of the "real world." But first let us take a look at the total system.

FOUNDATION OF THE PERFORMANCE AUDIT

There are two basic concepts underlying the performance audit: behavior and economics. The audit is a set of procedures for examining behavior and the impact of behavior on the economics of an organization. Each of these underlying concepts will be discussed in turn.

Behavioral Foundation Of The Performance Model

The performance audit is a system for examining performance problems. In order to make such an examination, a theory for looking at performance is required.

We look at performance problems from the vantage point of a rather simplistic model of human performance. We identify what we call the performance *system.* This means that any desired performance is part of a performance system, which has the following components:

1. The job *situation,* or occasion to perform
2. The *performer*
3. The *behavior* (action or decision) that is to occur
4. The *consequence* of that behavior to the performer
5. The *feedback* of the consequence back to the performer

Schematically, the relationship is:

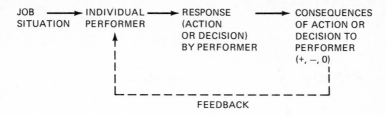

That is, in any job there is a *situation* or occasion requiring a particular *performer* to make a particular *response* or take some action, which results in some consequence to the performer. The performer may consider that consequence to be positive, or negative or to have little value. And last, information on that consequence is fed back to the performer.

For example, when you are charging a plane ticket at the air terminal (situation), the ticket agent (performer) should, among other things, check your credit card with the book to see whether it is all right (described action); as a result, she learns the status of your credit card (a consequence), and this is fed back to her immediately.

The overriding and simplistic "law" governing this system is that behavior is explained by its consequences. People tend to avoid doing things that result in negative consequences and to do more often things that lead to positive consequences. Given the general law of the performance system, we find specifically that a desired job behavior may fail to occur in any job situation because of a break-down in any of the five components of the performance system.

This can be illustrated with the ticket agent example. Assume that the airline is concerned with the failure of ticket agents to check credit cards of passengers. Each component of this performance system can be examined as follows:

1. *The Job Situation.*   Perhaps it is not clear that the situation merits the desired action:

(In the credit-card check, it may be that the occasion to perform—check all passengers regardless of amount of purchase—was not made clear.)

2. *The Performer.*   Perhaps she is physically or mentally incapable of performing, or she may be uninterested (the consequences of performing are insufficient):

(The ticket agent is physically incapable of reading the credit-card book.)

3. *The Behavior (response or action).*   Perhaps the performer does not know she is supposed to make the response, does not know how to make it, or it is physically impossible to make, or she does not have the necessary tools or support:

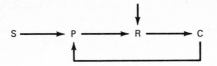

(The ticket agent does not know how to look up credit cards correctly in the book.)

4. *The Consequence.*   Perhaps the consequence is punishing or nonexistent:

(Perhaps the agent has a conflict in consequences. That is, every time she has walked to the end of the counter and looked up a credit card, she has found nothing. That provides no strong motivation for continuing to do this every time a customer presents a credit card. In addition, frequently customers are aggravated by the time this step takes and by the apparent questioning of their honesty. They frequently express this hostility to the agent. This hostility (negative consequence) can be avoided by *not* checking the credit card. In addition, supervision is *always* concerned with the length of passenger lines waiting to be served and with pushing the agents to handle passengers faster. The consequence of a harping supervisor may tip the scales in favor of not performing as desired.)

5. *The Feedback.*   The performer receives no information about her response— whether it was adequate or inadequate; if it was inadequate, how to improve it; etc.

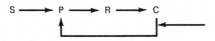

(If an agent fails to check a credit card and the passenger's credit was in fact no good, the agent may never learn of this.)

According to our performance system, getting the desired human behavior to occur in a situation is the result of a number of conditions' being right. Therefore, the failure of a behavior to occur can be the result of any one of these conditions' not existing. This performance system gives us a framework for viewing human performance — for diagnosing and correcting performance problems.

This model has a number of important applications, but its contribution to the performance audit is the framework it provides for diagnosing performance problems and prescribing solutions. The model can be used as a conceptual "template" to lay over a problem—forcing identification of the components (i.e., situation, performer, desired performance, etc.) and suggesting questions to ask about each component. A representation of this template, along with "trouble-shooting" questions, appears in Fig. 14-1. Application of the model in this way isolates which components of the performance system might be "faulty" (e.g., unclear statement of the desired behavior or poor feedback to the performer on her performance) and need correcting before the desired behavior can be expected. It is an invaluable tool for determining when training is an appropriate solution to a performance problem.

The performance model can be used to troubleshoot performance problems of any size. It can be used to diagnose the failure of an individual—of a subordinate manager to delegate responsibility, for example. It can be used to analyze a position or a group of performers, such as salesclerks not approaching customers, foremen handling grievances, or salespeople handling a new product. And finally, it can be used to probe entire organizations— a plant with high costs, low productivity, and "poor morale."

In summary, the performance model is a framework which allows us to discrimi-

---

S ──────────────────────────► R   C

SITUATION   RESPONSE   CONSEQUENCE

Does performer know when to respond?   What are the consequences of R?

Does performer know how to respond?   Are they positive or negative?

Does performer know criteria for   Of no value?
proper response?
                                           How immediate are they?
Does performer have resources neces-
sary to respond?   Does another R have more positive
                                        consequences?

                                        Does performer receive adequate
                                        information on the consequences?

                                           Correct variable

                                           Frequent

                                           Immediate

                                           Specific

                                           Interpretable

                                        Can performer detect incorrect R?

                                        Can performer interpret feedback
                                        and correct problem?

Fig. 14-1   Troubleshooting performance. *(Copyright © 1973, Praxis Corporation.)*

nate between problems or deficiencies which can be best corrected through training and those which require changes in the "environment." For the latter, it also helps determine precisely what changes are required to correct the deficiency or to support the recommended training.

Economics And Behavior

The performance audit concerns itself with the economics of the organization being analyzed. There are two reasons for this:

1. To determine whether the deficient behavior really makes a difference; that is, is there any value in improving that particular behavior, or could the time and energy be better spent correcting some other behavior?
2. It tells us something about what is important (or should be important) to the organization and therefore is most likely to receive positive consequences from all levels of management. For example, in the private sector, profits are the ultimate consequences at all levels. Behavior which cannot be observed to contribute to profits or other economic measures will not be supported. Also, there is frequently a conflict between levels or subsystems centered around economic measures, and once this comes to light, a number of problems and deficiencies are often explained.

A brief example will make the point: The marketing function of a bank decided that it would launch a major training program for tellers in all its branches. The objective was to have tellers "sell" additional bank services, with particular emphasis on personal loans. Although the marketing staff was convincing in its argument that personal loans were extremely profitable, the program was doomed to failure because of the existing structure of consequences (economic and other) in the branches. First, there were immediate negative consequences to the tellers for errors in handling money, failure to balance out at the end of the day, and taking bad checks. This, coupled with long lines, kept the tellers' minds on the essentials: no fancy stuff. Second, there was no support from branch management for the personal-loan emphasis. The positive consequences for the branch manager (attracting attention downtown) were for building up a sizable loan portfolio—which could be done quicker and at less cost by making a $1-million loan to a small corporation. It takes a lot of $3,000 personal loans (and considerable expense per loan) to equal $1 million. Given these two sets of consequences, 30 weeks of training in "selling services" would have a negligible effect on personal loans as long as the balance of consequences itself was unchanged.

This example illustrates both reasons for an economic analysis. First, no attempt was made to determine the value of correcting the "deficiency"—selling services. (Indeed, it was subsequently determined that many of the services were of considerable marginal return, once the actual cost of the service was calculated.) Second, we see that the large loan portfolio of the branch is going to be much more important to the branch manager than the effort of the tellers to sell high-cost, low-yield services.

Economic analysis takes place on several levels. At a general level, we attempt to do a "stakes" analysis—to find out what is at stake in the organization and what would be the impact of improving performance in a particular area. In the bank example above, we would ideally first look at the various sources of revenue and expense to the system and determine where improvement would be most beneficial (i.e., build an economic "model" of a branch). Then we would look to see whether the teller level in fact could impact those revenue or cost areas where it has been established that there is potential for improvement.

Let us look at another example: Figure 14-2 contains an economic "model" which was built as part of a performance audit of a food manufacturing plant. The organization (which had over 25 such plants in its system, all making basically the same products) wanted to do some training in its manufacturing operations. Although there was a budget of $255,000 for such training, they did not know who to train to do what. A performance audit was undertaken to determine what training, if any, would have the greatest impact on the performance of the plant.

One of the first steps in the audit was to build a facsimile of a "typical" plant on paper (a model plant) documenting critical dimensions such as the work flow, organization chart, and budget (Fig. 14-2). Next we began to look at the "stakes" of our typical plant. Given the budget that was assembled, we asked questions such as:

1. Suppose a packaging machine operator does not operate a machine correctly for 10 minutes. During this time, only empty bags are being made, and no product enters the machine. In which category would the largest dollar loss occur?
   a. Ingredients
   b. Labor
   c. Wrapping paper
2. Suppose a training program made the workers so efficient that the direct-labor budget was reduced by 10 percent. How many years would it take to recover the $255,000 invested in the development of the training if it were used in only one plant?

    a. One year
    b. Two years
    c. Three years or more
3. Suppose a training program reduced product waste to such an extent that the cost of ingredients was reduced by 10 percent. How many years would it take to recover the $225,000 invested in the development of training?
    a. One year
    b. Two years
    c. Three years or more

DESCRIPTION	TOTAL	PRODUCT A	PRODUCT B
Market Value	$16,000,000	$ 8,000,000	$ 8,000,000
Ingredient Cost	$ 3,600,000	$ 1,400,000	$ 2,200,000
Packaging Materials Cost	2,000,000	1,050,000	950,000
Total Materials Cost	5,600,000	2,450,000	3,150,000
Total Direct Labor	$ 760,000	$ 375,000	$ 390,000
Manufacturing Expenses (13+%)	2,200,000	1,100,000	1,100,000
Cost of Manufacturing	$ 8,560,000	$ 3,925,000	$ 4,640,000
Pounds Produced	22,400,000	12,000,000	10,400,000
Equipment			
Fryer (large)	6	4	2
Packaging Machines	16	8	8
Relevant Personnel			
Machine Operators	16	8	8
Cooks	12	8	4
Other			
Two 8-hour shifts; 5-day week; 52 weeks per year; 260 days per year.			

Fig. 14-2 Manufacturing economics of a typical plant.

    The answers to these questions indicate that the big stakes are in ingredient and packaging materials and that the recommended improvements must result in reduced packaging and ingredient waste rather than a more efficient work force.
    Now that we know what is at stake, we next look to see who in the organization can best impact those high-stake areas. This is done by looking at the spread or variance in performance of a particular level of employees (e.g., operators, supervisors, department managers, district managers). We are looking for the difference between the performance of the poorest and the best employees. If that difference is large, the program's potential for improvement is great. But if the

poorest performer is *nearly* as good as the very best performer (assuming that the very best is really good), the potential impact on performance is quite low.

In our food example, management had expressed some interest in training supervisors. That being the case, we gathered and assembled data contrasting the "best" and "worst" supervisors. From this analysis it was concluded (1) that there was no significant difference between the day- and night-shift performance,

```
I.   AVERAGE MUFs

     1.  Packaging machine operator  =  $ 5.00

     2.  Product A cooks              =    12.00

     3.  Product B cooks              =     6.00


II.  FREQUENCY OF MUFs PER DAY FOR TYPICAL PERFORMERS
```

PERFORMANCE CLASS	PACKAGING MACHINE OPERATORS	PRODUCT A COOKS	PRODUCT B COOKS
High Performers	10	10	10
Standard Performers	40	25	30
Low Performers	60	30	40

Fig. 14-3 Summary of individual performance data—model plant.

factoring out certain advantages of the night shift, and (2) that if the best packaging machine supervisor is only 1 percent superior to the poorest and if each is responsible for $4 million worth of product a year, we could not make a strong argument for spending $225,000 on training that might at best reduce that difference by 25 percent.

It was also quickly discovered that improving the performance of unskilled employees would have little impact on production rate or costs. On the other hand, three groups of skilled employees—the packaging machine operators (PMOs) and the cooks for product A and product B—could make quite a difference in production.

To find some quantitative measure of the potential impact on performance of these three jobs, we first identified the critical ways in which the employees could fail. Then we asked which failures would cost money and how much.

To do this, we developed a convenient economic unit for these jobs: the cost of a *minute of unit failure* (MUF). For example, suppose a cook lets the frying oil get too hot. For each minute that this happens, $12 is lost in ingredients and labor.* If a PMO does not operate the machine correctly, sometimes losing product and bags, the average cost of this loss is $5 a minute. Referring to Fig. 14-3, you can see that:

---

*All figures appearing in this case are hypothetical and are used for purposes of illustration. They do not necessarily reflect the actual or relative costs of this industry.

1. In our model plant, a change in a single low-performing PMO into a high performer would result in a savings (or improvement) of $65,000 in a single year (260 working days).
2. The potential impact on performance of these skilled employees is greater than for supervisors.

I.   ECONOMIC IMPACT OF CHANGING INDIVIDUAL PERFORMANCE (ONE YEAR)

Change in Performance Level	Packaging	Product A Cook	Product B Cook
Low to Std.	$25,000	$15,000	$15,000
Std. to High	37,500	45,000	30,000
Low to High	62,500	60,000	45,000

II. ECONOMIC IMPACT OF CHANGING PERFORMANCE PROFILE IN THE PLANT

    A. Distribution of Performers

        -- At present vs. how Plant would like it --

CLASS	PACKAGING		PRODUCT A COOK		PRODUCT B COOK	
	Present	Planned	Present	Planned	Present	Planned
High	3	12	1	3	2	6
Std.	5	4	2	1	4	2
Low	8	0	1	0	2	0
TOTAL	16	16	4	4	8	8

    B. Ecomomic Impact of Changing Distribution of Performers

	Packaging	Product A Cook	Product B Cook	Total
SAVINGS	$537,500	$105,000	$90,000	$732,500

Fig. 14-4 Summary performance data—model plant.

Thus, we conclude that we should be concerned initially with the skilled-operator level. In addition, the MUF helps us determine in which group of operators there is the greatest potential impact on performance. Given the summary in Fig. 14-4, the client concluded that they wished to invest the $255,000 in improving the performance of the packaging machine operators.

Summarizing briefly, the analysis of economics tells us whether a problem is worth solving (or which deficiency is worth correcting), and it also tells us about the organizational consequences which may or may not support any changes of behavior. In the above case we illustrated several levels of economics analysis addressed at the "worth-it" question. We determined the stakes and who can best impact them. The matter of organizational consequences also emerges, but less directly. From this analysis we concluded that in addition to training, a performance feedback system should be developed and implemented which would provide all levels of plant management with daily waste and production data. Without an information system which apprises them of the improved performance, management will not be able to arrange the consequences necessary to maintain the desired improved performance. It is important to note that this economic analysis is done to get direction and set priorities. It is not meant to provide a guarantee that the training program will return $X per plant per year. However, this analysis *does* by its very nature specify where we can look to evaluate the results of the training or change program.

We have looked briefly at the foundation underlying the performance audit. It consists of (1) the performance system, which provides a framework for studying behavior and the influences on behavior, and (2) economics, which indicate the behavior that should be of concern and which provide insight into likely organizational consequences for various performance.

Now we shall describe a general framework for *conducting* a performance analysis—the levels of performance analysis.

Ideally, a performance audit involves the following three levels of analysis:[2]

Level I (Policy)	The structure and goals of the organization and the kind of environment it provides for the job	Which program will give the highest payoff for improving performance?
Level II (Strategy)	The theory and accomplishments of a job itself and how it helps fulfill the goals of the organization	What are the strategies of defining and improving a job?
Level III (Tactics)	The kinds of changes that must be made in the behavior of individuals if they are to accomplish the job	What specific things must you do to make people more efficient in doing a job?

There are three distinct phases of the analysis at each level, as summarized in Fig. 14-5. We shall briefly illustrate the levels of performance analysis using the food case as an example.[3]

Level I   As you will recall, the client asked for training in the area of manufacturing. But for whom, and in what? Therefore, a level I analysis was first conducted to determine *what* was at stake in the manufacturing organization (labor, ingredients, materials) and *who* in manufacturing impacted those high-stake areas the most. As you can see by referring to Fig. 14-5, this involves looking at the organization structure, the work flow, and the economics of the manufacturing plant. On the basis of this analysis (discussed earlier in the section on economics), we concluded that the high-stake areas were packaging and ingredient waste and that packaging machine operators had the greatest potential for improved performance related to these areas. The general program recommendation resulting from this level I analysis was that improvement of the packaging machine operators' performance should have first priority—probably through a combination of training and an improved performance information system.

Level II   A level II analysis is concerned with examining a specific job or function and determining how performance of that job can be improved. The basic sequence of analysis at this level is to:

Fig. 14-5 Levels of performance analysis. *(Copyright © 1974, Praxis Corporation.)*

	Stage A MODELS	Stage B MEASURES	Stage C METHODS

Level I
POLICY
	ORGANIZATIONAL MODELS
	1. Draw up an organizational model.
	2. Draw up a work-information flowchart.
	3. Draw up an economic model.
	To be sure these models are realistic and desirable, base them on a knowledge of the actual setups in the organization and on a knowledge of these setups in similar organizations.
		STAKES ANALYSIS
		1. Describe any performance problems noted in Stage A.
		2. Measure the economics at stake.
		3. Determine the value of correcting the problems.
		4. Rank the problems by priority for treatment; decide to concentrate on the job with the highest potential payoff.
			POLICY PROGRAMS
			1. Decide on some general programs to improve this job:
			  a. organizational programs
			  b. job programs
			  c. people programs
			2. Estimate the cost of these programs.
			3. Determine their worth.
			4. Reevaluate the programs and make recommendations.

Level II
STRATEGY
	JOB THEORY AND OUTPUTS
	1. Describe key outputs.
	2. Derive a job theory.
	3. Describe all job outputs that define this job theory.
	4. Determine the requirements for each output and set standards for these requirements.
		DEFICIENCY ANALYSIS
		1. Determine any deficiencies in job outputs.
		2. Estimate the causes of critical deficiencies:
		  a. a deficiency in the environment (D_E)
		  b. a deficiency in the individual's repertoire (D_K)
			PROGRAM STRATEGIES
			Determine strategies for treating deficiencies:
			  a. information program
			  b. training
			  c. guidance
			  d. motivation program (etc.)

Level III
TACTICS
	TACTICAL DESIGNS
	1. Develop knowledge maps, showing instructional strategies and subject matter inventories, to treat D_K's.
	2. Develop environmental designs, to treat D_E's.
	3. Develop designs for making changes in personnel, to treat DI's.
		BEHAVIOR ANALYSIS
		1. Determine appropriate media for developing designs.
		2. Determine schedules for developing designs.
		3. Determine the costs of implementation, including the cost of development.
			TACTICAL INSTRUMENTS
			Develop the necessary materials and tools, and try them out:
			  a. inductives
			  b. theory training
			  c. job aids and skill guides
			  d. performance indices
			  e. progress plotters
			  f. incentive systems (etc.)

1. Determine what is expected or desired of the individuals and functions being studied.
2. Identify the actual performance.
3. Analyze the discrepancy, if any, between what is desired and what actually happens to determine:
   a. The value of correcting it
   b. Its cause or causes
      Using the performance model, we classify performance deficiencies as *knowledge deficiencies*, which result from employees' not knowing what to do, how to do it, or when to do it, and *execution deficiencies*, which result from employees' failing to perform because of factors in the work environment. Execution deficiencies are further classified as resulting from *poor feedback* to employees on how well they are doing and what they might do to correct their performance, from *punishment* or *insufficient positive consequences* for doing as expected, or from some form of *task interference* resulting from poor or inappropriate job or system design. This entails a more detailed study of the existing communications network (paper, meetings), reporting relationships, relationships between functions, and management controls.
4. Recommend changes for improving performance. These changes include the following (where appropriate): training, modifying consequences for various performance, changing the information flow to provide better feedback on performance, and changing the design of certain jobs or functions.

These steps were followed with the packaging machine operator job, and the resulting strategies included training in such things as threading paper, adjusting weights, and troubleshooting breakdowns. Also, specific recommendations were made for improved performance feedback to operators and supervisors on productivity, weight, and waste in order to maintain the improvements in performance which would result from training.

Level III   Level III analysis involves those steps generally accepted as basic to developing effective training materials. We start by developing training objectives and end with a training program—an instrument for improving performance. The packaging machine operator training course was a combination of self-instructional booklets, demonstration, simulation, and guided practice which was easily administered in each plant by supervision. The result was to reduce the training time of new PMOs from six months to three weeks, with performance of trainees uniformly meeting standard within that time. The economic return to the organization was considerable because the analysis had assured us that we were training in areas where the resultant changes had significant impact.

In summary, the levels of performance analysis provide a structure for conducting a performance audit. They show that we move from the general to the specific, from policy (where and whom do we impact?) through strategy (how do we best impact what?) to tactics (designing the solution). As you will see next, the levels help you keep track of where you are in an analysis and of the scope of your analysis.

CONDUCTING A PERFORMANCE AUDIT

Now that we have discussed the underlying theory and the general levels of performance analysis, we can turn to the performance audit. However, in the "real world" it is frequently difficult to complete all the steps in the levels. Given that one may frequently have to compromise an analysis, it is important that one know the levels of performance analysis and at what levels one can operate as well as the behavioral theory or performance model in order to realistically assess what data on analyzing causes, setting priorities, and prescribing solutions will "sell." Three general conditions under which you might conduct a performance audit are described below.

Ideally, you might be asked to determine how you might best impact an organization or segment of an organization. In such a case, you should be able to conduct all three levels of performance analysis. As a guide to estimating the time required for such an analysis, the first two levels of analysis for a problem such as that in the food company example could be done in six to ten worker-weeks. The time necessary to complete level III would depend on the extent and nature of the proposed solutions.

However, organizations tend to classify or identify problems according to their proposed solutions, and therefore you might first become aware that a "problem" exists when you receive a request for training—in most cases what you would characterize as "fire-fighting" training. Referring to the levels, what is happening is that someone is specifying a particular solution or tactic (level III). In this case, the trainer must move up as many levels as possible to begin the analysis in an effort to get the answers to these questions:

1. Is the problem the result of a deficiency of knowledge (D_K) or a deficiency of execution (D_E)? That is, can training solve the problem (cell IIB, Fig. 14-5)?
2. Is it of value to solve this problem (cell IIB)?
3. What is the desired outcome? What *should* be happening (cell IIA)?
4. Could the effort be better spent impacting some other problem (cell IB)?

Minimally, it would be beneficial to begin with a level II analysis, determining the desired performance, the deficiencies, and the cause of the deficiencies. Better yet would be to start with level I, particularly economics.

Referring once again to the food company, assume that management had asked for human relations training for supervisors. Assume that management was recommending this in response to increased turnover among skilled operators. If no analysis was possible, a training department would have little choice but to conduct such training. However, a level II analysis, which starts with what is expected of a supervisor, might well turn up the fact that the supervisors have very little objective performance data with which to supervise (a D_E), resulting in oversupervising operators, which in turn causes operators to resign. A level II analysis might determine that the problem cannot be solved through human relations training at all, but through an improved management information system. With better performance data with which to evaluate and assist operators, "relations" would most likely improve. Finally, a level I analysis would show (per the example) that *plant performance* can be improved most by directing attention at a different level (operators) and a different problem (packaging machine performance) altogether.

When confronted by management with a "training problem" and little chance for much analysis, the following questions usually yield helpful information:

1. What is the desired performance (job outcome)?
   - What are the job standards?
   - Who says that these are the standards?
   - Does everybody agree on these standards?
   - Does everybody (anybody) know whether these standards are now being met?
2. What are specific differences between actual and expected performance?
   - Has anyone ever performed as required?
   - Who?
   - When?

3. Could employees perform properly if their lives depended on it?
   - Did employees perform properly when they first came on the job?
4. Do employees whose performance is deficient know:
   - What is expected of them?
   - That they are not performing correctly and exactly how far they are from expected performance?
   - How to perform correctly?
   - When to perform?
5. What positive and/or negative consequences of performing correctly or incorrectly can employees expect from:
   - Their bosses?
   - Their subordinates?
   - Their peers?

Finally, there is the situation in which training is clearly needed—say, the revision of an entry-level training course. The trainees are new to the fairly complex job and the organization. Given this obvious need for training, how is a performance audit appropriate?

Conducting a level I analysis will provide data on how the job impacts the organization—an important and often overlooked training point. These data also provide the key to how the training might ultimately be evaluated—how it impacted the organization. The food company example was such a case. Also, these impact data are frequently helpful later in the training design.

For example, a level I analysis conducted as part of revising a training course for new telephone operators showed that the rate at which new operators performed on the job had amazing economic impact (in terms of direct labor). However, the existing training course emphasized accuracy and assumed that the new operators' rate would increase on the job. Knowing the economic impact of this low rate and being aware that improving the rate on the job would be highly inefficient, the training staff was able to design a revised course so that new operators were performing at standard in both rate and accuracy when they completed the course. (This analysis showed that additional training time could be easily justified in order to improve the rate upon entry to the work force—although additional time was not necessary in this case.)

Finally, level I analysis provides a vantage point for determining what the job should or must be.

Level II analysis leads to specifying the training content and emphasis. First, it tells you what the master performer *does.* You learn what performance is required of the master performer by observing and interviewing, and then you determine what must be learned to become a master. This is in contrast to just studying the subject matter basic to the job and determining the training content without the reality of the job. Examination of the current deficiencies in performing the job—the differences between what should be and what is—provides data on difficult-to-learn (and apparently difficult-to-teach) aspects of the job, as well as on environmental factors which will interfere with or not support the trainee. The value analysis done at this level also helps set priorities. For example, in conducting a level II analysis for the revision of a training course for repair service clerks (take complaints of equipment failures over the phone; pass the information to a dispatcher, who directs a serviceman to call on the complaining customer), the value analysis showed that the most costly deficiency of the repair service clerk was the failure to ask what time the customer would be home so that the repairman could obtain access to the equipment. This resulted in double visits and irate customers. However, with these data, special emphasis was placed on this "learning objective."

To summarize, the result of level II analysis is distinguishing between D_K and

D_E and recommendations on the necessary environmental support for the training. It also provides a realistic appraisal of the performance which can be gained through training alone. The resulting course plans will reflect priorities established through value analysis and instructional strategies to deal with the hard-to-learn concepts and discriminations.

Level III analysis is done as part of any well-constructed training program and need not be discussed here.

As you can see, the performance audit is relevant whenever someone is seriously concerned with improving performance. A "quick and dirty" performance audit is preferable to no analysis at all. Of course, every additional level of analysis that can be conducted increases the probability that the resulting training will have a significant impact on the organization.

IMPLICATIONS

The performance audit is not a training technique, or another tool in the trainer's "bag of tricks," as some may want to say. It is a process of analyzing human performance problems which results in cost-effective solutions— one of which might be training. The performance audit should be the first phase of a training development activity.

The performance audit can be, and has been, adopted as the basis for training procedures for a training function, providing a useful guide for the development of training programs, It also has implications for the organization and staffing of the training function, suggesting functional organization (specialists in analysis and evaluation, development, and implementation) and a shift in the distribution of manpower from a heavy emphasis on development to at least an equal distribution between development and analysis or evaluation. The result of using the performance audit as the basis of training procedures will minimally be higher-quality (i.e., more relevant) training and the opportunity to demonstrate results to management through better evaluation of the impact of training.

The performance audit holds greater implications for the training function, however. The performance audit is more than just a technology of training—it is a technology of performance improvement. It is a comprehensive, objective system for analyzing human performance problems. As such, it provides the training function with an opportunity to change its role from a narrow one of "training solution designer" to the broader one of "performance improver." It provides the basis for a "performance" department or "performance improvement" department which initiates the analysis of performance problems and which, on the basis of this objective analysis, prescribes the most cost-effective solution. This significant change in the role of training has taken place in a number of companies in the past five years.

In conclusion, the performance audit is currently the operating training philosophy of a number of organizations and is having the impact described above. In most cases, implementation has been slower than desired. It takes time for management to realize that training wants to do business differently—that they want to ask some questions before churning out another course. It also upsets the standard method of evaluating the training department—the "heads-per-dollar" model—and instead suggests the need to evaluate the impact of training on the profits or operating budget of the company. The point is that even though use of the performance audit will enhance the quality of the work of the training function and will positively impact the economics of the organization, the change will be resisted by segments of management because it is not what they have come to expect from training. However, an increasing number of trainers are finding the results worth the battle.

REFERENCES

1. Gilbert, T. F.: *Praxeonomy: A Scientific Approach to Identifying Training Needs,* University of Michigan, Graduate School of Business Administration, Bureau of Industrial Relations, Ann Arbor, 1967.

   Mager, R. F.: *Analyzing Performance Problems* Fearon Publishers, Inc., and Lear Siegler, Inc., Education Division, Palto Alto, Calif., 1970.

   Rummler, G. A.: *Human Performance Problems and Their Solution,* University of Michigan, Graduate School of Business Administration, Bureau of Industrial Relations, Ann Arbor, 1972.

2. For further discussion of levels of performance analysis, see Gilbert, T. F.: *Levels and Structure of Performance Analysis,* Praxis Corporation, Technical Paper no. 1, Morristown, N.J., 1974.

3. For a detailed discussion of this topic, see ibid.

Chapter 15

Job Enrichment and Redesign

RICHARD O. PETERSON

BRUCE H. DUFFANY

Richard O. Peterson *and* **Bruce H. Duffany** *are both Managers of Research in Work Organization and Environment at AT&T in New York. They are responsible for conducting research in the Bell System on various aspects of work and organization design and for developing strategies which apply work design principles to the problems of utilizing human talent in a cost-effective manner, while at the same time ensuring that quality work is the management policy of the Bell System.*

Dr. Peterson began working for AT&T as a contractor, doing research on the training of telephone operators. Joining the staff in 1964, he assumed responsibility for further implementation of that training, as well as for research and development of training for other operator services jobs. He worked with the American Institutes for Research for about 10 years on such diverse projects as maintenance training, missile-system development, rehabilitation of the mentally retarded, and test development. Dr. Peterson was a member of the original research team with Frederick Herzberg on the studies of motivation to work. He has degrees in mathematics and in industrial psychology, all from Carnegie-Mellon University.

Mr. Duffany began his employment with the Bell System in the C&P Telephone Company of Maryland, where he held several line and staff management positions. In 1966 he conducted one of the original trials to find out whether job enrichment was an effective management technique. As a result of the success of that trial, Mr. Duffany was brought to AT&T to extend this success to other Bell System organizations. For two years he worked as a management consultant for Drake-Beam Associates in New York, and he helped to initiate job enrichment trials in General Foods, Standard Oil of Indiana, New York Life Insurance, and Prudential Life Insurance. In his Bell System assignments, he has initiated over 100 work design efforts on both management and nonmanagement jobs and has helped to train over 400 managers in work design concepts. Mr. Duffany is a graduate of Johns Hopkins University with a degree in industrial engineering.

Job redesign (and the other processes such as job enrichment which we include in this term) has evolved from a long and respectable history of concern for people at work and for the structure of work itself. Davis and Taylor present an excellent summary of the "genealogy of work design" and support it with extracts from significant contributors over the years.[1]

It is not really a product of recent declarations about "worker alienation," "blue-collar blues and white-collar woes," or the "changing work ethic." In fact, some overzealous articles and books have resulted in a sharpening of criticism about job redesign and its applicability. This has in turn led to a corresponding sharpening up of the techniques as well as to a stronger rationale for job redesign.

A manager concerned with individual and organizational performance has no need to participate in a debate over whether job redesign is appropriate for everyone or for every job, or in a debate over whether job redesign will resolve all work-related ills. A rational approach assumes that the effective manager confronts each organizational performance problem without a preconception about the solution. For example, in the analytic framework called the *performance audit,* advocated by Praxis Corporation in their Performance Analysis Workshop, solutions may include training, performance aids, more effective feedback, changes in consequences of actions, and also *job engineering* (their term).* We must consider job redesign from this larger perspective, as a solution to specific kinds of performance and personnel problems, not as the general solution to all kinds of problems.

Furthermore, when we start to solve a problem through job redesign, we should build into our solution process the means by which we can honestly evaluate the effect of the new design. This kind of "action research" is often difficult to design and control, and unequivocal proof is almost impossible to demonstrate. However, these potential deterrents should not prevent us from undertaking job redesign where it is appropriate. The techniques and the evidence are improving all the time.

Probably the most effective way to support our "rational" approach toward improving the quality of work is to define what we mean by "improvement." How will we know when jobs are better? What do we expect will happen when they are?

WHAT IS A "GOOD" JOB?

Criteria for job quality are neither universal nor absolute. Instead, every job redesign activity should begin with agreement on the objectives to be achieved by the process and the indicators of how well those objectives have been achieved.

Types of Objectives for Job Redesign   We encounter three reasons for undertaking job redesign.

1. *To solve a specific personnel or performance problem.*   Analysis of the problem may suggest that something in the job appears to cause errors or contribute to turnover, for example. Job redesign is anticipated. Objectives may thus be stated in terms of reductions in errors, decreases in turnover related to work, decreases in incidental absence, reduction in waste or rejects, improvement in job satisfaction, reduction in overtime, elimination of extra quality checks, etc.

2. *To achieve a new personnel or performance objective.*   Assume that someone decides to reach a new goal with job redesign—to increase the number of customers, to increase sales volume, to reduce cost per unit produced, or to increase employee mobility among jobs. These new goals can be stated in specific terms, just like the problem-oriented goals above. Included should be only those objectives which can reasonably be affected by change in the work design.

Another category of new objectives is created by the introduction of new technology or a major organizational change. Goals may be in terms of comparisons with present performance (e.g., current levels to be reached within three months or absence to be 10 percent less than present rates). Goals may also be in terms of the change process itself (e.g., all job changes completed within six weeks).

*See Chap. 14, "The Performance Audit."

3. *To improve the quality of work.* Even if there is no serious problem we presently attribute to our jobs and no new organizational objective to be achieved, we may still undertake job redesign to improve the "quality" of jobs and work. Our underlying goal would be better utilization of employee capabilities and motivation, or perhaps better matching of employee work preferences with employee work—not just because better utilization may lead to some other objectives, but because this is a worthwhile objective in itself.

Characteristics of Job Quality   When we refer to "good job quality," we must ask: "Good for whom?" or "Good in what way?" We risk overgeneralizing if we attribute to everyone a preference for the same characteristics in a job. If we carry that to its extreme, we have to join the critics who say there is no way to design a job so that it will become "good" to all employees performing it.

However, some research and considerable experience show that a few characteristics of work quality have a generally more favorable impact on people than others. Herzberg suggested that after basic "hygiene" needs for pay, working conditions, and benefits are assured, a good job must incorporate such "motivator" qualities as responsibility, achievement, recognition for achievement, growth, advancement, and interest in "the work itself."[2]

However, even Herzberg acknowledged that ". . . no job can provide all these ingredients at one time. Nor, perhaps, can all jobs provide all these ingredients at different times. However some of these components of psychologically rewarding jobs must be present."[3]

More recently, Ford recommended three fundamental aspects of any enriched or improved job.[4] As these three characteristics are referred to in this chapter, they are defined as follows:

1. *A meaningful module of work.*   This implies that the piece of work for which the employee is responsible has a clearly identifiable beginning and end. Hence the individual can tell where the work begins, where it ends, and in what ways it is separable from pieces of work being done by others. The activities or functions the employee performs must be complete. Furthermore, these functions will be performed for a clearly identifiable set of users or providers of work—the employee's "customers" or "clients."

An employee having such a *module* will know exactly what he or she is to do and for what clients the work will be done. The employee will also know that no one else is performing these same functions or activities for the same clients.

In summary, a well-designed module will make the following contributions to the work design:

a. A completeness or closure of work activities and functions, resulting in a product—preferably the largest product possible for the employee
b. Functional variety among work activities
c. A well-established group of customers for whom the products are produced
d. Identifiable results of an individual's efforts (the products themselves)
e. Cost-effective utilization of valued skills and talents
f. The foundation for developing the other characteristics of a well-designed job

2. *Employee's control of the module.*   Responsibility for decisions in carrying out the work is the heart of this characteristic. Once skilled in the basics of the job, the employee must be allowed the *power to act*—the opportunity to make decisions about how the work is done or in what sequence—or be permitted to use judgment in dealing with others.

3. *Direct feedback to the employee.*   Information must get back to the employee about his or her performance, preferably while performance is still going on or soon

after it is completed. This *feedback* will be more motivating if it comes directly from the task itself or the client served, rather than via the supervisor.

Dimensions of work quality such as these are useful not only in diagnosing problems in a specific job but also in redesigning it, as illustrated later. The three dimensions defined above attempt to incorporate factors identified by many other researchers.[5] Undoubtedly, continued research will result in a refinement of such dimensions and in techniques for their measurement.

Individual Differences   In our efforts to find solutions appropriate for the maximum number of employees, we must not ignore the important differences that exist between individuals in terms of work interests and motivations. For example, on the basis of several experimental studies, John Maher concludes that "There are some people who seek to minimize effort expended on the job and who would thus prefer to avoid enriched, more challenging work." Hulin also points out the fallacy of overgeneralizing to all employees.[6]

Situational Differences   Another series of variables which may affect how employees view the quality of work is in the job "situation," represented by such factors as geographic location (e.g., central city, suburban, rural), management atmosphere (e.g., willingness to take risks, management style, strength of organizational tradition), and ethnic and life-style composition of the work force (e.g., family economic background, acceptability of work-ethic values).

Future research and experience must clarify the impact of individual and situational differences on work preferences and therefore on methods for work design and redesign.

Effects on Personnel and Performance   The original question asked in this section was: What is a good job? Two of the suggested objectives relate to achieving specific performance goals (such as increasing efficiency or reducing errors) or personnel goals (such as decreasing turnover or improving job satisfaction). How good is the evidence that job redesign, for example, does in fact achieve such goals?

What sequence of events do we really expect when we improve the quality of work? In an oversimplification, we may be looking for the relationship shown in Fig. 15-1.

This assumes that two major types of goals (improved work performance and reduced absence and turnover) can be achieved only if work satisfaction improves.

Maher, previously cited, examined the linkage above and suggests instead that the middle link be omitted, as shown in Fig. 15-2. He reports that "Performance has been shown to increase in almost every single documented case of job enrichment," even when the enrichment does not result in measurable improvement in job satisfaction. Lawler also points out that most studies attempting to measure the effects of job enrichment "almost without exception . . . show that some positive gains are derived when jobs are enriched. In most cases, productivity is higher after enrichment." And in 10 out of 10 studies he reviewed, job enrichment resulted in higher work quality.[7]

As is suggested in the next section, we should set up our job redesign efforts with a clear indication of the performance we want to change and improve upon. We should not assume that such improvement necessarily comes by way of job satisfaction.

AN ACTION-RESEARCH STRATEGY

Anyone undertaking an activity as significant as job redesign will want to evaluate its impact, probably by taking a "snapshot" of the situation before redesign begins and comparing it with a similar snapshot taken some time after the redesign has been in effect. The two pictures should be as comprehensive as possible, including

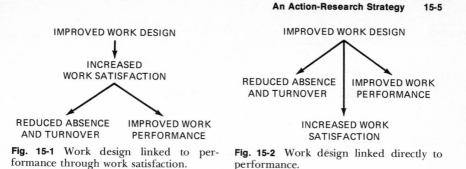

Fig. 15-1 Work design linked to performance through work satisfaction.

Fig. 15-2 Work design linked directly to performance.

measures of productivity, service, turnover, and attitudes, if they are all relevant. In some cases there will also be a "control" situation, much like the situation in which changes will be made, but kept without change for purposes of comparison.

Arranging for these before-and-after measurements in a systematic fashion is in fact a research approach to the activity. Since the strategy is being used to evaluate the effects of actions in a real-world setting, we refer to it as *action research*. Figure 15-3 summarizes many of the independent and dependent variables.

More complex models relating a wide range of variables to job design are proposed by Morse and by Monczka and Reif.[8] Both of these represent a contingency approach, based on the idea that the success of job redesign is contingent upon a number of other predisposing conditions being met.

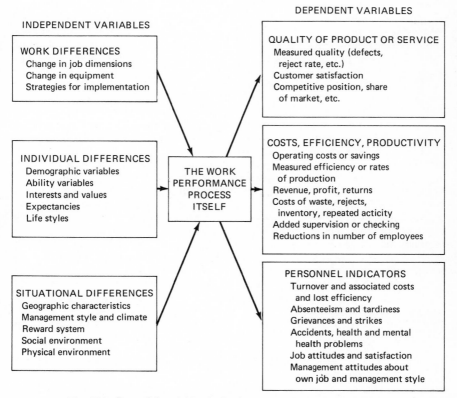

Fig. 15-3 Potential variables in "action research" on work design.

THE PROCESS OF JOB REDESIGN

The process to be described represents an average of successful experiences with job redesign in several organizations. The actual experiences, of course, lie somewhere on either side of the average.

Five major functions are recommended:

1. Identifying work design problems
2. Preparing the organizational climate
3. Developing the new job design
4. Implementing the new job design
5. Following up and extending

1. Identifying Work Design Problems   Earlier, we suggested that work and jobs might be redesigned to solve a specific problem, to achieve a new objective, or primarily to improve the quality of work. The first function thus becomes a matter of collecting information to determine whether one or more of these reasons exist. This function should also include a preliminary assessment of whether the problem is really worth trying to solve by redesign. The following are some tasks to be carried out within this first function.

1a. Reviewing standard personnel indicators.   One of the most extensive efforts to study and implement job redesign has been taking place in the Bell System. Ford begins his book about the first several years of this effort by saying, "The problem that precipitated the studies in this book is employee turnover."[9]

Analysis of turnover is a matter of determining not just how high it is on the average, but where it is concentrated. Are there similar characteristics in the jobs with higher turnover? Who is quitting? In a nutshell, search through the statistics and descriptive information for signs that any of the three kinds of independent variables in work performance (see Fig. 15-3) may be interacting to contribute to the turnover.

Similar analyses can be focused on absenteeism, tardiness, health problems, grievances, and other indicators of possible employee withdrawal from the job.

The products of these analyses are not explanations for the problem, but hypotheses for subsequent activities.

1b. Reviewing organizational performance results.   Here again, the objective is to find out whether a problem is concentrated in a particular area of work or group of jobs. The indication might come from performance measurements, such as reject rates, errors, supervisory ratios, efficiency measurements, sales volume, operating costs, or customer complaints. As with the personnel indicators, the analysis may identify patterns of jobs, people, or situations contributing to the performance problems.

1c. Identifying new objectives or requirements.   New objectives are often combined with problem objectives. For example, there may be an objective to introduce new work methods and increase output as a result, while trying to overcome a problem of rejects and waste. Such goals need to be specified if they might affect or be affected by job redesign.

1d. Sampling employee experiences and attitudes.   In addition to learning how satisfied employees are with their jobs as a whole, we can find out how they react to specific aspects of their work situation, such as supervision, pay, coworkers, promotions, and the work itself. The Job Descriptive Index is one standard instrument for this purpose.[10]

If we want to identify problems with the work itself, we need to get reactions to such characteristics of work as its modularity, employee power to act, and the availability of direct feedback. The Job Dimensions Checklist, developed by Suzansky, relates employee responses directly to six job dimensions, including these three.[11] Also, the "Reactions to Your Job" Questionnaire produces a profile of how employees view their jobs according to 10 factors, including interest, opportunities for growth and learning, degree of freedom, planning, feedback, and use of time and effort, for example.[12]

Employee attitude and experience data can also be gathered by individual and group interviews and by logs or other records in which employees describe specific work experiences and reactions at the time they occur.

1e. *Selecting the target jobs.*   At the end of step *d,* any "problem jobs" should be evident if they exist. If several interrelated jobs have apparent problems, the redesign should be addressed to the entire group of jobs and the work processes they represent. They may be those with the biggest performance problems, with the largest number of people, with the fewest restrictions in terms of equipment or operating methods, with the highest absence rates, with supervisors most interested in redesign, or with any combination of these criteria.

1f. *Estimating the payoff of redesign.*   The function of identifying problem jobs should include a preliminary evaluation of whether the problem is worth solving through job redesign. Where possible, the objectives to be achieved should be priced out in terms of new revenues, reduced costs, other savings, etc. Precision is less critical than the order of magnitude of moneys involved.

These estimates serve three purposes: first, to help in the decision to go ahead or not; second, to indicate which jobs to begin with; and third, to catch the attention of money-conscious management.

2. Preparing the Organizational Climate   This second function is as critical to the success of job redesign as any other. Need for management support is recognized whenever a new organizational concept is introduced. The steps below should help in gaining that support.

2a. *Identifying potential organization barriers and supports.*   This step should produce a description of facts, policies, opinions, and practices which could stand in the way of effective redesigns and those which would support a change. Deterrents include such things as inflexible personnel policies, previous negative experience with improving jobs, expectations of quick results, and equipment or operating practices which restrict job activities.

Special attention should be given to the impact of the current management measurement and reward system. For example, what indicators are used to identify top-performing managers and supervisors? What importance do personnel results have in their success or failure? If, for example, a manager's evaluated performance does not include such personnel-oriented items as turnover among employees or their job satisfaction, the manager will pay less direct attention to them than to matters of costs, sales, service, and productivity (even though the manager grants that the personnel items help in achieving the other goals).

One major factor to be considered is the potential impact of the union, if any is involved in the jobs under consideration. Experience suggests that unions are not against job redesign per se. But if contractual issues might be affected, the union will be more than casually interested.

Early consultation with key union personnel will help prevent sudden objections and roadblocks later and, in fact, may help to provide support for the redesign.

Sirota and Wolfson and Schappe identified categories of obstacles, which could well serve as checklists for examining the barriers in a specific organization.[13]

2b. *Developing strategy for preparing the organizational climate.*   There is a temptation when working in an operating environment to charge into action as soon as early roadblocks are cleared. Ultimate progress will be greater if that temptation is reduced by working from a strategy which keeps the immediate actions in the perspective of the long-range objectives.

Obviously, no single strategy suits all organizations and job redesign situations. Only a few additional principles can be suggested for designing a strategy to suit your own needs:

- Include top management of the specific organization to be involved (the division, department, or region) in early discussions of the proposed job redesign.
- Emphasize possible payoffs and show concern for "bottom-line" effects. Illustrate with examples and experiences, wherever possible.
- Keep meetings to the point and avoid the temptation to consume valuable time with more theory and opinion than needed to explain the basic ideas and intentions.
- Design the information and meetings for each specific audience. Do not assume that everyone at each level or in each part of the organization needs or wants the same information. To do so may cause them to tune out during the presentation or discussion.
- Do not force decisions or commitments too quickly or unnecessarily. Allow time in your schedule between meetings and the times when you need to take action. Furthermore, it may be appropriate not to require any specific decisions or commitments from top management at all, but simply to do what is necessary to arouse their positive interest and concern.

2c. Developing understanding and commitment.   This is essentially carrying out the strategy of step *2b,* Making necessary contacts, developing the informational materials, holding meetings, and making presentations. These activities may include management, the union, line and relevant staff personnel, headquarters, and field organizations.

2d. Finalizing objectives and committing resources.   The immediate products of establishing a favorable organizational climate are (1) getting the managers who are directly concerned with the target jobs to agree on the specific objectives to be met through the redesign, on how those objectives will be measured, and on any conditions limiting the redesign and (2) getting approval for the anticipated costs and other resources necessary to proceed, such as approval for the time to conduct data gathering and other activities, for the possible services of an outside consultant, and for the collection of special data.

It is helpful to prepare a statement of general intent, summarizing what is planned, the objectives, the requirements, the commitments, and the schedule. Such a document, even if informal, will help managers respond to questions from others and react to reports from the redesign. It should also remind them to discuss the process with their subordinates, emphasizing the importance of the effort in their overall priorities.

Once the commitments have been made and the project is to proceed, the key personnel must be assigned. The core of the project team should probably be two people: one individual representing the line organization in critical decisions and technical information and another representing the staff in matters of general coordination, methodology, and reporting. Either of these individuals might be the team leader, depending on such things as who initiated the idea, where the greatest credibility will lie, and who has more time. It may be appropriate to have the services of an outside consultant available to the team in matters of methodology and process, but the consultant should not have primary responsibility for the redesign activity. In redesign projects in organizations without access to qualified staff, the consultant may fulfill some of the functions of the staff.

3. Developing the New Job Design   This is the heart of the process and is characterized by both *analysis*—the systematic study of work content for problems of work quality—and *synthesis*—the rebuilding or reinforcing of work content to overcome those problems. The product will be recommendations concerning how one or more jobs should be redesigned.

3a. Specifying how work gets done.   The product of this step is a detailed description of how work flows to and from the target jobs and how it is handled in each job. Three kinds of work-related information will be helpful for this analysis.

- How work is actually done—from operating procedures, task analyses, flow diagrams, training content, interviews with incumbents, etc.
- How work and jobs are organized—from job descriptions, organization charts, etc.
- How work performance objectives are measured—from measurement and appraisal plans, target-setting methods, etc.

If possible, determine what reinforces the present structure of jobs. For example, if a lot of checking of work is done, what penalties are there in company measurements for errors, rejects, or other unchecked problems? If employees are not permitted to make many decisions on their own, find out what the penalties are for wrong decisions. This may point to the need to change the scoring system and its penalties and rewards before the job itself is changed.

If such work-related information does not exist in documented form, experts may be able to develop it collectively, sequentially, or individually. Consider having workers in the job participate in such information gathering. If workers are directly involved at this early stage, explain to them the purpose of the effort, without creating unrealistic expectations.

3b. Diagnosing specific problems.   The objective of this step is to identify elements of the work design which contribute most to the problems or goals of performance, attitude, or job quality.

In the early job restructuring activities in the Bell System, this activity was combined with the next step (*3c*), creating solutions to problems. Brainstorming, in a form called "greenlighting," jumped directly into trying to improve the work module and to increase the opportunities for responsibility, achievement, recognition, and growth. This early AT&T approach is described in detail as the "art of reshaping jobs" in Ford's book documenting the experience.[14]

Some alternative techniques have been designed to focus more attention on the specific problems that underlie the general indicators. For example, assume we are studying a job which seems to have a reasonably complete module but which rates low on power to act and feedback (one way of looking at job quality). If a workshop approach was used, participants would pinpoint instances of the employee's low control over the work and instances where feedback is needed. Ideas would be expressed with minimal evaluation and would be recorded by the workshop leader for later consideration and evaluation.

Following are some guidelines for a workshop with participants who are familiar with the target job:

- Develop a summary of the specific objectives to be achieved by the redesign and of the specific problems to be overcome. Review these with participants at the beginning of the workshop. Refocus the activity of the workshop with these when it goes astray. Add to or modify the lists, if necessary.
- Develop a summary of the functions of jobs being considered and a diagram of the work flow among functions and jobs. These can be used to make sure that participants are equally familiar with the technical details of the work, as well as to identify work-flow problems.
- Select for the workshop a series of dimensions of work quality especially relevant to the target jobs. "Module" may be one of the dimensions, for example, or you may prefer more specific elements such as these:

Module	*Feedback*
Wholeness	On quality
Closure	On efficiency
Meaningfulness	From clients
"Turf"	From supervisors
Client identity	Style of feedback
Control	*Skills*
Power to act	Use of valued skills
Decision making	Opportunity to learn on
Choices and alternatives	present job for other jobs
Control of pace, method, and type of work	

It does not matter if the dimensions overlap with one another. They will be used to stimulate thinking, and different words may trigger new ideas. Review the terms in the workshop so that everyone has a similar understanding of them.

■ Begin the analysis by considering the overall work flow within a job and the degree to which it enhances or hampers each of the work-quality dimensions in turn—first the module, then control, then feedback, and finally skills. This should help you develop insight not only into the overall quality of the job but also into the dimensions most in need of improvement. The results of this appraisal of work flow by quality dimensions can be compared with whatever evaluation was made earlier through questionnaires or interviews on work quality. The product of this activity would be a list of possible problems in the work flow, associated with specific dimensions.

■ The next step is to relate the suggested work-flow problems to the original list of personnel and performance problems or objectives.

Throughout these workshop activities, participants should express ideas freely, unevaluated by others at this time, as in brainstorming.

If this analysis step is combined with the next step, the participants can consider possible solutions, still in a brainstorming, nonevaluative fashion.

These steps are being described for workshop methods, but they can also be carried out by one or more job redesign specialists by themselves, if they have enough job information.

3c. Suggesting solutions to problems.   Here again, a modified brainstorming approach may be productive. Each of the tasks may be considered in turn, or the discussion may be freewheeling so that ideas are generated on any of the problems raised previously. The goal is to relate one or more suggested solutions or improvements to each of the identified problems. It may not be possible to do this, especially when problems are outside the realm of current solutions, as when the technology does not yet exist.

Figure 15-4 represents several general principles for improving quality, as proposed by Ford.[15]

In addition to the rich source of suggestions represented in the Ford publications, a wide range of ideas for work improvement can be found in the writings of many others with practical experience.[16]

3d. Considering related jobs.   Before completing a series of recommendations for redesigning any one job, it is necessary to examine the relationship between that job and the others around it: those which provide inputs, those which receive outputs, those which perform simultaneous or overlapping functions, supervisory jobs, or other related support jobs in clerical or administrative functions. Go back to the work flow with the new ideas from step 3c and see how the flow now relates to these other jobs. Ford describes the possibilities of clustering or "nesting" related jobs, for example.[17]

3e. Determining the impact of the suggested changes.   Up until now, the suggestions have been largely the result of nonevaluative brainstorming. Now is the time for considering systematically the realities of the organization, including the obstacles and barriers considered in step *2a*. Advantages and disadvantages of alternative

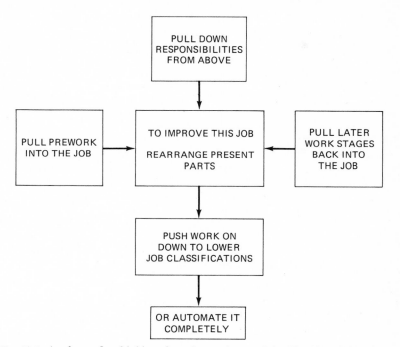

Fig. 15-4   A scheme for thinking about improving work itself. *(Adapted from Ford.)*

suggestions must be weighed, as they are affected by such issues as wage scales, work schedules, operating practices, equipment, the management "reward system," supervisory practices and styles, union agreements, customer expectations, overall efficiency and effectiveness, etc.

As part of this evaluation, identify those suggestions which may help to make an immediate impact, even though they are not likely to have a lasting effect. The workshop leader will need to move suggestions away from repeated efforts to solve basic job problems with superficial changes such as improved lunch facilities, parking lots, employee newspapers, and information meetings.

The final result of this step is a series of recommendations for the redesign of one or more jobs. The focus should be on what the end result of such redesign will be, rather than on "how to get there from here."

4. Implementing the New Job Design   Putting a recommended design into operation is the objective of this function. It is highly dependent on the organizational structure, on the manner in which line organizations assume responsibility for the changes, and on the degree of change required by the redesign.

4a. Designing strategy for implementation.   At one extreme, implementation may be a universal, one-time changeover from the present jobs to the redesigned jobs: Everyone is prepared at the same time for the complete change, which then takes place as soon as everyone can be trained, procedures modified, or other organizational conditions fitted to the redesigned situation. This kind of universal implementation is appropriate where functions of two or more jobs are closely interrelated, where it is not possible to have two employees in the same job working differently, or where there will be a simultaneous change in equipment or procedures.

At the other extreme, the redesign may be an alternative way for some employees to work when they become qualified for the improved jobs. In this case, if performance in present jobs is completely compatible with performance in the new jobs, not all employees may change over to the redesigned jobs. Not all employees may want the redesigned job, and not all of them may be qualified. Furthermore, the progression from the present jobs to the new jobs may be gradual, with only a few changes made at a time. Some changes may be used as new opportunities, or even privileges, and given to employees to reinforce good performance at the present job. This kind of implementation is successful when the same job can be performed at various levels of responsibility and completeness and when there are no major changes in equipment or procedures affecting all employees.

The strategy must be designed to fit one of these approaches or something in between them. Regardless of the extent of the change, plans must be made for training needed to meet the requirements of the redesigned job. If the change will be introduced selectively, then criteria must be developed for specifying how an employee becomes eligible for features of the redesigned job.

4b. Implementing. In some situations, the first steps of implementation will make some of the "showy" changes immediately and for everyone. These may be short-lived in their effects, but they will help to establish the fact that changes are occurring, in response—one would hope—to some of the ideas generated by employees themselves. These "broadside" changes, often primarily hygienic in nature, need to be followed soon by more substantive changes involving improvements in important job dimensions. If the changes are to be made selectively and progressively, the criteria must be discussed at least with those nearing qualification. Employees should be allowed the option of not adopting the redesigned job, if it is not necessary that they do so.

If at all possible, managers and supervisors who participate conscientiously in implementing the redesign should be reinforced by their bosses. Helpful questions and supportive comments will overcome some of the inertia which often makes people reluctant to leave the comfort of present conditions.

Implementation may start very small in one location and gradually prove itself there before managers are willing to extend it to other locations. A well-designed action-research type of data collection and analysis will expedite that expansion.

5. Following Up and Extending   The fifth function must continue long after the initial implementation and may lead to the redesign of other jobs. The following are several activities (not necessarily sequential) that will help perpetuate and extend a successful redesign.

5a. Maintaining ongoing records.   Keep continuous records of alternatives considered, decisions made, steps taken, and results achieved. Continue to track organizational performance even after everyone seems satisfied that success has been achieved.

5b. Maintaining ongoing communications.   Develop simple, frequent means of keeping key personnel and managers informed of progress without burdening them with details. This will reassure them that the effort is a serious, long-term process.

5c. Reinforcement by management.   Try to keep middle and top management periodically reinforcing the effort to analyze, explore, and change where necessary.

5d. Interviewing.   After the redesign has been implemented and has "settled in" for some employees, interview a sample of them to get their perceptions of the changes and their redesigned jobs. When employees resign or transfer, interview them to get their reactions to the quality of their jobs and to find out how their feelings relate to the decision to leave.

5e. Modifying policies and practices.   When redesign leads to greater power to act, for example, try to get organizational policies and operating practices to reflect the improvements. For example, where a selective approach is used, allowing greater discretion to some employees, recognize this in the operating practices; e.g., "If the employee is working under conditions of the expanded job. . . ."

5f. Perpetuating with new managers.   Include information about and provide skills in job redesign in the orientation and training of new managers and staff.

5g. Recycling difficult job problems.   Where a first attempt to improve a job is not successful or does not go far enough, return to some of the early steps of analysis, perhaps back to the function or work-flow analysis. Some jobs are highly resistant to redesign, including some which should simply be eliminated through mechanization or combined with others.

5h. Moving up the hierarchy.   Do not limit the restructuring to the craft, blue-collar, or other nonmanagement jobs. As responsibilities are drawn downward by redesign at the bottom, the next level of jobs becomes ripe for redesign, right on up the organizational ladder. In fact, if this is not done, many of the supervisors and lower-level managers will resist or undermine job redesign for their employees because it will tend to denude their own jobs.

5i. Evaluating.   One does not have to be a died-in-the-wool researcher to be curious about effectiveness and impact. So evaluate, evaluate, and evaluate. Keep looking back at objectives. When they change, modify the data collection accordingly. It is not necessary to keep large masses of data flowing at all times, but some carefully selected indicators, tied to instances of redesign, can do wonders to reinforce the entire effort and to maximize your own growth and understanding of the redesign process.

FINAL OBSERVATIONS

It must be obvious to the reader that there is no single way to redesign jobs. Some people are more experienced at it than others, but there are few real experts. Even the novice should experiment and be innovative. Then follow up and evaluate the results and make necessary adjustments. When you are asking others to hold nothing sacred in their views about work and jobs, you must be similarly flexible.

Above all, job redesign should not be introduced as a program or a panacea. Instead, with its early diagnostic steps, it must become a way of managing, a way of life in the organization. If we give the broadest possible definition to "organization development" as the improvement of the quality of working life and performance in an organization, job redesign must be one of the most potentially powerful approaches for achieving that objective.

REFERENCES

1. The "genealogy" is presented in Davis, L. E., and J. C. Taylor (eds): *Design of Jobs,* Penguin Books, Middlesex, England, 1972, Introduction, pp. 9–20.
2. Herzberg, F., B. Mausner, and B. B. Snyderman: *The Motivation to Work,* John Wiley & Sons, Inc., New York, 1959.

   Herzberg, F.: "One More Time: How Do You Motivate Employees?" *Harvard Business Review,* pp. 53–62, January–February 1968.
3. Herzberg, F.: *Work and the Nature of Man,* The World Publishing Company, Cleveland, 1966, p. 178.
4. Ford, R. N.: "Job Enrichment Lessons from AT&T," *Harvard Business Review,* pp. 96–106, January–February 1973.

5. A selection of significant contributors to these dimensions over the years includes: Walker, C. R.: "The Problem of the Repetitive Job," *Harvard Business Review,* vol. 28, pp. 54–58, 1950.

   Guest, R. H.: "Men and Machines: An Assembly-Line Worker Looks at His Job," *Personnel,* vol. 31, pp. 496–503, 1955.

   Turner, A. N., and P. R. Lawrence: *Industrial Jobs and the Worker,* Harvard University, Graduate School of Business Administration, Cambridge, Mass., 1965.

   Hulin, C. L., and M. R. Blood: "Job Enlargement, Individual Differences, and Worker Responses," *Psychological Bulletin,* vol. 69, pp. 41–55, 1968.

   Davis, L. E.: "The Coming Crisis for Production Management: Technology and Organization," *International Journal of Production Research,* vol. 9, pp. 65–82, 1971.

   Hackman, J. R., and E. E. Lawler III: "Employee Reactions to Job Characteristics," *Journal of Applied Psychology Monograph,* vol. 55, pp. 259–286, 1971.

   Herzberg et al.: op. cit.

   Ford: op. cit.
6. Maher, J. R.: "Job Enrichment, Performance and Morale in a Simulated Factory," in J. R. Maher (ed.), *New Perspectives in Job Enrichment,* Van Nostrand Reinhold Incorporated, New York, 1971, p. 71.

   Hulin, C. L.: "Individual Differences and Job Enrichment: The Case against General Treatments," in Maher, *New Perspectives in Job Enrichment,* p. 182.
7. Lawler, E. E., III: *Motivation in Work Organizations,* Brooks/Cole Publishing Company, Monterey, Calif., 1973, p. 152.

   Lawler, E. E., III: "Job Design and Employee Motivation," *Personnel Psychology,* vol. 22, p. 433, 1969.

   Herzberg, F., B. Mausner, R. O. Peterson, and D. F. Capwell: *Job Attitudes: Review of Research and Opinion,* Psychological Services of Pittsburgh, Pittsburgh, 1957, chap. 4, "Effects of Job Attitudes."
8. Morse, J. J.: "A Contingency Look at Job Design," *California Management Review,* vol. 16, pp. 67–75, Fall 1973.

   Monczka, R. M., and W. E. Reif: "A Contingency Approach to Job Enrichment Design," *Human Resource Management,* pp. 9–17, Winter 1973.
9. Ford, R. N.: *Motivation through the Work Itself,* American Management Association, New York, 1969, p. 13.
10. Smith, P. C., L. M. Kendall, and C. L. Hulin: *The Measurement of Satisfaction in Work and Retirement,* Rand McNally & Company, Chicago, 1969.
11. Suzansky, J. W.: *The Effects of Individual Characteristics as Moderating Variables of the Relation between Job Design Quality and Job Satisfaction,* Stevens Institute of Technology, 1974.
12. Ford, R. N., and E. F. Borgatta: "Satisfaction with Work Itself," *Journal of Applied Psychology,* vol. 54, pp. 124–135, 1970.
13. Sirota, D., and A. D. Wolfson: "Job Enrichment: What Are the Obstacles?" *Personnel,* pp. 8–17, May–June 1972.

    Schappe, R. H.: "Twenty-Two Arguments against Job Enrichment," *Personnel Journal,* pp. 116–123, February 1974.
14. Ford: *Motivation through the Work Itself,* chap. 7.
15. Ibid., p. 157.
16. Davis, L. E.: "The Design of Jobs," *Industrial Relations,* vol. 6, pp. 21–45, 1966.

    Greenblatt, A. D.: "Maximizing Productivity through Job Enrichment," *Personnel,* pp. 31–39, March–April 1973.

    Lawler, E. E., III, R. J. Hackman, and S. Kaufman: "Effects of Job Redesign: A Field Experiment," *Journal of Applied Social Psychology,* vol. 3, pp. 49–62, 1973.

Paul, W. J., Jr., K. B. Robertson, and F. Herzberg: "Job Enrichment Pays Off," *Harvard Business Review,* pp. 61–78, March–April 1969.

Powers, J. E.: "Job Enrichment: How One Company Overcame the Obstacles," *Personnel,* pp. 18–22, May–June 1972.

Sirota, D.: "Job Enrichment: Another Management Fad?" *The Conference Board Record,* vol. 10, pp. 40–45, April 1973.

17. Ford: "Job Enrichment Lessons at AT&T," p. 101.

Chapter 16

The Assessment Center Method

DOUGLAS W. BRAY

Douglas W. Bray *is Director, Management Selection and Development Research, for the American Telephone and Telegraph Company. Dr. Bray pioneered the development of the management assessment center in 1956 as part of ambitious longitudinal research into managerial careers under the title of the Management Progress Study, and he is an internationally recognized authority in the field of management selection. Dr. Bray holds a Ph.D. from Yale University, is a Diplomate in Industrial-Organizational Psychology of the American Board of Professional Psychology, and is past president of the Division of Industrial-Organizational Psychology of the American Psychological Association.* Formative Years in Business, *written by Dr. Bray and his colleagues, has recently been published by Interscience-Wiley.*

The recent spread of the assessment center method throughout business and governmental organizations has been phenomenal. In 1960 only one American business organization was using assessment centers, and even in the mid-1960s only a handful of companies were running them. By the early 1970s, however, the method was being applied in several hundred organizations, and many more were waiting in the wings to join the rush to add the technique to their personnel selection and development repertoire.

NATURE OF ASSESSMENT CENTERS

The term "assessment center" is somewhat of a misnomer since it implies that there must be a building or some other semipermanent physical location for the activity. Although this is often the case, there is nothing mandatory about it. What is really involved in assessment is the application of various methods of observing and evaluating behavior in a variety of situations. Such methods can be applied in nearly any location, including a business office set aside for a day for the purpose. The methodology is what is important, not the physical setting.

The purpose of an assessment center is to provide an objective off-the-job evaluation of developed abilities, potential, strengths and weaknesses, and motivation. (The degree to which evaluation of motivation is an aspect of assessment varies considerably from organization to organization.) The assessment center leads to these evaluations through the observation of behavior in a variety of standardized performance situations, the rating of that behavior on a number of predetermined dimensions, the drawing of conclusions concerning potential for certain levels and types of work, and the diagnosis of developmental needs.

EMERGENCE OF THE MANAGEMENT ASSESSMENT CENTER

The assessment center first came to public attention in the United States at the conclusion of World War II, when it was revealed that the method had been used during the war to select intelligence operatives for the Office of Strategic Services. This use was publicized in an article in *Fortune* magazine[1] and in a book entitled *Assessment of Men.*[2] These reports generated considerable interest because of the imaginative and exciting nature of many of the simulations used and also because the elaborateness of the method contrasted sharply with the simplicity of paper-and-pencil methods of selection so widely used in nearly all other contexts, military and otherwise.

The OSS reports led to a few other attempts to apply the method, notably to the selection of clinical psychologists at a time when great numbers of them were being trained for the Veterans Administration and to the selection of psychiatrists at the Menninger Clinic. The results of these applications, as well as several outside the United States, were summarized in the mid-1950s.[3] Most psychologists viewed the results reported as disappointing, and the assessment center appeared not to be destined to play much of a role in either personnel selection or personnel development. Certainly very few suggested that it was a promising method for business use.

In 1956 the American Telephone and Telegraph Company undertook a longitudinal study of the development of young managers.[4]

In order to form a base for the years of follow-up to come, it was necessary to determine the abilities, aptitudes, values, and motivations of the study sample at the time when they first became managers. A 3½-day assessment center process was designed, and the 422 subjects of the study were assessed in the years 1956 to 1960. The assessment center had been introduced into American business.

This first AT&T assessment center was staffed by professional psychologists and thus was similar to the OSS center and other professional centers which had preceded the Bell System application. An important breakthrough occurred in 1958, when Michigan Bell management suggested that the assessment center might be modified to make it usable by laypersons. The specific purpose in mind was to aid in making the promotion decision involving craftsmen nominated for first-line management. The proposed assessment center started operations in the fall of 1958 with a staff consisting entirely of laypersons. Thus the assessment center method was freed of its reliance on professional assessors and freed of the barrier to widespread use which this requirement imposed. The way was open for the assessment center movement.

There was little immediate reaction; other organizations were slow to follow the Bell System's lead. During the 1960s, however, several companies became interested and started making serious use of the assessment center method, although on a smaller scale than AT&T. The first of these was Standard Oil of Ohio,[5] followed by General Electric and IBM. Momentum gradually increased up to the rapid proliferation of the late '60s and early '70s. Such expansion was supported by basic scientific studies[6] and by popular articles in publications read by many business executives.[7]

THE TYPICAL ASSESSMENT CENTER

Since the assessment center is an extremely flexible method, a description of the typical center may be misleading. Centers may run from less than a day to three or more days, they may or may not involve paper-and-pencil testing or measures of personality, and, in special instances, they may not even include that staple of the assessment center method—a group exercise. There is, nevertheless, a model which is representative of most centers.

The usual center occupies two days of the subject's time. Subjects are assessed in groups of six or twelve because most group exercises are constructed to accommodate six participants. While at the center the subjects undergo an extensive interview, an in-basket, and two group exercises. These are the basics, frequently embellished with additional individual performance situations and by paper-and-pencil tests and questionnaires.

The Business Game

Most assessment centers include a business game which, surprisingly enough, requires extremely little knowledge of business. The participants, usually six in number, try to make a profit by buying materials, putting them together in prescribed combinations, and selling them back to the staff members administering the exercise. The first assessment center business game used Tinker Toys. Others have involved the buying of digits and the resale of two- or three-digit-number combinations, shares of stock in stock trading and conglomerate games, or simple electronic parts. The purpose of such games is not to determine business knowledge or experience, and a definite effort is made in designing games to keep them simple enough so that no assessee will have any particular advantage over the others because of past business experience. The game conditions are intended to be a stimulus for interpersonal behavior so that the assessors can observe evidences of leadership, decisiveness, resistance to stress, planning and organizing ability, and other characteristics relevant to performance as a manager. All the games have definite time limits and, in addition, include stressful or uncertain periods so as to heighten interest and involvement. The games are, in fact, involving, and many assessees report that they enjoy going through them.

The Leaderless Group Discussion

An extremely common component of the assessment center is a leaderless group discussion. The original and most common format called for the six participants to act as the members of a board or committee, each of whom had an assigned point of view concerning the matter up for decision. The assessee was to promote this point of view as successfully as possible in the discussion period. In one example the six participants adopt the roles of members of the city council of a small city. They are to meet to decide what to do with additional federal funds which have suddenly come their way. Each participant is told that he or she has looked into the needs of a different city department and is attending the meeting hoping to obtain as much of the money as possible for that particular interest. Each participant is provided with briefing materials which give needed information about the city, its budget, etc., and a special briefing sheet outlining his or her particular project. Once again, as in the business game, an effort is made to provide materials which will fall within the experience of all the participants so that no special advantage will accrue to any of them. Behavior in the presentations and discussion is observed for such dimensions as oral communication skill, leadership, planning and organizing ability, resistance to stress, interpersonal sensitivity, and judgment. Other group discussion exercises have the participants play the roles of members of school boards, scholarship committees, supervisors meeting on a possible promotion, compensation committees, etc.

Not all leaderless group discussions are of the assigned-role variety. In some the participants are told that they are members of a task force or a special committee of some sort considering one problem or a series of problems. In this type of discussion the participants come to their own conclusions about the issues involved and the extent to which they wish to make a forceful presentation of a particular point of view. The participants are therefore not required to be as definitely competitive as they are when individual roles are assigned. Both types of group discussions are useful, depending on the particular dimensions which one desires to observe.

The In-Basket

The in-basket presents management problems to the individual assessee in the form of written materials which might come across a manager's desk. These include letters, memorandums, notes from the boss, records of telephone calls, appraisal forms, routine reports, etc. The assessee is usually told that he or she has come into a new job which has been vacant for several weeks. Things have piled up, and the assessee has come in for the first time on a Sunday afternoon to spend a few hours getting on top of things. Some of the materials, which are in no particular order, are quite important and call for early action. Others are routine and may well be ignored. Assessees are instructed to deal with the materials as they think they would in the real situation except to make more of a record than they otherwise might of the actions they intend to take.

Although the in-basket can be treated simply as a written exercise, it is usually followed by an intensive interview. In this interview the assessor digs into the assessee's reasoning and perceptions about the various items in the basket and into the causes of his or her decisiveness or indecisiveness. The interviewer may also ask questions about the assessee's perception of the whole situation: How good a boss was the previous incumbent? What problems does the organization have? What does the assessee plan to do to correct them? The in-basket interview is often conducted as a third-party inquiry. In other applications the staff members may play the role of the assessee's new boss and thus introduce a power relationship and perhaps somewhat more stress. The interview and the review of the written material itself form the basis for evaluating such dimensions as planning and organizing skills, decision-making ability, judgment, attention to detail, and perception.

The Interview

An extensive interview is inevitably a part of the assessment process. Such interviews are usually quite lengthy, running from one to two hours, and often rove freely over many areas of the assessee's past and current life. Childhood and school experiences are, of course, prominent among the areas covered. Aspirations and expectations about the future are usually a matter of particular interest. In some centers interviews follow a prescribed format which specifies the questions to be asked. At the other extreme are interview methods which allow the interviewer complete freedom in formulating questions and interacting with the interviewee. In such cases the interviewer is expected to have a good grasp of the dimensions about which the interview is to provide information. A personal history blank is often administered early in the assessment process or even before the assessee reports to the center. The interviewer reviews this blank prior to the interview to help formulate the general approach and specific questions. Although some of the dimensions for which the interview provides good data are observable elsewhere in the assessment process, such as personal impact and oral communication skills, the interview makes a unique contribution in respect to some dimensions not easily observed elsewhere.[8] These include advancement motivation, the importance of job security, goal flexibility, and range of interests.

Paper-and-Pencil Tests

Although many assessment centers rely entirely on simulations and interviews, a considerable number include at least some paper-and-pencil testing as part of the battery of techniques. The Bell System assessment centers for the selection of first-line supervisors, for example, have long included a test of general mental ability and a current-events test. Centers elsewhere have used similar tests, and some have also used personality and motivational inventories. The cognitive instruments are used to obtain objective measures of learning capacity, range of interests, etc. The personality blanks are used for the purpose of evaluating motivational characteristics, an area which is tapped at most assessment centers only by the interview.

Other Methods

The above types of techniques—business games, group discussions, in-baskets, interviews, and paper-and-pencil tests—are those most commonly seen in the typical assessment center. Other types of simulations have, however, appeared and will no doubt be added to in the future. One of these is the analysis/presentation exercise, in which the assessee must do an extensive analysis of a problem (often as an evening assignment) and then make a formal presentation of recommendations. Another simulation—individual fact-finding and decision making—requires the assessee to dig out the facts in an ambiguous decision-making situation by face-to-face questioning and then defend the decision under vigorous cross-examination by an assessor.

A few centers have added projective personality tests, such as the Thematic Apperception Test. Such a step obviously requires the services of a professional staff member for the administration and particularly the interpretation of the responses to these instruments. The reason for adding such tests is, of course, to find out more about the motivation of the assessees. The techniques have been shown to be helpful in throwing light on dimensions such as achievement motivation, desire to hold a leadership role, and independence.[9]

Assessment-Staff Activities

The purpose of the assessment exercises is to elicit behavior so that the candidate can later be judged on a variety of characteristics. It is obvious, then, that a trained staff must be on hand to observe the behavior. Although, as has been noted, early assessment centers relied almost completely on professional observers, most business assessment centers are staffed entirely by laypersons. These individuals are usually managers in the assessee's own company two levels above the level of those being assessed. (This requirement may have to be relaxed at higher levels of the organization.) These managers are trained for three to ten days to administer the assessment techniques and, more importantly, to carefully observe and record behavior so that their observations can later be made available to all members of the assessment staff. Behavior in a particular exercise may be observed by only one or two assessors, who must then prepare a report on their observations for later use by the entire staff. The nature of this report varies according to the software used and the training of the assessor. In some instances, the assessor report form provides the framework for the report, and the assessor completes the final report by answering fully all the questions on the form. More experienced assessors may simply record behavior in any manner they wish and write a report which they structure and organize completely on their own.

After the assessees have returned to their jobs and all the assessment reports are written, a most important phase of the assessment process takes place. This is the assessment staff meeting in which the performance of each candidate in all the exercises is reviewed and rated. The consideration of each candidate never occupies less than an hour and frequently takes closer to two hours. One candidate at a time is considered. The entire assessment staff listens to the reports of the candidate's behavior in all the exercises, interviews, etc., and then rates the candidate on the dimensions around which the assessment center is organized. These dimensions, such as face-to-face leadership skill, proficiency in planning and organizing, and decision-making ability, usually number from 15 to 25. Differences in ratings are discussed and adjudicated with the goal of achieving as much consensus as possible.

Following the rating of the dimensions, the assessment staff turns its attention to final recommendations. These may have to do with selection, placement, advancement, or development. In the case of advancement, the assessors usually place the candidate into one of several categories depending on whether they consider him or her to be completely acceptable for promotion, questionable, or unacceptable. Once again, there is considerable discussion of differences of opinion among the assessors in an effort to make sure that the reasons for the final recommendation are completely clear.

USES OF ASSESSMENT

The first operational use of assessment centers in the Bell System was as an aid in determining the promotability of nonmanagement employees who had been recommended by their organizations as candidates for first-line management. Although this is still a very common application of the assessment center method, much experience has accumulated about its use for other purposes. Uses have differed in respect to the level of the employee evaluated, the type of job for which the person is being evaluated, and the general purposes of the assessment.

Employment

A few organizations have used the assessment center to aid in employment decisions. These applications have concerned themselves with recent college graduates being considered for general management employment and persons applying for sales jobs. Several Bell System telephone companies as well as Sears, Roebuck[10] have used assessment centers in the college employment process. These centers have been similar to the typical one described above or have been some condensation thereof. Of practical importance is the fact that candidates for employment not only are willing to undergo assessment but also are often greatly impressed that a company devotes so much care and attention to its employment process. Logistics are sometimes a problem; it may be difficult to assemble groups of candidates to undergo assessment at the same time. Some type of prescreening before assessment may also be necessary to reduce large pools of applicants to smaller numbers for more serious consideration. Applicants for sales positions, including experienced salespeople, have also shown a clear willingness to be assessed even when the process may require a day of their own time.

Early Identification

Although it is the newest application of the method, early-identification assessment is logically considered next since it concerns the employee who has been hired only recently. The purpose of early identification, as used so far, has been to uncover potential for management-level work among new nonmanagement employees. Assessment is condensed into one day, and staff procedures are much shortened so that a high volume of assessees can be processed. The purpose of the assessment is not to render a final judgment of the candidates' promotability to management levels, but rather to identify those who have promise for the future. The intent is to give those with high potential special development opportunities and accelerated treatment so that they can reach target positions significantly earlier then might otherwise be the case. Early-identification processes have been worked out not only for management and sales jobs but also for the job of engineering assistant. In this application the assessment techniques are all individual in nature. There are no group exercises.

Placement

Placement has been used only sparingly as a purpose of assessment. This is most likely because assessment has usually been done on a general management model rather than for specific jobs. Assessment does, however, influence placement decisions in some cases. In the Standard Oil of Ohio application an important aspect of assessment is to decide the next assignment an assessee should have, given the overall pattern of strengths and weaknesses revealed by assessment. The point here is that assessment often leads to an assignment for developmental purposes rather than because the person is a "better fit" in the job to which he or she is to be moved. Assessment has also played a role in interdepartmental transfers, where it has proved to be a powerful way of breaking down traditional barriers. This application is especially helpful in instances where some departments are rich in talent and others are hard up for managers. The New York Telephone Company used assessment in such a circumstance with the highly successful transfer of managers across departmental lines.

Advancement

By far the most frequent use of assessment is as part of the promotion process. The most usual pattern is for those who have been appraised by management as good candidates for advancement to go to the assessment center for a final check. This type of assessment is done at many different levels of management. It is probably most common at the lower levels, but many organizations restrict their assessment to middle managers. A few use it even at close to the vice-presidential level. Although attendance at the assessment center by nomination is by far the most frequent pattern, some organizations have assessed all incumbents at given levels of management to aid not only in selecting the most capable but also in evaluating the amount of potential available and in highlighting the developmental needs of the organization.

Development

Recommendations for development are nearly always one of the outputs of the assessment center process. Not only may new assignments and different career paths be indicated for a particular individual, but formal training may also be suggested. Assessment which is done purely for the purpose of development is, however, rare. The original General Electric program had a strong emphasis on development and currently involves the preparation of a developmental plan during the manager's week at the center.[11] Several other organizations have also combined assessment and development experiences. In one department of IBM, for example, those attending the sessions spend the first two days being assessed and the next three days in management development activities. It has proved difficult for organizations to stick to a strict developmental model in their assessment activities. Once extensive evaluative information on individuals is available, the pressure to use that information as a guide to advancement and placement is extremely strong.

Affirmative Action

A new purpose for assessment centers has been found in affirmative-action programs, which seek to speed the advancement of minority-group members and women. Early-identification programs are particularly relevant in this regard. Many organizations are hiring increased numbers of minority-group members into entry-level jobs. Normal processes of identification, development, and advancement are often lengthy, and it is particularly necessary to identify minority-group members with higher potential so that they can be moved along more quickly. The use of assessment centers (whether in early-identification programs or otherwise) can also serve to reduce the anxiety of some operating people that affirmative action may result in the advancement of individuals who are not fully capable of effective performance. Operating people tend to believe that nothing but the traditional approach of long service in a variety of jobs can produce a capable worker. Certification through an assessment center can provide evidence that the person really is capable of doing the level of work in question.

An interesting aspect of the consent agreement between AT&T and the EEOC and other government agencies was the provision of special regional assessment centers for women already in telephone company management. The problem consisted in the assertion by the government agencies that many women college graduates hired directly into management in the telephone business had not been put on the same "fast-track" program that many males had entered during the years in question. Since, however, many of the women managers had not been hired against the same standards as the men assigned to the special program, it was necessary to find a means of identifying those women of comparable potential. It was agreed that three regional assessment centers would be established to process all the 2,000 women who were covered by the agreement and who elected to attend.

ESSENTIALS OF ASSESSMENT

An obvious first step in starting an assessment center is to decide the level and type of job to which assessment is to be applied. Is the center to be used for employment or advancement, or will it be primarily developmental in nature? Is it to be concerned with lower-, middle-, or even upper-level management? Is the center to assess general management ability or certain specialist skills, such as sales? Answers to these questions will depend on a variety of factors including dissatisfaction with current methods, the importance of the job in question, resistances to certain applications, and the availability of appropriate staff.

Selecting Dimensions

Once the type and level of job are decided upon, the next most important step is identifying, defining, and getting organizational acceptance of the characteristics that the assessment center is to measure. These characteristics are called *dimensions, variables,* or *qualities.* It is these dimensions which will form the focus of assessment, will be reported on to management in terms of strengths and weaknesses, and will be discussed with assessees in feedback sessions. Obviously, the dimensions must make sense to the management of the organization, or management people—whether assessors, assessees, or supervisors—will not take them seriously.

Methods of identifying the dimensions to be used may include formal job analysis and descriptions, but they are most often based on special interviews with line and staff managers in the organization who supervise the level of work in question or who have special staff knowledge thereof. The process is often iterative in nature; that is, those building the assessment center construct a list of dimensions from the first round of interviewing and then play these back to management for revision. Second and third drafts may then be made until there is general satisfaction with the list.

With so many organizations now involved in assessment, the number of dimensions used somewhere or other is quite large. The following are some samples:

Oral communication skill
Leadership skills
Personal impact
Sensitivity
Flexibility
Independence
Work standards
Career ambition
Work involvement
Resistance to stress
Energy
Decisiveness
Planning and organizing ability
Tenacity

Choosing Exercises

A next step is the selection of assessment center exercises (including interviews and tests, if appropriate) designed to elicit behavior relevant to the dimensions around which the center is organized. Examples of the most common techniques have been given above, but it may be appropriate to design new ones for specific situations. For instance, one retail store chain has a special exercise known as the "irate customer phone call," and another organization has a special individual case for those to be employed as salespeople of printed advertisements. In planning the assessment center, there should be a good amount of redundancy between exercises so that a particular dimension can be seen in more then one setting. The more of this the better, since it adds to the reliability of judgments of the various dimensions.

Staffing

Although a few assessment centers depend heavily on professionals, nearly all are staffed by managers from the organization itself. These managers are usually two levels above the assessees in the organization; that is, they supervise the level of management for which the assessee is a candidate. This is not universal, however. In some instances the assessors are only one level above the assessees. An important decision relative to staffing is the number of times an assessor is likely to serve. In the original Bell System applications, it was anticipated that assessors would serve for several months or more. Few organizations have followed this lead, however, and many use assessors for only one or two assessee groups. Both extremes have their advantages. When assessors are to serve a long time, it is feasible to train them very thoroughly since the cost of training will be written off over many weeks of assessment. It is also likely that the more experienced the assessors, the better the quality of assessment. On the other hand, it may be very difficult to persuade management to release personnel for long periods, although they might be quite willing to have them serve a time or two. Considerable turnover of assessors also accomplishes the permeation of the organization with knowledge and sophistication about assessment since many managers will have been trained and will have served on the staff. They thus will be in a better position to appreciate assessment reports and to be guided by them.

Feedback

Once the assessment of a candidate has been completed, the ratings made, and the reports prepared, the findings must then be played back to the organization. This is clearly what the assessment center is all about, and although it comes at the conclusion of a description of the essentials of assessment, it is clear that what is going to happen at this point should be decided long before the assessment center is started. One aspect of feedback concerns the form of the report to management and the question of who in management should receive the report. The most usual form is a short summary of the assessee's performance at the assessment center, paying particular attention to strengths and weaknesses demonstrated. This report is often sent to a manager in the assessee's organization several levels above the assessee. In other instances, it is sent directly to the assessee's boss. It would seem to make most sense to send the report to that level of the organization which actually controls the promotion or transfer of people at the assessee's level. For development purposes, however, it is usually expected that the information will eventually reach the candidate's supervisor.

Nearly all assessment center applications provide for the feedback of the assessment results to the assessees themselves. This is often done by a member of the assessment staff, but is sometimes carried out by a specialist who has learned assessment center methods and who handles all feedbacks within the organization. This would seem to be especially appropriate if that person is also in charge of management development, career counseling, or some similar function. The report to the assessee is usually private, although some organizations permit—at the assessee's request—that his or her boss be present; some organizations even require this. A variation tried by a few organizations is to have the assessment center administrator and the boss agree on a feedback which encompasses both assessment results and job performance, and this feedback is given jointly.

Outside Assistance

The assessment center is a sophisticated intervention into an organization's personnel management system, both in the operation of the center and in its various impingements on the organization. It is therefore essential that advice and assistance be obtained from those experienced in the method during the process of introducing a center into a new setting.

A number of organizations have come into being in order to fill this need. Their services fall into one or more of three categories: (1) consultation and assistance in training assessors and assessment center administrators, (2) the provision of assessment center techniques on either a ready-made or a tailor-made basis, and (3) assessment of candidates on a per-head basis. Development Dimensions, Inc., provides services of all three types, has an extensive catalog of assessment exercises, and conducts regular conferences and workshops on the assessment center method. Cabot Jafee and Associates and an interlocking organization, Assessment Designs (both of Orlando, Florida), provide consultation services and materials. Personnel Decisions (Minneapolis) both assists organizations in installing centers and conducts "public" centers.

Other sources of assistance include Hilton Wasserman and Associates (New York), Assessment Associates (Baltimore), Consulting Associates (Southfield, Michigan), Humber, Mundie & McClary (Milwaukee), John Paisios & Associates (Chicago), and Canadian Management Assessment Centres Ltd. (Toronto). Some other consulting firms, originally established to provide different kinds of services, have now included assessment centers in their areas of work. The American Management Associaton has marketed a package including films and software to enable organizations to introduce centers for selecting first-level managers. Educational Testing Service has developed tailor-made in-baskets for a number of years.

The growing international scope of assessment center activities is creating a demand for consulting assistance overseas. For example, Development Dimensions has affiliates as far afield as Tokyo, Rio de Janeiro, and Johannesburg, and many of their exercises have been translated into French, Japanese, Portuguese, and Afrikaans.

VALIDITY STUDIES

The validation of the assessment center process poses special problems. Since most assessment centers have been used as the basis for decisions relative to advancement or development, criteria such as promotion soon after assessment are seriously contaminated. Comparing assessment results with ordinary management appraisals is not a good basis for validity studies; if one had confidence in management appraisals, one would not be conducting assessment centers in the first place.

In spite of these and other difficulties, however, there have been many convincing studies of the predictive power of assessment ratings. Assessment centers were introduced into business as part of the Bell System's Management Progress Study.[12] Individual assessment results in that study were fed back neither to management nor to the assessees themselves, and the data thus provide an excellent basis for the determination of long-term predictive validity. The study assessment staffs made a final rating of whether each subject would reach middle management within 10 years from the time of initial employment as a management trainee or, in the case of up-from-the-ranks managers, from the time of assessment. Eight years after the assessment of the candidates, the management level of each was determined. The results are shown in Table 16-1. Of the college

TABLE 16-1   Management Progress Study Predictions and Progress in Management

Staff predictions	Management level eight years later			
	Third level or higher	Second level	First level	Total
College recruits:				
Will reach third level	64%	36%	—	100%
Will not reach third level	32%	68%	—	100%
Non-college managers:				
Will reach third level	39%	61%	—	100%
Will not reach third level	9%	41%	50%	100%

graduate management trainees rated likely to reach middle management within 10 years, some 64 percent had, in fact, reached middle management. Of those not so predicted, only 32 percent had reached the target level. In the case of the non-college persons, the corresponding percentages were 39 and 9. These results show very definite predictive power for the assessment center in a situation in which assessment results were known to no one except the researchers.

In another Bell System study, of the personnel assessment program used to help select first-line managers, an attempt was made to overcome the contamination problem by using two or more promotions, rather then just the initial promotion, as the criterion.[13] A sample of almost 6,000 assessees was followed, with the results shown in Table 16-2. At the extremes of the table, those who were rated more than acceptable at initial assessment had received two or more promotions in slightly over 40 percent of the cases, while those who were rated not acceptable had been

TABLE 16-2   Percent of Nonmanagement Assessees Promoted to Second-Level or Higher Management

Assessment rating	Number of assessees	Number receiving two or more promotions	Percent receiving two or more promotions
More than acceptable	410	166	40.5
Acceptable	1,466	321	21.9
Questionable	1,910	220	11.5
Not acceptable	2,157	91	4.2
Total	5,943	798	13.4

promoted twice or more only about 4 percent of the time. A study of this sort does not completely overcome the contamination problem. However, it is argued that although assessment recommendations may play a considerable role in the decision to promote from nonmanagement into management, further advancement is unlikely to be very much affected because of the strong influence of perceived performance as a first-level manager and because of changes in supervisors from year to year.

Another Bell System study, this time of a sales assessment center,[14] used a carefully controlled research design. There was no feedback of assessment center results, and the criterion was observation of on-the-job performance by a team of trained managers. Seventy-eight men who had been hired by ordinary employment methods as communications consultants were sent to a sales assessment center, where they received a final rating as to their acceptability for sales employment. Six months or more after they had completed sales training and were out on the job, they were carefully observed by a team of specially trained sales managers who rated them dichotomously on whether they did or did not meet standards of sales performance. The raters had no knowledge of the assessment predictions. Table 16-3 shows the relationship between assessment judgments and the ratings

TABLE 16-3   Percent of Sales Assessees Meeting Field Review Performance Standards

Assessment rating	Number of assessees	Number meeting review standards	Percent meeting review standards
More than acceptable	9	9	100
Acceptable	32	19	60
Questionable	16	7	44
Not acceptable	21	2	10
Total	78	37	47

of job performance. It will be seen that there is a strong relationship, with all those few men who had been rated more than acceptable meeting performance standards, as compared with only 10 percent of the unacceptable group.

An IBM study[15] used the technique of following the later careers of assessment candidates who were promoted to first-line management. The promotion to first-line manager had been made partially as the result of an assessment center report. Table 16-4 shows the combined results for three departments—sales, service, and administration. The IBM center placed the candidate in one of six categories reflecting the assessors' opinion of the degree of management potential possessed. The top category, as the table shows, was that of executive management, and the lowest category was a recommendation that the person remain in nonmanagement. Once again a wide difference is observed between those in the higher and those in the lower assessment categories.

TABLE 16-4   Percent of Assessees Receiving Further Advancement after Becoming First-Line Managers*

Assessed potential	Number of managers	Number promoted a second time	Percent promoted a second time
Executive management	41	14	34
Higher management	85	27	32
Second-line management	110	30	27
First-line management	88	11	12
Remain nonmanagement	71	5	7
Total	395	87	22

*Adapted from data shown in the IBM study.

A unique criterion used by IBM for those of the above managers in the sales department was demotion after advancement to first-line management.[15] Table 16-5 shows the results, and it will be noted that demotion among those in the

TABLE 16-5   Sales Managers Demoted after Advancement to First-Line Management

Assessed potential	Number of managers	Number demoted	Percent demoted
Higher management	46	2	4
Second-line management	50	7	14
First-line or nonmanagement	71	14	20
Total	167	23	14

highest assessment ratings was strikingly less frequent than among those rated less optimistically.

A special type of validity study is that comparing the later performance of minority- and non-minority-group assessees. A recent doctoral dissertation used data from a Michigan Bell Telephone Company assessment program.[16] The study compared careful job performance and potential for promotion ratings with assessment ratings for black and white female assessees. Table 16-6 shows the

TABLE 16-6   Correlations between Overall Assessment Rating and Later Performance and Potential Ratings

	Whites (assessment rating with N = 91)	Blacks (assessment rating with N = 35)
Job performance	41*	35†
Potential for further advancement	59*	54*

†Statistically significant at the 0.05 level.
*Statistically significant at the 0.01 level.

resulting correlations. Very little difference, and certainly no statistically significant difference, between the two groups appeared. The dissertation also presents data showing that the supervisor's knowledge that his or her subordinate has been assessed does not affect ratings of performance or potential.

IMPLICATIONS FOR TRAINING AND DEVELOPMENT

The spread of the assessment center method has great implications for those concerned with training and development. One effect of assessment is the identification of those toward whom training should be directed and some good leads as to what their training needs are. Where successful performance at an assessment center is, for example, a precondition for training or for advancement to a job which will require training, trainers can expect to have more capable groups of trainees than they otherwise would. Training time can be reduced, or higher goals for training can be established. On the other hand, assessment often identifies a group of candidates who do not perform well enough at the assessment center to merit recommendation for immediate promotion, but who do not fail badly. This is a group that might profit from training enough so that they could qualify for advancement later. Since assessment centers rate a number of dimensions important to performance in management, the trainer can focus training more on the actual needs of the individual or groups of individuals. There is no point in providing leadership training for a person who has already achieved the highest possible rating on that dimension.

Not only can individual needs be targeted, but also the training organization can determine the needs of whole levels of individuals. In assessing a group of middle managers for one of its subsidiary companies, some 45 percent were judged not promotable by an AT&T assessment staff. A review of these cases showed five general categories of deficiency. Table 16-7 shows the percent of the group

TABLE 16-7   Deficiencies Manifested by Middle Managers Assessed as Having Low Potential for Further Advancement (*N* = 22)

Area of deficiency	Percent
Leadership skills	82
Administrative skills	73
Achievement motivation	45
Interpersonal conflicts	45
Intellectual ability	32

manifesting each weakness; many of these managers who were assessed poorly clearly had more than one deficiency.

The table suggests the uncomfortable observation that far from all these managers are good bets for development. How much can one hope to accomplish with a trainee who has distinctly less intellectual ability than those at his or her level and who also has little achievement motivation?

The possible motivational effects of assessment feedback have been noted earlier. If the assessee has received an objective statement of his or her strengths and weaknesses shortly before entering a training experience, it is reasonable to expect more motivation for profiting from the training experience.

A final and completely different opportunity which assessment gives training organizations is the use of assessment as a criterion. Reviewers of management training and development programs over the years have bewailed the lack of objective evidence that the programs accomplish anything. Trainers have often responded that they are, in fact, accomplishing something but that it is extremely difficult to trace the effects of the training into ultimate criteria such as turnover or productivity. Since many of the goals of management training parallel the dimensions utilized for evaluation in assessment centers, it seems logical that assessment may provide a criterion for the effectiveness of training. Managers could be assessed before and after training, or, in a more experimental design, they could be assigned randomly to training or no-training conditions, or to different types of training, and assessed some time after training. It may be that the assessment center approach can finally throw some light on the overall effectiveness of management training and assist in pinpointing its strengths and weaknesses.

REFERENCES

1. "A Good Man Is Hard to Find," *Fortune,* March 1946.
2. Office of Strategic Services Assessment Staff: *Assessment of Men,* Rinehart & Company, Inc., New York, 1948.
3. Taft, R.: "Multiple Methods of Personality Assessment," *Psychological Bulletin,* vol. 56, pp. 333–352, 1959.
4. Bray, D. W., D. L. Grant, and R. J. Campbell: "Studying Careers and Assessing Ability," in A. J. Marrow (ed.), *The Failure of Success,* AMACOM, New York, pp. 154–169, 1972.

   Bray, D. W., D. L. Grant, and R. J. Campbell: *Formative Years in Business: A.T.&T's Long-Term Study of Managerial Lives,* Interscience Publishers, a division of John Wiley & Sons, Inc., New York, 1974.
5. Finkle, R. D., and W. S. Jones: *Assessing Corporate Talent: A Key to Managerial Manpower Planning,* Interscience Publishers, a division of John Wiley & Sons, Inc., New York, 1970.
6. Bray, D. W., and D. L. Grant: "The Assessment Center in the Measurement of Potential for Business Management," *Psychological Monographs,* vol. 80, pp. 1–27, 1966.
7. Byham, W. C.: "Assessment Centers for Spotting Future Managers," *Harvard Business Review,* pp. 150–160, 1970.
8. Grant, D. L., and D. W. Bray: "Contributions of the Interview to Assessment of Management Potential," *Journal of Applied Psychology,* vol. 53, pp. 24–34, 1969.
9. Grant, D. L., W. Katkovsky, and D. W. Bray: "Contributions of Projective Techniques to Assessment of Management Potential," *Journal of Applied Psychology,* vol. 51, pp. 226–232, 1967.
10. Bentz, V. J.: "Validity Studies at Sears," paper presented before the American Psychological Association, annual convention, 1971.
11. General Electric Company, Corporate Education Services: *Talent Development Program,* January 1972. (Internal publication.)
12. Bray, D. W.: "The Management Progress Study," *American Psychologist,* vol. 19, pp. 419–420, 1964.
13. Moses, J. L.: "Assessment Center Performance and Management Progress," *Studies in Personnel Psychology,* vol. 4, pp. 7–12, 1972.
14. Bray, D. W., and R. J. Campbell: "Selection of Salesmen by Means of an Assessment Center," *Journal of Applied Psychology,* vol. 52, pp. 36–41, 1968.
15. Kraut, A. I., and G. J. Scott: "Validity of an Operational Management Assessment Program," *Journal of Applied Psychology,* vol. 56, pp. 124–129, 1972.
16. Huck, J. R.: "Determinants of Assessment Center Ratings for White and Black Females and the Relationship of these Dimensions to Subsequent Performance Effectiveness," unpublished doctoral dissertation, Wayne State University, Detroit, 1973.

Chapter **17**

Group Norms: Their Influence on Training Effectiveness

ROBERT F. ALLEN

STANLEY SILVERZWEIG

Robert F. Allen *is President of Scientific Resources Incorporated and the HRI Human Resources Institute of Morristown, New Jersey. He is also Professor of Psychology and Policy Sciences in the Graduate School of Kean College of New Jersey. He has been a consultant to a large number of major corporations and associations through the United States and Western Europe and has developed and implemented Normative Systems programs in a variety of organizational settings, including hospitals, prisons, universities, unions, and governmental agencies. He holds a Ph.D. from New York University.*

Stanley Silverzweig *is Executive Vice President of Scientific Resources Incorporated and the HRI Human Resources Institute. He has served as a consultant to over 200 organizations and governmental agencies on problems of training and organizational improvement. He is also a novelist and a specialist in materials development. He holds a B.A. from Clarke University.*

The authors, together with Saul Pilnick, are codevelopers of the Normative Systems approach to organizational change described in this chapter.

Norms of group behavior, or the expected behaviors of the individuals within an established group setting, are major factors in determining how that group performs. The effect of group norms should be taken into account in the design and implementation of training efforts intended to improve organizational performance. These norms, often elusive and unrecognized, have tremendous power. They can aid and abet, or drastically undermine, the work of the professional trainer.

This potent behavioral force is the product of the organizational culture itself. The culture might be a store, an office, a factory, a school—or, more correctly, the groups of human beings who work there. A basic understanding of the teaching role of this organizational culture is an important and frequently overlooked ingredient in the development of training strategies. Many, many programs have been rendered ineffectual because they have come into conflict with the *real* training being done by the people within the particular culture. What the culture supports and what it fails to support (and often actually attacks) provide the real curriculum for learning, regardless of what is "taught" in the seminar, class, or training session.

Astute trainers will be aware of the potent teaching force of the culture and will use it to make their programs work. They will be aware that they cannot hope to be successful if they are working at cross-purposes with their "shadow" trainer— those elusive group norms.

HOW DOES THE CULTURE TEACH?

A clear understanding of how the culture goes about its business quietly, insidiously training its people, is of prime importance to professional trainers. The first thing they will see upon examination of the shadow trainer at work is the relentless influence of group norms. It behooves them to understand thoroughly what norms are, how they operate in a culture, and how they can be changed. Our experience has been that when norms are considered, understood, and dealt with systematically, training programs can and will work.

WHAT ARE NORMS?

What the culture supports is passed on by examples set in people's behavior. The expected or anticipated behavior within a group are called *norms*. A norm for a group is not merely the behavior that you will see most people exhibit. It is an idea that exists in the minds of members of the group regarding the behavior that will be *expected*. The norms form a code of behavior established for the group, and they determine the behavior of members and the attitudes the group adopts.

Whether a norm is a matter of fashion (hairstyle) or a tradition (giving Christmas presents) or an expression of value ("do your own thing"), it must have group support to exist. Support may be in the form of encouragement from group members to adhere to the norm or in the form of rewards to members who do. The group has power to enforce its norms by applying pressure on members to conform.

This power is evident when a new behavior is taught and then comes into conflict with an old, established behavior. Experience shows that the old norm nearly always wins out.

NORMS IN CONFLICT

Let us look at two conflicting behaviors in a supermarket company. One has been taught in a training session; the other has been taught by the culture.

A young lady—Sally Jenkins—accepts employment as a cashier in the XYZ Supermarket Company. This company prides itself on the quality of its cashier training program, particularly in the area of customer courtesy. The program itself is well designed, is four days in length, costs a good deal of money, is led by skillful trainers, and uses the best equipment and best procedures possible. Sally Jenkins has enjoyed her training experience and feels that she has learned a great deal about customer service. Her first day on the job, however, leads her to question what she has learned. It is 10:30 A.M. that first day, and things have been going rather well. Two customers are lined up at Sally's check-out counter, and Jane, an experienced checker from the next register, calls over: "Sally! It's time for coffee. Let's go."

Sally looks at the two customers, turns to Jane, and says, "Jane, you go ahead. I'll finish up with these customers and be with you in a jiffy." But Jane's reply puzzles her because it contradicts what she has learned in the training program.

"Look, Sally, around here when it's coffee-break time, it's coffee-break time. They can find another line."

Sally is caught in a dilemma. If she follows Jane's suggestion, she will be ignoring / what she has been taught, she will disappoint two customers, and possibly she will also violate her own value system. If she does not go along, however, she may not receive a very friendly reception from her fellow checkers when she does take her break. She may not be invited to go to lunch or to join the bowling league. Sally may even appear on the turnover statistics in a few days, stating: "Somehow, this just isn't my kind of place."

The setting may change, but the problem of conflicting norms is the same. The expected behaviors of the culture form the training curriculum for the employee within the company, whether the newest recruit or the president of the corporation. When norms meet head on, the old norm, supported by the culture, is bound to win out. Training programs, so called, are valuable and successful only to the extent that they are skillfully used to seed new norms or to reinforce existing norms within the organization. In some cases our training programs actually ask people to behave in ways that would be harmful to them if they were to follow our instructions. Witness the young man who has been told in a sensitivity training session to be open, direct, and honest in providing feedback to his boss when this is contrary to the norms of both his boss and his department. Perhaps it is fortunate that people do not always follow the instructions that we give them in training sessions.

WHAT INFLUENCES NORM DEVELOPMENT?

The development of norms in organizations is affected by a number of key influences. They must be considered by the trainer if the training program is to be effective.

It is important for trainers to see how norms become established, for therein lies the answer to changing them. Although sometimes a group comes to an agreement about certain behaviors and establishes norms right there and then, most norms are established in a much more subtle fashion. They come into being over a period of time without anything actually being said, so that members of the group are hardly aware that the norms exist. They just become "the way things are done around here."

Following are some of the more important influences on norm development.

Leadership Commitment

One of the major factors shaping norms in an organization is the level of leadership commitment. This needs to be more than commitment to the training program: it must be commitment to the *desired behavior*. Unfortunately, too often a behavior like "teamwork" that is taught in a training program has little or no real commitment from the organizational leadership. In such a situation the teamwork norm may be verbally espoused but go no further. However, when leadership commitment to a behavior is visible and active and is backed up by realistic supports such as dollars and time allocation, the desired behavior is more likely to be reinforced and maintained.

Modeling Behavior

Prestigious members of groups often serve as models, and others readily copy their behavior. In this way, norms are established or reinforced. Any employee in a company may be involved in modeling behavior. Take, for example, the ease with which a "coming in late" norm can be established. Let one person come in late habitually, and other employees will begin to think, "If he can get away with it, I can too." When the person modeling the behavior has any special status—say it is the boss who comes in late—the behavior will quickly be accepted as bearing the stamp of approval, and a norm will be well on the way to being established. Although this example deals with a negative norm, trainers can see the lesson in it for them. If they wish to institute certain positive norms, the tremendous influence of modeling behavior should not be overlooked.

Information Feedback

Norms tend to be most readily reinforced in an organization where information feedback is provided. Where there is little information flow, norms tend to be rapidly extinguished. If productivity and cost effectiveness are regularly and widely communicated within a positive environment, norms relating to them are more likely to be developed and maintained. This applies to all operational areas and to human relations areas as well. Where employees and their managers are kept apprised of their success or lack of success in a given area, norms within that area are likely to be reinforced.

Trainers should also see that current information systems are examined to determine the normative impact of information being transmitted. We have found instances where weekly reports and ratings on individual and department sales foster competition—in conflict with the teamwork between departments that the store was trying to encourage. When these reports were modified, cooperation between departments was facilitated, and norms involving joint problem-solving efforts were made workable.

Provision must be made for ensuring that individuals have the needed information to support change efforts. For most organizations, this will require a wider distribution and broader sharing of relevant information.

After a training program is under way, it is essential to have feedback on the progress being made in the change effort. Those involved should be told how they are doing, for knowledge of improvement is a powerful reinforcement. The trainer, as well as leaders of operational units, can help this flow of information by setting up instruments of evaluation concerning member behavior as it detracts from or supports desired norms.

Recognition and Reward

"What's in it for me?" is a question that must be answered positively, and with tangible evidence, if a new behavior is to stick. Behavior that is rewarded will tend to be repeated over and over again. If the reward gives particular satisfaction, the behavior will be learned thoroughly. If it continues to be rewarded, it will gradually come to be performed regularly and thus will become a norm for the group in question.

The "payoff" for a desired behavior can take the form of supervisory acknowledgment and praise or of administrative decisions affecting pay, promotion, and other benefits.

Three aspects of the reward system should be considered. First, make sure there *is* a reward. Put yourself in the position of the individuals being asked to change, and make sure there is something in it for them.

Second, think in terms of short-term results and immediate payoff. If individuals suffer in the short run because they train people, use production time, maintain quality standards, or pass up an immediate sale for better customer relations, they will soon learn to choose whatever else keeps them out of trouble and gives them an immediate payoff—even if it deviates from the norms you are trying to establish.

Third, make use of team incentives and/or bonuses to encourage cooperation, mutual concern, and joint effort. Creative approaches to developing rewards based on group efforts that support goals are needed. Unless this is done, individuals may feel they are in competition for the money available for pay increases and merit boosts, and therefore they will not really want their associates' behavior to be consistent with norm goals. One approach is to key a bonus into total section performance, rather than to a smaller unit or to individuals.

Knowledge and Skill Development

Nothing will wipe out a norm more rapidly than lack of knowledge and skills to develop it. Witness the supervisor who has not been helped to develop the skills of leadership and the resultant tendency to downplay the importance of these skills within the organization. Too often we set up a situation where people are encouraged to develop a commitment to new norms but are not provided with an opportunity to develop the skills necessary for their implementation.

The development of improved job performance norms will be of little value if the people concerned with these norms are not given the opportunity to acquire the necessary job performance skills.

Orientation

One of the most teachable periods for all employees is the time when they join a new company or accept a new position. Too often the orientation they receive at this point is either nonexistent or counter to the norms that would be most useful. What passes for orientation is often nothing more than a review of company benefits, a routine rundown of the rules, and a halfhearted pep talk. The orientation program can, however, be utilized to introduce to the new employee the positive norms existing in the organization, as well as the organization's norm goals.

Work-Group Support

In carrying out norm-change programs, training directed at on-the-job teams helps assure that positive change will receive maximum support. Attention should be paid to the informal leaders or more influential team members, for they will be crucial to the group's acceptance of the norm, via their modeling behavior.

Through work groups, a seeding process can enhance norm development and change. For their initial placement new employees may be seeded into work groups that have strong positive norms. This is in contrast to what usually happens—the new employee is taken aside by an old hand and is told "how things really are around here."

In addition, positive employees can be "seeded" into work groups with poor norms. This is most effective when the group has undertaken a norm-change effort. Otherwise, the "positive" employee, because he or she is not given support, may be influenced by the "negative" majority.

Supervisory Follow-Through

The supervisor is a key to an effective norm-change program. What he or she supports is likely to be reinforced in an organization, while what he or she downplays has little chance for continuing growth. One of the most important responsibilities of a trainer is to see that the supervisor of the individual being trained is fully "on board" before the training is begun.

NORM INFLUENCES AS PRIMARY TRAINERS

These influences are the primary "trainers" in an organization, and good use of the knowledge about norm development and maintenance will be invaluable to the trainer.

None of what we have said here denigrates the value of a well-planned, well-executed training program. It points instead to the need for such training programs to be supported in the day-to-day experience of people on the job. A good training program can help seed new norms and refine old ones.

THE NORMATIVE SYSTEMS APPROACH

This focus on building a supportive environment has caused us to use the term "Normative Systems" to describe our particular approach to training and organizational development. This approach stresses the key influence of norms on personal and organizational effectiveness. It seeks to increase people's understanding of the influence of culture upon their lives and helps them to devise ways of making certain that the cultures of which they are a part reflect their highest goals and aspirations.

Possible Applications

Normative Systems has been applied to many different types of training situations. It has been employed in corporate offices, in migrant worker camps, in large community litter campaigns, in small rehabilitation centers, and in mammoth manufacturing corporations. Over the last 10 years, Normative Systems programs have been used in over 200 organizations—business and industrial, union and professional, private and governmental, educational and correctional.

The chief areas in which trainers will find the Normative Systems type of programs useful fall into five major categories.

Introducing New Organizational Programs

"How can we get this new program off the ground?"
"How can I successfully introduce this new training concept?"

When an organizational program is being introduced, it is important to see that its success depends almost entirely upon its ability to develop new norms or ways of behaving within the organization. A Management by Objectives program that remains "only a program" tends to use up large mounts of organizational time and energy, while contributing little to behavioral change.

When any new program seems to be hard to get going, chances are that old norms are getting in the way and need to be dealt with.

Strengthening Existing Programs

"How can we get the men to wear the proper safety equipment?"
"How can our orientation for new employees be made to stick?"

Sometimes programs already exist within an organization but are really not doing very well. Usually the failure can be traced to their inability to modify existing norms. We saw this in our example of the new checker in the supermarket. Here we can see the importance of modeling behavior. If influential members of the work group are practicing the desired norm, it will be picked up by new people coming in.

Many organizations have long-standing programs which exist well on paper but which never have really been practiced by the people. With a good understanding of the dynamics of norm change, the trainer can strengthen and make workable programs that already have management sanction and verbal backing.

Solving Perplexing Human Factor Problems

"How can we reduce absenteeism?"
"Why won't our employees work harder?"

Many times our most perplexing human factor problems are deeply embedded in norms. In a warehouse setting, low productivity may be supported by the culture. The person who breaks this norm and strives for greater productivity may be in serious difficulty with his or her fellow workers. Examining the norms and norm influences will help us deal with this problem.

Launching New Work Groups or Work Teams

"How can we make this new factory, store, or department even better than those we've had in the past?"

A golden opportunity exists for seeding positive new norms at the time a new work group or work team is being established. Positive employees can be seeded into the new work groups at this time. Training directed at on-the-job teams can help work groups get off to a strong start, with desired norms a part of the initial process.

It is important to remember that a short time after the new unit begins operation, it will have its own set of norms. Whether these norms are positive or negative can be determined to a considerable extent by the initial developmental process. It has been our experience that employees under these conditions will choose positive norms if they have an opportunity to consider the alternatives.

A Total System of Organizational Intervention and Change

"How can we increase the effectiveness of our total organization?"

Many trainers are interested in total systems of organizational development. By viewing the organization as a total culture, it is often possible to assist its members in bringing about change. In such a process our purpose is to help people modify the cultures of which they are a part so that these cultures can more accurately reflect individual and organizational needs and aspirations.

NORMATIVE CHANGE: A THREE-STEP PROCESS

When a trainer or an organization that he or she represents is interested in bringing about normative change, we recommend following a three-step process: understanding norms, identifying norms, and changing norms.

Understanding Norms

The first step in the process is to help as many people in the organization as possible to come to understand the immense influence that norms have upon their own effectiveness and the effectiveness of the organization. As part of this "understanding" process it is essential to make people see that many of the things they may have thought of in the past as "givens" or as "human nature" are really responses to cultural influences. The concept is a deceptively simple one because most of us find it easier to understand how norms influence other people than to realize that they influence us.

We often find that the main block to cultural change is the belief that such change is impossible. Understanding norms and how they operate helps to break through this barrier.

Much of the basic material for understanding norms has been touched on in the first part of this chapter. The concepts can be presented through lectures, audiovisual materials, group exercises, and discussions. Once the basic concepts are understood, we can focus on the particular norms that are crucial for the organization.

Identifying Norms

The next step is to identify specific norms of the culture we are dealing with. This is done with the help of the people who are actually participating in the establishing and reinforcing of the norms. With the trainer's help, they look at their own behaviors.

IF AN EMPLOYEE IN YOUR COMPANY WERE
TO:

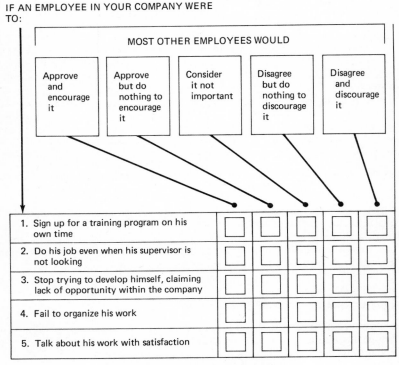

Fig. 17-1 Extract from norm indicator.

Our practice has been to make an analysis—an intensive and systematic study of the norms which define the particular organization and which significantly influence individual and organizational efficiency and goal attainment.

Normative analysis is rapid, and feedback on the findings can be provided quickly. Additional advantages are that the cost of the study is minimal and that very limited employee time input is required. It consists of three phases:

Information Gathering.   The technique here includes selected interviews with top management, on-site observations, and the administering of certain survey instruments. A Leadership Norm Indicator (Fig. 17-1) pinpoints who the leaders are and what type of leadership is operating, and an Associate Opinion Survey samples opinions of personnel, including lower-echelon employees. The information report includes identification of weak norm areas and recommendations for programs.

Normative Description.   A "norm pack" is developed which provides a description of those norms that make a crucial contribution to the success or failure of the organization. Actual examples of both positive and negative aspects in each of the critical norm areas are included. These samples are usually written in such a way as to reflect verbatim employees' statements and concerns. A normative profile is drawn as a graphic indication of the strength of the various norm areas in the organization. It shows both normative strengths as they actually exist and the strengths desirable or necessary for the organization to operate at minimal effectiveness. The "norm gap" is pinpointed. This is the difference between the existing normative profile in an organization and the profile desirable for peak effectiveness.

Norm-Gap Measurement.   Making use of the data gathered from various parts of the organization, a norm profile (Fig. 17-2) is developed. This profile shows the disparity between what the organization wishes and what actually takes place. Periodic evaluation of this norm gap provides an ongoing method of measuring the progress of the program.

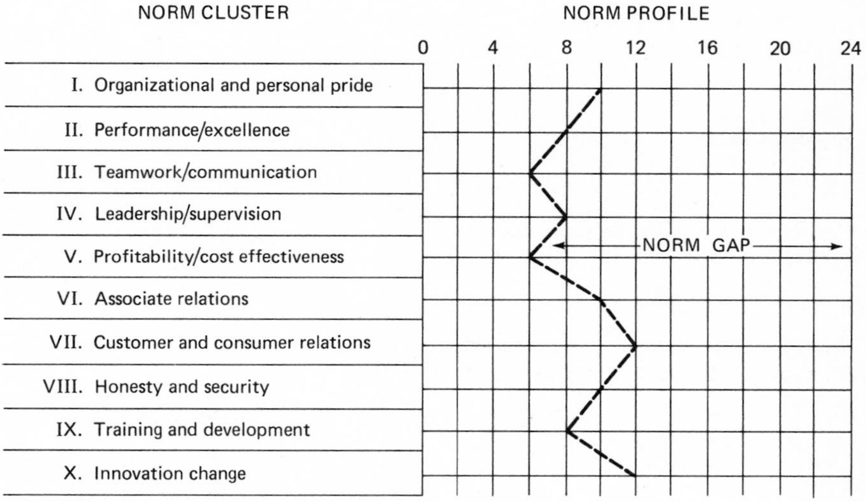

Fig. 17-2   Norm profile.

Common Critical Norm Areas   Experience has indicated that an organization will have approximately 10 to 12 critical norm areas that contribute to success or failure. Common to many organizations are the following:

Organizational and personal pride—a feeling that "this is our organization"
Performance and excellence—seeking out the best performance possible
Teamwork and communication—support of coordination of efforts
Leadership and supervision—supervision viewed as a constructive relationship and sharing of problems
Profitability and cost effectiveness—emphasis on assuring of profitability and on reducing unnecessary costs
Associate relations—concern for good relationships between employees and management
Customer and consumer relations—focus on high quality of customer service
Honesty and security—a high value placed on personal integrity and a concern for the organization
Training and development—importance placed on training and development activities
Innovation and change—actively seeking out positive continued improvements

Once the norms, positive and negative, have been identified and the distance between these norms and the goals has been determined, it is time to establish priorities and move into change strategies.

Changing Norms

In order to bring about change, it is necessary that people within the organization examine and modify each of the various norm influences that we have described. If a given change is not supported by these norm influences, it is not likely to last very long. If it is contradicted by the norm influences, it may never be practiced at all outside the training session. Norm influences such as management commitment, modeling behavior, and information and reward systems are a necessary prerequisite to any organizational change.

Working on a single norm influence is not likely to bring about change. It is necessary to work on many, if not all, of these influences simultaneously if significant change is to be developed and maintained. Too often we work on a single influence—by providing a pay raise or instituting a new training program, for example—and are then disappointed that the actions we have taken do not bring the desired results.

ORGANIZATIONAL CHANGE BEGINS AT THE TOP

It is also important that organizational change not be sought at the lower levels until it has been achieved at the level immediately above. Effective norm programs begin at the top of the organization and continue downward through all levels of the organizational structure. It is difficult, if not impossible, for planned change to be developed at the lower levels without the commitment, support, and visible modeling behavior of supervisory and management-level personnel.

NOT BLAME PLACING, BUT PROBLEM SOLVING

One of the most important by-products of a successful Normative Systems program is a reduction of negative blame placing and an increase in constructive problem solving. We have found that within the context of norm concepts, the issues are depersonalized, and discussion can deal with behavior without arousing personal defenses. "We all discovered an incredible thing," a corporate president stated. "No one felt threatened when we talked about norms. We forgot about the idea of telling people what *they* did wrong because the very word 'norm' implies shared responsibility."

In other words, it is less threatening and less accusative to focus on norms than to blame people for things for which the overall organization may well have been responsible.

FOCUS ON RESULTS

The focus in all normative programs needs to be on results rather than on words or activities. There also needs to be a balance between short-term and long-term achievements. Programs that do not provide some short-term results very seldom last long enough to demonstrate long-term effectiveness.

When there is a focus on results, it has been our experience that significant achievements are possible. A number of examples can be cited. In one case, a retail organization that placed high priority on honesty and security norms demonstrated a 40 percent reduction in retail shrink within three months. Impressive comparative figures are found in the statistics concerning litter campaigns in five major cities in 1974. The Normative Systems approach brought about a 40 percent reduction in litter, as compared with an 8 percent reduction using other campaigns. Assembly-line errors in a manufacturing plant were reduced by 60 percent. Breakage and theft of products in a retail chain were reduced by 70 percent.

Accidents in a construction company were cut in half. Sanitation standards in a food handling company were markedly improved. Average productivity of sales calls in a food service company were increased by 60 percent. Moreover, these improvements were lasting ones. In all cases the programs resulted in more income for workers and higher levels of job satisfaction and personal success.

THE TRAINER AS A CHANGE AGENT

In summary, what we are suggesting here is that trainers see themselves as *change agents*. Since the primary influences within organizations are those cultural differences which shape behavior, our role is to be certain that these influences work to the mutual benefit of the individual and the organization of which he or she is a part.

When each individual training program is being considered, it is important that certain questions be carefully considered. A beginning list of these questions would include the following:

1. ☐ Have we defined our training objectives in terms of the desired normative outcomes?
2. ☐ Do we have a workable approach to involving the people most directly affected?
3. ☐ Is there visible commitment by management to the behavior change being sought? If not, what do we need to do to build it?
4. ☐ Have we assured that management personnel and other key reference groups are prepared to model the desired behavior visibly?
5. ☐ Has a system been set up to keep people informed about how well they are doing in achieving the desired goals?
6. ☐ Have we checked to see that people will be rewarded or at least not penalized for the desired behavior?
7. ☐ Have we made certain that people will have an opportunity to develop the knowledge and skills that may be required?
8. ☐ Can the formal orientation program and procedures be used to recommend the desired behavior?
9. ☐ Are we prepared to make use of the informal leadership of the work group to strengthen the desired norms?
10. ☐ Have we developed the support of supervisory personnel for what we are trying to achieve?
11. ☐ Have we developed a systematic way of working on a number of influences simultaneously and in coordination with one another?
12. ☐ Has the program been designed in such a way as to assure that no level within the organization is asked to make changes until the level above has developed a full commitment to the change being sought?
13. ☐ Is the program designed in such a way as to avoid blame placing and constitute instead a constructive problem-solving approach?
14. ☐ Is the program results-oriented? Do we have a clear focus on what we are trying to achieve?

CONCLUSION

It is important that the information gained as a result of this work with group behavioral norms not be seen as a method of merely securing greater conformity to managerial directives. Rather, it is a method of helping people from all levels of an organization—from top management to the lowest and newest employee—to become involved in creating their own environments instead of being merely the victims of whatever currently exists. Because they are involved from the start, they are not conforming to outside pressures, but are taking an active part in the systematic norm-change process.

The basic question we have been attempting to answer here is one raised in executive suites across the country; it is a crucial question for all who are interested in developing effective training programs: "With all the dollars we've invested in training," the managers ask, "where is the payoff? Why don't training programs work better?"

The trouble with the traditional methods of training is that they have been dealing only with symptoms, without touching that underlying culprit that we mentioned at the start—the "shadow trainer." Negative organizational norms too often do their silent work, undermining hardworking trainers. But if this shadow trainer is understood and dealt with, the culture can be a positive force, adding strength to the professional trainer's efforts. Training *can* be successful and significant, even indispensable, if it is treated in the context of the organizational culture and its powerful norms.

BIBLIOGRAPHY

Allen, R. F., and S. Pilnick: *New Employee Orientation System,* Materials Division of Scientific Resources Incorporated and Supermarket Institute, Chicago, 1968.

Allen, R. F., and S. Pilnick: "Confronting the Shadow Organization: How to Detect and Defeat Negative Norms," *Organizational Dynamics,* Spring 1973.

Allen, R. F., S. Pilnick, and C. Park: "The Shadow Organization," *Management Accounting,* vol. 55, no. 7, National Association of Accountants, January 1974.

Allen, R. F., S. Pilnick, and S. Silverzweig: *Teacher Aide Training Systems,* The Macmillan Company, New York, 1968.

Allen, R. F., S. Pilnick, and S. Silverzweig: "The Influence of the Peer Culture on Delinquency and Delinquency Rehabilitation," *Psychiatric Outpatient Quarterly,* vol. 6, no. 3, Fall 1970.

Allen, R. F., S. Pilnick, and S. Silverzweig: *Normative Systems: An Approach to Increasing Organizational Effectiveness,"* SRI Press, Morristown, N.J., 1970.

Allen, R. F., S. Pilnick, and S. Silverzweig: *Norms in the Supermarket Industry: A Self-Instructional Program,* SRI Press, Morristown, N.J. 1970.

Allen, R. F., S. Pilnick, and S. Silverzweig: *Normative Systems in Union Organizations,* HRI Press, Morristown, N.J., 1972.

Allen, R. F., S. Silverzweig, and M. Schneider: *Changing Our Litter Culture,* Normative Systems action-research model for the reduction of litter in American communities—a report of a two-year project, Keep America Beautiful, Inc., New York, 1974.

The Coca-Cola Company: *A Piece of the Action,* a film report on the Agricultural Labor Project of the Coca-Cola Company, Atlanta Film Co., Atlanta, Ga., 1972.

"An Experiment in Problem-Solving through Personnel Involvement," *Chain Store Age,* May 1970.

Garner, Phil: "A New Life for Migrant Workers," *The Atlanta Journal and Constitution Magazine,* Jan. 23, 1972.

Larkin, Timothy: "Adios to Migrancy," *Manpower,* U.S. Department of Labor, August 1974.

Pilnick, S., R. F. Allen, H. Dubin, and A. Youtz: *From Delinquency to Freedom: A Report on the Collegefields Delinquency Rehabilitation Program,* U.S. Department of Health, Education, and Welfare, Washington, 1967.

Pilnick, S., R. F. Allen, and S. Silverzweig: "Guided Group Interaction," in *Encyclopedia of Social Work,* National Association of Social Work, New York, 1971.

Supermarket Institute: *Normative Systems in the Food Industry,* a series of films produced by Fred Niles, Inc., in cooperation with the Materials Division of Scientific Resources Incorporated, Morristown, N.J., 1970.

Chapter 18

Evaluation of Training

DONALD L. KIRKPATRICK

Donald L. Kirpatrick *is Professor of Management Development, Management Institute, University of Wisconsin–Extension, Milwaukee. Dr. Kirkpatrick's responsibilities include the planning, coordinating, teaching, and evaluation of conferences for managers from industry and government. In industry, he served as Personnel Development Supervisor with International Minerals and Chemical Corporation of Skokie, Illinois, and as Personnel Manager of Bendix Products Aerospace Division, South Bend, Indiana. He received his B.B.A., M.B.A., and Ph.D. from the University of Wisconsin. His Ph.D. dissertation was entitled "Evaluating a Human Relations Training Program for Industrial Supervisors and Foremen." He has conducted many ASTD national and chapter meetings on training evaluation. He is a past president of the Wisconsin chapter of ASTD, and he served as National Vice President from 1969 to 1972 and as national ASTD President for 1975. His 1971 book,* Supervisory Training and Development, *was published by Addison-Wesley. His Supervisory Inventories on communication, human relations, and safety are widely used as teaching and evaluation tools. His Management Inventories on leadership and motivation and on time and delegation were published in 1974.*

Effective training directors will make an effort to evaluate all their training activities. The success of these efforts depends to a large extent on a clear understanding of just what "evaluation" means. This chapter will attempt to accomplish two objects: (1) to clarify the meaning of evaluation and (2) to suggest techniques for conducting the evaluation.

These objectives will be related to "in-house" classroom programs, one of the most common forms of training. Many of the principles and procedures can be applied to all kinds of training activities such as performance review, participation in outside programs, programmed instruction, and the reading of selected books.

The following quotation from Daniel M. Goodacre III is most appropriate as an introduction:

Managers, needless to say, expect their manufacturing and sales departments to yield a good return and will go to great lengths to find out whether they have done so. When it come to training, however, they may expect the return—but rarely do they make a like effort to measure the actual results. Fortunately for those in charge of training programs, this philanthropic attitude has come to be taken for granted. There is certainly no guarantee, however, that it will continue, and training directors might be well-advised to take the initiative and evaluate their programs before the day of reckoning arrives.[1]

EVALUATION CLARIFIED

Nearly everyone would agree that a definition of evaluation would be "the determination of the effectiveness of a training program." But this has little meaning until we answer the question: In terms of what? We know that evaluation is needed in order to improve future programs and to eliminate those programs which are ineffective. The problem is how to begin.

Evaluation changes from a complicated, elusive generality into clear and achievable goals if we break it down into logical steps. These steps can be defined as follows:

STEP 1: *Reaction.* How well did the conferees like the program?

STEP 2: *Learning.* What principles, facts, and techniques were learned?

STEP 3: *Behavior.* What changes in job behavior resulted from the program?

STEP 4: *Results.* What were the tangible results of the program in terms of reduced cost, improved quality, improved quantity, etc.?

With this clarification of the meaning of evaluation, training directors can now begin to pinpoint their efforts at evaluation. They better realize what they are doing, and they recognize the limited interpretations and conclusions that can be drawn from their findings. As they become more experienced and sophisticated in evaluation design and procedures, they slowly begin to obtain more meaningful results on which future training can be based.

These four steps will now be defined in detail with examples and suggested guideposts. It is important to stress that the described *procedures* and *techniques* can be used in almost any organization. It is also important to stress that the *results* from one organization cannot be used in another organization. Obviously, there are many factors that would influence the results. These variables include the group, the conference leader, and the approach to the subject.

STEP 1: REACTION

Reaction may best be defined as how well the trainees liked a particular training program. Evaluating in terms of reaction is the same as measuring the feelings of the conferees. It is important to emphasize that it does not include a measurement of any learning that takes place. Because reaction is so easy to measure, many training directors do it.

Guides for Evaluating Reaction

1. Determine what you want to find out.
2. Use a written comment sheet covering those items determined in step 1 above.
3. Design the form so that the reactions can be tabulated and quantified.
4. Obtain honest reactions by making the forms anonymous.
5. Allow the conferees to write in additional comments not covered by the questions that were designed to be tabulated and quantified.

The comment sheet shown in Fig. 18-1 was used to measure reaction at an ASTD summer institute that was planned and coordinated by the staff of the Management Institute of the University of Wisconsin.

Those who planned this ASTD program were interested in reactions to subject, technique (lecture versus discussion), and the performance of the conference leader. Therefore, the form was designed accordingly. The conferees were asked to place a check in the appropriate spaces so that the reactions could be readily tabulated and quantified.

ASTD INSTITUTE

Leader _____   Subject _____

Date _____

1. Was the Subject Pertinent to Your Needs and Interests?

    ☐ No   ☐ To Some Extent   ☐ Very Much So

2. How Was the Ratio of Lecture to Discussion?

    ☐ Too Much Lecture   ☐ O. K.   ☐ Too Much Discussion

3. Rate the Leader on the Following:

	Excellent	Very Good	Good	Fair	Poor
A. How well did he state objectives?					
B. How well did he keep the session alive and interesting?					
C. How well did he use the blackboard, charts, and other aids?					
D. How well did he summarize during the session?					
E. How well did he maintain a friendly and helpful manner?					
F. How well did he illustrate and clarify the points?					
G. How was his summary at the close of the session?					

What is Your Overall Rating of the Leader?

    ☐ Excellent   ☐ Very Good   ☐ Good   ☐ Fair   ☐ Poor

4. What Would Have Made the Session More Effective?

    _____

    _____

    _____

    _____

                                    _____
                                    Signature (optional)

Fig. 18-1 Rating chart.

In question 3, concerning the leader, it was felt that a more meaningful rating would be given the leader if the conferees considered items A through G before checking the overall rating. This question was designed to prevent a conference leader's personality from dominating group reaction.

Question 4 allowed the conferees to suggest any improvements that came to mind. The optional signature was used so that follow-up discussions with conferees could be done. In this ASTD summer institute, about half of the conferees signed their names. With this type of group, the optional signature did not affect the honesty of their answers, in all probability. It is strongly suggested that unsigned sheets be used in most in-house meetings, however.

In most cases, a simpler comment sheet is sufficient. Figure 18-2 shows a form that provides maximum information on reaction and requires minimum time from participants. This form can be used for each leader. Of particular importance is the separation of "subject" from "leader."

To evaluate a total program that includes a number of sessions, a final comment sheet (Fig. 18-3) can provide additional valuable information for improving future programs.

So that "standards of performance" can be established for the quality of instruction, the reactions can conveniently be converted to numerical ratings. For example, on the forms shown in Figs. 18-2 and 18-3 the following ratings can be used:

Excellent = 5; very good = 4; good = 3; fair = 2; and poor = 1. An example of reactions from 27 participants might be:

10	Excellent	$10 \times 5 =$	50
10	Very good	$10 \times 4 =$	40
5	Good	$5 \times 3 =$	15
1	Fair	$1 \times 2 =$	2
1	Poor	$1 \times 1 =$	1

Total 27   Total points 108
Participants

Dividing 108 (total points) by 27 (total participants), we get a rating of 4. Experience in a particular organization can provide data for the establishment of a standard of performance for all instructors.

I firmly believe in getting a comment sheet on each subject and each leader. In the case where the same leader is conducting a series of meetings with the same group, it may not be necessary to get reactions after each session. In a nine-session program, for example, it may be sufficient to obtain reactions after the third, sixth, and ninth sessions. A final comment sheet should also be used to get an evaluation of the entire program.

How to Supplement the Evaluation of the Conferees

It has been emphasized that the form should be designed so that tabulations can be readily made. In my opinion, too many comment sheets are still being used in which the conferees are asked to write in their answers to questions. A form of this kind makes it very difficult to summarize comments and to determine patterns of reaction.

At the Management Institute of the University of Wisconsin, sessions are evaluated in terms of the reactions of the conferees. This has been done for more than 20 years. Occasionally the coordinator of the program felt that the group reaction was not a fair evaluation of the effectiveness of the program. Sometimes the staff people felt that the conference leader's personality made such an impression on the group that this person received a very high rating. In other sessions, the coordinator felt that the conference leader received a low rating because he or she did not have a dynamic personality. Therefore, some members of the Management Institute adopted a procedure by which the conference leader was rated by the coordinator as well as by the group. The form shown in Fig. 18-4 was used.

REACTION SHEET

Please give us your frank reactions and comments. They will help us evaluate this program for possible improvement in future programs.

Leader _____   Subject _____   Date _____

1. How do you rate the subject content?

    ☐ Excellent   COMMENTS:
    ☐ Very Good
    ☐ Good
    ☐ Fair
    ☐ Poor

2. How do you rate the conference leader?

    ☐ Excellent   COMMENTS:
    ☐ Very Good
    ☐ Good
    ☐ Fair
    ☐ Poor

3. What benefits do you feel you got from this session?

    ☐ New knowledge that is pertinent.
    ☐ Specific approaches, skills or techniques that I can apply on the job.
    ☐ Change of attitude that will help me in my job.

    OTHER:

4. What would have made this session better? (Use other side if necessary.)

Fig. 18-2   Reaction sheet.

This procedure, in which the coordinator of the program also evaluates each conference leader, was also used in an ASTD summer institute. It was found that a coordinator's rating was usually close to the group's rating, but in some instances it varied considerably. In selecting and orienting future conference leaders, both of the evaluations should be taken into consideration.

It is suggested that the training director in each company consider this approach. A trained observer such as the training director or another qualified person would fill out an evaluation form independent of the group's reactions. A comparison of the two would give the best indication of the effectiveness of the program.

FINAL REACTION SHEET

NAME OF PROGRAM _____ DATE _____

1. How would you rate the overall program as an educational experience?

☐ Excellent   Comments:
☐ Very Good
☐ Good
☐ Fair
☐ Poor

2. To what extent will it help you do a better job for your organization?

☐ To a large extent   Comments:
☐ To some extent
☐ Very little

3. What were the major benefits you received? (Check as many as you wish.)

☐ Helped confirm some of my ideas.
☐ Presented new ideas and approaches.
☐ Acquainted me with problems and solutions from other companies.
☐ Gave me a good chance to look objectively at myself and my job.

Other benefits:

4. How were the meeting facilities, luncheon arrangements, etc?

☐ Excellent   Comments:
☐ Very Good
☐ Good
☐ Fair
☐ Poor

(OVER)

Fig. 18-3   Final reaction sheet.

Measuring Reactions to Outside Training Programs

The forms and suggestions discussed above will apply best to an internal training program. Since many companies send their management people to outside training programs at universities, the American Management Association, the National Industrial Conference Board, etc., it is suggested that the reaction of each person attending such a program be measured. Lowell Reed, former training director of Oscar Mayer & Company of Madison, Wisconsin, used the form shown in Fig. 18-5 for evaluating the reaction to the University of Wisconsin Management Institute program.

In this situation, Oscar Mayer & Company was not interested in the reaction to

5. Would you like to attend future programs of a similar nature?

☐ Yes
☐ No
☐ Not sure

6. Other comments and suggestions for future programs:

Signature (optional) _____

Fig. 18-3 (Cont.)   Final reaction sheet.

specific leaders. They were interested in the reaction to the overall program to determine whether to send other foremen and supervisors. In other words, this particular questionnaire was designed to fit the need of Oscar Mayer & Company.

Another company used the form shown in Fig. 18-6 to evaluate the reaction of their managers who attended an outside program. Still another approach is suggested in Fig. 18-7. The evaluation of outside programs is of vital importance in selecting programs that will provide maximum benefits for an organization. The feedback from past participants is probably the best means of judging whether future attendance at these programs is worth the time and money. (The author's booklet entitled *Obtaining Maximum Benefits from Outside Management Development Programs* gives details.[2])

COORDINATOR'S RATING OF LEADER

Date _____

Rating _____ Name of Leader _____ Subject _____

	Very Much So	To Some Extent	No
A. PREPARATION			
1. Did he prepare for the meeting?			
2. Was his preparation geared to the group?			
B. CONDUCTING			
1. Did he read his material?			
2. Did he hold the interest of the group?			
3. Was he enthusiastic-dynamic?			
4. Did he use visual aids?			
5. Did he present his material clearly?			
6. Did he help the group apply the material?			
7. Did he adequately cover the subject?			
8. Did he summarize during conference and at end?			
9. Did he involve the group?			

C. CONSTRUCTIVE COMMENTS
   1. What would you suggest to improve future sessions?

   _____

   _____

D. POTENTIAL
   1. With proper coaching what would be the highest rating he could achieve? _____

E. ADDITIONAL COMMENTS

   _____

   _____

Fig. 18-4 Leader rating sheet.

Conclusions about Reaction

The first step in the evaluation process is to measure the reactions to training programs. It is important to determine how people feel about the programs they attend. Decisions by top management are frequently based on one or two comments made by people who have attended. A supervisory training program may be canceled because one superintendent told the plant manager that "this program is for the birds."

MANAGEMENT INSTITUTE PROGRAM QUESTIONNAIRE

Please circle the appropriate response

1. I thought the program was:
   A. Very well organized and helpful
   B. It was of some value
   C. It was poorly organized and a waste of time

2. In reference to the subject content:
   A. It was all theory and of little practical value
   B. It was both theoretical and practical
   C. It was very practical and useful

3. Concerning the quality of the instruction:
   A. The instruction was excellent
   B. The instruction was average
   C. The instruction was of poor quality

Fig. 18-5   Oscar Mayer & Company evaluation form.

Also, conferees who enjoy a training program are more likely to obtain maximum benefit from it. According to Spencer, "for maximum learning you must have interest and enthusiasm." In a talk given by Cloyd Steinmetz, of Reynolds Metals and past president of ASTD, he stressed: "It is not enought to say, 'Boys, here is the information, take it!' We must make it interesting and motivate them to want to take it."

To evaluate effectively, training directors should begin by doing a good job of measuring the reactions and feelings of people who participate. It is important to do this in an organized fashion, using written comment sheets which have been designed to obtain the desired reactions. It is also strongly suggested that the form be so designed that the comments can be tabulated and quantified. In the experience of the staff of the Management Institute, it is also desirable to have the coordinator, training director, or another trained observer make his or her own appraisal of the session in order to supplement the reactions of enrollees. The combination of these two evaluations is more meaningful than either one by itself.

Companies who send their people to attend outside institutes and conferences should make an effort to evaluate the reactions to these programs. Several suggested forms have been described.

A training director who has effectively measured the *reactions* of conferees and finds them to be very favorable can feel extremely proud. However, the director should also feel humble because the evaluation measurement has only begun. Even though he or she has done a masterful job of measuring the reaction of the

REACTION TO SUPERVISORY INSTITUTE BY FOREMAN AND SUPERVISORS
WHO HAVE PARTICIPATED

IN GENERAL

    1. How worthwhile was the Institute for you?
         _____ Very worthwhile
         _____ Fairly worthwhile
         _____ Not very worthwhile
         _____ A waste of time

    2. The Institute had:
         _____ Too much theory and not enough of the practical
         _____ Too much of the practical and not enough theory
         _____ About the right combination of theory and practice

HOW THE INSTITUTE WAS CONDUCTED

    3. On the whole, the course was conducted
         _____ Very well
         _____ Fairly well
         _____ Poorly
         _____ Very poorly

    4. Lecture and discussion
         _____ Too much lecture
         _____ Too much discussion
         _____ About the right amount of each

    5. Discussion leaders
         _____ Too many from the University
         _____ Too many from business and industry
         _____ O.K.

    6. Visual aids
         _____ Not enough movies, charts, etc.
         _____ Too much use of demonstrations, blackboards, movies, charts, etc.
         _____ O.K.

Fig. 18-6   Supervisor institute program evaluation form.

group, there is still no assurance that any learning has taken place. Neither is there any indication that the behavior of the participants will change because of the training program. And still further away is any realistic way of judging which results can be attributed to the training program.

STEP 2: LEARNING

It is important to recognize that a favorable reaction to a program *does not assure* learning. All of us have attended meetings in which the conference leader or speaker used enthusiasm, showmanship, visual aids, and illustrations to make a presentation well accepted by the group. A careful analysis of the subject content would reveal that the speaker said practically nothing of value—but said it very well.

APPLICATION OF THE COURSE

7. Did the Institute apply to your particular operations?

_____ Yes   _____ Partly   _____No

FOLLOW-UP

8. Would you like to attend another institute?

_____ Yes   _____ No

Comment

9. These Institutes should run for _____ 5 days, _____ 4 days, _____ 3 days.

10. Please list 3 of your main problems:

1. _____

_____

2. _____

_____

3. _____

_____

11. Comments or suggestions

_____

_____

_____

_____

_____

_____

Fig. 18-6 (Cont.)   Supervisor institute program evaluation form.

Learning Defined

There are several definitions of learning. For the purpose of this chapter, learning is defined as follows: the principles, facts, and skills which were understood and absorbed by the conferees. In other words, it does not include the on-the-job use of these principles, facts, and skills. This application will be discussed later in this chapter in the section on behavior.

Guideposts for Evaluating in Terms of Learning

Several guideposts should be used in establishing a procedure for measuring the amount of learning that takes place:

1. The learning of *each conferee* should be measured so that quantitative results can be determined.

EVALUATION OF OUTSIDE
MANAGEMENT DEVELOPMENT PROGRAMS

Name _____ Title _____ Date _____

PROGRAM ATTENDED:

Name of Program _____ Dates _____

Location _____ Fee _____

Organization Presenting Program _____

1. How accurately did the program announcement describe was what covered at the program?

   [ ] Very accurately   [ ] Fairly accurately   [ ] Inaccurately

2. To what extent did the subject content meet your needs and interests?

   [ ] Very well   [ ] To some extent   [ ] Very little

3. How effective were the speakers and conference leaders?

   [ ] Excellent   [ ] Very good   [ ] Good   [ ] Fair   [ ] Poor

4. How were the facilities, meals, etc.?

   [ ] Excellent   [ ] Very good   [ ] Good   [ ] Fair   [ ] Poor

5. What benefits do you feel you gained?

   [ ] Knowledge of what other companies were doing.

   [ ] New theory and principles that are pertinent.

   [ ] Ideas and techniques that can be applied on the job.

   [ ] Other (please explain).

6. How would you rate the entire program in relation to time and cost?

   [ ] Excellent   [ ] Very good   [ ] Good   [ ] Fair   [ ] Poor

7. Would you like to attend a future program presented by the same organization?

   [ ] Definitely   [ ] Possibly   [ ] No

8. Would you recommend that others from our company attend programs presented by the same organization?

   [ ] Yes   [ ] No   [ ] Not sure   If yes, who should attend?

9. Other comments.

Fig. 18-7   Outside program evaluation form.

2. A before-and-after approach should be used so that any learning can be related to the program.
3. As far as possible, the learning should be measured on an *objective* basis.
4. Where possible, a control group (not receiving the training) should be compared with the experimental group which receives the training.
5. Where possible, the evaluation results should be analyzed statistically so that learning can be proved in terms of correlation or level of confidence.

These guideposts indicate that evaluation in terms of learning is much more difficult than evaluation in terms of reaction, as described earlier. A knowledge of statistics, for example, is desirable. In many cases, the training department will have to call on the assistance of a statistician to help plan the evaluation procedures, analyze the data, and interpret the results.

Suggested Methods

Classroom Performance   It is relatively easy to measure the learning that takes place in training programs that are teaching skills. The following programs would fall under this category: job instruction training, work simplification, interviewing skills, induction techniques, reading improvement, effective speaking, and effective writing. Classroom activities such as demonstrations, individual performance of the skill being taught, and discussions following a role-playing situation can be used as evaluation techniques. The training director can organize these in such a way that he or she will obtain a fairly objective evaluation of the learning that is taking place.

For example, in a course that is teaching job instruction training (JIT) to foremen, each foreman will demonstrate in front of the class the skills of JIT. From their performance, the training director can tell whether the foremen have learned the principles of JIT and can use them, at least in a classroom situation. In a work simplification program, the conferees can be required to fill out a "flow-process chart," and the training director can determine whether they know how to do it. In a reading improvement program, the reading speed and comprehension of the participants can be readily determined by their classroom performance. In an effective speaking program, each conferee is normally required to give a number of talks, and an alert training director can evaluate the amount of learning that is taking place by observing the individual's successive performances.

Thus in situations like these, an evaluation of the learning can be built into the program. If it is organized and implemented properly, the training director can obtain a fairly objective measure of the amount of learning that has taken place. He or she can set up before-and-after situations in which the conferees demonstrate whether they know the principles and techniques being taught. In every program, therefore, where skills of some kind are being taught, the training director should plan systematic classroom evaluation to measure the learning.

Paper-and-Pencil Tests   Where principles and facts are taught rather than skills, it is more difficult to evaluate learning. The most common technique is the paper-and-pencil test. In some cases, standardized tests can be purchased to measure learning. In other cases, training directors must construct their own.

To measure the learning in human relations programs, two standardized tests are quite widely used in business and industry. The first is *How Supervise?* by File and Remmers. This is published by The Psychological Corporation of New York and has been used by a number of companies on a before-and-after basis to measure the learning that takes place. A newer test is the *Supervisory Inventory on Human Relations,* by Kirkpatrick and Planty. Sample test items from the latter are listed in Fig. 18-8 (answered by circling A for "agree" or DA for "disagree").

There are also standardized tests available in such areas as communications, labor relations, grievances, discipline, and safety. In following the guideposts that were suggested in the beginning of this chapter, this kind of standardized test should be used in the following manner:

1. The test should be given to all conferees prior to the program.
2. If possible, it should also be given to a control group which is comparable to the experimental group.

PLEASE ANSWER ALL STATEMENTS EVEN IF YOU ARE NOT SURE
Copyright © 1965 by D. L. Kirkpatrick

Published by Dr. D. L. Kirkpatrick, 4380 Continental Dr., Brookfield, Wis. 53005

1. Anyone is able to do almost any job if he tries hard enough.   A   DA

2. Intelligence consists of what we've learned since we were born.   A   DA

3. If a supervisor knows all about the work to be done, he is therefore qualified
   to teach others how to do it.   A   DA

4. A well trained working force is a result of maintaining a large training department.   A   DA

5. In making a decision, a good supervisor is concerned with his employees' feeling
   about the decision.   A   DA

6. The supervisor is closer to his employees than he is to management.   A   DA

7. The best way to train a new employee is to have him watch a good employee
   at the job.   A   DA

8. Before deciding on the solution to a problem, a list of possible solutions should
   be made and compared.   A   DA

9. A supervisor should be willing to listen to almost anything the employees want
   to tell him.   A   DA

Fig. 18-8 Supervisory Inventory on Human Relations.

3. These pretests should be analyzed in terms of two approaches. In the first place, the total score of each person should be tabulated. Second, the responses to each item of the inventory should be tabulated in terms of right and wrong answers. This second tabulation not only enables a training director to evaluate the program but also provides some tips on the knowledge and understanding of the group prior to the program. This means that in the classroom, the training director can stress those items most frequently misunderstood.
4. After the program is over, the same test or its equivalent should be given to the conferees and also to the control group. A comparison of pretest and posttest scores and responses to individual items can then be made. A statistical analysis of these data will reveal the effectiveness of the program in terms of learning.

One important word of caution is necessary: Unless the test or inventory accurately covers the material presented, it will not be a valid measure of the effectiveness of the learning. Frequently a standardized test will cover only part of the material presented in the course. Therefore, only that part of the course covered in the inventory is being evaluated. Likewise, if certain items on the inventory are not being covered, no change in these items can be expected.

Many training directors and others responsible for programs have developed their own paper-and-pencil tests to measure learning in their programs. For example, the American Telephone and Telegraph Company incorporated into its Personal Factors in Management program a short test measuring trainee sensitivity and empathy. First, each individual was asked to rank, in order of importance, 10 items dealing with human relations. The participants were then assigned to groups which worked 15 minutes at the task of arriving at a group ranking of the 10 statements. Following this 15-minute "heated discussion," each individual was asked to complete a short inventory, which included the following questions:

1. (a) Were you satisfied with the performance of the group?
   Yes ____ No ____
   (b) How many will say that they were satisfied with the performance of the group?
2. (a) Do you feel that the discussion was dominated by two or three members?
   Yes ____ No ____
   (b) How many will say that they thought the discussion was dominated by two or three members?
3. (a) Did you have any feelings about the items being ranked that, for some reason, you felt it wise not to express during the discussion?
   Yes ____ No ____
   (b) How many will say that they had such feelings?
4. (a) Did you talk as often as you wished to in the discussion?
   Yes ____ No ____
   (b) How many will say that they spoke as often as they wished?

The successive class sessions then attempted to teach each conferee to be more sensitive to the feelings and ideas of other people. Later in the course, another "empathy" test was given to see whether there was an increase in sensitivity.

In Morris A. Savitt's article entitled "Is Management Training Worthwhile?"[3] he described a program that he evaluated. He devised a questionnaire which was given at the beginning of the program "to determine how much knowledge of management principles and practices the conferees had at the beginning." At the end of the 10-week program, the same questionnaire was administered to test the progress made during the course. This is an example of a questionnaire tailored to a specific program.

Nile Soik, of the Allen-Bradley Company, described an additional evaluation procedure in his article in the March 1958 issue of the *Journal of the ASTD*. Not only did he use the *Supervisory Inventory on Human Relations* before and after the program, but he also administered it six months later. He was measuring the forgetting that took place in the period following the program.

And so we see that the paper-and-pencil test can be used effectively in measuring the learning that takes place in a training program. It should be emphasized again that the approach to this kind of evaluation should be systematic and statistically oriented. A comparison of before-and-after scores and responses can then be made to prove how much learning has taken place.

Conclusions about Learning

It is easy to see that it is much more difficult to measure *learning* than it is to measure *reaction* to a program. A great deal of work is required in planning the evaluation procedure, in analyzing the data that are obtained, and in interpreting the results. Wherever possible, it is suggested that training directors devise their own methods and techniques. As has been pointed out in this section, it is relatively easy to plan classroom demonstrations and presentations to measure learning where the program is aimed at the teaching of skills. Where principles and facts are the objectives of the training program, it is advisable to use a paper-and-pencil test. Where suitable standardized tests can be found, it is easier to use them. In many programs, however, it is not possible to find a standardized test, and training directors must use their skill and ingenuity in devising their own measuring instruments.

If training directors can prove that their programs have been effective in terms of learning as well as in terms of reaction, they have objective data to use in selling future programs and in increasing their status and position in the company.

STEP 3: BEHAVIOR

A personal experience may be the best way of introducing this section. When I joined the Management Institute of the University of Wisconsin in 1949, one of my first assignments was to sit through a one-week course called "Human Relations for Foremen and Supervisors." During the week I was particularly impressed by a foreman named Herman from a Milwaukee company. Whenever a conference leader asked a question requiring a good understanding of human relations principles and techniques, Herman was the first one who raised his hand. He had all the answers in terms of good human relations approaches. I was very much impressed, and I said to myself, "If I were in industry, I would like to work for a man like Herman."

It so happened that I had a first cousin who was working for that company. And oddly enough Herman was his boss. At my first opportunity, I talked with my cousin, Jim, and asked him about Herman. Jim told me that Herman might know all the principles and techniques of human relations, but he certainly did not practice them on the job. He performed like the typical "bull of the woods" and had little consideration for the feelings and ideas of his subordinates. At this time I began to realize there may be a big difference between knowing principles and techniques and using them on the job.

Robert Katz, professor at Dartmouth, wrote an article in the July–August 1956 issue of the *Harvard Business Review*. The article was called "Human Relations Skills Can Be Sharpened." In it he stated that those who want to change their job behavior must meet five basic requirements:

1. They must want to improve.
2. They must recognize their own weaknesses.
3. They must work in a permissive climate.
4. They must have some help from someone who is interested and skilled.
5. They must have an opportunity to try out the new ideas.

It seems that Katz has put his finger on the problems that exist in a transition between learning and changes in behavior on the job.

Evaluation of training programs in terms of on-the-job behavior is more difficult than the reaction and learning evaluations described in the two previous sections. A more scientific approach is needed, and many factors must be considered. During the last few years a number of attempts have been made, and more and more effort is being put in this direction.

Several guideposts are to be followed in evaluating training programs in terms of behavioral changes:

1. A *systematic* appraisal should be made of on-the-job performance on a *before-and-after* basis.
2. The appraisal of performance should be made by one or more of the following groups (the more the better):
    a. The person receiving the training
    b. The person's superior or superiors

    c. The person's subordinates

    d. The person's peers or other people thoroughly familiar with his or her performance

3. A statistical analysis should be made to compare performance before and after and to relate changes to the training program.

4. The posttraining appraisal should be made three months or more after the training so that the trainees have an opportunity to put into practice what they have learned. Subsequent appraisals may add to the validity of the study.

5. A control group (not receiving the training) should be used.

Some of the best evaluation studies of changes in behavior are briefly described below.

The Fleishman-Harris Studies[4]

To evaluate a training program that has been conducted at the central school of the International Harvester Company, Fleishman developed a study design and a battery of research instruments for measuring the effectiveness of the training. Seven paper-and-pencil questionnaires were used, and the trainees, their superiors, and their subordinates were all surveyed.

To supplement the data that Fleishman had discovered, Harris conducted a follow-up study in the same organization. He used a before-and-after measure of job performance and worked with experimental and control groups. He obtained information from the trainees themselves as well as from their subordinates.

Survey Research Center Studies[5]

The Survey Research Center of the University of Michigan has contributed much to evaluation of training programs in terms of on-the-job behavior. To measure the effectiveness of a human relations program conducted by Dr. Norman Maier at the Detroit Edison Co. and to measure the results of an experimental program called "feedback," a scientific approach to evaluation was used. A basic design was to use a before-and-after measure of on-the-job performance with experimental as well as control groups. The supervisors receiving the training as well as their subordinates were surveyed in order to compare the results of the research. The instrument used for measuring these changes was an attitude and opinion survey designed and developed by the Survey Research Center.

The Lindholm Study[6]

This study was carried out in the home office of a small insurance company during the period from October 1950 to May 1951. A questionnaire developed as part of the research program of the Industrial Relations Center of the University of Minnesota was used. It was given on a before-and-after basis to the subordinates of those who took the training. No control group was used. A statistical analysis of the before-and-after results of the attitude survey determined the effectiveness of the program in terms of on-the-job behavior.

The Blocker Study[7]

A different approach was used in the study conducted in an insurance company having approximately 600 employees. Fifteen supervisors who took a course on democratic leadership were analyzed during the three-month period following the course. Eight of the supervisors were classified as authoritarian on the basis of their behavior prior to the program.

During the three-month period immediately following the program, the changes in behavior of the supervisors were analyzed through a study of their interview records. They used standard printed forms which made provision for recording the reason for the interview, attitude of the employee, comments of the supervisor, and action taken, if any. Each supervisor was required to make a complete record of each interview. They did not know that these records were to be used for an evaluation study. There was a total of 376 interviews with 186 employees.

The interview records were classified as authoritarian or democratic. The changes in interview approach and techniques were studied during the three-month period following the course to determine whether on-the-job behavior of the supervisors changed.

The Tarnopol Approach[8]

In his article called "Evaluate Your Training Program," Tarnopol suggests the approach to use as well as a specific example of an evaluation experiment. He believes in the employee-attitude survey given on a before-and-after basis using control as well as experimental groups. He stresses that "in our experiences, five employees are a good minimum for measuring the behavior of their supervisor." He also stresses that "although canned questionnaires are available, it is advisable to use measuring instruments that are specifically suited to the requirements of both your company and your training program."

In his employee-attitude approach, Tarnopol has suggested inserting some neutral questions which do not relate to the training being given. This is an added factor in interpreting the results of the research.

The Moon-Hariton Study[9]

This study was made in an engineering section of a department of the General Electric Company. The staff of the General Electric Company was assisted by a representative of The Psychological Corporation.

Two years after the adoption of a new appraisal and training program, a decision was made to attempt to evaluate its effectiveness. It was felt that the opinion of the subordinates about changes in the managers' attitudes and behavior would provide a better measure than what the managers themselves thought about the benefits of the program. Thus a questionnaire was designed to obtain the subordinates' views about changes in their managers. Nevertheless, it was felt that the opinions of the manager would add to the picture. Accordingly, they were also surveyed.

The questionnaire asked the respondents to compare present conditions with conditions two years ago. In other words, instead of measuring the attitudes before and after the program, the subordinates and the managers were asked to indicate what changes had taken place during the last two years.

The Buchanan-Brunstetter Study[10]

At the Republic Aviation Corporation, an attempt was made to measure the results of a training program. The questionnaire was used, and an experimental and a control group were measured. The experimental group had received the training program during the past year, while the control group was going to receive it during the following year. The subordinates of the supervisors in each one of these groups were asked to complete a questionnaire which related to the on-the-job behavior of their supervisor. After answering the questionnaire in which they described the job behavior of their supervisor, they were asked to go over the questionnaire again and to place a check opposite any items "(1) which you think are *more* effectively done now than a year ago; (2) which you think are *less* effectively done now than a year ago."

In this experiment as well as in the Moon-Hariton approach, the subordinates were asked to indicate what changes in behavior had taken place during the last year. This was done because a measure of their preprogram behavior had not been made.

The Stroud Study[11]

A new training program called "Personal Factors in Management" was evaluated at the Bell Telephone Company of Pennsylvania by Peggy Stroud. Several different approaches were used to compare the results and obtain a more valid indication of on-the-job behavioral changes that resulted from the program. The first step was the formulation of a questionnaire to be filled out by four separate groups: (1) conferees, (2) controllees (supervisors not taking the course), (3) superiors of the conferees, and (4) superiors of the controllees.

The first part of the questionnaire was the consideration scale taken from the leader behavior description questionnaire originated in the Ohio State leadership studies. The second part of the questionnaire was called the "critical incident" section; the conferee and control groups were asked to describe four types of incidents that had occurred on the job. The third and final section of the questionnaire applied to the conferees only. They were asked to rate the extent to which they felt the training course had helped them achieve each of its five stated objectives.

It was decided to conduct an extensive evaluation of the training program after the program had begun. Therefore, it was not possible to make a before-and-after comparison. In this study, an attempt was made to get the questionnaire respondents to compare on-the-job behavior before the program with that following the program. According to Stroud, it would have been better to measure behavior prior to the program and then compare it with behavior measured after the program.

This study, called "Evaluating a Human Relations Training Program," is one of the best attempts I have discovered. The various evaluation results are compared and fairly concrete interpretations are made.

The Sorensen Study[12]

One of the most comprehensive research studies that has been done to evaluate the effectiveness of a training program in terms of on-the-job behavior was made at the Crotonville advanced management course of the General Electric Company. It was called the "Observed Changes Enquiry."

The purpose of the "enquiry" was to answer these questions:

1. Have manager graduates of General Electric's advanced management courses been observed to have changed in their manner of managing?
2. What inferences may be made from similarities and differences of changes observed in graduates and nongraduates?

First of all, the managers (graduates and nongraduates alike) were asked to indicate changes they had observed in their own manner of managing during the previous 12 months. Second, subordinates were asked to describe changes they had observed in the managers during the past 12 months. Third, their peers (looking sideways) were asked to describe changes in behavior. And finally, the superiors of the control and experimental groups were asked to describe the same changes in behavior. This gave Sorensen an excellent opportunity to compare the observed changes of all four groups.

In this extensive research, Sorensen used experimental as well as control groups. He also used four different approaches to measure observed changes. These include the person and his or her subordinates, peers, and superiors. In this research, he did not use a before-and-after measure, but rather asked each of the participants to indicate what changes, if any, had taken place during the past year.

The Kirkpatrick Study[13]

This study was conducted in 1969 to evaluate an institute on supervisory skills for foremen and supervisors. The institute covered six topics: order giving, training employees, appraising employee performance, preventing and handling grievances, decision making, and initiating change.

Research Design   A questionnaire was completed by each participant to obtain information on the participant, the company, and the participant's relationship with his or her immediate supervisor. Specific information was obtained on:

1. The participant. Job, experience, education, age, reasons for attending the program, and what he or she hopes to learn
2. The company. Size, type, and climate for change
3. The participant's boss. Years spent as boss, the climate he or she sets for change, and involvement in sending the person to the institute

Interviews were conducted with each participant within two to three months following the institute. The interviews were conducted in the participant's company to obtain information regarding changes in behavior that had taken place on the job.

In addition, interviews were conducted with the participant's immediate supervisor as another measure of changes in the participant's behavior.

Examples of specific questions are shown in Fig. 18-9.

In addition to measuring changes in behavior, an attempt was made to determine what results were achieved. Questions asked of both the participant and his or her boss are shown in Fig. 18-10.

Although the design of the evaluation was relatively simple, it provided data to indicate that significant changes in both behavior and results were achieved.

Conclusions about Behavior

These are some of the best approaches that have been used to measure effectiveness of training programs in terms of on-the-job behavior. Only the methods and instruments used in these studies have been mentioned. The results, although interesting, cannot be borrowed by other training directors, but the techniques can.

For those interested in evaluating in terms of behavioral changes, it is strongly suggested that these studies be carefully analyzed. The references in this chapter indicate where the detailed articles can be found.

Once more I would like to emphasize that the future of training directors and their programs depends to a large extent on their effectiveness. To determine effectiveness, attempts must be made to measure in scientific and statistical terms. Measuring changes in behavior resulting from training programs involves a very complicated procedure. But it is worthwhile and necessary if training programs are going to increase in effectiveness and their benefits made clear to top management.

It is obvious that very few training directors have the background, skill, and time to engage in extensive evaluations. It is therefore frequently necessary to call on industrial psychologists, research people and consultants for advice and help.

STEP 4: RESULTS

The objectives of most training programs can be stated in terms of results such as reduced turnover, reduced costs, improved efficiency, reduction in grievances, increase in quality and quantity of production, or improved morale, which, it is

Training Employees	Yes	No	Not Sure				
a. *Since* the participant attended the program, are his new or transferred employees better trained?							

Training Method	Participant Always	Participant Usually	Participant Sometimes	Participant Never			
b. *Before* the program, who trained the workers?							
c. *Since* the program, who trained the workers?							

Progress in Training Effectiveness	Does Not Apply	Much More	Some-what More	No Change	Some-what Less	Much Less	Don't Know
d. *Since* the program, if someone else trains the employees, has the participant become more observant and taken a more active interest in the training process?							
e. *Since* the program, if the participant trains the employees, is he making more of an effort in seeing that the employees are well trained?							
f. *Since* the program, is the participant more inclined to be patient while training?							
g. *Since* the program, while teaching an operation, is the participant asking for more questions to ensure understanding?							
h. *Since* the program, is the participant better prepared to teach?							
i. *Since* the program, is the participant doing more follow-up to check the trainees' progress?							

Fig. 18-9 Examples of supervisor interview questions in Kirkpatrick study.

hoped, will lead to some of the previously stated results. From an evaluation standpoint, it would be best to evaluate training programs directly in terms of results desired. There are, however, so many complicating factors that it is extremely difficult, if not impossible, to evaluate certain kinds of programs in terms of results. Therefore, it is recommended that training directors evaluate in terms of reaction, learning, and behavior.

Certain kinds of training programs, though, are relatively easy to evaluate in terms of results. For example, in teaching clerical personnel to do a more effective typing job, you can measure the number of words per minute on a before-and-after basis. If you are trying to reduce grievances in your plant, you can measure the number of grievances before and after the training program. If you are attempting to reduce accidents, a before-and-after measure can be made. One word of caution, however: E. C. Keachie stated, in an issue of the *Journal of Industrial Training* (July–August 1948), "Difficulties in the evaluation of training are evident at the outset in the problem technically called 'the separation of

---

1. To what extent has the program improved the participant's working relationship with his boss?

☐ To a large extent
☐ To some extent
☐ No change
☐ Made it worse

2. Since the program, how much two-way communication has taken place between the participant and his subordinates?

☐ Much more
☐ Somewhat more
☐ No change
☐ Somewhat less
☐ Much less
☐ Don't know

3. Since the program, is the participant taking a more active interest in employees?

☐ Much more
☐ Somewhat more
☐ No change
☐ Somewhat less
☐ Much less
☐ Don't know

Fig. 18-10 Interview questions for participant and boss in Kirkpatrick study.

variables'; that is, how much of the improvement is due to training as compared to other factors?" This is the problem that makes it very difficult to measure results that can be attributed directly to a specific training program.

Below are described several evaluations that have been made in terms of results. They do not offer specific formulas for other training directors to follow, but they do suggest procedures and approaches which can be effectively used.

Safety Programs

Many attempts have been made to evaluate the effectiveness of safety training programs in terms of lost-time accidents. One study was conducted by Philip E. Beekman, plant administrator of salaried personnel for the Colgate-Palmolive Company, Jersey City plant. This study was briefly described in *Supervisory Management Newsletter,* no. 3, 1958, of the American Management Association. A comparison was made of plant safety records for the nine-month period before the training program with a comparable period after the program. The frequency rate for lost-time accidents was measured along with the number of reported accidents. The frequency rate dropped from 4.5 to 2.9 percent, and the number of reported accidents dropped from 41 to 32. This improvement was credited directly to the training effort because no physical changes were made which affected the accident rate.

4. On an overall basis, to what extent has the participant's job behavior changed *Since* the program?

Supervisory Areas	Much Better	Somewhat Better	No Change	Somewhat Worse	Much Worse	Don't Know
a. Order Giving						
b. Training						
c. Decision Making						
d. Initiating Change						
e. Appraising Employee Performance						
f. Preventing and Handling Grievances						
g. Attitude toward Job						
h. Attitude toward Subordinates						
i. Attitude toward Management						

5. In regard to the following results, what changes have been noticed *since* the participant's attendance in the program?

Performance Bench Marks	Much Better	Somewhat Better	No Change	Somewhat Worse	Much Worse	Don't Know
a. Quantity of Production						
b. Quality of Production						
c. Safety						
d. Housekeeping						
e. Employee Attitudes and Morale						
f. Employee Attendance						
g. Employee Promptness						
h. Employee Turnover						

Fig. 18-10 (Cont.) Interview questions for participant and boss in Kirkpatrick study.

At a conference at the University of Wisconsin, Dr. G. Roy Fugal, of the General Electric Company, described a before-and-after evaluation of one of their safety programs. The purpose of the training was to reduce the number of accidents and to increase the regularity with which all accidents, major and minor, were reported. The training program consisted of the usual presentations, discussions, and movies, which were very dramatic in describing accidents and their implications. The comprehensive evaluation indicated that the training program did not have desirable results. Therefore, a new approach to training was adopted which was more oriented to the job relationship between the foreman and each worker. An evaluation of this kind of safety training program did indicate the desired results.

Postal Carrier Training

In the September–October 1957 issue of the *Journal of the ASTD,* John C. Massey described a program in which he evaluated in terms of results. Experimental group A received 35 hours of orientation training under the post office training and development program. A comparable group—control group B—did not receive any training. Results of this study are shown in Table 18-1.

TABLE 18-1   Results of Training

	Total number of incidents	
Category	Experimental group A	Control group B
Negligent accidents	5	8
Misdeliveries	21	33
Mishandling valuable mail	3	7
Late reporting	35	32
Absence without reporting	3	6
Abuse of sick leave	8	12
Errors in relay operations	13	22
Adverse Probationary reports	4	9
Discourtesy	4	5

The design of this evaluation study includes an experimental as well as a control group. The importance of using these was emphasized under Step 3: Behavior. A control group should also be used in evaluating results wherever possible to overcome the difficulty described by Dr. Keachie.

An Insurance Company Study

In a recent letter, S. W. Schallert, of the Farmers Mutual Insurance Company of Madison, Wisconsin, reported to me on an evaluation he had made. A number of their claims adjustors were enrolled in the Vale Technical Institute of Blairsville, Pennsylvania. The purpose of the three-week course was to improve the ability of adjustors to estimate and appraise automobile physical damage.

The specific technique used by Schallert was to have the adjustors keep track of their savings for approximately six months after returning from Vale. These savings were the difference between the estimate of damage by garages and the estimate of damage by the claims adjustors who had been trained at Vale. Where the final cost of the adjustment was the same as the estimate made by the Farmers Mutual man, this was considered the savings.

In other words, the purpose of the training was to prepare the adjustors to make estimates which they could justify and sell. Actual dollars-and-cents figures could then be used to determine whether the cost of sending these adjustors to Vale was justified.

A Cost-Reduction Institute

A number of years ago, two graduate students at the University of Wisconsin attempted to measure the results of a cost-reduction institute conducted by the Management Institute of the university. Two techniques were used. The first was to conduct depth interviews with some of the supervisors who had attended the course and with their immediate superiors. The other technique was to mail questionnaires to the remaining enrollees and to their supervisors. Following is a brief summary of that study:

DEPTH INTERVIEWS

Interview with Trainees

1. Have you been able to reduce costs in the few weeks that you have been back on the job?
    Replies: 13—Yes
               3—No
               2—Noncommittal or evasive
               1—Failed to answer

2. How? What were the estimated savings?
   Different types of replies indicated that the 13 people who said they had made cost reductions had done so in different areas. But their ideas stemmed directly from the program, according to these trainees.

Interview with Superiors   Eight of the cost-reduction actions described by the trainees were confirmed by the immediate superior, and these superiors estimated total savings to be from $15,000 to $21,000 per year. The specific ideas that were used were described by superiors as well as by the trainees.

MAILED QUESTIONNAIRES

Questionnaires were mailed to those trainees who were not contacted personally. The results on the questionnaire were not nearly as specific and useful as the ones obtained by personal interview. The study concluded that it is probably better to use the personal interview rather than a questionnaire to measure this kind of program.

Measuring Organizational Performance

Another sophisticated and penetrating article related to evaluation was written by Rensis Likert. It appeared in the March–April 1958 issue of the *Harvard Business Review*. It shows how changes in productivity can be measured on a before-and-after basis. Two different types of groups were used. The first was a group of supervisors trained in using a democratic kind of leadership in which decision making involved the participative technique. The supervisors in the other group were trained to make their own decisons and not ask subordinates for suggestions.

In addition to measuring the results in terms of productivity, such factors as loyalty, attitudes, interest, and work involvement were also measured. Where both training programs resulted in positive changes in productivity, the "participative" approach resulted in better feelings, attitudes, and other human relations factors.

The article described another excellent study from the University of Michigan. Dr. Likert concluded by saying that "industry needs more adequate measures of organizational performance than it is now getting."

Conclusions about Results

The evaluation of training programs in terms of "results" is progressing at a very slow rate. Where the objectives of training programs are as specific as the reduction of accidents, the reduction of grievances, and the reduction of costs, we find that a number of attempts have been made. In a few of them, the researchers have attempted to segregate factors other than training which might have had an effect. In most cases, the measure on a before-and-after basis has been directly attributed to the training even though other factors might have been influential.

Studies like those of Likert attempt to penetrate the difficulties encountered in measuring such programs as human relations, decision making, and the like. In the years to come, we shall see more efforts in this direction, and eventually we may be able to measure human relations training, for example, in terms of dollars and cents. At the present time, however, our research techniques are not adequate.

SUMMARY

One purpose of this chapter is to stimulate training people to take a penetrating look at evaluation. Their own future and the future of their programs depend to a large extent on their ability to evaluate and use evaluation results.

Another objective has been to clarify the meaning of evaluation. By breaking it down into reaction, learning, behavior, and results, the training person can begin to do something about it and can gradually progress from a simple subjective reaction sheet to a research design that measures tangible results.

Articles on evaluation will continue to appear in the *Training and Development Journal* and other magazines. Some of these articles are well worth studying because they describe effective principles, procedures, and methods of evaluation. One example of an excellent article is "Performance Oriented Training: Results Measurement and Follow-up," by Lerda and Cross, which appeared in the August 1962 issue of the *Journal of the ASTD*. Another fine article appeared in the October 1962 issue of the *Journal of the ASTD*. It was entitled "The Development and Evaluation of a Programmed Training Course for Sales Personnel," by J. S. Abma. These articles are worthwhile because they provide helpful principles and approaches which other training people can borrow. Likewise, many of the evaluation articles that continue to appear are not worth the time it takes to read them. A list of other worthwhile reading appears in the References.

This chapter has not provided the answers to the training director's problem of evaluation. It has attempted to provide an understanding of principles and methods. Better understanding will come from continued study of new principles and methods that are described in articles written in professional journals. Needless to say, skill in using proper evaluation methods can come only with practice.

REFERENCES

1. Goodacre, Daniel M., III: "The Experimental Evaluation of Management Training: Principles and Practice," *Personnel,* May 1957.
2. Kirkpatrick, Donald L.: *Obtaining Maximum Benefits from Outside Management Development Programs,* University of Wisconsin—Extension, Milwaukee, 1968.
3. Savitt, Morris: "Is Management Training Worthwhile?" *Personnel,* September–October 1957.
4. Fleishman, E. A., E. F. Harris, and H. E. Buntt: *Leadership and Supervision in Industry,* Personnel Research Board, Ohio State University, Columbus, 1955, p. 110.
5. Mann, Floyd: *Human Relations in the Industrial Setting,* University of Michigan, Survey Research Center, Ann Arbor.
6. Lindholm, T. R.: "Supervisory Training and Employee Attitudes," *Journal of the ASTD,* November–December 1953.
7. Blocker, C. E.: "Evaluation of a Human Relations Training Course," *Journal of the ASTD,* May–June 1955.
8. Tarnopol, Lester: "Evaluate Your Training Program," *Journal of the ASTD,* March–April 1957.
9. Moon, C. G., and Theodore Hariton: "Evaluating an Appraisal and Feedback Training Program," *Personnel,* November–December 1958.
10. Buchanan, P. C., and P. H. Brunstetter: "A Research Approach to Management Improvement," *Journal of the ASTD,* January–February 1959.
11. Stroud, P. V.: "Evaluating a Human Relations Training Program," *Personnel,* November–December 1959.
12. Sorensen, Olav: *The Observed Changes Enquiry,* General Electric Company, Manager Development Consulting Service, Crotonville, N.Y., May 15, 1958.
13. Kirkpatrick, Donald L.: "Evaluating a Training Program for Supervisors and Foremen," *The Personnel Administrator,* September–October 1969.

BIBLIOGRAPHY

Anderson and Anderson: "Human Relations Training for Women," *Training and Development Journal,* August 1971.
Barrett, James E.: "Can We Evaluate Training Expenditures?" *Training in Business and Industry,* January 1970.
Blumenfeld and Holland: "A Model for the Empirical Evaluation of Training Effectiveness," *Personnel Journal,* August 1971.

Catalanello and Kirkpatrick: "Evaluating Training Programs: The State of the Art," *Training and Development Journal,* May 1968.

Couch and Strother: "A Critical Incident Evaluation of Supervisory Training," *Training and Development Journal,* September 1971.

Crawford, H. E.: "A Note of Caution on Listening Training," *Training and Development Journal,* May 1967.

House, R. J.: *Management Development: Design, Evaluation, and Implementation,* University of Michigan, Graduate School of Business Administration, Bureau of Industrial Relations, Ann Arbor, 1967.

Kirkpatrick, Donald: *Supervisory Training and Development,* Addison-Wesley Publishing Company, Inc., Reading, Mass., 1971, chap. 9, "Evaluation of an Internal Training Program."

Kirkpatrick, Donald: *Evaluating Training Programs,* American Society for Training and Development, Madison, Wis., 1975.

Kohn, Vera: *A Selected Bibliography of Evaluation of Management Training and Development Programs,* American Foundation for Management Research (American Management Association), New York, 1970.

Lawrie and Boringer: "Training Needs Assessment and Training Program Evaluation," *Training and Development Journal,* November 1971.

Malouf, L. G.: "Managerial Grid Evaluated," *Training and Development Journal,* March 1966.

Miraglia, J. F.: "Human Relations Training," *Training and Development Journal,* September 1966 (extensive references).

Moffie, Calhoon, and O'Brien: "Evaluation of a Management Development Program," *Personnel Psychology,* Winter 1964.

Morrisey and Wellstead: "Supervisory Training Can Be Measured Objectively on the Job," *Training and Development Journal,* June 1971.

Murdick, R. G.: "Measuring the Profit in Industry Training Programs," *Journal of the ASTD,* April 1960.

Nevis, Smith, and Harper: "Behavior and Attitude Changes Related to Laboratory Training," *Training Directors Journal,* February 1965.

Norman, J. H.: "Dollars and Cents Evaluation of a Training Program," *Journal of the ASTD,* October 1959.

Soik and Kirkpatrick: "Effective Listening," *Training and Development Journal,* August 1968.

Stander, Townshend, and Swartz: "A Quantative Evaluation of a Motivational Training Program for Blue Collar Workers," *Training Directors Journal,* Nobember 1964.

Underwood, W. J.: "Evaluation of Laboratory Method Training," *Training Directors Journal,* May 1965.

Wakeley and Shaw: "Management Training: An Integrated Approach," *Training Directors Journal,* July 1965.

Chapter **19**

Statistical Methods
for Measuring Training Results

TREADWAY C. PARKER

Treadway C. Parker *is Director of Organization Development Services with the American Management Associations. In that capacity, he is concerned primarily with the design and development of performance improvement programs which utilize training as a major component. Prior to working with the AMA, Dr. Parker was Director of Research of the American Foundation for Management Research, and he has held various positions with Exxon and Dunlap and Associates, a consulting firm. In addition, he was an independent management consultant. He holds a Ph.D. in organizational psychology from New York University and M.A. and B.A. degrees from Washington University in St. Louis. Dr. Parker's main interests are in the areas of overall organization development, management training and development, training evaluation approaches, and the management of new business ventures. He has published articles in numerous business and professional journals.*

Systematic training and development activities are on the increase in business, government, educational, and military organizations. The increase in job-related educational programs is in response to the accelerating pace of change in the world, which in turn is causing an acceleration in obsolescence of job knowledge and skills. What is appropriate for today in the way of knowledge and skills is more and more likely not to be appropriate for tomorrow. The solution to this problem is increased training and development of all levels of the work force.[1]

Along with the increased amount of job-related education, there are mounting pressures to discover whether particular educational programs are effective. As job-related educational activities assume a more identifiable technology and account for a larger part of annual organizational expenditures, executives responsible for the performance of their organizations are more than ever asking questions about the tangible results of educational programs in relation to their costs. These questions are most often asked of the training or educational director in an organization, and there is little doubt that trainers will be under increasing pressure to provide answers in quantitative terms about the cost effectiveness of their existing and proposed educational programs.[2,3,4] The purpose of this chapter is to provide a discussion of some quantitative methods which may be useful to the training professional in measuring the outcomes of programs and relating these in some meaningful fashion to program costs. The author would be the first to say that the application of these methods in the operating organizational setting is often very difficult. But, difficult as it is, this writer also feels that it must be attempted if the training and development profession is to retain and increase its usefulness to productive organizations in the coming period.

Training Design and Evaluation Model   Any systematic discussion of quantitative methods must flow from an underlying model of the design of educational programs and the measurement of their results. Thus Fig. 19-1 is a diagram of

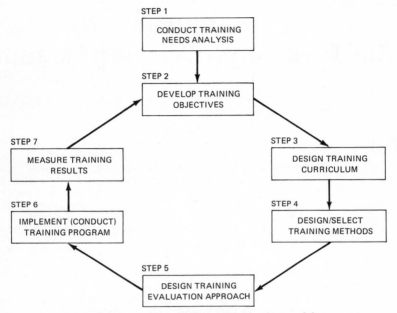

Fig. 19-1   Training design and evaluation model.

the seven-step model which the author has come to use over a period of time in his training and development activities.

In measuring the results of educational programs, we are concerned primarily with what takes place during steps 5 and 7 of the procedure outlined. However, it can be seen that it is impossible to conduct a proper measurement of results without paying careful attention to program objectives. Measuring results implies some criteria against which the obtained results can be compared, and in the case of educational programs such criteria are partly the outgrowth of the training objectives. Generally speaking, program results can be stated in terms of how well the training objectives were achieved. Thus there is a definite and most important linkage between educational objectives and measurement of results. In fact, in the author's opinion, proper measurement of results is not possible unless objectives are clearly stated beforehand.

The Central Problem in Educational Measurement: Measuring Change   When we conduct an educational program, the underlying assumption is that the participants in the program will learn something. Otherwise, there would be no point in expending the time, energy, and money necessary to design and conduct a program. So, for the purposes of this discussion, we shall assume that our basic problem in measuring training results is that of measuring the type and degree of learning exhibited by program participants. Therefore, the basic question is: How do we know when a person has learned something? In its simplest form, the answer is that we must be able to measure changes in personal characteristics in order to say that a person has learned something. The simple fact is that there is no other way to measure learning except to measure changes in behavior. For example, a training-program participant demonstrates learning by performing a task at a higher level of skill than previously, or a gain in knowledge by answering questions about a particular subject, or a change in attitude by making different statements or taking different actions regarding a particular matter. Thus the central problem in educational measurement is the measurement of change, which is a very difficult task requiring controlled experimental conditions.[5] Since such conditions are rarely possible to attain in operating organizations, we shall try to limit our discussion to methods which provide reasonable approaches to the measurement of training results in operating organizations.

Categories of Educational Measurement   The three areas where quantitative methods are most useful to training professionals are outlined below and further elaborated in the remainder of this chapter.

Participant Personal Characteristics.   This category of measurement is difficult to define precisely. Generally, it has to do with the effects of training in areas such as trainee knowledge, attitudes, and skills. It is differentiated from job performance because in many situations, the measurement of training effects on knowledge or attitudes may be more specific and more narrowly defined than the measurement of these effects in the area of job performance. Also, different measurement techniques may be necessary.

Participant and Organizational Performance.   This category is most important in terms of the end results of training in operating organizations. Here we are concerned with measuring the job performance of individuals, small work groups, and even fairly large segments of an organization. The measurements of performance in this category are often due to changes in participant personal characteristics. For example, a person may perform a job better because of increased job knowledge resulting from training. However, if improved job performance is the desired outcome of training (as it usually is, although this is not always made explicit), it is often possible to bypass the measurement of job knowledge improvements and go directly to job performance.

Return on Training Investment.   This category of measurement normally does not deal with the effects of training on individuals as such but is concerned with the overall costs and benefits of a given training effort measured in terms of improved performance. Often this type of analysis is applied to projected training programs to determine whether they make economic sense. The difficulties of measurement in this category stem from the fact that (1) training costs are usually much easier to identify than training benefits, and (2) overall performance results may not be demonstrated for some time after the actual training has taken place. The ability to do an adequate job of measurement in this category depends heavily on being able to measure the effects of training on job and organizational performance.

It should be pointed out that the categories outlined above are not intended to be exhaustive in terms of covering all measurement situations that will be faced by training directors, nor are they well defined and precise. Rather, they should be considered illustrative of measurement problems that are expected to become increasingly important over the next few years.

QUANTITATIVE APPROACHES TO MEASURING TRAINING RESULTS

In this section we shall discuss in some detail the three interlocking aspects of quantitative measurement and the application of these to the three measurement categories previously outlined. The three interlocking parts of a quantitative measurement system which are discussed below include (1) experimental design, (2) data collection, and (3) statistical analysis.

Experimental Designs

Once a clear statement of training objectives has been developed—e.g., reduce waste by 20 percent, increase the effectiveness of production scheduling, reduce employee turnover by 15 percent, increase supervisory human relations skills, or increase the effectiveness of management long-range planning—the training director has determined what should be measured to evaluate training results. Next the training director must determine how to measure the results as validly and accurately as possible. To do this, he or she must plan an experimental design and select data collection techniques and appropriate statistical methods.

In measuring changes resulting from training programs, there is one basic experimental model which has several variations for use under varying conditions and which provides varying degrees of accuracy. The model is simple in that it requires a measurement of participants before training to establish the level of knowledge, skill, performance, attitude, and the like prior to training and one or more measurements of participants after training to ascertain their new level of knowledge, skill, performance, attitude, etc. The model is diagramed in Fig. 19-2.

While the experimental design in Fig. 19-2 is the most basic one, several variations have been developed; these are categorized and discussed below.[3,6,7,8]

Fig. 19-2 Basic experimental design.

One-Group Designs   There are two common variations of this experimental design: (1) posttraining measurement without control group and (2) pre/posttraining measurement without control group.

The design of the posttraining measurement without control group is diagramed in Fig. 19-3. This design is the one most frequently used and is the weakest of those available. Its basic problem is that no performance base line is established prior to training, and this prevents measurement of change.

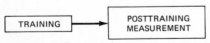

Fig. 19-3 Posttraining measurement without control group design.

Additionally, factors other than training could account for the behavior measured after training. This design is not suggested for serious measurement of training results.

The pre/posttraining measurement without control group is the model presented in Fig. 19-2. This design is probably the most widely used of the pre/postmeasurement designs. It represents some improvement over the design in Fig. 19-3, but it still leaves much to be desired. While this design does establish a pretraining base line so that changes can be measured, it is still not possible to determine whether factors other than training might have caused any changes in behavior. If only one group is available for measuring training results, this design is preferable over the first one presented. However, if more groups can be used, the next set of designs is considerably more powerful.

Two-Group Designs   As with the one-group designs, there are two variations of the two-group designs. The first is the posttraining measurement with control group, and the second is the pre/posttraining measurement with control group.

Figure 19-4 shows a diagram of the first of the two-group designs.

This design, while more powerful than the one-group designs, still suffers from the inability to measure changes from pretraining base line measures since they

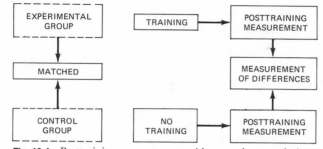

Fig. 19-4 Posttraining measurement with control group design.

are not part of the design. This is its major weakness. However, when the experimental and control groups are matched on factors such as age, education, experience, and intelligence level, which could influence any differences measured after training, this design can yield useful comparative information. If the two groups are not matched on these factors, the value of this design is greatly diminished. In any case, this design is recommended over either of the one-group designs.

The second two-group design is diagramed in Fig. 19-5.

The design shown in Fig. 19-5 is the most powerful discussed so far. If the

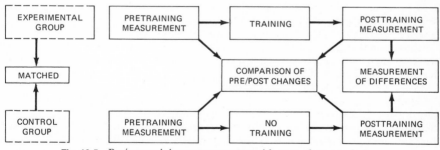

Fig. 19-5 Pre/posttraining measurement with control group design.

experimental and control groups are matched on background factors such as age, education, experience, intelligence level, and the factor for which training is conducted—e.g., work quality (waste)—this design overcomes the major weakness of the previous designs. It not only permits the comparison of posttraining differences in the experimental and control groups but also allows comparison of changes from pre/posttraining measurements. While this design is statistically powerful, it may not be practical from the administrative point of view. In the operating environment, it may be particularly difficult to match the experimental and control groups on a sufficient number of background and performance factors. However, the increased measurement power of this design over others seems well worth the administrative effort.

Three-Group Design   A three-group design utilizing one experimental and two control groups, which is an extension of the second two-group design, has been developed to control for the possibility of the "Hawthorne effect" in relation to the results of a trained group. This design is diagrammed in Fig. 19-6.

As can be seen from Fig. 19-6, the three-group design is rather elaborate and is intended to reveal whether the experiencing of a pretraining measurement by

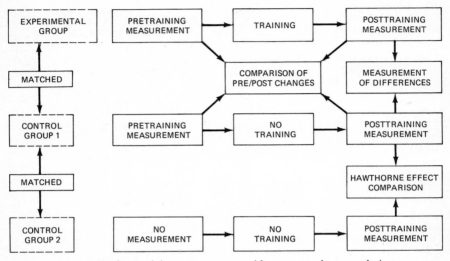

Fig. 19-6   Pre/posttraining measurement with two control groups design.

control group 2 is sufficient to cause a higher posttraining measurement even without training. While this design is a good one from the measurement point of view, its administrative difficulties will usually outweigh its advantages in the typical operating organization. However, its use is recommended where possible.

Four-Group Design   In the interest of thoroughness, we present a four-group design which is basically an extended version of the two- and three-group designs. It is diagrammed in Fig. 19-7.[9]

As can be seen from the diagram, the four-group design is really an extended two-group design which provides replication of the two-group design as well as the advantages of the three-group design in measuring for the Hawthorne effect. The idea here is that control group 2 is a control group for the first training cycle and then becomes an experimental group in the second cycle. In addition, the pretraining measurements for control groups 2 and 3 can be compared with the

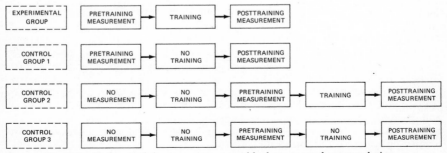

Fig. 19-7   Pre/posttraining measurement with three control groups design.

posttraining measurements for control group 1 to test for the Hawthorne effect. While this design may seem cumbersome administratively in that four groups must be matched, two groups out of four end up being trained, whereas only one out of three is trained in the three-group design. While we have described the three- and four-group designs here as possibilities, the decision as to whether to use either of these designs must weigh the on-the-spot balance between measurement power and administrative difficulties.

Extended Periodic Measurement Design   Before leaving experimental designs, we shall describe one additional type which can be very useful in measuring training results. This design is an extension of the two-group pre/posttraining measurement with control-group design. In the extended version of this design, the measurements of the experimental and control groups are taken for an extended period of time prior to and after the training. In this way a performance base line is established over several weeks or months before training and measurements of both groups are continued for several weeks or months after training of the experimental group. The expected result using this design is no difference between the groups prior to training and a divergence of the groups after training, with the trained group showing significant improvement over the control group. Some uses of this design will be discussed more fully later in the chapter.

Summary.   To summarize, we have described several experimental designs utilizing from one to four matched groups. From the measurement point of view, the more complex designs are preferable, but they are administratively cumbersome. In light of this trade-off we suggest that the two-group pre/post training measurement with control-group design shown in Fig. 19-5 represents the best balance between measurement power and practicality in the operating environment. Therefore, this is the design that we recommend for use in most situations. We have also described an extended periodic measurement version of this design which is useful in situations where measurements of experimental and control groups can be made over an extended period of time.

Data Collection Methods

The second category to be discussed under the heading of quantitative approaches is data collection methods. Let us assume that an experimental design has been selected. The next step will be to select the appropriate means of collecting the data on participant knowledge, attitudes, performance, and the like.[6] The data collection methods can be considered measurement techniques because whatever methods are used should yield numerical measures of the variables under consideration. The list of possible data collection techniques includes (1) questionnaires, (2) paper-and-pencil tests, (3) job sample (performance) tests, (4) interviews, (5) simulations, (6) visual observations, (7) rating forms, (8) individual and group performance measures such as productivity and work quality, and (9) individual and group behavior measures such as absenteeism, grievances, lateness, and morale.

Questionnaires   A questionnaire is a standardized instrument for collecting data because it measures responses to the same set of questions presented in the same way to all participants. It is systematic in the sense that it is preplanned and designed to measure the variables considered important. Questionnaires are often used to measure participant attitudes about areas which may be affected by training.

Care should be taken in the design of questionnaires to make the questions clearly understandable to respondents. The format should be designed so that responses are made on scales which will yield meaningful numerical scores. Multiple-choice and checklist formats can also be useful. Again, the watchword is clarity of wording so that clear interpretations of results can be made. Well-designed questionnaires are one of the most important techniques in measuring training results.

Paper-and-Pencil Tests Tests are another frequently used standardized measuring device. They are similar to questionnaires but differ in one important aspect. Questionnaires generally have no "correct" or "incorrect" answers, but tests usually do. Thus, while questionnaires generally measure attitudes or feelings, tests measure knowledge categories where there are definite correct and incorrect responses. Tests are often used to measure procedural knowledge of a task being learned—for example, the steps in troubleshooting machine malfunctions or in handling grievances. Areas in which there are clearly correct and incorrect ways of performing a task are usually measurable by tests.

Care should be taken in test design to ensure that the question and answer alternatives are clear and not subject to misinterpretation or controversy. To be useful as a measuring device, any test used must yield meaningful numerical scores. Much has been written about the techniques of test construction, which is a specialized field in itself. Space does not permit a full discussion of test design, and readers would be well-advised to familiarize themselves with some of the technical work in this field before attempting to construct and use a "homemade" test. There is a wide variety of published tests available, some of which may be appropriate for particular measurement situations. Tests are one of the most important and widely used devices for measuring training results. They have long been the standard measuring device used in school systems for tracking educational results.

Job Sample or Performance Tests Job sample or performance tests are another form of data collection which can yield numerical information about how well a training participant can perform a particular task. In this case, instead of measuring primarily cognitive knowledge, as with paper-and-pencil tests, we are able to measure performance skill levels by having the participant actually perform a task on a test basis. A good example of a performance test is a typing test. Here trainees are asked to actually type some standard letters, and their performance is measured in terms of speed and accuracy.

The job sample test is most useful in measuring training results when a skill is being learned since this type of test goes beyond job knowledge to measure actual performance. While job sample tests have been fairly widely used for measuring straightforward skills such as typing, this technique is by no means limited to simple skills. For example, the familiar driving test used to qualify people for driver's licenses is really a performance test which includes a variety of subtests such as backing up, parking, open-road driving, and driving in traffic. In the author's opinion, this form of measurement should and probably will be more widely utilized in the future.

Interviews The interview is probably the oldest and most widely used data collection method in existence. Unfortunately, the way it is often used makes it a relatively poor data collection method for yielding quantitative measures. However, this need not be the case if some thought is given to designing interview formats which will produce quantifiable data.

The central idea here is not new, but it is often overlooked in results measurement projects which use interviews as their primary data collection method. Simply stated, what is required is some preplanning of the interview structure so that it covers in specific terms those areas in which data are needed. For example, there is no reason why an interview cannot be structured in much the same manner as a questionnaire. The interviewer can use a response form keyed to the questions for recording responses on numerical scales or predetermined response categories. The response forms can then be utilized for quantitative analysis. In addition, the interview allows respondents to explain their answers and can often provide important insights which are impossible to gain using the questionnaire method alone.

The main drawbacks to the interview method are a lack of quantitative response data and the time consumed. A way around the first drawback has been discussed above, but the second remains. Since an interview by definition takes two people's time, it is a more expensive data collection method than the questionnaire method. However, if the project does not involve a large number of people and the interview is structured to yield numerical data, it can be a very worthwhile data collection method.

Simulation   Simulation of actual job tasks has come into increasing use as a training method in the past few years, and for certain complex tasks it has proved to be very effective. Less attention, however, has been devoted to using simulation as a data collection or measurement device.

When used as a measurement method, simulation is similar to the job sample or performance test method. The primary difference between the two methods is in the complexity of the tasks involved and the fact that a job sample is usually a part of the actual job, whereas a simulation is by definition an artificial representation of an actual task. Also, simulations are often more general in nature than job samples. For example, an in-basket exercise is a simulation if artificial but relevant materials are used.

Simulation typically involves performance on the part of the training participant, and it offers the possibility of measuring performances against a standardized set of requirements. For example, a decision simulation will normally involve a standard set of conditions about which the participant must make certain decisions. Typically, the outcomes of these decisions can be evaluated to yield (often but not always) some numerical scores which can be used in evaluating educational results. For example, it has recently been found that the increasingly popular "assessment center" approach, which is a form of simulation, can be used to measure the effects of training. At present, there is a wide variety of simulations (often called "games" or "exercises") available which can be readily used for measuring training results.

Visual Observation   Visual observation is another data collection method which has been neglected possibly because it has not been structured properly for quantitative data collection. There are many situations in which visual observation of trainees before and after training can provide quantitative measurements of behavior. Like interviews, visual observations can be standardized and systematized to provide numerical data. One of the best and most straightforward ways to find out whether training participants are behaving differently before as compared with after training is to observe them in a systematic way. Observation can be greatly systematized by preplanning what behaviors will be looked for and how these will be recorded to provide numerical data. As with the interview method, the key to systematic visual observation of performance is to prepare an observation checklist ahead of time which is organized around the categories of behavior to be observed and which provides a way for the observer to count the frequency of occurrence of each particular behavior.

Visual observation using organized checklists is particularly useful when complex performance which is difficult to assess by means of questionnaire, interview, or simulation must be measured. For example, visual observation is applicable to customer contact situations such as department store salesclerks, airline ticket agents, or bank tellers where behavior toward customers is to be evaluated. Visual observation can yield numerical measures on frequency of contact, time necessary per transaction, transaction tone, and other such behavioral variables which are important in measuring training results.

Rating Forms and Checklists   No discussion of data collection approaches would be complete without some attention to the use of rating forms and checklists. These types of forms are primarily methods for systematizing and structuring the collection of training-results data. Both types provide an observer with a way of organizing judgments about behavior and/or performance. To the degree that they are well designed, these tools can assist greatly in providing valid and accurate numerical indicators.

Rating forms are useful primarily when one or more people must make judgments about the degree, amount, or value of a particular type of behavior or performance. For example, some rating forms contain a series of statements about the behaviors to be measured with five-point "frequency" response scales running from "very seldom" to "almost always"; these allow the observer to indicate his or her judgment of the frequency of the behavior in question.

Other formats may include statements with response scales that enable the observer to indicate how much the statement applies to the person to be measured. Still other formats use scales which ask the observer to rate or evaluate the value or

Very seldom	Sometimes	A good deal of the time	Most of the time	Almost always
1	2	3	4	5

Fig. 19-8   Typical quantifiable response scale.

"goodness" of a series of behaviors. Rating forms are actually quite flexible in that various types of response scales can be used to measure whatever is desired. The important requirement is that the scales be designed, like that in Fig. 19-8, so that responses can be quantified.

Figure 19-8 illustrates a simple five-point response scale with definitions for each point. In addition, the numerical score for each scale point is shown below the scale. This is representative of the type of scale that will yield quantitative information.

Checklists represent a slightly different method of collecting data. With this format, the observer notes whether a particular behavior occurs and/or how often it occurs within a given time period. Checklists normally do not have response scales like those of rating forms. Instead, they contain a series of statements or behavior descriptions, and the observer is asked to check if the behavior occurs. The observation and checking may be keyed to a time period such as once each morning and afternoon or twice per work shift.

Individual and Group Performance Measures   Here we move into an area of discussion which is concerned not strictly with data collection but with describing some categories of data which can be useful in measuring training results. The category of individual and group performance is obviously very important in measuring training results. In this section we would like to mention briefly some performance measures to remind the reader of the wide variety of possible measures.

Both individual and group performance are typically measured in terms of quantity of work, quality of work, and time required to perform a given work task. At lower organizational levels, where work is usually more structured and defined, it is often possible to measure quantity of work by counting outputs such as number of units assembled, number of letters typed, number of forms processed, number of claims processed, number of calls made, and number of customers dealt with. When one looks at a particular job carefully, it is normally not too difficult to discover some reasonable measures of quantitative output.

Quality measures are also easier to come by at lower organizational levels where work is structured. In production operations, measures such as units rejected, rework percentages, and waste indices are often kept on a continuing basis. In clerical operations quality can often be measured by number of errors, particularly in large processing operations, where a quality-control check is a matter of course. As one moves upward in the organization, it becomes increasingly difficult to obtain objective measures of performance and increasingly necessary to rely on judgmental factors. Thus, as is well known to training professionals, measures of work performance become more nebulous and elusive at the supervisory and management levels.

One possible way to deal with this problem is to assume that a supervisor or manager is responsible and accountable for the work outputs of his or her particular unit. Thus at least part of the measurement of managers' performance could be on the basis of the collective performances of their subordinates. This suggests that group measures of work output and work quality at the lower levels, where they are better defined, can be useful as indirect measures of performance at higher levels.

To summarize, the basic categories of individual and group performance measurement are quantity, quality, and timeliness. Sometimes these are all combined in various ways into a single category labeled "effectiveness." In any measurement of performance, however, the primary concern should be for objectivity and accuracy. While there are some pitfalls to the use of production, waste, error, and other objective records, they are often more desirable than subjective ratings by supervisors as measures of results.

Individual and Group Behavior Measures   Another type of results data we would like to mention briefly is concerned with nonperformance categories of individual and group behavior such as lateness, absenteeism, voluntary quits, grievances, and morale. While these are not direct measures of work performance, they are often related to it.

We mention these categories because often training programs are specifically designed to affect the kinds of behaviors mentioned above. Where this is the case, the training officer should select measures that will reflect changes in these types of behaviors so that training results will be measurable in categories appropriate to the training program.

In summary, this section has described and discussed a number of data collection methods and categories of measurement which can be useful in measuring the results of educational programs. These are the methods by which behavior can be converted into the numerical format which is necessary for quantitative analysis of results. Once such measures are collected, the next step is the statistical analysis of the measures; this is discussed in the next section.

Statistical Analysis Methods

In this section we shall describe and discuss some of the more commonly used statistical techniques. We do not intend to deal with the more sophisticated, multivariate methods in any detail because of their complexity. Rather, we shall limit the discussions to the simpler, more straightforward techniques.

There are three basic types of methods to be discussed: (1) the statistical evaluation of group differences such as before and after training, (2) measures of relationship or correlation between two sets of data, and (3) graphic methods for displaying differences between two groups over a period of time. The statistical methods can be further subdivided into parametric and nonparametric methods. Parametric methods are generally used with larger samples such as 30 to 50 or more, and they have the added drawbacks of requiring a number of assumptions about scores representing normal distributions.[10] Nonparametric methods, on the other hand, can be used with small samples of data (fewer than 25) and are "distribution-free," which means they require no assumptions about the underlying score distributions. In situations where the technical assumptions underlying the parametric methods are valid, these tests will be the most powerful, but the assumptions are stringent enough so that they are not often fully met. This makes the use of nonparametric methods "safer" in most situations.

Group Differences—Parametric Methods   The basic parametric statistic used to evaluate group differences is called the t test. It has two forms which are used to test differences between independent groups and related groups. Independent groups are made up of *different* people, such as an experimental group and a control group. Related groups are made up of the same people, such as an experimental group which is measured before and after training.

Independent Groups.   Let us take a typical situation in which a training director wants to know how well his control and experimental groups are matched on age and education. He will first calculate the averages (means) and standard error of the means for age and education for each group. Then he will apply the independent-group t test formula below:

$$t = \frac{M_1 - M_2}{\sqrt{\sigma^2{}_{m_1} + \sigma^2{}_{m_2}}}$$

where M_1 = mean (group 1)
M_2 = mean (group 2)
σ_{m_1} = standard error of mean (group 1)
σ_{m_2} = standard error of mean (group 2)

In the problem under consideration, a "good" matching of the groups on age and education would be indicated by no statistically significant differences in the means for age and education. If the t values are less than 2.00, there are no significant differences between the two groups at the 0.05 level of significance, which indicates that the groups are not different in terms of age and education. On the other hand, if a t value is greater than 2.00, it would indicate a statistically significant difference between the groups on that variable. A table of t ratios should be consulted for exact significance values.[11,12]

The t test formula shown above would be used with independent groups of approximately 25 or more where the scores are considered to meet the underlying assumptions for parametric statistics.

The t test can also be used to evaluate differences in percentages between two independent groups. Let us say that you want to compare two work groups on their scrap rates, which are expressed as percentages. The procedure for doing this is the same as for group means except that percentages are substituted for the means in the formula above as follows:

$$t = \frac{P_1 - P_2}{\sqrt{\sigma^2{}_{p_1} + \sigma^2{}_{p_2}}}$$

where P_1 = percentage (group 1)
P_2 = percentage (group 2)
σ_{p_1} = standard error of percentage (group 1)
σ_{p_2} = standard error of percentage (group 2)

The interpretation of the resulting t value would be the same as described for group means. That is, if the t is 2.00 or greater, there is a significant difference. If it is less than 2.00, there is no difference.

Related Groups.   In evaluating measures from before and after training, the problem is one of differences in performance between the same group at two different points in time. In this case we are dealing with related or correlated groups since at each measurement point, the groups consist of the same people. For statistically evaluating differences in related groups, we need to use a slightly modified version of the t test.[11,12]

Let us suppose that you have given a knowledge test to a group of trainees both before and after training and that you want to find out whether the pre/posttraining mean scores are significantly different. First you would calculate the pre/posttraining means and standard deviations. Normally, this would be all the data necessary for a t test, but in this case, since the same people are involved in both groups, it is also necessary to calculate the correlation between the two sets of pre/posttraining observations for inclusion in the related-observations t test formula below:

$$t = \frac{M_1 - M_2}{\sqrt{\sigma^2_{m_1} + \sigma^2_{m_2} - (2r_{12} \cdot \sigma_{m_1} \cdot \sigma_{m_2})}}$$

where M_1 = mean (first set of observations)
M_2 = mean (second set of observations)
σ_{m_1} = standard error of mean (first set of observations)
σ_{m_2} = standard error of mean (second set of observations)
r_{12} = correlation between the two sets of observations

The inclusion of the correlation term in the formula corrects for the fact that the two sets of measurements are from the same people. Without this term, the t estimate would usually be lower than it should be. As before, a table of t ratios should be consulted to determine the statistical significance of any particular t value obtained.[11,12]

As in the case of independent groups, the t test can also be applied to evaluate differences in percentages between measurements of the same group on two different occasions. Let us assume that you have measured absenteeism rates of a group before and after training and that you now want to evaluate the results. You would calculate the pre/posttraining percentages and standard errors as with independent groups and also the correlation between the two sets of absenteeism figures. These would then be evaluated by using the formula shown below:

$$t = \frac{P_1 - P_2}{\sqrt{\sigma^2_{p_1} + \sigma^2_{p_2} - (2r_{12} \cdot \sigma_{p_1} \cdot \sigma_{p_2})}}$$

where P_1 = percentage (first set of observations)
P_2 = percentage (second set of observations)
σ_{p_1} = standard error of percentage (first set of observations)
σ_{p_2} = standard error of percentage (second set of observations)
r_{12} = correlation between the two sets of observations

The usual table of t ratios should be consulted to find the statistical significance of the resulting t value.[11,12]

Group Differences—Nonparametric Methods   As mentioned previously, nonparametric statistical methods should be applied when one is not sure that the assumptions underlying the use of parametric statistics are valid for a particular measurement situation. Since the validity of these assumptions very often becomes questionable when N drops below about 25, nonparametric statistics are often called *small-sample statistics*.[13]

In this section we shall deal with the same types of measurement situations described in the section on parametric methods.

Independent Groups.   A very powerful nonparametric test which is a good alternative to the parametric t test is the Mann-Whitney U test. Let us again take the case of two different groups and how well they are matched on age.

The first step is to take all the ages from the two groups and combine them into one rank order from low to high; that is, all the ages are arranged in order and then ranked. We then apply the two formulas below and pick the smaller of the two resulting values for U:

$$U = n_1 n_2 + n_1(n_1 + 1) - R_1$$
$$U = n_1 n_2 + n_2(n_2 + 1) - R_2$$

where n_1 = size (group 1)
n_2 = size (group 2)
R_1 = sum of ranks (group 1)
R_2 = sum of ranks (group 2)

The smaller U value is then used in conjunction with the appropriate statistical table(s) to determine the statistical significance of any differences in the groups.[13]

Related Groups.   As with the parametric t test, in measuring differences between the same group on two different occasions, we are dealing with related measures, and a different statistical test must be used. While there are several nonparametric tests for testing differences between related groups, the most useful for the typical pre/posttraining situation is the Wilcoxon Matched-pairs Signed-ranks test.[13]

Let us assume that a training director has given pre/posttraining tests to a group of participants and that she wishes to test the pre/posttraining differences. In using the Wilcoxon test she should follow this procedure: Arrange the pre/posttraining scores into one pair for each individual and obtain the difference score for each person. All the difference scores should then be ranked, beginning with 1 for the smallest difference and moving up in ascending order. Then assign to each rank the sign of its corresponding difference score. Then sum the positive and negative ranks separately and let T equal the smaller of the two sums. The T value is then used in conjunction with the appropriate statistical table to determine whether any observed difference is statistically significant.

The above procedure is illustrated in Fig. 19-9.

Measurement of Correlation—Parametric Methods   There are some measurement situations in which the training professional may wish to determine the degree of relationship between two or more variables. The statistical methods

Person	Pretraining Score	Posttraining Score	Difference Score	D Score Rank	Sum of Ranks +	Sum of Ranks −
1	10	14	+4	4	4	
2	12	10	−2	2		2
3	15	18	+3	3	3	
4	13	12	−1	1		1
5	9	14	+5	5	5	
6	14	20	+6	6	6	
				Sum	18	3
					T = 3	

Fig. 19-9   Example of Wilcoxon matched-pairs signed-ranks procedure.

used for this purpose are called *correlational* or *regression* techniques. As in the case of the methods used in evaluating group differences, there are both parametric and nonparametric methods of correlation; the most frequently used of these are presented below with brief explanations.

Continuous Variables.   Let us say that a training director has trained a group and has given pre/posttraining tests to each individual trainee. He has calculated a change score for each person and now wishes to know whether the degree of change is correlated with the educational level of the participants. He can tabulate the two variables—i.e., education and change score—for each person and then apply a statistical method known as the *product moment* or *Pearson correlation* to measure the degree of relationship between education and pre/posttraining change. Let us say he designates education as variable X and change as variable Y. He can then apply the following formula:[12]

$$r = \frac{\dfrac{\Sigma xy}{N} - (M_x)(M_y)}{\sqrt{\left[\dfrac{\Sigma x^2}{N} - (M_x)^2\right]\left[\dfrac{\Sigma y^2}{N} - (M_y)^2\right]}}$$

where Σxy = sum of all pairs of x and y scores multiplied together
M_x = mean (x scores)
M_y = mean (y scores)

The value resulting from this formula is called a *correlation coefficient*. It can range from -1.00 (which is a perfect inverse relationship) through 0.00 (which is no relationship) to $+1.00$ (which is a perfect positive relationship). The coefficient is used in conjunction with appropriate statistical tables to determine its statistical significance.[12]

Dichotomous Variables.   When the two variables to be calculated are dichotomous, i.e, expressed in two discrete categories such as male and female, the appropriate statistic to use is the phi coefficient. The frequencies for each variable are arranged in the fourfold table shown in Fig. 19-10.

The computation of phi is then as follows:

$$\text{Phi} = \frac{(AD - BC)}{(A + B)(A + C)(B + D)(C + D)}$$

The statistical significance of the phi coefficient can be estimated by converting the phi to chi square (χ^2) and using the appropriate statistical table.[12]

Variable 2

		Male	Female	Totals
	Pass	A	B	A + B
Variable 1	Fail	C	D	C + D
	Totals	A + C	B + D	N

Fig. 19-10   Fourfold phi coefficient table.

Measurement of Correlation—Nonparametric Methods   A training director who wishes to measure the relationship between two variables without making the assumptions required by the Pearson correlation can rank the data and use the Spearman rank correlation coefficient. Let us take the problem mentioned previously regarding the correlation between education and knowledge change of training participants. The education and change scores would be tabulated for each participant, and then both sets of scores would be ranked. Once the scores are ranked, the following formula can be applied to the rankings to yield a Spearman rank correlation:

$$r_s = 1 - \frac{6\Sigma D^2}{N(N^2-1)}$$

where ΣD^2 = sum of squared differences between ranks
     N = number of pairs of measurements

The resulting rank correlation coefficient is then used in conjunction with the appropriate statistical table to determine its statistical significance.[11,12,13]

While there are several additional nonparametric correlation methods in general use, either they offer no advantage over the Spearman rank correlation or they represent different correlation problems. Therefore, they have not been included in this section. The reader interested in a broader discussion of nonparametric correlation techniques should consult modern statistics textbooks on the matter.[8,11,12,13]

Graphic Display Techniques   Sometimes a training director is interested in showing in graphic form the results of a training program. While graphic display of results is not strictly statistical in nature, the author feels that some space should be devoted to it in this chapter.

One of the most common and effective uses of graphic methods is to show the effects of training over a period of time. This can be particularly effective when performance information can be continuously collected on both trained and untrained groups. Suppose that you have been asked to conduct a short training program to reduce the reject rate in an operating department. You want to measure the effects of the program on the reject rate to demonstrate the value of the program. You know that standardized weekly records are kept on rejects and that you can have access to them. This represents an ideal situation to use graphic as well as statistical methods. Let us say that there are four sections in the department doing identical work and that you are going to begin by training one of them. You construct the graph shown in Fig. 19-11 by plotting the weekly reject rates for all four groups for the past several weeks (say, 10 weeks).

The reject rates for the four groups are fairly stable and range from about 10 to 13 percent. You now train one group in techniques for reducing rejects and continue to plot the rates for all groups. As the training begins to take effect, the weekly rates for group 0 begin to decline and look like they will stabilize at about 4 percent. You have shown that training can reduce reject rates by more than half, and furthermore you can now estimate the dollar savings attributable to the training program.

Things do not always work out as neatly as portrayed in Fig. 19-11. However, if the necessary data are available, the construction of such a graph is a simple and effective method of displaying results. This graph also illustrates that pre/post-training measurements should not occur too close to the actual training. This is particularly true when performance is being measured because it usually takes a while for performance to change and stabilize after training.

Summary   In this section we have presented the most frequently used parametric and nonparametric statistical methods for evaluating training results. The methods described are the simpler and less complex of those available. There are many additional methods such as analysis of variance, analysis of covariance, multiple regression, factor analysis, and other multivariate techniques which in some situations are more powerful and appropriate than the ones presented here. However, the proper use of the more complex techniques requires a depth of statistical knowledge which goes beyond the scope of this handbook. In the more complex measurement situations, a competent behavioral scientist with statistical training should be considered for assistance in selecting and implementing the best approach. Also, for the reader who is interested, several statistics textbooks and handbooks are available which give thorough descriptions of the analytic methods which can be used.[5,8,11,12,13]

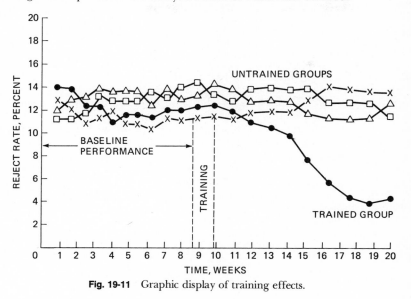

Fig. 19-11 Graphic display of training effects.

APPLICATION OF QUANTITATIVE APPROACHES TO THE MAJOR CATEGORIES OF TRAINING MEASUREMENT

In this final section of the chapter, we shall attempt to pull together what has already been said and to focus on the three major questions which were mentioned earlier:

1. The effects of training on participant personal characteristics
2. The effects of training on participant and organizational performance
3. The return on training investment

Effects of Training on Participant Personal Characteristics

Let us assume that a training director is going to conduct a course in reading skills improvement for employees and that she has proceeded through the steps of the training-design procedure outlined in Fig. 19-1. The objectives of the program are to increase (1) the reading speed and (2) the degree of comprehension of the participants over their level upon entrance into the program. The training director decides to measure the effects of the program before giving it to large numbers of people.[2,14,15,16,17]

First, she decides to use the two-group pre/posttraining measurement experimental design. She chooses two groups (experimental and control) of 20 people each and matches them as well as possible on age, sex, and education, which might have some effect on reading skills. She then tests the accuracy of her group matching by using the Mann-Whitney U test to evaluate differences in age, sex, and educational level between the two groups. She finds that none of the three U tests is significant, which indicates that the groups are not statistically different on the three matching variables. If a U test was significant, she would have to continue matching and testing until the test was not significant.

The training director uses a commercially available reading test as her measuring instrument. Once the groups are matched, she administers the test to both groups. Again, she tests for any differences in the pretraining reading skills scores using the Mann-Whitney U test and discovers no significant difference. Next she puts the experimental group through the training course, while the control group carries on with their regular work routine. A few days after the training course, the training director administers the posttraining reading skills test to both groups. If an alternative but equivalent form of the test is available, it should be used instead of the same form. However, the same form can also be used since any carryover from the pretest should be the same for both groups.

At this point, two types of evaluations can be performed. First, the posttest reading skills scores for each group can be compared using the Mann-Whitney U test. In this comparison the expectation is that the two groups are different in reading skills, with the experimental (trained) group the higher of the two. In addition, the pre/posttraining reading skills test scores can be compared for each group separately. In this case, it would be necessary to use the Wilcoxon Matched-pairs Signed-ranks tests for related groups. The expectation is that there would be no pre/posttraining difference for the control (untrained) group and that the pre/posttraining difference for the experimental (trained) group would show a significant improvement. If the above expectations are met, there is reasonable evidence that the reading skills training program does in fact improve reading speed and comprehension. The measurements outlined above could be continued with additional groups of trainees as a continuing check on training effects.

Effects of Training on Participant and Organizational Performance

The same procedure outlined above can be used to measure the effects of training on performance. However, the data collection method will be different from that used in the case where a commercially available test can be employed as the measuring instrument, and possibly it will be more difficult.

Let us take another example. A training director is asked to improve the productivity and work quality in a food packaging operation. He investigates and finds that the machine operators are not properly trained in how to run and maintain the machinery, and he concludes that a training course in machine operation is needed. The specific objectives are (1) to increase the productivity (output per shift) and (2) to reduce the percentage of rejects (defective packages). Both indicators are routinely recorded for each shift by an automatic counter, and so there are accurate measures of performance on a particular shift. Again, the training director wishes to demonstrate that training does improve productivity and work quality. He selects several groups of operators and matches two groups as best he can to provide an experimental and control group. He then collects baseline production and reject data for all work groups for the previous several weeks to establish typical performance levels for the groups over a period of time. When averaged over several weeks, these typical performance levels can be considered pretraining measures.

The experimental group is then trained, while the control group continues to work as before. The performance data are routinely collected for all groups as before. As time goes on and the training begins to take effect, the expectation is that the performance of the trained group will improve relative to that of the other groups. To note the effects, the training director plots a performance graph such as that shown in Fig. 19-11. As the performance of the trained group diverges (one hopes) from that of the untrained groups, the Mann-Whitney U test can be used to test differences between the trained and untrained groups, while the Wilcoxon Matched-pairs Signed-ranks test can be used to test pre/posttraining differences within the trained and untrained groups.

Measuring Return on Training Investment

One of the major measurement areas gathering momentum is that of analyzing training as an investment which produces a payout. For many years training and development have been considered by organizational managements to be a necessary cost of doing business. Beyond that, little attention has been given to the financial analysis of training as an organizational activity. With the recent attention given to human asset accounting and other methods for measuring human performance and development, there has been an increasing interest in estimating the financial returns of training. This section discusses some relatively simple ways of approaching this problem without going into the more elaborate estimating methods.

In doing a training investment analysis there are three basic sets of estimates to be gathered and combined: (1) program costs, (2) behavioral and performance improvement, and (3) time necessary for the system payout to occur. Each of these is discussed below.

Program Costs   Program costs are fairly easily identifiable and can be categorized into development and acquisition costs and operating costs.

If a training program is to be developed from scratch, the following categories should be considered in estimating costs:

1. Costs of training-staff design (salaries, benefits, etc.)
2. Costs of expert consultants (internal or external)
3. Materials costs
4. Equipment costs
5. Program-trial costs (facilities, materials, staff, trainee costs, equipment costs)
6. Program refinement or redesign costs (staff time, consultant time, etc.)

Sometimes a "packaged" program which will fit the projected training needs is available from an outside source. In this case, the following categories would apply in estimating acquisition costs:

1. Program purchase price
2. Training-staff familiarization time
3. Program-trial costs (facilities, materials, staff, trainee costs, equipment costs)

In terms of operating costs, the following categories should be considered regardless of the source of the program:

1. Instructional-staff costs
2. Materials costs
3. Facilities costs (including meals, etc.)
4. Equipment costs
5. Trainee costs (salaries, living costs if any, etc.)

Naturally, these operating costs are incurred only when the program is conducted.

Behavioral and Performance Improvements   This has been the most difficult area to measure, and its lack of measurement has been largely responsible for the perception of training as a "necessary cost" rather than an investment. However, as has been pointed out, there are various ways to measure results (however imperfectly), and reasonable estimates can often be made from some of the approaches outlined. Once estimates of performance improvement are made, monetary values can be placed on the improvements to permit comparison with program costs. The process of measuring behavioral and performance improvements and of assigning them values is much more difficult at management and supervisory levels than at the skill training levels, primarily because

COST CATEGORY	COST
Training Staff Time	
a. Training director—1 week @ $500	$500.00
b. Project leader—3 weeks @ $300	900.00
Consultant	
a. Production supt.—1 week @ $300	300.00
Materials	
a. Trainee manuals	100.00
b. Trainee materials	100.00
Equipment Costs	
None	0.00
Program Trial	
a. Facilities—1 week @ $100	100.00
b. Materials—flip charts, etc.	50.00
c. Instructor—1 week @ $300	300.00
d. Trainees—10 @ $180	1800.00
Program Refinement	
a. Project director—1 week @ $300	300.00
TOTAL DEVELOPMENT COST	$4450.00

Fig. 19-12   Hypothetical program development costs.

work performance is better defined and more measurable at the production level than at the managerial level. However, as mentioned previously, it is often possible to use work-group results or behaviors such as production, work quality, turnover, grievances, and absenteeism as measures of managerial performance. In any case, the two parts of the return side of the equation are (1) measurements of performance improvements and (2) conversion of these measures to dollar figures for comparison with costs.

System Payout Time   The final factor in the investment equation is an estimate of the payout time in terms of when it will begin, how long it may last, and how stable or predictable it may be. These estimates are based on program costs and anticipated returns. For example, with high development and/or operating costs and relatively low returns, the payout time will be long. Conversely, with low development and/or operating costs and high returns, the payout will be short. Generally speaking, the simpler the skills to be developed, the shorter and greater (relative to program costs) the payout will be. As job and skill complexity becomes greater, the payout will be longer, but financially it may be much greater for the total organization.

Let us now take an example of a specific training situation and see how a return on investment (ROI) analysis could be made. Consider the training situation discussed earlier in which a number of machine operators were to be trained in techniques for reduction of rejects. The program was developed internally by the training director and his staff by an on-the-spot analysis of the operator's job and the necessary skills. Figure 19-12 shows some hypothetical estimates of the development costs of the program.

On the return side of the equation, each operator (of which there are 40) produces about 100 units per day, and the reject rate has been averaging about 11 percent (see Fig. 19-11). Thus on a given day about 4,000 units are produced, of which approximately 440 are rejects. In a five-day week about 20,000 units are made, with about 2,200 rejects. Each unit produces $10 in revenues for the

COST CATEGORY	COST
Instructional Staff	
a. Instructor–1 week @ $300	$300
Materials	
a. Trainee manuals @ $10	100
Facilities	
a. Training room @ $100 per week	100
Equipment	
None	
Trainee Cost	
a. 10 @ $180 per week	1800
TOTAL COST PER CYCLE OF 10 TRAINEES	$2300

Fig. 19-13   Hypothetical program operating costs.

company, and so about $22,000 per week of revenue is lost because of rejects. Thus a small change in the reject rate can have a great effect on revenue. In fact, a 1 percent change in the reject rate is equal to about $2,000 in revenue per week. Immediately this can be recognized as a high-leverage situation if performance can be improved through training.

Estimated Return	
Revenue increase per week	$14,000
Revenue increase per year	$700,000
Estimated Cost	
a. Program development including training of 10 operators	$4,450
b. Operating costs for 3 additional training cycles	$6,900
	$11,350

Fig. 19-14   Hypothetical program return of investment.

You conduct the training program with one section (10 operators) of the department, and by reference to the training-effects graph (see Fig. 19-11), you see that the reject rate declines for the trained group and appears to stabilize in about 12 weeks at approximately 4 percent. Thus the effect on the trial group is to reduce their weekly rejects from about 550 to about 200, which represents additional weekly revenue of approximately $3,500. From this you can estimate that if all operators are trained, the weekly revenue should increase by about $14,000 within about three months after training.

You further calculate the operating costs for conducting each cycle of the program as shown in Fig. 19-13.

You can now make some reasonable estimates of the return on the training investment (see Fig. 19-14).

Thus, on a training investment of about $12,000, the estimated annual return is an additional $700,000 in revenue. This may seem to be an outlandish return to many readers, but we would say that it is certainly well within the realm of possibility in a high-volume, mass-production system. The leverage of training in the job skill area is often tremendous and should be considered very carefully along with other forms of capital investment.

SUMMARY

In this chapter we have discussed the measurement and analysis of educational and training results in a logical and coherent fashion. The author is strongly convinced that if this area is dealt with by training professionals in a careful, thoughtful, and logical way much of the mystery concerning the true measurement of results, and the apparent reluctance to attempt it, will disappear and be replaced by a constructive attitude of insistence on careful evaluation for purposes of improving training performance. Only through this constant attention to improvement will training continue to emerge and develop into the true profession that it is fast becoming. Experience has repeatedly shown that when measurement becomes possible in a given area, that area will progress and develop at an increased rate. The author feels that the training and development area is no exception to this general finding and that it is time to move strongly in the direction of thoughtful and practical measurement of results.

REFERENCES

1. Tracey, W. R.: *Managing Training and Development Systems*, AMACOM, New York, 1974.
2. Barrett, J. E.: "The Case for Evaluation of Training Expenses," *Business Horizons*, pp. 67–72, April 1969.
3. Tracey, W. R.: *Evaluating Training and Development Systems*, American Management Association, New York, 1968.
4. Wheeler, E. A.: "Economic Considerations for Industrial Training," *Training and Development Journal*, pp. 14–18, January 1969.
5. Harris, C. W. (ed.): *Problems in Measuring Change*, The University of Wisconsin Press, Madison, 1963.
6. McGhee, W., and P. W. Thayer: *Training in Business and Industry*, John Wiley & Sons, Inc., New York, 1961.
7. Underwood, B. J.: *Psychological Research*, Appleton-Century-Crofts, Inc., New York, 1957.
8. Winer, B. J.: *Statistical Principles in Experimental Design*, McGraw-Hill Book Company, New York, 1962.
9. Solomon, R. L.: "Extension of Control Group Design," *Psychological Bulletin*, vol. 46, pp. 137–150, 1949.
10. Boneau, C. A.: "The Effect of Violations of Assumptions Underlying the *t* Test," *Psychological Bulletin*, vol. 57, pp. 49–56, 1960.
11. Diamond, Solomon: *Information and Error*, Basic Books, Inc., Publishers, New York, 1959.
12. Guilford, J. P.: *Fundamental Statistics in Psychology and Education*, 2d ed., McGraw-Hill Book Company, New York, 1950.
13. Siegel, S.: *Nonparametric Statistics: For the Behavioral Sciences*, McGraw-Hill Book Company, New York, 1956.

14. Doty, J. H.: "Human Capital Budgeting: Maximizing Returns on Investment," *Industrial Engineering,* pp. 139–145, March–April 1965.
15. Lott, O. C.: "Evaluating to Reduce Training Costs," *Training and Development Journal,* pp. 38–41, January 1967.
16. Mincer, J.: "On-the-Job Training: Costs, Returns and Some Implications," *Journal of Political Economy,* pp. 50–73, October 1968.
17. Norman, J. H.: *Dollars and Cents Evaluation of a Training Program,* Temco Aircraft Corp., 1961.

BIBLIOGRAPHY

Barnes, R. M.: *Work Sampling,* John Wiley & Sons, Inc., New York, 1957.

Blumenfeld, W. S., and M. G. Holland "A Model for the Empirical Evaluation of Training Effectiveness," *Personnel Journal,* pp. 637–640, August 1971.

Bolar, M.: "Evaluating Management Development Programs in Industry," *Training and Development Journal,* pp. 34–39, March 1970.

Catalonello, R. F., and D. L. Kirkpatrick: "Evaluating Training Programs: The State of the Art," *Training and Development Journal,* pp. 2–9, May 1968.

Cote, D. P.: "Measuring Results of Supervisory Training," *Training and Development Journal,* pp. 38–46, November 1969.

Fergeson, W. C.: "Quantitative Evaluation of Training Using Student Reaction," *Training and Development Journal,* pp. 36–42, November 1968.

Harrison, J. A.: "A Price Tag for Training Services," *Training in Business and Industry,* pp. 41–44, February 1969.

Holder, J. J.: "Evaluation of an In-Company Management Training Program," *Training and Development Journal,* pp. 24–27, April 1972.

House, R. J.: *Management Development: Design, Evaluation and Implementation,* University of Michigan, Bureau of Industrial Relations, Ann Arbor, 1967.

Kohn, Vera: *A Selected Bibliography on Evaluation of Management Training and Development Programs,* American Foundation for Management Research, New York, 1969.

Kohn, Vera, and T. C. Parker: "Some Guidelines for Evaluating Management Development Programs," *Training and Development Journal,* pp. 18–23, July 1969.

Livingston, H. S.: "The Training Function: Overhead or Profit," *Training and Development Journal,* pp. 18–21, August 1970.

Miner, J.: *Studies in Management Education,* Springer Publishing Co., Inc., New York, 1965.

Reevers, E. T., and J. M. Jensen: "Effectiveness of Program Evaluation," *Training and Development Journal,* pp. 36–41, January 1972.

Rose, H.: "A Plan for Training Evaluation," *Training and Development Journal,* pp. 38–51, May 1968.

Roy, S. K., and A. M. Dolke: "Evaluation of a Supervisory Training Program," *Training and Development Journal,* pp. 35–39, December 1971.

Shaffer, D. E.: "Control through Measurement," *Training Directors Journal,* pp. 39–50, September 1969.

Travers, R. M. W.: *An Introduction to Educational Research,* 2d ed., The Macmillan Company, New York, 1964.

Wolfe, J.: "Evaluating the Training Effort," *Training and Development Journal,* pp. 20–27, May 1973.

Applications in Training

Chapter **20**

Organization Development

THOMAS H. PATTEN, JR.

PETER B. VAILL

Thomas H. Patten, Jr., *is Professor of Organizational Behavior and Personnel Management and Associate Director, School of Labor and Industrial Relations at Michigan State University, East Lansing, Michigan. Dr. Patten is a graduate of Brown University and Cornell University, where he received his Ph.D. in 1959. Prior to joining MSU in 1967, he taught at the University of Detroit and spent eight years with the Ford Motor Company in the personnel and organization staff. He is the author of two books:* The Foreman: Forgotten Man of Management *(American Management Association, 1968) and* Manpower Planning and the Development of Human Resources *(Wiley, 1971). He edited* Organization Development: Emerging Dimensions and Concepts *(ASTD, 1973), and he has also published many articles. He is a member of the International Personnel Management Association; the Industrial Relations Research Association; the American Sociological Association; the American Compensation Association; the NTL Institute for Applied Behavioral Science, Organizational Development Network; the Academy of Management, Organizational Development Division; and the ASTD Organization Development Division. In 1972, he was made National General Chairman of the ASTD OD Division. He is a member of Phi Kappa Phi, Phi Beta Kappa, and other honorary associations.*

Peter B. Vaill *is Dean of the School of Government and Business Administration and Professor of Management Science at George Washington University. He has done teaching and research in managerial behavior, organization development, and the interrelations of organization technologies and organizational behavior. He has published numerous articles, particularly in organization development. Dr. Vaill has had consulting relationships with a wide variety of organizations. He has conducted management training programs for many governmental agencies, private companies, and institutes. He has also presented papers at meetings of professional associations and societies, including the American Psychological Association and the American Institute of Industrial Engineers. He holds an A.B. from the University of Minnesota and an M.B.A. and D.B.A. from the Harvard Business School.*

This chapter presents a survey of the theory and practice of organization development (OD). It is organized around five major topics: (1) requisite concepts for conducting OD, (2) the nature of techniques employed in OD, (3) implementation of OD techniques, (4) the conduct of OD, and (5) the future of OD. For heuristic purposes, we define OD as planned efforts to improve the management of organizations.

REQUISITE CONCEPTS

There is no shortage of concepts and theories to draw upon as one considers going at the business of deliberately trying to change the way an organization is operating. There are, in fact, a number of "comprehensive models" of how the change process ought to go—models which summarize the work of one theorist or another and which crystallize that person's own normative view of how OD should be conducted. And yet practitioners report consistently that it is not possible to take a published model of the change process "off the shelf" and plug it in to a particular organization. Starting conditions vary too widely; organization histories and casts of characters have their own unique texture, which must be accommodated; the *reasons* for entering into a change program differ from organization to organization; and the motives, power, and role of those initiating change also vary widely. For such reasons as these, no existing model of the change process in an organization spans all the nuances and subtleties. All models have to be stretched, modified, or "fudged" to take account of local realities.

Thus a single change model is not presented in this chapter. Rather, the *issues* which *any* change model has to address are first described in the present section. Then some particularly effective techniques are described, following which some case studies of their actual use are presented. Lastly, we speculate about the future.

There are seven broad issues which any model of the process of organization development has to take into account. These are listed below. Each issue is then examined in more detail, and the key concepts OD has evolved for dealing with each issue are noted. The seven issues, phrased as questions, are as follows:

- What is the nature of the entity that is to be changed?
- What are the reasons for initiating change?
- How is the role of the person or persons initiating change to be conceived?
- How is the phenomenon of "resistance to change" to be conceived of at the level of the person, the group, and the collectivity?
- What view is taken of the *process* by which change will proceed?
- How will the effects of change efforts be determined?
- What larger philosophies of human beings and society undergird attempts to change a particular organization?

In response to each of these broad questions, OD has a set of "answers," so to speak—concepts, theories, research findings, and so forth—which form the basis of creating a particular strategy for changing a particular organization. We shall now proceed to analyze these answers.

Nature of the Entity to Be Changed

The great watershed concept which OD relies on to deal with this question is the idea of a *social system.* The idea has roots in sociology and anthropology stretching well back into the nineteenth century, but the first and still perhaps the most exhaustive statement of the manifestation of the social system in industry was made in the Hawthorne researches.[1] People do not exist as single units, nor are they related to one another only as some external authority like management says they should be related (i.e., through "formal organization"). Nor does the nature of the relations they develop with one another derive only from the activities required for survival in the particular environment in which they are located.

The idea of a social system presumes that people develop stable relationships with one another which have deep psychological meaning for organizational members and which are observable by those who are "outside" the system. Thus, says OD, in changing an organization one is not merely making some mechanical rearrangements of the activities people will perform. The context and texture of people's lives are being changed, and the internalized rules they have adopted for governing their own behavior and that of other members are being fundamentally altered.

Since the original social-system ideas were stated, an enormous amount of research and theory have been brought to bear on *how* social systems operate. Concepts of *norms* and *roles* have received major attention.[2] The idea of *interaction*—what members of an organization say and do, to and with one another—has come to be central.[3] Hitherto unguessed-at energies and creative potentials in all kinds of social systems have been discovered. It is probably no exaggeration to say that the whole movement known as "participative management" relies on the idea that a kind and quality of organization and wisdom exist in the social system that far transcend anything that can be arbitrarily *put* there by outsiders.

OD does *not* say that some human collectivities are social systems and some are not. Rather, it says that any human collectivity that one would consider altering significantly is usefully conceived as an ongoing social system with the properties which social systems have been found to possess. And the hallmark characteristics are the *feelings* members have developed for one another and the *interactions* through which feelings are expressed.

Reasons for Initiating Change

Wrapped up in this question are all the issues of goals, purposes, and objectives which are present in any system that has some formal mission. OD has a very mixed history on the question of the reasons for attempting to change an organization. It has been accused of being merely the tool of a repressive management or merely the latest velvet glove of paternalism.[4] It has been accused of attempting to bootleg idealistic values about human nature into the organization whether they pertain to organization needs and goals or not. It has been accused of being overly person-oriented at the expense of performance.

Gradually over the past five or six years, however, a consensus has emerged that OD has to focus on how the organization can be more effective in its environment—that this should be the overriding reason for instituting a change program.[5] Considerations of human welfare and betterment do not therefore take a back seat. Rather, they are kept *related* to performance issues. Philosophical debates about whether ultimately the needs of people are identical with the needs of the organization have been dropped as undecidable in favor of a more limited and practical approach which seeks to find ways in the particular organization at hand whereby both the people and the organization can be more effective and satisfy more needs.

OD has discovered another important facet of the goals issues—namely, that the *process* by which goals are formulated should *itself* be an object of change in many organizations. The clarification of the basic mission and the establishment of specific objectives that are consistent with the mission have more and more been processes receiving OD attention. Today it is a matter of course for OD specialists to assist the organization in clarifying why it wants to change before they do anything else—and an increasingly common reason for desiring organizational change is to enable the organization to pursue objectives it has not pursued before.

Role of the Change Agent

It is not an exaggeration to say that OD exists as an organized field today because of two broad answers to this question which have been evolving over the past 30 years or so. These two answers interlock and are mutually supportive:

1. Given the nature of social systems in the modern organizational world, the command/obedience style of management is less and less appropriate to changing an organization since research shows that this style has a high probability of producing unintended consequences that are often inimical to the goals of the change.
2. It has been found that people whose whole cultural experience has been an education in the rightness of the command/obedience style can rarely make significant modifications in their behavior to find new adaptive relations with their organization without the help of third parties who are professionally trained to give this kind of help.

In other words, we have a field of OD today because a centuries-old leadership style (command/obedience) has become obsolete. But we have not yet institutionalized the cultural and educational patterns to produce leaders in large numbers who are *naturally* adapted to the organizations they must lead. Adaptations must therefore be ad hoc and personal, and we have discovered that consultants are effective adjuncts to managers who find that they are going to have to make some of these adaptations themselves.

OD is thus at present a repository of new ideas about organizational leadership and of new ideas about how managers can be helped by consultants to change their styles. At the present time both sets of new ideas—about leadership and about consultancy—are extremely tentative, fragile, and undergoing constant change. Because of this, it is incorrect to say that one can learn a new managerial style and/or learn about consultancy and then simply perform the new techniques. What is equally important is to evolve a personal learning style that will sustain one through the continuous changes in ideas that will mark the next 30 years.

The death of command/obedience as the dominant management style traces from research about how effective leaders behave. Beginning in the early 1960s, a "situational" view of leadership emerged which says that effective leaders are those whose behavior is attuned to the needs and opportunities inherent in the situation in which they are immersed.[6] Their own feelings, ideas, and impulses are defined as part of the situation, and therefore "situational leadership" is not merely doing what others want. Rather, it is the ability to negotiate and mediate among different and often conflicting demands—of which the leader's own needs are one set. It is the ability to find and articulate consensus and to lead in translating consensus into action. As noted above, however, situational leadership is a fragile idea compared with the massive weight in our culture of the command/obedience style of behavior. Few good case studies exist of what good situational leadership looks like. We have practically no criteria that people can use to tell them when they are behaving situationally.

Therefore, to experiment with this style, managers need help in understanding its importance, and they also need support and feedback as they begin to change their own style. It is at this point that the consultant's role becomes important.

A great deal of theory exists today about how OD consultants can be of help to managers and to organizations. The growth of theory has accelerated dramatically in the past five years and is no longer merely a collection of dos and don'ts and rules of thumb.[7] In the early and middle 1960s it became clear that OD consulting is something quite different from technical advice giving, that the creation and maintenance of a genuine helping relationship with the client are the primary task, and that it is the client's needs—not the consultant's—which are of main importance. These insights developed hand in hand with the realization that in most situations, the client (a manager) was involved in changing both his or her own behavior and that of others—a process which could not be aided by a consultant who simply supplied formulas.

Another key development was the role of the *internal* consultant, someone who was on the payroll and who knew the organization from within. External, independent consultants can be crucial to getting a change process started and can offer valuable suggestions at strategic choice points, but the day-to-day support the manager and others need often can be supplied by an in-house consultant more effectively and cheaply.

The development of the internal role has been far from easy, however, for a myriad of complex questions regarding the internal person's responsibility and authority have had to be worked through. Nevertheless, this work has gone forward rapidly, and today there are probably at least 2,000 internal consultants around the world who can be said to have a sophisticated understanding of the role—with the number growing at a rate of 10 to 15 percent a year.

Internal consultants, by virtue of their continued access to the system, have moved consultancy well beyond a one-to-one relationship with a manager, to explore the ways the consultant can exert a supportive and facilitating force on the *organizational* processes which are in need of change. The internal consultant (or team of internal consultants) can work at several levels of the system and can focus on the crucial *linkages* between subunits of the organization, which often are not directly accessible to the line manager. To define the role of a consultant to an organization rather than to a single manager is the major frontier for today's internal OD consultants. This does not mean that they no longer work with single managers, but rather that their stance toward the manager is changing. The thrust is away from forming relations with managers to help them work on their interpersonal style, and toward forming relations with them in order that their key managerial functions of deciding, planning, organizing, and leading can be focused on.

And so the evolution of OD has been both a cause of, and a response to, two major and fundamental changes: for line managers, a trend away from the command/obedience model and toward an as-yet ill-defined role of participative leadership, and for consultants, a trend away from detached, external advice giving and toward an attached role of support and facilitation.

Coping with "Resistance to Change"

In the 1940s and 1950s, resistance to change was treated as a genuine force to be reckoned with and overcome. OD has made major contributions to understanding what is really going on when something we loosely call "resistance to change" manifests itself. OD now sees the organization as a *field* of interacting forces and processes rather than as a two-dimensional battlefield of forces for change and forces for resistance. Social-system ideas helped to clarify this. So too has the increasing understanding of the *culture* of a group or organization: patterns of behavior observed in the organization are functional for certain needs of members and of the system as a whole. Norms arise to buttress these patterns. To label these behavior patterns "resistances" is to risk overlooking their value and functionality for members.

Perhaps the body of theory of which OD has made the greatest use in understanding resistance is motivation theory. Beginning in the middle 1950s managers and human relations specialists began to realize that people behave as they do for reasons which have deep meaning for them, even if these reasons are not sanctioned or recognized by the organization. McGregor crystallized this in his statement of Theory Y, which summarizes the person's *own* reasons for acting as he or she does, in contrast to the reasons invented by some outsider who is trying to get the person to conform and obey. What is important about McGregor today is not so much the accuracy of Theory Y as the base his original statement provided for further research and theory about the needs, goals, and intentions of people in organizations.

When one grants that each individual's behavior makes sense to that person, it is clear that the negative label "resistance" may be missing the point. OD realizes this, and it has evolved a variety of approaches which have a common feature: No change should be installed which does not make sense to those who are affected by it.

View of the Processes of Change

For many years, in all management theory as well as OD in particular, a search has been going on for a useful way of thinking about the process of change through time in an organization. The operative questions are: How do initiatives for change "cascade" through the system? At what *rate* can we expect change to proceed? When can we expect to notice results? How long will the system be in a state of flux before it stabilizes in some new pattern of behaviors? How are we to regard apparent lapses and reversions to previous "outmoded modes" of functioning?

Kurt Lewin's original change model of "unfreezing-moving-refreezing" was an early statement about the process of change.[8] OD has subsequently placed most of its emphasis on the "unfreezing" portion of the Lewin model. What is meant by "moving" an organization and "refreezing" it in a more viable mode has received less attention. Some would even argue that the "refreezing" metaphor is misleading in today's turbulent world—that what is needed is to prepare the organization for a life of "organic flux" and for the possibility that truly *stable* patterns are a will-o'-the-wisp. Nevertheless, statements like Greiner's[9] are helpful in that they convey a sense of the sequence in which things happen in a change process.

Comments we have made earlier about the nature of the system being changed, about the role of initiators, and about the meaning of resistance are germane to this problem of the process of change. OD has come around to the understanding of the process of change as something that is *not a simple linear sequence*. Change initiatives occur on several fronts at once. Resistances and sticking points occur on all these fronts. Some thrusts occur quickly and easily, while others seem to occur with glacial slowness. Unexpectedly, the system may appear to revert to tried-and-true methods even though everyone agrees that these are bankrupt and discredited ways of doing business.

In OD thinking, the overall change process is increasingly being seen as a somewhat disjointed *political* and *opportunistic* process in which a multiyear time horizon must be taken and in which periodic reversions are not only inevitable but also possibly beneficial in that they help the system reaffirm its commitment to change: once new ways are glimpsed, it is often helpful to "fall back" to old ways to rediscover their inadequacy.

It is important to say that no universal and comprehensive theory of the process of change now exists. There is at the present time a good deal of theorizing about the stages and process of growth, but the major theoretical advances are yet to be made, and the wisest course of action is for an individual organization to develop its own model of the process of change.

The main contributions that OD theory can make at present are the ideas that (1) the change process is not a linear sequence, (2) it will almost always take longer to bring about significant change than one might assume at the outset, and (3) it seems to be useful to think of the change process in terms of broad phases which overlap and are interdependent but which nonetheless have a cumulative effect.

Determining the Effects of Change

Like the previous question, the problem of measuring change is one in which the important work is yet to be done. Human relations in industry, the precursor of OD, was fascinated all through the 1950s and early 1960s with scientific approaches in which independent variables were manipulated to produce effects on dependent variables. Attempts to control for the effects of other variables were sometimes made, as in the classical experimental approach.

However, this strategy is being questioned increasingly. In the real world, it is difficult if not impossible to *prove* what changed what. Many of the key dependent variables are hard to operationalize, e.g., "organization climate," "openness," and "innovation." What *causes* these variables to change is equally hard to pin down, especially if we are conceiving the organization as a field of interacting and mutually dependent forces.

So cause-and-effect approaches are being supplemented, and in some cases supplanted, by other approaches. One such approach we may call *perceptual tests*. Perceptual tests ask: Do the people in the system who are living with the forces and patterns which are the targets of change feel that change is occurring? Instead of asking for objective, scientific proof of change, we ask whether the patient "feels better." This is admittedly a less rigorous test, and risks of distortion are very real, but OD has found it a useful approach.

A second strategy is called *action research*. Action research asks: Do the results so far provide guidance for what should be done next? The word "guidance" is important, for action research does not insist that the next steps be crystal-clear, logically arrived-at deductions from results to date—something a classical scientific model would insist upon. Action research entails a process of cyclical intervention and feedback where the system itself is assumed to be in a process of continuous change.

Finally, OD has moved away from the classical role of science, which is to test and accept or refute hypotheses. To be able to accept or refute hypotheses is the whole point in classical science of defining variables and controlling their effects on one another. OD is less interested in proving and disproving hypotheses than in creating change in something like the desired direction. The assumption is that other researchers can go back over the results later to seek explanations for what happened.

This is not to say that OD is consciously or deliberately unscientific, but rather that OD is practical and results-oriented in the final analysis. It is interested, like management, in helping change to occur. Where OD people can see how to help change occur, they tend not to stop and convert their efforts into a controlled experiment.

Underlying Philosophy of People, Society, and Change

OD, like the human relations movement it grew out of, has been accused frequently of being overly idealistic and dewy-eyed about the potentialities of human nature. OD people are often pictured as soft, woolly-minded dreamers who do not really understand how the world is hooked together.

This caricature has little basis in fact, for the OD profession contains the same spectrum from tough- to tender-mindedness that any field does. It is true that OD people in general believe in, and are committed to, substantial change in the way our organizations operate. They certainly reject any suggestion that this is the best of all possible worlds—that no more human potential can be drawn on than is utilized at present, that no more adaptive structures can be fashioned than those we have, or that conflict can never be managed more smoothly than it presently is.

As is true of the other questions raised in this section, OD needs a view of people in the organization that both is *realistic* and *defines* the potential for change that exists in a particular setting. OD has tended to move away from universal theories of human nature, therefore, in favor of ways of thinking that help identify what is achievable in particular settings.

The universal theories as stated by people like McGregor, Argyris, and Tannenbaum and Davis[10] have not been thrown out. Rather, attention has shifted to what is practical and possible, with the universalistic statements forming a foundation.

One thing seems clear: OD will never be a technical exercise in which no broad philosophy of people in the organization is needed. This is because OD's *focus* is human beings—their feelings, needs, and relations with others. People are "valuing animals" who commit themselves. Without a clearly articulated value system of its own, OD cannot deal with the infinite variety of opportunities and constraints which the valuing animals create for themselves. OD is thus embedded in and chooses to address a matrix of human values in action. Thus it is confronted with all the dilemmas of choice confronting any action taker—dilemmas that can be worked through only with the aid of a basic set of values about people and about change.

OD's fundamental tenet is that organizations can do better and that the lives of those who inhabit organizations can be better.

To recapitulate up to this point, we have tried to characterize OD by discussing it in relation to seven issues which any system aimed at changing organizations must resolve for itself. We have avoided a tight definition of OD, not because there are no such definitions, but rather because OD people themselves like to keep their definitions loose. Given the variety they are dealing with, this is a wise decision, and we replicate the decision in this chapter by characterizing OD but not delimiting it.

TECHNIQUES, INTERVENTION STRATEGY, AND OD VALUES

Having identified seven key issues OD must deal with, we now become more specific. As we have seen, OD is clearly one of the most significant developments at the present time in training and, indeed, is inclusive of far more active and potent interventions than the word "training" or "education" ordinarily implies. OD is not a panacea for all the ills of a work organization,[11] and in turning to the remaining sections of this chapter on techniques and applications of OD in companies and governmental organizations, we try to avoid overselling or overembellishing inherently exciting but somewhat amorphous ideas. There is much evidence that OD has been oversold and misapplied by marginally qualified trainers functioning as entrepreneurs,[12] and lengthy, serious, and thoughtful treatments of the ethical questions in sensitivity training and OD are just now starting to become available in published form.[13]

Some Key Techniques

At the present time OD has progressed far beyond the omnibus and uncritical application of sensitivity training, although the latter is still widely used on an intraorganization basis in an OD effort when it is considered needed. The three main techniques (in the sense of OD facilitative-tactical modes) which we discuss are team building, Management by Objectives (and job enrichment, which we believe—to the extent that it is participative and problem-solving-oriented—is analogous to MBO for lower-level employees[14]), and internal consulting. (We omit discussion in this chapter of micro-level techniques or methods of learning about human relations such as T groups, fishbowls, confrontation meetings, Transactional Analysis, sensing, and all the similar methods and designs for learning utilized in OD efforts. This handbook contains a separate chapter on laboratory methods.) All three of the macro-level modes are closely interrelated, and, as some behavioral scientists have shown, they can be integrated to constitute a strategic model for organizational change.[15] However, if we were to survey the *Fortune* magazine top 500 and second 500 industrial companies, we would probably find only a handful that have introduced OD as a fully integrated strategic model for change.

CHOOSING THE POINT OF INTERVENTION

Ideally, OD should be introduced from the top of the organization and cascade downward through the various levels of management. It is much easier to gain acceptance and to achieve more fundamental results for managerial improvement by introducing OD at the level of the chief executive officer and assisting in building a "team at the top." We acknowledge that it is sometimes possible to intervene lower in an organization and build teams or transmit some OD values into the organization by carrying out a successful demonstration project or series of demonstration projects in parts of the organization which have systemic autonomy and a certain amount of budgetary and personnel integrity. It is to be hoped that these lower-level organizational interventions will act like brush fires and ultimately result in a conflagration that the team at the top cannot ignore. But the problem of starting an OD effort is reduced to a minimum when cultural changes flow down through the organization from the top.[16] Only salmon are notable for their records of success in swimming upstream to spawn. However, inasmuch as there is turnover at the top, a heavy time demand on top managers to implement OD, and a need to keep the impetus behind the OD effort at the top, merely starting at the top does not, of course, guarantee success.

Further Comments on Values

The practice of OD is based on several key values. These include acceptance of the organization's need to fulfill its responsibility to its various communities for interdependency and continuity, for increasing effectiveness in performance, and for development of an internal climate in which personal growth is supported. In the writers' view, the inculcation of values and means for fostering individual growth comes first.

To realize these values, OD employs its knowledge of behavioral science in planned interventions in the processes of the organization. These interventions may be concerned with the technical problems of the business, its administrative problems, and the human problems of its social system,[17] although we customarily think of OD as being concerned with the latter. We turn to these problems in more detail below.

OD must be a long-range, continuous effort enduring three to five years to be maximally effective because it must eventually come to grips with changing the norms and values in an organization, which are impervious parts of the culture. Changing an administrative practice or procedure may be accomplished in a short time and have some effect on organizational behavior, but fundamental cultural change takes longer and should begin with unblocking individuals and releasing their energy, a difficult but important prelude to team building and other typical OD facilitative-tactical modes.

OD is necessarily innovative because the problems with which it deals are seldom identical; each must be solved in its own special terms consonant with a specific work organization's culture. Moreover, the stream of new findings from research in the behavioral sciences provides a continuing opportunity as time goes by for more cogent interventions within and between all levels—individual, group, and organizational. The current theory and results of research should be evaluated and absorbed into the strategy of OD as a matter of accepted practice. The usefulness of these new ideas should be subjected to constant scrutiny; inappropriate ones should be discarded, and potentially effective ones should be tried out.

As a long-term, continuing effort with new ideas fostering innovative techniques, OD must continuously evaluate the results of its procedure. The feedback loops in the various subsystems of an organization provide a ready mechanism for this evaluation. If a technical, administrative, or human problem that has been solved has been treated in a way beneficial to organizational health and if the resulting performance of the organization shows improvement, the intervention may be considered to have passed the test of usefulness.[18]

The social system in an organization involves the relationships and interactions of employees and managers. As we have suggested above, OD specialists typically concern themselves with (but do not limit themselves to) the human problems of the social system. They can detect opportunities for improvements of various kinds by careful analysis of the transactions between people at the interfaces in an organization, as has been well described by behavioral scientists.[19] The results of their analyses, when transformed into planned interventions, can affect any of the major subsystems of an organization—the technical, administrative, or human. OD specialists may therefore recommend such interventions as installing MBO, revising the reward system by the introduction of a new pay plan, or introducing team-building sessions for top management or a newly formed project group.[20]

The technical, administrative, and social systems may be visualized as closed systems because they are bounded within the organization. MBO is a closed-loop internal planning and control system that provides a type of secondary regulation for the work organization by returning information through feedback loops to control the performance of the technical, administrative, and social systems. The essential difference between the open system of the whole organization and any closed-loop planning and control system that regulates internal performance lies in the quality of feedback information. A closed-loop system can provide feedback of performance on a timely, short-term basis. Corrective action to bring the overall system back into control can be taken quickly. On the other hand, the overall organization, because it is an open system, has no way of knowing its various points of no return. Consequently, it must rely on interim measures and the adaptability of its component systems to adjust to changes imposed by the environment.[21] MBO has been such a popular OD intervention because it can be a timely feedback regulator and can lead rather quickly and obviously to improved managerial performance.

The Special Problem of Strategic Models in OD

Previously, we discussed strategic models in OD, while suggesting that the use of most techniques has been tactical and opportunistic rather than strategic. Strategic organizational development does not start with acceptance or rejection of the status quo in an organization, but rather with an intellectual model of an ideal. The properties of the model are specified by theory, logic, and empirical data. The model's validity is pretested against probable circumstances projected over definite periods of time. In this sense, a strategic OD model is a blueprint of what should be, not what is. The use of a strategic model is not equivalent to installing MBO or any other closed system because these can be undertaken within the restraints of the status quo. Such installations need not involve an active process of learning to reject the outmoded aspects of the status quo, although they can be made into useful tools in the implementation of a strategic model of organizational excellence.[22]

In the first section of this chapter, we said that there are seven basic issues which any approach to changing an organization must deal with. The interrelation of those seven issues was not stressed at the time, but we should point out that a strategic model of an overall change program could be developed by formulating answers to those seven issues, which are interdependent with one another. For example, there is a clear opportunity to interrelate our model of the nature of the system being changed with our ideas about where resistance will come from. The persons initiating change are clearly the ones who need an overall philosophy of what they are doing. *The more an organization develops a deliberately consistent and integrated position on these seven issues, the more we can see that it has an overall strategy.*

The authors of this chapter take the position that it is desirable to strive for such coherence, but are quick to add that much organizational change has occurred without an overall strategy. Some major change efforts have been carried out in organizations where a clear position was held only on the goals question and the values question. A great deal of change has been created with a clear position on the leadership issue alone, with issues in all other categories left rather vague.

There are pros and cons on the question of how thoroughly answers to these seven issues need to be worked out before proceeding with a change effort. We think the degree to which an organization tries to proceed systematically should be a matter of choice rather than accident, and so we sketch below a few of the key considerations.

Systematic OD has several advantages. First, it relies on theory, logic, and empirical data. It can produce enthusiasm for change and participation in it, rather than resistance to change. The only limit to possible change stemming from strategic OD lies in the capacity of people to think, analyze, and reason (which we turn to in the last part of this section). Risk is reduced because the projected changes can be pretested for probable consequences of the OD efforts.

There are some disadvantages to systematic OD. The depth of intellectual endeavor requires rigorous thinking, which is both demanding and time-consuming. Many managers find it difficult to give up the fun and excitement of "fire fighting" to have time for conceptual reflection.[23] There is no one strategic OD model or system which has been universally endorsed and which points in the proper direction for an OD effort. Therefore, many OD efforts are necessarily innovative and experimental, if not downright opportunistic, because OD practitioners are reluctant to buy into grand, overall designs.

The Unblocked Person and OD Techniques

Turning back to the human limits on implementing strategic OD, we identify a conception of the nature of human beings that we hope is consonant with strategic OD and suggests what managers should resemble in a final form at a designated point in time, namely, at the end of an OD team-building effort which has unblocked them and freed them to use more of their own and others' resources in a managerial role. Such an effort will often mean that they have had a sensitivity training or encounter group experience somewhere along the line in the OD effort—and quite possibly as a part of, or prelude to, team building.

The theory of open encounter as it exists in sensitivity training and T groups is based upon the belief that the individual is a unified being and functions on many levels at once: physical, emotional, intellectual, interpersonal, social, and spiritual. These levels are considered to be intimately interrelated, and actions on any one level are accompanied by actions on all others. The theory assumes that there is a life flow in the human being on all these levels, an energy that flows through cycles of motivation, preparation, performance, and consummation. When these energy cycles are interrupted, physical blocks lead to physical illness, emotional blocks to underachievement, social blocks to incompatibilities, and spiritual blocks to postponement of the realization of the total person. Removal of the blocks is a therapeutic task, but development of the energy cycles is the task of education and fully living.[24] OD can provide this education and this new way of fully living as a "turned-on" manager when it results in culture change in an organization. Therapy can be sought from the relevant professional resources, as needed.

The life flow of the individual functions best in the presence of openness. Blocks can be removed when people are open to themselves and others. Achieving self-awareness and being open and honest with others allows the person's energy to flow freely, and it makes the individual more effective in problem solving and decision making, not only in managerial work, but also in everyday life. Self-deception and dishonesty block energy and take it out of the life flow potentially available to the person. In a word, the open encounter in everyday life in a work organization unblocks energy and allows it to be used for more productive purposes.

Our self-concept is enhanced when we take responsibility for ourselves in everyday life—at work or elsewhere. If we feel that we are responsible, competent, important, and likable, we will be more likely to express those parts of ourselves. If we have a weak and restricted self-concept, we will not live up to our full capacity. To the extent that our self-concept is expanded and enhanced, more of our potentialities will be utilized, and our life flow will be invigorated.[25] Thus successful team-building efforts which expand self-awareness, improve the individual's self-concept, diffuse openness, and enable people to be more effective in problem solving and decision making in a group situation are fundamental to starting on strategic OD, launching an MBO effort, or enabling the rewards system in an organization to act as an incentive for performance. We find few organizations "doing" OD today that seem to have linked these matters together to identify a clear-cut ideal model toward which they are moving by planned stages.

Instead, organizations tend to use the techniques described below piecemeal. Each technique derives directly from what we have just said about the process and importance of helping people become unblocked. It remains now for organizations to develop change strategies which link these techniques together into a more impactful effort.

Team Building

Turning to the specific OD techniques (in the sense of facilitative and tactical modes) presently used with some popularity, we indicated at the outset that all these were discussed at least 15 years ago by Douglas McGregor but have been elaborated upon and polished by numerous practitioners since then. For example, team building, MBO and JE (job enrichment), and internal consulting were described in characteristic terms by McGregor, and his descriptions bear repeating here because conceptually his overall characterizations appear to be as valid today as they were then. We merely identify and generally define in this chapter what these OD techniques are as a prelude to examining which companies and organizations are doing each at the present time. (Other chapters in the handbook provide additional information on these techniques which need not be repeated here.) It should also be understood that we use the terms "team building," "Management by Objectives," "job enrichment," and "internal consulting" generically, recognizing that organizations may have their unique names or designations for their own in-house versions of these modes. (For example, MBO is called "goal setting" in many organizations.)

Team building is an OD facilitative-tactical mode that is intended to make a group effective and achieve unity of purpose. Most managerial teams are not teams at all, but collections of individual relationships with the boss in which each individual is vying with the other for greater power, prestige, recognition, and personal autonomy. Under these conditions, unity of purpose is a myth, and the managerial team is inept at accomplishing objectives through group effort. A good group is one in which the atmosphere tends to be informal, comfortable, and relaxed; there is considerable discussion, in which virtually everyone participates; the tasks or objectives of the group are well understood and accepted by the members; the group members actively listen to one another; there is disagreement, but it is worked through to a consensus (with no formal voting as a cop-out); there is frequent, frank, and relatively comfortable criticism; people are free in expressing their feelings as well as their ideas and have no hidden agenda; clear work assignments are made and accepted; leadership in the group shifts as needed to draw forth and utilize all the human resources in the group; there is little or no struggle for power and control because the main concern is to get the job done consistent with cultural values in the organization; and, finally, the group self-consciously stops periodically to examine how well it is doing as a group in accomplishing its tasks and how the feelings and behaviors of members are contributing to the group and its work. In a word, team building as an OD technique attempts to move a group forward in all the aforementioned directions. It is based on the clear realization that the highest commitment to organizational objectives and the most successful collaboration in achieving them require unique kinds of interaction which can occur only in a highly effective group setting.[26]

Management by Objectives

Management by Objectives is a way of managing people that emphasizes the integration of personal objectives and organizational objectives and is built upon self-control. The purpose of MBO is to encourage goal integration, to create a situation in which a subordinate can achieve his or her own goals best by directing his or her efforts and energies toward the objectives of the enterprise or overall work organization. MBO is, in concept, a calculated attempt to link improvement in managerial competence with the satisfaction of higher-level ego and self-actualization needs. MBO does not tack a new set of duties on top of the existing managerial job. It is, rather, a different way of fulfilling one's existing responsibilities—of "running the job."[27] Put another way, MBO is a flexible, rational, participative way for the manager to plan and control the accomplishment of work.[28]

In practice, MBO is usually translated, as we have discussed, into a closed-loop system designed for managing managers and professional employees in which a superior and his or her subordinates sit down and jointly set specific objectives which are to be accomplished within a set time frame and for which the subordinate is then held accountable. But practice varies widely as to the degree of formalization and the quality of superior-subordinate goal negotiation, commitment, and participation.[29] Our hunch is that MBO works best after the groups which intend to use it have been developed into a team whose members openly encounter one another.

Job Enrichment

Job enrichment (or JE) started out as a limited tactical change in managing employees in which several well-known companies undertook to increase the duties and responsibilities of certain routine jobs as a way of minimizing some of their unpleasant features. The idea of redesigning jobs to include meaningful tasks rather than highly specialized repetitive operations appeared to offer vast possibilities for motivating employees with incentives in the jobs themselves.[30] A number of leading contemporary behavioral scientists have taken the position (based upon research and theory) that the factors which motivate are "growth" factors, or those which give the worker a sense of personal accomplishment through the challenge of the job itself. In other words, motivation is in the content of the work, the internal dynamics that the employee experiences in completing his or her task.[31]

In JE the emphasis changes from rigid management direction and control to more participative modes, where much of the planning and controlling associated with doing the work are restored to the employee. To this extent JE is akin to MBO for higher-level employees because lower-level employees are asked to make greater input into the conduct of their work and to link their goals and satisfactions to the attainment of organizational objectives. Both JE and MBO are fundamentally grounded on self-control and humanistic notions. Both can become important cornerstones of OD and bases for entirely new styles of organizational management.

Internal Consulting

Internal consulting as a facilitative-tactical OD mode is important for carrying out team building, for installing MBO and JE, and, in general, for redefining the role of the training specialist or manager (or whoever has the assigned role of bringing OD to the client organization). The proper role of the OD facilitator is that of internal consultant, and organizations are, increasingly, creating such positions or redefining traditional training positions so that the incumbents of them become internal consultants or change agents.

Internal consultants take a professional stance vis-à-vis their clients. They recognize (1) that help is always defined by the recipient and (2) that they can neither fulfill their responsibilities to the organization nor maintain proper ethical standards of conduct if they are placed in a position which involves conflicting obligations to their managerial clients.

Internal consultants play an organizationsl role in which they provide three important kinds of help. First, they help in strategic planning by being sensitive to management's needs and by contributing their knowledge. Second, they help in solving problems. They concern themselves with immediate and specific problems and provide help to managers on all organizational levels. Third, they help with managerial controls, but not as policemen running rigid systems. Rather, they act as diagnosticians who find practical ways to capitalize on self-control and build it into the way work is planned, assigned, conducted, and the like.[32]

Internal consultants in an OD effort possess the knowledge to make interventions in the organization and help management manage better. To be effective, they need to have a nontraditional role and the skill to carve out the type of role briefly described above. Obviously, there is no one proper OD internal consultative role that can be set forth in infinite detail here or anywhere else because of the vast differences in organizational cultures, environments, and situations. The essential point is that it is difficult, if not impossible, for an organization to undertake OD without redefining or establishing anew the role of the agent of change. Effective OD is not a program grafted on to an existing organization as an ornament, but rather movement toward a new way of organizational life. Consequently, installation of an OD internal consultancy has been widely recognized as an OD facilitative-tactical device at the macro level which is a prelude for all other organizational interventions.

THE CONDUCT OF OD

It is extremely difficult to summarize the kinds of OD programs in operation in the United States today or to provide any amount of descriptive detail. Table 20-1 shows data for 20 diverse organizations categorized according to the main facilitative-tactical modes of OD which we have been discussing. Obviously, there are many other prominent organizations which have been and presently are actively engaged in OD which are not shown, such as General Motors Corp., Dow Chemical Company, Aluminum Company of Canada, First National Stores, American Telephone and Telegraph Company, Procter and Gamble, Emery Air Freight, RCA, Union Carbide, and Donnelly Mirrors, Inc. Nor does the list include the Harwood Companies, Inc., and their efforts since the 1940s to build participative management as a modus operandi in their way of corporate life,[33] or

TABLE 20-1

	Organization	Team building	Management by Objectives	Job enrichment	Internal consulting
1.	Kaiser Aluminum & Chemical Corp.	x			x
2.	SmithKline Corp.	x			x
3.	American Airlines	x	x	x	x
4.	Boeing Co., Vertol Div.	x			
5.	Various New York banks	x	x	x	
6.	Guardian Life Ins. Co.			x	
7.	Mountain Bell Telephone	x	x	x	
8.	Federal Bureau of Reclamation, Region 2	x			x
9.	TRW Systems Group	x			x
10.	Saga Administrative Corp.	x		x	x
11.	Sonesta Hotels	x	x		x
12.	Exxon and Humble Oil	x	x		x
13.	Detroit Edison				x
14.	Armstrong Cork				x
15.	Corning Glass Co.	x	x	x	x
16.	Genesco, Inc.	x			x
17.	Raymond Corp.	x	x	x	x
18.	Steinberg's Ltd.	x	x	x	
19.	Syntex Corp.	x		x	x
20.	Texas Instruments Inc.	x	x	x	x

SOURCES: Items 1–8: J. Jennings Partin (ed.), *Current Perspectives in Organization Development*, Addison-Wesley Publishing Company, Inc., Reading, Mass., 1973, pp. 30–192. Items 9–13: Alfred J. Marrow, (ed.), *The Failure of Success*, AMACOM, New York, 1972, pp. 259–315. Items 14–20: Harold M. F. Rush, *Behavioral Science Concepts and Management Application*, National Industrial Conference Board, Inc., Personnel Policy Study no. 216, New York, 1969, pp. 59–171.

the innumerable Scanlon plans,[34] which are clearly outstanding examples of OD and cultural change in work organizations. The ones listed in the table have been recently reported in the literature, which the reader who wishes more detail can consult (although there is no reason to assume the reports are complete).[35] One other precaution in considering the list is that it does not reveal the range of OD technology used at the micro level, such as the Johari window, confrontation meetings, data gathering survey tools, Transactional Analysis sessions, fishbowls, and the gamut of similar tools. Organizations which use macro-level facilitative-tactical OD modes feel free to pick and choose from a growing armamentarium and to apply what they hope will be useful. Table 20-1 provides merely a glimpse of the macro modes that have become established (or have at least been given a trial) in a number of well-known organizations.

Several observations are worth making in respect to these organizations. First, in not all these cases were interventions made at the top-management level. Second, the OD efforts made in the organizations typically emphasized such interventions as team building, MBO, JE, and internal consulting, but the T group was by no means ignored as an important intervention. Third, most of the OD projects were in one form or another attempting to redistribute power and influences through-out the client organization. Fourth, the OD efforts described have been long-term, in some cases covering more than a decade (such as in the TRW Systems Group). This observation suggests once again that successful OD is not a program, but rather an effort or attempt at change in an organizational culture to create a new way of life at work. Fifth, OD is humanist and participative by its very nature. The OD ideal may thus perhaps be said to foster circumstances in organizational management so that the human being becomes a fully functioning person working in concert with every other member of the organization. Sixth, OD emerged out of the training function and is today much broader than the latter. OD is also often heavily interlarded with management development—as traditionally conceived. Training may be viewed as simply one type of OD intervention. However, OD tends to be administratively placed within the organization's personnel depart-ment and probably will remain there in the foreseeable future.[36] Hence, the top personnel and/or training manager is the logical prime candidate to become the work organization's OD internal consultant or change agent.

THE FUTURE OF OD: FOUR TRENDS

The OD field is in a state of flux all around the world. Every OD conference contains ringing calls for new approaches as well as solid contributions on the subject of how actually to conduct a program of changing an organization. At several points in this chapter we have noted that our theories and our data are improving all the time, but we have also called attention to some key issues which need a good deal more work. In this final section, we shall speculate briefly on where we think the field is going over approximately the next decade.

OD Strategy

We have already commented at some length on the difference between proceed-ing piecemeal and proceeding systematically. We think that more and more organizations will develop strategies for orderly change and that less and less will a kind of random jabbing at the system be seen as useful by OD people and line managers. Our basic reason for this prediction rests on the trend toward defining the organization as a whole as the "client," rather than subunits of it. The larger the entity to be changed, the more important it becomes to replace opportunism by strategy. As a concomitant of this trend, we think that OD will increasingly have to deal with accusations that it is a Machiavellian system and that the OD person is a would-be puppeteer who stands behind events and manipulates people's lives. Our assumption is that the basic OD value system has answers for such accusations, but it is worth noting that such assaults may well occur.

OD and the Human Potential Movement

We need not dwell on the enormous amount of current work on, in Maslow's phrase, "the farther limits of human nature."[37] We do not regard this basic thrust as chicanery or black magic, even though there are those in the field whose motives may be frankly exploitative. OD cannot help but be affected by the total movement, however, and it is our expectation that OD will have the opportunity to incorporate exciting new conceptions about the nature of the human being and about what he or she may become. Since Argyris's original observation that the needs of the healthy person and the demands of the organization may be fundamentally incompatible, we have seen 20 years' worth of attempts to avoid that—apparently—pessimistic conclusion. But with the rise of "alternative institutions" over the past 10 years, it may be that not all is lost, even if Argyris was right insofar as traditional structures are concerned. We note that serious students of human nature are taking a searching view of the experiments with alternative institutions which are going on.[38]

OD and the "Internal Transformation"

Related to the search for more humane institutions, but a separate trend in itself, is the work that seeks a fuller understanding of people and technology. The school of thought concerned with "sociotechnical systems" has sought for twenty years to document the interdependence between human social behavior and the technical and physical environment within which the behavior is occurring.[39] There is now a field known as "ecological psychology" which is investigating along similar lines. Popular phrases such as "office landscaping" also point out the growing awareness of the interaction between people and their immediate technical and physical environment.[40] The upshot of this work will be to change our ideas about the question raised earlier in this chapter: What is the "it" which we think we are changing? We predict that in order to remain relevant, OD will have to incorporate these new conceptions.

OD and Organizational Ecology

A final set of trends which we think OD will benefit from concerns the growing interest in organization-environment relationships.[41] Many of the organizations which have embraced OD most enthusiastically have been ones existing in turbulent environments—where it seemed that the only way to survive under such uncertainty was to undertake some process of building up internal strength, resiliency, openness to change, and tolerance for ambiguity. OD has therefore encountered the problem. The point we are now making is that we expect major theoretical advances on the question of just what it is that the organization is up against, with resulting clarification for OD people as to what it is that the organization and the individuals in it really need.

These four trends, taken together and along with other events, will combine to change the nature of OD fundamentally we think. The next 10 years in OD will therefore be a period of at least as much ferment and excitement as marked the 1960s.

CONCLUSION

OD is an exciting and rapidly growing phenomenon in the fields of training, personnel, and manpower management that is attracting the attention of training managers and training specialists all over the world. In its short life, OD has never been known to be easily pinpointed and summarily defined. This ambiguity has been a tragedy and a source of consternation for trainers. We hope that in this chapter we have clarified OD, identified its boundaries, pointed out its main modes, and indicated generally where it is being carried out in the United States today.

REFERENCES

1. Roethlisberger, F. J., and W. J. Dickson: *Management and the Worker,* Harvard University Press, Cambridge, Mass., 1939, especially chap. 24, "An Industrial Organization as a Social System," pp. 551–568.
2. See, for example, Katz, D., and R. Kahn: *The Social Psychology of Organizations,* John Wiley & Sons, Inc., New York, 1966, passim.
3. Homans, G. C.: *The Human Group,* Harcourt, Brace & World, Inc., New York, 1950, passim.
4. A point of view on OD which some have felt has a "union-busting" flavor to it is presented in Myers, M. S.: "Overcoming Union Opposition to Job Enrichment," *Harvard Business Review,* vol. 49, no. 3, pp. 37–49, May–June 1971.
5. Beckhard, R.: *Organization Development: Strategies and Models,* Addison-Wesley Publishing Company, Inc., Reading, Mass., 1969, pp. 2–8.
6. For a classic statement see Tannenbaum, R., and W. H. Schmidt: "How to Choose a Leadership Pattern," in R. Tannenbaum et al., *Leadership and Organization,* McGraw-Hill Book Company, New York, 1961, pp. 67–80.

   A recent empirical statement of great value is Fiedler, F. E.: *A Theory of Leadership Effectiveness,* McGraw-Hill Book Company, New York, 1967.
7. Argyris, C.: *Intervention Theory and Method,* Addison-Wesley Publishing Company, Inc., Reading, Mass., 1971.

   Schein, E. H.: *Process Consultation,* Addison-Wesley Publishing Company, Inc., Reading, Mass., 1969.
8. These ideas are nicely summarized in Bennis, Warren G., et al. (eds.): *The Planning of Change,* Holt, Rinehart and Winston, Inc., New York, 1961, pp. 237–238.
9. Greiner, L. E.: "Patterns of Organizational Change," *Harvard Business Review,* vol. 45, no. 3, pp. 119–130, May–June 1967.
10. Tannenbaum, R., and S. A. Davis: "Values, Man and Organizations," in W. H. Schmidt (ed.), *Organizational Frontiers and Human Values,* Wadsworth Publishing Company, Inc., Belmont, Calif., 1970.
11. Nadler, L.: *Developing Human Resources,* Gulf Publishing Company, Houston, 1970, pp. 245–246, 103–104, 159–160.
12. Back, K. W.: *Beyond Words,* Russell Sage Foundation, New York, 1972, pp. 159–173, 213–237.
13. Dyer, W. G.: "Here-and-Now Data versus Back-Home Personal Concerns: A Professional and Ethical Decision," in W. G. Dyer (ed.), *Modern Theory and Method in Group Training,* Van Nostrand Reinhold, Incorporated, New York, 1972, pp. 233–242.
14. See Beck, A. C., and E. D. Hillmar: *A Practical Approach to Organization Development through MBO,* Addison-Wesley Publishing Company, Inc., Reading, Mass., 1972, passim.

   Or, as Dale has put it: "Job enlargement varies the work but perhaps more important is the fact that when an enlarged job is put together, the worker has a greater opportunity to do everything that contributes to a clearly perceived result. In other words, it makes 'management by objectives' more practical." Dale, E.: *Organization,* American Management Association, New York, 1967, p. 133.
15. Blake, R. R., and J. S. Mouton: "Is the Training-Group Consultant Approach a Method of Organization Development?" in Dyer, op. cit., pp. 197–220.

   Patten, T. H., Jr.: "OD, MBO, and the Reward System," in T. H. Patten, Jr. (ed.), *OD: Emerging Dimensions and Concepts,"* American Society for Training and Development, Madison, Wis., 1972, pp. 3–10ff.

16. Kuriloff, A. H.: *Organizational Development for Survival*, American Management Association, New York, 1972, p. 40.
17. Ibid., pp. 40–41.
18. Kuriloff: op. cit., p. 41.
19. See Lawrence, P. R., and J. W. Lorsch: *Organization and Environment: Managing Differentiation and Integration*, Harvard University, Graduate School of Business Administration, Cambridge, Mass., 1967.
20. Kuriloff: op. cit., p. 34.
21. Ibid., pp. 34–35.
22. Blake and Mouton: op. cit., p. 201.
23. Ibid., pp. 202–203.
24. Schutz, W. C.: *Here Comes Everybody*, Harrow Books, New York, 1972, p. xviii.
25. Ibid., pp. xviii–xix, 116–117, 181–191.
26. McGregor, D.: *The Human Side of Enterprise*, McGraw-Hill Book Company, 1960, pp. 227–243.

   McGregor, D.: *The Professional Manager*, McGraw-Hill Book Company, New York, 1967, pp. 160–182, 106–111.
27. McGregor: *The Human Side of Enterprise*, pp. 61–76.
28. Lasagna, J. B.: "Make Your MBO Pragmatic," *Harvard Business Review*, vol. 49, no. 6, pp. 65–69, November–December 1971.
29. Thomson, T. M.: "Management by Objectives," in J. W. Pfeiffer and J. E. Jones (eds.), *The 1972 Annual Handbook for Group Facilitators*, University Associates, Iowa City, 1972, pp. 130–132.
30. McGregor: *The Professional Manager*, pp. 84, 95.
31. Jessey, F. V.: "Job Enrichment," in Pfeiffer and Jones, op. cit., pp. 127–129.
32. McGregor: *The Human Side of Enterprise*, pp. 163–175 and passim.

   See also McGregor's seminal article on the helping relationship, "The Staff Function in Human Relations," *Journal of Social Issues*, vol. 4, no. 3, pp. 5–22, Summer 1948.
33. Marrow, A. J. (ed.): *The Failure of Success*, AMACOM, New York, 1972, pp. 83–130.
34. McGregor: *The Human Side of Enterprise*, pp. 110–123.

   Frost, C.: *The Scanlon Plan for Organization Development: Identity, Participation, and Equity*, The Michigan State University Press, East Lansing, 1974, pp. 124–125.
35. Other sources for the latest reports on OD experiences are *Training and Development Journal, Journal of Applied Behavioral Science*, and, occasionally, *Harvard Business Review, California Management Review, Personnel, Personnel Journal, Human Resource Management*, and *Business Week*. The annual handbooks for group facilitators, published by University Associates (presently located in San Diego, Calif.), are virtual gold mines of information on OD resources, concepts, theories, and program and intervention designs. Still another source for a comparative analysis of 30 examples of redesigning work can be found in *Work in America*, report of a special task force to the Secretary of Health, Education, and Welfare, The M.I.T. Press, Cambridge, Mass., 1973, pp. 188–201.
36. Partin, J. J. (ed.): *Current Perspectives in Organization Development*, Addison-Wesley Publishing Company, Inc., Reading, Mass., 1973, pp. 270–276.
37. Maslow, A. H.: *The Farther Reaches of Human Nature*, The Viking Press, Inc., New York, 1971, passim.
38. See *The Journal of Applied Behavioral Science*, special issue on alternative institutions, Spring 1973.
39. Davis, L. E., and E. L. Trist: *Improving the Quality of Worklife*, University of Pennsylvania, Management and Behavioral Science Center, Philadelphia, June 1972.

   Trist, E. L.: "A Socio-Technical Critique of Scientific Management," paper contributed to the Edinburgh Conference on the Impact of Science Technology, University of Edinburgh, May 1970.
40. Steele, F. I.: *Physical Settings and Organization Development*, Addison-Wesley Publishing Company, Inc., Reading, Mass., 1973, pp. 21–145.
41. Emery, F., and E. L. Trist: "The Causal Texture of Organizational Environments," in F. Emery (ed.), *Systems Thinking*, Penguin Books, Inc., Baltimore, 1969.

   Thompson, J. D.: *Organizations in Action*, McGraw-Hill Book Company, New York, 1967.

Chapter **21**

Executive Development

WALTER R. MAHLER

Walter R. Mahler *is President of Mahler Associates. Mahler Associates has had two decades of experience in executive development, management development, organization planning, and personnel administration. The company has worked with many of the large companies in the Fortune 500 as well as with medium-sized and smaller organizations. Prior to establishing his own organization, Dr. Mahler served as a consultant for seven years to The Psychological Corporation. His experience includes several years in industry, in retailing, and in government work. His interests are revealed by his recent publications:* Executive Continuity, *Dow Jones-Irwin, Homewood, Ill., 1973;* Diagnostic Studies, *Addison Wesley Publishing Company, Inc., Reading, Mass., 1974;* Structure, Power and Results, *Dow Jones-Irwin, Homewood, Ill., 1975; and How Effective Executives Interview, Dow Jones-Irwin, Homewood, Ill., 1976.*

The first edition of *Training and Development Handbook* included a chapter on supervisory development and one on management development; it did not contain one on executive development. One of the significant changes which have taken place in recent years is the recognition of the importance of executive development. This recognition led the editor to ask that attention be given to that special type of development called *executive development.* Just what is so unique about executive development? It has several unique characteristics. The population we are concerned with is unique. We are talking about a small group of managers, occupying the top two or three levels of an organization. In an extremely large organization, we might well be talking about three levels. "Level" is one way of referring to executives. Another would be to say they have to do with making policy decisions, with setting the direction of the organization, with allocating resources, and with monitoring returns on these resources. Sometimes the term used for the individuals in this rarefied atmosphere is "institutional leaders." They are designing, building, and maintaining an institution. The contrast would be lower-level managers, who operate or run the organization.

The second unique aspect of development of the executive is that it must be viewed as a process extending over a period of years. The process provides opportunity for accelerated growth and for securing the experience, the special knowledge, and the special skills which will result in a broad-gauged individual capable of providing the leadership expected of a top executive. One observer has defined managers at the middle level of an organization as primarily problem solvers. Executives are problem recognizers and problem definers. From the point of view of competitors, executives are problem creators. In addition, they are opportunity recognizers and opportunity seekers. This definition helps to illustrate that unique features are required of an executive development program, in contrast with management development efforts.

REASONS FOR INCREASED CONCERN

The major organizational entities of society are becoming giant-sized: big government, big labor, big business, big education, big medical care, big social agencies. Increased size and a rapid increase in the speed with which change takes place mean that executive leadership has become a critical requirement for organizational success. It is a necessity.

The last decade has seen numerous corporate failures which provide a dramatic and tragic example of the importance of executive leadership. A recent study of 15 large business enterprises concluded that the development and selection of management was a top-priority responsibility of each chief executive. There is also concern about executive development on the part of major agencies in the federal government and major educational institutions.

There is another reason for increased concern. It was about a decade ago that certain executive development technology was introduced. Several techniques were widely used. One universally applied technique was the replacement chart, often a multicolored chart. As time went by, chief executives first became aware and then concerned that real executive development had not occurred. The paraphernalia was in place, and techniques were being carried out, but the expected results—namely, qualified executives ready when needed—often proved illusory. The failure techniques, in themselves, led to a keen interest in efforts which will truly result in *developed executives*.

FACTORS INFLUENCING GROWTH

We are concerned here with factors of importance in influencing growth of executives to fill the critical positions in the organization. More often than not, these positions will be general-manager-type positions. In some instances, they will be top-level functional positions. The following factors are of critical importance in influencing growth:

- Early opportunity to supervise, to take significant risk, and to take full responsibility
- A variety of models of executive competence to emulate
- Appropriate length of time in a given position
- An experience with adversity—learning by undoing
- Experience in more than one area of specialization
- Constructive coaching by a superior
- Periodic educational experience of short duration when one is "learning-prone"

IMPORTANCE OF A SYSTEMS APPROACH

Holden made a study of top management 25 years ago and just recently repeated the study.[1] He found that in spite of considerable divergence in methodology, there was a consensus among the executives visited that certain significant changes had taken place during the past few years in executive development programs within their corporations. The changes most frequently mentioned included:

1. Increased personal involvement and commitment by top management
2. More effective integration at the executive level of manpower planning and corporate long-range plans and operations

3. Greater use of an improved professional corporate staff service, including a more sophisticated information system for use in manpower planning
4. Improved selection and early identification of young men and women with top-management potential
5. A more realistic approach to executive appraisal encompassing separate evaluations of past performance and of long-term future potential
6. Increased emphasis upon development programs geared to the personal needs of each individual and including considerable personal involvement by top management

An intensive study of successful and unsuccessful company executive development programs was recently completed by Mahler and Wrightnour.[2] The study concluded that successful efforts would well be characterized as being comprehensive, system approaches. Ten major requirements for a systems approach were identified:

1. Top-management action
2. An effective staff contribution specifically for executive personnel
3. Identification of the kind and number of executives needed in the future
4. Objective, descriptive information about candidates for executive positions
5. Accelerated development of high-potential candidates
6. Specialized educational programs
7. An organization-wide approach to selection and placement

Let us examine these requirements in greater detail.

CRITICAL ROLE OF TOP MANAGEMENT

It is of considerable importance that a tradition be established that top management have executive continuity as one of its prime responsibilities. It is not sufficient for a chief executive to recognize or even be enthusiastic about an effort such as this. It must become a habitual part of the top-management role to carry out certain actions on a regular basis decade after decade. It must become "institutionalized"!

Let us consider an example of an organization in which attention to executive continuity has been institutionalized. For more than 25 years, Exxon has had a committee on compensation and executive development. The very top executives make up the committee. Once a year, the heads of each of Exxon's operating groups and functional departments are called before the committee to forecast movements within their managerial realm over the next five years and to recommend promotions for the top spots. This top committee concerns itself with the top 250 jobs in the company.

Much more typical of the type of top-management actions that are generally taken are the following:

- The top manager or management verbalizes great concern about a problem of executive continuity. This is not followed by any action.
- Top management encourages and supports the establishment of a management school or the extensive use of outside courses, but they do little or nothing else.
- Top managers avoid doing anything personally about the development of their own immediate subordinates. They shy away from having any dialogues with a subordinate about his or her performance or managerial effectiveness.
- Top managers quite often accept replacement plans as presented.

In summary, this first and most important requirement is not met in many organizations. Much can be accomplished by a deliberate effort to meet the other requirements, but optimum results require top-management interest and action on a regular and sustained basis.

The climate established by top management can either help or hinder when it comes to attracting, developing, and retaining high-potential personnel. Top management develops a reputation, an image, whether it likes it or not. A climate which contributes to executive continuity would have the following characteristics:

- Responsibility is delegated.
- Individuals are trusted.
- Individuals are given challenging opportunities to test themselves.
- Rewards go to those who produce.
- Individuals are treated with dignity and respect.
- Both individual performance and team performance are stressed.
- A consultative approach to problem solving and planning is used.

One action which has demonstrated its value in several large business organizations is an annual top-executive manpower review. General Electric, IBM, Johnson & Johnson, Exxon, and Uniroyal are examples of companies which have been making regular use of such reviews.

The review process contributes in several ways. Having a variety of management processes, such as budget preparation and monthly reporting, ensures that everyone recognizes that top management has a strong interest in cash-flow and other financial results. A formal executive manpower review makes it apparent that top management is concerned about "people flow" at the executive level.

The review process usually requires that the "visiting" executive share his or her thinking on subjects such as the following:

- Future plans for the structure of the organization
- Evaluation of individuals in critical positions
- Actions planned for individuals in critical positions
- Individual judged to have potential
- Recommended actions for those with potential
- Results of accelerated development effort
- Results of college recruiting effort

STAFF CONTRIBUTION

What constitutes an appropriate staff contribution? The basic responsibilities would include:

1. Designing an overall program. This involves designing a systems approach and establishing the timetable for the implementation of this approach.
2. Securing sound data. It is especially important that good descriptive information about all candidates for executive positions be secured.
3. Stimulating the necessary anticipatory actions and planning on the part of operating managers which are needed to implement the systems approach.
4. Facilitating a corporatewide approach to the selection decisions pertaining to key executives.
5. Implementing programs requiring a comprehensive or a corporatewide approach such as college recruiting, accelerated development, manpower inventory, manpower planning, and executive compensation.
6. Conducting organizational studies and participating in organizational planning processes.

It was argued earlier that a systems approach is absolutely necessary. Executive management must look to a specialized group to design an appropriate systems approach. Implementation of the design will require changing old habits and developing new ones at all levels of the enterprise. A change in habits is going to meet with resistance. A "gadfly" or "catalyst" staff contribution is needed if the organization is really going to change.

Qualifications of the Top Staff Person

Establishing the position of a top staff person to concentrate on the implementation of a systems approach is an important step. Equally important is the selection of a well-qualified staff person. Let us consider some of the major characteristics to be sought in this "water walker." He or she should:

1. Be able to understand and evaluate executive ability and performance
2. Have a keen understanding of people—their motives, interests, and values
3. Be able to establish and sustain effective working relationships with all levels of management
4. Have the courage of his or her convictions
5. Have a knowledge of managing as a process
6. Have an intimate knowledge of the organization
7. Have a sound grounding in organization planning
8. Have a knowledge of the major personnel functions, such as compensation, personnel development and personnel placement

Pitfalls to Avoid

There are several roles which could be described as pitfalls to be avoided. One role is the "king-maker" role. In this type of role the staff group is seen as being responsible for selections and appointments. Two cautions are in order here: (1) Avoid exercising the potential power inherent in this new position, and (2) avoid any appearance of taking on the king-maker's role.

The second type of role pitfall is that of becoming a "mechanic" or planner. Individuals in this role quite often become preoccupied with the mechanics, the processes, and the procedures, mistaking these for accomplishments. They have very complete books, usually in fancy colors, but they do not have *developed executives.*

EXECUTIVES OF THE FUTURE

A people flow of competent executives is needed for 5 years hence, for 10 years hence, and for 20 years hence. It is likely that the type of executive who headed companies 25 years ago would have difficulty being successful today. However, it seems to be less obvious, or at least to be of less concern, that the type of executive who will be successful 25 years from now will, in all likelihood, be quite different from executives of today.

Each organization will need to make judgments on both the number and, even more importantly, the type of executive needed in the future. This problem is a most complex one. Arriving at reasonable assumptions is frustrating. Again, it is necessary to arrive at some assumptions, for these assumptions are needed to guide decision making all along the people-flow system from recruitment to retirement. I would suggest that executives of the future need the following:

1. *Knowledge.* Executives will need a knowledge of world business conditions, and a knowledge of governmental affairs both United States and worldwide. They will need a knowledge of organization planning and of the intricacies of changing an organization in a dynamic worldwide operation. They will need to be able to master a knowledge of new markets, new products, and new developments, and they will especially need to have a knowledge of the entire sequence of events from the germination of new ideas to their conversion into products and subsequently into sales.

2. *Experience.*   Executives of the future will need certain types of experiences. They will need to have a depth of experience in several functions, one of which must be in the area of marketing. They will need to have an intimate exposure to top-level problems early in their careers. They should have had experience both as line managers and as staff managers. They should have had experience in several types of businesses and in a series of high-risk jobs.

3. *Abilities.*   Executives of the future will need to have certain abilities. They will need the ability to manage highly technical groups. They will need to be able to make effective use of numerous specialists. They will need to be able to master the art of delegating and controlling large organizations, and they will need to view problems broadly, avoiding a parochial attitude. They must be able to anticipate the future and to make firm decisions about the allocation of resources and adhere to these basic decisions. They must be able to view complex problems from the three points of view simultaneously: financial, technical, and human. They need to have the ability to plan and carry out changes in the organization in an effective manner. They need to be able to calculate risks and then take the calculated risk. They need to be able to secure effective teamwork in a complex organization. They need to be able to use the new tools of management, such as data processing, information systems, automation, new incentive methods, and mathematical models.

EFFECTIVE REPLACEMENT PLANNING

There are several characteristics of an effective replacement planning process. Many organizations ask for nominations of individuals for replacements for a specific position. When planning for replacements for future executives, this is a limitation that can and should be avoided. The first characteristic of an effective replacement planning process is that executives are asked to identify individuals under their supervision whom they believe to be currently qualified, or potentially qualified, for a higher executive level, Notice that we are not asking them to be identified as a replacement or backup for a specific position. The replacement planning process should call for a statement justifying the evaluation of the individual as now qualified or having potential to qualify. In addition, a specific plan of action should be required. This plan should ask for the next two desirable position moves for this individual, plus other special action such as course attendance or exposure to special task forces. The replacement plan should also call for the identification of individuals about 30 years of age who are deemed to have high potential.

Another characteristic of a sound replacement planning process is the repetition of the process each year. Organizations should also do their planning at successive levels so that it is possible to get independent judgments of at least two levels.

IMPORTANCE OF OBJECTIVE DATA

It is a very rare company that has accurate and useful information available on candidates for executive positions. In fact, it is ironic that many top-management people talk about their personnel as being valuable resources. One look at the data that executives in most large companies utilized in making critical executive-continuity decisions reveals that they had very little helpful information available to them.

Let us now consider how to go about securing objective, descriptive information. There are six basic sources of information:

1. A personal history record. This consists of such basic data as age, education, salary progression, and title of positions held.

2. A self-description or self-analysis; for example, individuals are asked to prepare a statement of their accomplishments during the preceding year.
3. Performance appraisals prepared by superiors. In some organizations, this information is collected by means of a group discussion. The written record is usually reflected as group consensus.
4. An evaluation prepared by a trained psychologist. Some organizations have their own internal psychologists, and others make use of outside professional organizations. This type of information is derived mainly from psychological tests and depth interviews. The information consists primarily of psychological observations and insights.
5. A reference check with former bosses.
6. The Accomplishment Analysis process. Developed by Mahler Associates, this represents an attempt to get information about the managerial abilities of candidates by means of a thorough exploration of past accomplishments, or lack of accomplishments, and the practices of management that were used in achieving these accomplishments.

Making decisions on appointments to key positions is a challenge for every top executive. Such decisions can have a critical impact upon the future success of the enterprise. Most experienced top executives have long sought multiple sources of information when faced with a critical decision. Here is where the Accomplishment Analysis process comes into play. The top executive has two sources of information: executives in the regular line of authority and the staff person or persons doing Accomplishment Analyses.

In our experience in numerous large organizations, about half of the names on replacement charts do not belong there. But which half? Here is a second purpose of the Accomplishment Analysis process—to "validate" the replacement chart. The staff person who studies 30 executives by means of the Accomplishment Analysis has one distinct advantage. No one else in the company has as sound a base for judging each of these individuals as the staff person. Staff people put their reputations on the line regularly by indicating whether they feel a given nominee has the potential to do a particular job.

Since this process usually takes place before critical decisions are made, differences between executives' replacement planning thinking and Accomplishment Analysis thinking can be discussed thoroughly. Differences can lead to an "alert" being set up to permit closer observation before a critical decision is made.

There is a third purpose served by the Accomplishment Analysis process, namely, that of stimulating growth and development. The Accomplishment Analysis process puts the staff person in an excellent position to identify important developmental needs and then do something about them.

Studying scores of executives who are about the same age permits insightful analysis of developmental needs. The chance to first interview in depth and then talk frankly with both a nominee and his or her superior makes for real ease in establishing an effective counseling relationship.

ACCELERATED DEVELOPMENT A MUST

As the overall system begins to come into focus, it becomes apparent that many developmental actions cannot be accomplished unless plans are undertaken early in the career of an executive. This leads to the requirement for an accelerated development program. Although the establishment of such a program does not necessarily guarantee good results, its absence greatly lessens the chances of success.

Let us consider three rather critical specifications which have previously been discussed as being important for future executives.

First, executives must think like generalists; in effect, they must be generalists before they are appointed to a general-manager position. Second, they must make decisions as an entrepreneur would. This means that they must calculate risks and then take these calculated risks. And, finally, they must be able to lead quite diverse groups of people.

If executives are going to meet these three requirements before being appointed general managers, then it becomes necessary to give them certain experiences early in their careers. An organization that is serious about having candidates meet these requirements for general-manager positions should provide early opportunities for risk-taking experiences. Some type of an accelerated development program becomes a necessity.

It is predictable that organizations will meet resistance when launching an accelerated development program. Few organizations actually endeavor to do this in a deliberate manner. It is necessary that top management decide whether this requirement is going to be a matter of policy. If it is, the policy must be encouraged. In some instances, considerable persuasion is necessary.

CONTRIBUTION OF FORMAL EDUCATION

Educational programs for experienced executives have been with us now for a quarter of a century.[3] Harvard held its first advanced-management program in 1945. General Electric can be credited with initiating the first long-term internal educational program for executives in 1955, when it established its own nine-week advanced-management course.

A diligent search of the literature and discussions with people in many large organizations suggest that we do not have sound data upon which to base an answer to the question of the value of formal classroom education for the executive. One astute observer has stated, with regard to educational programs for executives, that never has so much money been invested with so little evidence of an adequate return. Sterling Livingston and others have questioned the heavy reliance upon formal university education in developing managers.[4] They argue that formal education, in and of itself, is not really capable of developing managers. We would state our position a bit differently. A company should not expect a formal education program to produce future executives. Achieving this result requires a comprehensive systems approach. However, we see needed contributions which can best be provided by an effective educational program.

Potential Pitfalls

The prevailing practice of relying on educational programs, whether these are external or internal to the organization, has failed to produce the needed results because of recurring pitfalls.

The first pitfall is the absence of a thorough need-determination process which governs the choice of subject matter, size of group, educational method, and type of instructor.

A second pitfall has to do with the heterogeneous nature of participants. The instructor in the average university program is faced with 66 quite diverse students. They come from organizations differing greatly in size, they represent different types of businesses, and they have different backgrounds and unique personal needs. The instructor must strike a general pattern which appeals to most of the students, most of the time.

The third potential pitfall associated with both external and internal educational programs is that top management may assume that the educational activities will do the job of developing their future executives and may therefore neglect many of the other requirements identified as being necessary for the overall system. In effect, top management places too great a reliance on the educational process for developing executives.

A fourth pitfall has to do with the participant. In many organizations, the executive who can be made available for six weeks or longer is sent. This means that the real comers often miss out on an educational experience. In some instances, the entire process is done in such a way that the participant arrives at the course with a distinctly negative attitude.

A fifth pitfall is that the educational process may not be programmed as a continuous effort over the entire career of an executive. Once in a manager's career, usually at some randomly determined time, he or she is given an opportunity to participate in an educational program. Often this constitutes the first and last formal educational experience that this individual receives. Such a one-time-only exposure is unlikely to assist a manager in keeping up-to-date with either managerial or technological knowledge, both of which are rapidly expanding.

A sixth pitfall has to do with the need to improve managerial ability. Educational programs have as their avowed purpose that of "broadening" an executive's knowledge and awareness. Application of this knowledge calls for skills. These skills are almost never included among the objectives of advanced management programs.

Next we discuss some of the requirements for growth and development of executives in continuity programs which might be met by an educational program.

Requirements Which Might Be Met by an Educational Program

Let us consider four critical career crossroads for executives. They have to do with the transitions from:

1. Individual contributor to functional manager
2. Functional manager to general manager
3. Managing one business to managing several businesses
4. Managing several businesses to being an institutional leader

In making the initial transition, individuals have to change their self-concepts. They have to rely on others to do work they used to do. They have to become comfortable doing managerial tasks. They must derive satisfaction from others' good performance. They have to master supervisory skills and methods. This transition requires changes in attitude, acquisition of new knowledge, and development of new skills.

This transition requires a well-designed educational program for the new supervisor. It is amazing that even large companies seldom have regular programs which ensure that new supervisors do receive training upon being appointed. There is a need for an increasing number of young high-potential personnel to become supervisors before the age of 30. This group, as well as others, should have the benefit of education in supervision.

Once in supervision, individuals usually stay in one function for some time. They are expected to master this function. Here again is a need for the acquisition of specialized functional knowledge and skills. This type of instruction is best accomplished with some homogeneity of participants.

Let us consider the transition from functional-manager work to general-manager work. The individual has to understand each major function so that he or she can both direct the functional manager and integrate across functions, making appropriate and timely trade-offs. Often the individual has to recognize that his or her way of thinking, deciding, and managing has been strongly conditioned by previous experience in one function. This usually proves a handicap in managing several functions, and so unlearning—as well as learning—has to take place.

During this transition, the individual has to shift from a supportive role to the dominant role in direction of the business. Business judgment is required. The ability to understand and lead diverse groups becomes critical. Here again we see a real value in an educational program. Becoming a general manager requires becoming knowledgeable about other major functions. The processes of planning, organizing, and controlling become more critical. Leadership and application of behavioral knowledge become a necessity. We see many of the present university programs providing the needed broader knowledge about functions and business in general. The original General Electric program was designed to do just this.

However, as we noted in the discussion of pitfalls, few advanced-management programs really aim at skill development. We see a big need for skill training of general managers in management processes.

The transition to managing several businesses is a challenge to most executives. A shift has to be made from directing a business to leading, inspiring, and controlling general managers. The general managers are often more experienced in a given business than their supervisors.

Here again there is so much to be learned that a class or group effort becomes a necessity. There is an opportunity here for a specially designed program which relies heavily upon higher-level managers. Their prior experiences in managing several businesses can be shared with the newly appointed group executives.

Finally, a few individuals are asked to make the transition to the role of institutional leader. They must now set the direction and secure and allocate resources. They have to establish policies and values for the enterprise and protect the integrity of the institution. New learning, new attitudes, and new skills are required. Rarely are there models available to be emulated. Again, the amount of learning required of the institutional leader suggests that a group effort can make a real contribution.

MANAGEMENT BY OBJECTIVES IN EXECUTIVE DEVELOPMENT

Management by Objectives means different things to different people. As the term is used here, and MBO program has the following unique characteristics:

- Each individual in the program has his or her own objectives document.
- The document reflects, insofar as possible, the *end results* the individual *commits* himself or herself to achieve.
- The document includes a comprehensive set of objectives. It reflects the entire position.
- The primary use of the document is for self-management.
- The document also serves the individual as a communications device with superiors, subordinates, and colleagues.
- The program is primarily a personal management tool.
- The program can contribute to personnel decisions, but this is a secondary benefit.
- The program makes use of current planning methods; it does not duplicate them. (Methods might be budgets, forecasts, project descriptions, etc.)

Potential Benefits

The potential benefits of an effective MBO program are the following:

- Participants gain a much more precise understanding of what is expected of them.
- The planning function is improved, as stress on results replaces stress on tasks, activities, and effort. The superior is not a "puppeteer" to a manager.
- Managers are more likely to work at the level for which they are being paid.

Many managers are busy operating at a level (or two) below their own position.

- There is improved control and more confidence that results will be achieved, with the shift from control over people to control over results. There is also a shift from "boss" control to self-control.
- Superior-subordinate relationships are improved because less close supervision is needed.
- There is improved team spirit and team performance as variances lead to collaboration.
- Participants gain a much more precise knowledge of the basics upon which they will be judged.
- Managerial abilities are developed as a result of more effective coaching.
- The organization gains much better data on the capabilities of its talent, which aids in more effective manpower utilization.

It is apparent that these benefits constitute a significant contribution to executive development.

Participants have a chance to test themselves against a demanding set of objectives. The process makes it legitimate for the participants to have progress discussions with their superiors, thus gaining the benefit of the superiors' coaching. In addition, the MBO methodology is appropriate to the changes requested in providing leadership which is effective with the talented individuals supervised by top executives.

Examples of Objectives

Often, high-level executives list as a major responsibility that of identifying key personnel resources. Usually this involves personnel at the next two levels. An example of the objectives set for such a responsibility by the president of a manufacturing company follows:

RESPONSIBILITY	OBJECTIVES (3–5 Years)	GOALS (This Year)
1. Selection, Development, and Motivation of Key Executives (Key executives are those one and two levels removed.) *Indicators:*		
(a) Number of executives who quit	None	None
(b) Number of key positions filled with competent performers	All	Identify exceptions and program action
(c) Number of choices of qualified performers we have when making appointments to key positions	Eventually—two as a minimum	Replacement plans prepared
(d) Compensation competitive on appropriate comparisons (internal and external)	No major changes needed	Analyses made and any needed corrections made No exception
(e) Development action for each key executive implemented per schedule	No exception	No exception
(f) Number of key executives implementing a goals program	All	All
(g) Up-to-date basic data on all key personnel	No exception	Age study and personnel file on all

It becomes apparent that the above objectives are directly related to many of the requirements that are built into the system recommended for executive development. The MBO program is one way of making the requirements operational.

Another major responsibility included in an MBO document is that of self-improvement. An example of objectives for such a responsibility for a general manager follows:

RESPONSIBILITY	GOALS
2. SELF-IMPROVEMENT	
a. Knowledge of financial business management	1. Reading program set up and implemented
	2. Study the manufacturing variance area of the new reporting system; develop a comprehensive understanding of how to use this as a control tool
	3. Attend seminar on finance for nonfinancial executives
b. Knowledge of industry technology	1. Trade literature, trade shows, plant visits, on continuing basis
	2. Attend one technical seminar
c. Management	1. Attend key and critical objectives seminar in September
d. Extraneous assignment	1. Phase out of extraneous assignment by Nov. 15

Imagine the leverage gained by having every participant commit himself or herself to a set of specific self-improvement objectives. The periodic discussion of objectives such as those illustrated above permits an executive to contribute to the growth and development of each of his or her direct reports.

EVALUATION OF EXECUTIVE DEVELOPMENT

The current state of the art of executive development is a distinct cut above the prevailing practice of 10 years ago. However, significant advances are needed with regard to each of the basic requirements of the systems approach. We see a need for much more collaboration among all parties concerned with advancing the state of the art. Educators, business people, consultants, and governmental officers all need to undertake cooperative efforts. Such efforts can justify substantial support over a period of years. This will permit dealing with issues of consequence.

REFERENCES

1. Holden, Paul E., Carlton A. Pederson, and Gayton E. Germane: *Top Management,* McGraw-Hill Book Company, New York, 1968, pp. 203–208.
2. Mahler, Walter R., and William F. Wrightnour: *Executive Continuity,* Dow Jones–Irwin, Inc., Homewood, Ill., 1973.
3. Andrews, Kenneth R.: *The Effectiveness of University Management Programs,* Harvard Business School, Division of Research, Cambridge, Mass., 1966.
4. Livingston, J. Sterling: "The Myth of the Well-Educated Manager," *Harvard Business Review,* pp. 79–89, January–February 1971.

Chapter 22

Management and Supervisory Development

ANDREW A. DALY

Andrew A. Daly *is Director of Management Development, IBM Corporation. He joined IBM in 1943 in financial organization at corporate headquarters and has held a variety of positions with the company, including those of first Manager of Education at corporate headquarters and Manager of Education for the Kingston plant. He began the IBM Management School, which has been attended by over 6,000 managers. Nearly 25,000 managers have been enrolled in his course in the fundamentals of management. He was ASTD National President from 1956 to 1958; President and Chairman of the Board, New York metropolitan chapter; and Founder and Chairman of the Board for both the Long Island and Hudson-Mohawk chapters of ASTD. He received the Annual Distinguished Alumnus Award from Seton Hall University Business School in 1973 and an ASTD Author Award. He holds a B.S. degree in business from Seton Hall University.*

The words "foreman," "supervisor", "manager," and "executive" require definition in terms of the role, responsibilities, and duties within the organization. The meaning of effective supervision must be clarified. Where supervisory training stops and where management or executive development begins is a moot question. A similar confusion exists about the use of the words "education," "training," and "development."

For the purposes of this chapter, the concern is with the first level of supervision through the third level of management or supervision, including persons who plan, organize, direct, evaluate, and control the work of employees and who have the responsibility to employ, pay, promote, and/or release individuals. Not included are those who merely assign work and are not accountable for the productivity of the organization.

The term "development" encompasses all activities—on-the-job coaching as well as classroom training and education within and outside an organization—which are specifically planned to improve the job performance of the individual.

The training of the new supervisor or manager, the experienced first-level supervisor, the newly promoted manager of managers, and the experienced middle manager will be surveyed and reviewed.

GROWTH OF MANAGEMENT TRAINING

The growth of management development has not followed consistent patterns throughout the world, or even in a particular country. Large variations have evolved in the organization, the staffing, the philosophy, the content, and scope of these activities. There is a diversity of approaches, and what is right for one organization today might or might not be appropriate for another tomorrow or even in five years.

Supervisory and management development takes place in all types of industrial, business, and governmental organizations—big and small—in one location or in multilocation operations. There are one-person training departments and those with large professional staffs. Some staffs act primarily as consultants to managers, with little or no classroom effort, while others put heavy emphasis on highly formal classroom activity. Just as important, the people who fulfill this function vary tremendously in terms of education and experience. In addition, programs vary from those which provide basic company and supervisory information to those which are the equivalent of university graduate-level courses. In many organizations, increased attention is being given to presupervisory training.

Managing Change

At no time in the recent past has business and institutional management been more acutely aware of the need for training and development at the managerial level. Over the last 20 years, we have seen the need for this training grow as business systems have become more complex and competitive. Current literature—books and periodicals—has stressed the rapidity of change and the emerging complexity of organizational life. Alvin Toffler[1] describes the shattering stress and disorientation that we induce in people by subjecting them to too much change in too short a time.

The pace of social and technological change, coupled with the knowledge explosion and the population explosion, is so great that all organizations must inevitably be influenced by it. Changes are varied and fast-moving, and they require flexibility on the part of all managers. The job of the training department—that of helping prepare people at all management levels—is both difficult and demanding.

Changes seem to fall into the following general categories.

Environment
International interdependence
Increased affluence throughout the world
The expansion of multinational organizations
An increasing use of automation, computers, and management sciences and other aspects of information technology
Problems of the economy—inflation, unemployment, etc.
New views concerning the environment, pollution, energy, ecology, consumerism, etc.
An increase of knowledge and the rapid development of technology
A shift from a production to a service economy
A shorter working life, often with the individual pursuing two or three separate careers
Greater government influence

Changing Population
The mix in the work force
The "new" generation
Minority groups

An increased number of women employees
Older employees
A better-educated population

Changing Attitude and Values
Less respect for authority
Increased conflict and confrontation
A greater desire to influence organizations
A desire to be intellectually challenged and to make full use of one's talents
A tendency to be less patient and more easily bored
A greater credibility gap and less trust of upper management
Changing motivations and rewards—a decrease in the power of fear as a prime
   motivator
Concern for social improvement, the ecology, and conservation of energy
Changing attitudes about morality, country, and family
A greater influence of peer-group standards
Reduced organizational loyalty
A desire for a greater say in the management system

Other Changes and Challenges
Greater application of behavioral science research
More effective techniques of selecting managers
A need for new structures and processes that will help organizations cope with
   changes resulting from temporary systems and task forces

These changes make it critical that all levels of management—from the bottom
to the top—work together as a team. New employees have new attitudes, new
expectations, and new ideas. They want to change things for the better. Organizations and managers must demonstrate that they welcome change as a way of life.
Most first-line supervisors have come from the ranks, where they have usually
been well grounded in the technical aspects of the work but where very little of
their experience has prepared them to supervise other employees.

Adequate and well-planned selection for management and supervisory positions
is an essential first step if management development is to be effective. Most
organizations seek to provide management promotions to those persons who have
performed best in nonmanagement jobs. This is excellent. Unfortunately, however, success in nonmanagement work does not often predict success in management; more often, those who are promoted to management are apt to continue to
do the things that earned them the promotion and not give adequate attention to
the job of manager or supervisor.

The development of managers must be a continuous—not a one-time—process
throughout their careers. They must be kept current, vital, and active in their self-
development. Even if they are in the "penalty box" or in possible terminal
positions, they should not be permitted to retire on the job or settle into medioc-
rity.

SOURCES OF INFORMATION

In preparing this chapter, the author surveyed many training directors from
around the world and, in addition, either talked with representatives or received
materials of 20 other organizations. Many books, periodical articles, and other
writings were studied. All this made it possible to "take the pulse" of the here and
now and to make a projection into the future of formal management training
programs.

The training director who recognizes the large number of approaches and
variations which exist should be a student of the field in order to select the

approach, content, etc., which will be most appropriate for his or her organization in terms of its state of growth and its specific needs.

It was felt that such a survey and comprehensive overview were essential in order to best acquaint the reader with the development and application of management development within the constraints of different organizations having different histories, viewpoints, and management needs.

A balanced survey of the present state of the art is reported, rather than a promulgation of special strategy or philosophy in the very broad field of management development.

Among the items investigated were:

- The company policy or philosophy about management development
- The role, structure, staff requirements, and duties of the management development organization
- The techniques of determining the content and organization of the training
- The use of internal and external resources
- Instructor skills and ability
- The content of programs or courses
- The length and schedule of programs
- The methods used in their evaluation

It was apparent that the use and content of performance appraisals varied between organizations. Some companies made extensive use of job rotation, job enrichment, and the employment of management trainees. Management development was a voluntary activity for some, while others had rigid requirements.

Job Instruction Training, sensitivity training, Transactional Analysis, Management by Objectives, organizational development, life/career planning, problem analysis and decision making, the Managerial Grid, and equal opportunity programs were listed among the subjects or content. Programmed instruction, simulations, leaderless groups, video cassettes, closed-circuit TV, and learner-controlled instruction are some of the techniques used.

Management development objectives varied from platitudes to specific objectives which were stated in behavioral terms. Many of these items are described more fully in other parts of the handbook.

The survey of training directors throughout the world asked: What changes in the level of knowledge and skill will be required by managers in the future? Some of the areas in which improvement seems to be required are the following:

- Conference leadership and group dynamics skills
- Planning work and goal setting
- Organizational theory and application
- Role of the organization in dealing with social, political, and economic issues
- Use and control of leadership style
- Motivation theories and applications
- Teaching and coaching ability
- Life/career planning
- Job enrichment and development
- Managing individual differences
- Managing change

Many training directors appear to be indecisive in their approaches to management development. Some adapt a little bit from each area or use the most recent training fad or innovation, which may not always be related to the real needs of the individual organization. It seems that there should be greater insistence on the evaluation of training and development. The fact that an activity is popular does not constitute a valid recommendation.

SURVEYS ABOUT SUPERVISORY AND MANAGEMENT TRAINING

Several excellent surveys have been completed on the status, scope, content, methods, etc., of supervisory and management training. These surveys indicate that a high percentage of companies of all sizes have a well-defined system of management development. Highlights will be reported here.

The following are excerpts from a survey by The Conference Board:[2]

> Of the 228 participants in the study in companies having one to 25 supervisors to others having over 1,000 supervisors, 89% conduct some supervisory training and 72% ensure that all newly-appointed supervisors receive training before or immediately after assuming their new responsibilities.
>
> Companies were questioned about the problems that their first line supervisors had faced in their two years prior to the survey. About half report that they had had serious problems caused by the introduction of new production methods, technologies, or equipment, and by the lack of skills or poor job attitudes of younger workers.
>
> And, while the pressures for output, cost control and quality are mentioned by 116 organizations as the factor that tends to hinder supervisors in performing as they have been taught, the immediate supervisor and the higher management are the next most frequently mentioned by 58 respondents. For comparison, the third most frequent cause cited—the ingrained habits and prejudices of the supervisor, is mentioned by 22 of the respondents.
>
> Eighty respondents say that the supervisor's immediate boss promotes supervisory performance when the boss sets an example by managing the way the supervisor has been taught to manage.
>
> Sixty-two organizations—26%—however, say that their programs do not offer rewards to supervisors for doing what they are taught to do. "Compensations criteria are not congruent with the training objectives" says one. "Doesn't really pay for results" says another.
>
> In only 14% of the responding organizations is all training done on the job.
>
> Among the smallest respondents—those with 25 or fewer supervisors—only 31% have programs of classroom training. The proportion of organizations with programs rises steadily with size, up to 85% among the respondents with over 1,000 supervisors.

List of Subjects Covered in Initial Off-the-Job Training Programs

Subject Area   *Number of Times Mentioned*

Leadership, human relations, working with
  people, behavioral science, motivating
  employees 128
Management theory and practice, management
  concepts, the management process 62
Company policies, benefits, personnel
  procedures 47
Labor relations, labor laws and regulations,
  collective bargaining, union contracts,
  dealing with the union 42
Company organizations, role of the line
  departments, role of the staff, staff services 41
Problem solving, analyzing problems, decision
  making 41
Role of the supervisor, supervisory concepts 30
Safety, fire fighting, first aid, housekeeping, the
  Occupational Safety and Health Act 28
Company administrative procedures,
  mechanics, paperwork 27
Company nondiscrimination policy, equal
  employment opportunity regulations, the
  minority employees, deal with minorities 25

Of these organizations, about two-thirds offer their initial supervisory training only to persons who have already been promoted to a supervisory position. About half of the remaining organizations offer pre-supervisory training for persons with an interest in becoming supervisors who have not yet been finally selected.

Method   Group discussion is the most commonly used method; 95% of the organizations giving initial classroom training employ the discussion method. Furthermore, of the organizations that use it, almost half rely upon it for from 21% to 40% of the course time and almost another quarter devote from 41% to 60% of the course to group discussion.

The lecture is the next most frequently used instructional method, with 92% of the organizations incorporating lectures into their courses. However, less than half of them devote 20% or less of the course time to lecturing and only about one-fifth employ lectures for more than 40% of the program.

83% of the organizations report using case studies in their programs and 71% incorporate role playing situations. But, overwhelmingly, these account for 20% or less of course time.

Instructors   Of the organizations that conduct initial supervisory training, 112 (75%) use training personnel as faculty. Almost half of that number have from 81% to 100% of the instruction provided by trainers. Other staff personnel are called upon for instruction by 58% of the respondents, and their role tends to be more limited. 38% of the respondents report using the line organization as instructors.

Additional Off-the-Job Training   Almost three-quarters of the organizations conduct additional off-the-job training. While the practice becomes more frequent as the size of the organization increases—97% of the largest organizations do so—in even the smallest respondents, three out of five make specialized training available to their experienced supervisors.

Evaluation   149 organizations with initial off-the-job training programs give an overwhelming vote of their program having met its objectives.

Subjective criteria are used far more frequently as a basis for evaluating supervisory training programs than are more objective criteria. 49% of the organizations use the opinions of the trainees as to the worth of the training as the basis for judging their program. A quarter to a third of the respondents ask the immediate supervisors of the new supervisors for their opinions.

Only performance appraisal data and the department records are reported by more than 10% of the respondents as a basis for evaluations.

Other Surverys

Lundberg, Dunbar, and Bayless[3] report on a survey of the 50 largest (in terms of sales) companies. Of the 50 questionnaires sent, 31, or 62 percent, responded. The results are as follows:

Do you currently have a management training program?
     26   Yes   2   No
How long has the current program been in effect?
     Less than one year 2
     Two to five years 3
     Six to ten years 6
     Ten years or longer   12
Do you feel the program has been effective?
     Yes 21   No 0   Uncertain 2
Do you consider your present methods of measuring effectiveness reliable?
     Yes 10   No 3   Uncertain 10
How do you measure the effectivess of the program?
     Financial success of the trainees 2
     Achieving budget objectives 5
     Reduced manager turnover 6
     Formal testing during or at the end of the program 7
     Special survey, studies, interviews 9
     Advancement of trainees 12
     Achievement achieving performance goals   16

Martin and Kerney[4] report on the results of a national questionnaire sent to 300 organizations, of which 225—or 75 percent—responded. The chief results had to do with management development techniques. The results are as follows:

Technique or Tool	Number
On-the-job experiences and job transfers	200
Seminars	195
Conferences	193
Role playing	120
In basket	73
Quantitative techniques	67
Sensitivity training	57
Other	36

The rank order of effectiveness of management development tools is as shown below:

Technique	Effectiveness
On-the-job experiences and job training	158
Seminars	39
Conferences	23
Role playing	11
In basket	10
Quantitative techniques	6
Sensitivity training	10

MANAGEMENT PHILOSOPHIES AND MANAGEMENT DEVELOPMENT POLICY

A large majority of organizations have philosophies or policies that reflect their views about the management job and the commitment to management development. Many times, these take the form of the written word or a record of the spoken words of the chief executives. They become a creed or belief about management and are often translated into a plan for management development within the organization.

The following quotations reflect the attitudes or views of executives:

Management development must be a continuing process. Otherwise, the management in all probability will become static, and any company with a static management, in the future, will become a static company. It seems to me that management is the key to success of all business enterprises. If you look at companies that surround yours, I think you will find that those who will become the most successful spend a great deal of time in the management development function.

Paul A. Gorman
Chairman of the Board and President
International Paper Company

The fundamentals of good management, in my opinion, are enduring. But theory is one thing, practice quite another. Effective management demands continual refreshment, continual rededication, continual personal resolve.

F. T. Cary
Chairman
IBM Corporation

Policies for management development have also been described by many companies. The following description of the role of management development comes from the Addressograph-Multigraph Company:

The role of management development has been concentrated in the following major activities:

Assisting the divisions in the training of managers—requested by them

Developing a counseling relationship with key management in each operation-division on any performance, interpersonal, or intergroup problem

Developing a performance appraisal process and implementing it

Developing a planning system to encompass all personnel across divisions for the usual purposes of management planning, identifying candidates, and determining development needs

The Eastman Kodak Company has expressed the following goals of management and general education:

The overall goal of management and general education is to help Kodak people and departments find educational solutions to their operating problems.
In support of this overall objective, the following three working objectives apply:

1. Establish a liaison relationship with each operational unit
2. Provide training experiences in the most economical and efficient manner possible
3. Support and promote the principles of good management in all our activities

The IBM Corporation has described its attitude as follows:

The responsibility of the training and development of a manager is shared by the individual and his/her immediate manager.
Off-the-job management training and development is designed to supplement job experience and coaching by the immediate manager.
The development of a manager should begin immediately upon the first management appointment and be continuous, with job assignments as the focal point for the application of personal efforts in company-sponsored education.
Managers should receive adequate training to enable them to fulfill the responsibilities of their positions

1. *New First-Line Managers or Supervisors*
   - Immediately—an orientation normally conducted by the immediate manager to the position and to location practices and procedures.
   - Within 30 days—participation in a one-week IBM New Manager School. This school will provide basic knowledge and skills essential for managers.
   - Based on need, functional training within the location or division.
   - Within 18 months, participate in the Experienced First-Line Manager or Supervisor training program.

2. *Experienced First-Line Managers*
   - First-line manager should participate in a training program within his location or division every three years that includes the minimum established IBM curriculum.

3. *New Managers of Managers*
   - Participation in the first phase of the Corporate IBM Management School within one year of a promotion to be a manager of managers.

4. *Experienced Managers of Managers*
   - Participate in another phase of the IBM Management School every four years.

Each training director should be constantly aware of the management philosophy of the organization and should pay attention to the spoken and written word of executives and to the philosophy of—policies and practices—management development. If no printed statement about supervisory and management development exists, the training director should seek to create one.

QUALITIES OF GOOD MANAGEMENT DEVELOPMENT

Whether management development is considered a program or a process, on the job or off the job, it must have certain essential attributes.

Definite Objectives The program should be designed to bring about worthwhile improvements in the performance and productivity of the organization with aims sufficiently well defined to permit measurement of results.

Relevancy Program content should be pertinent to the participants' needs in relation to their particular jobs within the organization. The program should deal with what is germane and current, not with things that are merely nice to know.

Substantiality The program should treat subject matter in sufficient depth and with sufficient comprehensiveness to bring about appreciable behavior improvement. It should shun mere verbalization and orientation information unless absolutely essential. The natural resistance to change must be recognized.

Strong Leadership The program should employ instructors or discussion leaders who are competent in their particular fields, are skilled at imparting knowledge, and have the ability to communicate—individuals whose own performance sets examples worthy of emulation by others. The motivation of the manager to apply the learning on the job must be a key consideration.

Appropriate Level The program should be designed with a realistic awareness of the qualities, backgrounds, and capabilities of the participants. It should be neither too elementary nor too advanced. The principles of adult learning as described in this chapter should be utilized.

Sound Methods Instructional methods should be carefully selected to match the learning objectives; they should not be merely show items or gimmicks. The methods chosen should stimulate a desire to learn.

Active Participation Provision should be made for active learner involvement; participants should not just "put in time."

Validity The program should provide information which is reliable, factual, and valid and which encourages free and thorough exploration of the content.

Efficacy The objectives should be measured and accomplished. The program should hold up under critical scrutiny and evaluation by objective means. It should be worth more than it costs, and it should increase the value of the participants to the organization.

ADULT LEARNING

The person responsible for the development of supervisors and managers must be not only an educator but also an "adult" educator who understands the distinctions—as expressed by Dr. Malcolm Knowles[5]—between "pedagogy" and "androgogy" (adult learning). This person should provide an environment for learning by:

- Treating mistakes as occasions for learning
- Helping individuals to diagnose their own needs for self-improvement
- Involving participants in planning, carrying out, and evaluating their own learning activities
- Making use of the experience of participants for their learning
- Providing opportunities for participants to be exposed to "unfreezing" experiences
- Building training experiences around real-life problems, not predetermined subject content
- Providing immediate opportunities to practice new learnings with a sense of satisfaction

SUPERVISORY AND MANAGEMENT DEVELOPMENT STAFFS

As mentioned earlier, there are great variations among organizations in terms of the qualifications of persons in management development positions as well as in the way organizations develop their management development organization. The management development function may exist at a headquarters level or at a particular plant or local organization. Sometimes the function reports to the senior person or executive in the personnel organization, even though occasionally it reports directly to the senior line executive.

More and more, the trend seems to be toward having former line managers with good performance records and high potential act in this capacity. Naturally, they should have an instructional ability and a desire to be successful. It is also a good practice to use these capable line managers with high potential for limited tenures since they can instruct better on the basis of their experiences and practices than on the basis of theories. The career path in the function is rather limited and could easily become a terminal position for professional persons who have no other particular talents. Ideally, certain professional talent should exist to maintain continuity and to improve the quality of programs.

It is critical that the position level and the salary level be sufficiently high to attract capable persons. The visibility and contacts available in this type of work should not be overlooked as a means of recruiting capable line managers.

The roles of a management development person might be categorized as follows:

Program Planner
Determines needs
Sets objectives
Picks methods
Builds programs

Instructor
Conducts activities to meet program objectives
Conveys and interprets information and concepts
Uses appropriate instructional techniques
Evaluates and passes along feedback from trainees
Responds flexibly to the group
Sets an example and remains accountable for objectives
Manages the group

Consultant
Responds to requests for help from managers
Makes recommendations to the manager
Helps others to identify problems and find solutions in real time
Uses appropriate process techniques
Encourages exchange and facilitates feedback
Works with diverse elements and synergizes them

Administrator
Maintains hierarchy relationships
Develops overall strategy
Secures and arranges resources
Supervises program mechanics
Maintains statistics and records
Enrolls students and secures speakers
Schedules programs

No one person probably fulfills all the various functions; rather, the individual performs parts of each. Having a capable staff is essential to the training and development of supervisors and managers. Too often this role takes the guise of a clerical activity or is assigned to an individual who has not succeeded elsewhere in management. It is also very important that a plan for the development of training staff persons exist. Internally or through the use of professional societies, there are many ways of helping these persons to improve their ability in any of the above roles.

DETERMINING MANAGEMENT TRAINING NEEDS

Management training programs have varied goals, purposes, and objectives. However, they all need specific learning objectives which specify what is to be accomplished. The determination of the needs to be served requires research and study. There should also be an organized plan to evaluate the results in determining whether the needs have been served.

The programs could be preventative (designed to prevent errors or problems) or corrective (designed to help solve a business problem which has been identified). Examples of programs are as follows:

1. Programs that provide orientation or basic training for new supervisors or managers and teach them the mechanics, or basic knowledge and skills, necessary to do their jobs
2. Training programs for managers that provide the further training and additional skills necessary for the "people" side and administrative elements of their jobs
3. Programs that communicate information about the organization, and also enable trainees to discuss organizational problems
4. Programs that provide information about new management theories, concepts, and approaches, such as scientific management

Many sources exist that can help in determining management training needs, and the training director should be aware of all these inputs when determining the content of a particular program. They include:

Company philosophy and traditions
Management duties, responsibilities, and authority
Company operating plans and policies
The education and experience of managers
The history and size of the organization
The functions to be served
Operational and organizational problems
Past attitudes toward training
Evaluation of prior programs
Performance appraisal results
Opinion surveys and other such surveys and their results
Interviews and discussions with potential trainees, former participants, the supervisors of past and future participants, and line executives

The use of the above techniques will vary, depending upon the purposes of the program.

An example of a survey in which graduates designate in a priority order those topics which are "needed," "nice to include," and "not needed" is given in Fig. 22-1.

A survey of how the particular learning was applied on the job becomes not only an evaluation but also a means of determining the needs to keep a particular

MANAGER CURRICULUM SURVEY

Please designate by "letter code" for all <u>items</u>.

    A–"need to include"
    B–"nice to include"
    C–"not needed"

Also, insert other subjects or topics you feel are needed.

Letter ·
Code

A	B	C	
			Provide a greater understanding of the current environment.
			Marketplace
			Organization and Management Systems
			Technology
			Know the role of the first-level manager—the responsibilities and authority.
			Make managers aware of when and where they should seek assistance.
			Ability to provide appropriate recognition, rewards, and penalties.
			Ability to motivate, using both psychological and other forms of motivation.
			Knowledge of recent theories of motivation
			Knowledge of techniques for personal career planning.
			Knowledge of alternative theories of leadership.
			Ability to use natural leadership ability to get results.
			Ability to recruit and orient new employees.
			Ability to establish a budget and to interpret an operating statement.
			Knowledge of principles of delegation and management of time.
			Knowledge of problem-solving techniques.
			Understand the attitudes, interests, and be able to supervise the following groups:
			Young employees
			Women
			Older employees
			Marginal employees
			Employees with health problems
			Enhance the skills and abilities in the following areas:
			Develop fair and objective performance plans
			Appraisal performance and counseling
			Coach and instruct subordinates
			Conduct effective meetings
			Plan, organize, and control work
			Decision making and establishing priorities
			Introducing and managing change
			Controlling expense and maximizing revenue

Fig. 22-1 Manager curriculum survey.

program current. It is also very important that the training director have access to the results of performance appraisal results, opinion survey data, and operating plans as a regular means of improving the programs.

A statement of "basic management responsibilities" should exist or be created for the organization. This listing should define the responsibilities and authority, usually by level of management, and should apply to all members of the management organization. The list should define the supervisor's or manager's role in managing people, involving such basic duties as employment, training, supervising, promotion, and termination. It should also define the supervisor's role in planning, complying with company or organization policies and procedures, and budgeting security and protection, as well as his or her responsibility for production or results.

These basic responsibilities should be a part of each management performance plan and should be an addition to specific responsibilities assigned to a particular position. The existence of such a list can become the keystone of the management training and can also be the basis for determining needs or deficiencies.

Another approach to determining needs, particularly where an area of weakness seems to have been identified, is to make a performance audit in which you seek to:

Identify the problem
Determine the performance deficiencies
Establish the need to correct the deficiencies or the value of correcting them
Determine the cause—knowledge, skill, or organization

Another approach to determining management training needs is to survey the subordinates of potential trainees and have them report upon a management practice of the trainee manager. Typical questions in such a survey are as follows:

1. How often does your manager give you recognition and encouragement you feel you deserve?
   a. Seldom
   b. Sometimes
   c. Frequently
   d. Almost always
2. Has your manager had any discussions with you about ways in which you might improve your ability to appraise and counsel your employees?
   a. Has never done this
   b. Has rarely done this
   c. Does this now and then
   d. Does this quite often
3. How would you say your manager delegates?
   a. Too many controls
   b. Without adequate control
   c. With some control
   d. With adequate control

This type of survey information is fed back to the trainee manager in a confidential manner, with a designation of how his or her subordinates react to the supervision. It could also indicate those items which the subordinate would like to see improved or changed. This "moment of truth" is helpful to the manager in planning for involvement in the program. It also establishes common needs, using group norms which can become the basis for the entire program.

Also helpful are instruments that are completed by trainees in which they describe how they handle management situations such as reaching decisions that affect other supervisors at their own level and what they do when policies or procedures are not adhered to.

Task forces or advisory committees to determine content are also valuable. These groups are usually composed of individuals who are currently active in supervision or have already completed some phases of the program; they might even include the superiors of the persons to be trained.

One of the most comprehensive studies of management training needs was conducted by the Exxon Corporation. It defined the following objectives:

- Improve training relevance and acceptability through functional field and headquarters involvement in needs determination
- Verify effectiveness of existing supervisor program coverage
- Check for unfilled training requirements
- Apply measurement techniques to increase planning precision

Data Collection
1. Questionnaire method
   - Eighty-eight content items evaluated on a four-point scale
   - Content developed from internal and external practices
   - Areas covered
     - Management's contributions
     - Management's social and legal responsibilities
     - Business economics
     - Management science
     - Individual and group behavior
     - Leader behavior
     - Communications
     - Optimizing job performance
     - Support systems
     - Labor relations
     - Intercompany and interindustry relations
   - Comments encouraged (210 entries, many multiapplicable)
2. Five functions and over 600 participants and 1,200 evaluations:

   - Marketing
   - Production
   - Refining
   - Controller's
   - EPRC
3. Bench-mark positions evaluated by incumbent and superior
4. Percent return—99 (nonanonymous)

PROGRAM CONTENT

There is no curriculum or list of topics or subjects that is of equal value to all levels of supervision or is appropriate to the same extent for all organizations. Various surveys of needs should provide an indication of content together with a description of the knowledge or skill required. With this information the training director is in a better position to determine the time requirements or length of the program and its objectives, as well as the needed ability of the instructor and the most appropriate method.

In planning the program, consideration must be given to the amount of knowledge, skill, and attitude training that should be included in the program and to the requirements for personnel or supervisory skills, administrative ability, and self-development skills.

In developing a program, it is important that detailed outlines be prepared for each subject or topic. The program should not be merely a list of topics such as "managing change," "managing managers," and "managing individual differences." Too often a program is merely a list of topics which reads like the index of a book.

Each particular subject should be developed with a detailed outline so that someone other than the person who prepared the outline could provide the instruction. The outline should also be tested with a real audience before it becomes a part of a program curriculum. A typical outline should include:

The title

Objectives—what participants should know and be able to do as a result of the instruction

Description—a summary paragraph giving the content, methods, and results of the session or program

Materials or references to be used

Visual or audio aids as well as readings or study materials

A time schedule showing what occurs each 10 or 15 minutes

An instructor or discussion outline listing on the right-hand half of a page, in concise language, the topics to be covered in sequence and designating visuals to be used, questions which might be asked, and responses to be expected (The left-hand side of the page should be left for the instructor to insert his or her own comments.)

Suggested handout materials

Bibliography of books, etc.

Instructors

The selection of instructors is critical. Certain subjects can best be taught by training-staff members, and others by trained line management; some require the use of noncompany college professors or consultants. The use of line managers and executives certainly improves the communications process and enables the supervisors and managers to have a better understanding of the views of these operating executives. Having executives from different functions work with or instruct in the program broadens the knowledge and understanding that participants will have of all parts of the business, and it reinforces the commitment of the organization to management development.

TRAINING FOR NEW MANAGERS OR SUPERVISORS

Probably the most critical training is that which is provided to newly promoted supervisors or managers; it is essential that these people have proper viewpoints and attitudes and be provided with the tools of their new role so as to avoid making mistakes at an early stage. New managers should understand their role, their authority and responsibility, the performance that is expected ot them, the policies and practices of the company, their budget and operating responsibilities, legal regulations, and union relationships; they must also be familiar with the most current theories of motivation and leadership, and they must have had some practice in supervisory skills and in the management of human relations situations.

The role of new supervisory persons is difficult, and many are nervous and apprehensive about making mistakes. The role change from an employee to a member of management must be thoroughly discussed and understood because it creates many new relationships and because the individual is now responsible for "getting work done through others." The manager is now involved in making decisions that influence the productivity and profits of the business, as well as the careers, incomes, attitudes, and lives of the employees who are supervised. Some examples of programs for new supervisors or manager training programs are as follows:

Texas Instruments
   Civil rights and equal opportunity programs
   Attendance, salary, and wages
   Work performance and conduct
   Termination
   Performance review
   Security and safety
   Quality-minded supervisor
   Benefits
   Labor relations
   Motivation

The Ford Motor Company.   The Foreman Institute is a five-day development program focusing on the most critical problem situations encountered by a new foreman. These include person-to-person confrontations, administration of discipline, assignment of manpower, removal and replacement of defective materials, and prevention and correction of stock shortages and equipment failures. Utilizing a learning-by-doing approach, the Foreman Institute was developed to deal with handling these problem areas.

The Foreman Institute *will not* provide total development for a new foreman. Certain development needs are most effectively presented within an individual's plant environment. Consequently, the institute was designed to supplement, not replace, local plant training programs and on-the-job training.

IBM.   The IBM New Manager School, which is a week-long resident program at a central corporate location, includes participants from all divisions of the company and covers the following subjects:

   Basic beliefs and principles
   Managing people
   Company policy
   Communication
   Business conduct and ethics
   Technological trends
   IBM organization
   Medical
   Safety and security
   The marketplace
   Appraisal and counseling
   Planning, organizing, and controlling

There is also an "immediate orientation" given by the second-level supervisor directly after promotion dealing with the vital topics, reports, and personnel information which are needed for the new manager's immediate success. In addition, IBM provides functional training for new managers; this is given at their home location and is designed to prepare them to manage in the particular environment.

The Phillips 66 Company.   This program includes the following:

   Knowing your employees' individual differences
   Job satisfaction and morale
   Improving communications
   Maintaining effective discipline
   Guiding and developing employees

Each organization should give attention to the training of these critical management persons. The evolution of this type of training began with the three J programs—Job Instruction Training, Job Relations Training, and Job Methods Training. Too often training directors become enchanted with the training of middle managers or executives or with the use of new or sophisticated techniques. Such a concern can be very important, but it may lead to the neglect of the training of the new supervisor or foreman. Training directors must continually change and improve the curriculum so that it will be current with the needs of the individuals and the organization.

NEW MANAGERS OF MANAGERS

Equally important is the training of new members of middle management so that they will understand and be able to meet their responsibilities. The fact that their role is to instruct their subordinate supervisors should be made clear and meaningful, and they should be held accountable for this effort.

The training of the new manager of managers should have the same priority and be given the same amount of attention as the training of the new supervisor. This training should give greater attention to understanding the interaction between organizational units, resolving conflict, managing change and its implementation, organizing and controlling work, budgeting, and using numerical data as a management tool.

The members of middle management need greater organizational knowledge and information to better understand the interaction between functions and the impact of decisions upon other organization units. The skills of delegation, problem analysis and decision making, coaching subordinate supervisors, and conducting meetings need increased attention in middle-management training. There is also the responsibility to ensure uniformity in the supervision of people in different units, including the establishments of financial standards, performance standards, head count, operating results, the salary administration program at the management level, etc. Opportunity should be provided for a better understanding of current organization-wide problems and for participation in their solution.

In the organization of the training of middle management it is best to have the group composed of a cross section of the organization, with a good functional mix; this ensures a learning and sharing of experiences among the participants.

ADDITIONAL MANAGEMENT OR SUPERVISORY TRAINING

Management or supervisory training should not be a one-time activity. Most organizations do provide additional training beyond the basic training for new supervisors or new middle managers to provide new or additional skills and knowledge or provide added depth to the topics presented in the basic programs. It is important that there be an overall plan of development to ensure that training will be given periodically during the career of the supervisor. Supervisors should be kept current on, and fully aware of, policies and practices, and also should be taught new and improved skills and techniques designed to aid in their employee relations and in the solution of operating problems.

Supervisors should be stimulated to continue their self-development. Too often middle managers merely give lip service to the idea of management development, without really supporting it or becoming involved; this creates the typical "credibility gap" between their words and their actions.

Westinghouse Electric believes that every management and professional person in the organization should have at least one formal learning experience each year. This organization has established career pathways and has described a typical hierarchy of courses in general management for all levels of management from the first-level manager through upper management.

Some typical courses are categorized as follows:

1. *Conceptual Development*
   Human values and the executive role
   Human resource measurement seminar

2. *The Management Process*
   Models for management seminar—middle management
   Business management course
   Project management
   Motivation to work—applications of job enrichment
   Performance review—coaching and counseling

3. *The Rational Process*
   Problem solving and decision making
   Motivation—Transactional Analysis
   Management of change—a systems approach
   Productivity in the office
   Career planning workshop

4. *Finance and the Computer*
   Computer principles and applications
   Techniques of finance and accounting
   Profit planning and financial statements workshop

5. *Individual Skill Development*
   Business conference and discussion leader workshop
   Communications skills workshop
   Improving written communications
   Effective reading

The following courses are offered at the General Motors Institute:

Applied management (one week)
EEO—minority relations (three days)
Fire protection (one week)
Improving people performance (three days)
Interpersonal relations laboratory (one week)
Management problem solving and decision making (one week)
Managerial Grid seminar (one week)
Plant protection administration (one week)
Quality-control foreman (one week)
Technical-staff management (one week)
Woman supervisor (three days)

Eastman Kodak offers the following range of courses:

Basic English refresher
Communications workshop
Basic industrial relations practices
Creativity and problem solving
Interpersonal relations
Oral presentation
Effective reading and writing improvement workshops
Motivation and people interaction
Fact gathering and interviewing

Project management
Conference leadership
Job instructor training
Time management
Office-methods principles
Managerial economics
The tools of management science

The New York Telephone Company has developed a middle-management seminar known as the "Challenges of the Future," which permits managers to discuss the goals of the organization and the development of plans of action. This program does a great deal to ensure the commitment of all managers and their involvement in the process of planning change.

Mobil Oil Company has a program for corporate departments which includes the following subjects:

Management development in perspective
Planning and controlling
Organization: the foundation of effective management
The nature of leadership
Introducing change
Motivation
Employee communication
You and Mobil's future

As managers gain experience in management, they should be provided with greater information about the external environment and its influence upon the organization. Topics of possible interest could include:

Public policy and corporate power
Wage and price controls
Racial America
The legitimacy of business
United States foreign policy
Goals and means in our economy
National health
The humanization of management systems

Knowledge in these areas helps to make the manager a better-informed citizen, and it increases his or her understanding of the environment that affects the organization. Topics such as these are best taught by authorities from outside the organization.

In addition, many supervisory and management training courses are offered by the American Management Association, ASTD, and other professional associations; by colleges and universities; and by management consulting organizations. These cover a great range of subjects. Some companies, such as General Electric, Xerox, and Westinghouse, have developed their internal materials for purchase by other organizations.

Decentralized organizations or organizations with multiple locations should consider packaging their own training modules and securing and adapting other prepared programs. With adequate trainer outlines and the support of good audio and visual aids, line executives should be able to conduct such training at their locations.

Examples of such company-prepared training programs are:

First National City Corporation
   Conducting employee feedback meetings about opinion survey results

General Electric
  Career-action planning
  Effective management through work planning
IBM Corporation
  Transparent management
  Employee privacy

INSTRUCTIONAL METHODS

The surveys that have been reported show that the lecture-discussion method is the preferred method of instructing. However, more recently there has been increased use of video tape cassettes, computer-assisted instruction, simulations and exercises, audio cassettes, self-analysis and other instruments, and films with instructor outlines. Many of these films and video cassettes enable organizations to bring to their programs some of the foremost experts in the country, with accompanying lecture notes to be used by the location trainer.

We find that Transactional Analysis concepts are being used to assist in interpersonal skills. In addition, multiple levels of management are participating together in team-building or organization development programs to improve team effectiveness and organizational health.

Some companies have developed their own self-study materials which permit individuals to acquire the knowledge needed for management. Classroom sessions are then utilized for skill training that requires a professional trainer and interaction between individuals, such as role playing and cases.

There are many forms of programmed instruction, including those which are commercially available as well as those which have been developed internally within an organization. These texts are used primarily for self-study instruction and are designed more to present knowledge or information than to teach skills or provide opportunities for practice under the guidance of a trainer.

It does seem that more and more instructional methods are concerned with a quick and direct application to the work situation. The content should be based on real-world examples and personal experience, rather than merely presenting textbook theories which have not been validated for the specific organization.

LOCATION AND SCHEDULE OF THE PROGRAM

An increasing number of programs are scheduled as full-time activities, occupying at least one full week and thus completely separating participants from their work. The exceptions are those smaller companies in which it is difficult to replace the person while he or she is attending the program. The full-time nature of the program permits complete and undivided attention and allows the time necessary for study and work assignments, particularly in the case of resident programs which have the added advantage of providing evening sessions for discussion among the trainees.

The use of nonorganization facilities such as conference centers, motels, or even company centers has increased. The use of such facilities is educationally sound— a "cultural island" is created—and it also gives further proof of the organization's commitment to, and investment in, supervisory and management development.

It does seem that these special facilities should be reasonably close to the company location if company executives are to be used as speakers. Most of these facilities have the furniture and visual aids needed for a program, and they often include recreational facilities. Participants are increasingly engaging in physical fitness activities during the time of attendance, and thus recreational facilities and equipment are becoming more essential.

In developing the program schedule, the building blocks or units should have a flow of content which is related to, and works toward, the overall objectives. A variety of methods should be used to avoid an excessive dependence on motion pictures or lectures in consecutive time periods without providing for some participant involvement. Every effort should be made to give the participants a say in the selection of some of the content, such as through the use of electives, work problems which the participants bring with them, and the development of objectives or work plans for the future.

EVALUATION OF RESULTS

The evaluation of management training is the subject of many articles, publications, and books about training and is a topic in many programs, with speakers expressing their views. Considering the investments in dollars, worker-hours, and facilities, it does seem important to measure the results of a program in terms that are meaningful to the organization—increased work performance, profits and a significant effect on the "bottom line" of the operating statement. Admittedly, it is more difficult to measure the results of management training than those of skills training, sales training, or other technical programs which provide information or teach skills that can be assessed on a before-and-after basis.

The evaluation of most management training programs seems to rely upon the trainees' reactions—verbal feedback on "happiness sheets." The rationale behind this is that if the participants like the program, it must be good.

Why Evaluate?   Each training person has a responsibility to justify the results of the programs as they contribute to the organization's productivity and profits. In addition, an effective evaluation process should show how the training improves the performance of the managers.

What to Evaluate   Ideally, with an effective determination of needs, objectives, to be accomplished by the training program should have been established at the outset. These objectives should include the knowledge, attitudes, and skills to be improved and the habits to be corrected. The ability of the instructors, as well as the methods used, should be evaluated.

Who Should Evaluate?   The evaluation should be made by all persons who are involved in, or affected by, the particular program—the trainees, their superiors, and the training staff. It is even desirable to have persons in the organization who are not involved evaluate the results or audit the program.

When to Evaluate   Evaluation should be a continuous process; it should begin in advance of the training, when the training objectives are established, and a plan of evaluation should be prepared at that time. The evaluation should determine the trainees' ability before the program starts, continually monitor their progress during the course of the program, and evaluate the results immediately at the conclusion of the program, as well as at three-, six-, or nine-month intervals afterward.

One approach is to have the trainees develop at the end of the training a plan of activities to be accomplished within the next 90 to 120 days which apply to the training. There should be a follow-up to make certain that the planned activities have been completed. This is usually done by means of an interview by a staff member. It is also desirable for the training director to meet with the trainee's manager to determine the performance improvement.

The levels of evaluation should include both subjective and objective criteria:

Subjective
    Trainee's reaction
        During training and at the end
        Three to six months afterward
    Reaction of immediate superior

Reaction of subordinates
Evaluation of the trainer

Objective
Performance appraisals
Records of production, costs, and quality
Records of absence, turnover, and grievances
Opinion survey results
Accomplishment of objectives
Testing—before and after

Combinations of the aforementioned techniques are needed. However, always be aware that the style of the instructor can unduly influence the popularity of a subject. It is not unusual for students to enjoy and to report well on sessions in which the instructor is more an entertainer than an instructor and in which little content is presented.

On the other hand, there are occasions when the program content, even if the needs are well established and the training is effective, cannot be applied on the job. For example, principles of participative management cannot be applied in an environment that is conducive only to an autocratic style. The superior, the ability of subordinates, or other factors in the organizational climate or environment may hinder the performance of the trained manager.

There is a danger in being willing to take credit for the successes of a training program but being unwilling to accept criticism for its failures—either might be caused by activity outside the scope of the program. Programs that have a corrective goal such as reducing absenteeism, reducing grievances, or improving cost performance are more apt to have specific targets or goals. Preventative programs are designed primarily to maintain the status quo or to improve it and are concerned mainly with the development of proper attitudes or habits, which cannot be easily measured.

It is possible that the use of trained groups, as contrasted with control groups who are not trained, may provide some evidence of results.

The Postal Service Training and Development Institute made a conscious effort to relate management training experience to organizational indices of effectiveness in the field. Using the same management information data base and the same measurement of effectiveness employed by postal executives to judge unit output, the institute undertook to isolate and measure the impact of training on organizational performance.

In looking at or evaluating a program, the following questions should be asked:

Was the deficiency agreed upon?
Did the course offer a solution to the deficiency?
Did the students know the objectives?
Was there a plan of evaluation before starting?
Did the program have a trial or test?
Did the trainer follow the course design?
Did the students meet the course requirements?
Was the job environment conducive to application?
Has the deficiency been overcome?

Figure 22-2 shows an evaluation form that could be used for a program. An example of an open-ended postprogram evaluation is shown in Fig 22-3.

NONCLASSROOM MANAGEMENT DEVELOPMENT

This chapter has deliberately focused on programs of formal training for managers and supervisors. However, it is recognized that the majority of development

STANDARD EVALUATION FORM

Course Title: _____ Date: _____

Location: _____ Instructor: _____

To guide us in planning future training, please answer the questions below. You need not sign the sheet unless you so desire.

How would you rate the following?

	Excellent	Satisfactory	Unsatisfactory
Ability of Instructor	_____	_____	_____
Adequacy of Course Content	_____	_____	_____
Adequacy of Visual & Audio Aids	_____	_____	_____
Adequacy of Course Materials	_____	_____	_____
Application to Your Job	_____	_____	_____
Conduct of Session	_____	_____	_____
Length of Course	_____	_____	_____
Adequacy of Facilities	_____	_____	_____

If any factor is rated "unsatisfactory," please provide explanation:

_____

_____

_____

What was of most value to you?

_____

_____

What was of least value to you?

_____

_____

Additional comments would be appreciated.

_____

_____

_____

_____
Signature (Optional)

Fig. 22-2   Standard evaluation form.

occurs on the job in the coaching relationship between the superior and the subordinate as well as through planned job rotation activities.

The appraisal process, properly utilized, should be one of the key instruments

1. List the most valuable and least valuable aspects of your participation.

   Most valuable and why -

   _____

   _____

   _____

   Least valuable and why -

   _____

   _____

   _____

2. Considering the objectives of the entire program, how are they related to your own management development needs?

   _____ A.   Highly related

   _____ B.   Somewhat related

   _____ C.   Unrelated*

   *Comments

   _____

   _____

   _____

   _____

   _____

3. My feelings about this program:

   _____

   _____

   _____

   _____

   _____

Fig. 22-3   Postprogram evaluation.

of development. Normally, these programs, which may be identified as Management by Objectives, ask that the superior and the subordinate agree on a performance plan for a period of time; the plan includes activities as well as evidence of acceptable performance or standards of performance which represent the individual's work. This performance plan is evaluated periodically to determine the level of accomplishment, and it becomes the basis for a new performance plan. It also indicates those areas in which the individual must show improvement and will need coaching by his or her superior.

The training director should become involved in this nonclassroom training activity, working to improve performance planning, to establish objectives or standards of performance that will aid in the evaluation process, and to make the interviews two-way discussions that will result in plans for improved performance and career development. This role is a natural follow-on to the training in these areas within the classroom, and it enables the training director to assist in the application of content on the job.

Other job-centered development includes job enrichment and job development activities; task-force assignments are also effective development activities. In performing this work, the training director should seek to consider how best to motivate people and to ensure proper motivation and leadership behavior.

Trainers have certain ethical responsibilities, and they should also have a loyalty to the trainees and a respect for their confidences. Normally they should not give their views of the capabilities of a trainee as a manager, and they should not report on comments that a trainee makes during the course of a program. They should not criticize or disparage the policies of the organization or the executives of the business in the presence of trainees.

Mr. Charles Bowen[6] has as his central theme that "Management development must return to unadorned fundamentals and that takes place on the firing line." He is cautioning against the use of "cookbook" management or transparent management, which results in managers who:

- Abdicate or "cop out"
- Transmit instructions through an "open pipe"
    With no reason why
    With no value added
    With no tailoring to specific circumstances
- Publicly attribute to someone else the responsibility for a decision
- "Play it safe," or practice "no-risk" management

J. Sterling Livingston states:

> Many highly intelligent and ambitious men are not learning from either their formal education or their own experience what they most need to know to build successful careers in management.
>
> Their failure is due in part to the fact that many crucial management tasks are not taught in management education programs, but are left to be done on the job, where few managers ever master them, because no one teaches them how. It is also due in part to the fact that what takes place in the classroom often is mis-education that inhibits their ability to learn from their experience.[7]

SUMMARY

Members of the management development staff should be well informed, have credibility and acceptance, and be at a high-enough level in the organization so that they can impact and influence decisions. They should be capable of examining the programs in terms of whether they provide an adequate return on the investment to the organization. Too often in the past we have concentrated on elegant solutions to problems that are vaguely defined. Members of the management development staff should be consultants and advisers to managers at all levels. They should be learning and information specialists who are able to plan programs, determine needs, and establish objectives; who are concerned with both preventative and corrective development; who are current on learning systems technology; and, above all, who can continually evaluate and quickly change training efforts.

Organizations must be willing to invest money, resources, and manpower in these efforts, whether they occur within or outside the company. We cannot afford to do without training, nor can we provide merely lip service to these very important company and management responsibilities, nor can line managers abdicate their responsibility to the training department.

REFERENCES

1. Toffler, Alvin: *Future Shock,* Random House, Inc., New York, 1970.
2. *Supervisory Training,* The Conference Board, Inc., Report no. 612, New York, 1973.
3. Lundberg, Craig, Roger Dunbar, and T. L. Bayless: "Contemporary Management Training in Large Corporations," *Training and Development Journal,* September 1973.
4. Martin, Desmond D., and William J. Kerney: "The Current State of Management Development Participation and Methods," *Journal of Business,* Dec. 19, 1973.
5. Knowles, Malcolm: *The Adult Learner: A Neglected Species,* Gulf Publishing Company, Houston, 1973.
6. Bowen, Charles. P., Jr.: "Let's Put Realism into Management Development," *Harvard Business Review,* July–August 1973.
7. Livingston, J. Sterling: "The Myth of the Well-Educated Manager," *Harvard Business Review,* pp. 79–89, January–February 1971.

Chapter 23

Training for Special Groups: Minorities, Women, and the Disadvantaged

LEWIS M. RAMBO

Lewis M. Rambo *is Vice President, Personnel, Arthur D. Little, Inc., a research and management consulting firm based in Cambridge, Massachusetts. Prior to joining Arthur D. Little, Inc., Dr. Rambo was Manager, Organization and Manpower, Military Engine Division, General Electric Company, Cincinnati, Ohio. He has had extensive experience in personnel, labor relations, training and development, and organization development with General Electric Company and previously with the Ford Motor Company. Dr. Rambo served as personnel psychologist with the United States Army and as a consultant for many community-based organizations. He is a former Chairman of the Research Committee of ASTD.*

An increasing number of businesses and other institutions are coming to accept the fact that minority-group members, women, and the economically and socially and/or educationally disadvantaged are part of this country's human resources too. It is also being recognized that it is just not good business to neglect or underutilize any talent or manpower source. This acceptance stems in part from legislative edict and governmental pressure; many organizations are contractually obligated to make more aggressive efforts to bring larger numbers of minorities and women onto their payrolls. There is also a parallel realization in many institutions that affirmative action and equal opportunity have become a condition of doing business, not only with governmental agencies, but with the rest of society as well.

The resolve to open up organizations to all comers is a first step, but even after extensive recruiting efforts, careful screening and selection, and the revision of traditional hiring procedures, something more has to be done. These "special" hires (special in the sense that they previously had not been brought into the organization in comparable numbers) may require more extensive orientation to the details of their jobs and to specific work requirements, plus remedial education and training. They may also require supportive services, with priority being given to individual and group counseling. The Hawthorne studies[1] clearly demonstrated that even the whitest of the white respond more effectively to organizational requirements when they have the benefit of constructive, job-related counseling.

The particular combination of extra counseling efforts will depend upon the socioeconomic backgrounds, previous work experiences, and skill levels of these new employees.

It is a serious mistake to assume that all minorities or women will, on a prima facie basis, need a great deal more training or require closer supervision than other new employees. Often these special candidates are well qualified, but because of traditional and restrictive hiring policies, they may have been prevented from demonstrating their abilities. The care that a personnel office takes in interpreting the work experience, training, and skills of all those to be hired—whether they belong to a minority group or not—will be of great value in determining individual needs for prejob or on-the-job training. In many cases, managers and supervisors may be surprised and pleased to discover that so-called special hires become skilled and valued contributors to their organizations with minimal orientation and training.

UPGRADING THE UPGRADABLE

In most organizations there are undoubtedly a fair number of minorities and women with talents that have been underutilized because they were undetected or overlooked. Often little or no special training is required to accomplish meaningful upgrading of these individuals. What is really needed is active organizational support, managerial attention, and the revision of outmoded promotional policies. Much of the contemporary organizational thinking about upgrading and promoting minorities and women stems from strong reliance on some timeworn and questionable assumptions that have come to be accepted as axiomatic. Some of these assumptions are derivations from the socioeconomic and philosophical lore of this country, while others are myths and misconceptions about "what the world is really like."

The Job Opportunity Myth

One of the most widely held myths is that significant upgrading can occur without pump primers like substantial increases in profit levels, heightened company or organizational expansion, and unusual attrition. The truth is that no organization can undertake significant increases in the rate and direction of minority, female, or any other kind of personnel utilization unless the organization:

- Is growing, i.e., is expanding its range of operations and thus its need for additional personnel.
- Is experiencing considerable attrition—as a result of quits, retirements, etc.—which creates vacancies at several levels within the organization.
- Alters its promotional system, denying movement to individuals who might otherwise have been elevated under the old rules. In effect, this alteration shifts the focus of promotional opportunity to different people. Parenthetically, this kind of opportunity shift can create severe attitudinal problems among the members of previously favored populations.

Please understand that—without question—companies can improve the way they assess, evaluate, and promote their employees. They can work to minimize favoritism, bias, and prejudice, while at the same time placing more emphasis on performance, ability, and potential. Still, none of these steps will by themselves create a single new job opening! Only expanded operations and more business—or attrition—will create the need for increased numbers of people to fill higher-level jobs.

The Horatio Alger Myth

A second myth that follows from the "Horatio Alger" or "frontier" orientation of this country is that everyone wants to be upgraded—everyone wants to move up in the organization. Business magazines have been full of articles bemoaning the unwillingness of many employees to move into positions which ostensibly carry higher levels of authority and responsibility (e.g., foremen, supervisors, and work-team leaders). This unwillingness among some groups of employees to take leadership roles seems to be on the increase and suggests that significant changes are needed in the nature and requirements of the very jobs into which companies now want to promote minorities and women. It is obvious that many of these jobs involve little inherent challenge, autonomy, responsibility, or opportunity—or at least they are perceived that way. It is also obvious that a basic tenet of our system—"move up to get ahead"—is not presently viewed by many employees to be as valid as it once was.

While it is clear that, in theory, most people have the capacity to accept more responsibility, do more productive work, and make a more significant contribution to an organization, as a practical matter, not everyone views "moving ahead" as an absolute blessing.

The Upgrading Myth

A third widely accepted myth is that upgrading can occur only at relatively low levels within an organization so as not to disrupt the delicately balanced positions and organizational relationships at higher levels. The truth is that there can be no general upgrading anywhere in an organization without a disruptive chain of upward moves or the general erosion of the "distance" between position levels in terms of work content, authority, and power. This is not to say that some erosion is not desirable. Still, company management must recognize that giving more responsibility and authority to larger numbers of lower-level employees will ultimately affect them and the way they structure their own jobs.

The Responsibility and Money Myth

A fourth and final myth presumes that as you move up in the organization, you get more money. This assumption bears careful review, especially in middle- and lower-level jobs, given current compensation practices, overtime premiums, extra management and supervisory demands, additional uncompensated duties not expected of nonmanagement personnel, etc. Managers who compare their base salary relative to the number of uncompensated overtime hours, extra assignments, etc., with the pay of their skilled hourly operators find to their dismay that they have little or no financial advantage. (The fact that lead hourly operators and/or skilled employees can and often do make as much money as their supervisors, or even more, is an often-cited example.)

In many cases upgrading may be simply a matter of opening up higher-level positions to female and minority employees—positions that have historically been closed by reason of company promotional policies, union rules, past practices, etc. Possibly the most meaningful progress in the area of upward movement will be in the direct placement of promising or talented lower-level minority or female employees in more responsible, higher-paying jobs. These kinds of placements have been called "rifle shots" or "shooting star" promotions and have been tried with a fair amount of success in several companies—Ford, Xerox, GE, Chrysler, and IBM, to name a few. In many instances, these employees performed effectively because their skills and abilities were more closely matched to the real demands of the jobs than management had previously supposed.

Organizational Needs

The preceding myths underscore the issues and difficulties that surround the overall problem of upgrading. Considerable attention—based on the need to remove as many as possible of the barriers to constructive, meaningful promotional movement for all employees—must be given to the following requirements:

- In-depth analysis of existing organization structures to create alternative tracks, career ladders, or promotional chains that will provide substantial job challenge and incentive. Just as companies review their budgets, product lines, and capital expenditures each year, management is well-advised to review its human resource utilization posture regularly. All too often, managers accept without question long-standing promotional patterns, job specifications, and position descriptions. Although the company may have changed dramatically—its image, products, plant locations, etc.—managers fail to consider the effects of these changes on the organization's employees. These analyses will also furnish greater flexibility to company management in considering varied promotional opportunities.
- The careful development of inventories of existing skills or skill interests can be of value in determining where an employee or prospective employee might best be utilized. Objective skill patterns* for each position can then be established. These patterns may be operationalized into specific expected on-the-job behaviors and matched with each employee's range of abilities or interests. If the demands of a given job can be matched with a profile of an employee's abilities, a hiring manager has the advantages of:
  - An objective assessment of the employee's chances for succeeding on that job.
  - A "personalized" prescription for the employee's continuing skill development. This prescription could feature both short- and longer-term actions that the employee might undertake with company support to meet specific career goals. These actions need not spell commitment to a long course of study or an advanced degree. Rather, actions can be programmed in "bite-sized," "do-able" steps. Personalized prescriptions, when coupled with success on the job and sincere interest on the part of supervisors, can serve to reinforce the employee to contribute to the limits of his or her ability.
- Development of programs aimed at skill building and academic preparation. These programs should lay out in detail the objectives that must be reached and the proficiency levels that must be attained in order to be in line for promotion, e.g., the new apprentice training systems now offered by many industries.
- Experiments in the design and structure of jobs to make them more responsible, demanding, and interesting, while at the same time allowing the employee to participate in those decisions that bear on his or her own job performance. Equally important is the design of a "results reporting system" so that employees can assess their own performance on a realistic basis.
- Improvement of approaches to fair, unbiased, and systematic evaluation of the potential and performance of employees by management, moving the most deserving first.

*Objective skill patterns have been developed by James F. Weidig, training manager, and incorporated into branch operations with considerable success at Ford Motor Credit Company.

- Use of situational counseling when necessary for employees displaced or affected by changes in the organization. These resources might also be made available to those viewed as unable to move further in the organization as they reach their intellectual, skill, or emotional limits.
- Examination of the possibility of developing an adviser-counselor bank where employees near retirement would be paid to act as coaches, teachers, and/or advisers so that minorities and women at lower levels might be trained to move into better, higher-skill jobs sooner. This accelerated upgrading should be vital to a business whose skilled manpower resources are aging. For example, a skilled mechanic with one year to go before retirement could be assigned several "intern" mechanics. It would be his job to teach, advise, and possibly supervise these younger employees.

It should be recognized that fuller, more meaningful utilization not only of minorities and women but of all employees can be achieved. The challenge is that organizations must be serious and committed to making full use of human talent.

RECRUITING THE RECRUITABLE

We have discussed upgrading first, assuming that a number of minority and women employees are already in most organizations waiting to be discovered and to be offered more challenging job opportunities. This may not be the case with companies or institutions which, for various reasons, have resisted, avoided, or just started bringing minorities and women (in other than traditional clerical, service, or maintenance roles) onto the payroll. Many managers and personnel directors have been instructed to locate and hire more minorities and women only to discover that there are few highly qualified members of these groups standing in line anywhere in the United States looking for jobs—they have been snapped up long ago.

These managers have discovered that organizations must compete for a scarce personnel resource—women and minority workers with established skills and abilities—in a highly competitive market. In most cases imaginative, aggressive and intensive recruiting efforts will result at best in reasonable success at hiring above-average and talented minorities and women. Recruiting managers are discovering that they cannot locate minority or women candidates on predominantly white, male campuses or with blanket ads in newspapers. Top management is often surprised to discover that in prior years, few if any predominantly minority or female colleges were scheduled for visits by company recruiters. Companies are now visiting schools with large minority and female populations, establishing relationships with department chairpersons, college placement directors, and campus organizations.

Some companies are investing heavily in "growing their own" prospective employees, especially in areas of high demand and low supply like engineering, industrial management, and other technical fields. Companies such as General Electric have taken positive steps with activities like PIMEG (Program to Increase Minority Engineering Graduates), which works to stimulate minority-group interest in engineering and other technical specialties. Employee referral programs, the use of well-established personnel search firms specializing in women or minorities, and expanded community outreach efforts have also met with some success. Still, the number of these people is limited. Organizations wishing to implement "successful" affirmative action programs must be willing to substitute the word "qualifiable" for "qualified" in their recruiting and placement projections.

QUALIFYING THE QUALIFIABLE

Before an organization can begin the process of qualifying minorities, the disadvantaged, and women for entry-level and other positions, some real consideration must be given to the question: Qualified for what? A careful, thorough analysis of the various skills required for lower- and middle-level positions may reveal that really very little formal prework instruction is necessary. Further, a review of actual work specifications may lead to the admission by some members of management that the "real" concern surrounding the decision to require qualification training stems from the fear (actual or imagined) that the new hires will not adapt to or be easily accepted by the existing work environment.

The existence of sociopsychological considerations does not eliminate the need for traditional job analysis or position reviews of the various jobs on which newly hired qualifiable minorities and women are to be placed. A company's training director or administrator will be able to use this job-content information for training and for personnel development programs, in addition to the structuring of work orientation sessions for the newly hired special employees. Work analysis, if carefully and objectively done, may reveal that many entry-level and other beginning jobs are needlessly repetitive and dull. This lack of variety, interest value, and responsibility may help to account, in part, for the decline in work output and quality of performance from existing "qualified" workers. An open, concerted effort at restructure or redesign of work duties can often result in heightened challenge, increased job interest, and expanded opportunities for skill development.

A further outgrowth of a work review in these jobs will be the compilation of information about differences and similarities between jobs in the organization. The consolidation and recombination of position requirements can often result in jobs which allow more flexible assignment of employees, while at the same time giving workers the opportunity to expand their knowledge and skills in doing the organization's work. There are many other uses for job analysis information other than those stated. Most standard texts on industrial psychology or industrial management cover this vital subject in more detail.

In a review of hiring and training programs for the hard-core unemployed (disadvantaged), Goodman et al.[2] found that job structure and organization expectations have a significant effect on both job tenure and job performance. Quinn et al.[3] uncovered job factors which appear to be related to unwanted turnover and poor job attitudes. The assignment of boring work, the perceived inability to change from one job to another (now or in the future), the failure to outline the work routine, and the lack of orientation (how the new employee's work fits into the total picture) resulted in significantly higher turnover and negative job attitudes.

THE "NEW" WORKER

Rambo,[4] in a study of nearly 800 newly hired production workers (a significant number of whom were minority and disadvantaged), significantly predicted job stability by determining that the initial expectations concerning what the work and job environment would be like, prior to going on the job, exerted considerable influence on job perceptions after a 45-day work-adjustment period. In this same study, it was found that new employees with both high initial expectations and positive ratings of the work after being on the job for a trial period remained on the job longer than employees with other combinations of initial expectations and present job perceptions. Differing expectations and frames of reference as time on the job progresses are being given stronger consideration in the prediction of who will and who will not stay with the job long enough to be qualified and eventually upgraded.

By using the Goodman et al. expectancy-performance model as a reasonable approach for explaining not only the behavior of the hard-core unemployed (disadvantaged) but also the behavior of new workers in general, some tentative suggestions can be made about the structure and nature of training programs aimed at qualifying the qualifiable. The expectancy-performance theory suggests that behavior is a function of expectancies about behavior-reward outcomes and the attractiveness of these rewards. Research on the relationship between expectancies and rewards[5] has recognized that workers operate in a complex social system. The expectancies and rewards of such a system in turn combine with individual worker value systems to determine whether the new worker will remain on the job and will feel sufficient commitment to produce on that job.

Expectations Are Crucial

A growing body of evidence suggests that new workers (minorities, women, and disadvantaged) must view remaining on the job as leading to their desired and expected rewards. Most entry-level or beginning hiring programs have experienced excessive turnover. The job is not even half done when you hire—*hiring simply does not mean training!* Organizations must consider the implications of bringing new people into their work force when no systems have been designed for actually providing promotional opportunities, varied assignments, and clear career paths. Although economic conditions appear to have a significant effect on how various kinds of work are perceived, it may be unrealistic to expect young people reared in the relative affluence of the last 20 years to view work in the same perspective as their parents did.

O'Leary[6] found that a number of hard-core unemployed black women who had successfully completed an eight-week course providing basic education and occupational training quit the sponsoring company to accept more challenging and better-paying positions shortly after graduation. This evidence suggests that effective training programs must be immediately tied to expanded promotional opportunities and increasing amounts of responsibility. Any employee who finds that his or her skills and abilities have significantly increased will also experience a corresponding increase in expectation levels and accompanying "marketability." If the organization in question is not able to accommodate these higher expectations, such employees are likely to seek greener pastures.

Some Turnover Is Unavoidable

Companies must be willing to accept some unwanted attrition. Management must not become reactionary, attributing this kind of turnover behavior to ingratitude, opportunism, and needless job hopping. Some good people will remain! As long as the results of the training efforts are positive, and as long as those trained are effective while on the job, there is little more that management can expect. If people are leaving for the "right" reasons—namely, better job opportunities—the company has to be better off than it would be if the attrition were a result of inability to perform, high absenteeism, and needless discipline problems.

Good Supervisors Are the Key

Goodman et al. report that supervisors can play a key role as newly hired employees attempt to become qualified. Friedlander and Greenberg[7] found a strong relationship between successful on-the-job performance and the supportiveness of the supervisor. As Goodman reports, in general the studies seem to indicate that supervisory style does affect the behavior of disadvantaged workers. These findings suggest that supervisors who are to be assigned minority, female, or disadvantaged employees must themselves be trained, as well as their new charges. Managers need to be exposed to professional guidance techniques, the use of feedback methods, and knowledge of the potential positive and negative effects of their own personal verbal and nonverbal behavior on their subordinates.

Care must be taken to help these managers understand what is expected of them as well as what is to be expected of the newly hired or promoted minority or female employees. This kind of briefing is especially important for supervisors with known interpersonal problems with, or overt biases toward, minorities and/or women. All supervisory personnel must be kept informed of the organizational consequences of prejudicial or biased treatment of these employees.

This kind of orientation provides direction for supervisors so that they do not have to try to interpret management's expectations with few data or none at all. In most cases a simple message from top management is all that is necessary. It must be communicated that the organization is committed to affirmative action with regard to minorities and women. Further, it is important that corporate policy outline the reasons for the commitment. It would be wise for top management to stress the practical business considerations, as well as the legal and contractual obligations and the social and moral issues, when discussing equal opportunity policy.

Further, management's actions when problems arise must make it clear that unjust discrimination will *not* be tolerated. There is often some merit to stringent enforcement to demonstrate that the prescribed new expectations by the corporation are now the norm.

TRAINING, TRAINING, TRAINING: IS THAT THE ANSWER?

Success with special populations clearly requires more than training: Broad organizational commitment is needed. The long-lingering American problems of discrimination, apathy, and ignorance—not the individual minorities and women being hired—have created the challenge!

Considered and aggressive programs, not platitudes, will meet this challenge.

REFERENCES

1. Roethlisberger, F. J., and W. J. Dickson: *Management and the Worker,* Harvard University Press, Cambridge, Mass., 1939.
2. Goodman, P. S., P. Salipante, and H. Paransky: "Hiring, Training, and Retaining the Hard-Core Unemployed: A Selected Review," *Journal of Applied Psychology,* vol. 58, no. 1, August 1973.
3. Quinn, R., B. Fine, and T. Levitin: "Turnover and Training: A Social-Psychological Study of Disadvantaged Workers," unpublished paper, University of Michigan, Survey Research Center, Ann Arbor, 1970.
4. Rambo, L. M.: "Initial Job Expectations, Present Perceptions and Future Anticipations and Their Effects on Job Stability," unpublished doctoral dissertation, Wayne State University, Detroit, 1971.
5. Heneman, H. G., and D. P. Schwab: "Evaluation of Research on Expectancy Theory Predictions of Employee Performance," *Psychological Bulletin,* vol. 78, 1972.
6. O'Leary, V. E.: "The Hawthorne Effect in Reverse: Trainee Orientation for the Hard-Core Unemployed Woman," *Journal of Applied Psychology,* vol. 56, no. 6, December 1972.
7. Friedlander, F., and S. Greenberg: "Effect of Job Attitudes, Training, and Organization Climate on Performance of the Hard-Core Unemployed," *Journal of Applied Psychology,* vol. 55, no. 4, 1971.

BIBLIOGRAPHY

1. Doeringer, P. D. (ed.): *Programs to Employ the Disadvantaged,* Prentice-Hall, Inc., Englewood Cliffs, N.J., 1969.
2. Dunmore, A. J.: *Chrysler Update,* Chrysler Corporation, Department of Urban Affairs, Detroit, April 1973.
3. Fretz, C. F., and J. Hayman: "Progress for Women: Men Are Still More Equal," *Harvard Business Review,* September–October 1973.
4. Muth, Edmund H.: *Systematic Automotive Education Program Design,* Illinois Law Enforcement Commission, Correctional Manpower Services Unit, Chicago, 1973.
5. Wellman, D.: "The Wrong Way to Find Jobs for Negroes," *Trans-Action,* April, 1968.

Chapter 24

Scientist and Engineer Continuing Education

JOHN M. KINN

John M. Kinn *is Director of Educational Services of the Institute of Electrical and Electronic Engineers, Inc., in New York. He has done engineering work with Western Electric Company and Bell Telephone Laboratories, and he was on the editorial staff of* Electronics *magazine. At* IBM *he was Associate Editor of the* IBM Journal of Research and Development, *Manager of Scientific Information, and Manager of Technical Information and Liaison Services. He joined IEEE in 1965 and has been responsible for educational activities as well as intersociety affairs, professional relations, and other institute functions. He holds a B.S. in electrical engineering from the University of Missouri. He is a senior member of IEEE and a member of ASTD, the National Association of Science Writers, the Society of Photographic Scientists and Engineers, and the American Association for the Advancement of Science.*

The objectives of this chapter are to provide the trainer with insights into the character and makeup of scientists and engineers so that he or she can better evaluate proposed educational approaches and their potential for acceptance by these professionals; to give examples of current methodology and results of typical professional development programs; and to provide insights into trends in the professional environment external to the trainer's organization which may have a profound effect on further programs he or she elects to develop.

Throughout this chapter the fundamental concepts of continuing studies or lifelong learning will be stressed, inasmuch as the environment in which scientists and engineers work is one of constant change and advancement. As the evolution of scientific and engineering knowledge continues to accelerate, the need will continue unabated for imparting this new knowledge to those in the profession with little or no experience in a given specialty, as well as for updating those who are currently working in the field but who may not have kept up with the latest advances. Unlike traditional education, where each course builds upon its predecessor, the continuing education of scientists and engineers requires a vast array of independent, self-sustaining modules of learning. The presentation of this knowledge, in the classroom or via modern instructional technology, places extreme demands upon trainers. They must link scientific and engineering theory of a decade or more ago to today's new concepts, and they must render them understandable by distilling the true scientific and technical essence from this burgeoning fund of knowledge.

UNDERSTANDING SCIENTISTS AND ENGINEERS

Scientists and engineers consider themselves to be professionals in a very broad sense, as shown by the following quotation:

> A profession is man-centered in two ways: (1) a profession demands practitioners who are free and responsible individuals and who, through their personal integrity, dedication, and courage, can be depended upon to establish and maintain their personal standards of performance; (2) a profession, no matter how technical the procedures it employs, demands that its practitioners be primarily motivated by service to their fellow men.
>
> A learned profession is a still more demanding occupation. Two further ingredients are required: (1) a learned profession requires years of preparation of the whole man and of his knowledge and skills; (2) a learned profession requires the learning approach throughout life, as a means of fulfilling one's responsibility to one's fellow men, through the ready application of new knowledge.[1]

The concept of lifelong learning has been espoused for many years—but rarely honored in the breach. Yet it is precisely this lifelong need that trainers must be prepared to fulfill if they are to achieve the ultimate objectives of their organizations. Understanding the underlying motivations of scientists and engineers will enable trainers to pinpoint more accurately the type of educational offerings best suited to the lifelong learning needs of the particular constituency.

The Industrial Scientific and Technical Environment

Since the end of World War II, there has been a phenomenal growth within industry of programs oriented toward research and development, coupled with a concomitant growth in product engineering. This growth has been the subject of many studies, both formal and informal, which have attempted to gain a better insight into the factors affecting the productivity of scientists and engineers. It is safe to say that the knowledge gained so far, while of great help, is still in its early stages of formation.

At the outset one must recognize there are measurable differences between scientists and engineers in many aspects of their approaches to their life's work. Therefore, we should first try to differentiate those aspects of their work characteristics which might have meaningful application in the education and training process.

Workers in the scientific and engineering disciplines exhibit a spectrum of characteristics, which Ritti[2] carefully assessed, coalesced, and classified. He used the labels "local" and "cosmopolitan" to differentiate individuals whose primary goals are oriented toward self-fulfillment through achievement of organizational goals (locals, or engineers) from those who derive primary satisfaction from identification with their profession or field of specialty (cosmopolitans, or scientists). Caution should be used in applying these labels, for while these ideas about career orientation can be useful in thinking about organizational problems, they can also be misleading unless one recognizes that the majority fall somewhere between these two arbitrary ends of the behavioral spectrum.

However, one can generalize that basic research—the search for fundamental new knowledge—might be considered peripheral to the business goals of the company, and hence strains between business goals and the "cosmopolitan" scientific goals may easily arise. Engineering involves the creation of technology that is marketed or otherwise put to use; thus the "local" outlook of engineers tends to be in consonance with the business objectives of their organization.

Survey data accumulated by Ritti support the statement that the goals of engineers are generally in harmony with the aims of the business. Table 24-1 shows seven major clusters or dimensions of these goals, and the percentage of the total population indicating the goal is very important for them.

To further aid in identifying the goals and aspirations of these two groups, Tables 24-2 to 24-4 compare results of a nationwide survey on work goals with results obtained for a major corporation for (1) development engineers and (2) research scientists, development scientists, and development engineers; the tables also present a comparison between development engineers, junior development engineers, and senior engineering students.

In general, the tables emphasize that trainers in industry must develop educational offerings which take into account the differing work goals of these classes of scientific and technical personnel. In other words, courses, seminars, etc., on essentially the same topic must be tailored to a specific group (researcher, developer, designer, applications engineer, etc.), not just in terms of level but also in terms of the relation of the topic to company goals (for locals) or professional enhancement (cosmopolitans), as well as the spectrum in between.

Scientific and Technical Knowledge Acquisition

At this point one could describe a list of various techniques found most suitable for organizing scientific and technical knowledge, and such a treatment will indeed appear later in the section on methodology. But in order to judiciously select one or more appropriate delivery methods, the trainer should have additional insights into the ways in which scientists and engineers acquire information. In consonance with the local/cosmopolitan concept, other studies have been undertaken to determine the mechanisms scientists and engineers use when faced with the need for more knowledge either to solve a problem or to anticipate a further need.

Rosenbloom and Wolek[3] have found that there appears to be a significant dichotomy between the approaches taken by scientists as against those taken by engineers in this regard. They looked at the ways these groups communicated both inside and outside their companies and found two prevailing modes of acquisition of knowledge: the use of interpersonal relationships between knowledgeable individuals and the use of professional literature. They also concluded that, through the years, the professional communities of science and engineering have developed traditions and practices—indeed entire cultures—which have proved effective for the transmission of accumulated knowledge. However, these systems may not facilitate the transfer of knowledge between fields or into practice. For the latter to take place, it appears that one must rely on the basic training of all professionals and their perception as to how they should communicate within this culture.

Looking at this communication process in terms of the purposes of organizations, such as those in industry, one can surmise that the science-based corporation readily provides within itself the means of access to scientific and technical knowledge. A matrix of information networks develops between professionals within the firm, yielding a pattern of information exchange which becomes part of the main fabric of life within an organization. Thus trainers in less science-based organizations may well have to develop an internal climate which is more consistent with that of the science-based organization.

To help utilize the findings in this study, Table 24-5 will be helpful in interpreting the information in Figs. 24-1 to 24-4.

As Fig. 24-1 indicates, the incidence of the various modes of knowledge acquisition is similar for scientists and engineers, most probably the result of parallelism in their basic training.

When the respondents described the circumstances leading up to the acquisition

TABLE 24-1   Major Dimensions of Engineering Goals

	Percent indicating "very important"
I. Business Goals	
Have the opportunity to help the company build its reputation as a first-class organization	72
Have the opportunity to help the company increase its profits	69
Work on problems that have practical applications important to your company	67
Have the opportunity to see the concrete results of what you have done	65
Know what the goals of your division are	61
Work on projects that have a direct impact on the business success of your company	48
Participate in decisions that affect the future business of the company	41
Participate in decisions that set the direction of technical effort in the company	38
II. Technical Goals	
Have the opportunity to explore new ideas about technology or systems	61
Advance to a high-level staff technical position	57
Work with others who are outstanding in their technical achievements	54
Have the opportunity to work on complex technical problems	49
Work on projects that require learning new technical knowledge	47
Work on projects that utilize the latest theoretical results in your specialty	37
III. Security Goals	
Live in a location and community that are desirable to you and your family	82
Work in a cooperative, friendly atmosphere	76
Have stability in your life and work	54
Have adequate retirement, health insurance, and other company benefits	53
IV. Monetary Goals	
Receive better-than-average salary increases	54
Make more money than the average college graduate	42
Make a great deal of money	27
V. Managerial Goals	
Learn how the business is set up and run	45
Become a first-line manager in your line of work	43
Be the technical leader of a group of less experienced professionals	33
Learn administrative methods and procedures	33
Advance to a policy-making position in management	32
VI. Scientific Goals	
Establish a reputation outside the company as an authority in your field	29
Receive patents on your technical ideas	24
Publish articles in technical journals	15
Communicate your ideas to others in your profession through papers delivered at professional meetings	14
Be evaluated only on the basis of your technical contributions	13

TABLE 24-1 *(Cont.)*

	Percent indicating "very important"
VII. ANXIETY AVOIDANCE GOALS	
Work in a well-ordered job situation where the requirements are clear	26
Have few worries, tensions, and troubles	24
Have little tension and stress on the job	19
Be given clear, detailed instructions as to how to proceed with the job	11

SOURCE: R. R. Ritti, *The Engineer in an Industrial Corporation,* Columbia University Press, New York, 1971. Reprinted by permission.

of information, almost half reported that they had done specific search themselves. In nearly one-third of the cases the information was acquired because someone pointed it out, while in about one-fifth of the cases respondents intended to develop their general competence rather than to acquire some particular knowledge. From this, the authors concluded that information may be looking for the person as frequently as the person is seeking information. Thus trainers might

TABLE 24-2   Work Goals of Nationwide Sample Engineers Compared with Those of Company Development Engineers

	Percent indicating "very important"	
	National sample	Company
1. To have a position where people are interested in working		77
Work in a cooperative, friendly atmosphere		76
2. A large degree of freedom to manage my own work	62	
Have freedom to adopt your own approach to the job		67
3. To be able to advance and move ahead in my position	62	
Advance to a high-level staff technical position		57
4. To have the respect of my colleagues because of my technical achievement	42	
Be known in the company as an expert in your field of specialty		49
5. To have an opportunity to move into a management career	41	
Become a first-line manager in your line of work		43
6. To have a position where I know exactly what my work responsibilities are	40	
Work in a well-ordered job situation where the requirements are clear		26
7. Association with other engineers and scientists of recognized ability	35	
Work with others who are outstanding in their technical achievements		54
8. Membership in an organization that is highly regarded by people in my profession	19	
Work for a company whose reputation is respected by others in your field		64
9. To be free to publish nonconfidential scientific contributions	15	
Publish articles in technical journals		15

SOURCE: R. R. Ritti, *The Engineer in an Industrial Corporation,* Columbia University Press, New York, 1971. Reprinted by permission.

TABLE 24-3   Comparison of Work Goals of Research Scientists, Development Scientists, and Development Engineers

	Percent indicating goal is "very important"		
Work goal	Research scientists (N = 33)	Development scientists (N = 25)	Development engineers (N = 4,582)
How important is it to you to:			
Have the opportunity to explore new ideas in technology or systems	*	85	61
Have the opportunity to help the company increase its profit	28	44	69
Gain knowledge of company management policies and practices	19	32	60
Participate in decisions that affect the future business of the company	6	24	41
Work on projects that have a direct impact on the business success of your company	*	32	47
Advance to a policy-making position in management	6	36	32
Work on projects you yourself have originated	75	32	32
Establish your reputation outside the company as an authority in your field	84	72	29
Publish articles in technical journals	88	72	15
Be evaluated *only* on the basis of your *technical* contributions	*	28	13

*This item not included in survey of this group,
SOURCE: R. R. Ritti, *The Engineer in an Industrial Corporation,* Columbia University Press, New York, 1971. Reprinted by permission.

well look into their organizational situation with a view to facilitating this information transfer process as part of their program.

Turning now to the general sources used by professionals to gain the knowledge they seek (see Fig. 24-2), individuals in the life sciences and chemistry seem to make greater use of the formal literature than those in data processing. Similarly, interpersonal communication with sources outside their own firms seems more common among life scientists and computer scientists than among chemists or any of the engineering groups. Chemical and metallurgical engineers report a greater incidence of use of professional documents—and, correspondingly, a lesser reliance on sources within their own firms—than mechanical and electrical engineers. The latter two, in turn, are quite similar in the pattern of sources reported.

As an aid to further understanding the process of information transfer, Fig. 24-3 indicates that for "problem-oriented" modes of acquisition—that is, situations where the information was sought directly or was pointed out—local interpersonal communication is common. Engineers show more interpersonal communication with people in other parts of their own corporations, while interpersonal communication by scientists tends to be with individuals employed outside their own corporations. When using documents, engineers tend to consult corporate reports or trade publications, while scientists make greater use of the professional literature.

Reference to Fig. 24-4 will show how these two groups go about obtaining information in a competence-oriented mode. "Competence-oriented" communication includes browsing, reviewing new developments, brushing up, becoming

TABLE 24-4   Comparison of Work Goals of Development Engineers, Junior Development Engineers, and Senior Engineering Students

Work goal	Percent indicating goal is "very important"		
	Development engineers ($N = 1,315$)	Junior engineers only ($N = 174$)	Engineering students ($N = 447$)
How important is it to you to:			
Have the opportunity to help the company build its reputation as a first-class organization	67	68	75
Have the opportunity to help the company increase its profit	64	61	57
Have the opportunity to explore new ideas in technology or systems	57	61	72
Work on projects that have a direct impact on the business success of your company	42	39	48
Participate in decisions that affect the future business of the company	*36*	*40*	*64*
Participate in decisions that set the direction of technical effort in the company	*33*	*39*	*68*
Advance to a policy-making position in management	*29*	*36*	*55*
Establish your reputation outside the company as an authority in your field	*27*	*43*	*41*
Publish articles in technical journals	14	17	20
Be evaluated *only* on the basis of your *technical* contributions	12	12	14

SOURCE: R. R. Ritti, *The Engineer in an Industrial Corporation,* Columbia University Press, New York, 1971. Reprinted by permission.

familiar with a new area, etc. Thus documentary sources are dominant even for engineers. For scientists, the professional literature accounts for most of the written sources of information. Engineers rely more heavily on interpersonal communication and use trade sources fully as much as professional sources.

From the foregoing, one can conclude that trainers should seriously consider

TABLE 24-5   Categories for Sources of Information

A. INTERPERSONAL COMMUNICATION:
    1. LOCAL SOURCE: An engineer or scientist employed in the same establishment
    2. OTHER CORPORATE SOURCE: Another person employed by the same corporation
B. WRITTEN MEDIA:
    3. DOCUMENTS: Any written source originating in the same corporation

Sources outside the company:

A. WRITTEN MEDIA:
    4. TRADE DOCUMENTS: Suppliers' catalogs, trade magazines, unpublished technical reports, etc.
    5. PROFESSIONAL DOCUMENTS: Published books, journal articles, or conference papers
B. INTERPERSONAL COMMUNICATION:
    6. EXTERNAL: Interpersonal communication with any person employed outside the firm

ways in which they can adapt the behavior problems exhibited by these two groups of professionals within their organizations so they can optimize the information transfer process and hence achieve their ultimate training goal with regard to this constituency.

The basic nature of the individuals involved is such that trainers have both a

	Total N = 1852	Scientists N = 654	Engineers N = 966
Specifically sought	47%	42%	53%
Pointed out	32%	33%	30%
General competence	21%	25%	17%

Fig. 24-1   Circumstances of acquisition. (*From R. S. Rosenbloom and F. W. Wolek, Technology and Information Transfer: A Survey of Practice in Industrial Organizations, Harvard University, Graduate School of Business Administration, Division of Research, Cambridge, Mass., 1970.* © *The President and Fellows of Harvard College,* 1970. *Reprinted by permission.*)

challenge and an opportunity to devise educational offerings utilizing both the informal and formal modes of communication as they may dominate at a specific location and also utilizing the orientation of the individuals as either local or cosmopolitan to establish the best approach to facilitating their acquisition of knowledge.

The Scientist/Engineer Educational Pattern

The constant search for, and development of, new knowledge by scientists and the application of that knowledge by engineers have tended to create an environment in which these individuals are extremely mobile both geographically and techni-cally. The high degree of technical mobility presents both opportunity and chal-lenge to trainers inasmuch as they will frequently be called upon by management to develop programs to ensure the technical vitality of this group of professional employees. The results of a recent national sample survey of scientists and engineers by a major engineering society (the IEEE) might prove helpful in shedding additional light on the ways in which this group relates to education.

By a random selection process based on choosing about 1 out of every 20 members having United States mailing addresses, 5,000 members from all mem-ber grades except "student" were mailed questionnaires. A very surprising 3,279 responses were received and tallied, a much larger response than the typical 30 to 40 percent.

What kind of people are they? They range in age from 21 to 80 years, with a median age of 40. On the average, they have been society members (any grade) for 13.6 years. Somewhat more than half (54 percent) belong to at least one subgroup of the society, and 46 percent even belong to some other technical society. Since entering employment as engineers (or since receiving their first professional degree), they have on the average spent 16.7 years in practice.

Most respondents went to engineering school in the same part of the United States in which they grew up—a reflection of the fact that the United States is liberally sprinkled with first-rate engineering schools in all states. The highest degree they received was:

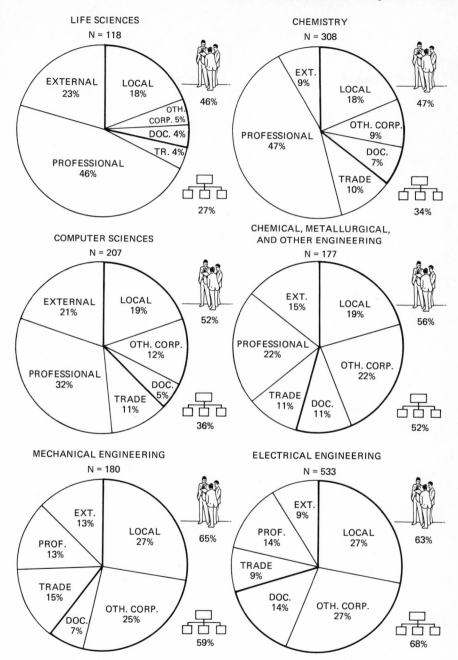

Fig. 24-2 Information sources by field. (*From R. S. Rosenbloom and F. W. Wolek, Technology and Information Transfer: A Survey of Practice in Industrial Organizations, Harvard University, Graduate School of Business Administration, Division of Research, Cambridge, Mass., 1970.* © *The President and Fellows of Harvard College, 1970. Reprinted by permission.*)

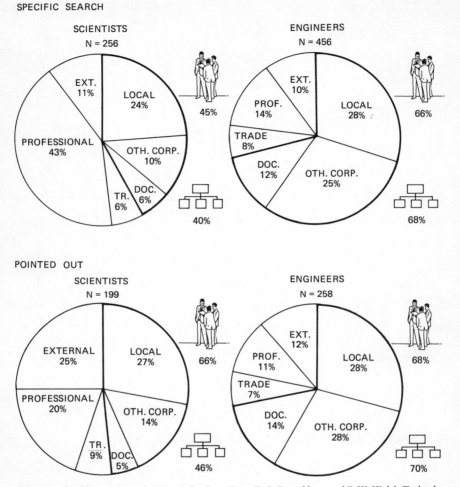

Fig. 24-3   Problem-oriented communication. *(From R. S. Rosenbloom and F. W. Wolek, Technology and Information Transfer: A Survey of Practice in Industrial Organizations, Harvard University, Graduate School of Business Administration, Division of Research, Cambridge, Mass., 1970. © The President and Fellows of Harvard College, 1970. Reprinted by permission.)*

Associate	....	3.4%
Bachelor's	....	53.1%
Master's	....	28.4%
Doctorate	....	11.2%
None	....	3.8%

Five out of six (82.7 percent) took an undergraduate degree. Of those who went on to graduate study, a surprising 46 percent did it full time, but almost as many (42.7 percent) went to graduate school while employed full time. As for the advanced degrees, they were not all in engineering:

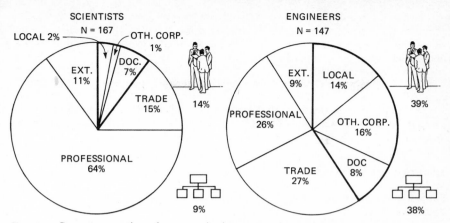

Fig. 24-4 Competence-oriented communication. (*From R. S. Rosenbloom and F. W. Wolek, Technology and Information Transfer: A Survey of Practice in Industrial Organizations, Harvard University, Graduate School of Business Administration, Division of Research, Cambridge, Mass., 1970.* © *The President and Fellows of Harvard College,* 1970. *Reprinted by permission.*)

Engineering	73.5%
Business	9.8%
Science	12.6%
Other	4.0%

Moving on to more recent educational activities, how recently did respondents take credit-bearing courses which could apply toward an advanced degree?

This year	14%
Within the past 3 years	18%
Within the past 10 years	31%
More than 10 years ago	37%

This suggests that although some of those who are past the age of 40 have done some college work well into their professional careers, formal education stops earlier for most. What about less formal education programs? How many have taken advantage of these?

Company programs	26%
College programs	14%
Home-study programs	4%
Professional society programs	4%
Variety of programs	23%

This leaves 30 percent of respondents who either do not bother about updating or extending themselves or depend upon less formal methods. Taking a finer-detail look at which members (by age) had availed themselves of special-education opportunities, we see:

Those now in their twenties	64%
Those now in their thirties	77%
Those now in their forties	73%
Those now in their fifties	55%
Those now in their sixties and up	78%

These data strongly suggest the mid-career "slump" between about 45 and 55 years of age, during which (according to psychologists) many individuals must go through a "rediscovery" phase. The data we obtained also show that home-study and society-sponsored programs are more popular with middle-aged engineers than college courses (in which they must compete with younger people).

From the foregoing it can be seen that scientists and engineers generally are in need of varied educational offerings and that motivation to achieve educationally, while high, still requires industrial trainers to seek out and include motivating elements in their educational offerings which are tailored to the age, background, and current occupational status of these professionals.

METHODOLOGY

Educational Delivery Methods: The Professional-Technical View

Modern technology has enabled educators to develop and implement new methodology for the delivery of educational offerings. While assessment of the effectiveness as well as the acceptance of these new techniques will require further extensive study, some initial information can be gleaned from numerous independent studies and reports now available.

A report[4] prepared for the IEEE, summarizes some current thinking on this subject which trainers may find useful in program development. In brief it states that during the last half of the 1960s, a dramatic expansion of educational methods began to evolve and was increasingly accepted by both the educational community and the scientists and engineers to whom these methods were directed. Thus the major thrust of organizational educational activities centered around developing both appropriate delivery methods and a continually expanding set of offerings. In all cases these methods have been evaluated from the standpoint of ease of use, economy, and ease of administration. Out of these efforts have evolved three classifications that make it possible to categorize educational activities: type, mode, and delivery method.

The types of educational activities center first on those which produce an *awareness* of a new (to the individual) body of knowledge with which he or she has not been conversant up to the present time. An example of this might be a series of presentations to power engineers on modern control theory, with some implication of where this new collection of thought can be employed in power generation, transmission, and utilization. In general, awareness presentations are surveys and do not cover the subject matter in depth.

A second presentation form deals with the *fundamentals* of a particular body of thought. Such a presentation generally correlates with a senior or first-year graduate elective and deals with the fundamental theory. For example, an in-depth presentation of the fundamental theory of solid-state switching devices for power-system engineers would provide them with the background needed to understand the state-of-the-art development.

A third presentation form would be the pulling together of the *engineering state of the art* of a particular phenomenon. This presentation might consist of both information at the cutting edge of science and engineering as well as quite old information. As opposed to the presentation of fundamentals, this presentation deals with engineering applications and emphasizes the use of fundamental theory and the state of development of particular devices, systems and materials.

There are two *modes* of educational presentations dealing principally with the number of participants present. Call the first of these *group interaction*. The classroom situation is an example.

Also in the group interaction mode are the subsets of the seminar, short course, symposium, lecture, workshop, and tutorial.

The second mode is *individual,* or noninteractive. Here the individual is remote from the others participating in the course and is unable to interact with them. The correspondence course represents this mode of educational presentation.

Finally, we should briefly mention the third classification—*delivery method.* Until the early 1960s, essentially all the delivery methods employed the instructor/chalkboard, the book, and the laboratory. As noted, during the 1960s new delivery methods were advanced, and many became generally accepted.

Given the foregoing summarization as generally applicable to the professional development of scientific and technical personnel, one can then establish an order of priority for the methodology to be employed, as well as an order of priority for the topics to be covered using such a methodology. Table 24-6 indicates the responses obtained from a random-sample survey of the IEEE with regard to these interests.

EMERGENCE OF INFORMAL SELF-STUDY

Woven into the results obtained in studies such as those summarized above is a pattern of change in emphasis in mode from the classical instructor/chalkboard format to informal self-study. In an attempt to further assess this growing area of educational opportunity, a special study was conducted by the IEEE to determine the extent to which such offerings would be acceptable to the scientific and technical specialists constituting the membership. The results of that study are discussed below.

Self-Study Questionnaire: Summary of Results

A total of 1,534 members out of 5,000 surveyed responded to the questionnaire. This response was analyzed in three ways: an overall tally of opinion, a cross-tabulation of response versus age and a cross-tabulation of response versus degree level. The overall sample size as well as the sample sizes of each age and degree group were large enough so as to produce statistically significant results with a 95 percent confidence level. This did not hold for the group above age 64 or for those who indicated their highest degrees as none, associate, or professional.

Course Topics   When presented with a list of 58 technical and 8 business or managerial topics, respondents indicated that they were "very interested" or "somewhat interested" or else made no response.

In order of acceptance, the following 17 technical topics received the highest percentages of "very interested" responses (an asterisk indicates a tie):

1. Communications systems
2. Minicomputers
3. Computer simulations of engineering systems
4. Logic design
5. Computer-aided design
6. Digital instrumentation
7. Commercial power systems
8. Industrial control systems
9. *Energy resources and consumption
9. *Computer architecture
11. Modern automatic control systems
12. BJT, FET, and operational amplifier circuits
13. *Displays—state of the art
13. *MOS/LSI computer processors

TABLE 24-6 Survey Results on Priorities of Subject Interest and Learning-Method Preferences (Total IEEE Questionnaires—1,026)

I. SUBJECTS: Weighted subject scores were generated by multiplying all "1" responses by 3, all "2" responses by 2, and all "3" responses by 1 and adding the resultant three numbers.

	Some interest	Important	Crucial	Weighted score
1. Effective management of projects	151	185	117	871
2. Business management for engineers	192	188	100	868
3. Starting your own business	180	143	133	865
4. Set up an operation as a consultant	135	135	145	740
5. Financial management for engineers	197	140	81	720
6. Management of organizations	151	142	83	684
7. Methods of supervision	129	143	87	676
8. Making effective presentations	107	128	91	636
9. Use of minicomputers	96	124	85	599
10. Avoiding technical obsolescence	115	136	66	585
11. Negotiating effectively	89	97	66	578
12. Person-to-person communication	109	116	72	557
13. Writing reports for results	105	118	70	551
14. Legal problems in electrical engineering	118	98	44	544
15. Creative problem solving	111	105	72	537
16. New-venture management	128	106	62	526
17. Digital signal processing	91	111	69	520
18. Increasing effectiveness of meetings	101	116	54	495
19. Logic design	93	100	66	491
20. Computer principles	110	117	49	491
21. Writing technical proposals	108	97	59	479
22. Medical applications of electronics	101	92	64	477
23. Balancing personal and professional life	110	83	59	453
24. Methods for self-renewal	95	86	53	426
25. Modern control theory and practice	86	89	51	417
26. Marketing engineering services	97	80	48	401
27. Computer applications in electronics	88	91	46	408
28. Utility systems	62	49	80	400

#	Topic				
29.	Application of electrotechnology to social problems	382	30	57	88
30.	Simulation	371	48	72	83
31.	Automotive electronics	365	30	86	103
32.	Developing control instrumentation	357	43	73	82
33.	Industrial applications of power	355	54	72	49
34.	Communications switching	349	41	73	80
35.	Transistors	340	51	62	63
36.	Engineering for reliability	329	28	88	69
37.	Human engineering	327	27	75	96
38.	Design of minicomputers	321	34	72	75
39.	Computer peripherals	318	33	69	81
40.	Optoelectronics	315	32	68	83
41.	Linear and nonlinear filtering	313	41	57	76
42.	Business applications of computers	312	34	62	86
43.	Avoiding overspecialization traps	311	27	69	92
44.	Microwave communication systems	309	37	61	76
45.	Artificial intelligence	304	33	65	75
46.	Engineering for maintainability	304	27	74	75
47.	Solid-state physics and electronics	303	39	61	64
48.	Command information and control systems	299	38	58	69
49.	Solving ecological problems	299	24	62	103
50.	Electrical engineering relevance to society	292	24	61	98
51.	Writing patent disclosures	289	31	55	86
52.	Teleprocessing	288	30	61	76
53.	Microelectronics	272	30	66	50
54.	Radar systems	271	38	46	65
55.	Transportation systems	270	34	47	74
56.	Data transmission capabilities and characteristics	265	42	85	69
57.	Applications of rotary machine	264	39	48	51
58.	Cable-TV systems	262	23	54	85
59.	Navigation and guidance systems	260	29	50	73
60.	Control of engineering quality	254	24	60	62
61.	Urban and social systems	243	22	50	77
62.	System identification	192	25	25	67
63.	Video cassette technology	160	15	31	53

TABLE 24-6 (Cont.)

II. LEARNING EXPERIENCES: Weighted subject scores were generated by multiplying all "1" responses by 11, all "2" responses by 10, etc., down to multiplying all "11" responses by 1 and adding the resultant 11 numbers.

	1	2	3	4	5	6	7	8	9	10	11	Weighted score
1. Learning by reading	159	167	128	128	100	79	53	35	26	17	15	7301
2. Learning by problem solving	229	157	132	87	75	56	37	35	26	12	2	7263
3. Learning by experimentation	118	118	127	105	87	83	43	32	14	22	6	6003
4. Learning by one-to-one dialogue with expert	150	104	84	86	73	80	49	49	37	26	5	5734
5. Learning by observation	38	57	83	79	90	70	98	85	60	39	17	5622
6. Learning by small-group discussion	113	93	88	91	74	84	77	64	34	25	8	5506
7. Learning by listening	75	91	75	92	116	90	92	64	49	31	27	5450
8. Learning by preparing a presentation on the subject	76	77	67	99	56	65	64	63	54	40	23	4621
9. Learning by gaming	53	68	67	52	54	42	51	36	51	74	69	3681
10. Learning by emulating an expert	13	34	25	25	25	43	52	51	84	103	86	2349
11. Learning by response to a deadline	21	27	34	28	35	27	36	36	45	75	168	2216

III. LEARNING SITUATIONS: Weighted subject scores were generated by multiplying all "1" responses by 16, "2" responses by 15, etc., down to multiplying all "16" responses by 1 and adding the resultant 16 numbers.

Rank

	1	2	3	4	5	6	7	8	9	10	11	12	13	14	15	16	Weighted score
1. Books	163	152	130	107	55	55	34	31	14	16	12	10	2	7	0	2	10360
2. Evening program	234	119	90	95	61	40	37	26	17	20	14	15	3	4	0	4	9683
3. Home-Study correspondence courses, etc.	179	131	114	71	60	25	32	17	18	13	20	11	7	11	10	4	9211
4. Periodical literature	103	123	119	83	62	57	34	29	19	18	13	9	14	3	10	9	7705
5. One-day live program	77	82	65	64	70	48	39	37	27	22	22	26	37	1	2	3	7101
6. Audio cassettes	39	60	65	80	56	42	37	26	27	26	21	13	9	10	8	2	5965
7. On-the-job training	103	56	34	39	39	30	32	35	19	26	15	21	11	9	12	33	5561
8. Two-day live program	28	59	67	43	36	40	40	33	28	41	20	26	29	41	3	1	5306

9. Audio cassette and slide package	42	48	54	47	68	47	45	26	36	26	17	16	10	11	5	2	5413
10. Live television	33	36	37	42	53	59	43	25	29	30	25	19	11	7	13	8	4858
11. Motion pictures	15	21	34	29	45	43	41	44	33	46	12	16	10	16	14	8	4089
12. Five-day live program	19	29	28	35	27	29	24	38	25	15	21	23	31	41	51	4	3710
13. Video tape and video cassette	13	24	23	22	37	44	29	34	26	26	23	19	19	13	20	14	3602
14. Computer-aided instruction	9	17	13	19	19	20	23	26	36	24	22	23	26	31	30	32	2732
15. Telephone contact	20	12	20	13	24	23	20	19	17	18	13	23	14	13	29	51	2520
16. Two-week live program	11	9	9	12	19	18	23	23	20	20	20	15	29	32	43	71	2430

15. Power Systems—dc and dc/ac systems
16. *Biomedical instrumentation technology
16. *Automotive electronic systems

The top five managerial topics, in order of acceptance, were:

1. Financial and business management for engineers
2. Methods of supervision
3. Entrepreneurship—getting started in business
4. Project management and proposal writing
5. Making effective presentations

Special Course Interests—by Age   More than 20 percent of the respondents in each group indicated that they were "very interested" in the following topics (an asterisk indicates a tie):

1. Age—less than 24 years
   a. Technical topics
      (1) Commercial power systems
      (2) *Communications systems
      (2) *Minicomputers
      (4) Logic design
      (5) *Computer-aided design
      (5) *Automotive electronic systems
      (7) *Computer simulations of engineering systems
      (7) *Energy resources and consumption
      (7) *Power systems—computer-aided operation
      (10) Color television theory and design
      (11) *Environmental pollution—sources and solution
      (11) *Power systems—dc and dc/ac systems
   b. Managerial topics
      (1) Financial and business management for engineers
      (2) Entrepreneurship—getting started in business
2. Age—25 to 34 years
   a. Technical topics
      (1) Logic design
      (2) Minicomputers
      (3) Computer simulations of engineering systems
      (4) Communications systems
   b. Managerial topics
      (1) Financial and business management for engineers
      (2) Entrepreneurship—getting started in business
3. Age—35 to 44 years
   a. Technical topics
      (1) Communications systems
      (2) Minicomputers
      (3) Computer simulations of engineering systems
   b. Managerial topics
      (1) Financial and business management for computers
      (2) Methods of supervision
      (3) Entrepreneurship—getting started in business
      (4) Project management and proposal writing
4. Age—45 to 54 years
   a. Technical topics
      (Fewer than 20 percent of the respondents in this age group indicated that they were "very interested" in any of the 64 technical topics presented.)

     b. Managerial topics
       (1) Financial and business management for engineers
  5. Age—55 to 64 years
     a. Technical topics
       (1) Communications systems
     b. Managerial topics
       (1) Making effective presentations
  6. Age—over 64 years
     (Sample size was too small for results to be statistically significant.)

Special Course Interests—by Highest Degree Level   More than 20 percent of the respondents in each degree-level group indicated that they were "very interested" in the following topics:

  1. Bachelor's degree
     a. Technical topics
       (1) Communications systems
       (2) Logic design
     b. Managerial topics
       (1) Financial and business management for engineers
       (2) Methods of supervision
       (3) Entrepreneurship—getting started in business
  2. Master's degree
     a. Technical topics
       (1) Computer simulations of engineering systems
       (2) Minicomputers
     b. Managerial topics
       (1) Financial and business management for engineers
       (2) Entrepreneurship—getting started in business
  3. Doctorate
     a. Technical topics
       (1) Computer simulations of engineering systems
     b. Managerial topics
     (Fewer than 20 percent of the respondents holding doctoral degrees indicated that they were "very interested" in any of the business or managerial topics presented.)
  4. Associate, professional, or no degree
     (Sample sizes of each category were too small for results to be statistically significant.)

Educational Materials   The percentage shown represents the total affirmative response—i.e., "essential," "very useful," and "useful"—to each item offered:

  1. Textbook—93.9 percent
  2. Study guide with workbook—92.2 percent
  3. Reprints of journal articles—71.7 percent
  4. Audio cassette lectures—50.6 percent

Results were very uniform regardless of age or degree level, with the exception that Ph.D.'s felt a lesser need for the study guide than was expressed by the overall group.

From the foregoing it can be seen that scientists and engineers are very interested in using the self-study mode for acquisition of the knowledge they feel they need; hence industrial trainers may well consider the possibility not only of providing such offerings but also of creating an internal climate for their most effective use—for example, the establishment of quiet conference areas where scientists and engineers could engage in self-study without the normal distractions of their work area. Such study areas could be available both during and after working hours to facilitate their optimum use.

MID-CAREER DEVELOPMENT

Technology Future Shock

In the past, most engineers and scientists employed in industry could look forward to both lifetime careers in the areas of science and technology they were educated in and lifetime careers in their corporations. Since the end of World War II and commencing especially in the 1950s, it has become increasingly clear that this situation no longer exists. In a recent major survey of one segment of the engineering profession it was found that average industrially employed engineers change jobs at least four times during the first 20 years of their working lives. Such changes may well reflect a desire on their part to advance technically and financially, as well as an increase in job opportunities available to them during an exceptional industrial growth period in the nation. The latter circumstance may not hold for the long-term future; hence many industrial organizations will be faced with the problem of restoring the technical vitality of their older (mid-career) scientific and engineering employees in order to maintain their rate of productivity consistent with the influx of new talent. The development of programs aimed at scientists and engineers in mid-career presents a great challenge to the industrial trainer inasmuch as the concepts and approaches normally used, and discussed previously, may have to be modified to take into account the difference in motivation and outlook of these individuals. This is not to say that education, retraining, etc., are the sole answer to this problem; rather, they are some of the many factors which a corporation must review in arriving at a viable program aimed at solving the problem.

Miller[5] has summarized some contributing factors in demotivation; these are discussed below.

Obsolescence Caused by Simple Lack of a Specific Skill   The best example is the engineer who thinks, "I am no longer capable at calculus because I never use it."

Functional or Organizational Obsolescence   This occurs when a function that the professional has performed over a period of time is no longer required. Rapid technical change can cause field or specialty displacement. An example might be an expert in glass technology who finds that the company's products no longer require his expertise. He is then faced with searching out someone else who needs his specialty or with retraining in a more useful field.

Energy or Motivational Obsolescence   This is best seen in senior professionals who realize they are not going to move farther up the ladder and work only hard enough to maintain their position. Such people sometimes become obsolete because of a lack of adaptability. They are simply not able to forget the past and adjust to a changed environment.

Obsolescence Caused by a Built-in Bias for Youth   The engineering manager who usually gives a challenging job to a younger person creates such obsolescence by depriving the senior person of a chance to learn, change, and grow. Managers often justify this by pointing out that experience causes obsolescence because it generally teaches us what we cannot do—it establishes limits. Managers are also reluctant to give the senior an assignment which is seen as a junior's job.

Miller proposes numerous approaches which corporations may pursue—emphasizing education, but indicating that it does not guarantee vitality. He points out the need for training to be part of the workday; packaging of educational offerings must be oriented to the individuals—i.e., busy people need to be taken away from the work environment temporarily to make the educational experience effective. Because principals should be included in the educational offerings, jobs should be deliberately designed to provide wider ranges of opportunity. Sabbaticals may be of help—an expression on the part of general management that human resources are vital to the corporation. Measurement of progress and performance should reflect these aspects of vitality and will also be of help.

Summarizing, Miller states:

> There is no single solution to extending the productive period for the professional. The range of activities necessary must include redesign of the environment to provide support for learning and growth, provision of appropriate rewards for those who remain vital, and a multitude of facilities and activities. A vital location is characterized by an important job, first-rate leadership, high productivity, excitement, sense of purpose, a feeling of accomplishment, a sense of personal opportunity, openness to change and new ideas, nearly unachievable goals, fair and thoughtful measurement and reward, and strong contacts to ideas and people outside. In such an environment, there is a high probability there will be a high percentage of vital people.[6]

Career Planning

Given the conditions described in the preceding section, one can also visualize the possibility of training programs within industry that emphasize the general principles of career planning. One such program, now in existence within the General Electric Company, offers promise of providing such an emphasis, for engineers and scientists.

A brief description of the process as given by the author of the program, W.D. Storey, should enable industrial trainers to evaluate the potential for this type of educational experience in their own work setting:

> Career Action Planning or CAP is a flexible, self-directed process guided by a workbook, which can be easily individualized to meet the needs, interests and commitments of individuals in a variety of situations. CAP is primarily designed for the career development of an individual within an organization; it does not deal with the details of changing employers. There is no enormous commitment required by the individual. He can spend as little as an hour learning about the process of career planning or as much as 10–12 hours to do all of the fourteen exercises, most of which can be completed in one-half to one hour or less. Neither the individual nor his manager has to exchange documents for administrative purposes.
>
> The individual may privately select only those exercises from the total CAP process which he thinks are helpful or interesting for (1) identifying his or her own learning needs; (2) planning actions for learning; (3) getting resources or support for implementing actions for learning; (4) evaluating progress and accomplishments; (5) testing the realism and quality of plans, expectations and potentials; (6) discovering alternative opportunities, constraints and possible risks and consequences; (7) learning how to make choices; and (8) finding out where he or she stands. A one-to-three-minute self-administered test helps the individual decide, without first doing an exercise, whether he needs to do such thinking and is ready to do it now.[7]

Storey expands on these eight exercises and provides insights into their general applicability to the working environment. He summarizes by stating:

> There are many important things, like sponsorship, political realities and being at the right place at the right time, which determine the course of our careers—things which we often attribute to luck, knowing the right person, or accidents which just happen to have influenced what we do. We cannot always influence such accidents, whether the accidents are desirable or unfavorable. However, getting better answers to the questions which have been considered does force one to deal with issues which he can control and which can help him increase the influence he has on the timing, quality and number of desirable accidents throughout his career.[8]

Outline of the General Electric Career Action Planning Program

Chapter I—What Is Your Career Plan?
A Ten-Question Test to Assess Your Current Plan
The Benefits Persons Report Who Do CAP

EXTERNAL FORCES AFFECTING PROFESSIONAL DEVELOPMENT

Certification

Within the scientific and engineering community, a dialogue has developed concerning the possible need for programs which may certify the competency of individuals to practice their profession. The ways in which such certification could be accomplished are numerous and include the maintenance of lifelong records of educational achievement.

Currently, most states have laws regulating the practice of engineering, and more than a majority have a clause in their laws exempting industrially employed engineers from licensing. However, many states are considering rescinding this clause, thereby opening the possibility that most industrially employed engineers may be required to become licensed and, upon applying for renewal of that license (usually every three years), may be required to show evidence of maintaining their competency by various means, including a record of their educational achievement during the period since the license was last renewed.

The concept of certification therefore represents a further challenge to the individual trainer to ensure that in evolving his or her programs, due consideration is given to the way in which the level, type, and duration of such offerings are usable in terms of certification programs which may be established by states, professional organizations, or the federal government.

Continuing Education Units

A need has long been felt for some system which would provide for the measurement of noncredit continuing education. Several organizations and institutions have initiated or are studying systems of measurement and awards that have little or no relationship to any other system in being. A uniform, nationally accepted unit holds promise of providing a suitable means of recognizing and rewarding individual effort in the pursuit of continuing education.

Definition of the CEU   The continuing education unit is defined as follows: Ten contact hours of participation in an organized continuing education experience under responsible sponsorship, capable direction, and qualified instruction.

Continuing education, for the purpose of this recommendation, includes all institutional and organizational learning experiences in organized formats that impart noncredit education to postsecondary-level learners. These properties of continuing education may be applied equally under the proposed system, regardless of the teaching-learning format, program duration, source of sponsorship, subject matter, level, audience, or purpose.

Specific Attributes of the CEU   The CEU has been designed to facilitate communication about continuing education from one person to another, from one institution to another, from employee to employer, from one area of the country to another, and from one time period to another. Some specific objectives which the CEU will fulfill are:

It will systematize the recording and reporting system for continuing education by establishing a uniform, nationally accepted unit of measurement of participation in noncredit continuing education.

It will provide a uniform system for accumulating statistical data at local, state, and national levels on the total amount of participation in continuing education.

It will permit the accumulating, updating, and transfer of the continuing education record of an individual.

It will encourage long-range educational goals and continuing education as a process of lifelong learning for individuals, for professional groups, and by institutions.

It will make the pursuit of knowledge more attractive as a way of personal and professional development and will provide a framework within which an individual can develop at his or her own pace.

It will permit and encourage adult students to marshal and utilize a host of continuing education resources to serve their particular needs.

In general, the CEU is intended to serve all interests in continuing education, whether public or private and whether individual, instructional, institutional, organizational, governmental, or societal. The unit is also applicable to the appropriate learning experiences of adults at all levels, from postsecondary to postdoctoral; for all classes of adult learners, whether the instruction is in vocational, technical, professional, or managerial fields or is designed for people bent on personal improvement; and in all formats of teaching and learning known to the field of education.

Criteria and standards deemed to be minimum essential guidelines in offering continuing education units to individual participants in continuing education activities are obtainable from the National University Extension Association, located in Washington, D.C.

Applications   The following suggestions for possible applications of the continuing education unit are offered as guidance and to serve as illustrations. These practical examples are considered to set limitations to the situations in which the CEU can be applied. Some possible applications of the unit are:

Continuing education intensive courses in technical and professional areas (i.e., for engineers, lawyers, doctors, teachers, etc.)

In-service training programs to improve competence in new techniques or technical areas

Courses or classes which may be used in partial fulfillment of certificate or licensing requirements

Programs, sponsored by technical or industrial societies through universities, which are designed to upgrade the performance of members in occupational or technical areas

Liberal education programs for the general public

Paraprofessional or subprofessional training programs

Vocational training programs, either in-service programs or programs that prepare students for job-entry positions

Limitations   Any program carrying academic credit, either secondary or collegiate

Programs leading to high school equivalency certificates or diplomas

Organizational orientation training programs

Short-duration programs only casually related to any specific upgrading purpose or goal

Determination of Units to be Awarded   The determination of the number of units to be awarded for a particular continuing education experience is the responsibility of the director of extension or continuing education or of the director of training; the determination is based on the recommendation of the program director immediately responsible for the activity.

SUMMARY

This chapter has attempted to provide a general overview of the characteristics of scientists and engineers, their working environment, and educational methodologies to which they are exposed: emerging educational techniques holding promise for the future; special problems involving changing technologies and the effect such changes have on the mid-career of scientists and engineers; and educational approaches being considered to help alleviate the problems created by technologies that are changing rapidly.

Industrial trainers who include in their planning the concepts described in the preceding pages, should be better able to serve the specific needs of this population group within their organizations. As they recognize the underlying differences between the approach of engineers to the acquisition of knowledge and the approach of scientists, they will be able to make more effective use of educational delivery methods appropriate to both the tasks at hand and the individuals with whom they are dealing. In addition, they will be better able to attend to the mid-career needs of these individuals by developing programs addressed to both their changing psychological needs and changing technological needs. Throughout this chapter, the concept of lifelong learning has been stressed in one form or another. The industrial trainer should continually evaluate the state and level of scientific and technical knowledge of this constituency in his or her organization. Application of the concepts outlined in this chapter will enable the industrial trainer to effectively serve the need of scientists and engineers throughout their career lives.

REFERENCES

1. Brown, J. D.: *The Role of Engineering as a Learned Profession,* Conference on Engineering Education, Princeton University Press, Princeton, N.J., 1962.

2. Ritti, R. R.: *The Engineer in an Industrial Corporation,* Columbia University Press, New York, 1971.
3. Rosenbloom, R. S., and F. W. Wolek: *Technology and Information Transfer: A Survey of Practice in Industrial Organizations,* Harvard University, Graduate School of Business Administration, Division of Research, Cambridge, Mass., 1970.
4. Saunders, R. M.: *The Role of IEEE in Continuing Engineering Studies,* ASEE Continuing Engineering Studies Series, Conference Report, no. 8, November 1973.
5. Miller, D. B.: *Technical Vitality of the Older Engineer in Industry,* Conference Report, American Society for Engineering Education, July 1973.
6. Ibid.
7. Storey, W. D.: *An Introduction to Self-directed Career Planning,* Conference Report, American Society for Engineering Education, July 1973.

Chapter **25**

Vocational and Technical Education

ARTHUR W. SALTZMAN

RAYMOND J. MALY

G. RICHARD HARTSHORN

Arthur W. Saltzman *is Centralized Industrial Relations Services Manager, General Services, Ford Motor Company. He previously served Ford as Manager of the Corporate-Level Training Department. He is a member of the Research and Evaluation Subcommittee of the National Manpower Advisory Council and of the Michigan Manpower Planning Council, and he is a past director of the Michigan Economic Opportunity Office.*

Raymond J. Maly *is Manager, Management and Technical Training, Ford Motor Company. His experience with Ford includes better than 20 years of operations and staff assignments in industrial relations, including labor relations, salary administration, and training. He has served as Supervisor, Salaried Personnel and Training, in a plant, and as Personnel and Organization Manager for one of the company's largest product engineering offices. Before entering industry, he was an Instructor at DePaul University. Mr. Maly has a bachelor's degree in philosophy from St. Mary's and a master's degree in economics from the University of Notre Dame.*

G. Richard Hartshorn *is Management Training Supervisor, Management and Technical Training, Ford Motor Company. During his 10 years with Ford, his assignments for manufacturing facilities at the plant and division levels have concentrated on technical and managerial training. Mr. Hartshorn's career includes positions as Manager, Personnel Research, Training and Services, for the finance and insurance subsidiaries of the Ford Motor Company, as well as five years in metallurgical research with the General Motors Corporation. He holds a bachelor's degree in vocational and technical education and a master's degree in instructional technology from Wayne State University, Detroit, Michigan.*

This chapter briefly surveys vocational and technical educational resources available to the training professional. It discusses special-purpose work-related programs offered by public and private educational institutions, with primary focus on public institutions. Such programs are designed both to qualify youth for entry-level positions in specific occupational categories and to meet the special skill training needs of designated groups of adults. Educational programs leading exclusively to college degrees are not discussed.

Four elements of the training professional's job will be considered:

1. Recommending policy for the organization relating to use of public funds and institutions
2. Establishing objectives that are mutually acceptable to the organization and the educational resource
3. Identifying and evaluating available community educational resources, including schools, programs, and services
4. Establishing mutually beneficial relationships with educational institutions

POLICY IMPLICATIONS

Policy considerations relating to the use of in-house and external training resources are, in part, "make-or-buy" decisions depending on available options and, in part, on philosophical inclination. The small business with limited space, overworked supervisors, and a part-time training staff obviously depends on external resources. Large firms, particularly those with sophisticated technical training support units associated with their sales or production activities, have other options. It is convenient and sometimes cost-effective for such firms to use these resources for in-house training.

There is no one best way, though, even for large companies. To illustrate, the Ford Motor Company has for many years followed a policy of using public educational facilities whenever possible to provide vocational and technical eduation. In contrast, the other two-thirds of the automotive "Big Three"—General Motors and Chrysler—operate large proprietary technical institutes.

As a result of changing manpower and vocational education legislation at all levels of government, the organization must decide (1) whether to use public educational services and, if so, on what terms and (2) how to respond to the pressures of immediate social priorities. These policy decisions must be made, if not deliberately, then by default. In either case, the recommendations of the training professional are usually critical.

In making recommendations about the use of public education, a rule of thumb is that older and better-established schools and programs are usually accepted by management, while newer institutions will be considered more carefully. Few managers remember that land-grant colleges were established to train specialists in the agricultural and mechanical arts under the Morill Act of 1862. Enrollments in apprentice-related classes and similar offerings of technical institutes and vocational high schools are rarely challenged. These are available largely as a consequence of the Smith-Hughes Act of 1917 and subsequent categorical vocational legislation.

Management may be more skeptical about the merits of more recent programs. Those offered by the community colleges, which emerged in the 1950s, may need aggressive sponsorship. Still more care may be required in drawing on the institutions of the 1960s: Job Corps centers, skills centers, and regional vocational schools. These developed as a result of such laws as the Manpower Development and Training Act of 1962, the Vocational Education Act of 1963, and the Economic Opportunity Act.

Policy recommendations concerning the potential use of public resources associated with social-priority programs have additional dimensions. These, too, have a long tradition—for example, programs providing training and jobs for the physically handicapped and for war veterans (the GI bill following World War II was probably the largest of all government-sponsored vocational education programs). However, recent programs transcend traditional training. They are designed to provide "equal opportunity" for blacks, women, older workers, youth, and other groups considered excluded under usual employment practices.

Participation in these programs means dealing with several basic policy questions. Traditional employment standards may have to be modified, entry-level jobs may have to be restructured under the Economic Opportunity program, and the propriety of accepting government subsidies under the Job Opportunities in the Business Sector (JOBS) program may have to be examined.

Legal, social, philosophical, and economic issues are involved in such decisions. The astute training professional will assess management's attitude toward each of these before utilizing the vocational and technical resources associated with such programs.

ESTABLISHING MUTUALLY ACCEPTABLE OBJECTIVES

Needs analysis and the setting of training objectives are particularly critical in the case of vocational and technical courses and programs; these vary widely in content, quality, and degree of relevancy. Properly designed behavioral objectives and related skill and knowledge standards can provide the basis for planning jointly with, and evaluating the effectiveness of, the educational resource used.

Task Analysis

Task analysis, behavioral objectives, and related skill and knowledge requirement techniques are some of the better by-products of the programmed learning movement. There are a number of approaches to task analysis. Figure 25-1 is an illustration from the Upjohn Institute program, How to Use the National Task Bank.

Most educators participate enthusiastically in setting objectives. Their importance for the training professional can be readily illustrated by a discussion of the way in which objectives are used in three of the major types of vocational and technical education programs.

Preemployment Education

Preemployment education is usually offered on a full-time basis. It is designed to qualify youth for entry-level jobs such as that of typist, computer operator, automotive mechanic, or assistant cook. Graduates acquire certification or, in the case of high schools or junior colleges, diplomas. Since training is completed prior to employment, the behavioral objectives become standards for employment decisions.

Preemployment programs provide the basis for answering three critical questions: Can the graduate perform the entry-level tasks to the specified standards? Can he or she perform better than new hires with less specific education? To what extent will the training enhance the graduate's career progress? If behavioral standards enable the placement activity to obtain systematic answers to these questions, preemployment programs can be used in a cost-effective manner.

Special-Group Education

A second type of training includes courses and programs tailored to the needs of specific groups of employees or organizations. Such training may be designed by the organization itself, or it may be purchased from private vendors or, in some

Data	People	Things	Data	People	Things		Reas.	Math.	Lang.	
WORKER FUNCTION – LEVEL			WORKER FUNCTION – ORIENTATION			INSTR.	GENERAL EDUCATION DEVELOPMENT			TASK NO.
3B	1A	2B	70%	5%	25%	2	3	1	4	
GOAL: (To be completed by individual user)					GOAL: OBJECTIVE: (To be completed by individual user)					

TASK: Types/transcribes standard form letter, including specified information from records provided, following S.O.P. for form letter, but adjusting standard form as required for clarity and smoothness, etc., in order to prepare letter for mailing.

TO DO **THIS** TASK

PERFORMANCE STANDARDS

DESCRIPTIVE:
- Types with reasonable speed and accuracy
- Format of letter is correct
- Any changes/adjustments are made correctly

NUMERICAL:
- Completes letter in X period of time
- No uncorrected typing, mechanical, or adjustment errors per letter
- Fewer than X omissions of information per X number of letters typed

TO THESE STANDARDS

TRAINING CONTENT

FUNCTIONAL:
- How to type: letters
- How to transcribe material, correcting mechanical errors
- How to combine two written sets of data into one

SPECIFIC:
- How to obtain records and find information in them
- Knowledge of S.O.P. for standard letter format: how/where to include information
- Knowledge of information required in letter
- How to use particular typewriter provided

THE WORKER NEEDS THIS TRAINING

Fig. 25-1 Task analysis. *(Functional Job Analysis. An Approach to a Technology for Manpower Planning. Reprinted by permission of the W. E. Upjohn Institute for Employment Research, Washington, D.C.)*

cases, the public schools. If objectives are accurately specified and can be met by the public schools, low-cost, effective training results.

For example, the Ford Motor Company and the Dearborn public schools have developed a program to qualify employees who have failed the selection test for a regular apprenticeship. In this program, the company diagnoses the employees' deficiencies. Each deficiency becomes an instructional objective and is corrected through an individually tailored learning plan. The employee uses self-instructional materials and studies segments needed to correct each specific deficiency. School counselors assist trainees with learning materials at the plant site to optimize employee involvement and commitment.

Trainees who satisfactorily complete the preapprenticeship program qualify for regular apprenticeship training without retaking the entire apprentice selection test battery. The program is of particular value for training disadvantaged employees who have inadequate educational preparation.

Individual Courses and Programs

A third type of training draws on individual courses and programs offered as part of standard curricula. Schools, both public and private, offer basic courses in newer occupations, such as those generated by the computer industry, as well as in traditional areas, such as supervisory training.

Courses are many and varied, and the training professional's challenge is to learn what subjects are offered, where they are offered, what the quality of the courses is, and how relevant they are. With so many courses in so many subjects, the training professional is dependent primarily upon participant evaluation.

The most feasible quality check usually involves a brief written report from employees who have completed a course. Employees who know the behavioral objectives (i.e., what they should learn) will be able to report on whether such learning took place and whether the knowledge acquired was useful on the job.

EDUCATIONAL RESOURCES

Schools

Public High Schools   There are several distinct kinds of public schools which the training professional can turn to for vocational and technical courses. General, technical, and vocational high schools exist in most large metropolitan areas. Most high schools have a division of adult education or a person designated to coordinate vocational training. These schools typically offer a variety of occupationally related courses to prepare full-time high school students for jobs. Most schools also offer selected groups of programs at night for adults.

Curricula usually fall into three categories: (1) commercial or business, including typing, shorthand, and home economics; (2) vocational, typically including machine-shop work, metalworking, and carpentry; and (3) agricultural. In addition, the range of schools includes the special-purpose institutions that exist in the larger cities, such as the High School of Needle Trades in New York City.

Area Vocational Schools   These schools are relative newcomers to the educational community and are usually strategically placed to serve smaller communities and rural areas which cannot support a technical high school of their own. Most of them were built with funds available under the Vocational Education Act of 1963. Consequently, they are newer, have modern equipment, and frequently offer more flexible and relevant courses. An example of this type of school is the St. Paul Area Technical Institute, which is referred to in the discussion of continuing vocational and technical training.

Junior Colleges   Many junior colleges offer excellent vocational education and are well equipped, not only with machinery and equipment, but also with qualified staff using contemporary training technology. In addition to providing classroom instruction for apprenticeship programs, junior colleges also offer technician training in areas such as hydraulics, electronics, industrial technology, tool and die design, drafting, and specialized fields of engineering.

Colleges and Universities   Four-year colleges and universities also offer a variety of resources to the training professional. Publicly supported colleges frequently sponsor specialized programs directed toward adults who need updating in a particular area. Some private colleges sponsor such programs as well. These courses are usually offered through the senior college's division of adult or continuing education. They require that the school substantially alter its usual approach, which centers on tightly structured, conventional degree credit programs. Some schools custom-tailor programs and offer them at the workplace or on the school premises, frequently using qualified members of industry as instructors.

Independent Study

Independent study programs have been used in industry for a considerable period of time. International Correspondence Schools points out that more than 3,500 business and govenment organizations are using ICS independent training materials, programs, and assistance as part of their formal training programs.

Some large corporations use self-learning programs coupled with special-purpose educational media to reduce instructional costs and avoid premium payments after regular work schedules. Such courses range from those using commercially published programmed texts to those using lessons prepared on video tape and supported by program books which parallel and complement the video presentations. Some training packages also include hands-on training on simulators, which are training aids closely resembling equipment on the factory floor.

Company-operated Institutes

Some companies, such as General Motors, RCA, IBM, and AT&T, have established special institutes, programs, or classes to tailor-make educational programs to their own needs. These programs usually complement the more general and theoretical classes presented by local educational institutions and are aimed at updating technicians, skilled craftsmen, and engineers. The content usually focuses on the specific application of theories, something which is not usually covered as well in traditional adult education at the secondary, junior college, or college level.

Courses Sponsored by Unions and Trade Associations

Unions and trade associations also are utilized by many employers as educational resources. Building and construction trade unions, for example, offer apprenticeship training in many large metropolitan industrial areas. Several unions, such as the UAW, offer training to disadvantaged persons. The building and construction trades sponsor dozens of apprenticeships covering a multitude of classifications from bricklayer and carpenter to plasterer and tile setter.

Proprietary Schools

More than 7,000 private "for-profit" schools offer vocational training. Most of this is full-time preemployment training in such trades as cosmetology, typing, or data processing. Many schools offer evening programs for upgrading employees as well. Since there is little published information available about the quality of such schools, each must be evaluated on its own merit. Specification of behavioral objectives and of systems through which participants can report is extremely important so that the training professional can separate the wheat from the chaff.

Skills Centers

These training institutions originated in the 1960s under MDTA to provide, in one school, both skill training and basic education for "disadvantaged" adults. The focus is on the adult; skills, job-hunting techniques, literacy, grooming, or whatever may be required is taught in modules with no fixed-time constraint. Centers now exist in many areas, and administrators usually willingly set up vestibule areas to meet the special needs of particular employers.

PROGRAMS AND SERVICES

Several factors affect the types of school programs and vendor training services and the terms under which they will be offered. Public school courses are usually structured to take advantage of funding available under law. Private technical institutes and colleges frequently separate vocational and technical programs to protect degree standards. Vendor offerings vary from straight classroom teaching to teaching-machine technology. Some of the most commonly used programs are apprenticeship, cooperative education, continuing vocational and technical education, and government programs for special groups.

Apprenticeship

A total of 264,122 persons enrolled in apprenticeship programs in 1972, with more than 60 percent in the building trades. Apprenticeship is the oldest continuing vocational and technical training system in American industry.

The importance of the apprenticeship training model transcends the program. It has evolved directly from the medieval guild system, as has training in the medical and legal professions. Further, the model has been extended and is used for a wide variety of vocational training: to develop foremen, technicians, and engineers, for example. The cooperative education program and that latest in federal manpower efforts, the "coupled work-study" program, are essentially variants of the same model.

In its present form, apprenticeship flourishes where unions flourish. The program is typically administered by a union-management joint apprenticeship committee (JAC). In essence, it is a system under which a trainee acquires vocational skills "on the job" by working with journeymen craftsmen for a designated period of time. In addition, the apprentice acquires related formal knowledge, usually in a classroom, but occasionally through self-study. Programs vary in length, typically from two to five years, and successful graduates are certified as journeymen in such trades as plumbing, electricity, die making, bricklaying, printing, and mechanics.

Both the federal and state governments supervise these programs and subsidize the related training aspects. The National Apprenticeship Act of 1937 (Fitzgerald Act) is the basic federal law, and the program is administered through the Bureau of Apprenticeship and Training (BAT) of the Department of Labor. In addition, 30 states have state apprenticeship councils (SACs).

Programs meeting BAT and/or SAC standards may be registered, and graduates are given certificates of completion by the appropriate agencies. Certificates are sought after since they assure the journeyman of greater job choice.

Standards include a minimum of 144 hours of related training per year, specified wage progress, and levels of supervision. Most related training is provided by public schools with designated subjects such as shop mathematics, blueprint reading, and electrical theory.

The effectiveness of the on-the-job learning phase can vary considerably. In small firms with few apprentices, success is obviously dependent upon the ability of journeymen and their willingness to share their skills. In larger firms, the training professional can help organize the work situation to increase program effectiveness. Apprenticeship assignments can be structured so that simple tasks are learned first and complex tasks later. Checks can be devised to assure that skills have been mastered.

In the Ford Motor Company an extensive task analysis of the nine most populated trades was undertaken. With this as a base, a vestibule school was established, and self-paced learning guides were designed. Apprentices perform each operation on production materials under the guidance of journeymen instructors until they demonstrate mastery. Tasks undertaken are increasingly complex, and skills are learned more quickly and completely. The task guide tells the apprentices what they must learn to do, and it lists the tools, materials, and equipment necessary to perform the task. It also defines when the task is being done correctly, directs apprentices to reference materials, and provides a check sheet on which apprentices record that they have learned to do each task. The task statement shown in Fig. 25-2 is from *Basic Training Guide: Tool and Die Making*.

The apprenticeship model is widely accepted. Training professionals interested in either improving present programs or initiating new ones can contact BAT personnel, who are located in every state, or any of the 30 state SACs.

Cooperative Education

Schools use federal funds to offer cooperative work-study programs. Local and state funds supplement federal subsidies in some districts. These are programs under which students spend some time at school and some time at work. Schools are interested in these programs because they smooth the transition from school to work. Employers, in turn, have the opportunity to evaluate potential employees before full-time job commitments are made. Students also find the arrangement very helpful because it enables them to apply theory to work situations much sooner than they could otherwise.

Typically at the high school level, seniors split their days between class and job, with a minimum of 15 hours of work per week. At the junior college level, split days or whole days at work alternating with whole days at school may be the pattern. At the college level (outside the purview of this chapter) students spend an academic quarter or semester on campus and an equal period of time on the job.

Federal subsidies are given for cooperative programs in areas involving the distributive, trade and industrial, and office occupations. Information about these programs is usually available from the Cooperative Education Association, which publishes the *Directory of Cooperative Education*.

Continuing Vocational and Technical Education

Public schools in many areas offer a variety of vocationally related technical courses during the evening. Schools receive federal funds for these courses too, and offerings usually include the same courses as those for apprentices supplemented by other, more advanced programs. Subjects vary from computer programming to financial analysis and plant layout, and the courses are designed to help adults qualify for advancement.

Courses are offered by high schools, area vocational schools, junior colleges, and university extension programs, frequently simultaneously, in the same city. They may be organized into curricula leading to certificates or, at the junior college level, to two-year degrees. For example, the announcement shown in Fig. 25-3 is from the catalog of the New York University School of Continuing Education, Division of Business and Management.

Figure 25-4 shows one section of a poster announcing the courses offered in the evening by the St. Paul Area Technical Vocational Institute (St. Paul, Minnesota).

Government Programs for Special Groups

Federal manpower policy has emphasized increasingly that the work-providing community has a social obligation to employ special groups of individuals. Traditionally, these groups have included returning war veterans and the physically handicapped. Recently, the "disadvantaged," including minorities and women, have been added. A variety of approaches have been tried. These include retraining and prevocational training at new types of institutions, such as the skills

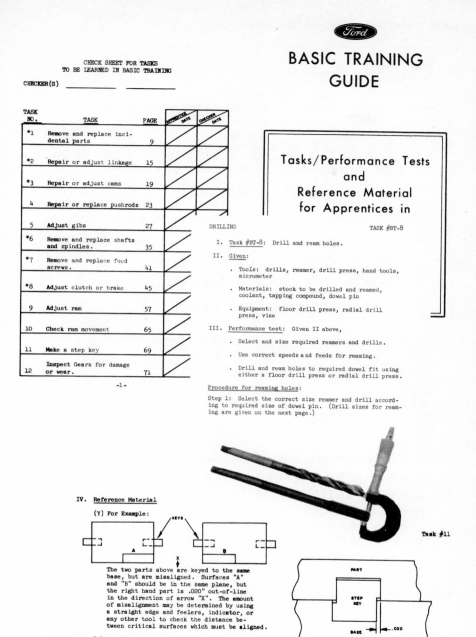

BASIC TRAINING GUIDE

CHECK SHEET FOR TASKS
TO BE LEARNED IN BASIC TRAINING

CHECKER(S) _____ _____

-1-

Tasks/Performance Tests
and
Reference Material
for Apprentices in

DRILLING   TASK #BT-8

I. Task #BT-8: Drill and ream holes.

II. Given:

- Tools: drills, reamer, drill press, hand tools, micrometer

- Materials: stock to be drilled and reamed, coolant, tapping compound, dowel pin

- Equipment: floor drill press, radial drill press, vise

III. Performance test: Given II above,

- Select and size required reamers and drills.

- Use correct speeds and feeds for reaming.

- Drill and ream holes to required dowel fit using either a floor drill press or radial drill press.

Procedure for reaming holes:

Step 1: Select the correct size reamer and drill according to required size of dowel pin. (Drill sizes for reaming are given on the next page.)

Task #11

IV. Reference Material

(Y) For Example:

KEYS

A   X   B

The two parts above are keyed to the same base, but are misaligned. Surfaces "A" and "B" should be in the same plane, but the right hand part is .020" out-of-line in the direction of arrow "X". The amount of misalignment may be determined by using a straight edge and feelers, indicator, or any other tool to check the distance between critical surfaces which must be aligned.

(Z) For Example Above:

(2) step keys can be made with a .020" step, as seen in end view on next page, which will move right hand part back so that Surfaces "A" and "B" will be aligned.

PART

STEP KEY

BASE   .020

Step keys are also used to re-time mechanical movements. For example, a press ram that is out-of-time due to a twisted crank may be re-timed by removing the gear key of the crank that is twisted. Rotate twisted crank in gear until aligned with other crank. Measure misalignment between gear keyway and crank shaft keyway. Make and install step key. Step keys for presses are not off-set more than .090" - .100".

Fig. 25-2 Portions of basic training guide for apprentices. *(Reprinted by permission of the Ford Motor Company.)*

Fig. 25-3 Continuing education announcement. *(Reprinted by permission of New York University, School of Continuing Education, Division of Business and Management.)*

centers. Included also are novel approaches such as the JOBS program, under which employers are asked to hire submarginal trainees and are subsidized until the trainees can perform to commercially acceptable standards.

A number of state, federal, and local departments are involved, ranging from the Veterans Administration through the Department of Health, Education, and Welfare, the Department of Labor, and the local prison and school system. The number of federal programs alone can be mind-boggling. A recent publication summarizing federally assisted manpower programs in tabular form listed 18 programs.[1]

Programs change as new laws are passed. Regardless, programs which train

No.	Class	Instructor	Room No.	Time	Days	Start Date	End Date	Hours	Fee

AIR CONDITIONING & REFRIGERATION

No.	Class	Instructor	Room No.	Time	Days	Start Date	End Date	Hours	Fee
1-01 710C4	Princ Refr & Elec I	Lawton	423/S-16	6:30-9:30	TH	1-24-74	5-16-74	48	15.00
1-01 715D3	Princ Refr & Elec II	Thomas	423 S-16	6:30-9:30	M	1-21-74	5-20-74	48	20.00
1-01 715D4	Princ Refr & Elec II	Vincent	423 S-16	6:30-9:30	W	1-23-74	5-15-74	48	20.00
1-01 721D2	Refrig & Elec III	Lawton	S-16/423	6:30-9:30	T	1-22-74	5-14-74	48	20.00
1-01 721D3	Refrig & Elec III	Dunbar W.	423/S-16	6:30-10:00	T,TH	1-22-74	3-14-74	56	20.00
1-01 726D2	Refrig & Elec IV	Vincent	S-16 423	6:30-9:30	M	1-21-74	5-20-74	48	20.00
1-01 726D3	Refrig & Elec IV	Caswell	S-16/423	6:30-9:30	W	1-23-74	5-15-74	48	20.00
1-01 730C2	Princ Air Cond V	Malaske	304	7-10	TH	1-24-74	5-9-74	45	15.00

CHEMICAL TECHNOLOGY

No.	Class	Instructor	Room No.	Time	Days	Start Date	End Date	Hours	Fee
1-03 720D1	Ind. Chemistry II	Bergstrom	327	6-10	T,TH	1-22-74	4-4-74	77	20.00
1-03 715D1	Organic Chemistry	Faye	325	6-10	T,TH	1-22-74	5-9-74	105	20.00
1-03 730C1	Polymer Chemistry	Various	325	7-10	M	1-21-74	5-13-74	45	15.00
1-03 725C1	Wastewater Lab Procedures	F. Osborn	327	7-10	W	1-30-74	5-15-74	45	15.00

CONSTRUCTION TECHNOLOGY

No.	Class	Instructor	Room No.	Time	Days	Start Date	End Date	Hours	Fee
1-04 710D3	Drawing	Tichich	331	6-9	M,W	1-21-74	5-8-74	87	20.00
1-04 710D4	Drawing	Schliek	201	6-10	T,TH	1-22-74	5-9-74	120	20.00
1-04 716C1	Adv. Construction Estimating	Roth	333	7-10	M,W	1-21-74	5-8-74	87	15.00
1-04 717D1	Advanced Surveying	Trence	203	6:30-9:30	M,TH	1-21-74	5-9-74	87	20.00
1-04 721C1	Basic Structural Design II	Tichich	331	6-9	M	1-21-74	5-6-74	42	15.00
1-04 726C1	Construction Model Building	Blesener	331	6-10	T	1-22-74	5-7-74	60	15.00

DESIGN TECHNOLOGY

No.	Class	Instructor	Room No.	Time	Days	Start Date	End Date	Hours	Fee
1-05 710D3	Fund Mech. Drafting	Spanovich	209	6-10	M,T	1-21-74	5-7-74	116	20.00
1-05 710D4	Fund Mech. Drafting	Raiche	205	6-10	W,TH	1-23-74	5-9-74	120	20.00
1-05 711C2	Assembly & Layout	Paulson	207	6-10	TH	1-24-74	5-9-74	60	15.00
1-05 717C1	Machine Design	Risch	203	6-10	T	1-22-74	5-7-74	60	15.00
1-05 745D1	Statics & Strength II	Skok	106	6-10	M,TH	1-21-74	5-9-74	116	20.00
1-05 746C1	Dynamics II	Reagan	226	7-10	T	1-22-74	5-7-74	45	15.00
1-05 742C2	Registration Refresher	Kallemeyn	208	6-10	W	1-23-74	3-3-74	44	15.00
1-05 723C2	Cost Estimating	Paulson	208	6-10	T	1-22-74	5-7-74	60	15.00
1-05 743C2	SME Certification Review	W. Schuldt	208	7-10	M	1-21-74	5-13-74	42	15.00

BASIC ELECTRONICS

BASIC ELECTRONIC SERIES: THESE INTRODUCTORY CLASSES ALSO START NOV. 5, JAN. 14, MAR. 13, 1974. Every other meeting is spent in the lab. Intended for the beginner, these courses also provide an excellent review of modern electronic principles and basic applications. Qualified students may enter the series at higher levels.

No.	Class	Instructor	Room No.	Time	Days	Start Date	End Date	Hours	Fee
1-08 710C4	Elect. Fund I	Alnes	426/421	6-10	M,W	1-14-74	3-11-74	64	15.00
1-08 711C4	Elect. Behavior II	Martinson	427/424	6-10	M,W	1-14-74	3-11-74	64	15.00
1-08 712C3	Reactive Comp. III	Mickelson	424/427	6-10	M,W	1-14-74	3-11-74	64	15.00
1-08 712C4	Reactive Comp. III	Deeg	424/427	6-10	T,TH	1-17-74	3-12-74	64	15.00
1-08 713C3	Elect. Devices IV	McKinnon	422/431	6-10	M,W	1-14-74	3-11-74	64	15.00
1-08 720C3	Small Signal Amps V	Breault	431/422	6-10	M,W	1-14-74	3-11-74	64	15.00
1-08 721C3	Power Amps VI	Ritchie	416/431	6-10	T,TH	1-17-74	3-12-74	64	15.00
1-08 722C3	Pulse & Digital Circuits VII	Berdahl	431/426	6-10	T,TH	1-17-74	3-12-74	64	15.00
1-08 723C3	Special Device Appl. VIII	Schilling	416/419	6-10	M,W	1-14-74	3-11-74	64	15.00

APPLIED ELECTRONICS

No.	Class	Instructor	Room No.	Time	Days	Start Date	End Date	Hours	Fee
1-08 729C1	Medical Elect. Fund	Snegoski	420	6-10	T	1-22-74	5-8-74	64	15.00
1-08 745C1	MSI/LSI	Khambata	432	6-10	TH	1-24-74	4-18-74	48	15.00
1-08 743C2	Operational Amps	Zander	419	6-10	W	1-23-74	4-17-74	48	15.00
1-08 757C1	Logic Circuit Appl.	Khambata	221	6-10	W	1-23-74	5-4-74	56	15.00
1-08 780C1	Electronics for Maintenance Men	Schilling	421	6-10	M	1-21-74	5-13-74	60	15.00
1-08 782C1	Digital Instrument Fund.	Schilling	429	6-10	TH	1-24-74	5-9-74	60	15.00
1-08 784D1	Logic Laboratory	Schilling	419	6:30-9:30	T	1-22-74	5-2-74	33	20.00

RADIO & TV

No.	Class	Instructor	Room No.	Time	Days	Start Date	End Date	Hours	Fee
3-32 721C1	Radio Service II	Cervenka	429	7-10	M	1-21-74	5-20-74	48	15.00
3-32 713C2	FCC License	Snyder	426	6-10	T	1-22-74	5-28-74	72	15.00
3-32 735D1	TV Service II	Freeborg	425	6-10	M,W	1-14-74	4-29-74	112	20.00
3-32 745C1	Color TV II	Rubbert	425	6-10	T	1-22-74	5-14-74	64	15.00
3-32 745C2	Color TV II	Rubbert	425	6-10	TH	1-31-74	5-23-74	64	15.00
3-32 712C2	Tape Recorder Serv.	Rubbert	429	6-10	W	1-23-74	5-15-74	64	15.00
3-32 711C1	FM Multiplex	Rubbert	429	6-10	W	1-23-74	5-15-74	64	15.00

INDUSTRIAL HYDRAULICS/PNEUMATICS TECH.

No.	Class	Instructor	Room No.	Time	Days	Start Date	End Date	Hours	Fee
1-10 710C3	Basic Hydraulics I	Minogue	220	6:30-9:30	TH	1-24-74	5-16-74	48	15.00
1-10 715C1	Basic Hydraulics II	Mahle	220	6:30-9:30	M	1-21-74	5-13-74	45	15.00
1-10 715C2	Basic Hydraulics II	Walraven	220	6:30-9:30	W	1-23-74	5-8-74	45	15.00
1-10 725C1	Design & Function of Hyd. Circuits	Minogue	222	6:30-9:30	W	1-23-74	5-8-74	45	15.00
1-10 726C1	Systems Control	Walraven	222	6:30-9:30	TH	1-24-74	5-9-75	45	15.00
1-10 735C1	Maintenance & Testing	Wickoren	220	6:30-9:30	T	1-22-74	5-14-74	45	15.00

INSTRUMENTATION TECHNOLOGY (These classes are sponsored by the Instrument Society of America)

No.	Class	Instructor	Room No.	Time	Days	Start Date	End Date	Hours	Fee
1-12 720C1	System Applications II	Keseluk	309	6-9	M-TH	1-21-74	4-22-74	72	15.00
1-12 715C2	Test Technology	Snegoski	420	6-10	TH	1-24-74	5-16-74	64	15.00

QUALITY CONTROL   (These courses are offered for the ASQC Certification Program) Obtain special registration form from ASQC or at TVI.

No.	Class	Instructor	Room No.	Time	Days	Start Date	End Date	Hours	Fee
1-15 711B1	Total Quality Control	R. Kane	206	6:30-9:30	M	1-21-74	5-6-74	42	
1-15 712B1	Inspection Engineering	McLellen	203	6:30-9:30	W	1-23-74	5-1-74	42	
1-15 713B1	Statistics in Q.C.	Hilliard	204	6:30-9:30	W	1-23-74	5-1-74	42	
1-15 720B1	Supervision for Q.C.	Schroeder	304	6:30-9:30	M	1-21-74	5-6-74	42	
1-15 731B1	Quality Costs & Audits	Sherwin	203	6:30-9:30	M	1-21-74	5-1-74	42	

DRAWING

No.	Class	Instructor	Room No.	Time	Days	Start Date	End Date	Hours	Fee
9-02 711B3	Related Drawing	Anderson	205	6-10	T	1-22-74	5-14-74	68	
9-02 711B4	Related Drawing	Anderson	205	6-10	M	1-25-74	5-20-74	68	

MATHEMATICS

No.	Class	Instructor	Room No.	Time	Days	Start Date	End Date	Hours	Fee
9-03 710B11	Basic Mathematics	Various	308	6-8	M	1-21-74	5-13-74	30	10.00
9-03 712B12	Adv. Mathematics	Various	308	8-10	M	1-21-74	5-13-74	30	10.00
9-03 710B13	Basic Mathematics	Various	102	6-8	T	1-22-74	5-7-74	30	10.00
9-03 716B14	Adv. Algebra	Various	102	8-10	T	1-22-74	5-7-74	30	10.00
9-03 710B15	Basic Mathematics	Various	103	6-8	W	1-23-74	5-8-74	30	10.00
9-03 714B16	Beginning Algebra	Various	103	8-10	W	1-23-74	5-8-74	30	10.00
9-03 710B17	Basic Mathematics	Various	204	6-8	TH	1-24-74	5-9-74	30	10.00
9-03 712B18	Adv. Mathematics	Various	204	8-10	TH	1-24-74	5-9-74	30	10.00
9-03 720B19	Metric Mathematics	Various		6-9	W	1-23-74	2-20-74	15	10.00

SUPERVISION & FOREMANSHIP

No.	Class	Instructor	Room No.	Time	Days	Start Date	End Date	Hours	Fee
1-18 710B1	Supervisory I	Various	326	6:30-9:30	TH	1-24-74	5-16-74	48	10.00
1-18 711B1	Supervisory II	Various	326	6:30-9:30	M	1-21-74	5-20-74	48	20.00
1-18 720B1	Supervisory III	Various	326	6:30-9:30	T	1-22-74	5-14-74	48	10.00
1-18 721B1	Supervisory IV	Various	326	6:30-9:30	W	1-23-74	5-15-74	48	10.00

Fig. 25-4   Course listing from technical institute announcement. (*Reprinted by permission of the Saint Paul Area Technical Vocational Institute, St. Paul, Minnesota.*)

individuals for vocations impact the work-providing community. Training professionals are well-advised to become familiar with current government manpower policy trends and areas of emphasis so that they can appropriately advise their management.

RELATIONSHIPS BETWEEN INDUSTRY AND SCHOOLS

Training professionals need to be aware of the special needs of the public vocational education system. Capital equipment is constantly replaced by industrial firms intent upon using new technology. Public schools do not have the money. Some reasonable system must be devised so that students do not find themselves trying to learn skills of questionable value on equipment which no longer is in use.

Some schools have difficulty getting business to provide work-related experience. This problem is not peculiar to vocational education. Schools of dentistry and medicine, for example, long ago faced the necessity of locating in or near hospitals so that interns could begin to apply the theories of the classroom to the ills of the hospital room.

Faculty members need to keep current. Their time is preempted by the demands of students, administrators, and research. Occupations, however, develop at the workplace, not in laboratoris or treatises. Somehow teachers must be given access to the workplace so that they can learn about new skill requirements and new technology. Several paths are open for building the necessary relationships. For one thing, teachers can be used as consultants. In this capacity, they may fill a real short-time need in organizations which have neither the expertise nor the manpower to provide training for themselves. A shop instructor, for example, who is an expert in electronics may be an invaluable asset to a plant struggling with the need for updating technicians to maintain and troubleshoot new equipment.

Joint committees of educators, industrial trainers, and engineers are another way of bringing education and occupation together. For example, in an industrialized Midwestern community, a technical school approached its local industrial and business committee for assistance in setting up an electronics program. As a result, an engineering manager was assigned to serve in an advisory capacity to the school. His contribution consisted of designing a curriculum and simulation equipment for classroom use.

Committees are also used to establish related classroom programs for apprenticeship training, to keep educators current on growing and contrasting career paths, and to develop awareness of equipment needs.

Training professionals play a pivotal role in these relationships, since they frequently interface with the schools. In addition, they have a vested interest in maintaining the competency of this lowest-cost educational resource.

REFERENCE

1. Levitan, Sar A., and Robert Taggart III: *Social Experimentation and Manpower Policy: The Rhetoric and the Reality,* The Johns Hopkins Press, Baltimore, 1971.

BIBLIOGRAPHY

Cooperative Education Association: *Directory of Cooperative Education,* Drexel University, Philadelphia, 1973.
    (A compendium of cooperative programs offered throughout the United States and

Canada. Provides detailed information on the institutions in terms of program type, enrollments, graduates, etc.)

Evans, Rupert N.: *Foundations of Vocational Education,* Charles E. Merrill Books, Inc., Columbus, Ohio, 1971.

(A well-organized, thought-provoking book extending from needs analysis and philosophical foundations for vocational education to teacher development and an examination of the future of vocational education.)

Evans, Rupert N., Garth L. Mangum, and Otto Pragan: *Education for Employment,* Institute of Labor and Industrial Relations, Ann Arbor, Mich., 1969.

(A reprint of a 1966 report of the Council on Vocational Education including a section on the 1968 vocational act amendments. The summary of vocational education in the United States was used for this chapter.)

Fine, Sidney A.: *Functional Job Analysis: An Approach to a Technology for Manpower Planning,* W. E. Upjohn Institute for Employment Research, Kalamazoo, Mich., 1973.

Hendershot, Carl H.: *Programmed Learning and Individually-Paced Instruction Bibliography,* Carl H. Hendershot, Publisher, Bay City, Mich., 1973.

(A comprehensive listing of programmed learning materials, classified by subject and publisher. It includes price, length, level, and content of each program and is updated periodically.)

Levitan, Sar A., Garth L. Mangum, and Ray Marshall: *Human Resources and Labor Markets,* Harper & Row, Publishers, Incorporated, New York, 1972.

(An excellent textbook combining traditional labor economics with newer manpower materials. This chapter used information from chaps. 11, 16, and 17, on apprenticeship and manpower programs.)

Levitan, Sar A., and Robert Taggert III: *Social Experimentation and Manpower Policy: The Rhetoric and the Reality,* The Johns Hopkins Press, Baltimore, 1971

(A reference—especially appendix, p. 108—for a list of federally assisted manpower programs.)

Lovejoy, Clarence: *Lovejoy's Career and Vocational School Guide,* Simon and Schuster, New York, 1967.

(Includes a description of more than 3,500 vocational schools.)

Mager, Robert F.: *Preparing Instructional Objectives,* Lear Siegler, Inc., and Fearon Publishers, Inc., Belmont, Calif., 1970.

(A programmed text to develop skills in defining and stating teaching objectives. Describes criteria for measuring learner accomplishment and determining what must be taught and discusses materials and procedures to improve instruction.)

Mager, Robert F, and Kenneth H. Beach, Jr.: *Developing Vocational Instructions,* Lear Siegler, Inc., and Fearon Publishers, Inc., Belmont, Calif., 1967.

(A programmed text which includes steps necessary to translate task analysis into instructional units. Provides examples and how-to methods for accomplishing job task analyses, designing measurement instruments, and preparing instructional units.)

Mangum, Garth, and John Walsh: *A Decade of Manpower Development and Training,* Olympus, Salt Lake City, Utah, 1973.

(Summarizes attempts to evaluate federal manpower programs and concludes that "MDTA has been worth the cost and effort." Chapter 3, on skills centers, was used as background to this chapter.)

Olean, Sally J.: *Changing Patterns in Continuing Education for Business,* Boston University, Center for the Study of Liberal Education for Adults, Boston, 1967.

(A survey of "higher-level" business programs which are or could be conducted at a college. Twelve firms and several educational consultants are included.)

Patten, Thomas H., Jr.: *Manpower Planning and the Development of Human Resources,* Wiley-Interscience Publishers, a division of John Wiley & Sons, Inc., New York, 1971.

(The most comprehensive book on manpower planning and development known to the authors. Particularly strong in industrial programs, including both historical background and present practice. Chapter 7, on apprenticeship and technical training, and chap. 13, on public policy, were drawn upon.)

Smith, Harold T.: *Education and Training for the World of Work: A Vocational Education Program for the State of Michigan,* W. E. Upjohn Institute for Employment Research, Kalamazoo, Mich., July 1963.

(An excellent study of vocational education in Michigan which also contains descriptions of vocational systems in 10 other states, including New York, California, Illinois, and Minnesota.)

Somers, Gerald G.: *The Effectiveness of Vocational and Technical Programs: A National Follow-up Survey,* University of Wisconsin, Center for Studies in Vocation and Technical Education, Madison, 1971.

Staley, Eugene: *Planning Occupational Education and Training for Development,* Frederick A. Praeger, Inc., New York, 1971.

Chapter 26

Sales Training

FRANCIS C. REBEDEAU

DANIEL A. TAGLIERE

Francis C. "Bud" Rebedeau *is President of Kielty-Rebedeau and Associates, developers of learning programs since 1947. The firm lists many of the continent's leading corporations and associations as clients. Mr. Rebedeau has designed and conducted workshops, conventions, and on-the-job programs that have helped thousands of salespeople and managers develop results-oriented skills. He is a recognized authority in the field of training and meeting planning. He has been guest speaker and seminar leader at hundreds of meetings for all kinds of groups and has received many awards for his programs. He was 1975 Chairman of the Sales Training Division of ASTD and served on the board of directors. He serves as an officer and/or on the boards of directors of several other professional organizations.*

Daniel A. Tagliere *is President of Organization Development Services Company, which provides a variety of skills, programs, and consulting services in the areas of organization development, management development, human relations, and sales training. ODS began operations in 1972 and lists many government agencies, associations, and industrial organizations as clients. Mr. Tagliere is a social and behavioral scientist, researcher, author, speaker, and consultant. He holds a graduate degree in social science from Northern Illinois University and frequently lectures at major universities and public seminars. He is the author of* People, Power and Organization, *published by the American Management Association in 1973. He has also published numerous articles.*

This chapter describes the sales training function in the modern corporation. It provides information on how sales trainers determine the training needed by the organization's salespeople, how they meet the needs, and how they evaluate the results in terms of increasing profitable sales and other factors.

SALES TRAINING IN THE MODERN ORGANIZATION

Any organization that employs people to promote the use of its goods or services could technically be defined as a sales organization. In the broadest sense, this definition could apply to governmental, religious, and charitable organizations, as well as profit-oriented companies. Sales training, however, is more at home in companies that openly recognize the need for capable people to promote and sell their services or goods.

The sales training function is most securely entrenched in companies that are marketing-oriented. Such companies recognize that their goal is to sell profitably. They realize that they can produce what they can sell. When marketing has the place of honor, sales training has a place of prominence.

In marketing-oriented companies the sales training function is almost always separate from other personnel training. And while the general training department may be concerned with greater numbers of people, the sales training department usually spends more money per trainee for training and for refresher or advanced training.

The makeup of the training department depends on several factors, including the size of the organization, the geography of the sales effort, the turnover of the sales force, and the attitudes of top marketing people.

In production-oriented companies where products are expected to "sell themselves," the sales training function may be handled on a part-time basis by a sales supervisor, or it may be ignored altogether. Even in companies where sales training is held in high esteem, however, the one-person department can still be found. In such cases, this individual may be a valuable professional with a sizable budget to hire outside resources as needed. In the very large organization with large and distinctively different sales groups, the sales training function may be supported by numerous writers, producers, directors, and instructors, using the full gamut of modern techniques and media.

Department Size

Here is a *broad* rule of thumb for determining the size of the sales training department:

1–15 salespeople—responsibility of the sales manager
16–50 salespeople—one person, half time
51–100 salespeople—one person, full time

The sales training director is currently gaining status among the other professionals in the typical corporate environment because of the explosive growth of the social and behavioral sciences. As these disciplines move steadily from the realm of the obtuse and the abstract to the more practical world of the measurable and the usable, the sales trainer as possessor of these concepts and skills has gained respect and power. Management increasingly asks sales trainers to contribute their judgment on matters of manpower planning, selection, motivation, promotion, and compensation. Sales trainers are coming of age and are being recognized for the important role they play in corporate growth and financial success.

Several basic facts become apparent to those responsible for the training of people in a selling organization:

1. The most effective training occurs day to day on the job. Trainers can provide the knowledge, tools, and practice to improve sales performance, but in most instances they must depend on sales supervision in the field to make sure that their programs are implemented properly.
2. Trainers can only partly solve training problems. They can help trainees to gain knowledge and improve their skills, but in most organizations they can only help influence changes in attitudes, habits, and morale. These three aspects of sales behavior are the result of overall organizational norms and first-line sales supervision.
3. Trainers will do well to separate product training (knowledge of the product or service) from sales training (interpersonal relationships between seller and buyer). Acquisition of extensive product knowledge does not ensure sales

success. Product knowledge must be combined with selling skills if a sales force is to realize its maximum potential.

An effective sales training program, therefore, must be results-oriented, involve organization management and supervision, and include both sales and product training. Figure 26-1 lists the things that a typical sales training manager should know and be able to do.

It is important to note that there are many ways to sell goods and services in our complex economic world and that many different kinds of sales organizations have evolved. Many chapters and perhaps many handbooks would be required to describe each variety. To provide an intelligent overview of sales training in modern times, we shall have to limit ourselves to the universal or very common elements. We can begin by defining what we mean by "selling," "sales training," and "product training."

Definitions

Selling has been defined as "an attempt to get others to do something when you lack the power to make them do it." Professional buyers, in particular, are fully cognizant of the fact that they have the ultimate decision power in a sales situation. There is a lot that salespeople can do to influence the buyer's decisions, but they cannot make him buy.

Sales training can be defined as anything done to help salespeople master the concepts, skills, attitudes, and habits that improve their proficiency in influencing prospects to make positive buying decisions and to fulfill their other organizational responsibilities. This definition is broad enough to cover the entire range of activities commonly grouped under the heading "sales training." It also covers the training and development efforts of sales trainers in most sales organizations.

Product training can be defined as the portion of the training program that teaches salespeople what they must know to persuasively present their product to buyers.

Almost everything you can mention could not have come into being without some form of selling. Whether you think of a soap product, an insurance policy, a new school, a symphony orchestra, or a war, somewhere the idea was conceived, and someone convinced one or more other people to accept it and act upon it.

In the world of commercial products and services, the marketing process, as it applies to sales, begins with the manufacturer and ends with the ultimate consumer. The product or service may be channeled through one or more intermediaries, variously called *jobbers, brokers, distributors, sales representatives, wholesalers,* or *retailers.* The intermediate steps in the channel of distribution each represent a need for selling and therefore a need for sales training and product training. The marketing approach for a product or service influences the nature of the selling effort and therefore the kind of sales and product training provided. Appeals when buying for resale are different from appeals to the consumer.

No matter which level of the distribution pattern is being trained, however, two facts remain: Sales training deals with persons interacting for the purpose of exploring and filling mutual needs or wants, and product training deals more with the actual product or service being sold—the inherent features and their benefits, the exclusives, the competitive advantages, and other properties.

Sales training therefore concentrates on how prospective sellers and buyers interact. Product training concentrates on dissemination of knowledge and tools regarding the product or service marketed.

The most effective product training formula used by contemporary trainers seems to revolve around features, advantages, benefits, empathetic sales stories, and demonstrations (where possible).

PLANNING

I. RESEARCH

    A. Evaluate the effectiveness of current training
        programs in terms of:

        1. What they are
        2. HOW administered
        3. Results being achieved

    B. Analyze training needs for sales personnel of
        the various departments as they relate to:

        1. Newly hired sales representatives
        2. Experienced sales representatives
        3. Supervisory personnel
        4. Management personnel

    C. Develop necessary sources of information with
        which to build effective training programs:

        1. Libraries
        2. Product data
        3. Laboratories
        4. Plants and installations
        5. Field studies
        6. Personal contacts
        7. Consultants
        8. Others

II. ORGANIZE

    A. Establish specific objectives for:

        1. Individuals
        2. Departments
        3. Projects
        4. Programs

    B. Check policies:

        1. Company
        2. Department
        3. Personnel

    C. Design training formats for:

        1. Individuals
        2. Groups
        3. Departments

    D. Organize liaison and communication with the:

        1. Field
        2. General office
        3. Plants
        4. Laboratories
        5. Supervisory personnel
        6. Customers

III. DEVELOP

    A. Provide for the time, talent, and information
        sources necessary to develop:

        1. Sales manuals
        2. Sales/product bulletins

    B. Implement system for supplying sales aids
        and equipment.

    C. Devise training schedules.

    D. Design training programs in the following
        categories:

        1. General business/marketing
        2. Sales techniques
        3. Product (own Company's and
            competitors')

        4. Policy
        5. Motivation
        6. Work habits
        7. Management
        8. Interpersonal skills

    E. Establish standards of performance.

    F. Assist in the development of supervision
        techniques and procedures.

IV. FOLLOW THROUGH

    A. Devise techniques by which the effectiveness
        of training programs can be measured.

    B. Establish use of information and materials.

    C. Provide facts on the achievement of training
        goals.

    D. Determine overall profit results by:

        1. Territory
        2. District
        3. Department
        4. Company

    E. Evaluate sales performance against standards.

Fig. 26-1 Job responsibilities for sales training managers.

PERFORMING	CONSULTING

PERFORMING

I. IMPLEMENTATION

   A. Determine WHERE to train.

      1. Group training

         a) General office
         b) Districts

      2. Individual training

         a) On-the-job
         b) Correspondence
         c) Informal

   B. Decide WHEN to train.

      1. Indoctrination/orientation
      2. Periodic/refresher
      3. Advanced

   C. Define WHO the trainers will be.

      1. Sales training manager
      2. General office staff
      3. District managers
      4. Technical personnel
      5. Product specialists

II. COOPERATION

   A. With sales personnel.

      1. Identify training programs as their own.
      2. Secure advice as to content.
      3. Appeal to self-interests.
      4. Sell the program

   B. With management.

      1. Achieve acceptance at all levels.
      2. Make management a part of all
          training programs.
      3. Establish liaison and communication.
      4. Promote programs.

III. CONDUCTING PROGRAMS

   A. When conducting programs with INDIVIDUALS,
      be sure to:

      1. Announce meeting place, date, time.
      2. Decide on objectives of the work-with.
      3. Review Curbstone Conference techniques.
      4. Prepare to follow up.

   B. Before conducting GROUP training sessions,
      make sure you:

      1. Prepare an announcement covering the:

         a) Purpose of the training
         b) Program outline
         c) Results to be achieved
         d) Materials required at the meeting

      2. Select an appropriate meeting place by:

         a) Inspecting the premises
         b) Checking facilities
         c) Determining equipment required

      3. Set up the meeting room and equipment.

      4. Conduct rehearsals, which includes
         the training of assistants in workshop
         procedures, techniques, and methods.

   C. During GROUP training sessions:

      1. Inform.
      2. Secure active participation.
      3. Assign projects to be completed in
         the field.

   D. After GROUP training sessions, follow through:

      1. On the program.
      2. On the results to be achieved.
      3. On the additional help required.
      4. On the topics to include in subse-
         quent training programs.

CONSULTING

I. MANAGEMENT

   A. Assist management with situations involving
      personnel:

      1. Recruiting
      2. Hiring
      3. Indoctrination
      4. Training
      5. Evaluation

   B. Provide help when new products are introduced.

   C. Handle instructions for application of new pro-
      grams or promotions at the field level.

   D. Analyze changes in organization to determine
      how they relate to training activities.

      1. Specialized training for new manage-
         ment personnel

      2. Group training in new organizational
         setups

II. THE FIELD

   A. Helping the field force with:

      1. Problem salesmen

      2. Sales problem areas

      3. Customer training

III. MEDIA

   A. Aiding in the development of:

      1. Meeting scripts

      2. Booklets, pamphlets, manuals

      3. Audio/visual aids

      4. Charts

      5. Sales presentation tools

      6. Use of ads, displays in the field by sales personnel

      7. Promotions

      8. Programs

      9. Customer training programs

    10. Sales meetings:

         a) National
         b) Local
         c) Customer

         .... with special emphasis on:

            Costs
            Production procedures
            Lead time requirements
            How-to-use

Fig. 26-1 (Cont.) Job responsibilities for sales training managers.

Feature   A property of the product or service that is important to the customer. ("Note that this model has two handles.")

Advantage   A positive interpretation of a feature. ("The two handles mean that you can hold it with both hands.")

Benefit   How the feature and its inherent advantages benefit the customer. ("The two-handed grip means safer, more accurate work and therefore fewer costly mistakes.")

Empathetic Sales Story   A word picture visualizing the benefit in the customer's terms. ("Imagine how your workers will increase their output using this model and how they will take more pride in their work.")

Demonstration   Proof of the benefit–sales-story claim. ("Let me show you how this model works right here on your production line.")

These five points apply to almost every product or service. They are presented to sales forces with as much variety, impact, repetition, and intensity as circumstances permit. Application of this formula can enrich every product training program.

Selling skill development has become more complex in recent years. Not long ago, it was not uncommon to teach salespeople universal steps for making a sale. The approach (or opening) was developed to apply to as many buyers as possible. Probing (or qualifying) questions were standardized on the basis of the broadest customer appeal possible. And so it was with trial closes, handling objections, etc.

Sales Interactions

Behavioral and social scientists have recently provided practitioners a simplified, easy-to-understand language, and with it, usable insights into interpersonal relationships as they apply to selling. It is now possible for sales trainers to teach salespeople to identify buying styles and to modify their selling styles to fit the buyer. We have learned to teach salespeople how to particularize presentations for maximum effectiveness, rather than build many appeals to fit every kind of buyer into every presentation.

It is useful for sales trainers to look at selling interactions in several ways when developing their programs. The usual "structure" of the sale will determine the need, or lack of it, for teaching flexibility and the extent of product knowledge and selling skills to be used. Understanding "power relationships" between buyer and seller is important, as can be the knowledge of ego states as explained in Transactional Analysis theory.

Sales interactions range from highly structured ones to those which are minimally structured. For example, the selling of many common items, such as newspapers and cigarettes, is highly structured by tradition. Buyers know just what they want and how to go about getting it. The salesperson knows just how to take the payment for the item, and the transaction occurs with an almost mechanical efficiency. This kind of selling requires training in how to be an order taker. The salesperson need only be trained to be quick, efficient, and reasonably polite.

A less structured sales interaction may also involve many mechanical elements and some unexpected ones as well. For example, a retail clerk or door-to-door salesperson may display his or her wares, emphasizing featured items and encouraging the prospect to sample the merchandise and to ask questions. In short, the salesperson helps the prospect to make a decision and, if possible, will try to expand the order by "selling up" or selling related items. The salesperson may also offer a package deal or a quantity discount to prompt the expanded purchase decision. Sales situations in which the opportunity to expand a sale is present require different sales skills and therefore different sales training objectives and procedures.

Still less structured sales situations are those in which prospective buyers are aware of their need or of an opportunity but are not at all sure how to meet the need to take advantage of the opportunity. In such cases, buyers may seek out those salespeople who seem to have something to fit their need, or they may be receptive to being approached by salespeople with something to say. In situations like these, salespeople usually modify a well-rehearsed sales presentation or procedure to fit what they perceive as the buyer's interest. Sales training for this type of sales interaction would most likely include techniques for finding and qualifying prospects, as well as artfully tailoring presentations and the closing.

The least structured type of sales interaction would be one in which neither the prospective seller nor the prospective buyer knows exactly how to help the other at the start of the interaction. Then, through mutual examination of the buyer's situation, they uncover a need or opportunity, and the salesperson creates a solution to the buyer's needs. This type of selling also requires special kinds of sales training, particularly in the area of problem solving, creativity, and sensitivity to others' needs and moods.

Any of the four sales interactions described above may be encountered in a particular sales job, and all may be present even during a single sales interaction. For the purposes of determining the sales training needed, however, it is helpful to generalize about the type of interaction most frequently encountered by the members of a particular sales organization. Ideally, salespeople will be taught to be flexible and to vary their behavior to fit the situation so that prospects can be sold in the manner in which they wish to buy.

Changing people, by means of training or any other strategy, is not easy. In some cases it is impossible. Yet in order to improve their performance, sales trainers must have faith in the ability of human beings to consciously and willingly modify their behavior, despite their programmed inclination to resist change.

Power Relationship

Another aspect of the interpersonal side of selling is the *power relationship*. It deals with the way two individuals see themselves, each other, and the situation they are in and with the way these elements interact and influence the final outcome of the interaction. Older theories of human behavior, human relations, and salesmanship tended to be one-sided. Salespeople, for example, were instructed to behave in a certain way and were assured that if they did, their sales would increase. Currently, more study and thought are being given to the interaction of personalities and to why one strategy or pattern of behavior may be effective with one prospect and not another.

The power-relationship theory holds that people tend consciously or subconsciously to size up themselves and others as they interact with them. A person may feel naturally superior to some people, (for example, when interacting with small children) or inferior to others (when confronted with those whom they see as superior because of any of a number of factors, such as physical size, wealth, or rank). In still other cases, a person may see another as equal in status. Finally, the power issue may never really arise in the conscious or subconscious mind of either party. How salespeople view themselves and the prospect in terms of power and how the prospect sees the situation can greatly influence the sales interaction.

In addition to the various power relationships, the element of like or dislike can complicate the sales interaction. It is possible to like and admire a superior person as a kindly father figure. It is also possible to dislike a superior person intensely. Salespeople who are aware of their own feelings toward a prospect and who are sensitive to the prospect's feelings toward them can adapt the sales approach to fit the relationship and can enhance the possibility that a sale will be made.

Transactional Analysis

The TA (Transactional Analysis) model of human ego states—Parent, Child, and Adult—can also help in understanding the interplay of personalities in sales situations. Also, the TA techniques called *hooking* and *stroking* can be useful to salespeople. Hooking is the technique of guiding another person to change his or her mood or shift to another ego state or power relationship. Acting humble with some individuals will hook their dominant, aggressive behavior. In others, it will elicit a supportive, protective reaction. Stroking is a message of recognition. Positive strokes are messages of approval that one person gives to another. We all need and want strokes, preferably positive ones. Knowing how and when to apply the right kind of stroke can be beneficial to salespeople when attempting to guide the behavior of the prospect toward making the right buying decision.

Some sales trainers are concerned about the moral implications of using hooks and strokes in sales situations, claiming that this is really manipulation and can be used to harm the prospect. Others see such techniques as just additional tools for influencing buyers that may be used callously and with contempt or with an honest hope of helping the prospect to make the right buying decisions. The issue is usually resolved, at least academically, by the claim that the use of behavioral science techniques for influencing behavior is intended to hook other persons into the adult state or to put them into a power neutral status, which enables two respectful individuals to explore a problem or opportunity objectively and come to a rational decision that is best for both. However the moral issue is resolved, future sales trainers will become more and more involved in the use of behavior-modification techniques.

DETERMINING SALES TRAINING NEEDS

Perhaps the greatest and most worthwhile movement to take hold in the world of education in general, and sales training in particular, is that toward training to achieve clear, measurable goals. Goals will vary by industry or company. Examples of clear, measurable goals could include sales volume, share of market, full-line sales (as opposed to selective selling), number of calls, cost of sales, etc.

While the current literature on sales training logically emphasizes the need to train toward specific objectives, many, if not most, sales training programs are still based on other criteria. Budget is one such criterion, and perhaps the most justifiable. Certainly it is more understandable than such factors as packaging, the reputation of the developer or vendor, or the "gut" feeling of influential executives in the organization.

A generalization to help determine budgets for sales training departments has been developed over the years. It depends on variables such as high turnover, individual sales volume, and kinds of selling (inside "clerk," outside "account maintenance," or outside "problem solver"). A starting point for computing annual budgets could be one week's pay per salesperson for training the salespeople and their supervisors and managers.

Normally, sales training objectives, whether they are for specific skills or for an entire program, are researched in one or more of the following ways: by observing how successful salespeople operate, by asking how management people want training done, or by relying on the judgment of an experienced sales training specialist. Some researchers will go to the marketplace and ask the potential buyers what they think is important in a salesperson's behavior.

A way to record estimates of the competency of the members of a sales organization is shown in Fig. 26-2. The members of the organization are listed down the side, and the critical skill or development areas are listed across the top.

The person doing the estimating—it can be the salesperson, the sales manager, the trainer, or another individual—indicates his or her estimation of competency by marking an X or an O in the appropriate squares or by rating them from 1 to 10. The composite of the estimators can then serve as a guide in planning a series of development programs for the sales group.

The end result of sales training research, whether it is conducted by means of surveys, interviews, or a study of other comparable organizations, is the development of a list of training objectives and priorities. The objectives may be in the form of a job description, a Position Responsibilities Chart, or simply a list of work tasks.

Performance Standards

The objective of the research is to establish an acceptable "standard" against which sales performance and selling skills are measured. By identifying what salespeople

X = Adequate or better O = Not adequate	Qualifying Prospects	Probing	Developing Presentations	Making Presentations	Trial Closes	Closing	Paper Work	Following Up	Repeat Sales	Keeping Records	Expense Control	Time Management			
Abraham	X	O	X	X	X	X	O	X	X	X	X	O			
Butler	X	O	X	X	X	X	O	X	X	X	X	X			
Cooper	X	X	O	O	X	X	X	X	X	X	X	X			
Davidson	O	X	X	X	X	O	O	X	X	X	X	X			
Enrietto	X	X			X	O	X	X	X	X	X	X			
Fowler	X	X		X	X	O	X	X	X	X	X	X			
Goodman	X	X								O					
Houghton	X	X			O					O					
Ingram	O	X	O								O				
Johnson	X	X			O					O					
Kelly	X	X													
Landon	X	X	O							O					
Morton	X	X													
Establish Training Priorities: What skills are inadequately mastered by a significant number of group members?															

Fig. 26-2 Sales training needs.

should know and be able to do, a standard is established. The difference between what they *should* know and be able to do and what the research reveals that they *do* know and *are* able to do determines the makeup and priorities of the training program.

Clear position responsibilities make it easier to communicate to trainees just what they are expected to know and be able to do in order to meet their employment obligations.

A list of job functions, responsibilities, or activities in chart form needs two other elements to make it usable for the sales trainer and the sales trainee. First, the chart must be approved by all concerned; this includes management, salespeople, and the training specialist. Second, the chart of activities must be recognized as a temporary effort and therefore must be systematically reviewed and updated, on an annual basis at least. When such a chart becomes an integral part of the system, it will constitute a vital element of the entire sales organization function, from the recruiting of new salespeople to the setting of quotas and work goals. New people are usually trained to master all the items on such a chart, and experienced individuals are trained individually or in groups to master those skills below standard and reinforce those at or above standard. Special programs may be developed to zero in on a particular responsibility. Prototypes of a salesperson's Position Responsibilities Chart are shown in Fig. 26-3.

Responsibilities Identification

The makeup of the Position Responsibilities Chart can take many forms, but the example shown has proved to be a convenient format. It has been used most frequently with industrial salespeople. This is why the column headings include the word "management." Many salespeople in modern sales organizations have responsibility for more than just selling, even though selling is the focus of their activity. Titles such as "territory manager" are becoming more widely accepted for this reason.

The Position Responsibilities Chart can be used for all types of sales jobs, however, and it is also widely used for management jobs both in and out of the sales area. Its chief value seems to lie in its simplified format. It allows anyone to quickly grasp the whole and the parts of the job and how they interrelate. The prime responsibility spells out in clear language that the jobholder is expected to sell profitably. The four sections (and there may be more or less) focus on a major group of responsibilities. The first three on the sample shown deal with the management of self, prospects and buyers, and organization responsibilities, and they tend to be somewhat universal for industrial salespeople. The last column deals with those responsibilities which must, by their nature, be highly tailored to fit the needs of the sales organization.

The Position Responsibilities Chart can be a highly useful device for both the salesperson and his or her manager. It can be used to help recruit new people, give specific assignments, and evaluate performance. It is, however, particularly useful for training salespeople. When an organization tells salespeople that this chart lists all the things they are expected to know and do to fulfill their employment obligations, it should also be prepared to train them to meet those obligations.

Many organizations hire salespeople and simply assume that they know how to sell successfully. In some cases this approach may be justified, and it may even be effective. But experienced sales managers expect to train and retrain their people constantly to do things the way the organization wants them done.

The Position Responsibilities Chart becomes an excellent guide for setting training objectives. Individual entries on the chart are not usually spelled out in behavioral terms and may therefore be insufficiently exact to serve as objectives for

PROTOTYPE: Salesperson's Position Responsibilities Chart

Prime Responsibility: To meet or exceed your sales quotas and other work objectives while keeping within the limits of company rules and policies, and in a manner that permits the company to earn an acceptable return on its investment in you and your work needs.

A. MANAGE YOURSELF	B. MANAGE YOUR PROSPECT/BUYERS	C. MANAGE YOUR RESPONSIBILITIES TO THE ORGANIZATION	D. MANAGE THE TECHNICAL ASPECTS OF THE JOB
1. Know and motivate yourself.	1. Know your sales style and how to modify it.	1. Know your leader as an INDIVIDUAL and how to best interact with him or her.	1. Know what you sell— features, advantages, and benefits.
2. Participate in setting your sales quotas and other work goals.	2. Know your prospects' buying styles and how to interact with them for best results.	2. Know your various types of job situations and how to modify or adapt to them.	2. Know your market.
3. Plan and schedule your work activities.	3. Know the various types of sales situations and how to adapt to them.	3. Know the organization's goals, strategies, problems, and opportunities.	3. Know your competition.
4. Develop and use your nonsales interpersonal skills.	4. Seek and qualify new prospects.	4. Know the organization's history and present makeup.	4. Know your territory.
5. Develop and use your communication skills.	5. Develop proposals and presentations.	5. Know the organization's rules and policies.	5. Interact with peers.
6. Develop and use your creative skills.	6. Conduct selling sessions and close.	6. Know the key people in the organization and their positions.	6. Handle technical procedures (must be tailored to individual organizations).
7. Develop and use your problem-solving skills.	7. Follow up sales efforts.	7. Maintain required records.	
8. Keep current on company developments.		8. Develop and submit required reports.	
9. Keep current on industry developments.		9. Serve as a source of information and judgment for the organization.	
10. Keep current on developments in professional salesmanship.		10. Work on team or committee assignments when requested.	
		11. Participate in meetings.	
		12. Seek ideas for helping the organization and "sell" them to management.	
		13. Help the organization with its public relations efforts.	

Fig. 26-3 Prototype: salesperson's position responsibilities chart.

a specific training program. But they can serve as a generalized target from which specific training objectives can be developed.

For example, item 5 under "Manage Yourself" on the sample Position Responsibilities Chart says "Develop and Use Your Communication Skills." A training program designed to help a salesperson master this position responsibility might have the following among its objectives:

> Upon completion of the Sales Listening course, trainees will be able to use the five key listening skills and demonstrate their proficiency by completing the Listening Skill Analyzer with 90 percent accuracy within 10 minutes.

Ideally, the more specific the training objectives are, the better. However, practicalities may suggest that they be more generally described in the interest of gaining learner acceptance. This is particularly true in the case of those "people-dealing" skills which cannot be dealt with as accurately as skills relating to inanimate objects.

PLANNING TO MEET SALES TRAINING NEEDS

Determining what training is needed for individual members of the sales organization, or for a particular group, to meet the responsibilities of the job naturally leads to filling the needs. However, for those in charge of the training effort of a complex sales organization, it is helpful to visualize the overall plan for the organization. This helps to explain the training effort to others, management in particular, and to explain budget requirements. The chart shown in Fig. 26-4 can be useful.

MEETING SALES TRAINING NEEDS

Sales training programs that cover all the needs of a salesperson, as well as those which concentrate on a specific knowledge or skill area, fall into three general categories:

- Original programs
- Packaged programs
- Modified existing programs

Original programs have the obvious advantage of being exactly tailored to the needs of the organization and the sales trainees. However, for a comparatively small sales force, they can be quite costly in terms of staff time if developed internally and in terms of money if developed with the help of an outside professional.

Packaged programs can be comparatively inexpensive unless the organization is so large that the total expenditure would more than pay for an original program. Packaged programs can be of great value if they fit the organization's needs because of their proved effectiveness.

The modified package is a compromise between original and packaged programs. Such programs usually carry a conceptual theme with universal application, but have participation sessions built around cases tailored to fit the sales organization's needs. This "marriage" can result in a professional course that costs a minimum amount and yet is tailored in the important essentials.

Techniques

The techniques and devices utilized in sales training efforts are naturally the same as those generally used in other forms of personnel training. Sales training techniques and devices are most similar to those used in supervisory and management training simply because those areas all rely heavily on working with or through others. Techniques commonly used by sales trainers fall into three broad categories:

1. Feed forward
2. Peer information exchange
3. Feedback

WHO Needs Training? (personnel categories)	WHAT Needs to be Taught?	WHEN Should Training Take Place?	WHERE Should Training Take Place?	HOW Should Training Be Accomplished?	WHO Should Do the Training?	Budget Needed

Fig. 26-4 Organization training needs.

Feed forward includes such techniques as lectures, films, manuals, textbooks, product specifications, and newsletters.

Peer information exchange includes formal and informal sharing of information among those with similar responsibilities through publications, meetings, etc.

Feedback is any communication from the field to the trainer or management—by means of reports, personal field contact, meetings, etc.—regarding successes, problems, or frustrations.

Effective sales or product training depends on all three techniques.

Large organizations often have a formal sales school for new salespeople. Currently, there seems to be a trend toward having new salespersons demonstrate ability before inviting them to attend the school.

Training by Objectives

One way to provide initial training for the new person when formal schools are not practical and also to screen out unacceptable candidates before enrollment in a central school is to use an individually administered Training by Objectives program. Such programs commonly use what is known as a *self-development guide*. It allows training to be particularized to the person, the position, and the current situation, and it is based completely on the idea that "all development is self-development."

Countless small companies have adopted self-development systems made available through their associations. By adopting self-development guides, these organizations demonstrate their belief that adults should train themselves, which means setting their own goals and directing their activities toward achieving those goals. When a person starts a new job, it is safe to assume that mastery of the job is his or her training goal. This heavy emphasis on goal orientation is the origin of the Training by Objectives appellation.

Goals are important for adults. Without a clear statement of training objectives, people in a new job—whether it is selling hardware or managing a regional office—are going to spend a lot of time "spinning their wheels." Whenever they are exposed to something related to their work, they have to determine whether the information fits into the job and, if so, how. If they have a clear understanding of what they are trying to master, every new fact, idea, or skill can be evaluated in terms of how it helps them get where they are going.

Position Responsibilities Charts have been found to be the most useful device for helping individuals accept their training goals. The charts, as mentioned, are simply a listing of the various things a person should know and be able to do in order to fulfill his or her occupational obligations.

For each of the specific responsibilities listed on the chart, there is a section in the self-development guide. These sections do not tell the trainees how to do what is required of them. If they did, they would constitute a reference manual, rather than being part of the self-development system.

When trainees are given the guide, and after they understand what the new job requires of them, they are told about their responsibility for training themselves. They are also given sufficient authority to accomplish this task of self-training. Depending upon their level, they are allowed a time period in which to train themselves and are given a budget for travel and expenses, if necessary; facilities are provided in which to do research, and they are encouraged to communicate with others in the organization who they feel can be of help.

The first section in most guides is concerned with what trainees can expect from the organization. Here they find information about paydays, benefits, vacation policy, and so on.

Performance Objectives   The following sections of the guide deal with what the trainee is expected to give in exchange for what he or she gets. They follow a pattern. First the objective of the section is spelled out. Naturally, these subobjectives are directly related to the overall objectives of learning the job. Next there is an introduction explaining the importance of the subject area to the person and the organization, followed by a series of questions that have been carefully designed to lead to mastery of the position requirement. When trainees can answer the questions or perform the activity, it is assumed that they are trained. An example of a typical activity for a sales trainee might be: "Secure a map of your territory, locate your major accounts, and plot the shortest possible route between them." Questions on this same topic might be: "How can you determine which accounts are to be contacted in person at least once each week?" or "What is the typical chain of command in the kind of organizations we service?"

You can see that answering the questions or performing the activities may take anywhere from a few hours to several weeks. Many factors will affect the length of the program, including the person's own interest and initiative. Trainees can proceed as fast or as slowly as they wish. The important thing is that they learn the job.

Implementation   The administration of the program may be strictly sequential or randomly mixed. Some companies use the sequential approach. New people are given a binder containing only the tabs, the first unit, and a recording of the company president welcoming them and their families to the organization. When they have completed the first section, they are given the next one, and so on until the binder is completed.

Other self-development systems operate differently. New people, with their supervisors, schedule a series of review meetings at the outset of the program. They then work on each section of the guide as they see fit. For example, when dealing with records and reports, the person may work on that section for a few hours a week. The sections may be finished completely out of sequence, depending on how the person schedules travel, reading, and meetings.

At each weekly review session the trainee and his or her supervisor check the trainee's responses to questions, and together they evaluate the exercises performed. Then they decide what the trainee should do during the next week; rarely do trainees perform the activities in the same order in which they appear in the guide.

Companies with Training by Objectives programs have all reported consistent good results with the approach. Typical comments from those in charge of the program include, "We found the self-development guide approach to be a thoroughly adult way to train new employees and retrain older ones." "It puts the responsibility for training right where it belongs—squarely on the shoulders of the person being trained—and it has greatly shortened the basic training period for new people." Other common remarks about the system include: "It saves a lot of expensive executive time and energy." "It is relatively inexpensive to develop and administer, and yet it particularizes training in a way that no other device can." "We have found that older employees appreciate the self-development guides even more than trainees."

Training by Objectives—by helping people to determine their training goals and then guiding them while they accomplish these goals—is not another theoretical stab at implementing a self-development approach. It has been field-tested for years by some of the most successful companies in the world. The approach is applicable to all but the most highly structured routine technical jobs. Ample proof of its efficacy exists both for the training of managers and sales personnel for new assignments and for the retraining of entire organizations.

"Work-with" Training

Another form of individual training is "work-with" training. Sales trainers and/or sales managers should work with their salespeople with some frequency. And after each sales call or other convenient break in the flow of work, the two should have what was called (before the day of the parking lot) a "curbstone" conference. This is the time when the trainer can reinforce the good part of the salesperson's performance and correct the less than adequate elements.

Whether trainers coach spontaneously as they see the need or set out to provide a one-time, very specific coaching session, it helps to have a formula or track to run on.

JIT in Sales Training

Probably the most widely practiced and most effective coaching formula dates back to World War II. The need to train large numbers of individuals in a tremendous variety of tasks spawned the development of what was known as Job Instruction Training (JIT). Since then, many variations have appeared, but they all follow the same logical procedure for helping individuals master skills, ranging from piloting a ship through stormy waters to sewing buttons on shirts. The formula is so wonderfully simple that after carefully following it a few times for special coaching purposes, an individual can commit it to memory and use it almost automatically when the need arises. While the formula is most often thought of as being used for technical training purposes, it can readily be adapted for management and sales skills as well.

One variation of the JIT formula is PEDOS (preparation, explanation, demonstration, observation, and supervision). An explanation of each step follows.

Preparation   The first step, preparation, applies to both the coach and the person who is being helped to master a specific skill or series of related skills. As always, the best way to prepare yourself to perform some function is to determine your objectives. What exactly do you want to achieve? An acronym that will help when determining objectives is SAM (specific, attainable, and measurable). Coaching objectives should be specific in terms of behavior. What do you want the trainee to be able to do, using what tools and materials, in what time frame, and under what circumstances? The more specific, the better, without going into endless detail: "Complete the company-approved cash requisition form in the prescribed manner." "Handle irate customers so that they agree to keep their purchases." "Handle a credit interview in such a way that all the desired information is obtained." "Conduct a sales meeting in the traditional format." All these are legitimate coaching goals.

The coaching goals should be attainable. Some people are inspired by lofty or even impossible goals. Most of us, however, are turned off when we are expected or challenged to achieve the impossible. Most people respond better to goals that they see as both challenging and possible. Such goals provide the reinforcement of accomplishment without the threat of failure. Admittedly, the setting of goals that are both challenging and attainable is a matter of judgment.

Finally, the job or the task should be measurable. You should have some way of determining whether your trainee is doing the job better than before. You may be content to judge on your own feel for the skill, but it will be easier to evaluate your coaching success if you can measure the skill development. Measure such things as the number of items completed, how long the job takes, the degree of accuracy, and the judgment of others concerning the trainee's performance. This last measure can yield a subjective evaluation. Anything that you can put a number on will tend to make the job measurable.

Also of concern when preparing to coach is having the right tools, facilities, and equipment ready for the session. In some cases this may mean a pencil, a pad of paper, and a few quiet moments. In others it may mean an elaborate set of props, a special room, and a considerable amount of certain materials.

The next step is to prepare the trainee for the coaching session. It seems to help if people are aware that they are about to be coached. If they get the feeling that the coaching session is a rather casual encounter, the effort will be wasted.

Explanation   The next step in the coaching formula is the explanation, which is started by telling the person what the final objectives of the coaching are. This gives both trainer and trainee a target to shoot for. Explanations should go from the simple to the complex, from the familiar to the unfamiliar. Start out on terms with which the person is conversant and then relate the new to the old. It is usually possible to explain a task in a series of steps. Give each step a number and a name to aid retention: "First, we review the customer file. Second, we establish call objectives. . . ."

Demonstration   The next step in skill development is the demonstration of how it should be done. For manual skills, let trainees look over your shoulder—from the viewpoint that they will have when they use their own hands to do the task. Show them as often as necessary. We all learn more by actual example than we ever do just by being told. Use exaggerated movement to help trainees picture the series of steps. Repeat the important steps and indicate by your voice and expressions that they are important. And while you are demonstrating the skill, you can add further explanations about the "why" of each step. Never assume that an explanation, no matter how complete, can take the place of the demonstration.

Observation   The next step in the PEDOS formula is observation. Telling and showing are not enough. The only really positive feedback is to see for yourself.

Even the simplest explanation can be misunderstood, and most trainees will not be insulted if you ask them to show you how they would perform a task, just so you will be sure that you have communicated clearly. While observing, maintain a positive and confident attitude, even if the trainee fumbles. Fumbling is natural when learning something new. Try to avoid making any negative comments.

When coaching a new hire on a sales call, for example, break the entire call into smaller, easy-to-recognize steps. These could be "approach," "qualify," "demonstrate," "trial close," "handle objections," "close." The coach explains and demonstrates each step before the call and instructs the trainee to pay particular attention to the first step. When the trainee feels confident enough, he or she approaches the customer, and then the coach takes over the sale. When the "approach" step has been mastered, the trainee takes over both the "approach" and the "qualify" steps before the coach steps in. This expanding procedure is repeated until the trainee is handling the entire call.

As you make your observations, try to communicate to the trainee that the task is a series of new but simple steps the trainee will master with time and practice—that the errors the trainee is making are quite natural and will gradually vanish with experience.

It is important to have preset ideas on what to look for while observing. Is the manner in which the trainee accepts questions from the customer crucial? Is the sequencing of steps in the presentation of prime concern? Observe any step that is really critical to mastering the skill.

Some skills have a high degree of inherent structure; i.e., the way they are to be performed cannot vary to any great extent. This may be due to legal requirements, such as requirements concerning the application for a license or permit. Other reasons may include safety precautions or the fact that experience has shown one way to be the best. Other skills are such that the procedure can vary and the end result still be attained. But even in less structured skills, like gathering information, developing reports, and planning special sales promotions, there are usually certain key steps that must be included. These are the things you would plan to observe when the trainee practices.

Supervision   The last step in the PEDOS formula is supervision. To supervise means to make sure the job gets done. After you have gone to the trouble of preparing yourself and the trainee and have explained and demonstrated the skill or task, it would be a mistake to forget about coaching sessions and assume that the job will be done right from then on. We are all creatures of habit, and the temptation to do things as we have previously done them is strong. Supervision is the only way to protect your coaching investment. The PEDOS planner is shown in Fig. 26-5.

Workshops

Some sales trainers believe that a professionally produced workshop is the best medium for stimulating, informing, training, developing, and motivating a group of experienced salespeople. "Professionally produced" means that the medium—rather than the technical information of the subject area—serves as the production orientation. While the technical matter is an essential part of the workshop, it is only part of the system. If this were not the case, an encyclopedia, film, recording, or manual in itself would be the best medium for instruction.

The first step in the production of a workshop involves research to determine the objectives and content, with consideration given to the needs and abilities of the participants.

Research is conducted through field checks by experienced interviewers and researchers with a representative group of key individuals to pick up materials for case situations, to acquire the jargon, and to become knowledgeable concerning current successes and frustrations of those in the field. In addition, materials published by other authorities are reviewed to supplement the acquired knowledge.

Surveys are extensively used to build a statistical base for the field observations and to provide substance for problem discussions. Care is taken that both the field-check guides and the surveys receive management approval before they are used.

```
Trainee_____    Date_____

Task or Skill_____


PREPARATION

    1.  Prepare Yourself:

        a.  Coaching objective:  What, in specific, attainable and
            measurable terms do you want this trainee to be able to do?

        b.  What equipment, materials, time, and facilities will you
            need?

    2.  Prepare the Trainee:

        a.  What is most likely to impress this person with the
            importance of this skill?

        b.  What appeal is most likely to motivate this trainee to
            want to master this skill?

EXPLANATION

    What is the logical sequence of steps in the execution of this skill?



DEMONSTRATION

    How, when, and where will you show this trainee how to perform this
    skill?



OBSERVATION

    What will you look for as the trainee practices the skill?



SUPERVISION

    How will you determine if the trainee continues to perform the
    skill adequately?
```

Fig. 26-5 PEDOS coaching planner.

The research stage leads to an expanded outline. This instrument spells out the specific objectives for the entire workshop, as well as those of each session. It outlines the content, topics, format, exercises, audiovisual media, handouts, staging, props, and both preworkshop and postworkshop assignments.

The expanded outline is another quality-control point for the trainer. The case histories must have an authentic ring, and the field jargon of the industry must be used. Salespeople who are "meeting-weary" automatically tune out workshop leaders who do not know their language and who think that the participants will forgive them for their lack of research effort.

The final developmental step in workshop production is the writing of a scripted or carefully outlined stage scenario. Every exercise for the participants is detailed, and all instructions for props, visuals, and handouts are specified; yet the end result gives the impression of informality. Complete planning is the only way to be sure that everything you plan to cover will be covered, in the way you want it covered, and in the time available.

Presentations   Does such elaborate preparation mean that the meeting leaders must monotonously read their scripts or outlines in front of the participants? Not at all. They are crutches, and there is danger of overreliance on them. Experienced meeting leaders, however, soon learn to use lines, dashes, circles, and a variety of other marks on their scripts that enable them to glance at the page only occasionally as they proceed through each session. They also know that nothing can replace adequate rehearsal.

The script provides another safeguard against having to cancel an expensive meeting because the meeting leader missed a plane or was otherwise detained. Several people have a copy of the script, and any of them can step in if an emergency arises.

When the script is approved, it is time to produce the materials. This involves the designing of printed items such as preparation guides, participation guides, and special handout pieces. Slides, films or video tapes, charts, signs, banners, or any of a great variety of audiovisual devices and materials are developed, and this entire effort must be synchronized to mesh smoothly with the overall project.

Staging   Staging the actual workshop is another area that sometimes requires special knowledge and talents. Seating, heating and ventilation, lighting, rest rooms, meals and beverages, sound systems, projection equipment, table numbers, storage areas, etc., are all highly vulnerable links in the workshop chain. Weakness in any one of these may well ruin the entire workshop. Many jobs in these areas cannot be delegated. They require personal, direct supervision. Otherwise, the result may be nonfunctioning sound systems, insufficient seating, or projectors that suddenly move out of focus, for example.

A full-dress rehearsal, completely set up in the meeting room, is the only safe way to make final preparations. Then the room must be sealed, and later opened, by the person in charge. Before the program begins, music may have to be started, and name badges handed out to the participants as they come in. All materials should be safely covered to dissuade the curious from sneaking a preview.

Ten Key Techniques   Research, outlining, scripting, producing, staging, and conducting are the essential, sequential steps in the production of a workshop. These steps, however, are similar to the steps to be taken for any meeting. What makes workshops so uniquely successful is the degree and kind of involvement of the participants. The following are 10 key techniques for ensuring the participants' full involvement—giving as well as getting—in the workshop.

1. *Tailored Lectern Presentation.*   This technique has already been mentioned, but since it is the heart of the workshop and perhaps its most essential feature, it bears further discussion. What the speakers say must be based on research into the topic, the needs and backgrounds of the participants, and the predetermined objectives of the entire workshop as well as the individual session. This requires research, scripting, and practice, practice, practice.

2. *Audiovisual Devices.*   Assuming that they are properly developed and used, AV aids lend color and variety, and they increase the effectiveness of whatever communication takes place. Audiovisual devices should never dominate the stage—they should always be subordinate to the speaker.

3. *Preparation Guides.*   All participants in a workshop should be required to have done something before they arrive—something that requires them to think and to act. For example, they may be asked to bring in certain reports, keep a log of their time, or complete a quiz. The activity must help them prepare to participate in the workshop. Most participants willingly do their preworkshop assignments when they are told that the others attending will be counting on them to be prepared.

4. *Seating.*   Different arrangements of tables and chairs are preferred for different types of gatherings. Seating arrangements deliver a nonverbal message to participants. Theater style tells them that they must sit and be talked at. Schoolroom arrangements tell them that they are expected to do some writing. Horseshoe, or U-shaped, conference seating indicates writing and minimal contribution from them to the entire group. For workshops, we have found nothing to equal round tables with seating for five to eight participants. Round-table seating allows a speaker to address a thousand people at one time, while the participants never deal with more than a handful. No other seating arrangement permits the participants to exchange ideas and information and to practice a skill with the frequency that round-table seating does.

5. *Rotating Seating Assignments.*   Four times every day, the participants move to a new table location, where they join a completely different group. The rotation is controlled by carefully developed formulas and through the use of table numbers and participant numbers. While the entire procedure is complex to set up, the participants merely sit where instructed according to a schedule. In effect, the "musical chairs" routine permits and encourages systematic brain-picking at a series of meetings—each with a different set of peers. No other medium or form of meeting allows participants to become exposed to so many others who can help them in such a brief period and under conditions so highly conducive to personal growth.

6. *Structured and Timed Participation Sessions.*   This workshop technique is greatly enhanced by the round-table and seating-rotation techniques. The speaker uses a timer, and workshop participants do nothing but listen for about 15 or 20 minutes. In addition to listening, they work alone on specific problems and exchange ideas and information either in turn (two or three minutes per person) or on an open-table discussion basis. Table reports from table chairpersons (a rotating assignment) allow the entire group to share the most significant developments at any one table. Action planning time—at the end of each session and at the end of the workshop—is designed to encourage the participants to make careful plans for applying what they learned during the session or the workshop.

7. *Participation Guide.*   This workshop technique is of particular importance. The participation guide is a complete binder, personalized if practicable with the participant's name and with tabs and all paper items in the proper sequential order. It has many advantages, such as obviating the need for constantly handing out paper items and eliminating time-wasting confusion and binder snapping.

The guide contains "feed forward" outlines enabling the participants to follow the speaker in the manner that concertgoers follow a musical score. Note taking is kept to a minimum because the participants do not have to bother writing down what the speaker says. Instead, they can confine their note taking to recording new ideas of their own or to expanding on what the speaker said. The content of the visuals may also be reproduced on paper and put into the binder to provide repetition and to help participants keep pace. Finally, the guides serve as a handy reference for use after the workshop.

8. *Recognition Award.*   This is a token in the form of a certificate, a plaque, or a trophy given to all participants or to just the outstanding ones. Most of us, it seems, derive at least some small measure of satisfaction when our efforts are recognized. We have seen participants work through the night to compete on a project that

promised only the reward of a small gilt plaque bearing the person's name. Never underestimate the value of symbols.

9. *Workshop Evaluation.* Asking the participants whether they believe the workshop's objectives were achieved lets them know that the workshop was developed for them. They are not children in the traditional schoolroom, hoping they performed up to the teacher's expectations. They are adults who have as much to contribute as they have to gain from the speaker or the other participants. Asking them to evaluate the workshop is the only way, short of an actual field performance evaluation, of providing the workshop producers with the feedback they need to improve their performance.

10. *Postworkshop Follow-up.* Participants may be asked to make a composite of all the plans they developed during the action planning times at the end of each session. They may then be invited to put their composite into an envelope and address it to themselves. These are sent as reminders to the participants within two weeks following the workshop.

Also, the participants may be asked to write a report for their immediate superiors on what they plan to do as a result of having attended the workshop. This is not advisable at all levels and in all organizations, but more and more managers are demanding that meeting attendance pay off in some concrete way. What better way than to have the person attending explain how the experience will affect his or her behavior?

Devices such as magic tricks, jokes, gags, puzzles, and trick quizzes ease the tension brought on by the intense activity of the workshop, and these should be employed with taste and moderation.

Workshop Principles Workshops are built on twin principles. The first is that "no one person knows as much as all others." This is particularly true when dealing with subject matter which is still relatively new and in the formative stage or which is noncumulative in nature, such as sales or management techniques. Product knowledge and technical material, of course, can also be taught in workshop format, with the participant practicing while the others at the table evaluate and discuss application of the newly acquired skill.

The second principle upon which workshops are based is that "all development is self-development." People, particularly adults, must train themselves. Sales trainers are limited to creating the environmental conditions under which salespeople are most likely to experience personal growth.

Dollar for dollar, professionally researched, developed, produced, and conducted workshops seem to provide the greatest return on the training-effort investment. Professionally developed workshops are complex and require a variety of professional skills, but the results are worth the effort.

Figure 26-6 shows a planning form for meetings. It will help you to remember and use the workshop principles discussed above.

TECHNICAL SALES TRAINING

Technical training for salespeople poses special problems. While all the traditional and modern training media have been and are being used—manuals, cassettes, video tape, and the great variety of sound-film devices—the results are often less than adequate. Part of the problem lies in the fact that technical materials are often developed by technical experts and not trainers.

Salespeople should be concerned primarily with selling, even when they must have considerable technical expertise to do their job. To help keep this fact in perspective, technical sales training should be presented in a way that simulates how the salespeople will seek and use the technical knowledge in their sales activities.

```
┌─────────────────────────────────────────────────────────────────────┐
│                                                                       │
│              G R O U P   M E E T I N G   P L A N N E R                 │
│                                                                       │
│     A.  DETERMINE YOUR OBJECTIVES                                     │
│         1.  Date, time, place of meeting _____  │
│             _____  │
│                                                                       │
│         2.  Audience _____  │
│             _____  │
│                                                                       │
│         3.  Objectives (what you want members of the audience TO DO   │
│             as a result of attending -- be specific)                  │
│             _____  │
│             _____  │
│             _____  │
│             _____  │
│             _____  │
│                                                                       │
│     B.  ORGANIZE YOUR AGENDA                       Time Schedule      │
│         Agenda (List Topics)_____   _____  │
│             _____   _____  │
│             _____   _____  │
│             _____   _____  │
│             _____   _____  │
│                                                                       │
│     C.  DEVELOP CONTENT OF EACH TOPIC                                 │
│         1.  Why_____   │
│             _____  │
│         2.  What_____   │
│             _____  │
│         3.  How_____   │
│             _____  │
│         4.  When_____   │
│             _____  │
│                                                                       │
│                  [KR]   Kielly-Rebedeau & Associates                  │
│                                                                       │
└─────────────────────────────────────────────────────────────────────┘
```

Fig. 26-6 Group meeting planner.

Inquiry Learning

A meeting technique for providing technical training that is currently gaining favor with sales trainers is called *inquiry learning.* The inquiry learning technique is based on the now apparent fact that "adult" learning is enhanced when learners learn what they want to learn, when they want to learn it—in other words, when they ask meaningful questions and get immediate answers.

The first obstacle that usually arises when people plan to implement the inquiry learning principle is that they do not know what questions to ask when they are required to tackle a new field of knowledge. People simply do not know what they

D. PREPARE THE PARTICIPANTS -- Send participants a pre-meeting assign-
    ment -- something to read, do, or bring to the meeting.

    _____

    _____

E. PLAN TO USE PARTICIPATION

    Some Forms of Participation

    Show of hands   Question-and-answer sessions
    Mental exercises   Pre-Meeting preparation
    Written tests, quizzes   Exchange sessions
    Call for volunteers   Work sessions
    Directed Writing   Practice sessions (plus evaluation)
                  Buzz groups -- Table rotation

    _____

    _____

    _____

    _____

    _____

F. MEETING MEDIA -- PLAN TO USE PROPS OR VISUALS

    Typical Forms of Visuals

    Chalkboards   Feltboards
    Generated charts   2 x 2 slides
    Prepared charts   Slidefilms
    Printed materials   Motion pictures
                 Tape recordings

    _____

    _____

    _____

    _____

    _____

    _____

    _____

    _____

Fig. 26-6 (Cont.)   Group meeting planner.

do not know. The solution is to give them the right questions to ask. This saves them a lot of frustration and unnecessary work, while keeping the impetus for learning where it belongs—with the learner. The following discussion explains how the inquiry learning principle can be implemented to train salespeople to learn a body of technical knowledge, then to identify prospects among both new and present accounts, and finally to approach prospects and close sales.

The first step is to develop the questions that, when answered, will lead to achievement of the objectives of the meeting. Each question is printed on a separate card. The questions are numbered according to the logic of the material; that is, they are arranged in a sequence that is most likely to lead to attainment of

G.   PLAN TO USE SHOWMANSHIP

Elements of Showmanship*

Mystery	Conflict
Realism	Beauty
Life	Dramatizations
Motion	Contrast (in size or time)
Timeliness	Demonstrations
Pictures	Costuming
Color	The Bizarre (tricks with
Sound	lights, magic, etc.)

H.   PLAN TO GET FEEDBACK -- Feedback Techniques: Tests and Quizzes
                                                      Action Plans
                                                      Meeting Evaluations

_____

_____

_____

_____

I.   FOLLOW THROUGH, PLAN A SPECIFIC ASSIGNMENT

Be specific
Be sure the men KNOW WHAT TO DO
Be sure they WANT TO DO IT
Be sure they are ABLE TO DO IT
Be sure they know WHEN and HOW TO REPORT RESULTS

_____

_____

_____

_____

_____

_____

_____

_____

*With credit to Zenn Kaufman, marketing consultant, 420 Lexington Ave.,
New York, N.Y.

Fig. 26-6 (Cont.)   Group meeting planner.

the objectives. The number of the question is on the back of the card. At the beginning of the meeting, the trainer shuffles the cards and deals them out to the participants, who are instructed to put them face down and to read them to the group when the trainer calls for them by number.

   Question Categories   The questions fall into three categories: reference questions, application questions, and administrative questions. The *reference* questions deal with general information that all salespeople should know, and the trainees should be able to answer them without hesitation. Examples of reference questions are: "What advantages does our product offer over other products for such and such application?" and "Where can I find a key to the code of

Meeting Room Requirements Summary

_____

YOUR COMPANY NAME

Date of Event:_____   Current Date:_____

Duration of Event:_____

Room:_____   Time:_____

Food or Beverage:_____   Time:_____

Stage Size:_____   Height:_____   Location:_____

Audience Seating:_____

_____

Head Table:_____   Table Lectern:_____

Room Lighting:_____

Stage Lighting:_____

Lectern:_____   Where?_____

Extra Microphones:_____

Special Drapery:_____

_____

Other Requirements:
  Water:_____

  Table Standards:_____

  Ashtrays:_____

Outside Elements:
  Projectors:_____

  Union Projectionist:_____

  Screen:_____   Who Provides?_____

  Exhibits:_____   Where?_____

Supervision:
  For the Company:_____

  For the Hotel:_____

  Checks to be signed by:_____

Fig. 26-6 (Cont.)   Group meeting planner.

the various product lines?" The reference questions are also printed on a form, with plenty of space for the participants to write in the answers. The forms are distributed at the start of the meeting; when a reference question comes up, the meeting leader reminds the participants to take notes. Poker chips, representing award points, may be given to the participants for completing the reference-question answer form; this adds color to the proceedings and provides an incentive to do well.

The *application* questions deal with specific, technical information that must be looked up in the product catalog or other source of technical data. Some common questions in this category are: "At how many revolutions per minute should you feed product X into a no. 10 machine?" Each time an application question comes up, the person who reads the card calls on one of the other participants to answer it. The meeting leader awards a poker chip for a correct answer. If the participant cannot answer the question, the reader can answer it or can ask another participant to do so.

The *administrative* questions—the third and last type of question in the deck—deal with the procedures of the meeting itself. One of the early questions in this category is: "What will we be able to do after this meeting that we cannot do now?" And one of the last questions in the meeting is: "When are we going to total the points, see who gets the prizes, and get the hell out of here?" The participants, in addition to reading the questions dealt to them, are encouraged to inject questions of their own at any time.

Using inquiry learning, salespeople may be guided in the meeting right up to the point of shaking the hand of the prospect. This is done through questions such as: "Who are the potential buyers of this new product line?" and "How can I tell which of my present accounts are likely prospects for this new line?" Primed with the answers to questions like these, the participants can be led through a series of exercises, each of which is designed to remove a reason for not asking for a sale. They may be asked to list, on a special form, the known prospects in their territory. A chip may be awarded for every entry they can list in a certain period.

Call Planning   Next the salespeople can be led to complete a Supplemental Call Planning Form, on which they are instructed to list the company, location, and call target date for each prospect. They can be told that they are not expected to follow this call plan in detail, but to use it to supplement their other planning activity. Copies may be given to the sales supervisor so that he or she can schedule joint calls.

The next step is to have the trainees develop their own "personal approach" statement and their close, or "request to quote on a specific order." They can be asked to write these statements silently and alone right at the meeting. The purpose is to arm them with a ready statement that is natural to them, but available on cue, when they are face to face with a prospect.

Practice   The final exercise in the meeting can be to have each participant practice his or her opening and closing statements in role-playing situations, with one of the other participants playing the part of the prospect. The others can be led to offer constructive criticism. The presentation can be rated in a manner that provides quantitative scores. The winners can then receive points toward the meeting awards.

Meetings in the inquiry learning format tend to move at a rapid pace. The inquiry learning cards, the reference sheets, the awards points, the prospecting exercise, the approach and close planning, the call target date list, and the peer-evaluated role playing all combine to produce a lively meeting that leads the participants right up to an introduction to the prospect.

One trainer reports that "the inquiry learning meeting format effectively combines both technical product training and sales practice. It is training in a thoroughly adult manner, enhanced by a unique and exciting entertainment element." The "adult manner" is a matter of creating conditions in which people can seek the answers to questions of importance to them—inquiry learning. The entertainment element is nothing more than our old friend—involvement.

EVALUATING SALES TRAINING EFFORTS

Some criteria should be used by sales training executives to rationalize the programs they present and to justify their expenses. It is impossible to compute the cost of *not* investing in a sales training program. But some criteria should be used,

```
                          ACTION PLANNER


1.    Some one idea, technique,or solution generated during this
      session is worth your taking some action on.  Please state
      it here.




2.    What deadline can you idealistically set for yourself to
      fully implement the idea?




3.    What is the very first step you must take to definitely set
      you on the path of meeting your deadline?  When do you plan
      to take it?




4.    If you do the above and the results are what you expect,
      what will it mean in added income or savings?  (Of course,
      you'll have to "guesstimate.")




5.    What did it cost you to participate in this session?




6.    Divide the figure from Question 5 into the figure from
      Question 4 to get your ROSTI -- Return on Sales Training
      Investment (a percentage figure).
                      Est. Profit
                      ──────────── = ROSTI
                      Investment




7.    Subtract 5 from 4 to get net gain figure.
```

Fig. 26-7 Action planner form.

despite the variables in product, pricing, promotion, and people that occur in the marketplace. "Before" and "after" comparators (other variables are minimized, and sales or share of market is measured before training and after training) and control groups (several similar groups are selected from similar markets, all variables except training are minimized, training is provided for one group and not the other, and the impact of training in terms of sales or share of market is measured) are most commonly used and accepted.

Traditionally, sales training efforts have been evaluated on a "gut feel" basis.

Usually the evaluation technique is no more critical than an evaluation questionnaire completed by the trainee immediately following completion of the training program.

Sales trainers are now seeking ways to justify their programs with more mathematical precision. In larger sales organizations, sales trainers are collecting and comparing before-and-after sales figures to validate their programs. Those who use outside programs are asking for demonstrated proof of effectiveness.

Consider each of the following characteristics of the training session and make a fair judgment regarding their quality by marking the appropriate square and totaling the points.

	Poor 1	2	3	4	5	6	7	8	Exceptional 9	10	
Preparation											
Training Objectives											
Presentation Content											
Delivery (voice, props,etc.)											
Participation											
Feedback											
Assignment											

TOTAL _____

Trainer_____

Topic_____

Fig. 26-8 Trainer performance rater.

In sales organizations where sales volume is not the only important measure of a salesperson's success or where the relationship between a specific training program and sales results is somewhat indirect, other evaluation techniques are used. One such technique is ROSTI—return on sales training investment. This technique, which can be used for individuals or for entire groups, works best for programs directed at experienced salespeople. When the program is over, the salespeople are asked to tabulate all the costs of getting them through it. They also systematically evaluate every action plan they developed during the program in terms of the probable payoff in sales increases, or expense savings, that will accrue to them if they do follow their own action plans. Figure 26-7 shows a form participants can use for this purpose.

By dividing their estimated dollar benefit by their actual expenses, trainees can arrive at the value of participating in the program. The same formula can be employed by the sales trainer, using the collective figure of his or her program participants, plus expenses for such items as the meeting room, meals, and mailings. It is common for such calculations to project a 1,000 percent return on the sales training investment. The figure is impressive and usually optimistic. While critics are sure to remind you that the income benefit is only estimated and that actual benefits are almost impossible to measure with precision, a variation of the ROSTI concept is the kind of talk financial management understands.

While sales trainees are not usually the best judges of the effectiveness or the professionalism of sales trainers, their opinions are important. Management does tend to value the opinion of those who participated in the training, and trainers usually value the opinion of the trainees. Some trainers prefer to have the trainees write narrative reports on the effectiveness of the training, while others provide structured forms. Still others provide open-ended statements that do not lead the participants to make either negative or positive comments—for example, "The meeting leader was ———" or "The training materials are ———." The Trainer Performance Rater shown in Fig. 26-8 can be helpful when several trainers are used in the same program.

SUMMARY

Today's effective sales training executive follows several basic steps:

1. Establishment of standards. What must a salesperson or sales manager know and be able to do to function successfully?
2. Analysis of needs. What does the sales force generally now know, and what skills do they now possess?
3. Development of programs. What is the most effective way to bring needed training to the sales force within budget?
4. Program validation. What is the best way to measure the effectiveness of the program?

Programs should be based on a knowledge of how people develop and on an understanding of the mechanical techniques for helping individuals toward self-development.

If properly managed, the sales training function can contribute significantly to the goals of any organization.

Chapter **27**

Secretarial and Clerical Training

CAROLYN E. IVES

Carolyn E. Ives *is an Assistant Secretary of the Individual Insurance Operations at the Connecticut General Life Insurance Company in Hartford. Since 1963, she has been responsible for the design and implementation of clerical and supervisory training programs interfacing organization development and MBO with technical skills training. She has been a member of ASTD since 1969, has held many chapter offices, and is currently President of the Connecticut chapter. She chaired the Site Selection and Arrangements Committee for the Region 1 1974 Conference, was a member of the 1974–1975 National Program Design Committee, and is a member of the Professional Development Committee. With the Life Office Management Association, she has served on the Examination and Curriculum Committees and was recently appointed to the Training and Management Education Committee. A graduate of the University of Connecticut, she holds a B.S. in Business Administration and is doing graduate work in organization behavior at the University of Hartford.*

All organizations have at least one thing in common: Clerical support services that must be performed regularly to ensure the smooth functioning of the organization. The following list is a representative sampling of clerical and secretarial responsibilities:

Typing from rough drafts, dictating equipment, or personal dictation
For data processing, performing repetitive, high-volume tasks such as keypunching and coding
Answering routine and nonroutine correspondence
Gathering statistical and general information
Receiving visitors and taking phone calls and messages
Arranging appointments, travel plans, and meetings
Filing, copying, collating, printing, and ordering supplies
Processing incoming and outgoing mail

These services may be provided by one secretary for one or more technical or management persons or by a group of people in a clerical pool.

An executive secretary's position will usually have multiple job qualifications such as an ability to type and take shorthand and the equivalent of a college-level knowledge of English and mathematics. Within the clerical pool, the positions may have no job qualifications beyond an ability to read. For example, a mail clerk's job might be to pick up and distribute the mail, make photocopies, collate, and run errands.

Most organizations also require typing as a basic entry-level skill. However, some organizations have developed basic training programs in typing, arithmetic, hygiene, English grammar, English as a primary language, English as a secondary language, etc. These programs are aimed at employees who enter the workplace needing remedial skill training. The programs are not intended to compete with those offered by the local business school or college. Instead, they are tailored to help the employee acquire minimum skills needed to get entry-level jobs done within that particular organization.

From the mail clerk or typist to the president's secretary, the clerical and secretarial positions provide support services for other people, with few decisions being made at the clerical level. For example, balancing workloads, scheduling deadlines, and establishing time and service standards are tasks usually done by management people and imposed on the clerical and secretarial work force. At the same time, secretaries who work for the top executives within an organization frequently enjoy management-level responsibilities. The quantity and quality of these responsibilities are usually in direct proportion to the number of years the secretary and executive have worked together.

The tasks done by a clerical employee frequently are written out on a job description in descending order of importance (see Fig. 27-1). The job description identifies what has to be done, how often it must be done, and whether the work has to be checked by anyone else.

These employees may not go through a formal training program. They may be given training on the job by an instructor, who might be the outgoing incumbent, a line trainer, or a supervisor.

Past Attitudes   Historically, very little effort has been made to encourage the clerical or secretarial employee toward a career orientation. Management and technical people's assumptions about this work force include:

- Has an extremely high annual turnover
- Will work only temporarily until marriage or birth of a child
- Resists taking on additional responsibility
- Prefers detailed, repetitive, routine tasks

Federal legislation, Supreme Court decisions regarding sex discrimination, women's organizations, and rising levels of self-awareness are beginning to bring about dramatic changes in the area of clerical career advancement. Most organizations are aggressively searching for promotional candidates within the clerical and secretarial population. Employees are being encouraged to participate in management development programs, to engage in outside study programs, and to apply for management or technical positions as openings occur.

This chapter presents a suggested career advancement training program which begins with the first day of employment. Each segment of the program is selected, scheduled, and conducted to coincide with the time an employee is ready to assume new tasks or responsibilities.

Two other topics have also been included in this chapter. Job enrichment and word processing have the potential to positively impact clerical upward mobility. Both require the endorsement of top management and represent a substantial installation cost. These topics are examined from the clerical and secretarial perspective.

The final paragraphs in this chapter deal with you—the trainer—and the qualifications you will need to design and implement these programs.

CAREER ADVANCEMENT CLERICAL TRAINING PROGRAMS

These programs should take the trainee through suggested career advancement steps, beginning on the first day of employment. They are divided into four segments:

- Determining training needs
- Designing a training program

CONNECTICUT GENERAL LIFE INSURANCE CO.
POSITION DESCRIPTION

TITLE OF POSITION	POSITION CLASS	POSITION NUMBER
Agent's Secretary		

DEPARTMENT	NUMBER IN POSITION	M	DATE
		F	

DIVISION	REPORT TO

GENERAL PURPOSE

To PERFORM secretarial duties for the Agent; to TRANSCRIBE and TYPE miscellaneous material. To ANSWER telephone calls; to HANDLE mail; to PERFORM duties to assist Agent in servicing policyholders.

PERCENT OF TIME SPENT

REGULAR DUTIES

1. PERFORMS secretarial duties for the Agent; TRANSCRIBES and TYPES correspondence, programs and miscellaneous material for Agent. COMPOSES, TYPES and SIGNS own name on routine correspondence.

2. RECEIVES and OPENS incoming mail; CALLS Agent's attention to any requiring his immediate attention. PREPARES outgoing mail.

3. RECEIVES Agent's telephone calls. TAKES messages; ACTS as his receptionist for visitors calling at office. MAKES appointments. MAKES routine telephone calls for Agent.

4. PERFORMS miscellaneous service duties; CONTACTS other Insurance companies to OBTAIN information regarding policy changes, coverages, etc. INITIATES work on claims; CONTACTS underwriting department regarding action on individual policies. MAINTAINS Term Conversion file; INITIATES action, PREPARES Term Conversion figures. Under Agent's direction, WRITES explanatory letters to policyholders. PREPARES Term and other product Conversion letters. PREPARES Contract Illustrations; CALCULATES Estate settlement costs; LISTS policies and RECORDS pertinent data from each.

5. ARRANGES client medical appointments and WORKS directly with clients on all requirements.

6. MAINTAINS files such as correspondence, Program, client, Prospect, Age Change, Term Conversion, etc.

7. MAINTAINS manuals, i.e. Blue Books, Technical Reporters, Announcements, Agent's Operations Manual, Rate Manual and Program construction manual.

8. PERFORMS miscellaneous related clerical duties to assist Agent in servicing policyholders; HANDLES accounting and tax records for agent and clients on interrelated activities; MAINTAINS mailing lists; PREPARES for mailing such material as Birthday, Anniversary and Christmas cards, memo blots, calendars, etc. May PREPARE agency meeting notes; may MAINTAIN contest records; HANDLES personal correspondence as required.

100%

OFFICE EQUIPMENT OPERATED (SHOW PERCENT OF TIME IN MARGIN)

THIS STATEMENT OF DUTIES IS FOR IDENTIFYING THIS POSITION. IT DOES NOT COVER IN DETAIL ALL OF THE DUTIES REQUIRED OF THE POSITION

B5291

Fig. 27-1 Clerical job description.

- Constructing an implementation plan
- Evaluating the program

How to Determine Training Needs   Begin by identifying promotional opportunities available for clerical and secretarial personnel. In some organizations jobs are structured, and so a move cannot be made out of the clerical area. Other jobs have qualifications that clerical employees rarely possess. For example, the manager's job may require an M.B.A. and an outstanding background in mathematics. Examine these barriers carefully. Remove artificial barriers and develop a valid list of promotional opportunities for the clerical work force.

Prepare a training survey to show how people are being trained now and the problems that exist and recommend a training program which will meet the current needs of your organization. A sample table of contents of a training survey is shown in Fig. 27-2.

Sample Table of Contents.   Sections 1, 2, and 3 are included to show why the survey was done, what kind of people are doing the work, and simple work diagrams.

Table of Contents

Section	Page Number
1. Why This Survey Has Been Done	3
2. Statistical Overview of the Work Force. .	5

°How many people are involved
°Lengths of service
°Educational backgrounds
°Age ranges

3. Work Flow Diagrams.	6
4. How Training is Currently Being Done. . .	10
5. Evaluation of the Training Program. . . .	25
6. Recommended Training Program.	30
7. Cost of Training Programs	48

°Present
°Recommended

Fig. 27-2   Training survey—table of contents.

Section 4 includes a comprehensive discussion of how employees are being trained at this time. This information is obtained from nondirective interviews with the line supervisor, the trainer, and the employees. Figure 27-3 includes a list of interview questions that are asked of the employees. The trainer and line supervisor's interview are modified slightly to show their roles, and additional questions are included to determine who designed the training program and when.

Section 5 is an evaluation of the present training program. Excerpts from the interviews with employees, trainers, and supervisors are used to reinforce observations made in the evaluation.

Section 6 must be separated into two sections: recommended training programs for present employees and recommended training programs for newly hired employees.

Section 7 is included to show the cost of the recommended training program versus the cost of the present training program.

Your discussion with your prospective client should lead to an agreement on how much of the recommended training program, if any, will be implemented.

---

1. What kind of work do you do each day? Perhaps you can describe a typical day's work for me.

2. Identify the most important things you do in your job.

3. What skills or previous work experience did you bring to this job?

4. How do you learn the work? What kind of written training materials, if any, were used?

5. Who conducted the training? Was this done on the job, in a classroom, or elsewhere? Where?

6. How do you learn when you have done a task correctly? Incorrectly?

7. What part of the training program did you especially enjoy? Why?

8. What part of the training program did you dislike? Why?

9. Are you finished with your training now? How did you know you were finished?

10. How do you view your future with this organization? What career path, if any, is available for you from this position?

11. If you had an opportunity to change the training you received in any way, how would you change it? Would you make it longer? Shorter? Why?

Fig. 27-3 Training survey—employee's interview questions.

Designing a Clerical and Secretarial Training Program The training program for the clerical staff must be designed with the knowledge that new clerical employees have very little overlap time with their predecessors. Therefore, these employees cannot take much time away from the work area for training programs.

The following is a list of eight suggested segments in a clerical and secretarial training program:

1. New-employee orientation
2. Basic task training
3. Technical refresher training
4. Time management
5. Written communications
6. Interpersonal relations
7. Life/career planning
8. Special outside training programs

The first day of work, the employee and supervisor should lay out a tentative training schedule for the first half year. Figure 27-4 shows an example of a program for a clerical employee. Joint setting of completion dates enables the supervisor to provide guidance while the new employee makes a personal commitment to get through the program.

1. *New-Employee Orientation.*   This orientation must be basic and should contain all information the employee needs to know to work satisfactorily in the organization. The following is a list of suggested items:

   a. Working hours
   b. Coffee breaks and mealtimes

TRAINING ENROLLMENT AND DEVELOPMENT RECORD

NAME	Gregory, Carol		EDUCATION	High School Graduate

JOB TITLE	1 Typist	2 Secretary	3
EFFECTIVE DATE	1 1-13-75	2 11-17-75	3

TRAINING PROGRAM	SUGGESTED COMPLETION DATE	ACTUAL COMPLETION DATE
1 New Employee Orientation	1-15-75	1-15-75
2 Product Training	2-15-75	2-10-75
3 Basic Task Training	4-2-75	4-3-75
4 Time Management	4-2-75	4-3-75
5 Written Communications	6-75	
6 Interpersonal Relations	1-76	
7 Black/White Workshop	7-76	
8 Male/Female Workshop	1-77	
9 Life/Career Planning	7-77	
10		

EXTRA JOB RELATED STUDY PROGRAMS

SCHOOL OR PROGRAM	COURSE	GRADE OR COMPLETION DATE
1 Life Office Management	Exam 1	P (June 1975)
2 Univ. of Cincinnati	English Composition	A (Aug. 1975)
3 Life Office Management	Exam 2	P (certificate - Dec. '75)
4		
5		
6		

Fig. 27-4   Training enrollment and development record.

   c. Emergency passes
   d. Schedule of paydays
   e. Medical privileges, if any
   f. Parking regulations
   g. Time off with pay
   h. Insurance benefits
   i. Attendance policy
   j. Salary administration program
   k. Tour of office facility
   l. Historical background and current description of the organization
   m. Counseling procedures, if any

This information can be put into a printed booklet or on a set of typed pages in an easy-to-read format. Give new employees individual copies, if possible. Otherwise, make copies available near the work area.

Ask the new employee to read the booklet or the typed pages. Schedule a session to discuss the contents during the first part of the first week. Use a classroom setting, if possible.

2. *Basic Task Training.*   The clerical or secretarial employee is usually given on-the-job training, and part of that training might better be done using a different technique. Video tapes, sound-slide programs, and programmed instruction have all been used successfully to show new employees how to do simple or complex clerical tasks. The number of students to be trained each year, the life expectancy of the course content, and the time available to develop the program are three factors that you will consider when determining which of the techniques is economically feasible.

If you must use on-the-job training for part or all of the program, give the new employees a detailed written training schedule. Some of the training will involve manuals, booklets, and sample work. When you are unavailable, the trainee can identify reading assignments from these written pages and can use the time productively.

Figure 27-5 is a sample training program for the secretary's position shown in Fig. 27-1. All the tasks to be learned have been included and are arranged in chronological learning order. The trainee is told what resource is needed to learn each task. The proposed completion date is shown so that the trainee will have an understanding of when training is supposed to be completed. The trainee is asked to fill in the actual completion dates throughout the program.

Certificates can be granted for some or all of the courses taken. The certificates will satisfy any adult who feels that something tangible should be awarded when a course has been completed (see Fig. 27-6).

3. *Technical Refresher Training.*   The clerical and secretarial work force must be given regular refresher training. Any changes in the organization usually impact this work force as soon as they occur. For example, a new record-keeping system or additional products and/or services will require the employee to follow different procedures.

Identify the topics that must be discussed. Ask employees to identify topics they want included. Keep the sessions brief—not more than two hours. Schedule the sessions on a bimonthly or quarterly basis as needed. A sample agenda is shown in Fig. 27-7.

The most appropriate technique will usually be informal discussion sessions between the employees and the trainer. Use the employees as discussion leaders whenever appropriate.

4. *Time Management.*   The new employee should be given time-management education during the basic task training period. From the first day, emphasis is placed on task organization, expedient work processing, etc. The employee can

also be taught to look at how time demands are made: what tasks have to be done, when, and for whom.

Line clerical employees often work in a tightly structured task environment and have little flexibility in managing their work flow. Staff clerical employees enjoy a slightly higher degree of flexibility in scheduling their own work.

	BASIC TASKS TO BE LEARNED		
ACTUAL COMPLETION DATE	TASKS (INCLUDING LEARNING STEPS, IF ANY)	RESOURCES NEEDED	PROPOSED COMPLETION DATE

1-14	1. Transcribe and type correspondence
	  a. Review typist's manual
	  b. Review sample work
	  c. Training session
		Typist manual
		Sample work
		Trainer
			1-14-75
			1-14-75
			1-14-75

1-14	2. Type programs
	  a. Review sample programs
	  b. Training session
		Sample prog.
		Trainer
			1-14-75

1-14	3. Answer telephone; take messages	Trainer	1-14-75
1-14	4. Receive visitors; make appointments	Trainer	1-14-75
1-15	5. Open incoming mail; prepare outgoing mail	Trainer	1-15-75

1-16	6. Identify items in mail requiring Agent's attention
	  a. Review sample work
	  b. Training session
		Sample work
		Trainer
			1-15-75
			1-16-75

1-16	7. Make routine telephone calls	Trainer	1-16-75
1-17	8. Make medical appointments for clients	Trainer	1-17-75
1-23	9. Maintain files and mailing lists	Trainer	1-24-75
2-1	10. Maintain manuals	Trainer	1-31-75

2-7
2-17
2-18
	11. Prepare sales illustrations
	  a. Take product training
	  b. Take illustration course
	  c. Training session
		Prod. training
		Illus. course
		Trainer
			2-7-75
			2-14-75
			2-17-75

2-21	12. Compose answers to routine correspondence
	  a. Review sample work
	  b. Training session
		Sample work
		Trainer
			2-21-75

2-25
2-27
2-27
	13. Term conversions
	  a. Review term conversion manual
	  b. Review sample work
	  c. Training session
		Term manual
		Sample work
		Trainer
			2-25-75
			2-26-75
			2-27-75

4-1
4-2
4-3
	14. Calculate estate settlement costs
	  a. Take technician course
	  b. Review sample work
	  c. Training session
		Tech. course
		Sample work
		Trainer
			3-28-75
			4-1-75
			4-2-75

Fig. 27-5 Task training outline.

In either case, the following technique is suggested for giving the clerical employee an introduction to time management.

Ask each employee to write out a list of tasks that must be done in the coming month (see Fig. 27-8). Give new employees guidance so that they can include tasks as yet unlearned. The list becomes a set of objectives for that period. During the month as each task is completed, the employee makes a notation to that effect. And as unexpected tasks come along, they are added to the end of the list (see Fig. 27-9).

At month's end, sit down with the employee to review the month's results. Give

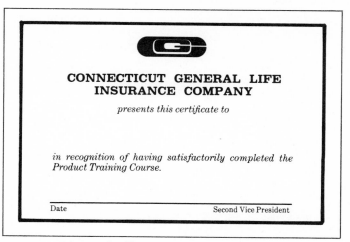

Fig. 27-6 Certificate: product training course.

the employee an opportunity to explain why some tasks did not get done and why new tasks were added. Also, point out to the employee what demands were made by other people. This information should be used to plan the next month's activity accordingly.

If the employee had a low-productivity month, the list represents an immediate source of direct feedback. If an unusual amount of additional work was done during the month, the employee has a logical way of bringing this to the supervisor's attention.

At appraisal time, the employee has accumulated a documented record of tasks completed. Attempts to improve management of time will be evident through the months.

Staff clerical employees frequently ask that this procedure be adopted as a normal part of the month's activities. The list acts as a discipline for unstructured jobs that require a high degree of initiative to perform. The procedure achieves its highest level of effectiveness when members of the clerical group begin to meet monthly to share the task lists with one another. Where tasks overlap or require cooperation between two people, mutual commitments are made to finish the tasks prior to the next meeting.

Line clerical employees usually do not like to follow this procedure more than once or twice. The flow of their work is steady and unending. The employee makes out a list of identical tasks each month, and the procedure seems like an unnecessary extra task. If the employee's production is satisfactory, the procedure does not have to be used. If either quantity or quality is less than satisfactory, ask the employee to follow this procedure once or twice. You will have enough specific performance data to conduct a productive session on time management with that employee.

5. *Written Communication.*   The clerical and secretarial employees share with technical and management people a need to write clear and concise notes, memos, letters, and instructions. Decide whether the program should be developed internally or purchased from an outside firm.

There are advantages and disadvantages to a program which has been developed internally. The examples used will deal specifically with your work, and the student will not have to transfer the knowledge because examples differ. However, the trainer should have an ability to write and experience in the field of communi-

---

Trainer: J. Peeples

Date: March, 1975

Discussion Items	Discussion Leader
1. Tour of new printing facility	Foreman, Printing
2. Use of new printing forms	J. Peeples
3. Communication difficulties with marketing clerical staff	Entire group
4. New products planned	Director of Marketing
5. 1975 holiday schedule	J: Peeples
6. Flexible working hours pilot	Director of Personnel
7.	
8.	
9.	

Fig. 27-7 Technical refresher training—sample agenda.

cations in order to be able to produce a program with credibility. That background may be inappropriate to meet the rest of your training needs.

Some excellent inexpensive courses prepared by well-qualified communicators are available. These courses offer your employees quality instruction; they are modularized and will fit conveniently into an organized training program.

Whether developed internally or externally, the program should consist of three parts:

- Learning. Written, spoken instruction on the basic steps to clear, concise writing.
- Doing. Practice at using the new knowledge.
- Monitoring. Having written work reviewed periodically for retention of new knowledge.

6. *Interpersonal Relations Training.*   This training concerns human interaction; it may focus on heightened self-awareness, team building, group feedback, etc. Further, the workshop may deal with only one issue, such as racism or sexism, and have consciousness raising as its primary objective.

Organizations do not usually include money in the budget for the clerical and secretarial work force to attend workshops of this kind. Interventions such as T groups, sensitivity training, and team building are normally reserved for managers and key technicians.

However, interpersonal relations training for the clerical and secretarial work

---

LIST OF TASKS for period beginning 1-6-75

                                         To be completed 2-7-75

1. Work with trainer on: Writing my job description

                         Earned Day survey

                         Group Product Training revision

2. Finish rearranging M. Folse's part of the files

3. Complete processing the Week-ending lists

4. Collate, staple, label, and mail the Supervisor memo

5. Revise enrollment instructions for all Product
   Training students

6. Conduct tour of the building for two visiting
   supervisors

7. Attend two birthday lunches

8. Take two vacation days in early February

9. Attend presentation of new fringe benefit
   orientation

Fig. 27-8 Time management—list of tasks at beginning of month.

force can be justified as a training expense. Begin by identifying the kind of interpersonal training needed and by determining the extent to which your organization is willing to consider this kind of training for the work force. Consider these factors:

- Employees may have constant interface with customers and could create serious public relations problems for the organization. The switchboard operator and the receptionist, for example, deal with the general public constantly.
- Employees who work under tight deadlines and have unusually heavy workloads may be able to perform their jobs only if team spirit is extremely high.

■ Promotional candidates with satisfactory organizational skills may need to become more aware of the impact they have on others personally in order to become effective supervisors.

The training can be offered internally or externally, but the organization must be especially careful to work with professional organization development consul-

---

LIST OF TASKS for period beginning 1-6-75

To be completed 2-7-75

		Date Completed
1.	Work with trainer on: Writing my job description	1-10-75
	Earned Day survey	Not done
	Group Product Training revision	1-31-75
2.	Finish rearranging M. Folse's part of the files	1-20-75
3.	Complete processing the Week-ending lists	3/4 done
4.	Collate, staple, label, and mail the Supervisor memo	1-24-75
5.	Revise enrollment instructions for all Product Training students	Rough draft
6.	Conduct tour of the building for two visiting supervisors	1-17-75
7.	Attend two birthday lunches	2-7-75
8.	Take two vacation days in early February	2/3 & 2/4
9.	Attend presentation of new fringe benefit orientation	1-17-75
ADDITIONAL TASKS DONE DURING THE SAME PERIOD:		
10.	Typed 20 job descriptions for Job Analyst	1-16-75
11.	Typed, printed, collated, stapled, labeled, and mailed LOMA test results to all supervisors	1-31-75
12.	Collected for Cheer Fund; completed status report	2-7-75
13.	Updated ASTD Newsletter Mailing List	1-10-75

Fig. 27-9 Time management—list of tasks at end of month.

tants. The Organization Development Division of ASTD has material available concerning this profession.

This part of the training program should probably be made available only on an optional basis. An employee who is trying to learn how to interact more successfully with a customer has several alternatives:

Gaining on-the-job experience
Reading published material
Attending formal classes
Participating in your workshop

The participants, together with supervisors, should be able to study the published objectives of a workshop and then decide whether that workshop will meet their needs. Some people know that workshop environments are inappropriate ways for them to learn.

7. *Life/Career Planning Workshops.* These workshops are designed to help individuals reach into their past experiences—both their successes and their failures—and think about the future: where they want to go and what resources they have for getting there. Using a series of activities, each participant identifies a variety of possible goals and lays out a tentative action plan for accomplishing them.

The workshop is usually appropriate only for large organizations. Employees have a wide range of promotional opportunities available within a large organization. Each employee can identify a possible career goal, investigate its attainability, and then adopt a realistic action plan to reach that goal.

The organization benefits in two ways by offering the workshop. First, employees step forward with tentative career goals identified. Management has only to match the employee with an appropriate career path. Second, employees who know where they are heading are capable of being highly productive. If the organization can match the employee to an appropriate career path, higher production should result.

Conversely, small organizations may lose employees because of this kind of workshop. A person may identify a career goal that is not attainable within that organization. Unless another goal is considered, the employee may decide to change organizations.

The workshop should be two to three days in length; it should be residential to ensure maximum group interaction and should be conducted by an experienced facilitator. It is best to mix the group in terms of age, experience, marital status, and race whenever possible.

The employee's supervisor should be aware of the workshop's objectives. The employee usually returns to the work area with a high level of enthusiasm and needs a supportive environment to cement the commitment made in the workshop.

8. *Special Outside Training Programs.* These programs are offered by business schools and colleges as well as by professional, trade and civic associations, and service organizations. The programs are designed to give the employee new knowledge, skills, and attitudes and to provide broader perspectives in areas beyond current job requirements.

Clerical and secretarial employees usually start with a career planning workshop or counseling session in order to establish some career goals. The career planning process enables the employee to identify the learning steps necessary to achieve career goals. Some of these learning steps may be available from in-house programs.

Other learning steps, such as a college degree in business administration or an associate degree in a paralegal or paramedical program, will have to be obtained outside the organization. If there is a tuition refund program, the employee will already have guidelines available for selecting the appropriate course or institution. But the trainer may have to develop guidelines to help the employee know where to go for programs. While the employees are participating in the outside programs, they can provide evaluations as to the quality and relevance of the programs.

Decisions as to who should participate, what programs should be considered, etc., are most easily made on the basis of the needs of employees who are trying to reach career goals.

Implementation When the training program has been recommended, reviewed, and agreed upon, a number of steps will be necessary to put it into operation (see Fig. 27-10). Manuals, materials, films, and tapes may have to be prepared. Facilities may have to be found. Both the trainers and the trainees will have to be identified.

After the program has been in operation for a short length of time, an evaluation of part or all of it should take place. Changes should be made, if necessary, to conform with the evaluations. Gantt charts (Fig. 27-11) or PERT and CPM, etc., may be used to show multiple task deadlines and to prevent overscheduling throughout the implementation phase.

Evaluation Evaluation is the feedback you need to determine the effectiveness of a training course or program.

Identify what you want evaluated and who is to do the evaluation, when it should be done, and whether it is to be written or oral. Also, determine how much, if any, of the evaluation will be shared with other people. For example, the management people may be interested only in whether improved performance has taken place and to what extent. The trainees may be interested only in how many people completed the course and program and how long it took for each. Your interest will include both of these and more.

Your evaluation should include the things you have learned while preparing

Item	Completion Date
1. New Employee Orientation (Trainer: M. Folse)	
a. Research and identify content	6-1-73
b. Content prepared and photocopied	8-1-73
c. Illustrations prepared and photocopied	8-1-73
d. Pilot orientation arranged	8-8-73
(1) Facilities reserved	
(2) Students identified, notified	
e. Content, illustrations revised	9-8-73
f. Pilot orientation evaluated	9-8-73
g. Orientation agenda revised	10-1-73
h. Booklet printed	10-1-73
i. Present work force orientation scheduled	11-1-73
j. Work force orientations completed	12-1-73
k. Orientations evaluated	1-15-74
2. Basic Task Training Program (Trainer: V. Cook)	
Etc.	

Fig. 27-10 Career advancement training program—implementation plan.

DESIGN AND IMPLEMENTATION OF NEW EMPLOYEE ORIENTATION PROGRAM

TRAINER: M. Folse

ITEM	MAY	JUNE	JULY	AUG	SEPT	OCT	NOV	DEC	JAN
Booklet Contents and Illustrations	Identify	Prepare	Photocopy	Revise	Print				
Pilot Orientation Facilities Students		Reserve / Identify	Invite	Attend / Evaluate					
Full Orientation Facilities Students					Reserve / Identify		Notify Attend	Evaluate	

Fig. 27-11 Gantt chart of implementation plan.

and conducting the course or program. The following are suggested steps for your evaluation:

1. Schedule a debriefing session immediately following the conclusion of the program. At the session discuss such items as logistics, training techniques, materials used, effectiveness of the staff, problems which arose, and situations which were unusually good.
2. Summarize the information. Then write a trainer's evaluation and file it for future reference.

This document, along with the participants' evaluation, should be used when you begin to schedule the courses or programs again.

JOB ENRICHMENT

This management strategy emphasizes job redesign. The process begins with an evaluation of current job design, organization structure, and management techniques being employed. Clerical jobs are ideal for the job enrichment process. The volume of work, the number of people doing the same kind of work, and the simplicity of the work being done all combine to enhance the consultant's chance to show dramatic increases in productivity, improvements in quality, and reductions in absenteeism and turnover. Secretarial jobs are less than ideal for the process. The items necessary to enrich a secretary's job are usually found on the boss's desk. Each secretary's job differs somewhat from others nearby. The enriching process almost has to be done on one secretary's job at a time, making results more difficult to see.

Jobs can be examined as to the strength of job design. Six characteristics considered necessary for a strong job design are outlined below:

1. Are clients readily identifiable? Are there few enough to get to know?
   SECRETARIAL: The boss is usually viewed as the client. The relationship can be excellent.
   CLERICAL: These jobs usually have little or no client identification. The relationship can be improved.

2. Does the work have meaning and worth to the employee?

SECRETARIAL: The boss's role in the organization usually determines the work's worth.

CLERICAL: The work is usually broken into simple, tedious, repetitive tasks that have little meaning to the employee.

3. Does feedback come directly from the client? Is feedback delayed or filtered?

SECRETARIAL: The secretary usually gets immediate, accurate feedback.

CLERICAL: The feedback usually comes in through supervisory people. It is usually delayed and filtered—if it gets through at all.

4. Are there tasks being done above or around the employee that can more effectively be done by just one person?

SECRETARIAL: Most secretaries are capable of handling part of the boss's job. The extent to which work is delegated varies greatly.

CLERICAL: Most clerical positions have the potential for considerable task combination. The assembly-line approach does not have to be used on clerical jobs.

5. How long will the employee continue to learn new things on the job?

SECRETARIAL: If the boss has a job that is growing, there is continuous opportunity for growth. Lacking that, by delegating over a long period of time, this job has an excellent chance of providing growth.

CLERICAL: Most clerical jobs can be learned in less than six months. Unless tasks are combined from the jobs surrounding the clerical job, the opportunity to learn new things is extremely limited.

6. What are the promotional opportunities available?

SECRETARIAL: Promotional opportunities are usually scarce unless the person is willing to make a career change. Also, top executives usually take their secretaries along as they move. Secretaries must succeed early and hope the boss will do likewise.

CLERICAL: Very few promotional opportunities are available. The job design keeps employees from being able to show promotional potential. Higher-level jobs are usually filled with people from the outside.

When an organization engages in job enrichment, clerical people in redesigned jobs find themselves planning and scheduling their own work. They concentrate on the needs of their customers and must demonstrate diplomacy and tact when explaining to their customers what can and cannot be done.

Employees in enriched clerical positions begin thinking about career orientation. As additional and more difficult tasks are learned, the employee demonstrates a capacity to grow. Promotional opportunities are usually designed to create a higher-level working relationship with the same customers.

Secretarial employees are not usually able to follow the same pattern. At some point in their skill development, secretaries must give serious consideration to making a career change. The number of high-level secretarial positions available is too small to encourage people in the secretarial occupation to compete for them. Further, every part of the secretary's job makes an excellent foundation for almost any kind of occupation.

WORD PROCESSING

This management strategy involves a change from the traditional one secretary/one executive working ratio. It also incorporates the use of automated word processing equipment, which includes power typewriters, central or remote dictating systems, and correcting mechanisms which permit editing of documents.

The secretary's job is divided into two parts: administrative work and typing or correspondence duties.

Administrative work is centralized so that one administrative secretary can process the work of several executives. These duties consist of making telephone calls and appointments, handling mail, doing routine letter writing, and performing simple tasks formerly done by the executives.

Typing duties are centralized and automated equipment is installed. One correspondence secretary can then process the work of several executives. These duties consist of transcription and power typing. Transcription typing includes recorded dictation and copy typing; the power-typing duties include rough drafts, edited drafts, and finished documents.

The word processing system usually has top management's endorsement from the beginning. The automated equipment represents a significant installation expense which can be offset only by sustained use of the equipment. When the system is enthusiastically supported by both management and the clerical staff, the organization may be able to get the work done with one secretary for every five executives.

Training Needs Four training needs appear at the inception of word processing. The administrative secretary may or may not find the newly designed job more interesting and challenging. The client relationship of one secretary/one executive is usually eliminated. This job design characteristic has had high appeal for many secretaries. Asking the administrative secretary to do the work for a group of executives may prove to be demotivational. Other characteristics of the job are usually strengthened by word processing. The opportunity for both continued learning and direct feedback is enhanced when a pool of executives must be served.

The correspondence secretary's position, however, may be very poorly designed. The word processing center may wind up with jobs that have no client relationship, a high volume of boring typing, very few new learning opportunities, and filtered feedback. Each of these weak job design characteristics should be minimized at the time the jobs are designed. Correspondence secretaries can be given a set of customers to serve. These customers will have tasks which will give the secretary a reason to get away from the automated equipment during the day. New learning opportunities should be methodically layered into the job. Customers can be asked to return the work directly to the secretary when corrections are needed.

Career Advancement New supervisory and management positions are usually created when word processing is installed in an organization. Eventually, these positions can be filled with people being promoted out of the secretarial positions. Allowing a secretary to move into a job that supervises secretaries requires less of an adjustment than moving the secretary into some kind of technical work. Administrative secretaries who successfully work for a pool of executives make excellent candidates when top-executive secretarial positions open up. A large number of executives have experienced the performance capabilities of this person and can recommend and/or sponsor the promotion. Correspondence secretaries should be considered eligible for promotion as soon as the skills of the job have been acquired. Emphasis should be placed on making the word processing center an entry-level career opportunity instead of a dead-end typing pool.

TRAINER QUALIFICATIONS

The qualifications you will need in order to design and implement these clerical and secretarial training programs include the ability to write programmed instruction and procedural manuals, an understanding of the adult learning process, a knowledge of how to write evaluation instruments, and experience with classroom instruction, process consultation, and consciousness-raising facilitation. Essentially, these are the same qualifications as those for designing and conducting technical training programs.

BIBLIOGRAPHY

Collins, M.: "Job Descriptions: Foundations of Successful W/P Management;" *Modern Office Procedures,* pp. 67–69, November 1973.

Ford, R. N.: *Motivation through the Work Itself,* American Management Association, New York, 1969.

Hackman, J. R., and E. E. Lawler III: "Employee Relations to Job Characteristics," *Journal of Applied Psychology Monograph,* vol. 55, no. 3, pp. 259–286, June 1971.

Herzberg, F.: *Work and the Nature of Man,* The World Publishing Company, Cleveland, 1966.

Herzberg, F., B. Mausner, and B. Snyderman: *The Motivation to Work,* John Wiley & Sons, Inc., New York, 1959.

Modern Office Procedures, January, March, June, September, October, December 1974.
    (A series of reports by the editors on word processing.)

Chapter **28**

Computer-Related Training

JOHN H. McCONNELL

FERDINAND J. SETARO

John H. McConnell *is President of both John H. McConnell Associates and McConnell-Simmons & Co. Inc., Morristown, N.J. Both organizations provide organizational development and training services and resources. Prior to entering the consulting field, Mr. McConnell held a variety of training, data processing management, and operating management positions in industry and government over a 20-year period. Mr. McConnell has been associated with Garan, Inc.; Universal Oil Products — Wolverine Tube Division, The J. L. Hudson Co., Detroit Edison Co., and other organizations, as well as the cities of Detroit and Highland Park, Mo. He holds a bachelor's and a master's degree from Wayne State University in educational psychology. He has done additional graduate work at the same university. Mr. McConnell has authored over two dozen articles on training and development (some of which have appeared in the* Training and Development Journal*), two dozen programmed instructions, and 50 multimedia training programs, and he has been the subject of a number of articles. Mr. McConnell and Mr. Setaro have coauthored two multimedia programs:* Using the Computer as a Management Tool *and* The AMA Conference Process.

Ferdinand Setaro *is Director of Management and Organization Development for Colonial Penn Group, Inc., of Philadelphia, where he is responsible for corporate education and training and serves as internal consultant to senior management. Prior to joining Colonial Penn in 1973, Mr. Setaro was with the American Management Association, where he served as Membership Administrator, Director of the Supervisory Management Association, Inc., and Project Director, Multimedia Management Education Systems. At AMA, Mr. Setaro helped develop the Management Internship Program and coauthored the AMA course* Using the Computer as a Management Tool. *A graduate of Columbia College, Mr. Setaro holds a certificate in systems analysis and programming from the Management Institute and has completed course work for the master of public administration degree at New York University. He is a member of the National Panel of the American Arbitration Association, the American Society for Public Administration, the Academy of Political Science, the Association of Internal Management Consultants, the Data Processing Management Association, the Society for Management Information Systems, and ASTD.*

Perhaps some people have not been affected by the computer, but certainly the authors of this chapter have been, as well as the reader. The computer and the current state of the art of data processing have drastically changed the way most organizations work, creating major challenges for many within the organization— including the training director. However, those very challenges now provide the training director with the opportunity to make a greater contribution to the organization's future success.

Areas of Training Needs It is our thesis that regardless of what the training director has done in the past, the most significant training opportunities in areas related to the computer lie ahead. In our experience, computer-related training needs have only recently been fully identified. True, training departments have done a good job in the area of data processing skills training. However, only in the past few years has there been any recognition of the areas in which training can make its most substantial contribution to computer-generated training needs. These areas are:

> Training the organization's operating personnel to make optimum use of computer services and to communicate successfully with data processing personnel
>
> Training data processing personnel to communicate successfully as an independent staff function with operating personnel

If necessity be the mother of invention, then we all know the maternity of the computer—we are just not sure about the paternity. A word used to refer to an illegitimate child, along with many of its four-lettered brethren, has often been used to describe the computer. Those who hurl such words at the inanimate machine include both data processing personnel—the people who try to make it work—and operating personnel—the people who try to work with what it makes. However, the fault lies not with input, output, manipulation, or control devices but rather with the way in which people introduced the machine into organizations.

HISTORY AND DEVELOPMENT

In its early stages the computer was seen as some kind of fast bookkeeping or record-keeping machine and was usually relegated to one of the subdepartments of the finance or accounting organization. In those first days of "business" application, very few people were trained in computer usage other than those who were going to work directly with it. For most people in an organization the only manifestations of the computer's existence were the appearance of reports in a slightly different format and the establishment of new positions and job titles.

Early Computer Skills Training The training in the skills necessary to operate the computer was supplied primarily by the computer manufacturer. Typically, an organization purchasing a computer selected appropriate personnel and sent them to the computer manufacturer for training as computer operators, keypunch operators, programmers, etc. In fact, some computer manufacturers went so far as to publish and administer aptitude tests designed to determine which of an organization's employees had the most potential for this new technology. With few exceptions, organizations did little, if any, internal training themselves. This generally held true for quite a few years. The computer was used mostly in the financial and accounting area, and most training was technical and was left to the computer manufacturer.

However, the needs of organizations to make faster calculations and to handle an increased amount of paperwork and data were continuing. At the same time, breakthroughs in electronic technology allowed the building of faster and smaller computers which handled more data, took up less space, and performed more administrative and management tasks.

Computer Usage Expansion   Other functions within the organization began to recognize that this fast-calculating machine used by the finance department had tremendous possibilities for improving their operations. In addition, the growing numbers of computer professionals began to look for new challenges from their base in the finance department. In many organizations applications outside the finance function were frustrated. Since the computer was first established in the finance department, it seemed that the accounting and finance work took priority over all other applications. As a result, in some organizations departments such as engineering and material control purchased their own computers and established their own data processing functions.

The growing importance of the services provided by the computer, the computer's initial relationship to the finance department, and the proliferation of computer facilities caused many organizations to begin to experiment with new reporting relationships. Sometimes the computer was placed under the control of an office services or general administrative department. Other times it was placed within an industrial engineering department. More commonly, it was moved up within the finance department to a higher reporting level.

Current Computer Organization   In recent years, we have seen many instances in which the computer function has been moved completely out of all other departments and established as a department of its own. In other words, it is a functional department equal within the organization to such other functional departments as personnel, purchasing, engineering, and accounting. In its new role, it has become a staff department similar to all other staff departments, providing a vital and needed service to the total organization. It is in this role that the training director must view the organization's computer-generated training needs.

COMPUTER-GENERATED TRAINING NEEDS

The Computer Mystique   Considering the computer department as a staff department is the easiest way to understand the training needs generated within the organization by the computer. However, in doing so, it is important to remember the history of its development within the organization and also the fact that in many people's minds a mystique has grown up around the computer.

The computer and its new technology and accompanying jargon have in some cases intimidated operating personnel. Many did not feel qualified to question some of the decisions made regarding the computer and its use. In fact, some operating managers all but abdicated their responsibilities to the computer and the computer professionals.

Paradoxically, the computer professionals have realized that to function successfully they cannot do both their job and the operating manager's. Now most computer professionals are anxious to have the operating managers and their people do their own jobs so that the computer professionals will be free to do theirs.

Computer-Generated Training Needs   Consequently, to counter the computer mystique and to get people to do their own jobs—neither abdicating nor usurping—one of the most pressing needs is training to establish a common ground where both operating personnel and data processing personnel can talk to each other in a common language. This means a language that is not colored either with computer jargon which the operating personnel do not understand or with operating jargon which does not make clear what is expected from the staff service provided by the computer.

The computer has generated needs for training in two broad areas within the organization. First, the training director must provide the training needed by data processing personnel—the people actually working with the computer and its peripheral systems. Second, the training director must provide training for operating personnel—the people within the organization who use the services provided by data processing personnel.

We shall now look at the types of training needed, the types of resources available, and implementation approaches within each of these areas.

DATA PROCESSING PERSONNEL

The training needed by data processing personnel can be classified into skill training and employee training. Skill training concerns itself with both the initial and the further development of the various data processing skills. Employee training is that training which normally is provided to employees of the organization no matter what their department. Skill training includes such things as keypunch and data entry training, machine operation training, programming training, and systems analysis training.

Skill Training Needs

Since skill training is technical training, it is usually difficult for the training director alone to determine the training needed. However, the training director can look to a number of sources which can assist in determining these training needs. First are the managers within the data processing function. These people are usually quite able to determine the skill needs of their employees. The training director should attempt to develop and implement training which meets the needs identified by the data processing department's management, as would be done with any other department.

Also available are services offered by the computer manufacturer and outside consultants. Both of these sources can be used to assist in determining the technical training needed by data processing personnel, but the training director should generally not turn to these sources without the cooperation of data processing management.

Training Resources

As with any other training, once training needs have been identified, the training director is faced with the task of designing or obtaining appropriate training programs and implementing them to fulfill these needs. Here again, since it is technical training, the training director is often not qualified to design and implement such programs without assistance. However, there is a broad spectrum of sources available.

Computer Manufacturers   For most organizations, computer manufacturers are still the primary source of technical and skill training, particularly at the basic skill level. Computer manufacturers have training programs available in data entry, computer operations, etc., but these programs may be limited to customers of the manufacturer. If the manufacturer cannot provide training, it is in the manufacturer's best interest to refer the request to someone who will assist the training director in providing effective skill training.

Private Schools   The many private schools that provide basic data processing technical training are another source for skills training. However, it is extremely difficult to generalize about the quality of these schools.

Some of these private schools turn out excellent graduates, but there have also been a number of complaints about such schools. They are primarily profit-making institutions with relatively little governmental or professional controls, and therefore the quality of the schools and their graduates varies tremendously. Thus when considering using such schools or hiring their graduates, it is wise first to investigate thoroughly both the curriculum and the performance of the graduates.

For such an evaluation, the training director can again turn to the organization's own data processing management or a representative of the computer manufacturer.

Public Schools   In addition to private schools, many of the public schools, particularly the community colleges and vocational high schools, have added training in various computer-related skills to their curricula. However, here again it is difficult to generalize about the quality of such schools. As with private schools, both the curriculum and the performance standards of each public school must be evaluated.

In the case of both public schools and private schools, many times incorrect training is worse than no training at all. Hiring someone who is incorrectly trained may require the training director not only to teach the basic needed skills (which the training director believed the employee already possessed) but also to teach the "unlearning" of incorrect skills.

On-the-Job Training   Not to be overlooked for training in computer-related skills is on-the-job training. Many basic skills can be taught on the job. This is usually most cost-effective where few people are to be trained at any one time or within a year. The only caution to be exercised in using the apprenticeship type of approach is to be sure that the person doing the instructing is not instructing in obsolescent or incorrect skills. In other words, regardless of how well the person doing the instructing performs the job now, he or she should also possess the type of skills and use the kind of approach which the organization desires for the future.

In-House Training Sessions   If the organization has a significant number of people to train in similar skills at one time, it is possible to bring these people together for in-house training sessions. There are a number of sources of materials and instructors to use in such situations. First, let us look briefly at the source of instructors.

One source is existing trainers, who can be trained in the subject matter to be taught. This approach enables the individual to concentrate training skills on the subject matter. Obviously, the reverse is also true—an existing subject matter expert can be taught training techniques.

Another source is outside trainers. A variety of people outside the organization possess basic subject matter and/or training skills and are available for conducting in-house courses—for example, university professors, consultants, and computer manufacturer representatives.

Purchased Training Programs   A final method is to buy a training program which furnishes your organization with both the content and training skills needed. Such programs are published by both management and data processing associations. In addition, training materials may be obtained to use alone or with one of the other training methods. Many computer manufacturers publish programmed instructions in data processing skills. Other materials are obtainable from publishers such as Wiley Systems, McGraw-Hill, AMACOM Extension Institute, and Auerbach.

Training-Resource Considerations   All the above are possible approaches. However, the training director must always remember to weigh the cost of such programs and the benefits provided in terms of the needs of the organization.

Skills Enhancement

Most of what has been covered so far can be applied to both entry-level skills training and skills enhancement. In the case of the latter, several resources are available to the training director which deal exclusively with the further development of existing skills.

Professional Associations   Many professional associations offer seminars and courses on the latest techniques and developments in computer-related technology. These organizations cover a wide variety of disciplines; some of the largest are such organizations as the Association for Computer Machinery, the Data Processing Management Association, the Association for Systems Management, the Society for Management Information Systems, and the American Management Associations. The training director's name should be placed on as many of these organizations' mailing lists as possible. This provides a current file, within the training department, of the various offerings. In addition, these organizations many times provide other materials and services which can be of assistance in actual in-house training.

Professional Journals   Although they do not in themselves provide training for continued development, professional journals are a prime resource. They probably are not needed as much by the training director as they are by data processing personnel. However, the training director may want to establish the training department as the source of such publications, and again his or her name should be placed on the mailing lists of these publishers.

General Employee Training

So far, this section of the chapter has dealt with the training and development of technical skills needed by data processing personnel. If this chapter attempts to make any one point regarding skill training, it is that the training director must view computer-generated training for data processing personnel in the same way that he or she would view training provided to any other staff department. The training director should not become enamored with the "mystique" that has grown up regarding the computer and data processing personnel.

It is because of this mystique that many organizations have forgotten that data processing personnel are also employees. Much effort and time have been spent in providing the basic technical and skill training needed, but sometimes, in the process, the general training normally provided to employees of the organization has been overlooked. This is the second area in which the training director must provide service to data processing personnel.

Employee Orientation   Orientation for new employees, benefit programs, and supervisory training all apply to data processing personnel as well as to any other employees within the organization. Failure to consider this aspect of the data processing personnel's training needs tends to set data processing apart from the rest of the organization.

Management Training   Within the area of employee training, management training is perhaps the most important element for data processing personnel. Data processing personnel need good management, and therefore data processing managers need management training, just as any other function within the organization does. Data processing management must learn how to direct, lead, and set performance standards. In this respect, they are the same as engineering managers, accounting managers, and sales managers.

When they join an organization, managers are usually associated with a given profession or specialty and grow to management positions within that profession or specialty. Unfortunately, often not much is done to prepare an individual for management. There is little the computer operator does in preparation for motivating people. There is little the systems analyst does in preparation for controlling the activities of people. There is little the programmer does in preparation for establishing meaningful performance standards.

Management training must be provided to these people, and this training should not be something unique; rather, it should be the same management training that is provided to all management employees within the organization. Management training is discussed elsewhere in this handbook, and so we end this section with a strong recommendation to think of those discussions as part of this chapter.

OPERATING PERSONNEL

Operating personnel, like data processing personnel, need training in all the usual employee and management activities. However, as was pointed out earlier, this is usually provided. This section concentrates on operating personnel's needs for training that is related to data processing.

First, let us define operating personnel. Since the subject of this chapter is computer-related training, operating personnel are defined as all those employees within the organization who utilize the services of the data processing personnel, but who themselves are not within the data processing department. Obviously, this definition includes people in such diverse functions as operations, sales, general management, personnel, purchasing, material control, engineering, accounting, and advertising.

Although people in these departments are not data processing professionals, many times they are involved in the processing of data. The secretary in a department who adds up a series of department costs for the manager is performing a data processing function. The manager who brings a number of reports together and summarizes them for the boss is performing a data processing function. Furthermore, these operating personnel many times are providing input or data to data processing.

Operating personnel must therefore be trained in understanding how to use the services of, communicate with, and interface with data processing. Failure to train from this perspective has caused many failures in the training of operating personnel in skills related to data processing.

As the computer became more integrated into organizational life, it was recognized that many operating managers and operating nonmanagement employees did not have an understanding of this new technology, exposing the need to provide some type of training for operating personnel. However, although the need was recognized and identified, it was defined incorrectly.

Early Training Attempts

Almost all initial attempts at training operating personnel revolved around training them to understand the basic technology and functioning of the computer. Training was given in such things as basic computer design, basic computer programming, and binary mathematics. In other words, training was given in understanding the operation and mechanics of the equipment, but there was no training in how to use the services of the equipment.

All such training was well intended, but it failed to accomplish its basic objective. Examining this kind of training closely shows that it is really training in basic computer-related skills. What have these skills to do with the needs of operating personnel? This is training needed by data processing personnel—the people who make the machine work. It is not needed by the people working with what the machine makes. This type of training has only contributed further to a misunderstanding of the computer and to the computer mystique.

After all, there is no way that a short training course can develop a skill in people who see no reason for learning it since they will not apply it on their jobs. The result is that they become more and more confused and frustrated. Operating personnel became convinced that this is a whole new technology that they could never understand.

Nevertheless, some computer manufacturers instituted programs with titles such as "Understanding the Computer for Noncomputer Executives." Some were multiweek programs in which executives of organizations purchasing computers were brought together by the computer manufacturer to learn how to use the new tool. Unfortunately, what was given was a training course in computer technology. The operating managers left such programs frustrated and confused. Rather than contributing to the successful use of the expensive machine, in many cases the course caused uncertainty as to how it could best be used to meet operating objectives.

Current Real Training Needs

Operating personnel's real need is to understand how to use data processing services. To put it another way "to assure that the people who make the machine work make what is needed come out."

Nonmanagement Employee Training Needs

Nonmanagement employees are regularly called upon to deal with the output of data processing. As a result, they need to know how to read and understand this output. They need to know how to read codes and abbreviations. They need to understand the formats of reports.

Sometimes operating personnel are called on to learn skills usually associated with computer-related personnel. For example, a typist may become a data entry clerk and learn to use a new piece of equipment. This is most often a straight manual skills training type of assignment and is handled like training for other, similar skills.

In addition, since operating personnel often provide the data which data processing personnel process, they also need to know what kind of questions to ask, when they are asked for data, so that they will know how to present these data and how to be sure that the data are accurate and error-free.

Identifying Training Needs   The first step in meeting the training needs of nonmanagement personnel is to determine their specific needs accurately. This is usually accomplished by questioning the nonmanagement employees themselves. They know best the type of reports they are asked to interpret and the type of data they are asked to furnish. They should be the primary source for identifying their training needs. However, the information obtained from them must be reviewed with appropriate data processing professionals and operating managers to ensure that there are no planned systems and procedural changes which would affect these training needs.

Many techniques are available for identifying these training needs. Fairly typical is a questionnaire used by a nonferrous metals fabricator. Annually this questionnaire is distributed to all nonmanagement employees who interact with the data processing function. This means that questionnaires are sent to nonmanagement employees receiving reports from the data processing department and to nonmanagement employees supplying data to this department. The completed questionnaires are categorized by the type of training need expressed, and a representative of the training department meets with selected employees from each group to further specify the training need. Finally, the results of the survey are reviewed with the data processing function and operating management, and specific training objectives are established to meet these identified needs.

Training Resources   Unfortunately, not much is being done to meet specifically identified nonmanagement employee training needs, and few prepared training resources are available. At this time, probably the best way to meet these training needs is through training seminars by data processing professionals under the training director's control. In these seminars data processing professionals can explain what they need from operating personnel. However, any such training must be under the training director's control to ensure that it does not degenerate into a technological course in "how the computer works" by the data processing professionals.

Data processing professionals are not the only people who have a propensity to do this. It is something that happens whenever experts begin talking about their subject area—their area of expertise. It becomes very difficult to remain at the level of someone who needs only a basic understanding, but unless this is done, operating personnel will be exposed to much they do not need to know and little which will help.

Operating Managers

Training nonmanagement operating personnel is generally concerned with how to feed data to data processing and/or what to do with the output from data processing. Training of operating managers is different, and to comprehend it fully, the relationship between data processing professionals and operating managers must be understood.

Operating Manager's Role in Data Processing   Basically, for the operating manager, the function of data processing is to take data (facts and figures) and process them into information (data in a form needed by the manager). The operating manager then combines this information with knowledge and experience to arrive at decisions, make plans, and develop controls.

Note the distinction between the operating manager and the data processing professional. The operating manager is the individual who processes information, along with knowledge and experience, into the decisions necessary to run the organization. The data processing professional processes data into the information that is used by the manager. The connecting point between the data processing professional and the operating manager is information.

Note that information is not data. Data are facts and figures—any facts and figures. They do not become information *until they are in a form needed by the manager*. This means that data processing's job is to provide the *information* needed by the manager—to process data into that information. The data processing professional is not performing this function effectively unless the output is information.

Types of Training Needs   It is the operating manager, then, who should call upon data processing to provide information. To do so, the operating manager must understand (1) how to identify information needed and (2) how to communicate those information needs to data processing. This may sound like a simple procedure, but if it is, why do experts consider that failure to carry it out properly is the reason most computers are less than 50 percent effective in achieving managerial objectives?

Identifying Information   The operating manager's first training need is to learn how to identify needed information. What is the information needed to arrive at a decision? What is the information needed to make a plan? What is the information needed to develop a control?

Such information must be stated accurately and specifically. It must be stated in a way that is understandable by anyone who reads it. Ambiguous words and jargon do not help the situation.

Therefore, when it comes to training the operating manager to use the computer, the training director should put the greatest emphasis on identifying information needs, while at the same time avoiding the trap of talking about how the computer works, what programming it needs, etc.

The operating manager has a job to do and needs information to do that job. Data processing supplies that information. Keeping this in mind, it becomes apparent that the operating manager must learn to correctly and accurately identify information needs and then state them specifically so that the information to be provided can be completely understood by data processing.

Communication   The interface between the operating manager and data processing personnel is information, and, as has already been indicated, the need to communicate between the two is essential. Since communication demands a sender and a receiver, both the data processing professional and the operating manager must develop the ability to communicate with each other successfully.

When the operating manager attempts to describe information needs to the data processing professional, he or she needs to be able to communicate in a way they both understand. In the same way, the operating manager needs to be able to understand the data processing professional when the latter attempts to provide that information. Therefore, the final element of training for operating managers is also needed by data processing professionals. Probably the training director's greatest challenge, with respect to computer-generated training needs, is teaching data processing professionals and operating managers how to communicate with each other.

Identifying Training Needs   Unless an organization believes that its operating managers are efficiently obtaining the information they need to make decisions, the training needs described above exist, and in all probability the operating managers themselves feel that service provided by data processing could be better. In such situations, the task for the training director is to assist operating managers in recognizing these training needs.

This has been accomplished in a number of ways. A New England-based metal fabrication company used the services of an outside consultant to review the use of the data processing function by operating managers. The result of this study was a report which identified the training needs. An insurance company used a different technique. Part of its annual long-range planning meeting was devoted to identifying and stating the needs of operating managers with respect to the various service departments, including data processing. This portion of the meeting was conducted by the organization's management development director, using a conference-style format. The operating managers first identified their problems and then stated solutions to those problems. Finally, these were translated into specific training and organizational development needs.

Training Resources   The American Management Associations has recently published an in-house training program, which, to the authors' knowledge, is the first such program available that attempts to teach operating managers how to identify and communicate their information needs to data processing professionals and also attempts to improve communication between data processing professionals and operating managers. Integrated into the program is an opportunity for the organization's data processing professionals to work in a seminar structure with the operating managers.

This program is working successfully, and the training director might consider a similar approach, that is, development of opportunities for data processing personnel and operating personnel to meet in a seminar or conference environment to discuss areas of similar interest and needs in a way that will improve communication and understanding. Communication can be accomplished at the nonmanagement level by mixing employee training groups from both areas. Then, through discussion—formal and informal—and the learning process that occurs, participants will gain a certain degree of appreciation for one another's problems and will also come into direct contact with one another as individuals. This should contribute greatly to further understanding.

While this last suggestion may sound elementary, the communication problems that tend to exist between line and staff departments have been so exacerbated vis-à-vis the computer that building human contacts can very often be a major step toward engendering the cooperation that is so often missing between operating managers and data processing professionals.

SUMMARY AND CONCLUSION

The computer has changed all our lives, and it will continue to do so as it becomes more widely used. This creates a tremendous challenge for the training director—a challenge that he or she can meet, thus contributing greatly to the organization's success.

To do so, the training director must first recognize data processing as another staff department—a staff department that provides a service to the organization by processing data into information that the organization needs. It provides information either as an end product or as input for decision making.

The computer adds, subtracts, multiplies, divides, prints, etc. It does this with great speed, and it generates larger quantities of figures than have ever before been available. However, it does this only to meet the needs of operating personnel. It should provide only information that is needed by the organization. It should never determine what information is needed. The determination of needed information and the making of decisions using that information are the responsibilities of operating management.

The training director should analyze the training needs of the organization. Meeting with the management of data processing will enable the training director to identify the basic data processing skill training that is needed and the areas that require continued professional development. These needs should be clearly identified and stated before the training director takes the next step of beginning to find ways to meet these training needs. Where the technological or skill needs are beyond the scope of training personnel, the training director should look to outside resources for assistance.

In other areas of general employee and management training, the training director should treat data processing personnel like any other group of employees within the organization. They need the same training in these areas, and the training director should identify those needs in the same way that needs in the rest of the organization are identified.

Operating personnel training needs with respect to data processing should likewise be well identified and stated. However, here the training director may find that operating personnel are not really sure of their needs. In such a case, the training director would do well to implement training programs that provide for an increased understanding of the services provided by data processing and of operating management's role in using those services, that is, identifying and communicating information needs.

The training director should look further for every possible opportunity possible to bring data processing personnel and operating personnel together—at all levels within the organization—to exchange information and increase understanding. Training programs requiring group discussion provide excellent opportunities to do this. Used in this way, all training can help build understanding and communication between operating management and data processing professionals—the two partners in the use of data processing to successfully achieve meaningful objectives.

BIBLIOGRAPHY

The following books provide general background information on the computer and its introduction and implementation within organizations. In addition, most of them touch on the training generated by the computer.

General Management

Bremer, R. W., and Susan Brewer (eds.): *Computers and Crisis: How Computers Are Shaping Our Future,* Association for Computer Machinery, Inc., New York, 1971.

Grindley, Kit, and John Hunkle: *The Effective Computer: A Management by Objectives Approach,* AMACOM, New York, 1974.

Hertz, David B.: *New Power for Management: Computer Systems and Management Science,* McGraw-Hill Book Company, New York, 1969.

Smith, Paul T.: *How to Live with Your Computer: A Non-Technical Guide for Managers,* American Management Association, New York, 1965.

Stewart, Rosemary: *How Computers Affect Management,* The M.I.T. Press, Cambridge, Mass., 1972.

Technical

Brandon, Richard H.: *Management Planning for Data Processing,* Brandon/System Press, Inc., New York, 1970.

Gregory, Robert H., and Richard L. Van Horns: *Business Data Processing,* Wadsworth Publishing Company, Inc., Belmont, Calif., 1965.

Krauss, Leonard L.: *Administering and Controlling the Company Data Processing Function,* Prentice-Hall, Inc., Englewood Cliffs, N.J., 1969.

Laden, H. N., and T. R. Gildersleeve: *Systems Design for Computer Applications,* John Wiley & Sons, Inc., New York, 1967.

Making the Computer Work for Management, Programmed Instruction PRIME Course, AMACOM, New York, 1967.

The Prentice Hall Editorial Staff: *Encyclopedic Dictionary of Systems and Processing,* Prentice-Hall, Inc., Englewood Cliffs, N.J., 1971.

Proceedings of the Fifth Annual Conference of the Society for Management Information Systems, Society for Management Information Systems, Chicago, 1974.

Chapter 29

Training in
the Health-Care Field

ARTHUR S. KING

Arthur S. King *is Director of Education and Training at the American Arbitration Association. Until recently, he was Director of Manpower Development for the United Hospital Fund of New York where he was responsible for researching, planning, designing, and coordinating educational, training, and counseling programs for hospitals in New York City, including UHF member institutions. Mr. King was previously Director of Training and Development at Long Island Jewish–Hillside Medical Center, New Hyde Park, New York. He has a B.A. in anthropology and political science from Queens College and an M.A. in sociology and political science from City College, New York. He is currently completing Ph.D. course work in education at New York University. He is a member of ASTD and has been active nationally on the Program Design Committee and the Publications Committee. He is past chairman of the Hospital and Health Services Special Interest Group. He is also a member of the American Society for Health Manpower Education and Training.*

The health-care industry that we are familiar with today is undergoing very significant changes. It is presently the third largest industry in the United States and is soon to be the second largest. Many of the changes it faces are based on various social, political, and legislative processes. While these processes move forward at varying paces, the education and training field within this industry must continue to develop along rapid but unique lines in accord with this unique industry.

In the past, the health-care industry was composed primarily of custodial enterprises to which ill people—the patients—were brought in the hope of curing infirmities. As times and techniques of handling patients have changed, the health-care industry has improved its delivery of service to a point where patients are almost invariably cured. In the change process, the hospital has emerged as the key institution in illness curing. The hospital has become the place where you must go if you are to take full advantage of the total potential of medical services which modern technology and science have made possible. Although the hospital is the key institution in health-care delivery, many other organizations and institutions are deeply involved in facets of health-care service. In almost every large company of every industry, there is a form of clinic or medical station which provides some type of immediate, direct health service, such as caring for those who suffer minor accidents or illnesses on the job or conducting physical examinations required for employment. In addition, because of their product or service, many industries employ medical and/or health-care professionals to consider or negate the hazardous effects of this product or service on their consumers. This is true for the manufacturing, construction, food-producing, recreation, and service industries, among others. In essence, the health-care industry has come to encompass every facet of every process dealing with living things.

Since the primary focus of this chapter is training in the direct patient-care service aspect of health-care delivery, we shall dwell specifically on the hospital and medical service facilities and their unique training requirements, as opposed to those of other facilities or industries alluded to above.

HEALTH-CARE MANPOWER

The hospital is a complex social, economic, and technological institution whose primary concern is delivering high-quality care to patients. Although the hospital or health-care institution contains vast amounts of complex machinery and equipment, the large labor force is the major component of its expense budget. Currently employing in excess of three employees per bed (the accepted unit by which the size of the institution is measured), it is a labor-intensive industry with a tremendous range and variety among the personnel working in the institution, According to current projections, the wages and salaries of the hospital's labor force account for approximately 70 percent of its operating budget. (This figure is increasing to 75 percent.)[1]

As a result of the large labor force and the nature of the service delivered, the management of the modern health-care institution has become an exceptionally challenging task—a process which is responsible for one of the hospital's unique features. This feature will be explored at another point.

Another unique feature of the delivery of health and medical care is the extent to which services must be individualized. Despite the size and specialty of the various health-care institutions, the organization and management must be combined with the technical and professional services to design a personal pattern of care for each patient. Although ways of doing so are continuously explored, health care cannot be mass-produced like the services of other major industries. Even the delivery of health-care services through organized programs such as clinics or mobile care stations must be custom-tailored for specific groups and then again for the individual patients.

Effect of Professionalism

Professionalism is another key feature underlying the delivery of health care. The health- and medical-care industry is probably one of the most professionalized industries in American society. Within the health system there are a number of professional societies and associations which either license or accredit the members of the various clinical practices. Inherent in the associational credentialing is the requirement that the constituent members undergo specialized training or experiences prior to being allowed to practice. In addition, the professionals and paraprofessionals involved in patient care must, in one way or another, relate to, or be responsible to, the architect of the medical program, namely, the physician. The physician is therefore presumed to be the most influential, authoritative, and, in many cases, imperious member of the health-care team.

Lately, with the vast emerging specialization of the other interrelated segments of the health-care delivery field, the traditionally "ordained" authority of the dominant physician has become an area of significant challenge. We note from the focus of national legislation that various approaches and mechanisms are being established to shift the thrust of the primarily physician-oriented dominance of the field to the results-oriented patient care or consumer-directed dominance. This challenge to an almost 200-year history of the physician-dominated health-care practice will probably result in a slow but revolutionary change in the delivery of health care as it is presently known,

HEALTH-SYSTEM COMPONENTS

A direct result of these unique features of health-care delivery is the complex nature of the system and its administration. Basically, despite the varying types of health institutions—hospitals, long-term care facilities, etc.—the system has three components: (1) the deliverers or providers (hospitals), (2) the users (primarily patients), and (3) the mechanisms which bring the providers and users together. The very nature of the process whereby the providers and users are brought together accounts to a great extent for the complexity of the system. Since the cost of providing health care is, in the main, financed indirectly through third-party payers, such as Medicare, Medicaid, Blue Cross, and other insurance mechanisms, intricate relationships have been established which consider and pay respect to interests and obligations within the industry. Here again, one notes that the management and administration of the health-care institution differs to a significant degree from that of the other major industries. The imposition of special requirements, standards, and practices on the part of the third-party payers is, in and of itself, an area for volumes of discourse and fortunately is inappropriate for discussion here, Nevertheless, these complexities must be realized by the individual involved in training and education in the health-care field.

The relationship of ownership patterns and the variety of institutions that exist in health-care delivery is another area for consideration. Health-care providers may exist as group practices, community mental health centers, partnership practices, teaching hospitals, extended care facilities, or special disease agencies, to mention a few. In addition to those previously mentioned, other types of health-care facilities exist which have special policies and requirements affecting everything from the type of care rendered to the methods of financing and operation. Commercial and nonprofit health insurance plans, union health plans, and local and regional health authorities provide various levels of care, each in many cases interfacing with some or all of the other elements previously mentioned. Because of these diverse programs, health-care delivery has been considered to be, in many respects, uncoordinated and fragmented. While attempts are currently under way to sort out and rearrange the order of health-care delivery, the present management process required to operate the programs and institutions remains peculiarly dissimilar to that in existence in any other industry.

The administrative situations of the health-care institutions are further complicated by the involved financial reimbursement arrangements alluded to earlier. Because payment for services delivered is derived from a variety of sources—direct payments from patients or payments from prepaid insurance plans, commercial insurance companies, the government (through Medicare and Medicaid), and Blue Cross and Blue Shield—traditional financial arrangements characteristic of other industries tend not to be the regular practice. A direct result of this is the creation of relationships and procedures requiring a high level of administrative layering or stratification. The resulting coordination between the health-care providers and the external agencies, most of which invoke a myriad of regulations and accreditation requirements, is unrivaled in any other industry. It is reasonable, therefore, to assume that some facets of the classical concepts of management and organization theory may not always be practiced or universally applied. In fact, we find many of the newer concepts of management and organizational structure at work here. These concepts call for greater emphasis on responsibility or accountability, with the influence shifting to external public accountability relationships. On the internal management side of health-care delivery, the elements of conflict resolution between administrative goals and professional prerogatives directed toward public accountability are emerging as the single most important challenge facing health-care management and administration today.

ROLE OF TRAINING

With all these special problems at all levels of the health-care delivery system, how does the trainer perform within such an intricate system? What are the issues to which the trainer, with an esoteric job preparation and experience, must address himself or herself? Like trainers in all other industries, the health-care trainer must necessarily relate to the following essentials:

- Becoming aware of, and defining, the need for improvement of some aspect of the institution's operation
- Choosing from among alternative solutions for overcoming the deficiency
- Implementing a planned program to correct the deficiency
- Following up to evaluate whether desired outcomes are achieved

Although these essentials underlie the activity of any trainer in any field, the unique qualities of the health-care delivery system put the health-care trainer in a separate class.

Legislative and Social Factors

Because of the rapid growth of all services and industries, including the health-care delivery industry in the United States, there has been a major national emphasis on the propagation of the increasingly needed numbers of skilled workers. Simultaneously, there has also been a thrust toward the elimination of poverty and the improvement of the economic and social conditions of the American people. Various legislative mandates concerning manpower development supportive of the latter condition have been enacted during the past 10 to 15 years. While most industries have taken advantage of the funding enacted through the MDTA-type programs, the specialized qualities of the health-care industry have, in many cases, precluded full and active involvement in those programs. The training and development of health professionals and paraprofessionals, with their associated licensure and credentialing requirements, has prompted the need for special legislation. The trainer involved in the health-care field quickly becomes aware of the shortcomings of the U.S. Department of Labor MDTA programming and the special requirements of the health manpower training legislation provided through the various programs of the U.S. Department of Health, Education, and Welfare Public Health Service and other branches of the federal government. Aside from the resources available through the federal government, many state and local governments have addressed themselves to the issues of manpower development, oriented primarily to the non-health-care delivery industries.

While manpower legislation has been and will be a major concern for the trainer in the health-care delivery industry, certain other bodies of law, particularly in the areas of education, human welfare, health reimbursement, occupational health and safety, labor and employment, and tax levies may be of specific interest, too.

Professional Societies   Another major factor that the trainer in health care must consider is the effect of the authoritative role of the professional associations and societies on the professional and paraprofessional employees. In the health-care delivery industry, probably more so than in any other field, professional organizations have a heavy impact on level of education, standards, and definition of service rendered—not to mention salary and benefit levels.

These associations, of which there is probably one for each of the 250 or more job categories, have served in the past and do currently serve an important role in assuring the minimum level of proficiency required of personnel in a particular job category. They do so by identifying the task, skill, and educational requirements that are necessary for the professional to perform a prescribed service. In doing this, many of the associations have worked with the professional licensing agencies of the state education departments to crystallize the prerequisites for employment and job performance. In addition to standardizing training and performance prerequisites, many of the professional associations have been successful, where it is advantageous, in establishing equivalency standards and conditions of reciprocity of training and service with other states. While the professional associations do assist in assuring a uniform level of basic training for job entry, they have also been able to operate, in many instances, as labor organizations similar to unions. Because of their ability to define educational and licensure requirements, they have also been able to stipulate wage levels, performance levels, tasks, duties, qualifications, etc. In addition, of major significance is the effect of these organizations on the type of programming that the health-care trainer may consider in resolving or removing institutional deficiencies.

Educational Institutions   As a result of the strength of these organizations, the educational enterprises (colleges and universities), which are the prime developers of paraprofessional and professional health manpower, have been affected to the point that the schools must not only design and implement didactic programs for content and background but must also involve themselves in affiliation relationships with health-care delivery institutions. These affiliations are necessary because of the mandatory clinical practice inherent in the professional and paraprofessional training programs. As the technology of health-care delivery improves, more and more training programs are moving away from the in-service training departments of the health-care facilities into the two- and four-year colleges. As the concept of licensure and/or credentialing has increased as a prerequisite for employment in the various health-care delivery occupations, the educational requirements have also increased, and vice versa. What we have here is essentially an unusual cycle which, while removing facets of manpower propagation from the industry, has also removed certain elements of control from the institution's management.

Unions   In a similar vein, labor and collective-bargaining organizations are active in the health-care field. The health-care delivery industry, during the past 15 years, has experienced considerable labor organizing. Starting in major cities in the Northeast and the Southwest, a number of unions have been formed. (In New York, for example, almost every category of health employee, including physicians, nurses, technicians, and security guards, has been organized.) The advent of unions in health care, as in other industries, has to a significant degree affected hiring practices, discipline and grievance mechanisms, promotion practices, working conditions, and wage and benefit packages. Because unionism is relatively new to the industry, response and receptivity on the part of management to the labor organizations (and vice versa) have been mixed. Although the arrival of the union at health-care institutions is in many cases beset with problems, the eventual benefits derived therefrom are soon realized. Generally, the methods of handling discipline situations become formalized, wage and benefit packages are stabilized, and communication with employees usually tends to improve. Despite the pros and cons of unions in health care, one finds it somewhat difficult to imagine the effects of a labor-management altercation on patient care. Nevertheless, such altercations have occurred and will probably continue as unionism becomes more entrenched in the industry.

To help minimize the effects of possible labor-management problems, legislation on a national level has been enacted recently to cover the health-care industry. Realizing the growth of health labor organizations on a national basis, the Taft-Hartley law was amended during the summer of 1974 to cover the health-care delivery field. At present, because of the newness of the legislation, test cases have not been heard.

From the vantage point of the health-care trainer, the whole area of labor relations and supervisory development has become one of major interest and activity. Because of the recent legislation, the trainer would do well to obtain a thorough grounding in this area to be effective in his or her job.

From another vantage point, the unions in health care, like the professional associations, have expressed a major concern about becoming involved in the education and training of their constituent employees. An example of this is the Hospital League/District 1199 Training and Upgrading Fund. These training programs, for the most part, are oriented toward prerequisite training for promotions and career mobility. Here is another key area that the health-care trainer must explore when establishing a program at his or her institution.

Third-Party Payers   Earlier, when we described the nature of financing health care, we made mention of the important role of the third-party payers. Because of the significance of their role, we feel that it warrants further discussion. The third-party payers—Blue Cross and Blue Shield, Medicare, Medicaid, and insurance carriers—require in their financial reimbursement programs certain standards of accreditation and levels of quality of care. Inherent in these accreditation standards and quality levels are issues of medical practice, accounting, specific categories of credentialed employees in certain numbers, and facility utilization requirements. Involved in the preceding practices are additional areas that the health-care trainer would do well to investigate and address. Certain training areas such as nursing in-service education and patient education, among others, have emerged as mandated areas for health-care training. These areas, because they are mandated and reimbursible, are programs which generally elicit strong support from the administrative personnel in the health-care institution.

Community Relationships   In the age of accountability, the community has become a viable force in shaping some of the activities of the health-care trainer. In almost every part of the country, local residents living near a health-care institution have become keenly aware of many issues, ranging from postnatal training for new parents to weight-control classes to stop-smoking programs open to the general public. These community programs take a lecture approach as well as a disease- or illness-screening approach. In all cases there is an ample opportunity, as well as a necessity, for the trainer in the health-care industry to be involved.

On the other hand, some communities are eager to see major changes in the way the hospital or health-care facility relates to them. Local residents have stormed the executive offices of an institution, demanding major revisions in its policy. While such occurrences may be few and far between, they must be recognized and dealt with. An area of recent concern is patients' feelings of impersonality when dealing with various nonmedical (and, in some instances, medical) personnel. A result has been a slow but increasing push toward employee-patient relations training programs.

Since hospitals and health-care facilities are generally located in or near residential communities, the institution is looked upon as a source of employment. This being the case, the health-care trainer would do well to work out relationships with community groups, and particularly schools, as a source of new employees and/or volunteers.

The technological revolution prompted by major research undertakings and the information explosion, along with the space exploration program, has considerably benefited the health-care industry. A direct result has been the major involvement of all types of industries, particularly the learning-systems divisions of major companies, in health, occupational safety, metric conversion, human relations, and executive development areas. Most of the industries which supply health facilities with everything from furniture to linens to foodstuffs to life-support systems have developed approaches to increase the efficiency, economy, and longevity of their supplies, materials, and equipment. Along with their products and/or services they offer informational and educational programs that provide operating instructions as well as background and related information. The health-care trainer can benefit considerably by contacting the suppliers of hospital and health-care equipment. Also, as equipment changes, different relationships are established with governmental agencies because of ordinances and regulatory requirements.

THE HEALTH-CARE INSTITUTION'S TRAINING DEPARTMENT

Generally, the training department in the health-care institution is a small department or a subsection of the personnel department. While the department size and reporting relationships vary with the type of institution, usually the department consists of a training director or manager, two or three staff trainers, and a secretary. Occasionally, one notes that the relationship of the training process may vary with the internal or external resources available.

Since the training department in the health-care facility may be separate from the nursing in-service education department, the activity of the former may take on different proportions. Probably the most common form of departmental setup is to have a hospital-wide training department and a separate nursing in-service education department, the latter being totally and solely responsible for training and orienting nursing personnel. The training department's relationship to the nursing in-service education department ideally should be close so that either element can share resources, thereby reinforcing the other.

In reporting relationships, the personnel director has generally been the person to whom the training director reports. In some cases, however, the training director might report to an administrator in charge of manpower and/or human resources. In the latter instance, the training director would presumably be a fullfledged department head on a par with other department heads. Ideally, the training director should be at least a department head reporting to an administrative person.

Since the training specialist is in a staff position, it is expected that he or she will plan learning experiences that will be helpful to the administrator who is in charge of the entire work force.[2] In addition, it is expected that the trainer will assist not only the administrator but also the other department heads and supervisors in achieving their goals. When the training specialist performs, he or she should be accountable for whether or not the employees are able to perform their tasks or jobs. The trainer is not and cannot be accountable for the day-to-day performance on the job. The maintenance of adequate job performance on a day-to-day basis is the role of the supervisor.

In addition, assigning the training specialist primarily to conduct classroom experience severely limits the trainer's activity. To gain the maximum benefit of the trainer's services, his or her skills as a planner, evaluator, consultant, and resource person must be utilized.

Administrative Environment

The activity of the training specialist in health care, like that of the training specialist in any other industry, is directly related to how supportive the climate is, which in turn is dependent largely upon the expectations of the administrator. If the administrator believes that performance improvements can be made through the training process and backs this belief by maintaining an open line of communication and other appropriate resources, then the required positive climate is established. An open line of communication is one which is established between the administrator and all the institution's departments, including, of course, the training department. Maintaining this kind of atmosphere makes it possible for the necessary give-and-take regarding problem identification and information sharing to occur. Issues relating to internal and external matters, expansion prospects, productivity, efficiency, economy, institutional accreditation, and reimbursement can be exposed and carefully worked out. The administrator, as well as the individual department heads, can avail himself or herself of the specialized skills and expertise of the training specialist. The role of the training specialist as an internal consultant becomes quite evident at this point.

Facilities   The provision of appropriate resources to the training specialist by the administrator would necessarily include, aside from positive climate, certain situations within which the trainer must operate. To perform in its many roles, the training department, in addition to its offices, should have an area of space set aside for classroom activity and physical work, or a workroom. Realizing that space in health-care institutions, as well as in other types of organizations, is at a premium, conference room space could be shared with other teaching or educational segments of the institution, such as specialized nursing and medical education programs for physicians in which the training specialist may not be involved. The training workroom would double as a training resource library and an audiovisual workshop, storage, and viewing room. In addition, because considerable material must be gathered and collated for training sessions and conferences, the workroom would include a worktable on which to spread out the materials so that they can be observed from a viewpoint of sequence and flow. Reproduction equipment, such as a copying machine, is exceptionally beneficial to the training specialist. If such resources are not available to the training department per se, the allocation of a sufficient budget for copying as well as printing services is essential.

Equipment   Additional resources that the training department requires include an array of audiovisual equipment. Such basic equipment as a 16mm sound movie projector (equipped with either a zoom lens or a long-throw lens for the auditorium and a short-throw lens for the small conference rooms), an overhead projector, a 35mm slide projector, a cassette recorder equipped with cuing or programming capabilities, and an automated filmstrip projector is essential. Extra bulbs for all the equipment and extension cords are required. Video tape recording and playback equipment, while not an initial essential, is exceptionally useful in the hands of a creative training specialist. Not only does video equipment assist the trainer by instantaneously capturing situations for immediate feedback and for future use, but it also can be useful for recording programs helpful to the administrative and medical staffs, among others.

If the teaching program at the institution is to be extensive, then at least a duplicate set of all the aforementioned equipment is needed. Some institutions solve this problem by establishing an audiovisual department where such equipment is loaned on a scheduled basis, maintained, and serviced (see also Chapter 43, "Audiovisuals and the Training Process").

Trainer Strategy

Aside from supportive climate and certain equipment, the trainer should be able to set up and operate his or her department in such a way that its use can be increasingly productive and helpful to the institution. Much of the thrust toward this end comes from the energy and ingenuity of the training specialist and his or her staff. Before discussing the kinds of programs and services offered by the training department, it is appropriate to comment briefly on the trainer's energy and ingenuity.

One of the chief complaints and problems of the training specialist in the health-care delivery industry, and probably of training specialists in other industries, concerns the type and level of administrative support and backing that they, the training specialists, do not receive. While a major component of this problem may be the lack of the administrative staff's recognition of the training department's use and potential, the training specialist is probably the key element in resolving this problem.

Process versus Performance   All too often one finds the trainer almost totally preoccupied with a training-process orientation instead of a results or performance orientation. Training-process orientation is characterized by the training staff's being busily concerned with the nature of outlines, techniques, films, and other things which will demonstrate the esoteric nature of their expertise. Frankly, this is not a bad approach to take in program development, but unfortunately it uses up valuable time. In many instances the effort devoted to dealing with training-process activity is not commensurate with the expected outcomes of the program. When such a situation occurs frequently, the administrator, a results- or performance-oriented person, becomes increasingly distressed about the output of the training staff. In fact, when budget revision time comes, a question that the administrator frequently raises is: To what extent has the training department demonstrated its value by reducing costs and simultaneously improving performance, productivity, and patient care on an institutional basis? Another question raised is: In what ways has the training department (generally a negative cost factor) been successful in defraying its operational costs and changing to a positive or income-producing cost center?

Administrative Support   To address itself favorably to these two questions and, in turn, automatically obtain the needed administrative support, the training department must necessarily orient itself to productivity, performance, and results. Earlier, we pointed out that there must be a close relationship between the training department and the administrator and his or her staff. This being the case, the training staff becomes aware of the issues of chief concern to the administrator in the operation of the institution. Additionally, the trainer, being alert and enterprising, is able to bring contingent knowledge concerning employee relations and performance, thereby, whenever possible, identifying areas in which the training approach is the most feasible. In many cases feasibility may mean training employees in a new area rather than hiring, instituting a new process or technique, or conducting a research project to identify or crystallize a problem or deficiency. Of course, the effort does not end there. After the performance deficiency has been identified and it appears that a training strategy is appropriate, the training specialist then presents a proposal to the administrator detailing the problem and the proposed solution. When presenting the proposed solution, the trainer clearly and logically stipulates the approach to be taken, including time, personnel, and material requirements; expenditures; and evaluation strategy. If the trainer's solution can demonstrate the benefit of removing the deficiency while proving economical from a time, personnel, and fiscal point of view, then the program would presumably be acceptable to the administrator. Assuming that the trainer and the training staff follow through effectively and completely with that program and continue to operate according to that scheme, support from the front office will never be a problem.

Trainer Qualifications

To move quickly into the results or performance orientation, the trainer should, of course, come to the job having had as much of the required preparation as possible. Although trainers cannot always meet all the requirements, they should make every effort to develop themselves adequately. Optimally, the trainer's preparation would include a background in psychology, sociology, economics, statistics, and management. In addition, the health-care trainer should have:[3]

1. A general knowledge of the health-care industry and its constituent elements
2. A knowledge of the purpose of training and its use as a management tool
3. A knowledge of management and supervisory skills, including labor relations
4. An ability to conduct learning-needs analyses, analyze jobs and operations, and perform job breakdowns for teaching purposes
5. An ability to prepare course outlines and lesson plans, write manuals, and draw from other sources in the development of the abovementioned
6. An understanding of the learning process, with particular emphasis on adult education
7. A knowledge of teaching methods, including procedures for preparing and presenting subject matter, instruction analysis, and curriculum development, and an ability to construct education and training measurement instruments to evaluate performance
8. A knowledge of various training techniques, including (but not limited to) role playing, incident process, conference leadership, group dynamics, design and use of gaming and simulation techniques, and design and utilization of audiovisual aids
9. An ability to conceptualize, utilize, and develop reinforcement and training transfer exercises
10. An ability to select and train teachers and instructors in methods of instruction, conference leadership, and use of aids
11. An ability to counsel individually with employees as well as with the administrative staff
12. An ability to plan new programs and revamp old ones
13. An ability to seek funds and prepare funding proposals
14. An ability to plan, supervise, and administer a training department, including budgeting and the maintenance of materials and a resource library
15. An ability to furnish and equip a training department and conference room with appropriate materials and equipment
16. An ability to publicize, sell, and stimulate the use of the training service; win employees', supervisors', and department heads' confidence; and assist in maintaining a high level of employee morale

These requirements may sound somewhat overwhelming, but the typically small size of the health-care training department necessitates this kind of background. Also, considering the large variety of occupations in the health-care institution, the training specialist must be able to cope with numerous unusual situations.

Internal and External Relationships

When the training specialist establishes the department, he or she must take considerable care to develop a working relationship with all other departments immediately, particularly with the nursing department (also with the nursing in-service education department, should it exist as a separate entity). The nursing department is singled out here because it naturally interfaces with the patients and all other departments every minute of every day of the year. In addition, the nursing personnel can be quite helpful in orienting the training specialist to the major issues relating to employee-patient relationships, a key feature in quality care delivery.

Once the internal relationships are established, certain external relationships should also be developed. Of paramount importance are relationships with the union (should there be one—or more), other local health-care training personnel, local and regional training personnel, health-service organizations (state hospital associations, the American Hospital Association, etc.), and local colleges and universities. As program development begins, other appropriate relationships should be explored and developed.

Another important issue that the health-care training specialist should address is the identification and statement of the role of the training department. Interface with the administrator and the various departments will be helpful in stipulating the elements of the training department's role. The following, which is adapted from an article by Neal D. Clement,[4] is an example of a statement of the role of a training department:

1. Coordinate the total education program for the hospital and represent the hospital in its liaison with other educational institutions, other hospital education programs, and other appropriate resource agencies
2. Provide, or assist in providing, indoctrination (orientation) programs for new employees
3. Support and act as coach or consultant to line and staff management personnel who desire and/or need such assistance
4. Keep informed concerning educational resources and programs on both a local and a national level and utilize and disseminate such information as appropriate
5. Provide and recommend teaching materials
6. Assess educational needs of the employees and the hospital and coordinate the employees' needs and the hospital's needs in the development of educational programs
7. Develop (and stimulate the development of) sound education programs and the total education program
8. Assist in the review and evaluation of specific education programs and of the total education program
9. Initiate and promote the development of appropriate research programs
10. Identify, evaluate, and cooperate with pertinent resource agencies (schools, universities, other hospitals and health agencies, etc.) to promote and develop programs of basic and continuing education for hospital and related health personnel
11. Help individuals, institutions, and related organizations in accomplishing for themselves appropriate functions of continuing education and complement such efforts
12. Cooperate with pertinent resource agencies in the promotion and development of health-career programs and stimulate interest in health careers

In addition, Clement also points out that the training department should promote continued efficiency and improved patient care in the hospital operation by appropriately developing and fostering the required atmosphere, programs, and work environment suitable to the changing conditions. He also mentions the need to continually upgrade the skills of the training department staff and finally to periodically review and update the role and objectives of the training department.

PROGRAM DEVELOPMENT

Program development from the health-career trainer's point of view is an interesting and rewarding, but complicated, area to deal with. The health-care trainer invariably becomes involved with the following programs as a necessary part of the department's repertoire:

1. Orientation programs—primarily for new employees
2. Skill training—including JIT and other approaches
3. Management and supervisory training—including labor relations
4. Tuition assistance and external continuing education
5. Employee-patient relations training
6. Patient education

Needs Analysis

When involved in program development in health care, as in any other industry, the training specialist must demonstrate the need for the program by identifying an actual or potential deficiency. Because the health-care institution has so many intricate contingencies related to it and because all the more than 50 to 70 departments are so closely interrelated around the individualized services required for each patient, a very careful needs analysis must be performed. In the process of performing the needs analysis, it is appropriate to assess the effects of a possible program in one department on the other departments. It is also helpful to check with other institutions and health organizations to identify possible unknowns and side effects not immediately realized. If the deficiency involves some aspect of equipment and its use or misuse, the equipment supplier might suggest a solution or an approach that another institution has developed or used. In addition, there might be some training resource material already developed that addresses the problem. Because health-care trainers' activities encompass such a vast area, the less time they spend "reinventing the wheel," the more effective they can be.

Using Resources

Wherever possible, the trainer should look for external funding resources to help defray the costs of conducting the program. If external funds or free services and materials are available, the training specialist should concentrate his or her efforts on developing refinements in the program that will maximize its success potential.

The use of government resources through individual agencies or the Veterans Administration hospitals can prove exceptionally helpful. The VA hospitals are generally quite large and filled with every kind of procedure for almost every service or activity. Tailoring of procedures from any resource, or course, is necessary to help relate the material or approach to the trainer's institution.

In certain instances information, support, and resources may be available through the labor union affiliated with the health-care institution. While some trainers or their superiors may feel uncomfortable in certain relationships with the union, this resource should be explored where appropriate. In fact, all available external community and internal resources should be searched out in program development.

As indicated earlier, the health-care industry is presently undergoing major changes. Many of the changes will be coming as a result of federal legislative activity. The recent enactment of the Professional Standards Review Organization (PSRO) and the impending national health insurance concept will have a major impact on health-care institutions and, of course, on the activity of the health-care trainer. Such situations rearrange the power structure of internal and external forces in the health-care delivery field. As a result of continuing changes, new or different areas of emphasis will develop, and the trainer must be especially alert to impacts on manpower performance needs. Other areas in which changes affecting health-care training will probably occur include quality-assurance programming, comprehensive health planning, and mandatory continuing education units for continued licensure. To address these potential changes, the health-care delivery trainer must be continually exposed to the literature in these areas. Subscriptions to relevant newsletters and journals are a must.

Finally, aside from doing extensive reading, the training specialist should develop and maintain a library of quality resources. Although many resources are cited throughout this handbook, the texts listed in the Bibliography for this chapter should be in every health-care trainer's library.

REFERENCES

1. Austin, Charles J.: "What Is Health Administration?" *Hospital Administration,* vol. 19, no. 3, Summer 1974.
2. *Training and Continuing Education: A Handbook for Health Care Institutions,* Hospital Research and Educational Trust, Chicago, 1967, chap. 1.
3. Adapted from Whitlock, Gerald, H.: "Trainer Education and Training," in Robert L. Craig and Lester R. Bittel (eds.), *Training and Development Handbook,* McGraw-Hill Book Company, New York,1967, pp. 527–555.
4. Clement, Neal D.: "A statement of Training Philosophy and Goals," *Training and Development Journal,* April 1969.

BIBLIOGRAPHY

The Audio-Visual Equipment Directory: A Guide to Current Models of Audio-Visual Equipment, National Audio Visual Association, Fairfax, Va.
    (An annual audiovisual equipment directory.)
Bennett, Addison C.: *Methods Improvement in Hospitals,* J. B. Lippincott Company, Philadelphia, 1964.
    (An organization development text for health care.)
Catalog of Federal Domestic Assistance, Executive Office of the President.
    (A catalog of all United States federal grant mechanisms and services.)
Desatnick, Robert L.: *A Concise Guide to Management Development,* American Management Association, New York, 1970.
    (A how-to guide for management development.)
Getzels, J. W.: *Learning Theory and Classroom Practice in Adult Education,* University College of Syracuse Unitersity, Syracuse, N.Y., 1956.
    (A text on learning theories.)
Haimann, Theo: *Supervisory Management for Hospitals and Related Health Facilities,* Catholic Hospital Association, St. Louis, Mo., 1965.
    (A supervisory management text for health-care institutions.)
Kemp, Jerrold E., Willard R. Card, and Ron Carraher: *Planning and Producing Audio Visual Materials,* Chandler Publishing Company, San Francisco, 1968.
    (A complete audiovisual design resource.)

Knowles, Malcolm S.: *The Modern Practice of Adult Education*, Association Press, New York, 1970.
    (A text-on adult education principles.)

Lewis, Marianna O., and Patricia Bowers (eds.): *The Foundation Directory*, Columbia University Press, New York, 1971.
    (Deals with funding resources through private foundations.)

McLarney, William J.: *Management Training: Cases and Principles*, 5th ed., Richard D. Irwin, Inc., Homewood, Ill., 1970.
    (Management cases and their analyses.)

Mager, Robert F.: *Preparing Instructional Objectives*, Fearon Publishers, Inc., Palo Alto, Calif., 1962.
    (A text on writing objectives.)

Making the Most of Training Opportunities, American Management Association Bulletin no, 73, New York, 1965.
    (A bulletin on training techniques.)

Murphey, Robert W. Howard: *Where to Look It Up*, McGraw-Hill Book Company, New York, 1950.
    (A resource for resources.)

Patten, Thomas H.: *Manpower Planning and the Development of Human Resources*, John Wiley & Sons, Inc., New York, 1971.
    (A text on manpower development principles.)

Pfeiffer, J. William, and John E. Jones: *Structural Experiences for Human Relations Training*, University Associates Press, Iowa City, Iowa, 1969. vols. 1–4.
    (An array of training techniques and exercises.)

Tracey, William R.: *Evaluating Training and Development Systems*, American Management Association, New York, 1968.
    (A text on evaluation techniques.)

Tracey, William R.: *Designing Training and Development Systems*, American Management Association, New York, 1971.
    (An all-around training resource.)

Training and Continuing Education: A Handbook for Health Care Institutions, Hospital Research and Educational Trust, Chicago, 1970.
    (An all-around health-care training text.)

U.S. Civil Service Commission: *Assessing and Reporting Training Needs and Progress*, Personnel Methods Series no. 3, Government Printing Office, Washington, 1956.
    (Deals with training-needs assessment techniques.) .

Chapter **30**

Training in International Cultures

ROBERT H. WILSON

Robert H. Wilson, *a recently retired foreign service technical assistance officer, served as Vocational Education Adviser, Chief Education Officer and Director, Human Resources Development in the U.S. Agency for International Development Missions in Bolivia, Brazil, and Venezuela, and also as International Training Adviser and Chief of Planning and Evaluation, Office of Labor Affairs, AID, Washington. He organized and administered formal and nonformal international training programs in cooperation with the International Labor Organization, the Organization of American States, the Economic Commission for Africa, and private-sector organizations. He was instrumental in the USAID/ASTD program, which resulted in the organization of the International Federation of Training and Development Organizations. Mr. Wilson obtained a B.A. in vocational education and an M.A. in education administration while working as an apprentice, mechanic, and equipment maintenance supervisor in private industry and as a teacher, supervisor, and director of vocational training at the city, state, and national levels.*

ACKNOWLEDGMENT: The author wishes to acknowledge the assistance of Richard McGuerty, an international training expert, in the preparation of material for this chapter.

The purpose of this chapter is to explore those cultural and environmental factors which can influence training programs at the international level. This international training context includes training programs conducted by multinational organizations, (manufacturers, oil companies, banks, construction firms, etc.) and technical assistance programs sponsored by universities, foundations, and government agencies. The chapter is directed primarily to those trainers who are responsible for the design and implementation of training programs in countries other than their native countries.

FACTORS IN INTERNATIONAL TRAINING

Training professionals are aware that one difficulty in training is creating an environment or climate in which learning can take place effectively. Further, an ability to identify the factors which control the environment and to deal with them constructively is the mark of a professional trainer. The experience of the United States technical assistance program has shown that many trainers who are successful in the United States have difficulty in an international environment. The orverriding cause of this failure is the inability to adapt to new learning environments. Primarily for this reason, most international assignment contracts have a probationary clause, often for two years. Those who succeed are those who identify the new factors, evaluate their influence, and take appropriate action. This chapter will provide some guidelines for training personnel to use in dealing with these factors.

The following are some of the major factors to consider in planning international training programs:

Learning habits
Vocabulary, language, and terminology
Labor laws and regulations
Human behavior and attitudinal influences
The structure of educational and training systems
Funding and administrative arrangements

Learning Habits

The individual's learning habits result chiefly from school and work experience. They may differ considerably from country to country and even between communities within a country. Learning-habit differences are the result of formal educational philsophy, teaching practices, different reading materials, parental influence, etc.

Knowledge of learning habits is essential when planning any training program. The challenge to the international trainer becomes more complex, particularly in developing countries. Often workers have been exposed to a wide variety of education and training by such agencies as religious organizations, foreign governments (through their technical assistance programs), foreign private corporations, the United Nations, and other international and regional organizations. These wide variations are reflected in indigenous learning habits.

Vocabulary, Language, and Terminology

The international trainer must be sensitive to the noninterchangeability of many technical terms. In South America, until only recently, there were no generally accepted words for commonly used English terms such as "manpower," "vocational guidance," "automobile tires," "high school," and "training." In each of four different Spanish-speaking countries, training was expressed as *adiestramiento, capacitacion, formacion,* and *entrenamiento.* A series of conferences was necessary to arrive at universal agreement on terminology and a glossary to use in the preparation of training manuals, correspondence courses, etc., for the region.

As another example, there are no Arabic words for "metal tubing" or "jet propulsion." Translation of instructional materials, particularly in the nonformal areas, often becomes difficult when new words and phrases must be formulated to accommodate both good language usage and the functional needs of the training program. The international trainer will often encounter this problem when attempting to use home-office or off-the-shelf instructional materials. The International Labor Office (ILO) has published a series of glossaries for technical and general vocational education and training in French, English, Spanish, and some Asian languages.

A significant constraint on training and development internationally is the low universality of instructional materials, which indicates a need for serious research and planning in this area.

Labor Union Roles

Labor unions in the more industrialized countries have often become quite involved in training workers. This is logical; not only are workers the consumers of training, but also their living standards and general welfare tend to be directly related to the skills and knowledge they develop. Further, particularly in the skilled occupations, most training is conducted on the job and in off-the-job skill improvement programs with skilled workers as instructors. Thus an increasing number of work contracts with training clauses concerning wages, hours of work, length and scope of programs, and ratio of trainees to skilled workers has resulted from national legislation and labor-management bargaining.

Generally, employers are interested in a surplus of trained workers, while labor organizations prefer a dearth. An effective solution to this problem often is joint training committees to formulate training policy and operating procedure. International trainers will also find wide variations in labor organizations, interest in training and in their ability to participate in it. In the more developed countries, labor unions, particularly craft-type organizations, have a long tradition of training. In fact, some labor unions conduct programs for teaching apprentices and upgrading skills at their own expense, while others cosponsor programs with employers as well as formal or nonformal training institutions.

Labor organizations in the less industrialized countries lean more to the vertical, or noncraft, type and have shown less interest in cosponsoring training. This situation is changing rapidly as a result of programs for labor union leadership training. In the past five years, either by decree or by legislation, most Latin American countries have made joint participation of workers and employers mandatory in the design and conduct of vocational training.

Labor Laws and Regulations

Two categories of labor laws and regulations are of concern to the international trainer: (1) those pertaining to supervisory and administrative responsibilities which may be included in management training programs and (2) those relating to apprenticeship or preemployment training for young adults and on-the-job and off-the-job skill upgrading. Some items usually regulated by a ministry of labor are:

- Apprentice selection and certification procedures
- Work permits for trainees
- Work permits for nonnationals
- Safety regulations for trainees (minors)
- Pay scales for in-service trainees
- Worker seniority: upgrading, layoff, retirement, tenure, reemployment rights
- Equal pay and work opportunities for women and minorities
- Skill achievement examinations, occupational classification, and related pay scales
- Pay bonuses, gratuities, and family planning incentives and disincentives
- Social security, medical and clinical services, housing, and transportation
- Welfare of women and children laborers
- Labor union affiliation

Most European countries and countries formerly under their control have some form of mandatory standardized skills and achievement testing system to qualify workers for occupational status and related pay scales. Usually the ministry of labor establishes the standards and administers tests. The trainer should be aware of the standards and testing requirements when designing training courses for occupations covered by such regulations.

When vocational training does not meet realistic worker performance requirements, ministries of labor, particularly in Latin American countries, often coordinate training activities between employing establishments and training institutions. Labor ministries have a definite role in the development and utilization of the work force, and trainers should establish cooperative relations with appropriate ministry representatives.

Human Behavior and Attitudinal Influences

As mentioned previously, economic and human resource development policies have generally been presumed to be in conflict. Historically, production establishments resort to worker behavior controls to produce quality goods and services at an optimum level. Characteristics of these behavior controls can be evaluated as being indicative of the extent to which the establishment has progressed from the economic to the human resource philosophy or, perhaps, the extent to which it has been able to integrate the two philosophies for mutual benefit.

Getting useful work accomplished through human effort requires effective management of human behavior. The purpose of developing appropriate controls is to create an environment or "climate" that is conducive to production. For the lack of better terminology and to meet the need for a readily understood and usable vehicle for accommodating change, the word "subculture" is used here to denote employee grouping within an employing establishment. Some people may refer to the subculture as a work-oriented culture, but regardless of what it is called, it is made up of identifiable factors that can influence the success or failure of production. Since this action is possible, the training professional in the role of a behavior change agent can approach a humanistic production problem more scientifically.

Dr. Phillip Harris, in his manual *Organizational Dynamics,* identified some of the characteristics of cultures and subcultures as follows:[1]

- Language and communication
- Dress and appearance
- Food and feeding habits
- Time and time consciousness
- Rewards and recognition
- Relationships
- Values and standards

In every national culture there are many subcultures whose members may share common traits with the national group but have certain behavior characteristics that distinguish them from members of another group. For example, members of sex groups; racial, ethnic, or tribal groups; and labor unions or employer organizations may have some similar traits nationally or regionally, but they may have sets of quite different values, learning habits or work attitudes resulting from local environmental influences.

International trainers will be in contact with workers in a variety of environmental settings and must be sensitive to a wide range of environmental factors that can influence the success or failure of training programs. Basic techniques found to be effective in domestic training and development generally will also work at the international level. The challenge for international trainers is to use their behavioral science knowledge and skills to cope with cultural influences which affect human performance (see also Chapter 17, "Group Norms: Their Influence on Training Effectiveness").

Some humanistic relationships which can be sources of potential conflict and which require specialized understanding and action to achieve teamwork and mutual benefit are management-worker, worker-worker, union-management, union-worker, and employing establishment/community.

Structure of Educational and Training Systems

Trainers in a foreign country will find it useful to develop a working knowledge of both the formal and nonformal educational and training systems. In most coun-

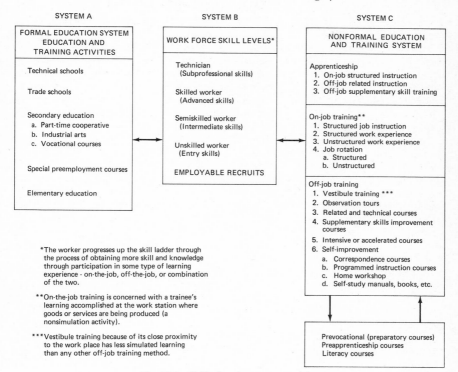

Fig. 30-1   Skills development model.

tries, programs for training the work force at the skilled and semiskilled levels vary widely.

A balanced program for work-force development is usually made up of two distinctly different establishments. The "formal" educational or primary learning establishment is concerned with the production of learning and is engaged primarily in providing situations in which learning can take place. The other establishment is concerned primarily with producing goods and services and is only secondarily concerned with producing learning, and then normally only when additional knowledge and skills are needed to support a desired level or quality of production. The latter establishment is the end consumer of the learning establishment's products, and the degree to which it must resort to educating and training—its secondary activity—depends to a large extent on how well the primary learning establishment gears its output to the input needs of the production establishment (see Fig. 30-1).

In virtually all countries, the diversity and multiplicity of jobs and the ever-changing characteristics of the work force make it essential that training be closely coordinated with realistic worker performance requirements. And since the formal educational establishment cannot effectively arrange its program to meet total job performance requirements, job training and retraining have become an integral function of the establishment responsible for the production of goods or services.

This is no indictment of formal education, except where it tries unsuccessfully to deviate from development of basic capability or fails to recognize and provide support for nonformal training and development systems. Preemployment education and training by the formal educational establishment have a different set of goals and objectives from those of job performance education and training for employed adults.

In France and Japan, all vocational training below the technical level is administered by the ministry of labor, while the ministry of education is responsible for occupational training in the technical and professional areas. Generally in Europe, ministries of labor, because of their relation to the worker through enforcement of labor laws, are responsible, in cooperation with employers and labor organizations, for the training of workers. Often the formal vocational education systems are administered by the ministry of education.

In the lesser-developed countries, particularly in Latin America, the International Labor Organization has been very influential in structuring nonformal education and training systems. Since the ILO works with ministries of labor and not with ministries of education, most formal worker training systems either are administered by the ministries of labor or are semiautonomous organizations administered by national councils composed of government, employers, and labor union officials.[2]

Increasingly, society demands that formal education be more suited to the individual's needs for working and living in the economic and social environment of the future. Young people tend to perceive most of their learning as being for later use in life; their time perspective is one of postponed application. Adults, on the other hand, particularly employed persons, are engaged in learning largely in response to pressures they feel from current life problems. They regard learning as a process of improving their ability to deal with problems that confront them now or in the immediate future.

This situation is only one of the factors, but a very important one, that have influenced the structuring of two distinct patterns or systems for educating and training the work force.

Funding and Administrative Arrangements.

In the process of economic development, various systems for training the work force have been developed. A significant consideration is funding, and a variety of arrangements have been devised for the collection and use of funds for skill and knowledge training of the work force.

The general concept in most countries is that education and training provided by the formal educational system are financed by public money. In the nonformal system, however, the employing establishment generally is responsible for financing work-related training. In some instances, though, depending on manpower development priorities, public money is used to subsidize worker training, particularly preemployment training and retraining for unemployed workers. Another general rule is that public money is used for training government employees, the military, physicians, teachers, and others who provide a professional or semiprofessional service to the public, while private-sector money supports training for workers producing goods or services which the consumer purchases. The cost of training is thus reflected in the selling price of the goods and services.

Latin America Structure   Most Latin American countries have generally followed the pattern set by Brazil which formalized its system for training the work force in 1942. Servicio Nacional Apprentendizacem Industrial (SENAI), an autonomous nonformal educational institution consisting of a national network of 42 centers, is supported by a 2 percent payroll tax levied on all nongovernment employing establishments with 25 or more employees. By law, employers are required to maintain a designated percentage of employees in a training status. National and regional councils with tripartite representation—labor, employers, and government—establish policy and administrative procedures for the program. A 1959 amendment to the law reduced the tax to 0.02 percent for establishments which organized their own training programs in accordance with SENAI guidelines.

Instituto Nacional de Cooperacion Educativo (INCE), a Venezuelan semiautonomous institution established in 1960, is patterned after SENAI except that the vice president must be a member of organized labor, and funds are directly collected and disbursed by INCE. Administrative arrangements for collection of funds and implementation of programs vary between each of the 20 Latin American national manpower training institutions.[3]

African Structure   Nigeria, the first African country to institutionalize its nonformal system by forming the Industrial Training Fund (ITF), followed the pattern of INCE for collection and disbursement of funds, tripartite representation on the National Council, and reimbursement up to 60 percent to employers for the cost of training programs. However, there is one significant difference: ITF does not operate vocational training schools. Its basic policy is to help employer establishments organize and operate their own training programs and to cooperate with existing educational institutions in improving and expanding their training services and contracting for training services not currently available.

In general, the African nonformal training systems seem to be less legalistic and less competitive with the formal system and are patterned more like the United Kingdom's Industrial Training System than the Latin American versions.

Advanced Countries   The United Kingdom's 1964 Industrial Training Act, which is administered by the Ministry of Labor, provides for Industrial Training Boards (such as Engineering, Construction, Textile, etc.). The boards determine the tax levy for their respective fields, administer training programs carried out in government centers, and set standards for on-the-job training by employers.

A general system of government subsidy is used in Belgium, Italy, Japan, the Netherlands, Norway, Sweden, and Switzerland; this system reimburses employers for training expenses and offers free training in public or private training centers. In West Germany and Austria, industry chambers bear the administrative and organizational cost of training from funds collected from employers under a levy imposed on the establishment's payroll.[4]

For information on African countries, contact the Division of Manpower and Training, Economic Commission of Africa, Addis Ababa, Ethiopia. For information on Latin American countries, contact CINTERFOR (ILO), Montevideo, Uruguay. For information on European and Asian countries, contact the Division of Vocational Training, International Labor Organization, Geneva, Switzerland.

NATIONAL MANPOWER PLANNING

Manpower Policies Affect Training

Manpower planning by employing establishments is undergoing change and warrants increasing attention. Formerly, the Training Within Industry job analyses–training timetable approach, which is familiar to trainers, was sufficient. But as management becomes more conscious of its social responsibility as related to the welfare of the worker, the role of the trainer as a change agent and expert on human resource development becomes more significant. Internationally, the role becomes even more comprehensive, complex, and challenging.

The lesser-developed nations particularly, and from necessity, are doing more manpower planning. In the past 10 years more than 500 economists, educators, and related professionals from 92 countries have received training in manpower planning at the AID's International Manpower Institute. Most of these people are involved in developing manpower programs in their respective countries and have a direct influence on national manpower development and utilization.

Employing establishments use the knowledge and skills of the work force to produce goods and services. Thus they are directly affected by manpower programs of national agencies. This is especially true in countries with such problems as:

- Introduction of modern production technology
- Change from a capital-intensive to a more labor-intensive development policy
- Reform of formal education and increasing emphasis on nonformal employer-supported training systems
- Reduction in numbers of expatriate workers, with indigenous job creation for nationals

Scope of National Manpower Planning

Manpower planning in most countries is becoming more comprehensive and complex and goes further than establishing needs. It provides a strategy for integrating education, training, health services, and monetary considerations for both economic and social development.

Manpower planning is in a transition period, not only between countries, but also within many national planning agencies. This situation, which results from conflicting development policies for economic and human resources, is well described by Dr. Fred Harbison in his book entitled *Human Resources as the Wealth of Nations*.[5] He says that economic policy and planning are concerned centrally with such things as rate of economic growth, income distribution, balance of payments, material capital accumulation, consumption, and investment and that the human element is evaluated in terms of its contribution to achievement of economic goals. In contrast, the human resource policy and planning activity is concerned with such goals for development as the maximum utilization of human beings in productive activities and the fullest development of the skills, knowledge, and capacities of the work force. Although these two policies are generally presumed to be in conflict, there is a growing belief among national planners that integration of them is the key to more effective development. Thus the problem facing national planners is how and to what extent the two policies can be integrated effectively and economically.

Training Professional's Role

Changes in development policy or manpower planning at national or community levels can create problems that are far-reaching, abrupt, and upsetting to employing establishments' training. Thus it is essential that the training manager understand manpower planning activities and develop an appropriate plan of action. One effective approach to training people individually or as representatives of professional training organizations is to have them act as consultants or advisers in the planning and development of manpower programs.

TECHNICAL ASSISTANCE FOR HUMAN RESOURCE DEVELOPMENT

Influences on the Work Force

In most countries, development of the work force is influenced by external as well as internal factors. One significant external force during the past 25 years has been technical assistance provided by another country, a foreign company or university, or organizations such as the United Nations and the Organization of American States (OAS).

Work-force characteristics are favorably influenced by such assistance programs. In São Paulo, Brazil, a staff of 55 United States and Brazilian personnel trained over 26,000 industrial supervisors and foremen; about 3,000 specialists; and 500 industrial trainers, supervisors, and directors, as well as an equal number of industrial safety supervisors and coordinators.

At the peak of the technical assistance program, 81 countries in Asia, Latin America, and Africa were involved in cooperative programs with one or more of the aid donor organizations. Hundreds of vocational schools were built, and thousands of people were being trained in these schools and abroad in cooperating countries. For example, a total of 106,538 people were trained in the United States between 1944 and 1970. About 10,000 of these participants were enrolled in programs in the industrial vocational training field. Vocational training schools provided by the governments of countries such as the United States, the United Kingdom, Japan, Germany, France, and Spain usually are equipped with machinery, instructional materials, and instructors from the aid donor country. Further, many equipment manufacturers are motivated to make gifts of training equipment to local training institutions with the expectation that when trainees become members of the work force, they will use their influence to purchase familiar equipment.

Changing Roles in Technical Assistance

Many developing countries are now able to establish their own development priorities and have a strong and understandable determination to do so. Competent indigenous professionals and technicians have been trained to help their countries help themselves. The policies they pursue will be the most important determinant of their success or failure. What other industrial countries do will have only a secondary influence on the outcomes.

Many industrialized countries, some of which were former recipients of technical assistance, have steadily expanded their own development programs. The trend is to work more in consortia with the United Nations family to provide assistance to a decreasing number of developing countries. In this respect, the United Nations organizations, foundations, and multinationally supported banking institutions are increasing their activites and assuming a larger share of the technical assistance load, thus decreasing the need for binational assistance programs.

SUMMARY

Some basic concepts in the area of international training are:

- The fundamentals for the design of management of work-force training are basically the same from country to country.
- The most difficult problem facing the international trainer is adjusting to the cultural variations of the people and establishing a climate conducive to the learning process.

- Instructional materials that relate to the environmental and cultural conditions are essential.
- Educational and training customs and practices and labor union and employer relationships are important factors in designing work-force training.
- A knowledge of the degree of social recognition for the dignity and welfare of the worker can be most helpful.

The following is a listing of some specific environmental conditions that can influence work-force training. Determine whether and to what extent:

- Public or private training institutions for upgrading the skills of the work force are available
- Workers are required by legislation to be members of a labor organization
- Workers in an employing establishment have an opportunity to choose the labor organization that will represent them
- Labor unions are organized by craft (horizontal structure) or by types of industry (vertical structure)
- Labor unions normally participate in development and operation of training activities and in what manner
- Workers (not through a formal organization) normally participate in the development and operation of training activities and in what manner
- Workers and/or their organizations are required by law to participate in the planning, organization, and operation of training programs
- National family planning programs provide incentives or disincentives for control of population growth
- Employing establishments are required to cooperate in population and family planning programs
- Employing establishments are required by law to provide training for workers
- Labor regulations affect wages, hours, working conditions, numbers of trainees and apprentices, classifications, restrictions according to age or sex, selection, and upgrading of workers by on-the-job and off-the-job training
- Records and reports are required and by whom
- Maximum effort is being made to identify and make use of existing local expertise in the design, organization, and operation of training programs
- Imported or other off-the-shelf programs and instructional materials are being adapted for local vocabulary and other cultural differences
- Local or national organizations such as safety councils, chambers of commerce, employer groups, labor unions, women's societies, and religious and professional societies conduct, support, or participate in education and training
- The status of women in the development process and the establishment of equal pay and work opportunities are matters of official policy
- Labor-intensive development takes priority over capital-intensive development in national economic development planning
- Indigenization of the work force employed in multinational organizations is required by official policy

Professional trainers should be well acquainted with economic and social trends that can influence employment and production activities within their organization. Because of frequent changes in the political, economic, and social characteristics of countries, this statement is especially significant to trainers employed by multinational organizations.

The following is a listing of several recognizable trends in international manpower development:

- Worldwide there is more concern about human resource problems—unemployment, underemployment, job creation, income distribution, social security, and adequate working conditions.
- The movement by national and international agencies to improve the status of women and integrate them into the development process creates a need for updating training programs for supervisors and managers who must find ways and means to integrate more women into a broader scope of work activities.
- The growing concern that the traditional formal educational system is too expensive and not flexible enough to accommodate the changing characteristics of the work force has resulted in a significant movement toward more nonformal education and training, particularly at the workplace.
- The worldwide population control and family planning movement is having a significant impact on the role of training professionals, primarily because national population legislation and policies affect not only the characteristics of the work force as the producer of goods and services but also personnel policies and practices pertaining to employment and training.[6]
- A worldwide activity dedicated to the development and improvement of professional training organizations has resulted in a network of national and regional training organizations affiliated with the International Federation of Training and Development Organizations (IFTDO). This organization can make an important contribution to training professionals by providing a service for training trainers, establishing standards for professional training courses and institutions, sponsoring research, and providing for exchange of methods and materials.[7]

CONCLUSION

A well-managed training program is a basic element of a foreign enterprise. It is one of the best and most readily recognized demonstrations of the enterprise's willingness and desire to develop local employees. An effective training program can serve two functions: develop an effective work force and establish a favorable relationship with the local community.

Local societies look with favor on a foreign enterprise when it provides employment for local workers, when the jobs entail responsibility and offer pay comparable to those of jobs in other societies, and when the enterprise reduces the number of foreign specialists it employs as quickly as possible.

A. K. Alford, Jr., in his presentation at the First International Conference of Multinational Organization Training Directors, said that the selection of foreign national trainers is a most critical part of a program.[8] He also said that from his experience, foreign national trainers must be of an even higher caliber and have greater potential than their domestic counterparts. He told the group that the basis for his statement was the fact that international trainers not only must learn all that domestic trainers have to know but also must do so in a second language, learning from people who live in another culture and have different customs, values, and thought patterns. Not only must international trainers translate materials, programs, and the like, but they must also transpose all that they have learned to a new total environment and gain acceptance in the native culture.

REFERENCES

1. Harris, Phillip R.: *Organizational Dynamics: An Instructor's Manual for Human Resources Specialists,* Management and Organizational Development, Inc., La Jolla, Calif., 1970.

2. For more detailed information, see *On-Job Training and Wage Hour Standards in Foreign Countries,* U.S. Department of Labor Bulletin no. 1610, 1968.
3. Belcher, Forrest, R. H. Wilson, and James Pearson: *A Manual on Forming National Training and Development Organizations,* American Society for Training and Development, Madison, Wis., 1971.
4. For additional information about administrative arrangements for funding training, see *Training Methods for Skills Acquisition,* American Society for Training and Development, Madison, Wis., chap. 9.
5. Harbison, Frederick H.: *Human Resources as the Wealth of Nations,* Oxford University Press, New York, 1973.
6. Report and studies—family planning and population control:
    (a) *Asian Symposium on Labour and Population Policies.* Sponsored by ECAFE, 1969.
    (b) *Asian Employers' Seminar on Population and Family Planning.* Sponsored by ILO, 1971.
    (c) *Asian Study of Family Planning Services in Industry.* Sponsored by ILO, 1970.
    (d) *Asian Seminar on Trade Unions, Workers' Education and Population Questions.* Sponsored by ILO, 1973.
    (e) *Family Planning in Industry: Some Company Profiles.* Sponsored by FICCI, Federation House, 1972.
7. IFTDO Secretariat: *Conference Checklist and Organizational Manual,* American Society for Training and Development, Madison, Wis., 1974.
8. *Report of International Conference Multinational Organization Training Directors,* American Society for Training and Development, Madison, Wis., 1973.

Organizations and Addresses

IFTDO—International Federation of Training and Development Organizations, PO Box 5307, Madison, Wis. 53705
ECAFE—Economic Commission for Asia and the Far East, Bangkok, Thailand
ILO—International Labor Office, Ch 1211, Geneva, Switzerland
FICCI—Federation of India Chamber of Commerce and Industry, Federation House, New Delhi, India

BIBLIOGRAPHY

The following materials provide basic information on international manpower development and utilization and are suggested reading for the international trainer.

Belcher, Forest, R. H. Wilson, and James Pearson: *A Manual on Forming National Training and Development Organizations,* American Society for Training and Development, Madison, Wis., 1971.
   (Practical steps and guidelines for organizing a training society are suggested. A national training society can solicit national and community support for human resource development. For the trainer, it can provide programs, information, bibliographies, and idea exchange. For the professional, it can provide standards and establish a code of ethics. A training society can be of immense value in the total educational system of a nation as it moves toward more effective use of its human resources. Available in English, French, and Spanish.)
Brennan, Ted, and Frank Hodgson: *Overseas Management,* McGraw-Hill Book Company, 1965.
   (This book deals with management's understanding of special problems in applying modern management concepts in situations in which a substantial portion of the work force has very little appreciation of concepts of advanced technology, efficiency, and methods of cost control.)
Educational Technology and the Developing Countries, Information Center on Instructional Technology, Washington, 1972.
   (Ideas about educational development, technology, change, and improvement of learning in developing countries are examined. All countries of the world are confronted by a crisis in education. This crisis involves enrollment, costs, shortage of teachers, manage-

ment problems, changing curricula, and teaching methods. Available in English, French, and Spanish.)

Harbison, Frederick H.: *Human Resources as the Wealth of Nations,* Oxford University Press, New York, 1973.

(Presents an approach to national development based upon the simple idea that human resources are the ultimate basis of the wealth of nations. From this perspective, the goals of development are the maximum possible utilization of human beings in productive activity and the fullest possible development of the skills, knowledge, and capacities of the labor force.)

Harris, Phillip R.: *Organizational Dynamics: An Instructor's Manual for Human Resources Specialists,* Management and Organizational Development, Inc., La Jolla, Calif., 1973.

(A manual complete with subject matter and supporting charts, work assignment topics, illustrations, and evaluative material required to train trainers concerned with cross-cultural human behavior-modification objectives.)

Hilaski, Harvey: *On-Job Training and Wage Hour Standards in Foreign Countries,* U.S. Department of Labor, Bureau of Labor Statistics, 1968.

(A report of a study about on-the-job training provided by employers and supported by governments in 16 countries. It discusses classroom instruction as related to on-the-job training and also covers labor legislation, wages, ages for workers, and funding schemes.)

How to Make an Inventory of High-Level Skilled Manpower in Developing Countries, U.S. Department of Labor, Bureau of Labor Statistics, Washington, 1968.

(This manual is a composite of methods and techniques used in determining high-level skilled manpower requirements in several industrialized countries. Standard occupational classifications are defined and used in the charts, tables, and sample questionnaires suggested for use in making skilled manpower studies for employing establishments and government agencies.)

IFTDO Secretariat: *Conference Checklist and Organizational Manual,* American Society for Training and Development, Madison, Wis., 1974.

(A manual for organizing national and regional conferences. It presents guidelines, statements of goals, organizational procedures, funding sources, staffing, program outlines, etc.)

Journal of European Training, MCB (European Training) Limited, Yorkshire, England.

(This periodical, started in 1970, provides professional training for managers with ideas and information on major training issues.)

Kleiner, Joseph: *Establishing a Correspondence Teaching System,* USAID/Venezuela, Office of Labor Affairs, Agency for International Development, Washington, 1965.

(Covers basic theory, course assignments, and correspondence teaching systems. Details on lessons, assignments, student help, and examination methods are given. Available in Spanish, French, and English.)

Laird, Dugan: *Training Methods for Skills Acquisitions,* American Society for Training and Development, Madison, Wis., 1972.

(Provides information about domestic and international training systems. Guidelines for planners in the design of appropriate training systems are given, and such methods as on-the-job, apprenticeship, correspondence, formal, and nonformal systems are covered. Available in English, French, and Spanish.)

Non-Formal Education Bibliography, Agency for International Development, Bureau for Technical Education, Washington, 1973.

(A 70-page annotated bibliography of 195 publications which reflects a large measure of the experience accumulated on nonformal education and training systems.)

Polcyn, Kenneth A.: *An Educator's Guide to Communication Satellite Technology,* Information Center on Instructional Technology, Washington, 1973.

(Ways in which communication satellites have opened extraordinary possibilities for worldwide spread and enrichment of human learning are demonstrated. Present educational systems will have to abandon the traditional practices in favor of more effective new technologies.)

Proceedings of International Federation of Training and Development Organizations International Conferences, Development Digest, Los Angeles, Calif.

(Audio tape cassettes of speaker presentations and panel discussions for the IFTDO conferences in Geneva. (1972) and Bath (1973).

Proceedings of International Manpower Institute on Manpower Development Program for the Seventies, U.S. Department of Labor, Washington, 1971.

(This annual seminar featured daily lectures and discussions on broad economic, demographic, political, and social questions, with particular emphasis on the relationship of these characteristics to the building of an effective manpower program. Questions of broad manpower policies and manpower development planning were considered, and more specific matters of development implementation were discussed.)

Report of Accelerated Vocational Training for Adults, Organization for Economic Cooperation and Development, Paris, 1965.

(A comparative study of the methods and areas of accelerated vocational training for adults in France, Great Britain, The Netherlands and Belgium.)

Schwartz, Paul A., and Robert E. Krug: *Ability Testing in Developing Countries,* American Institute for Research, Washington, 1971.

(Presents techniques of aptitude testing for application in cultures in which standard ability tests are not effective. The applications of these techniques to human resource development programs in developing countries is covered. The handbook serves as a comprehensive overview of the technical and organizational issues that require resolution in programs of testing reform in a developing country.)

Sheffield, James R., and Victor P. Diejomaals: *Non-Formal Education in Africa Development,* African-American Institute, New York, 1972.

(An in-depth study of 15 African countries as related to nonformal or out-of-school education-apprenticeship systems, in-service training activities, and on-the-job training methods. Part I treats preemployment activities; part II, on-the-job and skill upgrading training; part III, training programs for rural youth; and part IV, rural adult training.)

Teaching and Training Methods for Management Development Manual, International Labor Office, Management Development Branch, Geneva, 1972.

(A comprehensive introductory-level manual on teaching and training methods for management development prepared for international use. It is presented in the form of a five-day introductory course for the training of management trainers and includes case studies, handouts, checklists, and charts.)

Wilson, R. H.: *Technical Assistance Project with the Venezuelan National Institute of Cooperative Education (INCE),* Office of Labor Affairs, Agency for International Development, Washington, 1967.

(INCE, a nonformal educational institution, contributes to the accelerated development of human resources in Venezuela. It designs, organizes, and conducts on-the-job and off-the-job training programs from literacy to executive levels under a payroll tax deduction system in the private sector.)

Wilson, R. H.: *Implementation of Training for the Maintenance Work Force,* Office of Labor Affairs, Agency for International Development, Washington, 1971.

(A publication of materials used in seminars about training plant maintenance workers, conducted in Kuala Lumpur, Bangkok, and Singapore. It covers assessing training requirements, developing a training plan, and choosing training methods and on-the-job training versus institutional training. The goal of seminars conducted by the U.S. Department of Commerce was to improve the capability of plant engineers, maintenance supervisors, and trainers in managing training programs for maintenance personnel.)

Chapter 31

Communications Training

THOMAS E. ANASTASI, JR.

Thomas E. Anastasi, Jr., *has been involved in communications training for over 15 years. He has conducted programs for clients throughout the United States and Canada and in Iran. In 1969 he began the Communication Training Group in Medfield, Massachusetts, which provides training and consulting services in all aspects of written, oral, and organizational communication. He was Director of the United States Civil Service Commission's Communication Training Institute in Boston, Assistant Professor of Adult Education at Northeastern University, and Management Development Specialist with Bethlehem Steel. Mr. Anastasi has published widely. His books include* How to Manage Your Reading, How to Manage Your Writing, How to Manage Your Speaking, Face to Face Communication, A Secretary Is a Manager, Communicating for Results, *and* The Desk Guide to Communication. *He is a graduate of Holy Cross College and holds an M.Ed. from Northeastern University.*

At least a half dozen cartoons in the popular press have been captioned, "What we have here is a failure to communicate." The artwork has depicted scenes ranging from the domestic to the military and political. But when communication fails in the real world, the world that you must train and develop people to cope with, it is seldom funny.

Who needs communications training? The answer to that question is almost as broad as the answer to the question: Who in our organization needs to communicate? Anyone who does is a possible candidate for skill development in the several forms of communication. The need for communications skill is universal. And good communications skill training, like good communication, is simple and is most effective when kept simple. But useful simplicity takes work and planning. It is easy to complicate communications training, to work out convoluted designs and programs that are self-satisfying to the trainer but confusing and of little value to the participants. So let this be our first observation as well as our continuing criterion as we plan and evaluate our communications training: *Keep it simple.*

Effective communications training is skill training when it is best done. It gives its participants increased skills in the communication medium they are studying. It does not give them a mere awareness of the medium and of its literature and artifacts. A good report-writing program produces people who can write better reports than they could before they took the course. It does not merely produce people who know more about report writing. And beyond that, it produces people who can produce those better reports back on the job and not merely in the classroom. So as you plan your communications skill program, as you select participants and resources, as you conduct it, and as you evaluate it, keep the objective in mind. And the objective should be to develop useful skills.

Communications skill can easily be confused with glibness. We often think of a good speaker as one who can crank out pleasing words on demand, or of a good writer as one with a pleasant, readable, enjoyable, fluid style. Style for speakers, writers, interviewers, conference participants, and the like is a nice thing. But it can be deceptive if it is a hollow style, camouflaging a lack of useful content in the message. Communications training in your organization should be training to produce people who can generate useful messages—messages with a useful, thoughtful content expressed in a useful style. Or, if the training is in a receiving skill—reading or listening—it should produce people who can dig for meaning, useful meaning, in what they read or hear. It is not sufficient to turn out people who can merely read at a great rate or listen with acuity.

Program Objectives A good program will do more than teach skills in the medium which is its subject. It will help participants to see that medium and their developed skill in the context of the entire communications situation. It will teach them when to use that medium. Let us take a writing course for an example. Writing is useful for some messages, but not for others. Sometimes we may write to a customer or colleague, and other times we would do better to call the person on the phone or arrange a face-to-face meeting. An effective writing program will explore that. It will show participants how to write, but it will also lead them to consider when to write, just as an effective program in employment interviewing will acquaint participants with the limitations of the interview as an information-gathering device.

Any training experience is finite and short-lived; thus an effective program will provide an immediate skill-building experience, but it will go beyond that to give participants guidance and criteria for long-range skill development so that they can, when they are on their own after the program, continue to develop their skills. Skill can be developed, and bad habits extinguished, only by long-term practice and application. Thus an effective program will allow and encourage the participant to continue his or her skill development.

Communications Objectives In recent years, much has been published about communications theory, as behavioralists, information theorists, semanticists, and others have struggled to explain that which has been happening without explanation for thousands of years. Communications theory has been boomed to fad status. But does it have any role in organizational communications skill programs? I suspect that it does, and I have found it a useful part of many programs. Communications skill is more than a facility for stringing words together in a pleasing way. Communication is a human interaction. Reader and writer, speaker and listener, act, react, and interact dynamically to produce meaning. The theory gives a conceptual base to practitioners which, thoughtfully applied, can help them to operate more effectively. It can help them to see the people and the symbols of communication in context; it can give them a perspective on overall effectiveness and a standard for comparison. So theory has its place, even in the short communications course. But a little good theory, well presented and explained, can go a long way. Figure 31-1 is a graphic example of simple theory, simply presented. In all too many academic programs, theory has replaced application, and some colleges are turning out well-grounded theorists who cannot write, speak, listen, or read, but who know why and how all these processes occur. That, I think, will not do for your program.

So, with all these general observations in mind let us turn to a practical consideration of how your communications training programs might proceed.

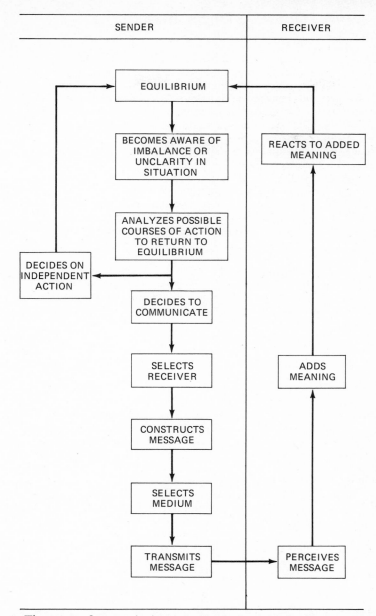

Fig. 31-1 The process of communication. *(From Thomas E. Anastasi, Jr., A Secretary Is a Manager, Devlin House, Medfield, Mass., 1976. Used with permission.)*

COMMUNICATIONS TRAINING AS PART OF OTHER PROGRAMS

Communications training can, of course, be conducted by itself and most often is, and yet it can be successfully integrated into other programs. Indeed, it should be part of many. Management and supervisory development programs most often include some work on communications. Sometimes this is of a general sort, such as discussion of organizational communication, and sometimes it moves into direct skill areas such as appraisal interviewing and employee development counseling. Well done, it can be a valuable adjunct to other training.

In management and supervisory development, communications used to be part of every course. A course was usually subtitled "How to Give Orders," or if some other phrase was used, giving orders was the thrust of the coverage. Now, of course, we are more enlightened—at least one hopes that we are. But skill in giving instructions is useful for managers and supervisors. So too, however, is skill in listening. Managers, regardless of their hierarchical level, must make decisions, and information is the raw material out of which decisions are made. Listening is a dandy way to get information, and thus some development of a manager's listening skills should be useful.

As you consider your total catalog of training programs and development activities, look closely at those which are related to human skills, to dealing with people in any way. "Communication" is another word for dealing with people. Could communications skill training make these training experiences more useful to their participants? If so, include it.

Communications training has been usefully incorporated into programs in management, sales, secretarial skills and development, customer relations, and countless others.

Program Planning

In planning such a course, consider your objectives. What are you trying to accomplish? What skills will successful participants need to do their jobs better? What are the problems, if any, which prompted the course?

Are you, for instance, planning to conduct a management course? Have you been prompted to do this because the company has an unacceptable turnover rate? If so, why do you have such a high turnover? This awareness, in itself, should not be enough to institute training in communications. If your turnover is due to a lower wage rate than that offered by neighboring competitors or to dissatisfaction with working conditions, then better communications, while nice, will do little to remedy the underlying causes of your turnover.

But if you have reason to believe that some organizational lack is at the root of your troubles, you might consider what better communications would do for your managers and thus for your employees and your organization.

If you do not know why people are leaving, you must explore the reasons. Are your supervisors conducting exit interviews? Do you have an exit-interview program? Should you? Do supervisors need training in how to conduct an effective exit interview? Would this produce better exit interviews, and would it provide the organization with better management information? If the answers to questions like these suggest an affirmative trend, then perhaps you should think of including some work on exit interviewing in your management and supervisory training.

Performance Orientation

Are you getting the most productive performance from your secretarial force? Are the secretaries using their abilities fully? Could they, for instance, make a productive contribution by writing for their managers or by editing what comes to them for signature? Would this be a more satisfying kind of work for the secretaries? Have they the time to do it? Would it help them grow? Again, if you notice an affirmative trend in answers to questions like these, you should consider including some skill training in writing and editing in your secretarial programs.

How are things in the sales force? Do your outside representatives need any skill work? What makes a successful salesperson in your organization? Is communications skill in any particular form critical? Do your salespeople have those critical skills? Can you teach these skills as part of your regular sales training? Should you?

Identifying Needs In deciding whether to include communications training as part of your other programs, the best approach is to identify skill needs. Talk to the potential participants and their supervisors. Talk, if you can, with the people with whom they relate. Do your interviews reveal any specific skill deficiencies which can be eliminated by training? If so, try to include this as part of your regular training for these people. Communications skill training, offered as part of another program, is best conducted as closely job-related specific training in specific skills. It should emphasize a skill-building, workshop approach that will allow real skill to develop. If you find that your potential training population has broader skill needs, then you will probably have to plan a program devoted to skill building alone. Only discrete, specific objectives can be usefully met in communications training which is conducted as part of another program.

Unfortunately, just the opposite approach is most often taken by trainers who include a survey course on communications as part of other programs. This, even if it is well done, will produce awareness but not skill. If awareness of the nature of communication or if consciousness of its importance is your goal, this may help. But if skill at communicating is what you were trying to achieve, once-over-lightly surveys are not likely to help much.

DETERMINING COMMUNICATIONS TRAINING NEEDS

Communications training needs can be determined much as other needs are by the normal routine of surveys, analyses, and investigations that are part of any systematic approach to training. Managers can often spot skill needs in their staffs and can relay these to you for action. You may also find felt needs among people in other courses. And, of course, people may tell you that they need skill training. Your analysis of appraisal forms and career planning guides may show patterns of need. But all that is a routine part of training-need assessment.

Performance Analysis

Beyond these normal practices and procedures, there are other ways to determine communications training needs. One way is an analysis of communications results. Does your company, for instance, communicate with consumers about problems and complaints? If so, you might want to analyze the results of these activities. One company did so and found that in many cases, it took more than one message to a customer to resolve a great number of the complaints. This organization handled most of its customer contact through letters. Their analysis of several cases showed that repeated contacts were necessary because the first letter to the customer was, in many cases, unclear or unacceptable. Customers wrote again because they felt that their problem had still not been resolved, and thus the company had to bear the expense of still another letter, not to mention the cost in customer annoyance. The analysis identified causes for the lack of clarity or the unacceptability of the company's letters. A training program was then set up for the letter writers. The result: fewer messages, more satisfied customers, *and* letter writers who approached their jobs with greater confidence and skill and who finished their work with a greater sense of achievement.

However, you must be careful with this kind of analysis. Not every communications problem is solvable by training. The United States Social Security Administration conducted letter-writing training for years without really solving its basic problems. The letters got better as a result of the training, but the basic problem—that of clear, effective communication with clients—did not drastically improve until the system was changed. Someone realized that the basic problem was the fact that the letter medium was the wrong one for much of the Administration's work, and a telephone procedure was instituted for answering letters from social security clients. Two-way communication was necessary to clarify clients' questions and to assure that useful answers were given. This procedural change did more to improve communications than any amount of training would have. Of course, the change in procedure made it necessary to train personnel in telephone interview techniques. But this was the right training for the solution of the problem.

Another kind of analysis can be done by someone skilled in communications. A staff member or consultant can analyze your organization's writing to see whether there are factors which suggest training needs. The same can be done with your meetings or other oral presentations. This sort of quality-control check can be made routinely if a staff member is competent to do it. If a consultant must be hired for the job, then you should be pretty sure that a problem exists before you call on such a person for diagnosis—unless your budget has provisions for prophylaxis.

Problem Definition Essential

In any case, you should attempt to define the problem as specifically as you can. If, through any process, you determine that you have a "writing problem" and attempt to solve it by conducting or sponsoring a "writing course," you are not likely to do much to solve the problem. There are many standard courses and programs in the several communications skills. Some are good; others are asinine. But not even the best of the good ones is always good for all needs at all times.

If you are not capable of defining the problem, and many trainers are not, then get someone who is. Perhaps a colleague can help you. Perhaps you will need an outsider. But someone must do it. If an outsider does it, be sure that he or she explains the problem in concrete terms before attempting to suggest the remedy. As you well know, training, in and of itself, is neither good nor bad. It is the relationship of the training to the objective that provides a sound foundation.

You may choose to consult a colleague in the training field about his or her experience in meeting a communications training need, and he or she may, in all good conscience, recommend a program that worked well in another instance. But unless those needs parallel yours, any recommendation may be invalid.

If, for instance, you are dealing with a proposed writing program, what changes in writing behavior do you want? And, beyond that, what changes are possible in your organization? Until you have determined that, you are unlikely to present a truly effective program.

Specificity in Objectives

Let your statement of need read, "We need a training program which will. . . ." Then fill in the blank with specifics. Do not be satisfied with "We need a writing course," "We need a course in conference leadership," or anything that general. These last general statements indicate an awareness of a problem area and should represent the beginning of your need definition, not the final determination.

In other words, you should write the specifications before you design the product, and you should make sure that those specifications will, if met, help solve the problem.

Results, Not Entertainment

Effective communication is results-oriented. A good piece of business writing is one which allows and stimulates readers to respond as the writer wanted them to, not one with an effective style or an acceptable "fog count." Sound business presentations provide useful information in a useful way. They are not necessarily the ones that sound good or even those which are effectively delivered. Someone with good rhetorical skills, a pleasant voice and appearance, and a winning delivery can make something that lacks content sound good—and can make the audience enjoy it. But if results, and not entertainment, was the goal, this person is not likely to be successful. The point of all this, as it relates to determining communications training needs, is that you should look at the results of your organization's communications activities:

Do your reports contribute to sound decisions?
Do your oral presentations inform and persuade?
Are your manuals and procedures useful to their readers?
Are your customer contacts supportive of good customer relations?
Do your managers and executives have all the information they need?

These questions and others like them will help focus your attention on areas in which communication is weak. Then you must ask yourself whether lack of skill contributes to the problems. If it does, then possibly you have a training need, if the people with the lack of skill can reasonably be expected to develop the requisite skills. If not, you may have a selection problem, for it may be easier and more effective to hire better communicators than to train them.

Figure 31-2 shows a device we have used to guide management discussions in search of training needs. Working with appropriate functional managers and executives, we discuss their perceptions of communications effectiveness within the organization. We ask them to do this from several points of view and then to validate or to attempt to validate their replies. This form focuses on internal communication. We use a similar form for discussions of the effectiveness of external communication.

However you do it, look at communications from the viewpoint of the results. What results are you getting? Are those results acceptable? If not, can training be reasonably expected to give you those results? If it can, what kind of training?

Program Design Questions

When you have the answers to these questions, then you are ready to begin work on the design of your program. If you are ready for that next step, you should have answers to these questions:

- *Who are the proposed trainees?*
- *What are their training needs?*
- *Do the proposed trainees have similar training needs?* If they do, you can conduct one program for the entire population. If they do not, you should be thinking of more than one program. If you put all the proposed trainees through the same experience and if you try to cover everyone's needs, you will be wasting much of the participants' time as you address their colleagues' needs. If you have a fairly large group of people with some needs in common and other needs not in common, you might think of a branching pattern which will present part of the course to all; then you can go on to offer "elective" sections to the trainees who need special coverage.

I. <u>Opportunities for Communication</u>. What should be communicated upward in this organization?

    A. In top management's view?
    B. In middle management's view?
    C. In first-line supervision's view?
    D. In the employee's view?

II. <u>Opportunities for Communication.</u> What should be communicated downward in this organization?

    A. In top management's view?
    B. In middle management's view?
    C. In first-line supervision's view?
    D. In the employee's view?

III. <u>Opportunities for communication</u>. What should be communicated from line management to staff management?

    A. In line management's view?
    B. In staff management's view?

IV. <u>Opportunities for communication</u>. What should be communicated from staff management to line management?

    A. In staff management's view?
    B. In line management's view?

V. <u>Analysis</u>. Look at your answers to each question above. From the point of view expressed in the questions, ask: <u>Are we taking adequate advantage of this opportunity for communication</u>?

    A. If the answer is "yes" ask:
       1. <u>How do we know that we are</u>?
       2. <u>Could we do it better</u>?
       3. <u>Should we</u>?

    B. If the answer is "no" ask:
       1. <u>How do we know that we aren't</u>?
       2. <u>Why aren't we</u>?
       3. <u>What can we do to improve this situation</u>?
       4. <u>What results will this improvement show</u>? <u>What if we fail to improve</u>?

    C. If the answer is "we don't know" ask:
       1. <u>Why don't we know</u>?
       2. <u>How can we find out</u>?

Fig. 31-2 Analysis of organizational communication. (© *1970 by The Communication Training Group.*)

- *What are the specific objectives of the training program?*
- *What, if any, are the other considerations?* These may be elements like time, money, resources, organizational barriers, personal idiosyncrasies, and the like. You will probably learn more about these as you go along through the program design phase, but it is well to begin considering them early. This lets you think about alternatives and strategies as soon as possible.

DESIGNING COMMUNICATIONS TRAINING PROGRAMS

This section should probably be titled Selecting or Designing Your Program. If you have an internal capability to conduct your own program, you will be concerned with design; if not, you will be concerned with selecting a commercial package or a resource to design a program for you.

If you have the internal capability, you probably need little guidance in the particulars of design, and so most of this section will deal with design criteria and with the processes involved in coming to a good design or a good selection of a well-designed program—all of which means, I think, extensive work with the potential population and their managers. Skill training should lead to behavior change, and the forces which inhibit or enhance that behavior change come from the people and customs of the organization.

Need for Change in Climate

We could design a splendid program which should improve performance in a given skill area, but it will all come to naught if the participants refuse to change or if their managers—or what we might euphemistically term the "organizational climate"—militate against change (see also Chapter 17, "Group Norms: Their Influence on Training Effectiveness").

Case in Point   Everyone at the Bonjour Tristesse Negligée Company agreed that the reports within the company were poorly written. Everyone agreed that a report-writing course would be a good thing to have. And so they set one up—and it was pretty good. Everyone had a nice time. But the participants kept pointing out that the course material, while splendid, was not appropriate. "Sure," they said, "we should write that way. But *they* won't let us. You should have our bosses in this course, not us."

So most of the participants made no attempt to change their writing outside the course, though all did rather well on the workshop exercises in the class. One or two people did try to change their writing style. Two actually. One was very secure and the other was new to the company. And their bosses said to them, "What the hell are you writing like that for? That's not the way we do it here."

Sound familiar? It should. That sort of response is not at all atypical. But with careful planning, things do not have to be that way. To avoid such a result, you must involve participants and their managers early in the design phase of the training program.

The trainer's goals will be of little use unless they match the behavior which the trainees are willing and able to emit and which the organization will allow them to emit. Discussion and negotiation of acceptable behavior change should take place at the beginning of the design phase, not during the training program or after it.

Participant Inputs

This is not to say that the trainees alone should design the program; rather, the trainer should be familiar with their perceptions of the training needs and of the program's objectives. The trainer may decide to go ahead with aspects of the program which the participants will resist, but if he or she has explored this ahead of time, the resistance will not come as a surprise, and the trainer will plan a training strategy to counter that resistance. This precourse discussion with participants should not be centered on resistance—it may not even be a problem. What is more likely is that the participants, who know their own communications opportunities and problems quite well, will be able to give valuable inputs to the course designer.

Manager Inputs

The precourse meetings with the participants' managers are of a different order. The managers can make valuable inputs to the design process because they are familiar with the communications behavior of the participants. Unlike the participants, they can see that behavior in a wider organizational context. But beyond that, it is they who must support and reinforce any lasting behavioral change. And it is they who can advertently or inadvertently thwart anything that happens in the training experience.

The aimed-for behavioral change does not take place in the training room. It occurs back on the job. And the manager, to a very great extent, determines what behavior may be emitted on the job. The manager may accept or reject the trainer's concepts for the program. If the manager accepts them, this can be a strong force for achieving the program's goals, particularly if the program has, as it should have, a follow-up phase. If the manager rejects the trainer's goals, the trainer has an opportunity to sell his or her concepts and to convince the manager to support the course objectives. If that fails, the trainer can either scrap the program or change it to accommodate the behavioral change that the manager will support.

In either case, the trainer will not be presenting training that has no chance of succeeding. This is why specific course objectives are necessary. They allow the trainer to discuss the proposed course with proposed participants and managers alike to ensure the most productive training.

If the trainer goes to the manager with generalized statements about better communications skills, the manager is likely to accept them, only later to reject the specific behaviors which the program fostered.

Get support from the top. If possible, it would be well to have nominating managers take the course before enrolling their subordinates.

If you are dealing with a large population of managers and participants, you may have to conduct your predesign conferences with a representative sampling of managers and participants. That is fine, but even a well-chosen sample yields truths about only some of the total population. If you use this method to develop a course design, realize that it makes another step necessary. That step is accurate, concrete communication of the course objectives to the whole population before nomination. Thus you would conduct your predesign conferences with a sampling of managers and participants. From this you would plan a course. Then you must prepare a course announcement that will accurately describe the course and its methods and objectives and the precise communication behaviors which are its goal. This must be done in concrete, communicative terms so that both nominating managers and prospective nominees can make their judgments about the course on the basis of reality.

Build on Existing Skills

As you design a course or select an already designed course, realize that the participants are experienced communicators. They have been communicating all their lives and have built up a fund of habits and experiences. Take advantage of their experience. If, for instance, you will be training report writers, realize that they have written reports and that many, if not most, of the reports that they have written have been acceptable. Your task is not to turn "bad" writers into "good" writers. That approach may well put them in a hopeless condition. Your job is to help them to take better advantage of their report-writing opportunities. It is not to give them skill where they have none; it is to help them to improve the skills they have. Take advantage of their writing experience. They will probably be sensitive to their problem areas and most receptive to your positive suggestions for dealing more effectively with those problem areas. Reports, for instance, are often poorly organized, not because writers like to write poorly organized pieces, but because they have never had any opportunity to learn how to organize a report properly. If you can give them positive guidance in organization, they will be receptive. But in teaching this skill, as in teaching all others, make sure that you give adequate instruction. If you present the techniques and patterns of organization in only a cursory way, you may encounter resistance to the idea—not because your writers do not want to organize, but because a cursory treatment fails to teach them the skills that they need to do the job. Being still unskilled, they will be resistant.

Skill Building

In training people in any of the communication skills, it is never enough to give expository treatment to the subject matter. That would be adequate if you were trying to get your students to *know about* the subject. But that is not what you should be trying to do. If you are doing your communications training job the way it should be done, you will be giving your trainees an opportunity to learn *how to communicate*. Let the design of your program teach skill and ability, not merely knowledge and awareness. As you design your training program, design it to teach skill.

Your prospective trainees have another kind of experience you should take advantage of. They have seen the other side of the coin. People whom you are training to interview have been interviewed many times—sometimes well and sometimes poorly, but well enough and poorly enough often enough so that they are able to form judgments as to what makes an effective interview. People whom you train to speak have listened. Those whom you train to listen have spoken. Readers write. Writers read. Counselors have in turn been counseled. Take advantage of this experience to train effectively. Let the trainees reflect on their own experience to develop criteria of effective performance.

Good communication is *other-centered*. Good writing is reader-centered. Good listening is speaker-centered; good listeners try to listen through their own biases and to pay close attention—to think along with the speaker and to get at his or her meaning. Your trainees have been in the role of the "other." Make use of that experience.

People are often insecure about their abilities to communicate. They realize that communications skill is an important part of their jobs. They know that they should communicate better than they do, and this can make them defensive and insecure. Most people have learned their communications skills erratically. Many (most?) professionals and semiprofessionals have had little training or education in the communications skills. It is quite possible to go all the way through postdoctoral studies in any discipline without taking a single course in communications. But what happens when one first takes a job? Within days, one is assigned a report or memo to write, a conference to attend, or a presentation to give. And where does one find the skill to attack the assignment? From whatever experience one has had up to that point. And who has taught physicists to write? Other physicists, from their writing. And often these physicists have been similarly untrained and have learned to write from still other physicists. In this way the formulas and jargons of each trade and discipline are perpetuated, and thus each professional and semiprofessional comes to believe that the style of writing common to his or her trade is the only proper and acceptable one—because the tribal elders said so.

What Not to Do

Where does that leave you, who must train people to write differently from the way they do? You may have a rough row to hoe, but you can do it. The stylistic convictions of these folk are not too solidly based in logic. Theirs is an emotional tie grounded in the desperation engendered by an inability to write any other way. They know that poor writing is poor writing. They have to read it and try to make sense of it. So you can bring them to the light and the truth. But how you do this is important. Remember the base in desperation: Do not take away the habits of a professional lifetime unless you are prepared to substitute something else; otherwise, you will leave your trainees with nothing at all to sustain them in the writing jobs that will persist.

Some writing training, for instance, has consisted of the instructor's demonstrating how bad the process of writing can be. Horrible examples are chosen from the field—though usually not from the trainees' own writing—and everyone has a jolly time kicking the hell out of the examples. Such sessions are usually very pleasant and fun to teach. The instructor's wit and sense of comedic timing can come to full fruition. Having shown the students many examples of poor writing, the instructor concludes by telling them not to write like that and sends them on their way with a benign exhortation to go and sin no more.

So, now they know what not to do—well, they sort of know what not to do. But what should they do? How should they write? That, somehow, is never covered in these sessions. And the same is quite often true of courses in the other communications skills: They are negative in content. Trainees need to know what to do to communicate more effectively—not what not to do.

Positive Content

Of course you can use examples of poor communication as a training device, often quite effectively. But that should not be the main focus of the training experience. Give the trainees a majority of positive content. Build skill in effective communications. And maximize their positive experiences in using and developing positive skills.

Some training seems to follow the "puppy-training" process of pushing trainees' noses into their mistakes so that they will not repeat them. This, at best, stimulates aversive behavior. It does not lead to skill development. Your skill training program should be designed so that your trainees can leave the course having had the maximum number of positive experiences with the skill. Design your program in such a way as to allow the trainee to succeed often.

Program Components

Analyze the skill to be developed. Break it down into the smallest useful bits and give the trainees positive experiences in each one. Writing skill offers a good example. Writing style is a complex subject, but it can be seen as a network of components such as:

Skill with verbs
Skill with modifiers
Skill in transition
Skill in paragraphing

The above is, of course, just a partial list. A well-designed program would see the skills in such a network and would develop each separately. It would not tackle the subject of style as a whole. Some of the skills above would break down further into other components. Skill with verbs, for instance, can be further broken down to:

Mood
Voice
Strength of verbs and verbal nouns
Parallel use of verbs and verbals

Consistency of tense
Problems of agreement
Concreteness of verbs

For some kinds of skill training, there will be still other subdivisions of skill with verbs. Each of these divisions and subdivisions should be separately treated at first to give the trainees the component skills that will later be integrated into a sense of style. Each of these subdivisions will require some expository treatment in which the terms are defined and the stylistic considerations discussed. The extensive use of examples should help here. You will probably find that adults who have been away from grammar and the academic consideration of the elements of writing and structure will need even the most basic terms explained. They may, for instance, need to be reminded of what a verb is. If they are going to work with verbs, they should know what they are. They should understand transitive versus intransitive verbs, simple predicates, and the like. This coverage should not take long, and it should not be done "grammar school style." But it should not be left out either. All adults would profit from a reacquaintance with "voice." Most do not remember the difference between the active and the passive voice. And many will be reluctant to ask. Thus they will learn nothing as you try to show them how to substitute the active voice for the passive one.

Put Learning to Work

After you have given the subject matter adequate exposition and illustration, give the trainees an opportunity to put their learning to work. Let them convert some passive constructions to active ones. Let them recast some sentences and explore for themselves the difference that their revisions make.

Take away their old behaviors and their old writing habits, but give them new behaviors and new habits—new skills to replace the old.

As you design your communications training sessions, keep another point in mind: Communication is not a precise science. There is no one right way to communicate in any given situation, and attempts to force right answers and limited behaviors upon the trainees will probably fail, as they should. And if they succeed, they will produce shallow automatons.

Help your trainees to develop their own styles. Give them guides to effectiveness, but do not allow your training program to function as a cookie cutter, mass-producing like after like. Effective communicators think. A program with strict rules and prescriptions of style prevents prethinking and says to its alumni, "Don't think. Just do it our way."

I suspect that few trainers would ever consciously conduct a program that way. But it can happen unconsciously if the trainer is only casually grounded in the skill which he or she is teaching. The trainer will be tempted, if not forced, to hold the students to what he or she understands. And often the shallowly prepared instructor will understand only a few "hows" and no "whys." If you would instruct in any skill of communication, then prepare yourself broadly so that you can help your trainees to develop their own styles and so that you will not be tempted or forced to try to get them to copy yours.

A CHECKLIST FOR PROGRAM DESIGN

As you design or select a program, compare it against this brief checklist:

- Are your program goals consistent with behavior change that is:
    - Likely to be acceptable to the trainees?
    - Likely to be reinforced by their managers?

- Are the skills which will be learned in the course likely to be useful to the trainees when they are back on the job?
- Do you have enough support from the top to assure that the *organizational climate* will be receptive to the trainees' new skills?
- Does your course announcement accurately communicate the course content and objectives?
- Does the course design take advantage of the trainees' precourse experience?
- Is the main thrust of the course directed toward positive skill building?
- Will the course allow the trainees to develop skill or will it simply inform them about the subject?
- Does the course give an *other-centered* orientation to skill application?
- Does the course permit individual style development?
- Does the course maximize successful learning experiences?
- Are the skills broken down into the best useful units?
- Is there adequate explanation of terms and principles?
- Is there adequate opportunity for application of the skill?
- Is the proposed instructor broadly enough prepared to make the learning experience one that will be useful in the individualized development of style and skills?

IDENTIFYING AND USING RESOURCES

Human Resources

A communications skill trainer—whether it is you, a training colleague, a colleague from elsewhere in your organization, or a consultant from the outside—should, as noted in the last section, have sufficient background to see the skill in its context within the trainees' job responsibilities. He or she should have sufficient depth and skill to develop the trainees' individual styles.

Experience is vital. Members of a training staff who will be called on to conduct communications training sessions should, in my opinion, serve an apprenticeship with an experienced trainer. Their apprenticeship would logically progress from observation accompanied by out-of-class discussion with the experienced trainer, followed by team teaching with the trainer and, ultimately, teaching on their own.

Academic preparation is, in my experience, an undetermined variable. Some course preparation in the skill area is helpful, but experiences may easily substitute for it. A fluency in at least the basics of human behavior seems essential. Communication is a social process, and it must be taught with that understanding, or else the training will produce word arrangers who will operate in a vacuum. Naturally the trainer should have a sound grounding in the philosophy and practice of adult education and industrial training. Someone whose teaching experience has been solely with children will likely fare ill with a group of adults with a background of experience in the skill and an immediate need for useful, immediately applicable skills. This does not mean that the local high school English teacher cannot teach an industrial writing course, but it does mean that his or her qualifications must go beyond those which the school board requires.

The instructor should be *adept* in the skill which he or she is teaching. That, of course, does not mean that the best report writer in the house should be chosen as the instructor for the report-writing course. Your experience has no doubt shown you the differences between being able to use a skill and being able to teach others how to use it. But it does mean that the interviewing instructor should be a good and experienced interviewer and that the oral communications teacher should speak well.

An *outside* source should be experienced in the kind of training that he or she will be doing for you. If you are offering a letter-writing course, then someone whose experience has been exclusively in training report writers or advertising copywriters may not fill the bill. If you are selecting an outside resource—or an inside resource, for that matter—it would be well to observe this person working with another group if that is possible. Contacts with colleagues in the training profession who have observed the prospective instructor may be helpful if you yourself cannot observe the candidate.

Other people may help you in several ways. By "other people" I mean *consultants*. Consultants may be fee-paid outsiders, or they may be colleagues within your own organization who, though they do not work in training, may have valuable skills that you can use.

A consultant may take care of your entire program for you, from needs determination, through program design and presentation, to program evaluation and follow-up. Or the consultant may work on only one of those phases or on several.

A consultant may serve as a guest lecturer for a part of your program. You may have internal capabilities to handle the program design and presentation in all but a few topical areas, and you may find it helpful to have the consultant work for you in just those few areas. In a technical writing course, for example, you may have the internal capacity to cover everything but the subject of graphics and may employ someone to cover that topic for you. Or your oral presentation program may need a little beefing up in the audiovisual area.

You may choose to use a consultant to design a program for you and your staff to present. Consultants often get assignments like this when working for clients who have large populations to train and who cannot afford to have the consultant conduct all the training. In that type of relationship, the consultant would custom-design a training package and all its supporting material for you and would then pilot or field-test it with your trainees. When the course package was finally developed and firmed, the consultant would train your trainers to present future offerings of the course.

Even the reverse of that process is possible. If you have a course all developed, but have no instructor or have insufficient instructors for your training schedule, then you can hire someone from outside your training department to conduct some or all of the training for you. Government agencies frequently have packaged courses which their employees are required to take. Local activities which lack qualified instructors have frequently hired outsiders to conduct the training using the package.

Commercial Packages

Some are good. Some are bad. Some are always bad for any possible use. But none are always good. Before selecting any package, plan your requirements. Know what you want the package to do before you check to see what is available. The package should fit your training needs. Your training needs should not fit the available packages. Sometimes, of course, you may have to trade off a requirement against availability, but those trade-offs should be made only for less important requirements. Your basic purposes should remain intact.

Commercial packages, by their very nature, must be prepared to meet *general training needs*. But your needs are specific. Still, there can be a use for them. Some of your specific needs may be common to many other programs, including those offered in commercial packages. Often a creative blending of commercial packages, perhaps with some of your own instructional material added, can produce an excellent program at a low cost.

And it is quite possible that your training need may be such a common one that a commercial package will be readily found to do the entire job. For any training need of any considerable dimension, however, this is unlikely. Communications skill usually needs the assistance of a *talented instructor* for in-training application and guidance, and a package cannot give that. Packages are best suited for expository treatment of information; they are usually less suited to personal skill development.

Training packages, particularly *programmed instruction* and other *self-paced* learning tools, are quite well suited for tutorial situations in which a given trainee or trainees will need special work to remedy deficiencies in background or to bring the individual to the conceptual level of the rest of the class. Because students can follow these courses of study on their own time and at their own pace, the courses may be particularly helpful.

Be wary of packages or people who hawk a gimmick or formula as the universal solution to all trainees' communications problems and training needs. Communication is too broad a process to admit of resolution through narrow techniques.

Part of a package can often be *combined* with parts of other packages or with your own instructional material to produce a useful learning experience. Do not be afraid to be innovative or to approach a packager to ask for only part of the package at only part of the price. Many packagers will, at an additional cost of course, tailor their packages to meet your needs. This is usually too costly unless you have a large population to train.

Textbooks

As with commercial packages, plan your objectives first and then seek a text. Do not do it the other way around. Your objectives, and not text availability, should determine course content and method. The instructor, of course, should have final text decision authority. It is this person who will have to work with it and with the trainees.

A text should not duplicate the course content exactly. If it does, the instructor will be in the position of one who simply reads the text to the student. Rather, the text should amplify and expand the in-class coverage. The text should also be chosen to serve as a reference for postcourse use. Used as a reference and a refresher, it will best serve the trainees' needs. For that reason it is usually unwise to try to save on text costs by collecting them at the end of the course to use with subsequent classes.

CONDUCTING COMMUNICATIONS TRAINING

We shall look at this in more detail in the next section as we examine various communications skills and typical programs. In general, though, we might make these observations:

1. *Keep class size small.*   Groups of 12 to 18 are best. They provide a sufficient number for spirited discussion, and they allow each trainee to have ample opportunity for skill-building practice.

2. *Emphasize workshop sessions.*   The majority of sessions, particularly when the subject is any form of oral communications skill, should be practical sessions in which the students practice the skill under the guidance of a skilled instructor. The comments of their fellow trainees are a valuable contribution and allow all participants to make use of their experience. In many such sessions, we have found it most useful to confine lecture to the first session of the course. The rest of the instructor's contribution can be best made in the form of comments on trainee performance or impromptu minilectures as they are warranted by the progress of the class. Other instructors may prefer to operate differently, but however they do it, they should maximize trainee participation.

3. *Maintain an informal setting.*   The skills of communication are those which many

trainees associate with English classes in school, and for many people this does not seem to have been one of life's high points, perhaps because so many teachers devoted most of their attention to form and little to content.

That ratio of attention has no place in a communications skills course. In business, industry, and public service, the content is far more important than the form. The form is merely a vehicle for the content. And while instructors may quite correctly be concerned with the vehicle, they should also recognize the value of the content. Instructors should also realize that form is a changeable thing and that innovation, particularly where it promotes clarity and effectiveness, should not be condemned.

Realize, too, that you are dealing with individual differences. In any communications class you will find people who, before the first session begins, already have more skill than some of their fellow trainees will have when the course is over. Both kinds of trainees must be helped to grow in skill. The better students can get better still, and the less skilled can develop within their own potentials to develop. An informal atmosphere will help to dispel the idea that the class is really the National Indoor Communications Championships. Each can be encouraged to compete with himself or herself, but not with colleagues.

A communications skills class can be a dangerous place for marginal communicators. They know that they are not very skilled, and a poorly conducted class can act to reinforce their feelings of inadequacy and destroy any confidence that they might have had. Far too many people have left speech or oral presentation classes vowing never again to open their mouths where they could be heard by another living soul.

None of this should be taken to mean that you should withhold honest, helpful criticism. Not at all. But it does mean that sessions like this are best conducted in a businesslike, but informal and spontaneous, atmosphere which encourages growth in skill rather than progress toward some arbitrary goal. Emphasize individual growth.

4. *Allow adequate time for skill development.* We have found that it is usually better to spread instruction over a long period of time. If you were to present 24 hours of instruction, it would probably be best to do so in two- to three-hour sessions held once a week rather than to schedule the 24 hours in three or four consecutive days. This allows the students to apply skills back on the job during the course. This suggestion cannot, though, be taken as a hard-and-fast rule, for excellent training has been offered in a variety of schedules including the compressed kind. A case may be made for the intensity of concentration in a class conducted over a short period. Trainee progress has more to do with the quality of the experience than with time frame in which the course is conducted.

SOME TRAINING PROGRAMS IN COMMUNICATIONS SKILL

In this section we shall look at some typical programs in the various skill areas. These programs are not presented as models for general use, for every communications skill program should be prepared and conducted to meet the specific training needs of the group for which it is conducted. Those presented are general and basic. In some cases and for some needs they may be seen as a foundation in basic skills upon which individual trainers could compose variations to meet specific needs.

Writing Skills

This sample program focuses on no particular written medium and might be presented to trainees who must write in several mediums. Letters and reports are treated, as they are the most common mediums. Workshop and illustrative material should be prepared from a sampling of the trainees' own writing, or at least from the files that are typical of the subject matter and forms of writing commonly written by the trainees. Use of forms, situations, and language that are typical brings the course closer to the reality that the trainees deal with and may help to reduce or eliminate the force of objections that "This is OK, but it wouldn't work for the kind of writing that we have to do."

FOUNDATIONS OF EFFECTIVE WRITING

This program is arranged in six 3-hour sessions. Other scheduling patterns that would total about 18 hours of instruction could be arranged.

Session 1

1. Writing problem and opportunity census.
   (A written or oral discussion of trainee writing problems and opportunities. Presentation of their questions and problems. Can be combined with a brief pretest.)
2. Foundations of communication.
   a. Assumptions about communication.
   b. The process of communication.
   c. How writing differs from speech.
   (To begin discussion on this point, an experiment is often helpful. Prepare three simple drawings in advance. The drawings should each be an arrangement of simple geometric figures.

   Ask for a pair of volunteers and give them these instructions: One is to tell the other how to draw one of the drawings on a flip chart. The drawer and the describer must stand back to back so that they cannot see each other. The describer will tell the drawer what to do using any words that he or she might choose, but the drawer may not speak to the describer. When they have finished, ask for a second pair of volunteers.

   The second pair will have the same task with another drawing. This time, however, they may talk to each other. The drawer may ask for clarification or amplification of the instructions. When they finish, ask for a third pair of volunteers.

   The third pair has the same task with another drawing. This time, the describer may watch the drawer and they may communicate freely.

   When they have finished, you may point out that with the first pair, the describer "wrote" to the drawer, since it was one-way communication. The second pair "telephoned" (two-way verbal communication), and the third pair met in two-way, face-to-face communication. This experiment can form the base for a class discussion of their communications opportunities and of the importance of medium selection. This leads to the next point.)
   d. When to write and when to speak. How to choose the best medium for the task at hand.
   e. Introduction to reader-centered writing.
   (A useful exercise at this point is an extension of the last experiment. Divide the class into two groups. Give each a drawing and ask each to write to someone in the other group, telling how to draw the drawing. Then have each make a drawing based on a set of written directions given by someone in the other group. Show each person the results of his or her writing in the form of the drawing based on it. Use this as the basis of a class discussion of the elements that produced effective and ineffective writing in the exercise.)
   f. What better writing can do for you.

Session 2

1. Why we write as we do.
   a. How you can develop your writing ability.
2. Formula writing and how to avoid it.
3. How to keep writing simple, clear, and direct.
4. How to use verbs.
   a. Voice. Prefer the active voice. Exercise.*
   b. How to avoid verbal nouns. Exercise.
   c. How to use concrete, specific verbs. Exercise.
5. How to write concisely.
   a. Circumlocution and how to avoid it. Exercise.
   b. How to avoid abstraction. Exercise.
   c. How to use modifiers.
      (1) Concrete modifiers and concrete nouns. Exercise.
      (2) One-word substitutes for phrases and clauses used as modifiers. Exercise.
6. How to edit and revise your own writing.
   (As an exercise, the trainees can work on their drawing instructions from the first session.)

Session 3

1. Report writing.
   a. Functions of reports.
   b. Steps in report writing.
      (1) Plan your purpose in terms of reader response.
      (2) Define.your scope.
      (3) Identify information needs.
      (4) Organize the approach.
      (5) Make an outline.
      (6) Decide when and how to hold a preapproval conference.
      (7) How to use the expanded outline.
         (*a*) To improve paragraphs.
         (*b*) To overcome inertia.
      (8) How to write the rough draft.
      (9) The final draft.

Session 4

1. How emphasis guides reader response.
   a. What denies emphasis.
      (1) Mechanical emphasis and careless patterns.
      (2) Improper subordination.
      (3) Passive voice, abstraction, wordiness, clichés.
   b. How to write emphatically.
      (1) Pause in pattern and punctuation.
      (2) Word order.
      (3) Proportion and emphasis.
      (4) Repetition and flat statements.
2. Parallelism.
   a. Defined.
   b. Within a sentence.
   c. In larger elements. Paragraphs. Overall parallelism.
   d. Exercise in emphasis and parallelism.

*These exercises should be given after adequate explanation and illustration of the style element involved.

  3. Transition.
     a. Defined and illustrated.
     b. Exercises in transition.

Session 5

  1. Form, appearance, and layout.
  2. Use of graphics.
  3. Tone: Sometimes it is *how* you say it.
     a. Exercises in tone.
  4. A brief review of punctuation and usage.
     a. Exercises in punctuation and usage.
     (This section is optional. If your pace of instruction to this point allows it, this section could be quite useful. Many people shy away from writing because they are afraid they will make a mistake in grammar or usage. It has been awhile since most trainees studied these subjects, and so an updating may give them the confidence they need. If you do not have time to cover this, refer the trainees to a standard reference source or to a programmed instruction text.)

Session 6

  1. How to write effective letters.
     a. Criteria for effectiveness.
        (1) Creative.
        (2) Personal.
        (3) Valuable to the reader.
        (4) Correct in form and style.
     b. How to begin a letter.
     c. How to develop the body.
     d. How to end a letter.
     e. Exercises in letter writing.
        (1) Revision of typical letters.
        (2) Writing letters from typical cases.
     f. Discussion of letter-writing problems.
     g. How to continue your writing skill development.

These six sessions represent a compact coverage of the basics of business writing. They could easily and profitably be expanded by additional application. More exercises could be added in the present format, and additional workshop sessions could be added at the end. These workshops should be of two types. At first, give the trainees writing to discuss and revise. (This writing should be typical of the trainees' own writing opportunities.) Then give them writing cases.

Sessions on organization could be added as well, but these are often better reserved from more specific writing courses such as those in report writing, letter writing, technical writing, and the like.

However you handle any exercise, remember not to get trapped in the one-right-answer syndrome. Teach the trainees to write and to think about writing as a means to effective results.

Oral Communications Skills

The program outlined below is, in general, suitable for two kinds of training: oral presentation or briefing and public speaking. With augmentation in sales techniques it could also be a suitable base for a course in sales presentation.

Oral presentation and public speaking are often treated as though they were synonymous. They are not. Any competent person can be trained to give a good oral presentation. The same is not true for public speeches or presentations. The difference between the two is this: An oral presentation is a useful presentation of useful information. It is the way that a competent business or government person shares his or her ideas through the spoken word. It is judged by results. Good content, effectively organized and presented, distinguishes it. Public speaking, on the other hand, places greater stress on delivery and on the entertainment value of the presentation. The content should be good, and it should be well organized, but that is not enough in itself.

Oral presentations are given to inform and to persuade people to adopt a point of view or take a course of action. They may be given internally or to customers, clients, or the profession at large in professional and industry meetings.

Public speeches are given as part of an organization's public relations program, to the internal or the external public. They require much more polish and style in delivery. And they frequently must entertain. Examples are speeches to the community, to service and other groups, to stockholders, and to consumer groups.

It is sometimes hard to differentiate between oral presentations and public speaking. But you can do so if you consider whether the emphasis is on content (oral presentations or briefings) or on the image and entertainment engendered (public speaking).

The principal difference to the trainer is in the selection process. Any competent member of an organization can give a sound oral presentation if he or she has been taught the necessary skills. Candidates for courses in this skill may be chosen on the basis of need for the skill.

Candidates for public-speaking courses, on the other hand, should be chosen on the basis of need, but after an audition. If they do not come to the course with the basics of voice, polish, appearance, and verbal fluency, then they are not likely to develop these qualities in any course of reasonable length. Given unlimited time and resources, many people could acquire this skill. But within the normal limitations of industrial, business, and governmental training, the best approach would be a strict selection process—and that means auditions. With that in mind, let us take a look at a typical program:

EFFECTIVE ORAL COMMUNICATION

This sample outline is for a program of 16 three-hour sessions. The scheduling pattern can be varied to meet your own requirements. It also assumes a class of 12 to 15 trainees.

Session 1

1. The process of communication: how an audience finds meaning.
    a. Semantics: the imprecise nature of the words you will be using.
    b. "Communication" is a word we use to describe all the ways in which people affect one another.
        (1) Verbal communication.
        (2) Nonverbal communication.
    c. Results-oriented speaking.
2. First impromptu speeches. The members will introduce themselves, describe their oral presentation experience, and tell about the opportunities that they will have to use the course in their jobs. These first speeches should be given without critique.
3. Overview of the course and its methods and objectives.
    a. Overview.
    b. Description of methods and of assignments to be given. Emphasis in the course is on participation and on skill building by doing.

    c. Discussion of the procedures and purposes of the critiques. Importance of everyone's participation.
        (1) The instructor can bring only a limited viewpoint to his or her own comments. The class as a whole is more typical of the audiences that the trainees will face in actual speaking situations. Therefore, there will be more useful comments, and the experience will be more rewarding, if everyone openly and honestly participates in the critiques.
4. Assignment of brief prepared presentations for the next session. Each participant will be required to present a three- to five-minute description of his or her function in the organization.

Session 2

1. Trainee presentations followed by critiques. The instructor should lead the critique discussions for this first group of presentations, but it would be well to assign a trainee discussion leader for each of the following sessions. In this and in the other critique discussions, the instructor may, of course, offer comments as he or she sees fit.
2. How to organize ideas.
    a. Expository patterns.
        (1) Chronological.
        (2) Illustrative.
        (3) Descriptive.
        (4) Analytic.
        (5) Definition.
        (6) Impressionistic.
    b. Logical and persuasive patterns.
        (1) Inductive.
        (2) Deductive.
        (3) Cause and effect.
        (4) Topical.
        (5) Alternative.
    c. The values of organization.
    d. How to organize.
3. Assignment for the next session: Each participant is to prepare a brief presentation (five to eight minutes), using a subject of his or her own choice and employing one of the expository patterns.

Session 3

1. Trainee presentations and critiques.
2. How to prepare for a presentation.
    a. What an oral presentation really is.
        (1) Focus on the quality and usefulness of ideas.
    b. How to analyze an audience.
    c. How to speak for results. The importance of audience-centered speaking.
3. Assignment for the next session: Each participant is to prepare a five-minute presentation giving an analysis of an audience that he or she would be likely to address.

Session 4

1. Trainee presentations and critiques. The critiques may comment on both the style of presentation and the usefulness of the analysis.
2. How to plan an effective presentation.
    a. How to plan a purpose.
    b. How to set a scope.

    c. How to begin an effective presentation.
    d. How to develop the body.
    e. How to end for effect.
3. Assignment for the next session: Each participant is to prepare a brief presentation (three minutes) using one of the logical or persuasive patterns.

Session 5

1. Trainee presentations and critiques.
2. How to use communication (audiovisual) aids.
    a. When to use them and when not to.
      (1) The dangers of overuse.
    b. Description and demonstration of the more commonly used visual aids. (Selection of the aids to be discussed should be based on the kinds of speaking that the trainees will do on the job and the kinds of aids most likely to be useful to them.)
      (1) Boards and charts: flip charts, chalkboard, charts, display boards.
      (2) Models, mockups, and objects.
      (3) Projectors: overhead, slide, opaque, movies.
      (4) Tapes: audio, CCTV.
      (5) Handouts.
    (The discussion of each aid may include a demonstration and should include a discussion of its advantages, limitations, and suggested uses.)
      (6) How to present statistical, numerical, and quantitative data.
    c. How to work with communication-aid artists and artisans.
3. General discussion of the uses and abuses of communication aids.
4. Assignment for the next session: Each participant is to prepare a 10-minute presentation of his or her choice using appropriate communication aids.

Session 6

1. Trainee presentations and critiques.
2. Techniques of delivery. (Much of the instructor's inputs on this subject will have been made in the form of comments on the trainees' delivery in their in-class presentations. The instructor will continue to offer additional comments in the sessions to come. This session, however, provides the opportunity to put those comments together in a cohesive presentation.)
    a. Script, memory, or notes.
    b. Eye contact.
    c. Voice contact.
    d. Gesture and movement.
      (1) Control.
    e. Nervousness and readiness.
    f. Nonverbal behavior.
3. General discussion of problems with delivery
4. Assignment for the next session: Half of the trainees are to prepare 20-minute presentations on subjects of their own choosing.

Session 7

1. Trainee presentations and critique.
2. Assignment for next session: The other half of the trainees are to prepare their 20-minute presentations.

Session 8

1. Trainee presentations and critique.
2. Assignment for the next session: Each trainee is to prepare a five-minute persuasive presentation.

Session 9

1. Trainee presentations and critique.
2. General discussion of progress to this point.
3. Discussion of problems and questions. Open forum.
4. No assignment for the next session.

Session 10

1. Techniques of impromptu presentation.
   a. Special delivery considerations.
   b. How to organize the unprepared presentation.
   c. Impromptu presentations from subjects assigned by the instructor. Critiques.

Session 11

1. Additional impromptu presentations and critique.
2. Team presentations.
   a. The need for unity. How to achieve unity.
   b. Transition.
3. Assignment for the next session: Divide the class into teams of three or four. Each team is to prepare a 30-minute team presentation. Half will speak at session 12, and the other half at session 13.

Session 12

1. Team presentations and critique.

Session 13

1. Team presentations and critique.
2. Assignment for the next session: Each trainee is to prepare a 10-minute expository or instructional presentation.

Session 14

1. Trainee presentations and critique.
2. How to handle questions and discussion.
3. Assignment for the next session: Each trainee is to prepare a five-minute logical or persuasive presentation on a subject of his or her choice.

Session 15

1. Trainee presentations and critique. Each presentation should be followed by a brief period of questions from the floor.
2. No assignment for the final session.

Session 16

1. Review of the course.
2. Final trainee comments in brief impromptu presentations.
3. How to continue your skill development.

For amplification of any of the points mentioned in this outline, you may find it helpful to consult my *Communicating for Results* (see the Bibliography at end of the chapter).

The key to a successful oral presentation program will be the practice in the trainee presentations. Honest, helpful critique on these from trainees and the instructor will make these most useful as a skill-building tool.

Some instructors may prefer video and audio taping, but my experience has been that these add an undesirable artificial element. They are useful, however, for remedial work in special problems. The decision to use or avoid these aids will, of course, depend on your objectives—used to amplify and reinforce, they can have their place in an effective program.

Listening Skills

By now, everyone is aware of the differences between listening and hearing, but many listening courses are little more than hearing drills, a sharpening of auditory perception. This can be useful; many people perhaps do need to have their auditory acuity strengthened. But this should not be considered listening training.

There is another problem with listening training. In many programs, the trainees are acquainted with the major barriers to listening effectiveness and with the problems that listeners have. Then they are told, "Don't listen that way." But they are given no positive skills.

Hearing is the physical apprehension of sound. *Listening* is the search for meaning in what we see and hear—and in what is not said as well. When we hear, we observe someone else's thinking. When we listen, we think along with the speaker. Hearing is passive. Listening is active. A good listening program should deal with listening and should not be concerned primarily with hearing. And it should present a positive approach to listening skill and not be merely a recitation of proscriptions. It should allow trainees ample opportunity to practice their listening skills. A listening program is costly to develop because it requires extensive audiovisual support. The audio support should be of professional quality if the listening experience is to be of maximum value.

Listening skills can be built in another way. The principles of listening can be presented in lecture form, and the reinforcement can be offered in role-playing and similar experiences in a program designed to build other skills such as interviewing, employee counseling, or conference participation. The basic listening coverage could also be offered in one of the packaged programs and reinforced through application in a program designed to build one of the other communications skills that emphasizes listening.

For examples of two approaches to the packaged program, check the Xerox *Effective Listening* program and the packaged course *Listening on the Job,* which Sid Diamond and I prepared for Addison-Wesley.

If you choose to prepare your own listening program, the following outline should give you a sound base. Unlike the other outlined programs, this one is topical and will not be developed in sessions, as its form and length will be determined by the illustrative and workshop support you can and do give it. If this were used as the outline for a lecture, the lecture would probably last about three hours.

EFFECTIVE LISTENING

1. Your listening skill background. Contrast with education and training in other communications skills.
2. The role of listening skill in your job.
3. What you can get out of better listening.
4. You can listen better than you do.
   a. Listening is a skill.
   b. It is a skill that can be developed.
   c. It must be applied to be useful.
      (1) Listening is not a character trait but a skill.
5. Active listening.
   a. Listening is more than hearing. It is multisensual.
   b. Listen for meaning.

  c. Listen for what you can get out of what you hear.

  d. Listen actively.

 6. Listen aggressively.

  a. Eliminate distractions.

  b. Seek clarification or repetition when necessary.

 7. Speech-thought speed differential.

  a. What it is.

  b. How to use it for better listening.

 8. Questioning and summarization techniques.

 9. Eye contact.

10. The process of communication.

  a. How to find meaning.

  b. The listener's semantic input.

  c. Charged words and charged situations.

  d. The dynamics of dispute.

  e. How to listen through your own responses.

11. How to differentiate content and delivery.

  a. What delivery does to a listener.

  b. How to listen to a poor delivery.

  c. How to listen critically to a good delivery.

  d. How good listening can improve a poor delivery.

  e. How to listen for the feelings expressed by the speaker.

12. Nonevaluative listening.

  a. What evaluation, positive or negative, does to the speaker.

  b. How to listen nonevaluatively.

13. Defensive listening: why and how to avoid it.

14. Communication as a shared experience.

  a. How to listen acceptively.

15. How to develop and apply your listening skills.

Interviewing Skills

An effective program in interviewing skills should do two basic things: It should teach the trainees the skills needed for effective interviewing, and it should make them aware of the benefits and limitations of the interview as a communications tool. Too many people use interviews to achieve unrealistic aims. In countless seminars and courses I have asked participants what they could expect to learn from an employment interview. I have asked that question of many groups in many places from Texas to Teheran. The people in those groups have been managers, supervisors, executives, personnel specialists, recruiters, and employment specialists. And from almost every group I have gotten an impressive list of goals such as the candidate's personality, motivations, willingness to work, health, reasons for wanting the job, domestic tranquillity, and countless other similarly unlikely expectations. People who interview like to think that they can, in 20 minutes or an hour or two, learn everything possible about another human being except possibly his or her views on a life hereafter—and many would like to know about that.

  Interviewing skills training should give the trainees a realistic expectation of what an interview can do and what it cannot do, and the trainees should then be taught skills for making their interviews productive sessions for the sharing of information.

  The outlined program below focuses on one type of interview: the employment interview. It could be adapted to train in the skills needed to conduct exit, counseling, and appraisal interviews. This outline is for five 3-hour sessions. This course could be expanded by adding more practice sessions. Another five practice sessions would greatly increase the value and improve the skill-building experience of the course.

EFFECTIVE EMPLOYMENT INTERVIEWING

Session 1

1. Nature of the employment interview.
   a. To gain information.
   b. To give information.
2. Discussion of what we can expect to learn from an employment interview.
   a. Ask the trainees to list what they would expect to learn from an employment interview. List their responses on a board of flip chart. Then discuss each response. Help them to eliminate the unrealistic responses and to arrive at a useful list. If any of the responses relate to another information source such as the application, transcripts, the physical exam, or reference checks, point that out.
3. What we cannot expect to learn from the interview.
4. Importance of listening skill in interviewing.
   a. If the trainees have already had listening training, review the main points with them and point out applications in the interview situation. If they have not, then you should give them the major points covered in the Effective Listening outline presented in the last section.

Session 2

1. Openness and honesty: how to build rapport.
2. How to structure the purpose of an interview.
3. Environmental factors: the interview setting.
4. How to encourage communication.
   a. Questioning techniques.
   b. The directive approach.
   c. The nondirective approach.
   d. The eclectic approach.
5. How to open the interview.
6. How to close the interview.
7. Demonstration interviews. (For these you can use film, video tape, or scripted role plays. Or you can have experienced interviewers conduct them live and spontaneously. Make the situations typical. Avoid the "horrible-example" technique; you want to build positive skills, not produce comedy.)
   a. One or more demonstration interviews as time allows. Follow each with an open discussion of points raised during the interview.

Session 3

1. How to give information in an interview.
   a. What does the candidate need to know to make an effective employment decision?
   b. Unpleasant facts and how to handle them.
   c. Fact or assumption: the need for accuracy.
2. Profiles of the prospective clientele.
   a. If the trainees will be interviewing a discrete group or groups (women, minority-group members, physicists, college students, recent high school graduates, handicapped persons, veterans, or any other identifiable

group or groups), they should be given information about those groups and their special needs and interests.

Session 4

1. Practice interviews and critiques.
   a. The interview situations should be typical, and the trainees should be given adequate information on their practice interviewees. It can sometimes be helpful to let the trainees see the other role by letting them alternate as interviewees for their fellow trainees' practice interviews.

Session 5

1. More practice interviews.
2. General discussion of problems and opportunities in employment interviewing.
3. How to continue your skill development.

Reading Skills

It is difficult to present a *typical* reading skills program since each trainer seems to have his or her own approach to the subject and each is quite sure that his or her approach is the only tried-and-true method. Some use machinery to promote better perception; others do not. And the machinists and nonmachinists are often somewhat less compatible than the Hatfields and the McCoys. Some instructors have special perceptual techniques to impart; others scorn those techniques. So where does that leave you who must design or select a reading skills program?

Let us look at some criteria for an effective program. First, the machines. Are they useful? Let me avoid that controversy with a few observations. Effective programs have been conducted with and without mechanical devices, but if you are considering the adoption of a device-based program, you should determine whether the program teaches your trainees to read better with the machines or without them. If the machine is used to develop skills that are useful without the machine, then it may be an acceptable program. If it teaches people to read better with the device only, then it is not useful. Machines and devices are useful tools for remedial reading programs, but they are less likely to be useful in a developmental program.

Machines and devices may be useful in special perceptual training programs such as those which might be offered to telephone information operators, proof clerks, or others who might need to be able to pick out discrete data quickly.

An effective program should present reading as an intellectual process as well as a perceptual one. Trainess should be taught techniques of finding meaning in their reading rather than simply techniques of apprehending words. Speed training may be helpful, but trainees should be taught skill in using a variety of reading rates, each suited to the purpose of the reading and the type of material to be read. The training, in brief, should develop skills that will be useful on the job and not merely in the classroom.

The outline below is for a basic, general business reading skills program. It consists of twelve 75-minute sessions offered at the rate of two or three sessions per week.

EFFECTIVE READING SKILLS

Session 1

1. Rate and comprehension pretest.
2. What promotes effective reading?
3. How to grow in skill.

4. How the eye and the mind take in information.
   a. Fixation skills. The eye constantly moves across the page. It makes brief stops to take in information. These brief stops are called *fixations*. The skilled reader will take in several words with each stop, or fixation. The poor reader will take in only a word or part of a word.
   b. Regression and how to avoid it. Effective readers read something once, confident of their skill. Ineffective readers constantly look back at what they have already read. They flounder. Effective readers do not look back, or regress. They read with skill and confidence.
   c. Vocalization and subvocalization. To vocalize is to read aloud and to confine your reading speed to your speaking speed. To subvocalize is to lip-read or to use any of the organs of speech while reading. Subvocalization also occurs when we read aloud to ourselves inside our heads—when we "hear" what we read in our minds.
5. Speed and comprehension practice.

Session 2

1. How to read for main ideas.
2. When to read for main ideas.
3. Practice in reading for main ideas.
4. Speed and comprehension drills.

Session 3

1. Organizational patterns in writing.
2. Paragraph structure. How to recognize topic focus.
3. Practice in organization and paragraph structure.
4. Speed and comprehension drills.

Session 4

1. Skimming and scanning skills.
2. When to skim or scan.
3. Practice in skimming and scanning.
4. Speed and comprehension drills.

Session 5

1. How to read a book.
2. How to read a periodical article.
3. Prereading.
4. Speed and comprehension drills.

Session 6

1. How to read graphics and statistics.
2. Speed and comprehension drills.

Session 7

1. How to evaluate what you read.
2. Speed and comprehension drills.

Session 8

1. How to read a letter.
2. How to read a report.
3. How to manage your in-basket.
4. Speed and comprehension drills.

Session 9

1. How to remember what you read.
   a. How and when to use notes.
2. Speed and comprehension drills.

Session 10

1. Open forum: questions and problems.
2. Speed and comprehension drills.

Session 11

1. Special reading techniques. If the trainees regularly read special formats such as contracts, proposals, or specifications, show them techniques for reading these most effectively.
2. Speed and comprehension drills.

Session 12

1. Course review.
2. Posttest: final speed and comprehension check.
3. How to continue your reading skill development.

Multiple Skills Programs

If you have read all the course outlines presented in this chapter, you have probably noticed that some topics return again and again to the outlines. This makes multiple skill programs possible and even desirable if trainees need skill in more than one medium of communication.

Communications theory forms the base for any skill, and an understanding of the communications process is essential to the effective employment of any skill.

Patterns of organization are useful to the writer, speaker, listener, and reader. Transition is vital to all these skills. Speaker and writer must be able to use these skills, and reader and listener should be alert to the significance of transition in the messages they receive. Listening, of course, is an essential skill for an interviewer, a counselor, or a conference leader or participant.

Effective communicators will be able to choose the proper medium for their message and will then have the writing or oral skill to put their message across effectively. Writers may well need to know how to interview, and thus to listen, as they gather information to write about; and, of course, the writer who cannot read effectively cannot effectively or efficiently gather data.

Readers, writers, speakers, and listeners should know how to understand and use graphic and statistical data. There are many skills that are vital parts of overall communications skill, and effective communicators will have mastered all of those skills so that they fully share the information they must give and get.

The common threads running through the several skills make it possible for the creative trainer to design an overall communications skills course that will enable trainees to function fully in all the skills that are part of the communications process. This overall training can be accomplished in less time than it would take to train in the several skills one by one, and it can be accomplished more effectively because the several skills reinforce one another.

Even if the trainer chooses not to offer an overall communications skill program, he or she should consider some combinations. Listening training should certainly be included in any course on interviewing, counseling, oral presentation, conference participation, or reading. Reading and listening training blend together beautifully, as do writing and oral presentation skills training.

As you analyze your training needs, try to do so in terms of the total spectrum of communication opportunities in which your prospective trainees may need skill and offer them training which will allow them to function fully in taking best advantage of all their opportunities.

EVALUATING COMMUNICATIONS TRAINING

These programs are centered about skill development, and thus the programs are best measured by the skills they result in on the job. This means long-term evaluation for the best and most reliable results. You may choose to conduct an evaluation at the end of each course, and for this you can use a trainee reaction sheet or ask the trainees to give oral evaluations of the training experience they have just finished. This can often be productive of useful comments and observations that can help you to revise your course for maximum learning. But this immediate evaluation, as most trainers have found out, quite often produces trainee reactions to the pleasingness of the course rather than to its skill-building value.

Skill takes time to develop—time and application. Trainees must have time to try the course principles and techniques back on the job and to adapt them to their own unique opportunities for communication. Thus a delayed evaluation conducted two to four months after the course is completed can be very helpful to the trainer who wants to keep his or her training program most responsive to trainee needs.

This delayed evaluation should be of two types: trainee reaction and communications skills analysis. For the first type, trainees should be asked to give their impressions of the course and its usefulness on the job. For the second, the trainer should analyze examples of the trainees' current communication behavior for comparison with their precourse behavior and with the goals of the course.

If the training experience has been a letter-writing course, an analysis of letters written by the trainees will be the best indicator of their skills. If the results are positive, you have a reasonably reliable indicator of the course results. If the results of the analysis are negative—if they show no progress in skill—some other checking is in order before the trainer decides that the course methods or content was inadequate. One of the elements which most often inhibit skill application is what we have previously called the *organizational climate*. More bluntly stated, people or policies which have inhibited or forbidden skill application may have kept the trainees from applying skills that they learned. If this should prove to be the case, the trainer will have to revise his or her course selection procedures or will have to act to remove or change the inhibiting factors.

To get the most reliable evaluation of any communications skills program, evaluate the trainees' postcourse behavior. Skill in communication, not knowledge about skill, should have been the goal of your training program. That skill is, then, not just the best measure of your program—it is the only real measure of it.

BIBLIOGRAPHY

The books and training materials in this list are intended as a twofold guide. Some of the material will be useful in giving prospective communications skills trainers a useful background to prepare them for their training role. Some of the material will be useful as text and training materials for class use. The list is necessarily brief, but many of the works cited contain excellent bibliographies which can suggest further material. The works cited are grouped according to the skills which they support. Some of the works can be used in several areas; these have been listed under the primary area which they support. Works in the first section support no particular skill, but are listed as generally helpful to trainers and trainees alike.

Foundations of Communication

Anatasi, Thomas E.: *Desk Guide to Communication,* Devlin House, Medfield, Mass., Rev. Ed., 1976.

Burby, Raymond J.: *Communication with People: The Supervisor's Introduction to Verbal Communication and Decision-Making,* Addison-Wesley Publishing Company, Inc., Reading, Mass., 1970.

Fabun, Don: *Communication: The Transfer of Meaning,* The Glencoe Press, Beverly Hills, Calif., 1968.

Giffin, Kim, and Bobby R. Patton: *Fundamentals of Interpersonal Communication,* Harper & Row, Publishers, Incorporated, New York, 1971.

Hall, E. C.: *The Silent Language,* Doubleday & Company, Inc., Garden City, N.Y., 1959.

Haney, William V.: *Communication and Organizational Behavior,* Richard D. Irwin, Inc., Homewood, Ill., 1967.

Hayakawa, S. I.: *Language in Thought and Action,* 3d ed., Harcourt Brace Jovanovich, New York, 1972.

Mortenson, C. David (ed): *Basic Readings in Communication Theory,* Harper & Row, Publishers, Incorporated, New York, 1973.

Oral Presentation and Speaking Skills

Anastasi, Thomas E.: *Communication for Results,* Cummings, Menlo Park, Calif., 1972.

Howell, William S., and Ernest G. Borman: *Presentational Speaking for Business and the Professions,* Harper & Row, Publishers, Incorporated, New York, 1971.

Scott, Robert L. (ed.): *The Speaker's Reader: Concepts in Communication,* Scott, Foresman and Company, Glenview, Ill., 1969.

Listening, Interviewing, and Conference Skills

Anastasi, Thomas E.: *Face to Face Communication,* General Electric Educational Publications, Schenectady, N.Y., 1971.

Anastasi, Thomas E., and Sidney A. Dimond: *Listening on the Job,* Addison-Wesley Publishing Company, Inc., Reading, Mass., 1972.

Duker, Sam (ed.): *Listening: Readings,* Scarecrow Press, New York, vol. I, 1966, vol. II, 1971.

Gordon, Raymond L.: *Interviewing: Strategy, Techniques, and Tactics,* The Dorsey Press, Homewood, Ill., 1969.

Nichols, Ralph G., and Leonard A. Stevens: *Are Your Listening?* McGraw-Hill Book Company, New York, 1957.

Steinmetz, Lawrence L.: *Interviewing Skills for Supervisory Personnel,* Addison-Wesley Publishing Company, Inc., Reading, Mass., 1971.

Zelko, Harold P.: *Successful Conference and Discussion Techniques,* McGraw-Hill Book Company, New York, 1957.

Writing Skills

Baldauf, Richard B.: *A Handy Guide to Grammar and Punctuation,* Addison-Wesley Publishing Company, Inc., Reading, Mass., 1965.

Gallegher, William J.: *Report Writing for Management,* Addison-Wesley Publishing Company, Inc., Reading, 1969.

Perrin, Porter G., et al.: *Writer's Guide and Index to English,* Scott, Foresman and Company, Chicago, 1965.

Strunk, William, and E. B. White: *The Elements of Style,* The Macmillan Company, New York, 1959.

Reading Skills

Anastasi, Thomas E.: *How to Manage Your Reading,* General Electric Educational Publications, Schenedtady, N.Y., 1971.

Leedy, Paul D.: *Read with Speed and Precision,* McGraw-Hill Book Company, New York, 1963.

Lewis, Norman: *How to Read Better and Faster,* Thomas Y. Crowell Company, New York, 1958.

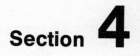

Media and Methods

Chapter **32**

Job Instruction

BIRD McCORD

Bird McCord *is a consultant and doctoral candidate in Personnel Psychology at Columbia Teachers College. Her experience includes Director of Training and Executive Placement, Famous-Barr, a division of The May Department Stores Company, St. Louis, Missouri; Personnel Director for May Merchandising, a subsidiary of The May Company; Training Director, Gimbels, New York; and she has been a frequent discussion leader at training workshops and management seminars. She holds a B.S. degree from New York University and an M.A. from Columbia University.*

In 1940, the need for trained defense workers caught American industry off guard. The World War II emergency called for developing shortcuts for assimilating new recruits into the nation's work force.

Some defense contractors felt that the shortage of manpower was not the most critical factor, but rather the lack of skill in supervising and managing workers. The typical foreman snapped, "Do it my way or else." Recruiting and training a largely inexperienced work force meant that the foreman's job changed from one of driving subordinates to one of achieving results and, at the same time, keeping production moving and workers satisfied.

Training Within Industry (TWI), an advisory service formed by the National Defense Advisory Commission, was given the responsibility for finding ways to help contractors achieve maximum utilization of manpower resources. As a result, TWI developed three training programs designed to solve production problems and to be used by operating personnel. All were developed because of demands for assistance with real needs, all were tried out in numerous situations and settings, and all were a mergence of ideas among numerous people.

Much of the credit for the industrial job during World War II was rightfully given to the work done by Training Within Industry. But TWI did far more than enable American industry to meet its wartime production needs. New ideas and new ways of viewing the human side of an organization resulted. Management, preoccupied with production needs, suddenly became aware of the relationship between the development of products and the development of the people who did the work.

American industry needed help with problems affecting production, turnover, morale, absenteeism, costs, and waste. Particularly, help was needed in finding ways of using people to their maximum potential. This was a whole new concept. The development of people as the responsibility of management made the supervisor accountable for training subordinates and for finding solutions to his or her own problems. New meaning was given to training and its role in helping management solve its production problems. Advances in training were achieved as programs that solved production problems for both supervisors and workers were developed. Learning by doing resulted in significant advances in the saving of training time. Ways of measuring and evaluating training resulted.

By the end of the war, training had become an accepted tool for management in American industry. In 1945, C. R. Dooley, director of Training Within Industry, wrote, "We have learned so much about the techniques of training that what we knew before is as nothing."[1]

ESTABLISHMENT OF TRAINING WITHIN INDUSTRY

Training Within Industry was established in August 1940 by the National Defense Advisory Commission. On April 18, 1942, by Presidential order, TWI became part of the War Manpower Commission and operated under the Bureau of Training until its close in 1945. Although no long-range objectives were set at the time of its founding, TWI started as an emergency service to defense industries. The first bulletin issued by TWI, on September 24, 1940, announced: "The underlying purpose of this activity is to assist defense industries to meet their manpower needs by training within industry each worker to make the fullest use of his best skill up to the maximum of his individual ability."

At the beginning of defense contracting, few plants had training directors or any other means of training the thousands of new, inexperienced workers who would be hired. By 1942, the increased number of shifts in plants resulted in new positions, each day, for 6,000 workers and 400 supervisors. When TWI ceased operation, it had been instrumental in training 23,000 persons as instructors and had awarded nearly 2 million certificates to supervisors who had gone through TWI programs in more than 16,000 plants, services, and unions.

The TWI Policy

The three fundamental principles of TWI, which carried through its five years of operation, were that it (1) convinced management that training is an everyday operating tool, (2) helped industry to instruct its supervisors, and (3) served as a clearinghouse of information on ways industry could meet production problems through training.

During the first year of operation, TWI acted primarily as an advisory service to defense contractors. By August of 1941, it had shifted its emphasis: influencing industry to do its own instruction through supervisory training and improvement.

Organization of TWI

The staff, composed of executives from industry, brought to TWI the experience of all that had developed in industrial training since the end of World War I. In particular, the staff members were aware of the difficulties involved in trying to convince management that production problems could be solved through training. Collectively, they contributed their experience in vestibule training, apprentice and craftsman training, foremanship development, accident prevention, work measurement, and elimination of waste.

The director of TWI was Channing R. Dooley, an engineer by training, who was lent in 1940 to TWI by Socony-Vacuum Oil Co., where he was industrial relations manager. The associate director, Walter Dietz, was personnel relations manager of the Manufacturing Department of Western Electric. Assistant directors were Michael Kane, of AT&T, and William Conover, of U.S. Steel. These four men had been acquainted for years and shared similar outlooks toward training. All, save Conover, had been on loan to the government during World War I.

In addition to the headquarters staff in Washington, D.C., the field organization was built on decentralization with officers in more than 20 districts. Each district was headed by a director on part-time loan from his company. The district representative was the full-time paid head. Staff members were borrowed on either a full- or a part-time basis from industry. Both the headquarters and district offices had officers and advisers from both management and labor.

TWI's Method of Operation

Since TWI was an advisory service, its personnel did not have the authority to enter a plant without the approval of management. TWI required that, when it started a program in a plant, one person must be charged with responsibility for training. In smaller plants, TWI made arrangements for outside trainers to be used.

At the beginning of TWI's existence, staff members presented TWI's capabilities and programs according to their own backgrounds and, consequently, often contacted the wrong people in a plant. They talked in terms of the program and how it operated, rather than the results that might be achieved. Gradually, TWI became aware of management needs, and by 1943 it had instigated a policy of initiating a program only after management and supervision had been informed.

In reporting the closing of the TWI field service, *The New York World–Telegram* cited (September 29, 1945) the following example: When Mr. Collin, TWI's upstate New York director, approached the president of a company, he was asked, "What do you want?" "I don't want anything," Mr. Collin answered, "but if I had a dozen toolmakers I'll bet you'd give me a warmer reception. I don't have the toolmakers, but I have something that will help you get along without them."

By 1944, TWI had adopted an "operating plan": A program could not be started in a plant without a definite plan, aimed at the continuation of the use of principles of the program.

The *TWI Bulletin* began placing emphasis on management involvement and on how a training director might "sell" a program to management. In bulletin after bulletin, TWI insisted that more programs failed because they were poorly presented to management than for any other reason. It constantly reminded training people that when training can offer something to the line organization, the program of selling is simplified.

Background of Job Training

Vocational training began in the earliest civilization when parents gave job instruction to their children. Apprenticeship training can be traced to ancient times. It was brought to the American colonies from Western Europe. Later, when the growth of the factory system gave rise to tyrannical bosses, it became evident that better methods of industrial training were needed. Gradually, as a result of the influence of Frederick Taylor in the early 1900s, developments in education and psychology, and what had been learned during World War I, direction shifted from driving workers to produce to viewing the supervisor's role as one of obtaining production through people.

Influence of Frederick W. Taylor The major thrust of Taylor's work was to increase production. By talking with managers and workers, he discovered that managers often did not know what they wanted from workers and that workers, in turn, did not know what managers wanted. Taylor studied methods and equipment and analyzed the steps important in doing a job. He divided the work into simple, elementary movements and discarded the ones he considered useless. Then, by observing the fastest and most skilled worker and by using a stopwatch, he recorded each motion. Thus, through mathematical calculations, he could determine the proper length of time required to do almost any job. This process enabled him to establish standards for both quality and quantity.

Taylor's critics thought him preoccupied with equipment because they considered workers only in terms of skill and production. However, Taylor placed emphasis on standardization and development of superior methods, and he believed that it was possible, scientifically, to select and train workers. He developed an instruction (or method) card which gave a worker each specific part of the job to be performed, together with the time required for each step or operation.

Influence of Educators and Psychologists   Johann Friedrich Herbart, a nineteenth-century German psychologist, sought to prove that education is a science. In teaching that the student's learning is the result of the teacher's instruction, he influenced educational methods in the United States. Herbart believed that the mind receives and assimilates new ideas in a certain pattern. Therefore, any subject might be presented to the student according to a standard format. He outlined four steps of instruction in the learning process:[2]

Clearness . . . . Analysis and synthesis
Association . . . . The ability to build on what
                                                       is already known
System . . . . Organizing new information
                                                       with what is already known
Method . . . . Practice

A number of American educators influenced the development of industrial training methods. Among these were Horace Mann, who taught that useful knowledge was more important than philosophic wisdom, and John Dewey, who saw learning as an orderly process and placed emphasis on practical experience.

Edward Thorndike, experimenting with animals, developed two fundamental laws of learning: (1) the law of habit formation, which states that the right movements can be put in the proper sequence and practiced until they become routine, and (2) the law of effect, which states that a response is strengthened when a task is performed correctly, while annoying or less satisfying responses are weakened.[3]

These and others contributed to the development of a method of training which uses procedural steps to condition the learner; this method presents one step at a time, demonstrating and explaining it until it is done correctly.

Training in World War I   In 1917, the Emergency Fleet Corporation of the U.S. Shipping Board needed 450,000 additional workers. A former vocational instructor of the Massachusetts State Board of Education, Charles R. (Skipper) Allen, aided by his group in the Emergency Fleet Corporation, developed a method to train shipbuilders. It was based on Herbart's four steps of instruction. Allen named these:

Preparation . . . . Show
Presentation . . . . Tell
Application . . . . Do
Inspection . . . . Check

From Allen's findings, and those of the Army during World War I, the following principles were developed for use in industrial training:

- Training should be done within industry.
- Training should be done by supervisors. (The ability to instruct is an important part of the supervisor's job.)
- Supervisors should be trained in how to instruct.
- The best group size for training is 9 to 11 people.
- The preparation of a job breakdown is an important step before training.
- Break-in time is reduced when training is done on the job.
- When given personal attention in training, the worker develops a feeling of loyalty.

Allen foresaw the need for the TWI programs:

> We would have the best conditions if 1) Each man was trained to do his job in the best possible way; 2) Each man was trained to do his job in the least possible time compatible with training; 3) The experience of each man during the training period had been such that he stayed through the training period and did not quit when only partly trained.[4]

Although some discussion did take place as the result of Allen's work and although a few books on how to instruct did appear during the '20s and '30s, not until the need for defense production became serious in 1940 were steps taken to develop a method of instruction.

Development of Job Programs

The programs that TWI developed tended to serve two purposes: They solved new or recurring production problems, and they gave a sense of satisfaction to supervisors who participated. In all, three job programs were developed, based on the same fundamentals. Each was:

1. Subjected to extensive tryouts and revisions to make it simple and practical, using shop rather than theoretical terms.
2. Developed to help supervisors solve their own problems.
3. Standardized so that large numbers of persons could be reached—a task which otherwise might have been impossible. (Standardized materials were developed in the form of manuals which frequently directed the instructor to illustrate major points on a blackboard. Other audiovisual devices had been considered and discarded because in 1940 they were not readily available in most organizations.)
4. Based on learning by doing, using actual case problems. Each case involved instruction, action, drill, improvement, training, and checking. (Of these, drill became the most important. "What to do" is not enough. Only when people are drilled in "how to do it" does action result.[5])
5. Founded on a "multiplier principle": training persons who, in turn, could train others.
6. Dependent upon creating the proper atmosphere by setting a tone of informality. (Terms such as "class," "teacher," and "student" were avoided. Instead, "meeting," "instructor," and "learner" or "worker" were used.)
7. Planned for 10 persons in 5 two-hour sessions, scheduled within a two-week period—on company time and at company expense.

As TWI worked with training directors, it discovered five relative needs of all supervisors. These are shown in Fig. 32-1.

This helped clarify the role of training by showing that certain supervisory needs, unique to a specific situation, would have to be met by the plant. TWI developed programs only in those areas which were consistent in all industries.

Acceptance of Programs   TWI gained wide approval for developing Job Instruction as an effective method of teaching. The acceptance of this and other TWI programs was due, in part, to the way they were developed: All were the result of demands from the districts and were based on common needs. The sheer size of the job of training vast numbers of inexperienced workers, and the fact that few contractors had training capabilities, undoubtedly contributed to TWI's acceptance. In addition, the programs were adaptable to most industries and jobs. Plant personnel liked the TWI staff, many of whom, like themselves, were from industry.

From its inception, TWI worked with organized labor. Before any job program was introduced into a plant, the union was informed.

Measurement of Effectiveness   Prior to 1943, there had been little attempt to measure training results. When the Job Methods program was introduced, the savings in both cost and labor soon became evident. In addition, the House

Appropriations Committee asked for figures to back up the claims made by TWI concerning reductions in training time and increases in production. Since total figures were not available, 600 plants volunteered statements, from which the

---

EVERY SUPERVISOR HAS FIVE NEEDS

Needs	Provided by
1. Knowledge of the work Materials, tools, processes, operations, and products used	Plant
2. Knowledge of responsibilities Policies, agreements, rules, regulations, schedules, interdepartmental relationships	Plant
3. Skill in instructing Increasing production by developing a well-trained work force	Job Instruction Training
4. Skill in improving methods More effective utilizations of materials, machines, and manpower by having supervisors study each part of the job in order to eliminate, combine, rearrange, and simplify details	Job Methods Training
5. Skill in leading Assisting supervisors in improving their understanding of individuals, their ability to size up situations, and ways of working with people	Job Relations Training

---

Fig. 32-1 Supervisor needs. (*Training Within Industry Report, 1940–1945,War Manpower Commission, Bureau of Training, Washington, September 1945, p. 48.*)

first report was compiled. From this beginning, reports continued to be used to interest management in the results achieved through use of the programs.

The major contribution of TWI during its lifetime was making American industry aware that it could solve its production problems through training.

The lasting contributions of TWI are that it proved to management what training is and what benefits can be achieved from its use. It instructed line executives and supervisors in the use of training methods, it made the training staff responsible for the planning and development of training, and it proved that production problems can be solved through training.

JOB INSTRUCTION TRAINING (JIT)

During the first week of operation, TWI received an assignment. One of the most critical manpower shortages was in skilled lens grinders and polishers for government arsenals and Navy yards. Fulfilling its role as an advisory service, TWI held a conference with representatives from the major lens-grinding and precision instruments plants. Twenty separate jobs were involved in grinding, and it was considered necessary for each operator to learn all of these, requiring approximately five full years.

The outcome of the conference was a recommendation to upgrade the present workers in precision optical work to the most highly skilled jobs and to break in new workers on one simple job. This required that a number of jobs and operations be broken down, job specifications written, and a training program developed.

The government borrowed Michael J. Kane from AT&T to visit defense contractors and to develop materials for a training program. As a result of Kane's program, mastery of one of the simpler jobs could be acquired within a few months.

In breaking down each part of the job, Kane discovered that it was possible to identify a few critical points. Since these areas were the keys to good work, he called them "key points." They later became the basis for the job breakdown. In developing the lens-grinding program, Kane used the instruction steps developed by C. R. Allen during World War I. However, he expanded Allen's four-step method to a *seven-step method of instruction:*

1. Show workers how to do it.
2. Explain key points.
3. Let them watch you do it again.
4. Let them do the simple parts of the job.
5. Help them do the whole job.
6. Let them do the whole job—but watch them.
7. Put them on their own.

At a meeting of the New Jersey district TWI group in the spring of 1941, Glenn Gardiner, New Jersey's district director and vice president of Forstmann Woolens, stated that he believed the four basic steps of Charles Allen could be used in developing a standard program on "How to Instruct." The program was developed by the New Jersey group and reviewed by the district committee in June of 1941. "If the learner hasn't learned, the teacher hasn't taught" was the slogan.[6]

Within a month, New Jersey plants were requesting the use of the program, and by August of 1941 it was presented to TWI district directors and adopted for national use. The use of the word "job" in Job Instruction Training indicated that the program was simple, fundamental, and on the job level.

In August 1941, at a meeting of district directors, came a decision to change TWI's direction from that of an advisory service and to focus on supervisory improvement, particularly on the most acute problem faced by plants: that of training new workers. As a result, it was decided to develop a nationwide JIT program to give the supervisor practice in how to break in the new worker.

In perfecting the JIT program, TWI combined the best of Kane's program— the job breakdown consisting of steps and key points—with the four-step method of instruction used by Gardiner. The program required 10 hours of instruction for a group of 10 supervisors (see Fig. 32-2).

JIT was introduced in October 1941 and was rapidly accepted by management. By the fall of 1945, over a million persons—supervisors and instructors—had been trained in JIT. Its acceptance was due to the fact that it was a fast solution to the problem of training new workers. It was interesting to watch and to take part in, and it related directly to the needs of supervisors.

Although the Job Instruction program, as developed by TWI, was not new, it put into standard format the already existing principles of good instruction. It became an organized method of training based on supervised instruction, enabling the employee to perform specific skill while actually working on the job.

Major Points of JIT

Job Breakdown The manual required that before instructors developed the job breakdown in the first JIT session, they explain, verbally, how to tie a fire

STANDARD 10-HOUR JOB INSTRUCTION PLAN

SESSION I. 2 hours

    Introduction
    Importance of training to production
    Instructing ability as a personal asset
    Demonstration of faulty instruction
    Demonstration of correct instruction
    The FOUR BASIC STEPS
    Distribution of "How to Instruct" cards
    (Selection of two volunteers for the next session)

SESSION II. 2 hours

    Two volunteers "instructing" demonstration to bring out the NEED for the four things an
      instructor must do to "get ready"

    Practice in making Job Breakdowns of:
      (a) The fire underwriters' knot
      (b) The two jobs presented during the first hour
    Summary: The four things an instructor does to "get ready"

SESSION III. 2 hours

    Drill on training time tables
    Three practice instruction demonstrations with coaching on Job Breakdowns

SESSION IV. 2 hours

    Four practice instruction demonstrations with coaching on Job Breakdowns

SESSION V. 2 hours

    Three practice instruction demonstrations
    Conclusion and Summary:
      (a) Questions
      (b) Importance of good Job Instruction to production
      (c) Necessity of using the Job Instruction Plan

ADHERE STRICTLY TO THIS PLAN—DO NOT DEPART FROM IT OR CHANGE IT

Fig. 32-2 Supervisory instruction. (*Job Instruction, War Manpower Commission, Bureau of Training, Training Within Industry Service, Washington, 1944.*)

underwriter's knot. Since tying this knot is somewhat complicated and since few, if any, of the participants knew how to do it, the point was apparent: Simply telling someone how to do a job is not enough. This was an appropriate lead-in to having the group prepare a job breakdown (see Fig. 32-3).

There was considerable disagreement among plants over the selection of the underwriter's knot for demonstration. Many felt that it was obscure and unrelated to their type of production. (The underwriter's knot is so named because of its specification in insurance policies. It is used in most electrical fixtures and appliances, and it helps relieve the strain on wire connections.) In adapting the program to peacetime use, many organizations substituted other tasks, not widely known to participants, for demonstration purposes.

SESSION OUTLINE

Timetable 5. Break down the fire underwriters' knot.   References

    a. Here's a quick simple way to make a breakdown.

    b. Explain that here is what you did to get fire underwriters' knot clear in your mind before instructing.

    NOTE: Pass out blank Breakdown Sheets and explain headings, important steps, and key points.

    c. Take wire and go to board.

      +Write down headings PART and OPERATION. FILL in.

      +Do the first important step, then write it on the board.

      +Do the second important step, write it down, and so on through.

      +Then tie the knot again, step by step, bringing out each key point.

      +Ask yourself aloud the three questions for each step and answer them yourself.

    d. Establish the breakdown on the board in numbered steps as follows:

Part: Twisted Lamp Cord	Operation: Tie Fire Underwriters' Knot
Important Steps	Key Points
(1) Untwist and straighten	6 inches
(2) Make r.h. loop	in front of main strand
(3) Make l.h. loop	pull toward you
	under stub
	behind main strand
(4) Put end through loop	
(5) Pull taut	end even,
	knot snug

WORK FROM THIS OUTLINE—DON'T TRUST TO MEMORY

Fig. 32-3 Job breakdown procedure. (*Job Instruction, War Manpower Commission, Bureau of Training, Training Within Industry Service, Washington, 1944.*)

The instructor or supervisor prepared a job breakdown on the job while watching an experienced worker perform each step of the job. The preparation of the breakdown ensured that supervisors covered all the steps in the job, helped them organize their thinking so that they introduced each step of the operation in the right sequence, and required that they become familiar with all aspects of the job, particularly the mechanical operations, with which they may have had little or no previous experience. As they observed each step, they recorded it on a breakdown, sometimes called a *blueprint* (see Fig. 32-4). (A well-written job breakdown should be detailed enough to serve as a step-by-step procedure so that an

---

JOB BREAKDOWN SHEET FOR TRAINING PURPOSES

DEPARTMENT _Lens Grinding_   JOB _Centering_

BREAKDOWN MADE BY _Joseph Nelson_   DATE _Sept. 2, 1941_

IMPORTANT STEPS (WHAT TO DO) A logical segment of the operation, when something happens to advance the work	KEY POINTS (HOW TO DO IT) Anything that may: Make or break the job Injure the worker Make the work easier to do
1. Place piece on plate against regulating wheel	Knack - don't catch on wheel
2. Lower level wheel	Hold at end of stroke (count 1, 2, 3, 4) Slow feed. Watch - no oval grinding
3. Raise lever - release	
4. Gauge pieces periodically	More often as approach tolerance
5. Readjust regulating wheel as required	Watch - no backlash
6. Repeat above until finished	

Fig. 32-4 Job breakdown blueprint

individual, unfamiliar with the job, can perform each step satisfactorily.) The operation was recorded in a single, brief statement; for example, "Adjust the tension."

Next, the key point was recorded. This was the part of a step that was the "key" to doing it correctly—to making it easier to perform. Instructors were taught to ask three questions in determining the key points: Is there anything in the step that will make or break the job? Hurt the worker? Make the work easier to do? Key points did not include every possible thing that might be done. The purpose of the list was to make certain that the supervisor did not overlook the key points which were crucial in training a new worker. Knowing what the key points were and

Fig. 32-5 Job Instruction card.

being able to identify them quickly constituted one of the most important aspects of the Job Instruction process. For example, when using a knife, a key point is "Cut away from you."

The Four Basic Steps   The four steps in a Job Instruction pocket card format were first used by C. R. Allen during the 1920s. The four steps of "How to Instruct," introduced during session I, appeared on one side of the card, and the four-step method on "How to Get Ready to Instruct," introduced during session II, appeared on the reverse side of the card (see Fig. 32-5).

Training Timetables   It had been assumed that each supervisor would set a date by which time each worker should have developed a specified amount of skill. Later, the development of the training timetable was included as a part of session III in the JIT program (see Fig. 32-6).

Induction Outline   The June 1943 *TWI Bulletin* introduced the need for the development of an introductory outline for newly hired workers. A sample outline was developed for the first week of employment, indicating the major topics and responsibility for each (see Fig. 32-7). The development of a plan of induction then became part of the JIT program for any new worker.

JOB METHODS TRAINING (JMT)

After the JIT program had been in existence for a year, TWI undertook, as its next task, the development of a program to conserve manpower, machines, and materials. Glenn Gardiner (the New Jersey district director of TWI) set the requirements for the program: It should be practical, have everyday use, and be based on simplified principles of industrial engineering. Moreover, it should follow the same pattern as JIT: five 2-hour sessions for 10 supervisors. The initial name on the first four-step cards was "How to Improve War Production Methods," but it was soon changed to "How to Improve Job Methods."

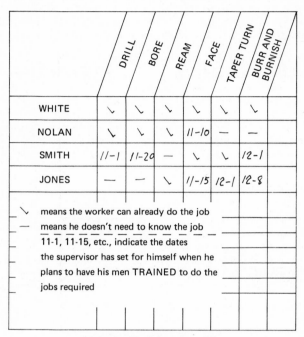

	DRILL	BORE	REAM	FACE	TAPER TURN	BURR AND BURNISH	
WHITE	＼	＼	＼	＼	＼	＼	
NOLAN	＼	＼	＼	11-10	—	—	
SMITH	11-1	11-20	—	＼	＼	12-1	
JONES	—	—	＼	11-15	12-1	12-8	

＼ means the worker can already do the job
— means he doesn't need to know the job
11-1, 11-15, etc., indicate the dates
the supervisor has set for himself when he
plans to have his men TRAINED to do the
jobs required

Fig. 32-6 Training timetable.

The overall objective was to help supervisors improve and simplify their job and the jobs of their subordinates by designing a better method or process. The program emphasized that through improved job methods, supervisors could eliminate the unnecessary parts of a job while making the necessary parts easier and safer to perform. JMT was the first attempt to make supervisors responsible for improving job methods. It was influenced by earlier work, done by Taylor and other industrial engineers.

Unlike JIT, JMT was based on improving or changing certain aspects of the job. This required that ideas and suggestions be approved by the organization. Therefore, management as well as labor had to be notified before the program could be offered in a plant. The new plan changed TWI's operating policy and required that a representative of management sponsor every TWI program. JMT was introduced to a conference of district directors in May 1942 and was adopted for national use.

Major Points for JMT

Demonstration To show the application of the four steps of Job Methods, a problem involving unnecessary movements was presented. The instructor demonstrated the making of a radio shield in session I.

Although many industries criticized the use of this particular demonstration, it was retained because of the ease of shaping a portable replica. (Any similar demonstration might be presented.)

Job Breakdown Participants were required to develop two breakdowns: one on the "present method" and the other on the "proposed method." In developing the present-method breakdown, supervisors learned to challenge the way the job was done. A brief statement of action was entered on the breakdown in column 1. (This is step 1 on the Job Methods card.)

In illustrating the steps in the four-step process, the instructor told the group to cross off all unnecessary details on the present-method breakdown and to combine any details that seemed practical. The instructor illustrated the four-step method (as shown in Fig. 32-8) on the blackboard.

In the second column, supervisors were instructed to make notes on any particular facts about the detail of the action. In the third column, participants developed new methods for doing the job by using steps 2 and 3 on the Job Methods card (see Figs. 32-9 to 32-11).

Sessions II to V At the conclusion of session I, participants were asked to select a small job in their department that had given them difficulty and to apply the four-step method in developing a present-method and a proposed-method breakdown. During sessions II to V, participants were asked to present their breakdowns according to the following format:

The Eight Steps of a Practice Demonstration

1. Describe the job.
2. Demonstrate the method.
3. Read the details—present.
4. Use information from step 2.
5. Show how information is used in step 3.
6. Demonstrate the proposed method.
7. Sum up.

When calling on volunteers to present their ideas, the JMT manual advised instructors to:

- Ask the volunteer, "Is this idea new?" "Have you made a present and a proposed breakdown?"
- Call on the next volunteer if the answer to either of the above questions was "no."
- Have the volunteer follow the demonstration procedure outlined above.

In commenting on each demonstration, instructors were advised to:

- Compliment the volunteer on the good points that showed application of the Job Methods plan.
- Ask members whether they had any questions about the demonstration or any suggestions for further improvements.
- Discuss the application of each part of the four steps and exactly how each helped the supervisor make improvements.
- Stress the questions, "Was it worked out with the operator(s)?" "How was credit given (or planned)?"
- Not assume the attitude of an "expert"—to lead the discussion only.
- Sum up (using the blackboard) the results of the improvements in terms of increased production and machine use, savings in materials, better quality, safety and housekeeping, etc.

Job Methods Proposal In session II, participants were asked to develop a Job Methods proposal form. This was submitted to management along with the breakdown forms in order to obtain approval on job changes (see Fig. 32-12).

INDUCTION OUTLINE

WHEN & WHERE?	WHAT & HOW?	BY WHOM?
First Day		
1. On arrival in plant	1. Introduce to working supervisor	1. By person hiring
2. On arrival in dept., 15 minutes	2. Information needed in daily routine +Any information new employee may need on getting to and from work, parking regulations, etc. +Starting time, lunch period, quitting time, hours per week +Review of compensation items (when will employee be paid, where, how much?) +Opportunity for questions	2. By supervisor
3. Following preliminary interview, 1/2 hour	3. Meeting other workers, getting to know layout of building +Take trip through dept. with general explanation of product +Show him where he is to work and meet neighboring workers +Tell him about any special rules on smoking, leaving dept., etc.	3. Supervisor or group leader
4. Following until noon	4. Job instruction	4. By person who is to handle training
5. Noon	5. Show location of cafeteria and lunch with him +Show recreation facilities +Introduce him to others	5. Neighboring worker
6. After lunch until 1/2 hour before quitting time	6. Job instruction	6. Trainer
7. 1/2 hour before closing	7. Give pass, explain use and regulation in case of absence. Give book of rules and regulations	7. Supervisor
Second Day		
1. At a convenient time, 1/2 hour	1. Review booklet of rules and regulations +To see that he understands subjects covered in booklet +To give opportunity to ask questions	1. Supervisor

| 2. At a convenient time, 15 minutes | 2. Check through job with safety engineer and review policies and procedures on safety | 2. Safety engineer |

Fifth Day

| | 1. Interview with worker
+Find out what he is thinking
+Clear up any misunderstanding
+Give opportunity for questions | 1. Supervisor |

Within First Week

| | 1. Meet with other new men from other depts.
+Tour plant
+Have organization setup described
+Have mutual benefit and other organization plans described | 1. Personnel |

Fig. 32-7 Induction outline. *(TWI Bulletin, War Manpower Commission, Washington, June 1943, pp. 6–7.)*

JOB RELATIONS TRAINING (JRT)

Prior to the start of World War II, human relations programs developed by industry varied widely.

In August 1941, TWI mailed a questionnaire on supervisory needs to several hundred supervisors and executives. The replies indicated weaknesses in handling people. As an advisory service, TWI had suggested that training in supervisory skills should be done by the individual plant, since specific duties and responsibilities within the plants varied. It did not seem feasible to develop a single program for all industries. As a result of the survey, TWI organized a 10-hour intensive program, following the same format as JIT and JMT. The program was designed to further skill and practice in handling human problems. The words "job relations," rather than "human relations," emphasized that the program was directed toward the job.

JRT was based largely on the results of the Hawthorne study, conducted at the Western Electric Hawthorne plant. The program was developed under the supervision of Walter Dietz, who was on loan from Western Electric and was experienced in human relations. F. J. Roethlisberger, who had written *Management and the Worker*, was made responsible for the initial plans, including determining the direction of the program.[7] Dietz and Roethlisberger sought to answer the question: What can be done to increase knowledge and improve understanding of supervision at the work level?[8]

JRT was not intended to give training in specific job responsibilities; TWI maintained that this was the duty of the individual plant. It also assumed that supervisors knew the job.

Job Relations was presented as an everyday relationship between supervisors and those whom they supervised. Poor relationships caused poor results; good relationships lead to good results. The JRT program placed emphasis on making supervisors aware that because they were managers, their best results came through good relationships with those whom they supervised.

JRT was by far the most comprehensive of the TWI programs. It required longer than two years to research, develop, and try out. In the fall of 1941 the first 10-hour program was completed, and during 1942 it was tested. In all, 10 revisions were made, and in February 1943 it became available to industrial plants.

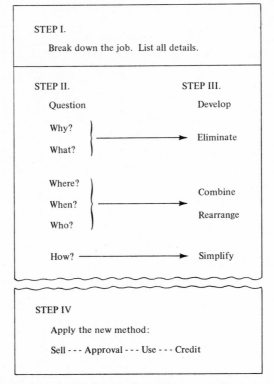

STEP I.

    Break down the job. List all details.

STEP II.   STEP III.

    Question   Develop

    Why?   Eliminate

    What?

    Where?

    When?   Combine

    Who?   Rearrange

    How?   Simplify

STEP IV

    Apply the new method:

    Sell - - - Approval - - - Use - - - Credit

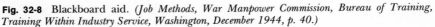

Fig. 32-8 Blackboard aid. (*Job Methods, War Manpower Commission, Bureau of Training, Training Within Industry Service, Washington, December 1944, p. 40.*)

Only the chart in the first session remained unchanged throughout the 10 revisions. During the first few revisions, problems were used that revealed the use of both good and poor supervisory methods. TWI felt that management and supervisor would object to the discussion of actual problems. However, TWI discovered that supervisory situations, with clearly denoted errors, proved more beneficial than those which seemed contrived. The final versions of the program required supervisors to present at a session any problem for resolving within their scope of responsibility.

Session I The first session developed supervisory responsibility. The members of the group were asked to state the duties for which they were accountable. The instructor filled these in on the circular chart under "A Supervisor Gets Results through People" (see Fig. 32-13).

Next, the group was asked to state the factors affecting each employee as an individual. These were filled in on the chart under "People Must Be Treated as Individuals." Then the instructor developed the points of the four-step method for Job Relations (see Fig. 32-14).

The session was concluded by the instructor's reading a case illustrating step I of the four-step method. Participants were requested to bring in their own problems and present them to the class.

Sessions II to IV A standard format was used during these sessions. The instructor reviewed the four-step method and read aloud a problem illustrating one of the steps. After the reading, the group was expected to determine the objective, that is, what the supervisor should try to achieve. The instructor used

Operation   Inspect, Assemble, Rivet, Stamp, and Pack   Product   Radio Shields

Your Name   Bill Jones   Operator's Name   Jim Brown   Department   Packing   Date   June 16, 1974

List of all details for Present / ~~Proposed~~ Method	Notes	Ideas
Every single thing that is done. Every inspection. Every delay.	Reminders. Tolerance. Distance. Time used, etc.	Don't trust your memory. Write them down.
1. Walk to box of copper sheets	Placed 6' from bench by handler	
2. Pick up 15 to 20 copper sheets		
3. Walk to bench		
4. Inspect and lay out 12 sheets	Scratches and dents. Scrap in bins	
5. Walk to box and replace extra sheets		
6. Pick up 15 to 20 brass sheets		
7. Walk to bench		
8. Inspect and lay out 12 brass sheets	One on top of each copper sheet	
9. Walk to box and replace extra sheets		
10. Walk to box of brass sheets	One on top of each copper sheet	

Fig. 32-9 Present-method breakdown. (*Training Within Industry Report, 1940–1945, War Manpower Commission, Bureau of Training, Washington, September 1945, p. 228.*)

the four-step method by asking the group to state the facts of the problem. Then he or she wrote on the blackboard the group's responses to each step (see Fig. 32-15).

The original Job Relations program was used with union stewards. A later version, Union Job Relations, was released early in 1945.

WHAT THE J PROGRAMS CONTRIBUTED

Lasting Influences

JIT Since it is based on a mechanical-step procedure, JIT is difficult to apply to certain jobs, such as sales and clerical positions; however, although variations of the original four-step, seven-step, and nine-step methods have evolved, the essential principles remain the same.

Job Instruction gives an individual a sense of performing a meaningful job while learning, whereas classroom training may tend to prolong the "trainee" stage. Based on performance rather than subject matter, Job Instruction is relevant in an era concerned with increasing productivity. It plays an important role in industries where it is difficult to keep workers informed, where technology is changing

Operation   Inspect, Assemble, Rivet, Pack   Product   Radio Shields

Your Name   William Brown   Operator's Name   Sam Oats   Dept.   Packing   Date   June 17, 1974

List of all details for Proposed Method	Notes		Ideas
Every single thing that is done.	Reminders.	Tolerance.	Write them down. Don't trust your memory.
Every inspection. Every delay.	Distance.	Time used, etc.	
1. Put pile of copper sheets in right jig	Boxes placed on table by handler		
2. Put pile of brass sheets in left jig			
3. Pick up 1 copper sheet in right hand and 1 brass sheet in left hand			
4. Inspect both sheets	Scratches and dents. Drop scrap through slots		
5. Assemble sheets and place in fixture	Fixes, lines up sheets, and locates brass sheet		
6. Rivet the two bottom corners			
7. Remove, reverse, and place sheets			
8. Rivet the two top corners			
9. Place shield in front of fixture	Repeat #3 to #9 eight times		
10. Put 20 shields in shipping case, 200/case	Cases placed by handler		

Fig. 32-10   Proposed-method breakdown. *(Training Within Industry Report, 1940–1945, War Manpower Commission, Bureau of Training, Washington, September 1945, p. 229.)*

WMC-T-4

HOW TO IMPROVE
JOB METHODS

A practical plan to help you produce GREATER QUANTITIES of QUALITY PRODUCTS in LESS TIME, by making the best use of the **Manpower, Machines and Materials**, now available.

STEP I—BREAK DOWN the job.
1. List **all** details of the job **exactly** as done by the **Present Method**.
2. Be sure details **include all:—**
   - Material Handling.
   - Machine Work.
   - Hand Work.

STEP II—QUESTION every detail.
1. Use these types of questions:

   WHY is it necessary?
   WHAT is its purpose?
   WHERE should it be done?
   WHEN should it be done?
   WHO is best qualified to do it?
   HOW is the "best way" to do it?

2. Also question the:
   Materials, Machines, Equipment, Tools, Product Design, Layout, Work-place, Safety, Housekeeping.

16—31488-2

STEP III—DEVELOP the new method.
1. **ELIMINATE unnecessary** details.
2. **COMBINE** details when practical.
3. **REARRANGE** for better sequence.
4. **SIMPLIFY** all **necessary** details:

   To make the work **easier** and **safer**
   - **Pre-position** materials, tools and equipment at the best places in the **proper work area**.
   - Use **gravity-feed** hoppers and **drop-delivery** chutes.
   - Let **both hands** do useful work.
   - Use **jigs** and **fixtures** instead of hands, for holding work.

5. **Work out your idea with others.**
6. Write up your proposed **new method.**

STEP IV—APPLY the new method.
1. Sell your proposal to your **"boss."**
2. Sell the new method to the **operators.**
3. Get final approval of all concerned on Safety, **Quality, Quantity, Cost.**
4. Put the new method to work. Use it until a **better** way is developed.
5. Give **credit** where credit is due.

JOB METHODS TRAINING PROGRAM
Training Within Industry Service
BUREAU OF TRAINING
War Manpower Commission

G∩O 16—31488-3

Fig. 32-11 Job Methods card.

JOB METHODS PROPOSAL

To _____ Date _____

From _____ Department _____

Product or Part _____

Following is my proposal for improving the method for doing the work:*

_____

_____

_____

_____

_____

_____

_____

_____

_____

_____

_____

_____

*Note. Tell exactly HOW you believe this improvement can be accomplished. Use another sheet for additional information or sketches if needed. Attach Present and Proposed Breakdown sheets.

Fig. 32-12 Job methods proposal. (*Training Within Industry Plan for Improving Job Methods, War Manpower Commission, J-M 10, Washington, September 1943.*)

rapidly, and where diversification and geographically widespread organizations make centralized training impossible. Companies which are too small to have other means of training or which employ too few people to warrant the use of other types of training benefit from its use. Also, JIT has played an important role as an easily implemented method of training and upgrading workers in underdeveloped countries.

However, in the United States, Job Instruction is only one means of instruction (not the only one, as it was in the '40s), and it should be selected for use only where it is best suited.

Job Instruction fails when there is no follow-up coaching or where a supervisor merely leaves an employee to learn on the job without instruction.

JMT Through experience with JMT, TWI learned the importance of securing management involvement and support before introducing any training program. The need for regular coaching by the instructor was necessary for the program to be effective on an ongoing basis. With regular follow-up, JMT furnished a fast yet practical method of analyzing a job, helped build morale by

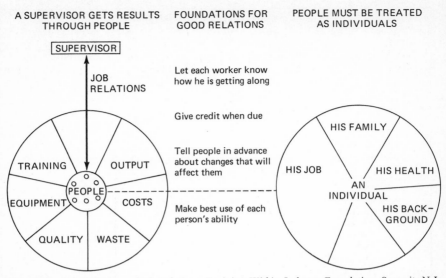

A SUPERVISOR GETS RESULTS
THROUGH PEOPLE

FOUNDATIONS FOR
GOOD RELATIONS

PEOPLE MUST BE TREATED
AS INDIVIDUALS

Fig. 32-13 Job Relations. (*Job Relations, Training Within Industry Foundation, Summit, N.J. 1947, p. 31.*)

giving supervisors a means of receiving recognition for improvements, and laid the framework for continued improvement.

Of the three programs, JMT probably contributed the least as far as lasting influence is concerned. It was criticized for being too technical for the average supervisor to use.

JRT The development and design of supervisory and leadership training in the late 1940s and 1950s were greatly influenced by JRT. Although no longer called "job relations" or "human relations" programs, training programs for

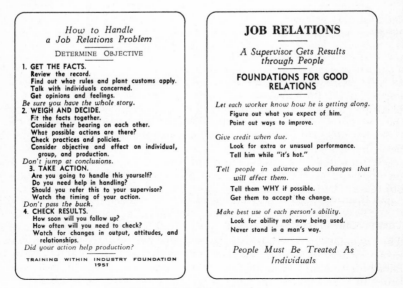

Fig. 32-14 Job Relations card.

first-level supervisors remain influenced by the approach developed by TWI: presentation of real-world problems and discussion of actual supervisory situations.

What We Have Learned Since All three J programs placed emphasis on teaching, rather than on learning. Today, the focus is on the learner, rather than

---

BLACKBOARD GUIDE—TOM—PROBLEM NO. 2

Just what is Tom's supervisor trying
to accomplish?

1. Get the facts
2. Weigh and decide
3. Take action
4. Check results

To make Tom a safe
worker and get work
back to normal.

Weigh and decide

Possible actions
Warn about rules on care of equipment
Give penalty layoff

Facts

Report bad cards
Tell him losing girl isn't your fault

Was good worker
Quality and quantity down
Careless

Action

Warned before
Barked back
Lost his girl
Felt nobody cared
Cards bent

Told Tom he was sorry
Asked Tom's help
Checked cards
Reported faulty cards

Fig. 32-15 Job Relations session II. (*Job Relations, Training Within Industry Foundation, Summit, N.J., 1947, p. 65.*)

the instructor. JIT does not give the learner the reasons for performing a job in a particular way. In wartime, correct performance was emphasized as something all workers should strive for in order to further defense efforts. Today, it is important for the employee to understand the reasons for doing a job in a particular way and to understand the importance of his or her contribution to the overall functioning of the organization.

We have learned the importance of analyzing performance deficiencies before designing a training program. We know the importance of writing behavioral objectives stated in performance terms. We have learned to use a number of methods and to decide which one is best—only after a careful analysis of the objectives. The J programs, particularly JIT, prescribed the method of instruction before determining the problem.

Contributions to the Training Field

The most important contributions of the J programs were their influence in professionalizing the field of training. TWI discovered two major reasons for the failure of training. First, where there is a history of a training department's promoting generalized training programs, unrelated to the problems of the organization, management fails to see training as an effective tool. Second, when a training staff is preoccupied with means—how the program is to operate and the methodology to be used—rather than with the results, management fails to see a relationship between training and its ability to solve operating problems.

Perhaps the single outstanding accomplishment was that training became inherent in management and, when properly used, an effective tool of management.

REFERENCES

1. *Training Within Industry Report, 1940–1945,* War Manpower Commission, Bureau of Training, Washington, September 1945, p. v.
2. Ibid., pp. 185–186.
3. Garrett, Henry E.: *Great Experiments in Psychology,* Century Company, New York, 1930. p. 120.
4. *Training Within Industry Report,* War Manpower Commission, Bureau of Training, Washington, September 1945, p. 188.
5. Ibid., p. xi.
6. Ibid., p. 193.
7. Ibid., p. 200.
8. Ibid., p. 204.

BIBLIOGRAPHY

AMA Encyclopedia of Supervisory Training, American Management Association, New York, 1961, pp. 156–174.

AMA Programmed Instruction for Management Education, Prime 8: On the Job Training, American Management Association, New York, 1965, Panels 1–3, Programmed Notebooks 3–5.

Brown, Leonard.: *Job Instruction: The Communication of Ability,* Roundtable Films, Beverly Hills, Calif., 1967.

Button, William H., and William V. Wasmuth.: *Employee Training in Small Business Organizations,* New York State School of Industrial and Labor Relations, Cornell University, Ithaca, N.Y., 1964, pp. 24–32.

Gomersall, Earl R., and M. Scott Meyers: "Breakthrough in On-the-Job Training," *Harvard Business Review,* pp. 62–72, July–August 1966.

Halsey, G. D.: *Training Employees,* Harper & Brothers, New York, 1949.

Harger, Howard E.: "Job Instruction Training," *Training Directors Journal,* pp. 39–44, October 1964.

Lovin, Bill C., and Emery R. Casstevens: *Coaching, Learning and Action,* American Management Association, New York, 1971.

On-the-Job Training: An Answer to Training Needs of Business, Chamber of Commerce of the United States, Washington, June 1963.

On-the-Job Training: Guide for Planning and Conducting, Air Force Manual, U.S. Department of the Air Force, August 1966, pp. 23–50.

Sandell, Roland E.: "Making Job Training Effective," *Personnel Journal,* pp. 571–573, November 1964.

Standard Brands, Inc.: "Guides for On-the-Job Training," *Supervisory Management,* pp. 35–40, August 1957.

Suessmuth, Patrick.: "Training Ideas Found Useful," *Canadian Training Methods,* pp. 20–22, May–June 1972.

Wenig, Robert E., and William D. Wolansky: *Review and Synthesis of Literature on Job Training in Industry,* U.S. Department of Health, Education, and Welfare, Educational Resources Information Center, Washington, June 1972.

Wikstrom, Walter S.: "On-the-Job Training," *Supervisory Training,* The Conference Board, Inc., Report no. 612, New York, 1973, pp. 20–35.

Chapter 33

Classroom Instruction

MARTIN M. BROADWELL

Martin M. Broadwell *is Corporate Partner and Director of Training and Educational Services for an Atlanta-based firm, Resources for Education & Management, Inc. In this position, he is responsible for national and international consulting activities in the fields of training, management, supervision, and manpower development. Before joining Resources in 1970, he was with the Bell System as an engineer and for several years was Director of Engineering Training for Southern Bell. Prior to that he taught mathematics and science in Xenia, Ohio. He is the author of four books on training and supervision and has written over 50 articles for magazines in the United States, Australia, and England. He is a frequent lecturer and consultant on university campuses, and he has consulted for foreign firms in India, Switzerland, Australia, England, Northern Ireland, Venezuela, Mexico, and South Africa. He holds degrees in physics, mathematics, and management.*

Informal studies show that perhaps 95 percent of adult training is done in the classroom, and in many organizations the figure is 100 percent—and all this in the face of such advances as computer-assisted instruction, closed-circuit television, teaching machines, self-instructional devices, and the newer learner-controlled instruction. Why, then, is so much still going on in the classroom? There are many reasons; neither time nor purpose permits listing all of them here, but a few are important. There is an ease and convention about the classroom that does not exist with the other techniques mentioned. It is easy to do classroom instruction, for all one has to do is find a room, assemble an instructor and students, and have all the ingredients for carrying on instruction—not necessarily the *best* instruction, but instruction nevertheless.

This ease of operation is perhaps the main reason for the popularity of the classroom. After all, a "room" can be a storage room, a motel room, a banquet room, a conference room, or a training room. There are other reasons why the classroom is popular. Everybody is exposed to the same message at the same time in the classroom setup. Everyone gets to start and stop at the same time and see the same film at the same time, and they are all there to interact with the same people at the same time. All this can be done with just one instructor, and once a course gets under way, it is possible to continue without revision. (Remember, we are talking about what can be done, not necessarily what *should* be done or what produces the best results.)

A typical classroom has the advantage, too, of being flexible. There is an opportunity for small-group activity, individual work, and total-group work. There can be screens, chalkboards, and easels at the front of the room, as well as models and demonstration gear. Tables can be provided and rearranged, allowing the trainees to work around them or on one side of them, or the tables can be removed and an auditorium arrangement set up. Also, facility costs can be kept to a minimum, with the classroom arrangement, as opposed to many other styles of instruction or techniques. As long as the rooms are occupied to their fullest, the cost per trainee is minimal. When the room is not being used for training, it can be used for other purposes, and this keeps the training costs down.

Disadvantages There are disadvantages, however, and we should mention them early in the chapter. While the classroom method of instructing is the most popular with training people, it is also perhaps the most *ill used* of all the possible techniques. Anything that can be put together as easily as we talked about earlier is bound to have drawbacks. The drawback is simple: It is just as easy to have *bad* training in a classroom as it is to have *good* training. It may even be easier. A room, a group of trainees, and an instructor guarantee only a classroom situation, not success. In fact, the ingredients mentioned lend themselves to poor instruction. When there is a teacher who knows the subject and learners who do not, the most natural thing for the instructor to do is to start to tell them what he or she knows. When this happens, and it often does, we have one of the oldest and poorest forms of teaching there is. We can expect very little learning to come from this kind of situation, at least not for long, anyway. There is another drawback which will be covered in more detail later. That is the matter of the difficulty of getting feedback from *all* the learners. When there are 10 to 20 trainees in the room and the instructor has much to cover, before long many of the learners will be at different points, but the instructor may not know it. Unless there is frequent feedback, the instructor will be unable to tell where the learners are. It is difficult to get this feedback when all learners have equal time to listen and respond if they want to. Worse, *there may be no requirement to respond at all.*

We should also know the limitations of the classroom. There are things the classroom can do quite adequately and other things it cannot do. It can provide a situation for getting people together who need to be together to learn. It can provide an atmosphere for learning using the stimulation of an effective instructor and of the students themselves. It can bring together people with like problems and let them share their solutions. It can bring together cross sections with different problems. It can create and encourage furtherance of interactions between people who would never get this type of interaction in other teaching-learning situations. But there are some things the classroom is limited in doing well or at all. It cannot guarantee that 95 percent of the people entering will make 95 percent on a given test, as programmed instruction might be able to do. It does not promise to allow each student to progress at his or her own pace, as self-instruction does. It cannot let each learner follow his or her own learning paths, as computer-assisted instruction can do. It cannot let each student negotiate for specific learning goals, as the open classroom allows. So there are limitations. All we have to do is admit them, work around them, and determine those things the classroom can do best. We also need to avoid trying to make the classroom do things *it does not do very well.*

ELEMENTS OF THE CLASSROOM

Let us look now at the elements that make up any classroom. It is easier to talk about the components of the classroom than about the classroom situation as a whole. The first element is the *instructor*. Not that the instructor is the most important factor, but it is his or her presence that makes the classroom different from most other forms of training. We shall have more to say later about the selection and training of instructors, but in this section we want to see the influence this element has on the learning process.

The instructor brings to the classroom a certain amount of knowledge and experience—usually more than learners possess. If the instructor has not had more actual years of experience, probably he or she has had more *meaningful* experience—experience that is organized and prepared for sharing with others. The students may or may not respect this experience or knowledge, but it is there nevertheless and influences the outcome of the teaching-learning activity. Usually, the instructor is not one of the gang, nor should this be the case. This is not to say that there should be an aloofness, but rather a degree of commitment. There is generally nothing wrong with an instructor's sharing pleasantries with the group, but to overdo this just to get in "good" with the class will usually lessen his or her effectiveness.

Most people like to think of the instructor as being the great leader and producer of learning. We would like to soften that considerably by suggesting that the best way to think of the instructor is as a *facilitator of learning.* It should be the aim of every instructor to provide opportunities for learning, whatever it takes. If it means getting little or no credit for the outcome, then that should not be a consideration. Those instructors who find the classroom a place for an ego trip are *misusing* the students, not helping them.

The Trainees

The next ingredient is the group itself, those trainees who make up the class to be trained. It is this ingredient that makes the training necessary. Without them, there would be no need for either the instructor or the classroom. The best instructors remind themselves of this fact frequently! No two trainees are alike, Each has a different ability to learn, a different desire to learn, a different background to build upon, and a different environment to go to after the training is over. No one technique will work equally well with all the trainees. What motivates one may turn another off. What is exciting to one may bore the other. A learner may try to find excuses for not performing well, such as a dull teacher, a hot room, or hard chairs, and indeed these will hurt learning. Another may ignore these things or even try to defend them. The point is that the learner is an individual, and in a classroom situation it is difficult to be treated as one; it can be done, however, as we shall see later.

The Material

Another ingredient is the material to be taught. The purpose of training is to overcome a deficiency, to produce behavior change. The ideal situation is one in which both the trainer and the trainees know exactly what the deficiencies are and what the specific behavior change is going to be. In other chapters this is spoken of as setting *behavioral objectives.* For our purposes, let us just say that it is best when the learner knows where he or she is going, since this can be of some help in getting there. Without a set of directions, training is like driving a car blindfolded, waiting for someone else to say when to start, stop, turn, and so on. Many classrooms give this impression, as the learners grope for meaning in the instructor's discussion.

There has been quite a shift in thinking about preparing material over the years. Most training people now recognize that the material is just a means to an end. They no longer talk about "covering material." Rather, they talk about reaching objectives and overcoming deficiencies. But the material to be taught is an integral part of the teaching-learning situation. Material should be selected on the basis of its contribution to the behavior change required, rather than its presence in other, similar courses. The "We've *always* taught this material to this group" syndrome is to be avoided.

The Environment

The last ingredient we need to mention is the *environment*. This includes the tables and chairs and room temperature and ventilation, of course, but much more than these things. It includes also the *climate for learning,* which is difficult to measure but is a very significant part of the learning situation. Do the students feel free to ask a question? Do they feel free to experiment with an answer? Is it punishing to question the teacher? Are there leaders in the group who keep others from participating? These are all part of the environment and need to be taken into

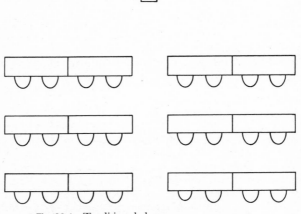

Fig. 33-1   Traditional classroom arrangement.

consideration when deciding how well the training is going. Poor results may be due not to poor teaching and poor learners or to the selection of the wrong subject matter but rather to the fact that the environment for learning was poor. We shall discuss some things that produce and change the environment later on in this chapter. Let us not forget, however, that the physical things mentioned do affect the learning and have to be considered. Even with the best instructor, it is difficult to concentrate if the room is smoky, hot, or noisy or if the chairs are too hard or too soft.

CLASSROOM ARRANGEMENTS

Having mentioned the physical aspects of the classroom, let us look now at the various designs for setting up a classroom and see what effect classroom arrangement has on learning. In the *traditional* arrangement (Fig. 33-1), the trainees sit in rows facing the front of the room. They may be at tables which are lined up across the room, or they may be seated theater style without tables. Much training is done in this fashion, and it has some advantages and some disadvantages. For example, it is a very efficient arrangement as far as use of space is concerned. It requires only space for an aisle up the middle. The tables or chairs can come right up to the front of the room within a foot or two of the instructor's equipment and can extend to the back wall. An aisle in the middle allows for projection equipment; an overhead projector can be used without blocking much of the view, and so all the space is accounted for. All the trainees are in full view of the screens and easels and can see the instructor equally well, except for the heads in front of them, of course.

The disadvantages of this arrangement are not as obvious as the advantages. The traditional arrangement is essentially teacher-oriented, with the teacher completely in control. The likelihood that the learners will voluntarily respond is small, and the possibility that they will talk and exchange ideas with one another is even smaller. When interactions do occur, they are likely to be between the teacher and an individual student. When there is a series of exchanges, they usually go from teacher to student to teacher to another student to teacher to still another student, and so on, with the instructor being the focal point all the time. The instructor also can determine the direction of the discussion by choosing to respond to a certain

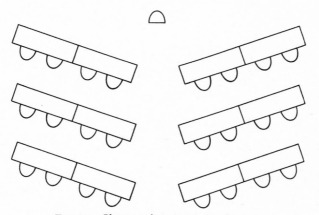

Fig. 33-2   Chevron classroom arrangement.

question or statement or to let it drop. New instructors tend to like this approach because it gives them some security and makes up for a lack of confidence.

Another arrangement may be called the *chevron* design (Fig. 33-2). This is a variation on the traditional arrangement in which the tables are moved back slightly down the middle at an angle so that the students can see one another as well as the instructor. This arrangement is to be preferred over the traditional one because it produces much more voluntary responding from the trainees. There is still the advantage of being able to see the front visuals and the instructor, there is still the aisle for projection equipment, and there is still a strong element of control available to the instructor, though perhaps this is less obvious than in the traditional arrangement. Informal studies indicate that the flow of conversation is across the aisle and that the learners tend to talk to the people they can see, rather than the ones behind them.

This matter of visibility is important in the classroom because whatever arrangement the instructor chooses will result in the learners' either being able to see the front of the room well, and fellow students not so well, or being able to see one another well, but not the front of the room. In the *circle* arrangement (Fig. 33-3) nearly half of the group cannot see the front of the room without moving their chairs and/or tables. A good compromise is the *U-shaped* arrangement (Fig. 33-4), which allows the learners to see one another fairly well and at least the center of the front very well. This limits the use of the front of the room to the center because the sides are obscured by students. Another problem with this arrange-

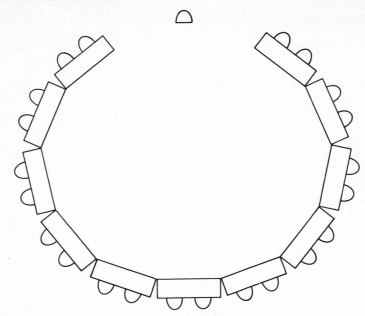

Fig. 33-3 Circle classroom arrangement.

ment is that the students along each edge of the U cannot see the others in that row, and so they tend to talk across the opening. The trainees at the back tend to interact more with the instructor than with the other trainees. A *V-shaped* arrangement (Fig. 33-5) makes more of the front of the room available, but the students see less of one another. In this arrangement, there are fewer people across the back and more down each side, which conserves space across the room. Obviously, the circle and the U- and V-shaped arrangements are the least efficient in terms of use of space, since the entire center is generally unused.

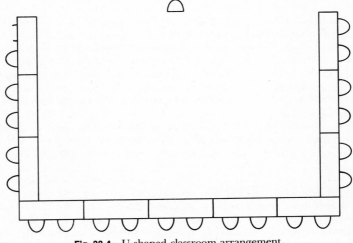

Fig. 33-4 U-shaped classroom arrangement.

PSYCHOLOGY OF DESIGN

Several things are obvious in a discussion of classroom arrangement. First, there is no perfect system for all training needs. Next, how they are seated makes a difference *to the learners* in terms of whom they talk to, how they feel about the

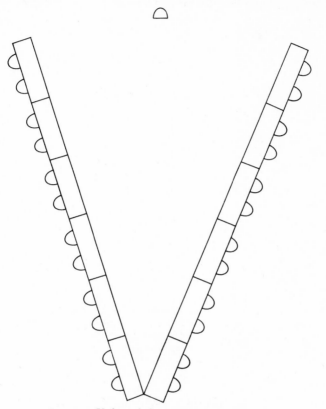

Fig. 33-5   V-shaped classroom arrangement.

instructor's role, and how well they can see the visuals. It should also be obvious that the availability of space will determine the arrangement to a certain extent. Another consideration that needs to be expanded, however, is that we can divide the types of arrangements roughly into two categories: teacher-centered and learner-centered. Those arrangements which tend to limit participation (by their design) are essentially teacher-centered. This means that the teacher controls the activities. The teacher directs the flow of the conversation and the learning patterns. The teacher is very visible in the sense that the learners have a greater dependency on the instructor and must get their instructions constantly from him or her.

Learner-centered Arrangements

The arrangements that allow for the learners to participate and to interact easily with the others in the group are considered learner-centered. The visibility of the instructor is reduced considerably as far as controlling the step-by-step processes toward learning is concerned. The flow from one activity to another is more natural, and the learners are generally less aware of the change. The instructor has not lost real control—just some of the visibility in exercising control. For example, when the arrangement is in a U shape, the instructor can regain attention simply by moving slightly into the U and taking over. The learners will immediately be quiet since they will not want to talk around the instructor. Again, this arrangement makes use of the instructor's visibility as a means of keeping control, especially where the learners are very dependent on the instructor. What we have done is to convert the U shape from a learner-centered arrangement to an instructor-centered one.

When the learners are gathered around tables in small groups, there is an even more learner-centered situation. The teacher will find it harder to get back into the center of things, especially when the students are busily engaged in a discussion that is meaningful and relevant to them. One way for the instructor to regain control is to have each group report on something. When the groups have finished talking, it is easy for the instructor to take up where he or she had left off in the planned program. The instructor can also regain control by beginning some instruction—perhaps merely calling the students' attention to a common problem that the instructor has observed while listening to the groups. He or she can use the chalkboard, an overhead, or an easel to point up the problem, and that action in itself will bring the control back to the instructor. This same process may be used with the circle arrangement. This is a very hard student-centered situation to break at times, since the learners have gotten themselves into a very comfortable process of sharing equally with one another and with the instructor. Turning control over to one person—the instructor—may not please them very much. Often, though, the instructor can regain control by simply standing up or going to the board, as just mentioned with respect to the U-shaped configuration.

Teacher-centered Arrangements

Teacher-centered arrangements do not suffer from the problem of getting the learners to relinquish any control, since they rarely have any under these arrangements anyway. The traditional "all-seats-facing-the-front" arrangement is the best example of this. The instructor is more highly visible than in any other teaching design, standing in the front of the room with all the students looking in his or her direction. Even the chevron design loses very little of the teacher-centered aspect, although the learners do get to see one another and to talk more in this design. The instructor can simply begin to do something at the front of the room, and all the learners will direct their attention there.

CLASSROOM TECHNIQUES AND SYSTEMS

Involvement

Let us look now at some basic requirements for successful classroom instructing. There are three characteristics to look for in a successful situation. First, there is the matter of *involvement*. Since none of us ever learn much without being involved in the learning situation, it is most important that the learners be involved as much as possible. They must not be just killing time or participating without having set a specific learning goal. Their involvement must be meaningful and well directed. The learners, as much as possible, should see where their involvement is taking them and why they are doing the particular thing they are doing that has gotten them involved.

The involvement can be of several kinds. A small group of students may work together on a common problem; individual learners may work on problems separately; or the instructor may mention a problem and ask the students to think about it. There does not have to be physical involvement in order to get mental involvement, but many a good instructor has been fooled by thinking that what he or she is saying is so provocative that all the learners are mentally engrossed in every word—hence involved—when in reality they are bored, confused, or thinking about something else altogether. It is an assumption at best to think that learners are involved mentally when there is no concrete evidence of this. Only when they have *said* something or are *doing* something can the instructor be sure of the extent of their involvement.

Accountability

The second ingredient to look for in a successful classroom teaching-learning situation is student *accountability* for the learning activity. Since learning is a *self*-activity, the students need to know that they are responsible for learning. When there is a specific objective, they need to think of it as an objective *they* must reach, not one the instructor must *make* them reach. In the case of a small-group activity, homework, or outside reading, the learners must feel that they have the responsibility for reaching the particular learning goal in the assignment. The instructor should plan activities that will let the learners take on some of the responsibility for the learning—hence the term "accountability." If the learners know the objectives ahead of time and see that a certain assignment will allow them to reach that goal, they will more readily accept the accountability for performing the activity. This places a burden of responsibility on the instructor to see that the learners really do take the responsibility for the learning, however. Often, instructors tend to overprotect the learners by accepting the accountability for the learning themselves. They say things like, "You'd better listen to this because it's important." An instructor may reach all the conclusions for the learners, rather than risk letting them do it. The successful instructor will present just enough information to allow the conclusion to be reached and then will let the students reach that conclusion themselves. This approach makes the learners, rather than the teacher, accountable for the thought processes required to reach the conclusion. If the instructor presents all the facts and then reaches the conclusion, the learners really have little or nothing to do during the teaching-learning process.

Feedback

A final characteristic of a good classroom situation is a high amount of *feedback* from the learners. Feedback is that ingredient which allows the instructor to know just where the learner is at any given time during the instruction. There is an obvious truism here: The more feedback there is, the more the instructor will know about the success of the instruction. Feedback can be obtained in many ways. Unfortunately, many instructors tend to depend upon watching the *faces* of the learners for a large amount of their feedback. If the students look fairly pleasant or satisfied, if they seem interested, or if they smile and nod their heads positively, the instructor reads this as feedback that says, "Things are going great." Experienced instructors have usually learned not to be surprised when they finally ask for some verbal feedback from a group such as this and hear a student say, "Uh, I don't know . . . I haven't been able to follow you very well."

Successful instructors have learned to depend only upon that which they *hear* for sure, or *see* for sure, to tell them what they *know* for sure about the class. Feedback in a class can be compared with instruments or dials on a machine that tell us how a particular operation is going. The more accurate the feedback, the better the control. The lights and meters on the dashboard of a car are there to tell the driver how well the car is functioning. Without them the driver would worry about the oil pressure, the fuel level, and overheating. The same is true in the classroom: Without feedback, the instructor worries constantly about how well the students' minds are functioning. As we look at the various systems for teaching, it will be obvious how large a part feedback plays in determining what we *call* the "system."

When we talk about techniques, it is easier to think in terms of the three characteristics just discussed than to classify the techniques. For example, it is meaningless to speak of the "discussion method" unless we know what is going on during the discussion. The method is one in which the students and the instructor engage in discussions of some sort about some subject. Neither the amount of talking done by the students nor the number of students doing the talking is defined, but we know we need that information if we are to judge the effectiveness of the teaching. Are the students being asked to reach conclusions as they "discuss" the topic? Is the instructor getting feedback from the students in such a way as to test the success of past teaching or set the direction for future instructing? Are all the students offering feedback, or just one or two? We can say the same for the "question and answer" technique. What are the questions doing for the instructor? Is there usable feedback? What is the learner getting out of the question and the answer? How much responsibility—accountability—does the individual learner have for the answers? How involved are the students as a whole? Is the questioning and answering just between the instructor and one or two students, or are there small subgroup sessions in which the individuals give their inputs; a consensus opinion or answer is arrived at, which is in turn presented to the whole group; and a final conclusion is reached that represents all the thinking of all the learners? Any instructor can evaluate the processes being used by applying these three criteria to the situation: involvement, accountability, and feedback. It is better to use these as a measure of a particular method, rather than whether the instructor "feels comfortable" with it or even whether the students like it. Rather than list different methods and comment on them, let us look at different systems of instruction and see how it is possible to introduce methods into these systems.

TEACHING-LEARNING SYSTEMS

We can best understand what is happening in the classroom if we divide the possibilities into three different systems or formats. These systems are not absolute. Not everything that happens in the classroom can be said to be a part of one of these systems, nor can a teacher stay only in one of these systems all the time. The important thing is to begin to think about what is happening in the classroom in terms of what the student is doing and what the instructor is doing.

Direct Teacher Input Systems

The first system is the *direct teacher input system*. As the term implies, the inputs to the class come directly from the instructor or from some source other than the learner. This system has the lowest possible amount of involvement. There is no feedback, and the accountability must consist in something other than the learner's responses or their work on a project. The simplest form of this system is the lecture, but this is not the only form. Anytime there is a complete input of new information from an external source (other than the learner), we have this system. Showing a movie, a filmstrip, or a series of overhead transparencies or slides is an example of this system *if nothing else happens during the time of the showing.* If there is just the presentation of the material, with no accountability during the presentation, then all the input is directly from a teaching source. Building in the subtlety of having the students look for points of disagreement, requiring role playing at the completion of the showing, or listing the key points on the board as the students call them out from their notes results in a different system.

The important thing about this system is that it requires nothing of the viewers or listeners, other than their presence. Any conclusions that are reached, any new information that is brought out, and any discoveries that are made are all due to the instructor, not the students. The students may like this, by the way. There is something that we may call the "podium syndrome" that makes some students feel very comfortable when the instructor is talking. For some, it is a kind of "security blanket" in the classroom—they like to feel that things are well organized and that the instructor will cover all points clearly and precisely, with the students staying out of it to prevent confusion. This is not to say that all students are like this, but perhaps too many are. Such students do not take too well to doing work on their own or to reaching their own conclusions. Unfortunately, they do not retain nearly as much as they need to of what they *hear* the instructor say during these comfortable moments, and so they do not make very good learners from this point of view. Even when the instructor gets them involved and they come up with their own conclusions and thus are in a position to learn more and remember more, they may still end up saying, "Why didn't the instructor just tell us that without going through all that effort to get us involved?" This does not remove the instructor's responsibility to do the best possible job of instructing, even though the students may not recognize the instructing as being the best.

Teacher Modification System

The next system, which moves up a level in student involvement, we call the *teacher modification system* In this system the teacher provides the original inputs of new information or conclusions, but does some questioning of the learners to see whether they interpreted the information correctly. If they did not, the teacher "modifies" their words or ideas to make sure they hear the correct information again. This is a superior system to the first one because the learners are likely to take more home with them—since they got involved—than they would under the direct teacher input system. When the instructor gets the learners involved in a discussion of the material presented, whether presented on film or in a lecture, and when they review what has already been said without drawing new conclusions, the teacher is operating in the teacher modification system or mode.

We must remember, though, that if the learner comes up with any *new* conclusions, the instructor is no longer operating in this system. Only when the instructor puts in all the new material, ideas, and conclusions, either in lecture form or by some other means, and then gets the learners to feed this information back through some form of questioning or discussion can we describe the process as teacher modification. We use the term "modification" because if the feedback shows that the learner does not have all the information or has the wrong idea on some things, the teacher "modifies" the learner's perceptions and presents the correct idea or concept. The process is simply one of the teacher giving out new information, having the learner feed that information back, and then making a correction if necessary. The instructor has all the control and all the responsibility for what gets corrected and what does not. The instructor—and usually *only* the instructor—knows the specific learning objective. Only the instructor can "pass" on the success of the learning experience. While this system helps the learners retain some of the information better, expecially information with which they became involved, it still lacks the degree of accountability that ensures the greatest amount of learning.

Learner Discovery System

A still more effective system is called the *learner discovery system,* in which the learner begins to draw conclusions and supply some of the learning activity under teacher *guidance* rather than *control.* The idea is for the teacher to supply only those facts which the learners cannot find themselves and for the learners to come up with their own discoveries as much as possible. Instead of feeding "old" information back to the teacher—as in the teacher modification system—the learners furnish new conclusions or concepts and even new factual information they have found on their own. Here we have a much better situation for retention to take place, since the learners are accountable for the learning and must know where they are going in order to see whether they have gotten there. This is a more effective type of involvement, and the instructor gets very good feedback.

One thing to notice here, however, is that the teacher still determines whether there is just modification or actually discovery. A case study, for example, is an excellent way to get a group involved in coming up with some good conclusions that they might have missed if the teacher had just told them about a management principle or described an abstract situation. Some instructors, however, are so afraid that the students will miss the point that they provide the conclusions themselves instead of waiting for the learners to come up with them. In this case— even though the learners may have been involved in role playing during the learning experience—the teacher is still operating in a teacher modification system or maybe even direct teacher input system. If all the new conclusions come from the teacher, who ends up by saying something like, "Now, are there any questions?" little more than a glorified lecture has taken place.

The same is true if there is a video tape made of the salesperson's performance in a simulated sales effort. If the instructor ends up telling the salesperson all the things he or she did wrong and right and why, then the instructor just took a long time to get around to the lecture. The learner was not allowed to learn anything alone. The feedback went to the learner in the form of seeing the video tape replay, but the conclusions that could have been reached by the salesperson were reached instead by the instructor, and so the instructor got no particular feedback on how the learner saw the situation. We could make the same illustrations with in-baskets and management games.

Just having the learners go through some involvement does not automatically get the teaching process into the highest order of teaching, no matter how sophisticated the equipment used or the method employed.

Learner-controlled Instruction

Another system, which will be discussed in detail in a later chapter, is the open-classroom system, or learner-controlled instruction. This is quite different from the systems talked about here, in that it takes an altogether different approach to the learning process. It is concerned less with technique or methodology than with obtaining the desired performance through a "contracting" process that gets the instructor and the learner agreeing on several things before the training begins. They agree on the goals—objectives in behavioral terms— and they agree on the measuring devices for seeing whether these goals are actually met. Since the learner and the instructor agree on the goals, the learner is obligated to do the tasks assigned; the instructor is obligated to see that the assignments will guarantee that the learner gets to the goals if the assignment is completed. From a mental standpoint, there is total accountability and involvement. Since there is constant measuring, feedback is always individual and accurate. Above all, the majority of the instruction (and learning) is self-paced.

EVALUATION

Evaluation of instruction is complicated by the fact that we often evaluate the wrong things. For example, we tend to evaluate the instructor when we are talking about classroom teaching. But if we have failed to choose the correct material to teach, we are looking at the wrong thing when we look at (evaluate) the teacher.

The best instructor available cannot produce employees who can perform correctly if the subject matter does not deal with their deficiency on the job. By the same token, we cannot expect the best instructor in the world to help improve the organization if the wrong students are selected. So part of our evaluation has to do with the organization's skill in selecting subject matter, setting specific objectives, and getting the proper employees to the training location. Even then, we may evaluate the wrong thing. We may watch an instructor in action and decide that he or she is doing a good job because there is a lot of action, movement, and variety. The instructor is a good performer: he or she does not lean on the podium, does not talk while facing the board, and gets a lot of eye contact. We have to remember that what we are looking for is not a good public speaker, but a good *facilitator of learning*. So far we have pointed out the characteristics of a good learning situation: accountability, feedback, and involvement. We can best judge the worth of an instructor by the extent to which these things are present in the classroom. The amount of accountability, feedback, and involvement in the learning situation tells us whether the instructor is doing the job required. It may be that these things are present to the point where the learners are not even aware of the instructor's position at the speaker's stand or of the amount of eye contact. The students are too involved in the learning process to observe the teacher's actions on the platform. When this happens, we can say that the instructor has developed a good classroom technique.

Chapter 34

Group Methods: Conferences, Meetings, Workshops, Seminars

JACK REITH

Jack Reith *is a consultant in organization and management development. After 20 years as an executive in business and industry, he established his own consulting firm, Lindley & Company, in southern California in 1970. Mr. Reith's business and consulting experience includes the electronics, aerospace, and public utility industries, as well as banking. In the field of organization development, he has also worked with public agencies, churches and small business. Mr. Reith is a graduate of Yale University. In addition to graduate studies at UCLA and Claremont Colleges, he has received special training from the NTL Institute for Applied Behavioral Science. He has published many articles in various professional journals and was a contributing author to the first edition of the* Training and Development Handbook.

This chapter will discuss the forms and purposes of group sessions and the use of group methods in conferences, workshops, seminars, and other types of meetings.

Next, 16 types of structured meetings will be defined. The mechanics of structured meetings will be described, and guides for effective planning, design, implementation, and evaluation of such meetings will be provided.

Next, group methods will be defined, and group process and group dynamics will be explained. Premises underlying the use of group methods will be described, and guides for effective use of these methods will be provided. Suggestions for the training of group leaders will be included.

GROUP METHODS: WHAT ARE THEY?

The term "group methods" is often used to describe any one of a number of popular techniques such as team building, brainstorming, role playing, simulation, and management games. It is more accurate to speak of "group process" or the change which takes place when the dynamics that occur within a group cause the desired growth and development. Too often the growth is attributed to the technique rather than the dynamics; hence, in this chapter, all kinds of group meetings will be described, but special attention will be given to describing and then differentiating between the methods used to effectively plan and conduct structured, task-oriented meetings and the group process which occurs in all meetings and which, with a trained leader, can be used to achieve defined objectives.

Group Methods versus Structured, Task-Oriented Meetings.

Any time two people are called together by one of them (leader) there is a meeting. For meetings there are always two dimensions:

1. The task or goal
2. The process—what is happening within the group (of two or more people)

The task or goal may be all that the leader recognizes, and he or she may be willing and able to achieve this goal without interest in, attention to, or recognition of the process.

As leaders become trained, they can learn to understand the dynamics which occur in any group and to use them to help attain the task goals.

As leaders become more thoroughly trained, they may be able to plan their training to utilize the group dynamics entirely as the learning/growth/change technique.

A matrix may be developed to represent the two dimensions as shown in Fig. 34-1.

The omega (Ω) dimension is the task-accomplishment dimension and is exemplified by a highly structured meeting with strong leader control, which (when accomplished effectively) results in the achievement of task goals on a perfect time schedule.

The delta (Δ) dimension is the group-centered dimension, in which the meeting fulfills the needs of the individuals (and group) without necessarily accomplishing a task or achieving an objective. Maximum change is effected because attention is given primarily to individual needs. Different kinds of group meetings fall into different positions on the matrix.

If the task can be achieved with maximum development and self-fulfillment of each individual and the group as a whole, then group methods (the group process) will have been effectively utilized. This is difficult and rarely achieved because of conflicting needs. But the more able the leader is in planning, in observing, in understanding, in interpreting, and in providing leadership for the group process, the greater the probability of growth, learning, and change in the individual and the group, as well as accomplishment of the task.

In discussing group methods, it is most important to recognize:

- That the task (Ω) and process (Δ) dimensions are different
- That underlying premises and values are different
- That the leader must be especially trained to utilize group methods

Essential to effective use of the group method as a tool in teaching is an understanding of the premises and values underlying the group methods, group process, and group dynamics. These will be discussed later in this chapter.

KINDS OF STRUCTURED MEETINGS

There are many different kinds of structured meetings. The person responsible for planning a meeting or a learning experience or a problem-solving session must arrange the principals and participants, and the physical resources, so as to best accomplish the objectives defined for the meeting. Planning and design of meetings and other group activities will be covered later in this chapter. Here, the objective is to define the many kinds of meetings. The definitions come primarily from the work accomplished at the Bureau of Studies in Adult Education at Indiana University and from the books written by the members of that organization. Sixteen kinds of meetings will be defined.[1,2,3]

Speech-Lecture   A speech or lecture is a carefully prepared oral presentation of a subject by a qualified individual. It is generally characterized by formality. It is an easy type of program to organize. However, it provides no opportunity for audience participation, and hence it provides for communication in one direction only.

Speech-Forum   The speech-forum is a learning method which consists of an organized speech given by a qualified person and a period of open discussion immediately following the speech. The speech-forum provides for minimal two-

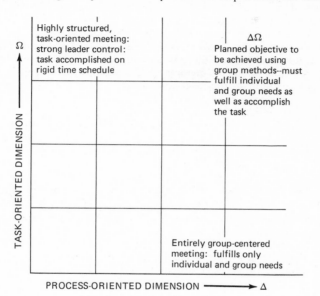

Fig. 34-1   Meeting matrix.

way communications. In addition to the speaker, there is usually a chairperson on the stage or podium to act as moderator during the discussion period.

Panel.   A panel is a group of three to six persons who carry on a purposeful conversation on an assigned topic. The panel members are selected on the basis of previously demonstrated interest and competence in the subject to be discussed as well as their ability to verbalize in front of an audience. The panel members are usually seated at a table in front of the audience. Conversation among panel members is started by a moderator, who usually prepares questions in advance which he or she uses to start and sustain the discussion. In the strictest definition, there is no audience participation in the panel.

Panel-Forum   A panel-forum is a panel which is immediately followed by an audience-participation period involving free and open discussion by the panel members on questions submitted by the audience. A moderator usually acts as a go-between for panel members and the audience. Questions can be presented directly from the floor by members of the audience, or they can be written on cards collected and read by the moderator. Sometimes questions are collected from the audience in advance by the moderator.

Symposium (Ancient Concept)   A symposium (ancient concept) is a group of 5 to 20 persons who meet in a private dining room to enjoy good food and fellowship and who desire to discuss, informally, a topic of mutual interest. During dinner, the previously selected topic is introduced by the moderator (symposiarch). Group members are then free to talk informally about the topic if they wish. When everyone has finished eating and the table has been cleared, the group carries on a more systematic (but still informal) discussion of the topic under the guidance of the moderator. As a rule, this technique is used for leisurely exploration of a topic, rather than for problem solving or discussion of highly controversial issues.

Symposium (Modern Concept)   A symposium (modern concept) is a series of related speeches by two to five persons qualified to speak with authority on different aspects of the same topic or on closely related topics. The speeches vary in length from 3 to 20 minutes, depending upon the number of speeches, the amount of time available, and the topics to be treated. The speakers do not converse with one another. They make presentations to the audience. A chairperson is usually in charge of the symposium.

Symposium-Forum (Modern Concept)   A symposium-forum (modern concept) is a symposium which is followed immediately by an audience-participation period of free and open discussion. A moderator acts as a go-between for the speakers and the audience. He or she is skilled in the techniques of handling an audience and stimulating group participation. Like the panel-forum, the symposium-forum provides for a limited degree of two-way communication.

Colloquy   A colloquy is a modification of the panel, using six to eight people. Three or four of the people are resource persons or experts, as in a panel. However, in addition to the experts, three or four people representing the audience also sit on the stage. These people ask questions, express opinions, and raise issues to be treated by the experts. A moderator usually directs the proceedings. The moderator may sit at a small table in the center of the stage, with the three or four experts behind a table on the left side of the stage facing the audience, and the three or four audience representatives behind a table facing the audience on the right side of the stage. Usually the members of the audience just listen, but occasionally they may participate under the guidance of the moderator. A particular advantage of the colloquy is the opportunity it provides to reduce the natural barriers that usually stand between a large audience and the experts up on the stage, thereby helping to establish rapport between the audience and those on the platform.

Group Discussion   As defined by Bergevin, Morris, and Smith,[2] group discussion is purposeful conversation and deliberation about a topic of mutual interest among 6 to 20 participants under the guidance of a trained participant called a *leader.* Maximum opportunity is provided for the individual participant to share his or her ideas and experiences with others. The discussion method is often used as a part of education and training programs and courses of all sorts. The leader is particularly important in group discussions; special training for leaders is desirable wherever possible.

Conference   A conference is a group composed usually of 2 to 50 persons who represent different organizations, departments, or points of view but who have some common interest or background. They gather information and discuss mutual problems, with a reasonable solution as the desired end. Problem identification and solution is often the objective of a conference. However, the conference is also used to interchange information and to improve cooperation.

Convention   A convention is an assembly of representatives or delegates from local units of a parent organization who have a common interest or an assembly of representatives or delegates from different organizations or professions who have a common interest. These persons meet together to explore and act on problems of common interest. A convention is a medium which often uses a combination of other group activities, such as speeches, panels, forums, and group discussions. Planning is essential to successful conventions. Careful attention must be given to the selection of a chairperson, to the appointment of a planning committee, and to the selection of speakers and group discussion leaders. Often a large convention will involve many committees covering all pertinent responsibilities, from finance to hospitality.

Committee A committee is a small group of individuals appointed or elected to perform a task that cannot be done efficiently by the entire group. A committee is usually appointed and authorized by, and responsible to, the parent group; there is a presiding officer, who is usually designated, but sometimes elected by the group. The powers and duties of a committee are often fixed by the parent organization or by the constitution and bylaws of the parent organization. Committees are usually established to study a particular problem (including carrying out research essential to the solution of the problem), to reach a conclusion on the basis of study of the problem, and to act if action is indicated and authorized. A report is usually prepared as the final act of a committee. The report is submitted to the parent group which established the committee.

Institute An institute is a series of meetings arranged for a group of persons who come together to receive instruction in, and information about, a specific field of work. The series may be held on one day or may continue for weeks, months or years, in a planned and organized manner. Authoritative instruction is emphasized. An organized body of knowledge is presented to the learners, or issues are raised for their consideration. Often various group activities are utilized: speech, symposium, panel, group discussion, etc. The participants learn in groups, but individual study is also involved.

As discussed later in this chapter, institutes have been established by the practitioners of certain group methods. These institutes run from a few weeks to years, and the longer ones often qualify the participants to carry on work within the discipline. Usually a certificate is awarded at the end of an institute.

Seminar A seminar is a group of persons gathered together for the purpose of studying a subject under the leadership of an expert or learned person. Often the procedure followed is to identify the problem, explore the problem, discuss or lay out necessary research involved in the solution of the problem, conduct the research, share the findings with others in the group, and reach a conclusion on the basis of the research.

Workshop A workshop is a group of persons with a common interest or problem, often professional or vocational, who meet together for an extended period of time to improve their individual proficiency, ability, or understanding by means of study, research, and discussion. The workshop allows considerable flexibility, and the emphasis is on improving individual proficiency and understanding. Theory and practice are often treated concurrently. The learner is encouraged to work out a program of personal study and receives help with this program from the other participants and resource people. The learning situations tend to be based on interests and needs identified by the participants themselves, rather than by experts.

Clinic A clinic is a meeting of a group of people with common interests; it is established for the purpose of diagnosing, analyzing, and seeking solutions to specific problems. The group usually confronts real-life situations in order to establish a manner and method to meet them more successfully. Oftentimes case studies, demonstrations, role plays, speeches, field trips, and shared real-life experiences form the basis for the diagnosis and solution of problems.

CONDUCTING THE STRUCTURED MEETING

Planning the Meetings

The success of almost any meeting depends, in large part, upon the amount of planning and preparation which preceded it. The first step suggested for planning a meeting is to define the objective or objectives for the meeting.[4] Objectives may take whatever form most readily fits the needs of the participants, the subject matter, and the circumstances of the meeting. The objectives can be simply a statement of what you hope to accomplish by having the meeting.

Much has been written about defining objectives for organizational management,[5,6] as well as objectives for learning experiences.[7] Equally important is defining objectives for meetings. The following list may be of help in defining objectives for business meetings of various types. Meetings are often held to:

1. Inform
2. Instruct
3. Define and plan
4. Clarify
5. Create
6. Resolve and decide

It is interesting to note that as you proceed from the top of this list to the bottom, the number of attendees for an efficient meeting will tend to decrease. For example, large numbers of people may attend a meeting where the primary objective is to inform. On the other hand, only a handful of people may be efficiently and effectively involved in a meeting called to resolve a difficult problem.

A meeting, of course, may be designed to accomplish a number of objectives. After an objective has been defined, it should be examined to see whether having a meeting is the best way to accomplish it. A meeting may not be needed at all![4]

Prior Contact with Participants

A very effective way to start the planning of a meeting is to contact participants before objectives for the meeting have been completed. Contact with participants will help clarify meeting objectives, will begin to prepare the participants to actively participate in the meeting, and will possibly identify needs of the individual participants which may be met in part during the meeting, thus moving the meeting in the delta direction on the meeting matrix.

Caucusing

Some very effective meeting leaders consistently have prior meetings or caucuses with those attendees whose opinions or recommendations will significantly affect the results of the meeting. I have found this approach to be particularly effective when new ideas, proposals, or plans are being submitted for approval at a meeting. Usually among the meeting participants will be formal or informal leaders whose understanding and approval of the proposal will greatly influence its acceptance by the group at the meeting. Prior understanding of the proposal may put these people in a position to render positive opinions regarding the value of the proposal.

Of special importance is a premeeting with speakers and presenters to discuss the material which they will be presenting, to plan the sequence of events, and to correlate the material they will present with the total meeting agenda. This can be done most effectively in person, but the telephone can be used if person-to-person contact is impossible.

Soliciting Agenda Material

As mentioned earlier, participants will feel more a part of the meeting, and will move further toward the delta position on the meeting matrix, if they are asked to review the planned agenda and to make recommendations for changes or additions. Again, this is most effectively done in person, but of course the telephone can often save a great deal of time.

Developing the Agenda

In any event, the preparation and mailing of an agenda *in advance* will greatly help all participants know what the objectives and sequence of items to be covered are for a planned meeting. One exception to this is when it is decided to build the agenda at the beginning of the meeting. This technique will be described later in this chapter.

A meeting agenda should include a statement of the objectives of the meeting, the time of the meeting, the location of the meeting, the participants' names and identifications, and a list of subject matter or problems to be discussed or presentations to be made. Also, an agenda may include a definition of expected actions to be taken by participants following the meeting.

Timing of Agenda Items

Effective meeting leaders have developed different ideas about the sequence of items on a formal agenda. Some feel that the most important items should be put first. Others feel that the first items on the agenda should be warm-up items to get the group started toward active participation.

Certainly attention should be given to the location on the agenda of complex items so that the group will be fully alert and capable of understanding the problems discussed; otherwise, Mr. Parkinson's prediction may become a reality: The same amount of time may be spent on a $10-million decision and on one costing $10.[8]

I have heard some people who conduct high-level meetings state that they often intentionally place controversial items at the end of a long agenda, when people will be tired and presumably more willing to approve these items. This is certainly a decision that you can make, if you are willing to risk having a matter approved by people who do not fully understand the nature of their decision.

The Meeting Room

Certainly the selection of the meeting room is a very important part of the planning of a meeting. The meeting room should be convenient to the participants, it should be quiet, and its selection should be planned so as to minimize (even discourage) interruptions by those not scheduled to attend the meeting. Preparing a meeting room is also important. The following items should be considered when preparing the room:

1. Will a speaker's table, podium, or lectern be required?
2. Will adequate lighting for notes on the lectern be available?
3. Will a microphone be necessary?
4. Is there a wall- or ceiling-mounted projection screen available?
5. Will at least one easel or blackboard be available?
6. Will the speaker need auxiliary tables on which to place display material?
7. What is the most effective design for room arrangements? That is, should the chairs be placed in classroom-style format, should an "executive square" be arranged with the tables, would the meeting leader or leaders prefer an open U shape, etc.?
8. Are various types of projection equipment needed for the meeting— overhead projector, 16mm projector, 35mm slide projector? Have you tested the equipment and film? Are extra bulbs and extension cords available? Can the room be adequately darkened?
9. Have name plates and tags been prepared?
10. If they will be needed, are pads and pencils available for the participants to use?
11. If appropriate, have you made arrangements for water glasses, water pitchers, coffee, etc.?

12. If smoking is to be permitted, are there sufficient ashtrays available for the participants?

A comprehensive checklist for large meetings, conferences, and conventions is included later in this chapter.

Beginning the Meeting

I have been conducting meetings of various sorts and sizes and types for nearly 25 years. If there is one error I make most frequently, it is that of assuming that everyone at a meeting knows the other people there. I urge that at the beginning of any meeting, the meeting leader be *certain* that all those present know one another or have been introduced. The meeting leader can accomplish this simply by introducing people he or she is sure have not met. Often it is a good warm-up for a meeting to ask the participants to introduce themselves. Name tags that attach to the participants' clothing are helpful, and "table tents" placed in front of each meeting participant will aid not only meeting participants but also the speakers or conference leaders as they talk with the meeting participants.

Next, at the beginning of the meeting the agenda should be reviewed, particularly the objectives of the meeting. If an agenda has not been prepared, the objectives of the meeting should be stated at this time, and an agenda may be "built" at the meeting.

Building an Agenda at the Meeting

As mentioned earlier, some meeting leaders like to use an agenda-building technique as a method of getting early involvement of participants. Experience has shown that this sort of approach does tend to move the meeting to an effective delta-omega position on the meeting matrix. Agenda building consists of getting the recommendations from meeting participants as to what the agenda items should be. The meeting leader can, of course, include his or her own. This can be done on a blackboard or newsprint chart by first listing all the recommendations made by the group and the meeting leader and then obtaining group agreement as to the sequence in which the agenda items will be covered.

If desired, in order to assure coverage of the entire agenda, the meeting leader can obtain concurrence from the group as to the amount of time which will be spent on each item.

Although this may seem like a time-consuming approach, those who use it believe that overall it creates a more effective meeting and reduces the total meeting time.

Techniques for Keeping on Schedule

As mentioned in the previous paragraph, obtaining the concurrence of the meeting participants as to the amount of time to be spent on each agenda item is one way of keeping on schedule. As a minimum, the meeting leader can place on his or her copy of the agenda a time objective for the conclusion of each agenda item.

Keep the meeting focused on the agenda items. Stimulate discussion, but watch your time schedule. Call a coffee break if a hot argument goes on too long.

A technique I have seen used effectively for long meetings with large numbers of speakers is to provide more than adequate time for coffee breaks. This effectively provides a "pad," which is often needed during such long meetings.

Above all, the leader should never lose control of a meeting.

Recognizing or Restraining the Individual

The most skillful meeting leaders seem to have an uncanny talent for leading a group in such a way that the people who really should participate in the meeting do participate, while those who tend to "overparticipate" are restrained from doing so. Part of this talent consists in being sensitive to where individuals are at every moment, and to where the group is at every moment, during the meeting. This sensitivity can be developed and improved through training, particularly training in the group process, as discussed later in this chapter.

Quiet individuals must be invited to participate by the meeting leader, often repeatedly during a meeting. Those individuals at the meeting who tend to talk at every opportunity must be restrained. Often if the right atmosphere is created by the meeting leader, others at the meeting will tactfully "turn off" the overcontributors. If it does not turn out this way, the meeting leader must speak up, saying something like, "Bill, let's hear what John has to say on this subject before we go on."

Meeting Dynamics: Task versus Process

This is an appropriate point at which to refer back to the meeting matrix of Fig. 34-1. Many of us have attended meetings which were highly structured, which had strong leader control, and which accomplished tasks on a regular time schedule. Sometimes we left with the feeling that something was missing, that it was a painful meeting, or that the results or tasks accomplishe¹ did not represent the best judgment of each of us. This is what often happens when the meeting leader conducts a meeting at a maximum omega level on the meeting matrix.

Sometimes a meeting has to be conducted this way, but experience has shown that just a small movement in the delta direction on the matrix will often accomplish the tasks just as speedily but with more enthusiasm, and later support, from the participants. The more an individual is trained in group methods, the more he or she is able to accomplish the task and at the same time fulfill individual and group needs during the meeting.

Meeting Control

Although some of my colleagues believe that meetings or groups can function effectively without a leader, such meetings and groups are rare indeed. I believe that all meetings, and most group activities, require a leader and that the leader has considerable responsibility. People who attend meetings are, in effect, delegating to the meeting leader a part of their valuable time to be used effectively, during the meeting, in order to accomplish the objectives for which the meeting is held. This delegation charges the meeting leader with responsibility for efficient utilization of their time.[4]

An awareness of group dynamics and an understanding of group process will certainly help a leader become more effective. Often, however, a meeting leader must simply confront time itself and direct the meeting toward a conclusion.

Summarizing

Summarizing is a key responsibility of meeting leaders; it helps them to effectively control a meeting and to facilitate the accomplishment of meeting objectives. The summary may cover where the meeting is with reference to the agenda, it may cover where the leader thinks the group is in reference to a decision on an agenda item or the solution of a problem, or it may cover the position taken by one of the participants. In any event, mastery of this technique can help a meeting leader be most effective in his or her management of the meeting.

Action Items

What I call the "assignment" and "commitment" aspect of a meeting is one that has not been adequately covered in many discussions of meetings. Both the assignment of responsibility for the solution of a problem and the commitment by the individual or individuals responsible at the meeting are extremely important. Too often a great deal of the value of a meeting is lost because it is not clear who will take responsibility for significant actions which the group has agreed upon and which will make the time spent at the meeting worthwhile. It is the meeting leader's responsibility to assure that the assignment is clear and that the commitment is made.[4]

Minutes of Meetings

Minutes seem very formal and time-consuming to some people, but they are the assurance to all concerned that the objectives of a meeting were achieved and therefore that the time devoted to the meeting was well spent. Furthermore, when more than one person is involved in any communications process, there is not only the chance for error in understanding but also the probability of it. Therefore, minutes of meetings are an essential part of the follow-through to see that meeting objectives are achieved.

Some minutes include simple statements of the following:

1. Conclusions reached
2. Action items and assignment of responsibility
3. Matters unresolved

More complete minutes will include a statement of:

1. Date, time, and location of the meeting
2. Objectives of the meeting
3. List of the participants
4. Matters discussed, item by item, including the expressed opinions of the people who attended the meeting
5. If the meeting involved voting, the names of those making motions and seconding the motions, as well as the result of the vote
6. Action items assigned, with expected results and dates
7. Matters not covered, or postponed, with an explanation

Follow-Up

Some of the most effective leaders it has been my pleasure to work with over the years are those who personally follow up on action items and decisions made at meetings they have held. Not only do most of us appreciate a reminder, but the personal contact made by the meeting leader completes the communications loop and prepares the meeting leader to build the agenda for the next meeting, as suggested earlier in this chapter.

MEETING, CONFERENCE, AND CONVENTION CHECKLIST[9]

Accommodations

Agreement with Hotel or Facility before Meeting

1. Approximate number of guest rooms needed, with breakdown on singles, doubles, and suites
2. Room rates
3. Reservations confirmation
4. Copies of reservations to those concerned
5. Date that majority of group is arriving
6. Date that majority of group is departing
7. Date that uncommitted guest rooms are to be released

8. Understanding regarding rooms to be assigned to VIPs, special guests, etc.—those to be paid by company and those complimentary by hotel
9. Hospitality suites needed
10. Checkrooms, gratuities, bars, snacks, service time, and date

Meetings

Check with Hotel before Meeting

1. Floor plans furnished
2. Correct date and time for each session
3. Room assigned for each session: rental
4. Headquarters room
5. Seating number, seating plan for each session, and speakers' tables
6. Meetings scheduled, staggered for best traffic flow, including elevator service
7. Staging required—size
8. Equipment for each session (check against equipment and facilities list)
9. Other special requirements (check immediately before meeting.)
10. Checkroom open and staffed
11. Seating style as ordered
12. Enough seats for all conferees
13. Cooling or heating system operating
14. PA system operating; mikes as ordered
15. Recording equipment operating
16. Microphones—number and type as ordered
17. Lectern in place, light operating, gavel, block
18. Water pitcher, water at lectern
19. Water pitcher, water, and glasses for conferees
20. Guard service at entrance door
21. Ashtrays, stands, matches
22. Overhead projector and screen
23. Teleprompter operating
24. Pencils, note pads, paper
25. Chart stands, easels, blackboards, related equipment
26. Piano, organ, signs, flags, banners
27. Lighting as ordered
28. Special flowers and plants as ordered
29. Any other special facilities
30. Directional signs if meeting room is difficult to locate
31. If meeting room is changed, notice posted conspicuously
32. Stenographer present
33. Photographer present
34. Assignment of someone to remove organizational property after the meeting
35. Check for forgotten property

Equipment and Facilities

1. Special notes to be placed in guest boxes
2. Equipment availability lists and prices furnished
3. Signs for registration desk, hospitality rooms, members only, tours, welcome
4. Lighting—spots, floods, operators
5. Staging—size
6. Overhead projector and screen

7. Blackboards, flannel boards, magnetic boards
8. Chart stands and easels
9. Lighted lectern, teleprompter
10. Gavel, block
11. PA system—microphones, types, number
12. Recording equipment, operator
13. Motion picture, filmstrip, or slide projection equipment; blackout switch
14. Special flowers and plants
15. Piano (tuned), organ
16. Phonograph and records
17. Printed services
18. Dressing rooms for entertainers
19. Parking, garage facilities
20. Decorations (check fire regulations)
21. Special equipment
22. Agreement on total cost of extra services
23. Telephones
24. Photographer
25. Stenographer
26. Flags, banners—whether hotel furnishes United States, Canadian, and state flags
27. Radio and TV broadcasting
28. Live and engineering charges
29. Closed-circuit TV

Registration

1. Time and days required
2. Registration cards—content, number
3. Tables—number, size
4. Tables for filling out forms—number, size
5. Chairs
6. Ashtrays
7. Typewriters—number, type
8. Personnel—own or hotel's
9. Water pitchers, glasses
10. Lighting
11. Bulletin boards—number, size
12. Signs
13. Notepaper, pens, pencils, sundries
14. Telephones (check immediately before opening)
15. Personnel—their knowledge of procedure
16. Information desired on registration cards
17. Information on badges
18. Handling of guests, dignitaries
19. Program and other material in place
20. Emergency housing
21. Hospitality desk
22. Wastebaskets
23. Mimeograph registration lists

Speakers

Check before Convention

1. Have speakers been invited early?
2. Have speakers been informed of length of time available to them?

3. Have speakers been informed of type of talk desired?
4. Are financial arrangements understood? Fee or expenses only? Fee or fee plus expenses? When is payment to be made?
5. Are biographical material and photos available for publicity and introduction?
6. Is speaker's wife coming along?
7. Has hotel reservation been made?
8. Will speaker require special equipment?
9. Has speaker been furnished with program or tentative program as early as possible?
10. When is majority of group arriving?
11. Are any local people closely related (personally or businesswise) to speaker, and should they be invited to hear him or her speak?
12. Has someone been designated to meet speaker upon arrival in city?

Check immediately before Meeting
1. Has speaker been personally introduced to officers and head table? Have special needs been met?
2. Is blackboard or easel in place?
3. Are pointers and chalk in place?
4. Will help be needed in turning charts?
5. Is projector on hand?
6. Is projector stand available?
7. Is projectionist on hand?
8. Is material to be passed out?
9. Will speaker need assistance?

Other Important Points
1. Is emergency speaker available in case of a "no-show"?

Miscellaneous

Decorations
1. Have decorations and storage space for decorations prior to use been arranged for?
2. In case of elaborate decorations, have fire regulations and hotel policy been checked?

Entertainment
1. Has an interesting entertainment program been planned for men, women, and children?

Guests
1. Have local dignitaries been invited and acceptance received?
2. Have they been provided with tickets?
3. If expected to speak even briefly, have they been forewarned?
4. Have arrangements been made to welcome them upon arrival?

Publicity
1. Has an effective publicity committee been set up?
2. Have city editors and radio and TV program directors been personally called on?
3. Has an integrated attendance-building publicity program been prepared?
4. Have newsworthy releases been prepared?
5. Have arrangements for photographs for organization and publicity been made?

Recording
1. Have arrangements been made to take minutes of the meeting, to type resolutions, to mimeograph proceedings?

Registration List
1. Have arrangements been made to mimeograph registration lists?

Sign Checklist
1. Registration desk, hospitality room, tickets, information, members only, special events, hospitality committee, special tours, ladies' committee, no smoking, welcome, advance registration

Signs
1. Have adequate signs been prepared to assure smooth operation, and is masking tape available for mounting?

GROUP METHODS AND PROCESS DEFINED

What Happens in Groups

Any time two or more people get together, a group is formed. Each individual brings to the group what Athos and Coffey[10] describe as a *personal system* of values, beliefs, knowledge, ways of thinking, and sentiments.

According to Athos and Coffey, there must also be a *required system* in order for the group to survive. By this they mean those activities, interactions, and sentiments which are essential or "required" from a group *if it is to survive as a group*.

From the interaction of the personal system and the required system emerges the group dynamic, or what Athos and Coffey call the *emergent system*.

The Roles People Play

When in groups, people tend to fulfill roles related to their personal system, to the required system of the group, and to the emergent system or dynamic which results from the interaction of the first two systems.

Careful observation of the emergent system will reveal three roles fulfilled by the participants. These roles may be called *group task roles, group building and maintenance roles,* and *self-centered roles.* They were first described by Kenneth D. Benne and Paul Sheats in 1948.[11] Others, such as Brilhart, have incorporated these roles into complete books covering the interaction process.[12]

Group Task Roles

Group task roles are behaviors that help the group solve its problems or accomplish its tasks. Group task roles include:

1. *Initiator.* Proposes new ideas, new goals, procedures, methods, solutions.

2. *Information Seeker.* Asks for facts, clarification, or information from other members; suggests that information is needed before making decisions.

3. *Information Giver.* Offers facts and information, personal experiences, and evidence (note that information is useful to accomplishing the task only when it is both pertinent and valid).

4. *Opinion Seeker.* Draws out convictions and opinions of others and asks for clarification of position or values involved.

5. *Opinion Giver.* States own belief or opinion and expresses a judgment.

6. *Clarifier.* Elaborates on idea expressed by another, often by giving an example, illustration, or explanation.

7. *Coordinator.* Clarifies relationships between facts, ideas, and suggestions or suggests an integration of ideas and activities of two or more members.

8. *Orienter.* Clarifies purpose or goal, defines position of the group, and summarizes or suggests the direction of the discussion.

9. *Energizer.* Prods group to greater activity or to a decision, stimulates activity, or warns of need to act while there is still time.

10. *Procedure Developer.*   Offers suggestions for accomplishing ideas of others or performs such tasks as handling seating arrangements, running the projector, and passing out papers.

11. *Recorder.*   Keeps written records on paper, chart, or blackboard, serving as group's "memory."

Group Building and Maintenance Roles

Group building and maintenance roles are behaviors that help members to function together, as a group, and to maintain constructive interpersonal relations while doing so. Group building and maintenance roles can be defined as follows:

1. *Supporter.*   Praises, agrees with, and indicates solidarity with others or goes along with them.

2. *Harmonizer.*   Mediates differences between others, reconciles disagreements, and conciliates.

3. *Tension Reliever.*   Jokes or brings out humor in a situation, reduces formality and status differences, and relaxes others.

4. *Gatekeeper.*   Opens channels of communication, brings in members who otherwise might not speak, and sees that all have an equal chance to be heard.

Self-centered Roles

Self-centered roles are behaviors directed toward satisfying the individual's own need without regard for the need of the group as a whole. These needs can serve only individual aims, often at the expense of the group. Personal or self-centered roles include:

1. *Blocker.*   Constantly raises objections, insists that nothing can be done, brings up the same topic after the rest of the group has disposed of it.

2. *Aggressor.*   Deflates status of others, expresses disapproval, jokes at expense of another member, and expresses ill will or envy.

3. *Recognition Seeker.*   Boasts, calls attention to self, relates irrelevant personal experiences, and seeks sympathy or pity.

4. *Confessor.*   Uses group as an audience for his or her mistakes, feelings, and beliefs, which are irrelevant to the group task, or engages in personal catharsis.

5. *Playboy.*   Displays a lack of involvement in group task by making jokes and cynical comments and indulging in horseplay and ridicule.

6. *Dominator.*   Tries to run the group by giving directions, ordering, flattering, interrupting, and insisting on his or her own way.

7. *Special-Interest Pleader.*   Speaks up primarily for the interests of a different group, acting as its representative, apologist, or advocate.

Interaction of Roles Gives Us the Group Process

Value judgments ("good" or "bad") should *not* be applied to the roles. In fact, part of the training of an effective leader of groups includes his or her development of a value system which recognizes the importance of the expression of these roles by each member of the group. Each individual in the group is important. Each individual has needs, just as the group itself has needs. The interaction of these needs, roles, or behavior is what gives us group dynamics and the group process.

Definition of Group Dynamics, Group Process, and Group Methods

Group dynamics consist of the interaction of individual and group needs. These dynamics can be identified by observing the roles described above.

Group process is the process of interaction of these roles. Group process is how things are happening, rather than what is being talked about. Group processes are thus going on all the time, not just when the leader decides to "use group methods." The trained leader can facilitate the group process by creating the proper environment so that the interaction of needs will occur and the group process will proceed in a constructive manner toward the maximum attainment of individual and group objectives. This leads to a definition of group methods.

Group methods are the techniques used by a trained leader to effectively facilitate group process in order to accomplish training and development objectives. In meetings where learning is not the objective, observation and identification of group dynamics, and effective facilitating of group process, will permit the leader to accomplish task objectives more effectively and more expeditiously, with greater satisfaction on the part of the individual participants. This is the underlying reason for the success of the delta-omega position on the meeting matrix.

Basic Premises and Values Underlying Effective Use of Group Methods

Effective use of group methods requires the understanding, acceptance, and application of a number of premises and values.

1. *Role of the Leader.* The leader is a facilitator or enabler. For most effective use of group methods, the leader must be more participative than authoritarian. The role of the leader will be further discussed later in this chapter.

2. *Respect for the Individual.* The personal worth and intellectual value of each individual in the group and of the group as a whole must be recognized.

3. *Recognition of Needs.* Each person in the group has individual needs. The group itself has needs. Effective use of group methods aims at maximization of fulfillment of individual and group needs within the parameters of the situation (a meeting, conference, seminar, etc.—which usually includes a task dimension). Where the objective is maximum development and self-fulfillment of the individual, we are in the maximum delta position on the meeting matrix.

4. *Individuals Respond to Their Environment.* We are all social and emotional beings. Our relationships to others around us and near us influences our growth and development, as well as our total adjustment. Peer-group pressure, evident in the interaction of roles in groups, indeed can powerfully affect the learning process.

5. *Expression of Thoughts and Feelings.* The right to express thoughts and feelings, and the encouragement of such expression, constitute human values important to the group process. Differences of opinion and attitudes must be recognized, accepted, and encouraged. The group process will prosper (group methods will work) only in such an environment.

6. *Individual Differences.* Individual differences must be accepted and respected.

7. *Cultural Differences.* Individuals and groups are part of cultures and subcultures which influence or determine the way they act and react.

8. *Attitudes.* The attitudes of individuals, the attitude of the group, and the attitude of the leader significantly affect the group process and the success of application of group methods. More will be said later in this chapter on the importance of the attitude of the leader.

9. *Resistance to Change.* Resistance to change is a natural human tendency. Verbalization of the desired change by the individual or group is in no way an indication that the resistance to change has been overcome and the change has been made. *Practice of the new behavior will tend to help overcome the resistance to change.*

10. *Observing Stages of Change.* Individuals and groups go through various changes of feelings during meetings. The leader must be observant and sensitive to where the individuals are and where the group is.

11. *Individual Resources.* Individuals in the group represent a very valuable resource; in fact, in adult groups they are the most valuable resource in the learning process.

12. *Uniqueness.* Each individual in the group is unique to the time and place and

circumstance which precipitated the group's formation. The group will behave accordingly, i.e., will be different from any other group, or even from that group at a different point in time. Each group becomes a unique dynamic within itself.

13. *Evaluation Is a Continuum.* This must be the case for effective application of group methods. Since it is the dynamics in the group (what is happening) which creates the process of change, the leader must be constantly assessing the dynamics of both the individual and the group.

GROUP METHODS: PROGRAM DESIGN, METHODOLOGIES, EVALUATION

As we begin a discussion of the design of programs using group methods and as we review the methodologies and special techniques involved, it is desirable to further refine our definition of group methods. Earlier, we defined group methods as the effective facilitating of group process to produce change through group dynamics.

I would like at this time to further define a group method as any methodology or technique which facilitates change through group dynamics. This leads us directly into program design and the identification of methodologies and special techniques.

Program Design

Program planning and design are covered extensively elsewhere in this handbook. It will be sufficient here to review some basic steps involved in program design:

1. Identify the need or problem.
2. Clearly define objectives in writing. For training and development programs, the objectives are often written in terms of changes in participant behavior expected to occur during the program.
3. Develop a preliminary design—plan the program and select the methods which will most effectively achieve the defined objectives. Here is where a determination must be made as to whether the utilization of group methods is the most effective way to meet objectives or whether you should plan to use lecture methods, a written case study, or other approaches.
4. Next, test the design against the original objectives to give preliminary validation to the design and selection of the methods.

Methodologies for Change

Using our refined definition—that a group method is a methodology or technique which facilitates change through group dynamics—we find a large number of methodologies available for use by the trained leader. For purposes of description, I shall divide these methodologies into two categories: (1) methodologies and disciplines and (2) methodologies and special techniques.

Methodologies and Disciplines

The methodologies and disciplines which I shall identify here are not intended to be a complete list by any means. Characteristics of disciplines include the following: a somewhat unique or different language, extensive training requirements for training leaders, certification of leaders on completion of training (and in some cases internship), and research and writing in the discipline. Particularly because of the last—research and writing—some of these disciplines have strongly influenced the development, understanding, and use of group methods. This is true particularly of the first discipline discussed below.

1. *Laboratory Training and the T Group.* Laboratory training provides a learning experience in which each participant can try out new behavior in a setting where experimentation is safe—and encouraged. In other words, the immediate behavior of participants is the basic subject matter.

The basic learning unit is the T group (training group guided by a trained leader). Members of the group have an opportunity to create a productive work group out of an unstructured situation. In the process of creating direction, order, and leadership from their own resources and in the process of making decisions, dealing with conflict, and working on tasks, participants gain, often for the first time, a clear view of the impact of their own characteristic method of working with people. Thus, in a unique way, these groups provide each participant with a microcosm for studying and understanding his or her interpersonal behavior.

Some background on the development of T groups is appropriate at this point because it will help explain the origin of many of the other group methods utilized today.

In 1946 Kurt Lewin, Kenneth Benne, Leland Bradford, and Ronald Lippitt developed the concepts that led to the first T group type of meetings, which were held in Bethel, Maine, in 1947, shortly after Lewin's death. The summer groups at Bethel came to be well known. An organization—the National Training Laboratories—was formed. Now called the NTL Institute for Applied Behavioral Science, it has offices in Washington, D.C.* This organization provides a wide variety of extensive training opportunities.

The primary thrust of the NTL groups has been in industry. This direction developed primarily because industry could afford the expense of such groups for its top personnel. The groups initially fit the T group description of their name. They were training groups in human relations skills in which individuals were taught to observe the nature of their interactions with others and the nature of the group process. It was this observation of group dynamics and study of group process which led to the development of many of the group methods used in business and industry today. From these experiences, executives and managers returned to their jobs with a better understanding of their own way of functioning in groups and on the job and with a greater awareness of their impact on other people.[13]

Leaders trained by NTL in the following years became leading practitioners of the use of group methods in business, industry, churches, civic organizations and in the new discipline of community development and organization development. A new leader certification organization was established in 1972. It is known as the International Association of Applied Social Scientists, Inc. (IAASS). The association is located at 6170 East Shore Drive, Columbia, So. Car. 29206.

2. *Psychodrama and Role Playing.* Another chapter in this handbook discusses role playing extensively. Psychodrama was originated by Dr. J. L. Moreno around 1910, and it became more systematized and publicized in the early 1930s, after Moreno came to the United States from Vienna. He developed concepts of group "play," role theory, and the use of creativity and spontaneity in therapeutic and educational contexts.

3. *Transactional Analysis.* Transactional Analysis was brought to popular attention by a book entitled *Games People Play: The Psychology of Human Relationships,* by Dr. Eric Berne; the book was in its eighth printing with the 1964 edition.[14] Transactional Analysis was also described by Dr. Thomas A. Harris in *I'm OK— You're OK: A Practical Guide to Transactional Analysis,* published in 1969.[15] It is a thesis of Transactional Analysis that three parts of persons exist within each of

*The address is 1815 North Fort Myer Drive, Arlington, Va. 22209.

us: Parent, Adult, and Child. These are known technically as *ego states.* The interaction of these three ego states within the individual affects his or her communications with others. The study of communications through Transactional Analysis techniques can be effective in facilitating change.[16] The International Transactional Analysis Association (ITAA) is located at 3155 College Avenue, Berkeley, California 94705.

4. *Other Disciplines.*   These include organization development and management development, as well as more therapeutic disciplines such as gestalt psychology and behavior modification. Organization development and management development are covered extensively elsewhere in this handbook.

Methodologies and Special Techniques

One of the reasons why disciplines are defined in the context of program design and methodology is that most disciplines have spun off some special techniques which are useful to the practicing leader or facilitator. Many of these special techniques are covered effectively in *Managing with People: A Manager's Handbook of Organization Development Methods,* by Jack Fordyce and Raymond Weil.[17] Others are discussed in works listed in the References at the end of this chapter. The following are only a few of these special techniques:

1. Use of subgrouping
2. Special uses of diads and triads
3. Discussion method[12]
4. Recognition of nonverbal communications[18]
5. Growth groups[19]
6. The case study workshop
7. Use of tape and video tape
8. Team building
9. Trust building[20]
10. Sociometrics and debriefing technique
11. Brainstorming[21]

Which to Use?

The selection of which methodology or special technique to use in the design of a training program, conference, workshop, seminar, or meeting rests with the leader. Some leaders become specialized in one methodology or discipline. Others utilize a variety of techniques and methods. Which to use depends on the training and experience of the leader.

GROUP METHODS: LEADER DEVELOPMENT

Role of the Leader

The leader's role in any group situation is to facilitate the attainment of the objectives defined for the meeting. When group methods are used, the most effective leaders tend to recede from a position of active leadership. They do not entirely join the group, but rather facilitate group process. In his book entitled *Learning to Work in Groups,*[22] Matthew B. Miles states: "The leader is not precisely a member of the group—yet he must retain some membership in the group or his efforts will be fruitless. He is certainly not a leader or discussion chairman (in the usual sense of the word)—yet his acts do influence the group in moving toward shared goals."

Miles continues: "When the training group gets bogged down or becomes apathetic, or is full of fight, the leader's job is not necessarily to help the group get out of the mess, but to help them learn from the mess." To do this, the leader must thoroughly understand and accept the premises and values described earlier in this chapter and must also have had considerable training.

Miles describes four functions of the leader:

1. The leader as a planner
2. The leader as a guide in building group norms
3. The leader as a guide in developing specific behaviors
4. The leader as an evaluator

The Leader as a Planner

During the early stages of planning and conducting a meeting or program, the leader's role is primarily that of helping the group head in the direction which will produce results in terms of attaining the objectives defined. Whether this is done with a complete training-program design, with an agenda sent out before the meeting, with an agenda built at the beginning of the meeting, or through an assessment of the needs and expectancies of participants at the meeting, this role is an important responsibility of the leader.

Defining the methodologies and techniques which may be most effective is usually a planning role of the leader. Also, the use of auxiliary equipment such as video tape recording and playback can be defined by the leader prior to the meeting.

The leader is responsible for providing an effective environment for the meeting or program and for providing an environment which is effective both physically (e.g., quiet) and psychologically.

During the meeting or learning experience, the leader must continue his or her attention to the group, asking questions such as:

1. Is the group moving in the direction of the objectives?
2. Are individual needs being met, as well as group needs?
3. Is the meeting climate psychologically safe for change?
4. Are the members getting an opportunity to practice new kinds of behavior (if this is an objective)?
5. Are people getting a chance to think about what they are doing, as well as experience it?
6. Is the group developing as a group?

The leader must keep these concerns constantly in the forefront of his or her thinking, says Miles, and must also help the group members pay attention to them from time to time.

The Leader as a Guide in Building Group Norms

During the actual meeting, conference, or learning experience, the leader's basic role is to keep things moving toward the attainment of objectives. The leader's behavior during the session helps to set group norms, that is, informal standards and ways of behaving that are highly valued by members of the group.

In a training group, certain norms are needed if growth and change are to take place. These have been described by Jack Gibb [23] and are discussed below.

1. *People are important.*   Leaders have a basic feeling of respect for the worth of others. They do not interrupt; they listen. They occasionally reject ideas, but never people. They show they believe that persons are ends, and all else is means. As they demonstrate their belief, they serve to some degree as a model for other group members, and the norm of basic respect for persons gradually becomes established in the training group.

2. *It is safe to try things out here.*   Trainers create a physical and psychological

environment that facilitates learning. They indicate by their actions that things are off the record here—that trying new things is, if this is a learning experience, the name of the game. They permit and invite discussion of their own behavior. They do not criticize anyone for expressing any feeling or idea. Gradually, willingness to experiment becomes a group norm.

3. *Feelings are important.* Trainers take expressions of feelings seriously. When people say they feel mad, bad, or glad, trainers help the group see that these are basic and important data for the group to consider. Feelings of members tell us how well progress on the path is going. Feelings represent the dynamics of group action discussed earlier in the chapter. The leader's observation of these dynamics and playback to the group is often extremely meaningful in the attainment of the objectives and in the learning process. Frank expression of feelings is essential if group members are to learn and grow.

4. *Things are not taken personally.* Trainers respond objectively to the expression of feelings. The expression of feelings is normal and natural in the group environment.

5. *We are learning from doing things and analyzing them.* From the start, trainers indicate by their actions that they see learning as beginning with experience. Unless an introduction is necessary, they do not lecture the group, but help the members examine their own experience. They help the group members set up trials of particular approaches to problems—trials which will lead to the solution of the problem and to the attainment of the group objective.

6. *What happens here and now is the important thing.* Trainers do not usually encourage the group members to talk about the past, other groups, back-home experiences, or things they have read, unless these are pertinent to the accomplishment of the task which has been given to the group. Mostly, leaders address themselves directly to what is going on in the training group, that is, the group process.

7. *We plan together.* Finally, trainers show the group members that they believe the training group is basically a shared, planful enterprise. They do not spring things on the group. They do not attempt to pull rank. They do not direct the group and hence do not take sole responsibility for the group's success in attaining its objectives.

Miles believes that it is far more important for leaders to accept and demonstrate these norms than it is for them to be especially proficient in a specific method or technique of group methods.

The Leader as a Guide to Specific Behaviors

As trainers encourage the development of norms like those suggested above, they must also perform certain functions in the training group during a training activity, or see that they are performed. Miles lists six functions which the leader may perform from time to time as the group session progresses.

1. *Providing Methodological Help.* The trainer must be able to help the group invent, construct, or adapt learning activities that will enable the members to learn what they want to learn. The methodologies referred to here can include such things as forming dyads and triads, setting up role-playing situations, or utilizing any of a great variety of methodologies effective to the attainment of meeting objectives.

2. *Guiding Analysis.* Here the trainer comments on, generalizes from, raises questions concerning, and in general helps the group members think explicitly about the experiences they have been going through. This is sometimes called the "making-visible" function or the "playback" function. It can also include the guidance of thoughtful discussion. Typical analysis behaviors might include making interpretations about what is happening in the group, asking why something is or is not going on, introducing a social science concept for discussion, asking for implications of the preceding statement or experience, and pointing out some-

thing that has just been happening and inviting analysis of it. Trainers may also find themselves helping to analyze the nature of the group itself, that is, where the group is as a group.

3. *Giving Support.*   As the meeting or training program continues, it is important for group members to have support from the leader as they work or learn. Where the nature of the group method requires the members to expose their own behavior to analysis as they try out new behavior, the support which the leader gives is often emotional support that will help them try out new things to see what happens. At the beginning of the group's activities together, support may come mostly from the leader. As the group continues to work together, support comes more and more from other group members, through the development of the norms discussed earlier.

Most effective leaders of groups also receive support from the group and are not hesitant to ask for this support when it is needed.

One of the leader's key responsibilities, particularly in T groups, is to be alert to individuals who may be having difficulties. Quick support of an individual who is beginning to have trouble adjusting to a concept or to statements made by others in the group will prevent the individual from getting into further difficulty. However, unless support is needed by an individual in the group, the objectives are best served if the leader's intervention and comments concern the group as a whole.

4. *Encouraging Group Growth.*   As the leader suggests training methods, helps the group think, and gives emotional support, he or she also needs to encourage group members to join in taking responsibility for these matters. For example, rather than setting up roles for the role players, the leader may suggest that the group do this as the members gain experience.

The leader may not always give the first interpretation of what has been happening, but may wait for the opinions of the group. Rather than answering questions, the leader may turn them back to the group as a whole.

5. *Controlling Group Movement.*   The fact that Miles has placed the control of group movement here is especially interesting. It ties in directly with my earlier comments on the leader's responsibility for control. Suffice it to say here that the nature of this control relates to the objectives of the meeting, workshop, T group, or seminar. As stated earlier, participants in any group are entrusting the leader with their time—with expectations that objectives will be accomplished. Control is important and yet can be the most delicate of all functions performed by the leader. Certainly group dynamics will be inhibited by overcontrol of the leader.

6. *Maintaining Membership in the Group.*   Obviously, the leaders must be seen as having some membership in the group; otherwise, what they say and do will have little impact. They must indicate that they value membership in the group. Leaders who try to remain too emotionally aloof or who demand special status may find themselves in trouble. The group may well isolate such a leader, and he or she will be unable to lead.

Conversely, the leader cannot afford to be "only a member of the group." He or she cannot give up the responsibility for helping the group attain the objectives for the meeting and/or for helping the group attain its learning objectives. There is a very delicate balance here.

The Leader as an Evaluator

As stated earlier in the chapter, the evaluation of group process is a continuum; this must be the case if effective results from group methods are to be obtained. The leader must constantly assess the feelings of the group, as well as the group's progress toward accomplishing the task. The leader must be open to, and encourage, continuous feedback on the group's evaluation of the group's progress and of the leader and his or her role. Also, feedback is helpful on such matters as the group's opinion of the values of the activities the leader helped to plan and which of these activities needs to be expanded or reduced through new planning.

Leader Development: Self-Awareness

The first step in becoming an effective leader of groups is to develop self-awareness. This is important because leaders bring to the group their own feelings, prejudices, and hand-ups, and if they are not aware of these factors, they will not become effective facilitators. Some additional insight into the importance of self-awareness may be gained from Carl Rogers's *On Becoming a Person,* particularly the chapter entitled "This Is Me."[24]

Leader Development: Interpersonal Awareness

The leader's awareness of his or her own interaction with others is essential to effective leadership of groups. In his chapter entitled "On Becoming a Trainer" (in *Modern Theory and Method in Group Training*[25]) William P. Golden identifies what he calls *core dimensions* in the interaction process which facilitate growth and development through group dynamics. A review of his chapter will be helpful in further understanding the importance of interpersonal awareness.

College and University Training

Study in the behavioral sciences is very helpful in the development of a leader. Most colleges and universities throughout the country offer courses in psychology, sociology, and related fields; many business schools have programs in human relations for business and industry. Some colleges and universities now have programs in group dynamics and group leadership development. Many of these same universities and colleges offer extension courses, which can be taken in the evening.

Seminars and Workshops

A variety of private organizations, consulting firms, and institutes offer courses and programs aimed at helping develop leaders of groups.

Special Institutes

As described earlier in this chapter, many disciplines have established their own special institutes in which they provide in-depth training (one to three years).

Reading

An extensive list of references is provided at the end of this chapter. Each of the books cited, in turn, contains its own list of references. This great source of learning is as close to us as our local library.

Above All—Experience!

In my own development as a leader of groups, I was guided by two nationally known and thoroughly experienced trainers. Both of these men stressed, above all, that experience is the best teacher. I was urged by both to participate in as many group experiences as possible, in addition to taking courses in subject matter related to human behavior and group leadership. In the final analysis, *the leadership of groups is as much an art as a science,* and the art is learned and improved only through experience.

REFERENCES

1. Bergevin, Paul, and Dwight Morris: *Group Processes for Adult Education,* Community Services in Adult Education, Bloomington, Ind., 1951.

2. Bergevin, Paul, Dwight Morris, and Robert M. Smith: *Adult Education Procedures,* Seabury Press, Inc., New York, 1963.
3. McKinley, John, and Robert M. Smith: *Guide to Program Planning,* Seabury Press, Inc., New York, 1965.
4. Reith, Jack: "Meetings Cost Money—Make Them Pay Off!" *Training and Development Journal,* October 1970.
5. Odiorne, George S.: *Management by Objectives,* Pitman Publishing Corporation, New York, 1965.
6. Morrisey, George L.: *Management by Objectives and Results,* Addison-Wesley Publishing Company, Inc., Reading, Mass., 1970.
7. Mager, Robert F.: *Preparing Instructional Objectives,* Fearon Publishers, Inc., Belmont, Calif., 1962.
8. Parkinson, C. Northcote: *Parkinson's Law,* Houghton Mifflin Company, Boston, 1957.
9. Reprinted by permission of AMACOM, a division of the American Management Associations, Licensee, from Auger, B. Y.: *How to Run Better Business Meetings,* © 1972 by Minnesota Mining and Manufacturing Company, pp. 156–161.
10. Athos, Anthony G., and Robert E. Coffey: *Behavior in Organizations: A Multidimensional View,* Prentice-Hall, Inc., Englewood Cliffs, N.J., 1968.
11. Benne, Kenneth D., and Paul Sheats: "Functional Roles of Group Members," *Journal of Social Issues,* vol. 4, no. 2, pp. 42–46, 1948.
12. Brilhart, John K.: *Effective Group Discussion,* Wm. C. Brown Company Publishers, Dubuque, Iowa, 1967.
13. Tannenbaum, Robert, Irving R. Weschler, and Fred Massarik: *Leadership and Organization,* McGraw-Hill Book Company, New York, 1961, chap. 9, "Looking at Ourselves: A New Focus in Management Training," pp. 123–140.
14. Berne, Eric: *Games People Play,* Grove Press, Inc., New York, 1964.
15. Harris, Thomas A.: *I'm OK—You're OK,* Harper & Row, Publishers, Incorporated, New York, 1969.
16. Campos, Leonard, and Paul McCormick: *Introduce Yourself to Transactional Analysis,* published by San Joaquin TA Institute, Stockton, Calif., 1972.
17. Fordyce, Jack K., and Raymond Weil: *Managing with People,* Addison-Wesley Publishing Company, Inc., Reading, Mass., 1971.
18. Nierenberg, Gerard I., and Henry H. Calero: *How to Read a Person Like a Book,* Hawthorn Books, Inc., New York, 1971.
19. Clinebell, Howard J., Jr.: *The People Dynamic,* Harper & Row, Publishers, Incorporated, New York, 1972.
20. Lewis, Howard R., and Dr. Harold S. Streitfeld: *Growth Games,* Harcourt Brace Jovanovich, New York, 1970.
21. Clark, Charles Hutchinson: *Brainstorming: The Dynamic New Way to Create Successful Ideas,* Doubleday & Company, Inc., Garden City, N.Y., 1958.
22. Reprinted by permission of the publisher from Matthew B. Miles, *Learning to Work in Groups,* Teachers College Press, copyright 1959 by Teachers College, Columbia University, New York, pp. 205, 206, 209–213.
23. Gibb, Jack R.: *A Norm-centered View of T-Group Training,* Jack R. Gibb, LaJolla, Calif., Unpublished monograph.
24. Rogers, Carl R.: *On Becoming a Person,* Houghton Mifflin Company, Boston, 1961.
25. Golden, William P.: "On Becoming a Trainer," in William G. Dyer (ed.), *Modern Theory and Method in Group Training,* Van Nostrand Reinhold, Incorporated, New York, 1972.

Chapter 35

Case Method

PAUL PIGORS

Paul Pigors *is Professor Emeritus, Massachusetts Institute of Technology, where he has been a faculty member since 1941. He has also taught at Tufts College, the University of Rochester, and Harvard. With his wife, Faith, Dr. Pigors originated the "incident process," a variant of traditional case method designed to help students search for meanings at various levels of abstraction as they analyze actual situations, formulate issues, and generalize from experience. This method of self-education makes extensive use of group dynamics. It has won wide acceptance at home and abroad as a tested approach to achieve learning-as-changing and to stimulate productive interaction with other people. Dr. Pigors has written and lectured extensively and is continuing his work as a case writer, discussion leader, arbitrator, and consultant.*

A good stance for reaching toward the stars is to have one's feet firmly planted on the ground. Practical judgment enables a person to do this. And one objective of case method is to cultivate this skill. Getting down to cases develops situational insight, building on one's own tested experience and that of others.

In talking with others about experience as a case, one can learn to benefit from two essential features of case method: *the case discussed* and *group discussion*. A person who reads and thinks about a case by himself or herself is using two features of case method: *the case report* and *case analysis*. Looking into a case situation to seek out its meaning as practical experience is close to the heart of case study. But even then, a study group may not have begun to work on the case which is, potentially, most significant for them: *the case of the study group itself*.

DIFFERENT OBJECTIVES AND VARIETIES OF CASE METHOD

The Harvard Method

This technique is mentioned first. It is the oldest and most respected form of case method. Also, to many people, it is *the* case method. First developed in the 1880s by Christopher Langdell at the Harvard Law School, this nondirective way of helping students to think for themselves slowly won acceptance in law, medicine, business administration, and social work.

Objectives   A major objective of the Harvard method has always been to help students learn for themselves by independent thinking, discerning in "the ever-tangled skein of human affairs"[1] principles and ideas which have lasting validitv and general applicability. A collateral objective is to develop skill in using knowledge. At the Harvard Graduate School of Business Administration, a constant aim has been to teach

> ... administration as a skill (i.e., 'art') linked inseparably to knowledge. Knowledge, without the skill to use it, is inert and surplus baggage to the practitioner. Skill without the continual infusion of new knowledge leaves its possessor practicing in the grip of unmodified routines ... or certain of seeing the skill he uses outmoded by men able to alter, elaborate, and extend their skill with new knowledge.[2]

Nondirective Leadership   In the Harvard method, teachers function as a catalyst. They assign cases for study and provide a permissive environment for group discussion. They guide the learning-teaching process. They do not attempt to cover a subject by "telling 'em" (the lecture method). Instead, they help students to discover for themselves the facts and ideas—displayed in case reports—which are most meaningful to them.

The role of a Harvard teacher, in such a course, has been described operationally by Glover and Hower as follows:

> "Let me summarize what I think I heard you say, to see if I caught what you were driving at."
> "Would you mind elaborating that? I'm not sure it is clear to most of us."
> "Is this what you mean?"
> "I think I see your point, but I am having difficulty relating it to your previous interpretation (or to what Mr.——has just said, or to the situation as developed in the discussion so far)."[3]

Harvard Cases   Other hallmarks of the Harvard method are the excellence, variety, and number of their published case reports.[4] For case writing, few institutions can equal the research division of the Harvard Business School. Members of its staff spend years in the field and in writing case reports which faithfully represent actual situations.

However, to some people the Harvard reports seem unnecessarily detailed and time-consuming.

FABRICATED AND ABBREVIATED CASES AS SHORTCUTS TO PROBLEM SOLVING

An easy way to get around this difficulty is to invent a case, either out of whole cloth or by piecing together fragments from reading and experience. However, no training director can afford to overlook the costly disadvantages of fictitious or doctored case material. As discussants set to work on a fictitious case, some of them will ask for more information. But discussion leaders who try to ad-lib, however adroit they may be, are likely to become entangled in the web they weave. At that point, members of the discussion group lose confidence in such a leader's integrity and ability. Worse still, their interest in the problem—now evidently unreal—evaporates.

Another undesirable consequence of using invented "facts" as starting points for discussion is that a bad example is set. Members of a study group may be encouraged to make unwarranted assumptions, to state opinions as facts, and to jump to conclusions. In such ways, a discussion leader may serve as a misleader.

Abbreviated case reports represent another attractive shortcut. The objectives are similar to those mentioned in connection with the fictitious (problem) case. An advantage is that like fictitious cases, authentic case reports (one or two pages is enough) focus attention on a given problem.* But unlike fictitious cases, abbrevi-

---

*One source of such reports is the American Arbitration Association. Their Education Department publishes monthly summaries of awards and opinions that were rendered under the rules of the association and were released for publication. Its Case-of-the-Month series provides excellent examples of abbreviated case reports.

ated reports of actual situations can be developed into full-length cases by anyone who has the time and interest to study the complete record.[5] (Of course, when that has been done, the case material being worked with is no longer an abbreviated report.)

Oversimplification   When a greatly abbreviated case report is presented for analysis, however, there remains the serious disadvantage that the case has been oversimplified. Students are not looking at a true-to-life situation. For practice in problem solving, too much has been done for them, and too little is asked of them. Life does not present anyone with neatly packaged problems. Essential problem-solving skills entail learning how to identify a problem in the making and how to prevent it from turning into a major difficulty. A person who wants to enhance these skills needs opportunities (such as can be gained by analyzing Harvard-type cases) to see (1) how problems look in their early stages, (2) what factors in the total situation might aggravate or alleviate them, and (3) what might be done to prevent further complications. For such purposes, a greatly abbreviated case report, like a fabricated case, is too flimsy to work with.

Audiovisual Presentations and Recorded Cases

These approaches to case study offer important advantages. The research and writing required in preparing comprehensive written reports are unnecessary. A taped case is economical to prepare and offers case material (usually in dialogue) in a lively form. A film (although more expensive) shows characters in a specific setting. Therefore, it can be an economical and interesting way to provide background information. To students, the element of entertainment may seem like the most important advantage. They do not have to start on a case by doing a lot of reading. But those advantages are outweighed by inherent disadvantages. Nothing is made available in writing, and so there is no memory aid. And many films are marred by flaws in the script or acting which make the situation untrue to life. Nevertheless, such audiovisual presentations provide evidences of social interaction—in expressive behavior such as tones of voice, gestures, and facial expressions—enabling case students to test their own powers of perception and insight. And as they try to read signs of inner motivation—in filmed and recorded characterizations—students quickly develop feelings of identification.

But anyone who wants to help conferees get the benefit of dramatic presentation, with the additional advantages which come only from a do-it-yourself twist, can resort to a device which is effective, inexpensive, and enjoyable: role playing.

ROLE PLAYING AS A TEST OF SKILL IN CASE ANALYSIS

Two important objectives, which can be realized when role playing is combined with case method, represent significant advantages over viewing films or listening to tapes. Role playing calls for active participation. And it provides opportunities for case students to show how they would practice what they preach.

Similarities between Case Method and Role Playing   Allen Solem[6] has compared the objectives of case study and those of role playing as follows: Both methods (1) provide a means for presenting one situation to all students; (2) make provision for a free exchange of views through discussion; (3) reflect a high interest factor through personal involvement; (4) offer stimulating ways for presenting problems; (5) are taken from real-life situations; (6) are geared to skill development as an important objective of training; (7) share the attribute of enabling the course director to avoid giving specific answers to the problem, thus encouraging the development of a variety of possible solutions; and (8) make it possible for participants to practice skills without anyone getting hurt in the process.

The Wharton School Method: "Live" Cases

A "live" case is a report of events that have just happened or are still in process. At the Wharton School such reports are presented by an executive from the organization where the case situation developed and where the problem was (or is being) tackled.

Major objectives of the live case method include giving students up-to-date factual information to start from, providing an interim exercise in problem solving (both in working committees and by writing individual reports), and offering opportunities to compare and appraise a variety of solutions for each problem analyzed (hypothetical solutions worked out in the study group and management solutions that have actually been applied).

Advantages   This method saves discussion leaders and conferees alike from the pitfalls encountered when taking illegitimate shortcuts. Other advantages include a short homework requirement to start with, a leader with firsthand knowledge of the facts to talk with (in developing an oral case report), and live problems to work with.

The implementing procedure[7] is as follows:

Advance Homework.   The day before the first classroom session to be led by the executive, students are given a short written statement of a case problem. This statement is sometimes supplemented by pertinent information about the company.

First Classroom Exercise.   When the executive presents the case to the group (usually at noon to about 30 students and an instructor), he or she reviews the problem in about 10 minutes and spends the remaining 45 minutes or so answering questions.

Second Homework Assignment.   In the six days before the next classroom discussion, students meet informally—in small groups—to discuss their proposed solutions. Each student then writes his or her own analysis and solution of the problem, summarizing the report in a one-page letter to the executive.

Second Classroom Exercise.   At the second meeting of the whole group, a student leads the discussion of the reports, forwarding to the executive the 10 which he or she considers best.

Homework for the Executive.   The executive studies the 10 reports and adds written comments.

Third Classroom Exercise.   At noon on the eleventh day after the first meeting, the executive again meets with the entire class and tells them about his or her solution. The executive also comments on the written reports, mentioning individual students by name. The session ends with a general discussion of solutions by management and/or students.

The Henley Syndicate Method[8]

The British have another system for using live case material. They do not regard it as case method, presumably because it differs considerably from the Harvard method. But it is outlined here because its objectives and techniques are much like those of the Wharton School method. The outstanding feature of the Henley method is its emphasis on sharing experience by participation in small groups, or syndicates.

Objectives   Advocates of the "syndicate"method in case study are convinced that this is the best way of helping managers to increase their knowledge, change their attitudes, and enhance certain skills such as those of oral and written communication, suitable committee behavior, and making group decisions.

Organization and Procedures   The syndicate method was developed by the British Administrative Staff College, at Henley-on-Thames. As in the Harvard executive program, "students" are managers in residence (12 weeks at Henley and 13 at Harvard). But the Henley system is quite directive. For example, before the group (66 members) arrives, the composition of each syndicate has already been determined, and chairpersons have been appointed for each subject. "Briefs" have been prepared on each topic to be discussed, though these are "suggestive rather than directive."[9]

Group work on briefs proceeds as follows: First an entire syndicate, consisting of 10 members, discusses the brief, breaking down the various problems raised into specific assignments which are "allotted to individuals or small teams of syndicate members; later a full meeting of the syndicate is convened to consider their findings. These are then incorporated in a [written] report which is presented to a plenary session of the course where it is again discussed, together with reports from other groups."[10]

Each syndicate always has a chairperson and a secretary, positions that are rotated with each brief. "Normally, syndicates are required to deal with a number of briefs at a time . . . to foster quick decisions and flexibility of mind."[11]

Written case material, used in connection with some subjects, is taken from actual situations. Some of this material contains a certain amount of "superfluous matter so that participants have to decide what is relevant to the problems they are considering."[12]

Centre Européen d'Éducation Permanente (CEDEP)[13]

This Center for Permanent Education, founded in 1971, is located in Fontainbleau (near Paris) adjacent to the European Institute of Business Administration (INSEAD). It constitutes a major development in the training of European executives and is a departure from the formal lecture method used in French *lycées* and universities. The principal teaching methods are participative—for example, the Harvard case method and various forms of group dynamics.

The most significant innovative feature of this cooperative endeavor by professional teachers from both organizations (INSEAD and CEDEP) and executives from six major industrial concerns is a 90-day residential teaching program spread over two years. Each two-week training period at CEDEP is followed by a three-month recess, during which participating executives return to their respective companies. Each of the eight 2-week training periods is built around a special theme as follows:

The company and its market resources . . . . 42 classes over 14 days
Operational resources—analysis and management . . . . 30 classes over 10 days
The external and internal environment of the company . . . . 30 classes over 10 days
Introducing new products . . . . 30 classes over 10 days
Performance evaluation and control . . . . 36 classes over 12 days
Logistics and distribution . . . . 30 classes over 10 days
The institutional role of the company . . . . 30 classes over 10 days
Integrated management of the company . . . . 42 classes over 14 days

One objective of CEDEP is rapidly to create a "critical mass" of executives, each of whom has participated in the same type of management development. Total enrollment is limited to 60 participants. Teaching units are subdivided into two sections of 30 each or 10 work groups of six.

During the three-month recesses, participating executives keep in close touch with one another and with CEDEP staff members. INSEAD provides backup services such as library and duplicating facilities.

The governing principle is to stimulate a continuing process of self-education. Each time participants return to their company, they can apply and test ideas and practices acquired at the centers. On their return after each recess, they bring with them information as to the productive results achieved or difficulties encountered in implementing new managerial ideas or practices. Thus executives continually provide new case material and evaluative information, and CEDEP works toward its major objective: to stimulate and follow up the development of each executive and, in this way, to foster the integrative development of each participating company.

THE INCIDENT PROCESS[14]

Objectives The central aim in this variant of the Harvard method is to stimulate self-development in a blend of understanding that combines *intellectual ability* (the power to think clearly, incisively, and reasonably about specific facts and also about abstractions); *practical judgment* (the capacity to modify conclusions, arrived at intellectually, so that they meet the test of common sense, including organization sense); and *social awareness* (the ability to appreciate the force of other people's feelings and the willingness to adjust or implement a decision so that it will be acceptable to persons who are affected by it).

A Five-Step Cycle for Working on Cases

1. *Starting with an Incident.* Group work on each case begins* when the group meets. The members, working alone for a couple of minutes, study a written incident. They then ask themselves: What seems to be going on here? What leads can I find here toward facts of the case and issues that stirred people up?

Appended to each incident is an invitation to make a short-term decision in the role of a person who had to cope with the incident when it actually happened.

2. *Getting and Organizing Factual Information.* During this phase (20 to 30 minutes) group members address questions to the discussion leader—the person with the facts. (The leader either prepared the case or has mastered information given in a comprehensive case report written by someone else.) The general tenor of questioning is directed, at first, toward finding out about the "what," "when," "where," and "how" of the situation in which the incident developed and about who was there. Clues are also tracked down if they seem to offer reliable insight into the "why" of behavior. When a mass of factual information has been assembled, it needs to be summarized. This suboperation highlights key items for decision making—in the organizational role from which the case is being analyzed.

3. *Formulating an Issue for Short-Term Decision.* During the next 5 to 10 minutes the group as a whole considers two questions: What is at stake here organizationally and for the persons immediately concerned? How shall we state the critical question for action, now? (Perhaps it is a multiple issue.)

4. *Making, Crystallizing, Presenting, and Testing Decisions.* This four-part phase may take 20 to 30 minutes. The suboperations are: (a) Each member writes his or her own answer to the question: How would I handle the incident (if I used my best judgment), and what reasons support my decision? These papers are signed and turned in to the discussion leader. (b) According to differences in written decisions, opinion groups of like-minded members select a spokesperson or a role player. Each spokesperson polls subgroup members and works with them to answer the question: What is the strongest case that we can put together to support our joint decision? (c) Next, decisions are put to the test of a brief debate between spokespersons, or in role playing. Subgroup decisions and reasoning are presented, compared, and appraised. (d) Then the discussion leader provides information

*There is *no required* homework, although after the group gets the hang of the method, voluntary work between meetings is done by students as discussion leaders and participant observer-reporters.

about another kind of test—the test of history. What actually was done by the person in whose role discussion group members have been analyzing the case? How did that decision work out in the immediate sequel? No attempt is made to teach a class solution.

Having thus disposed of short-term issues raised by the incident, the group is ready to ask the kind of questions which can be most productive for them.

5. *Trying to Learn from the Case as a Whole.* As groups gain proficiency during earlier phases, it often becomes possible to reserve a whole hour (in a two-hour study period) for reflective analysis. Characteristic general questions for this culminating phase of case analysis are: After the immediate incident had been coped with, what more needed to be thought about, and done, by insiders in that case situation? Which of the long-term goals that are obviously worth working for in that case are of special interest to members of this study group because the same goals are equally important in our everyday work situation? But apparently many training directors have shared the experience of the Pigors team that after short-term decisions have been discussed, most members of a study group feel a sense of letdown when they are asked to enlarge the scope of their thinking, To obviate this difficulty, small-group work has proved effective. It stimulates active participation from almost every member of a study group. The procedure is to present "buzz groups" with specific, but different, assignments:

   a. What shortcomings (or flaws in the case situation) seem to have been account-able for difficulties that showed up in the incident? (These are *factors to work on.*)
   b. What factors (personalities, organizational relationships, previous manage-rial actions, etc.) can be identified as actual or potential forces that would tend to favor productive interaction in such a situation? (These are *resources to work with.*)
   c. What kinds of long-term action might alleviate current difficulties and/or tend to prevent the recurrence of such an incident? (This kind of planning concerns *goals to work toward.*)

Such questions can also profitably be asked periodically about the situation of the study group itself in a series of meetings. They can be answered most productively if group members take turns in two leading roles, as discussion leader and as observer-reporter, and if such questions form the chief items on the agenda for stock-taking and planning sessions.

Learning by Leading — in "The Case of the Work Group Itself" According to standard practice by the incident process, the whole group subdivides early in a series of meetings into two-member teams. If time allows, each team leads the group twice. The first time, one teammate serves as discussion leader for the day, while the other functions as participant observer-reporter. When their second turn comes, they exchange roles.

In the role of discussion leader, a conferee prepares or studies a comprehensive, written case report and works with his or her partner to make a detailed plan for presenting the case by the incident process. During a group session, the conferee leads the discussion and has a chance to test his or her own plan for helping associates to learn about the case and from it.

The role of participant observer-reporter for the day requires the conferee to make advance preparation with his or her teammate, keep track of what is said and done during group discussion, and write a report which is distributed to the whole group.

Stock Taking and Planning Progress in "the case of the work group itself" depends in part on effective performance appraisal by participants, as members of a study group compare past performance with objectives and set new targets.

LABORATORY EXERCISES

In executive development programs sponsored by the Graduate School of Business Administration, University of Washington, course directors have used a great variety of structured problem situations. Two-hour laboratory sessions, devoted to the study of relevant management functions, provide participants with an opportunity to "experience" managerial concepts under consideration.[15] This problem-solving approach calls for skill in mathematical analysis, evaluating logical relationships, and solving riddles or puzzles. However, as in the incident process, primary emphasis is on *the learning situation of the group itself*. Instructors provide for immediate feedback. After each session, and in periodic reviews, participants are asked to assess their learning (or nonlearning) experiences. During such appraisals, students are urged to adopt a realistic, person-centered approach and to consider what they have learned and what it means to them as individuals and as managers.

Shared experience is encouraged by team relationships and reliance on small-group work in each session, as well as by periodic critiques by the study group as a whole.

CONSTITUENT ELEMENTS OF CASE METHOD: INTERACTIVE VARIABLES

Despite differences in objectives and techniques, all serious case methods have the same constituent elements. These variables are the case report (in some form), *case analysis* (systematic or otherwise), and the current learning situation (where group members and a course director are participants).

Case Report

A case report is always a picture that is presented in one of several ways: orally, in writing, on film, by means of television, or through role playing. Regardless of the medium used, case students try to connect with the case situation as presented. If studying case reports is to result in greater knowledge, more understanding, enhanced skills, and a more appreciative response to other people, certain standards of case reporting must be met.

Criteria A case report should be realistic—*show* rather than *tell*—so that case students can form their own opinions of its meaning. For students of human relations or of administration, a case report should indicate interpersonal relationships, both formal and informal, providing the kind of information given on organization charts and in position descriptions. It should also indicate something of the human quality of relationships between key persons in the case.

A case report should depict process. To qualify as a realistic picture, the report must reveal changes. And a case writer should try to make clear that the situation was still changing at the point where he or she stopped observing it.

Finally, a case report should indicate something of what seems to have been happening *in* people—at the level where outward events are transmuted into personal experience. This kind of case material can best be provided by aptly quoting what was said—at critical moments—and by accurately and vividly describing body language. (To meet this criterion in verbal reporting requires consummate skill. Here is one place where presentation on film or by role playing has distinct advantages.)

Limitations But even the best case reports have serious limitations. No picture, however realistic, is identical with what it portrays. No matter how experienced a case writer may be, his or her perceptions of facts are different from the facts themselves. All reporting is interpretive—inevitably biased and selective.

Special Opportunities However, some of these difficulties have been overcome by departures from traditional case method. For instance, at Harvard and in the incident process, it is standard practice for students to do fieldwork and write their own case reports. At the Wharton School, students often analyze cases that are still in the making. Furthermore, whenever the course director focuses attention on the learning situation of the study group itself, case students have a priceless opportunity to examine their own experience.

Case Analysis

If case analysis is to result in enhanced skills, modified attitudes, and learning-as-change, it should approximate what has to be done by thoughtful people in everyday life. To be of practical value, case analysis must include identifying difficulties: trying to understand how they developed (seeing not merely *who* was to blame but chiefly *what* was accountable), disentangling related difficulties to consider them separately as well as in relation to one another, and deciding which need to be tackled first (because they are serious and urgent, but can be remedied and seem likely to get worse if ignored).

Case Analysis Should Be Comprehensive   It should be much more thorough than the quick and superficial way in which most of us look into a situation when called on to make everyday decisions. For example, according to the plan of the incident process, case writers and case students systematically gather and verify information on three typical factors: (1) the behavior of human beings involved in the case (who did what, with what observable effects on other people?); (2) space-time dimensions (such things as significant changes and the "when," "where," and "how long" of it); and (3) the technical aspect (methods, procedures, and equipment used, etc.). In getting such information to prepare a case report, we urge students to interview more than one person. Even an inside view is always multiple.

Case Analysis Should Be Flexible   It would be misleading to prepare a check-list of questions (however comprehensive) and tell interviewers or observers that these questions could unlock the secrets of every case and lead to right answers for every problem. Any system for exploring actual situations (through the medium of case reports or by firsthand observation) should be used as a flexible plan. It indicates the need to ask a variety of questions and to get around in the situation—mentally—seeing it from many angles.

Case Analysis Should Always Culminate in Reflection: What Is at Stake Here in the Situation as a Whole?   How might long-term goals best be approached? And if studying relatively remote cases is to develop into a case-minded approach to everyday events, reflective analysis should frequently be extended toward the future of those who are doing the reflecting. What might be learned from the case we have been talking about, and from our group dynamics experiments, which could profitably be translated into action by members of this group?

Limitations of Case Analysis   What seems to have been accountable for the relatively meager results—to judge by subsequent behavior—that have so often been achieved by case study?

One inherent difficulty is built-in bias. Even a case student who is, in fact, an outsider in relation to a given case that he or she analyzes cannot achieve a perfectly objective attitude. His thinking is inevitably warped and limited by prejudices, habits of thought, and preconceptions of which he may be unaware. Stumbling blocks which trip many of us when we attempt case analysis as a solitary exercise are these: We assume that our own way of thinking about a case is the best way. We judge our own coverage of a case to be adequate. And we take it for granted that our own assumptions and conclusions are correct. One reason why group work on cases can be so unsettling at some times, and so fruitful at all times, is that what one member takes for granted is often questioned by others.

Another limiting factor is often brought to case study as an expectation. Many case students start with the assumption that nothing more arduous will be expected of them than (in effect) throwing a few stones at "those people in cases," after which they will be treated to a complete analysis by an expert—who will tell them what the case means. But until such expectations have been replaced by a more realistic understanding of what case method can be, students will miss the major benefits of case analysis.

A third serious barrier to productive case analysis, especially in solitary thinking, is that it calls for skill with language. But many people are sent to case-study courses primarily because they seem to lack communications skills. Such people are likely to bog down in inaccurate, unclear thinking unless they listen with understanding to what other course members have to say. Fortunately, much of the work in analyzing cases can be done during group discussion. Some of this analysis is best done in small subgroups. If a full measure of learning is to be derived by case analysis during discussion, experience suggests that the following criteria need to be met.

Case Discussion*

Discussion Should Always Be Focused   When a group is talking about a case, everyone at any given time, should be centering attention on the same item. And all members should be working, as teammates, at the same level of abstraction. For example, it is unproductive to have talk swing back and forth between getting information and comparing opinions. Usually, the most productive discussion takes place in small groups. But whatever the size of the discussion unit, the subject of talk should be sufficiently clear-cut, and the language sufficiently precise, so that everyone can know just what is being talked about.

Discussion Should Achieve Coverage   There should be coverage, for instance, of general ideas and issues raised by the case being studied. Discussion thus qualifies as "talk that gets somewhere." And talk must keep moving if it is to get around. Talk that stays too long on dead center gets boring. But how fast must talk move not to seem boring? There is no single answer to that question. However, an instructive exercise in management—especially for a student who is leading a discussion—is to try to make the answer approximately right for all members of a group.

Discussion Should Be Characterized by a Free, Informal, and Experimental Atmosphere   Four freedoms which can and should be made available during case discussion are (1) the freedom to try out ideas for size; (2) the freedom to cite firsthand experience; (3) the freedom to speak one's mind (when necessary even in disagreement, without regard to the status of the speaker with whom one disagrees); and (4) the freedom to propose and lead experiments in conference method (experiments to clarify the nature and origin of disagreements and to establish common ground). Talk among group members can be fully productive for human relations only when differences of opinion, feelings, attitudes, and values can be *worked through*.[16] Some groups start by shying away from all controversial topics. And some training directors encourage that tendency or even make it a rule. But where, when, and how can differences be worked through more productively than in a study group that is committed to learning-as-change?

*The word "discussion" denotes an interchange of opinions, a free give-and-take of views. There has been considerable misunderstanding on this point by persons who have used the incident process and written about their experience. For example, in the incident process, mere fact-finding does not qualify as discussion. Genuine discussion takes place as attitudes and feelings *toward* facts are expressed and as opinions *about* facts are clarified and compared.

IMPORTANCE OF THE CURRENT SITUATION: THE
CASE OF THE STUDY GROUP ITSELF

Some training directors (and university professors, too) seem not to have taken full advantage of the fact that much of the work done by case method takes place *in a social situation.* Variables in this situation—as in all other cases discussed—include *human nature* (manifested in the behavior and interpersonal relationships of participants), the technical factor (methods of work), and *space-time dimensions.*

Outward changes come about in the ongoing case of the study group itself ("this case") as participants learn how to work together. Subjective changes come about as case students modify their attitudes toward one another and toward people in "those cases out there." Other significant advances occur in "this case" as participants become more case-minded. A special combination of altered attitudes and enhanced skills can be especially productive. At first, members of a case-study group are apt to see themselves as critics. Professor Lee[17] put it this way: "They begin with what is easier, judging, approving, condemning. . . . [But gradually] the easy praising and blaming give way to asking, searching, listening. . . . [In this way, meetings] can become a testing ground on which each member can measure the reach of his own arts and habits in communication." What will be learned on this testing ground depends on a number of interacting variables. These include the skill and experience of the official leader, the readiness of participants to engage in the arduous process of learning-as-change, and the length of the course.

Planning, both before and during a case-study course, is essential to progress in managerial skills. If some of the planning, preferably near the start of the course, can be done *with* group members, they are more likely to participate wholeheartedly in carrying out the plans. But planning is not the only leadership function in regard to which group effort can pay off in group performance. Group members can benefit by taking a share in leading discussions, observing what is said and done around the conference table and in small-group exercises, reporting their observations, helping to set new targets, and appraising group performance. In these ways, skills acquired in discussing "those cases" can be developed into a case-minded approach to "this case" (the learning situation of the study group itself). That development comes about as case students repeatedly shift their attention back and forth between "those cases" and "this case," applying in their own behavior, here and now, some of what they have recommended for persons "out there." In this way, case students are *actually doing* what they are talking about.

REFERENCES

1. Redlich, Josef: *The Common Law and the Case Method in American University Law Schools,* a report to the Carnegie Foundation for the Advancement of Teaching, Bulletin no. 8, New York, 1914, p. 12.
2. Bailey, Joseph C.: in Faculty of the Graduate School of Business Administration, Harvard University, *Organizational Behavior and Administration: Cases, Concepts and Research Findings,* The Dorsey Press and Richard D. Irwin, Inc., Homewood, Ill., 1961, p. xx.
3. Glover, John D., and Ralph M. Hower: "Some Comments on Teaching by the Case Method," in Kenneth B. Andrews (ed.), *The Case Method of Teaching Human Relations and Administration: An Interim Statement,* Harvard University Press, Cambridge, Mass., 1953, p. 20.
4. For examples, see Glover, John D., and Ralph M. Hower: *The Administrator: Cases on Human Relations in Business,* 3d ed., Richard D. Irwin, Inc., Homewood, Ill., 1957. Particularly useful to a training director are the excellent bibliographies compiled by Lindfors, Grace V.: *Intercollegiate Bibliography: Cases in Business Administration,* Intercollegiate Clearing House, Soldiers Field, Boston. See especially Burleson, Jean (ed.): *Case*

Bibliography and Index: Management of Organizations—Europe, 1973. This is published as a service to management education on behalf of an emerging European confederation of such language centers as Case Clearing House of Great Britain and Ireland, Centrale de Cas, Italian Case Clearing House, Nordic Management Board, Spanish Case Clearing House, Turkish Case Clearing House, and Zentrale fuer Fallstudien, with cooperation of The European Institute of Business Administration (INSEAD) European Foundation for Management Education.

5. For an example, see in Pigors, Paul, and Charles A. Myers: *Personnel Administration: A Point of View and a Method,* 7th ed., McGraw-Hill Book Company, New York, 1973, case 19, "Fear or Featherbedding?" pp. 563–565.

6. Solem, Allen R.: "Human Relations Training: Comparison of Case Study and Role Playing," *Personnel Administration,* vol. 23, no. 5, pp. 29–37, 51, September–October 1960.

7. Murphy, Walter B.: *Industrial Policy: The Purposes and Operations of the Course,* mimeographed outline of the live case method, Wharton School of Finance and Commerce, Philadelphia, 1952.

8. Hall, Sir Noel Frederick: "The Henley Experiment," in *The Making of Higher Executives: The Modern Challenges,* New York University, School of Commerce, Accounts, and Finance, New York, 1958, pp. 31–67.

9. Negley, Glenn R.: "The British Administrative Staff College: Training for Executive Responsibility," *Personnel Administration,* vol. 25, no. 1, pp. 35–42, January–February 1962.

10. Argyle, Michael, and Trevor Smith: *Training Managers,* The Acton Society Trust, London, 1962, p. 18.

11. Ibid.

12. Ibid., pp. 18–19.

13. *CEDEP: Centre Européen d'Éducation Permanente,* syllabus published by the European Institute of Business Administration (INSEAD), Fontainebleau, France, October 1972.

14. For more on the theory of this method, see Pigors, Paul, and Faith Pigors: *Case Method in Human Relations: The Incident Process,* McGraw-Hill Book Company, New York, 1961, especially part three, "The Incident Process and a System of Job Rotation," pp. 139–215. The Bureau of National Affairs has also published a manual for training directors and 42 cases as follows: Series I—Practical Supervisory Problems; Series II—Government Cases: Federal, State and Local; Series III—White Collar Cases.

15. Knudson, Harry R., Robert T. Woodworth, and Cecil H. Bell: *Management: An Experiential Approach,* McGraw-Hill Book Company, New York, 1973.

16. For the rationale of "working through," see Jacques, Elliott: *The Changing Culture of a Factory,* Tavistock Institute of Human Relations, The Dryden Press, Inc., New York, 1952.

17. Lee, Irving J.: *Customs and Crises in Communication: Cases for the Study of Some Barriers and Breakdowns,* Harper & Brothers, New York, 1954, preface, p. xii.

Chapter 36

Role Playing

WALLACE WOHLKING

Wallace Wohlking *is on the faculty of the New York State School of Industrial and Labor Relations, Cornell University. Since 1960 he has regularly conducted, under Cornell University auspices, workshops on role playing for training specialists. His articles on role playing, conflict resolution, and learning theory have appeared in a variety of journals. He is the coauthor of a business-game series entitled* Handling Conflict in Management, *and published by the American Management Associations.*

According to surveys conducted in recent years, role playing is used by 15 to 20 percent of the organizations which conduct in-house training programs.[1] By far its two most common uses are for (1) training supervisors in human relations skills and (2) training sales personnel in sales techniques. Also, role playing is used often in training programs in the areas of interviewing, grievance handling, group problem solving, performance review, conference leadership, and decision making. Role playing may be used to develop or increase skills in any interaction between human beings, e.g., banking transactions, the transactions of complaint and return departments, the issuance of traffic tickets, and the handling of drunks.

Role playing may be defined as an educational or therapeutic technique in which some problem involving human interaction, real or imaginary, is presented and then spontaneously acted out. The enactment is usually followed by a discussion and/or analysis to determine what happened and why and, if necessary, how the problem could be better handled in the future.

Role playing is a technique which offers an opportunity for practicing skills in "doing" and implementing. With role playing, individuals can practice handling a wide variety of problems which confront them in carrying out their organizational responsibilities.

Role playing is used best as a tool to develop "implementation" skills. As Norman Maier has pointed out, there is often an important gap between the ability to develop a good solution or decision related to a problem and the ability to implement and carry out the solution at the point of face-to-face interaction.

LEARNING THEORY AND ROLE PLAYING

Malcolm Shaw[2] has theorized four kinds of learning that can take place through role playing: (1) learning by doing (practice of desired skill), (2) learning through imitation (participants can imitate desirable behavior), (3) learning through observation and feedback (participants can learn about their own effectiveness and weaknesses when class members feed back observations on role-play behavior), and (4) learning through analysis and conceptualization (repeated experience with role-play problems allows participants to learn principles of human relations or management).

TRAINING OBJECTIVES AND ROLE PLAYING

Role playing is a method which lends itself to teaching either "content" or "process" objectives. In training settings, content has to do with the substance of the training presentation. Process has to do with the manner in which a situation is dealt with or is responded to.

For example, if a role play has been constructed to teach supervisors how to handle an employee's discipline problem, the content of the role play of an interview between the supervisor and the employee will relate to such matters as: (1) What discipline infraction took place? (2) What were the extenuating circumstances, if any? (3) What would be a good decision in handling this particular type of discipline case?

In general, content focuses on such matters as: (1) an analysis of *what* was said, (2) an examination of the *quality* of any decision that was made in a role play, and (3) clarification of the *facts* in the role-playing case.

By contrast, process matters in the interview role-play example above have to do with such questions as: (1) Why did the employee respond the way he or she did? (2) What attitudes were present in the role players? (3) What techniques did the supervisor use to obtain a full explanation of the employee's discipline infraction? (4) What kind of eye contact took place between the supervisor and the employee? (5) What did the supervisor do to create a climate of trust?

In general, process issues in role-playing situations have to do with such matters as the attitudes, motivations, body language, and facial expressions of the role players. Basically, the trainer explores the psychological dynamics and tone of the role play when he or she examines process issues.

In any role-playing interaction, content and process material are simultaneously being created. Postenactment discussion of role plays will normally tend to focus on one of these two areas.

TYPES OF ROLE PLAYING

Because some forms of role playing are more appropriate than others for certain training objectives, the effective use of role playing within a training program is predicated on a clear understanding of its various forms.

There are two basic types of role playing: structured role playing and spontaneous role playing. The most commonly used form in organizational training is structured role playing. It is characterized by the use of written cases. These cases may be selected from texts or written specifically to meet organizational training objectives. The most widely used written cases are those of Norman Maier.[3] Another source of role playing cases is Scott Parry's *Using Role Playing in the Classroom.*[4]

There are three basic subcategories of structured role playing: the single role play, the multiple role play, and role rotation.

Single Role Plays

This type of role playing typically consists of two or three people playing out roles in front of a class. It is the form of role playing which is perhaps most widely used by trainers.

The single role play is best used when the training objective is primarily that of *demonstrating* how certain types of problems can be dealt with or of looking at the complications which may ensue if a problem is not well handled. It is valuable for the class as a shared experience that can be discussed and analyzed because it has been seen by all class members. It is quite an appropriate choice where the trainer is attempting to develop analytic skills as well as a better understanding of process issues.

The basic advantage of the single role play is that it allows the entire class to examine in depth all the dynamics and complexities involved when individuals attempt to solve a problem and/or better understand one another.

It has two basic disadvantages: (1) Some players tend to feel embarrassed performing in front of the entire class, and (2) if the players do badly, it may be difficult for the trainer to handle the negative comments about them that are likely to emerge in the discussion that follows the role play. Thus the single role play should be used only after an adequate trust level has been built up in the group and when negative feedback is given in a climate where norms of openness and mutual concern have been established.

A cautionary note about the single role play: Many trainers use this form when they intend to give practice to trainees in developing skills. It should be pointed out, however, that normally in any written role play, there is a skill burden placed on only *one* of the players, regardless of the number of roles in the case. In the typical role play, one person is attempting to deal with the problem, and the others are contributing to the problem. In other words, in the standard written role play, regardless of the number of roles, all the role players except one act as foils to that one person. The person who is dealing with the situation, be it one of attempting to elicit some important information or solve a problem, has the skill burden. Norman Maier's term for this is "sitting in the hot seat." As a consequence, only one person actually gets any real practice in the single role play. Therefore, trainers who desire to give trainees actual practice in implementation skills should give greater consideration to using the multiple role play or, possibly, role rotation.

Multiple Role Plays

In the multiple role play all trainees are players. The class is broken up into groups of two, three, or whatever number of roles are called for by the particular role play. Each player is given a written role (or an assignment as an observer), and then the entire class role-plays at the same time.

The multiple role play should be used when the instructor desires to give the entire class a chance to *practice* in dealing with a problem related to the training objective.

The advantages of the multiple role play are that it (1) allows all class members to participate; (2) demonstrates the broad variety of conclusions and decisions that may be reached by many individuals, all starting with the same data; and (3) causes almost no embarrassment to the players and sharply reduces the problems related to negative comments about ineffective role-playing behavior.

The disadvantages of multiple role playing are minor in nature: (1) Some groups will finish before others, and (2) very little time can be allowed for the discussion of process experiences of each individual group because, in general, the process discussions of what happened in the role play are of great interest to the individual group but of limited interest to the class as a whole.

Role Rotation

Role rotation consists typically of having one person play a role, usually that of an individual who has a problem or is creating a problem, and having several class members attempt to use their skills to handle the situation. The role rotation is done in sequence. After one participant finishes dealing with the problem presented by the role player, another volunteer is requested by the trainer to respond to the same situation until three to five persons have had a chance to role-play the situation.

In outward appearance, role rotation is similar to the single role play. However, when a number of persons rotate in one role, participants tend to feel less embarrassed and are more willing to participate in the exercise.

Role rotation is particularly effective for teaching the techniques related to various forms of interviews involving discipline, grievance handling, and communications misunderstandings. It is also appropriate when the trainer would like to teach certain key points that should be included in interviews related to handling customer complaints, sales approaches, and other relatively standardized interview situations.

This method also demonstrates the wide variety of styles in which different individuals will deal with the same problem. The difference in style will usually generate considerable discussion among trainees about the relative effectiveness of various styles and approaches to handling problem situations.

Spontaneous Role Playing

Spontaneous role playing can be used to achieve any of the objectives which a trainer may attempt to obtain with structured role playing. However, in practice, spontaneous role playing tends to be used more often to help participants acquire insight into their own behavior and attitudes or the behavior and attitudes of others. This is in contrast to structured role playing, in which emphasis is usually on *skill* development. Spontaneous role playing requires that the trainer elicit some problem from the group and then direct an enactment of the problem. No written roles are used; the material for the role play is obtained directly from the group itself.

The trainer in the spontaneous role play is usually more active and intervenes more than the trainer in the written role play. Through the use of such techniques as role reversal, the auxiliary ego, and the soliloquy, the trainer can usually generate a very deep involvement of the role players in the enactment, thus developing levels of feeling and insight not normally achieved with structured role plays. Although the postenactment discussion of structured role playing may focus on either process or substantive issues, the postenactment discussion of spontaneous role playing focuses almost exclusively on process factors, e.g., motivations, attitudes, and defense mechanisms.

The major advantage of spontaneous role playing is that it tends to delve more deeply into the motivations and assumptions that influence a role player's behavior. Its disadvantages are that (1) it requires extremely high skill on the part of the trainer; (2) like the single role play, it may embarrass the players; and (3) because only a few persons actually get an opportunity to role-play, most of the class learning is from observation rather than the practice of a skill.

It should be pointed out, however, that those rare trainers who are highly skilled in both structured and spontaneous role play can often effectively blend the two role-playing approaches. For a more complete discussion of concepts and techniques used in spontaneous role playing, see Zerka Moreno's work.[5]

STEPS IN THE ROLE-PLAYING PROCESS

The typical role play (whether structured or spontaneous) usually involves three phases: (1) the warm-up, (2) the enactment, and (3) the postenactment discussion.

The Warm-up

It is necessary to develop some class motivation for any planned role-playing activity. Warm-ups for the use of structured role plays take considerable planning.

In contrast, warm-ups for conducting spontaneous role play take considerably less planning but require a high degree of skill in moving class members toward revealing their problems and/or basic feelings. These "revelations" become the basis for the spontaneous role play.

The objective of the warm-up is to get the trainees to participate in a constructive manner in the role-play experience. To achieve this end, the trainer must deal with two elements: (1) any possible anxiety the trainee may have about role playing and (2) the level of the motivation of the trainee.

There are several ways of reducing possible trainee anxiety relating to role-playing situations. The first technique is to so structure the role-playing experience that the trainee does not feel "on the spot"; therefore, the initial role-playing experience should be with multiple role plays. Second, it is important to inform the role players of what will happen in the role-play session. Usually some discussion of the process itself will serve to minimize trainees' anxieties, especially with groups that are relatively unsophisticated in training settings. It is also important to conduct the role play in a setting which is quiet and private. No one should be able to eavesdrop on the role players.

Ideally, chairs should be arranged in a circle or in a U shape so that all the trainees can see one another's faces. This arrangement will tend to allow the trainees to communicate more rapidly and with greater effectiveness with one another and with the trainer.

As part of the trainer's approach to assure trainee involvement in the role-playing exercise, the session should be introduced in such a manner that it becomes clear to the trainee that the exercise is somehow related to his or her on-the-job needs or is otherwise intrinsically interesting. The most typical and usually the most productive approach is to encourage the group to discuss their own experiences with the given problem under consideration. For example, if the role play that the trainer plans to present is on a performance appraisal, he or she may want to get a list of problems from the group which they encounter in handling a performance appraisal. This normally would provide increased motivation for the trainees to participate in the role-playing experience.

In addition to the problem census described above, there are other techniques available for warming up groups where the structured case is to be used. They include (1) a brief lecture or reading assignment on the key topic related to the role-playing case and (2) a presentation of a model of desired behavior, for example, a film which demonstrates how to conduct a nondirective interview.

At this point it is appropriate to comment on the question as to when to use role playing in a training program and on the relationship of role playing to conceptual learning.

Some trainers favor a "deductive" style of teaching. They tend to go from the general to the particular, from principle to application. Consequently, a trainee with such an orientation would tend to precede role-playing activity with theoretical inputs and/or demonstrations related to the training objective. Trainers who are more oriented to "discovery" learning methods (simulations, business games, etc.) may start off with a role-playing exercise and then attempt to have the trainees develop generalizations or principles based on the role-playing experience.

Another factor of importance in determining how role playing is to be used relates to the nature of the group to be trained. If the group is resistant to cognitive teaching approaches or if it learns better from specific experiences than from the presentation of abstract concepts, then it would appear useful to utilize a discovery learning approach. In other words, the role playing should be used first, and then the theoretical material should be allowed to emerge in the discussion which follows the role play.

The Enactment

Structured Role Plays Before conducting the single role-play enactment, the trainer should carry out the following procedures:

1. The trainer should read aloud the general instruction sheet or any similar background statement which gives facts that all the role players would normally know. If there is no general instruction sheet related to the role play, this step is omitted.
2. Those persons who have volunteered or have been selected to play the roles should be sent out of the room and told to read their role briefing sheets. They should be told not to converse with one another about the information on their briefing sheets.

   While the role players are briefing themselves, the instructor should pass out any observer sheets which he or she may have designed to bring out data relevant to the teaching objectives. If the trainer does not have the observer sheets, he or she should pass out a full set of the roles which are about to be enacted in front of the class.
3. While the class is reading the observer sheets or the briefing sheets, the instructor should check with the role players and clarify any questions they may have about their briefing sheets.
4. The trainer then has the role players take their positions in front of the class (usually they would be seated facing one another) and advises them that under no circumstances should they step out of the role.
5. To begin the role play, the trainer sets the scene by restating the identity of the roles being enacted and making a brief statement about what has just happened as the action begins. For example, "Lee Baker, the supervisor, has just called Bob into his office to discuss the situation."

Most written role plays which focus on communications skill problems or deal with process issues are designed to take 10 to 12 minutes. A role play will generally take longer if more than two people are involved or if it is designed to improve problem-solving skills. This type of role play takes more time because it is usually built around substantive issues which may involve technical matters related to the work process. A widely used role-playing case which deals with both process and content issues is Norman Maier's "Change of Work Procedure." This role play (four roles) requires the mastery and understanding of technical data, and, as a partial consequence, about 25 minutes is required for its enactment. Maier recommends that between 25 and 30 minutes be allowed for the enactment of his role play entitled "The New Truck Dilemma" (six roles).

In single role plays and role-rotation role plays (as contrasted to multiple role plays) the trainer should generally allow the role play to come to a conclusion. However, if the same points are being made repetitively, the trainer should not hesitate to terminate the case and start a discussion of the role play. This can be done by saying something like, "I feel we've covered the main points, so let's end it here."

The most serious problem which confronts the trainer in conducting the single role-play enactment occurs when the role player with the skill burden is getting into serious trouble. The trainer then can aid the role player by using an "intervention interview."

The instructor stops the role play and asks the role player who is having trouble the following questions (allowing the player time to respond to each one): (1) How well do you think you are doing? (2) What do you think the problem is? (3) What change in your approach might help things go better? Typically, this pause allows the role player to pull himself or herself together and to continue the role play in a more effective manner. If this procedure does not work because the troubled role player is coming up with inadequate responses, the trainer can then shift the burden of devising a more effective approach to the class. This is done by telling the role player that at this point, if he or she has no objections, the class will be used as a group of consultants. The trainer then turns to the class and asks questions similar to those originally put to the role player, such as: (1) What problem is occurring here? (2) What other approach or approaches might be more effective? The player will usually then take the advice of the class and proceed on a different tack. The approach of using the class is especially valuable in helping a player who is in trouble because if the advice from the class works, the role player has gained insight into a different way of handling a problem. If the advice fails, the role player will be less vulnerable to criticism, feeling that he or she was only attempting to carry out the class's suggestions.

The procedure for preparing a class for a multiple role play varies slightly from that for preparing a class for a single role play:

1. The trainer divides the class into whatever group sizes are required by the role play. Persons left over should serve as observers.
2. The trainer reads aloud any set of general instructions that may accompany the role play.
3. The roles are passed out to each of the role players.
4. The trainer asks whether there are any questions about the role-play process itself (as opposed to the role content). Typical questions in this category will include, "How long will I have to role-play?" "When do we start?" "May I look at my briefing sheet during the role play?"
5. The trainer asks the role players who have questions about the content of their individual roles to raise their hands so that he or she can go over to them and answer their questions privately. This procedure allows role players to ask for a clarification of their role without revealing critical information to the other role players they are about to engage.
6. The role players should then fold their briefing sheets and print their role names on the back; then they place the sheets in front of themselves or attach them to their clothing so that the other members will know who they are. This also serves the purpose of preventing rereading of role sheets during the role playing.
7. The trainer starts the role play.

During the multiple role play the instructor should monitor the role-playing activity. About five minutes after the start of the role play (the wait is desirable so that role players can feel free to warm up to their roles), the trainer should unobtrusively circulate among the role-playing groups and listen in. This is done for two reasons: (1) Listening will give the trainer an idea about how the class is handling the role plays and will provide some data upon which to draw during the postenactment discussion, and (2) it will also give the trainer an indication of how long the enactment will take. When one or two groups have finished and the majority are about to finish, the trainer should give the entire class a two-minute warning prior to the end of the enactment.

As a general rule, the instructor never intervenes in a multiple role-play enactment. This is in contrast to the single role play, where he or she may intervene if the circumstances require it.

Spontaneous Role Plays Role-playing techniques used in spontaneous role-play enactments include role reversal, auxiliary ego, soliloquy, and numerous others. For a more complete discussion of the techniques used in both spontaneous and structured enactments, see the article by Wohlking and Weiner on this topic.[6]

Postenactment Discussion   Each role-playing situation requires some degree of closure. The issues and problems that develop during the enactment should be brought out in such a manner that both the role players and the other group members have a better understanding of the implications for them of the role or roles in which they have participated or which they have watched.

Single Role Play   In conducting the postenactment discussion of the single role play, reactions to the role play should be obtained first from the person who had the skill burden, then from the other participants, and finally from the audience.

In the single role play it is important to allow the person who had the most difficult role (the player in the "hot seat") to comment first on his or her own performance. This allows the player to acknowledge certain deficiencies that may have been exposed and to explain his or her thinking about the problem.

After debriefing the protagonist, obtain reactions from the other role player or players in the enactment. For example, ask: "What did you like about the boss's approach? Did he do anything to make you comfortable?"

It is then appropriate to ask the remainder of the class for reactions. It is desirable that the trainer have a set of discussion questions prepared for the postenactment discussion. These questions can focus either on the substantive issues, (e.g., "What factors went into the final decision?" "How good was the decision?") or on the process issues, (e.g., "How well did the supervisor communicate with the employee?") To facilitate discussion, the trainer may provide class members with observer sheets prior to the enactment. When making references to the enactment, trainees should be asked to use the names of the fictional roles rather than those of participants playing the roles.

Multiple Role Play   The multiple role-play postenactment process is characterized by the following sequence:

1. A data roundup, in which each role-playing group is asked to state the outcome of the role play (usually tallied on a blackboard as each group reports). Examples of the questions asked are: "What decision was made?" "Were the subordinates less satisfied or more satisfied than at the start of the role play?" "Was the decision made by the leader, by a group, or by both?"

2. A report from each group on the reasons and/or the rationale for the outcome.

3. A class discussion in which the varying outcomes and their supporting reasons are compared and contrasted.

A fourth step can be taken in one-to-one role plays which are designed to improve communications effectiveness or to sensitize trainees to the feelings of others. The trainer instructs the person who had the problem or was creating the problem to act as a consultant to the person who carried the skill burden in the role play. For example, if an individual playing the role of supervisor in a role play has had to handle a grievance from an employee, the employee is asked to be the consultant following the role play. As the consultant, the player is instructed by the trainer to deal with such questions as: How well was the complaint handled? To what extent did the player, as an employee, have an opportunity to explain his or her problem fully? To what extent did the player, as an employee, feel that the supervisor was concerned about the employees? Questions like these are designed to give persons playing the supervisor's role feedback about their personal style and about how other people experience them within the context of a superior-subordinate relationship.

Role-Rotation Role Play   In conducting postenactment discussions for role-rotation exercises, trainers should ask questions that focus on certain elements of all the role plays rather than on any individual role play. A trainer who is attempting to achieve certain process objectives should focus on broad categories of behavior. For example, if the objective of the role play is to improve communication skills, the discussion which follows the role play can focus on effective communication techniques versus ineffective communication techniques, rather than on the performance of specific role players.

If the role play is designed to teach a relatively standardized method of dealing with a problem such as handling grievances, typical discussion questions might include: To what extent did those who played the role of supervisor ask the grievant to state the contract clause which management allegedly violated? Did the supervisors always obtain all the key facts relevant to the grievance? If not, what should the supervisor have done to obtain all the facts? The basic idea in all the discussion questions related to role-rotation role plays is to keep the focus on those elements or techniques which contribute to performance effectiveness, rather than focusing on the excellence or inadequacy of the behavior of individual role players.

PROBLEM AREAS IN CONDUCTING ROLE PLAYING

Trainer-based Problems

Trainers encounter two major problems when conducting role-playing sessions: (1) failure to distinguish between content and process training objectives and (2) failure to establish a supportive climate when moving into postenactment discussions focusing on the attitudes and behaviors of role players.

Setting Clear-cut Targets   Trainers who are unclear in their own minds as to the nature of their key training objective allow comments on process as well as substantive issues. For example, a trainer might permit a discussion on the quality of a decision (and its implications for the role player) to become mixed with such considerations as the effectiveness of the communication styles of the role player on the cause of certain attitudes, which results in the participants' becoming confused as to what they are expected to learn from the session.

This problem can be avoided if the trainer clearly determines in advance the training objectives of the sessions:

1. If the training objective is to improve the quality of decision making, the discussion should focus on the implications of the decisions made and the standards by which the decisions can be evaluated.
2. If the training objective is related to improving process skills (for example, communication skills), the postenactment discussion questions should focus on process questions (for example, how effectively the supervisor communicated with the employee).
3. If the trainer wants to handle both process and substantive (content) issues, he or she should clearly conduct the postenactment discussion in such a way that each area is discussed separately. Either process or content issues may be discussed first, but it is important to summarize the first discussion before going on to the second. Following this procedure will make clear the training objectives of the session.

Creating a Supportive Climate   The failure to achieve a climate in which players are supportive of one another can result in unhappy consequences for a role player who does badly in front of a class. The normal instinct of most trainees is to concentrate on the inadequacies in behavior which are displayed by the role player. During this process two phenomena may occur: One of the role players may receive criticism in a way that is hurtful, which in turn makes the other class members less willing to participate in role plays or inhibits their behavior in other role plays that the trainer may want to conduct later in the session.

There are three things the trainer can do to develop a supportive climate and improve the trust levels when conducting a single role play or a role-rotation exercise: (1) develop earlier favorable and "safe" experiences with role playing, (2) set down ground rules prior to conducting a single role-play postenactment discussion, and (3) utilize a nondirective discussion technique.

Therefore, it is recommended that the trainer conduct one or more multiple role plays at some time prior to the single role play. This will allow class members to become more comfortable with the role-playing process, and it also will allow them to get to know one another.

In conducting the postenactment discussion for a single role play, the trainer should set down several ground rules for the class:

1. Participants should be told to make their comments in a self-oriented manner. Basically, this means that the only kind of comments that should be made by a trainee in reaction to a single role play should be related to the kinds of feelings that he or she experiences while watching the role play. For example, a trainee might comment, "I was very uncomfortable when the subordinate was asked a question about his attitude toward the company. I like to keep my personal feelings to myself, and I am generally reluctant to express them to such people as bosses."

2. Trainees should be told that their comments should be descriptive of what happened in the single role play rather than evaluative. For example, the trainer should encourage observations such as, "I noticed that the supervisor almost never looked at the subordinate during the entire course of the interview." This type of comment is to be preferred to something like, "I felt the supervisor tended to be evasive during the interview."

3. Second-guessing the protagonist should be discouraged. Trainees should be encouraged to concentrate on describing the behavior they observed or how they experienced the behavior they observed, rather than make statements such as, "The supervisor should have handled the role play in an entirely different style. She should have been more direct and asked more specific questions."

The trainer should attempt to be as nonevaluative as possible in conducting the postenactment discussion of the single role play. The trainer should exercise his or her skill in using a nondirective discussion approach with the group when dealing with trainee comments about a given role play. For example, an exchange might go something like this:

TRAINER (to trainee group): What special feelings did any of you experience while the role play was under way?

TRAINEE I was really irritated when the subordinate challenged the supervisor's authority.

TRAINER You say that you were somewhat angry when the subordinate questioned the supervisor's prerogatives. Could you expand on that?

TRAINEE More and more in my business I run into people who won't take orders. They don't seem to understand that I'm paid to give orders and that they're paid to take them.

Handling the discussion in this manner usually moves the trainee group into a deeper level of feeling and of greater openness. Moving the discussion to this "feeling" level allows trainees to see more closely the connection between certain statements and the emotions that they are likely to trigger in people.

Student-based Problems

The three most common student problems encountered by the trainer are (1) burlesquing of the role, (2) making up facts not in the role, and (3) stepping out of the role.

Burlesquing of the Role   It is important to understand that when players burlesque their role or make a caricature of the role they are assigned, their actions are not usually directed against the trainer. More typically, this behavior is a defense against playing the role or playing it badly. The role player thinks, "If I really ham it up, people will know that this is not the way I behave in real life." So, in effect, the role player "cops out." If this occurs, the trainer should step in and use the intervention interview technique described earlier in the section on the enactment.

Making up Facts Not in the Role   Most role players make up some facts which are not in the role. Generally this does not affect the role play. However, if the facts which are created develop situations that undermine the basic purpose of the role play, the trainer should intervene, saying, "Let's stop the interview for a moment and just review and clarify some of the key facts." Then the trainer should ask the role player in question to review some of the key points which have been distorted. After this clarification, the role play may be resumed. It is important *not* to intervene unless the distortion truly changes the training objective.

Stepping out of the Role   Despite the instruction not to step out of the role, which should be given just prior to the start of an enactment, it is common for role players to stop in the middle of the role play and say something like, "In real life I would do this differently." The trainer should be very firm with the role player at this point and say, "Do not step out of the role. Just act out the part as if it were you in this situation. Do whatever would be natural for you." It is important for the trainer to do this in a firm, unequivocal manner. This strategy almost invariably puts the role play back on course.

VIDEO TAPE PLAYBACK AND ROLE PLAY

In recent years much publicity has been given to the concept of using video tape in role playing. Typically, the idea is to play the video tape back and then to critique the performance of the role players. Despite the amount of attention this has received in the training publications, its actual practice is limited. Video tape playback in training is probably best used in areas not related to role playing. For example, it would be helpful to persons learning specific motor skills, such as machine operations, to have video tape playback on their performance. Some aspects of sales training may also be appropriately combined with video tape playback in which physical demonstrations of certain equipment are required. However, where the role play focuses on dealing with process issues, the role players become too exposed to negative criticism.

When role play is used in connection with video tape in process training, it is usually the intention of the trainer to demonstrate to the trainee certain behavior that the trainee has engaged in. The trainer's motive is to show clearly and unequivocally that the trainee behaved in a certain manner which was probably counterproductive to the trainee. This has enormous appeal to the trainer, but often the trainee reacts poorly to this type of feedback about his or her behavior.

If video tape is used in conjunction with role playing, the following guidelines should be considered:

1. During the taping process itself, use only a fixed camera or cameras (two or three cameras are preferable to one), as the roving camera is very distracting and usually will inhibit the role players by making them even more aware of the video taping process.
2. Play back the video tape of the role play only in a private consultative situation and allow the role players to initiate the critiquing with the consultant.
3. If there is to be any class discussion of the video tape playback, it is extremely

important that the trainer follow the guideline suggested earlier in the chapter under Creating a Supportive Climate. Speculation about why a role player behaved as he or she did in the exercise should be discouraged. Emphasis should be placed on having trainees describe their own feelings as certain events occurred, rather than analyzing and dissecting the behavior of the role players.

4. When video tape is used in conjunction with role plays dealing particularly with process training, genuine consent for taping and playback should be obtained from the group prior to the taping.

WRITING ROLE-PLAYING CASES

After trainers have used standardized cases, they may find it desirable to write role-playing cases specifically tailored to the training needs of their own organization. The following guidelines are suggested when writing a case:

1. The case should be relevant to the trainee's needs. This means that the problems should be related to the trainee's immediate job or to a job he or she is likely to have in the near future.
2. The case should be written in language readily understood by the trainee. This factor assumes greater importance as the trainer works further down in the organizational hierarchy.
3. The case should be concisely written. The trainee usually has only about five minutes to study his or her role briefing sheet. Thus the style should be simple, and unnecessary facts and data should be omitted.
4. In plays which are particularly complex or are designed primarily to develop analytic or problem-solving skills, the individual role briefing sheet may need to be supplemented by a page entitled "General Instructions" or "Background Information." This page can contain facts that would ordinarily be known to everyone—the nature of the organization, the job duties of the role players, technical details of the work process, etc. It is designed to be read aloud to all participants just prior to a role play. Using this device reduces the amount of information that individual roles contain. As a consequence, the individual role briefing sheets need contain only such information as (a) the identity of the role player, (b) his or her attitudes toward a certain issue or problem, and (c) any extenuating circumstance related to the individual role.
5. The case should allow ample *role maneuverability*. The case should be written so that the role players can respond creatively to problems. The role-play briefing sheet should state the problem, but not suggest how it should be handled.
6. In describing the behavior of other persons in the role play, words like "jealous," "selfish," and "greedy" should be avoided. The use of such terms tends to elicit stereotypical responses from the role players who have the burden of dealing with the problem situation.
7. If cases are to generate interest, some degree of conflict must be present. The term "conflict" is used here to encompass a broad range of differences between people in terms of both intensity and quality. Types of conflicts which can be used to generate interests include:
   a. Conflicts in loyalties; e.g., a supervisor feels a conflict between his allegiance to his work group and his loyalty to management.
   b. Divergent goals; e.g., a supervisor's personal career goals may be at variance with the task that management would like handled.
   c. Perceptual differences; e.g., the same problem is seen in two entirely different ways by two people.

    d.　Allocation of limited resources; e.g., two department heads fight over their share of an annual allocation of budget money.

    e.　Structured interaction; e.g., the quality-control department head and the manufacturing unit's department heads are in chronic conflict because of their "adversary" relationship.

Ideally, all role plays should contain the above elements. Trainers should start off by writing fairly simple cases and then work their way up to more complex ones.

A typical mistake that the writer of role plays makes is to create a problem which cannot be solved by the role players themselves. For example, the trainer might write a role play in which the only way an adequate resolution can be achieved is through an action by the president of the company or through a major revision of organizational policies.

Another typical problem involves the kind of information put into the role players' briefing sheets. A common error is to tell only one role player about a prior event. For example, in a case involving the disciplining of an employee, the supervisor's briefing sheet might contain information that the employee was warned about lateness two months ago, and yet the same information is omitted from the employee's briefing sheet. Although it is true that a given event may be perceived differently by different people, it is necessary that all role briefing sheets state that the event occurred.

A third common error that writers of role plays make is to include too many conflicts. As a consequence, the case becomes all but unresolvable in the time which can be allocated to the role players. In this situation the opportunity for a successful learning experience is almost eliminated before the role play ever starts.

For a more extensive treatment of how to write roles, see the article by Wohlking on this topic.[7]

REFERENCES

1. Utgaard, S. B., and R. V. Davis: "The Most Frequently Used Training Techniques," *Training and Development Journal*, pp. 40–43, February 1970.

   Foreman, W. J.: "Management Training in Large Corporations," *Training and Development Journal*, pp. 11–17, May 1967.
2. Shaw, M. E.: "Role Playing," in Robert L. Craig and Lester R. Bittel (eds.), *Training and Development Handbook*, McGraw-Hill Book Company, New York, 1967, pp. 206–224.
3. Maier, N. R. F., A. R. Solem, and A. A. Maier: *Supervisor and Executive Development: A Manual for Role Playing*, John Wiley & Sons, Inc., New York, 1957.
4. Parry, S.: *Using Role Playing in the Classroom*, Training House, Inc., New York, 1973.
5. Moreno, Z.: "A Survey of Psychodramatic Techniques," *Group Psychotherapy*, vol. 12, pp. 5–14, 1959.

   See also Weiner, H. B., and J. S. Sacks: "Warm-up and Sum-up Techniques," *Group Psychotherapy*, vol. 22, pp. 1–14, 1969.
6. Wohlking, W., and H. B. Weiner: "Structured and Spontaneous Role Playing: Contrast and Comparison," *Training and Development Journal*, pp. 8–14, January 1971.
7. Wohlking, W.: "Guide to Writing Role Playing Cases," *Training and Development Journal*, pp. 2–6, November 1966.

BIBLIOGRAPHY

Corsini, R., M. Shaw, and R. Blake: *Role Playing in Business and Industry*, The Free Press of Glencoe, Inc., New York, 1961.

Maier, N. R. F.: *Principles of Human Relations*, John Wiley & Sons, Inc., New York, 1952.

Maier, N. R. F.: *Psychology in Industrial Organizations*, 4th ed., Houghton Mifflin Company, Boston, 1973.

Maier, N. R. F., et al.: *Supervisory and Executive Development: A Role Playing Manual,* John Wiley & Sons, Inc., New York, 1957.

Moreno, J. L.: "Psychodrama," in S. Aneti (ed.), *American Handbook of Psychiatry,* Basic Books, Inc., Publishers, New York, vol. II, 1949, chap. 68.

Parry, S.: *Using Role Playing in the Classroom,* Training House, Inc., New York, 1973.

Zoll, A. A.: *Dynamic Management Education,* 2d ed., Addison-Wesley Publishing Company, Inc., Reading, Mass., 1969.

Chapter **37**

Human Relations Laboratory Training

VLADIMIR A. DUPRE

Vladimir A. Dupre *is a consultant in organizational behavior. He was formerly President of the NTL Institute for Applied Behavioral Science, Arlington, Virginia. He has been involved in laboratory education since the early 1950s, both as a laboratory trainer and organizational development consultant and as the organizer and director of the Midwest Group for Human Resources (MGHR). MGHR was an organization of trainers that became the Midwest division of NTL in 1967. Dr. Dupre received his Ph.D. in human development from the University of Chicago and taught for 20 years in a number of colleges and universities in the Midwest. His special professional interests, in addition to laboratory education, are in psychotherapy, the social psychology of power, and public policy.*

Organizations use human relations laboratory training to improve the quality of individual leadership and membership. A major problem in organizations (educational, industrial, governmental, or service) is the management of human resources to achieve organization goals and to provide individual work satisfaction. Human relations training is one method of addressing this problem. It does so by applying scientific knowledge in the behavioral sciences to leadership training.

In an organization setting, individuals work with and through people to get tasks accomplished and to carry out the processes which operate organizations: decision making, problem solving, conflict resolution, communication, motivating, etc. These are most frequently conducted in a variety of interpersonal and group situations. Thus from a human relations training viewpoint, educating individuals for leadership and membership involves developing (1) self-understanding, (2) the ability to listen and to communicate, (3) an awareness of interpersonal and group dynamics, and (4) the capacity to diagnose and solve interpersonal, group, and organization problems.

This type of behavioral learning is not usually accomplished by the addition of knowledge alone. It requires the integration of knowledge with experience and practice. Human relations training is designed to provide such a total learning experience. Its method is to build from scratch an organization for learning. The laboratory, in becoming an organization, generates the same kind of human problems encountered elsewhere in organizations:

1. Tensions between people and between units
2. Establishing and maintaining status

3. Power and status struggles
4. Rewarding and punishing behavior
5. Controlling and regulating
6. Managing resources to accomplish tasks
7. Developing teamwork and support systems

These issues become the laboratory for learning as participants become aware of them and work on them. When laboratories are arranged for members of an organization or have a management focus, the design is built to heighten organization-type problems, and the staff intervenes to analyze the experience more from the framework of organization leadership. The subject for analysis and learning is the "here-and-now" behavior of the people in the laboratory. In a well-run laboratory, help is provided in translating learning that is useful in the here and now into learning that is useful in outside organizations.

Laboratories are not designed to provide the participants with a set of specific technical skills or methods for becoming effective leaders and members, though skills may be learned. Rather, the emphasis is upon learning a process essential to the continued learning that is required for effective leadership in contemporary organizations. Learning from experiences involves becoming more diagnostically competent about the social environment, more aware of one's behavior and its impact and consequences, and more able to try out and evaluate new behavior. This learning cycle includes (1) the presentation of self, (2) diagnosis from feedback, (3) experimentation, and (4) evaluation. It is this continuous process that laboratories are designed to help people learn and manage more effectively.

The training laboratory has become a highly respected and widely used learning method since its inception at Bethel, Maine, in 1947. A broad, diverse movement was spawned by this powerful approach to learning about oneself and groups.

ORIGINS AND DEVELOPMENT

Laboratory training's central processes of exposing behavior, data collection, feedback, and generalization reflect its academic and research origins. It grew from Kurt Lewin's experimental work in group dynamics and the efforts of behavioral scientists to apply knowledge to the solution of social problems. In 1946, a Connecticut Interracial Conference was designed to focus on "ways of teaching individual and group skills required for harmonious and productive living in modern society."[1] In this instance, the objective was to improve leadership skills for people working in community problem areas. Through a combination of accident and planning, it was discovered that the examination of personal and interpersonal behavior in a group setting is a powerful method for getting people involved and motivated, for expanding individual consciousness, and for teaching people how to work together. This initial experience introduced the methods of stopping ongoing action to look at what is happening in a group (here-and-now data), of using feedback as a learning device, and of applying research to the world of practical affairs. This interest of the founding professionals in using action research as a method of dealing with social issues continues as a major force in laboratory education, though it has come to have many other objectives and uses.

Led by Leland P. Bradford, then director of the Division of Adult Education Services of the National Education Association; Ronald Lippitt, of the Research Center for Group Dynamics of the University of Michigan; and Kenneth D. Benne, then at Teachers College, Columbia University, the NTL Institute of Applied Behavioral Science (originally the National Training Laboratory for Group Development) was founded in 1947 and conducted its first summer session at Bethel, Maine.

Since 1947, human relations laboratory training programs have spread throughout the world, developing a diversity of objectives and method that reflects the significance of this powerful experiential learning approach. The basic learning method is increasingly used for organization and community development programs, moving well beyond its original focus on individual leadership training. Large numbers of training organizations have grown from NTL Institute activities as participants have acquired professional skills and set up their own organizations. As professional training has spread, the techniques of laboratory education have been incorporated into teaching, psychotherapy and counseling, administration, management, and other professional practice.

Early human relations training centered on leadership skills and group relations. However, as participants became aware of the intense emotional involvement associated with sharing a group experience, the support afforded in a close set of relationships, and the value that laboratory training placed on self-examination, there was an increase in this kind of training for personal development. Given the social values and norms of the 1950s and 1960s, people were seeking authenticity and openness in a setting which valued community, participation, freedom of choice, and emotional involvement. For many, groups were used in the quest for identity, meaning, and self-esteem, making training groups more therapeutic than originally intended.

Countering the personal-growth focus has been the increased use of laboratories for managers and other organization personnel. Research on the human side of enterprise has led to a social-systems-theory approach in which the individual is viewed within his or her interpersonal environment, the group is viewed within the formal organization, and the organization is viewed within the larger social context. Training has become geared to improving leaders and their organizations. Laboratories are now frequently one part of an organization development (OD) effort.

The laboratory method has also come to be applied to more specific problem areas such as team development, conflict management, negotiation processes, consciousness raising, and career development. Also, laboratories are designed for homogeneous populations as well as the original heterogeneous groupings. As a result of the dramatic increase in the demand for laboratory training, the training of professionals in its uses has become a major recent development.

WHAT IS LABORATORY EDUCATION?

Laboratory education creates a special environment for learning about oneself, interpersonal relations, and group and organizational dynamics. It is designed to improve the way an individual understands his or her social environment, develops alternative behaviors for relating to that environment, and chooses from among these alternatives. It is an engrossing, demanding, and valuable process that provides the individual with a method of "learning how to learn."

Conditions for Learning The laboratory develops a special set of conditions necessary to this type of learning. According to the NTL Institute's *Reading Book for Laboratories in Human Relations Training*[2] these include the following.

Presentation of Self. Until individuals have (and use) the opportunity to reveal the way they see and do things, they have little basis for improvement and change.

Feedback. Individuals do not learn from presentation of self alone. They learn by presenting themselves as openly and authentically as possible in a situation in which they can receive from others clear and accurate information about the effectiveness of their behavior—a feedback system which informs them of how their behavior is perceived and of what the consequences of their behavior are.

Atmosphere. An atmosphere of trust and nondefensiveness is necessary if people are to feel free to present themselves and to accept, utilize, and offer feedback. The establishment of this psychologically safe environment is one of the primary tasks of the staff and participants.

Experimentation.   Unless there is an opportunity to try out new behaviors, individuals are inhibited in utilizing the feedback they receive.

Practice.   If their experiments are successful, individuals then need to be able to practice new behaviors so that they become more comfortable with the changes they have decided to make.

Application.   Unless learning and change can be applied to back-home situations, they are not likely to be effective or lasting. Attention needs to be given to helping individuals plan for using their learnings after they have left the laboratory.

Relearning How to Learn.   Because much of our traditional academic experience has led us to believe that we learn by listening to experts, there is often a need to learn how to learn from this experiential mode: presentation—feedback—experimentation.

Cognitive Map.   Knowledge from research, theory, and experience is needed to enable the participant both to understand his or her experiences and to generalize from them. Generally this information is most useful when it follows or is very close in time to the experiences.

The laboratory, especially the T group, creates a situation in which these conditions come into being, allowing each member to participate in his or her own learning experience and to play a part in the learning experience of others in the group. The conditions are therefore especially created to serve the learning goals of individuals. They are not ends in themselves, nor are they intended for replication outside the laboratory in back-home situations.

Underlying Assumptions   According to Charles Seashore,[3] underlying laboratory training are the following assumptions.

1. *Learning Responsibility.*   All participants are responsible for their own learning. What people learn depends upon their own style, their degree of readiness, and the relationships they develop with other members of the group.

2. *Staff Role.*   The staff person's role is to facilitate the examination and understanding of the experiences in the group. He or she helps participants to focus on the way the group is working, the style of an individual's participation, or the issues that are facing the group.

3. *Experience and Conceptualization.*   Most learning is a combination of experience and conceptualization. A major T-group aim is to provide a setting in which individuals are encouraged to examine their experiences together in enough detail so that valid generalizations can be drawn.

4. *Authentic Relationships and Learning.*   People are most free to learn when they establish authentic relationships with other people and thereby increase their sense of self-esteem and decrease their defensiveness. In authentic relationships persons can be open, honest, and direct with one another and thus can communicate their feelings, rather than masking them.

5. *Skill Acquisition and Values.*   The development of new skills in working with others is maximized as people examine the basic values underlying their behavior, as they acquire appropriate concepts and theory, and as they are able to practice new behavior and obtain feedback on the degree to which their behavior produces the intended impact.

VALUES IN HUMAN RELATIONS TRAINING

Crucial to the success of human relations training is the demonstration of a set of values through the behavior of the training staff, the design of the components of training, and the interventions used by the staff in operating the experiences.

There must be congruence between what is being taught and how the teaching process occurs. Since the training is directed toward educating individuals to make free choices on the basis of data, to be open and authentic, to be aware of feelings and relationships, and to experiment, the staff members act openly and authentically, talk straight, are willing to accept and use feedback, search for data, and support the process of making choices. Out of this value position, they avoid being manipulative or controlling, setting themselves up as authority figures, or advocating a dogma.

One of the staff's major tasks is to create with the participants a special learning climate that in itself models the human relations values. By confirming individuals as unique, self-respecting people, a sense of trust is developed. This is furthered by staff commitment to educational inquiry, to supporting the individual's right to choice, and to experimenting with new behavior. Much of the criticism leveled at human relations training is the result of staff members' unprofessionally violating these values by using their authority to force participants into activities either overtly or covertly. Coercion of any kind has no place in human relations training. The quality of the relationship between the staff and the participants has a great influence on the success of the experience.

GOALS AND OUTCOMES

Because a human relations laboratory is an organization in itself, learning goals can be categorized in terms of learning about individuals, groups, and organizations.

Individuals

A 1965 NTL statement of goals indicates the emphasis on personal development as follows:

1. "Introspectiveness" or "awareness"—the ability to reflect on feelings and ideas within ourselves, including feelings and ideas about others
2. Openness—the ability to be open to feelings and ideas of our own, reflected in the ability to be more expressive and more receptive to a wide range of expressive behavior in others
3. Awareness of feelings—developing a high regard for the significance of feelings in living and working
4. Recognition of, and concern about, feeling-behavior discrepancies—developing an ability to diagnose the relation between how we feel and how we behave and to move toward greater congruence between these
5. Flexibility—expanding the repertoire of behavior; developing skill in behaving in new and different ways
6. Integrating into a more coherent whole the various parts that make up our personalities so that our identity is clear and more complete

Groups

The laboratory can center more on dimensions of group life such as power distribution, communication networks, interpersonal or intergroup conflict, stages in group development, and the influence of norms and structure on group life. Though individual learning occurs, the emphasis is on helping participants become more effective problem solvers, group discussion leaders, organizers of work groups, and builders of group cohesion. Here the T group, as a microcosm of the world, focuses on conflicting choices concerning such dimensions as authority and control, group membership and leadership, assertion and passivity, and other existential dilemmas posed by freedom of choice.

Organizations

A laboratory has a wide range of experiences well beyond the core T-group experience. These can include task groups, simulations of organizations, team-building and intergroup exercises, and other experiential events designed to facilitate an aspect of learning. These experiences view the total laboratory as a complex organization with concepts such as division of labor, styles of managing, competitiveness, and status. Recently, a particular laboratory design has developed around the uses and consequences of power. The opportunity to test management philosophy and style against concrete behavior makes a laboratory relevant to understanding organizations.

Table 37-1 outlines the differences between laboratories designed for individual, group, and intergroup goals, pointing out their respective individual and organizational relevance and indicating some of the experiences to be expected in each.

Illustrating laboratory learning goals are the comments made by a participant, Fred Ambellan, who was superintendent of schools in Sayville, Long Island, at the time he attended a program for school administrators in Bethel. He reviews his experience:

> The back-home executive sees an almost agonizing change in his associates. They're saying things he never expected them to say. They differ with him. They have ideas of their own. It takes time for him to realize they're saying no more than they ever said. It's he who has learned to listen. It takes a stout heart to accept and adjust to such new realities. He needs all his new-found skills to take and give, to deal with, to amplify the kind of feedback he should have encouraged long, long ago.
>
> He realizes how many of his assumptions about communication must be re-examined. He learns that: (1) what he means to say and what he actually says are not the same, (2) what others hear and what he thinks they hear varies, and (3) what others say and what he thinks they say are different. He is aware, suddenly, that "telling" is not "communicating."
>
> He is aware of the multi-level nature of communication. When the climate or topic is inappropriate or threatening, he sees that even his most forthright central-staff friends won't say what they mean or mean what they say. He notes how they "pull down the conversational curtain" when the discussion turns to areas they would like to avoid. They resort to a "silent language" of averted faces, glassy eyes, or flushed cheeks if they are disinterested or disturbed. Even such silent signs, he finds, are eloquent when noted.
>
> He finds in individuals, groups, and himself a vast difference between an intellectual and an emotional reaction. He realizes that there is "head" thinking and "gut" thinking. He no longer assumes it's simple for the individual and group to become clear about goals. He finds it takes time, training, and security-giving experiences before members of a group will "level" with each other.
>
> He is aware of the status concerns of himself and others. He notices and recognizes emerging patterns of participation and leadership. He is more conscious of the vital housekeeping chores which can maintain effective group efforts.
>
> He finds he has become a far more effective contributor, whether as a leader or member of a group, now that he has learned to engage in this much broader band of listening, contributing, collecting data, analyzing, and servicing. He is more "with" the group as a total person. He no longer needs to "leave" in order to think up his next "brainy" contribution.
>
> He notices there are both formal and informal structures in his back-home bailiwick. He is conscious of where people go when they want to get things done. He begins to see such official or unofficial subgroups as big organizations in microcosm, each with its own social system of independent and corporate activity.
>
> He sees that "feelings" are the fuel which keeps individual and subgroup efforts in motion. Whether such feelings result in flight, fight, dependency, independence, or interdependence has much to do with the success of the enterprise.
>
> Hierarchies and power structure assume different implications. Most men bring back

TABLE 37-1   Basic Laboratories in Human Interaction

Design focus	Individual and organizational relevance	Experiences
Personal and Interpersonal	More openness and honesty in dealing with self and others; reduced defensiveness and game-type behavior; increased ability to learn from one's own behavior; expanded awareness to growth potential; increased awareness of racially conditioned feelings and attitudes	T groups Nonverbal Painting Improvisation and fantasy Body movement Interpersonal confrontation Racial confrontation
	Improved communication with others; development of new ways of working with others; locating feelings that block satisfactory and effective relationships and bringing these out for examination; working for creative resolution to conflict	
Intergroup	Effects on your behavior when your group is working with another group; looking at your loyalties in multigroup operations; diagnosing intragroup problems brought on by intergroup work; examining the effect of different racial mixtures	T groups Competitive and collaborative exercises Observation of groups Conflict models Multiple loyalty simulations Construction of conceptual models
	Examining intergroup consultation, cooperation, and competition (corresponds to interdepartmental relationships in a firm); how changes can be made between groups; looking at payoffs for collaboration and competition; conceptualizing and confronting conflict, including that generated by racial differences	
Group	Increasing ability to act in different ways in a group and to live with different types of group climate, including that in which race is a problem; getting feedback on your group style and work methods; using your own feelings to help understand group process; feeling freer in groups	T groups Role analysis Cluster and large groups Team building Consultation Helping relationships Construction of conceptual models Group problem-solving exercises
	Understanding stages of group life and development; leadership and membership in groups (such as departments, task forces, teams, classes; learning why some problems get "solved" over and over and why some decisions do not stick; constructive methods for dealing with problem members; experimenting with different methods for handling racially generated problems	

an enhanced respect for total staff involvement and improved skills for developing it. They also return with some notion of how to develop leadership "in-depth." Without such concerns and skills, many phases of the educational enterprise can be stalemated by informal or formal hierarchies among employees. He sees that the organizational chart is not the organization. Until hierarchies are brought into orchestration, more effort is spent keeping another person or group from operating than is spent planning for children.

He has important new ideas about change. Although no institution of learning is exempt from change, too many leaders think that change is a drive toward a goal similar to a touchdown play. In the training laboratory, the educational executive learns that an organization's practices are "a dynamic balance of forces working in opposite directions within the social-psychological space of the institutions." Driving forces and restraining forces keep an organization's program (or production level) at what Kurt Lewin calls a "quasi-stationary equilibrium." Change is effected when individual driving and restraining forces are altered. Not all factors can be isolated or altered, but many can be.

He has new insight into leadership roles. He realizes that administrators too often allow issues to become "win-lose" in character. When this occurs in a staff or community situation, people tend to park intelligence at the door.

To sum up, the human relations training laboratory helps the school executive set up a climate which is not "win-lose" structured. It shows him that issues need not be polarized. It charts some pathways toward building role congruency instead of interpersonal conflict. Some persons (after Bethel) even give up the idea that they must always be alone in their struggle. Instead, they become "change agents" and "linking agents" in a more cooperative social setting.[4]

METHODOLOGY

The method used in laboratory education to encourage learning is Lewin's unfreezing-changing-refreezing cycle process. The application of this method is a complicated task, one that is done well only by specially trained professionals who understand learning theory and dynamics and individual anxieties and defenses; group dynamics, research, evaluation, and experimentation have been the basis for refinements in laboratory training leading to highly predictable success in behavioral learning experiences.

Human relations laboratories generally are residential, lasting from one to two weeks. The core training takes place in a T group ("T" for training), made up of from 10 to 12 people, which meets for a minimum of 60 percent of the laboratory time. In this unstructured group, the staff and participants face an ambiguous situation in which the normal givens (agenda, structure, norms, leadership) are absent. It is their task to build a system for learning. Out of the initial tensions, people move to fill the vacuum, to provide the necessary structures, norms, and procedures. As people act, their behavior becomes the subject matter of learning. Other laboratory activities are designed to clarify, extend, and support the T-group experience, all being submitted to the same process of inquiry and scrutiny for learning.

Stages of Change

Using Lewin's theory of stages of change,[5] the T group provides the conditions for (1) unfreezing, (2) changing, and (3) refreezing.

Unfreezing occurs best when:

1. Normal routines are removed so that we can take stock in a process of self-diagnosis
2. Usual social supports are shifted to create a disequilibrium
3. Discrepancies between intended and actual behavior become known through feedback in an open, supportive environment
4. Anxiety is induced by these discrepancies to an extent that motivates an

individual to consider change but not to the extent that it threatens or immobilizes

5. Conditions are psychologically safe through reduction of threat and barriers to change
6. Willingness to change is seen as rewarded in some way

If individuals begin to feel safe under circumstances where disequilibrium has produced sufficient motivation, they will search for new information, alternative actions or beliefs, or new ways to behave and relate. One method is to scan the social environment for relevant cues; another is to identify with a person whose beliefs or behavior seems to be more appropriate. The T group encourages both methods. As individuals' perspectives open up as they scan or identify, they develop new behavioral responses and feelings.

Finally, refreezing occurs when these new feelings and behaviors are tried and reinforcement occurs. Social support is needed before there can be an integration of newly acquired behavior into the personality of the individual. The unfreezing-changing-refreezing cycle is endless in a growing person.

A human relations laboratory made up of strangers facilitates the unfreezing and changing phases, but refreezing occurs best in familiar relationships. For this reason, training directors often recommend stranger laboratories away from familiar surroundings and people. By the same token, laboratories within organizations pose problems in unfreezing people—the process occurs more slowly. To facilitate refreezing, it is desirable to have a plan for follow-up, and it is helpful to send a team from an organization to a stranger lab.

This basic learning theory illustrates why the group setting is so important to human relations training. The group provides the forces required for learning:

1. Forces producing disequilibrium and hence motivation
2. Forces for support through feedback so that risk can be taken
3. Forces for identification
4. Forces for reward and reinforcement

The trainer's role in modulating and regulating these forces is critical since it is his or her design and behavior which set the process in motion and which model the values that are needed to create the appropriate learning conditions. As the members of the group learn and internalize these values and learning methods, the trainer becomes less central. During the course of a laboratory, dependency on the staff decreases as participants acquire the skills, values, and attitudes needed to operate the learning process themselves. To the extent that individuals learn how to learn (that is, learn how to carry the responsibilities of human relations training), they are better equipped to transfer the learning to their lives.

As a participant goes through a human relations training laboratory, he or she experiences a reeducation process and thus can become a change agent as a result of examining and using the derived learnings. Since managers and supervisors are involved in producing improvement and change among those with whom they work, learning how to initiate change through the unfreezing-changing-refreezing cycle is an important objective for training. To know how to motivate, to reduce defensiveness, to create a learning environment, and to build support for change—all part of T-group skills—can be very useful to the trainee as he or she returns to organization work.

FACTORS AFFECTING HUMAN RELATIONS TRAINING

No two training programs are alike, since there is always variation in the purpose, composition, and staff of a laboratory. Lippitt and This[6] have outlined these forces, indicating that the mix of these forces usually results in successful training experiences (see Fig. 37-1).

DESIGNING A TRAINING LABORATORY

The principles and orientations of laboratory method and the conditions for laboratory learning determine the curriculum and shape the training activities. Benne, Bradford, and Lippitt identify five major curriculum elements or "experience continuities essential to laboratory experience."[7] These are discussed below.

The Here-and-Now Focus   Immediate experiences of participants furnish the basic ingredients for laboratory learning. The struggles of groups to achieve satisfactory organization and forward movement, the strivings by members to find a place in the formation and functioning of their groups, and the efforts of members to integrate discrepant demands stemming from multiple memberships, within and without the laboratory—all these experiences yield vivid and personal content for learning. Such learning can be accomplished best if participants are assisted in collecting data about their efforts—personal and collective—and in analyzing these data collaboratively. A major focus in every laboratory program is on releasing significant here-and-now experiences for analysis, conceptualization, practice, and generalization.

The There-and-Then Focus   At appropriate times, attention needs also to be directed to situations away from the laboratory, more particularly to those situations in which participants have lived and will live again after the laboratory is ended. If learnings and behavioral gains begun in the training program are to weather transplanting from the laboratory island to the mainlands of life and work, participant attention needs to be focused on the relations between here and now and there and then. This ordinarily involves the diagnosis of forces at home which are resistant to, or supportive of, better ways of functioning. It includes assistance in developing realistic commitments to continue such diagnosis in collaboration with associates at home.

Focus on Social and Value Perspectives   In the associational life of the laboratory, participants are challenged to reassess the adequacy of their value orientations and social perspectives as well as their motivations, knowledges, and skills. This may deeply threaten their self-concepts. Participants ordinarily need support in focusing reconstructive attention upon discrepancies among the differing values they live by in various parts of their lives or between their interpersonal values and the values implicit in this orientation to larger social issues and problems.

Focus on the Use of Tools and Skills of Inquiry   Learning and growth can be materially advanced as individuals improve their skills in inquiry—in data collection, data analysis, diagnosis, experimentation, and evaluation. As these inquiry skills are developed, individuals become less dependent upon authority figures to teach them what they need to learn and better able to use peer resources in clarifying and solving problems in their lives. Skills of inquiry may also help them to be more competent in assessing forces which affect change in situations away from the laboratory and in enlisting others in joint assessment and modification of these forces.

Focus on Self as an Agent of Change   Unless individuals perceive their need for continued learning and growth and accept personal responsibility for initiating steps toward learning, unless they have reduced internal barriers and blocks to their learning, and unless they have learned to receive help from others and to give help to others in processes of changing, little continuing learning or change will take place within them or within the social systems of which they are a part outside the laboratory. The training laboratory assists participants to see themselves, actually and potentially, as agents of change.

MISUNDERSTANDINGS ABOUT HUMAN RELATIONS TRAINING

The popularity, power, and intensity of laboratory education, plus its "mystique," have led to several misunderstandings about its purposes and methods. Chris Argyris, one of laboratory education's most active theorists and practitioners, as well as one of its critics, has succinctly outlined the major areas of confusion:

1. Laboratory methods in general, and T-groups in particular, are not a set of hidden, manipulative processes by which individuals can be "brainwashed" into thinking, believing, and feeling the way someone might want them to without realizing what is happening to them.
2. A laboratory is not an educational process guided by a staff leader who is covertly in control and who by some magic hides this fact from participants.
3. The objective of laboratory education is not to suppress or induce conflict, and

PRETRAINING INFLUENCES

1. Purposes of program
2. Training design
3. Trainee expectations and goals
4. Planners' expectations and goals
5. Past experiences of those at the conference
6. Staff expectation and goals
7. Cultural setting

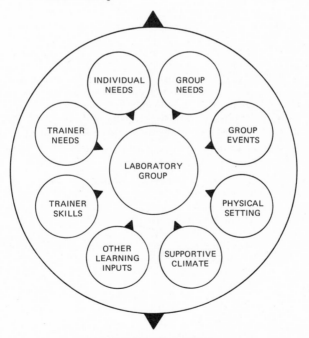

LEARNING APPLICATION

1. Direct transfer to back-home situation
2. Cognitive and skill application to other situations
3. Application of "how to learn" ability to new situations
4. Reinforcement and follow-up with back-home training
5. Personal goals and achievement experiences

Fig. 37-1 Forces in human relations training.

neither is it to get everyone to like one another, nor hate one another. Rather the focus is on understanding whatever does happen.

4. Laboratory education does not attempt to teach people to be callous, disrespectful of society, and to dislike those who live a less open life. Rather the issue is how to make use of all group resources.
5. Laboratory education is neither psychoanalysis nor intensive group therapy.
6. Laboratory education does not have to be dangerous, but it must focus on feelings.
7. The objective of laboratory education is to develop effective reality-centered leaders.
8. Change is not guaranteed as a result of attending a T-group.[8]

Since laboratory education is a controversial and misunderstood training tool, its use should be very carefully scrutinized and planned. Both the exaggerated claims of overzealous practitioners who are inadequately trained and the sensationalized descriptions of sensitivity groups by the press should be overlooked. When carefully used by qualified professionals in the context of a thoughtfully designed training program, laboratory education can make a significant contribution. But training personnel making decisions about its use need to know its purposes, the values on which it is based, the methods it employs, the organization or individual providing the professional service, and the "fit" with the organization for which the services are being provided.

Some of the organizational and/or individual conditions indicating the possible usefulness of laboratory education experiences are:

1. People are not talking or listening to one another.
2. Individuals need help in recognizing and using social and emotional learning.
3. Knowledge of interpersonal and group forces in organization life is either lacking or ignored.
4. People agree that problems exist and that they are frustrated and unhappy, but nothing is being done to improve the situation.
5. Work is not getting done because people are confused and are expending energy to deal with their frustrations and feelings.
6. Individuals are having difficulty living with change and ambiguity.
7. People need freeing up to release creativity and energy.
8. Leadership is not producing ideas for coping with organization problems.

Once organizational or individual needs have been identified, the training director needs to examine the following issues:

1. Is laboratory education the method of treatment for the problems identified?
2. How does it fit into an overall plan or strategy for organization improvement?
3. Is competent training leadership available, and can an explicit contract be developed specifying outcomes and an evaluation process?
4. Are the laboratory values sufficiently congruent with organization values to maximize chances for success?
5. Is organization support sufficient and at high-enough levels of power?
6. Will participants be sufficiently informed, and will they attend voluntarily?
7. Has preparation been made for reentry from the laboratory into the organization, and will there be the internal support needed to make the transfer of learning possible?
8. Do staff members understand the organization—its special needs, culture, and problems?
9. Are you aware that laboratory training is not a "quick-fix" or a shortcut first-aid measure—that the process is difficult and is merely an initiation to a learning process that must be sustained in order to have a lasting effect?

In selecting participants for human relations training, the training director should consider (1) the individuals' ego strength; (2) their ability to hear, without undue threat, what others say to them; (3) their ability to communicate thoughts and feelings with minimal distortion; and (4) their awareness of what will take place and their free decision to attend. No one should be sent in order "to get him straightened out."

In selecting staff members for human relations training, careful attention needs to be given to their professional experience and training. Trainers are in a powerful position that can be misused either intentionally or inadvertently. The growth of the profession has raised questions concerning their competence, personal motivation, and ethical responsibilities. Trainers' responsibilities are complex and demanding. Not only do they initiate action to develop a learning group, but they also help the group set appropriate limits, protect individual rights against group coercion, respond sensitively to individual stress, and act as models of openness and authenticity. Their own personal security and self-knowledge are crucial to their ability to serve the group's needs rather than their own.

PROFESSIONAL STANDARDS FOR TRAINERS

In the late 1960s the tremendous expansion of the human relations movement led to widespread concern with professional standards and training for laboratory educators. The NTL Institute's international network of trainers, the only reservoir of carefully selected professionals, represented an increasingly small proportion of the growing number of practitioners, many of whom were inadequately prepared to assume complex trainer responsibilities. To meet public needs and to protect the profession, the NTL established the International Association of Applied Social Scientists in 1971 as a professional accrediting organization.

The purposes of IAASS are to (1) establish standards of competence for the emerging profession of practitioners who work with small groups by using the methods of laboratory education and persons who work with larger social systems to facilitate system changes through the use of behavioral science, (2) develop a certification process for these practitioners, and (3) educate the public regarding appropriate use of the applied social sciences. Several hundred professionals are now accredited members of the IAASS Divisions of Laboratory Education, Organization Development, Community Development, Personal Growth Group Counseling, Third World Consultants, and Internal OD Consultants. Information about standards and certified members may be obtained from the IAASS office at 6170 East Shore Drive, Columbia, So. Car. 29206. Persons planning for human relations training should consult with IAASS to assess trainer competence. Committees on standards and admissions, ethics, and discipline are actively seeking ways to better serve the public and the profession.

FUTURE DIRECTIONS

The development of the laboratory method of human relations training has been characterized by ferment, experimentation, and expansion. While the vitality of the movement continues as it spreads throughout the world, recent developments suggest several new directions.

Increased Emphasis on the Transfer of Learning   The short-term laboratory has not produced sustained learning and growth as the individual returns to the familiar situation. Increasingly, efforts are being made to provide follow-up experiences to sustain initial learnings and to assist the individual in integrating laboratory learnings into the work setting. A related aspect is the embedding of the human relations training into an ongoing organization development program. As a result of such efforts, individual change becomes more closely related to organization goals and change.

Extended Use of Laboratory Methods Laboratory methods are being used by other professionals in the development of their practice. These include particularly the traditional helping professions such as psychotherapy, counseling, ministry, and education, but recent extensions are into public administration, law, urban planning, and community development.

Applications to Social Issues. The movement began with a commitment to social problem solving, and while this has continued, the major thrust through the 1950s and 1960s was toward personal-growth and organization applications. As issues of racism, sexism, family breakdown, and personal alienation confronted society in the late 1960s and 1970s, laboratory education methods began to be used in helping people cope with changing social and personal values. An awareness that in order to cope with the modern world, a person must be educated for insecurity—able to face new problems without precedent by innovating, improvising, and problem solving—has increased interest in laboratory approaches which are designed to give practice in just such skills.

Professionalization The development of IAASS and the public concern with professional quality have created a new profession with graduate academic programs and advanced professional training offered by such organizations as the NTL Institute, the New England Center for Personal and Organizational Development, Esalen Institute, the Association for Human Resources, Explorations Institute, and University Associates. The challenge for the future is in developing and using appropriate standards without stifling the needed experimentation.

Expansion of Research and Theory Vigorous research through the 1950s and into the 1960s has been replaced with strong emphasis on the development of practice skills and technology. New theory is now needed to move the field forward, and research of a different order needs to supplant earlier work.

The continuing success and development of the laboratory method depend upon the way these matters are handled by the profession. To continue without new energy, new theory, new applications, and new methods would ultimately result in the death of the movement by absorption into existing practice and institutions. It is a time for change.

REFERENCES

1. Lippitt, Ronald: *Training in Community Relations,* Harper & Brothers, New York, 1949.
2. *Reading Book for Laboratories in Human Relations Training,* NTL Institute, Washington, 1972.
3. Seashore, Charles: *NTL Institute News and Reports,* April 1968.
4. *Overview,* November 1962.
5. Lewin, Kurt: *Field Theory in Social Science,* Harper & Brothers, New York, 1951.
6. Lippitt, Gordon L., and Leslie E. This: "Leaders for Laboratory Training: Selected Guidelines for Group Trainers Utilizing the Laboratory Method," *Training and Development Journal,* March 1967.
7. Benne, K. D., L. P. Bradford, and G. L. Lippitt: "Designing the Laboratory," in. L. P. Bradford, J. R. Gibb, and K. D. Benne (eds.), *T-Group Theory and Laboratory Method: Innovation in Re-education,* John Wiley & Sons, Inc., New York, 1964.
8. Argyris, Chris: "In Defense of Laboratory Education," *Training Directors Journal,* vol. 17, pp. 25–30, October 1963.

BIBLIOGRAPHY

The most useful books and articles in the field of laboratory education are the following:

Appley, Dee G., and Alvin E. Winder: *T-Groups and Therapy Groups in a Changing Society,* Jossey-Bass Publishers, San Francisco, 1973.

Argyris, C.: "In Defense of Laboratory Education," *Training Directors Journal,* pp. 25–30, October 1963.

Argyris, C.: *Integrating the Individual and the Organization,* John Wiley & Sons, Inc., New York, 1964.

Argyris, C.: "T-Groups for Organization Effectiveness," *Harvard Business Review,* March–April 1964.

Back, Kurt W.: *Beyond Words: The Story of Sensitivity Training and the Encounter Movement,* Russell Sage Foundation, New York, 1972.

Benne, K.D., W.G. Bennis, and R. Chin: *The Planning of Change,* rev. ed., Holt, Rinehart and Winston, Inc., New York, 1969.

Bradford, L. P., J. R. Gibb, and K. D. Benne (eds.): *T-Group Theory and Laboratory Method: Innovation in Re-education,* John Wiley & Sons, Inc., New York, 1964.

Buchanan, P. D.: "Evaluating the Effectiveness of Laboratory Training in Industry," *Explorations in Human Relations Training and Research,* no. 1, National Training Laboratories, NEA, Washington, 1965.

Burke, R., and W. Bennis: "Changes in Perception of Self and Others during Human Relations Training," *Human Relations,* vol. 2, pp. 165–182, 1961.

Burke, W. W., and H. A. Hornstein: *Social Technology of Organization Development,* NTL Institute, Washington, 1972.

Dyer, William: *Modern Theory and Method in Group Training,* Van Nostrand Reinhold, Incorporated, New York, 1972.

Eddy, W. B., W. W. Burke, V. A. Dupre, and O. South: *Behavioral Science and the Manager's Role,* NTL Institute for Applied Behavioral Science Washington, 1969.

Fordyce, J., and R. Weill: *Managing with People,* Addison-Wesley Publishing Company, Inc., Reading, Mass., 1971.

Golembiewski, R. T., and Arthur Blumberg: *Sensitivity Training and the Laboratory Approach,* F. E. Peacock Publishers, Itasca, Ill., 1970.

Johnson, David W.: *Reaching Out: Interpersonal Effectiveness and Self Actualization,* Prentice-Hall, Inc., Englewood Cliffs, N.J., 1972.

Journal of Applied Behavioral Science, NTL Institute, associated with the NEA, Washington, published bimonthly.

Lippitt, G. L.: *Organizational Renewal,* McGraw-Hill Book Company, New York, 1960.

Lippitt, G. L., and Leslie E. This: "Leaders for Laboratory Training: Selected Guidelines for Group Trainers Utilizing the Laboratory Method," *Training and Development Journal,* March 1967.

Lippitt, R.: *Training in Community Relations,* Harper & Brothers, New York, 1949.

McGregor, D.: *The Human Side of Enterprise,* McGraw-Hill Book Company, New York, 1960.

Seashore, C.: "What Is Sensitivity Training?" *NTL Institute News and Reports,* vol. 2, April 1968.

Social Change (formerly *Human Relations Training News*), NTL Institute, associated with the NEA, Washington, published quarterly.

Underwood, William J.: "Evaluation of Laboratory Method Training," *Training Directors Journal,* pp. 34–40, May 1965.

Chapter **38**

Correspondence Study*

RUTH D. SALINGER

Ruth D. Salinger *is a personnel psychologist with the Bureau of Training,
U.S. Civil Service Commission. She is engaged in research and development projects to improve the management of training in the federal government. Her efforts have included determining the factors which prevent
effective training and development from taking place. This project won her
an award for best contribution to training research from the Washington
chapter of ASTD and Training Officer's Conference. Mrs. Salinger has
also assisted in the development of a training cost model designed to predict
the cost of training courses. She has written on the subject of the role of the
trainer as a professional manager. Mrs. Salinger received her bachelor's
degree from Cornell University and her master's degree from the George
Washington University, where her thesis was concerned with intrinsic
motivation. She has researched the area of sleep and dreams, from the
historical perspective to the modern-day physiological studies. This information will be published as a chapter in an introductory psychology textbook.*

Technology in the training field has greatly expanded in recent years. Traditional
instructional methods and media have been supplemented by a number of new
techniques, such as computer-assisted instruction. One training strategy which has
existed for a number of years, but which is flexible enough to incorporate many
new approaches, is correspondence study. The purpose of this chapter is to
acquaint the training specialist with correspondence study—to define it, describe
its advantages and limitations, discuss efforts made to evaluate its effectiveness,
and provide guidelines for the use of this technique as part of an organization's
training program.

CORRESPONDENCE STUDY DEFINED

Correspondence study is a systematic method of training in which an exchange of
materials and examinations, usually by mail, is the main means of interaction
between the student and the source of instruction. Other commonly used terms
are "correspondence education," "correspondence instruction," and "home
study." In this discussion, these terms will be used interchangeably. One type of
program which does *not* fall into this category is self-study; here the student
receives learning material from an institution, but does not submit any responses

*Portions of this chapter have been adapted, with permission, from "Correspondence
Study: A Review for Trainers," *Training in Business and Industry,* June 1973.

to be evaluated.[1] Some sort of exchange between student and "teacher" is, by definition, a part of correspondence study.

The basic components of traditional correspondence study have been itemized in the Encyclopaedia Britannica: "(1) specially prepared materials, written in self-explanatory fashion and arranged in a series of lessons; (2) supplementary printed and other materials; (3) a series of exercises to be worked out by the student; (4) the evaluation of these exercises by a competent instructor with the student being informed of the evaluation . . . and (5) a final examination over the whole course."[2]

This description, however, is a general one; there are a number of variations, which will be noted later in the chapter. What follows is a brief discussion of the present scope of correspondence study in this country.

How Big Is It?   In 1970, over 5 million Americans were studying by correspondence, according to the National Home Study Council. This figure includes new enrollments for that year as well as carryovers from previous years (some courses require more than one year to complete, and some students may take more than one year to complete a course). Table 38-1 shows the breakdown of enrollment by type of organization.

TABLE 38-1   Correspondence Study in 1970*

	Number of schools reporting	1970 student body	1970 enrollment
National Home Study Council (NHSC member schools†	156	1,630,128	649,913
Other private home-study schools	99	220,069	140,579
Total private schools	255	1,850,197	790,492
Federal and Military	23	2,185,701	1,851,493
Colleges and universities	53	312,592	234,212
Religious	13	323,720	307,717
Business and industry‡	11	68,891	43,671
Total of all schools	355	4,741,101	3,227,585

From past knowledge about schools not responding, the NHSC estimated the total student body for 1970 to be at least 5,018,630.

*From a 1970 survey conducted by the National Home Study Council (NHSC), an organization of private home-study schools. Its Accrediting Commission is recognized by the U.S. Office of Education as a national accrediting agency for private home-study schools.

†All schools reported.

‡Many firms prefer to contract for courses already offered by accredited home-study schools, rather than preparing and conducting their own. About 10,000 of these contracts are in effect with NHSC member schools.

A survey taken by the Correspondence Education Research Project (CERP) in 1965 estimated the number of people enrolled in home-study courses of all types to be 2,935,000. The military and civilian government accounted for about 65 percent of those taking correspondence courses (the military's training courses accounted for 60 percent alone), and private home-study schools accounted for over 22 percent.[1]

It is difficult to obtain precise data in these surveys, but the figures from these two sources do give the reader some idea of the extent of home-study use. As a comparison, there are about 7½ million students in undergraduate college and university programs in the United States today.[3]

Why do some organizations and individuals use home study as an instructional technique while others do not? The following review of the advantages and limitations of home study, especially as seen from the trainer's point of view, will help answer this question.

ADVANTAGES

There are two major advantages associated with the correspondence method: (1) flexibility and (2) economy and efficiency. The flexibility aspect includes the lack of place and time constraints, the lack of a restricted pace of work, and the possibility of combining the home-study method with other methods.

Thus the home-study student does not have to be in a specific place at a specific time, but can study when and where desired. This is particularly advantageous for people who are not close to a residence school, who move frequently, or whose schedule conflicts with that of a residence school. Correspondence study may be more convenient than residence study for the physically handicapped person, the convalescing patient, and the confined prisoner.

Another aspect of flexibility concerns the pace of the residence class. Correspondence students are not bored by a class that is too slow for them, nor do they have to worry about keeping up with a class that is too advanced. They can work at the pace which allows them to master a particular lesson or subject.[1]

The correspondence method is also flexible enough to be used in combination with other instructional approaches, such as classroom training, on-the-job training (OJT), or self-study, and with various media other than straight written material—television, for instance. One type of strategy commonly used in home-study programs is known as *group instruction* (also called *directed study* or, on the high school level, *supervised correspondence study*).[4] In this approach, students taking the same home-study course meet periodically. Their instruction can be informally organized and run by the members themselves; it can be informal, with periodic visits by an instructor; or it can be formally organized and directed by an instructor.

A second general advantage of correspondence study is that it can be an economical and efficient means of instruction. Correspondence study can be economical because of the relatively low costs of giving correspondence courses. This is especially the case if an organization uses home-study courses from outside sources, rather than developing and conducting its own. The use of home study eliminates the travel and parking expenses which may be a part of residence programs.

Home study is an efficient way to provide training in that it can be undertaken by any number of people at a time, whenever the training is needed. Organizations whose employees are in small offices scattered geographically, for instance, may find that home study is the most appropriate training approach available.

Other advantages of the correspondence method are the following:[1]

- Classes do not have to be scheduled.
- The need to provide a certain number and type of classroom facilities is eliminated.
- Employees do not have to wait until there is room for them in a course before they can take it.
- Employees do not have to wait until they are able to take time off from their work to attend a course.
- After a course has been established, a minimum number of enrollees is not required in order for the course to be run at a particular time.

Also, employees may be able to apply what they are learning while they are learning it, which may reinforce the learning and improve work at the same time.

LIMITATIONS

The user, or potential user, of home-study courses should be aware of the problems and limitations of this method: time delay, lack of interaction and feedback, difficulty in changing materials, limited subject matter, dependence on the written word, difficulty in testing, lack of motivation, noncompletion of courses, and resistance to accepting the method. These problems are not insoluble, however, and some possible ways of overcoming or minimizing the disadvantages associated with correspondence instruction are discussed, along with the limitations.

Time Delay

Correspondence students have to wait for their lessons and examinations to be received and graded and for their questions to be answered. Although one survey showed that a number of correspondence course suppliers provide feedback in seven days or less from the time they receive the student's lesson, not all schools are able to do this, especially when their students are geographically dispersed and when subjective questions are used. Delay may result in the student's losing enthusiasm and interest.[1]

The home-study instructor should therefore grade lessons and examinations and return them to the student as quickly as possible. Objective questions facilitate this grading, but they may reduce the personal contact between instructor and student and may not be appropriate for certain subject areas.

Other ways to minimize the time delay include using the programmed instruction (PI) format, using group study, and having individuals familiar with the course material available to help the student in person.

Lack of Interaction and Feedback

There are several problems associated with the lack of personal contact which is characteristic of the home-study method. There is a limited amount of feedback to the instructor concerning both the performance of the student and the effectiveness of the instruction. In addition, the student lacks interaction with other students and with the instructor, which may be a problem not only from an instructional standpoint but also from a motivational one.[1]

A partial list of methods to overcome this problem area includes:

- Alternating home study with residence training or on-the-job training
- Using group instruction
- Having the home-study instructor provide personal written comments in place of, or in addition to, standard answers
- Providing resource people to whom the student can turn for guidance and feedback
- Using media which can provide varying degrees of interaction and feedback

Some of these media which can now be combined with traditional home-study programs or which will be available in the future are broadcast media (radio and television), projection media (films, slides, etc.), audio media (records and tapes), graphics (diagrams, maps, etc.), three-dimensional media (actual items and models, cutaways, etc.), computer-assisted instruction (CAI), written material in the programmed instruction format, and the telephone.[1,4,5,6,7]

For example, the telephone can be used not only on a one-to-one basis, as is usually done now, but also in a conference format such that a group of people—students only or students and an instructor—can be on the phone at the same time.

A technique used by the 3M Company, while not home study in the strict sense, demonstrates this application of the telephone in a learning situation and also the use of some elements of group study. In this case, instruction in basic systems was requested of the 3M training department in St. Paul, Minnesota, by a 3M subsidiary in Chattanooga, Tennessee. The subsidiary could not afford to send its employees to St. Paul, nor could it afford to bring in an instructor from St. Paul to Chattanooga. The solution to the problem was to use a WATS telephone line to transmit the instructor's lectures to the students; illustrations in the form of overhead transparencies are shown in the room where the students assemble. The students have a chance to ask questions as the instructor proceeds.[8]

Private home-study schools are making increased use of WATS lines to answer administrative questions and also to motivate students to begin their lessons and continue them.

Difficulty in Changing Materials

Change in home-study materials is sometimes desirable, and yet the materials may be expensive to change once they have been developed and printed.

One format which is frequently used in home-study courses and which facilitates this change of materials is that of separately packaged lessons rather than comprehensive, bound texts. By sending the student only one or two lessons at a time, changes can be made continually.[9]

Limited Subject Matter

Some subject areas, at least at this time, cannot be taught effectively through the *exclusive* use of the correspondence-study method. This is particularly the case where physical performance is essential. The use of home study is also limited when the learning process requires, for instance, complex equipment or interaction with others.[1]

On the other hand, the combination of various methods and media can expand the potential role of correspondence instruction. Residential training, for instance, can be combined with home study in various ways. Ryder System, Inc., a truck renting and leasing corporation, operates a number of training schools. One course for truck drivers consists of a home-study portion in which students learn about truck systems, making pretrip inspections, troubleshooting, etc., followed by three weeks of practical training.[10]

A private home-study school which specializes in dental and medical assistant programs has an independent study program along with a 60-hour in-residence terminal training session.[11]

A 1970 U.S. Civil Service Commission survey of government agencies* revealed that a number of agencies which use home study do so by combining home study with either classroom study or on-the-job training. The military is a particularly big user of this approach, as it is of the group-study method of correspondence instruction.

Kits to be assembled or manipulated can be combined with written home-study materials to expand the range of subjects for which correspondence instruction can be applied. Types of kits used include television- and radio-set kits; compressor components for refrigeration servicemen; upright and grand action models for piano tuners; secondhand typewriters for repairmen; hat components for millinery designers and chairs for upholsterers; locks, key blanks, tools, and a key-making machine for locksmiths; and stained swatches for dry cleaners.[9]

While a wide variety of courses can be taught by home study, including those in the supervisory, technical, and clerical areas, organizations may have a need for very specialized instruction applicable to their unique functions. Thus the existing home-study courses which can be useful to an organization may be limited. If an existing course cannot be used and if the organization's staff is not able to develop its own course, contracting for a specific type of course may be the answer.

*The survey was conducted by the author, and the data are unpublished. Every branch of the military was contacted, as well as 42 civilian federal government bureaus.

Dependence on the Written Word

Correspondence study depends mainly on the medium of writing. This causes a number of problems, some of which have already been mentioned. The subject matter which can be taught is limited, and changes in materials may be costly. Also, students are limited to those who can learn well through reading and can effectively express what they have learned in writing.[1]

Like the problem of limited subject matter, that of dependence on the written word in home study can be partially solved through the addition of various methods and mediums.

Difficulty in Testing

Another major problem is in the area of testing. Exercises and examinations are usually in written form. Since grading subjective responses is time-consuming, objective questions are often used. If they are returned without remarks, the student is deprived of feedback from the instructor in the form of comments and suggestions.[1]

When written lessons and examinations are used, whether objective or subjective, feedback should be provided in some form—personal comments, references back to instructional materials for questions answered incorrectly, or standard answers for missed questions.

Lack of Motivation

One important problem of the correspondence method of instruction is that of motivation. Students usually have to fit their correspondence study around other activities—their job, residence courses, and homelife. The scheduling and the supervision connected with other kinds of training are not usually a part of home study. Thus self-discipline and persistence are particularly crucial for the successful completion of home-study courses.

There are several sources of motivation which can be built into home-study programs. One is an arrangement such that completion of courses leads to a degree or at least to some academic credit. A warning here, however, is that correspondence courses are not always transferrable to a residence degree program, and a degree that a person acquires using correspondence courses may not be an accredited one according to the standards of some professional associations.[1]

The National University Extension Association stresses that "whenever independent study is used or expected to be used in an academic program at any institution of higher learning, prior approval should be obtained from the resident college or university before enrolling in the independent study course." The amount of home-study credit which can be applied to a degree usually varies from the equivalent of less than one semester's on-campus work to three years of residential study.[12] Several colleges offer special degree programs for adults with a minimum of residence requirements.

Course Credit   Information gained through correspondence courses may enable a person to earn a high school equivalency certificate on the basis of general educational development (GED) tests. On the college level, the college-level examination program (CLEP), developed by the College Entrance Examination Board and the Educational Testing Service, measures an individual's competence in several major subject matter fields. At some colleges and universities, appropriate test scores allow students to skip courses in which they would otherwise have to enroll. The tests also provide a standardized measure for employers or schools of individual achievement, whatever the person's background education and experience. The College Proficiency Examination program in New York State operates in a similar fashion to CLEP.[1]

Taking a correspondence course may equip a person to pass an examination qualifying that person for certification or licensing in such fields as accounting or engineering. Motivation may also be provided by the fact that a course or courses are required by the organization.[1] Or, if the course is not officially required, completion of the course may still be helpful to an employee when being considered for promotion.

The U.S. Civil Service Commission accepts successfully completed home-study courses as credit toward meeting qualifications requirements for federal positions, on this basis: Correspondence courses may be substituted for required experience to the extent that such home-study education is accepted for credit as the equivalent of residence study by accredited residence colleges and universities, state universities, or state departments of education, or as specifically provided in the qualification standard. The Commission also notes that even when home study cannot be substituted for required experience, it is proper for an agency to weigh and credit successful completion of relevant home-study courses along with other evidence of abilities in ranking candidates for positions. The use of correspondence courses is also appropriate when an agency desires to provide employees with additional abilities beyond the minimum requirements in the Commission's qualification standards.[13]

Tuition Reimbursement   Another source of motivation is a tuition reimbursement plan whereby the employer does not pay for the agreed-upon portion of the costs unless the employee completes the course and earns a satisfactory grade.[14]

Follow-up   Home-study instructors may send letters to their students to remind them about lessons which are overdue, to congratulate them when progress is made, or to encourage them generally throughout the progress of the course.[1] The use of the telephone for these purposes was mentioned earlier. Supervisors and subject matter specialists may directly encourage, advise, or prod employees taking courses. Several military branches send out monthly progress reports which identify for the commanding officer of a unit the students who need motivation; people in the unit can then counsel and encourage those students.

Program Formats   Finally, as discussed earlier, the format of the lessons and the program—the particular combination of mediums and methodology used—can be such as to help reduce motivational problems.

Here are some examples of how organizations successfully use correspondence instruction, employing a variety of incentives.[3] Republic Steel Corporation, which has used mail studies for apprentices since 1947, deducts $10 a month for four years from the apprentice's pay in order to fund the course. The company provides a supervised classroom which an apprentice can use for study on company time. At the end of the apprenticeship, those who are still at Republic receive a bonus which more than covers the cost of lessons.

The International Typographical Union (ITU) has each apprentice working in a commercial job shop or on a newspaper finish 10 volumes of correspondence studies. The material is linked to daily shopwork so that apprentices have a chance to master all the fundamentals of their trade. The local labor-management committee keeps an eye on the progress of the students.

The International Printing Pressmen and Assistants' Union of North America has 5,500 apprentices combining study by correspondence and job experience. Lessons are free and are mailed at regular intervals during the four-year apprenticeship program.

Noncompletion of Courses

Another major problem with this method is the high rate of noncompletion of home-study courses.[1] Several studies have attempted to discover the reasons for noncompletion of courses.[15,16] These studies, all concerned with college-level programs, came up with similar findings: As judged by the students, factors contributing to noncompletion are mainly lack of time (because of a job or residence classes especially) and lack of interest (because of the absence of instructor contact, for instance).

In the 1970 CSC survey, a number of government agencies mentioned the problem of noncompletion in their correspondence courses, especially where the courses were not required. The reasons for the noncompletion were not always given, but several agencies did point out that motivation is an important factor and that initial enthusiasm often did not last. For agencies that stated they did not have a noncompletion problem, one reason given was that the people who take the courses are ambitious and are interested in them—otherwise they would not sign up in the first place.

In sum, while the factors which contribute to course completion are not clear, motivation is probably an important one. The motivational problem may be alleviated by tying course completion to external factors (such as those discussed above) and by identifying individuals who need additional counseling and guidance and providing them with it.

The time problem in the noncompletion of courses may be alleviated by giving employees a certain amount of time on the job to work on their home-study courses. If lack of ability is a factor in noncompletion, this problem may be dealt with by screening employees for their capacity in relation to the level of the course. In addition, the problem of noncompletion may be traced to the course design— its content, sequencing, method of presentation, etc.

Another strategy, aimed at the makeup of the course enrollees, is called *selective recruiting*.[17] With this approach, an attempt is made to identify the characteristics of people likely to complete specific courses ("high-yield" group) and those likely to drop out ("low-yield" group). Several techniques may be used to determine these characteristics. One is to follow up enrollees in a course and to correlate different factors (reason cited for enrolling, current job status, future plans, educational level, etc.) with the high-yield and low-yield groups. From this, a screening device may be developed such that only high-yield people are likely to be accepted.

Another approach, which can be taken in conjunction with that described above, is to develop materials directed at an identified population, particularly along the dimensions of background, ability, and specific need, rather than using the same materials for all who enroll or who desire a course.[4]

A final point which should be made concerning the noncompletion of correspondence courses is that courses do not necessarily have to be completed in order to be effective and worthwhile. A person may find that only a portion of a course needs to be completed in order for the objective of taking the course to be met.[1]

Resistance to Acceptance of the Method

Correspondence study suffers from a lack of acceptance by a number of people, who consider this method to be second-rate in comparison with residence courses.[1] If we look back at the foregoing discussion of the limitations of home study, we can see that many of these limitations can be traced to one particular problem— limited motivation and self-discipline. This factor in turn influences the high noncompletion rate often found with home-study courses. The experiences of home-study users with this dropout rate, plus the general reputation of home study as a second-rate method of instruction, have resulted in a resistance to acceptance of the method.

While the mistrust of correspondence instruction may not be fully justified, the problems with the method are real. This does not mean, however, that trainers should avoid the use of home study or, if they use it, that they should do so reluctantly. There are problems associated with all teaching approaches, and there are ways to overcome the specific limitations of correspondence study, as suggested above. A little imagination and inventiveness on the part of trainers may be what it takes to make effective use of correspondence instruction.

EVALUATION

Evaluation of correspondence courses should be performed to determine the benefits yielded versus the costs. In the 1970 Civil Service Commission survey on home study in the government, information was obtained on the evaluation process used by agencies for their home-study courses. Of the agencies that have more than just infrequent use of home study, about half have no systematic method of evaluating the effectiveness of their courses. A common type of feedback for these agencies is in the form of comments, either solicited or unsolicited, from the students or from the field office administering the courses. Other agencies have no evaluation as such, or if they do, the results do not come into the central office.

Some agencies, however, do plan a more formal means of evaluation. One agency, for instance, has an evaluation form to be sent out six months after a course is completed, although use of the form is optional. It inquires about benefits derived from the course and asks for recommendations; there is also a place for supervisors to comment on any changes in their employees as a result of training. The agency also talks to people to get additional feedback. Similarly, another agency mails out a questionnaire for an end-of-course evaluation; then six months later another questionnaire is sent to find out how the training has helped the employee. Also, supervisory opinions are compared with those of the employee. This procedure is carried out for a sampling of trainees; if the course proves to be worthwhile as indicated by the feedback, the sampling is discontinued.

Another organization analyzes student grades; if there is an increase in the number of failures, the agency tries to find out the cause. If a student does not turn in a lesson within three months, a letter and questionnaire are sent to the student. The main purpose of this is to encourage completion, but the tactic also helps the agency improve the program. This agency also sends out a questionnaire at the end of the course, filled out by the employee and the supervisor. Changes are made if the results indicate the need for them.

One agency had an analysis made of its accounting correspondence program, covering both the nature of the program today and alternatives to the program for the future. Specific areas included in the study were the need for program revision, pattern of course completions, cost, type of grading, use of media, comparison with college courses, and various implications of program changes.

Most military functions evaluate their programs; some do so informally through general questionnaires, while others use more systematic means. As examples of the latter, two of the techniques used by one branch of the military are the analysis of noncompletions to trace the origin of a problem and the comparison of material in programmed instruction and regular format. One particular military facility compared the use of supervised correspondence study and conventional classroom apprenticeship training. A follow-up study was done by comparing the correspondence program at that facility and a classroom program at another apprenticeship facility.

Effective as a Learning Medium

The empirical research which has been done in the past on the effectiveness of home study versus other techniques has been concerned mainly with home-study programs at the high school and college levels. A variety of subjects have been investigated at these levels, and comparisons have been made of the achievement of correspondence-instruction students and that of students studying by other means. In summary, "It is clear that students who receive instruction by correspondence study achieve at least as well as students who study by other means, including classroom instruction, programmed instruction, and television, or by the use of kinescopes or videotapes."[18]

Additional research studies have made comparisons between instructional methodologies other than home study—between the use of televised and face-to-face lectures, for instance. Childs concludes that:

> On the basis on the evidence available now the only reasonable conclusion that one can reach is that there is no measurably demonstrated superiority that can be attributed to one general method of instruction over another, including correspondence study, programmed instruction, classroom instruction, independent study, tutorial instruction, or instruction where television is a major component. People can, and do, learn adequately and according to all evidence about as well under each method.[15]

What is important for learning to take place is the sending of information which is received and processed by the learner. However, in what Childs facetiously calls his "first law of impact of method on the human organism . . . insofar as general educational methodology is concerned, the brain doesn't give a damn."[18]

The kinds of things which *do* make a difference, as far as which general method a person might choose, include accessibility, cost, and personal preference. Also, there should be correspondence between the specific objectives of the teaching and the means of reaching those objectives. Some subject matters may lend themselves to being taught better by one method than another. And few people would dispute the dependence of the effectiveness of instruction on the quality of both the instructor and the materials.

Finally, motivation is essential to the process. "With it, learning can hardly be prevented. Without it, learning will not occur, at least in any important degree. And because interest is such a fragile thing it must be nurtured to insure its growth and protected to prevent its demise."[18]

Having looked at evaluation by reviewing what agencies are currently doing and by considering what past research has shown, we can summarize by noting what organizations should undertake in this area. If an organization currently using home study has a high rate of noncompletion or failure, efforts should be made to discover the reasons for this situation and, if it is worth doing, to correct the problem. If an organization is going to begin using correspondence study, it should take into account the factors involved in course noncompletion, especially that of motivation.

As with other types of training, a systematic means of evaluating training by correspondence should be developed and used as an integral part of the correspondence program. Pretests and posttests, questionnaires, or other measuring devices can be given, as well as follow-up measurements after the employee has been at work for a certain length of time after completing the course. Both supervisors and employees can provide input to the evaluation process.

GUIDELINES FOR USE

The decision to use or not use correspondence instruction should be a part of the total planning for an organization's training. This requires a systems approach, where needs and problems are analyzed and possible solutions are compared to arrive at a combination of training programs predicted to be effective. Follow-up efforts will confirm or refute these predictions.

In making this analysis, the trainer can consider a number of key points in order to determine the role that correspondence instruction might play.

Work Location and Work Facilities   How isolated is the agency from residence training facilities, such as government training or university training? What are the travel costs of sending students to these facilities? What is the capability of the organization's own facilities for conducting residence training?

Job Characteristics   What are the characteristics of the job along such dimensions as the following:

- Skills and knowledges needed.
- Potential methods of teaching these skills and knowledges.
- Frequency of updating required.
- Uniqueness of job skills and knowledges to a particular organization. To what extent does the training need to be fitted to the organization's specific function?

Work Force Characteristics   What are the characteristics of the work force along such dimensions as the following?

- Present type and level of skills and knowledges held, as compared with what is needed now or in the future
- Ability for self-discipline
- Ability to handle additional workload

Work-Schedule Flexibility   How convenient is it for the employee to be absent from the job for a certain length of time, as demanded by a formal training program? How convenient is it for the employee to be absent from the job during the specific period in time that a formal training course is scheduled?

Instructional Factors   What is the need for, or the ability to make use of, these instructional strategies?

- Group study
- Other special methods and mediums
- Time off during working hours to spend on home study
- People available at work to give guidance and feedback to home-study participants
- Combination and integration of home study with other types of training

Additional Incentives   What is the need for, or the ability to make use of, these motivational strategies?

- Having the course required
- Giving students tuition reimbursement
- Being able to use home-study courses for academic credit
- Being able to use home-study courses for licensing or certification
- Contributing toward promotions

Alternative Sources   Examples of various sources of home-study courses are the organization itself, universities, and private home-study schools. The sources an organization uses depend on factors such as these:

- Availability of home-study courses to meet organizational needs
- Availability of staff to develop and administer the organization's own correspondence courses
- Comparative cost/benefits among alternatives

Information on Availability   Are there methods available to disseminate information on home-study courses to employees?

Support by Management   Does top management support the use of correspondence study? Do trainers support the use of this technique? Are the attitudes prevailing in the organization such that correspondence study is considered potentially as effective as any other instructional method?

INFORMATION SOURCES

For trainers considering the use of correspondence study as part of their training program, it is important to know what is available and who can provide guidance in the area. The following is a description of organizations which in some way are involved with, or have information on, home study.

Council of Better Business Bureaus, Inc.   This organization publishes a pamphlet concerning home study as part of its Consumer Information Series. It provides advice and information for those who are considering taking a home-study course. This pamphlet, entitled *Tips on Home Study Schools,* is available through Better Business Bureaus.

Federal Trade Commission (FTC)   The Federal Trade Commission published *Guides for Private Vocational and Home Study Schools* in May 1972 in order to provide advice to *schools* in this field as to the legal requirements which apply to them. More recently, the FTC's Bureau of Consumer Education has written a brochure for prospective *students* and *counselors* of students, providing advice on what to look for, and look out for, when choosing a vocational course (resident or correspondence). This latest brochure, Consumer Bulletin no. 13, can be obtained by sending 40 cents to Superintendent of Documents, Government Printing Office, Washington, D.C. 20402.

National Institute of Education (NIE)   Part of the Department of Health, Education, and Welfare, the NIE has as its mission the improvement of American education through research and development activities. In order to be included on the NIE's mailing list and receive information on its programs, including grant procedures, one may write to The National Institute of Education, Office of Public Information, Washington, D.C. 20202.

National University Extension Association (NUEA)   In 1973, the NUEA's Independent Study Division (formerly called Division of Correspondence Study) contained 62 colleges and universities with correspondence-study departments. Each member school is accredited by the educational accrediting agency of its particular region or state. Courses range from the elementary level to the graduate level. The NUEA *Guide to Independent Study through Correspondence Instruction,* which lists the available courses, can be purchased for $1 from National University Extension Association, Suite 360, 1 Dupont Circle, N.W., Washington, D.C. 20036.

National Home Study Council (NHSC)   This group's Accrediting Commission is recognized by the U.S. Office of Education as a national accrediting agency for private home-study schools. The NHSC also has received the recognition of the National Commission on Accrediting and is the first agency representing private proprietary schools to be so recognized. In 1973, there were over 180 member schools of the NHSC. A directory of accredited private home-study schools, a description of the accrediting procedure, and other information is available from National Home Study Council, 1601 Eighteenth Street, N.W., Washington, D.C. 20009.

United States Department of Agriculture (USDA) Graduate School   The Graduate School, a private, nonprofit institution, offers a program of independent study for people inside and outside the federal government, throughout the world. Included in the course offerings are English, mathematics, supervision, and technology. For information, write Head, Independent Study Program, Graduate School, USDA, Fourteenth and Independence Avenue, S.W., Washington, D.C. 20250.

PART OF THE SYSTEM

In this chapter, the advantages and the limitations of correspondence instruction, and suggestions for overcoming the limitations, have been discussed, along with some examples of current usage of the method in government and industry. Guidelines were presented to help trainers determine whether home study is appropriate for their organization. Also, references to individuals and organizations concerned with home-study were provided.

It is important to keep in mind that correspondence study, like other training techniques, should be used only if it can contribute to the effectiveness of an organization's training program—ultimately to the effectiveness of the organization. With the systems approach, the needs are established first, and then the means to meet those needs are determined. Specifically, if analysis indicates that training is appropriate to meet certain organizational requirements, alternative training approaches should be considered. The appropriate strategy, or combination of strategies, is then chosen, with appropriateness being determined by factors such as cost, trainee characteristics, and subject matter.

Thus home study, like other training approaches, should not be used in isolation and for its own sake, just as it should not be rejected outright. Rather, it should be considered a potential part of the total training system.

REFERENCES

1. MacKenzie, O., E. L. Christenson, and P. H. Rigby: *Correspondence Instruction in the United States,* McGraw-Hill Book Company, New York, 1968.
2. "Correspondence Instruction," *Encyclopaedia Britannica,* 14th ed., 1964, vol. VI.
3. Marshall, P.: "Training by Mail," *Manpower Magazine,* vol. 2, no. 3, pp. 8–12, 1970.
4. Wedemeyer, C. A., and G. B. Childs: *New Perspectives in University Correspondence Study,* The Center for the Study of Liberal Education for Adults, Chicago, 1961.
5. *Computer-assisted Instruction: A General Discussion and Case Study,* U.S. Civil Service Commission, Training and Systems and Technology Series, no. V, Government Printing Office, Washington, August 1971.
6. Eurich, A. C.: "Home Study in the 21st Century," *National Home Study Council News,* January 1970 (Supplement).
7. *Report of the Conference on Newer Media in Correspondence Study,* University of Texas, Division of Extension, Austin, 1962.
8. "WATS Is Their Line," *Training in Business and Industry,* vol. 10, no. 7, pp. 30–31, 1973.
9. Fowler, W. A.: "Varied Techniques: Better Home Study Courses," *National Home Study Council News,* July 1972 (Supplement).
10. *National Home Study Council News,* pp. 9–10, December 1972.
11. *National Home Study Council News,* pp. 13–14, July 1972.
12. *Guide to Independent Study through Correspondence Instruction: 1973–1975,* National University Extension Association, Washington.
13. *Qualification Standards for White Collar Positions under the General Schedule,* Handbook X-118, U.S. Civil Service Commission, Bureau of Policies and Standards, March 1970.
14. *Accredited Home Study Courses for Industry Training,* National Home Study Council, Washington.
15. Childs, G. B.: "Recent Research Developments in Correspondence Instruction," paper presented at the Eighth International Conference on Correspondence Education, Paris, 1969. (Mimeographed.)
16. Sloan, D.: *Survey Study of Correspondence Dropouts and Cancellations,* Correspondence Study Program, University of Kentucky, Lexington, December 1965.

17. Hosmer, C. L.: "Dropout Rates and Attracting Quality Enrollees," *The Home Study Review,* pp. 35–37, Winter 1965.
18. Childs, G. B.: "Correspondence Study: Concepts and Comments," paper presented at the National University Extension Association Annual Conference, Omaha, Nebr., 1973. (Mimeographed.)

BIBLIOGRAPHY

Childs, G. B., et al.: *An Annotated Bibliography of Correspondence Study: 1897–1960,* prepared by the Committee on Research, Division of Correspondence Study, National University Extension Association, University of Nebraska, Lincoln, 1960.
Mathieson, D. E.: *Correspondence Study: A Summary Review of the Research and Development Literature,* National Home Study Council, in cooperation with ERIC Clearinghouse on Adult Education, Washington, March 1971.

Chapter 39

Programmed Instruction

KAREN SEARLES BRETHOWER

Karen Searles Brethower *is Assistant Professor of Psychology at Cleveland State University. Prior to joining CSU in 1972, Dr. Brethower was a member of the Education and Training Department of the Ford Motor Co., working on performance management systems and behavioral technology. From 1962 to 1969 she was at the University of Michigan, Bureau of Industrial Relations, where she helped design and conduct workshops on the training systems approach, programmed learning for business, and the management of behavior change. At CSU, she teaches organizational and industrial psychology. She works as a consultant to organizations in the development of training programs and changes in management practices to improve performance. Performance feedback systems, applied behavioral analysis, and general systems theory applied to organization policy have been of particular interest to her. A member of ASTD, she was President of the Greater Cleveland ASTD chapter for 1975, was cochairperson of the Region 3 ASTD Conference in 1973, and served on the Educational Services Task Force and the Research Committee of national ASTD. She has been Secretary of the National Society for Programmed Instruction and a member of the NSPI Awards Committee, the Midwest OD Network, the American Educational Research Association, and the Training Research Forum. She has published in the areas of educational technology and behavioral technology applied to management, and she has also written a number of proprietary instructional programs.*

DEVELOPMENTS DURING THE PAST 10 YEARS

Programmed instruction is both easier and harder to discuss than it was 10 years ago. In the early and mid-sixties, great promises were being made about programmed instruction. Many different things were subsumed under the label "programmed instruction," and arguments flared about the optimum length of a frame (a unit of material seen by a student at one time) and about how many "m's" should be in "programmed."

Today, programmed instruction has passed beyond the "fad" stage and is reaching early maturity. Other fads have taken its place. It is still being used in many organizations. However, there is far less accompanying publicity than there used to be. There are fewer programmed instruction companies. Many developers and vendors went out of business. Those which survived broadened in one direction or another. If PI is less in vogue than it was, why include the topic in a reference book such as this—one which should help *advance* the field of training, not shore up the boundaries of the status quo or, worse yet, the past. PI is included here because the process and the principles involved in it continue to be very important to any training effort and to many other behavior-change efforts. It is not passé, but often it is traveling incognito.

A picture of the current status of PI makes a reasonable starting point:

- Tailor-made PI programs are in use in many companies.
- Off-the-shelf PI programs are available on many topics.
- Principles of PI are incorporated into many training activities in the following ways:
  - Empirical development of materials
  - Setting behavioral objectives
  - Attempts to provide the trainee with frequent feedback
  - *Performance*-based requirements rather than *time*-based requirements for jobs

PI is being used today for the right reasons far more often than it was 10 years ago. Today, the reason is likely to be effectiveness or efficiency; 10 years ago it was likely to be the hope that PI would be the panacea to solve all human performance problems.

The process of developing programmed instruction broadened in focus over time. Initially, the process often went quickly through these four steps:

1. Deciding what should be programmed
2. Deciding who should do it
3. Developing the program (objectives, instructional analysis, designs, and empirical testing)
4. Implementing the program

As it became clear that there was available an instructional technology which allowed one to deliver trainee performance that met prespecified objectives, developers were faced with a new problem. Up until PI, a major problem for the training field had been *how* to increase the chances that a given trainee would be able to do whatever the training was supposed to equip him or her to do. Then, by setting precise objectives for trainee performance, analyzing that performance, and empirically testing and revising materials, it became possible to deliver trainee performance much more predictably than before. Once an instructional technology existed which allowed for the delivery of trainee performance to prespecified objectives, the new problem concerned what those objectives should be. The focus changed from the training per se to the larger question of how training can most effectively contribute to on-the-job performance. The relationship of training and job performance is shown in Fig. 39-1.

This broader focus led to analysis of the job environment in which the trained skills were to be used. It was found that all too often, training (PI or any other) was conducted when the environment into which the trainee was going would ignore or punish the use of the newly trained behaviors. Such analysis of the job environment yielded many benefits:

1. Refinement of the *symptom* statement to a *problem* statement (which allowed some estimate of the value of solving the problem)
2. Avoidance of training which would not be supported by the environment (cost savings realized)
3. Consideration of alternatives for solving the problem, which went beyond PI to include other forms of training and nontraining behavior-change techniques such as job aids, standards clarification, and systems changes
4. A basis for discussing with line managers what employee performance would be valuable to them on the job, the role that formal training could play in

achieving that employee performance, and the environmental on-the-job conditions that would have to be present for those trained behaviors to continue on the job

The expansion of focus from PI → training →behavior change → performance maintenance on-the-job is one of the most important developments arising out of the PI movement. Those interested in pursuing this further should consult Chapter 14, "The Performance Audit," as well as WOMCE on front-end Analysis,[1] performance analysis,[2] and maintenance.[3]

Today, there is less interest in the difference in format of programs and more interest in the developmental process which underlies any programming effort.

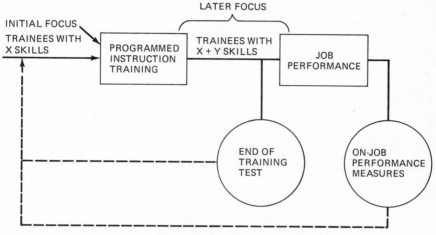

Fig. 39-1 Focus of PI development process.

Early emphasis on format and the *product* has shifted to emphasis on the *process*. Before, a program used to be defined as sequenced self-instruction presented in small steps and requiring active student involvement (the student filled in blanks). Now, a program is defined as the product of a process of empirical development and validation. The product might be in the form of a film, an audio tape cassette, a book, a set of role plays, or any combination of training methods. That which defines a program is the process by which it was developed rather than the form of the final product. The steps in the programming process are illustrated in Fig. 39-2.

HOW PROGRAMMED INSTRUCTION HAS INFLUENCED TRAINING

Programmed instruction has contributed significantly to changes in three important roles in training:

- The role of the trainer
- The role of the trainee
- The role of the developer

Trainer Becomes Resource Manager

The role of the trainer has changed from that of conference leader and/or source of all wisdom to that of manager and/or designer of resources. Most PI is self-instructional. Thus trainees are relatively self-sufficient and independent of the

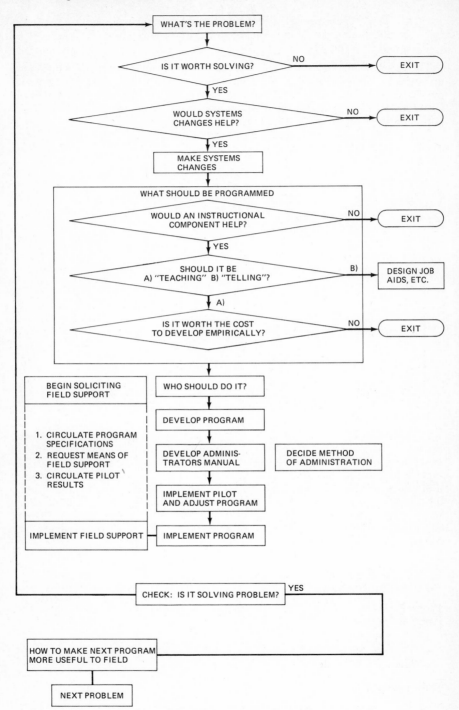

Fig. 39-2 The programming project.

trainer. They proceed at their own pace with the materials and usually are able to evaluate the accuracy of their performance via an answer key or comparison of their performance with an acceptable model. The trainer is asked not to lecture, except at points designated as guided discussions or some similar activity. The trainer does, however, have some very important responsibilities:

- Providing instructional materials
- Providing practice materials
- Using space such that students are not interfering with one another's performance
- Providing individual tutorial service where needed
- Sometimes administering or evaluating final criterion exams

In short, the trainer has become a resource and environmental manager rather than a delivery system for subject matter.

Trainee Becomes Active

The role of the trainee changed also. Previously, the trainee had frequently been a passive recipient of information. Programmed instruction changed this in several ways. First, the trainee had to be active in interacting with the material, or no progress was made. While it is possible to sleep through a lecture unnoticed, it is far more difficult to get away with sleeping through an hour during which you are supposed to be working on programmed materials. Second, since the trainee was responding frequently with PI (as opposed to infrequently with lecture), the distinction between what was *presented* and what was *learned* became very apparent. As a lecturer, I can maintain the illusion that my audience "learned" everything I presented if I do not require that they demonstrate that learning. With PI the requirement to demonstrate learning is almost continuous; so thus if there is a discrepancy between what is presented and what is learned, it shows up quickly and dramatically.

Developer Changes from Writer to Designer

Prior to PI, there had been relatively little empirical development of instructional material. For the most part, materials were written by a subject matter expert in whatever subject was being taught or by a trainer relying on expert sources. The material was edited for grammar, continuity, and accuracy and then was printed. In the development of programmed materials, the instruction is tried out on a trainee. If the trainee cannot perform as designed, the material is changed and tried again. The blame for end-of-training performance failure shifts from the trainee (he or she is unmotivated, stupid, or unsuited) to the material (it needs further development). In fact, one of the best methods for developing instruction with the *optimum* amount of teaching material relies heavily on tryout and revision. The method is called *lean programming*[4] and recommends that the first materials you give the trainee for tryout should be less than you estimate that he or she needs. This is done because (1) developers typically underestimate what their trainees already can perform and (2) if the materials are insufficient, the trainee can be used as a source of information on *what* needs to be added. The opposite is not true. If you present a trainee with excessive training material, it is very difficult to determine, after the fact, what could have been omitted without detracting from performance. While PI was an important partner in these changes, it was not the only area affected by them. They showed up in various ways:

1. Sales meetings which used to be presentations on product knowledge by headquarters personnel are now changed in format. The attendees are

polled in advance as to their highest priority concerns. These are compiled, and the attendees set the agenda for the meeting, run the meeting, and use headquarters personnel as one resource (among many) in meeting their needs.

2. Learner-controlled instruction (LCI) allows adult employees to temporarily become students on a schedule best suited to their needs and to actively take part in the diagnosis of their learning needs (see Chapter 42, "Learner-controlled Instruction").

Sherwin-Williams is using LCI as an integral part of career planning.[5] In the financial functions, job titles have been analyzed in terms of major performance requirements. These performance requirements have been converted to modules, each of which contains an objective and identification of resources for enabling one to meet that objective if he or she does not already meet it. This combination of (1) jobs described in terms of performance requirements and (2) learning modules (that guide a learner in meeting the performance requirements) is being used to better communicate what it takes to get transferred from one job to another. Further, it is used to facilitate self-development on the part of employees who have identified a position they would like to hold and for which they are not currently qualified. This is only one part of a total career planning system. It epitomizes the characterization of the adult learner as someone who must be actively involved in identifying his or her own goals and in meeting them. It also illustrates the role of trainer as manager of resources, rather than conference leader.

RESULTS FROM PROGRAMMED INSTRUCTION

Early claims overinflated what programmed instruction could deliver. Nonetheless, impressive results have been obtained. Some examples are cited for illustration.

Computer Input: Retail Stores A large retail chain had horrendous problems in opening new stores since switching over to cash registers tied directly into computers. The first day's tapes would invariably be rejected by the computer, and the work required to analyze the tapes and correct the errors consumed many hours of valuable time on the part of management personnel and computer personnel. The delay would sometimes run several days, and in the meantime there would be no information on first-day sales. After a programmed instruction course was developed, the next store opened with all tapes accepted by the computer at the end of the first day. This improved performance represented a savings in salary costs, better information, and less frustration.

Price Marking: Grocery Chain A grocery chain administered a programmed instruction course to employees responsible for marking prices on items. They did a "before-and-after" sample of 6,000 items in each of three stores. The average percentage of unacceptably marked items was 20.1 before training. After the programmed instruction was used to train employees, the average percentage of acceptable markings was 5.5, a reduction of 14.5 percent. Since the problem was calculated to be costing the chain more than $1 million a year, the savings were considerable.[6]

Sales Training: Ethical Pharmaceutical Company An ethical pharmaceutical company converted their training on an existing product from a standard lecture and study course to programmed instruction. The sales impact of the program was so much better than expected that the company sold out of the product—a very unusual event.

Temporary Employee Systems Training: Retail Store   A retail chain which always used a three-day group training course to train Christmas rush employees converted the training to programmed instruction. The instruction was self-paced and included a diagnostic pretest which allowed trainees to skip portions on which they could demonstrate proficiency. Since a large number of employees returned from year to year for the Christmas rush, many of them could demonstrate proficiency on some portion of the training. As a result, the chain was able to get 90 percent of the trainees on the floor and selling within the first day. The savings of two days of training time over several hundred employees not only saved money but also was motivationally desirable. It removed the requirement that adults sit through training on material they already knew. It allowed them to start the work for which they had been hired.

Packaging Machine Operation: Food Manufacturer   Packaging machine operators were trained using programmed instruction. As a result, the training period was reduced from six months to one month, yielding a labor savings across the company of $1,280,000 ($2.50 per hour × 40 hours per week × 16 weeks × 800 operators). During the training period some packaging material was rendered unusable due to operators using it improperly. This packaging material waste was estimated to be reduced from 73 to 5 percent, for a $2-million annual savings. The cost of developing the program was approximately $25,000.

It should be noted that the entire *process* of developing appropriate validated instruction was used in these cases, as opposed to changing format and delivery but not content. For instance, in the last example—that of packaging machine operators—a value analysis was carried out to determine which of several jobs in the manufacturing and packaging system had the greatest potential for improvement. Equally good programmed instruction on one of the other jobs would not have yielded as great a payoff. Also, programmed instruction does not necessarily mean paper-and-pencil presentations. The packaging machine operator program included many guides that the operator used initially for guided practice on the machine and later while actually running the machine. Limiting the program to a paper-and-pencil format without machine practice and job aids would have severely reduced the effectiveness of the program.

Many times the most powerful results of programmed instruction are realized from what is *not* in the final product. Limiting instruction to only performance which can be measured and will be used, rather than excessive information, makes the learner's task much easier. Excising extraneous content can go a long way toward buying the time to teach performance crucial to job success.

The determination of what performance *is* crucial and what the performance standards are yields benefits even without any instruction. It is one example of the power of the management adage, "Let people know what you expect of them, and you are more likely to get it." Many times management thinks the standards are clear until they themselves are presented with criterion (test) items that require application of those standards to situations. When faced with situations such as employees are required to handle, they find it much more difficult to specify the performance necessary so as to comply with the standard. An example of this occurred with a housekeeping program. Faced with a set of photographs and asked to sort them into acceptable and unacceptable housekeeping practices, managers (1) disagreed among themselves as to what was acceptable and (2) in many cases said, "It depends—on the time of day, percentage of production quota met, etc." This kind of discussion can generate standards which are much more refined and realistic than most that are on the books. In some cases, simply distributing the newly refined standards to employees and supervisors has been sufficient to obtain the desired performance improvement.

GUIDANCE IN THE USE OF PROGRAMMED INSTRUCTION

When to Use Programmed Instruction

One way to get the most out of PI is to use it only when appropriate. Programmed instruction as a process involves unusual developmental investment. The analysis, criterion items, and draft of instructional materials all must be carried out for any new project—they cannot be transferred from one situation to another. For instance, a safety program developed for postal inspectors will not work equally well when applied to safety problems of stamping machine operators.

The high developmental cost of programmed instruction is sometimes considered in isolation. In order to make a more informed decision about whether it is "worth it" to invest in the development of a program, one must consider two other factors:

1. Administrative costs
2. Probable benefits (which would be derived from the improved performance of employees upon completion of the program)

Programmed instruction should be evaluated (as should any other training effort) in terms of return on investment (ROI) rather than some partial measure, such as cost per hour or cost per trainee.

Administrative costs are often underestimated because they are hidden or absorbed into multiple budgets rather than being charged directly to the training program. Administrative costs would involve such items as:

Trainee travel costs
Trainee costs per diem
Trainee wages or salaries
Instructor salaries
Facilities costs
Costs of lost production time

For a complete discussion of training costs, refer to Chapter 4, "Budgeting and Controlling Training Costs." If the administrative costs can be reduced significantly through a shorter training period with no lowering of performance standards or distribution to trainees rather than centralized training, it is frequently sufficient to pay for the developmental costs several times over. The other potential means of offsetting the high developmental cost is the value of the improved job performance that will accrue as a result of the improved training. The situations in which programmed instruction is indicated are those in which there is a savings or benefit which offsets the developmental cost. Figure 39-3 shows some situations in which the programmed instruction process has been found to be worthwhile.

Each of the situations in Fig. 39-3 spreads the cost over large numbers or a long time period or justifies the high cost on the critical or potentially lucrative nature of the performance.

Motivation and Programmed Instruction

One of the early promises made for PI was that it had fantastic motivational effects on the trainees. Once they picked up a program, they just could not put it down. Apparently some trainees did not read the publicity because they could and did put the programs down. In part, the problem was one of assuming that there was some magic in PI that made it unnecessary to set up conditions to motivate trainees to complete the work. In part, trainees had to learn a new role in being responsible for their own learning. The important question for an organization using or considering the use of PI is: Has everything that could be done to induce trainees to work on the program in fact been done? Listed below are some questions one might ask about the PI application:

1. Do trainees know *why* they are taking the program?
2. Do supervisors know why their subordinates are taking the program?

Situations where PI may be indicated	What offsets developmental cost?
wide geographical spread of students	reduced travel expenses
large volume of students	developmental cost amortized over many students
stable subject matter	developmental cost amortized over moderate number of trainees for each of a number of years
crucial requirement for standardized performance (such as change over to computerized systems)	cost of <u>not</u> having predictable performance ability is very high
population doesn't need training in batches but in dribbles	avoids cost of untrained employees until enough for batch training or the cost of very low trainee: instructor ratio
high potential benefit from performance improvement	production improvement benefits greater than combined developmental and administrative costs

Fig. 39-3   When to use programmed instruction.

3. Will successful completion of the PI enhance trainees' performance on the job?
4. If so, is there any payoff (formal or informal) for enhanced performance?
5. Can a trainee in the middle of the program tell what progress has been made and what remains to be completed?
6. Does the program recognize the incoming knowledge of trainees by starting at an appropriate level or by allowing more experienced trainees to test out of sections in which they already are proficient?
7. Is time made available to work on the program? What else competes for that time (family, TV, doing required paperwork, demands made by fellow workers)?
8. How long is it between the time one starts the program and the time the material learned can be used outside the program?
9. Will anyone notice or care if a trainee simply quits? (If so, that communicates the low priority of the program.)
10. Do trainees know the rate at which they are expected to work on the program?

If the trainees know what is expected of them, if the environment and resources are conducive to working on the program, and if both the trainees and their supervisors benefit by completing the program, then there are likely to be relatively few "motivation" problems associated with the program.

Evaluation of Programmed Instruction

For many training courses the only evaluation that can be garnered is the happiness index—How did people like it? For programmed instruction there should be an additional question: How well did it work? There are several components to the answer:

1. End-of-training performance against objectives
2. On-the-job performance
3. Administrative ease

End-of-Training Measures   These indicate whether the program delivered what it promised to deliver. For a programmed instruction course you can look at the criterion exam and the performance levels on that exam. You are then in a position to ask yourself the question: What is the value of that performance to my organization?

Let me extend a word of caution: The *90:90 criterion* has become a sacred cow in the PI field and requires some explanation. It came into being with very good intentions. The 90:90 criterion requires that at least 90 percent of the students complete the final exam 90 percent or more correctly. It was set up to avoid the problem of relying on averages or means. To report performance as a mean—of, say, 90 percent—was felt to be inadequate. Why? Because one could achieve that 90 percent if each student scored 90 percent on the test or if there was a wide distribution of scores from very high to very low. This distinction was felt to be crucial for a product PI that was promising predictability. So what are the problems of the 90:90 criterion? In summary, problems exist only when the 90:90 criterion is assumed to replace common sense.

First, you may not need 90 percent performance by 90 percent of your trainees. You may need 98 percent performance by 70 percent of them if the program is coupled with a selection procedure, or you may need 80 percent performance by 100 percent of the students. The performance criteria might reasonably be expected to differ between a program on company history and one on OSHA (Occupational Safety and Health Act) violations that could close the company down. Thus the validity of 90 percent performance for 90 percent of the population must be examined in light of the specific program, its use, and its audience.

Second, in addition to questioning the performance and population percentages, there is the situation in which one is not willing to treat all items on the test as equal. It could be that for one section of the test you want the cutoff for "acceptable" performance to be 100 percent because this is required to perform adequately on the job, whereas on another portion of the test you would be willing to accept a much lower performance level. An example might be a program for surgical technicians in which it is crucial that they recognize instruments by name (100 percent performance required) because doctors call for them by name, but far less crucial that they be able to list locations of supplies because that is something with which they can get assistance and, furthermore, because past experience suggests that they learn it within the first few days on the job. Also, there is the hazard that in an effort to cut developmental costs and meet marketing deadlines, one could delete the item which had the highest error rate and/or add very easy items to inflate performance. So one must look at the actual items on the test and ask whether meeting the 90:90 criterion on this test would be valuable.

On-the-Job Performance Measures   Measures of production, (quantity or quality), absenteeism, tardiness, accidents, and other factors are the second point at which to evaluate a program. The effect that a programmed instruction effort has had on such measures is usually the real payoff to the organization. I strongly recommend that when considering an existing program, one ask previous users in what ways the program impacted job performance. However, in so doing, some limitations must be kept in mind. If they are not, one might be trapped into assuming that the on-the-job benefits realized by one company will accrue to another one—without considering all the conditions necessary for that to occur.

The instructional program is just one part of a system. Other parts of that system are:

1. The population taking the program
2. The method of introducing the program
3. The job environment (whether it is conducive to on-the-job application of skills learned in the program)
4. Supervisory follow-up after the program
5. Other communications related to subjects taught via PI
6. The degree of the training manager's active involvement in, and support of, the program

Therefore, all elements of the system (not just the instruction) must be considered when evaluating results achieved.

Comparison of job environments is probably more difficult than comparison of training environments in that job environments are more complex and less under the control of the person who would usually make the comparison, such as a personnel officer. Unless the entire system is assessed in terms of its contribution to changes in job performance, an important element may be overlooked, and the performance changes may not occur. An example of the importance of factors other than the program itself is provided in a study which illustrated that without supervisory follow-up, benefits realized from a program were temporary, whereas with supervisory follow-up, they were long-lasting.[6]

Administrative Ease   This becomes an important evaluation point since PI casts the instructor in the role of manager of resources. It is important to determine how difficult or easy this role is for the particular program. There have been cases in which a program has ceased being used because the resource managers were unable or unwilling to make necessary resources available. This occurred even in the face of evidence that when the resources were made available, the program produced results valuable to the organization. This is less likely to occur if the resources are limited to materials, and it is more likely to occur when the resources include access to people in the organization, equipment, supplies, work-in-progress samples, and other resources which require a large amount of energy to free, maintain, and make available for learning purposes.

Choosing a Source

Once you decide to use the process of programmed instruction, you are faced with a decision: What means do you want to use to obtain the program? There are four options: (1) You can buy an off-the-shelf program from a publisher if one exists that meets your needs, (2) you can hire a contractor to develop the program exclusively for you, (3) you can train your own personnel in the programming process and develop the program internally, or (4) you can combine the last two options and hire a consultant to develop the program while concurrently training some of your personnel in some phases of programming. Each of these has its advantages and disadvantages. Yaney provides a sound set of considerations for the choice of a source[7] (see Fig. 39-4).

In addition to these guidelines, I would suggest that since many of the principles involved in programming are being used today in other areas of training, the consideration of concurrent staff training or developing programming skills internally becomes particularly important. These skills then become part of the resources of the organization and can be generalized for use in other types of training.

Advantages	Problems

1. Contract Programming

Advantages	Problems
1. A package price and time set	1. Additional coordination costs
2. A completed programming effort	2. High cost for the initial hours
3. Prime responsibility in the firm	3. Less staff training

2. Off-the-Shelf Programming

Advantages	Problems
1. Readily available	1. Too general in many cases
2. Modification possible	2. Quality evaluations difficult
3. Wide price range	3. Less staff training

3. In-Plant Programming

Advantages	Problems
1. Customized programs	1. Difficult to predict costs
2. More internal control	2. Need to train own personnel
3. Subject matter experts available	3. Competing duties of programmers

4. Consultant Programming

Advantages	Problems
1. Negotiated fee and time	1. Additional coordination costs
2. Some staff training	2. Danger of overreliance on outsiders
3. Available as troubleshooter	

Fig. 39-4 A summary of the advantages and problems associated with the alternative methods.

Examples of Programs

Some examples are presented in Figs. 39-5 to 39-7. They are all taken from off-the-shelf programs. They have been chosen as examples of high-quality programs illustrating the variety of content and training techniques which can be used in programmed instruction.

The first sequence (Fig. 39-5) is taken from the middle of *A New Approach to Management's Role in Back Safety;* the objective of this sequence is for the learner to identify safe versus unsafe lifting practices. This portion is an example of *discrimination programming.* The program goes on to teach managers how to increase safe lifting and decrease unsafe lifting.

The second sequence (Fig. 39-6) is taken from *Labor Relations for the Supervisor,* and it is an example of *concept programming* in which various attributes of concept are successively taught through example and nonexample.[9] The sample shows two steps in the teaching of the concept of labor-law discrimination. There are more steps in the sequence which have not been included. The part titled "Question 4" is from the final exam and illustrates the requirement to apply a concept to situations which is one of the objectives of the program.

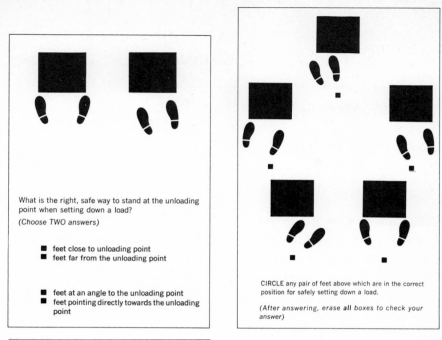

What is the right, safe way to stand at the unloading point when setting down a load?

(Choose TWO answers)

- ■ feet close to unloading point
- ■ feet far from the unloading point

- ■ feet at an angle to the unloading point
- ■ feet pointing directly towards the unloading point

CIRCLE any pair of feet above which are in the correct position for safely setting down a load.

*(After answering, erase **all** boxes to check your answer)*

The man on the left is setting down his load **safely, without twisting.** His "footprints" show how he has placed his feet.

The other man is in great danger of back injury because he has to **twist** as he sets down his load. NOTICE how his feet are placed.

TWISTING, as you set down, is:

- ■ dangerous
- ■ safe

A man can **avoid** twisting if his feet are:

- ■ at an angle to the unloading point
- ■ directly facing the unloading point
- ■ off to the side

Fig. 39-5 Sample problems from *A New Approach to Management's Role in Back Safety.*

2. TYPICAL UNION-MANAGEMENT PROBLEMS

I. DISCRIMINATION

Read the following two cases.

Case A

The union steward in the paint shop had been doing such a good job of presenting grievances that the union was winning most of the cases. His work record was excellent. He was demoted and placed on the night shift. (unacceptable)

Case B

In May, the supervisor told a union member and the general foreman that the member's work was not up to standard. The man's work remained consistently poor, and in December he was demoted and placed on the second shift. The normal procedure is to give a man a warning first, and, if he doesn't improve, to discharge him. (acceptable)

1. Read the following situations and decide which are unacceptable actions.

   _____ a) When the men in the shop received raises, the very anti-union men were always first in line.

   _____ b) Anyone familiar with Union X knows it is dishonest. All employees who recommend joining Union X have been reprimanded.

   _____ c) The union steward was very conscientious in doing his duty toward the union members. He felt that the company would understand that if his work slipped a little sometimes, it was because he was doing his best for the men. He was given a warning for bad work.

Fig. 39-6 Sample problems from *Labor Relations for the Supervisor.*

*****

(a) and (b) are unacceptable. Company action must be related to on-the-job circumstances and facts.

Read the following cases.

Case C

John had been very active in the union and, because he was skillful in negotiations, had helped the union considerably. His work record, which was normally good, fell off during the contract negotiations time and he was discharged. Normal procedure is to give a warning before a discharge can be made. (unacceptable)

Question 4

At the beginning of the union organizational campaign, the company announced a policy of protection of the union organizers' rights. One of the supervisors, who had intended to observe this policy, grew angry while talking with an organizer about the union when they met accidentally at a bowling alley. The supervisor struck the organizer. The company reprimanded him verbally for this and took no further action. The supervisor also recommended that John L., an outspoken opponent of the union, receive a raise. John had been working for a year and was in line for a raise; he got the raise.

What, if any, unacceptable actions are described above?

_____

_____

_____

_____

Which of the company's actions were acceptable?

_____

_____

_____

_____

Case D

Joe's work record was mediocre until the time he started becoming active in the union. He was extremely able and did a good job for the union, which upset the management. The normal procedure for bad work was a warning, but when Joe's work slipped below standard, he was discharged. (unacceptable)

2. Which, if any, of the following situations are unacceptable actions?

_____ a) A union member showed variations in the quality of work he performed for the company. The company didn't say much about it until he was elected union steward. The next time his work fell below par he was discharged.

_____ b) During a company layoff period, two men were laid off; one was very active in the union and the other not active. They had the same seniority. The man who was recalled to full-time work was the nonactive union employee. Usual practice is to recall each man on a half-time basis.

*****

(a) and (b) are unacceptable.

_____

The third and last example (Fig. 39-7) illustrates the design concept of moving from the simple to the complex. The progression from simple to complex in this case parallels a chess game.[10] The beginning of the program presents the board as it would look near the end of the game, when there are few pieces on the board and one (or few) moves to predict. Toward the end of the program the board is presented as it would appear at the beginning of the game, with many pieces and many possibilities to predict, evaluate, and choose between.

This order from the last task in a series backward through earlier tasks has proved to be useful in teaching many skills. One application of this concept has been made to the training of interviewers for a governmental agency. Initially the content to be included seemed so complex and overwhelming that a very long training period was predicted. However, upon examining interviewers' output (what action they could take upon completion of the interview), the training became simpler. Why? Because interviewers had a limited number of choices: They could send the client to the office dealing with (1) employment, (2) alcoholism, (3) psychological problems, or (4) welfare, or they could ask their supervisors for help in deciding where to send the client. Designing the program to teach the possible actions and decision rules for those actions first meant that the interviewing skills became much easier to teach. The training time was reduced drastically.

How to Increase Power of Off-the-Shelf Programs

Programmed instruction involves relatively high developmental costs since it is tried out and revised until it enables trainees to perform at the prespecified levels.

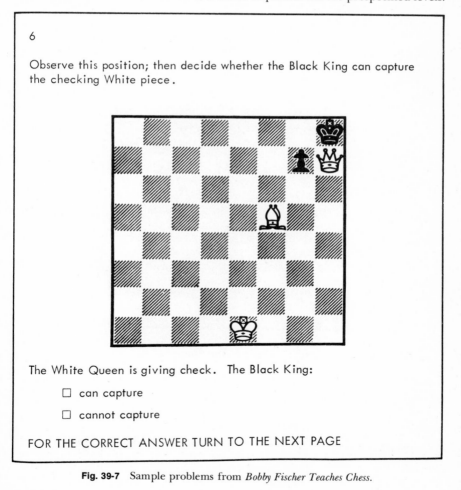

6

Observe this position; then decide whether the Black King can capture the checking White piece.

The White Queen is giving check. The Black King:

☐ can capture

☐ cannot capture

FOR THE CORRECT ANSWER TURN TO THE NEXT PAGE

Fig. 39-7 Sample problems from *Bobby Fischer Teaches Chess.*

6

cannot capture

(NOTE: The Queen is protected by the Bishop; therefore the King cannot capture. In fact, the King has no safe place to move to. So Black is checkmated.)

6

Observe this position; then decide whether the Black King can capture the checking White piece.

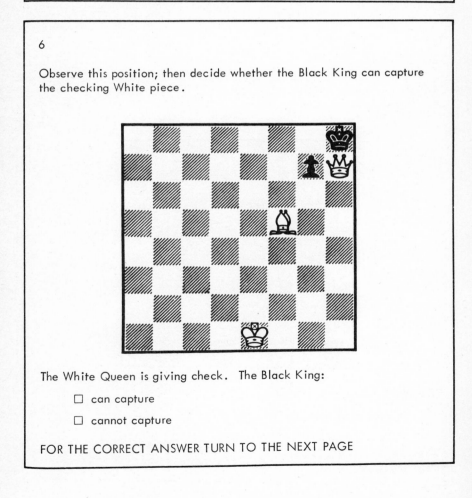

The White Queen is giving check. The Black King:

  ☐ can capture

  ☐ cannot capture

FOR THE CORRECT ANSWER TURN TO THE NEXT PAGE

232

Queen-takes-Rook-check

(After King-takes-Queen, Rook down mates. Note that here the Knight check fails because Black can reply with Rook-takes-Knight-check.)

232

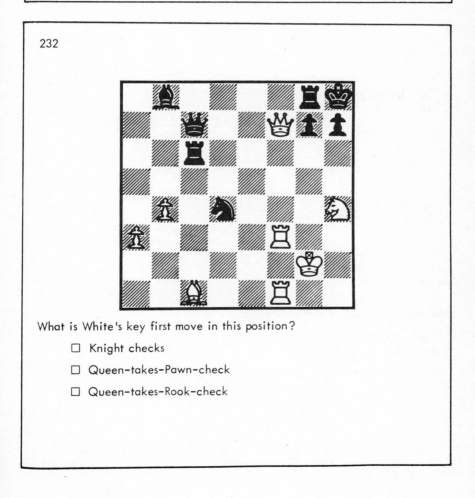

What is White's key first move in this position?

☐ Knight checks

☐ Queen-takes-Pawn-check

☐ Queen-takes-Rook-check

For programs developed under contract or by personnel internal to the organization, the developmental costs are borne by the organization which plans to use the program. For off-the-shelf programs, however, the developmental cost is carried by the publishers as an investment until such time as they can recoup the cost through sales. This makes the off-the-shelf program the least expensive alternative. In order to get their developmental costs back, the publishers would like the largest possible market for their programs. One way to increase the market is to produce a program on a general topic, such as safety or salesmanship, rather than a specific one, such as the implications of OSHA for oil refinery safety directors or how to get waitresses and waiters to increase wine sales. Therefore, the market abounds with programs on general topics which (1) *usually* teach vocabulary, (2) *sometimes* teach concepts, and (3) only *rarely* teach application of the concept. If the

---

1. Internal: Design some application tasks which require applying the general concepts to the specific situations your trainees will face on the job.

2. Contract: Find out if the developer of the general program would design a second program which would deal with the specifics of your situation for a price that is acceptable to you.

3. If portions of the program are not relevant to your situation or suggest actions contrary to your practices, design a learner's guide which tells trainees to skip those sections. Then cover these topics by some other means or develop a programmed unit on them.

Fig. 39-8   Ways to adapt off-the-shelf programs.

program on a general topic teaches part of what you wish to teach, you can tailor it to your needs in the ways indicated in Fig. 39-8. There are instances in which the off-the-shelf program is a worthwhile component of training even though it will not completely meet your needs. In any situation in which learners will be going from general to specific material, it makes the relevance of the general material clearer if they are given specific examples of how they will be expected to apply it later on and if they are allowed to practice in similar situations.

COMPUTERS, MEDIA, AND PROGRAMMED INSTRUCTION

Computer-related Instruction

Computer-assisted instruction (CAI) and computer-managed instruction (CMI) have been the basis for as many promises as programmed instruction was. They are supposed to reduce learning time, increase flexibility, and assure standardization of training. At the present time most computer-assisted instruction systems deliver very little flexibility and may or may not reduce learning time and assure standardization of what is *presented* to the trainee, but not necessarily standardization of the trainee's end-of-training performance. However, CAI and CMI *do* have many advantages: (1) They allow for interaction between the presentation device and the trainee, (2) they facilitate updating material which rapidly becomes obsolete (a problem with widely distributed paper-and-pencil programs), (3) they theoretically allow for individualization of amount and/or difficulty of material and learning strategy,[11] and (4) they allow for generating cumulative learning histories.

The three major components of CAI are hardware, software (computer programs) and courseware (instructional materials).

The aspect of CAI and CMI that is logically most closely related to programmed instruction is the courseware, or instructional materials. To date, most of the attraction of CAI has been in the hardware and software. The gleaming terminals and the ability to impress VIPs or trainees with the capability of the software have taken precedence over the less glamorous development of validated instructional materials. In some cases, it is only after the hardware and software are on site that courseware is given any consideration. Poorly designed, haphazard, after-the-fact courseware is not going to work much better in an expensive delivery and feedback system (CAI) than it is when presented by an instructor using practice exercises. The same care is needed to avoid training on an irrelevant objective, regardless of whether the end product is CAI or PI. There is great potential for application of what has been learned about developing validated instruction in the PI field to the courseware of computer-based instruction systems (see also Chapter 41, "Computer-assisted and Computer-managed Instruction").

Media Selection

In the early days of programmed instruction there was little problem with media selection. Everyone assumed that programs were of the paper-and-pencil type, and the only question was whether the paper would be presented in pages (bound or loose-leaf) or in some teaching machine (a presentation device). With the advent of the hardware branch of educational technology, many other options became available—computer terminals, cathode-ray tubes, rear-screen projectors, continuous-loop tapes, and cassette video playback units, to mention only a few. In the same way that PI was a fad in the mid-60's, these systems had their day as a fad, and some are still in that stage. Many such systems have a great deal to offer in the learning situation, but each must be evaluated on the merits of what it can do, rather than as a panacea that will replace paper and pencil and thereby necessarily and automatically improve learning.

The decision as to which medium (or combination of media) is most appropriate is often made prematurely. In order to make the decision wisely, the trainer must have already answered many questions. Some of these are listed below:

1. What will trainees have learned that they will use on the job?
2. Under what conditions will the new learning be used on the job (environment, time pressures, decisions as to when to use it)?
3. What are the relevant standards of the performance (rate, quality, quantity)?
4. What is the closest simulation possible of the on-the-job performance application?
5. What is the most inexpensive test of the on-the-job performance application?
6. What are the intermediate levels of simulation? What is the incremental benefit probable for each of these levels?
7. In terms of economics only, what would be the optimum simulation (best cost-benefit ratio)?
8. Are there reasons to go to some other level of simulation?
   a. Political: "The V P is hot on video tape."
   b. Practical: "We have to justify last year's purchase of x-T300 machines."
   c. Marketing: Packaging is important, and some other level of simulation will make a jazzier package.

A very practical and successful application of the above procedure has been carried out and written up by David G. Markle in the preparation of a "First Aid and Personal Safety Course."[12] The final product includes 20 film segments, 17 practice sessions, and 13 workbook lessons. A series of approximations to final 35mm color motion pictures were each tested against students' ability to perform to criterion in actual physical tasks and on a paper-and-pencil test. Approximations included (1) criterion test items, (2) resequenced criterions items, (3) script and slides plus criterion items, (4) black-and-white silent (motion picture) footage plus criterion items, (5) narrated black-and-white footage plus criterion items, and (6) narration and 35mm color footage plus criterion items.

Each version was tested and revised on the basis of error rate, completion time, and student comments. In the final product, some of the first-aid procedures are described with words only, while other procedures required a combination of motion picture and narration to demonstrate adequately. The transition from black-and-white to color film was based primarily on marketing considerations. The client predicted that the trainee audience would consider a black-and-white film unprofessional.

The decision as to which medium to use and the decision concerning whether to use the programming process to develop the instructional material are independent decisions. There is no reason why the PI process cannot be used to develop instructional packages in any medium or combination of media. One should be especially careful to guard against the illusion that using a new medium (video tape rather than paper and pencil) removes the need to carry out careful analyses, design, and testing of materials against trainee performance criteria.

CONCLUSION

Programmed instruction has delivered on its promise to produce prespecified trainee performance for many organizations. The best results have been achieved when PI was viewed as a process which includes an analysis stage *prior* to specifying objectives and developing the program itself and a maintenance stage which concerns itself with the support system to increase the likelihood that the trained behaviors will continue. Beyond the value of a programmed instruction unit, the principles underlying the process of programmed instruction are of great value in other areas of training. The References and the Bibliography provide sources of information for those interested in pursuing programmed instruction in more detail.

REFERENCES

1. Harless, J. H.: "An Analysis of Front End Analysis," *Improving Human Performance,* vol. 2, no. 4, winter 1973.
2. Mager, Robert F., and Peter Pipe: *Analyzing Performance Problems,* Lear Siegler, Inc./ Fearon Publishers, Inc., Belmont, Calif., 1970.
3. Brethower, Karen S.: "Maintenance: The Neglected Half of Behavior Change," in G. Rummler et al. (eds.), *Managing the Instructional Programming Effort,* University of Michigan, Bureau of Industrial Relations, Ann Arbor, 1967, pp. 60–72.
4. Rummler, Geary A.: "The Economics of Lean Programming," *Improving Human Performance,* vol. 2, no. 3, pp. 211–216, Fall 1973.
5. Maine, Arthur: "Educational Technology and the Changing Role of Training," presentation to the Greater Cleveland ASTD chapter, February 1974.
6. Brethower, op. cit.
7. Yaney, J. P.: "Choosing a Source," in G. Rummler et al. (eds.), op cit., pp. 190–203.
8. *A New Approach to Management's Role in Back Safety,* Advanced Learning Systems, Hicksville, N.Y., 1966, pp. 20, 21, 25.
9. Yaney, J. P., and Geary A. Rummler: *Labor Relations for the Supervisor,* Addison-Wesley Publishing Company, Inc., Reading, Mass., 1968, pp. 29–31, 84–85.

10. Fischer, Bobby, Stuart Margulies, and Donn Mosenfelder: *Bobby Fischer Teaches Chess*, Bantam Books, Inc., New York, 1972, pp. 24–25, 279–280.
11. Loftin, Mark M.: "Whatever Happened to CAI?" *Training in Business and Industry*, vol. 11, no. 6, pp. 26–29, 55, June 1974.
12. Markle, David G.: *Final Report: The Development of the Bell System First Aid and Personal Safety Course: An Exercise in the Application of Empirical Methods to Instructional Systems Design*, American Institutes for Research, Palo Alto, Calif., April 1967.

BIBLIOGRAPHY

The following resources are suggested for those interested in further information on programmed instruction.

Anderson, Richard C.: "Educational Psychology," *Annual Review of Psychology*, 1967.
Brethower, Dale, et al.: *Programmed Learning: A Practicum*, Ann Arbor Publishers, Ann Arbor, Mich., 1965.
Geis, George L.: "Premature Instruction," *Educational Technology*, vol. 10, no. 4, pp. 24–30, April 1970.
Harless, J. H.: "An Analysis of Front End Analysis," *Improving Human Performance*, vol. 2, no. 4, pp. 229–244, Winter 1973.
Harless, J. H.: *An Ounce of Analysis (Is Worth a Pound of Objectives)*, 2d ed., Harless Performance Guild, McLean, Va., 1974.
Mager, Robert F.: *Measuring Instructional Intent*, Lear Siegler, Inc./Fearon Publishers, Inc., Belmont, Calif., 1973.
Mager, Robert F., and Peter Pipe: *Analyzing Performance Problems*, Lear Siegler, Inc./Fearon Publishers, Inc., Belmont, Calif., 1970.
Markle, Susan M.: *Good Frames and Bad*, John Wiley & Sons, Inc., New York, 1969.
Markle, Susan M. (ed.): "Special Issue from the Past," *Improving Human Performance*, vol. 2, no. 3, National Society for Performance and Instruction, Fall 1973.
      (Reprints of selected NSPI journal articles.)
NSPI Newsletter and *Improving Human Performance*, The National Society for Performance and Instruction, Catholic University, Washington.
Shoemaker, Harry A.: "Standards for Training Development," *Improving Human Performance*, vol. 2, no. 1, pp. 68–75, Spring 1973.
Skinner, B. F.: *The Technology of Teaching*, Appleton-Century-Crofts, New York, 1968.
Warren, Malcolm: *Training for Results*, Addison-Wesley Publishing Company, Inc., Reading, Mass., 1969.

Chapter 40

Gaming Simulation and the Training Process

LARRY C. COPPARD

Larry C. Coppard *is a Research Associate and Special Assistant to the Dean at the University of Michigan's School of Education. In this position he is conducting research and developing programs in nonschool education. For the past two years, Mr. Coppard has directed a research program which is exploring the application of gaming simulation to training governmental and community leaders. Mr. Coppard is also President of Urbex Affiliates Inc., a training consultant and publisher of educational materials, including gaming simulations. Before coming to the University of Michigan in 1971, Mr. Coppard did consulting work with a wide variety of business, community, and educational institutions on the development of training and planning systems.*

Gaming simulation is a training methodology that is enjoying a great deal of popularity. Commercial airlines and NASA are using flight simulators for training new pilots and maintaining and improving the skills of experienced ones. Business students at many universities are developing managerial skills by working with simulated corporations. Planners are using policy games to explore alternative courses of action. Foremen and supervisors are becoming more sensitive to minority-group feelings through the use of specially designed games. Simulated cities are being used to train urban managers and to develop citizens' civic awareness.

BACKGROUND OF GAMING-SIMULATION USE

Gaming simulation is far from a new technique. It began thousands of years ago with such games as Chess and Go, which depict strategic military problems. Applications to training situations began in the early 1800s, when the Prussian army used games consisting of large, highly detailed maps, together with color-coded wood blocks to represent troops. Players determined troop movements, formations, and appropriate armaments. Following the use of the game, the players' decisions were discussed and critiqued. While the early military gaming faced some criticism, it became very popular and was adopted widely in military training throughout the world, particularly in the United States. Much of the current work done with gaming simulation is based on techniques which were developed for the military.

Business gaming was not common until the mid-1950s. One of the first business games to be widely used was the Top Management Decision Simulation, developed by the American Management Association. This game consisted of five teams of five players, each team representing the officers of a different firm manufacturing a similar product. Each of the firms competed for sales within a common market. After the appearance of this game, hundreds of others were developed that covered all aspects of business practice. In the late 1950s, due in large part to the work of Harold Guetzkow at Northwestern University, a number of games began to appear in the political science and international affairs fields. The Inter-Nation Simulation, developed at Northwestern, is a large model of international and national politics. Players assume the role of national leaders of a variety of nations, attempting to manage their own countries while at the same time developing workable relationships with other nations. Applications to the field of urban planning began to appear in the mid-1960s with games like Allan Feldt's Community Land Use Game.

Gaming-simulation applications can now be found in almost every field as a component in teaching, planning, and research processes. Trainers wishing to use gaming simulation in their work are wise to explore all fields in looking for a gaming simulation that may be suitable for a particular application. Often some of the most appropriate games are not found in one's own field, but instead were developed for another purpose and may be easily adapted to similar applications in a different field.

The popularity of gaming simulation today can be traced to a number of trends which have supported it. In recent years there has been increasing utilization of systems analysis and computer applications in dealing with complex problem situations. Gaming simulations often use systems analysis and computer assistance, and they have therefore benefited greatly from this trend. Educational methods have changed in recent years. The trend now, although not entirely adopted, is toward more open teaching styles in the classroom. Group process, peer-peer learning situations, and participative and action-oriented teaching methods are considered desirable. Also, gestalt-field learning theories have been widely adopted by educators. Gaming simulation provides a teaching method that is consistent with these trends. Starting with the work of Herbert Simon in the 1940s, there has been an increasing interest in understanding and molding decision-making processes. This trend toward the development of decision science has been supportive of gaming, as games tend to focus attention on the decision-making process and often provide a laboratory for consideration of decision-related issues. Finally, trainers have turned to gaming simulation in an attempt to improve the low quality and interest levels common in many training programs.

WHAT IS A GAMING SIMULATION?

Partly as a result of gaming simulation's current popularity, virtually any form of interactive training device is often called (although technically this is wrong) a *game*, a *simulation*, or a *gaming simulation*. Because of this rather imprecise use of these terms, a few definitions might be helpful. The reader should, however, note that these terms may be defined differently by professionals in other fields, although those listed are widely accepted by training practitioners.

Game   A game is a formalized activity consisting of two or more participants who attempt to meet their objectives within the limitations imposed by a set of rules, which determine the game activities and termination.

Simulation   A simulation is a representation of a real-life situation which attempts to duplicate selected components of the situation along with their interrelationships in such a way that it can be manipulated by the user.

Gaming Simulation A gaming simulation is the wedding of a game and a simulation; the game players act within and upon the simulation and receive feedback from it which affects the game activity.

The trainer has thousands of published gaming simulations from which to choose. While each exercise has its own characteristics, most gaming simulations have simular structural elements. Robert Armstrong and Margaret Hobson have suggested that gaming simulations are composed of three elements: a set of roles, a scenario, and an accounting system.

Roles The roles define the actors and decision makers in a gaming simulation. Roles may be developed which are similar to those of real-life decision makers, or they may be generalized into interest groups which represent a number of real-life decision makers who have common objectives. Roles are usually described in greater or lesser detail depending on whether the intent is to force the players to deal with highly defined situations or to have them develop and explore various interpretations of roles.

The Scenario The scenario is the basic description of the system or situation which is the subject of the gaming simulation. This description can be very simple or highly sophisticated. It may be conveyed to the players by means of a variety of methods including maps, charts, statistical reports, balance sheets, and histories. Some of these materials are included in a game manual and are usually supplemented by room displays and presentations by the game operators. The scenario sets the stage for the gaming simulation, describes the state of the system, and provides the basis for evaluating the players' actions during the game. Part of the definition of the scenario is the statement of the resources the roles have with which they can take action and a statement of the rules they must adhere to during the course of the exercise.

Accounting System The accounting system is a set of procedures which are developed for monitoring and recording the status of the system being explored in the gaming simulation. This system records the effects of role decisions and provides feedback appropriate to the individual roles and to the system as a whole. The accounting system may be simply a person or a group of people who react to game progress, or it may involve highly sophisticated computer models which contain built-in assumptions that predetermine the effect of decisions.

An Example

The wide variety of available gaming simulations makes it impossible to present an example which does justice to the whole field. A brief examination of one game which has had wide application in the training field should be helpful, however, in showing how the basic structural elements function in an actual game.

Policy Negotiations was developed by Frederick L. Goodman to teach the process by which a variety of systems function. The game requires 9 to 27 players and is usually begun by playing an introductory priming game so that the players can learn the structure of the game and, on the basis of this understanding, build a game around an issue of their choosing. Priming games on different issues are also used solely as an instructional component in training programs. This model has been used to explore school planning and credit union activities and as a device for retraining aerospace workers.

In one of the priming games available—The Industrial Park Game, developed by Margaret W. Monroe and Mike Raser—players are presented with a scenario which describes Berkeley, California, and the status of industrial development in that city. Players are told that the trend is for industries to move into industrial parks and that Berkeley must either provide such a park or suffer additional losses from its industrial base. The problem posed by the game is whether such a park should be established and, if so, how it should be designed. A map is provided to players to further elaborate the scenario.

Roles in the game include a redevelopment agency, business people, the white middle class, the black middle class, white activists, and black radicals. Each of these roles has a special stake in the outcome of the issue. Roles are given differing amounts of influence, symbolized by plastic pieces, which are used as the medium of exchange during the course of the game. The object of the game is for players to adequately represent their constituency group by arriving at a set of decisions that are in keeping with the group's interest. Players also try to raise the level of their prestige in the community. In addition to the main roles, there is a group of social forces which are represented by roles for the mass media, the chamber of commerce, and an environmental group.

The game begins with the consideration of a list of 29 issues, ranging from a requirement that any industrial park built can contain only "clean" industry to requirements for housing and shopping facilities. Players use their influence to bring desired issues to the top of an agenda for consideration in a public referendum. When an issue reaches the referendum, a vote is taken using the units of influence held by each role, and the issue is either passed or rejected. Influence is also invested so as to build coalitions among the roles and social forces and to raise the level of prestige of the roles.

The accounting system for Policy Negotiations is a set of plastic playing boards. Each role group has a small board on which the members indicate how they desire to expend their influence in any given cycle. In the center of the room is a large master board which is used to record the status of the agenda and the results of votes on issues. Space is also provided on the board for recording the levels of prestige and influence for each of the roles. An additional feature of the accounting system is a feedback matrix, prepared in advance by the game designers, which determines the effect that passage or failure of an issue has on the level of prestige and influence of each role and the effect it has on the likelihood of other issues passing or failing in the future. The master board is revised at the end of each of the play cycles to reflect changes. Play continues for 8 to 10 cycles, by which time the players have made a set of decisions which can be examined.

GAMING-SIMULATION TYPES

Gaming simulations are often classified as simple or complex, computer-operated or manually operated, media- or player-dependent, or rigidly programmed or flexible. All these distinctions may at times be important to the user of games, but their significance depends greatly on the instructional purpose to which the game is being put. The following list is intended to provide an overview of the most common game types currently available. Because of the nature of particular gaming models, an individual game may at times fall into more than one category.

General-Systems Games   These games are the most complex and comprehensive. They attempt to model the major components of a total system, such as an industry, a business, or a city. A series of theoretical models is often integral to these games and serves to define the various subsystems of the total simulation game. Because of the complexity of these games, a computer-assisted accounting system is usually required. General-systems games tend to be highly structured and are rarely flexible enough for player-initiated redesign. In fact, any redesign is often costly and time-consuming. The Management Game, by McFarlen, McKenny, and Seider, is an example of this game type. The game requires at least 20 players and from 3 to 10 days of playing time. A manufacturing firm is simulated, and players manage the company by establishing production levels, marketing strategies, and financial policy. Metro Apex, another game of this type, was developed at the University of Michigan. This game is a simulation of Lansing, Michigan, in which players manage the city by playing the roles of developers, industrialists, air pollution control officers, and city and county politicians and planners. Each cycle lasts four hours and represents one year in real time. With computer assistance, two additional hours are required for processing the decisions of each cycle.

Group-Interaction Games Games that focus on group interaction are often indistinguishable from role-playing exercises. Their purpose is less to simulate a system than to create a human relations problem that can be demonstrated in the process. The game is structured so that players can explore their feelings about, and responses to, the problem and their fellow players, as together they attempt to cope with the gamed situation. These games tend to be simple, are rarely computerized, and are usually quite flexible. Examples of this game type would include structured role plays and the many available group-process exercises such as those described in *A Handbook of Structured Experiences for Human Relations Training* by I. William Pfeiffer and John E. Jones. Starpower, a game by Gary Shirts, is also a good example. In Starpower, a society is built in which some people have a great deal of power, while others have little. Players experience the plight of the powerless and the corruption of the powerful, as those players with the most amount of power are given control of the game and are allowed to set the rules.

Resource-Allocation Games These games typically present players with a problem-laden situation or function to perform in which demands exceed available resources. Players must make the choices necessary to allocate these limited resources in the "best" manner. The scarce resource depends on the subject of the game, but many games center on allocation of personnel, use of space, production capacity, and land. One example of this game type is Planned Maintenance, developed by Didactic Systems Inc. In this game, maintenance managers in a manufacturing firm concern themselves with small equipment maintenance. Players determine criteria for inspections, scheduling, and use of time. In the Procter and Gamble Inventory Control Exercise, players maintain inventory levels, or at least try to, by setting levels of production. The Community Land Use Game, designed by Allan Feldt, is a manual game which simulates the development of a city. In this game, players have to allocate the scarce resource—land—in a way that encourages the healthy growth of a city.

Budget-Allocation Games These games are actually resource-allocation games in which the scarce resource is money. They are discussed separately because of the large number of games of this type, particularly in the field of business. While the game style can differ, these games typically present a problem situation to the players where their response can be, either totally or in part, the structuring of a budget for the agency which is the basis of the simulation. The U.C.L.A. Executive Decision Game is an example of this game type. In it players represent competing firms. By manipulating the budgets of their respective firms in areas such as marketing, design and styling, production, and capital investments, they attempt to improve their competitive advantage. Marketing a New Product, by Zif, Ayal, and Orbock, is a similar game in which players represent competing firms in a common market area and try to capture the market for their firm through setting their advertising and promotion budgets, together with various other considerations.

Influence- and Power-Allocation Games In this game type, decision-making situations are constructed in which role groups have differing amounts of power and influence. These games usually require that roles make certain decisions to address issues which are the subject of the game. Negotiating, compromising, and coalition building are common activities. Games of this type are often highly competitive. The Policy Negotiations game, described above, is an example of an influence-allocation game.

Non-simulation Games   These games do not simulate any particular system, but instead attempt to involve the participant in using concepts and principles from formal disciplines in a game exercise. The Wff 'n Proof game, by Layman Allan, is an example of this type. It is a game of logic in which players use abstract thinking and math logic to build logical systems. The assumption is that formal disciplines can be learned in this way and then used in other settings.

Gamut-Running Games   Many games are built on a format similar to Monopoly. Players move around a board, traveling a path on which they encounter a series of obstacles until some goal is reached by at least one player. Moves in these games are determined almost totally by chance. While the subject of these games can be serious, their use is probably most appropriate for entertainment, although with proper design this format can be a useful training device. The most widely known games of this type are Blacks and Whites, Smog, Dirty Water, and Women's Liberation, available at many bookstores.

Communication Games   While there are only a few examples available, some games contain structures which are specifically designed to facilitate communication between players and designers and among players. Examples of this game type are model-building exercises. The Truax Housing Simulation was developed by the Dade County Social Planning Agency. In this model-building game, residents of a low-income housing project were given materials and staff assistance to build a model of their apartment as they would redesign it. These player-developed models were used in subsequent plans for remodeling of the project. Another communication game uses visual display and data analysis techniques to facilitate communication. In Policyplan, a planning model developed by the author, players load the model with data relevant to their issues. Once loaded, the model is used to develop planning options. By means of visual displays, impact matrices, and computer-assisted data analysis, players can examine the perceptions of members of their organization regarding the impact and feasibility of policy decisions.

"Pure" Simulation   Simulations are often built which have no game component. In these applications the simulation, which is usually computerized, is used to explore the modeled system. Flight training simulators are examples of this use of simulation. Also, corporate planning officials often use computerized economic models as a means to explore the consequences of alternative planning strategies. When these simulations are used in an interactive mode, the user changes variables in the model to explore the effect of these decisions. "Pure" simulations are often used where the system being molded is well understood and the purpose in using it is to acquaint the learner with the system's characteristics.

WHEN TO USE A GAMING SIMULATION

Gaming simulations have been utilized in a variety of settings. Most applications, however, have been for educational and training purposes. While it is these applications that are of interest here, it is well to be aware of the other uses to which the technique has been put. Increasingly, gaming simulations are being built as an aid to planning processes. By building a gaming simulation of a system or subsystem for which planning is being done, a number of benefits can be derived. The building of the gaming-simulation model and the subsequent play of it often result in the identification of relationships that might have been unseen before.

Information needs can be identified, problem areas located, and assumptions examined. Policyplan, mentioned above, is a planning model that has been used with public and private organizations and community groups to structure a planning program. The gaming simulation simply provides the structure; users provide the information. The military has for years used gaming simulations, both in training and as part of their planning processes. Another application of gaming simulation which deserves review is in research. Gaming simulations have been used as structures for data gathering and as environments for testing theory. Space does not permit listing examples of research applications, but the interested reader is encouraged to look at John R. Raser's *Simulation in Society: An Exploration of Scientific Gaming,* which provides a number of examples of research done with gaming simulations.

Because gaming seems to be very "in," the claims for its usefulness are often exaggerated. The wise user will, however, weigh the appropriateness of gaming simulation against that of other methodologies that might be considered. Aside from its current popularity, there are some characteristics of gaming simulation that do recommend its use over other techniques in training applications:

1. Gaming simulations are particularly useful in exploring a process or relationships between elements in a system. While it is usually difficult to deal with process and relationships in presentational styles of instruction, gaming simulations actually allow the process to be brought into a training program. Participants not only see the process in action but also have an opportunity to participate in it and experience it. The process being considered may be one that is well understood and clearly defined, such as those modeled in a flight simulator or a specialized business game or those designed to teach a particular company's practice regarding a process such as inventory control. The process may also be one that consists of many variables which are not fully understood, such as the supervisory process between black foremen and white workers.

2. While gaming simulations may be used in situations where systems and processes are well understood, the technique is particularly useful for exploring problems, issues, and systems where hard information is scarce. On many questions there is little consensus regarding appropriate action. In these situations gaming simulation allows the trainer to develop a system which can serve as a basis for discussing issues which need clarification. Obviously, if a system or issue is not well understood, the gaming simulation that is developed will be an inadequate representation. This is both inevitable and helpful to the training environment because as the simulation is used, the trainer and trainee identify problems in the model and revise it as better understandings are developed.

3. Not all people learn in the same way. Gaming simulation provides an active, verbal, and at times physical learning environment. For those who learn better in a face-to-face interactive situation than through reading and lectures, gaming simulation may be the appropriate methodology.

4. Often the trainer is faced with a need to facilitate communication. Gaming simulation can provide a nonthreatening medium for discussing controversial issues. The gaming model provides a bridge for people to express points of view that they might not normally express. This is made possible because the rules and roles of the game allow participants to express themselves in ways which do not appear to be personal.

5. Sometimes training and educational programs become unproductive simply because the use of the same methodology becomes boring. Gaming simulation can provide an alternative format for considering material.

WHY USE A GAMING SIMULATION?

The field of gaming simulation is not yet completely developed, and very little evaluative research has been done on why gaming simulation seems to be an effective technique. Practitioners in the field have, however, identified a few characteristics of gaming simulations which seem to recommend their use. A list of the most common observations follows. It must be left up to the reader and further research to determine the validity of these observations:

1. Users of gaming simulations seem to find that the technique is useful in increasing the motivation of learners. Participants in gaming simulations often want to explore more issues and seek new information relative to the experience they have been through. The high level of motivation generated may be due both to the immediate feedback which is often a part of gaming simulation and to the competitive nature of many of the exercises.
2. Gaming simulations provide a systemic method of exploring issues. This characteristic allows for visualizing and demonstrating cause-and-effect relationships and interconnections between elements in a system in a way which is difficult or impossible with other methods.
3. Gaming simulations provide an opportunity to learn skills in a context similar to that in which they will be used. This fact seems to encourage transfer to real-life applications of these skills. Gaming often includes opportunities for decision making, resource allocation, communications, persuasion, compromise, and negotiations—all of which can be explored rationally and emotionally.
4. Gaming simulations require the players to make decisions and commit themselves to a course of action. This process helps learners state and probe their aims and intentions. The procedure seems to increase the productivity of discussions, and "rapping" is replaced by specific considerations of reflection on actions taken by participants in the gaming process and the resulting effects of those decisions.
5. Gaming simulations seem to provide a concrete reference point for use in discussing complicated concepts and ideas. It has been said that gaming simulation is similar to a language. Gaming language may be the one most appropriate for discussing systems and processes.
6. Gaming simulations provide a risk-free environment which encourages experimentation. When gaming models are designed to permit it, they can be excellent laboratory settings for testing ideas and assumptions and asking questions.
7. In using gaming simulations, learners seem to develop empathy for real-life decision makers as they have an opportunity to see situations from other points of view. Perceptions of roles, problems, and systems often seem to be broadened as a result of gaming experiences.
8. When a gaming simulation can be used as a substitute for certain types of real-life experience (i.e., field experience), training time may be shortened, and costs reduced.

Just as practitioners have seen many advantages to using gaming simulations, they also would point out a few common cautions:

1. Because gaming simulations provide for interaction between learners and often create an exciting competitive environment, learners are generally enthusiastic about the experience. This enthusiasm can lead to games' overselling themselves. If learners become blindly enthusiastic about a game and do not reflect carefully upon the experience, they can become overconfident

of their abilities as demonstrated in the gaming environment. Another problem for the trainer is that the high level of enthusiasm can make the learner feel bored with other training experiences.

2. A gaming simulation has to be a simplification of the real-life situation which it represents. A danger of simplification is that many variables important in a real-life decision-making situation are left out. Simplification also means that the range of choices available to a player in a game is invariably much narrower than that available in real life. However, if the variables and decision options are carefully chosen, this does not have to be a problem.

3. The cost of gaming simulation is often underestimated. Unless a gaming simulation is used as it comes from the publisher, the trainer should carefully evaluate how much time it will take to redesign it. Except in formal teaching applications, only a small number of gaming simulations can be used as published. The time required to train staff members in the use of the game and to provide an appropriate instructional context also should be considered.

4. Very little evaluation of gaming-simulation models has been done. Because of this, it is not possible to make a specific case for what it is that gaming simulations do. While other methodologies have not received a great deal of evaluation either, because of the unconventional learning format in gaming simulations, sponsors often want some assurance that they will work. If research evidence must be shown before games will be adopted, there is not a great deal of help that can be offered at the present time.

5. Gaming simulations, particularly computer-assisted ones, can become very rigid. Because the development costs are high, there is often resistance to changing a gaming model even though repeated runs of the exercise reveal design problems. There is a tendency to discount these problems because to deal with them would require the expenditure of money, which is often unavailable. Some games have been developed with this problem in mind and contain mechanisms for revision. This design characteristic is much easier to incorporate if the gaming model is relatively simple.

6. Participants in gaming exercises at times get into a gaming mentality and do not take the exercise seriously. When this happens, the learner's objective is often just to win, rather than to learn. The game operator's attitude toward the experience is often the critical element in determining whether this problem occurs.

7. Gaming simulations often emphasize quantitative considerations and provide little opportunity to consider qualitative issues. Therefore, players manipulate budgets, assign staff, set production rates, and decide on capital expansion, but they rarely deal with such issues as the nature of working conditions and social values. The reason for these omissions is that such considerations are difficult to model.

THE GAME DESIGN PROCESS

While gaming simulation has existed for a long time, it is still more of an art form than a science. Because of this, any attempt to outline a precise set of procedures by which games are built would result in an inaccurate picture of how this is really done. In spite of this, some have attempted to develop detailed procedures by which a gaming simulation might be built. For those who are interested, one source is *A Guide for Simulation Design*, by Charles Adair and John Foster.

A few guidelines can be stated which are generally faced by all designers. Actually, few gaming simulations are built which are totally new. The trainer is normally advised to first identify the problem or issue that must be considered and then look around for an already-existing game which deals with the issue or is at least close to what is needed. Gaming simulations can often be redesigned to meet different instructional requirements. If this procedure does not work and gaming simulation is clearly the best instructional methodology available, a new model must be built.

Actually, the best preparation anyone can have for game design is to have played a wide variety of gaming simulations. New gaming simulations can often be built using ideas and components taken from already-existing games. Another help to the game designer is to have colleagues who can assist in the early days of conceptualizing the idea and testing rough prototype models. In the final analysis it is the creativity and imagination of the game designer which will be the critical element in whether a successful game is developed. Regardless of the procedure used, there are at least nine basic tasks that any game designer should deal with in building a gaming simulation; these are discussed below.

Instructional Objectives for the Gaming Simulation Should Be Established   In some cases the exercise will have very precisely stated behavioral objectives, and in other situations the objectives may have to be quite broad. It is important in stating objectives that they not be defined too narrowly. The richness of gaming simulation is that learners can bring a variety of personal objectives to the exercise, and in many cases they meet those objectives if the gaming simulation is built in such a way that it will allow for learners with different expectations.

The Perimeters of the System Being Simulated Should Be Defined (e.g., a Corporation, Process, or City Government)   When the system is defined, a scenario can be written which describes the system in appropriate detail for the players.

Roles Should Be Defined   Roles should be developed only for those decision makers who are important to the issue under consideration. While there always is a tendency to include large numbers of roles, this should be avoided so as not to make the game too complex. A decision should be made as to whether the roles will be identical to those of real-life decision makers or whether they will represent interest groups. Descriptions of the roles should be written, and a decision made as to whether to define objectives for the roles or leave objective settings up to the players. Finally, the resources available to the roles should be outlined so that those assuming the roles know what it is they can do.

The Pattern of Interaction between Players Should Be Defined   Relationships between players and specialized functions that will be performed by particular roles should be identified. Also, procedures for passing information and resources among the players should be constructed.

An Accounting System Should Be Designed   The method of displaying the current status of the system should be established. Procedures for receiving decisions from the roles and methods of providing feedback and displaying the results of decisions should be established. Some decision should be made as to whether the game will use computer or noncomputer accounting procedures. Finally, charts, graphic displays, and any other artifacts should be designed.

The Steps of Play Should Be Developed   The actions that roles will be allowed to take and the timing of these decisions should be agreed upon.

Rules Guiding the Game Activity Should Be Established   These rules may represent external factors determined by the nature of the system being modeled. Rules might also be procedural and simply give structure to the activities of the exercise.

A Prototype Version of the Game Should Be Built   As soon as the basic decisions listed above are made, a working model of the proposed gaming simulation, with all required materials, should be constructed for testing.

A Few Trial Runs Should Be Conducted   A gaming simulation rarely works the first few times it is employed. Experience suggests that about five trial runs are required, with adequate time provided between runs for making necessary revisions.

In addition to the game design tasks listed above, there are a number of general principles that should guide the overall design or redesign process. These principles may also serve as a starting point for the evaluation of all gaming simulations.

Simplicity Whenever a gaming simulation is being built, there is always a tendency to include too much detail. The playability and success of the gaming simulation will depend greatly on the simplicity of the design. A good rule of thumb is that an exercise that is to be played in about an hour should have no more than 7 to 10 variables, and a full-day exercise should probably not exceed 50 variables. The more complex a model is, the more likely individual players are to confine their activities to one aspect of the exercise and not get a comprehensive picture of the system being modeled.

Revising the Model Provision should be made wherever possible to design into the gaming simulation a way to revise the exercise as it is used. A time might be provided at different points during the exercise for players to challenge the rules and the underlying assumptions in the model. Sometimes this is accomplished by the inclusion of man-made and natural laws. The natural laws are ones which cannot be challenged and which represent basic principles about the way the world functions. Man-made laws, on the other hand, are open to challenge because they are interpretations of the way things should be done and, at best, represent one person's or one group's viewpoint.

Graphic Support Graphics and other visual displays can greatly enrich the gaming process. Closed-circuit television, for instance, can be used as a communication device within the gaming exercise. Wherever possible, variables should be visualized on a chart or by means of artifacts such as wood blocks or colored pins. In all cases an attempt should be made to convert abstract concepts in the game to physical objects, graphic representations, or active procedures. This principle can be demonstrated by a situation in which the trainer is trying to deal with the problem of the handicapped versus nonhandicapped people doing certain manual tasks. The game designer might have the handicapped people in the game wear large gloves and perform the same tasks as the nonhandicapped people, which would concretely demonstrate the idea of being handicapped.

Personal Choice and Chance A balance should be maintained between personal choice and chance elements in a gaming situation. If a game is centered completely on personal choice or strategy, then early in the exercise those who are skillful in manipulating the simulation will be identified as winners, and the less competent players will lose interest, since they will know there is no way for them to move ahead. Some element of chance can keep this problem from occurring. If the game is all chance, the players will also lose interest, since they will assume that the outcome of the game has little or nothing to do with their actions.

Interaction A high level of interaction between the players should be encouraged. To do this it is generally advisable to have role groups composed of an uneven number of players. Having an uneven number (three seems to be best) means that discussions can be carried out throughout the exercise but that when a decision has to be made, a deadlock can be avoided. Careful attention should also be given to creating ways in which individuals within roles and players in different roles can debate issues and decisions and thereby learn from one another.

Timing As games increase in complexity, there is the danger that some players will have a great deal of work to do, while other individuals or roles will have very little. Attention should be paid to distributing the required activities as evenly as possible among all players. Decision cycles should also be timed so that there is sustained action throughout the game. This can be a serious problem in computer-assisted exercises, in which computer processing often takes a great deal of time. These lulls should be anticipated, and appropriate arrangements made for use of the time.

SUGGESTIONS ON USING GAMING SIMULATIONS

The successful use of gaming simulations is highly dependent on the way in which they are conducted. Because of this, a few generally recognized principles of game use should guide their application in training situations.

The Trainer Some people have a teaching style and personal abilities that are compatible with the use of games, while others will have little success with them. Everyone knows some people who are superb lecturers and others who can put an audience to sleep dealing with the same material and using the same format. This is also true of trainers. While each trainer has to experiment to see whether the technique is compatible with his or her style, it is safe to say that gaming simulations are generally most successful in the hands of people who are comfortable with flexible, unstructured, interactive learning situations and who have a slight disposition toward the theatrical.

The Instructional Context Gaming simulations should be placed carefully within the context of other training activities. While the exercise can often stand alone, the payoff from its use generally comes as the gaming simulation provides an environment for dealing with already-considered material and a basis for new learning activities. It is not uncommon for the real payoff of a gaming simulation to be felt days and weeks following the play of the game, as the exercise is referred to in light of new experiences.

Learning by Designing Often, as much is gained from designing gaming simulations as from playing them. Thus it is generally desirable, wherever possible, to involve learners in the design of games before their use and to provide opportunities for the players to be involved in revising the model during the course of using a game.

Game Introduction The rules and procedures for gaming simulations are often complex. Thus game users often feel compelled to give a long, comprehensive introduction to players before the start of play. This is usually a mistake. Generally, players should be given only enough information to start playing; then, in the process of playing, asking questions, making mistakes, and reading the player's manual, they will find out how the game works. In that the rules and processes of the game are its "content," to present everything verbally is to negate one of the basic reasons for using a game. Obviously, enough information should be given so that the level of player confusion does not hinder learning.

Debriefing Probably the most critical time in gaming simulation is the period of discussion and reflection about the game. These reflective times can be built into the game at various points, or, as is most commonly done, they can follow the game session. During these periods, players should be encouraged to explain their actions in the game, to critique the simulation and its assumptions, and to explore the ways in which the game was and was not like a real situation—to name but a few of the most common areas of discussion.

Space Gaming simulations cannot always be conducted in space designed for lectures and audiovisual presentations. Games usually are noisy and require room in which people can move around and meet in groups. The game user should carefully examine the available facilities to see whether the space will assist the gaming process or make it impossible.

GAMING-SIMULATION RESOURCES

The numbers of games, books, and articles available on gaming simulation run into the thousands. The following books and periodicals represent some of the best general sources in the field. The serious reader who wants detailed information on particular fields of application should find useful starting points for further investigation in this list.

Gaming simulations are produced by a large number of companies, many of which are quite small. Because of the reluctance of publishers to produce games except those of wide general appeal, games are often published privately by their authors. For this reason it is wise to consult one of the sources listed below to determine the games that may be of use in your application; then you can write the supplier of the game. Almost all the games mentioned in this chapter are described, and suppliers listed, in *The Guide to Simulations/Games for Education and Training*, by Zuckerman and Horn. The following are a few of the major game designer-suppliers who furnish catalogs: Abt Associates, Inc., 55 Wheeler Street, Cambridge, Mass. 02138; Didactic Systems Inc., Box 4, Cranford, N.J. 07016; Learning Activities and Materials Inc., P.O. Box 2198, Ann Arbor, Mich. 48103; and Simile II, 1150 Silvarado, La Jolla, Calif. 92037.

Books

Abt, Clark C.: *Serious Games,* The Viking Press, Inc., New York, 1970.
  (A general source on application of games in government, industry, and education.)
Adair, Charles H., and John T. Foster: *A Guide to Simulation Design,* Instructional Simulation Design Inc., Tallahassee, Fla., 1972.
  (A detailed technical consideration of the game design process.)
Armstrong, R. H. R., and Margaret Hobson: *An Introduction to Gaming/Simulation Techniques,* University of Michigan, Division of Management Education, Ann Arbor, 1971.
  (A brief introduction to gaming simulation.)
Babb, E. M., and L. M. Eisgruber: *Management Games for Teaching and Research,* Educational Methods Inc., Chicago, 1966.
Barton, Richard: *A Primer on Simulation and Gaming,* Prentice-Hall, Inc., Englewood Cliffs, N.J., 1972.
  (An introduction to computer simulation.)
Boocock, Sarane S., and E. D. Schild, (eds.): *Simulation Games in Learning,* Sage Publications Inc., Beverly Hills, Calif., 1968.
  (General consideration of gaming and education.)
Carlson, Elliot: *Learning through Games,* Public Affairs Press, Washington, 1969.
  (An introduction to simulation gaming; emphasis is on school applications.)
Coplin, William, (ed.): *Simulation in the Study of Politics,* Markham Publishing Company, Chicago, 1967.
  (A collection of readings on simulation in the field of political science.)
Graham, Robert G., and Clifford F. Gray: *Business Games Handbook,* American Management Association, New York, 1969.
  (Includes readings on business-game applications, an extensive review of many business games, and a long bibliography.)
Greenlaw, Paul S., Lowell W. Herron, and Richard H. Rawdon: *Business Simulation in Industrial and University Education,* Prentice-Hall, Inc., Englewood Cliffs, N.J., 1962.
  (Design and application of business games in university and management training.)
Hickok, W. H.: *A Bibliography of Research Studies on Games and Simulations,* Northwest Regional Education Laboratory, Portland, Ore., 1967.
Inbar, Michael, and Clarice S. Stoll: *Simulation and Gaming in Social Science,* The Free Press, New York, 1972.
  (A book of readings.)
Klietsch, Ronald G.: *Directory of Educational Simulations, Learning Games and Didactic Units,* Instructional Simulations Inc., St. Paul, Minn., 1969.

(A review and descriptions of a variety of instructional models, including applications to the military, business, and education.)

Klietsch, Ronald G.: *An Introduction to Learning Games and Instructional Simulations,* Instructional Simulations Inc., St. Paul, Minn., 1969.
(A theoretical analysis of simulation techniques.)

Lewis, Darrell R., and Donald Wentworth: *Games and Simulation for Teaching Economics,* Joint Council on Economic Education, New York, 1971.
(Oriented toward classroom application.)

Pfeiffer, J. William, and John E. Jones: *A Handbook of Structured Experiences for Human Relations Training,* University Associates, Iowa City, Iowa, vol. 1, 1969, vol. 2, 1970, vol. 3, 1971.
(A description of 74 human relations exercises.)

Raser, John R.: *Simulation and Society: An Exploration of Scientific Gaming,* Allyn and Bacon, Inc., Boston, 1969.
(Considers the scientific basis of simulation and research applications in the social sciences.)

Shaftel, Fannie R., and George Shaftel: *Role-Playing for Social Values,* Prentice-Hall, Inc., Englewood Cliffs, N.J., 1967.
(Explores the use of role playing in value clarification.)

Taylor, John L.: *Instructional Planning Systems: A Gaming/Simulation Approach to Urban Problems,* Cambridge University Press, New York, 1971.
(Gives background and current applications of gaming simulation and urban planning.)

Taylor, John L., and Rex Walford: *Simulation in the Classroom,* Penguin Books, Inc., Baltimore, 1971.
(Applications to teaching social studies.)

Zoll, Allen A.: *Dynamic Management Education,* Addison-Wesley Publishing Company, Inc., Reading, Mass., 1969.
(A general treatment of interactive methods in management education.)

Zuckerman, David W., and Robert E. Horn: *The Guide to Simulations/Games for Education and Training,* Information Resources, Inc., Lexington, Mass., 1973
(Descriptions of over 600 gaming simulations in all forms of education and training.)

Periodicals

Simulation and Games: An International Journal of Theory, Design, and Research, Sage Publications, Beverly Hills, Calif.
(Published four times a year; includes scholarly articles and book reviews.)

Simulation Gaming News, Alohn and Hyer Publication, Box 3039, University Station, Moscow, Idaho.
(Published five times a year in newspaper format. Provides latest news on gaming simulation in most fields of education and training.)

Chapter 41

Computer-assisted and Computer-managed Instruction

ALBERT E. HICKEY

Albert E. Hickey *is a consultant and publisher in the fields of education and training, especially programmed instruction, computer-assisted instruction, and computer-managed instruction. Founder and President from 1961 to 1974 of ENTELEK Incorporated, Dr. Hickey previously directed human factors and training research at Boston University Physical Research Labs, the Office of Naval Research, General Dynamics Corp. Electric Boat Division, and the Itek Corporation, and he was a member of the National Research Council Vision Committee. Dr. Hickey has recently been a consultant to the Defense Advance Research Projects Agency, RAND Corp., and Educational Testing Service, as well as a number of companies in the private sector. Dr. Hickey received his degrees in engineering and experimental psychology from Tufts, Columbia, and Boston University and is a member of the American Psychological Association, the American Educational Research Association, ASTD, and other bodies. He is the author or coauthor of more than 100 research papers and instructional programs.*

The woman in Fig. 41-1 is being trained by a computer to be a bank teller. The computer is the same computer that processes routine teller transactions and performs many other information processing tasks in the bank. Functioning part time as a "trainer," it displays information to the trainee, asks questions, accepts and evaluates her responses, and keeps track of her progress. In this particular case, the teller terminal has been augmented by a computer-driven audiovisual display, but this is not always required.

Teller training is just one example of computer-assisted instruction (CAI) in business, industry, and the military. Many companies have large computer-based management information systems (MIS) which send and receive information from terminals that may be located halfway around the world. These systems perform a wide variety of information handling tasks, including credit checking, reservations, order entry, inventory management, manufacturing control, traffic control, maintenance scheduling, etc. Training can now be piggybacked on most of these MIS systems. In fact, as computer-based MIS systems become more common, more and more employees are required to furnish information to a computer via a computer terminal and to interpret and respond to the output. So it is logical to

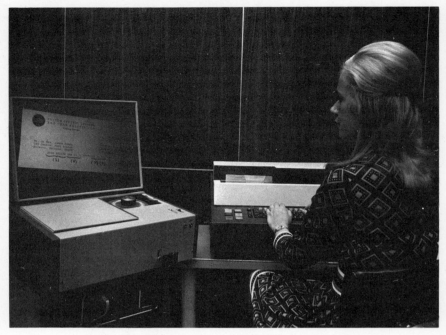

Fig. 41-1   Using a computer for bank teller training.

have a training mode for each application. Many other employees who do not normally use a terminal nevertheless have ready access to one and can take advantage of CAI.

Advantages   Although CAI was first introduced in schools, colleges, and universities over a decade ago, it may well have a greater payoff in industry and the military, where many of its advantages can be quickly translated into cost savings. These advantages include:

- Individualized instruction
- Reduced training time
- Elimination of travel for training
- Standardized training
- Quick updating of courses from a central location
- Elimination of the "transfer-of-training" problem
- Better training evaluation

Most of the above advantages, obtained by extending the use of an existing computer-based MIS to training, will be quickly appreciated by industrial trainers. Individualized instruction and easy transfer of training may require more explanation. In an individualized instruction system each trainee should be able to:

1. Work at his or her own pace
2. Begin and end the lesson when convenient
3. Begin at a point appropriate to his or her past achievement
4. Pursue his or her interest options or tailor instruction to a particular application

Furthermore, an individualized instruction system should:

1. Provide the trainee's preferred mode of presentation (graphics, verbal, aural, etc.)
2. Provide his or her preferred type of reinforcement
3. Diagnose and remedy deficient skills and knowledge
4. React to the immediate past history of responses
5. Follow the most effective presentation strategy for each trainee

Working with one trainee at a time, the skilled trainer can achieve many of the above objectives. But the task of providing individualized instruction to several trainees at the same time quickly creates a difficult information management problem. As in other data processing applications, the computer can be a great help in coping with this problem.

First of all, the computer can help the trainer to manage an individualized training program in which instruction is delivered to a number of trainees via *conventional* media, including manuals, programmed instruction, television, audio tape, etc. The trainer, or the trainee, inputs status information to the computer, and the computer prescribes what the trainee should do next. The process is called *computer-managed instruction* (CMI). In other cases, at least some instruction may be delivered to the trainee via a terminal on the computer system itself. Then the term *computer-assisted instruction* (CAI) is used. CAI and CMI are not competitive techniques. In fact, CAI can be incorporated with other media in a CMI system. For example, a student in a CMI environment may receive prescribed instruction from a PI module, TV, or other medium and then sit down at a computer terminal to be tested, the computer basing its prescription on the test results.

When a company hires new employees or introduces a new service or procedure, it is standard practice to assemble the affected employees at some central training location for lecture or video presentations and some practice. At the end of the intensive training session, the trainees return to their work locations. It may be several days or longer before employees get a chance to put into practice the knowledge or skill they acquired at the training center. Furthermore, their work environment may be quite dissimilar from the environment in which they were trained. Both of these factors tend to undermine the learned behavior. This transfer-of-training problem can be almost completely overcome if employees can be trained as required at terminals at their work stations. In fact, it is possible to switch employees from the training to the operational mode as soon as they meet certain performance criteria stored in the computer, and they may be virtually unaware of the transition.

HOW THE TRAINEE INTERACTS WITH THE COMPUTER

Let us move in a little closer and take a look at the way the trainee interacts with the computer. The interaction can be of several kinds:

1. Problem solving
2. Data reduction
3. Simulation
4. Testing
5. Drill
6. Practice
7. Tutorial
8. Inquiry

In the problem-solving mode, the trainee programs the computer so that it will perform the steps necessary to solve some numerical problem. From this experience, the trainee learns (1) how to sequence the solution steps using flow-chart language, (2) a computer language such as BASIC or FORTRAN, and perhaps (3) a generalized skill of problem solving. When used in this way, there is no burden on the trainer to preprogram the computer, but he or she should have a carefully graded set of problems to assign to the trainee. These problems may be drawn from the traditional mathematics or data processing curricula,[1] or from games of chance and strategy.[2] Although problem solving is the most common form of CAI in high school and college, it has been used very little in business and industry except to train computer programmers or simply to increase computer literacy.

In the second kind of interaction, the trainee uses the computer to perform tedious and repetitive calculations. This might occur, for example, in a course in engineering or sales forecasting. When the trainee uses a computer to *reduce data* in this manner, the computer is programmed, usually by someone other than the student, to do the necessary computations and format the output in an easily interpreted table. The principal purpose in having the trainee use the computer to reduce data is to expedite his or her training. Like problem solving, data reduction is widely used in high schools and colleges, but is less common in business and industrial training. The next four modes of interaction are the ones heavily used in industrial training.

The use of *simulation* by the military can be traced back before World War II, when primitive analog computers were used to simulate the tasks confronting artillerymen or aircraft pilots. Today the general-purpose digital computer is used to simulate the behavior of many dynamic systems that occur in nature, in business, or in warfare—systems that would not otherwise be economically or safely accessible. For example, at short intervals a computer can simulate to a management trainee the quarterly results obtained in the branch office of an insurance company. Or the computer may simulate a passenger making an airline reservation and the functions of the reservation system itself.

The computer can be used for the "on-line" *testing* of the trainee's knowledge of a subject that he or she may have acquired by studying more conventional training materials. Computer-based testing is a particularly good way to collect performance data to be used in a computer-managed instruction (CMI) system.

In the *drill, practice, and tutorial* modes of interaction, the computer asks a question of the trainee, waits for the answer, and then compares the trainee's response with a criterion prestored in the computer. On the basis of the outcome of this evaluation of one item, or a series of items, the computer will choose the next item or bit of information to be presented to the trainee. All three strategies therefore follows a pattern of *diagnosis and prescription*. They differ, however, in that practice exercises assume that trainees have already learned the necessary rule or principle in a lecture, textbook, or programmed instruction module—and that they require the practice to increase the reliability of their performance over a wide range of applications, concentrating their effort on those component concepts or skills which appear to be hindering their progress. In the tutorial mode, on the other hand, trainees learn the principle from their interaction with the computer. Most of the CAI programs currently used in industry are of the tutorial variety.

In the tutorial mode, the computer asks the questions. In an *inquiry* type of program, the trainee can ask a question, venture a diagnosis of a malfunction, etc. The computer interprets the trainee's question within the context of a limited vocabulary and some syntax prestored in the computer by the author. While such programs are understandably more difficult and costly to prepare, they do make better use of the rich potential of the computer.

A CAI program need not be limited to a single mode of interaction between trainee and computer. On the contrary, a well-designed program will involve a mixed strategy of simulation, testing, tutorial, and inquiry modes.

CAI DELIVERY SYSTEMS

The essential elements in a CAI or CMI system are the same ones required for most other computer applications:

1. A central processing unit (CPU)
2. Storage (or memory)
3. Terminal(s)
4. Communications

These basic elements can be assembled in many different configurations. The principal types of system configuration are listed below, with one or more examples of each:

1. Large dedicated systems .... PLATO
2. Small dedicated systems .... HP 2000, IBM System 1500
3. Commercial time-shared systems .... GE/CAISYS
4. Networks .... Health Education Network
5. CAI piggybacked on MIS systems .... ITS, TIME
6. Interactive cable TV .... TICCIT
7. "Smart" terminals.......................... LTS
8. CAI in a partition of a general-
purpose system .... Coursewriter III

With the exception of the Health Education Network, each one of the systems listed above is currently used in business, industrial, or military training. The Health Education Network serves a majority of the country's medical schools. Number 5 on the list, ITS and TIME, are not hardware systems, but software systems which enable users, especially in business and industry, to use their existing computer-based management information systems (MIS) for CAI on a part-time basis.

PLATO IV: A Large Dedicated System

The PLATO project was launched at the University of Illinois in 1960. When fully implemented, the current PLATO IV system will have about 1,500 terminals located in many parts of the country, all controlled by a computer system at the University of Illinois campus. It is classified as a dedicated system because the original system is used only for CAI. A PLATO IV terminal consists of a typewriter-like keyset and an ingenious display which can simultaneously show computer-generated graphic information and computer-selected photographic color slides to the user. Magnetic disks can contain a library of many lessons. Auxiliary equipment, controllable by the computer, can be added to the system, including audio cassette units, film projectors, tape recorders, etc.

Designed originally to provide instruction in college and university settings, a number of PLATO terminals have been installed by Montgomery Ward and by the Army, Navy, and Air Force to teach retail mathematics, truck maintenance, health care, and many other subjects.

IBM System 1500: A Small Dedicated System

Not all dedicated systems need be as large as PLATO. In the mid-1960's, IBM manufactured a limited edition of two dozen relatively small systems to explore CAI applications. The systems, each with 8, 16, or 32 terminals, were selectively marketed to a variety of institutions, including Army and Navy training activities. Some of the best evaluations of CAI were conducted on the IBM System 1500.

Like the PLATO system, the System 1500 features a terminal especially designed for instruction, combining an electronic (CRT) display, computer-selected photographic color slides, audio, light pen, and keyboard. The displays of electronic and photographic information are side by side, however, not superimposed, as on the PLATO IV terminal.

Pennsylvania State University makes ingenious use of one IBM System 1500. The computer and 16 terminals are installed in a 40-foot trailer. The trailerized CAI system is towed from one rural site to another so that teachers in these remote areas may receive continuing education on the identification and treatment of special students.

GE/CAISYS: A Commercial Time-shared System

In about 1964, techniques were developed to give a relatively large number of users access to a single computer in such a manner that each one thought he or she was the sole user. More than 100 companies now offer time-sharing service (TSS) commercially, the largest system being the worldwide General Electric Time-Sharing Service (GE TSS). Although business, industry, and the military have been heavy users of time-sharing services for engineering and scientific calculations, commercial time sharing has not been used for CAI in training and development until recently. To meet its internal needs, the Toronto Dominion Bank developed a CAI capability called CAISYS, which now resides on the worldwide General Electric Time-Sharing Service and is available to any company with access to the GE TSS.

The Health Education Network

What is a network? If we have one supplier of computer services and one user at a time, we have a batch processing system. This is the type of system most commonly found in the small or medium-sized company. If we have one supplier and many simultaneous users, we have a time-sharing system (TSS). The GE TSS described above is a good example. If we have many suppliers and many users at the same time, we have a computer network. Computer networks are not generally used in business and industry, but they are becoming very important in higher education. For example, in 1972 the Lister Hill National Center for Biomedical Communications established a CAI network now used by most of the medical schools in the United States.

ITS and TIME: CAI Piggybacked on IMS

Business, industry, and the military have a unique advantage over schools, colleges, and universities in adopting CAI and CMI. As we have observed, many companies already have large computer systems which accomplish a wide variety of information handling tasks at remote locations. These functions include reservations, order entry, credit checking, etc. It is relatively inexpensive to add training—CAI, CMI, or both—to the existing array of computer applications. Both IBM and the McDonnell-Douglas Automation Company have come forward with software packages which make it easy to piggyback CAI and CMI on an in-house computer-based management information system.

The McDonnell-Douglas TIME system was developed originally for the Bank of Montreal, which used it to superimpose a CAI teller training capability on its centralized computer-based teller transaction system. IBM developed a program product called the Interactive Training System (ITS) after successfully piggybacking CAI on its own order-entry system and on its own Field Instruction System (FIS). FIS provides instruction to customer engineers at more than 500 terminals in the United States, Canada, and (via satellite) Puerto Rico and Hawaii, all supported by an IBM computer in Poughkeepsie, New York. Over 2 million study hours are logged on FIS annually. More than 200 courses are available, and more than 30 percent of field engineering training is accomplished using FIS.

TICCIT: Interactive Cable TV

Most of the systems so far described rely on large computers designed for scientific or business applications. CAI and CMI do not, however, make heavy demands on the computer's logical ability, although they do require extensive memory for course material and student performance data. Furthermore, in many CAI applications it is desirable to have more versatile terminals than are customarily used with scientific and business systems. Recognizing these differences, in 1972 the MITRE Corporation undertook to design a CAI system from the ground up, making optimum use of television and computer technology. Called the TICCIT system (Two-way, Interactive Computer Controlled Informational Television), the system utilizes a commercially available color television set for display, two-way television cable for communications, and two minicomputers with added disk and tape memory. The only custom element in the system is the keyboard and the image refreshing system.

The TICCIT system was originally intended to deliver instruction in the two-year college, but one of the first TICCIT systems was acquired by the Navy to provide transition training to the air crews of the S3A, a new antisubmarine aircraft, thereby reducing the load on the overtaxed and extremely costly high-fidelity aircraft simulators. The cost of instruction on the TICCIT system is estimated at less than $1 per contact hour, not including the cost of developing the required courseware.

As with PLATO, adoption of the TICCIT system commits a company to a second computer system, one dedicated to training. This is a major decision that must be carefully rationalized.

LTS: A "Smart" Stand-Alone Terminal

All the CAI and CMI systems described so far have included multiple terminals connected by telephone wire, cable, or satellite to one or more computers. In some cases, the cost of communications becomes a very large factor in the overall cost of delivering CAI. It may be more economical to install at each site a training terminal that contains a small special-purpose computer and sufficient storage to present one lesson at a time.

The Lincoln Training System (LTS), designed with Air Force support by the Lincoln Laboratory of the Massachusetts Institute of Technology, is an example of a "smart" stand-alone terminal. It is a computer-driven microfiche system in which the visual images, audio, and computer control logic are all included on the same microfiche. Each microfiche contains 10 to 30 minutes of instruction.

PREPARING CAI COURSEWARE

The Course Development Process

The first 10 years of CAI research and development were devoted almost entirely to perfecting the delivery systems, some of which we have just described. Now that CAI has moved into the applications phase, it is apparent that the bottleneck in the widespread use of CAI and CMI is not low-cost delivery of instruction to the trainee, but the creation of the instructional programs themselves. CAI and CMI programs take more time to develop than conventional training materials. Estimates of the number of hours required to develop one hour of instruction range from 10 to 444. A sensible average for initial budgeting is probably 100 development hours per hour of instruction. Some of the reasons for the wide variation in preparation time are (1) the complexity of the subject matter; (2) the mode of interaction, e.g., drill or practice versus tutorial; (3) the complexity of the displays; and (4) the number of branches.

Figure 41-2 is a flow chart for the development of CAI courseware.[3] It begins in the upper left-hand corner with the recognition of the need for a course of instruction and the decision that the need should be fulfilled internally utilizing CAI. It might, after all, be met by sending the employee to an outside training activity on a released-time basis.

Setting Goals   The next step is the specification of training objectives. What is the desired learning outcome? What information, concepts, skills, etc., is the trainee to acquire? To what level of mastery? What prerequisite relevant information, concepts, skills, etc., can candidates for the course be expected to possess? What variability is to be expected in these entering abilities? What constraints must be accommodated? For example, if the goal is transition training for the introduction of a new manufacturing process or a new management information system, when will the new system become operational?

Learning outcomes can be classified in five categories: cognitive strategies, intellectual skills, information, attitudes, and motor skills. Troubleshooting a complex system is an intellectual skill; inventing a new system requires a cognitive strategy. In schools and colleges, most instruction is devoted to teaching cognitive strategies—teaching the students how to think. The development of cognitive strategies is also an important part of management development. In training, however, the emphasis is on teaching intellectual skills, information, and motor skills. A CAI system designed to teach cognitive strategies may be poorly adapted to teaching motor skills or even intellectual skills.

Task Analysis   In computer-based training, as in all other computer applications, the computer is a very demanding employee. Whether you program the computer to schedule deliveries or program it to teach clerks how to process insurance claims, the task itself must be completely defined. Unlike a human trainer, the computer cannot "finesse" a question, answer, or action by the trainee that it has not been programmed to handle.

There are three things you must tell the computer in detail: (1) all aspects of the task to be mastered by the trainee, (2) differences to be expected among trainees, and (3) how to sequence its instructions to the trainee. Defining the structure of the task or subject matter to be learned, together with the specification of the differences to be expected among learners, is the principal characteristic which distinguishes the preparation of adaptive, computer-based instructional programs from that of more conventional media, such as textbooks, motion pictures, stand-up lectures, and audio tapes.

Most task structures consist of two or three levels of phenomena. As shown in Fig. 41-3, the top level (level III) contains the concepts, rules, and principles: the *generalizations*. The lower two levels contain *instances*. An instance may be either a specific, concrete example of a concept or rule in operation (level I) or a verbal or graphic description of that concrete example (level II).

Take the case of the law of supply and demand. The verbal statement of that rule or generality resides on level III. A concrete example of that rule can be observed in the local market (level I). When the author of a textbook considers it impractical to send readers out into the real world to observe such a concrete event, he or she may describe it verbally or may refer readers to a video tape which shows a market transaction (level II). By presenting—directly or vicariously—one or more examples, the author is striving to have the student acquire a concept or generalization called the *law of supply and demand* which covers all market transactions. When

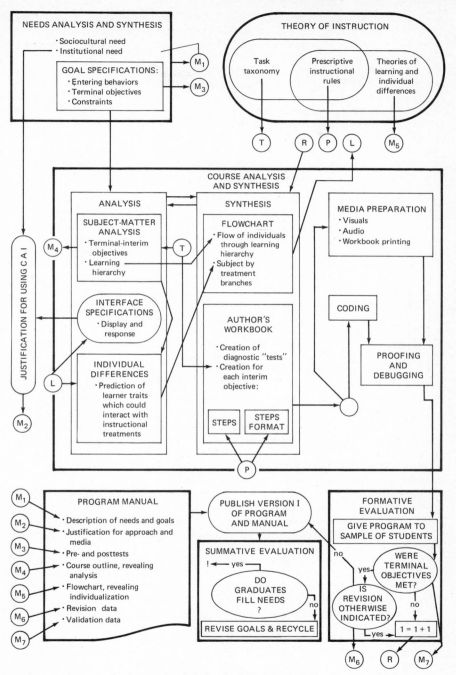

Fig. 41-2 A system for instructional design in CAI: *(C. Victor Bunderson, May 15, 1967).*

the author presents an instance to illustrate a generality, it is called an *example*. When the author requires the student to use the rule or generality to solve a problem based on the same instance, or to classify the instance, the instance is called a *practice* item.

Human beings are serial processors; that is, they can attend to only one thing at a time. Therefore, the learner cannot comprehend at once the whole multidimensional structure of the task to be mastered. He or she must cope with it one rule, one example, or one practice item at a time. It is the responsibility of the instructor, or author, to arrange these events in the most effective sequence for any given learner. As an alternative, it can be left to the learner to pick his or her own way through the task structure, or the two parties can work together.

Task analysis is generally a matter of collaboration between you as the instruc-

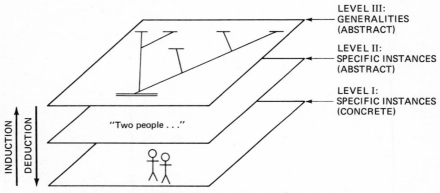

Fig. 41-3   A model of subject matter or task structure.

tional designer (ID) and a subject matter expert (SME). Ask the SME to list the concepts, rules, skills, and information to be learned and to furnish instances of each, both easy and difficult. Then help the SME arrange the concepts or skills in a learning hierarchy, stating which skills, rules, or concepts are prerequisites to the learning of any other.

Specification of Individual-Difference Variables   Earlier, we listed nine ways trainees may differ: learning pace, starting and finishing time, previous achievement, interest or application, preferred mode of presentation, preferred type of reinforcement, deficient skills and knowledge, response history, and presentation strategy. Some of these differences can be easily accommodated in a CAI or CMI system. Others are more difficult to handle because of a dearth of research information.

Preliminary testing of the population from which job candidates are to be drawn will help identify the individual differences to be expected. These may occur in reading or computational ability, in experience with similar tasks, etc. You must then decide which individual differences it is worthwhile accommodating.

Traditional tests of mechanical aptitude, clerical aptitude, etc., used for years to *select* those applicants who will be hired or those employees who will receive further training, may not be useful in designing an *adaptive* training program—one that will take all comers, identify their deficient skills and knowledge, and then provide individualized remedial instruction which will enable all trainees to perform the task successfully. Traditional aptitude tests mix the things we have listed as learning outcomes (cognitive strategy, intellectual skill, information, attitude, and motor skill). The fact that aptitude-test items are mixed does not diminish the value of the tests as predictors of success on the job because the task for which you are selecting the individual may also be mixed and because performance on the test items, since they are a sample of the task behavior, will correlate highly with job performance. But the tests do not diagnose competence on component behaviors, and that is essential to the prescription of alternative treatments in individualized instruction. Many psychologists feel that we need to develop new kinds of aptitude tests that test the information processing skills of storage, coding, and retrieval.

Flow Charting Your Instructional Strategy   Once you have a multidimensional task structure and have identified the several dimensions along which the individuals to be trained may vary, there must be a controller in the instructional system to draw events from the task structure and arrange them in a sequence that will optimize learning for each individual. In conventional instruction, it is the trainer who must make these rapid-fire decisions: picking certain kinds of examples for some trainees and repeating certain practice items for others. The computer, properly programmed, is a much more efficient controller in most cases. But the computer will only follow the instructions or rules given to it by the instructional designer or computer programmer.

Most CAI and CMI programs are totally prescripted. That is, the author inserts in the program a rule dictating what is to happen to each student at a given criterion point in the program as a consequence of the response the student makes at that point or as the result of a computer analysis of his or her recent response history. The rule may be very simple; e.g., if the word typed in by the trainee matches the word prescribed by the author, the trainee goes on to the next frame. Decision rules become more complex when a history of responses is to be analyzed for particular characteristics, such as repeated spelling, filing, or computation errors.

A sequence of choices among instructional alternatives is called an *instructional strategy*. A flow chart is a very useful tool for representing an instructional strategy. Each diamond in the flow chart of a CAI lesson represents a point at which a decision must be made about the student's path. The system may make the decision on the basis of the student's performance, the student may make the decision, or they may make it jointly.

As you build the flow chart, you must determine the number and kind of examples and counterexamples to be shown to each trainee. You must determine the number, difficulty, and frequency of practice items, etc.

Learner Control   Only rarely will you, the ID, convert the flow chart into a computer program; that is best done by a computer programmer. But once it is done and the program is loaded into the computer, the sequence of displays shown to the trainee is entirely under machine control. There is a growing trend to restore at least some control over the instructional sequence to trainees, allowing them to decide on the number and relative difficulty of practice items, for example.

The Navy compared learner and program control of CAI and found no difference in the students' achievement. Furthermore, the trainees preferred learner control by a factor of 4 to 1. These findings, plus the fact that learner-controlled programs are less costly to prepare, justify the interest in them.

The Terminal

In any interactive training system, there must be some display of information to trainees and some opportunity for them to respond. This interaction takes place at the terminal. A central problem in instruction is the fact that trainees are not directly coupled to the terminal. The reliability of instruction drops because the input to students is not highly reliable. You have to find ways to get them to attend to what you are showing them. You are concerned with formating information in the display, how rapidly you present it, etc. Thus far, the display and response requirement has been dealt with almost entirely as an engineering problem: making the best of the communications equipment available for training purposes. The following discussion has meaning only if special terminals are procured for CAI; otherwise, already-justified terminals are used.

Display Devices The "Model T" of computer terminals is the Teletypewriter Model KSB33. It is inexpensive and reliable, and good service is readily available. But it is also slow and noisy. The typical Teletypewriter terminal presents instructional material at approximately 125 words per minute, far below the average reading speed of a high school or college graduate.

In many industrial applications the Teletypewriter has been replaced by a general-purpose cathode-ray tube (CRT) terminal. These terminals are quiet and are rapidly approaching the Teletypewriter in cost, but they do not produce hard copy for the learner to tear off and take away.

Speed. Teletypes run at 110 baud. Baud rate is the rate at which binary digits appear on communication lines. The word "baud" commemorates the scientist Baudot. The maximum rate at which it is currently feasible to transmit over ordinary telephone lines is about 1,200 baud. Any terminal displaying alphameric information should be operating at at least 300 baud.

Speed often has distinct *dis*advantages. For example, if a CRT is operating in a "scroll" mode at 1,200 or 2,400 baud, the print is rolling off the top of the CRT screen before the trainee has a chance to read it. Reading is unpleasant, or even impossible, because the lines keep moving up.

Hard Copy. Hard copy is extremely valuable in training. When CRT terminals are used, hard copy can be obtained by installing one hard-copy device that is fast enough to serve several CRTs.

Supplementary Optical Displays. Training often requires a display with greater graphic and pictorial capability than one can achieve on Teletypewriters or CRTs. Thus these devices are often supplemented by random-access slide projectors under computer control or by microfiche projectors. Relatively static information is presented with the projector, and relatively dynamic information stemming from the interaction between the student and the computer is presented on the CRT or Teletypewriter.

In the widely admired terminal for the PLATO CAI system, an electronic display is superimposed on an optical display. The relatively persistent information is stored on microfiche for optical projection, and the more transient information is displayed electronically on a laminated glass panel. The photographic images on the microfiche are positioned under the optical projection system in response to signals from the computer.

Color. There is no doubt that color is an important display variable, but for all practical purposes it is available only on terminals which include a slide or microfiche projector or which utilize color TV. In slide systems, color cannot be used to code variables or transient information, but this can be done on TV displays. An excellent example of the use of color TV in CAI is to be found in the TICCIT system, and the instructional programs written for that system make elaborate use of color coding.

Audio. In many training applications it is desirable to have an audio as well as a visual channel to the trainee because the student's visual channel may be fully occupied in searching a visual display. Some interface systems therefore include a random-access tape cassette audio device under computer control.

Response Devices The most common way for the student to input information to the CAI system is via a keyboard. The keyboard allows the student to either construct a verbal or numeric response or select a response from several alternatives presented in a multiple-choice format.

Another response technique that is becoming more common is the light pen used in combination with a CRT display. The student can select a response from a display on the CRT by pointing to it with the light pen. This is particularly useful for identifying a point on graphic display, e.g., "Please point to the condenser." The PLATO display and some CRTs are touch-sensitive, eliminating the need for the light pen.

Voice-to-voice. The ultimate in student-computer interaction would be voice-to-voice communication. Although the computer is now capable of generating speech using small digital voice synthesizers, it is not yet capable of speech recognition. This limitation, however, is a problem not only for CAI but also for many other computer applications and will probably be solved within the next 10 or 15 years.

Response Analysis

Using the keyboard, the trainee can construct a verbal response. The computer may then check for the exact spelling of the constructed response or for just the presence of certain letters or consonants. Or it may search for key words, with or without regard to the order in which they appear.

The computer is very good at analyzing errors and retaining history. You just have to tell it what to do. For example, two stenographers may make the same number of errors in a spelling test. In one case, however, the errors are randomly distributed, while in the second case the trainee is regularly making the same mistake—for example, "i-e" inversions. The remediation prescribed for one student should be different from that prescribed for the other.

Do not limit your thinking to a combination of CRT and keyboard. In many tasks the learner must ultimately turn a knob, use an oscilloscope, or do something other than construct words using a keyboard. It may be desirable to have the operational equipment or a simulator next to the CAI terminal. For example, when CAI is used to teach basic electronics at the Army Signal School, the students, seated in front of terminals, are equipped with a small kit of components which they assemble into a circuit under guidance from the computer. Then, using conventional test equipment, they measure the outputs obtained from the circuit given certain inputs. When they type the readings into the computer, it decides whether they assembled the circuit correctly; if they did not, it may venture a diagnosis.

Feedback You must decide what information about trainees' performance should be fed back to them in order to bring their performance up to criterion with the least expenditure of time and effort. The computer has a great advantage over a noncomputer system in this respect. In a noncomputer system, such as programmed instruction, learners have to make their own confirmation of a correct answer or infer something from some other kind of signal. A CAI system can and should do something relevant. It should not just say "OK" or "Wrong" or flash a red light. The feedback should be diagnostic.

Design of Individual Steps Now you come to the point at which you design the individual frames, including content, format, and graphics, and prepare the artwork, tape the audio, and write any auxiliary material. These are AV techniques that most trainers are thoroughly familiar with.

At the same time, the computer must be programmed using a language it can understand. Computer languages developed for other applications, such as APL, BASIC, or FORTRAN, can be used to program CAI courses, but they take more author time than languages especially designed for CAI, such as Coursewriter and PLANIT. Even these specialized CAI languages can place a noisome burden on the author. It is much more desirable to let the author write in a natural language, such as English.

Worksheets: Off-Line Support for Authors One step in this direction is the development of "macros," which permit the subject matter specialist to input data, frame by frame, in a fairly limited set of formats without having to learn a CAI language. ITS includes such a facility, called the Expanded Course Structuring Feature. The author prepares the course using fill-in-the-blank worksheets. There are nine different worksheets:

Framework: Used by the author to specify the course structure, including the structure of each session and quiz

Common Message/"GO TO": Used by the author to specify branches

Glossary Definition: Used by the author to build a glossary accessible to the student

Text Display: Used by the author to input a frame of text at a point in the course where there is no need to solicit a response from the student

Question: Used by the author to structure a question to be used in a tutorial or test unit, including the single-character or single- or multiple-word responses The author also specifies:

- Replies to wrong answers—replies to unanticipated answers
- Replies to correct answers—hints when requested by student
- Branch-to instructions

Matching Question: Used by the author to present two columns of items to be matched by the student as part of a tutorial or test unit

True-False Question: Used by the author to structure true-false or yes-no questions to be used in tutorial or test units

Field Analysis: Used by the author to format displays

Screen Summary: Gives the author, for example, the ability to position a cursor on the display

Having filled in the worksheets off-line, either the author or an assistant sits at a terminal on the CAI system and types in the contents of each worksheet, or the information may be punched on cards. The computer automatically generates the necessary Coursewriter processing code. The author may also work directly in Coursewriter code if more flexibility is desired. A copy of the ITS Question Worksheet is shown in Fig. 41-4.

By providing a space in which the author can insert the reply to a specified wrong answer, the ITS Question Worksheet prompts the author to anticipate that possible outcome. It is but a short step from that kind of off-line author prompting to interactive on-line author prompting by the computer itself. Hewlett-Packard and other systems now offer such software. The author is first given a list of features that he or she may or may not choose to activate in an instructional process. The features are explained in plain English. The author is asked, for example, "What criterion do you want to set for mastery? One right, five right, etc.?" After the author sets these parameters, the computer asks such questions as, "What do you want to teach? Is it a concept? Is it vocabulary? Do you want to see some strategies for teaching that sort of thing? Now, is this the way you want to teach? If not, what don't you like about it?"

Formative Evaluation   While the program is in the gestation phase, it is desirable to do some formative evaluation with a small sample of "trainees," people who know nothing about the subject matter but who do know enough about the instruction process to be able to describe their hang-ups to the authors. Then a sample of representative trainees should be run through the revised program to see whether they can pass the mastery tests corresponding to the terminal objectives for the program. If they cannot, back to the drawing board.

Summative Evaluation   Once the course passes the field tests, it can be placed in service. But over a period of time it is necessary to conduct a second kind of evaluation to answer the question: Do the trainees who successfully pass the

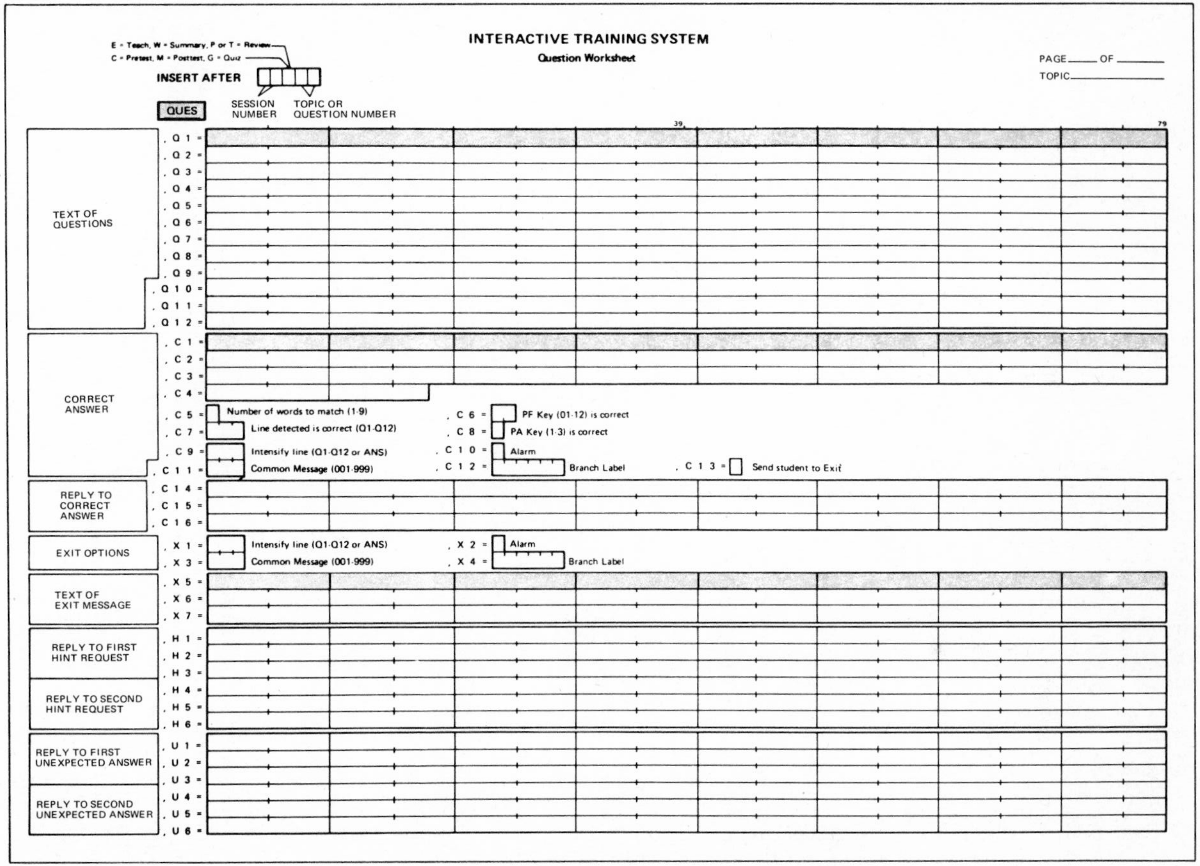

Fig. 41-4 Interactive training-system question worksheet.

course in fact perform satisfactorily on the job? If they do not, back again to the drawing board.

Documentation   Throughout the development process it is imperative to keep detailed records of each step. Computer programs are much easier to change and keep up-to-date than training manuals, but if the change has to be made at a later date by someone other than the author, he or she will be at a serious disadvantage if such things as a flow chart of the program organization and a file of subject matter data are not available.

Experienced trainers will recognize that there is little in this courseware development procedure that has not been advocated for the preparation of other kinds of training materials, especially programmed instruction. The difference lies in the complexity—particularly in the number—of alternative paths. If there are five alternative examples of a rule or if there are practice items at five levels of difficulty, then there are five branches to debug: five hours of author time per hour of student time.

Composition of the Authoring Team

Many university professors have developed single-handedly a CAI course in a subject—say, introductory German. But when it is necessary to produce curriculum material in quantity, as is the case in industrial and military training, a team approach is required. The minimum team is an instructional designer (ID) and a subject matter expert (SME). You may also include an instructional design technician (IDT), an evaluation technician (ET), and a packaging specialist (PS).

The instructional designer (ID) should have a general background in educational psychology and related subjects, including experimental methodology, human learning, measurement, and statistics, as well as experience in computer uses. In addition to this general background, he or she should have experience in instructional systems design and be a student of the growing literature on instructional theory.

The subject matter expert (SME) should be selected on the basis of knowledge of the subject matter to be taught, experience and interest in training, and openness to innovative, machine-mediated approaches to instruction.

The weakest point in the CAI effort is simply identifying who will make a good ID or SME. Traditional classroom experience does not ensure that a teacher will be able to conceptualize the design for highly adaptive CAI courses.

The instructional design technician (IDT) develops sequences of examples and nonexamples, matched and paired, having a range of divergency and difficulty. He or she also lays out specifications for display and response and for answer processing. The evaluation technician (ET) works with the ID to develop an evaluation design and evaluation instruments, and he or she collects data. The packaging specialists include artists, coders, and typists, who may serve more than one team. Much of the talent required to produce conventional AV materials of good quality is useful here.

The Future: Generative CAI

There are several drawbacks to the present frame-by-frame approach to authoring CAI training material. First, it is difficult to see how the requirement for CAI courseware can be met if the authors have to prepare the material frame-by-frame. Furthermore, the frame-by-frame approach to authoring implied by the worksheet encourages the author to continue thinking of his or her product as something like a book, except that it asks questions and scores responses. Finally, storing in the computer all the text and questions to be used in a course is not an elegant use of the computer's potential.

Generative CAI is an alternative to the frame-by-frame approach in which the computer contains (1) its own model of the subject matter, (2) a model of the student, and (3) an "intelligent" monitor based on developments in the field of artificial intelligence. The intelligent monitor constructs questions during the interaction between the computer and the student. Generative CAI is now in use for some training applications. It seems likely that before this edition of the handbook goes out of print, it will be more common.

AVAILABLE COURSEWARE

Although a tremendous amount of effort has gone into the authoring of CAI courseware, that effort has not had a widespread effect because much of the courseware cannot be readily transferred from one system to another. Programs written for the PLATO system will not run on an IBM 370, for example. But training programs developed to run on the IBM Interactive Training System should be transferrable from one ITS system to another. An ITS user group within the IBM GUIDE organization will facilitate this exchange.

"Turnkey" hardware and software packages are available to deliver instruction in subjects for which there is widespread demand. For example, Computer Curriculum Corporation sells a turnkey package in adult skills and general education development (GED), or they will recode the program to run on your system. This is a fundamental skills program with many applications in the military establishment, penal institutions, and industry.

A CMI program developed by the Navy and written in standard COBOL is now available, and a number of computer-based management games written in FORTRAN, BASIC, or other widely used languages are available. Simulations and business games are covered in detail in another chapter of the handbook.

DEVELOPING CAI AND CMI CAPABILITY

The first step in acquiring a CAI or CMI capability is, of course, to become as well informed as possible about the new field. Since it is new, there are no textbooks to turn to, but there is an extensive "fugitive" literature. You can maintain a complete and continuing surveillance of the literature by subscribing to the ENTELEK CAI/CMI Abstract Service.[4]

Two professional organizations conduct meetings and publish journals that are helpful. The Society for Applied Learning Technology (SALT) deals specifically with applications of computers to training, especially in the military. The membership of the Association for the Development of Computer Based Instructional Systems (ADCIS) is heavily weighted toward representatives of public education, colleges, universities, and professional schools, but many of the problems discussed are common to training applications.

It is essential to become acquainted with your data processing department. It is unfortunate, but true, that in most companies a breach exists between the corporate training department on the one hand and the data processing department on the other. The fact that most data processing departments conduct their own training is mute testimony to this schism.

Before opening that door into the DP area, it will help you to communicate with the computer people if you know some of their jargon. It will also help to know how the computer is being used in other parts of your organization. The American Management Association publishes a programmed instruction text that can be helpful to non-DP managers.[5]

Computers are generally crowded with work, and it is likely that your interest in using the computer to teach will not strike a sympathetic chord in the DP department unless you pick a training objective that will yield a direct payoff to that department. This suggests that your initial CAI venture should be aimed at improving the performance of an existing computer-based management system—for production and inventory control, credit clearance, manufacturing information, order entry, reservations, teller transactions, etc. Many of these DP systems suffer from a common ailment—GIGO, or "garbage in, garbage out." In other words, the DP systems do not produce good results because the people who enter the data at the terminal do not use the terminal properly or do not understand the purpose and function of the overall system. CAI can help your friends in DP improve the performance of these workers, even if they come under the jurisdiction of other departments.

Second, computer-based management systems are frequently being upgraded, not only in small, easily assimilated steps, but also in big jumps every five years, as new computer technology becomes available. The transition training required on these occasions can be staggering and is often best accomplished, at least in part, by adding a CAI capability to the system itself.

When you piggyback CAI on an existing MIS, you can be 99 percent sure that you will not find an off-the-shelf courseware package that will do the job. You will have to build it yourself. Begin by finding out what CAI language will run on your information management system. If it is an IBM system, you can probably rent the ITS package or the Coursewriter language. If it is a UNIVAC system, the CAI language is called ASET. If it is any other system, the McDonnell-Douglas TIME system may serve the purpose. From that point on, development of the courseware itself follows the cycle shown in Fig. 41-2.

GLOSSARY

ADAPTIVE TRAINING: A training process which accepts all applicants and adapts instruction to their individual differences.

BASIC: An easy-to-learn computer language used primarily for programming solutions to mathematical problems.

BAUD RATE: The rate at which bits of information appear on a communication line.

BIT: A unit of information: a binary choice between two alternatives, represented by the digits 0 and 1.

BYTE: A subdivision of a computer word; e.g., a 32-bit word may be divided into four 8-bit bytes.

COMPUTER-ASSISTED INSTRUCTION (CAI): Any situation in which the trainee interacts directly with the computer to achieve a learning objective.

COMPUTER-MANAGED INSTRUCTION (CMI): The use of the computer to analyze the results of instruction that takes place either off-line using conventional media or on-line (CAI) and to prescribe individualized instructional treatment.

COURSEWARE: As distinguished from software, courseware consists of computer programs for achieving particular learning objectives, e.g., a CAI lesson in algebra.

COURSEWRITER: An IBM computer language designed for writing instructional programs.

CPU: The central processing unit or "main frame" of the computer, containing the logic units and core memory.

CRT: Cathode-ray tube. An electronic, TV-like display.

CURSOR: A short horizontal line that moves about on a CRT display to indicate where the next character typed in by the terminal operator will appear.

DISPLAY: Any output of information to the trainee by the system, particularly on a CRT.

DRILL: A diagnosis-and-prescription type of instructional strategy characterized by presentation of instances as practice items, without statements of generalities.

FORMATIVE EVALUATION: Evaluation of an instructional program carried on during development.

FRAME: A unit in an instructional program. A conventional CAI program consists of a sequence of frames of information displayed to the student.

GENERALITY: A concept, rule, or principle.

GENERATIVE CAI (GCAI): In GCAI an "intelligent" monitor embedded in the computer software system constructs displays during the interaction between student and computer, based on models of the subject matter and the student. This is in contrast to the traditional frame-by-frame design of instructional sequences preactively by the course author.

INDIVIDUAL DIFFERENCE: A difference between individual trainees, e.g., anxiety level.

INPUT: Any information communicated to the system by the operator by typing on a keyboard, pointing with a light pen, etc.

INSTANCE: A specific application of a concept, rule, or principle. May be either an example or a practice item.

INSTRUCTIONAL STRATEGY: A sequence of choices among instructional alternatives or the decision rules governing the choices.

INTERACTIVE: A condition in which computer and human being exchange information at a relatively high rate.

ITS—INTERACTIVE TRAINING SYSTEM: An IBM software system or program product that enables the user to piggyback a CAI capability on an existing MIS.

LIGHT PEN: A device for inputting information to a computer system by pointing to information displayed on a CRT.

MACRO: A frequently repeated set of instructions, or program module, embedded in the computer software system, which can be triggered by one instruction, thus saving author time.

MANAGEMENT INFORMATION SYSTEM (MIS): A system, usually computer-based, to process information—teller transactions, orders, reservations, etc.

MEMORY: Any place where information is stored in the system. May include core, disk, drum, magnetic tape, etc.

OFF-LINE: To accomplish some task without using the computer, e.g., viewing a TV lesson.

ON-LINE: Using the computer.

OUTPUT: Any information communicated to the operator by the system by a CRT, Teletypewriter, high-speed printer, etc.

PLATO: A coast-to-coast dedicated CAI system based on a computer at the University of Illinois. A similar system is available for any large Control Data Corp. computer.

SMART TERMINAL: A terminal which contains some logic and memory capability used to do some local processing of information before communicating with a CPU.

SOFTWARE: The computer programming, or instructions to the computer, which establishes its capabilities, e.g., its ability to understand commands in FORTRAN, BASIC, Coursewriter, etc.

SUMMATIVE EVALUATION: Long-term evaluation of an instructional program to determine whether it is valid, i.e., to determine whether people trained in the program are competent on the job.

TICCIT: Two-way Interactive Computer-Controlled Informational Television. A CAI system designed by the MITRE Corp.

TIME: A software system or program product of the McDonnell-Douglas Co. that enables the user to piggyback CAI on an existing IMS.

TIME SHARING (TS): A technique which permits many users to use one computer simultaneously in such a way that each user thinks he or she is the sole user.

TUTORIAL MODE: A diagnosis-and-prescription type of instructional strategy characterized by the presentation of generalities as well as instances in the instructional sequence. Frequently simulates human tutorial interaction.

WORD: A standard number of bits grouped in sequence, usually 32.

REFERENCES

1. Sage, Edwin R.: *Problem-Solving with the Computer,* ENTELEK Inc., Newburyport, Mass., 1970.
2. Sage, Edwin R.: *Fun and Games with the Computer,* ENTELEK Inc., Newburyport, Mass., 1974.
3. Bunderson, C. Victor: "The Computer and Instructional Design," in Wayne Holtzman (ed.), *Computer-assisted Instruction Testing and Guidance,* Harper & Row, Publishers, Incorporated, New York, 1970.
4. *CAI/CMI Abstracts,* ENTELEK Inc., Newburyport, Mass., 1965 et seq.
5. *Computer Fundamentals for the Manager,* Cassettes—Workbook Program, American Management Association, New York, 1973.

Chapter 42

Learner-controlled Instruction

DUGAN LAIRD

Dugan Laird *is a consultant, writer, and speaker who entered industrial training in 1952. Previous to his work in industry, he was a high school and a university instructor. His industrial training experience includes nineteen years at United Air Lines, plus consultancies with the training and development activities at banks, insurance organizations, food manufacturers and distributors, hospitals, and nearly all branches of the United States government. Dr. Laird has worked in both the United States and Europe and has conducted seminars in Asia and Africa. He earned a bachelor's degree from Northern Iowa University and master's and Ph.D. degrees from Northwestern. In his current consultancies and research, he is especially interested in integrating younger workers and managers with existing value systems; in extending communications between the academic, governmental, and industrial training communities; and in improving the quality of learning designs. Dr. Laird writes a monthly column for the magazine* Training in Business and Industry *and is the author of several books on business writing and industrial training systems.*

Designers of learning systems for adults constantly seek ways to utilize the unique "adultness" of the learners. One recent development in this direction is the "open classroom," or learner-controlled instruction.

Learner-controlled instruction (LCI) is merely a learning-teaching system which involves the learner in a number of key decisions about how learning will take place. These decisions involve such issues as the pace at which the learning progresses, the sequence in which learning steps are achieved, the methods and materials used in this process, the objectives of the learning, and the measurement and evaluation of the learning.

It is probably most helpful to visualize these five decisions on a continuum—a continuum on which it is possible to involve the learner in as few as one or as many as all five of the decisions.

RATIONALE FOR LCI

Probably the first question one asks about LCI is "Why?" Why not continue traditional systems in which program designers or instructors make all the decisions about what the training will achieve, how it will be accomplished, and how it will be measured? The answer lies basically in the nature of adult learners—and there is new and considerable evidence that traditional systems are not producing behavioral change in the directions and to the degrees desired by organizations sponsoring the training.

When one examines adult learning theory, the names of Carl Rogers and Malcolm Knowles immediately appear. One of Rogers's statements indicates why this eminent psychologist believes that learners themselves must make the critical decisions: "Significant . . . learning has a quality of personal involvement—the whole person in both his feeling and cognitive aspects being *in* the learning event. It is *self*-initiated."[1] Many leading industrial trainers seek such involvement as a partial antidote to the indifference ("But I can't use this in *my* work") with which incumbent employees often greet totally structured learning designs.

Androgogy

The science of adult learning is called *androgogy,* a term used by the German Alexander Kapp in 1835 and further developed by Eugen Rosenthal in 1921 and by Van Enckevort in Holland.[2] In the United States, Malcolm Knowles has led inquiries into androgogy, explaining why adults need to become involved in learning decisions if the learning is to be significant and lasting. He contends (1) that adults see themselves as owners of unique experience which they wish to invest in learning, (2) that they desire an immediate application of the learning (in contrast to the promise of future relevance, which children accept), and (3) that adults profit more from self-directed than from authoritarian learning designs.[3]

People like Kohl point out that the notion that learning is orderly and identical for all "is wrong and in many ways pernicious."[4] Probably the most eloquent rationale for LCI appears in *Freedom To Learn,* where Rogers points out that (1) human beings have a natural potential for learning; (2) significant learning occurs when the subject matter is relevant to the student's purposes; (3) learning which involves a change in self-organization is threatening and tends to be resisted; (4) self-threatening learnings are most easily perceived and assimilated when external controls are at a minimum; (5) much significant learning is acquired through doing; (6) learning is facilitated when the student participates responsibly in the learning process; (7) self-initiated learning which involves feelings as well as intellect is more lasting than other kinds of learning; (8) independence, creativity, and self-reliance are facilitated when self-criticism and self-evaluation are basic and evaluation by others is secondary; and (9) the most socially useful learning consists in learning the process of learning, developing a continuing openness to experience, and incorporating into oneself the process of change.[5]

DEFINITION OF LCI

In applying this theory, designers of LCI typically supply the learner with:

1. A clear statement of the objectives to be achieved.
2. An explanation (or sample) of the evaluation that will be used to demonstrate satisfactory achievement of the objective.
3. A list of the resources (materials, activities, and people) available to help the learner master the objective. This list may be referred to as a "learning map" since it describes useful "stopovers" on the route from the trainee's position at the start to his or her ultimate goal.

Because of this learning design, the typical "open" classroom looks remarkably different from the traditional schoolroom. There are rarely rows of seats; seats are rarely assigned to specific trainees. There is no position of influence for the teacher at the front of the room or on an elevated platform. In the LCI scheme the room is a learning center. Within it there are resources arranged in smaller "centers." These will include a library (with audiovisual references and games as well as books); places for small groups to meet for discussion, case studies, or games; and places for individual study—including carrels for audiovisual playback. Assuredly, there is a convenient place where learners can access the instuctor, who becomes a major "resource" for learning. Weisberger gives a good example of a typical learning center.[6]

LCI PRECEDENTS

Where has LCI been attempted? Probably the most widespread effort has been made in the British infant schools, equivalent to the United States elementary schools.[7] Kohl, in *The Open Classroom,*[8] and Rogers, in *Freedom To Learn,*[9] chronicle some American examples, as does *Perspectives in Individualized Learning.*[10] An early industrial application took place at Varian Associates in 1960,[11] when Mager and McCann adapted a cadet program to LCI. Other cases include the Allied Supermarkets program for new managers, United Air Lines flight attendant training, some sections of upper- and middle-management training at Eastern Airlines, and Bell Labs in New Brunswick. An ASTD Institute on Determining Training Needs and Measuring Results and the July 1973 National Society of Sales Training Executives used LCI formats.[12] The Calhoun School of New York City employs LCI at its Middle School Center for Inquiry.[13]

DELEGATED DECISIONS IN LCI

In existing systems, two key variables emerge. First is the instructor's commitment to the approach. Trainers who reject the Rogers or Knowles psychology inevitably preordain failure for learners in LCI systems. A second variable is the ability of the learner to "get started." Special counseling during early phases seems vital for learners who are still dependent upon structure and who feel threatened by the decisions which LCI requires them to make.

By examining each of five decisions, we may get a clearer and more detailed comprehension of what LCI is and why it generates learning.

Self-Pacing

Pacing decisions have been made by learners (with or without instructor encouragement) for as long as learning has existed. In programmed instruction, adult educators began to stress the wisdom of self-pacing; indeed, they cited self-pacing as one big advantage of that method.[14] This need to set one's own learning speed may be especially significant with adults: Irving Lorge reports a difference between the speed of adult learning and that of children. Sight, hearing, and reaction are sufficiently slower in adults—and so the quantity (but not the quality) of performance is altered.[15] In LCI it is imperative that learners decide for themselves when they are ready to take an examination on material they are currently studying and when they are ready to take the next step on a learning map—to start on the next goal. Indeed, differentiated pacing is probably the most widespread form of individualization. Even in non-LCI systems where the goals of instruction are the same and the materials are the same, learners can move along their common tracks at different rates of speed.[16]

The advantages of this self-pacing accrue to the total organization as well as to the student: Learners who complete their training in less than the standard time can return to their workplace. At Varian, the first learner-controlled class completed a six-month cadet program in three months; a second group met the objectives, reported to work, and was appraised as equal or superior to conventional graduates after only two months of study.[17]

Sequence Control

Control of the sequence is another dimension of LCI. The traditional rationale for sequencing the stimuli in a teaching design is that people learn best when they go from the simple to the complex or from the familiar to the unfamiliar. That is probably a good assumption, but the inherent fallacy is that what is simple to one learner may be very complicated to another; that which is "familiar" in my experience may be totally alien to anything in your life. As Thorwald Esbensen has pointed out:

> If a sequence which the teacher thinks is absolutely necessary is *really* necessary, that conclusion will emerge as a result of the student's actual experience with choosing a pattern of tasks. As a matter of fact, there is a growing body of evidence that a teacher's predetermined sequence is sometimes mistaken from a standpoint of what the student is able to achieve when he is able to establish his own order of things.[18]

If we recall Knowles's point that adults bring unique experiences to the learning situation, we can see why threat levels are lowered if adult learners are permitted to make their own decisions about what is simple and familiar and are permitted to start learning where they are most confortable.

Variable Materials

Even methods or materials may be learner-selected or learner-produced. Esbensen cites cases where "the materials of instruction vary according to the different needs or preferences of the students."[19] British infant schools learned that "the best stuff is often homemade. Books made and illustrated by the children are coming to be a regular part of the curriculum in some schools."[20] With industrial participants, the early development may be slow and painful, but once they are launched in developing their own case studies, role plays, or questionnaires, they find this facet a useful way to inject their own unique problems and experience into the learning.

This variation in materials also impacts on the methods through which learning is achieved. Planning in nonauthoritarian classrooms must be based on the distinct possibility of abrupt changes. Kohl explains, "Subjects arise or are dropped or develop in many different ways."[21]

Because of this learner involvement, trainees often find ways to use old materials in meeting unexpected objectives. At the Calhoun School, the game of Monopoly (introduced by the staff to help provide an understanding of economics) was amended by the girls themselves to give empathic insight into life in the ghetto and membership in social minorities.

By creating items for their own learning maps or by adapting existing materials to reflect their own experience, learners achieve a great deal of the process that we call *motivation*. Learners who develop materials and methods are to a large extent determining the content of their learning, and they are so involved in this process that there can be no question of their motivation.

Objective Setting

What about the objectives of the learning? Is it truly appropriate for learners to determine their own learning goals? In many public schools, the objectives must reflect standards on state achievement tests; in most industrial or agency settings, management insists upon retaining its right to set the objectives of the training. "After all," they reason, "we must set production and performance standards which ensure achievement of organizational goals. Since the performance standards equate to training objectives, we—not trainees—must be responsible for setting those objectives." There is unquestionable validity in this viewpoint. Thus many LCI training programs do not delegate standard setting; rather, they delegate decisions about how those standards will be achieved by the performers.

However, the position occupied by the trainee may involve wider parameters and greater ambiguity. (Most of our supervisory and management posts do!) The learner must develop the judgment to cope with the variables inherent in the position. Here it may be appropriate for the learners themselves to make decisions about the knowledge they need to acquire and the skills they need to develop. As even the public schools have discovered:

> Although it is reasonable to assume that many of the basic skills we emphasize are appropriate to virtually all students, it is less evident that all of what we teach is necessary or best for all. . . . Individualizing objectives, then, means varying the goals of learning for students depending upon what seems to be needed in each case.[22]

One strategy used when LCI faces this issue is to prepare a list of objectives and let students select the ones they regard as relevant to their own needs. This is not truly LCI, but it is analogous to the "electives" offered in academic curricula. In some programs (as in the ASTD Institute on Determining Training Needs and Measuring Results) the list of preplanned objectives may be supplemented with learner-designed goals. The learner submits these original goals to the staff, who then design a learning map (invariably involving personal consultation) which should get the learner to the desired learning objective.

Measurement

Finally there is the issue of measurement. How can we trust the learners to measure their own achievements? Carl Rogers has pointed out that in the case of mature human beings, measurement by anyone else is secondary.[23] In any true LCI format, inputs by the learners about how well they have learned are vital. In LCI systems, inputs by both the trainee and the immediate supervisor are of primary impact; inputs by the instructor can be, at best, of secondary importance in measuring the success of the training.

Nearly all organizations would desire learners who can say, "Yes, I can meet these objectives; I'm ready to do this job out there in the 'real world'!" Such evaluation is often part of the LCI "contract." In most LCI systems, a contract is a definition of what the learner will have to do to demonstrate to himself or herself and to the instructor (and to the supervisor?) that the objective has indeed been met.

TWELVE GUIDELINES FOR LCI

In any LCI system, certain guidelines emerge:

1. It is necessary to mediate a great deal of the instruction. In the first place, many materials are necessary to meet the differing needs of different learners. In the second place, auto-instructional presentations free the instructor to be a facilitator of the learning rather than a mere mouthpiece for the content of the program. Thus the instructor helps the trainee define the precise question which is troublesome or motivating and then directs the learner to the probable source of assistance. The trainer is free to work with other trainees if the resources are mediated. There are many available media: books, films, filmstrips, audio tapes, video tapes, directions for group discussions, games, puzzles, programmed instruction, cases, simulations, field trips, meditation. If the resource involves interactions between people, then other learners are important resources to the learning. (Indeed there may be significant learnings for the trainee who must secure participation from peer learners in mediated group activity!)

2. A variety of media is recommended, how else can LCI respond to the individuality of the learners?

3. The learner must feel accountability for the learning. LCI is not permissive education! The learner, once pledged to an objective, has in effect signed a contract. The only escape from that contract is by renegotiation. On the other hand, when learners feel they can demonstrate mastery of the objective, they may omit or terminate activities on the map leading to that objective. If they satisfactorily meet all the standards for the contract, they proceed to another objective—and a new map.

4. Start small. To adopt LCI for an entire curriculum (or even to an entire existing program) may be threatening to the participants, the instructors, and the organization. In his book, in the chapter entitled "Ten Minutes a Day," Kohl counsels: "For ten minutes, cease to be a teacher and be an adult. . . . Make it possible for the ten minutes to grow to fifteen, twenty, so long as it makes sense to you and your pupils."[24] What happens in these few minutes? "Present the class with a number of things they can choose to do. Present them with options you feel may interest them. Allow them the option of sitting and doing nothing if they choose. . . . That ten minutes is to be their time and is to be respected as such."[25]

5. Minimize the lectures. Even if the instructor is lecturing to just one listener, the very existence of the lecture indicates that there is an instructor in charge rather than learner control.

6. As an instructor, step out of the way, but do not disappear. "Make it clear that you won't tell people what to do or how to do it, but that you will be available to help in any way you can, or just to talk."[26]

7. Instructors need to develop a sense of "suspended expectation."[27] This means not believing that a reportedly dull person is actually dull—or a bright person bright. It means avoiding the "Pygmalion" syndrome about classes and individuals, about subjects, about methods, and about organizational units. It means letting the learners find out for themselves about their own interests and potential—and about what does and does not work in achieving their goals. If instructors can achieve this suspended expectation and still be true to themselves, learning will increase.

8. The teacher must be as much herself or himself as possible—every bit as much as the learners. This means "that if the teacher is angry, he ought to express that anger, and if he is annoyed at someone's behavior he ought to express that too."[28]

9. Do not assign seats. To do so is to betray that the control still belongs to the teacher.[29] Just show people where the resources are.[30] This implies the next guideline.

10. There is no need to preach a long nonauthoritarian sermon. In fact, there are many reasons for not doing so. Learners tend to mistrust all sermons—regardless of their length or message. Open classrooms develop through the actions of the teacher—not because of his or her words.[31] In training adults (who have traditionally expected structure and authority in the learning situation), this may be a particularly important guideline—and it reveals why the trainer must have faith in the ability of the learners to face and solve the fundamental learning decisions by themselves.

11. Instructors should evaluate and criticize only when asked by learners for a judgment about a product or a problem. In no case does the instructor take sole responsibility for an evaluation of student accomplishments.[32]

12. Commitment by the instructor is essential. To Carl Rogers, the proper word is "facilitator." He stresses that in an LCI approach, "A facilitator is not a teacher and is not simply giving lip service to different approaches to

learning."[33] Many industrial trainers do not believe that Rogers is correct—they do not approve of delegating the learning decisions to the learner. As one has said, "For the industrial trainer, Rogers is not that well received."[34] Trainers who do not support LCI naturally tend to avoid using learner decisions in administering training programs.

SUMMARY

In its ultimate form, LCI is seen by people like Carl Rogers as an entire new context—not just a new arrangement of learning stimuli, resources, and relationships. Rogers once stated that LCI is not a technique or a method of facilitating learning; instead, he said, it is "a personal context, a context of values, a view as to the goal of personal development."[35]

In less extensive applications, industrial trainers have found it useful to delegate to learners one or more of the basic decisions about what, when, and how to learn the behaviors required by the organization. To the degree that they have used LCI approaches, they are trying to involve the learner in ways which produce more extensive, more lasting, and more relevant learning experiences.

REFERENCES

1. Rogers, Carl R.: *Freedom to Learn,* Charles E. Merrill Books, Inc., Columbus, Ohio, 1969, p. 5.
2. Van Enckevort, G.: Untitled article submitted to the *Journal of Adult Education* in Ireland, 1971.
3. Knowles, Malcolm S.: *The Modern Practice of Adult Education,* Association Press, New York, 1969.
4. Kohl, Herbert R.: *The Open Classroom,* The New York Review, New York, 1969, p. 52.
5. Rogers: op. cit., pp. 157–163.
6. Weisberger, Robert A.: *Perspectives in Individualized Learning,* F. E. Peacock Publishers, Itasca, Ill., 1971, p. 336.
7. Featherstone, Joseph: "The Primary School Revolution in Britain," *The New Republic,* Aug. 10, Sept. 2, and Sept. 9 1967.
8. Kohl: op. cit.
9. Rogers: op. cit.
10. Weisberger: op. cit.
11. Mager, Robert F., and John McCann: *Learner Controlled Instruction,* Varian Associates, Palo Alto, Calif., 1960.
12. *Sales Meetings,* Bill Communications, Philadelphia, October 1973, pp. 327ff.
13. "The Calhoun Middle School Center for Inquiry," unpublished prospectus, 1971.
14. Hawley, William E.: "Programmed Instruction," in Robert L. Craig and Lester R. Bittel (eds.), *Training and Development Handbook,* McGraw-Hill Book Company, New York, 1967, pp. 225–250.
15. Lorge, Irving: "Capacities of Older Adults," in *Education for Later Maturity,* Whiteside, Inc., New York, 1955.
16. Esbensen, Thorwald: "A Game For Enhancing Learner Responsibility," *Independent Study in Science,* National Science Teachers Association, 1970; reprinted in Weisberger, op. cit., p. 270.
17. Mager and McCann: op. cit.
18. Esbensen: op. cit., p. 268.
19. Ibid., p. 270.
20. Featherstone: op. cit., p. 4.
21. Kohl: op. cit., p. 56.
22. Esbensen: op. cit., p. 271.
23. Rogers: op. cit., p. 163.
24. Kohl: op. cit., p. 71.
25. Ibid.

26. Ibid.
27. Kohl: op. cit., p. 20.
28. Ibid., p. 15.
29. Ibid., p. 20.
30. Ibid., p. 33.
31. Ibid.
32. Rogers: op. cit., p. 144.
33. Ibid.
34. Shelton, H. R.: Unpublished letter to R. L. Craig, Dec. 27, 1973.
35. Rogers: op. cit., p. 217.

Chapter 43

Audiovisuals and the Training Process

KEVIN O'SULLIVAN

Kevin O'Sullivan *is the Executive Director of ASTD. Mr. O'Sullivan's professional background spans 15 years in the field of instructional technology and communications—first as a broadcaster and narrator and then as a writer, director, consultant, and teacher. After graduating from Dartmouth College, Mr. O'Sullivan served three years in the United States Navy, followed by professional assignments with General Electric Company, General Learning Corporation, ARIES Corporation, and, most recently, the National Audio-Visual Association as Director of Professional Development. His professional credits include the Freedom Foundation's Honor Medal for Literature; award-winning motion pictures; over 100 titles encompassing journal articles, textbooks, audio cassettes, and multimedia programs; and a wide array of distinguished service citations from the fields of government, business, and education.*

This chapter provides an overview of the role of audiovisuals in the training and instructional process. It is not intended to be totally comprehensive; the subject area would require a library shelf of volumes to treat in full detail. Instead, we shall scan several generic topics informally, describing the rationale and applications of various categories of AV media—and their logical place and function within the cycle of instructional development.

Before we begin, a few definitions will be helpful within the context of our overview.

Audiovisual communications is, in general terms, the application of technology to the art and science of transmitting ideas.

Technology implies the selection of a communications medium (or channel) to meet specific objectives of message transmission, in a system of elements which includes the sender, receiver, and environment (or setting) for reception.

Multimedia means simply that we select more than one presentation element to accomplish any single communications task. We base our choice on the objective, the audience, and the instructional strategies employed—plus practical criteria such as time and cost. The *media mix* may include a variety of presentational modes, including charts, texts, models, and the voice of the presenter. In short, any device or activity which contributes to the communications process can be properly classified as a useful element in *multimedia* or multimodal environments for learning.

HISTORICAL REFLECTION: FROM CAVE WALLS TO CENTER STAGE

Most scholarly dissertations on the history of communications usually begin with a description of early cave-wall drawings—which served as the documentary record and textbook of their time. The etchings and paintings were also effective *instructional* illustrations, orienting primeval youngsters to such skills as fishing and hunting and the avoidance of being stomped on by woolly mammoths.

But because this chapter is not intended as a historical treatise, we shall skip ahead several thousand years, to the period from 1935 to 1945, when most historians agree that "modern" communications technology began to establish a measurable impact in the instructional classroom. Chalkboards (in one form or other) had existed for centuries, and "magic lanterns" (kerosene and electric) and "talking machines" (cylinder and disk) had been used by a few pioneering instructors for several years, but it was the *widespread use of the 16mm sound motion picture projector* which first brought audiovisual technology into practical prominence in the classroom.

Instructional motion pictures of the '30s were largely travelogues, theatrical releases (used for discussion and analysis), and primitive lectures on film. But this *was* a start. Then, in 1941, wartime trainers suddenly needed to move vast numbers of people through orientation, attitude-building, and technical instruction which was both consistent and time- and cost-effective. To achieve their goal, they turned increasingly to training films and filmstrips, simulators, and a variety of "visual aids" (such as charts, flip charts, flannel boards, and models) in support of instruction at all levels. The success of media-augmented training was soon well documented, and concurrent research revealed that instruction *was* positively enhanced through audiovisual presentation and reinforcement of essential teaching points.

The Emergence of Instructional Technology

In the years that followed, audiovisual media maintained a generally accepted secondary status as "aids" to live instruction—until the emergence of instructional technology theory in the 1950s and 1960s. Because the new instructional environment was to be *learner-centered, any* presentational strategy was worth consideration, as long as it proved to be cost-effective and measurably efficient. In some cases, AV media began to assume a center-stage role for content presentation— freeing the instructor to concentrate on monitoring, tutoring, and evaluating trainee performance.

Many instructors were not comfortable with AV media for several reasons. Sophisticated programs were often complex to write and to produce; the additional cost factors of a media-intensive presentation were often prohibitive; and the presentation systems were not always completely reliable. Further, the end product was very, very visible—subject to instant criticism—and, in many cases, not equal in quality to what audiences had come to expect through contact with professional mass-media standards of television and film. And finally, many instructors and teachers were simply afraid to share their center-stage role with "one of those aids" or "one of those machines."

The "Software Gap"

As a result, the residual attitude toward AV media was: "We know audiovisuals have their place for enrichment on the fringe of the curriculum—but let us go slowly on further commitment until there is more reliable 'hardware' (equipment) and 'software' (programming) which is proof-tested, supportive, and readily available."

On the other hand, AV publishers, experiencing only modest purchaser interest in what was available, hesitated to produce more materials until they were certain that a substantial and growing buying market existed.

This "software gap" standoff existed throughout the '60s and into the '70s—and is only now easing. Several factors have brought about the change: (1) less expensive, more reliable AV systems entering the marketplace; (2) the availability of in-house production techniques which make program creation easy and inexpensive; (3) the accumulation of thousands of AV titles which have been well tested in the field; and (4) successful applications of media which, in turn, have encouraged additional applications.

The power of audiovisual communications is well documented, but as with any powerful instructional tool, each medium must be handled and directed with skill, planning, and an understanding of its strengths and limitations.

In the sections to follow, we shall discuss the classic place of media selection in the instructional design cycle—and then look at the various categories of tools available in a trainer's audiovisual arsenal.

AV MEDIA AND THE INSTRUCTIONAL DESIGN CYCLE

A common mistake made by trainers (or their managers) is to say, "We have a training problem; let's make a film." or "That video tape recorder is gathering dust; let's use it for our new orientation program." Each medium has its own distinct characteristics, advantages, and limitations—and the only way to ensure that you have chosen the appropriate medium for your message is to answer several questions first:

- What is the experience profile of your audience, and what must they be able to do, *know,* or *feel* upon completion of instruction?
- What is the nature of the content of instruction? Will sound, motion, color, animation, etc., be required to present the instructional message effectively? And what is the *minimum* content needed to accomplish established objectives?
- Where will instruction take place—and under what conditions?
- What sequencing and strategies of presentation, feedback, and evaluation appear to be most appropriate?
- Do you have the expertise and resources to develop a program which will use the appropriate medium to its best advantage?

It is also helpful to know as much as you can about the attention span of your viewers or listeners. How can you best catch and hold your audience's interest and willingness to learn? Some well-known learner types are portrayed in Fig. 43-1.

Media Selection

The point to be stressed here is that the selection of the "best" medium should come *after* the planning process described above. Shown schematically, the cycle of decision includes a chain of questions and events which *precedes* final media selection and subsequent program development (see Figs. 43-2 and 43-3).

The use of such decision charts can help in choosing the best medium for your particular communications mix. But it is well to remember that there is seldom a cookbook answer to the question: Which medium do I choose? There is simply no one best medium.

A good film is probably going to be better than a poor book—just as a well-written magazine article *may* be better than a so-so filmstrip. But what about the *perceptual preference* of the individuals in our audience? We know from experience that the "cognitive style" of a group of students may vary widely—some preferring print, and others preferring audiovisuals. And their relative level of achievement will vary in direct relation to the media mix we select or prescribe for each, assuming that content and presentation effectiveness are essentially equal.

A recent note from a veteran colleague in media put it this way: "The search for a fail-safe formula to make media selection easy simply has not produced much tangible result. Each study falls back on such terms as 'intuition' or 'empirical trial and error' or 'the systems approach.' Perhaps the most workable ground rule for media selection is that *the 'best' medium is simply the cheapest and simplest one that works.*"

Production Guidelines

Underscoring the "Keep it simple" concept of media selection, here are suggestions to bear in mind with your next project involving audiovisuals:

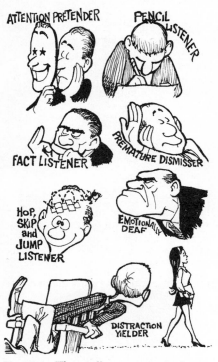

Fig. 43-1 The audience: some basic categories. *(Courtesy Association for Educational Communications and Technology.)*

1. Remember always to match media options against these criteria: relative reliability, ease of presentation, effectiveness, and cost.

    Remember that presentational complexity and author loss of control often go hand in hand. Programs sometimes skew off the track simply because producers do not fully understand the presentational power they are dealing with.

2. A "storyboard" is a *visualized* method of organizing the elements of a script, consisting of sketches representing images to appear on the screen. It is an essential planning device for seeing in advance what the program will look like — before smooth production begins (see Fig. 43-5).

It has been said that no one ever sets out to make a bad AV presentation, and yet many achieve that unfortunate distinction. Why? Most often because (*a*) the medium itself was incorrectly chosen and was asked to carry a message better suited to another, (*b*) the production techniques were substandard, or (*c*) too much content and superfluous effects crowded out the basic objectives of the transmission and overloaded the viewer's natural capacity to assimilate and process the information presented (compare the two examples in Fig. 43-6).

In AV production, the whole is always greater than the sum of the parts. As one veteran producer remarked, "You never *really* know what you have created until you see it on the screen. That first run-through is always an experience all its own! All elements together; ideas and images juxtaposed and flowing, affecting each idea and image which follows; and all mixed in unique combination with the perception and chemistry of the individual viewer. There are always surprises—some good, some not so good, as an AV

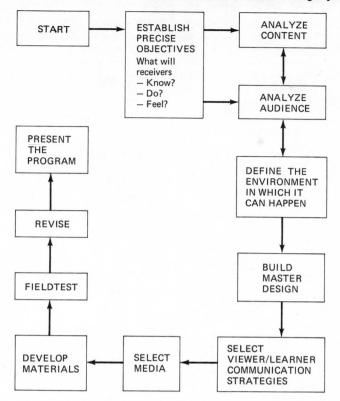

Fig. 43-2 Media selection and the instructional design process. *(Courtesy National Audio-Visual Association.)*

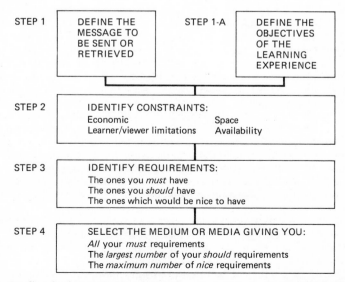

Fig. 43-3 Media selection: some questions to be asked. *(Courtesy National Audio-Visual Association.)*

show comes together. It is part of the fun. But *not* if you have not allowed enough production hours to make changes before the premiere!"

In preparing any slide (or filmstrip) presentation, it is always advisable to place all visuals on a "light table"—a back-lighted glass or plastic viewing surface—which permits you to see all slides in sequence. Then, reading the narration aloud, ensure that there are enough visuals to carry the message clearly and maintain a consistent, interesting rhythm and sequencing of graphic presentation. Although most producers try to introduce a new visual

Fig. 43-4 The importance of visuals in a presentation. *(Courtesy Association for Educational Communications and Technology.)*

every 8 to 15 seconds, there are many exceptions, depending on the slide's relative complexity—and the pacing desired for dramatic effectiveness. But in all cases, be sure to avoid a visual that "hangs" on the screen too long!

The eyes should keep moving over and through the visual. Once they *fix*— for lack of guidance by the visual itself or the narrative—a kind of hypnosis sets in, and the mind may turn off.

Conversely, remember that a powerful visual tends to impact with greater psychological force than spoken narration—and too much action on the screen will tend to subvert and drown out the audio portion of the program.

Professional AV scriptwriters concentrate on limiting the amount of spoken narrative to essential ideas only, written in a terse, conversational style. They realize that they are creating a *visual* presentation—and that the screen will be the focal point for the message they wish to convey. The professionals also avoid the use of "word slides" whenever possible, seeking instead a symbol, photograph, or other graphic to carry an idea with greater impact.

Music, well chosen, will add greatly to recorded sound tracks—and can provide smooth bridges between sequences of narration, allowing your audience to concentrate on the visual reinforcement of your message while they—and the narrator—catch their breath!

3. Keep in mind that audiovisual presentations are art forms in their own right. As in painting, it is best to start with simple images and uncomplicated conceptions. Then, as your skillfulness grows, new elements can be added to enhance the canvas. And certainly, if you are ever called upon to produce an AV masterpiece well beyond your natural level of comfortable experience, *seek help at once.* Talented resource and production professionals are available in almost every city. Call on one! It is well worth the investment to ensure that you—and what appears on the screen–*both* look good!

AV MEDIA: CAPSULE PROFILES

The following descriptions of individual AV media are provided through the courtesy of the National Audio-Visual Association, and most are adapted from the NAVA publication entitled *A User's Look at the Audio-Visual World* (see the Bibliography).

16mm Film Motion Pictures

AV users probably spend more dollars for 16mm projectors and films than for any other single kind of equipment. The medium has a long history of success; it is a familiar vehicle to both the viewer and the presenter. Many communicators rely on this medium because it can combine multiple elements (color, motion, action, plot, musical scoring)—all of which can contribute to the presentational effect.

There is a huge and growing library of films in the training and development field. Topics range from sales training to arc welding to the building of communications skills for managers. Some industrial concerns use so much 16 mm film that they have organized their own production units, although an increasing number now prefer to produce their in-house programs on video tape, for subsequent transfer to film (either 16mm or Super 8mm).

16mm Projector Types

- Totally manual threading requires the operator to loop the film by hand through the projector to the take-up reel.
- Semiautomatic methods permit operators to press a single lever which opens up an unobstructed path to thread and remove the film.
- Automatic loading permits the operator simply to insert the film into an entry slot; the machine will then propel the film around the proper path to the take-up reel.

Fig. 43-5 A typical form of visualized storyboard. *(Courtesy Association for Educational and Communications Technology.)*

Film Sound Systems   Sound is recorded on film by two methods (see Fig. 43-8).

- Optical sound tracks are composed of the same photographic emulsion as the picture portion of the film and are printed along the edge opposite from the sprocket holes. A small exciter lamp is used to project a beam of light through the track. The varying light patterns are "read" by a photoelectric cell—and converted to electronic signals fed to the audio amplifier.
- Magnetic sound tracks utilize a magnetic oxide strip bonded to the edge of the film. The sound is recorded on this track as in any other audio tape magnetic recording.

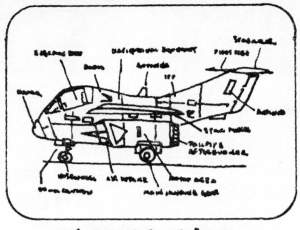

OVERCROWDED

8000-LB THRUST
TURBOJET ENGINE

SIMPLIFIED

Fig. 43-6 Two approaches to graphic representation. *(Courtesy Association for Educational Communications and Technology.)*

How much sound do you need? You will want at least 3 watts for an average meeting room, conference room, or classroom. All projectors have at least this much. For an auditorium of 500 seats, 10 watts probably will be sufficient.

Most projectors have a small built-in speaker system, but a remote speaker near the screen is almost always preferable for improved fidelity—and mental synchronization with the picture. Elevate the speaker to at least screen height and be sure to have masking tape on hand (or, better yet, 3-inch-wide carpet tape) to cover wires leading to the projector—or, sure enough, someone is bound to eventually trip over them in the dark.

Image Speed Control A special feature available on some motion picture

Fig. 43-7 Audiovisual presentation: some of the choices. (*Courtesy Association for Educational Communications and Technology.*)

machines is *analysis:* the capability to move the film through the projector at varying speeds so the viewer can analyze the action or the details of the image. Speeds range from very slow to total stop action—so you can examine individual frames. If you need this capability (as you might if you are documenting minute processes or teaching motion or movement), then be sure the machine you buy can deliver analysis capabilities. And check the films you plan to analyze: If the camera speed was not fast enough to record all the detail, no machine on earth can put that detail back in—no matter what the playback speed may be.

Super 8 and 8mm Film   An increasingly popular film format—especially for small audiences—is Super 8mm. Though we frequently call it 8mm, in truth

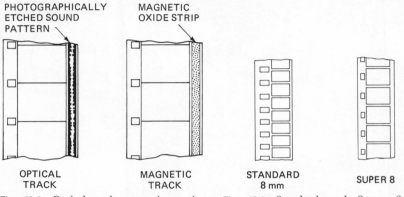

PHOTOGRAPHICALLY ETCHED SOUND PATTERN

MAGNETIC OXIDE STRIP

OPTICAL TRACK

MAGNETIC TRACK

STANDARD 8 mm

SUPER 8

Fig. 43-8 Optical and magnetic motion picture sound: a comparison.

Fig. 43-9 Standard and Super 8 film formats: a comparison.

Super 8 has really superseded it. Super 8's picture is larger and provides superior images and color—three-eighths the size of 16mm versus one-fourth for 8mm (see Fig. 43-9).

Super 8 is a common vehicle for single-concept films (often silent) and is extremely useful in one-to-one installations—where a single viewer is learning from the film.

What are the advantages of the format? What are some things to watch for? Here are some of them:

SUPER 8 CONSIDERATIONS

Advantages	*Things to watch for*
Cartridge loading or simplified reel-to-reel threading generally available	Less light output
	Less sharpness and clarity in large-screen projection
Small size	Greater visual "noise" in large-screen projection (because the frames are generally magnified proportionately larger than 16mm; thus flaws in the film are magnified on the screen)
Lightweight	
Fits single-concept presentation needs	
Readily adaptable to small rear-screen or front-screen applications	
	Fewer library titles available than with 16mm (although many can be special-ordered)
Lower equipment and print costs than 16mm (for both original production and purchase off the shelf)	

Some projectors have automatic controls which, on signal, can shift to slow motion, single-frame sequencing, or stop-action. Such features are especially valuable for use with programmed individual study.

In the Super 8 format, both optical and magnetic sound systems are side by side in the marketplace, with advocates for each. The compatibility question is contested and continuing. In many *small-screen* applications, Super 8 is supplanting 16mm—but the compatibility problem continues to hamper the growth of large 8mm libraries.

How Many Millimeters? For presentation purposes, which is better—16mm or

Fig. 43-10 35mm filmstrip. (*Courtesy National Audio-Visual Association.*)

Super 8? Here again there is no cookbook answer. But as openers, the following questions will be relevant:

1. How big is my group? (Does it go beyond a small projector's capability?)
2. Am I going to use front-screen or rear-screen projection, or maybe both? If a rear screen will be used, will it be a full-size screen or a miniscreen?
3. Is all the material I need available in the format I am considering?
4. Will I be producing my own films, or will I be buying or renting from outside sources?
5. Do I want magnetic sound systems so that I can record my own sound tracks directly on the film? (16mm magnetic sound projectors are rare—and dual-system machines are comparatively expensive.)

Filmstrips

A filmstrip is a series of still pictures on a strip of film (usually 35mm, but increasingly 16mm or Super 8mm), often accompanied by a sound program (see Fig. 43-10). The accompanying sound track may be on records, audio cassettes, or conventional ¼-inch audio tape.

"Automatic advance" projectors are increasingly popular—utilizing inaudible pulses on the record or tape to call up the next visual automatically, instead of the audible bell or beep required by manual systems. Virtually all professional filmstrip programs today are published with both automatic and manual cue systems available to the user.

The cost of producing a filmstrip is usually considerably less than that of producing a motion picture—and so this approach is appealing whenever it will adequately convey the message. Another factor of new technology is the rise of cassette-based systems: they now represent more than half of the filmstrip projectors sold with sound, and they are increasing in sales percentages each year. (A plus for cassettes: high-quality sound which can be both conveniently played with the picture and studied later without the picture on portable cassette playback machines.)

In the past, filmstrips were often an alternative medium when the communicator could not afford more expensive motion pictures. And all too often, early products were little more than illustrated lectures. But a new generation of programming has begun to offer excellent presentational values, including modern scoring and narration with high-impact graphics and photography.

FILMSTRIP CONSIDERATIONS

Advantages	Things to watch for	Tips to the user
ECONOMY Filmstrips are comparatively inexpensive AV communications tools The user can accumulate a large library	Request previews (when offered) prior to purchase	
EASE OF TRANSPORTATION The projector is lightweight, portable, and self-contained	Can easily be misplaced (especially the 16mm filmstrips)	Buy files and reference drawers for your library
WIDE RANGE OF PROGRAMS NOW AVAILABLE	May need adaptation to fit your particular situation	Create presentation guides which apply to your own needs
CONTROL OF CONTENT Every audience sees the same program	Must always be shown in the same sequence (unlike separate slides, which can be edited and rearranged)	Add discussions after showings Insert case studies before or after showings Design interactive texts for use with the filmstrip Record multiple narrative audio tracks for different audiences

The effective use of the filmstrip boils down, as is true of just about every medium, to the skill of the planner and developer—and their ingenuity in maximizing:

1. The strengths of the medium itself
2. The impact of the messages selected for presentation
3. The accompanying content (pre- and postpresentation discussion) which makes the program relevant and meaningful to particular audiences

Slide Projectors

A slide projector is basic equipment in most AV installations. Of the several sizes and formats, 2 × 2 (35 mm), is most common. Nowadays, 3½ × 4 lantern slides are seldom used except when projecting on very large screens or when extremely fine image detail is needed. New minislide formats appeal primarily to the home market (see Fig. 43-11).

"Slide-tape" presentations are growing more and more popular. In these packages, the projector is advanced automatically by an inaudible pulse on one stereo channel; the second channel of the tape presents the audio message, narration, or music. Several excellent self-contained machines are now on the market, in addition to separate synchronizers which can be interconnected with stereo tape and projector components.

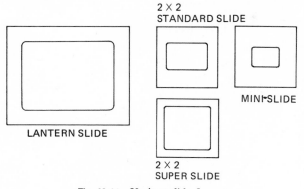

Fig. 43-11   Various slide formats.

Tips for Projector Users

1. Buy a full selection of lenses (including zoom) for varying room and screen sizes.
2. Everyone worries about lamp failure. As a simple antidote to the worry, note the date of installation on the lamp housing. Then replace the lamp on a regular basis *before* it blows. Excessively darkened filaments and glass housing indicate the lamp has burned for several hours—and should probably be replaced. Keep the old lamps for backups (in noncritical situations).
3. Buy a carrying case for your projector; cases give you both portability and protection. (And, of course, get a case big enough to hold those spare lamps, extra cords, and adapters you should always carry!)
4. Consider a projector table—particularly one with telescoping legs to elevate the light beam over the audience.
5. Beware of supercapacity trays, which may jam when slides warp or fray slightly at the corners. Thicker slides are not compatible with these large-capacity trays.
6. Protect the cardboard mounts of your slides with metal or plastic sleeves. Be cautious when using glass-mounted slides in high-intensity light projectors. In some models, the lamp heat may "cook" or blister the film emulsion.
7. Provide drawers and cases to store your slides. Systematic filing systems are a good investment—and especially popular are clear plastic sheets which hold several slides per page; these give quick visual access in loose-leaf notebook binders.
8. Your presentations can be enhanced by the addition of a dissolve system which alternates two projectors focused on the same screen, creating a smooth visual transition between slides by fading on and overlapping their images during the change from one to the next (see Fig. 43-12). Additionally, a two-projector dissolve system is especially useful in longer presentations because it doubles the carrying capacity for slides (two trays instead of one).

9. A "special-effects" technique used by some presenters: slides incorporating a light-polarizing film, projected through a revolving polarized filter—to create the illusion of motion. The effect is particularly useful in animating diagrams, schematics, and dramatic visuals designed to capture attention.

Overhead Projection

An overhead projector places an image on a screen by passing light through a transparent acetate, or other cell, which lies on the horizontal glass face ("stage") of the projector.

To create colorful visuals prior to or during a presentation, one can use water-soluble pens, wax pencils, and permanent felt-tip pens. (Not just any wax pencil or

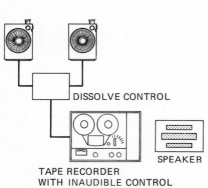

Fig. 43-12 Tape recorder utilizing inaudible central pulser to advance projectors.

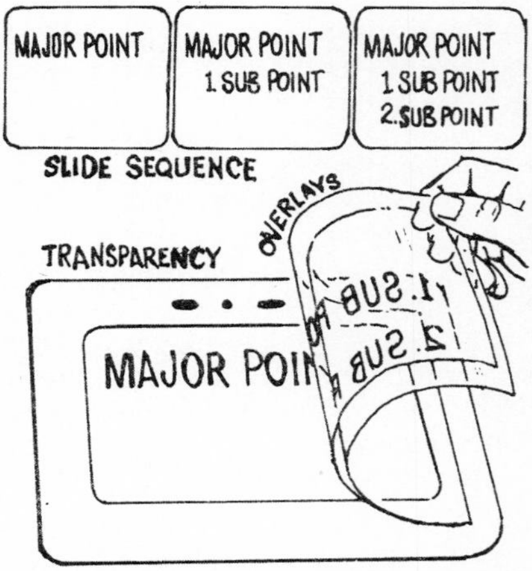

Fig. 43-13 Building a visual with acetate overlays. (*Courtesy Association for Educational Communications and Technology.*)

felt-tip pen will project color; they tend to "break up," fade, or project a black image unless specially designed for overhead projection.)

Overhead presentations are often improved by such techniques as:

- Acetate overlays which build a complex visual one step at a time (see Fig. 43-13)
- Translucent plastic models to show interaction of moving parts
- Negative acetates with brightly colored images against a black background
- Color photograph "lifts" transferred from clay-based paper (frequently used in pictorial magazines) to special clear acetate designed for projection
- Polarized light transparencies with a rotating filter to create the illusion of motion

Some important advantages of the overhead projector are:

1. The presenter or instructor can face the audience.
2. Both the sender and receiver can work in an undarkened room, with ample light for two-way communication, eye contact, and note taking.
3. Transparencies are generally easy to make.
4. The machine is relatively simple, and maintenance is not a problem if users take proper care of their equipment.

Opaque Projection

One big advantage of an opaque projector is its ability to project an image of any flat opaque object—such as a map or a page from a book. The user need not convert to any other format; it is a one-step process.

Utilization of opaque projectors nowadays tends to occur in special applications where intricate drawings need to be examined by a group. Some people use the projector to trace drawings onto chalkboards before the regular session—or to trace drawings onto larger charts for repeated future use.

One caution when using the opaque projector: There is an ever-present temptation just to insert an overloaded page into the projector—and to think you have a visual aid. Tiny lines in complex drawings may not communicate, and so users of opaque projectors would do well to keep the material so simple that every element, when projected, will be big enough and clear enough for every viewer to see it. But then, of course, that is true for every good visual, regardless of the projection technique.

Projection Screens

A media user should know about the two categories of projection: front-screen and rear-screen:

Front-screen projection utilizes an image projected on the front surface of a light-reflecting screen—from a projector within or behind the audience.

Rear-screen projection utilizes an image projected on the back surface of a semitranslucent screen placed between the viewer and the projector. Mirrors into which the projector is aimed, and which reverse the image for normal viewing in front of the screen, are a typical component of rear-screen systems (see Fig. 43-14).

Front-projection screens are of four general types:

FRONT-PROJECTION SCREENS

Type	Advantages	Things to remember
Beaded	Brightness	The beads may rub off
	High light return	Narrower viewing range than Matte White
		Highly reflective of ambient light; thus stray light must be controlled
Matte White (vinyl laminated to fiber glass or cheesecloth	Most accurate sharpness and color of image	Lower light return than beaded screen
	Wider angle of view than beaded screen	
Lenticular	Brightness; return light with sharpness nearly equal to beaded screen	Some problem with light falloff for audiences on side angles from screen
	Rejects ambient light from some angles	

FRONT-PROJECTION SCREENS   *(Continued)*

Type	*Advantages*	*Things to remember*
Superbright	Brightest of all; can even be used in some outdoor daylight conditions	Narrowest viewing angle of all (viewing clarity from the sides falls off sharply)

Rear projection is becoming increasingly popular for installations ranging from large, permanent in-the-wall settings (see Fig. 43-15) to tiny portable screens used on tabletops for sales presentations or individualized study.

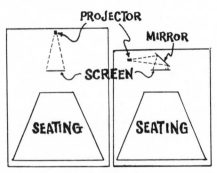

Fig. 43-14   Rear-screen projection: two methods. *(Courtesy Association for Educational Communications and Technology.)*

Fig. 43-15   Modern presentation room utilizing rear-screen projection. *(Courtesy National Audio-Visual Association.)*

The materials for rear-projection screens tend to fall into three types. The chart below lists them and tells a bit about each.

REAR-PROJECTION SCREENS

Material	Common uses	Advantages and features
Glass	Large screens Permanent location	Easy to clean Good sound isolation
Plexi/acrylic	Small- or large- screen locations	Lightweight Resistant to breakage
Flexible	Small screens Portable equipment	Portable Lightweight

In rear-screen installations, the projection booth design is a key factor—even if it is just a simple box to house a projector for a student-learning carrel or display unit. The critical elements to provide are:

1. Space to accommodate all system elements
2. Lamp power for comfortable viewing
3. Adequate noise control
4. Good ventilation
5. Control of ambient light within the booth, which can diminish the light quality on the screen

Regardless of whether front-screen or rear-screen projection is utilized, here are two classic formulas which will be helpful:

1. How big a screen do I need? The width of the screen should be at least one-sixth the distance that the farthest viewer is seated from the screen.
2. How close to the screen can I place my viewers? The nearest viewer should be two widths away from the screen to avoid eye fatigue and discomfort.

Audio Tape

Four general types of audio tape systems are now on the market: (1) the reel-to-reel tape deck, (2) the compact cassette, (3) the eight-track cartridge, and (4) the continuous cartridge (see Fig. 43-16).

Reel-to-reel is the senior member of the quartet, utilizing ¼-inch tape and running at speeds which may vary, depending on the playback machine and application, from $^{15}/_{16}$ inches per second to 15 inches per second.

Marketing trends indicate growing acceptance of the internationally standard compact cassette. Literally hundreds of millions of cassettes have been sold recently throughout the world. Directly related to their success are their unique advantages: playback machine portability, relatively low cost, range of program flexibility, and the ease with which they can be stored, played, and replayed—anytime and anywhere.

The cassette's running time is determined, of course, by the length of its tape. But cassette casings are all the same size. Thus the longer the running time, the thinner the tape. A C-60 cassette plays for 60 minutes (30 minutes on each side); a thinner-tape C-120 cassette provides two hours of recording (60 minutes on each side). Many cassette users feel that any tape thinner than C-60 stock increases the chances of stretching or jamming—although recent breakthroughs in tape technology promise improving reliability and fidelity for virtually all configurations.

Compact cassettes use $\frac{1}{8}$-inch-wide tape, moving $1\frac{7}{8}$ inches per second from one spindle to another. Up to four separate tracks can be recorded across the width of the $\frac{1}{8}$-inch tape.

Eight-track cartridges utilize $\frac{1}{4}$-inch-wide tape running at $3\frac{3}{4}$ inches per second. Thus the tape is wider and moves more rapidly than in the cassette format. The faster speed provides somewhat better sound reproduction fidelity (associated equipment permitting), and consequently the cartridge has remained the first choice of the music industry. Up to eight separate tracks can be recorded across the width of the $\frac{1}{4}$-inch tape.

Continuous cartridges employ a tape loop for repeated playback of a relatively short recorded message—usually for displays and exhibits. The tape width can be either $\frac{1}{8}$ or $\frac{1}{4}$ inch—and tape length varies with the total time of the recorded program and the carrying capacity of the cartridge itself.

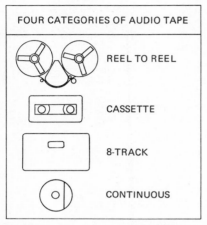

FOUR CATEGORIES OF AUDIO TAPE

REEL TO REEL

CASSETTE

8-TRACK

CONTINUOUS

Fig. 43-16   Four categories of audio tape.

Tape Duplication   When you need tapes in large quantities, you may consider purchasing an in-house duplicator. In this case, your main buying criterion should be quality control: assurance that every tape will be a valid reproduction of the master. Few areas in the AV field have grown as rapidly as tape duplication, and the market today offers many excellent duplicators.

When problems arise, they usually stem from the speed at which tapes operate while being duplicated; such high speeds necessitate high-quality materials plus close attention by skilled operators.

Do you need duplication equipment in your AV tool kit? The primary question is volume: Do you duplicate so many tapes that it would be cost-effective to make your own, or would outside vendors be a more economical alternative?

Remember, too, that there are legal implications. Professional tapes are protected by copyright: to duplicate them is to break the law! The Educational Media Producers Council policy statement explains: "We are not against the duplication of our materials; we are against unauthorized duplication."

Video

The potential applications of video technology are virtually limitless: to share messages from management, to capture visualized lectures for training programs, and to monitor remote workplaces, for example. Video tape can serve in support of training which otherwise might be impractical or uneconomical—as feedback for sensitivity and group dynamics sessions, and as reports from remote project management, and as profit centers which produce tapes for other uses.

Video is especially useful because of its instant-replay capabilities: for speech/sales/instructor role playing and self-critique, for time and motion studies, and even for rehearsals for productions which will subsequently be recorded in final form on motion picture film.

But as with all good things, there are also some negative factors to consider when contemplating a major investment in present-day video systems.

As one sadder but wiser media specialist remarked recently, "Video technology is a popular bandwagon to jump on—but look before you leap. The wagon is moving very fast." Any experienced user will tell you that this is a real danger zone—not because video capabilities are overestimated, but because the equipment is so very sophisiticated and the technology is in flux and moving in new directions.

There are two essential considerations: (1) that the system you install will fully fit your needs, and (2) that the budgeting you plan will maintain the system you install. This takes us to a major point: The greatest single mistake made by

Fig. 43-17   Television sound stage. *(Courtesy National Audio-Visual Association.)*

purchasers is a commitment to hardware before they clearly formulate its utilization and effectiveness. The financial commitment only barely begins with the purchase price. In fact, the front-end investment is, in the long run, the least of the video expenditure. The budget must include plans for secondary expenditures: the operating personnel; maintenance, repair, and production costs; distribution, updating, and inventory; scripts, sets, and creative consultants; etc. Old-timers point out that without the cash to support the system, the investment is like buying a rocket without fuel. A tried-and-true maxim, equally applicable to both yachtsmen and video specialists, is "Start small and achieve success—then buy up."

This definitely does not mean buying piecemeal. Since the buying decisions in video equipment do indeed represent major financial commitments, they deserve time—they deserve the systems approach, in which you define the ultimate output first and then identify the components and capabilities required to produce that output.

When you invest in a video tape system, be certain that it will be the medium for many messages—that you have access to (or a staff that can produce) tapes for many programs—for a good many years to come.

The "Video Revolution"   Millions of words have been generated in the trade and popular press recently about the "video revolution"—made possible by the advent of new easy-to-use cartridges, cassettes, and disks. At the moment, the marketplace is filled with competing formats, and the number is growing. Some of the new entries are promising; others may never reach the production line. It is well for the prospective buyer to step carefully—and to ask such questions as:

1. Is the equipment design stable and not likely to become obsolete—at least for the life of my purchase?

2. What is the equipment performance record—and is adequate, trained service help available when needed?
3. Is required software on the shelf? Will there be more?
4. Is compatibility with other video systems in my AV network an important consideration?
5. Is there a competitive system on the way which may dominate the market and force others to change or leave the field? Where will I be then?

In the final analysis, video tape recording is simply another means of extending our ability to communicate—nothing more, nothing less. There is no magic in machines. The skill and imagination of the communicators behind the cameras make the magic happen!

Easel Graphics

Before leaving our capsule review of media categories, a few words are certainly in order for training's classic *visual aids*—generally referred to as *easel graphics.*

Easel graphics are the most commonly used aids—and possibly the most commonly misused. As one red-eyed speech critic once said, "If all the poorly done charts in the world were taken from speakers and laid end to end—it would be a blessing!"

W. J. Connelly, writing for the Association of National Advertisers, suggests that "The most common fault is for a speaker to go on the assumption that if he or she can read the chart from 3 feet, the back row of the audience can read the chart from 100 feet." Some basic rules for all easel graphics, whether the device be a flip chart, chalkboard, magnetic chalkboard, or hook-and-loop board, are:

- Do not use more than four or five words per line.
- Do not have more than three vertical columns.
- Do not use vertical dividing lines—use space.
- Do condense information.
- Do use large symbols and abbreviations.
- Do eliminate every unnecessary word or figure.
- Do design your material so that it can be read easily in the back row of the audience.
- Do remember that the larger the symbol, the greater its visual impact will be.

Flip Charts   Flip charts are well known: a series of visual sheets (usually paper or plastic) hinged together as a display unit. Their name comes from the fact you flip the separate sheets into view as you progress through the presentation. They are usually associated with tabletop or small-group presentations, rather than with large audiences.

Chalkboards   These are, for presentation purposes, in the scope of "easel graphics" because in portable form they generally use an easel stand for support. A very old and familiar presentation technique, chalkboards are contemporary and effective in the hands of a person who will take the time to plan ahead. They give a special emphasis:

1. When they punctuate a presentation with specific visual reinforcement, *not* the presenter's doodles
2. When all images are large, clear, and fully readable

Chalkboards are now available in several pastel shades, and many have metal backing to permit magnets to be used to attach visuals and symbols to the surface during presentations.

A new type of write-on "chalkboard" has been developed which uses colored ink pens instead of chalk—and a specially treated surface which can be cleaned with a single wipe of a felt eraser.

Slap Boards Flannel or hook-and-loop boards, magnetic boards, and similar display boards are classified as "slap boards" because the speaker "slaps" or places pieces of printing, drawings, or photographs on the surface of the display board.

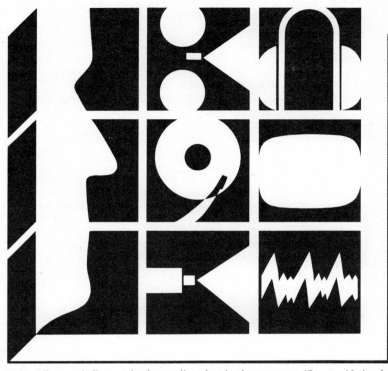

Fig. 43-18 The magic lies not in the medium but in the message. *(Courtesy National Audio-Visual Association.)*

With the hook-and-loop (or Velcro) board, small adhesive strips are placed on the back of the object to be displayed (words, symbols, photographs, etc.). The front surfaces of the strips are covered with many tiny nylon fiber hooks which grab the looped surface of a flannel-like display board. The bonding principle has remarkable holding power—and is rapidly replacing older-style flock boards, which for years were a presentation-room staple.

Magnetic boards are made with a write-on metal face or are sometimes covered with a surface of thin, soft fabric. Display pieces (words, symbols, objects) are prepared with magnetic backing—for instant cling to the board.

End results with both types of board are the same. The speaker can create an effective and occasionally dramatic presentation by adding each display element, step by step, visually as the narrative progresses.

POSTSCRIPT: THE MEDIUM, THE MESSAGE, AND THE MASTER PLAN

"Telling-showing-doing" is considered a basic formula for effective instructional sequencing. And it is well documented that audiovisual communications can do much to achieve the telling and showing in consistent, compelling ways.

The magic lies not only in the *medium* but equally in the *message:* one which is responsive to objectives, appropriate to the target population, and presented with style and professionalism.

The evolution of effective audiovisual communications has directly paralleled the growth of the training and development profession itself—advanced in like measure by individuals who realize that their craft must be at all times a blend of science, art, and understanding.

BIBLIOGRAPHY

Textbooks, Booklets, and Magazine Articles

Anderson, Ron H.: "Selection of Media: Another Perspective," *Improving Human Performance,* vol. 3, no. 3, Fall 1974.

The Audio-Visual Equipment Directory, National Audio-Visual Association, Fairfax, Va., 1974.

Bretz, Rudy: *A Taxonomy of Communications Media,* Educational Technology Publications, Englewood Cliffs, N.J., 1971.

Broadwell, Martin M.: "The Use and Misuse of A-V," *Media,* October–November 1971.

Brown, J. S.: *A-V Instruction: Technology, Media, and Message,* 4th ed., McGraw-Hill Book Company, New York, 1973.

Dale, Edgar: *Audiovisual Methods in Teaching,* McGraw-Hill Book Company, New York, 1973.

Designing for Educational Technology, Educational Facilities Laboratories Monograph, New York, 1971.

Educational Facilities with New Media, Educational Facilities Laboratories Monograph, New York, 1966.

Hays, Robert: *Practically Speaking: In Business, Industry and Government,* Addison-Wesley Publishing Company, Inc., Reading, Mass., 1969.

Index to Kodak Information, Eastman Kodak Co., Pamphlet L5, Rochester, N.Y., 1970.

Instructional Hardware: A Guide to Architectural Requirements, Educational Facilities Laboratories Monograph, New York, 1970.

Kemp, Jerrold E.: *Planning and Producing Audiovisual Materials,* Intext, Scranton, Pa., 1968.

Kemp, Jerrold E.: *Instructional Design: A Plan for Unit and Course Development,* Fearon Publishers, Inc., Calif., 1971.

McLuhan, Marshall: *Understanding Media: The Extension of Man,* McGraw-Hill Book Company, New York, 1964.

McVey, G. F.: "Television: Some Viewer-Display Considerations," *A-V Communications Review,* vol. 18, no. 3, Fall 1970.

McVey, G. F.: *Sensory Factors in the School Learning Environment,* National Education Association, Washington, 1971.

The Message Is You, Association for Educational Communications and Technology, Washington, 1971.

   (A booklet containing articles and additional bibliography of commercial pamphlets on preparing and projecting visual aids.)

Minor, E. O., and H. R. Frye: *Techniques for Producing Visual Instructional Media,* McGraw-Hill Book Company, New York, 1970.

Multimedia Classrooms Revisited, Educational Facilities Laboratories Monograph, New York, 1971.

New Spaces for Learning, Educational Facilities Laboratories Monograph, New York, 1966.

O'Sullivan, P. Kevin: *The Psychology of Sound,* National Audio-Visual Association, Fairfax, Va., 1974.

Quick, J., and Herbert Wolff: *Small Tape Video Production,* Addison-Wesley Publishing Company, Inc., Reading, Mass., 1972.

Rigg, Robinson P.: *Audiovisual Aids and Techniques,* Hamish Hamilton Ltd., London, 1969.

   (Distributed in the United States by Olympic Film Service, 161 West 22d Street, New York, N.Y. 10011.)

Smith, Welby, and Grayson Mattingly: *Introducing the Single Camera VTR System,* Smith-Mattingly Productions Ltd., Washington, 1971.

Tickton, Sidney G.: *To Improve Learning: An Evaluation of Instructional Technology,* R. R. Bowker Company, New York, 1970.

Tremaine, H. H.: *Audio Cyclopedia,* 2d ed., Howard W. Sams & Co., Inc., New York, 1969.

Vetter, Richard H.: "A Study of the Significance of Motion in Educational Film Communication," doctoral dissertation, University of California at Los Angeles, June 1959.

Wadsworth, Raymond: "1W, 2W, 3W, 4W, 5W, 6W: Law for Audio-Visual Presentations," *American School and University,* October 1971.

Yerges, L. F.: *Sound, Noise and Vibration Control,* Van Nostrand Reinhold, Incorporated, New York, 1969.

Periodicals

American School and University, North American Publishing Co., 134 Thirteenth Street, Philadelphia, Pa. 19107.

Audio-Visual Communications, United Business Publications, 450 Third Avenue, New York, N.Y. 10017.

Audio-Visual Instruction, Association for Educational Communications and Technology, 1201 Sixteenth Street, Washington, D.C. 20036.

Biomedical Communications, United Business Publications, 750 Third Avenue, New York, N.Y. 10017.

Business Screen, Harcourt Brace Jovanovich Publications, 757 Third Avenue, New York, N.Y. 10017.

Educational and Industrial Television, C. S. Tepfer Publishing Co., Inc., 607 Main Street, Ridgefield, Conn. 06877.

Educational Broadcasting, Acolyte Publications Corp., 825 South Barrington Avenue, Los Angeles, Calif. 90049.

Educational Technology, Educational Technology Publications, Inc., 140 Sylvan Avenue, Englewood Cliffs, N.J. 07632.

Film News, 250 West 57th Street, New York, N.Y. 10019.

Industrial Photography, United Business Publications, 750 Third Avenue, New York, N.Y. 10017.

Media and Methods, 134 North Thirteenth Street, Philadelphia, Pa. 19107.

Meetings & Conventions, Gellert Publishing Co., 1 Park Avenue, New York, N.Y. 10016.

National Report for Training and Development, American Society for Training and Development, P.O. Box 5307, Madison, Wis. 53705.

Nation's Schools, McGraw-Hill, Inc. 230 West Monroe Street, Chicago, Ill. 60606.

NAVA News, National Audio-Visual Association, 3150 Spring Street, Fairfax, Va. 22030.

Previews, R. R. Bowker Co., A Xerox Education Co., 1180 Avenue of the Americas, New York, N.Y. 10036.

Sales Meetings, Bill Communications, Inc., 1212 Chestnut Street, Philadelphia, Pa. 19107.

School Product News, 614 Superior Avenue, West Cleveland, Ohio 44113.

Training, Lakewood Publications, Inc., 731 Hennepin Ave., Minneapolis, Minn. 55403.

Training and Development Journal, American Society for Training and Development, P.O. Box 5307, Madison, Wis. 53705.

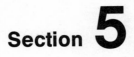

Section **5**

Training and Development Resources

Chapter **44**

Literature Searching and Surveillance

STANLEY M. GRABOWSKI

Stanley M. Grabowski *is Professor of Education and Chairperson, Department of Community Colleges and Continuing Education, School of Education, Boston University. He is also Vice Chairperson of the Commission on Planning Adult Learning Systems, Facilities, and Environments of the Adult Education Association of the U.S.A. Formerly he was Director of the ERIC Clearinghouse on Adult Education at Syracuse University. The preceding year he spent as Director of Training and Curriculum Materials at the Gerontology Center at Syracuse University. For eight years he was Director of the Institute of Adult Education in Bayonne, New Jersey. He received his undergraduate degree from Seton Hall University, South Orange, New Jersey, and an M.S. and a Ph.D. in adult education from Syracuse University. He has written more than 400 articles, reviews, and books. Besides being interested and experienced in adult education and information science, he has over 20 years of experience in teaching and conducting seminars and institutes in leadership training and motivation in education and industry.*

The years which have elapsed since the first edition of Training and Development Handbook was published have been marked by vast changes in society. It is a commonplace to say that only change is unchanging in our times. Mirroring the changes of society at large have been the changes in the field of training and development.

Patrick Farbro, writer of the Foreword to the first edition, was well aware of the many changes taking place and anticipated that even greater and more rapid changes would affect training. He noted:

> When this handbook is revised sometime in the future, or when another one is prepared, it will no doubt be drastically different. If not, directors of training and development will not be integrating into their practice the research results coming from the social and behavioral-sciences laboratories, or the social and behavioral researchers will not have produced results significant to organizational training and development or communications between the two will not have been effective.

The 1967 handbook was a product of its time and reflected this in what it covered and what it omitted. For example, the subject of this chapter was not included, but there was a chapter on related reading, which dealt with reading as a way of learning, changing, and developing within a training program. It outlined the purposes of reading, motivation, the need for improving reading ability, kinds of reading, and the evaluation of reading. That chapter contained nothing about literature searching and surveillance.

It was only in the late 1960s that information storage and retrieval systems began to spring up with the newer, more sophisticated computer programs. Since then, the information explosion, especially of educational material, has reached such staggering proportions that only a complex computer system can keep track of everything.

If there ever *was* a time when trainers could get by with a few standard textbooks, surely they no longer can be effective unless they stay abreast of current literature in their field as well as in related fields. They must search the literature on a regular basis if they are to know about the latest research findings and current practices relevant to their needs.

Trainers cannot afford to feel complacent about their competence acquired through formal education and training. The reality of life is such that they, like all other professionals, are prone to obsolescence. Past knowledge becomes quickly outdated, and even the best-trained trainers are in danger of losing their effectiveness.

Samuel Dubin, a psychologist at the Pennsylvania State University, figured out that the half-life of most professionals varies between five and ten years, depending on their professions. Half-life is the time after finishing formal training when professionals become only half as competent as they were upon graduation if they have not continued to learn about new developments in their field.

Another reason a trainer must be conversant with literature searching and surveillance is economy. Cost is always a factor in figuring training budgets. One way to keep costs down is for the trainer to know how to search the literature efficiently.

A cursory search of the literature, especially if it is not orderly, will waste a lot of precious time and yield inadequate results—or, worse, misleading information. Trainers must search thoroughly in the literature to find exactly what they need. In addition, their search must be so structured that it will allow them to select from among several alternatives. Otherwise, they run the risk of accepting a program which is neither valid nor reliable. The end result of a poor search will be wasted time at a huge cost of money.

HOW TO KEEP UP WITH THE LITERATURE

Systematic Scanning   No one book or even a catalog of resources suffices to keep trainers well informed about all the developments in their field. On the other hand, there are so many information sources today that trainers are hard put trying to decide what to read. A time factor also dictates some kind of selectivity. Even if trainers wanted to read everything, they just would not have the time to do so.

One way trainers can stay on top of the literature—at least to the extent of becoming aware of what is available—is to get into the practice of scanning a wide range of materials. The importance of this function could be underscored by saying that trainers ought to be almost compulsive in this regard if they want to be on top of the latest developments reported in the literature.

Some of the suggestions listed below will not require any efforts out of the ordinary for conscientious trainers. In many instances they will already be doing some of these things in the course of their regular reading. The point to be made here is that trainers would do well to set time aside at least once a month to follow as many of the listed suggestions as possible.

Book Reviews   One of the first things that come to mind when a trainer thinks of scanning the literature is to follow book reviews in professional journals and periodicals. These reviews will normally cover a handful of the most talked-about, if not the most important, books appearing in the field. The limited amount of space in most journals and periodicals precludes extensive book-review sections. The preferences of the editor in the selection of titles limits the number and kind of books reviewed. Although book reviews provide a very limited resource to the literature, they are a good starting point.

Book Advertisements   Another source of information about the literature is advertisements. Some publishers advertise their latest books in professional journals and periodicals. They also issue lists of their books, often categorized by subjects. While book advertisements and publishers' lists give very little critical insight into the contents of the books and their quality, they do serve the purpose of alerting the trainer to their availability. Trainers do not have to read all the books they see advertised, nor do they have to buy them all. Even if they had the time to read all the books advertised, they would find many of them not worth either the time or the money. Still, knowing that some of the books are available adds to a trainer's bank of resources.

Footnotes and References   A highly rewarding activity—one which many trainers are apt to skip—is scanning footnotes and references in journal articles and books. Authors often do extensive "homework" in preparation for their writing. They may have read many more documents than they actually used for quotations. Their footnotes and references may include some "fugitive" documents, the kind which are not readily available through normal publication channels. For example, they may include speeches, reports, and unpublished papers that might otherwise never come to the attention of the reader.

Bibliographies   Similarly, scanning bibliographies can reveal documents that might otherwise evade a trainer. Bibliographies on specific topics may be somewhat lengthy if they purport to be comprehensive in coverage. Such bibliographies can provide several options for trainers, giving them an opportunity to select exactly the one or two books dealing with a rather discrete issue.

Abstract Catalogs   An excellent way to find out what is appearing in the literature is to scan some of the abstract catalogs such as *Research in Education, Current Index to Journals in Education, Education Index,* and *Current Contents Education.*

Research in Education and *Current Index to Journals in Education* are published monthly for the Educational Resources Information Center (ERIC) of the National Institute of Education. *Research in Education* carries abstracts of about 1,000 documents each month and covers a wide range of education, including adult education and training. A companion catalog, *Current Index to Journals in Education,* carries annotations of journal articles, covering some journals regularly on a cover-to-cover basis and many others on a selective basis. In all, more than 500 journals are indexed in *Current Index to Journals in Education.*

Another journal catalog is *Education Index,* which does not provide annotations and which covers far fewer journals than *Current Index to Journals in Education.*

Current Contents Education is a weekly guide which provides tables of contents in the original form of 600 foreign and domestic journals.

Sometimes colleagues can be of help in directing a trainer to such valuable journals. Sometimes university professors can suggest useful journals in their areas of specialty. But these are complementary resources, at best. Trainers would profit more by looking at *Current Index to Journals in Education* to discover for themselves the variety of journals in their fields of interest as well as the kinds of articles these journals carry. Using this catalog, trainers can decide for themselves what journals they would actually like to see.

Contact with Colleagues   Every profession generates literature that never gets published. Some of it consists of reports and so-called in-house studies that are not deemed to be of general interest to others. As a result, these documents are not circulated through ordinary channels, such as journals and periodicals. Some of these fugitive documents may find their way into an information system such as ERIC and become readily accessible to those who know that the system exists and know how to use it. But there are numerous documents that stay with an individual trainer who has generated them. The only way such documents are made known to others is through informal contact with colleagues.

This informal network, sometimes called the "invisible university," consists of colleagues with similar or complementary interests who exchange their writings. Sometimes these documents are at draft stages, but often they are completed documents not intended for general circulation. In addition, this informal interpersonal network of trainers is a means of exchange of information in which interested individuals meet together to discuss emerging topics of mutual interest. Such meetings of colleagues may take place at conferences as well as through direct personal contact.

Trainers can learn about new knowledge, ideas, and practices through the invisible university, as well as test out some of their new theories and approaches with their colleagues. The additional advantage of discussing an idea with a colleague who has written it up is the direct confrontation about its implementation, implications, and evaluation with the author. The opportunity to ask an author questions can help to clarify issues and discover the little tricks, hints, and techniques which can be very helpful but which sometimes are left out of the writing.

HOW TO USE PERIODICALS

Different Kinds and Uses

All trainers are familiar with several journals and periodicals they judge necessary to read. They have their own reasons for selecting the journals, depending on their job and their needs.

Some of the journals they select will be directly connected with training and development. For example, a trainer might choose to read the following journals regularly: *Training and Development Journal, NSPI Research Quarterly, Training in Business and Industry, Personnel Journal,* and the *International Journal of Continuing Education and Training*. A trainer may find that all the articles are relevant to his or her needs and will read these journals from cover to cover. After reading them, the trainer will tend to file the entire journal for future reference.

In addition to the journals dealing directly with their field, trainers may peruse other journals which are in another field but which have a tangential relationship to training and development. For example, a trainer might look at *Adult Education, Adult Leadership, Journal of Extension,* and *Educational and Industrial Television*. Trainers probably would read these journals selectively, choosing only those articles which they consider pertinent to their work or interest. Because trainers do not need to keep these journals for reference, they might do best to tear out only those occasional articles they want to save and file and then throw away the rest.

Even when reading so-called popular journals, trainers ought to be on the lookout for pertinent material they might use in their work. Surprisingly, they may come across useful material in the most unlikely sources. Trainers would do well to tear out such material to add to their files.

Where to Find Periodicals

Busy trainers are hard pressed for time and recognize that they must use it most efficiently to stay on top of the literature. At the same time, they may be overwhelmed by the vast amount of journals published.

Most trainers quickly fall into a definite pattern of reading several favorite journals in the field. Often their selection is based on familiarity with only a handful of journals or on the advice of colleagues.

This kind of journal selection may provide trainers with a fairly good overall base of coverage, but it is hardly adequate for those who want to perform above average. These trainers need to look at a wider range of journals, or at least know what the journals are covering that could be useful for them.

In addition to journals published exclusively for trainers, such as the *Training and Development Journal,* trainers ought to be familiar with journals dealing with specialized areas they may need in their work. For example, a trainer who has to be proficient in educational and instructional technology covering both the hardware and software involved in training will have to keep up with some journals in that area, such as *Audiovisual Instruction.*

Also, there are several tangential but related areas of education that appear to be "musts" for a trainer—specifically, adult education and training in the military. The journals in such fields carry a wealth of information pertinent to training and development.

There are several international journals as well as English-language journals published in other countries that can be a rich source of information for a trainer, such as *Industrial Training International.*

MAKING AND MAINTAINING FILES

Many trainers leave all the filing to their secretaries. However, trouble sometimes arises when secretaries do not know how to file training materials. Most secretaries are quite capable of keeping good files when it comes to correspondence, budgetary items, and other routine clerical housekeeping matters, but when it comes to filing subject content material—the kind a trainer would use in his or her work— only an exceptional secretary would know where to begin filing.

Asking secretaries whether they know how to file such material may be no solution. Often they will say that they do know, but the real test of filing ability comes when they are asked to locate something a trainer needs. It is then too late to do anything about the material lost in the files. Trainers ought to avoid such disasters by making sure their secretaries know how to file their material properly.

A trainer cannot ordinarily expect a secretary to be knowledgeable about training and development, at least not when the secretary is first hired. Yet a good filing system demands a certain amount of subject knowledge.

Very often a secretary's inability to file training material properly is compounded by a trainer's own inability in this area. For example, some trainers, taking no chances, tell their secretaries exactly under what heading each piece of material goes. I recall one secretary who used to get thoroughly upset whenever her boss asked her to retrieve some material from the files because she was unable to find it where he told her to look. In desperation, she devised her own system to keep track of the trainer's system.

Developing a System

Trainers are not information science specialists or librarians and are not expected to know the complexities of setting up a comprehensive filing system. But if they are to have a file that will be useful, they must develop a system that they or their secretaries can use with relative ease.

In developing a filing system, a trainer should begin with the understanding that a filing system is good if it serves his or her needs. Trainers must devise the kind of system that will be responsive to their special needs. This means that they ought to pick and choose those elements of filing technology that can do the job adequately.

From the start, trainers ought to know that there are several ways they can approach the task of developing a filing system. Also, they ought to realize that there is not one system which meets all possible needs. Every system has advantages and disadvantages. A trainer must make the trade-offs in choosing a system.

The suggestions for developing a filing system given below are based on the best principles of information storage and retrieval science. The kind of system proposed here can be used by a trainer in almost any configuration of quantity of material and degree of sophistication. The basic system can be designed to fit complex needs or relatively simple ones. It can be useful whether a trainer's entire file consists of one filing-cabinet drawer or a vast array of cabinets, bookshelves, and computer tapes.

In-Depth Indexing

Most libraries use a broad category catalog system, together with title and author indexes. Titles can be misleading, and author names are useless when a searcher does not know any in the specific area in which he or she is looking. Besides, broad categories will uncover a huge amount of material, but not necessarily dealing with the specific issues a trainer needs. Then, too, no trainer wants to plow through a hundred documents to get at one small piece of information if it can be obtained more easily in another way.

In-depth indexing is a system that uses key words or phrases to tag documents. These words or phrases are called *descriptors* because they label or describe the contents of a document. Several descriptors are used to index each document—as many as are needed to label the document adequately. Most journal articles can be indexed sufficiently with four or five descriptors, while a book might need many more. Since the filing system is being designed for the use of the trainer, he or she can decide how many descriptors to use and which ones. Where wider use of the filing system may be made, a more complete indexing with descriptors may be necessary to ensure that the major points in the document will be covered.

For example, this chapter might be indexed with the following descriptors: *indexes, information systems, files, literature searches, periodicals, bibliographies,* and *abstracting services.* If someone other than a trainer were indexing this chapter for a wider audience, some additional descriptors might be added, such as *training and development, libraries,* and *thesauri.*

Assigning Descriptors

Trainers who decide to use descriptors in establishing a filing system ought to get in the habit of jotting down key words or phrases or of underlining them in the text as they read or scan a document. When the trainer has finished going through the document, he or she will have a list of descriptors from which to select the ones to use for filing purposes. After highlighting the key descriptors on the document, a trainer can then have a secretary follow through with the rest of the filing process. A by-product of selecting descriptors is improved reading comprehension on the part of the trainer. Being forced to read in such a way as to search for key words will help the trainer grasp the main ideas in a document.

The next step in the filing process using descriptors is to prepare filing cards. For this purpose either 3×5 or 4×6 index cards can be used. All the descriptors assigned to a document are typed on an index card, together with the title of the document and its source or location. In addition, the trainer can include any other pertinent information he or she wants (see Fig. 44-1). As many index cards will have to be prepared as there are descriptors assigned to the document. Using the descriptors mentioned for this chapter as an example, seven index cards would be typed, with the same information on each card.

indexes, information systems, files,

literature searches, periodicals,

bibliographies, abstracting services.

. . . .

"Literature Searching and Surveillance,"
In "Training and Development Handbook," 2nd edition.

Fig. 44-1   Descriptor file card.

Filing

The typed cards are then filed, one card under each of the seven descriptors. It is a good idea to highlight the descriptor on the card under which it is being filed. A special highlighting pen can be used for this, or the descriptor can be simply underlined or circled (see Fig. 44-2). Highlighting will facilitate the replacement of cards in their proper places if they have to be taken out of the file for any reason.

indexes, information systems, 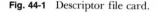(files,)

literature searches, periodicals,

bibliographies, abstracting services.

. . . .

"Literature Searching and Surveillance,"
In "Training and Development Handbook," 2nd edition.

Fig. 44-2   Highlighted descriptor file card.

As the file of descriptors is being developed, it is good to keep an alphabetical listing of all the descriptors being used. One descriptor per card can be arranged at the beginning of the file for quick reference. This listing can be helpful when searching for documents in the file. It enables trainers to translate their search into the specific terms they used to file the material. This listing of descriptors will become, in time, a thesaurus tailored to the needs of the trainer.

Coordinate Indexing

Trainers who have an extensive collection of documents or who are in charge of a library of training materials might consider using the basic in-depth indexing in an expanded version in order to gain the capacity to search for information combining descriptors. To do so, a trainer would have to add some means other than index cards for storing the information.

One variant to index cards in coordinate indexing is the use of computer-type cards which can be used as a needle sort. This kind of system is rather limited in the number of descriptors that can be used.

A more inclusive way to use coordinate indexing is by means of "optical coincidence," a sort of "peek-a-boo" system. In this kind of system, one card is used for each descriptor, and holes are punched or drilled into a matrix or grid on the card. Each hole in the matrix represents a code number of a document (see Fig. 44-3). To search the system, cards representing the descriptors to be searched are aligned and placed over a light source. The place where the light shines through the stack of cards shows the position in the matrix representing a document which includes all the descriptors being searched.

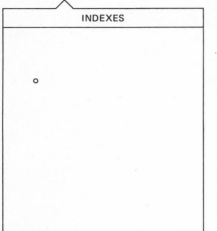

Fig. 44-3 A descriptor card with hole drilled to indicate a document code number.

Using the previous examples for this chapter, the seven descriptor cards would all have a hole punched in the same location in the matrix representing the document code number. When all seven cards were overlaid on a light source, the light would shine through in that position showing that all seven descriptors applied to the document (see Fig. 44-4).

Some optical-coincidence systems can be used with rather extensive collections of documents. A system using 8 × 10 cards can accommodate 10,000 holes, each representing a document code number. Additional sets of cards can extend the number of documents the system can handle.

Using the File

A trainer who has collected a large number of documents can store them in filing cabinets or on shelves. They can be arranged in any convenient way, such as according to the most important descriptor, according to originating source of the documents, or simply according to a sequential number assigned to the document when it is acquired.

Using descriptors allows a trainer to use any kind of filing or shelving arrangement of the documents. Sequential numbering of the documents is easy and does not require any additional time to try to figure out under what category to file them. This can be a great time-saver, especially when dealing with documents concerning several areas of interest to the trainer.

Of course, sequential numbering of documents does not lend itself to browsing under subject categories. But browsing is not the purpose of developing a filing system that is efficient in its retrieval capacity.

SEARCHING FOR LITERATURE

Searching for literature is both a science and an art. There are definite procedures that trainers can follow to find the information they need, but even knowing these procedures does not ensure that trainers will obtain everything they need or exactly what they need. Several individuals can search for the same information and come up with different results. The critical difference is not in the information available but in the searching strategies.

Stating the Problem

It is important for trainers to ask the right questions if they are going to get the right answers in their search for literature. This means that they must think

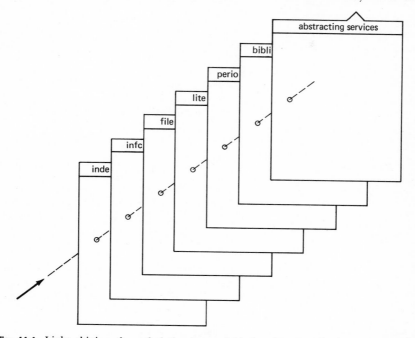

Fig. 44-4 Light shining through holes in overlaid descriptor cards showing coordinate indexing using an optical-coincidence search system.

through what they are looking for. Often, it turns out that a trainer has a broad topic or more than one problem. The first step in this case is to break down the problem into subproblems. The trainer can do this by asking specific questions to get the precise information needed. Otherwise, searching too broadly will result in a hit-and-miss mass of material at a great cost of time and money.

One of the quickest and most rewarding ways to begin a search is for a trainer to write down key words and their synonyms which best describe his or her problem. For example, a trainer who was looking for information about management development might come up with the following list of descriptors: *leadership training, professional continuing education, supervisory training, management systems, management games,* and *problem solving.*

Once a trainer has spelled out the problem in terms of key words or descriptors, he or she can begin to look for documents. If the trainer has developed a filing system such as the one using descriptors explained above, the next step would be to look up the descriptor cards in the file to match those on the search list. The descriptor file cards will help the trainer decide whether the document really zeroes in on the specific need because of the other descriptors which the trainer used to tag the document in preparing it for filing. In using an optical-coincidence system or a computer tape search, a trainer can refine his or her search by combining descriptors.

An additional advantage of checking the descriptors on file cards is that it can provide clues for further searching. For example, a trainer who has searched under the descriptor term *systems analysis* and found a document which is pertinent to the problem might find that the other descriptors on the file card, such as *cost effectiveness, critical path method,* and *systems concepts,* can lead to a search under those descriptors as well.

Using a Thesaurus

To form questions and to refine searches, a trainer will find that a thesaurus, such as the Thesaurus of ERIC Descriptors, is invaluable. This thesaurus is a key for unlocking information as well as for developing one's own approach to solving documentation problems. It is helpful in formulating search questions, whether the ERIC system is used in making a search or not, but it is indispensable when a trainer uses a computer to search for documents in the ERIC system.

A special feature of this thesaurus is a "Rotated Descriptor Display," based on KWIC (Key-Word-in-Context) indexing. In the "Rotated Descriptor Display" every word of multiword descriptors serves as an entry point in the index, with the entire descriptor printed at each entry point. For example, the descriptor term *management information systems* appears three times in the "Rotated Descriptor Display." Every word is alphabetized separately, and the full descriptor appears as context each time a word is entered in its alphabetical position. The first entry is under "Information" and appears as "Management *Information* Systems." The second entry is "Management" and appears as "*Management* Information Systems." The third entry is "Systems" and appears as "Management Information *Systems.*"

Using Experts

A trainer who is going to search for some specialized information or who is going to use one of the computer search services may find it useful to ask an expert for help in framing a question for the search. This may be a librarian or an information science specialist.

Using Libraries

Very few local libraries, and not even many university libraries, have the capacity to retrieve documents beyond the traditional catalog system. However, even in traditionally organized libraries trainers can find their way around the literature if they use the index and abstract catalogs mentioned above.

Using Search Services

In today's rapidly expanding information base trainers must go beyond the usual library resources to find the most current information. They will have to turn to one or more search services now available. These services range from performing single, on-demand searches to providing regular subscription search services right on through having direct access to a data storage computer bank with an on-line terminal.

Several search services are listed in the Directory of References at the end of this chapter. Most of these services will give a searcher either an annotated listing of titles or a listing of abstracts. A trainer must then obtain the documents from their originating sources or through a library.

Two information systems not only provide abstracts of documents but also have available a microfiche and hard-copy reproduction service for all the documents that they abstract not restricted by copyright. The ERIC system sells microfiche and hard-copy reproductions of documents announced in *Research in Education* through the ERIC Document Reproduction Service. Documents announced in the *Government Reports Announcements* are sold in microfiche, and hard-copy reproductions through the National Technical Information Service.

Microfiche

A note ought to be added about microfiche. Microfiche is a sheet of film which contains microimages. Both the ERIC and NTIS microfiches are standardized 4 × 6 with up to 100 images, each representing a page of the original document. The titles are eye-readable, but a standard microfiche reader is required to enlarge the

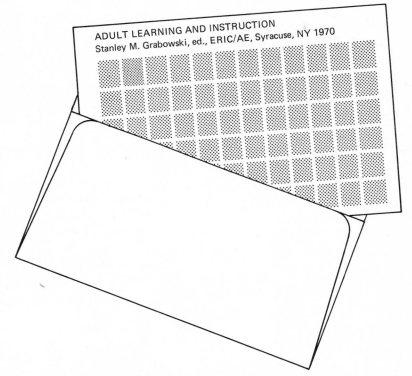

ADULT LEARNING AND INSTRUCTION
Stanley M. Grabowski, ed., ERIC/AE, Syracuse, NY 1970

Fig. 44-5   Microfiche—a 4 x 6 sheet of film—and a paper jacket.

images for reading purposes. More sophisticated microfiche reader-printers have the capacity to reproduce single frames in enlarged versions equal to the size of the original printed page.

Some people are reluctant to use microfiche because of their dislike for reading machines. Their objections are justified when the microfiche readers are of poor quality. However, microfiche has several advantages which make it highly utilitarian.

Microfiche is easy to store. It can be filed in a standard filing drawer used for 4 × 6 index cards. It saves a lot of space, as compared with that required for the actual documents. One file drawer can hold several hundred microfiches representing as many documents, which might occupy shelving on an entire wall. Microfiche is inexpensive. The ERIC microfiche costs 65 cents per title, while the NTIS microfiche costs 95 cents per title (see Fig. 44-5).

DIRECTORY OF RESOURCES

The following list of resources is merely indicative of the kinds that are available; it is by no means comprehensive or exhaustive. The journals listed here are only those mentioned in this chapter. Brief annotations are added under the abstracting and search services. Prices have been omitted because they are constantly changing, and listing them would serve no meaningful purpose in a handbook that will be used for several years.

Journals

Adult Education
Adult Education Association of the
U.S.A.
810 Eighteenth Street, N.W.
Washington, D.C. 20006

Adult Leadership
Adult Education Association of the
U.S.A.
810 Eighteenth Street, N.W.
Washington, D.C. 20006

Audiovisual Instruction
1201 Sixteenth Street, N.W.
Washington, D.C. 20036

*International Journal of Continuing Education
and Training*
Baywood Publishing Company, Inc.
43 Central Drive
Farmingdale, N.Y. 11735

Journal of Extension
807 Extension Building
832 North Lake Street
Madison, Wis. 53706

Educational and Industrial Television
C. S. Tepfer Publishing Company, Inc.
607 Main Street
Ridgefield, Conn. 06877

Industrial Training International
MGS Publications Ltd.
17 Crouch Hill, Finsbury Park
London, N4 4AP
England

Personnel Journal
100 Park Avenue
Swarthmore, Pa. 19081

NSPI Research Quarterly
National Society for Programmed
Instruction
P.O. Box 127
Cardinal Station
Washington, D.C. 20017

Training and Development Journal
P.O. Box 5307
Madison, Wis. 53705

Training
731 Hennepin Avenue
Minneapolis, Minn. 55403

Abstract and Index Catalogs

Abstracts of Instructional Materials in Vocational and Technical Education.   This includes abstracts of materials typically designed for teacher use or student use in the classroom, annotations of bibliographies, or lists of instructional materials. The following educational areas are covered: agriculture, business and office, distribution, health occupations, home economics, industrial arts, technical education, trade and industry, and general vocational and technical education. Personal author, institutional source, document number, conversion of document number, subject and identifier indexes, and a source list are included. The publication appears quarterly and may be ordered from The Center for Vocational and Technical Education, Ohio State University, 1900 Kenny Road, Columbus, Ohio 43210.

Abstracts of Research and Related Materials in Vocational and Technical Education.   This publication announces the availability of documents of interest to a wide audience—researchers, supervisors, teacher-educators, education specialists, etc. Subject categories include administration and supervision, curriculum, employment and occupations, evaluation and measurements, facilities and equipment, individuals with special needs, philosophy and objectives, research design and research development, students, occupational guidance and other student personnel services, and teachers and teacher education. Instructions are given for ordering documents. Indexes to personal and institutional authors, document numbers, vocational and supporting services, and document retrieval (subject headings and identifiers) are also included. The publication appears quarterly and may be ordered from Center for Vocational and Technical Education, Ohio State University, 1900 Kenny Road, Columbus, Ohio 43210.

CIRF Abstracts.   Abstracts are presented of periodical articles and books selected, on a worldwide basis, from several thousand current publications in the areas of vocational training and relating to operative personnel, supervisors, and technical staff in all sectors of economic activity. They are classified under vocational training systems; economic, technical, and social aspects; relationship between education and training; organization; vocational guidance and selection; prevocational training; programs of basic and further training, retraining, and career schemes; trade descriptions; teaching methods, examinations, and research methods; and training facilities, equipment, and teaching aids. The journal is published by CIRF Publications, International Labour Office, CH-1211, Geneva 22, Switzerland.

Current Contents Education.   This is a weekly guide which provides tables of contents in the original form of 600 foreign and domestic education journals, many in advance of publication date. An author index and address directory are included. The journal is published weekly by the Institute for Scientific Information, 325 Chestnut Street, Philadelphia, Pa. 19106.

Current Index to Journals in Education.   This monthly index covers over 500 journals in the field of education and, in addition, important articles in periodicals outside the scope of education-oriented literature. It is a companion piece to *Research in Education* and is indexed with the same subject descriptors, taken from the *Thesaurus of ERIC Descriptors.* It includes a listing of descriptor groups, a classified main-entry section with citations and descriptors, a subject index, and an author index. Semiannual and annual cumulations of the subject and author indexes are available from Macmillan Information, 866 Third Avenue, New York, N.Y. 10022.

Education Index.   This is a monthly index of over 250 educational journals and periodicals with an annual cumulation. It is available from Wilson Company, 950 University Avenue, Bronx, N.Y. 10452.

Government Reports Announcements.   This semimonthly abstract journal announces reports of United States government-sponsored research and development released to the public through the Clearinghouse by the Atomic Energy Commission, the Department of Defense, the National Aeronautics and Space Administration, and other United States government departments and agencies; United States government-sponsored translations; and some foreign reports written in English. Reports are announced in 22 subject categories and include military training, human factors, training devices, evaluation of training, learning, cross-cultural training, leadership, management development, job analysis, industrial training, urban planning, and community development. They are indexed by subject, personal author, corporate author, contract or grant number, and accession or report number. The index is sold by subscription or single copy. Quarterly and annual cumulations are also published. Order from National Technical Information Service, Springfield, Va. 22151.

Manpower Research Inventory.   This annual publication of the ERIC system presents and indexes résumés prepared under the sponsorship of the government's Interagency Committee on Manpower Research. A single volume encompasses material for fiscal years 1966 and 1967; beginning with 1968, a separate volume covers each fiscal year. It is available from the Superintendent of Documents, Government Printing Office, Washington, D.C. 20402. Prices vary for each volume.

Research in Education.   This monthly abstract journal announces recently completed research and related reports and current projects in the field of education, as well as a wide range of other literature of practical use to educational agencies in business and industry, churches, the military, and other governmental and community organizations, as well as in schools and universities. It is made up of abstracts and indexes. The abstracts highlight the significance of each document and are numbered sequentially; the indexes cite the contents by subject, author or investigator, institution, and accession numbers. There are semiannual and annual indexes. The journal is available from the Superintendent of Documents, Government Printing Office, Washington, D.C. 20402.

R & D Abstracts. This guide to available research and development reports from the United Kingdom and elsewhere presents abstracts and annotations analyzed under subject headings of the COSATI Subject Category List. It includes 22 broad scientific and technological categories, such as aeronautics; agriculture; behavioral and social sciences; biological and medical sciences; earth sciences and oceanography; mechanical, industrial, civil, and marine engineering; military sciences; and nuclear sciences and technology. All reports are listed and cataloged by author, originator, report number, contract number, title, and subject. The journal is published semimonthly by the Ministry of Technology, TIL Reports Centre, Station Square, St. Mary Cray, Orpington, Kent, England.

Training Abstracts Service: Notes for Users. This is a service prepared by the British Ministry of Labour to reduce to manageable proportions the relevant published material on techniques, methods, new equipment, and other matters pertinent to industrial training. The service provides wide coverage of British sources and some other English-language material, but it gives no systematic coverage of developments overseas. It includes abstracts, summaries, and annotated bibliographies appearing in periodicals, journals, and abstract services. Abstracts are printed on standard 6 × 4 cards and thus may be filed according to a classification scheme. In addition to its own 10 main schedules, it uses major groups in the summary of the International Standard Classification of Occupations, Universal Decimal Classification numbers for subject matter, and Standard Industrial Classification numbers for 24 orders of industry. The pamphlet contains a list of the 62 periodicals scanned, a list of the 10 organizations which have granted permission to reproduce their abstracts, and the classification schedules with their nine-page alphabetical index. It is available from Training Dept. (TD2), 168 Regent Street, London, W1, England.

National Search Services

Lockheed Information Retrieval Program
West Coast: 3251 Hanover Street
            Department 52-08, Building
            201
            Palo Alto, Calif. 94304
East Coast: 405 Lexington Avenue
            New York, N.Y. 10017

The New England Research Applications
Center
The University of Connecticut
Storrs, Conn. 06268

NTISearch—Abstract Retrieval Service
National Technical Information Service
Springfield, Va. 22151

PHI Delta Kappa, School Research
Information Service
Eighth and Union
Bloomington, Ind. 47401

PROBE
Education Library, Room 30
School of Education
Indiana University
Bloomington, Ind. 47401

Research and Information Services for
Education
198 Allendale Road
King of Prussia, Pa. 19406

San Mateo Educational Resources Center
333 Main Street
Redwood City, Calif. 94063

Systems Development Corporation, SDC/
ERIC Search Service
West Coast: 2500 Colorado Avenue
            Santa Monica, Calif. 90406
East Coast: 5827 Columbia Pike
            Falls Church, Va. 22041

Other Resources Educational Resources Information Center (ERIC) is a national network of clearinghouses providing ready access to educational literature; it is sponsored by the National Institute of Education.

Each of 15 decentralized clearinghouses collects, selects, and processes information about research studies and other literature in an area of education.

The total input of the ERIC system is announced in a monthly abstract catalog, *Research in Education,* with many of the documents available in microfiche and hard-copy reproductions through the ERIC Document Reproduction Service.

The ERIC clearinghouses also cover journal literature in a companion monthly catalog, *Current Index to Journals in Education.*

The clearinghouses most pertinent to training needs include the following:

ERIC Clearinghouse in Career Education
204 Gurler
Northern Illinois University
DeKalb, Ill. 60115

ERIC Clearinghouse on Information
  Resources
Stanford Center for Research and
  Development in Teaching
School of Education
Stanford University
Stanford, Calif. 94305

ERIC Clearinghouse on Counseling and
  Personnel Services
School of Education Building, Room
  2108
East University and South University Streets
Ann Arbor, Mich. 48104

ERIC Document Reproduction Service
  (EDRS)
P.O. Drawer 0
Bethesda, Md. 20014

University Microfilms
300 North Zeeb Road
Ann Arbor, Mich. 48106

Thesaurus of ERIC Descriptors
Macmillan Information
866 Third Avenue
New York, N.Y. 10022

Chapter **45**

The Role of Universities, Colleges, and Other Educational Institutions in Training and Development

GERALD H. WHITLOCK

Gerald H. Whitlock *is Distinguished Service Professor of Management and Psychology at the University of Tennessee. He received his doctorate in psychology from the University of Tennessee in 1954. After a period of employment with Union Carbide in personnel training and development, Dr. Whitlock returned to teach at the University of Tennessee. He is past chairman of the Committee on Industrial and Organizational Psychology, which administers the master's and doctoral programs, has been on the National Committee on Programmed Learning of ASTD, was chairman of the National Research Committee of ASTD, is a past trustee and chairman of the Board of Trustees of the ASTD Research Fund, and for eight years was editor of* Training Research Abstracts. *He has published a number of research papers in training and development, and he authored a chapter on training education in the first edition of* Training and Development Handbook. *He is a past member of the National Advisory Board for the ERIC Clearinghouse on Adult Education at Syracuse. He is a member of ASTD, the American Psychological Association, the American Association for the Advancement of Science, the Industrial Relations Research Association, and the Southern Society for Philosophy and Psychology. Dr. Whitlock was elected to the honorary societies of Phi Kappa Phi, Beta Gamma Sigma, and Sigma Psi. He was 1967 Phi Kappa Phi Lecturer at the University of Tennessee and in that year was appointed Distinguished Service Professor.*

The purpose of this chapter is to describe and evaluate the many services available for training and development through formal educational institutions and faculties. More and more, training directors have become educational as well as training consultants to their organizations, and performance in that role requires a working knowledge of the myriad of educational programs presently offered by colleges and universities, junior colleges, evening schools, and correspondence study. Cooperative efforts on the part of such institutions with business and government organizations are growing in number, rather than diminishing, and it can be foreseen that an increasing proportion of the training director's time will be taken up with such efforts.

COLLEGES AND UNIVERSITIES

The history of the growth of university-sponsored executive development programs has been presented elsewhere[1] and will not be repeated in detail here. Patton presents the founding dates for 41 such programs, beginning with the Sloan Fellowship program at M.I.T., which was started in 1931 and is considered to be the oldest continuing management education program in existence.[2] Of course, the Wharton School of Finance and Commerce at the University of Pennsylvania was begun in 1881, but this was an undergraduate program rather than a program designed specifically for working managers. Although Harvard offered summer courses for executives in 1928 and 1929, it was not until 1945 that its famous Advanced Management Program was begun.[3] From this beginning, the number of "live-in" university-sponsored executive development programs continued to grow steadily; in 1974 Bricker reported and described 54 independent, full-time, in-residence programs geared to accommodate 5,300 executives. Of these, 53 are sponsored by universities. While at the time of this writing there is no way to determine actual attendance by executives in 1974, it was observed that the attendance in 1973 was up 17 percent over that in 1972.[4]

The above programs last from 2 to 14 weeks and cost (tuition, room, and board) from $750 to $6,800.[5]

Why do companies spend that kind of money on university-sponsored management development programs? Apparently, impetus was given to utilizing university resources in the early 1940s, when the faculties of Harvard and Stanford were asked to develop courses to help meet the demand for managers of war production. While the emphasis in the program initially was on learning the managerial skills required for war production, by the end of the war, 80 percent of the enrollees were sent by their companies as part of their preparation for promotion.[6] As noted earlier, by 1945 Harvard had initiated its Advanced Management Program to accommodate senior executives not necessarily associated with war production, and soon other universities followed suit.

When participants in these programs are asked what they perceived to be the objectives of such programs—or when company executives are asked why they send their managers to these programs—many different answers are obtained. But there is one recurring theme: that of broadening. This doubtless reflects a realization on the part of participants of the near-inevitable narrowing effect of sustained membership in a particular organization—in terms of both interests and perspective. This effect, in the face of a business environment in which adaptability and flexibility are essential to survival, quite naturally caused organizations to turn to universities to do the job of intellectual retreading and revitalization. As has been noted, programs for this purpose typically range from 2 to 14 weeks. Some of the exceptions have been notable, however, such as the one-year AT&T program at the University of Pennsylvania and the one-year Sloan Fellowship program at M.I.T. Also, too numerous to count are the one- or two-day seminars and symposia on selected topics held on nearly every large campus throughout the year. Also, many universities offer management education programs through their evening schools. These usually meet once or twice a week at night and may or may not be degree-granting programs. These various types of programs will now be considered separately.

Live-in Programs

The best single source of information concerning university-sponsored programs of the live-in type is *Bricker's Directory of University-sponsored Executive Development Programs.*[7] The programs included in the directory meet the following criteria:

1. They are sponsored by a university or a management group.
2. They are concerned with the broad aspects of management rather than confined to specific functions.
3. They deal with the problems of industry generally and are not confined to a specific industry.
4. They require at least two weeks of in-residence attendance.

For each program included in the directory, the following information is provided: (1) the name of the program and the year it was started, (2) the name and location of the sponsor, (3) the duration of the program and the dates, (4) the tuition and type of living accommodations, (5) the level of management the program is principally designed for and the number of participants admitted, and (6) a description of program content and instructional method. Figure 45-1 is a reproduction of one of the program descriptions in the directory.

A number of other information sources exist. Some of them which would be of interest to the training director are discussed below.[8]

Seminar Directory: Industries' Guide to Short Courses, Seminars, Conferences and Workshops. Formerly called *The Continuing Education Handbook,* this directory provides national coverage of university and college noncredit seminars, short courses, conferences, and workshops of interest to industry and professional societies. Location, subject identification number, institution, department, and type of offering are indicated for seminars, conferences, and similar programs. Subject or course titles and the names of contact persons are given under specific institutions. Addresses and affiliations of instructors and leaders are also cited. Date and subject indexes are included, followed by instructions to institutions wishing to be listed. The directory is issued quarterly by, and available from, Stemm's Information Systems and Indexes, P.O. Box 42576, Los Angeles, Calif. 90050.

A Selected List of Professional Training Programs and Internships. This contains a list of major training and internship programs with all information pertinent to application for them, a list of short workshops for administrators, and the names of other groups that might provide more information on these subjects. It is available from the American Association of University Women, 2401 Virginia Avenue, N.W., Washington, D.C. 20037.

Continuing Education. This quarterly digest is a supplement to *World Meetings: United States and Canada* and provides information on short courses, seminars, workshops, and other offerings in selected fields of interest to technical and managerial personnel. Material is indexed by subject, location, and date. Reader service cards are included in order to obtain more detailed, up-to-date information between *Continuing Education* issues. The digest is published in January, April, July, and October by Data Bases, Division of Pennsylvania Research Associates, Inc., 101 North 33 Street, Philadelphia, Pa. 19104.

Journal of Continuing Education and Training. This journal addresses itself to training directors, instructors, and academic personnel; it presents new ideas, developments, and experiences in the field of continuing education and training. It is applicable to the educational process involving individuals of all age groups and backgrounds in the fields of technology and management through formal academic classwork, in-plant training, and self-study. The journal is published quarterly (May, August, November, and February) by Baywood Publishing Company, Inc., 1 Northwest Drive, Farmingdale, N.Y. 11735.

Federal Educational Policies, Programs, and Proposals: A Survey and Handbook, part II, Survey of Federal Educational Activities. This report, second in a three-part series, surveys the educational activities administered by federal agencies. It describes each program and summarizes the activities, including data on funds obligated for them. Such

UNIVERSITY OF TENNESSEE
Tenneseee Executive Development Program

Inaugurated 1972

SPONSOR: College of Businese Administration

PROGRAM LOCATION: Knoxville, Tennessee

DURATION: 4 spaced weeks over 3 months plus
a Capstone session 5 months later

1975 SESSION:
January	12 —	January	18
February	9 —	February	15
March	9 —	March	15
April	9 —	April	12

September 11-13 (The Executive Seminar)

TUITION: $2050 including room and meals
(Also covers wife's attendance in April session, and
attendance of participant and wife at Executive
Seminar in September.)

LIVING QUARTERS: Sheraton Campus Inn
Single rooms

PARTICIPANTS:

Number:	Not over 32
Age:	30-56 Average 44
Position:	Middle to top management
Industry:	Broad
Geography:	Mostly Tenneseee

FACULTY: University of Tennessee and other leading universities, as well as lecturers from industry.

OFFICIAL CONTACT: Dr. John A. Bachmann, Director
Management Development Programs
71 Glocker Administration Building
College of Business Administration
The University of Tennessee
Knoxville, Tennessee 37916
Telephone 615-974-5001

SUBJECT MATTER

The curriculum is grouped by weeks as follows:

First Week: The Executive

                      Creativity
                      Leadership
                      Systematic Problem Solving and Decision Making
                      Management Styles
                      Administrative Practices
                      Motivation
                      Communication Skills
                      Self Management
                      Organizational Behavior

Second Week: The Executive in the Firm

                      Financial Manmagement
                      Cash Flow and Capital Management
                      Tax Planning
                      Marketing
                      Labor/Management Relations
                      Managerial Accounting
                      Quantitative Decision Tools

Third Week: The Executive, The Firm, and the Operating
                  Environment

                      The Environment—Legal, Social, Cultural,
                          Technological, Political, and Economic
                      Corporate Planning
                      Strategy Formulation

Fig. 45-1   Sample program description in Bricker's directory.

Fourth Week: The Executive in Action

                 A Business Simulation
                 Self Development and Personal Values

Capstone Session: The Executive Seminar

                 Relevant Topics
                 Current Key Issues

METHODS OF INSTRUCTION

Instruction is by a variety of methods including lecture, case study, discussions, seminars and workshops. The fourth and final week of the program is devoted to a business game entitled "The Tennessee Management Simulation".

Classes meet for four 90 minute sessions between 8:30 a.m. and 5:00 p.m. on weekdays, and for two sessions each on Sunday afternoon and Saturday morning. Contemporary Issues are discussed at dinner two or three days a week. Small discussion groups meet each evening from 8:00 to 10:00 p.m.

Readings and cases are assigned for analysis prior to each week's session.

FACULTY

Faculty for the program includes key University of Tennessee professors, nationally recognized professors from other universities, and high level executives from industry.

PARTICIPANTS

Participants are from middle to top management of local enterprises and divisional operations of national enterprises in the textile, paper, printing, utility, transportation and other industries.

Salaries range from $15,000 to $40,000 with an average of $25,000.

SPECIAL FEATURES

Wives' Program

Wives are invited to be present during the fourth week of the program.

A planned program includes seminars and workshops on:

        The Enterprise System
        Urban Issues
        Investment/Estate Planning
        Executive Family Health
        Business Ethics and Social Responsibility
        Changing Values of Youth
        How Changing Behavior is Changing Our Institutions
        Self Development and Personal Values

Continuity of Development

Participants and wives of all TEDP classes are invited back to campus each Fall for The Executive Seminar on relevant topics and current key issues.

FACILITIES

Accommodations are in single rooms on the top floors of the Sheraton Campus Inn, adjacent to the UT Knoxville campus.

Meals are served at the University Faculty Club, the Hermitage Room of the University Center, and the Campus Inn. Food is good.

The University's athletic and recreational facilities are available.

RECOMMENDATION

This program has considerable merit for executives in middle management from any part of the country who can be spared from their jobs for only short periods of time, or who prefer to digest the material of the program in small doses over an extended period.

activities are construed to include (1) educational activities which are a federal responsibility, as indicated by statute or other authority; (2) educational or training programs which the federal government operates or supports; and (3) federal activities which provide education similar to that offered by other institutions. Included also are the educational programs of international organizations in which the United States participates. Two types of research programs are covered: (1) those carried out entirely or partly by institutions of higher education under contract with federal agencies and (2) those carried on by institutions, particularly land-grant colleges through their experiment stations, in cooperation with federal agencies, or vice versa. The appendix is a chart of federal moneys for educational programs administered by the Office of Education during fiscal year 1967. The report is available from Superintendent of Documents, Government Printing Office, Washington, D.C. 20402.

Expectations. What do companies expect to get out of university-sponsored management education programs? According to a study conducted in 1973 by Powell and Davis[9] of 100 of the largest United States business corporations known to be regular users of university programs, the reasons for their utilization, in order of rated importance, were as follows:

1. To broaden the interest in or awareness of, the individual—that is, to widen his or her business perspectives
2. To expose an already competent manager to new hypotheses or avenues of management thought
3. To prepare the individual for greater responsibility, but not necessarily promotion
4. To provide management training or education to an individual who rose through technical channels
5. To permit managers to interact and compare problem solutions with managers in other areas
6. To prepare an individual for imminent promotion
7. To provide opportunity for subordinate development while the supervisor is away at a program
8. To check the competency of a potential successor

All but the last two of the above reasons could be included under the "broadening" objectives noted earlier as being the common thread running through the numerous program objectives. It is perhaps gratifying to note that in a study of the reactions of over 6,000 participants in these kinds of programs, Andrews found that "it is the unquestionable message of these questionnaires that broadening is what men in the program most want."[10] While it may be a source of satisfaction to both company and university that program participants perceive good agreement between what the university offers and what companies want, this is due largely to the fact that the goals of such programs are so amorphous that scientific evaluation is almost impossible. However, as will be noted later, the reactions of mature, experienced participants may not be the flimsy basis for program evaluation they are often assumed to be.

The most extensive study of the impact of university-sponsored live-in executive education programs is that by Andrews of the reactions of over 6,000 participants. This was an in-depth study and would be of great interest to a training director.

Part-Time Nondegree Programs

Also of interest would be the study of the U.C.L.A. part-time program by Reed Powell.[11] Participants are employed executives and attend classes once a week from 4 to 9:15 P.M. (including a dinner meeting) for two semesters. The participants are selected by their companies and do not receive a degree (as contrasted with the University of Chicago MBA program). Powell, who earlier had worked with Andrews on the massive study of the live-in programs, sought to answer these questions:

> Can the executive be motivated to effective learning week after week particularly when he comes to school at the end of the day with his mind filled with business problems?
> Can the stimulus of the program overcome the physical fatigue which the day's work and the task of commuting to the university has left upon the man?
> Can the instructor open a subject area, move deeply into it and hope for continuity of developing interest and understanding in the follow-up sessions over a period of several weeks or every month?
> Does the minimal commitment made by the company on behalf of the participant have much less of a positive implication relative to the administrator's future in the company and is thus likely to be reflected in the participant's interest and willingness to become involved in the program?
> Is there a loss of valuable cross-fertilization of ideas when the program is limited to local participants who work and live within commuting distances?
> If physical setting, food, and the status of the program affect the program's impact upon participants, do these factors provide live-in courses of study with an advantage over their part-time counterparts?
> In short, can a university expect to provide an optimal, educational growth experience to executives on a part-time basis.[12]

To find the answers to these questions, Powell obtained the reactions of 181 participants who attended the U.C.L.A. part-time program. Of particular value in this study is the fact that Powell utilized the same procedure Andrews used in order to make specific comparisons between the reactions of live-in versus part-time participants.

The striking thing about the results of Powell's study was the similarity of responses of the participants in the two kinds of programs. In general, the answers to the questions Powell intended to answer were favorable to the part-time program. Obviously, the company makes less financial commitment in the case of part-time programs, and the time commitment is so spaced as to be less obvious, although in total amount it would be equal to the time commitment involved in many of the live-in programs. Powell has summarized the role of the part-time program as follows:

1. Managers of business concerns cannot always be away from their jobs for the period of time required by the live-in program. Particularly in medium-sized and small firms where the need for management development is often greatest, the key individuals cannot be spared for any length of time.
2. The higher costs of live-in programs (when tuition, board and room, travel, and salaries of the men while at the program, are considered) also make it impractical for many firms to utilize them as a source of management development.
3. It is increasingly recognized that good top management capability does not emerge with the sudden promotion of an individual. If he is to be an effective administrator, the process of development must begin long before the top executive positions are reached. Yet there is almost a complete lack of university-sponsored management development programs for lower-level supervisors, and only a few courses of study are aimed at the middle level of administration.

   The time, cost, and number of persons involved at the middle and lower levels of management make it prohibitive for many of the supervisors to attend live-in programs. However, part-time programs could be developed to aid a large proportion of people at these lower and middle levels towards greater managerial capability.
4. Another advantage of the non-residential program is its applicability to the education of senior-level executives in the large industrial centers of the country. The opportunity provided for the interchange of ideas and understandings among top managers living in a common geographical area has considerable potential value for the executives themselves, their firms, and the larger community.

5. An advantage of considerable importance to participants in the part-time program is the opportunity it provides for an active, educationally-oriented alumni to carry on post-program activities. The Executive Program Alumni Association of UCLA, for example, plans a series of events each year which not only maintains and furthers friendships among program participants, but also affords a stimulus for continued growth in management.
6. The part-time program does not have the social problems (drinking and parties) which often plague live-in efforts. In the research it became evident that the tendency towards social excesses at some live-in courses could present dangers to the reputation of the program, the quality of the educational experience, and the health of the executives.
7. The part-time program possesses a potential incentive which is of considerable value to many administrators. It can build toward the satisfaction of their needs for educational achievement and management sophistication at the same time by offering a degree-granting program in Business Administration such as the one at the University of Chicago.
8. The opportunity of an executive education while on the job afforded by the part-time program, and the relatively larger time span required to complete the class sessions, as compared with the live-in course, offers a number of advantages to participants:
    a. The longer intervals between class sessions allows for greater assimilation and integration of the learning experience.
    b. Executives have the opportunity of applying at work the things learned at the program and discussing the results at later class sessions. This provides a further understanding and evaluation of the material under study.
    c. A realistically-oriented environment is produced in which the theory, principles and practices of management are all interrelated elements.[13]

Part-Time Degree-Granting Programs

The major differences between the part-time programs described above and those described in this section are: (1) The company typically pays only a portion of the costs; (2) the participant earns a graduate degree, usually an M.B.A. or a master's of science in business administration; (3) the participant attends on his or her own initiative rather than being selected by the company. The course work might even be identical to that in a nondegree program if the program is sponsored by a college of business. It is not unusual for even this kind of program to have its beginning at the instigation of company officials. There are obvious advantages to the company that has a conveniently available means whereby its employees, particularly new ones, can pursue a graduate degree. The University of Tennessee, for example, offers master's degrees in both engineering and business administration at centers over 100 miles from the main campus. These programs are manned by regular faculty—some of whom travel once weekly to the off-campus centers and some of whom teach by tele-lecture each week and visit the center in person only once a quarter. All these U.T. programs were begun in response to requests by companies in the particular location. Under these circumstances the requesting company may actually bear the major costs of the program. The graduate degree-granting programs have most of the advantages of the part-time programs, plus the added incentive of a graduate degree.

Short Courses and Seminars

It is probably safe to say that every institution of higher learning which offers a degree in business administration will have faculty members who periodically offer on-campus seminars, workshops, or conferences for managers. These are usually from one to three days in duration, and particular topics are offered in nearly every area of management specialty. Such offerings provide a convenient means for management specialists to keep abreast of latest developments. In the absence of any company feedback to the contrary, the university faculty will tend to offer programs in accordance with their own interests. Of course, the program offerings of some universities—e.g., Michigan—are so extensive that there is something for everybody, but typically this is not the case. In all likelihood, company training directors will find the coordinators of these university programs quite responsive to their suggestions as to program content. It is also important to note that faculty members who conduct these seminars and conferences on campus are usually willing, on an individual consulting basis, to offer special in-plant seminars. The advantages of this arrangement are obvious, but not so obvious is the disadvantage of losing the opportunity to share experiences with members of other organizations attending campus seminars.

COMPANY POLICIES

Programs like those described above exemplify the major role of universities and their faculties in management education. Each has some advantages with respect to the others as well as some disadvantages, depending on the company's objectives. That these objectives may not always be precisely delineated is suggested by the following findings of Powell in his survey of corporation executives:

> There were several specific shortcomings on the part of organizations participating in university executive development programs:
> There is a definite lack of written policy about corporate participation in executive development programs.
> The selection of program participants is made primarily by staff executives, rather than the line executives most responsible for the performance of the person selected.
> No real effort is being made to specifically identify the developmental needs of the individual with respect to his current or future assignment and to match these needs with an appropriate educational program.
> Evaluation of performance after program participation is not generally accomplished, or, if so, is done subjectively, informally, and at the initiative of the participant himself.
> Positive means for the introduction and implementation of new ideas gained from the program are lacking.[14]

Perhaps the training director can provide truly valuable service to his or her organization in the areas of (1) policy regarding the use of a university program, (2) selection of participants, (3) preparing for the participants' return, and (4) evaluation of the program.

Policy Regarding Use of University Resources

Powell found that 75 percent of the companies in his survey had either no policy in this regard (on-campus, full-time programs) or an unwritten one.[15] Clearly this is an area in which the training director could be making some inputs. Some relevant policy areas would be the following.

1. *Extent of Usage.*   While there is no limit to the number of executives who might attend part-time programs, clearly there is a definite limit to the numbers of executives from a particular organization who can be in attendance at a full-time on-campus program. Hence there should be a policy regarding extent of participation. Noting that fewer than one-fourth of past participants have had less than 16 years of experience in their company and, similarly, that fewer than 20 percent were under 41 years of age, it is apparent that this means of executive development has been generally reserved for the more senior executives. At this point in the manager's career, he or she has almost surely succumbed to some extent to the narrowing effects of prolonged membership in the same organization. Hence, probably all such executives would benefit from the broadening effect of university programs. However, aside from budget considerations, there are those having

to do with the consequences of "passing over" executives when selecting participants, the "status" implications of being selected, and other such considerations.
Probably the best advice is to write the policy regarding attendance at university
live-in programs so as not to be inconsistent with policies concerning participation
in other types of development programs, e.g., rotation programs. Also, policy
concerning usage of university live-in programs should be written so as to complement the other executive development programs in the organization—particularly
those with emphasis on individual career development.

2. *Who Selects the Participants?*   The policy here should be clear and should provide
for heavy input from the prospective participant's immediate superior. Also, the
policy should specify what criteria are to be used, e.g., performance evaluations.
Of particular importance for certain types of programs, e.g., sensitivity training, is
a stated policy emphasizing freedom of choice and absence of adverse impact in
the event the offer of attendance is declined.

3. *Reimbursement.*   Finally, the policy should be clear concerning reimbursement
of expenses incurred as a result of attendance—including any family expense
involved.

Policy Regarding Selection of Participants

The overriding consideration here is to select only those participants who can and
will benefit from the program. Although it is almost universally stated that the
primary objective of development programs is to increase the effectiveness of
current performance, it is also generally true that promotions are based on quality
of current performance. Hence it is seldom possible to separate those two objectives entirely. This means that selecting "problem" managers or (as a form of
reward) managers who have outstanding records of company service or who are
near retirement constitutes not only a disservice to the company but usually also a
disservice to the sponsoring university's program. The policy should make it clear
that selection for attendance is based on demonstrated past job performance and
represents a prediction concerning the quality of future performance in whatever
capacity.

Preparing for the Participants' Return to the Organization

If it is company policy to select program participants on the basis of the quality of
their past performance with the expectation of improved future performance,
then the stage may be set for some rather difficult problems of accommodation.
Powell has expressed the problem as follows:

> Being selected to attend a university program is generally regarded as a positive
> occurrence and one having career implications, varying according to the particular
> university program selected for the individual. There is a status hierarchy among these
> programs, and they have different meanings for those within the company. If the
> program is successful in terms of providing an educational stimulus for the executive
> attending, he then returns ready to implement new ideas and changes in his organiza-
> tion. However, his company probably has not anticipated this result and is not prepared
> for it. Therefore, the more effective the university program, the more frustrated the
> executive participant is likely to become when he returns to his company environment.
> One might even conjecture that university programs could get into serious trouble if
> they become more effective in creating energized "tigers," who return to their firms
> anxious to ignite the spark of new opportunity and change within their organization.[16]

Anyone who has spent some time in organizations (any kind) has probably
observed or experienced the gap between knowledge and practice—between
conceiving and implementing. The point is that this kind of dissonance on the part

of the returned participant can be expected and thus managed. But it takes a policy which ensures access to appropriate authority, sympathetic consideration of proposals for change, and organizational flexibility. If any one of these is absent, then the university experience may become merely the occasion for frustration.

Policy Regarding Evaluation

The literature concerning the evaluation of university-sponsored management education programs reveals quite clearly the following: (1) Most companies, as well as most universities, make little or no attempt to systematically evaluate the effectiveness of such programs; (2) the evaluation that does take place consists almost exclusively of participants' reactions to the program, most of which are favorable; (3) few, if any, companies systematically measure behavioral changes resulting from program attendance; and (4) the literature remains full of admonitions to company directors to apply the same rigor to the evaluation of management education programs that they do to the evaluations of their training programs.

Although the literature is by no means replete with examples of well-designed training evaluation studies, such studies are plentiful as compared with those in which evaluation of management education programs is attempted. The latter are practically nonexistent—and for good reason.

In the case of training activites as well as education and development activities, a set of stimuli are chosen and presented for the purpose of producing certain responses which are the objectives of the program. The difference between training and education is in the specifiability of those responses. To the extent that stimuli can be related to specific responses, the activity may be termed "training." To the extent that only classes or responses can be related to the stimuli, the activity may be termed "education." In other words, there is a continuum of specifiability of responses or objectives, with training activity on one end and education on the other.

One could also call this a "specifiability-of-stimulus" continuum since the harder it is to specify the response, the more difficult is it to identify its stimulus. Thus no matter where on the continuum a particular learning activity is placed, there is a stimulus-response equation. First, consider this equation at the training end of the continuum in the context of evaluation of the training activity, a good example being a training program designed to teach typing. How would such a program be evaluated? The first thing that occurs to most people is to measure the response side of the equation—in other words, test the participants' achievement at the end of the program. If the results were satisfactory, then the program would be considered successful; i.e., the stimulus elements constituting the training program would be evaluated only in terms of the response. And this makes sense with activities on the training end of the continuum because of factors such as the following: (1) The response is easily related to the stimulus elements in the training program; (2) criterion performance levels are readily specifiable, understandable, and measurable—e.g., typing at the rate of 60 words per minute for three minutes with no errors; (3) the response is readily produced in the presence of appropriate stimuli; and (4) practice during training is very similar to final performance. These are just four reasons why, in the case of activities on the training end of the continuum, it is appropriate to evelute the stimulus (i.e., training) in terms of the response (i.e., achievement).

Moving to the other end of the continuum, e.g., a university-sponsored management development program, how much sense now does it make to evaluate the stimulus only in terms of the response? Consider the four conditions which characterize the typing example above:

1. The response is easily related to the stimulus elements in the training program. In the case of the university-sponsored program, the desired responses are expressed in such broad terms that it is all but impossible to relate them to specific stimulus elements. Indeed, even where broad aims are expressed, little agreement exists concerning the stimulus elements which will produce them, e.g., the stimuli which elicit the following responses: "increased insight and self-knowledge," "an expanded consciousness about the effects of behavior and a sense that more alternatives are available," "more effective functioning in one's present position and increased chances for promotion," or "a broader understanding of the economic, political, and social environment of business."

2. Criterion performance levels are readily specifiable, understandable, and measurable. The response (criterion performance) in the case of education and development programs is difficult to specify, almost unrecognizable, and unreliably measured. As to being understandable, it is probably a rare executive who leaves such management education programs with a clear notion of what responses he or she is expected to produce to which stimuli.

3. The response can be readily produced in the presence of the appropriate stimuli. Even if the participants in such programs do learn to produce certain responses in the presence of certain stimuli, it is the rare organization to which the "educated" executive can return and produce his or her newly learned responses at will—a multitude of organizational constraints prevent an easy transformation from knowing to doing. Also, the time at which the newly learned responses might occur following the education and development program ranges from immediately to never.

4. Practice during training is very similar to final performance. To what extent are the responses produced in the management education program similar to those characterizing the final desired responses, i.e., the behaviors constituting the program objectives? Compared with the typing situation, not very similar. Rather, it is hoped that classes of stimuli will be related to classes of responses; i.e., stimuli are often in the form of concepts which may elicit any one of a multitude of specific responses. And to complicate matters even further, it is typical in management development programs for the desired response on the part of the manager to be the stimulus for behavior change on the part of his or her subordinates.

For the above four reasons alone one would exercise the greatest caution in evaluating the quality of the stimulus elements only in terms of the response in the case of management education and development programs. In short, it is suggested here that in the case of education and development programs, it is unrealistic to insist that all teaching be evaluated only on the response side of the equation. And to state further that in the teaching–learning-on-the-job–performance situation, one can evaluate the quality of the program stimuli only in terms of the on-the-job performance is almost equivalent to saying that such programs cannot be evaluated. It is necessary to assess the consequences of each stage of the chain, beginning with the presentation of program stimuli and ending with the final responses which are the objectives of the program. If the program content was not learned, then the intended responses cannot be performed. If the program content was learned but organizational constraints prevented putting what was learned into practice, then one can hardly assess the quality of the program stimuli in terms of on-the-job behavior. If there were no such organizational constraints and the desired responses did in fact occur and if these responses were intended to be the occasion for behavior change on the part of other members of the organization (superiors, peers, subordinates), then it would appear that only the most temerarious training director would be willing to equate the degree of such behavior changes to the quality of the original program stimuli. In short, it hardly makes sense to evaluate the stimulus in terms of the response.

More systematic effort toward the evaluation of the stimulus side of the equation is one possible solution. It is not that one does not know how to evaluate the stimulus in terms of the response—indeed, all the developments in experimental design in this area are intended to ensure that the observed responses were in fact due to the program stimuli and not to preexisting or extraneous factors. The means are known, but the problems simply will not accommodate themselves to those techniques. The result is that there is not one instance in the literature of a scientifically sound experimental evaluation of a management education and development program—one where all the relevant variables are brought under statistical or experimental control and related in a precise way to relevant and reliable performance criteria.

Evaluation Techniques   Therefore, one must resort to other means of evaluating education and development programs, and it is suggested that more useful information concerning the quality of the program stimulus elements can be obtained from the participants than has typically occurred. In experiments at the University of Tennessee it has been discovered that students do know what effective teaching is, from the standpoint of learning, and can identify those stimulus elements which are productive and preventive of learning. Other studies have demonstrated the positive relationship between teacher ratings and student achievement.

If college students can do this, executives can probably do it even better. If this assumption is correct, then one way to evaluate the quality of the stimulus elements in management development programs is as follows: First, collect from a large group of participants incidents which elicited positive and negative judgments regarding the effectiveness of development programs, i.e., elements in the program which in their judgment were definitely productive or preventive of learning. These will be such things as "used case materials which were superficial," "demonstrated the relevance of new cost-saving techniques," "failed to exert sufficient control over the conferees and thus wasted time," "made naïve application of behavioral science theory to organizational problems," "required readings in sources which were obsolete," or "devised simulation exercises which nearly duplicated the real world." Second, edit and compile these responses into a checklist for use by trainees at the end of the program. Probably, the large proportion of management development programs could be covered by only a few checklists. The advantages of such a procedure are: (1) It permits some early assessments of programs in which objectives are so future-bound or environment-dependent that on-the-job behavioral measurements are impracticable or meaningless; (2) it has built-in relevance by virtue of the way the instrument is constructed; (3) it will yield a numerical score which can provide a basis for comparative studies; and (4) it is diagnostic of specific strengths and weaknesses of the development program.

In addition, after an appropriate time interval, the executives could be asked to identify specimens of effective (and ineffective) performance on their part which in their judgment was the result of attendance at the university program. Thus the program as a whole could be evaluated in terms of reported job performance. This particular evaluation activity could best be accomplished by a cooperative effort on the part of the appropriate company and university representative, e.g., the company training director and the university program director. The interviews should be conducted by the company representative to avoid the "basis of auspices" which might result otherwise. They should be conducted after the participant has "settled" back into his or her organization—e.g., one month after return—in order to allow for a "cooling down" of participants' characteristically positive reactions immediately following such programs. Finally, arrangements should be made for sending the learning specimens to the university representative, who sees that they are sorted, edited, etc., and compiled into a checklist which can be used to evaluate future efforts. The above process is continuous, thus providing the university representative with a continuing basis for updating the checklist. The responses to the checklist for each group of participants should be made available to each participating company. As a result of this procedure, the company has a better basis for making decisions concerning future participation, and the university has a means of diagnosing the specific strengths and weaknesses of each program.

The above approach, or some variation, will ensure a meaningful analysis of program strengths and weaknesses, but it will supply little information concerning the effect of particular program components on the participant's job performance upon return to the organization. For reasons stated earlier in this section, a meaningful cause-and-effect mapping of program components into job performance elements is all but impossible using typical experimental designs. Hence it is again suggested, in the absence of proper experimental designs and their attendant controls, that a pragmatic approach be taken to evaluating behavioral consequence (the response side of the stimulus-response equation mentioned earlier). If one is willing to make the assumption that mature, experienced managers can make their own linkages between the program components and their subsequent organizational performance, then it follows that a sensible approach to program evaluation is to systematically sample their judgments in this regard. This could be done at various time intervals following the program.

Although the above suggestion may seem rather nonrigorous, insistence on sophisticated experimental designs results in no evaluation at all since such designs are all but impossible to implement in typical organizations. On the other hand, useful evaluative information *can* be systematically obtained from executives who participate in these programs.

OTHER PROGRAMS

Cooperative Programs   One of the oldest forms of cooperation between institutions of higher education and industry is the cooperative education program. Such programs have been popular for 75 years and continue to grow in number; in recent years they have been extended even to graduate schools.

While most companies probably consider the major advantage of these programs to be in the area of recruiting, it is also true that well-planned cooperative programs provide excellent training and development opportunities for students. The training specialist is in an excellent position to ensure that such opportunities exist because he or she monitors the experiences of the students, making sure that they are assigned tasks at an appropriate level of difficulty and challenge.

In 1970 there were over 100 colleges and 300 organizations engaged in cooperative programs. There is even a professional organization—the Cooperative Education Association—whose members are involved in cooperative education, as well as the *Journal of Cooperative Education.*

Specifics of programs vary widely across colleges and universities. Training specialists should contact the appropriate university or college official if they wish to explore such involvement.

Departmental Programs   Countless seminars, conferences, symposia, and the like are offered continually by colleges and universities. Whether they are coordinated by a single division of the university (e.g., the department of conferences) or sponsored by a particular department (e.g., the department of management), such programs are numerous indeed and cover an entire gamut of topics of interest to the members of nearly every kind of organization.

Every training specialist should arrange to receive program announcements from nearby colleges and universities. For information concerning other programs, there is a quarterly publication, *Continuing Education,* each issue of which is a directory of over 2,000 United States and Canadian seminars and short courses covering the fields of science, technology, management, medicine, health, law, and government.

Faculty in various departments of the university frequently offer both "in-plant" and on-campus courses of this type. There are obvious advantages to both approaches.

Evening School   University evening schools provide the training specialist with a particularly valuable resource in the area of career planning. The vast number of organizations providing some form of educational assistance to employees attests to the popularity of this means of employee development. Obviously, utilization of this resource requires educational facilities within commuting distance, but the training director should not overlook the possibility of, in effect, bringing the campus to the organization—a practice not uncommon these days.

Correspondence Study   The National Home Study Council reported a student body of slightly over 5 million in 1970. This is total enrollment, including students in university correspondence courses. Such courses offer a high degree of flexibility to the training specialist and can be a valuable addition to the total training program. Detailed information regarding this resource can be found in Chapter 38, "Correspondence Study."

Community and Junior Colleges   With the increasing number of junior and community colleges in recent years, there has emerged yet another important resource for the training specialist. While there is typically a heavy emphasis on vocational and technical education at these institutions, the faculty frequently conduct supervisory and management training on a consulting basis. Some actually conduct on-campus vocational and technical training for requesting community organizations or help staff such programs at the plant site. It behooves training specialists to acquaint themselves with the resources available in their communities.

High Schools   The increased emphasis on the training of the disadvantaged has resulted in numerous and unusual cooperative efforts between companies and community high schools. A detailed description of a sample of 15 such programs is contained in *Industry and Schools Cooperate in 15 Different Ways,* compiled by Linda G. Douglass.[17] In general these programs are designed to minimize the number of high school dropouts and maximize suitable job placement of the culturally and educationally disadvantaged.

CONCLUDING REMARKS

If nothing else, this chapter suggests an almost infinite variety of ways in which educational and noneducational organizations can work to mutual benefit in the areas of training and management education. The life-span of both managerial and technical know-how decreases as society becomes more complex. University faculties are broadening the scope of their activities in the management and technical areas. One can therefore expect an even greater variety of mutually facilitative effort than has occurred in the past. Some writers talk seriously about interchanging university faculty and managerial personnel. It has even been suggested that beginning now, managers can expect to spend one out of every ten years in an educational institution because of the increasingly rapid obsolescence of knowledge. And when one considers what is happening in the field of educational technology, limiting factors to cooperative endeavors—such as space and time constraints—are soon to become very minor considerations. One can probably conclude that the only limit to new and innovative modes of cooperative effort on the part of university and nonuniversity organizations is the imagination of organizational and university personnel.

REFERENCES

1. Patten, Thomas H., Jr.: *Manpower Planning and the Development of Human Resources,* John Wiley & Sons, Inc., New York, 1971.

   Andrews, Kenneth R.: *The Effectiveness of University Management Development Programs,* Harvard University, Graduate School of Business Administration, Boston, 1966.
2. Patten: op. cit.
3. Ibid.
4. Bricker, George W.: *1974 Executive Development Programs,* Prentice-Hall, Inc., Englewood Cliffs, N.J., 1973.
5. Ibid.
6. Andrews: op. cit.
7. Bricker, George W.: *Bricker's International Directory of University-sponsored Executive Development Programs plus Marketing Management Programs,* Bricker Publications, South Chatham, Mass., 1975.
8. Abstracts prepared by ERIC Clearinghouse on Adult Education, Syracuse, N.Y.
9. Powell, Reed M., and Charles S. Davis: "Do Executive Development Programs Pay Off?" *Business Horizons,* p. 84, August 1973.
10. Andrews: op. cit.
11. Powell, Reed M.: *The Role and Impact of the Part-Time University Program in Executive Education,* University of California, Graduate School of Business, Division of Research, Los Angeles, Calif., 1962.
12. Ibid.
13. Ibid.
14. Powell and Davis: op. cit., p. 87.
15. Ibid., p. 84.
16. Ibid.
17. Douglass, Linda G.: *Industry and Schools Cooperate in 15 Different Ways,* University of Tennessee, Occupational Research Coordinating Unit, 1969.

Chapter **46**

Using Outside Training Consultants

SCOTT B. PARRY

JOHN R. RIBBING

Scott B. Parry *is a consulting psychologist and President of Training House, Inc., in New York City. A former Director of Sterling Institute and President of Training Development Center, he has personally handled more than 100 client accounts during the past 10 years. Dr. Parry is on the board of directors of ASTD's metropolitan New York chapter and on the faculty of the Management Institute of New York University, where he teaches courses on needs analysis, instructional system design, and organizational psychology.*

John R. Ribbing *is Manager of the Training Department, Coca-Cola U.S.A., in Atlanta, prior to which he was Brand Manager of Fanta and Advertising Manager for overseas sales of Coke and allied brands. Before joining the Coca-Cola Company in 1965, Mr. Ribbing managed an advertising agency; thus he is "at home" on both sides of the consultant-client desk. He typically makes use of at least a half dozen outside consultants at any given time.*

During the past decade, there has been a tremendous increase in the number of organizations that buy professional training services from outside sources. As a result, we have seen a marked growth in the number of firms providing these services. While companies pay substantial fees to training consultants, the dollar amount is small compared with the moneys at stake when clients follow the advice of consultants or put to use their programs and experience. In short, the hiring of consultants must be done on the same basis that any other sound purchasing decision is made: through cost-benefit analysis. A client invests in training to help his or her people perform in ways that are clearly beneficial to the people and to the enterprise. Consultants who cannot earn or save an organization more money than they cost should not be retained.

Consultant Defined Let us start by agreeing on what a consultant is—and is not. You are already familiar with some of the tongue-in-cheek remarks that are frequently made:

- A consultant is someone who borrows your watch, tells you what time it is, and then keeps it.
- Those who *can,* do; those who *can't,* consult.
- A consultant is someone who can help you go wrong with confidence.

Fortunately, similar derogatory comments are made about doctors, lawyers, and other professionals, and so we need not take them too seriously. They are, in fact, symptomatic of a universal problem that all of us face: knowing when we do and do not need outside help, be it the help of a consultant, doctor, lawyer, or TV repairman. Because we lack the knowledge and experience that professionals bring us, we are uncertain about how to utilize their services and how to evaluate their performance.

For our purposes, let us agree to define a training consultant as any outside individual or firm who is paid *primarily* for the delivery of professional training advice and/or service. This definition excludes outside suppliers of films, public seminars, cassettes, audiovisual hardware or software, tests, and other training products or services that are purchased "off the shelf." Of course, our definition does not bar consultants from having a product line. Indeed, those who have been in the consulting business for at least several years are likely to have favorite activities and exercises that they bring to new clients. Experience in using these is one of the consultant's main assets (provided they fit the client's needs).

In short, a consultant may offer both products and services, but the primary emphasis must be on the delivery of performance, not products. And, unlike the vendor of training products, the consultant has the ability to measure human performance, carry out needs analysis, prepare and conduct courses, train the client's trainers, and provide the other services necessary to assure delivery of the trainee's performance as specified.

Although our definition and discussion so far have been based on the assumption that the consultant is an outsider, an increasing number of organizations now have internal consultants—specialists in organizational development, human resource utilization, technical training, and so on. An increasing trend is to charge their services to the using department through a system of cross-budget credits and debits. These staff specialists often have more in common with the outside consultant than they do with training director who is still functioning as principal of an internal "little red schoolhouse."

WHEN TO USE A CONSULTANT

There are three major reasons, or needs, that prompt companies to use training consultants:

- The need to expand capability on a "crash" basis—when time is short and stakes are high (e.g., using office temporaries to supplement your own staff on a crash project). Many organizations keep a lean training department whose staff members are problem solvers, internal consultants, or project managers who call on outsiders to create and/or deliver courses.
- The need for specialized *expertise* or *facilities* (e.g., calling in the doctor or TV repairman). The design or selection of needs-analysis instruments and/or specialized instructional techniques may require professional skills that can be purchased from an outsider as needed for much less than it would cost to recruit or develop and maintain this expertise internally.
- Need for the "intangibles" of *objectivity* or *corporate leverage* to get a job done. This is a political reason for using an outside consultant whose neutrality and/or credibility is an asset in terms of seeing the problem in a fresh perspective and getting top management to listen. Training directors know all too well

that prophets are never heeded in their own country. Outsiders may command attention and be catalysts in getting things done, whereas insiders would have difficulty (either because their personal stakes in the outcome render them suspect or simply because they lack experience, credentials, or leverage).

Given these reasons for employing outside help, let us examine some of the major types of client engagements that consultants accept. Some training consultants are specialists, and others are generalists who have competence in a broad range of activities. Surveying the range of firms and individuals that identify themselves *primarily* as training consultants, we find their activities falling into one or more of the categories listed in Fig. 46-1.

Note that we have avoided any reference to the consultant's area of expertise—sales management, bank teller training, etc. A company seeking outside help should look for a consultant with experience in the same industry or functional area (sales). Of course, it is often not possible to find a consultant who is both the subject matter expert (SME) and the behavioral technologist. In most engagements, the client provides the SME who works with the outside consultant. This kind of partnership usually produces a more satisfactory and more cost-effective end result than is possible when the client and consultant work separately on the assumption that the consultant possesses all the subject matter expertise needed to fill the engagement. (Even if the consultant does, the client or the client's staff experts may be unwilling to admit it and may even engage in a variety of

---

a. ANALYSIS—analysis of human performance and assessment of organizational and individual needs. Includes task analysis, systems analysis, behavioral analysis, establishing behavioral objectives and performance criteria, and use of tests and survey research.

b. DESIGN—design of training programs. Includes research to determine course content and a design rationale for selecting methods and media, instructional strategies, criterion test, and decisions on administering the instructional—when, where, how often, for whom, by whom, etc.

c. PRODUCTION—preparation of instructional materials. Writing of training manuals, programmed instruction, cases, role plays, instructor guidelines, games and simulations, script for tape, creation of slides, film, videotape, flip charts, wall charts, etc.

d. PRESENTING—teaching. Giving in-company courses (either public, tailored, or homegrown) in such areas as sales training, management by objectives, problem solving, management development, transactional analysis, sensitivity training, "train-the-trainer" workshops, and EEO implementation.

e. IMPLEMENTING—installing instructional systems. Tailoring of the consultant's existing courses to meet the needs of client, and training of client's instructors in how to administer the course(s) on a continuing basis.

f. EVALUATING—evaluation and/or design of performance development systems. Performance appraisal, job analysis, preparation of job descriptions, assessment labs, skills inventories, placement, career planning succession programs, and OD work.

Fig. 46-1 Major types of activities of training consultants.

interesting behaviors calculated to undermine or disprove the consultant's expertise in his or her area of specialization.) This happens when the client's staff and the consultant see one another as competitors rather than as team members; building the team relationship on a task-focused basis is essential. It is the operational key to success for the task and to the operation of any long-term relationships in a constructive mode.

Defining the Job

From the client's viewpoint, our "inventory of activities" listed in Fig. 46-1 should help you to identify the nature and scope of services you are looking for. Thereafter, it is much easier to *select* the type of consultant who can best meet your needs and to agree on the division of labor between your staff and the consultant's.

Let us illustrate this:

- If you are interested in carrying out a needs analysis and in receiving professional advice on systems design (items a, b, e, and f in Fig. 46-1), then you should seek a consultant who has problem-solving skills, research design experience, maturity, and a following of clients for whom these services have been performed satisfactorily.
- If you are interested in finding outside help in putting together a course (items b and c), then you should find a consultant who has experience and creative skills in the various instructional methods and media, including both *presentation systems* (film, slides, overhead, etc.) and *practice and feedback systems* (role play, case method, games and simulations, etc.).
- If you are interested in finding a consultant to teach in-company courses for you (item d), then you will look for someone with a dynamic personality, subject matter expertise, and a catalytic teaching style that produces a high degree of learner interest and participation.

These three examples illustrate the same point: You must know what you want done before you seek out a consultant, and you should look for and be able to identify a consultant who has the skills to do the job. This sounds like a truism, and yet we could all point to examples of firms that have engaged consultants without first establishing the nature and scope of their involvement and the performance criteria against which they would be evaluated. Figures 46-2 and 46-3 might be useful to client and consultant alike in helping them to define what work is to be done and by whom. Figure 46-2 shows the training cycle in flow-chart form; Figure 46-3 is a "checklist" expansion of the major steps in the training cycle.

GUIDELINES FOR SELECTING CONSULTANTS

Unlike the purchase of tangible goods, the selection of a consultant carries with it a mystique that often finds buyers putting their trust in the seller's hands. To a certain degree this is true—much as you trust your doctor, lawyer, or TV repairman. What we are discussing, of course, is *trust* and *confidence*. This is perhaps the first quality to look for.

Does your consultant inspire confidence, or do you think twice about giving out information and being completely candid? A professional consultant will protect the interest of your company; a nonprofessional may carry tales outside the company, steal key people from you, or work for your competitor immediately after completing your contract. (You may want to include a "noncompetitive work" clause in your contract.)

The client should examine the consultant's desire for a long-term relationship— many consultants develop a pattern of going from client to client rather than building longer relationships with a base group of clients.

Is your consultant a professional who can build trust and confidence, or are you likely to be less than open and continue to regard your consultant as an outsider?

A second quality you should look for in a training consultant is a solid *understanding* of your problem or need. Listen to the questions your consultant asks and the manner in which he or she goes about testing you and your assumptions

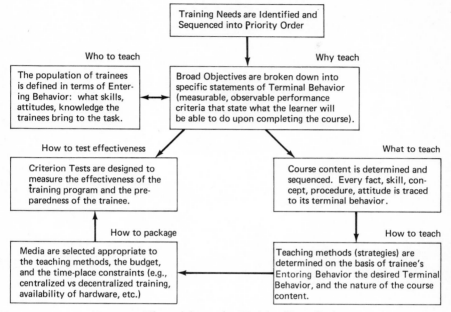

Fig. 46-2   The training cycle. *(Training House, Inc.)*

relating to the need. Some consultants have one or two techniques, instruments, or methods which, they will assure you, are just what you need. Others may focus on the abilities or experience of key persons in their firm. Still others spend much of their time describing specific problems they solved for other clients relating an impressive array of success stories.

However useful it might be to have a consultant that can bring you proved methods, key people, and success stories, the real test of professional consultants is their ability to listen, probe, test, analyze, and thereby come to grips with *your* problem. Listen to see how much time the consultant spends discussing his or her satisfiers versus your needs. What is the ratio between the two? Which does the consultant want to talk about first? The answers to these two questions can be quite revealing, and they may help you to separate professionals from those who have solutions in search of problems.

The outstanding training consultants are those who have sold their services and proved their worth on the basis of their understanding of the client's problems, needs, resources, and constraints. In entering a new engagement, they bring with them experience, but they reserve judgment on what is called for until they have first listened to the client and done their own independent data gathering. Professionals know that their objectivity is a major part of their value.

A third quality to look for is the consultant's ability to *reduce uncertainty*. Uncertainty always accompanies change. Often the solving of one set of problems or needs may produce another set. We identified earlier the three most common reasons for engaging a consultant: shortage of *time*, shortage of *expertise*, and

PLANNING
AND
DEFINING

1. Specify organizational objectives.
2. Perform a needs analysis. (Identify the problem; is it a training problem? a manpower distribution problem? an equipment problem? etc.)
3. Specify human learner performance objectives.
4. Specify terminal behaviors.
5. Specify entering behaviors.
6. Develop a criterion test.

STRUCTURING
AND
ENLARGING

7. Determine course contents: facts, skills, procedures, attitudes, concepts, principles, etc.
8. Organize material in a "teachable" way:
   a. Progression from simple to complex.
   b. Relate the new to the old; build a web of learning.
   c. Organize material in a "logical" way: chronological and psychological, in addition to the "logical" order in which it has always been done.
9. Flesh out the content outline: draw examples from the real world of behavior, illustrations, anecdotes to bring things to life.
10. Ask management to review materials developed to this point: make revisions, if necessary, and obtain go-ahead.

STRATEGY
AND
METHOD

11. Determine instructional strategies—concepts vs. rote (RulEg, EgRul). Keep in mind, "We learn not by being told, but by experiencing the consequences of our actions."
12. Decide on instructional methods—lecture, text, slides, photos. Both presentation and response methods must be built into the instructional system, so that the learner may respond in an audial mode (discussion, question and answer, cases) or a visual mode (draw diagram, make visual discrimination).
13. Packing or media for the course is determined.

DEVELOPMENT
AND
TESTING

14. Write the course (or supervise the writing of it).
15. Review by management and SME's of the material in as close to finished production form as possible. (This review is for content—not format.)
16. Developmentally test the course with 1, 2, or 3 trainees at a time.
17. Revise accordingly.
18. Prepare a field tryout edition of the course.
19. Select a sample of the population of trainees to try out the course.
20. Train the administrators of the field test.
21. Conduct the field test.
22. Analyze the data from the field test.
23. Revise accordingly (Another tryout necessary?)

PRODUCTION
AND
EFFECTING

24. Prepare final version of course, using professional narration, artwork, etc. Order in quantity (or schedule seminars, etc.).
25. Distribute materials and train administrators (provide administrator's guide, test score key, data collection forms).

Fig. 46-3 Steps in the design of an instructional system. *(Training House, Inc.)*

shortage of *objectivity* or *corporate leverage*. Behind each of these is the client's desire to reduce uncertainty. This is the fundamental service that the experienced, professional consultant can provide. The novice can bring specialized knowledge and skills to a client, but an inexperienced consultant is often unable to reduce risk for the client (and, in many cases, may actually increase the probability of failure).

In selecting a consultant, find out how he or she proposes to reduce risk or develop benefits. What controls and check points will be used to measure progress? What prior successes and failures (with reasons why) has the consultant had with other clients? Does the consultant talk about results and successes, or does the talk center on products and services to be provided? In selecting a consultant, you should check with two or three current clients to get the answers to these questions.

There are many other factors to look for in selecting consultants, of course. Here are a few:

- Is your consultant concerned with making you and your program a success, or is he or she on an ego trip, using your organization to meet personality needs? (Many consultants have strong ego needs; the issue is whether these needs are satisfied as a by-product of meeting the needs of your organization.)
- How fast does the consultant grasp your operations, the opportunities and constraints, and the nature of the interpersonal relations (company politics, personal rivalries, etc.)? Are the consultant's people-handling skills equal to his or her task-handling skills?
- How will your fellow managers perceive the consultant? Will the consultant make friends for you in making contacts with other employees, or is there a danger that he or she will embarrass you or cause others to wonder why you brought in such a person?
- How much time will the principal or principals in the consulting firm be spending with you? Do you know who will be assigned to the contract? Are you getting the "first team" or "second stringers"?
- Are you seeking a "bargain" or a "value" in selecting a consultant? Can the consultant contribute ways that will build the success of your own organization while adding to his or her own business strength? Is the consultant a good business person?

THE NEEDS ANALYSIS

Realizing the importance of getting the answers to these questions *before* entering into contract with a consultant, many firms begin the needs-analysis phase of a project on a per diem basis, reimbursing the consultant for labor and out-of-pocket expenses while they work together in establishing the need and in defining the nature and scope of the project. The major kinds of activities that go into a needs analysis are listed in Figs. 46-4 and 46-5.

Typically, a needs analysis may last from several days to several months. It gives both client and consultant the opportunity to see one another at work, to decide how they can work together to best advantage, and to establish criteria for evaluating the success of the project. It is extremely important that this be a joint activity of both parties; the consultant should not be expected to go back to his or her office and write up a program or proposal until this dual investment is made.

The end product of the needs analysis is a blueprint—a plan of action that both parties feel is appropriate to pursue. This plan of action usually lists the behavioral objectives (terminal behaviors, performance criteria) that trainees will have reached upon completion of their training. In smaller engagements, the needs

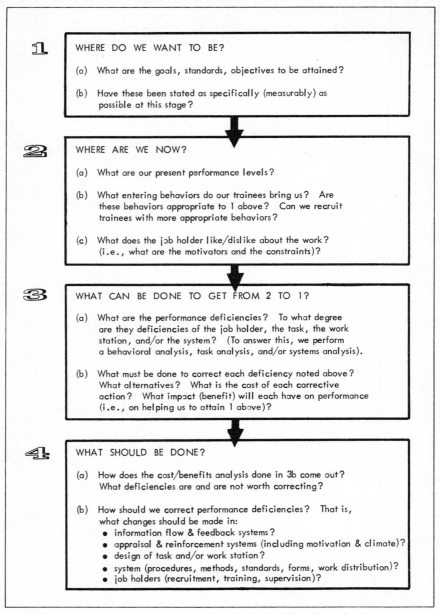

1   WHERE DO WE WANT TO BE?

(a)   What are the goals, standards, objectives to be attained?

(b)   Have these been stated as specifically (measurably) as possible at this stage?

2   WHERE ARE WE NOW?

(a)   What are our present performance levels?

(b)   What entering behaviors do our trainees bring us?   Are these behaviors appropriate to 1 above?   Can we recruit trainees with more appropriate behaviors?

(c)   What does the job holder like/dislike about the work? (i.e., what are the motivators and the constraints)?

3   WHAT CAN BE DONE TO GET FROM 2 TO 1?

(a)   What are the performance deficiencies?   To what degree are they deficiencies of the job holder, the task, the work station, and/or the system?   (To answer this, we perform a behavioral analysis, task analysis, and/or systems analysis).

(b)   What must be done to correct each deficiency noted above? What alternatives?   What is the cost of each corrective action?   What impact (benefit) will each have on performance (i.e., on helping us to attain 1 above)?

4   WHAT SHOULD BE DONE?

(a)   How does the cost/benefits analysis done in 3b come out? What deficiencies are and are not worth correcting?

(b)   How should we correct performance deficiencies?   That is, what changes should be made in:
  • information flow & feedback systems?
  • appraisal & reinforcement systems (including motivation & climate)?
  • design of task and/or work station?
  • system (procedures, methods, standards, forms, work distribution)?
  • job holders (recruitment, training, supervision)?

Fig. 46-4   Conducting a needs analysis. *(Training House, Inc.)*

analysis may take only a few weeks to complete and may be paid for under a per diem arrangement. (Fees and billing will be discussed later.) When the consulting engagement and training project are more ambitious in nature, the needs analysis may make use of a combination of research techniques (see Fig. 46-5) and may require many months. In such cases, the client and consultant usually enter into contract to cover the needs-analysis phase of the work (with a subsequent contract to cover the materials development phase). Their preliminary per diem time is then spent together in determining what information they want and why and how they plan to get it during the needs analysis.

A word of caution regarding the needs analysis: Many training directors (or their top management) are action-oriented and do not enjoy seeing a lot of time

---

SURVEY RESEARCH

Interviewing – present job holders, new trainees, supervisors, etc.

Questionnaire—mailed or filed at work, alone or in researcher's presence

"Climate survey"—measure morale, commitment, work environment

Tests of proficiency—writing skill, knowledge of supervisory practices

Attitude survey—management style (Theory X and Y), women in management

Human relations, etc.

"Critical incident" research

TASK ANALYSIS AND SYSTEM ANALYSIS

Flow charting and procedure and work flow

Work distribution study and analysis of time sheets

Methods improvement and work simplification

"Present vs. proposed" analysis of work elements

Operation analysis, man-machine analysis

FIELD OBSERVATION

Participant observer (as "coworker")

Nonparticipant observer: obtrusive and unobtrusive

Observer rating sheets, McBee cardsorts, etc.

"Shopping survey"—retail sales, banks, airlines, etc.

RECORD CHECK

Study production standards, quotas, appraisals, call reports

Systems and procedures documentation (flow charts, etc.)

SOP manuals, training guides, etc.

Complaints, error rates, rejects, "squeaky wheel" data

Job descriptions, performance appraisals, etc.

Library research-trade association data, competitor's data, studies by industry, use of experts, commercially available courses, etc.

SIMULATION AND ASSESSMENT LABS

Performance assessment in managerial skills

In-basket and managerial appraisals

Role playing—selling skills, interviewing

Case analysis in problem-solving and decision-making skills

Fig. 46-5 Methods and techniques of conducting a needs analysis.

and money spent on research to determine the need. "We *know* we need training," they are quick to tell the consultant. "So why spend a lot of time carrying out a needs analysis?" A little selling (educating, if you prefer) may be called for to make sure that client and consultant are agreed on the values obtained. A list of the major reasons for doing a needs analysis is shown in Fig. 46-6. But all these reasons can be summed up in Bob Mager's delightful parable of the seahorse who observed that "if you don't know where you are or where you want to be, you're not very likely to get there."[1]

Note our sixth reason in Fig. 46-6. This is the one that enables client and consultant to make decisions regarding the design and implementation of the instructional system: Who will be trained? Where, when, and in what sequence will they be trained? What criteria, standards, objectives, etc., will be used to measure performance? What course content, methods, media, and instructional strategies will be employed? How will the system be administered? Who will teach, who will

---

1. To find out <u>what</u> the present level of performance is. By establishing a "bench level" of present behavior (performance), we can measure change over time. That is, a needs analysis will give us pretraining measures which we can compare with our posttraining measures (assuming we give training. . . there may be other ways besides training to improve performance).

2. To determine <u>why</u> present performance is what it is. Why are those whom we'll be training performing as they are? What reinforcers are maintaining their behavior? What contingencies and constraints are preventing better performance? What is the relative strength of each of the factors affecting human performance, both positively and negatively? What can be done to increase the positive and reduce the negative?

3. To find out <u>who the trainees are</u>. What entering behavior do they bring to the job? What strengths can we build on? What deficiences do they possess? How universal are these? How homogeneous or heterogenous is our population of trainees? Should they be subgrouped for ease of administering different modules of training to deal with individual differences?

4. To <u>assess the organizational climate</u> or work environment within which the trainee operates. Will it support and nourish the behavior we will shape through training, or will it discourage and cause it to die? What can we do to improve climate? How can we prepare the trainee, his or her boss, customers, etc., to maintain a supportive climate?

5. To <u>examine the systems and procedures</u> employed with a view toward identifying ways of working smarter instead of harder. Can steps, tasks, forms, etc., possibly be eliminated, resequenced, combined, simplified to produce better behavior (increased output, reduced error, easier work, etc.)? Methods improvement and work simplification should always be examined as a possibility throughout your study of tasks performed, work stations, work flow, and who does what.

6. To <u>establish behavioral objectives</u>. . . measurable, observable, specific performance goals that each trainee must achieve as a result of training and/or whatever other changes (e.g., organizational, motivational) you identify as essential to producing and maintaining the desired behaviors. These objectives can be analyzed and sorted into subcategories for convenience in designing our subsequent behavior-shaping strategies. For example, behavior might be classified as cognitive, affective, and psychomotor (knowing, feeling, doing). . . or as knowledge, attitudes, skills (since not all skills are psychomotor—e.g., interviewing, proofreading). Skills might be further classified as task-handling and people-handling.

7. To <u>establish policy and make decisions</u> regarding the length, scope, format, location, cost, frequency, etc., of training. Examples of these decisions: initial vs. continuation (i.e., how much or how little to teach initially vs. subsequently); formal vs. OJT (i.e., "vestibule" and classroom vs. training by supervisor on the job); make vs. buy; head vs. book (must know "cold" vs. can look up or ask someone); centralized vs. decentralized training; individual vs. group (self-instruction vs. group-based); etc.

8. To <u>involve line managers</u> and others in your organization whose support and whose inputs are important to the success of your training efforts (e.g., the bosses of your trainees, the subject matter experts, the influentials. By getting them ego-involved at the start and forming a "partnership" with them you can rely on them to promote and sell training (or make changes in procedures, systems, reinforcement schedules, etc.).

Fig. 46-6   Reasons for conducting a needs analysis. (*Training House, Inc.*)

1. The supervisor's unwillingness to rate employees who may be virtually unknown.

2. The supervisor's unwillingness to take the time or make the effort to analyze the employee thoroughly.

3. Differences in temperament between raters—some are overfriendly, others are overcritical.

4. The "halo effect"—if the man is liked, he is seen as excelling in every trait; if disliked, as deficient in every trait.

5. The overweighting of recent occurrences, either favorable or unfavorable.

6. The need to give superiors information which will not embarrass the rater ("None of my people are less than 100 percent—I wouldn't keep such a person").

7. The need to use the ratings for personal gain—to win a subordinate's favor, or to hold back a subordinate whose progress threatens the rater.

8. The need to play politics and tell superiors what they want to hear.

9. The reluctance to make adverse ratings for fear they might have to be discussed with the employee.

10. The use of ratings for an ulterior purpose—to justify giving or withholding raises or promotions.

11. The lack of uniform criteria or standards of performance from rater to rater.

12. Personal prejudice or bias on the part of the rater—"All Swedes are squareheads."

13. Extreme rater indecisiveness—the inability to make a categorical judgment.

14. Lack of analytical ability on the part of the rater—the inability to see cause-effect relationships.

15. "Central tendency"—the reluctance of the rater to rate either high or low, the wish to stick to the safer middle ground of a "good" or "average" rating.

16. A proneness to wishful thinking—"Everyone is promotable, perhaps in five years."

17. The tendency to generalize from an inadequate or unrepresentative sampling of the employee's behavior.

18. The lack of companywide agreement as to what criteria and standards must be met to obtain a given rating.

19. The universality of rating forms that were designed to evaluate all employees in the company (with broad categories like "Quantity of Work" and "Knowledge of Job" that apply to everyone but are therefore job-specific to no one).

20. The belief by many supervisors that performance appraisal is done mainly to let the Personnel Department know who should and shouldn't get raises. (This leads many supervisors to "work backward" from the amount of pay raise they want to recommend to a rating that would justify it.)

Fig. 46-7 Problems with performance rating systems.

collect performance data, who will promote the program and enroll the trainees, etc.? These are the questions that should be answered at the end of the needs-analysis phase. These answers mark the beginning of the materials development and systems design phase.

Those who have been in the field of training for some time have learned, often painfully, that not every problem is a training problem. We could point to courses we have put together which were very good training programs (from an instructional systems design standpoint) but which failed to produce the desired terminal behavior in the trainee. A consultant who has (1) experience working with many firms, (2) a behavioral sceintist's outlook, and (3) an understanding of the many organizational factors affecting human performance (see Fig. 46-7) can be especially helpful in counseling a client on the degree to which training per se will and will not be useful in producing behavior change. The research tools used to carry out a needs analysis (Fig. 46-6) are valuable in helping a firm to identify the factors that are at work in producing or hindering the desired performance (organiza-

---

Statement of Objectives: How will the performance of the consultant and her or his products and our services be measured? If behavioral objectives do not yet exist, who is responsible for preparing them?

Scope of Work: How is the work divided in the phases (e.g., needs analysis, design of instructional system with selection of methods and media, creation of course materials, instructor time evaluation and follow-up)? What are the limits of responsibility, both for client and consultant?

Obligations of Both Parties: What will the client provide? What will the consultant provide? This should be as specific as possible, down to estimated man-days with names of person(s) who will be working on the project. In other words, who are the players on the client consultant team and what specific role will each fill?

Time Frame: This should include both calendar time (duration of project) and man-days of time, as described above. Due dates for each phase of the work should be stated.

Costs and Payment Schedule: What is the overall price of the contract? What will the payment schedule be? For example, an initial payment upon signing the contract with subsequent payments based on monthly billing or completion of each phase of work. Are travel costs included or will they be billed seperately? How about out-of-pocket expenses (e.g., printing costs, duplication of slides, use of professional voices or actors)? Is the client expected to submit an accounting with each bill of the time worked against the contract?

Discussion for Nonacceptability: If performance criteria have been spelled out in detail, the client may want to build into the contract some measures that terminate payment to the consultant for failure to deliver. Some contracts also have reward and penalty clauses for early or late delivery.

Noncompetetive Assurance: In highly competitive industries a client sometimes has a consultant agree to do no work for competitors (these must be defined, of course) throughout the period of the contract or for one or two years thereafter.

Fig. 46-8   Factors to be considered in a contract or letter of agreement.

tional climate, reinforcement and feedback systems, work-station design, work flow, design of forms and procedures, recruitment and placement policies, etc.; see Fig. 46-7).

FEES AND BILLING

As discussed earlier, consultants generally charge for their services on either a project basis (i.e., fixed-fee) or a time-plus-expenses basis (i.e., per diem). Either way, charges are based primarily on the consultant's time (see Fig. 46-8). When the nature and scope of the work to be done can be defined very specifically in advance, with agreement between consultant and client on the amount of time each will spend on the project, then it is appropriate to have a fixed fee for the project. However, many consulting engagements are subject to the "iceberg" phenomenon: Neither client nor consultant knows what lies beneath the surface— they can see only a small fraction of the mass. Projects of this nature should be priced on a per diem basis; otherwise, one party will inevitably end up being "short-changed."

For this reason, many consulting engagements are planned in two phases, with phase 1 being the needs-analysis phase (the activities described in Fig. 46-4). Here it is appropriate for the consultant to bill on a per diem basis. One of the objectives of a needs analysis, of course, is to define in precise terms the kinds of activities (courses, materials, etc.) that are needed. Once client and consultant have defined these, a fixed-fee contract is usually desired by both parties: *Clients* must budget specific amounts and are glad to have the "open-ended" phase 1 behind them, and *consultants* like the incentive of performing within the time estimates on which the fixed fee was based, thereby increasing the profit margin.

Both client and consultant have cash-flow needs, and it is important for both to agree on how and when fees are to be paid. Some contracts simply divide the total contract price into equal payments payable monthly (or at equal time intervals) throughout the contract. Others will make payments contingent on delivery of the specified products or services. Thus a contract covering the production of a course to be done in eight modules (lessons, cassettes, weeks, locations, etc.) might be billed in nine equal payments: the first is payable upon signing the agreement, the second is payable upon delivery of module 1, and so on.

REFERENCE

1. Mager, Robert F.: *Preparing Instructional Objectives,* Lear Siegler, Inc./Fearon Publishers, Inc., Belmont, Calif., 1962, preface.

Chapter **47**

Using External Programs and Training Packages

J. A. CANTWELL

D. J. HOSTERMAN

H. R. SHELTON

John A. Cantwell *is a member of the instructional development staff of the Engineering and Science Education Division, Sandia Laboratories, Albuquerque, New Mexico. He has served as a management consultant to various educational research and development organizations and for two years was on the staff of the National Center for Educational Research and Development, U.S. Department of Health, Education, and Welfare.*

Donald J. Hosterman *is a member of the instructional development staff of the Engineering and Science Education Division, Sandia Laboratories, Albuquerque, New Mexico. He has worked professionally in technical writing and in various phases of education, including instruction in basic Russian and sociology, and in educational television (KNME-TV, University of New Mexico). He has served as consultant to numerous universities in the establishment of cooperative educational and research problems sponsored by Associated Western Universities and the AEC's Division of Nuclear Education and Training.*

Howard R. Shelton *is Supervisor, Engineering and Science Education Division, Sandia Laboratories, Albuquerque, New Mexico. He has served as chairman of the Continuing Engineering Studies Division of the American Society for Engineering Education and as president of the New Mexico chapter of ASTD. He has served as technical and vocational education consultant to the Electromechanical Technology Project sponsored by the Technical Education Research Center in conjunction with Oklahoma State University. He has also served as consultant to the Technical-Vocational Institute, Albuquerque, New Mexico. He was chairman of a recent Engineering Foundation conference on the engineering and psychological aspects of maintaining the professional and technical competence of the older engineer. He was also coeditor of the conference monograph, published by the American Society for Engineering Education.*

The purpose of this chapter is to discuss various issues associated with the use of external programs and training packages. There is little information on this topic in the literature, and yet it is a major consideration in the trainer's day-to-day responsibilities.

This chapter discusses guidelines for selecting, working with, and judging the effectiveness of the external resource. In addition, it addresses the role and responsibilities of the various individuals in an organization who are involved in planning and conducting training and the issues which need to be faced before the decision is made to use an external resource.

To provide more clarity to the discussion, it is necessary to define some terms. Throughout the chapter, "trainer" refers to any individual in an organization who has responsibility for providing education, training, and development for the employees of the organization, although he or she may not be the person doing the instructing. "Organization" refers to the trainer's company, institution, or agency. "External resource" refers to all programs and training packages which are obtained from outside the organization, whether conducted on the organization's site or at another location.

Certain assumptions form the basis for the concepts presented in this chapter.

It is more economical to obtain a program from an external resource than to develop the program in-house. The reason is that the external resource can distribute the development costs across a large number of users. Most organizations cannot match this reduction in development costs when offering the programs only to their own employees.

The primary goal of training is to bring about measurable changes in job performance. Off-the-shelf programs developed without regard for specific organizational needs may not be adequate to meet this kind of goal. If they are not, the economy of obtaining the external resource is greatly diminished.

The trainer is accountable for the effectiveness of training, whether done by an external or an internal resource. The level of effort that the trainer expends to assure the effectiveness of the training at reasonable cost is essentially the same when using an external resource as when developing instruction in-house.

ROLES AND RESPONSIBILITIES

When external programs are used, there are specific roles and responsibilities of the trainer, the line organization, and the external resource.

Trainer

The trainer should be involved directly in decisions concerning the use of an external program. It is his or her responsibility to provide the perspective on how the external program fits into the total training program of the organization.

The trainer has the responsibility of gathering evaluation data from employees who attend training conducted off-site (short courses, seminars, conferences, etc.) as well as on-site. This information should be made available to management and other employees who may be interested in attending in the future. The trainer also has a responsibility to recommend alternative external resources where data suggest that they may be more appropriate.

The trainer is responsible for assuring that the external program meets the needs of the organization, is reasonable in cost, and incorporates an effective instructional design.

Line Organization

It is the primary responsibility of the line organization to determine what changes in job performance should occur. Since the line organization is the customer (the party seeking improvement in performance), it must be involved in all decisions concerning use of an external resource.

External Resource

The external resource is responsible for delivering the training program as agreed upon with the trainer and the line organization. In order to accomplish this, the external resource must work with both the line organization and the trainer to understand the job performance deficiencies identified by the line organization and to establish an instructional design which will achieve the desired performance changes.

IDENTIFICATION OF TRAINING NEEDS

When supervisors and executives analyze problems of inefficiency and low productivity, training is often proposed as the answer. Unfortunately, this solution may be chosen only because of the pressure to do something quickly. It would be more reasonable to withhold a decision until the problem has received careful examination and other alternatives have been considered. Training can be an expensive proposition and will lead to payoff, in the sense of an investment, only if it can correct specific deficiencies.

There are many reputable external organizations which advertise that their training packages will correct specific deficiencies. Unfortunately, a one-week MBO workshop for executives is not likely to cure internal confusion about organizational priorities. The 42-year-old design engineer is not likely to be technically retreaded by a two-week conference on microelectronics. Such expectations are developed, and thousands of dollars are invested in the hope that these changes will occur. Training may start the processes of updating hoped for, but even that may be questionable.

It takes time and money to investigate causes of organizational inefficiency, employee obsolescence, or whatever the symptomatic ill may be. If causes are not investigated, there is the strong probability not only of wasting the dollar cost of the training but also of jeopardizing future training plans if a given course fails to solve any problems. For example, an executive leaves an MBO workshop frustrated because the concepts discussed bear no relationship to the power and jurisdictional disputes of his or her organization. Everyone is angry—the person trained, line management, and the training organization's management. After the training, it is impossible to answer questions as to what is different if there has not been extensive prior analysis of problem causes and of expected performance changes.

In such situations, trainers' only defense may be that they have been forced to operate in a crisis-response environment. The decision has already been made to conduct training; the trainer is called upon to make the necessary arrangements, and fast. He or she has little or no opportunity to argue for a more deliberate pace in the decision process or a more thorough analysis of the problem.

Data Collection

One way to escape the crisis-response mode is to systematically collect data about problem areas. This does not require thousands of survey forms or computer runs. The organization's executive might periodically ask managers and supervisors what they think are the most pressing deficiencies and problems facing the organization. This source of data can be used to further define what problems warrant training and will usually provide the time to implement the more deliberate approach suggested in this chapter.

There are some traps to be avoided in surveys. Check-off lists of courses or topics of potential interest may not answer the question of what is really needed. For example, a checklist-type survey which indicates some interest in a course on racial or sex discrimination is not evidence that the organization does in fact have a discrimination problem. And if there is a discrimination problem, the form does not indicate the specifics which will help in selecting an external resource that will meet this need. Many organizations have sent first- and second-level managers to courses where they were lectured about the detailed clauses of Title VII of the 1964 Civil Rights Act. Unfortunately, such knowledge does not solve problems such as unequal pay for women.

Survey Formats

In contrast to checklists, survey forms which ask the manager or employee to respond to open-ended questions will usually turn up areas which need attention. It is difficult to summarize such data, and so the trainer may prefer to use a combination check-off list and open-ended questionnaire as an alternative. A modified checklist can help trigger ideas on problem areas; the respondent can expand the specifics in the open-ended section of the form. The survey form should be limited to one or two pages, since lengthier forms tend to be postponed to a more convenient time. More complete questionnaires can be utilized later, after interest has been kindled in a specific problem area.

Another caution relates to the originator of the form. A question-and-answer or checklist survey not only implies the existence of problems but also suggests solutions. If the trainer sends the forms out, the effort may appear self-serving and lack credibility. To prevent this, an appropriate line organization manager should "sponsor" the survey effort and sign correspondence which accompanies the survey forms. Management involvement in a survey should consist of more than endorsing a form. A management group should assist in preparing the survey and analyzing the data.

Problem definition may require more time and effort than either the line organization or the trainer is willing to commit. Yet if adequate time is not devoted to problem definition, there is the risk that training will be planned as the solution, when in fact the answer lies elsewhere.[1]

The most trying situation that the trainer faces occurs when he or she is notified that line management has contracted for a particular external training resource and requests that the trainer arrange for facilities, equipment, coffee, etc.—the "room service" training request. There is no evidence that the proper foundations for training have been laid, and yet the trainer is ultimately unaccountable for its success or failure. Trainers in this situation must grit their teeth, provide the service, and hope that some minor miracles occur. Their only recourse is the systematic surveying of line problems already suggested. The surveys not only will encourage earlier diagnosing of problems but also may give the trainer a role in the decision process at a time when he or she can exercise some influence.

DEVELOP IN-HOUSE OR OBTAIN EXTERNALLY?

When all agree that some form of training is needed, there may be a tendency to make a premature decision between the alternatives of in-house development and use of external resources. The presence of technical experts within an organization may lead to the quick decision to utilize them for training purposes without regard either to the extent of their availability for proper planning and conducting of training or to their abilities as instructors. No firm decision regarding the type, format, or source of training should be made unless sufficient attention has been given first to identification of the trainee population and the establishment of instructional objectives; and even with this attention, the decision will be obscured by factors which may have little to do with training. The trainer needs to consider each of these factors carefully.

Time If the pressures of a situation do not allow time for laying the firm foundation for training discussed earlier, training probably should not be attempted at all; hastily assembled or prematurely purchased training packages which miss the mark are worse than no training at all. In addition, the foundation-laying process will reveal other factors which the trainer needs to consider in his or her decision process.

In-house development of training requires a considerable investment of staff and management time. Lack of time for in-house development may force the trainer to look externally for a training package. But this decision should not be made hastily. Pressure situations in an organization sometimes, over a short period, provide a greater commitment of time and effort from line management and the in-house instructors than will be available in a relaxed, long-schedule situation. Hence the trainer needs to consider not only the time available but also the degree of support he or she will receive from in-house management and the instructional staff.

Technical Expertise, Equipment, and Facilities The influence of these factors in the training decision process becomes clear in the initial planning. Lack of any one or all three can force an early decision to seek an external resource for part or all of the training.

When planning training in new or unique theoretical concepts in such areas as management techniques, sensitivity training, personnel evaluation, and business methods, the trainer should be aware of possible "Cassandra" effects. Prophets are not accepted in their own country, and even though an organization may have in-house experts who are eminently qualified to handle such training, it may be necessary to contract externally if for no other reason than to give credence to the training.

Cost and Company Policy The cost of training and company policy regarding it are two nebulous factors which are difficult to assess. The trainer may encounter the misconception that in-house development and conducting of training is almost free; during low-budget periods, this belief may even grow into a policy which opposes purchase of any external resource. Under these conditions, it will behoove the trainer to think in terms of in-house development for all training, which is not a bad situation as long as the technical expertise, facilities, and development time are adequate.

Less easy to deal with is the opposite conviction, prevalent especially during periods of heavy workload, that external ready-made resources will meet training needs perfectly without any investment of management or staff time for planning and development. The trainer needs the support of line management and other technical staff not only for laying the proper foundations but also in working with the external resource to ensure a format which will achieve the planned instructional objectives. This support is difficult to get when line management argues lack of time, especially if they also believe that such guarantees are "bought" with the package.

There are some techniques the trainer might consider for overcoming the jamming effects of the cost and policy factors. If the organization is large (e.g., government agencies or companies with many branches), training packages may be available for borrowing at little or no cost from another agency within or closely related to the organization. This is especially true of video tape packages which involve no copyright complexities. The trainer needs to maintain open lines of communication with such sources on a continuing basis to ensure their availability when the need arises.

In all training, whether developed in-house or obtained externally, the cost and policy factors are intimately linked with the visible effects of past training efforts. Dollars for training are rarely plentiful, but the cost factor seems to dissolve when there is clear evidence of improved employee performance from past training. And improved employee performance is not the only visible effect of good training. Many supposedly minor considerations—establishing good relationships with trainees and their supervision, efficient course administration, making training courses easily available to all concerned employees, publicizing results, and many others—must be the concern of the trainer if he or she is to be successful in "shaking the money tree" in future training efforts.[2]

Combination Programs   In whatever direction other factors are tending to direct the trainer's decision regarding in-house versus external resources, the trainer should always consider the possibility of a combination package. Where lack of time or other factors prevent complete in-house development, perhaps an external resource, supplemented by some in-house instruction to ensure attention to local applications, will adequately satisfy training needs.

SOURCES OF EXTERNAL PROGRAMS AND TRAINING PACKAGES

Colleges and Universities   Most colleges and universities provide training programs for organizations through an extension service, a continuing education program, and regular academic degree curricula. The trainer should be knowledgeable about the capability of schools in his or her particular geographic area (and, to a somewhat lesser degree, about the capability of schools elsewhere) to provide appropriate credit courses, degree programs, continuing education programs, noncredit courses, short courses, seminars, workshops, symposia, and correspondence courses. Many colleges and universities offer both on-campus programs and programs conducted at the organization's work location.

Professional Societies   Professional societies offer continuing education programs as a prime service to their membership. Courses, workshops, seminars, symposia, independent study, and journals are available. The main advantage of these materials is that they relate directly to the professional field (engineering, law, medicine, etc.) and are available to society members at low cost.

Companies   Many companies have developed training programs as a customer service. These sources tend to be low-cost and practical because they deal specifically with the company's equipment or products and in a subject matter area where they have expertise.

Entrepreneurs   There are individuals and educational consulting firms which provide external programs and packages to organizations. Many of these are leading experts in their specialty areas and can be valuable to an organization. Short courses, workshops, seminars, symposia, noncredit-type courses, independent study materials, and individualized instruction packages are available from entrepreneurs. There are some advantages offered by the entrepreneur because of his flexibility in offering his resources in many different modes.

The trainer should maintain a file of information about programs offered by all the above sources. Such a file would consist of university catalogs, advertising brochures, short-course announcements, journals, publications, clearinghouse directories, and training directories.

FINAL SELECTION OF EXTERNAL RESOURCES

At this point, the reader might be wondering whether there are one or two key questions which can be used to decide which of several available external resources should be selected. Frequently, the basis for making this decision is simply subject matter competence: Who seems to know the most about the topic? A second basis for judgment is ability in course development and instruction: Who seems best at incorporating learning and instructional design considerations in the training? Rather than making a final selection on the basis of the answer to only one of these questions, both issues must be addressed.

Subject Matter Competence

Selection of an external resource, based on its subject matter competence, may be reliable and valid; however, there are some cautions. The organization or individuals who appear to be experts may be everything they or others say about them, but they may have had absolutely no experience with specific organizational applications or problems. If all parties involved are willing to spend the time and effort to correct this deficiency, then subject matter competence can be used effectively.

In addition to the problem of tailoring to specific organizations, there is also the matter of verifying the qualifications of the proposed external instructors. There are many organizations doing MBO and Transactional Analysis training. Slick brochures with pictures and résumés of "qualified" experts are not necessarily reliable evidence. Trainers should not hesitate to contact other organizations who have used the proposed external resource and ascertain the quality of what was done. If the proposed training is critical to improving operations or represents a major cost investment, the trainer should sit in on one or more sessions of a regular course offering conducted by the external resource.

Instructional Design Competence

The research, literature, and practice associated with instructional objectives, self-pacing, criterion testing, task and goal analysis, and a number of related matters are significant. Respected organizations in the industrial community, e.g., American Telephone and Telegraph and the Bank of America, are focusing attention on the design and execution of instruction according to a set of principles which have been undergoing review and development for many years.[3] These organizations have made this commitment on the basis of the results of instruction designed according to the principles suggested by Mager, Briggs, and others. This form of instruction produces better results than the predominantly lecture and conventional-classroom format.[4]

Given this evidence that there are better ways to design instruction, the trainer should first become familiar with some of the data and experience in this area. He or she is then in a position to assess whether the external resource has incorporated recent advances in instructional design. The prospective external resource should be able to document specific instructional objectives, a rationale for how the instructional activity relates to the objectives, and criterion tests which will indicate whether the student can perform as intended. With this documentation, the trainer can be reasonably assured that the prospective resource will provide instruction that leads to changes in employee performance.

NEGOTIATING AND IMPLEMENTING THE AGREEMENT

Usually there is a need for a formal contract, an agreement, or a purchase order when using an external program. In the case of an on-the-shelf program, the decision concerns whether to bring the program into the organization's work location or send people to the resource location. If people are to be sent to the resource, a registration fee is usually all that is required. However, if the program is to be brought to the organization, a more formal agreement is required to establish program and material costs, extent of instructional help from the external resource, constraints of using the resource materials in subsequent training sessions, and need for additional development to meet organization applications. It is recommended that the trainer and a line representative visit with the external resource in his or her place of business to establish a satisfactory line of communication, to provide an opportunity for the external resource to become better informed as to the needs of the organization, and to give the trainer a chance to better assess the capabilities of the external resource.

The content of the contract must cover agreements about the instructional design, evaluation techniques, equipment and supplies, schedule, and costs. In each of these areas it is important that the external resource know exactly what is to be done. The trainer then monitors and assures that the outside program is being delivered as agreed.

Course administration and logistics (costs, method of payment, schedule, class size, facilities, supplies needed, etc.) will occasion most of the contacts between the trainer, line representative, and external resource. However, the trainer should utilize these contacts to the fullest extent possible to discuss course development.

Course Development

Even before the external resource is contacted, the trainer and line representative should establish preliminary instructional objectives on the basis of an analysis of job needs and desired changes in performance. These must be discussed with the external resource before any mention of the administrative and logistics problems, for the trainer needs to know early to what extent the external resource is willing or able to shape the course to fit the organization's needs. The degree of influence the trainer has in course development will vary depending on the nature of the external resource.

Meetings   Short courses, seminars, and conferences conducted off-site by universities, professional societies, or entrepreneurs for numerous different organizations offer little opportunity for addressing specific organizational needs. Nevertheless, it does no harm to discuss these with the external agency. The trainer may learn that his or her organization's problems are similar to those of other organizations the agency has talked to, possibly leading to modifications of the course in order to address specific problems. If the trainer's organization is supplying all or most of the attendees at an off-site course, the external agency may be willing to give major attention to specific needs, especially if the course is new and is in the process of development. In all cases, it must be assumed that external training agencies are interested in the specific job applications of the organizations represented in their classes and that they would prefer getting this information prior to the course rather than in discussion or question-and-answer sessions during the course.

Materials Packages   Media-oriented training packages (video-taped courses, filmstrip and cassette packages, computer-aided instruction, programmed texts, etc.) also provide little or no opportunity for input regarding specific organizational needs. Pre-prepared packages are developed to sell as is; any alterations, modifications, or extensions to answer specific needs must be supplied by the purchaser. Although there are exceptions, the purchaser usually does not deal with the individuals who have developed the package; rather, contact is ordinarily with members of a sales force, who are not necessarily familiar with the facets of instructional design. Previewing the package may be the only reasonable means of making sound judgments regarding its suitability; however, external agencies which design and sell media packages are sometimes reluctant to supply more than a few representative samples for previewing. Purchase of such packages may amount to nothing more than a calculated risk, and it is a risk that should be taken only after careful analysis by both the trainer and the line organization based on all available information. In addition, there are techniques for assuring partial if not complete attention to specific training needs. For example, video-taped courses can be successfully supplemented by on-site experts who serve as "proctors"; they preview the tapes, determine to what extent they satisfy the preestablished instructional objectives, and prepare lectures, problem sets, tests, etc., as necessary to make up for any deficiencies of content or instructional design.

Tailoring to Specific Needs   When dealing with an external resource (entrepreneur, lecturer, etc.) that is to be brought to the organization to conduct training, both the trainer and the line representative should plan extensive communication regarding course development, including specific organization applications and instructional design. Fortunately, many entrepreneurs have incorporated some of the newer instructional design techniques in their programs; dealing with these can make the trainer's burden lighter. A comparison of content needs and preestablished instructional objectives, as worked out by the trainer and the line manager, with those announced by the entrepreneur will indicate to what extent the course answers specific organizational needs. Entrepreneurs of this type are capable of making minor changes in content and format and are willing to do so. However, the trainer should be aware that the economics of professional training packages dictate purchase of the package essentially as developed and that making extensive modifications may involve additional costs, if time permits it at all. A compromise on this score may be effected, as long as it does not jeopardize the preestablished instructional objectives.

The trainer will find that entrepreneurs who have developed their instruction in accordance with the newer techniques of instructional design welcome discussion on this topic; in fact, tailoring to specific local applications is an essential part of proper instructional design, and the information regarding local needs can come only from the trainer and the line representative of the organization. On the other hand, those whose instruction has been designed in the more traditional educational format seem to regard discussion of instructional design issues, e.g., instructional objectives, as an intrusion.

Contacts with the entrepreneur should cover all facets of the instructional design, including general biographical data on the prospective trainees and the diversity of their backgrounds, methods of screening attendees, and proposed methods of evaluating trainee progress. Open communications on all these topics indicate recognition of the entrepreneur's professionalism and may heighten his or her interest in specific training needs to a point which could not be achieved in a noncommunicative atmosphere.

Course Administration and Logistics

Although proper instructional design and application to local job needs are the main target of precourse negotiations, there are numerous administrative and logistic items which need to be discussed in detail with the external agency. No attempt will be made here to cover all areas of course administration which require the attention of the trainer (most are obvious or must be handled differently depending on circumstances), but some comments should be made regarding class size, facilities and supplies, trainee selection, and trainee tutoring.

Class Size   No attempt will be made here to specify an ideal number of trainees for any particular type of training, although obviously the physical limitations imposed by equipment need to be taken into account. The problem which requires the attention of the trainer is how to arrive at a compromise between line management and the external resource when their opinions regarding desirable class size differ radically.

Frequently, line managers will apply pressure to accommodate as large a group of trainees as possible. They may wish to reduce cost per capita to the lowest figure possible, they may be seeking to achieve quick upgrading of the educational status of their organization, or they may be desirous of completing the program as soon as possible to minimize the work-disruptive effects of training. In some cases, staff are assigned to training, regardless of its applicability to their jobs, to provide activity during low-workload periods or as a kind of reward for past meritorious performance. The resultant overstacking of classes, plus the poor motiviation of some trainees, can destroy a training program which otherwise might have been successful.

On the other hand, external resources may prefer small classes and will argue for limited attendance, especially if they know that results will be measured. Not only do small, informal classes increase the odds of successful completion by all attendees, but also the closer personal relationships between the instructor and trainees encourage favorable participant critiques.

Arguments that limited class size is an important facet of the instructional design of the course may fail to impress line managers, especially if they can cite examples of university lectures or conferences they have attended which involved hundreds of students. Perhaps the trainer's only recourse is to notify line management that the external resource has structured his or her course for a certain class size and that a major deviation from this may make the course ineffective; often a suitable compromise may then be effected.

Also, it can be argued that assigning one or two individuals from a particular organization to each of four successive courses is probably less disruptive of work schedules than sending four or eight from the same organization to a single course, especially if all assignments are to be done on the trainees' own time. Homework policies are difficult to enforce when a whole organization, or the majority of it, is attending a course at the same time.

External resources generally will go along with a larger class than they consider ideal, as long as it does not exceed an absolute maximum. Occasionally the trainer can sell the idea of shorter instruction periods (half days for two weeks, for example, rather than full days for one week), assigning the balance of time for individual tutoring and consultation. This program format can allay the instructor's fears that a larger-than-ideal class does not permit the personal interaction often necessary for successful training. This format is most workable with those external resources whose additional charges include only living expenses for intervening weekends. Others, especially those whose rates are based on the usual daily consultant fee schedule, will charge proportionately more on an extended schedule, probably making costs prohibitive.

Facilities and Supplies   When approximate class size has been determined, the trainer needs to give attention to reserving adequate facilities and providing needed supplies. In these preparations, all the needs of the external resource must be attended to, including adequate writing surfaces for participants, lab facilities (if needed), projection equipment and other media devices, reproduction services for class notes (either in advance of, or during, the course), the ordering of textbooks and other resource materials (if these are not supplied by the external resource), transportation and hotel accommodations (if help is needed here), and transportation of equipment from receiving areas to class sites.

One item that tends to be overlooked is the fact that external instructors may need access to the facilities the day before the first class in order to familiarize themselves with the setup or to prepare training aids. The rigid schedule of short courses does not generally allow for informal familiarization and orientation on the first morning of classes. Trainers may find their Sunday evening plans unexpectedly interrupted if they have not arranged for instructor access to the facilities in advance of Monday morning's classes.

A number of seemingly minor items, if properly attended to, can greatly enhance the overall "feeling" about training. Binders or other hard covers should be provided for class notes, especially if bulky, and notes should be preassembled to avoid wasted class time. Projection screens for overhead projectors should be tilted to eliminate keystoning, and spare bulbs should be made available for all projection equipment. Facilities should be arranged so that audiovisual equipment, while convenient for the instructor, does not at the same time interfere with trainee viewing. Soft fluorescent chalk should be available to ensure that board work is visible to all participants. Blank notebook paper and pencils should be provided. In short, the trainer should inquire about, and attend to, all details which are not the external agency's responsibility.

Trainee Selection   Trainee selection and screening may be a problem if course announcements are given wide distribution and the number of trainees signing up exceeds the planned attendance limit. For in-house-developed courses, trainee screening can be accomplished by an initial announcement, an orientation meeting, and personal interviews, each of which provides increasingly in-depth information about course content, prerequisites, and instructional objectives to the prospective participants and also allows the instructor, line managers, and trainer to make judgments regarding the capabilities and needs of the trainees. Every attempt should be made to duplicate this procedure for training packages obtained externally. If at all possible, the external resource should be brought on site in advance of the course to perform the orientation and interviewing. This type of visit has the added advantage of allowing the external resource person to gain some firsthand knowledge of the organization's job applications, as well as to become familiar with the training facilities. However, if costs or schedules prevent this prior visit, alternative procedures will have to be devised.

Line management and the trainer can substitute for the instructor in the orientation and interviews if they are sufficiently knowledgeable about the course material and objectives to give guidance to the prospective trainees. This will not be effective if trainees are unwilling to admit background deficiencies or lack of interest to a member of their line of management.

Extensive oversubscription can be prevented by assigning a limited number of "slots" to those organizations most in need of the training. The course announcement then is sent only to the supervisors of designated organizations, who are asked to do the screening on the basis of the number of slots allowed to each. The disadvantages of this procedure are that some organizations which have a real need for training may be overlooked, and supervisors may screen their staff on the basis of current workload rather than need.

Admittedly, the trainee selection and screening process cannot be as well controlled for training packages obtained externally as for training developed in-house. But the trainer should try to do as much as possible to ensure that the right training gets to the right people.

Session Scheduling   When scheduling training by an external resource, there is a tendency to fill all available work time with classroom activities. Indeed, external resources usually develop their packages on the assumption that customers want as much training time for their dollar as they can get in a fixed period.

However, experience has shown that full-time classroom schedules for short courses not only are overtaxing for the instructor and trainees but also result in the loss of some valuable benefits. During prior discussions with the external resource, the trainer and line representative should investigate other possible areas of benefit and should arrange the schedule as necessary to allow for it. At the very least, some time (one to two hours per day) should be allowed for private tutoring of individual trainees, especially those having difficulty with the course. Arrangements should also be made for informal discussions between the external resource and line management. Such sessions apprise management of the content and directions of training and also can provide some additional feedback to the instructor as to whether the course is meeting organizational needs.

EVALUATION DURING AND AFTER THE COURSE

Much has been written about the importance of evaluating training programs. Evaluation is often dismissed simply because it seems to be either too expensive or too complex. A modified version of an evaluation model proposed by Donald Kirkpatrick is outlined in Fig. 47-1[5] It has three major components—trainee critiques, assessing trainee achievement of instructional objectives, and applications on the job.

Evaluation Guidelines

Some general comments about evaluation may be of interest. Experience suggests that evaluation efforts are most effective if the trainer does the following:

1. Avoid numerous questions which ask trainees to rate environmental conditions and the instructor's personality, e.g., room temperature, comfort, and instructor friendliness. Such things influence learning, but they may not be factors which the trainer or instructor can change. The most helpful information is that which relates to the trainees' interest in the material and to the effect of various instructional components, e.g., readings, homework, and quizzes.
2. Act quickly on the data. There should be a mechanism for immediately summarizing the data and feeding these data to the individuals who can bring about timely changes and revisions. If it is a one-week program, data from the first day can be used to make the remaining days of the course more productive, assuming that the instructional and administrative staff assigned to the course have the data in time to do something with them.
3. Document any changes or revisions which come about as a result of acting on the evaluation data. This information will be helpful in future courses.

Trainee Critiques

The most common evaluation form asks trainees to give their opinions about various aspects of a course. Although some would discount this type of evaluation, it can be useful.[6]

Figure 47-2 is a sample of a trainee critique form. Trainees are asked to rate various aspects of a course and provide written comments. This information can be summarized and reviewed with the instructor and management associated with the course. Immediate action can be taken on problem areas that are evident from the data. Such a form can be administered periodically during a course, depending on its length and stage of development. Opinion data such as those collected on critiques are helpful in highlighting such factors as excessive reading or homework, absence of instructional objectives, and failure to relate instruction to job needs. High ratings of these items can be a source of reinforcement for the instructional staff.

Program Component and Purpose	Administered	Type of Data Collected	Who Makes What Kind of Decisions and Reporting of Data
I. TRAINEE CRITIQUES Obtain trainee views on course organization and administration	Periodically during course	Trainees rate various aspects of the course, e.g., relationship of course to job, homework, and quality of instruction	Management, instructor, and trainer Review data and decide what changes should be made, if any, to improve course Summarize data and provide information on changes to trainees, e.g., addition of job applications examples in the homework
II. HOMEWORK/QUIZZES AND EXAMS Obtain trainee performance data on instructional objectives	Daily and biweekly homework and/or quizzes	Information regarding such matters as (a) the effectiveness of the lecture/print/or video-tape presentation of material, (b) appropriateness for homework, (c) trainee mastery of specific concepts and skills	Course instructor Reviews individual performance of each trainee and decides (a) which trainees need special help and (b) which concepts and skills need additional review
	Midterm and end of course exams	Obtain information on the trainees' mastery of major instructional objectives	Provides solution sheets and/or written comments concerning incorrect answers to trainees
III. APPLICATIONS QUESTIONNAIRE Obtain trainee data on job applications of course material	Six to eight weeks after end of course	Obtain information (specific examples) on the extent to which trainees are actually applying skills and concepts learned in the course to their job assignments	Management, instructor, and trainer Review data and decide what changes are required, if any, in the content and instructional objectives of the course

Fig. 47-1 Course evaluation model.

32.

Course No: _____

Course Title: _____

Date: _____ (Mo.) _____ (Yr.)

This form is intended for wide use, and some items may be inappropriate. Circle a number for each appropriate item.

BACKGROUND
1. Job Title
2. Highest education level
3. Year last academic degree/certificate completed: 19_____
4. Average time spent on homework _____ hours/week

	VERY LOW	LOW	OK	HIGH	VERY HIGH
GENERAL					
5. Degree to which this course is meeting announced goals and content.	1	2	3	4	5
6. General interest value of the course material to you personally.	1	2	3	4	5
7. Applicability of the material learned to your work.	1	2	3	4	5
CONTENT					
8. Portion of the material that is really new to you.	1	2	3	4	5
9. The general difficulty or technical level of the material presented.	1	2	3	4	5
10. Up-to-dateness, factual accuracy, and reliability of information.	1	2	3	4	5
INSTRUCTION					
11. Apparent degree of effort and preparation made by instructor.	1	2	3	4	5
12. Apparent technical competence of instructor in material taught.	1	2	3	4	5
13. Ability of instructor to effectively communicate material covered.	1	2	3	4	5
14. Ability of instructor to handle questions and side-issues.	1	2	3	4	5
15. Your satisfaction with amount and type of discussion allowed in class.	1	2	3	4	5
16. Degree to which quizzes (and instructor correcting comments) are helpful.	1	2	3	4	5
MATERIALS					
17. Value to you of the textbooks used in this course, if any.	1	2	3	4	5
18. Value of any notes and handouts provided by the instructor.	1	2	3	4	5
INTERACTIONS					
19. Adequacy of instructor help received outside class.	1	2	3	4	5
20. Adequacy of notes and comments returned to you on homework and quizzes.	1	2	3	4	5
MOTIVATION					
21. Degree of supervisory pressure that you felt to take this course.	1	2	3	4	5
22. Degree to which taking this course interferes with your regular work.	1	2	3	4	5
23. Pressure you feel to perform or to compete with others in this course.	1	2	3	4	5
24. The level of effort that you personally are putting forth in this course.	1	2	3	4	5
HOMEWORK					
25. The amount and difficulty of homework or self-study expected of you.	1	2	3	4	5
26. Relationship of homework assignments to material covered in course.	1	2	3	4	5
27. Degree to which homework (and instructor correcting comments) are helpful.	1	2	3	4	5
VIDEO TAPES					
28. Over-all quality of video presentation.	1	2	3	4	5
29. Degree to which video tapes are helpful in mastery of course objectives.	1	2	3	4	5

COMMENTS:
Please indicate any general suggestions or comments that will improve this course. *(Continue any comments on back of paper)*

Fig. 47-2   Trainee critique form.

Assessing Student Mastery of Instructional Objectives

Despite the widespread use of critique and opinion instruments, they have one serious shortcoming: They do not indicate whether the trainee is achieving the instructional objectives for the course. Even though a trainee can give an instructor, the text, media, and facilities high ratings, he or she may be learning very little. To assess achievement of instructional objectives, careful attention needs to be focused on individual performance on tests and quizzes. Criterion-referenced measurement offers the following advantages:

1. Tests and quizzes are tied directly to instructional objectives. Trainees know exactly what they are expected to do in demonstrating their achievement of the instructional objectives.[7]
2. When a trainee is having a problem, criterion-referenced measurement provides a means of assessing the problem so that appropriate help can be provided.

There is little evidence that the traditional testing and normative grading practices are relevant to industrial training. If the primary goal is to bring about measurable changes in employee performance, it is pointless to fail trainees.[8]

Applications on the Job

Trainee ratings can be high, and quiz performance outstanding; yet when the trainee returns to the job, nothing changes. Since the ultimate payoff of training is improved job performance, it is not unreasonable to require the external resource organization individual to provide a scheme for assessing this.

One approach is to ask trainees to provide specific examples of what they are doing differently as a result of a course. The responses will cover a range of applications. For instance, one trainee may indicate an improved ability to understand control mechanism terminology in a maintenance handbook. Another may report acquisition of skills which led to solving a chronic equipment failure. All such information is significant in indicating whether a course did or did not lead to changes in job performance.

One reason more applications evaluation is not done is that few trainers want to get involved in expensive data collection efforts, statistical validity problems, etc. However, rigorous control groups and sampling schemes do not have to be established to find out whether trainees can or cannot do something as a result of a course. This is not to say that one should make absolute claims about the effects of training on the basis of such evidence. In spite of obvious qualifications, even general applications data are better than no evidence at all. For a review of this topic, see the article by Webb.[9]

Evaluation, especially of programs brought into an organization, is not easy. As suggested by the foregoing, there may be three different levels of evaluation (critique, achievement of objectives, and applications) which the trainer can use. There are more complex levels; for example, one can attempt to assess actual dollar return due to changes in productivity. Whichever level the trainer chooses to pursue, it should be manageable and provide data which are effective in strengthening his or her training programs.

REFERENCES

1. Mager, R. F.: *An Ounce of Analysis,* Harless Educational Technologists, Inc., Falls Church, Va., 1972

   Mager, R. F.: *Analyzing Performance Problems,* Fearon Publishers, Inc., Belmont, Calif., 1973.
2. Wilkins, H. T.: "How to Shake the Money Tree, Bask in the Warmth of Administrative Support, and Enjoy the Respect of Your Faculty Colleagues," *Audio-Visual Instruction,* vol. 18, no. 4, pp. 32–34, April 1973.
3. Shoemaker, H. A.: "The Better to Serve," *Bell Telephone Magazine,* American Telephone and Telegraph Co., New York, March–April 1972, May–June 1972.

   Mager, R. F.: *You Can Hear the Learning Happen* (tape-filmstrip), Mager Associates, Inc., Los Altos Hills, Calif., 1974.

Kapfer, M. B.: *Behavioral Objectives in Curriculum Development,* Educational Technology Publications, Englewood Cliffs, N.J., 1971.

4. Geis, G. L.: "Behavioral Objectives: A Selected Bibliography and Brief Review," an ERIC paper, ERIC Clearinghouse on Media & Technology, Stanford University, Stanford, Calif., 1972.

   Rothkopf, E. A., and R. Kaplan: "Exploration of the Effect of Density and Specificity of Instructional Objectives on Learning from Text," *Journal of Educational Psychology,* vol. 63, no. 4, pp. 295–302, 1972.

   Popham, W. J., et al.: "Instructional Objectives," *AERA Monograph Series on Curriculum Evaluation,* Rand McNally & Company, Chicago, 1969.

5. Kirkpatrick, D. L.: "Techniques for Evaluating Training Programs," *Journal of the ASTD,* December 1959 and January 1960.

6. McNeil, J. D., and W. J. Popham: "The Assessment of Teacher Competence," in R. W. Travers (ed.), *Second Handbook of Research on Teaching,* American Educational Research Association, Rand McNally & Company, Chicago, 1973, pp. 218–244.

7. Butler, F. C.: "The Criterion Test," *Instructional Systems Development for Vocational and Technical Training,* Educational Technology Publications, Inc., Englewood Cliffs, N.J., 1972, pp. 96–102.

8. Mager, R. F.: *Measuring Instructional Intent,* Fearon Publishers, Inc., Belmont, Calif., 1973.

   Briggs, L. J.: "Constructing Tests," in *Handbook of Procedures for the Design of Instruction,* American Institutes for Research, Pittsburgh, Pa., 1970, pp. 46–72.

   Jackson, R.: *Developing Criterion-referenced Tests,* ERIC Clearinghouse on Tests, Measurement and Evaluation, Princeton, N.J., 1970.

   Kriewall, T. E.: *Aspects and Applications of Criterion-referenced Tests,* Institute for Educational Research, Downers Grove, Ill., 1972

   Smith, R. G., Jr.: "The Quality-Control Function: Concepts," in *The Engineering of Educational and Training Systems,* D. C. Heath and Company, Lexington, Mass., 1971, pp. 97–108.

9. Webb, W. B.: "Measurement of Learning in Extensive Programs," in P. H. DuBois and G. D. Mayo (eds.), *AERA Monograph Series on Curriculum Evaluation,* Rand McNally & Company, Chicago, 1970.

Index